The Legal
Environment
of Business

The Legal Environment of Business

Herbert M. Bohlman
Associate Professor
Arizona State University
Judge Pro Tempore, Maricopa County Superior Court

Mary Jane Dundas
Associate Professor
Arizona State University

Gaylord A. Jentz
Herbert D. Kelleher Professor in Business Law
Department of MSIS, University of Texas at Austin

West Publishing Company
St. Paul   New York   Los Angeles   San Francisco

Composition: Parkwood Composition
Copyediting: Nancy Palmer Jones
Artwork: Miyake Illustration

Cover Photograph: Photograph courtesy of Image Bank © 1989;
by John Neubauer

COPYRIGHT 1989   By WEST PUBLISHING COMPANY
                   50 W. Kellogg Boulevard
                   P.O. Box 64526
                   St. Paul, MN 55164-1003

96 95 94 93 92 91 90 89   8 7 6 5 4 3 2 1 0

Library of Congress Cataloging-in-Publication

Bohlman, Herbert M.
  The legal environment of business.
  Includes index.
  1. Industrial laws and legislation—United States.
2. Commercial law—United States.   3. Business
enterprises—United States.   I. Dundas, Mary Jane.
II. Jentz, Gaylord A.   III. Title.
KF1600.B64 1989   346.73' 07   88-33915
ISBN 0-314-47212-6   347.3067

Contents In Brief

v

Part III
Business Formation   393

Part IV
Business and Government Regulation   447

Contents

Preface

The American legal scene has changed tremendously during the 1980s, and even more change is expected as we approach the 21st century. As a result, the effect of the legal environment in which business operates has changed and will change dramatically. THE LEGAL ENVIRONMENT OF BUSINESS was written with two goals in mind— to present to the student the breadth of the legal environment of business and to provide a legal foundation that can be used in his or her business or government career.

To accomplish these goals, we have presented materials that cover both the private and public regulation of business. Legal topics discussed in the first area include contracts, sales, secured transactions, negotiable instruments, property, agency, partnerships, and corporations. Legal topics covered in the second area—public regulation—are labor law, securities law, antitrust, consumer rights, and environmental law.

Although private and public regulations are easily divided in theory, in real life these two areas are often blended. Students need to understand both forms of law so that they are aware of their rights and recognize possible liabilities.

Total Learning/Teaching Package

This text constitutes what we believe to be a total learning/teaching package. The text contains numerous pedagogical aids and high-interest additions.

Case Selection and Presentation

Each chapter has five to eight cases to illustrate the application of the law to specific business problems. We have tried to create a balance between classic cases that are well recognized and recent cases that have changed the law significantly. Each case starts with the citation that includes the court, the date, the state reporter (if available), and the West reporter. The *Background and Facts* focuses on the setting in which the case arose and identifies the plaintiffs and defendants. The actual court case is presented in an edited manner. Finally, the *Decision and Remedy* clearly states who won the case and why. When appropriate we have a *Comment* section that presents additional material not available from the case itself or that notes future trends.

Features of Each Chapter

Each chapter has an example of one or more of the following special sections that are designed to instruct as well as to interest the student.

Quotations

Each chapter opens with a brief quotation that is appropriate to the chapter material.

Exhibits

Most chapters have at least one exhibit to illustrate important aspects of the law. Some exhibits are charts, such as the one setting out the federal court system; others focus on classifications or summaries; and others set out forms used in the legal or business world, such as the one presenting an example credit sale contract.

Legal Highlights

Nearly all chapters have legal highlights in which the student is presented with practical advice, such as how to check on a social security account, or with examples of how the law was applied in an unusual situation, such as the one on the cross-cultural conflict on the Texas Gulf Coast.

Facing A Legal Issue

Located at the end of each chapter is material entitled *Facing A Legal Issue*. In each discussion, we have attempted to present a factual situation which a business person could confront in his or her career. These situations concern problems that are collateral to the rest of the material contained within the chapter. They are an attempt to give students practical factual advice on how to apply the law.

Key Terms

Each chapter ends with a list of key terms first identified by bold-faced type in the text.

Questions and Case Problems

At the end of each chapter, five to ten *Questions and Case Problems* are set out. The questions are a mix of hypotheticals and problems taken from actual cases for which full citations are given. Complete answers to all of the *Questions and Case Problems* are found in a separate booklet entitled *Answers to Questions and Case Problems*.

Appendices

So that this book can serve as a reference, we have included a full set of appendices. They are as follows:

A   The Constitution of the United States of America
B   The Uniform Commercial Code (Excerpts)
C   Restatement of Torts, Second (Excerpts)
D   The Sherman Antitrust Act (Excerpts)
E   Clayton Act (Excerpts)
F   The Federal Trade Commission Act (Excerpts)
G   National Labor Relations Act (Excerpts)
H   The Federal Civil Rights Laws (Excerpts)
I   The Uniform Partnership Act (Excerpts)
J   Spanish Equivalents for Important Legal Terms in English

Supplements

Study Guide

The *Study Guide* was written by Thomas Brierton of Northern Illinois University. Each chapter reinforces what the text has presented. The *Study Guide* consists of descriptions of general principles discussed in each chapter, chapter summaries in sentence outline form, and true-false, fill-in-the-blank, and multiple-choice questions to test students' comprehension.

Instructor's Manual with Test Bank

The *Instructor's Manual* was written by Lou Ann Simpson of Drake University. Each chapter includes a chapter overview, case comments, and discussion questions and teaching suggestions. The *Test Bank* has been prepared by Larry D. Strate of the University of Nevada at Las Vegas. Each chapter of the *Test Bank* has a minimum of 15 true-false questions and 35 multiple-choice questions with many chapters having more items.

The *Test Bank* is available on WESTEST, which offers computerized testing for IBM-PC and compatible microcomputers or the Apple II family of microcomputers. WESTEST allows instructors to create new tests, modify existing tests, change the questions from West's original *Test Bank,* and print tests in a variety of formats. Instructors can add questions of their own to the *Test Bank.* Instructors should contact their West sales representative to inquire about acquiring WESTEST.

Educational Legal Software

LEGAL CLERK—A Software Package For Research And Learning is new to this edition and is the highly acclaimed West Publishing LEGAL CLERK Research Software System. LEGAL CLERK is a user-friendly, interactive software package that simultaneously introduces students to the rudiments of computer-aided legal research and reinforces the underlying concepts of business law. LEGAL CLERK provides a valuable learning tool to help your school meet AACSB recommendations for using microcomputers in business law courses.

LEGAL CLERK enables students with access to IBM-PC and compatible personal computers to retrieve specific cases found in THE LEGAL ENVIRONMENT OF BUSINESS for extensive study. To provide instructors with maximum flexibility, LEGAL CLERK covers three major subject areas of business law and legal environment—UCC Article 2 Sales; Government Regulation and the Legal Environment of Business; and Contracts. Instructors may select one or all three versions for their classes. Cases appearing in LEGAL CLERK are clearly identified in the text with a computer logo. The logos are color coded to help users easily identify which version of LEGAL CLERK contains specific cases.

 Uniform Commercial Code Article 2 Sales—Version 1.0

 Government Regulation and The Legal Environment of Business—Version 1.0

 Contracts—Version 1.0

A site license for all three versions of LEGAL CLERK is free to qualified adopters. Each version is accompanied by an *Instructor's Resource Guide* and, for student purchase, a *Student User's Guide.*

West's Book of Forms

West's Book of Legal Forms by Robert McNutt, California State University of Northridge, is also available for student purchase. It provides 40 samples of often-used business forms.

Transparency Acetates

The supplements package contains a set of approximately 40 transparency acetates.

Acknowledgments

Many people are involved in the production of a new textbook. The initial impetus for THE LEGAL ENVIRONMENT OF BUSINESS came from Clyde Perlee, Jr., who has been a strong supporter of this project. We acknowledge the guidance, insightful critiques, and suggestions provided by Roger LeRoy Miller. A hearty thanks to Denise Simon, our executive editor, who kept the project moving in a timely manner, and Robert Jucha, our development editor, who coordinated all the reviews and provided expert analysis. We thank Rose Gruenhagen and Eric Hollowell who helped to proofread this project.

A number of reviewers were kind enough to give us their ideas and comments on various drafts of the manuscript. They are:

Reviewers for Bohlman/Dundas/Jentz

David L. Baumer, North Carolina State University
Katherine Beebe, Salt Lake Community College
Thomas H. Brucker, University of Washington
Mark A. Buchanan, St. Cloud State University
Daylin J. Butler, Kansas State University
Lawrence S. Clark, Louisiana State University in Shreveport
Gamewell D. Gantt III, Idaho State University
John Geary, Appalachian State University
Amy Zoe Gershenfeld, University of Kentucky
Martin F. Grace, Georgia State University

Gerard Halpern, University of Arkansas

Marsha E. Hass, College of Charleston

James P. Hill, Central Michigan University

E. C. Hipp, Clemson University

David D. Jaeger, University of Cincinnati

Marianne M. Jennings, Arizona State University

Jack E. Karns, University of North Dakota

Nancy P. Klintworth, University of Central Florida

Paul Lansing, University of Iowa

Andrew Laviano, University of Rhode Island

F. Raymond Lewis, Northeastern Illinois University

Nancy R. Mansfield, Georgia State University

S. Scott Massin, Emory University

John E. McDonald, Jr., University of North Carolina at Charlotte

Sheel P. Pawar, Idaho State University

Jordan B. Ray, University of Florida

Lim Razook, University of Oklahoma

Daniel L. Reynolds, Middle Tennessee State University

Rene Sacasas, University of Miami, Florida

Scott Sibray, California State University, Chino

Lou Ann Simpson, Drake University

S. Jay Sklar, Temple University

Lucy L. Spalding, Illinois State University

Larry Strate, University of Nevada at Las Vegas

Donald J. Swanz, St. Bonaventure University

Irvin Tankersley, Memphis State University

Bernard F. Thiemann, Bellarmine College

Daphney Thomas, James Mason University

Wayne R. Wells, St. Cloud State University

We wish to thank our fellow colleagues who encouraged us, supported us, and spent hours reviewing our rough drafts: Professors Louie Aranda, Ethan Lock, Claude Olney, and Peter Reiss of Arizona State University. They were extremely helpful with our initial drafts and giving us their creative ideas and thoughts. They also gave us the motivation to keep going.

As careful as we have attempted to be, there are, no doubt, errors in this text for which we take full responsibility. We welcome comments from all users of the text, for it is by incorporating such comments that we can make this text even better in future editions.

Mary Jane Dundas
Herbert M. Bohlman
Gaylord A. Jentz

DEDICATION

M.J.D. dedicates this book to her parents, R.J. and Maria A. Dundas, and her sisters Jean and Marilyn, and their families.

H.M.B. dedicates this book to his wife, Mimi, and his children, Bill, Patti, Mike, and Laura.

G.A.J. dedicates this book to his wife, JoAnn, and his children, Kathy, Gary, Lori, and Rory.

UNIT I   INTRODUCTION TO LAW

Chapter 1   Introduction to Law and Its Sources

The educated citizen has an obligation to uphold the law. This is the obligation of every citizen in a free and peaceful society—but the educated citizen has a special responsibility by the virtue of his greater understanding. For, whether he has ever studied history or current events, ethics or civics, the rules of a profession or the tools of a trade, he knows that only a respect for the law makes it possible for free men to dwell together in peace and progress.

He knows that law is the adhesive force of the cement of society, creating order out of chaos and coherence in place of anarchy. He knows that for one man to defy a law or court order he does not like is to invite others to defy those which they do not like, leading to a breakdown of all justice and all order.

He knows, too, that every fellow man is entitled to be regarded with decency and treated with dignity. Any educated citizen who seeks to subvert the law, to suppress freedom, or to subject other human beings to acts that are less than human, degrades his inheritance, ignores his learning and betrays his obligations.

Certain other societies may respect the rule of force—we respect the rule of law.

John F. Kennedy, Speech at Vanderbilt
University, Nashville, Tennessee, May 13, 1963,
quoted in the *New York Times,* May 19, 1963, p. 62.

OUTLINE

Introduction

Law pervades all of our lives. The law affects an individual in many ways, but its effect on the business world is multiplied many times. This book provides an overview of the multiple and complex laws with which businesses must contend. Understanding the basic concepts of the law is essential to being a good businessperson.

In this chapter we will examine the definitions of law and discuss the various schools of legal philosophy. The history and sources of American law and the various classifications of law are reviewed. We will study the courts of law, the courts of equity, and administrative agency regulations.

Definition of Law

The word **law** defies a simple definition. Unfortunately, when the English language evolved, only one word was developed to cover three different concepts: First, law means a system designed to give order to society. Second, it means a system of moral conduct that ensures justice in society. Third, it means a principle represented by a rule or rules. When we speak of *the* law, we are using the first and second meanings, and when we say *a* law, we are using the third meaning.

Roscoe Pound, an early twentieth-century legal philosopher, thought that man established an ordered society using two fundamental sets of ideas. Society's moral ideas are taken from ethics; its political ideas are taken from political science. Moral ideas give us *the* law, while political ideas give us *a* law or *a* rule. A sovereign political authority is needed to enforce rules, while the principles of law (that is, the moral ideas) need judges who interpret the law based on experience, reason, and prior case law.

Schools of Legal Philosophy

Jurisprudence is the science or philosophy of law. The cases you will read in this book reflect the judge's opinion. But what is the judge's opinion based on? It is based in part on a person's philosophy of law, his or her reasoning abilities,

and his or her personality, as well as on custom, logic, and history. Other than personality, all these components of decision making can be developed through study. Such study includes the discovery of the various legal philosophies.

The Natural Law School

The **natural law school** holds that there is an ideal state of being that is either part of human nature or that comes from a divine source. This ideal state presupposes a definite right or wrong, which constitutes national law. Society does not create this natural law; it is discovered through the use of reason and the knowledge of good and evil. The natural law school emphasizes ethics as the source of law's authority. Basic ethical values are used to make legal decisions.

Documents such as the Magna Charta, the Declaration of Independence, the United States Constitution (see Appendix A for the complete text), and the United Nations Declaration of Human Rights reflect natural law ideals in phrases like: "We hold these truths to be self-evident, that all men are created equal, that they are endowed by their Creator with certain unalienable Rights * * *."

An example of the natural law school of philosophy is the civil rights movement. In the 1960s, when blacks sat at lunch counters or sat in the front of buses—areas that had been reserved for whites only—the blacks were arrested. At their trials, the common theme for the defense was that segregation is inherently wrong. Therefore, the defendants' acts of defiance could not be wrong because a higher law gives real meaning to the words of the United States Constitution. Although these blacks were convicted, society eventually changed the laws in this area, as we will see later.

The Historical and Sociological Schools

The **historical school** concentrates on the origin and history of the legal system and looks to the past to discovery what the principles of contemporary law should be. The legal principles that have withstood the passage of time are best suited for shaping present laws. Thus, law develops in and with the social environment.

Tied to the historical school is the **sociological school.** This philosophy depends on observation of social science principles as to which laws work. The sociological school emphasizes how people ought to conduct themselves within society. While the historical school is descriptive in nature, the sociological school is based on observation.

The legal field of **probate** uses the philosophy of the historical school. Probate is the court process of settling a person's estate by collecting all the debts owed to the deceased, by paying all the debts the deceased person owed, and by transferring ownership of the decedent's property to the heirs. The probate court will follow the deceased person's wishes expressed in his or her will, or, if there is no will, the court will follow the state statutes that determine who will receive the property.

The right to determine through a will who will receive a person's estate after death was granted by the English Parliament in 1540 in a law known as the statute of wills. Some version of this English law has been adopted through statutes in each of the fifty states. In making determinations in probate law, a probate judge relies almost exclusively on the rules that have developed historically and not on what she or he believes to be right or wrong in a particular case.

For example, in many states if you are married to someone for one hour and died before you can make out a will, your spouse will inherit everything. On the other hand, you may have lived happily with your lover as if you were husband and wife for fifty years. If you die without a will in a state that does not recognize a common-law marriage (if you live together as husband and wife you are deemed by law to be married), your lover will not inherit anything because you were not legally married. The historical approach is used here because our legal system does not want to change the law in the absence of a legislative act.

The Analytical School

Logic shapes the law. A member of the **analytical school** examines the structure and subject matter of a legal code and analyzes it logically to extract the underlying principles. By analyzing cases and rules, the analytical school formulates general principles. These principles are the starting points for legal reasoning.

The American Law Institute (ALI), through its **Restatements,** represents this philosophy. The ALI has written Restatements of various areas of the law, such as torts, trusts, contracts, and agency law. The people who developed and wrote the Restatements have reviewed the thousands of cases decided in the last 200 years to establish the **common law** in a particular area. Common law is a body of law developed from custom and from judicial decisions (that is, from cases) in English and American courts.

Although the Restatements themselves are not the law, they are statements of what the law is. They, in effect, have pulled together the cases on a particular topic and placed them in logical order in a series of volumes. The ALI sets out a particular law and gives the reason for it. Today, judges rely on the Restatements and cite them in case opinions.

The Legal Realists

Law is shaped by social forces and is an instrument of social control. **Legal realists** stress the pragmatic and empirical sides of law; because they see law as a means to a social end, they try to predict and influence lawmaking. In the legal realist school, despite moral law, historical development, and logical analysis, the same set of facts will not always result in the same conclusion. A reviewing court often views the law differently than a lower court, for example. For the legal realist, the legitimacy of law and of legal institutions is measured by how well they serve the needs of society.

The decision by the United States Supreme Court in *Roe v. Wade*[1] that recognized the constitutional right of a woman to decide whether to end her pregnancy by abortion is an example of legal realism. This decision might not have been the same if the court had applied any of the other philosophies.

The Economic School

The **economic school** of thought was developed in the 1970s by Richard A. Posner.[2] This theory

---

1.   410 U.S. 113, 93 S.Ct. 705, 35 L.Ed.2d 147 (1973).

2.   A former law professor at the University of Chicago Law School, Mr. Posner was appointed by President Reagan as a judge to the United States Court of Appeals, Seventh Circuit, on December 4, 1981.

holds that most laws may be evaluated in accordance with economic theory. For analytical purposes, it is assumed that everyone in the legal system is rational and will act in order to maximize his or her welfare. For example, a person who has been injured in an automobile accident, although he or she may file a lawsuit, will usually settle the claim because a settlement is faster and less costly than waiting for a courtroom trial.

Sources of American Law

American law has been evolving ever since the first landings in Jamestown, Virginia, in 1607 and in Plymouth Rock, Massachusetts, in 1620. At first, the colonies relied heavily on the English legal system, but during the early decades of the new nation the Americans also borrowed from the French and the German legal systems. These borrowed ideas and philosophies helped to shape the current sources of American law: the Constitution, the statutes passed by the legislatures, and the common law.

Constitutions

Each state and the federal government have a constitution. The constitution is the highest source to which a court will look when deciding law. The United States Constitution is the supreme law of the land. A law in violation of the Constitution, no matter what its source, will be declared unconstitutional and, thus, cannot be enforced. Similarly, each state constitution, although supreme within the respective state's borders, cannot conflict with the United States Constitution. The United States Constitution has two functions, described in the sections that follow.

Creation of Powers, Structure, and Limitations of the Federal Government   The Constitution creates the powers, structure, and limitations of the federal government. All powers not retained by the federal government reside in the states or the people. For example, the Constitution gives the federal government the power to regulate interstate commerce—that is, the commerce among the various states or foreign nations. The states retain the power to regulate intrastate commerce—

that is, commerce that is strictly within each state's geographic boundaries. Another example is that the federal government is given the exclusive right to coin money; the states cannot make their own money.

The Constitution also outlines the structure of the federal government. It establishes three branches of government, creating a system of **checks and balances** in which each branch ensures that the other two branches do not abuse their powers. The legislative branch (Congress) passes statutes; the executive branch (the president) enforces the laws; and the judicial branch (the courts) determines the validity of the laws and applies them to specific cases. Even though these three branches of government are separate, their powers do overlap at times.

The limitations of the powers of the federal and state governments are also contained in the Constitution. For example, no titles of nobility may be granted. Another section of the Constitution limits states to impose export and import taxes except for executing its inspection laws. (See Article I, sections 9 and 10 of the United States Constitution)

Guarantee of Freedoms   The Constitution guarantees the citizens of the United States (and often aliens) various individual freedoms. Most individual rights are set out in the first ten amendments, now called the **Bill of Rights.** The government is prohibited from infringing on these freedoms by specific restrictions expressed in the Bill of Rights. For example, the Fourth Amendment ensures that every person is free from unreasonable (but not all) searches.

Congress may on rare occasions pass a statute contrary to the Constitution, or, indeed, the president may act counter to the Constitution. The process of deciding whether a law is in conflict with the mandates of the Constitution is known as **judicial review.** The power of judicial review was first established in 1803 in the case of *Marbury v. Madison.*[3] The Supreme Court determined that it had the power to decide that a law passed by Congress violated the Constitution. Thus, the power of judicial review, residing in the judicial

---

3.   5 U.S. 137, 2 L.Ed. 135 (1803). See Chapter 2 for the case.

branch, is part of the system of checks and balances. Judicial review is examined in more detail in Chapter 3.

Statutes and Ordinances

Laws enacted by Congress or a state legislature are called **statutes. Ordinances** are laws enacted by cities and counties. Both statutes and ordinances must be in compliance with the United States Constitution and the relevant state constitution.

Because the states have retained many powers, Congress can pass only the legislation that falls within the range of power granted to it by Article I of the United States Constitution.[4] Many of the cases coming before the courts today involve statutes. Much of the work of the courts involves interpreting what the legislators meant when the law was passed and applying that interpretation to a present set of facts. In large parts, statutory law has replaced common law. For a particular case, the court looks first for a statute, ordinance, or regulation on which to base its decision. If none is found, the court looks to common law.

Common Law

The origins of common law lie in the ancient unwritten law of England. In 1066 the Normans, led by William the Conqueror, were the last invaders to conquer England. William and his successors began the process of unifying the country. One of the means used was the king's court. Before the Norman Conquest, disputes were settled locally according to local custom. The king's court sought to establish a common or uniform set of customs for the whole country and gave a person the right to appeal a local decision to the king.

The body of rules that evolved under the king's court was the beginning of the common law. As the number of courts and cases increased, the more important decisions of each year were recorded in year books. Judges, settling disputes similar to ones that had been decided before, used the year books as the basis for their decisions. If a case was unique, judges had to create new laws, but

they based their decisions on the general principles suggested by earlier cases. The body of judge-made law that developed under this system is still used today in England and the United States and is known as the common law.

Today, common law is derived from the usages and customs of society and from the judgments of the courts recognizing, affirming, enforcing, and sometimes changing those usages and customs. These judgments constitute case law. If the legislature believes it necessary, it can pass statutes that embody the common law; it can also pass statutes that completely change—or at least modify—the common law.

If a case before the court involves an issue for which no legislation exists, the court will refer to the common law to make its decision. Where it does not conflict with a statute, common law has the same force as statutory law. Even where statutes have been substituted for common law, courts often rely on common law to interpret the legislation on the theory that the people who drafted the statute intended to codify a previous common-law rule.

Most states have adopted common law by legislative decree. For example, the California Civil Code, Section 22.1, states that the "common law of England, so far as it is not repugnant to or inconsistent with the Constitution of the United States, or the Constitution or laws of this State, is the rule of decision in all the courts of this State."

Stare Decisis

The practice of deciding new cases with reference to former decisions is a cornerstone of the American judicial system. This practice is called *stare decisis* ("let the decision stand"). The use of a prior case decision, similar in facts or legal principles, in deciding a present case is referred to as **precedent.** Judges usually follow the precedent established by the decisions of previous courts. *Stare decisis* reflects the experience and wisdom of the past.

Functions of *Stare Decisis* The rule of *stare decisis* performs many useful functions. First, it allows the courts to be more efficient. A judge needs only to look at previous court decisions that set out the policies for a particular law; if other

---

4. Article I, Section 8, gives eighteen specific powers to Congress. The Tenth Amendment reserves all other powers to the states or to the people.

judges have confronted the same issue as that before the court and if they have reasoned through the case carefully, their opinions can serve as guides. This process saves the valuable time it would take for judges to reason out each and every case as if no other case like it had ever been decided.

Second, *stare decisis* results in a more just and uniform system of decision making. The rule of precedent works to neutralize the personal prejudices of individual judges. Judges are not required to, but usually do use precedent as the basis for their decisions. Some variations in rules of law still occur, however, because judges in different states and regions will apply different precedents in accordance with local law. Reasonable judges can differ in their interpretation and application of the law.

Third, precedent makes the law more stable and predictable. If the law on a particular subject is well settled, people will abide by the law and not bring cases involving that law to court. For example, no one today would think of bringing a lawsuit to have schools segregated on the basis of race. A law that is stable encourages people to settle their differences peaceably without using the court system.

Flexibility of *Stare Decisis*   *Stare decisis* gives the law stability, but it is also flexible. Judges depart occasionally from the rule of precedent because the precedent is incorrect or no longer applicable. For example, changes in technology, business practices, or society's attitudes necessitate changes in the law.

If courts were not able to depart from precedent, all legal thinking and reasoning would be frozen in time. Judges are reluctant to overthrow precedent; whether they do or not depends on the subject of the case, the number and prestige of prior decisions, the degree of social change that has occurred, and the identity of the deciding court. The Supreme Court of the United States is the highest authority in the land and is, therefore, freer to reverse the direction of the law than a lower court.

Judges sometimes find themselves faced with making a decision on a case of first impression. In this type of case, no precedent exists because there is no law on the topic. For example, in the 1960s judges were uncertain about how a person could steal time from a computer. Some courts held that the unauthorized use of the computer was not a crime. Today, many states have statutes that make the theft of computer time a crime.

At other times, judges find conflicting precedents or no precedents. In these situations, courts use one or more of the following to aid in making a decision: First, they refer to previous decisions that are similar in nature to the current case, and they use analogies to decide the case. Second, courts look at social factors and develop a policy. For example, state legislatures in the mid 1980s had not developed statutes concerning surrogate mothers; this left it up to the courts to develop policy concerning the contracts and legal relations involved among the surrogate mother, the child, and the biological father. Third, courts balance the interests of the parties involved.

Cases that overturn precedent often receive a lot of publicity. For example, the case of *Brown v. Board of Education*[5] overturned sixty years of segregation in schools and set the stage for integration of all peoples into U.S. society on an equal basis. The case of *Roe v. Wade*[6] overturned a century of laws that made an abortion a crime. The publicity that surrounds these cases makes it seem that case law is frequently overturned. In reality, the majority of cases are decided according to precedent by the rule of *stare decisis*.

Sources of Commercial Law

Commercial, or business, law is the body of law that governs commercial transactions. Commercial law covers such topics as contracts, partnerships, corporations, and agencies. Many of the principles of business law were developed centuries ago from what was known as the **law merchant.**

The Law Merchant

A system of mercantile courts existed in England and the rest of Europe well before the advent of the common-law courts. These mercantile courts administered the law merchant, which was de-

---

5.   347 U.S. 483, 74 S.Ct. 686, 98 L.Ed. 873 (1954).
6.   410 U.S. 113, 93 S.Ct. 705, 35 L.Ed.2d 147 (1973).

LEGAL HIGHLIGHT   A Paddling Precedent

In 1837 the state of North Carolina prosecuted and convicted a schoolmistress of assault and battery for whipping a student with a switch. The switching left marks, but these disappeared after a few days. The teacher appealed her conviction.[a]

The appeals court reversed the teacher's conviction. The court found that the welfare of the child was the main purpose for which the pain was inflicted. Any punishment that would endanger life, limb, or health, would disfigure the child, or would result in permanent injury would be unnecessary and inconsistent with the purpose of the switching. The teacher's judgment was presumed to be correct.

According to the appellate court, a jury could find that the pain inflicted was too severe and was disproportionate to the offense for the age of the child. If the jury also found that the switching did not leave any permanent marks and if they found that the teacher was acting in accordance with her sense of right, the teacher should be acquitted. The appellate court reasoned that it could not decide otherwise, or it would be interfering with the authority necessary to preserve discipline. If the teacher acted beyond her power, the parents and the public would act as a check. If they failed to act, the punishment "must be tolerated as part of the imperfections and inconveniences, which no human laws can wholly remove or redress."

Has our thinking on this matter changed in the last 150 years? What would the United States Supreme Court have to say about corporal punishment today? Would the Supreme Court follow the thinking of the North Carolina court?

In 1977 the United States Supreme Court had a chance to review a Florida statute that permitted corporal punishment of students in school.[b] The court said:

The use of corporal punishment in this country as a means of disciplining

schoolchildren dates back to the colonial period. It has survived the transformation of primary and secondary education from the colonials' reliance on optional private arrangements to our present system of compulsory education and dependence of public schools. * * * [W]e can discern no trend toward its elimination.

At common law a single principle has governed the use of corporal punishment since before the American Revolution: Teachers may impose reasonable but not excessive force to discipline a child. * * * * * * *

Because it is rooted in history, the child's liberty interest in avoiding corporal punishment while in the care of public school authorities is subject to historical limitations. * * * * * * *

Florida has continued to recognize, and indeed has strengthened by statute, the common-law right of a child not to be subjected to excessive corporal punishment in school. * * * [T]he teacher and principal * * * decide in the first instance whether corporal punishment is reasonably necessary under the circumstances in order to discipline a child who has misbehaved. But they must exercise prudence and restraint. For Florida has preserved the traditional judicial proceedings for determining whether the punishment was justified. If the punishment inflicted is later found to have been excessive * * * [those] inflicting it may be held liable in damages, and if malice is shown, they may be subject to criminal penalties.

Notice how the United States Supreme Court's reasoning followed closely that of the North Carolina Supreme Court. Although the North Carolina decision was not binding on the United States Supreme Court, the latter followed the precedent established by the earlier court. Common law was used to uphold the Florida statute.

[a]State v. Pendergrass, 19 N.C. 365, 31 Am.Dec. 416 (1837).
[b]Ingraham v. Wright, 430 U.S. 651, 97 S.Ct. 1401, 51 L.Ed.2d 711 (1977).

veloped from the uniform customs of the merchants, many of whom traveled from place to place to do business. The law merchant was important during the Middle Ages when the fair, or market, was the primary commercial event. In fact, the Magna Charta made special provisions for merchants. Section 41, for example, states that all merchants should "have safe and secure conduct, to go out of, and to come into England, and to stay there, and to pass as well by lands as by water, for buying and selling by the ancient and allowed customs." The law merchant eventually became part of the common law and was incorporated into American law.

Codification of Commercial Law

The United States from its very beginning as a nation adopted the English common law covering commercial transactions. In the early days, when commerce was just beginning to develop, there were many gaps in the body of this law. Different states took opposing positions on many commercial issues, leaving businesspeople in New York, for example, uncertain as to what the law would be in another state. Both the legal and the business professions over the years realized that uniform laws covering commercial transactions were necessary.

In order to achieve this uniformity, the legal profession, through the National Conference of Commissioners on Uniform State Laws in conjunction with the American Law Institute, has developed model codes of commercial law. Once a model code is completed, it is sent to each state. The state may choose to adopt the model code completely, may change parts of it to make it compatible with local law, or may choose not to consider or adopt the model code. Today, these codes are continually being developed as business needs change. Of all the model codes, the most important is the **Uniform Commercial Code** (UCC).

Uniform Commercial Code

During the 1930s, in order to create uniform commercial laws, some members of Congress proposed a statutory scheme that would cover all interstate commercial transactions. The bills were never passed. Congress realized that this area really belonged to the individual states, since Congress cannot control intrastate commerce. The National Conference and the ALI began work on the Uniform Commercial Code in 1942 and completed the final draft in 1952. All fifty states, the District of Columbia, and the Virgin Islands have adopted the Uniform Commercial Code.[7]

The UCC consists of ten articles:

1. General Provisions.
2. Sales.
3. Commercial Paper.
4. Bank Deposits and Collections.
5. Letters of Credit.
6. Bulk Transfers.
7. Documents of Title.
8. Investment Securities.
9. Secured Transactions.
10. Effective Date and Repealer.
11. Effective Date and Transition Provisions.

The Code does not greatly change the basic principles of commercial law derived from the law merchant or common law. The UCC expands these principles and places them in a comprehensive order to modernize, clarify, and standardize the rules. The UCC also clarifies the legal relationship of the parties in modern commercial transactions. The Code is designed to help determine the intentions of the parties to a commercial contract and to give force and effect to their agreement. Businesspeople are assured that their contracts, if validly entered into, will be enforced; this, in turn, encourages further business transactions.

Classification of Law

The law is classified by its various topics, although there is no way to prevent the overlapping of various aspects of the law. For example, contracts are generally classified as private law; a contract with a government agency, however, is classified as public law. These classifications are, of necessity, somewhat arbitrary.

Substantive Law Versus Procedural Law

Substantive law defines, describes, regulates, and creates legal rights and obligations. An example

---

[7]Louisiana has adopted only Articles 1, 3, 4, and 5.

of substantive law is the contract law that determines whether a minor can enter into a contractual agreement. Although a minor may enter into many types of contracts, he or she still cannot sell real estate without the help of a legal guardian or the court. Another example of substantive law is the rule that a person who, through his or her own fault, injures another must pay damages.

Procedural law establishes the methods of enforcing the rights created by substantive law. For example, how a lawsuit begins, how to select the court in which the lawsuit should be filed, how a jury is selected, how judgments are enforced, and which legal papers need to be filed are all questions of procedural law. Substantive law sets out our legal rights; procedural law sets out the process to enforce our legal rights.

Exhibit 1–1 lists legal subject matter according to its classification as substantive or procedural laws.

Public Law Versus Private Law

Public and private law are both subdivisions of substantive law. **Public law** addresses the relationship between people and their government; **private law** addresses direct dealings among individuals. **Criminal law** is classified as public law because, although a criminal act may involve only one victim, it is also an offense against society as a whole; thus, these acts are prohibited by governments in order to protect the public. The criminal act usually violates a civil right, as well. For example, drunk driving is a criminal act; if an accident occurs, the injured person can sue in civil court and recover damages.

Constitutional law is classified as public law since it involves questions of whether the government—federal, state, or local—has the power to act. The United States Constitution empowers the government to perform certain acts. Often the issue is whether the government—that is, the legislative or the executive branch—has exceeded the limits set by the Constitution. In addition, constitutional law limits the exercise of governmental power in ways usually designed to protect a person's life, liberty, or property from improper governmental action. For example, the Fourth and Fifth Amendments to the United States Constitution protect individuals from unreasonable searches and coerced confessions.

Administrative law is another example of public law; it governs the activities of various businesses. Whether a regulated business may stop a proposed regulation by the Occupational Safety and Health Administration (OSHA) that will require all noise to be reduced to very low decibels but that will raise costs excessively is an administrative law problem.

Other areas of the law, such as contract rights and duties, fall within the private law category. A businessperson who sues a supplier for breaking a contract or a pedestrian who sues a motorist for running into her or him is using private law. If a

Exhibit 1-1 Subject Matter Divided Into Substantive Law and Procedural Law

SUBSTANTIVE LAW	PROCEDURAL LAW
Administrative law	Administrative procedure
Banking law	Appellate procedure
Computer law	Civil procedure
Contract law	Criminal procedure
Constitutional law	Rules of evidence
Corporate law	
Criminal law	
Domestic relations law	
Estate law	
Media law	
Partnership law	
Property law	
Tax law	
Tort law	

state government contracts to have a classroom building erected at the state university, this contract will fall under public law because the government is involved. Public law is involved if a gardener employed by the state university, while driving a university truck, hits a pedestrian. See Exhibit 1–2 for some examples of public and private law.

Civil Law Versus Criminal Law

Civil law encompasses the legal rights and duties that exist among persons or between citizens and their governments. Corporation law, partnership law, and contract law, for example, are part of civil law. Civil law is concerned with a person's legally recognized rights and duties in relationship with others.

Criminal law involves a violation or wrong committed against society as a whole. Acts that are criminal are defined by statutes enacted by the local, state, or federal government. Criminal law is always public law, whereas civil law is sometimes public and sometimes private. In a criminal case, the government seeks to impose a penalty, such as a fine, a term of imprisonment, or even the death penalty, on an accused person. In civil law the person is seeking damages and/or other remedies. All law that is not classified as criminal is civil.

Courts of Law Versus Courts of Equity

Today the distinction between law and equity is primarily of historical interest, but understanding the differences between these two concepts is essential to understanding the modern court system and its remedies.

Courts of Law: Remedies at Law

The difference between **courts of law** and **courts of equity** evolved over a long period of time. The early English courts were severely restricted in the kinds of **remedies** (legal means to recover a right or redress a wrong) that they could grant. The **plaintiff** (the person seeking relief from a harm) would sue the **defendant** (the person accused of causing harm) by going to court to claim what was rightly his or hers.

The court could award land, items of value, money, or any combination of these three as compensation to the plaintiff. The courts that awarded these compensations became known as courts of law, and the three remedies were called **remedies at law.** Over the centuries, the courts of law became so strict that the only means of appeal was to petition the king.

Courts of Equity: Equitable Remedies

Unable to hear all the appeals, the king appointed an adviser, called a **chancellor,** to hear the petitions. The chancellor had the ability to grant new and unique remedies that fit the facts of the particular case. Eventually, a new body of rules and remedies was established. These courts in time became known as courts of equity and the relief granted as **equitable remedies.** Equity courts were grounded in justice and fair dealing; these courts furnished more equitable and adequate remedies than the remedies available in courts of law.

Plaintiffs had to decide whether they were going to file a lawsuit in a court of law or in a court of

Exhibit 1-2 Examples of Public Law and Private Law

PUBLIC LAW	PRIVATE LAW
Administrative law	Agency law
Appellate procedure	Commercial law
Civil procedure	Computer law
Constitutional law	Contract law
Criminal procedure	Corporation law
Rules of Evidence	Mining law
Tax law	Property law
	Tort law

equity based on the remedy they were seeking. Courts of law could grant only damages. Courts of equity could force a person to do or not to do something. The effect of the strictness of the courts of law several centuries ago still lingers in the consciousness of society through such adages as "You must cross every *t* and dot every *i*" when dealing with legal matters.

Merging of the Two Court Systems

In most states the courts of law and the courts of equity have merged. In these states most distinctions between the two have disappeared. A plaintiff may request both legal and equitable remedies in the same action, and the trial court judge may grant either or both forms of relief.

Yet the merging of the courts of law and equity has not diminished the importance of distinguishing legal remedies from equitable remedies. To request the proper remedy, students of the legal environment must be aware of the various types of equitable and legal remedies available.

Distinctions

Three distinctions exist between courts of law and courts of equity. First, courts of law award money damages while courts of equity grant other types of relief, such as **specific performance** (the contract must be specifically performed according to its terms) and **injunctions** (usually to prohibit someone from doing something, such as going on strike). In the end, the person seeking equity may end up with a money award, but that was not the primary relief he or she originally sought.

Second, a jury is allowed in a court of law, while in an equity court the judge makes the decision. Historically, juries were never used in courts of equity. Today, an advisory jury is available when equitable relief is sought, but its decision is not binding. The right to a jury in a court of law in a civil suit is preserved by the Seventh Amendment of the Constitution.

Third, the courts of law are bound by the **statute of limitations,** which sets out a specific time period during which a lawsuit must be filed or forever barred. The statute of limitations is measured in specific years. For example, if a contract has been broken, the person may be able to sue

anytime during a four-year period. If the person sues one day after the four years have passed, his or her case will not be heard by a court.

Courts of equity are bound by the **doctrine of laches.** This doctrine holds that individuals who fail to act promptly to protect their rights will not be helped by the court. (See Legal Highlight, maxim number six.) In other words, a person must sue within a reasonable time period or be forever barred from suing. For example, if a business is seeking an injunction to prevent the labor union from striking, the management must act within a reasonable time, usually a few days. Because of the nature of the cases heard, it is impossible to set specific time limits. A reasonable time may range from a few days to several decades.

Specific Types of Equitable Remedies

Equitable remedies try to correct a situation so that the harmed party may find relief.

Specific Performance A plaintiff may ask a court of equity to issue a decree of specific performance, which orders a defendant to perform the acts that he or she promised in a contract. The subject matter of the contract must be unique before a court will order specific performance. For example, in most states, land is considered to be unique. So is personal property that is, considered one of a kind, like the Hope diamond. A court of law can only order payment of money or property for damages; in many cases, this is not a satisfactory remedy. The buyer of the Hope diamond, for instance, wants the gem, not money damages. A court of equity can order the seller of the diamond to turn over the diamond to the buyer.

Injunctions A plaintiff may want to prevent or to stop a certain activity from happening. For example, a corporation may want to stop a union from striking. The corporation can file a lawsuit in a court of equity requesting that the union be ordered not to strike. The order is called a negative injunction. A negative injunction is an order to any person to refrain from or to stop doing a particular act.

Rescission A person signs and performs a contract because of the other party's misrepresentations. Once the misrepresentation is discovered,

LEGAL HIGHLIGHT   Equitable Maxims

When making a decision with regard to equitable remedies, judges are guided by equitable principles. These principles were developed over the past centuries and are based on common sense. Examples of equitable maxims are:

1. Whoever seeks equity must do equity.
2. Equality is equity.
3. Where there is equal equity, the law must prevail.

4. One seeking the aid of an equity court must come to the court with clean hands.
5. Equity will not suffer a right to exist without a remedy.
6. Equity aids the vigilant, not those who rest on their rights.

The last maxim means individuals who fail to look out for their rights until after a reasonable time has passed will not be helped. It forms the doctrine of laches discussed in the text.

---

the injured party wants to return to the position she or he had before signing the contract. The equitable remedy of **rescission** is available. Rescission cancels the agreement and reinstates the parties to the contract to the status quo. Before rescission will be granted, the injured party must show that she or he relied on the misrepresentations when signing the contract. If the equity court grants rescission, the plaintiff is entitled to any property or money that changed hands because of the contract returned to her or him. All duties created by the agreement are rescinded.

For example, a sales agreement is made because the seller misrepresents the quality of goods. If the fraud is discovered before any money changes hands, the buyer will want to have the agreement rescinded—an equitable remedy. If, however, money has been exchanged and the buyer has already resold some of the goods, the buyer will want a remedy at law and will seek money damages for harm suffered.

Administrative Agency Regulations

An **administrative agency** is created when the executive or legislative branch of the government delegates some of its authority to an appropriate administrative body. Since the days of President Franklin Roosevelt's New Deal, government agencies have proliferated in the United States. Federal agencies include the Federal Communications Commission, the Federal Aviation Administration, the National Labor Relations Board, the Occupational Safety and Health Review Commission, the Environmental Protection Agency, the Internal Revenue Service, the Food and Drug Administration, and the Interstate Commerce Commission. There are also state and local boards and agencies, such as environmental agencies, public utility commissions, and pardon and parole boards. Many agencies are found in the executive branch of government.

These agencies exercise legislative, executive, and judicial power. In making rules, the agencies are using legislative power; in enforcing their rules, they are using executive power; and in their adjudication procedures, they are using judicial power. Unlike legislators, presidents, governors, and many judges, administrative agency personnel are rarely chosen by popular elections, and most do not serve fixed terms. As a result, great power is given to people who may not be responsive to the public.

Federal, state, and local administrative agencies have expanded the number of their rulings at what appears to be an exponential rate. Some observers and citizens believe that the United States is in danger of having an overly bureaucratic government. We will examine administrative agencies in more detail in Chapter 4.

Locating Case Law

Except for the federal courts, New York, and California, few states publish the opinions of their trial courts. Decisions of trial courts are filed in the offices of the clerks of the courts but are available for public inspection. Most decisions of state trial courts are not published in any reporting system.

Appellate Court Decisions

Most decisions by courts of appeals are published and distributed. **Appellate courts** hear the appeals of decisions made by the trial courts. These reported cases make up the common law. Appellate court cases that are concerned with legal issues of great importance to society are published. The other appellate court decisions (approximately 40 percent of all decisions) are not reported, although they are available to the public. The cases in this book have been taken from reported appellate court decisions. It is, therefore, important to understand the case reporting system.

Reporter **Systems for Case Decisions**   The reported appellate decisions are published in volumes called *Reports* or *Reporters,* which are numbered consecutively. Many state appellate court decisions are published by the state governments. These state-published *Reports* are called "official reports"; however, they usually are about a year behind in publication. State cases also appear in regional units of the *National Reporter System,* published privately by West Publishing Company. These are called "unofficial reports."

Most lawyers and libraries have the West reporters because cases are published more quickly and are distributed more widely than the state-published reports. Because of the completeness of the *National Reporter System* and the quick publication of the latest cases (usually two weeks), many states have eliminated their own reports in favor of West's *National Reporter System.* These states have designated the *National Reporter System* as the official reports for their state cases.

West Publishing Company has divided the states into geographical areas (see Exhibit 1–3): Atlantic (A. or A.2d), South Eastern (S.E. or S.E.2d), South Western (S.W. or S.W.2d), North Western (N.W. or N.W.2d), North Eastern (N.E. or N.E.2d), Southern (So. or So.2d), and Pacific (P. or P2d). The first set of initials in each pair represents the first series; the initials that have 2d behind them are known as the second series. All of the regional *Reporters* are now in the second series, where all the new cases appear.

In addition, West Publishing Company distributes a number of specialized *Reporters.* United States court of appeals decisions are found in the *Federal Reporter* (F. or F.2d), while federal district court decisions are printed in the *Federal Supplement* (F.Supp.). Decisions concerning the federal rules of procedure are given in the *Federal Rules Decisions* (F.R.D.). Bankruptcy cases are reported in the *West's Bankruptcy Reporter* (B.R.).

Decisions made by the United States Supreme Court are found in the official reports printed by the United States Government Printing Office and called *United States Reports* (U.S.). Two unofficial reports publish privately these same decisions, *Supreme Court Reporter* (S.Ct.), published by West Publishing Company, and *Lawyers' Edition of the United States Supreme Court Reports* (L.Ed.), published by Lawyers Co-operative Publishing Company and Bancroft-Whitney Company.

How to Read a Citation   After appellate decisions are published, they are normally referred to (or cited) by giving the name of the case; the volume, name, and page of the state report (if any); the volume and page of the *National Reporter;* and the volume, name, and page of any other selected case series. For example, consider the following case: *Friedman v. C & S Car Service,* 108 N.J. 72, 527 A.2d 871 (1987). After the names of the parties, we see that the opinion in this case may be found in volume 108 of the official New Jersey *Reports* (published by the state of New Jersey) on page 72 and in volume 527 of the *Atlantic Reporter,* Second Series (published by West Publishing Company), on page 871. The year of filing of the appellate court decision is 1987.

In the title of a case, *Friedman v. C & S Car Service,* the *v.* or *vs.* stands for versus, which means against. When the case is appealed, the appellate court will sometimes place the name of the party appealing the decision first. In some states the appellate courts retain the trial court

Exhibit 1–3 *National Reporter System—Regional/Federal*

Regional Reporters	Coverage Beginning	Coverage
Atlantic Reporter	1885	Connecticut, Delaware, Maine, Maryland, New Hampshire, New Jersey, Pennsylvania, Rhode Island, Vermont, and District of Columbia Municipal Court of Appeals
North Eastern Reporter	1885	Illinois, Indiana, Massachusetts, New York and Ohio
North Western Reporter	1879	Iowa, Michigan, Minnesota, Nebraska, North Dakota, South Dakota and Wisconsin
Pacific Reporter	1883	Alaska, Arizona, California, Colorado, Hawaii, Idaho, Kansas, Montana, Nevada, New Mexico, Oklahoma, Oregon, Utah, Washington and Wyoming
South Eastern Reporter	1887	Georgia, North Carolina, South Carolina, Virgina and West Virginia
South Western Reporter	1886	Arkansas, Kentucky, Missouri, Tennessee, and Texas
Southern Reporter	1887	Alabama, Florida, Louisiana and Mississippi

Federal Reporters		
Federal Reporter	1880	United States Circuit Court from 1880 to 1912; Commerce Court of the United States from 1911 to 1913; District Courts of the United States from 1880 to 1932; U.S. Court of Claims from 1929 to 1932 and since 1960; the U.S. Court of Appeals from its organization in 1891; the U.S. Court of Customs and Patent Appeals from 1929; and the U.S. Emergency Court of Appeals from 1943.
Federal Supplement	1932	United States Court of Claims from 1932 to 1960; United States District Courts since 1932; United States Customs Court since 1956.
Federal Rules Decisions	1939	United States District Courts involving the Federal Rules of Civil Procedure since 1939 and Federal Rules of Criminal Procedure since 1946.
Supreme Court Reporter	1882	U.S. Supreme Court beginning with the October term of 1882.
Bankruptcy Reporter	1980	Bankruptcy decisions of U.S. Bankruptcy Courts, U.S. District Courts, U.S. Courts of Appeals and the U.S Supreme Court.
Military Justice Reporter	1978	United States Court of Military Appeals and Courts of Military Review for the Army, Navy, Air Force and Coast Guard.

NATIONAL REPORTER SYSTEM MAP

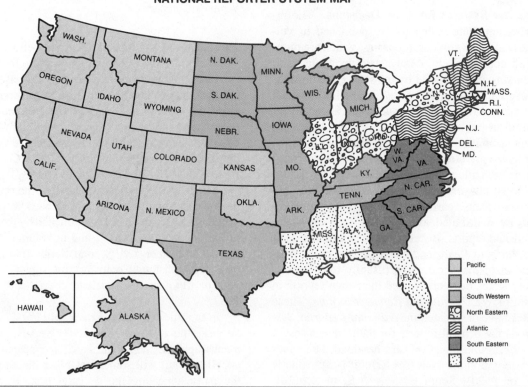

order of names; thus, it is impossible to distinguish the plaintiff from the defendant in the title of a reported appellate court decision. The facts of each case must be read carefully in order to identify each party; otherwise, the discussion by the appellate court will be difficult to understand.

Statute Publications Statutes are also published, but they are published by topic, while cases are published in chronological order. The citations for statutes are also different from those for cases. In a case citation, the first number is the volume number, and the last number is the page where the case is found. In a statutory citation, the first number is the title number, and the second number is the section number.

Federal statutes are found in the *United States Code* (U.S.C., published by the United States Government Printing Office) and the *United States Code Annotated* (U.S.C.A., published by West Publishing Company). The annotated statutes provide a summary and a list of cases decided under that statute.

For example, the federal criminal statutes are found in Title 18. Coincidentally, eighteen volumes comprise Title 18. A citation to a particular statute reads 18 U.S.C.A. § 2113. The number 18 is the title number, not the volume number. Section numbers are printed on the binding of statute volumes. You look for the volume that contains Section 2113, which is the federal criminal statute entitled "Bank Robbery and Incidental Crimes." The statute itself takes up only two pages; a one-paragraph discussion of the appellate court cases that have been decided involving Section 2113 follows the statute. Then, it takes 258 pages to list all the cases that have been decided under this particular section. In contrast, some statutes do not have any related cases because these laws are not controversial; the statutes requiring a birth certificate are examples.

Legal Research by Computers

Technology has developed computers large enough to handle the memory and the storage data bases (collections of information) necessary for computerized legal research. The two most widely used high-speed data-delivery systems are WESTLAW and LEXIS. WESTLAW is a computer-assisted legal research service of West Publishing Company. LEXIS, provided by Mead Data Central, Inc., provides a similar service. Each system has data-base-access software that allows researchers to interact with the delivery system.

In the WESTLAW data-delivery system, data are stored at West's headquarters in Saint Paul, Minnesota. User interaction with the data-delivery system can be initiated anywhere in the world from a computer terminal or a personal computer running a special WESTLAW access program. The WESTLAW user sends a query, or message, to the computer. The query is processed, and information stored in the computer is identified to answer the message. The information is transmitted back to the user where it is seen on a video display terminal (VDT) and can be printed as "hard copy" on paper. The information displayed on the VDT can also be stored on the user's storage equipment, such as a diskette.

WESTLAW, LEXIS, and similar computerized data-search systems are able to access virtually every case, statute, or regulation in the United States with a minimum of time and effort. Today, the latest cases are available within three days on the computer, far in advance of the printed copies that are sent to law libraries and subscribers.

Analyzing Case Law: A Supreme Court Case

The study of reported cases requires an understanding and application of legal analysis. The following excerpt is part of a case that was decided by the Supreme Court in 1985. Each of the different sections of the case are described in order to help you read the other cases in this book. All the cases have been edited. Three asterisks (* * *) indicate that part of the opinion within a paragraph or sentence has been deleted to make the case more concise and readable. Four asterisks (* * * *) mean that one or more paragraphs have been omitted. Any citations by the court of other cases have been omitted to make the case more readable.

The following case involves a federal question. The Supreme Court granted a **writ of *certiorari.*** This writ is the decision by an appellate court to hear an appeal. In this case, the Supreme Court had the discretion to decide whether it would hear the appeal. (Writs of certiorari are discussed in more detail in Chapter 2)

The Supreme Court had to determine whether a student had the right to retake an examination that he had failed. He was required to pass the examination in order to continue his studies toward a medical degree. The student took the legal position that he had a property right in his continued enrollment. He further argued that his dismissal was arbitrary and capricious and therefore his substantive due process rights were violated.

In its analysis, the Supreme Court used prior case decisions (precedent) to resolve the issues before the Court: What authority did a university have in dismissing students, and what procedure did the university have to follow?

1 — **REGENTS OF THE UNIVERSITY OF MICHIGAN v. EWING**

2 — Supreme Court of the United States, 1985.
474 U.S. 214, 106 S.Ct. 507, 88 L.Ed.2d 523.

3 — Justice STEVENS delivered the opinion of the Court.

4 —
Respondent Scott Ewing was dismissed from the University of Michigan after failing an important written examination. The question presented is whether the University's action deprived Ewing of property without due process of law because its refusal to allow him to retake the examination was an arbitrary departure from the University's past practice. The Court of Appeals held that his constitutional rights were violated. We disagree.

In the fall of 1975 Ewing enrolled in a special 6-year program of study, known as "Inteflex," offered jointly by the undergraduate college and the Medical School. An undergraduate degree and a medical degree are awarded upon successful completion of the program. * * *

In the spring of 1981, after overcoming certain academic and personal difficulties, Ewing successfully completed the courses prescribed for the first four years of the Inteflex program and thereby qualified to take the NBME Part I. Ewing failed five of the seven subjects on that examination, receiving a total score of 235 when the passing score was 345. (A score of 380 is required to state licensure and the national mean is 500.) Ewing received the lowest score recorded by an Inteflex student in the brief history of that program.

5 —
On July 24, 1981, the Promotion and Review Board individually reviewed the status of several students in the Inteflex program. After considering Ewing's record in some detail, the nine members of the Board in attendance voted unanimously to drop him from registration in the program.

In response to a written request from Ewing, the Board reconvened a week later to reconsider its decision. Ewing appeared personally and explained why he believed that his score on the test did not fairly reflect his academic progress or potential. After reconsidering the matter, the nine voting members present unanimously reaffirmed the prior action to drop Ewing from registration in the program.

In August, Ewing appealed the Board's decision to the Executive Committee of the Medical School. After giving Ewing an opportunity to be heard in person, the Executive Committee unanimously approved a motion to deny his appeal for a leave of absence status that would enable him to retake Part I of the NBME examination. In the following year, Ewing reappeared before the Executive Committee on two separate occasions, each time unsuccessfully seeking readmission to the Medical School. On August 19, 1982, he commenced this litigation in the United States District Court for the Eastern District of Michigan.

* * * *

The District Court held a 4-day bench trial at which it took evidence on the University's claim that Ewing's dismissal was justified as well as on Ewing's allegation that other University of Michigan medical students who had failed the NBME Part I had routinely been given a second opportunity to take the test.

* * *

Ewing discounted the importance of his own academic record by offering evidence that other students with even more academic deficiencies were uniformly allowed to retake the NBME Part I. * * * The statistical evidence indicated that of the 32 standard students in the Medical School who failed Part I of the NBME since its inception, all 32 were permitted to retake the test, 10 were allowed to take the test a third time, and 1 a fourth time. Seven students in the Inteflex program were allowed to retake the test, and one student was allowed to retake it twice. Ewing is the only student who, having failed the test, was not permitted to retake it. Dr. Robert Reed, a former Director of the Inteflex program and a member of the Promotion and Review Board, stated that students were "routinely" given a second chance. * * *

* * * *

* * * The District Court, however, found no violation of Ewing's due process rights. The trial record, it emphasized, was devoid of any indication that the University's decision was "based on bad faith, ill will or other impermissible ulterior motives"; to the contrary, the "evidence demonstrated[d] that the decision to dismiss plaintiff was reached in a fair and impartial manner, and only after careful and deliberate consideration." To "leave no conjecture" as to his decision, the District Judge expressly found that "the evidence demonstrate[d] no arbitrary or carpricious action since [the Regents] had good reason to dismiss Ewing from the program."

Without reaching the state-law breach-of-contract and promissory-estoppel claims, the Court of Appeals reversed the dismissal of Ewing's federal constitutional claim. * * *

[I]t concluded that the University had arbitrarily deprived him of that property in violation of the Fourteenth Amendment because (1) "Ewing was a 'qualified' student, as the University defined that term, at the time he sat for NBME Part I"; (2) "it was the consistent practice of the University of Michigan to allow a qualified medical student who initially failed the NBME Part I an opportunity for a retest"; and (3) "Ewing was the only University of Michigan medical student who initially failed the NBME Part I between 1975 and 1982, and was not allowed an opportunity for a retest.'' * * *

8 —

We granted the University's petition for certiorari to consider whether the Court of Appeals had misapplied the doctrine of ''substantive due process.'' We now reverse.
* * * *

9 —

Ewing's claim, therefore, must be that the University misjudged his fitness to remain a student in the Inteflex program. The record unmistakably demonstrates, however, that the faculty's decision was made conscientiously and with careful deliberation, based on an evaluation of the entirety of Ewing's academic career. When judges are asked to review the substance of a genuinely academic decision, such as this one, they should show great respect for the faculty's professional judgment. Plainly, they may not override it unless it is such a substantial departure from accepted academic norms as to demonstrate that the person or committee responsible did not actually exercise professional judgment.
* * * *

10 —

This narrow avenue for judicial review precludes any conclusion that the decision to dismiss Ewing from the Inteflex program was such a substantial departure from accepted academic norms as to demonstrate that the faculty did not exercise professional judgment. Certainly his expulsion cannot be considered aberrant when viewed in isolation. The District Court found as a fact that the Regents ''had good reason to dismiss Ewing from the program.'' Before failing the NBME Part I, Ewing accumulated an unenviable academic record characterized by low grades, seven incompletes, and several terms during which he was on an irregular or reduced course load. Ewing's failure of his medical boards, in the words of one of his professors, ''merely culminate[d] a series of deficiencies. . . . In many ways, it's the straw that broke the camel's back.'' Moreover, the fact that Ewing was ''qualified'' in the sense that he was eligible to take the examination the first time does not weaken this conclusion, for after Ewing took the NBME Part I it was entirely reasonable for the faculty to reexamine his entire record in the light of the unfortunate results of that examination. Admittedly, it may well have been unwise to deny Ewing a second chance. Permission to retake the test might have saved the University the expense of this litigation and conceivably might have demonstrated that the members of the Promotion and Review Board misjudged Ewing's fitness for the medical profession. But it nevertheless remains true that his dismissal from the Inteflex program rested on an academic judgment that is not beyond the pale of reasoned academic decisionmaking when viewed against the background of his entire career at the University of Michigan, including his singularly low score on the NBME Part I examination.

11 — ⌐ The judgment of the Court of Appeals is reversed, and the
└ case is remanded for proceedings consistent with this opinion.

Review of the Case

1. The name of the case is *Regents of the University of Michigan v. Ewing*. The names are in this order because the case was appealed to the United States Supreme Court by the regents of the University of Michigan after they lost in the lower appellate court. You never can be sure what the role of the party is unless you read the case. The only exception is that all lawsuits filed at the trial court level will have the plaintiff listed first.

2. The Supreme Court of the United States heard this case in 1985. This court is the highest appellate court in the United States. The citation (the information below the case name) discloses the name and level of the court. The numbers and letters found below the court name indicate to lawyers and researchers how to find the case in the library or computer. This case can be found in volume 474 of *United States Reports* on page 214; it can also be found in volume 106 of the *Supreme Court Reporter* on page 507; and it can be found in volume 88 of the Lawyer's Edition on page 523.

3. Justice Stevens delivered the opinion of the Supreme Court. The United States Supreme Court has a chief justice and eight associate justices.

4. The opinion begins with a recital of the facts, followed by a discussion of the law.

5. In this opinion, the Court first reviews the procedure followed by the university before Ewing filed a lawsuit in federal district court (the trial court).

6. Then the Court discusses what transpired during the trial in district court. Normally, the trial court decides all the facts that are being contested.

7. The United States Supreme Court states in a very brief summary on what basis the court of appeals reversed the trial court's decision.

8. The loser of that decision, the regents, petitioned the United States Supreme Court for a writ of *certiorari*. The Court granted the writ, which means that the Court agreed to review the lower court's decision. At this point, the Supreme Court gives its **holding**—that is, the decision of the case. The decision of the appeals court was reversed, and the district court's decision was affirmed.

9. The Supreme Court gives the legal reasoning that supports its decision. The Court reasons that, in reviewing an academic decision, courts must give great respect to faculty judgment. A substantial departure from academic norms must exist to warrant a reversal of a faculty decision.

10. The Court applies its rule of law to the facts of the case. The findings of fact by the district court were very persuasive in the Supreme Court's reversal of the court of appeals' decision.

11. Appellate courts generally do not have the power to enter a judgment for either party. Judgments are rendered by trial courts. This is why the Supreme Court remands (sends back) the case to the district court and does not enter a judgment.

How to Brief a Case

In order to understand the law and its implications with respect to business, you must be able to read and understand court decisions. One method of case analysis, often referred to as a briefing, facilitates such an understanding. There is a fairly standard procedure that may be followed when briefing a case in this book or in any other book. First, read the case carefully. When you believe that you understand the case, you can prepare a brief of it. Briefing a case while reading the case for the first time does little to enhance your legal education.

Although the format of a brief may vary, it will typically contain the following essentials:

1. Full case citation, including the name of the case and the date it was decided.
2. Facts.
3. Issue(s).
4. Holding.
5. Reasoning (including policy).

In preparing a brief, you should incorporate all the important facts, but a brief should of course, be short. The following illustrates a brief of the case we have just analyzed.

CASE CITATION:

REGENTS OF THE UNIVERSITY OF MICHI-
GAN v. EWING
Supreme Court of the United States, 1985.
474 U.S. 214, 106 S.Ct. 507, 88 L.Ed.2d 523.

FACTS:

Ewing was disqualified from continuing his education because he failed an examination. His prior
academic record was weak. He was, however, the
only student out of thirty-three students not allowed to retake the examination.

ISSUE:

Did the university action deprive Ewing of his
property without due process of law?

HOLDING:

A court cannot override a university decision concerning academic affairs unless it is such a substantial departure from academic norms as to demonstrate an absence of professional judgment.

REASONING:

The Supreme Court held that the university had
handled Ewing's dismissal in a professional manner. His academic record was very weak, and this
fact could be taken into consideration when deciding not to allow him to retake the examination.

Traditional Versus
Environmental Approach to the Law

We can begin to understand something about the
nature of law by looking at two approaches to the
study of it. The traditional approach sees law as
a body of principles and rules that courts apply in
deciding disputes. The study of law, then, is the
study of these rules and the general principles of
right and wrong on which the rules are based.
Reason and logic tell how the rules should be
applied in specific cases. The traditional approach
is based on the idea that the principles of right
and wrong change, if at all, less rapidly than society changes. This approach fulfills one of the
important functions of law—to provide stability,
predictability, and continuity so that people can
know how to order their affairs.

The environmental approach sees law as only
one part of the total environment of society. Law
is the institution that specializes in social control,
and other parts of society act on and influence it.
Studying the process by which the broader society
shapes the rules to govern itself is part of the study
of law. In the legal world, this approach is known
as sociological jurisprudence. The legal environmentalist emphasizes how social change is accomplished by using the legal system and how law
functions to provide an orderly process for social
change. The environmentalist believes that, if law
fails to adapt to changes in technology, attitudes,
and organization, social change may become violent.

In this book, you will be using the legal environmental approach to study business. You will
be studying the breadth of the law as it applies to
business as opposed to studying business law, which
focuses in depth on only certain laws. The business world and the principles on which it is based
are shaped in part by the legal environment. Other
outside forces also help to shape the rules by which
business is conducted. The interplay between logic
and social pressure, the tension between stability
and change, and the strain between predictability
and flexibility—all affect both the legal and business worlds. Neither world is wholly independent
of the other.

How To Find An Attorney

How do you find a competent attorney when you need one? the best method is the oldest method, asking your friends and acquaintances. A good attorney has a good reputation; word-of-mouth recommendations, even in this age of high technology, are still very reliable.

The yellow pages of your telephone directory provide a second method. Most attorneys specialize in a certain legal area, such as real estate, bankruptcy, or taxation. Many lawyers indicate their specialty in advertisements. Unfortunately, very few bar-certified specialties are actually authorized. A licensed attorney can place his or her name under most of the headings without having passed any special examinations and without having any length of experience in that particular field. You will have a better chance of finding a knowledgeable attorney if you find a lawyer who is bar certified or who is not listed under any other heading than the specialty you need.

Most local bar associations have a referral service. Attorneys register their area of expertise with the bar association. For a small fee you can have an initial interview with these attorneys. Last, certain books, such as the **Martindale-Hubbell Law Directory,** list attorneys and their specialties. These books are found in local libraries, and they list the lawyer's specialty, age, sex, years of practice, the schools from which the lawyer graduated, and a list of the partners in the law firm.

Lawyers may be hired on a contingent-fee basis. If the lawyer wins the case for the clients, his or her fee is taken from the amount of the award. Thus, the fee is contingent on the lawyer winning an award, either in court or through negotiations, for the client. Often this is the only way a person can afford an attorney. Lawyers may also be hired on an hourly rate, or for a fixed fee (such as $500 for handling a noncontested divorce without property settlement).

A good practice is to speak with several attorneys before deciding which one you want to retain. It is very important that you and the attorney have a good working relationship. Ask about the attorney's fees and the costs involved, the time required to resolve the case, whether the case will go to court or be settled, and what the settlement terms should be. Go prepared with a list of questions just as you would for any other business appointment.

Summary

What is law? No one definition of the law exists, and law is only one part of the total environment of society.

Several schools of legal philosophy exist. The natural school presupposes an ideal state of being in which there is a definite right or wrong and on which law is based, while the historical school emphasizes the evolution of the law based on its origins and history. The sociological school emphasizes discovery of the law through observation of society. The analytical school uses logic to shape the law, while legal realists view the law as a means to a social end. The economic school holds that laws may be evaluated in accordance with economic theory.

The courts examine various sources of the law when making a decision. If applicable, the state or federal constitution, statutes, and regulations are examined. Additionally, the courts review the case law.

The law can also be classified in several ways: substantive law or procedural law, public law or private law, and civil law or criminal law. Finally, the remedies that a court can apply can be divided into remedies at law and equitable remedies. Courts of law allow monetary damages, use juries, and apply the statute of limitations. Courts of equity are able to grant remedies other than monetary damages, have no right to use a jury, and apply the doctrine of laches.

Key Terms

administrative agency (**14**)	equitable remedies (**12**)	procedural law (**11**)
administrative law (**11**)	historical school (**4**)	public law (**11**)
analytical school (**5**)	holding (**21**)	remedies (**12**)
appellate courts (**15**)	injunctions (**13**)	remedies at law (**12**)
Bill of Rights (**6**)	judicial review (**6**)	rescission (**13**)
chancellor (**12**)	jurisprudence (**4**)	Restatements (**5**)
checks and balances (**6**)	law (**4**)	sociological school (**4**)
civil law (**12**)	law merchant (**8**)	specific performance (**13**)
common law (**5**)	legal realist (**5**)	*stare decisis* (**7**)
constitutional law (**11**)	*National Reporter System* (**15**)	statute of limitations (**13**)
courts of equity (**12**)	natural law school (**4**)	statutes (**7**)
courts of law (**12**)	ordinances (**7**)	substantive law (**10**)
criminal law (**11**)	plaintiff (**12**)	Uniform Commercial Code
defendant (**12**)	precedent (**7**)	(**10**)
doctrine of laches (**13**)	private law (**11**)	writ of *certiorari* (**17**)
economic school (**5**)	probate (**5**)	

Questions and Case Problems

1. Define the word law.

2. What is the difference between common law and statutory law? Judges are able to overrule common law by making a different decision in a later case based on similar facts. Should judges have the same authority to overrule statutory law?

3. Explain the following philosophies of law:
  a. natural law school
  b. historical school
  c. sociological school
  d. analytical school
  e. legal realists
  f. economic school

4. What are three differences between courts of law and courts of equity?

5. What are remedies at law? What are equitable remedies?

6. Discuss fully which of the following breach-of-contract situations warrants specific performance or only money damages as a remedy.
  (a) Norma signs a contract to sell her house and lot to Jethro. A few days later she finds another buyer who is willing to pay a higher price. Norma now refuses to sell to Jethro. What remedies are available to Jethro?
  (b) Y–U, a rock-and-roll group, contracts to appear for a week at a Las Vegas hotel showroom for a month. Two days before the scheduled engagement, the group informs the management that it refuses to appear. What remedies are available to the Las Vegas hotel?
  (c) Ronald signs a contract to purchase a rare stamp owned by George, who is breaking up his stamp collection. Before the stamp is turned over to Ronald, George decides to keep the stamp collection and refuses to deliver the stamp to Ronald. What rights does Ronald have to the stamp?

7. Laurel offers to sell his automobile to Hardy. Laurel tells Hardy that the car has been driven only 25,000 miles and has never been in an accident. Hardy hires Mike, a mechanic, to appraise the condition of the car. Mike believes that the car has been driven at least 50,000 miles and appears to have been in an accident. In spite of Mike's report, Hardy decides the car is a good buy for the price and purchases the car. Later, the car develops numerous mechanical problems. Hardy seeks to rescind the contract on the basis of Laurel's misrepresentations of the car's condition. Will Hardy be able to rescind the contract? Please explain your answer.

Chapter 2   The Judicial System and Litigation

It is the fundamental obligation of every civilized government to provide a system of impartial courts which can fairly adjudicate disputes involving its citizens.

Islamic Republic of Iran v. Pahlavi,
94 A.D.2d 374, 464 N.Y.S.2d 487 (1983).

OUTLINE

Introduction

Why does a businessperson need to understand the judicial system and how cases are litigated? First, everyone should have a basic working knowledge of the structure of the court system, both at the state and federal level. This knowledge leads to a better understanding not only of how the system operates but also of the flaws in the system that need correction. Second, basic knowledge of how a trial proceeds is necessary in order to understand the reports of trials covered in the newspapers and on television.

Third, as taxpayers, businesspeople have an interest in whether the system works as efficiently as possible without sacrificing the protections it should provide. Finally, the businessperson needs to understand what he or she will confront when involved in litigation. In our society, almost all businesspeople will be involved in litigation at some point in their careers.

This chapter will look at both the state and federal court systems and will follow a sample case from beginning to end. In studying the courts and their procedures, the first question is which court has the power to decide a particular case—that is, which court has jurisdiction.

Jurisdiction

Juris means law; *diction* means to speak. Thus, the power to speak the law is the literal meaning of the term **jurisdiction.** Before any court can legally hear a case, it must have jurisdiction—the power to decide that case. In order for a court to exercise valid authority, it must have jurisdiction over the person against whom the suit is brought and over the subject matter of the case. Without jurisdiction, a court has no power to act, and any judgment it enters is null and void.

Proper jurisdiction ensures that a judgment obtained in one state is enforceable in all other states where the defendant may be located or owns property. The **full faith and credit clause** of the Constitution mandates the enforcement of judgments made in sister states.

Jurisdiction over the Person and Property

In order to consider a case, a court must have power over the person or, in some cases, the property of the person against whom a suit is brought. A state court's power is limited to the territorial boundaries of the state in which the court is located. Therefore, a court has jurisdiction over anyone who can be served with a summons within those boundaries, unless that person's presence was obtained by fraudulent means. Jurisdiction over the person is known as *in personam* **jurisdiction.**

First, the court has jurisdiction over any resident of the state and over any person who does business within the state. Second, the court has jurisdiction over a nonresident who has committed a wrong within the state, such as being at fault in an automobile accident or having sold defective goods within the state. The court can exercise jurisdiction over the nonresident person by using the authority of a **long arm statute.** A long arm statute allows a state, through its courts, to obtain jurisdiction over a defendant who lives beyond its geographical boundaries when two conditions are met: The person committed the wrongful act within the state, and the traditional notions of fair play and substantial justice are met.

Third, a court can exercise jurisdiction over any corporation that has been incorporated in that state, even if the corporation has its main plant or office in another state. The state also has jurisdiction over any corporation that does substantial business within the state, even if the corporation does not have an office in that state.

In all cases where a court exercises personal jurisdiction, the defendants must be served with actual notice that they are being sued (usually by service of a summons and complaint). If the defendants are out of state, they may be served either by a person or by a certified letter which the defendant must sign and which contains the summons and complaint.

When a person cannot be located but owns property in the state, *in rem* **jurisdiction** applies.

A court has jurisdiction over **real property** (land and anything permanently fixed to the land) within its boundaries and generally has jurisdiction over other types of property also located within the state. If an individual owns property within a state and the property is the subject of the lawsuit, a court in that state can exercise jurisdiction even if the owner is outside the state. A court can also use property within a state to help satisfy a judgment debt. The court may render a decision covering the property but cannot impose liability on the owner when it has only *in rem* jurisdiction.

Subject-Matter Jurisdiction

Subject-matter jurisdiction imposes a limitation on the types of cases a court can hear. The limitation is set by the constitution or statute creating the court. A court's subject-matter jurisdiction can be limited not only by the subject of the lawsuit but also by the amount of money in controversy, by the type of criminal case, or by whether the proceeding is a trial or an appeal. Probate courts (courts that handle only matters relating to wills and estates) and small-claims courts (courts that handle cases involving small amounts of money) are examples of courts with limited subject-matter jurisdiction.

Subject-matter jurisdiction may limit the court's authority strictly to the property that is before the court. This is called **quasi in rem jurisdiction.** For example, in a divorce case, a court obtains jurisdiction over the marriage (the property) if one person (the plaintiff) resides within the state. *Quasi in rem* jurisdiction allows the court to grant a divorce but without personal jurisdiction over the defendant. This type of jurisdiction permits the court to order child support or alimony payments be paid by the divorced spouse out of property under the court's jurisdiction. (In certain cases involving children, statutes enable a plaintiff to reach out-of-state property of a divorced parent who is not meeting court-ordered support obligations.)

Venue

Jurisidiction is concerned with whether a court has authority over a specific subject matter or individual. **Venue** is concerned with the particular geographic area within a judicial district where a suit should be brought. The concept of venue reflects the policy of convenience. A trial court should be in the geographic neighborhood where the incident leading to the suit occurred or where the parties involved in the suit reside. Pretrial publicity or other factors may require a change of venue— that is, moving the trial to another community. A change of venue is used frequently in criminal cases if the defendant's right to a fair and impartial jury is impaired.

Court Systems in the United States

Today in the United States, at least fifty-two separate court systems are functioning. Each of the fifty states, the District of Columbia, and the federal government have their own fully developed and independent court systems.

The federal court system is authorized by Article III, Section 2, of the United States Constitution. The federal courts—that is, the system as a whole—are not superior to the state courts; they are simply an independent system. The United States Supreme Court is the final controlling voice over all the court systems, at least when questions concerning the Constitution, federal statutes, or treaties are involved.

A Typical State Court System

Most court systems, including the federal system, are based on a three-tiered model. Any person who is a party to a lawsuit typically has the opportunity to **plead** (or present) the case before a trial court and then, if he or she loses, before two levels of appellate courts. In other words, a case first proceeds through a trial court, which is, as its name implies, where trials are held and testimony is taken. The loser has the legal right to appeal the case to an appellate court. These courts review the decision of the lower court only on points of law; the facts of the case are not retried. The loser of the decision by the appellate court may appeal to the state supreme court. If a federal issue is involved in the decision of the state supreme court, that decision may be appealed to the United States Supreme Court.

Exhibit 2–1 depicts a typical state court system. It has three main tiers: (1) the trial court of general or limited jurisdiction, (2) the appellate court, and (3) the supreme court.

General and Limited Jurisdiction Trial Courts Trial courts that have **general jurisdiction** can hear cases on a variety of subject matters. Other trial courts have **limited jurisdiction** and can hear only cases on a specific subject matter. For example, a probate court, family court, criminal court, municipal court, or small-claims court cannot hear cases that go beyond its stated jurisdiction. A criminal court can hear only criminal

Exhibit 2–1 Hypothetical State Court System

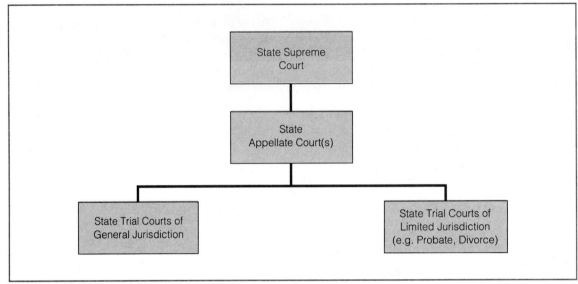

cases; the judge has no authority to make decisions in a divorce case, which must be heard by a family court. Trial courts have **original jurisdiction**— that is, cases in trial courts are coming before a court for the first time to be resolved.

The state constitution and statutes determine how a court system will work in that particular state. Trial courts are called by many names, such as county, district, superior, or circuit courts. For example, in Ohio the trial court is called the court of common pleas, while in New York the trial court is called the supreme court.

Appellate Courts In some states, trial courts of general jurisdiction also have limited jurisdiction to hear appeals from the lower judiciary, such as small-claims court or traffic courts. Generally, the term appellate court refers to the higher reviewing courts and not to trial courts with limited appellate review.

Appellate courts are also called courts of appeal or courts of review. Every state has at least one appellate court. The appellate court has **appellate jurisdiction**—that is, the court hears appeals only on issues of law. Many states have intermediate reviewing courts and one supreme court. The intermediate appellate court is often called the court of appeals, while the highest court of the state is normally called the supreme court.

New York, however, calls its highest court the Court of Appeals.

Appellate courts do not try cases that they are reviewing. Examination of the written record of the case on appeal is made by the justices to determine whether the trial court committed an error of law. The appellate courts look at questions of law and procedure, not questions of fact. The only time an appellate court disagrees with a trial court's findings of fact is when the finding is clearly erroneous—that is, when it is contrary to the evidence presented at trial or when there is no evidence to support the finding. Otherwise, the trial court determines all questions of fact.

The decisions of each state's highest court in all questions of state law are final. It is only when questions of federal law are involved that a state's highest court can be overruled by the United States Supreme Court.

The Federal Court System

The federal court system is similar in many ways to most state court systems. Also three tiered, it consists of: (1) trial courts, (2) intermediate courts of appeal, and (3) the Supreme Court. The federal government also has special courts. Exhibit 2–2 shows the organization of the federal court system in some detail.

Exhibit 2-2 Organization of the Federal Court System

CLAIMS COURT

Original Jurisdiction
1. Claims against the United States government except for tort claims.

COURT OF INTERNATIONAL TRADE

COURT OF APPEALS FOR THE FEDERAL CIRCUIT

Appellate Jurisdiction
1. Appeals from the Court of International Trade except where direct review may be had by the Supreme Court.
2. Appeals from the Patent and Trademark Office and the International Trade Commission, and review of certain findings of the Secretary of Commerce (28 U.S.C.A. § 1544) and the Secretary of Agriculture (7 U.S.C.A. § 2461).
3. Appeals from district courts in cases relating to patents or plant variety protection, and in cases related to claims against the United States government except for Tort Claims Act cases and internal revenue cases.

COURTS OF THE TERRITORIES AND INSULAR POSSESSIONS

Puerto Rico — Guam — Virgin Islands — Northern Marianas.
Mixed local and federal jurisdiction.

SUPREME COURT OF THE UNITED STATES

Original Jurisdiction
1. Cases in which a state, ambassador, public minister or consul is a party.

Appellate Jurisdiction
1. Cases from any federal court in which an act of Congress is held unconstitutional in a civil action to which the federal government or one of its employees is a party.
2. Cases from a federal court of appeals in which a state statute is held to be invalid because it violates a federal law.
3. Cases where the highest court of appeals of a state holds a federal law invalid or upholds a state law that has been challenged as violating the U.S. Constitution, or other federal law or treaty.
4. Appeals from certain orders of three judge courts.
5. Cases on writ of certiorari involving important federal questions.

COURTS OF APPEALS OF THE UNITED STATES AND THE DISTRICT OF COLUMBIA

Appellate Jurisdiction
1. Appeals from decisions of district courts except where direct review may be had by the Supreme Court.
2. Review of decisions and enforcement of orders of federal administrative agencies.

DISTRICT COURTS OF THE UNITED STATES

Original Jurisdiction
1. Federal questions (cases arising under the Constitution, laws, or treaties of the U.S.).
2. Diversity of citizenship cases where the amount in controversy exceeds $10,000.
3. Federal crimes and criminal proceedings against federal officers.
4. Judicial review of actions of administrative agencies.
5. Admiralty and Maritime cases.

Appellate Jurisdiction
1. Cases appealed from the bankruptcy court unless (a) the circuit court has created a three judge bankruptcy panel to handle appeals or (b) both parties consent to take the appeal directly to the circuit court.

Three Judge District Courts
1. Actions required by Congress to be heard by a three judge court.

U.S. TAX COURT

U.S. BANKRUPTCY COURT
11 U.S.C.A. § 11

HIGHEST STATE COURTS

SPECIAL COURT REGIONAL RAIL REORGANIZATION
45 U.S.C.A. §§ 719, 743.

UNITED STATES COURT OF MILITARY APPEALS

Appellate Jurisdiction
1. All cases in which sentence affects a general or flag officer or extends to death.
2. All cases sent by the Judge Advocate General.
3. All cases in which review is granted.

DEPARTMENTS, AGENCIES AND OFFICERS

Administrator of Environmental Protection Agency
Administrator of Federal Aviation Administration
Attorney General
Benefits Review Board
Longshoremen's and Harbor Workers' Compensation
Civil Service Commission
Commissioner of Administration on Aging
Commodity Futures Trading Commission
Comptroller General
Consumer Product Safety Commission
Copyright Royalty Tribunal
Federal Communications Commission
Federal Deposit Insurance Corporation
Federal Election Commission
Federal Energy Regulatory Commission
Federal Home Loan Bank Board
Federal Maritime Commission
Federal Mine Safety and Health Review Commission
Federal Reserve System, Board of Governors
Federal Savings and Loan Insurance Corporation
Federal Trade Commission
Foreign Trade Zones Board
Immigration and Naturalization Service
Interstate Commerce Commission
Maritime Administration
National Labor Relations Board
National Transportation Safety Board
Nuclear Regulatory Commission
Occupational Safety and Health Review Commission
Postal Services, Board of Governors
Railroad Retirement Board
Saint Lawrence Seaway Development Corporation
Secretary of Agriculture
Secretary of Commerce
Secretary of Defense
Secretary of Education
Secretary of Energy
Secretary of Health and Human Services
Secretary of Labor
Secretary of Housing and Urban Development
Secretary of Transportation
Secretary of the Treasury
Securities and Exchange Commission
Small Business Administration
Subversive Activities Control Board

Article III of the United States Constitution establishes the one Supreme Court. Congress is empowered to create such other inferior courts as it deems necessary. Inferior courts include the United States courts of appeal, the district courts, and the other courts of limited, or specialized, jurisdiction.

District Courts   At the federal level, the trial court of general jurisdiction is the district court. Every state has at least one federal district court located within its boundaries. Congress has divided the states and territories into ninety-five federal judicial districts, a number that will be reduced to ninety-four when the district court in the Canal Zone has been phased out. The number of judicial districts varies over time primarily because of population changes and corresponding caseloads.

An entire state can comprise a single district, or a state can be divided into several districts. Large states, such as California, have more than one judicial district. With one exception, the districts do not cross state lines; that exception is the district of Wyoming, which includes sections of Yellowstone National Park located in Montana and Idaho. The number of judges assigned to a district will likewise vary based on population and caseload.

Most federal cases originate in the United States district courts. Whenever there are two or more district courts within a single state, there is limited geographical jurisdiction in each court. The state of Florida, for example, has district courts for northern, middle, and southern Florida; thus, a case that arises in the southern Florida district cannot be tried by a court in the northern district, unless a motion for a change of venue has been granted.

United States district courts have original jurisdiction in federal matters—that is, federal cases start in the district courts. Other trial courts with original, albeit special or limited, jurisdiction are the United States Tax Court, the United States Bankruptcy Court, and the United States Claims Court (which hears claims against the United States on federal contracts). Certain administrative agencies and departments with quasi-judicial power also have original jurisdiction. These agencies and departments are listed in Exhibit 2–2.

Courts of Appeal   Congress has established twelve judicial circuits; each hears appeals from the district courts located within its respective circuit, or region. There is also a thirteenth circuit, the Federal Circuit, which has national jurisdiction limited by subject matter. Exhibit 2–3 shows these judicial circuits. The courts located within a judicial circuit are called courts of appeal or circuit courts. The decision of a court of appeal is final unless the Supreme Court accepts the case on appeal. Appeals from decisions made by federal administrative agencies, such as the Federal Trade Commission, are also heard by the United States courts of appeals.

Supreme Court of the United States   The highest level of the federal court system is the Supreme Court of the United States. The Supreme Court consists of nine justices. This number is not set by the Constitution, but it has been nine ever since the Civil War. All federal judges are appointed by the president of the United States and confirmed by the Senate. Under Article III, they "hold their Offices during Good Behavior"; Congress does have the power to impeach judges but rarely has this been done. All federal judges (with few exceptions—such as Bankruptcy judges) hold virtual lifetime appointments.

The Supreme Court has original, or trial, jurisdiction in rare instances as set forth in Article III, Section 2. Most of the time it operates as an appellate court. The Supreme Court can review any case decided by any of the federal courts of appeals; it also has appellate authority over cases decided in the state courts that involve a federal issue.

Jurisdiction of Federal Courts

Because the federal government is a government of limited powers, the jurisdiction of the federal courts is limited. Although the Constitution sets the outer limits of federal judicial power, Congress sets other limits on federal jurisdiction. The courts themselves can also establish rules that limit the types of cases they will hear. Federal courts hear cases that have certain characteristics, which the following subsections examine.

Exhibit 2-3 Judicial Circuits for the United States Courts of Appeals

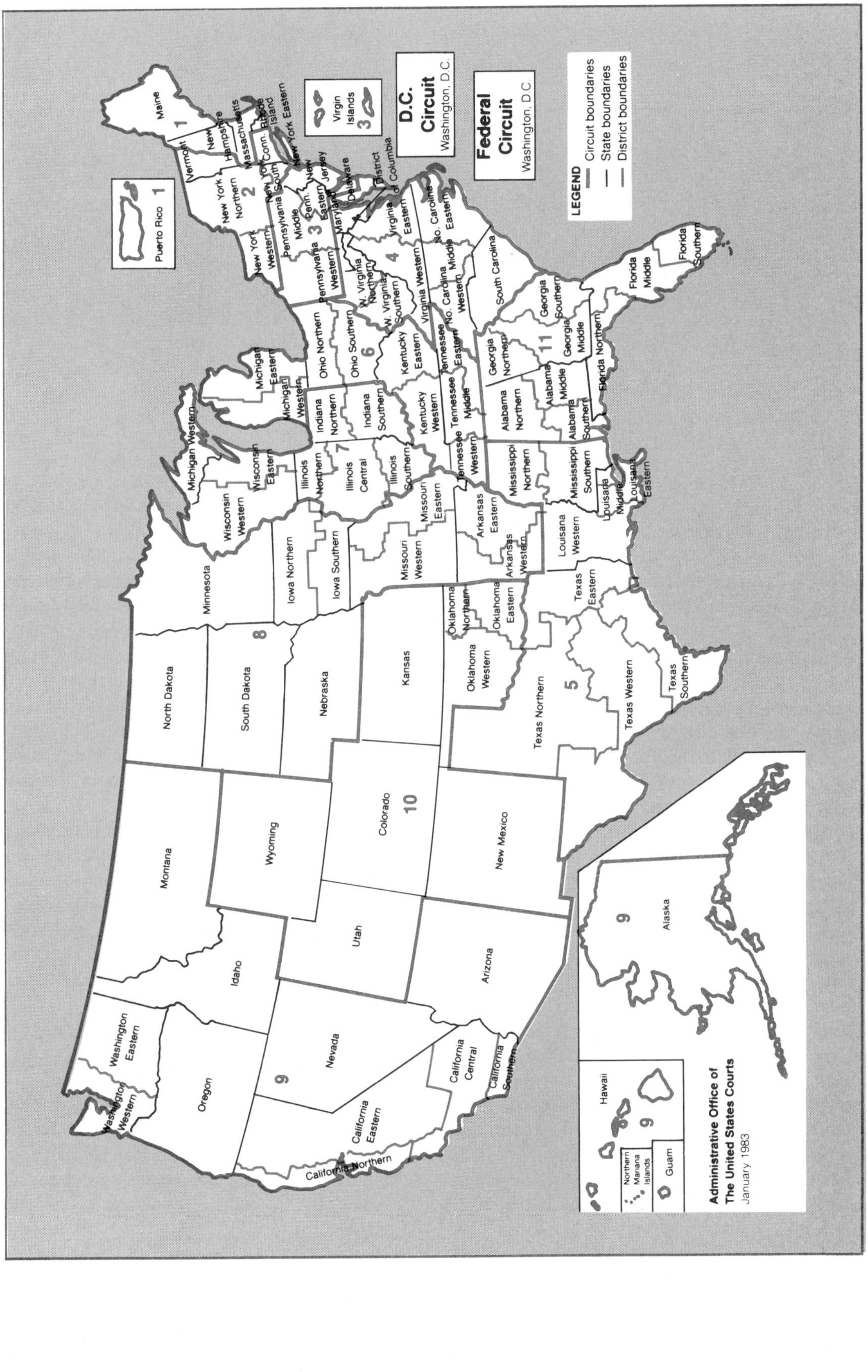

LEGEND
— Circuit boundaries
— State boundaries
— District boundaries

D.C. Circuit
Washington, D.C.

Federal Circuit
Washington, D.C.

Administrative Office of
The United States Courts
January 1983

| LEGAL |
| HIGHLIGHT   **Another Level of Appeals Court?** |

Of the over 5,000 cases appealed each year to the Supreme Court of the United States, the Court will decide approximately 200. Leading jurists are considering the establishment of a new national appellate court. In particular, the new court would hear cases from the various courts of appeals that have reached opposite decisions on similar cases. For example, the Second Circuit (which includes New York) may have decided that computer equipment is deductible for income tax purposes, while the Ninth Circuit (which includes California) may not allow this deduction. As a result, citizens are treated differently under the same federal income tax rules.

Cases of this type need to be resolved by one court but do not demand the attention of the Supreme Court. If another court were created, the Supreme Court would have more time to hear cases that have important public policy implications. Former Chief Justice Warren Burger has been extremely active in supporting the creation of this new court.

Which Cases Reach The Supreme Court?

No absolute right of appeal to the United States Supreme Court exists. Its jurisdiction is appellate "with such Exceptions, and under such Regulations as the Congress shall make." Thousands of cases are filed with the Supreme Court each year; yet it hears, on average, only about 200. To bring a case before the Supreme Court, a party requests the Court to issue a writ of *certiorari*.

Federal Question Lawsuits   Whenever a plaintiff's cause of action is based, at least in part, on the United States Constitution, a treaty, or a federal law, a **federal question** arises, and the case comes under the jurisdiction of federal courts. People whose claims are based on rights granted by an act of Congress can sue in a federal court along with those who claim that their constitutional rights have been violated. Any lawsuit involving a federal question can originate in a federal court. For example, all bankruptcy cases must be brought in federal court. No minimum dollar amount in controversy is required where federal courts have exclusive jurisdiction—that is, where the suit must be brought in federal court.

Diversity of Citizenship Lawsuits   **Diversity of citizenship** cases involve: (1) citizens of different states, (2) a foreign country as plaintiff and citizens of a state or different states, and (3) citizens of a state and citizens or subjects of a foreign country. In diversity of citizenship cases, however, the amount in controversy must be more than $50,000 before a federal court can take jurisdiction. Diversity of citizenship lawsuits do not involve a federal question.

Consider this example: Smith is driving from his home state, New York, to Florida. In Georgia he runs into a car owned by Able, a citizen of Georgia. Able's new Mercedes is demolished, and, as a result of the personal injuries she sustained in the accident, Able is unable to work for six months. The property damage is $35,000, and her loss of income for the six months is $18,000. Thus, this case involves more than $50,000 worth of damages. Able can sue Smith either in Georgia or in the federal district court. Georgia has *in personam* jurisdiction through its long arm statute. By driving on the Georgia highways, Smith has consented to Georgia jurisdiction. If Smith is sued in Georgia, Smith can have the suit removed to a federal district court on the basis of diversity of citizenship.

LEGAL HIGHLIGHT   **The Friday Conference**

On Friday mornings promptly at nine-thirty a buzzer summons the nine justices to an all-day meeting. Entering the conference room, each justice shakes hands with the other eight, a ritual started in the 1880s to symbolize harmony. The nine justices are William J. Brennan, Jr. (1956), Byron R. White (1962), Thurgood Marshall (1967), Harry A. Blackmun (1970), William H. Rehnquist, chief justice of the United States (1972), John Paul Stevens (1975), Sandra Day O'Connor (1981), Antonin Scalia (1987), and Anthony Kennedy (1988).

Once the door is shut, no one else is allowed in the room—no law clerks, no secretaries, no pages, no security personnel— another custom, started in 1907. The junior justice takes care of the coffee, answers the door (should anyone dare to knock), and handles all messages and documents.

The justices have assigned seats based on seniority; the chief justice sits at the east end of the table, and the senior associate justice sits at the west end. Behind each justice is a cart that holds his or her books and papers. The

volumes of the *United States Reports,* containing every decision made by the body since its first decision, line the walls.

The conference has two purposes: to vote on the cases already argued during the week and to select new cases for the Court to review. Only a few cases make it to the "Discuss List." Every justice has already screened each case, so the cases are processed quickly. Of the cases originally on the Discuss List, rarely more than six survive to be heard by the Court. During these conferences, each justice tries to persuade the others of his or her point of view; in the effect, the other justices serve as a jury. It is this persuasion process that eventually produces the consensus for a coherent Court decision.

Although much is known about the procedure of the Friday conference, the heart of the conference—the exchange of ideas and arguments among the justices—is not revealed. The justices customarily destroy their conference papers, and they rarely talk about the sessions.

Concurrent Versus Exclusive Jurisdiction

When both federal and state courts have the power to hear a case (such as in diversity of citizenship cases) there is **concurrent jurisdiction.** When cases can be tried only in federal or only in state courts, there is **exclusive jurisdiction.** Federal courts have exclusive jurisdiction in cases involving federal crimes, bankruptcy, patents, copyrights, and in lawsuits against the United States. States have exclusive jurisdiction in some other types of legal matters—for example, divorce, probate, or adoption cases.

Writ of *Certiorari*

When a writ of *certiorari* is granted, the Supreme Court orders a lower court to send the record of

a case to it for review. Parties may petition the Supreme Court to issue a writ of *certiorari.* Whether the Court will issue the writ is entirely at its discretion; it is not required under any circumstances to issue a writ of *certiorari.*

The Court has the discretion to issue a writ in the following situations:

■ When a state court has decided a substantial federal question that has not been determined by the Supreme Court before or when the state court has decided it in a way that is probably in disagreement with the trend of the Supreme Court's decisions.
■ When two federal courts of appeals are in disagreement with each other.
■ When a federal court of appeals has decided an

important state question in conflict with that state's law, has decided an important federal question not yet addressed by the Court but that should be decided by the Court, has decided a federal question in conflict with applicable decisions of the Court, or has departed from the accepted and usual course of judicial proceedings.

■ When a federal court of appeals holds that a state statute is invalid because it violates federal law.

■ When the highest state court of appeals holds a federal law invalid or upholds a state law that has been challenged as violating federal law.

■ When a federal court holds an act of Congress unconstitutional and the federal government or one of its employees is a party.

Most petitions for writs of *certiorari* are denied. A denial is not a decision on the merits of a case,

nor does it indicate agreement with the lower court's opinion. Denial of the writ has no value as precedent. The court will not issue a writ unless at least four justices approve it. Typically, only the petitions for cases that may raise important constitutional questions are granted writs of *certiorari*.

Judicial Review

Very early in the history of our country, the United States Supreme Court decided that it had the power of judicial review, as mentioned in Chapter 1. The Constitution does not provide for the courts to declare a statute unconstitutional; through the decision in the following case, the Supreme Court decided it had such power.

Case 2.1
MARBURY v. MADISON
Supreme Court of the United
States, 1803.
5 U.S. (1 Cranch) 137,
2 L.Ed. 60.

BACKGROUND AND FACTS *As a result of the national elections of 1800, the political party controlling the White House and Congress changed from Federalist to Republican, and President John Adams lost his bid for reelection to Thomas Jefferson. Believing that the Republicans would weaken the national government, Adams, during the final hours of his administration, made fifty-nine midnight appointments to the judiciary. He hoped to "pack" the court with loyal Federalists before Jefferson took office.*

Adams nominated William Marbury as a justice of the peace for Washington, D.C. The United States Senate ratified the appointment, and the commission was signed by Adams. Adams's secretary of state, John Marshall, delivered forty-two of the fifty-nine appointments before he left office. Under Jefferson's administration, however, the new secretary of state, James Madison, refused to deliver the commission to Marbury. Marbury, along with three others, decided to sue.

Before the government changed, the Federalist Congress had passed a law (the Judiciary Act of 1789) concerning, in part, the issuance of a **writ of mandamus**—*that is, a writ to enforce the performance of a public duty. The writ was to be issued directly by the United States Supreme Court, effectively making it a trial court. This statute greatly expanded the powers of the United States Supreme Court. It was on the basis of this new law that Marbury sued.*

In an unusual turn of events, John Marshall had gone from being secretary of state under Adams to chief justice of the United States Supreme Court (appointed by Adams). Today, any judge would remove himself or herself from the case because of conflict of interest, but Marshall heard the Marbury *case and wrote the opinion.*

Chief Justice MARSHALL delivered the opinion of the Court.

*   *   *   *

The act to establish the judicial courts of the United States authorizes the supreme court, "to issue writs of *mandamus,* in cases warranted by the principles and usages of law, to any courts appointed or persons holding office, under the authority of the United States." The secretary of state, being a person holding an office under the authority of the United States, is precisely within the letter of this description; and if this court is not authorized to issue a write of *mandamus* to such an officer, it must be because the law is unconstitutional.

*   *   *   *

The question, whether an act, repugnant to the constitution, can become the law of the land, is a question deeply interesting to the United States; but, happily, not of an intricacy proportioned to its interest. It seems only necessary to recognize certain principles, supposed to have been long and well established, to decide it. That the people have an original right to establish, for their future government, such principles, as, in their opinion, shall most conduce to their own happiness is the basis on which the whole American fabric has been erected.

*   *   *   *

It is emphatically the province and duty of the judicial department to say what the law is. Those who apply the rule to particular cases, must of necessity expound and interpret that rule. If two laws conflict with each other, the courts must decide on the operation of each.

So if a law be in opposition to the constitution; if both the law and the constitution apply to a particular case, so that the court must either decide that case conformably to the law, disregarding the constitution; or conformably to the constitution, disregarding the law; the court must determine which of these conflicting rules governs the case. This is of the very essence of judicial duty.

If, then, the courts are to regard the constitution, and the constitution is superior to any ordinary act of the legislature, the constitution, and not such ordinary act, must govern the case to which they both apply.

Those, then, who controvert the principle that the constitution is to be considered, in court, as a paramount law, are reduced to the necessity of maintaining that courts must close their eyes on the constitution, and see only the law.

This doctrine would subvert the very foundation of all written constitutions. It would declare that an act which, according to the principles and theory of our government, is entirely void, is yet, in practice, completely obligatory. It would declare that if the legislature shall do what is expressly forbidden, such act, notwithstanding the express prohibition, is in reality effectual. It would be giving to the legislature a practical and real omnipotence, with the same breath which professes to restrict their powers within narrow limits. It is prescribing limits, and declaring that those limits may be passed at pleasure.

*   *   *   *

Thus, the particular phraseology of the constitution of the United States confirms and strengthens the principle, supposed to be essential to all written constitutions, that a law repugnant to the constitution is void; and that courts, as well as other departments, are bound by that instrument.

The rule must be discharged.

DECISION AND REMEDY

The Court held unconstitutional the provision of the Judiciary Act of 1789 that gave original jurisdiction to the U.S. Supreme Court to issue writs of mandamus.

COMMENT   *Marshall was faced with a dilemma. If he exercised the authority given the Court by Congress to issue the writ of* mandamus *and thus order Madison, the new secretary of state, to deliver the commissions, Madison could refuse. The Court has no way to enforce its orders because it has no enforcement machinery. If Marshall did not issue the order, the secretary of state would end up being allowed to choose which acts he would perform.*

Marshall took another approach altogether: He found the act of Congress unconstitutional. The Constitution clearly sets out the cases over which the Court has original jurisdiction. No power was given to Congress to expand the Court's original jurisdiction. Since Congress did not have that power, the congressional act was declared unconstitutional by the Supreme Court. Marshall went on to say that Jefferson and Madison had acted incorrectly in refusing to deliver Marbury's commission, but the Supreme Court did not issue any order because it found that it did not have that power.

Marshall avoided a confrontation with the president by not ordering him to do anything, found that the president had acted incorrectly, and firmly established the doctrine of judicial review. Marshall did not create this doctrine; it was based on previous English and American legal decisions. The case also illustrates that a situation revolving around an insignificant fact, such as an appointment as justice of the peace, can lead to a monumental judicial decision, in this case the establishment of judicial review.

Judicial Procedures: Following a Case Through the Courts

American courts use the **adversary system** of justice. The judge plays an unbiased and mostly passive role. The lawyer functions as the client's advocate; he or she presents the client's version of the facts in order to convince the judge or the jury (or both) that the client's version is true.

Judges do not have to be entirely passive. They are responsible for the appropriate application of the law. They do not have to accept the legal reasoning of the attorneys; they can base a ruling and a decision on their own study of the law. Judges sometimes ask questions of witnesses and even suggest types of evidence to be presented. For example, if an indigent defendant chooses to act as her or his own counsel, the judge will often play more of an advocate role, intervening during the trial proceedings to help the defendant.

Procedure

Procedure involves the way disputes are handled in the courts. Procedural law establishes the rules and standards for resolving these disputes. The rules are very complex and vary from court to court. There is a set of federal rules of procedure, and there are various sets of procedural rules in the state courts. In addition, rules of procedure differ between criminal and civil cases.

A Sample Case

We will now follow a civil case through the state court system. The case involves a standard collection account by Acme Copiers, Inc. Lakin, the owner of a small accounting firm, has used Acme copies for several years. Acme believes that Lakin owes it money on a copier that it sold to Lakin. Lakin and Acme are unable to agree on a settlement through an alternative dispute resolution method, which we will discuss in Chapter 5. As a result, Acme files a lawsuit against Lakin; this makes Acme the plaintiff and Lakin the defendant in the case. Both parties have lawyers.

Pleadings and Process   A **pleading** is a document that is written by one of the parties to the lawsuit and is sent to the other party (or parties) and to the court to be included in the judge's case file. The purpose of a pleading is to provide information to the other parties. The following are the more well-known pleadings:

1. A complaint
2. An answer
3. A counterclaim
4. A cross-claim
5. A replay
6. A third-party complaint

Process is an order that comes from the court and is signed by the judge or judge's representative, such as the clerk of the court. A piece of process (the actual document) goes through three steps: issued, served, and filed. A judge *issues* a piece of process that orders a person affiliated with the case to do something. A copy of the process is *served* on the person by a process server, usually a marshal or sheriff, or an authorized private party. A party to the lawsuit cannot personally serve any papers involved with that suit. The process server *files* the process by returning it to the court case file with a notation as to when, where, and how the process was served.

The following is a partial list of documents that are known as process:

1. Summons—requires the defendant to defend against the claim of the plaintiff (pretrial).
2. Subpoena—requires the attendance of a witness (pretrial or during trial).
3. Subpoena *duces tecum*—requires evidence to be brought to court (pretrial or during trial).
4. Writs of attachment.
5. Writs of garnishment.
6. Writs of execution.

⎫
⎬ These are issued to assist a party in the collection of his or her claim after that party has received a judgment in his or her favor.
⎭

A **complaint** is one type of pleading, while a **summons** is one type of process. In our case, Acme's lawsuit (or action) against Lakin will start when Acme's lawyer files a complaint (sometimes called a petition or declaration) with the clerk of the trial court in the appropriate geographical area (the proper venue). The summons will then be issued by the court. The complaint informs the defendant why he or she is being sued, while the summons notifies the defendant how many days he or she has to file an answer or response.

The complaint contains: (1) a statement alleging the facts necessary for the court to take jurisdiction, (2) a short statement of the facts necessary to show that the plaintiff has been harmed by the defendant and is entitled to a remedy, and (3) a statement of the remedy the plaintiff is seeking. A typical complaint is shown in Exhibit 2–4.

The complaint states that Acme is a duly organized corporation within the state and that Lakin is a resident of that county and state. Next, the facts are recited: Lakin agreed to purchase the copier, and he has not paid the monies he owes for it. The complaint goes on to state that Acme is entitled to $3,500 to cover the cost of the copier.

After the complaint has been filed, the process server will serve a summons and a copy of the complaint on the defendant, Lakin. This is the only time a pleading is served by a process server. Usually pleadings are mailed by the parties to each other or are personally delivered by messenger service.

A typical summons is shown in Exhibit 2–5. It notifies Lakin that he is required to prepare an answer to the complaint. The summons also informs Lakin that failure to file an answer will result in a judgment by default for the plaintiff. A copy of the answer must be filed with both the court and the plaintiff's attorney within a specified time period, usually twenty to thirty days after the summons has been served. If Lakin does not file an answer within the time period, Acme will win a **default judgment**.

Rules governing the service of a summons vary, but usually service is made by handing the summons to the defendant personally or by leaving it at the defendant's residence or place of business. In a few states, a summons and complaint can be served by mail. When the defendant cannot be reached, special rules sometimes permit serving the summons by publishing it in the newspaper or by leaving it with a designated person, such as the secretary of state. If the defendant has received technical notice through a mailing or by publication, the court usually will not have personal jurisdiction over the defendant but will have au-

Exhibit 2–4 A Typical Complaint

IN THE SUPERIOR COURT OF THE STATE OF ARIZONA
IN AND FOR THE COUNTY OF MARICOPA

ACME COPIERS, INC., an Arizona corporation,)))	No. _____
Plaintiff,)))	C O M P L A I N T
vs.)))	(Contract)
PAUL L. LAKIN, a single person,)))	
Defendant.))	

COMES NOW, the Plaintiff, ACME COPIERS, INC., by and through its attorney, I. M. GOODGUY, and for its cause of action against the Defendant claims and alleges as follows:

I

The Defendant, PAUL L. LAKIN, is a resident of Maricopa County, Arizona. The said Defendant caused events to occur within Maricopa County, Arizona, which gave rise to this Complaint. The Plaintiff is a duly organized corporation within the State of Arizona.

II

The Defendant, PAUL L. LAKIN, contracted with the Plaintiff to purchase a copy machine for $3,500.00. The copy machine was delivered by Plaintiff to the Defendant. Plaintiff then billed the Defendant on May 16, 1988, in the amount of $3,500.00. No payments have been received, which conduct constitutes breach of contract by the Defendant, PAUL L. LAKIN.

III

Plaintiff has made all demands or performed all other acts necessary to mature or accelerate the aforesaid amount. The Defendant is liable for the Plaintiff's reasonable attorney fees under Arizona Revised Statutes, Section 12-341.01.

WHEREFORE, Plaintiff respectively demands judgment against Defendant as follows:

1. For the sum of $3,500.00 as compensatory damages.
2. For reasonable attorney fees under Arizona Revised Statutes, Section 12-341.01, plus Court costs in bringing this action.
3. For interest on all said sums from May 16, 1988, until paid.
4. For such other relief as the Court deems just and proper.

DATED this _____ day of January, 1989.

I. M. GOODGUY
2001 N. Winning Trial Lane
Tempe, Arizona 85281
Attorney for Plaintiff

Exhibit 2–5 A Typical Summons

IN THE SUPERIOR COURT OF THE STATE OF ARIZONA
IN AND FOR THE COUNTY OF MARICOPA

ACME COPIERS, INC., an Arizona corporation,	))))	No. _____
Plaintiff,	))	S U M M O N S
vs.	)))	
PAUL L. LAKIN, a single person,	)))	
Defendant.	))	

THE STATE OF ARIZONA TO THE DEFENDANT:

PAUL L. LAKIN

If served within Arizona, you shall appear and defend within 20 days after the service of the Summons and Complaint upon you, exclusive of the day of service. If served, out of the State of Arizona— whether by direct service, by registered or certified mail or by publication—you shall appear and defend within 30 days after the service of the Summons and Complaint upon you is complete, exclusive of the day of service. Where process is served upon the Arizona Director of Insurance as an insurer's attorney to receive service of legal process against it in this state, the insurer shall not be required to appear, answer to plead until expiration of 40 days after date of such service upon the Director. Service by registered or certified mail without the State of Arizona is complete 30 days after the date of filing the receipt and affidavit of service with the Court. Service by publication is complete 30 days after the date of first publication. Direct service is complete when made. Service upon the Arizona Motor Vehicle Superintendent is complete 30 days after filing the Affidavit of Compliance and return receipt or Officer's Return.

YOU ARE HEREBY NOTIFIED that in case of your failure to appear and defend within the time application, judgment by default will be rendered against you for the relief demanded in the Complaint.

YOU ARE CAUTIONED that in order to appear and defend, you must either appear in person or file an Answer or proper response in writing with the Clerk of this Court, accompanied by the necessary filing fee within the time required, and you are required to serve a copy of any Answer or response upon the Plaintiff's attorney. Rules of Civil Procedure 10(d), Arizona Revised Statutes, Section 12-311; Rules of Civil Procedure 5, Arizona Revised Statutes, Sections 22-215, 22-216.

The name and address of the Plaintiff's attorney is:

I. M. GOODGUY
2001 N. Winning Trial Lane
Tempe, Arizona 85281

SIGNED AND SEALED this date: _____

JUDITH ALLEN
Clerk Superior Court

By _____
Deputy Clerk

LEGAL HIGHLIGHT   Singing the Courthouse Blues

Appearing at a concert in Portland, Oregon, on November 9, 1981, the Beach Boys—Al Jardine, Bruce Johnston, Mike Love, and Dennis Wilson—were provided security by off-duty deputies. Three of these deputies—Fred Byler, Donald Kerr, and Kevin McVicker—later sued the Beach Boys for $5.4 million. The deputies claimed they were battered and falsely imprisoned when they tried to take photographs of the musicians.

The Beach Boys were properly served with a summons and a copy of the complaint at another concert they were playing in Portland in February 1983. No appearance was made or answer filed, and in August 1984 a default judgment was entered against the Beach Boys for $5.4 million. Each deputy was granted an award of $300,000 in general damages and $1.5 million in punitive damages. That award was upheld in December 1985 by a judge in the Multnomah County Circuit Court.

The lesson: Never ignore a summons and complaint. If you do, you may be liable for the full amount of damages alleged in the plaintiff's complaint.

thority over the property the defendant owns that is located within the court's jurisdiction.

Choices Available after Receipt of the Summons and Complaint   Once the defendant is served with a copy of the summons and complaint, the defendant must file a responsive pleading. This filing must be done within the stipulated time period. Among the choices are: (1) to file a **motion to dismiss,** (2) to file an **answer** containing an **affirmative defense,** (3) to a file **counterclaim,** (4) to file an answer containing both an affirmative defense and a counterclaim, or (5) to do nothing and have a default judgment entered against the defendant.

Motion to Dismiss   If the defendant decides to challenge the sufficiency of the plaintiff's complaint, the defendant can present to the court a motion to dismiss, also called a demurrer. The motion to dismiss is an allegation that, even if the facts presented in the complaint are true, their legal consequences are such that there is no reason to go further with the suit and no need for the defendant to present an answer. It is a contention that the defendant is not legally liable even if the facts are as the plaintiff alleges. If, for example, Acme's complaint alleges facts that exclude the possibility of any breach of contract by Lakin, he can move to dismiss, and he will not be required to answer because his motion will be granted.

If Acme wants to discontinue the suit because, for example, an out-of-court settlement has been reached, Acme can move for dismissal. The court can also dismiss on its own motion. If the court grants the motion to dismiss, the judge is saying that the plaintiff has failed to state a recognized cause of action. The plaintiff generally is given time to correct the problem and file an amended complaint.

If the plaintiff does not file this amended complaint, a judgment will be entered against the plaintiff solely on the basis of the pleadings, and the plaintiff will not be allowed to bring suit on the matter again. On the other hand, if the court denies the motion to dismiss, the judge is indicating that the plaintiff has stated a recognized cause of action, and the defendant is given an extension of time to file a further pleading. If the defendant does not file the answer, a default judgment normally will be entered for the plaintiff.

Answer and Counterclaim   If the defendant does not choose to file a motion to dismiss or has filed a motion to dismiss that has been denied, an answer must be filed with the court. This document either admits the statements or allegations set out in the complaint or denies them and sets out any defenses that the defendant may have. In most answers, the defendant admits to part of the allegations, such as admitting venue, and denies other parts of the complaint, such as denying any breach of contract in this case.

If Lakin admits all of Acme's allegations in his answer, a judgment will be entered for Acme. If Lakin denies Acme's allegations, the matter will proceed to trial. If Lakin admits the facts but denies owing the money, no actual trial will take place. A trial is to determine the facts; since no facts are in dispute, the judge hears only arguments on the legal issues—in this case, the legal determination of whether there was a breach of contract by Lakin. If there was a breach of contract, he owes the money. If, however, Lakin can successfully raise an affirmative defense, he will win the case.

Lakin can admit the truth of Acme's complaint but raise new facts that will result in dismissal of the action. This is called raising an affirmative defense. For example, Lakin could admit that he was liable but plead that the time period for raising the claim has passed. Acme's complaint must therefore be dismissed because it is barred by the so-called statute of limitations. The factor that determines whether there will be a trial is whether both parties agree to the facts. If they do, no trial will be held, as the judge will only need to determine the law as to whether the money is owed.

Lakin can deny Acme's allegations and set forth his own claim against Acme, alleging that Acme's copy machine never functioned properly. This is called, appropriately, a counterclaim. If Lakin files a counterclaim, Acme will have to answer it with a pleading, normally called a reply, that has the same characteristics as an answer.

Dismissals and Judgments Before Trial   After the pleadings are finished—the complaint, answer, and any counterclaim and reply have been filed—either of the parties can file pretrial motions. A lawsuit can be shortened or a trial can be avoided by the use of motions. In fact, most lawsuits that are filed never come to trial. Numerous procedural avenues are available for disposing of a case without a trial. Usually a party attempts to have the case dismissed through the use of pretrial motions.

In order for a judge to grant a pretrial motion that would avoid a trial, there cannot be any genuine issues of fact in the case; the only question must be one of law. If there are any facts in dispute, there must be a trial. Only a fact finder, a jury, or a judge sitting alone (if the parties do not want a jury) can decide the facts of the case. If the motion is denied by the judge, the case proceeds to trial.

Motion for Summary Judgment   Either party may move for a **summary judgment.** When the court considers such a motion, it can take into account evidence outside the pleadings. Most of the time, the lawyers do not appear in person to argue the legal aspects before the judge; rather, they submit written legal briefs (arguments) that set out the law. The judge can then read these briefs in between court appearances and make her or his decision. For example, one party can bring in a sworn statement or affidavit that refutes the other party's claim. Unless the second party brings in affidavits of conflicting facts, the first party will normally receive summary judgment. Again, if the judge grants the motion, one party will have a judgment. If the judge denies the motion, the case continues.

Lakin, for example, can bring in the sworn statement of a witness that Lakin did not purchase a copier and that Acme has served the wrong Lakin. Unless Acme can bring in other statements raising the possibility that Lakin was the purchaser, Lakin will be entitled to dismissal on a motion for summary judgment. Motions for summary judgment can be made before a trial, but they will be granted only if it is truly obvious that there are no factual disputes.

Discovery   Before a trial begins, the parties can use a number of procedural devices to obtain information and to gather evidence about the case. Acme, for example, will want to know whether Lakin admits he received the copier, what malfunctioned on the copier, and why a rental unit was necessary. The process of obtaining information from the opposing party or from other witnesses is known as **discovery.** Discovery includes gaining access to witnesses, documents, records, and other types of evidence. The rules governing discovery are designed to make sure that a witness or party is not unduly harassed, that privileged material is safeguarded, and that only matters relevant to the case at hand are subject to the discovery.

Discovery serves several purposes. Evidence is preserved from witnesses who might not be available at the time of the trial or whose memories will fade as time passes. A witness's testimony is established so that the witness's credibility can be challenged at trial if that testimony changes. If discovery reveals that both parties agree on all the facts, a motion for a summary judgment may be made. If one party finds that the opponent's case is too strong to challenge, discovery can lead to an out-of-court settlement. Even if the case does go to trial, discovery prevents surprises by giving parties access to evidence that might otherwise be hidden. Also discovery serves to narrow the issues so that trial time is spent on the main questions in the case.

Discovery can involve the use of **oral depositions, written interrogatories,** or both. Oral depositions are sworn testimony by the opposing party or any witness, recorded by a court official. The person being deposed appears before a court officer and is sworn in. The person answers questions asked by the attorneys from both sides. The questions and answers are taken down and later transcribed by the court official. Today depositions may sometimes be videotaped. Even satellite transmission is used to allow a busy witness to stay on her or his job while answering questions for attorneys a continent away.

Written interrogatories consist of a series of written questions normally sent to the opposing party. The person, with the aid of an attorney, prepares written answers that are then signed under oath. The scope of interrogatories is broader than that of oral depositions; parties are obligated to answer questions even if the answer involves the disclosure of information from their records and files. Uniform interrogatories for specific types of cases, such as automobile accidents, have been developed to make the process more efficient.

Pretrial Hearing   Either party or the court can request a **pretrial hearing,** sometimes called a conference. Usually the hearing consists of an informal discussion between the judge and the op-

posing attorneys after discovery has taken place. The purpose of the hearing is to identify and narrow the amount of subject matter that is in dispute and to plan the course of the trial. The pretrial hearing is not intended to compel the parties to settle their case before trial, although judges may encourage them to settle out of court if circumstances suggest that a trial would be a waste of time.

The Trial   A trial procedurally consists of several steps from start to finish; it results when the parties are unable to reach a settlement. Although many trials are started, a large percentage are settled prior to their conclusion. About 95 percent of the lawsuits filed are settled out of court, mainly because of the time and expense of trying a case. Furthermore, of those cases that do finally go to trial, about 97 percent are resolved at the trial court level; relatively few trial court decisions are appealed, and even fewer are changed on appeal.

Jury Selection   A trial can be held with or without a jury. If there is no jury, the judge determines the truth of the facts alleged in the case. The right to a trial by jury does not have to be exercised, and many cases are tried without one. In most states and in federal courts, one of the parties in a civil trial must request a jury or else the right to a jury is waived.

If a jury is requested, the jury members are selected from a panel of citizens who have been ordered by the court to jury duty. The jury panel is subject to *voir dire* (questions) from the judge and from the attorneys for the parties. The questions are asked to determine if any potential jury member has a bias toward one side, has any connection with the parties, or is unable to serve for the whole time of the trial. In significant cases, attorneys may use a psychologist to help them select members of the jury. Jurors who are selected to hear the case are paid a small daily fee and mileage. The losing party normally must pay these costs.

In the case between Acme and Lakin, both parties want a jury trial. After the jurors are selected, they are impaneled, sworn in, and the trial is ready to begin.

Opening Statements   Both attorneys are allowed to make opening statements concerning the facts that they expect to prove during the trial. The plaintiff's attorney gives the first opening statement, followed by the defendant's opening statement.

Plaintiff's Case   Since Acme is the plaintiff, it has the burden of proving that its case is correct. After opening statements, Acme's attorney calls the first witness for the plaintiff and then examines the witness in what is called direct examination. After Acme's attorney has finished, the witness may be cross-examined by Lakin's attorney. After *cross-examination,* Acme's attorney has an opportunity to ask the witness further questions call redirect examination, and Lakin's attorney can follow with *recross-examination.* When both attorneys have finished with the first witness, Acme's attorney calls the succeeding witnesses in the plaintiff's case; each is examined first by Acme's attorney and then is subject to cross-examination by Lakin's attorney (and redirect and recross, if necessary). For both attorneys, the type of question asked and the way in which it is asked are governed by the rules of evidence. After the last of the plaintiff's witnesses has been examined, the plaintiff rests its case.

Defendant's Case   Lakin's attorney then presents the evidence and witnesses for Lakin's case. Witnesses for the defense are called and examined, and the attorney for Acme has a right to cross-examine them. There is also the right to redirect and recross-examine each witness. Evidence favorable to Lakin is introduced. After all evidence has been presented and all witnesses dismissed, the defendant rests its case.

When the defendant's attorney has finished the presentation of evidence, the plaintiff's attorney can present additional evidence to refute the defendant's case in a rebuttal. The defendant's attorney can meet that evidence in a rejoinder.

Burden of Proof   During any trial, the plaintiff always has the burden of proof. There are three standards of proof. If Acme is seeking monetary damages, the plaintiff's burden is to establish its case with a preponderance of the evidence. If, however, Acme were seeking an equitable remedy, it would be required to prove its case with a higher degree of evidence, sometimes called clear and convincing evidence. In order to prove a defendant guilty in a criminal case, the prosecution must prove its case "beyond a reasonable doubt."

Motions for Directed Verdicts   After the plaintiff's case has been presented, the defendant's attorney may ask the judge to direct a verdict on the grounds that the plaintiff has failed to present a sufficient case for jury consideration; thus, there can only be one verdict as a matter of law—for the defendant. This is referred to as a motion for a directed verdict. It is rarely granted at this stage of the trial.

After the defendant's case has been presented, either attorney may move for a directed verdict. If the judge determines that the evidence presented by either side is so persuasive that a reasonable jury could only decide for that party, the motion will be granted. Frequently these motions are denied, and the case proceeds to a jury verdict.

Closing Arguments   After both sides have rested their cases, each attorney presents a closing argument, urging a verdict in favor of his or her client. The judge instructs the jury (if it is a jury trial) in the law that applies to the case. The instructions to the jury are called charges. Then the jury retires to the jury room to deliberate and deliver a verdict (that is, to make the decision).

Jury Verdict and Judgment   In the *Acme v. Lakin* case, the jury will have to weigh the evidence and not only decide for the plaintiff or for the defendant but also, if it finds for the plaintiff, decide the amount of money owed. The jury's decision is called a verdict. The verdict is made into a judgment once the judge signs the document that states who won and what amount is to be paid if an award was made.

Motion for a Judgment Notwithstanding the Verdict (j.n.o.v.)   Motions for directed verdicts are frequently denied, and the case proceeds to a jury verdict. After the jury verdict is returned, a motion can be filed with the trial judge to overturn the jury's verdict. This is in the form of a motion for a judgment notwithstanding the verdict ren-

LEGAL HIGHLIGHT   The Legacy

From 1981 to 1988, President Reagan named over 345 federal judges—28 women and 20 minority group members—to the 761-member federal judiciary. He also named the majority of justices on seven of the thirteen courts of appeals, including the influential District of Columbia Circuit Court of Appeals. Three of the Supreme Court justices are Reagan appointees: Sandra Day O'Connor (1981), Antonin Scalia (1987), and Anthony Kennedy (1988). The chief justice of the United States, William H. Rehnquist, was selected by Reagan, although the chief justice was originally appointed to the Court by President Nixon in 1972.

President Reagan, during his presidential campaigns, promised to appoint conservatives who would practice "judicial restraint." Because these appointments are in effect, for life, President Reagan has assured that his conservative philosophy will be represented on the federal judiciary for decades. By the end of his second term, President Reagan had appointed over 45 percent of the federal judiciary. All these appointments had Senate confirmation.

dered by the jury. This gives the judge the opportunity to decide by law that after consideration of all the evidence the jury erred in its decision. This motion is usually denied by the trial judge, but if granted a judgment will be entered for the party filing the motion.

Motion for New Trial   At the end of the trial, the loser can move to set aside the adverse verdict and to have a new trial. The motion will be granted if the trial judge is convinced, after looking at all the evidence, that the jury was in error. A new trial can also be granted on the grounds of newly discovered evidence, misconduct by the participants during the trial, or error by the judge.

The Appeal   A notice of appeal must be filed within the prescribed time. If Acme loses at the trial and decides to appeal, Acme becomes the appellant. Its attorney files in the court of appeals the record on appeal, which contains the following: (1) the pleadings, (2) a transcript of the trial testimony and copies of the exhibits, (3) the judge's rulings on motions made by the parties, (4) the arguments of counsel, (5) the instructions to the jury, (6) the verdict, (7) the posttrial motions, and (8) the judgment order being appealed. Acme may be required to post a bond for the appeal.

Appellate courts do not hear any evidence. Their decision concerning a case is based on the abstracts, the record, and the briefs. The attorneys can present oral arguments, after which the case is taken under advisement. When the court has reached a decision, the decision is written. It contains the opinion (the court's reasons for its decision), the rules of law that apply, and the judgment.

In general, the appellate courts do not reverse findings of fact unless the findings are unsupported or contradicted by the evidence. Rather, these courts review the record for errors of law. If the reviewing court believes that an error was committed during the trial or that the jury was improperly instructed, the judgment will be reversed. Sometimes the case will be remanded (sent back to the court that originally heard the case) for a new trial. In many cases, the decision of the lower court is affirmed, resulting in enforcement of that court's judgment or decree.

The Judiciary

On center stage in any trial or appeal is the judge, the person responsible for overseeing the proceedings and for making the final decision in the case.

State Judicial Selection Procedures

Judicial selection varies from state to state; however, all judges are selected either by election or by merit. Many states still elect judges to the bench. Opponents of this process claim that it introduces politics into the judiciary.

Judicial merit systems were created as an alternative to elections in order to ensure a more independent judiciary. Under a judicial merit selection system, applicants apply for an opening on the bench. After a committee reviews the applications, several names are sent to the governor, who then appoints one person from the list. State judges, whether elected or selected by the merit system, serve for specific time periods.

Federal Judicial Selection Procedures

When a vacancy occurs in the federal court system, the senators and others recommend candidates for the position to the president. No formal requirement, such as being a lawyer, exists for a person who wishes to serve as a judge at the federal level. The president nominates a person for the vacancy from the list of candidates. The name is sent to the Senate, which will either confirm or deny the appointment.

A federal judge holds office for as long as he or she exhibits good behavior. Since it is very rare for a federal judge to be impeached, confirmation is in effect a life-time appointment.

United States Magistrates

The concept of a magistrate has been embraced in the federal judiciary since the Judiciary Act of 1789. Today, the United States magistrate is a special jurisdiction judge, and he or she holds a position created by the Federal Magistrates Act of 1968.

A U.S. magistrate is a judicial officer appointed by the federal district courts to assist the district court in administering some of its functions. The magistrates have authority to try minor federal criminal offenses. They conduct many of the courts pretrial proceedings and preliminary criminal proceedings. For example, a person arrested for speeding in a national park would fall under a magistrate's jurisdiction.

FACING A LEGAL ISSUE   **Using a Small Claims Court**

Many times disputes occur over small sums of money. For example, your former roommate owes you for the last month's rent or for a telephone bill. Lawyers are expensive; it is not practical to hire one for such a small sun. Most states have small-claims courts. The amounts that can be in controversy will vary from one state to another, but small-claims courts offer an expeditious way to seek these smaller sums.

You can bring an action against your former roommate by filing a complaint. The service of the complaint and summons normally can be accomplished by certified mail. This alleviates the need to pay for a process server. The defendant must file a written answer to your complaint; otherwise, you can obtain a default judgment.

If an answer is filed, the case proceeds to trial before a judge. In some small-claims courts, a jury is not allowed, nor are lawyers allowed to represent either party. The hearing is usually very informal, with each party presenting his or her side of the case. The judge makes his or her decision based on the facts.

Small-claims courts provide a quick and inexpensive way to resolve minor disputes involving money damages.

Before a court can act, it must have jurisdiction. Personally serving a defendant grants a court *in personam* jurisdiction over that individual. Occasionally, a defendant cannot be located, and service must be accomplished in some other way. This grants a court *in rem* jurisdiction but does not allow a judgment to be rendered against an individual for money damages.

Within the United States, there are fifty-two separate court systems: one for each of the fifty states, for the District of Columbia, and for the federal government. The United States Constitution provides for the Supreme Court and such other federal courts as Congress shall designate. Congress has created a federal system with at least one federal district court in each state and U.S. courts of appeal to handle their appeals. To fall under the jurisdiction of the federal courts, a case must involve either a federal question or diversity of citizenship involving $10,000 or more in controversy.

Actions are instituted by filing a complaint and having a summons issued by the court. Once these are served on the defendant, the defendant must file an answer within a specific period of time or have a default judgment rendered against him or her. The defendant may also bring a counterclaim against the plaintiff, which, in turn, requires a reply. During the course of the lawsuit, either party may bring appropriate motions.

Prior to trial, discovery occurs by either oral depositions or written interrogatories. The plaintiff must carry the burden of proof at the time of trial. The plaintiff always introduces evidence first. Once both parties have presented all the evidence, the case is submitted to the jury for a verdict or to the judge if there is no jury. The jury or judge is the trier of fact. The losing party may appeal the decision. The reviewing court usually will not reverse the trial court unless there has been an error of law in the trial process.

Two methods are used to select state judges: election or merit. Federal judges are nominated by the president and are confirmed by the Senate. The conduct of a state judge is monitored by the population and through peer review. If any judge fails to perform as mandated, she or he may be removed from office.

Key Terms

adversary system (**36**)
affirmative defense (**40**)
answer (**40**)
appellate jurisdiction (**28**)
complaint (**37**)
concurrent jurisdiction (**33**)
counterclaim (**40**)
default judgment (**37**)
discovery (**41**)
diversity of citizenship (**32**)
exclusive jurisdiction (**33**)
federal question (**32**)
full faith and credit clause
    (**26**)

general jurisdiction (**27**)
in personam jurisdiction (**26**)
in rem jurisdiction (**26**)
jurisdiction (**26**)
limited jurisdiction (**27**)
long arm statute (**26**)
motion to dismiss (**40**)
oral depositions (**42**)
original jurisdiction (**28**)
plead (**27**)
pleading (**36**)
pretrial hearing (**42**)
process (**37**)

quasi in rem jurisdiction (**27**)
real property (**26**)
subject-matter jurisdiction
    (**27**)
summary judgment (**41**)
summons (**37**)
venue (**27**)
voir dire (**42**)
writ of *mandamus* (**34**)
written interrogatories (**42**)

Questions and Case Problems

1. The American court system has two types of courts—courts with original jurisdiction and those with appellate jurisdiction. What is the difference between the two court systems?

2. Discuss the difference between pleadings and process.

3. Discuss the method of appellate review that the Supreme Court exercises.

4. Discuss judicial review.

5. In state judicial systems, judges serve specific terms in office, while federal judges serve for a term of good behavior. Should both systems be the same? Which system is better on constitutional and public policy grounds?

6. Before the two parties go to trial, pleading must be exchanged and discovery must take place. Until recently, pleadings were very formal, and trials frequently turned on elements of surprise. Often the plaintiff would not know the nature of the defendant's case or who the witnesses would be. Should there be an exchange of information, gathered through the discovery process, prior to trial to eliminate surprises during the trial from either side? Please explain your answer.

7. Marvin, a resident of Alabama, was walking near a busy street in Birmingham when a large crate fell off a passing truck and hit him. Marvin suffered from numerous injuries that resulted in large medical expenses, a great deal of pain and suffering, and in his being off work for six months. He wants to sue the trucking firm for $300,000. The firms' headquarters are in Mississippi, although the company does business in Alabama. Where should Marvin bring his lawsuit—in an Alabama state court, a Mississippi state court, or a federal district court located in Alabama or Mississippi?

8. Colleen Cote, who lived in Wisconsin, brought a lawsuit in the federal district court located in Wisconsin. She sued Peter Wadel, a lawyer in Michigan, for legal malpractice in representing her in a case she had in Michigan. Wadel claimed that the federal court in Wisconsin did not have jurisdiction over him. Wadel did not have an office in Wisconsin. At this point, Cote could not file a lawsuit in the federal district court in Michigan because the statute of limitations had run out, and the Wisconsin court refused to transfer the case to Michigan. Should the case be dismissed? Please explain your answer. [Cote v. Wadel, 796 F.2d 981 (7th Cir. 1986)]

Chapter 3   The Constitution and the Regulation of Business

The Constitution of 1789 deserves the veneration with which the Americans have been accustomed to regard it. It is true that many criticisms have been passed upon its arrangements, upon its omissions, upon the artificial character of some of the institutions it creates. * * * Yet, after all deductions, it ranks above every other written constitution for the intrinsic excellence of its scheme, its adaptation to the circumstances of the people, the simplicity, brevity, and precision of its language, its judicious mixture of definiteness in principle with elasticity in details.

Lord Bryce
The American Commonwealth, 1888

OUTLINE

Introduction

Why does a businessperson or an individual need to know and understand the United States Constitution? First, it governs our personal and business lives as the supreme law in this country. All statutes passed by Congress or by any state legislature, all decisions made by judges in the federal and state courts, and all actions by the president or by the governor of a state must be in accordance with the Constitution. If there is any conflict, the United States Constitution will prevail. The Constitution serves as a limitation on the power of the government.

Second, we must read the Constitution in order to understand court decisions and why Congress acts or does not act in different situations. Third, every businessperson should appreciate the impact on business of the interstate commerce clause contained in the Constitution.

Articles of the Constitution

The Constitution has two functions: It creates the government and it sets out an individual's rights in relation to that government. The first three articles of the Constitution establish the framework of the government. Article IV gives direction to the states through the full faith and credit clause. This clause requires that each state respect the laws of the other states. Article V sets out the methods of amending the Constitution. Article VI ranks the order of the laws, giving highest priority to the Constitution itself and lowest priority to the laws of a local government. Article VII, the last article, provides for the ratification of the Constitution.

The Supremacy Clause

Article VI provides that the Constitution, laws, and treaties of the United States are "the supreme Law of the Land." The **supremacy clause** governs the relationship between the states and the federal government. When the Constitution specifically delegates a power to the federal government, any state law that conflicts with a federal law in that area is prohibited. If the conflict in the laws is taken to court, the state law will be rendered invalid. For example, only the federal government can coin money or pass naturalization laws.

In other areas, however, the state and federal governments may share powers—that is, they have **concurrent powers**. If Congress chooses to act exclusively in one of these areas, the federal government has preempted the area. For example, the federal government has preempted the areas of aviation and nuclear power.

Congress rarely preempts an entire subject area by prohibiting state regulation. If a state law and a federal law conflict in an area of concurrent powers and if Congress has not been clear as to its intent, the courts must determine whether Congress intended to exercise exclusive dominion over the given area.

Federalism is the organizational system of the United States government. Under this system, state governments share powers with the federal government, and neither government is superior to the other except within the particular area of authority granted to it by the Constitution. Federalism appreciates that society is best served by distributing various functions among local governments and the national government based on which government is best able to perform each function. For instance, the federal government can best handle national defense and foreign relations, while state and local governments are best able to handle traffic tickets, domestic relations, and probate.

Exhibit 3–1 depicts this division of powers.

Separation of Powers

The main body of the Constitution creates the federal government by dividing it into three branches—the **executive branch**, the **legislative branch**, and the **judicial branch**. The rights, duties, and powers of the legislative branch are set forth in Article I. Article II creates the executive branch and establishes the powers of the president. The federal judicial system is created by Article III.

Each branch of the government fulfills a separate function. Although no branch may exercise the authority of another branch, each branch has some power to limit the actions of the other two

Exhibit 3–1 **The American Federal System—Division of Powers Between the National Government and the State Governments**

Powers Granted by the Constitution

NATIONAL GOVERNMENT	NATIONAL AND STATE GOVERNMENTS	STATE GOVERNMENTS
Implied "To make all laws which shall be necessary and proper for carrying into execution the foregoing powers, and all other powers vested by this Constitution in the Government of the United States, or in any Department or Officer thereof" (Article 1, Section 8:18)	**Concurrent** • To levy and collect taxes • To borrow money • To make and enforce laws • To establish courts • To provide for the general welfare • To charter banks and corporations	**Reserved to the States** • To regulate intrastate commerce • To conduct elections • To provide for public health, safety, and morals • To establish local governments • To ratify amendments to the federal constitution
Delegated • To coin money • To conduct foreign relations • To regulate interstate commerce • To levy and collect taxes • To declare war • To raise and support military forces • To establish post offices • To establish courts interior to the Supreme Court • To admit new states		

Powers Denied by the Constitution

National	National and State	State
National • To tax articles exported from any state • To violate the Bill of Rights • To change state boundaries	**National and State** • To grant titles of nobility • To permit slavery • To deny citizens the right to vote	**State** • To tax imports or exports • To coin money • To enter into treaties • To impair obligations of contracts • To abridge the privileges or immunities of citizens or deny due process and equal protection of the laws

---

LEGAL HIGHLIGHT   **A Funny Thing Happened on the Way to Amend the Articles of Confederation**

The Articles of Confederation, in effect since 1781, were not working. Although there was a federal government, all the power was held by the states. Unfortunately, the states were not working together; each state based its decisions on its own best interests and not on the best interests of a unified thirteen colonies. After extended deliberations, Congress, meeting on Wall Street in New York City, called a federal convention to amend the Articles. If anyone had called this meeting a constitutional convention, no meeting would have taken place. The delegates were to meet only to amend a couple of sections of the Articles of Confederation. Many people were vehemently opposed to the idea of a strong central government.

Seventy-four delegates were named to the convention. Fifty-five delegates from twelve states attended. Rhode Island disagreed with the whole procedure and did not send any delegates. The convention started on May 14, 1787, in Philadelphia. These men labored through a hot, humid Pennsylvania summer. Working secretly, they wrote guarded letters to friends and rarely spoke of the business at hand during their leisure hours.

Instead of amending the Articles of Confederation, the delegates drafted a completely new constitution that would replace the Articles. The document created the strong central government so feared by many. Of the fifty-five delegates who started the work, forty-one were present when the Convention ended on September 17, 1787, and only thirty-nine signed the document, the Constitution of the United States of America.

The Constitution was then submitted to the states. Heated debate in the newspapers and in meetings followed. Arguing for the adoption of the Constitution was a series of newspaper articles that have become known as the *Federalist Papers*. These articles were written by James Madison, Alexander Hamilton, and John Jay. Before the Constitution could take effect, it had to be ratified by three-fourths of the states (nine out of thirteen).

After intense debate, the ninth state, New Hampshire, ratified the Constitution on June 21, 1788. Article VII of the proposed constitution stipulated that the Constitution became effective (on those who ratified) when ratified by nine states. By 1790 all thirteen states had ratified the Constitution. This document is now the oldest constitution in the world in continuous use. The genius of the writers lay in creating a mechanism that could translate theory into reality.

Many people observed that the Constitution did not list any personal freedoms. Before ratifying the Constitution, a number of states made it clear that amendments containing the rights of the people in relation to the government would be necessary. The first ten amendments, known as the Bill of Rights, were adopted in 1791.

---

branches. This scheme creates a system of checks and balances, as mentioned in Chapter 1, so that no one branch of government is able to accumulate too much power. For example, the executive branch is responsible for foreign affairs, but treaties with foreign governments require the advice and consent of the Senate. Congress has the power to tax, but the president can veto a tax bill. Congress determines the jurisdiction of the federal courts, but the Supreme Court has the power to hold acts of the other branches of the federal government unconstitutional.

The specific powers granted to Congress are listed in Article I, Section 8. Among those powers are the power to regulate commerce, the taxing power, and the spending power.

The Commerce Clause

Congress has the power "to regulate Commerce with foreign Nations, and among the several States, and with the Indian Tribes. * * *'' No other clause in the Constitution has a greater impact on business. Because the federal government is able to regulate commerce, the rules governing the movement of goods through the states are uniform.

Congress has the power to regulate any activity, interstate or intrastate, that affects interstate commerce. For example, wheat that a farmer grows strictly for his or her own consumption is still subject to federal regulation. The federal regulation allows only so many acres of wheat to be grown. A farmer cannot grow the allowed acreage of wheat, *plus* enough for his or her own consumption. If enough farmers grew excess wheat for home consumption, it would reduce the overall demand for wheat because these farmers would not need to buy it. Thus, even one farmer may have a substantial economic effect on interstate commerce; if he could grow excess wheat, others could, too, and the goal of the federal regulation would be defeated.[1]

---

1. Wickard v. Filburn, 317 U.S. 111, 63 S.Ct. 82, 87 L.Ed. 122 (1942).

State Regulation of Commerce States have a strong interest in regulating activities within their borders. States are sovereign governments; as part of their inherent sovereignty, they possess **police powers**. The police power gives the states the authority to regulate private activities in order to protect or to promote the health, safety, morals, or general welfare of their citizens. States, for example, have a strong interest in making sure that the trucks and automobiles on state highways are safe. Most state regulations place some burden on interstate commerce.

When a state regulation encroaches on interstate commerce, the courts must balance the state's interest, reflected in the merits and purposes of the regulation, against the burden it places on interstate commerce. A state law enacted pursuant to a state's police powers and affecting the health, safety, and welfare of local citizens carries a strong presumption of validity. Because courts balance the interests between the state and federal governments, the outcome in a particular case cannot be predicted. In the following case, the Supreme Court considered whether Iowa could impose stringent requirements on trucks that were passing through the state and were part of interstate commerce.

BACKGROUND AND FACTS *Unlike all other states in the West and Midwest, Iowa prohibited by statute the use of sixty-five-foot double-trailer trucks within its borders. Use of fifty-five-foot single-trailer trucks and sixty-foot double-trailer trucks was allowed. The appellee, Consolidated Freightways, owned sixty-five-foot double-trailer trucks. It was prohibited from using them to carry commodities through Iowa on interstate highways. Consequently, Consolidated filed suit, alleging that Iowa's statutory scheme unconstitutionally burdened interstate commerce.*

POWELL, Justice delivered the opinion of the Court.
* * * *

Because of Iowa's statutory scheme, Consolidated cannot use its 65-foot doubles to move commodities through the State. Instead, the company must do one of four things: (i) use 55-foot singles; (ii) use 60-foot doubles; (iii) detach the trailers of a 65-foot double and shuttle each through the State separately; or (iv) divert 65-foot doubles around Iowa. * * *
* * * *

In a fourteen-day trial, both sides adduced evidence on safety, and on the burden on interstate commerce imposed by Iowa's law. On the question of safety, the District Court found that the ''evidence clearly establishes that the twin is as safe as the semi.'' * * *
* * * *

Case 3.1
KASSEL v. CONSOLIDATED FREIGHTWAYS CORPORATION OF DELAWARE

Supreme Court of the United States, 1981.
450 U.S. 662, 101 S.Ct. 1309, 67 L.Ed.2d 580.

The Commerce Clause does not, of course, invalidate all state restrictions on commerce. It has long been recognized that, ''in the absence of conflicting legislation by Congress, there is a residuum of power in the state to make laws governing matters of local concern which nevertheless in some measure affect interstate commerce or even, to some extent, regulate it.''
* * * *

But the incantation of a purpose to promote the public health or safety does not insulate a state law from Commerce Clause attack. Regulations designed for that salutary purpose nevertheless may further the purpose so marginally, and interfere with commerce so substantially, as to be invalid under the Commerce Clause.
* * *

* * * *

Applying these general principles, we conclude that the Iowa truck-length limitations unconstitutionally burden interstate commerce.
* * * *

DECISION AND REMEDY *The Supreme Court held that the Iowa statute prohibiting the use of certain large trucks within the state unconstitutionally burdened interstate commerce.*

COMMENTS *Iowa's police power argument concerning highway safety—namely, that long trailers are unsafe when the trucks back up, are dangerous when turning in intersections, and are difficult to pass on the highway—was found insufficient by the Court. The Court stated, however, that Iowa had hoped merely to deflect some of the traffic just passing through the state by these regulations. The purpose of the law was not consistent with the free movement of goods throughout the United States.*

As the court in this case stated, its decision did not mean that the states have no rights. Often it is difficult to determine whether certain conduct is subject to federal control or is regulated only by the states. This is true even when we are discussing the commerce clause. For example, would a city-owned mass-transit system be subject to federal law, or is this type of conduct left solely to the control of the individual states? Are there ''areas of traditional governmental functions'' that should be left to the states to regulate?

The following case involved the San Antonio Metropolitan Transit Authority (SAMTA), which provides mass transportation. The United States Department of Labor issued an opinion that SAMTA's operations were subject to the federal minimum-wage and overtime requirements. SAMTA filed legal action to set this ruling aside. The United States Supreme Court supported the Department of Labor.

Case 3.2
GARCIA v. SAN ANTONIO METROPOLITAN TRANSIT AUTHORITY
Supreme Court of the United States, 1985.
469 U.S. 528, 105 S.Ct. 1005, 83 L.Ed.2d 1016.

BACKGROUND AND FACTS *The Federal Labor Standards Act (FLSA) was passed in 1938, and part of its provisions regulate minimum wage and overtime. The San Antonio Metropolitan Transit Authority (SAMTA) did not want to be subject to this statute and took the position that the operation of a mass transit system in a local district was a traditional function of local government, and thus, the federal government had no power to regulate the district's employment practices.*

BLACKMUN, Justice delivered the opinion of the Court.
*   *   *   *

In the present cases, a Federal District Court concluded that municipal ownership and operation of a mass-transit system is a traditional governmental function and is exempt from the obligations imposed by the FLSA. Faced with the identical question, three Federal Courts of Appeals and one state appellate court have reached the opposite conclusion.

Our examination of this "function" standard applied in these and other cases over the last eight years now persuades us that the attempt to draw the boundaries of state regulatory immunity in terms of "traditional governmental function" is not only unworkable but is inconsistent with established principles of federalism. *   *   *

*   *   *   *

Appellees have not argued that SAMTA is immune from regulation under the FLSA on the ground that it is a local transit system engaged in intrastate commercial activity. In a practical sense, SAMTA's operations might well be characterized as "local." Nonetheless, it long has been settled that Congress' authority under the Commerce Clause extends to intrastate economic activities that affect interstate commerce. *   *   *
*   *   *   *

*   *   *   [F]our conditions must be satisfied before a state activity may be deemed immune from a particular federal regulation under the Commerce Clause. First, it is said that the federal statute at issue must regulate "the States as States." Second, the statute must "address matters that are indisputably 'attribute[s] of state sovereignty.' " Third, state compliance with the federal obligation must "directly impair [the States'] 'ability' to structure integral operations in areas of traditional governmental functions." Finally, the relation of state and federal interests must not be such that "the nature of the federal interest *   *   * justifies state submission."

The controversy in the present cases has focused on the third *   *   * requirement—that the challenged federal statute trench[es] on "traditional governmental functions." The District Court voiced a common concern: "Despite the abundance of adjectives, identifying which particular state functions are immune remains difficult." Just how troublesome the task has been is revealed by the results reached in other federal cases. Thus, courts have held that regulating ambulance services, licensing automobile drivers, operating a municipal airport, performing solid waste disposal, and operating a highway authority, are functions [reserved to the states] *   *   *. At the same time, courts have held that issuance of industrial development bonds, regulation of intrastate natural gas sales, regulation of traffic on public roads, regulation of air transportation, operation of a telephone system, leasing and sale of natural gas operation of a mental health facility, and provision of in-house domestic services for the aged and handicapped, are not entitled to immunity. We find it difficult, if not impossible, to identify an organizing principle that places each of the cases in the first group on one side of a line and each of the cases in the second group on the other side. The constitutional distinction between licensing drivers and regulating traffic, for example, or between operating a highway authority and operating a mental health facility, is elusive at best.
*   *   *   *

We therefore now reject, as unsound in principle and unworkable in practice, a rule of state immunity from federal regulation that turns on a judicial appraisal of whether a particular governmental function is "integral" or "traditional." Any such rule leads to inconsistent results at the same time that it disserves principles of democratic self-governance, and it breeds inconsistency precisely because it is divorced from those principles.

DECISION AND REMEDY *The Supreme Court held that San Antonio Metropolitan Transit Authority employees were subject to the protection of the wage and hour provisions of the Fair Labor Standards Act.*

COMMENTS *The Supreme Court by its ruling has effectively held that the states are subject to the commerce clause in any aspect of governmental functions for which there is a federal statute regulating such function.*

The Taxing Power

Congress has the "Power to lay and collect Taxes, Duties, Imposts and Excises * * * but all Duties, Imposts and Excises shall be uniform throughout the United States." Congress may not tax some states while exempting others. All states must be treated in an equal manner. The courts examine whether Congress is actually attempting to regulate an area indirectly through taxation. If Congress is empowered to regulate the area, the tax is valid. On the other hand, if Congress is attempting to regulate an area over which it has no authority, the tax law is void.

Federal taxes can be supported as a valid exercise of federal regulation. The Supreme Court has upheld taxes imposed on the transfer of firearms, on the transfer of marijuana, and on the income of persons who are gambling. Taxes can also be upheld if they comprise a revenue-raising measure; that is, when a tax produces revenues, it is generally held to be within the national **taxing power**. Moreover, the expansive interpretation of the commerce clause usually provides a basis for sustaining a federal tax.

The Spending Power

Congress has the power "to pay the Debts and provide for the common Defense and general welfare of the United States. * * *" In other words, Congress can spend the monies collected under the taxing power. The **spending power** unavoidably involves policy choices. Some taxpayers object to the government spending money on a particular program. For example, some people object to Congress spending money to support national defense. It is, however, nearly impossible to object to specific government spending because of the **standing to sue** requirement.

The doctrine of standing to sue requires a litigant to demonstrate a direct and immediate personal injury due to the challenged action. A litigant must show that the injury is directly related to the particular government spending program and that the court can give the litigant relief from the harm alleged. Rarely is a taxpayer directly harmed by any government spending program. As a result, the spending power is seldom challenged. Communicating directly with members of Congress is a more efficient method of influencing spending policies.

Bill of Rights and the Other Amendments

The Bill of Rights was added to the Constitution in 1791. Specific protections for the individual against the government are set out in these first ten amendments.

Among the guarantees provided for by the Bill of Rights are:

1. The First Amendment protections of religion, speech, and assembly.
2. The Fourth Amendment provisions regarding arrest, and search and seizure.
3. The Fifth Amendment.
    a. Protection from **double jeopardy**—a person cannot be tried by the same level of government more than once for the same crime.
    b. Freedom from **self-incrimination**—a person cannot be forced to testify against himself or herself.
    c. Right to **due process**—a person has the right to timely notice of a trial and to a fair hearing.

LEGAL HIGHLIGHT   The Rising Sun

On Monday, September 17, 1787, the delegates met for the last time at Independence Hall in Philadelphia, Pennsylvania. James Madison penned an eloquent paragraph concerning that day:

> Whilst the last members were signing, Doctor Franklin, looking toward the President's chair, at the back of which a rising sun happened to be painted, observed to a few members near him that painters had found it difficult to distinguish in their art, a rising, from a setting, sun. I have, said he, often and often, in the course of the session, and the vicissitudes of hopes and fears as to its issue, looked at that behind the President, without being able to tell whether it was rising or setting; but now at length I have the happiness to know, that it is a rising, and not a setting, sun.

---

4. The Sixth Amendment rights to a speedy and public trial, to an attorney, to confront witnesses, and to cross-examination in criminal prosecutions.
5. The Seventh Amendment guarantee of jury trials in civil suits.
6. The Eighth Amendment provisions for bail and prohibitions against cruel and unusual punishment.

The Fourteenth Amendment was passed after the Civil War. This amendment includes a due process clause, like the one found in the Fifth Amendment; it also includes an **equal protection clause**, not found in any other part of the Constitution. Under the Fourteenth Amendment, people are protected from specific actions by the state governments.

Over a long series of cases, the Supreme Court adopted the **doctrine of selective incorporation**. Through the use of this doctrine and the due process clause of the Fourteenth Amendment, specific individual rights guaranteed by the first ten amendments are now applicable to the state governments as well as to the federal government. Those guarantees of individual liberty that are fundamental to the American system of law must now also be protected by the states.

Delegated Powers

The Tenth Amendment delegates certain **enumerated powers** to the federal government and re-serves all other powers to the states or to the people. This amendment limits the power of the federal government by stating that "the powers not delegated to the United States by the Constitution, nor prohibited by it to the States, are reserved to the States respectively, or to the people." The federal government has no powers apart from those specified in the Constitution; it holds only enumerated powers, since it can exercise only those powers that are expressly or implicitly granted to it.

The term "expressly" was not included in the Tenth Amendment. This word was found in the Articles of Confederation in a similar provision. By not having the word "expressly" in the amendment, the federal government is able to find *implied* federal powers. Thus, it is implicit in the Constitution that the federal government may do whatever is necessary to follow through on the specific powers granted it.

Bill of Rights in a Business Context

A business may be conducted by one person operating under her or his own name, a common name, or a fictitious name. Other types of businesses are conducted by partnerships or by corporations. Corporations and some types of partnerships exist as separate legal entities. As a legal entity, a business is entitled to some of the same

---

LEGAL HIGHLIGHT   Twenty-Six of 5,000 Proposed Amendments

The delegates to the constitutional convention did not believe that any protections of individual freedoms should be included in the document. Very shortly it became evident that the people had other ideas; indeed, they demanded constitutional protections.

Over the past 200 years, more than 5,000 amendments have been proposed. The first ten amendments came as a package, but the next sixteen amendments span the years from 1798 to 1971. Of those sixteen amendments, one canceled an earlier one: The Twenty-First Amendment repealed the Eighteenth

Amendment on liquor prohibition. One early proposed amendment was intended to ban constitutionally the act of dueling. Another attempted to prohibit Congress from abolishing slavery—ironically, it would have been the Thirteenth Amendment. Instead, the Thirteenth Amendment abolishes slavery. Over 200 proposed amendments attempted to stop the Civil War. More recent proposals include the Equal Rights Amendment, Right to Life Amendment, and a Balanced Budget Amendment.

---

rights and privileges as an individual citizen. For example, a legal entity can sue and be sued in a court, pays taxes under the legal entity status, and holds title to property. The Bill of Rights guarantees persons certain protections. The Supreme Court has recognized corporations as persons in very specific areas of the Constitution, while, in other areas, corporations do not qualify for constitutional protection.

Business and the First Amendment

The First Amendment to the Constitution states:

> Congress shall make no law respecting an establishment of religion, or prohibiting the free exercise thereof; or abridging the freedom of speech, or of the press; or the right of the people peaceably to assemble, and to petition the government for redress of grievances.

Freedom of expression is one of the foundations of our society. Our forefathers believed that the ability and the right to exchange ideas allow for the development of a free and open society. Armed with knowledge, the citizen has the ability to make better decisions.

The freedom of speech is not an absolute right. No one has a basic right to speak to another about

planning a murder. A person does not have a right to spread lies about others, nor does anyone have a right to yell "fire" in a crowded theater. Although we have the basic right of freedom of speech, there are limits to it.

The problem is establishing these limits. Everyone is in favor of freedom of speech for himself or herself. The difficulty occurs when an attempt is made to limit the freedom of speech of others. Should the American Nazi Party be allowed to hold a parade in a predominantly Jewish neighborhood? Should antinuclear demonstrators be allowed to block the entrance to nuclear plants? Should a large corporation be required to include in its annual meeting a proposal not to do business with South Africa?

The limitations on freedom of speech have varied over the years. This book focuses on defamation and commercial speech in looking at how these limitations affect businesses. You must recognize, however, that this is an extremely wide-ranging issue. Almost 200 years after the adoption of this amendment in 1791, society is still deciding what is meant by freedom of speech and what limits should be placed on that freedom.

Defamation   **Defamation** is discussed in greater detail in Chapter 12. For the moment, defamation is defined as the act of making any untrue statements that impinge on the integrity or character of another person or corporation.

Historically, defamation has never been protected by the First Amendment. During the civil rights actions of the early 1960s, the *New York Times* printed articles of a defamatory nature against an elected Southern official. The United States Supreme Court held that public officials seeking to recover for defamation relating to their performance of official duties must prove **actual malice**.[2] Actual malice means that a statement must be made with the knowledge that it is false or with reckless disregard of whether it is false or not.

Public figures and officials are covered by the First Amendment. A public official is a person who is elected or appointed to government service. A public figure is a person, such as an actor or an athletic coach, who seeks public recognition or a person who is thrust into the limelight, such as a person accused of a crime or a survivor of an airline crash.

Commercial Speech   In the past, the United States Supreme Court drew a distinction between freedom of speech as to political views or individual expression and freedom of speech in commercial statements. For example, political speech could not be restrained, but commercial advertising was subject to government control. This view continued until the case of *Virginia State Board of Pharmacy v. Virginia Citizens Consumer Council, Inc.*[3] This case, along with several others, challenged a legal ban on advertising the price of prescription drugs. Justice Blackmun held, "It is clear * * * that speech does not lose its First Amendment protection because money is spent * * * as in a paid advertisement. * * *"

After this case, several cases arose confronting the issue of **commercial speech**. One of the leading cases was *Bates v. State Bar of Arizona*.[4] The State Bar of Arizona refused to allow any attorney to advertise for services or to advertise the price of those services. Advertising was not considered professional. Two attorneys advertised quoting prices for routine legal work. The advertisements did not include anything that might commonly be called trade puffing. Because of this advertisement, the State Bar of Arizona suspended the attorneys from the practice of law. The United States Supreme Court held that the attorneys' freedom of speech had been violated.

Eventually the United States Supreme Court was confronted with additional problems of fact. How far should professionals be allowed to go in advertising? How much information must be contained within the advertisement? One of the most recent cases on this issue was *Zauderer v. Office of Disciplinary Council,* wherein the United States Supreme Court discussed commercial speech as it applies to advertising legal services.

---

2. New York Times Co. v. Sullivan, 376 U.S. 254, 84 S.Ct. 710, 11 L.Ed.2d 686 (1964).

3. 425 U.S. 748, 96 S.Ct. 1817, 48 L.Ed.2d 346 (1976).
4. 433 U.S. 350, 97 S.Ct. 2691, 53 L.Ed.2d 810 (1977).

BACKGROUND AND FACTS   *Zauderer was a licensed attorney in Ohio. He placed several advertisements in the local media advising readers that his firm would represent defendants in drunk driving cases and that his clients' full legal fees would be refunded if they were convicted of drunk driving. He did not disclose in the advertisements that many cases would be plea-bargained to a lesser offense. Later, Zauderer ran another newspaper advertisement publicizing his willingness to represent women who had suffered injuries resulting from their use of the Dalkon Shield. The advertisement featured a line drawing of the device and stated that the cases would be handled on a contingent-fee basis and that, if there was no recovery, no legal fees would be owed. Nothing was mentioned about the client being responsible for court costs. This advertisement attracted 106*

 Case 3.3

ZAUDERER v. OFFICE OF DISCIPLINARY COUNCIL OF THE SUPREME COURT OF OHIO

Supreme Court of the United States, 1985.
471 U.S. 626, 105 S.Ct. 2265, 85 L.Ed.2d 652.

clients. A complaint was filed with the state bar association claiming that Zauderer's advertisements were deceptive.

WHITE, Justice delivered the opinion of the Court.
* * * *

* * * [T]he decision in *Virginia Pharmacy Board v. Virginia Citizens Consumer Council, Inc.,* held for the first time that the First Amendment precludes certain forms of regulation of purely commercial speech. * * * This case presents additional unresolved questions regarding the regulation of commercial speech by attorneys: whether a State may discipline an attorney for soliciting business by running newspaper advertisements containing nondeceptive illustrations and legal advice, and whether a State may seek to prevent potential deception of the public by requiring attorneys to disclose in their advertising certain information regarding fee arrangements.
* * * *

There is no longer any room to doubt that what has come to be known as "commercial speech" is entitled to the protection of the First Amendment, albeit to protection somewhat less extensive than that afforded "noncommercial speech." More subject to doubt, perhaps, are the precise bounds of the category of expression that may be termed commercial speech, but it is clear enough that the speech at issue in this case—advertising pure and simple—falls within those bounds. Our commercial speech doctrine rests heavily on "the 'common-sense' distinction between speech proposing a commercial transaction * * * and other varieties of speech," and appellant's advertisements undeniably propose a commercial transaction. * * *

Our general approach to restrictions on commercial speech is also by now well settled. The States and the Federal Government are free to prevent the dissemination of commercial speech that is false, deceptive, or misleading, or that proposes an illegal transaction. Commercial speech that is not false or deceptive and does not concern unlawful activities, however, may be restricted only in the service of a substantial governmental interest, and only through means that directly advance that interest. Our application of these principles to the commercial speech of attorneys has led us to conclude that blanket bans on price advertising by attorneys and rules preventing attorneys from using nondeceptive terminology to describe their fields of practice are impermissible. To resolve this appeal, we must apply the teachings of these cases to three separate forms of regulation Ohio has imposed on advertising by its attorneys: prohibitions on soliciting legal business through advertisements containing advice and information regarding specific legal problems; restrictions on the use of illustrations in advertising by lawyers; and disclosure requirements relating to the terms of contingent fees. * * *

The interest served by the application of the Ohio self-recommendation and solicitation rules to appellant's advertisement is not apparent. The advertisement's information and advice concerning the Dalkon Shield were * * * neither false nor deceptive: in fact, it was entirely accurate. The advertisement did not promise readers that lawsuits alleging injuries caused by Dalkon Shield would be successful, nor did it suggest that appellant had any special expertise in handling such lawsuits other than his employment in other such litigation. Rather, the advertisement reported the indisputable fact that the Dalkon Shield has spawned an impressive number of lawsuits and advised readers that appellant was currently handling such lawsuits and was willing to represent other women asserting similar claims.
* * * *

* * * The application of * * * [Ohio's r]estriction on illustrations in advertising by lawyers to appellant's advertisement fails for much the same reasons as does the application of the self-recommendation and solicitation rules. The use of illustrations or pictures in advertisements serves important communicative functions: it attracts the attention of the audience to the advertiser's message, and it may also serve to impart information directly.

*   *   *   *

Appellant, however, overlooks material differences between disclosure requirements and outright prohibitions on speech. In requiring attorneys who advertise their willingness to represent clients on a contingent-fee basis to state that the client may have to bear certain expenses even if he loses, Ohio has not attempted to prevent attorneys from conveying information to the public; it has only required them to provide somewhat more information than they might otherwise be inclined to present.

*   *   *   *

The Supreme Court of Ohio issued a public reprimand. That judgment is affirmed to the extent that it is based on appellant's advertisement involving his terms of representation in drunken driving cases and on the omission of information regarding his contingent-fee arrangements in his Dalkon Shield advertisement. But insofar as the reprimand was based on appellant's use of an illustration in his advertisement and his offer of legal advice in his advertisement the judgment is reversed.

The Supreme Court held that Zauderer did violate disciplinary rules by not disclosing material information concerning costs and plea bargaining. The Supreme Court continued to allow commercial speech to be protected by the First Amendment. Within the legal profession, however, a high disclosure requirement of all material facts exists.	**DECISION AND REMEDY**

Today, there is no question that commercial speech is protected by the First Amendment; however, advertisements must not be deceptive, misleading, or fraudulent. In addition to advertisements, corporations may also want to make known their positions on various topics. At times it is difficult to determine when a corporation is advocating a public or political position and when it is using commercial speech. For example, a bank wants to spend money to present its views opposing a referendum that would allow a grad-

uated personal income tax. A corporation has as much right to publicize its views as an individual, even though these views promote the corporation's own profit or some other benefit. Moreover, the public is enriched by being exposed to all views, whether they are those of an individual or of a corporation.

Can a corporation be required to present an opposing viewpoint when it is advocating a certain position? The United States Supreme Court was recently confronted with this issue.

BACKGROUND AND FACTS *Pacific Gas and Electric Company has distributed a newsletter in its monthly billing statements for many years. The newsletter has included such items as political editorials, feature stories of public interest, and tips on energy conservation. The state regulatory commission decided that the envelope space was the ratepayers' property and ordered the company to allow an independent organization to publicize information contrary to that of the position of Pacific Gas and Electric. The company took the position that its First Amendment rights had been violated.*

 Case 3.4

PACIFIC GAS AND ELECTRIC COMPANY v. PUBLIC UTILITIES COMMISSION OF CALIFORNIA

Supreme Court of the United States, 1986.
475 U.S. 1, 106 S.Ct. 903, 89 L.Ed.2d 1.

POWELL, Justice, delivered the opinion of the Court.
* * * *

Compelled access like that ordered in this case both penalizes the expression of particular points of view and forces speakers to alter their speech to conform with an agenda they do not set. These impermissible effects are not remedied by the Commission's definition of the relevant property rights.

This Court has previously considered the question whether compelling a private corporation to provide a forum for views other than its own may infringe the corporation's freedom of speech. [A] Florida law provided that, if a newspaper assailed a candidate's character or record, the candidate could demand that the newspaper print a reply of equal prominence and space.

We found that the right-of-reply statute directly interfered with the newspaper's right to speak * * *. [W]e noted that the newspaper's "treatment of public issues and public officials—whether fair or unfair—constitute[s] the exercise of editorial control and judgment."

The concerns that caused us to invalidate the compelled access rule apply to appellant as well as to the institutional press. Just as the state is not free to "tell a newspaper in advance what it can print and what it cannot," the State is not free either to restrict appellant's speech to certain topics or views that others may hold.
* * * *

The Commission's order is inconsistent with these principles. * * *

DECISION AND REMEDY *The Supreme Court held that the public utility did not have to include in its billing envelopes any statements by third persons that were contrary to the positions held by the utility.*

COMMENTS *By its ruling, the Supreme Court restricted the right to reply. The end result is that a corporation is not required to present views that are contrary to those of the corporation.*

Freedom of Religion

The government cannot establish any religion nor can it prohibit the free exercise of religious practices. Any government action, both federal and state, must be neutral toward religion. Although a statute may have some impact on religion, as long as it does not promote or place a significant burden on religion, the statute is constitutional.

Sunday closing laws, for example, forbid the performance of certain business activities on Sunday. The closing laws have been found to be constitutional because the government has a legitimate interest in providing workers a day of rest. Although closing laws originally were religious in character, they have taken on the secular purpose of promoting the health and welfare of workers. Even though closing laws admittedly make it easier for Christians to attend religious services, the

Court has viewed this effect as an incidental, not a primary, purpose of Sunday closing laws. Today, the few closing laws that still remain generally allow the businesses of people of other religious faiths to be open on Sunday so long as they observe a day of rest.

Title VII of the Civil Rights Act of 1964 prohibits government and private employers and unions from discriminating against individuals because of their religion. Businesses must accommodate and not discriminate against their employees on the basis of religious beliefs.

The United States Supreme Court recently addressed this issue in *Estate of Thornton v. Caldor, Inc.*[5] In this case, the Court held that a Connecticut statute granting employees the absolute right not

---

5. 472 U.S. 703, 105 S.Ct. 2914, 86 L.Ed.2d 557 (1985).

to work on their Sabbath had the effect of advancing religious practices in violation of the establishment clause of the First Amendment. This type of statute discriminated against employees who might want a day off during the weekend for secular reasons.

In *Trans World Airlines, Inc. v. Hardison,*[6] the United States Supreme Court reviewed the case of a former airline clerk who brought a lawsuit against the airline and the union, claiming religious discrimination. He sought to have Saturday, his Sabbath, off. Neither the union nor the airline could work out a solution to the problem because he had low seniority, while those of higher seniority also wanted Saturdays off. Eventually he was fired for refusing to work on Saturday. The Supreme Court held the airline and the union had made reasonable efforts to accommodate his religious beliefs and that all the proposed solutions to his problem worked an undue hardship on the airline, the union, and his fellow employees. The operation of the seniority system was agreed to by both the airline and the union. As long as the seniority system did not have a discriminatory purpose, it was not an unlawful employment practice, even though the operation of the seniority system was discriminatory in its effect.

Search and Seizure

Before any governmental agency may search a place, that agency must obtain a search warrant from the court. The Supreme Court has found some exceptions, such as limited searches of automobiles or any place where the suspect may reach for a weapon. The search warrant must be based on **probable cause**. The Fourth Amendment states that the "right of the people to be secure in their persons, houses, papers, and effects, against unreasonable searches and seizures, shall not be violated, and no Warrants shall issue, but upon probable cause * * *." Probable cause requires law enforcement officials to have objective evidence that would convince a neutral magistrate that the proposed search is justified.

The warrant must particularly describe the place to be searched and the persons to be arrested or the things to be seized. General search warrants are prohibited. For example, a general search through a person's belongings is impermissible. Nothing is left to the discretion of the officer executing a search warrant; the search cannot extend beyond what is described in the warrant.

Constitutional protection against searches and seizures is extremely important to businesses and professionals. With increased federal and state regulation of commercial activities, frequent and unannounced government inspection to ensure compliance with the law would be extremely disruptive. In *Marshall v. Barlow's, Inc.,*[7] the Supreme Court held that government inspectors do not have the right to enter business premises without a warrant. In this case, the purpose of the law (Occupational Safety and Health Act of 1970) was to provide a safe workplace. If the business was found to be in violation of the government requirements, the government could impose fines for violations. Businesses have a right to require the government to obtain a warrant from a neutral magistrate. This case is discussed in greater detail in Chapter 4.

The Supreme Court reviewed the following case, which involved a public employer's search of the office of an employee. The Court held that a search warrant is not required, at least in the case of a public employee, as long as the search is for work-related purposes and is conducted reasonably.

BACKGROUND AND FACTS *Dr. Ortega was a physician and psychiatrist. He was chief of professional education at Napa State Hospital for seventeen years, until his dismissal in 1981. In July 1981, Dr. O'Connor, the executive director of the hospital, became concerned with possible improprieties in Dr. Ortega's work. In particular, he was concerned with whether Dr. Ortega had acquired an Apple II computer by donation or*

Case 3.5
O'CONNOR v. ORTEGA
Supreme Court of the United States, 1987.
480 U.S. 709, 107 S.Ct. 1492, 94 L.Ed.2d 714.

---

6.   432 U.S. 63, 97 S.Ct. 2264, 53 L.Ed.2d 113 (1977).

7.   436 U.S. 307, 98 S.Ct. 1816, 56 L.Ed.2d 305 (1978).

whether the funds were raised by coercion of the residents in Dr. Ortega's program. Dr. O'Connor was also concerned with possible sexual harassment of two female employees.

Dr. Ortega was placed on paid administrative leave pending the investigation of these charges. He was not allowed into his office. The hospital searched Dr. Ortega's office. The specific reason for the entry was unclear, but the hospital claimed it was to inventory and secure state property. At first the hospital claimed it was a routine inventory, but later it admitted having no policy of inventorying the offices of those employees placed on administrative leave. The hospital finally ended up seizing several items from Dr. Ortega's desk, including a Valentine's Day card, a photograph, and a book of poetry, all sent to Dr. Ortega by a former resident physician. These items were used against Dr. Ortega in the administrative personnel hearing. Attempts to separate Dr. Ortega's personal property from state property were given up, and no inventory of his office was ever made. His papers were placed in a box and put in storage for Dr. Ortega to retrieve. As a result of the personnel hearing, Dr. Ortega was discharged.

He brought this lawsuit alleging that the search of his office violated his Fourth Amendment rights and that he had a reasonable expectation of privacy in his office.

O'CONNOR, Justice delivered the opinion of the Court.
* * * *

The strictures of the Fourth Amendment, applied to the States through the Fourteenth Amendment, have been applied to the conduct of governmental officials in various civil activities. Thus, we have held in the past that the Fourth Amendment governs the conduct of school officials, building inspectors, * * * and Occupational Safety and Health Act inspectors. * * * As we observed, * * * "[b]ecause the individual's interest in privacy and personal security 'suffers whether the government's motivation is to investigate violations of criminal laws or breaches of other statutory or regulatory standards,' . . . it would be anomalous to say that the individual and his private property are fully protected by the Fourth Amendment only when the individual is suspected of criminal behavior.' " * * * Searches and seizures by government employers or supervisors of the private property of their employees, therefore, are subject to the restraints of the Fourth Amendment.
* * * Our cases establish that Dr. Ortega's Fourth Amendment rights are implicated only if the conduct of the Hospital officials at issue in this case infringed "an expectation of privacy that society is prepared to consider reasonable." * * *
* * * *

Within the workplace context, this Court has recognized that employees may have a reasonable expectation of privacy against intrusions by police. As with the expectation of privacy in one's home, such an expectation in one's place of work is "based upon societal expectations that have deep roots in the history of the Amendment." * * *
* * * *

Given the societal expectations of privacy in one's place of work * * * we reject the contention made by the Solicitor General and petititoners that public employees can never have a reasonable expectation of privacy in their place of work. Individuals do not lose Fourth Amendment rights merely because they work for the government instead of a private employer. The operational realities of the

work place, however, may make *some* employees' expectations of privacy unreasonable when an intrusion is by a supervisor rather than a law enforcement official. Public employees' expectations of privacy in their offices, desks, and file cabinets, like similar expectations of employees in the private sector, may be reduced by virtue of actual office practices and procedures, or by legitimate regulation. * * *
* * * *

The legitimate privacy interests of public employees in the private objects they bring to the workplace may be substantial. Against these privacy interests, however, must be balanced the realities of the workplace, which strongly suggest that a warrant requirement would be unworkable. While police, and even administrative enforcement personnel, conduct searches for the primary purpose of obtaining evidence for use in criminal or other enforcement proceedings, employers most frequently need to enter the offices and desks of their employees for legitimate work-related reasons wholly unrelated to illegal conduct. Employers and supervisors are focused primarily on the need to complete the government agency's work in a prompt and efficient manner. An employer may have need for correspondence, or a file or report available only in an employee's office while the employee is away from the office. Or, as is alleged to have been the case here, employers may need to safeguard or identify state property or records in an office in connection with a pending investigation into suspected employee misfeasance.

In our view, requiring an employer to obtain a warrant whenever the employer wished to enter an employee's office, desk, or file cabinets for a work-related purpose would seriously disrupt the routine conduct of business and would be unduly burdensome. Imposing unwieldy warrant procedures in such cases upon supervisors, who would otherwise have no reason to be familiar with such procedures, is simply unreasonable. * * *
* * * *

* * * We hold, therefore, that public employer intrusions on the constitutionally protected privacy interests of government employees for noninvestigatory, work-related purposes, as well as for investigations of work-related misconduct, should be judged by the standard of reasonableness under all the circumstances.

DECISION AND REMEDY

The Court concluded that a search of an employee's office by a supervisor will be justified at its inception when there are reasonable grounds for suspecting that the search will turn up evidence that the employee is guilty of work-related misconduct or when a search is necessary for a noninvestigatory work-related purpose such as retrieving a needed file. The Court sent the case back to the district court to determine the justification for the search and seizure and to evaluate the reasonableness of both the inception of the search and the scope of the search that included the seizure of Dr. Ortega's personal belongings.

Self-Incrimination

The Fifth Amendment guarantees that no person "shall be compelled in any criminal case to be a witness against himself." An accused person cannot be made to confess or to give any evidence that might be used against him or her in any criminal prosecution. An accused person is protected by the Fifth Amendment from the actions of the federal government. The Fourteenth Amendment due process clause incorporates the Fifth Amendment provision against self-incrimination and protects an accused from any illegal action by the state government. The accused, however, has this protection only for himself or herself. He or she may be forced to testify against others.

The Fifth Amendment's guarantee against self-incrimination extends only to natural persons and not to legal entities. Corporations and partnerships are legal entities; therefore, they do not have the protection of that clause of the Fifth Amendment. When records of these organizations are ordered by the court to be produced, the information must be given even if the evidence is incriminating.

The protection from self-incrimination does not apply to an individual's business records if they are being sought by the government through the use of a warrant. As discussed previously, before a warrant will be issued, probable cause must be established. The items must be produced under the warrant even though they might incriminate the person. What are the rights of a businessperson when she or he has turned over incriminating papers to an accountant or lawyer? This question was answered in the following case.

Case 3.6
FISHER v. UNITED STATES
Supreme Court of the United States, 1976.
425 U.S. 391, 96 S.Ct. 1569, 48 L.Ed.2d 39.

BACKGROUND AND FACTS *In two cases, taxpayers were under investigation for possible civil or criminal liability under the federal income tax laws. The taxpayers obtained from their accountants certain documents relating to the accountants' preparation of their tax returns and transferred these documents to their attorneys. The Internal Revenue Service attempted to obtain these documents by serving summonses on the taxpayers' attorneys. The attorneys refused to comply based on their clients' Fifth Amendment rights against self-incrimination and the attorney-client privilege.*

WHITE, Justice delivered the opinion of the Court.

In these two cases we are called upon to decide whether a summons directing an attorney to produce documents delivered to him by his client in connection with the attorney-client relationship is enforceable over claims that the documents were constitutionally immune from summons in the hands of the client and retained that immunity in the hands of the attorney.

* * * *

* * * [P]etitioners' appeal raised only their Fifth Amendment claim, but they argued in connection with that claim that enforcement of the summons would involve a violation of the taxpayers' reasonable expectation of privacy and particularly so in light of the confidential relationship of attorney to client. * * *

* * * *

All of the parties in these cases have concurred in the proposition that if the Fifth Amendment would have excused a taxpayer from turning over the accountant's papers had he possessed them, the attorney to whom they are delivered for the purpose of obtaining legal advice should also be immune from subpoena. Although we agree with this proposition, we are convinced that it is not the taxpayer's Fifth Amendment privilege that would excuse the attorney from production.

The relevant part of that Amendment provides:

"No person * * * shall be *compelled* in any criminal case to be a *witness against himself.*" (Emphasis added.)

The taxpayer's privilege under this Amendment is not violated by enforcement of the summonses involved in these cases because enforcement against a taxpayer's lawyer would not "compel" the taxpayer to do anything—and certainly would not compel him to be a "witness" against himself. The Court has held repeatedly that the Fifth Amendment is limited to prohibiting the use of "physical or moral compulsion" exerted on the person asserting the privilege. In *Couch v. United States*, we recently ruled that the Fifth Amendment rights of a taxpayer were not violated by the enforcement of a documentary summons directed to her accountant and requiring production of the taxpayer's own records in the possession of the accountant. We did so on the ground that in such a case "the ingredient of personal compulsion against an accused is lacking."

Here, the taxpayers are compelled to do no more than was the taxpayer in *Couch*. The taxpayers' Fifth Amendment privilege is therefore not violated by enforcement of the summonses directed toward their attorneys. *   *   *
*   *   *   *

Confidential disclosures by a client to an attorney made in order to obtain legal assistance are privileged. As a practical matter, if the client knows that damaging information could more readily be obtained from the attorney following disclosure than from himself in the absence of disclosure, the client would be reluctant to confide in his lawyer and it would be difficult to obtain fully informed legal advice. However, since the privilege has the effect of withholding relevant information from the factfinder, it applies only where necessary to achieve its purpose. Accordingly it protects only those disclosures—necessary to obtain informed legal advice—which might not have been made absent the privilege. This Court and the lower courts have thus uniformly held that pre-existing documents which could have been obtained by court process from the client when he was in possession may also be obtained from the attorney by similar process following transfer by the client in order to obtain more informed legal advice. *   *   * It is otherwise if the documents are not obtainable by subpoena *duces tecum* [subpoena used to obtain evidence in the hands of another] or summons while in the exclusive possession of the client, for the client will then be reluctant to transfer possession to the lawyer unless the documents are also privileged in the latter's hands. *   *   *

*   *   * We accordingly proceed to the question whether the documents could have been obtained by summons addressed to the taxpayer while the documents were in his possession. The only bar to enforcement of such summons asserted by the parties or the courts below is the Fifth Amendment's privilege against self-incrimination. *   *   *
*   *   *   *

A subpoena served on a taxpayer requiring him to produce an accountant's workpapers in his possession without doubt involves substantial compulsion. But it does not compel oral testimony; nor would it ordinarily compel the taxpayer to restate, repeat, or affirm the truth of the contents of the documents sought. Therefore, the Fifth Amendment would not be violated by the fact alone that the papers on their face might incriminate the taxpayer, for the privilege protects a person only against being incriminated by his own compelled testimonial communications. The accountant's workpapers are not the taxpayer's. They were not prepared by the taxpayer, and they contain no testimonial declarations by him. *   *   *
*   *   *   *

Whether the Fifth Amendment would shield the taxpayer from producing his own tax records in his possession is a question not involved here; for the papers demanded here are not his "private papers[.]" *   *   *
*   *   *   *

The Supreme Court held that nontestimonial business records not prepared by the taxpayer in the custody of third parties, including lawyers and accountants, must be surrendered when a search warrant is issued for them.

DECISION AND REMEDY

COMMENT   *This case did not confront the issue of whether the individual would have to produce his or her own records. Other tangible evidence, such as a blood sample, sperm sample, or clothing, must be surrendered when a warrant is issued. But would personal business records prepared solely by the taxpayer be required to be surrendered?*

Due Process

Under our Constitution, no person shall be deprived ''of life, liberty, or property, without due process of law.'' This clause is contained in both the Fifth and the Fourteenth Amendments and thus is applicable to both the federal and the state governments. The due process clause has two aspects: procedural and substantive. **Procedural due process** requires that any government decision to take a person's life, liberty, or property must be made fairly.

    Substantive due process focuses on the content, or substance, of legislation. Every statute and regulation, and every government act must be in compliance with the Constitution; otherwise, substantive due process has been violated. For example, Congress passes a statute imposing a $1 million fine and mandatory five-year prison term without a trial on any university professor who appears as an expert on a television news program. The law would be unconstitutional on both substantive and procedural grounds.

    A court would invalidate this legislation because it abridges freedom of speech, a violation of the First Amendment. A denial of substantive due process requires a court to overrule any state or federal law that violates the Constitution. Pro-cedurally, the law is unfair because the penalty is imposed without giving the accused a chance to defend her or his actions. A court will invalidate any statute or court decision because of the lack of procedural due process.

Equal Protection

Under the Fourteenth Amendment, a state may not ''deny to any person within its jurisdiction the equal protection of the laws.'' The Supreme Court has used the due process clause of the Fifth Amendment to make the equal protection guarantee applicable to the federal government. Equal protection means that the government must treat similarly situated individuals in a similar manner.

    Equal protection is concerned with whether there is a rational and legitimate purpose for applying different rules to people. For example, Congress passes a law that provides employment benefits for pregnant women for two weeks prior to delivery and for six months after the baby's arrival. The court would have to determine if there is a rational basis for this law. Similarly, if Congress passed a statute that exempted all men who play football from paying personal taxes, the courts would examine the facts to determine whether there was a rational basis of the law.

FACING A LEGAL ISSUE Stopping Employee Theft

You are in a business that employs a large number of people. You have noticed recently big increases in lost inventory, which often indicates that employees are pilfering inventory. You have no idea who these employees may be or how many are involved. After considering this problem, you decide to listen to your employees' telephone conversations.

In absence of state law to the contrary, it is generally recognized that a business may listen to conversations of their employees. The business owns the telephone service and may have a wiretap that is not considered illegal because the business is consenting to the tap. A wiretap becomes illegal when a third party listens to a conversation without consent from either one of the persons speaking or from one of the owners of the telephone service.

You also decide that, once the number of employees under suspicion is narrowed, you will administer a polygraph test to the suspected ones. Whether the use of polygraphs by businesses is legal is a more difficult question. Most courts will not allow the results of a polygraph into evidence because of the unreliability of the tests. The results depend greatly on the analysis of the person giving the test.

Estimations show an error rate of 16 percent in polygraph tests given. In other words, nearly two out of every ten persons will fail the test when they should have passed it. But these tests are utilized by many businesses. Twenty-one states prohibit polygraphs, and Congress has adopted a law governing their use. In the absence of state law limiting these tests, courts have held that a business can force its employees to take them. This is particularly true if an employee is informed about the tests prior to his or her employment and also is informed as to the questions that will be asked. Nevertheless, under the federal statute, a business may be liable for substantial damages if an employee passes the test.

Summary

The United States Constitution is the oldest active constitution in the modern world. The reason it has lasted so long is that our forefathers had the insight to produce a document that accomplishes three major objectives. First, the Constitution creates three branches of government, each independent of the other but with the ability to limit the powers of the other two branches through a system of checks and balances.

Second, it creates a central government that derives its power from the states but that is supreme. Federalism is the basic structure of our government. Certain powers are given to the federal government while other powers are shared with the states. The Constitution delegates certain powers or rights to the federal government; these are called enumerated powers. For example, the commerce clause of the Constitution allows the federal government to regulate all interstate and foreign commerce. Any commerce, considered cumulatively, that has a substantial economic effect will be considered interstate commerce and subject to regulation. Occasionally, there can be conflicts between federal and state law. The federal law will be upheld under the supremacy clause of the Constitution.

Third, it guarantees the people certain basic rights that neither local nor federal governments can abridge. These rights are set out in detail in the first ten amendments to the Constitution, called the Bill of Rights. These amendments have particular applications to business. For example, under the First Amendment, commercial speech is protected as long as it is not false, deceptive, or misleading. Under the Fourth Amendment, businesses are protected from illegal search and seizures in the absence of a valid warrant. However, corporations or partnerships are not protected from self-incrimination under the Fifth Amendment.

Businesses are also protected by the due process clause in the Fifth and Fourteenth Amend-

ments. There is a distinction between substantive and procedural due process. Procedural due process involves the methods used in protecting legal rights, while substantive due process involves protecting the basic legal rights themselves. The equal protection clause applies to both federal and state governments, which must give equal protection of the laws to all persons.

Key Terms

actual malice **(59)**
commercial speech **(59)**
concurrent powers **(50)**
defamation **(58)**
doctrine of selective
    incorporation **(57)**
double jeopardy **(56)**
due process **(56)**

enumerated powers **(57)**
equal protection clause **(57)**
executive branch **(50)**
federalism **(50)**
judicial branch **(50)**
legislative branch **(50)**
police powers **(53)**
procedural due process **(68)**

probable cause **(63)**
self-incrimination **(56)**
spending power **(56)**
standing to sue **(56)**
substantive due process **(68)**
supremacy clause **(50)**
taxing power **(56)**

Questions and Case Problems

1. A business has a backlog of orders. In order to meet its deadlines, management is considering running the firm seven days a week, eight hours a day. What issues of constitutional law might the management consider in making this decision? Is it possible to terminate someone for refusing to work more than forty hours a week? Is it possible to terminate employees for refusing to work on their religious holy day?

2. Renton, Washington, passed an ordinance that prohibited showing adult motion pictures within 1,000 feet of any residential zone. There were two theaters within 1,000 feet of a residential zone that wanted to exhibit adult films. The owners took the position that the ordinance violated their rights granted them by the First and Fourteenth Amendments. Is this a valid argument? [City of Renton v. Playtime Theaters, Inc., 475 U.S. 41, 106 S.Ct. 925, 89 L.Ed.2d 29 (1986)]

3. A Wisconsin statute prohibits persons or firms that have violated the National Labor Relations Act (NLRA) three times within a five-year period from doing business with the state. Gould, Inc., was not allowed to do business with the state after having three violations of the NLRA within a five-year period. The NLRA has substantive requirements that are in conflict with the Wisconsin statute. Is this statute constitutional under the supremacy clause? Is the Wisconsin statute displaced by the NLRA? [Wis-

consin Department of Industry v. Gould, Inc., 475 U.S. 282, 106 S.Ct. 1057, 89 L.Ed.2d 223 (1986)]

4. Puerto Rico passed a statute and regulations restricting casino gambling advertisements that were aimed at Puerto Rican residents. The operator of one of the casinos sought a declaratory judgment to have these restrictions declared null and void as violating freedom of speech. Puerto Rico took the position that it had a "substantial governmental interest" and the restrictions on such advertising "directly advance[d]" the Commonwealth's asserted interest. How would you hold in this situation? [Posadas de Puerto Rico Associates v. Tourism Co. of Puerto Rico, 478 U.S. 328, 106 S.Ct. 2968, 92 L.Ed.2d 266 (1986)]

5. The owner of a motel who refused to rent rooms to blacks, despite the Civil Rights Act of 1964, brought an action to have the act declared unconstitutional. The motel owner alleged that Congress, in passing the act, had exceeded its power to regulate commerce. The statute was upheld. What legal arguments were used to validate it? [Heart of Atlanta v. United States, 379 U.S. 241, 85 S.Ct. 348, 13 L.Ed.2d 258 (1964)]

6. New Jersey enacted a law prohibiting the importation of most wastes into the state. Some of the landfill operators in New Jersey, however, had agreements with out-of-state residents to dispose of their solid and liquid waste. Philadelphia brought an action claiming that this statute violated the commerce clause by discriminating against interstate commerce. New Jersey asserted that its statute was justified since its landfills were inadequate to dispose of its own waste and importation had a significant and adverse potential effect on the environment. Is this state regulation of interstate commerce permissible? [Philadelphia v. New Jersey, 437 U.S. 617, 98 S.Ct. 2531, 57 L.Ed.2d 475 (1978)]

7. The Mineral King Valley, located in the Sierra Nevada Mountains, is an area of great natural beauty. The United States Forest Service began to give consideration to Mineral King as a potential site for recreational development by Walt Disney Enterprises, Inc. In June of 1969 the Sierra Club filed a suit seeking a declaratory judgment that various aspects of the proposed development contravened federal laws and regulations. The Sierra Club sued as a membership corporation with a special interest in the conservation of national parks. There was, however, no allegation that the members of the Sierra Club would be affected by the proposed action. Has the Sierra Club demonstrated a direct and immediate personal injury due to the challenged action for standing to sue as is required by Article III of the Constitution? [Sierra Club v. Morton, 405 U.S. 727, 92 S.Ct. 1361, 31 L.Ed.2d 636 (1972)]

8. The plaintiffs, Americans United for Separation of Church and State, Inc., as taxpayers, brought an action to challenge a conveyance of land from the Department of Health, Education, and Welfare (HEW) to Valley Forge Christian College, the defendant. The plaintiffs alleged that such a conveyance violated the establishment clause of the First Amendment to the Constitution. The district court dismissed the complaint on the ground that the plaintiffs lacked standing to sue. What was the result on appeal? [Valley Forge Christian College v. Americans United for Separation of Church and State, Inc., 454 U.S. 464, 102 S.Ct. 752, 70 L.Ed.2d 700 (1982)]

9. Congress passed a law making it a federal crime for a person to steal any merchandise from any commercial truck that is part of an interstate shipment. Faulkner was a truck driver. In San Diego, California, he picked up 105 refrigerators that he was supposed to drive to Hartford, Connecticut. In Las Vegas, Nevada, he attempted to sell them to an undercover agent and was arrested. He claimed that he was innocent because the refrigerators never left his truck, and, therefore, no theft took place. Is he correct? Please explain your answer. [United States v. Faulkner, 638 F.2d 129 (9th Cir. 1981)]

Chapter 4   Administrative Agencies and the Regulation of Business

What the Court forgets is that, if government is to work, policy implementation is just as important as policy making. No matter how wise the chief, he has to have the right Indians to transform his ideas into action, to get the job done.

Charles Peters[1]

OUTLINE

---

1. Charles Peters, ''A Kind Word for the Spoils System''
Washington Monthly, September 1976, p. 30.

Introduction

Why should businesspeople know about administrative agencies? When most people think about enforcement of the law, they think about the courts. In actuality, most will never see the inside of a courtroom, and, if they do, it will probably be for a traffic ticket. In contrast, most people have already dealt with an administrative agency.

Today's business decisions are restrained by congressional statutes and by the interpretation and enforcement of those statutes through rules made and enforced by administrative agencies. The study of the powers, procedures, and practices of these administrative agencies is called **administrative law**. Since the late 1960s, the regulation of business has dramatically shifted from the courts applying statutory and common law in order to resolve problems to the more direct and comprehensive controls of administrative agencies. The current constraints placed on business transactions by regulatory authorities have a great impact on the economy. (See Exhibit 4–1 showing how administrative agencies fit into the organizational structure of the federal government.)

We will be studying five areas in this chapter. First, we will review the areas of business that administrative agencies regulate. Second, we will look at the features embodied in administrative agencies that allow them to handle problems more effectively than the legislature or the courts. Third, we will study the Administrative Procedure Act, its amendments, and the three types of power of an administrative agency: quasi-legislative, quasi-judicial, and quasi-executive. Fourth, we will discuss the constitutional, statutory, and judicial limits of an administrative agency's power. Fifth, we will briefly review the deregulation process.

Areas of Regulation

Administrative agencies handle two areas of public concern: **economic regulation** and **public welfare,** which in turn is broken into two parts—protection and **entitlement programs**. (See Exhibit 4–2 for some examples of different types of regulation.)

Economic Regulation

Economic regulation covers the following areas, among others. First, administrative agencies approve the entry into certain types of business; the Federal Aviation Administration, for example, certifies airlines and airports for operation. Second, securities and financial businesses are regulated; for instance, the Federal Reserve System regulates the banking industry. Third, agencies regulate rate control, as when the Federal Energy Regulatory Commission oversees the setting of rates for natural gas and electricity. Fourth, some business activities are entirely subject to regulation, such as the broadcast media, which is regulated by the Federal Communications Commission.

Other agencies have regulatory powers that cut across all types of businesses. For example, the Equal Employment Opportunity Commission has responsibility for all compliance and enforcement activities that work to eliminate discrimination in business, in labor unions, and in government.

Public Welfare

For regulation purposes, the term public welfare refers to programs that benefit the public at large; it does not mean only government aid to lower-income people. For example, the Occupational Health and Safety Administration (OSHA) protects all workers in the workplace. OSHA provides for the public welfare of all by ensuring safety in the work area. All citizens benefit if workers have a safe workplace because the time and money lost from injuries and death decrease.

An example of an agency that handles entitlement programs for the public welfare is the Social Security Administration. Employed persons contribute to social security; if they become disabled or if they retire and they meet the eligibility criteria, they are entitled to receive social security benefits. Social security benefits are not based on income; even millionaires may receive social security if they have contributed to it during their working days.

Features of Administrative Agencies

Several features allow regulatory agencies to deal with problems more effectively than the legisla-

Exhibit 4–1 Chart of the United States Government

This chart seeks to show only the more important agencies of the Government.

THE CONSTITUTION

LEGISLATIVE BRANCH

THE CONGRESS
Senate   House

Architect of the Capital
United States Botanic Garden
General Accounting Office
Government Printing Office
Library of Congress
Office of Technology Assessment
Congressional Budget Office
Copyright Royalty Tribunal
United States Tax Court

EXECUTIVE BRANCH

THE PRESIDENT

Executive Office of the President

White House Office
Office of Management and Budget
Council of Economic Advisers
National Security Council
Office of Policy Development
Office of the United States
Trade Representatives

Council on Environmental Quality
Office of Science and Technology Policy
Office of Administration

THE VICE PRESIDENT

JUDICIAL BRANCH

The Supreme Court of the United States
United States Courts of Appeals
United States District Courts
United States Claims Court
United States Court of Appeals for the Federal Circuit
United States Court of International Trade
Territorial Courts
United States Court of Military Appeals
Administrative Office of the United States Courts
Federal Judicial Center

DEPARTMENT OF HOUSING AND URBAN DEVELOPMENT

DEPARTMENT OF AGRICULTURE

DEPARTMENT OF COMMERCE

DEPARTMENT OF DEFENSE

DEPARTMENT OF EDUCATION

DEPARTMENT OF ENERGY

DEPARTMENT OF HEALTH AND HUMAN SERVICES

DEPARTMENT OF INTERIOR

DEPARTMENT OF JUSTICE

DEPARTMENT OF LABOR

DEPARTMENT OF STATE

DEPARTMENT OF TRANSPORTATION

DEPARTMENT OF THE TREASURY

INDEPENDENT ESTABLISHMENTS AND GOVERNMENT CORPORATIONS

ACTION
Administrative Conferene of the U.S.
African Development Foundation
American Battle Monuments Commission
Appalachian Regional Commission
Board for International Broadcasting
Central Intelligence Agency
Commission on the Bicentennial of the United States Constitution
Commission on Civil Rights
Commission of Fine Arts
Commodity Futures Trading Commission
Consumer Product Safety Commission
Environmental Protection Agency
Equal Opportunity Employment Commission
Export–Import Bank of the U.S.
Farm Credit Administration

Federal Communications Commission
Federal Deposit Insurance Corporation
Federal Election Commission
Federal Emergency Management Agency
Federal Home Loan Bank Board
Federal Labor Relations Authority
Federal Maritime Commission
Federal Mediation and Conciliation Service
Federal Reserve System, Board of Governors of the
Federal Trade Commission
General Services Administration
Inter-American Foundation
Interstate Commerce Commission
Merit Systems Protection Board

National Aeronautics and Space Administration
National Archives and Records Administration
National Capital Planning Commission
National Foundation of the Arts and the Humanities
National Labor Relations Board
National Mediation Board
National Science Foundation
National Transportation Safety Board
Nuclear Regulatory Commission
Occupational Safety and Health Review Commission
Office of Personnel Management
Panama Canal Commission

Peace Corps
Pennsylvania Avenue Development Corporation
Pension Benefit Guaranty Corporation
Postal Rate Commission
Railroad Retirement Board
Securities and Exchange Commision
Small Business Administration
Tennessee Valley Authority
U.S. Arms Control and Disarmament Agency
U.S. Information Agency
U.S. International Developemnt Cooperation Agency
U.S. International Trade Commission
U.S. Postal Service
Veterans Administration

Source: Office of the Federal Register, *U.S. Government Manual, 1987–88*, Washington, D.C., 1986.

Exhibit 4–2 Types of Regulation

Advertising Regulation	Cigarette, cigar, and liquor advertisements and sexually explicit material are controlled for the broadcast media.
Contract Regulation	Private contracts must follow certain regulations, such as the format for interest rate disclosures, language requirements, and the consumer's right to rescind the contract within three days in some situations.
Disclosure Regulation	These regulations require health and nutritional information on food labels, fuel consumption labels on automobiles, and warning labels on dangerous products; in addition, information on securities must be filed with the Securities Exchange Commission.
Licensing Regulation	Bank charters must be issued by the state banking departments, insurance business charters issued by the state insurance departments, and certificates of operation to railroads, trucking companies, and bus lines issued by the Interstate Commerce Commission.
Material and Process Regulation	Materials and processes of manufacture are regulated. The Food and Drug Administration can ban the use of additives to food. The Environmental Protection Agency regulates the use and disposal of hazardous chemicals.
Quota Regulation	The importation or exportation of certain products is limited. The sale of computer components to Soviet bloc countries is not allowed. The importation of oil is subject to quotas.
Rate Regulation	Where the government has granted a monopoly, it controls the profit returned. Utilities, electric, gas, water, and nuclear energy rates are controlled. Rates charged common carriers are regulated by the Department of Transportation when buses, railroads, or trucks are involved. The Federal Maritime Commission governs rates charged by common carriers using the waters.
Standard Regulation	Standards are set by various agencies. The Department of Agriculture sets the standards for meat and poultry. The Federal Aviation Administration sets the standards for airplane certification.

ture. First, because an agency regulates only a specific subject-matter area, it develops expertise in that area and is able to adopt detailed regulations. The legislature, with its limited resources and competing demands, is simply unable to develop the detailed plans needed to implement and monitor all the policies it establishes.

Second, a regulatory agency consists of a very well-developed hierarchy. A government employee generally will work for a particular agency for long periods of time, if not her or his entire career. The employee is promoted and rewarded within that structured bureaucracy. In contrast, the legislature consists of elected representatives and thus does not have continuity in its personnel.

Third, an agency has more flexibility than the legislature. If a business wants Congress to pass a certain law, the process is tedious and the results tenuous at best. Agencies, on the other hand, have been granted by Congress the ability to change regulations in a quick and efficient manner. Some regulations may be redrafted by the agency as soon as it sees the need for the change. Other regulations take longer to change because of the requirement to hold formal, public hearings, but, even with this requirement, it is a faster method than Congress adopting or changing statutes.

Criticisms

Some observers believe that the growth of administrative agencies has limited the ability of elected officials to effect change. In the past, political power and influence were in the hands of the legislative and executive branches of government, but recently they have been moving into the bureaucracy. Political power and influence are, to a substantial degree, wielded by quasi-permanent, unelected, nonpartisan administrative officials. The existing constraints on agencies' powers are gen-

erally seen as ineffective. The administrative agencies are now recognized by some as the fourth branch of the government. (See Exhibit 4–3 which shows the growing number and distribution of Federal employees for the years 1980 and 1986.)

Delegation of Power to Administrative Agencies

Administrative agencies are the primary interpreters and enforcers of congressional statutes that focus on business regulation. Created by Congress, an agency derives its authority from its enabling legislation. Four types of agencies can be created.

Exhibit 4–3 Distribution of Employees in the Federal Government

Branch of Government	1980	1986
Legislative	39,710	36,490
Judicial	15,178	18,966
Executive Office of the President	1,886	1,492
Executive Departments	1,716,970	1,761,644
Agriculture	129,139	113,147
Commerce	48,563	34,397
Census	19,925	8,539
Defense	960,116	1,067,974
Education	7,364	4,554
Energy	21,557	16,657
Health and Human Services	155,662	133,842
Housing and Urban Development	16,964	11,843
Interior	77,357	73,980
Justice	56,327	65,529
Labor	23,400	17,487
State	23,497	25,325
Transportation	72,361	61,281
Treasury	124,663	135,628
Independent Agencies	1,101,089	1,203,587
Federal Reserve System	1,498	1,520
Environmental Protection Agency	14,715	14,021
Federal Trade Commission	1,846	1,079
National Aeronautics and Space Administration	23,714	22,244
U.S. Postal Service	660,014	790,960
Veterans Administration[b]	228,285	240,423
All Others	171,017	133,340

Source: U.S. Bureau of the Census, *Statistical Abstract of the United States, 1988* (108th Edition), Washington, D.C., 1987.
[b]Given Cabinet status effective 1989.

Line Agencies, Independent Agencies, Government Agencies, and Quasi-Official Agencies

When an agency is under the direct control of the president, it is known as a **line agency**. A line agency is headed by one person who is appointed by and serves at the pleasure of the president but who must be confirmed by the Senate. The members of the president's cabinet are heads of line agencies. For example, the Secretary of the Department of Labor (a line agency) is a member of the cabinet who serves at the pleasure of the president. Exhibit 4–4 shows the structure of a sample line agency.

Congress also has established administrative agencies that are independent of the executive branch. If an agency is freestanding from the president and Congress, it is known as an **independent agency.** Many independent agencies have a commission created by Congress. The head of the agency, who is the chair of the commission, has the responsibility of setting the policy of the agency and of running the daily operations of the agency. The Federal Trade Commission and the National Aeronautics and Space Administration are independent agencies.

The commission is a group usually ranging in size from three to fifteen people; the number is determined by Congress. When appointing people to the commission, the president is required to be bipartisan, which means that both political parties must be represented. The length of service on the commission varies from agency to agency, but all terms are staggered and are longer than the four-year term served by the president. Each commissioner is equal to each of the other members. Although commissioners are appointed by the president, they act independently of the president and cannot be removed unilaterally by the president. See Exhibit 4–5 for the structure of a sample independent agency.

A **government agency** is created by Congress to administer a quasi-business venture. These agencies have three similar elements: (1) Each conducts a businesslike activity that (2) produces revenue to continue its own existence and, as a result, (3) needs greater flexibility than is usually given to other types of agencies. The major government agencies are the Tennessee Valley Authority (TVA), the Federal Deposit Insurance Corporation (FDIC), the Pension Benefit Guaranty Corporation, and the United States Postal Service.

A **quasi-official agency** is created by Congress but does not have the same authority as other agencies. These agencies must publish notice and information about certain types of activities in the *Federal Register,* and the members of the agency are appointed by the president, subject to approval by the Senate. Only four quasi-official agencies exist: Legal Services Corporation, National Railroad Passenger Corporation (Amtrak), Smithsonian Institute, and United States Railway Association.

Enabling Legislation

Most administrative agencies are created by Congress when it passes an **enabling act**. This act: creates the agency; sets out its structure; gives it the authority to make rules, investigate problems, and adjudicate cases; and defines what other powers it will have. Congress decides whether the agency will be under the control of the executive branch, whether it will be an independent agency, or a government corporation.

Chapter 6 explains that Congress at one time reserved to itself the right to veto specific actions taken by an agency. The Supreme Court held that it was unconstitutional for Congress to exercise the legislative veto. Congress still has some control over the agencies, however. First, Congress creates and defines the powers of the agency. Second, the Senate must confirm the appointments of the head of the agency and the commissioners. Third, although the president sends to Congress the budget, only Congress, through its constitutional ability to tax and spend, controls the appropriations to the agency. Fourth, Congress may reorganize or abolish the agency. For example, Congress passed the Airline Deregulation Act of 1978. Part of the act abolished the Civil Aeronautics Board, effective January 1985.

After the agency has been created, it must adopt a **general policy statement.** The statement sets out, in broad terms, the philosophy of that particular agency; it describes the mission and objectives of the agency. For example, the general policy statement for the Federal Trade Commission reads that "[i]t is responsible for the admin-

Exhibit 4–4 A Line Agency: Department of Commerce

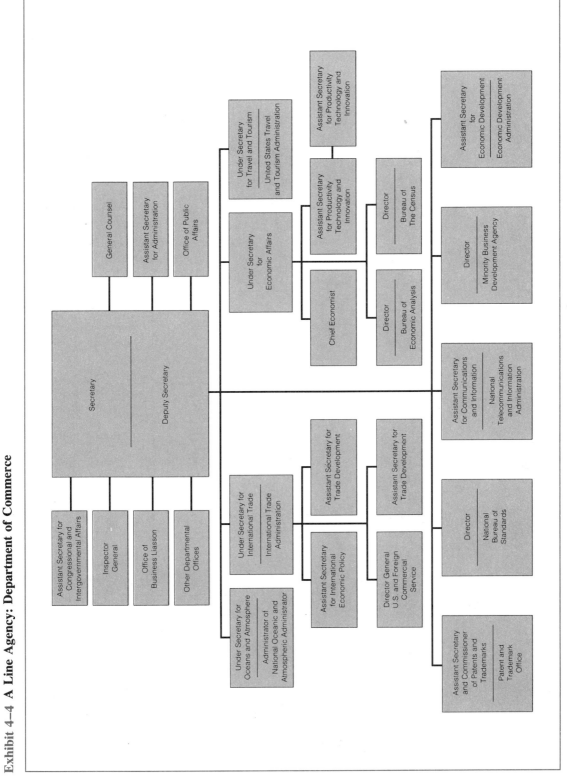

Source: **Office of the Federal Register,** *U.S. Government Manual, 1987–88*, **Washington, D.C., 1986.**

Exhibit 4–5 An Independent Agency: Federal Trade Commission

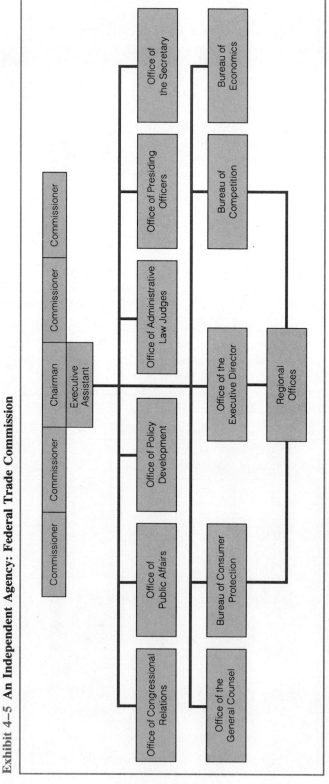

Source: Office of the Federal Register, *U.S. Government Manual, 1987–88,* **Washington, D.C., 1986.**

istration of a variety of statutes which, in general, are designed to promote competition and to protect the public from unfair and deceptive acts and practices in the advertising and marketing of goods and services.''[2]

The statement must also be politically astute; it must satisfy both the political atmosphere that created the agency and those who might curb its powers, if not outright abolish the agency. The authority of different agencies occasionally overlaps. The courts allow this overlapping as long as the actions taken by the agencies are consistent with their respective enabling statutes.

Administrative Procedure Act

The **Administrative Procedure Act (APA) of 1946** standardized many practices of the agencies and now governs how all federal agencies must conduct their business. The APA does allow for differences among the agencies, however, because each agency has a different enabling act. The APA sets out the procedures that an agency must follow when making rules, when acquiring and investigating information, and when adjudicating. The APA ensures that the agency adheres to constitutional requirements.

Three Areas of Power

Administrative agencies have three prime areas of activity: to make rules, to acquire and act on information, and to judge cases. These activities are carried out through the legislative, executive, and judicial powers that an agency possesses. Any one agency may possess a combination of all three types of power. These powers are really quasi-powers. For example, an agency with quasi-legislative power does not have the actual power to pass legislation; only Congress has legislative power. The agency does, however, have a power to adopt rules that is very similar to legislative power; this gives it the name ''quasi-legislative power.''

Agencies are able to promulgate rules that have the effect of law (a **quasi-legislative function**). They have policing powers to ensure compliance with those rules by acquiring information through

recordkeeping and investigations (a **quasi-executive function**). They prosecute violators, render judgments, and impose penalties in an administrative hearing (a **quasi-judicial function**). Congress, however, has not given all three powers to every agency.

Legislative Function The first function of an administrative agency is the legislative function. Operating in a similar manner to a legislative body, the administrative agency must adopt rules so the public knows how to conduct itself when dealing with the items regulated by the agency. For example, if the Environmental Protection Agency has set out rules on how to dispose of asbestos found in a building, any contractor who agrees to remodel a building containing asbestos must follow those rules or face possible fines.

Purpose of Rulemaking A rule adopted by an administrative agency is like a statute passed by Congress. A rule is designed to implement, interpret, or prescribe a law, policy, or practice of an agency. When an agency announces a broadly applicable, prospective policy, the agency uses the mechanism of a rule. Based on future standards of conduct rather than a past or current act, a rule is more appropriate and efficient than applying regulations in a case-by-case approach. A rule is often more specific and easier to follow than agency case decisions.

Ministerial Powers The ministerial powers are a very important part of an agency's activities. Most members of the public have their only contact with an agency when it is exercising its ministerial powers. For example, when a person visits a social security office for information, the agency is using its ministerial powers. Often a business will request an agency's opinion as to whether an action contemplated by the business will be legal under a certain regulation. The agency will give an opinion and offer the business informal advice.

Misinformation Members of the public rely on the agency to give them correct information. Based on that information, individuals and businesses carry out plans, knowing that their action complies with the agency rules. What happens, however,

---

2. 16 C.F.R. Ch. 1, § 0.1 (1-1-88 edition).

if an agency employee gives out inaccurate or wrong information? Public policy dictates that an agency is not bound by or liable for the incorrect information given by its employees. The real meaning of this statement is that a person cannot successfully sue the government.

Why is an agency not liable for the misinformation given by an employee? If it were, an agency could assume powers that Congress had not authorized nor did Congress want the agency to have. The agency is also responsible for spending the public monies entrusted to it in accordance with the law; the agency has no authority to do otherwise. Therefore, even if one individual is devastated by incorrect information given by the agency, the government's duty is to the public and to the protection of the public's trust and monies.

The agency rules are available to the public through the *Federal Register* and through the **Freedom of Information Act (FOIA) of 1966** (discussed later in this chapter). The courts have held that ignorance of the agency's rules or reliance on the agency's information is no excuse for not knowing, not understanding, and not complying with those rules. A person may be able to alleviate the harshness of the rule that ignorance of the law is no excuse if she or he fits into one of the following categories.

First, Congress can authorize an agency to stand behind the advice it gives in specific situations. For example, the Internal Revenue Service (IRS) may issue a binding-opinion letter to a business about a question on a specific tax issue. The IRS must stand by the advice given in that type of letter.

Second, a person may incur a debt to the government because he or she relied on incorrect information given by an agency employee. The harmed person is not able to sue the government, but in certain types of cases the government has the power to grant a remission of indebtedness if the person is qualified. In other words, the person may ask the government to forgive the debt based on hardship and poor advice.

Third, a person who has been harmed by incorrect advice given by a government employee may also apply to Congress for a private bill of relief. The person's congressional representative drafts and submits a bill to Congress to compensate the person for the error of the government. This route is long and difficult and not often successful.

Discretionary Rulemaking Powers Congress has authorized administrators to formulate rules and guidelines under a general (discretionary) authority granted to administrative agencies. For example, the commissioner of Social Security has the discretionary authority to make rules that specify who is eligible for Medicare benefits. This rulemaking authority, authorized by Congress, grants quasi-legislative powers to administrators.

The three types of agency rules are: **procedural rules**, **interpretive rules**, and **substantive rules**. Procedural rules govern the internal practices of an agency. An agency inherently has the power to determine its own goverance. In accordance with the APA, procedural rules must be published in the *Federal Register,* but no other hearings need be held. An agency must follow its own procedural rules; a court may overturn any action that violates a procedural rule.

Remember that an agency is created by a statute. An interpretive rule allows the agency to interpret the statute that it is charged with administering. When an agency issues an interpretive rule, the only public action it must take is to publish the rule in the *Federal Register*. For example, the Federal Reserve Board is charged with enforcing the Truth-in-Lending Act. The Federal Reserve Board published in the *Federal Register* an interpretation of the criteria for determining when a late charge would be considered a ''finance charge.'' No prior notice or opportunity to comment was given. An agency's definition of a term is considered an interpretive rule.

A substantive rule is based on a specific statutory authority to issue rules that create and manage programs. All rules that are not procedural or interpretive in nature are deemed substantive. APA procedural requirements for rulemaking vary, depending on whether an agency engages in **informal** or **formal rulemaking**.

Informal or formal rulemaking is used when an agency adopts a substantive rule. In informal rulemaking, the agency must publish notice of the

---

LEGAL HIGHLIGHT   "Governmentese" and Plain English

The contorted language used by the regulators has jokingly been called "governmentese." For instance, in the 1970s the Occupational Safety and Health Administration published standards concerning the ability of a ladder to hold a "live load unit ascending and descending the ladder with additional weights." Translated, the regulators were talking about a person—the "live load unit"—climbing up and down the ladder with something in his or her hand. Regulators are now required to write in "plain English." Here is the Consumer Product Safety Commission's description of a book of matches.

§ 1202.3 Definitions.

In addition to the definitions given in section 3 of the Consumer Product Safety Act (15 U.S.C. 2052), the following definitions apply for the purpose of this standard:

(a) "Bookmatch" means a single splint, with a matchhead attached, that comes from a matchbook.

(b) "Bridge" means the matchhead material held in common by two or more splints.

(c) "Broken bridge" means a bridge that has become separated.

(d) "Caddy" means a package of two or more matchbooks wrapped or boxed together at a production plant.

(e) "Comb" means a piece of wood, paper, or other suitable material that has been formed into splints, that remain joined at their base, and that are designed to have matchheads attached to their tips.

(f) "Cover" means the paperboard or other suitable material that is wrapped around and fastened to the comb(s).

(g) "Friction" means the dried chemical mixture on the matchbook cover used to ignite the bookmatch.

(h) "Match" means a single splint with matchhead attached.

(i) "Matchbook" means one or more combs with matchheads attached and a cover that is wrapped around and fastened to those combs.

(j) "Matchhead" means the dried chemical mixture on the end of a splint.

(k) "Splint" means the support for the matchhead or that portion normally held when using the bookmatch

§ 1202.4 Matchbook general requirements

A matchbook shall meet the following general requirements:

(a) The friction shall be located on the outside back cover near the bottom of the matchbook.

(b) The cover shall remain closed without external force.

(c) No friction material shall be located on the inside of the cover where possible contact with the matchheads may occur during ordinary use.

(d) There shall be no bridge(s) or broken bridge(s).

(e) No matchhead in the matchbook shall be split, chipped, cracked, or crumbled.

(f) No portion of any matchhead shall be outside the matchbook cover when the cover is closed.

(g) No part of a staple or other assembly device for securing the cover and combs shall be within or touching the friction area.

(h) A staple used as an assembly device for securing the cover and combs shall be fully clinched so that the ends are flattened or turned into the cover.

§ 1202.5 Certification.

Certification shall be in accordance with section 14(a) of the Consumer Product Safety Act (15 U.S.C. 2063(a)). Under this provision, manufacturers and private labelers of products subject to safety standards must certify that their products conform to the standard, based on either a test of each product or on a reasonable testing program.

Continued on next page

LEGAL HIGHLIGHT   **"Governmentese" and Plain English—Continued**

---

§ 1202.6 Marking.

(a) The manufacturer's or private labeler's name and city or a symbol which will identify the name and city shall appear on the matchbook. In addition, every private labeler must label the matchbook with a code which enables it to identify, if requested, the manufacturer of the product.

(b) Boxes or cartons in which two or more caddies are shipped shall be marked "For safety, store in a cool, dry place."

Source: 16 C.F.R. §§ 1202.3–1202.6, Ch. II (1-1-87 edition).

---

proposed rule, give interested persons an opportunity to participate in the rulemaking, and incorporate in the rule a concise general statement of its basis and purpose. Informal rulemaking is frequently referred to as notice-and-comment rulemaking.

In formal rulemaking, an agency must conduct hearing before it can adopt a rule. The parties for and against the rule are entitled to present their case or defense, to submit oral and documentary evidence, to present witnesses, and to conduct examinations of the various witnesses who testify before the agency. Although the parties do not have a right to an attorney, most parties, more often than not, employ an attorney to represent them. In many respects, a formal rulemaking hearing is similar to a trial.

Agency rules have the same legal effect as a statute; in other words, these rules are the law. Ignorance of these rules is no excuse when a person is accused of violating an administrative rule. These rules are made available to the public in the *Federal Register* and in the *Code of Federal Regulations*.

Once a rule has been adopted, the agency can rescind the rule. The agency's action is reviewable by a court, as seen in the following case. The rescission cannot be arbitrary or illogical and cannot be contrary to the will of Congress.

Case 4.1
STATE FARM MUTUAL AUTOMOBILE INSURANCE v. DEPARTMENT OF TRANSPORTATION
United States Court of Appeals, District of Columbia Circuit, 1982.
680 F.2d 206.

BACKGROUND AND FACTS *Congress enacted the National Traffic and Motor Vehicle Safety Act in 1966. The purpose was to reduce the number of deaths and personal injuries resulting from traffic accidents. The act directed the secretary of transportation to issue motor vehicle safety standards. Under the congressional guidelines, the Department of Transportation (DOT) issued a regulation in 1967 that required seat belts in all cars. By 1969 DOT had concluded that the level of seat-belt use was too low to reduce traffic injuries. DOT issued a notice of proposed rulemaking to consider the development and installation of passive restraint systems. In 1972, after extensive hearings and modifications of the original proposed rule, DOT adopted the final standard (Standard 208). The standard called for complete passive restraint protection on vehicles manufactured after 1975. The standard was changed after a further series of hearings and modifications. Now called Modified Standard 208, it extended the deadline to 1984.*

In February 1981, only one month after taking office, the new secretary of transportation, appointed by President Reagan, reopened discussion of the standard. In April, DOT announced it had rescinded the standard through what became known as Notice 25. The reasons given were that the automobile industry was not in good shape economically, sales were depressed, and unemployment high. State Farm and other insurance companies petitioned the court for review of the rescission of the standard.

MIKVA, Circuit Judge.
* * * *

* * * NHTSA [National Highway Transportation Safety Administration] artificially narrowed its analysis of Modified Standard 208. Although that regulation is a performance standard, the agency offered no evidence that certain technology would fail to perform. More important, it then rescinded the standard without analyzing it in terms of technology that clearly would comply.

By any measure of reasoned decisionmaking, NHTSA's action was arbitrary and capricious. Despite carefully issuing notice on an array of possible changes to Modified Standard 208, NHTSA proceeded as though the only question were whether to implement or rescind the safety standard exactly as that standard was first written five years ago. "It is easy enough for an administrator to ban everything." * * *

On balance, it is difficult to find anything positive to say about NHTSA's decisionmaking in this case. After conducting an elaborate quantitative analysis in a 280-page Regulatory Impact Analysis, NHTSA essentially rejected much of this analysis as "hypothetical": * * *

In other words, the analysis to support Notice 25 has not yet been undertaken. Moreover, several of the explanations stated in Notice 25 fly directly in the face of the agency's own analysis. In stating that the standard would raise equity problems, for example, because current users of manual belts would "subsidize" the nonusers who "will generate all of the benefits that result directly and solely from this regulation," * * * NHTSA ignored the fact that high insurance savings could be realized *even by regular users of manual belts.* * * * It is difficult to avoid the conclusion that NHTSA's analysis in Notice 25 has been distorted by solicitude for the economically depressed automobile industry—which is not the agency's mandate—at the expense of consideration of traffic safety, which is.

We do not hold, of course, that an agency charged with promulgating safety standards may never rescind those regulations once promulgated. But rescission must be supported by rational explanations, after a reasoned and good-faith effort to consider alternative means of advancing the agency's purpose. If Congress chooses, it has the authority to override Modified Standard 208 or any other regulation. * * * But NHTSA may not confuse its role with that of Congress. Based on the record and the statements in Notice 25, we must conclude that NHTSA has acted capriciously, wearing blinders that prevented it from reasoned evaluation of methods to fulfill the purposes of the Safety Act.
* * * *

At the same time, we should not simply remand this petition to the agency so that recalcitrance might succeed where rational decisionmaking might not. The implementation of a passive restraint standard has already been delayed without acceptable reasons, perhaps unconscionably so. Our decision does not foreclose rescission, but requires simply that the agency analyze obvious technological alternatives for compliance before doing so. * * *

DECISION AND   *The Court remanded (returned) the case to DOT. Its decision to rescind*
REMEDY   *the safety standard was arbitrary and capricious and not supported by the*
evidence in the record.

Judicial Function   Any problems that a person has with an agency can usually be resolved within the agency's judicial courts. The ability of the administrative agency to resolve internally most of the disputes that arise relieves the judicial court system of many cases. Not all agencies have this function.

Purpose of Adjudication   Administrative agencies develop policy through adjudication as well as through rulemaking. Adjudication is often appropriate when a decision relates to specific facts and to particular parties or when an agency is not ready to announce a rule and wants to take a more cautious, case-by-case approach. The number of adjudications each year is substantial.

Rulemaking is a legislative power, whereas adjudication is a judicial power. Agencies use either rulemaking or adjudication depending on the circumstances. If the future consequences of conduct are to be prescribed and the application will be general, rulemaking is proper. If liability is to be determined based on present or past acts concerning a specific individual, the case should be subject to adjudication.

Administrative Law Judge   An administrative agency adjudicates an individual case in a hearing conducted by an administrative law judge (ALJ) assigned to the agency. As an employee of the agency, an ALJ is not a member of the federal judiciary. The ALJ is authorized to perform a variety of judgelike functions in the judicial hearing. The ALJ issues subpoenas, administers oaths to witnesses, conducts hearing conferences, regulates the conduct and course of the hearing, rules on admissibility of evidence, and makes other procedural rulings.

Outside the hearing, an ALJ may not talk with anyone on any issues before him or her in order to remain as insulated as possible from all external influences. After the hearing, the ALJ issues a decision with the findings and conclusions that support it, just as in a court judgment.

Procedures for Administrative Adjudication   Administrative adjudication begins with the issuance of a complaint to a business that the agency believes has violated a particular rule or standard. After a complaint is served on an alleged wrongdoer, the party is given an opportunity to answer. Eventually, the complaint is heard by an administrative law judge, who conducts the hearing, rules on all motions, and decides both the facts and the law. In an agency hearing, no right to a jury exists.

After considering all the evidence and law, the ALJ issues an **order** that is subject to review by the head of the administrative agency. An order is defined as the final disposition of the case between the government and the party. An order is similar to a judgment by a court.

Most agencies have an appeal route built into the system. For example, a person audited by the Internal Revenue Service may appeal the auditor's decision to the Tax Court, a quasi-judicial court within the Internal Revenue Service. In some cases, the party can engage in an informal settlement process or agree to a **consent decree**—an agreement by the parties that carries the sanction of the court. After the final hearing, the affected party can appeal to the judicial courts.

Executive Function   Through the executive function, administrative agencies are able to ensure that their rules are followed.

Acquisition of Information   The bureaucracy is an information-gathering instrument of the government. The acquisition of information enables an agency to become an expert on the subject matter it regulates.

Most of the information the agency gathers is obtained voluntarily. On occasion, information must be obtained through compulsion. Agencies gather the information in one of three ways: record keeping and periodic reports, subpoena power, and power to conduct physical inspections. The first method obtains information through voluntary co-operation, while the latter two methods use compulsion to obtain the information.

Record-Keeping and Reporting Requirements Federal agencies that regulate businesses require those businesses to keep specific records and to make periodic mandatory reports based on those records. For example, a whiskey manufacturer must keep and maintain records for the Bureau of Alcohol, Tobacco, and Firearms. This information

allows the agency to study problems and to promulgate, amend, or delete rules as necessary.

Investigatory Powers Other executive functions performed by an administrative agency are investigations and prosecutions. When performing these functions, an agency follows procedural rules prescribing its conduct. Sometimes an agency fails to take any action. The following case concerns the refusal of an administrative agency to conduct an investigation.

BACKGROUND AND FACTS *The National Traffic and Motor Vehicle Safety Act of 1966 states that, if the secretary of transportation makes a determination that a safety-related defect exists, the secretary, through the National Highway Transportation Safety Administration (NHTSA) must order the manufacturer to recall and remedy the defect. It was alleged that between 1966 and 1979 defects in automatic transmissions built by the Ford Motor Company caused cars to disengage from "Park" and to roll without warning.*

A 1982 NHTSA investigation ended without a final determination on the existence of a defect because NHTSA and Ford entered a settlement agreement that required Ford to notify owners about the possibility of a defect. NHTSA explicitly reserved the right to commence a new proceeding on the alleged defect if additional facts warranted. In March 1985, the Center for Auto Safety petitioned NHTSA to reopen the hearing because of additional evidence. The NHTSA administrator denied the petition after reviewing the administrative record. She was not convinced that a final defect determination would be warranted even if a further investigation was undertaken. The Center for Auto Safety appealed the denied petition. The district court denied the review, and the Center appealed to the court of appeals.

Case 4.2
CENTER FOR AUTO SAFETY v. DOLE
United States Court of Appeals,
District of Columbia Circuit,
1987.
828 F.2d 799.

WALD, Chief Judge.
*   *   *   *

Because this case involves "informal agency action," *   *   * judicial review of NHTSA's denial of appellants' petition under the APA [Administrative Procedure Act] is limited to whether the decision was "arbitrary, capricious, or abuse of discretion, or otherwise not in accordance with law." *   *   * Judicial review *   *   * determines whether the reasons for the agency's decision were legally permissible and reasoned one, and whether there was adequate factual support for the decision. *   *   * The reviewing court may not consider new evidence that was not before the agency when it made its decision.

Here, we can identify no congressional objectives of the Motor Vehicle Safety Act with which the normal level of judicial review would interfere. The basic congressional objective underlying the Motor Vehicle Safety Act is stated simply and clearly in the Act's first section: "Congress hereby declares that the purpose of this chapter is to reduce traffic accidents and deaths and injuries to persons resulting from traffic accidents." *   *   * To the extent that judicial review helps to assure that factual support exists for NHTSA decisions denying enforcement petitions, it helps to reduce the threat of traffic accidents, and aids, not hinders, the basic congressional purpose of the statute.

Moreover, the Motor Vehicle Safety Act expressly contemplates extensive citizen involvement in enforcement of the Act by providing for citizen petitions for enforcement of safety standards, by expressly authorizing public hearings on allegations of safety-related defects, and by requiring the agency to publish a statement of reasons for denying a petition.

* * * *

By contrast, the administrative decision in this case concerns the possibility that certain kinds of cars are defective and unsafe. This possibility, in turn, depends on an evaluation of "technical" evidence about the cars which the agency's own regulations prescribe. * * * Of course, the reviewing court may not substitute its judgment for the agency's but it certainly is possible for the court to review the administrative decision for factual support without an impermissible substitution of judgment, in the same way we review agency factual determinations * * * thousands of times every year.

* * * *

While this court cannot, and should not, second-guess the agency's safety determinations, this court can and should assure that the agency has *some* factual support for those safety determinations. Making sure that the agency's stated reason for denying an enforcement petition is in truth the lack of a "substantial safety issue" guarantees that the responsible administrative agency has given at least a minimum amount of consideration to the citizens whose safety Congress has entrusted to the agency.

Our holding then is this: When Congress grants citizens the right to petition administrative agencies for enforcement on an issue of public safety, and the relevant substantive statute sends out no identifiable signals on the availability or scope of judicial review of an agency's denial of that petition, but the agency has bound itself by a legal rule to grant the petition unless it makes a finding of "no reasonable possibility" of a safety defect, then a petitioner is entitled under the APA to judicial review of a decision denying the petition to assure that the agency had some factual support for its "no reasonable possibility" finding. In such circumstances, the arbitrary or capricious standard of review in * * * the APA functions as usual, and is not limited to examining merely the stated reasons for the agency's decision. Therefore, * * * we hold that NHTSA's determination that no "reasonable possibility" of a safety-related defect exists in this case is subject to judicial review on the basis of the evidence that the Administrator had before her when she made her decision.

DECISION AND REMEDY   *The court reversed the decision of the district court and remanded the case to the district court. The court of appeals held that the Motor Vehicle Safety Act allows judicial review of NHTSA decisions, even those denying a citizen's petition. The district court has the "reasonable possibility" standard with which to review the decisions. The reviewing court must examine the administrative record in order to make its decision.*

Enforcement Powers Enforcement powers are also delegated to agencies. All final orders issued by an ALJ carry the weight of statutory law and can result in penalties if violated. These penalties are enforceable, unless a reviewing court reverses the agency decision. Failure to comply with the penalties is treated like any other violation of the law.

In most cases, violations are considered to be a civil matter. A business is held liable for money damages or is required to take some specific ac-tion, such as the installation of pollution-control equipment. In recent years, there has been a trend toward issuing civil penalties, such as fines.

The following case examines the right to a jury trial when fines may be levied as punishment.

BACKGROUND AND FACTS   *Two firms were cited by Occupational Safety and Health Administration (OSHA) inspectors for having unsafe workplaces. The first firm was cited for failing to have the sides of trenches shored and was fined $7,500. The second firm was cited for failing to have roof-opening covers installed to prevent accidents. The fine was $600. Both firms appealed the fines. They were given a hearing before an administrative law judge, who affirmed the findings of the OSHA inspectors. The fine of $7,500 was reduced to $5,000, but the second fine was affirmed at $600. Both firms appealed to the court of appeals, challenging the constitutionality of OSHA's enforcement procedures. The court of appeals affirmed the decision of the administrative law judge and found the enforcement pro-cedures to be constitutional. Both firms appealed to the United States Su-preme Court. The defendants argued that they were entitled to a jury trial under the Constitution.*

 Case 4.3

ATLAS ROOFING CO., INC. v. OSHA

Supreme Court of the United States, 1977.
430 U.S. 422, 97 S.Ct. 1261, 51 L.Ed.2d 464.

WHITE, Justice delivered the opinion of the Court.
*   *   *   *

We granted the petitions for writs of certiorari limited to the important question whether the Seventh Amendment prevents Congress from assigning to an admin-istrative agency, under these circumstances, the task of adjudicating violations of OSHA. *   *   *

The Seventh Amendment provides the ''[i]n Suits at common law, where the value in controversy shall exceed twenty dollars, the right of trial by jury shall be preserved. *   *   *'' The phrase ''Suits at common law'' has been construed to refer to cases tried prior to the adoption of the Seventh Amendment in courts of law in which jury trial was customary as distinguished from courts of equity or admiralty in which jury trial was not. *   *   * Petitioners claim that a suit in a federal court by the Government for civil penalties for violation of a statute is a suit for a money judgment which is classically a suit at common law, *   *   * and that the defendant therefore has a Seventh Amendment right to a jury determination of all issues of fact in such a case. *   *   *

*   *   * [W]hen Congress creates new statutory ''public rights,'' it may assign their adjudication to an administrative agency with which a jury trial would be incompatible, without violating the Seventh Amendment's injunction that jury trial is to be ''preserved'' in ''suits at common law.'' Congress is not required by the Seventh Amendment to choke the already crowded federal courts with new types of litigation or prevented from committing some new types of litigation to admin-istrative agencies with special competence in the relevant field. This is the case even if the Seventh Amendment would have required a jury where the adjudication of those rights is assigned to a federal court of law instead of an administrative agency. *   *   *

More to the point, it is apparent from the history of jury trial in civil matters that factfinding, which is the essential function of the jury in civil cases, was never the exclusive province of the jury under either the English or American legal systems at the time of the adoption of the Seventh Amendment; and the question whether

a fact would be found by a jury turned to a considerable degree on the nature of the forum in which a litigant found himself. Critical factfinding was performed without juries in suits in equity, and there were no juries in admiralty, nor were there juries in the military justice system. The jury was the factfinding mode in most suits in the common-law courts, but it was not exclusively so: Condemnation was a suit at common law but constitutionally could be tried without a jury[.]
* * *

Thus, history and our cases support the proposition that the right to a jury trial turns not solely on the nature of the issue to be resolved but also on the forum in which it is to be resolved. Congress found the common-law and other existing remedies for work injuries resulting from unsafe working conditions to be inadequate to protect the Nation's working men and women. It created a new cause of action, and remedies, therefor, unknown to the common law, and placed their enforcement in a tribunal supplying speedy and expert resolutions of the issues involved. The Seventh Amendment is no bar to the creation of new rights or to their enforcement outside the regular courts of law.

DECISION AND REMEDY   *The decision of the court of appeals was affirmed, and the fines for both firms were upheld. More importantly, the Supreme Court found that Congress had the power to create statutory rights without providing that juries be available to decide the facts. Congress is free to create new methods to resolve problems between disagreeing parties.*

Limitations on Administrative Agencies' Powers

Most limitations on administrative agencies' powers arise from one of three sources: (1) the Constitution, (2) congressional statutes, and (3) judicial review. Constitutional limitations typically relate to the substance of administrative agency behavior; any procedural inadequacies are subject to judicial review.

Major Constitutional Limitations

Amendments to the Constitution provide the most important limitations on administrative agency actions. Although most constitutional rights, such as due process and unreasonable search and seizure, are regarded primarily as rights of individuals, businesses also have some constitutional rights.

Both procedural and substantive due process protect businesses against arbitrary, capricious, and unreasonable administrative agency actions. Substantive due process applies when issues arise that involve property or other rights affected by government. Procedural due process focuses on

power notice and hearing procedures. Enforcement of due process rights through the Fifth and Fourteenth Amendments, however, follows a double standard. Whenever government action directly affects economic activity, courts usually find it to be constitutional. On the other hand, courts are generally suspicious of government actions that might limit basic human freedoms.

Fourth Amendment Limitations People are protected from unwarranted intrusions into their personal privacy by the Constitution. In civil and criminal cases, businesses are also protected from unreasonable searches. The Fourth Amendment has been used to prohibit building inspectors from looking for building-code violations against the desires of the owner of the premises when the inspectors do not have a warrant. On the other hand, an agency may make an unannounced inspection of those businesses that traditionally have been heavily regulated, such as the alcoholic beverage industry, the firearm industry, the fishing industry, and the meat-packing industry.

In the case that follows, the United States Supreme Court held that government safety inspectors must have a warrant to make a routine inspection of work areas in a private business.

BACKGROUND AND FACTS *Prior to this case, inspectors of the Occupational Safety and Health Administration (OSHA) were not required to obtain permission to enter the work areas of firms under OSHA's jurisdiction. In 1975, an OSHA inspector entered the customer service area of Barlow's, Inc., an electrical and plumbing installation business. After showing his credentials, the inspector informed the president and general manager, Barlow, that he would be conducting an inspection of the working areas of the business.*

On inquiry, Barlow learned that no complaint had been received about his company. The inspection was simply the result of random selection. The inspector did not have a search warrant. Barlow refused to permit the inspector to enter the working area of his business, relying on his rights guaranteed by the Fourth Amendment.

OSHA filed suit in the United States District Court, which issued an order compelling Barlow to admit the OSHA inspector for purposes of conducting an occupational safety and health inspection.

The OSHA inspector, now armed with a court order, when back to Barlow's, Inc., and Barlow again refused admission. This time, Barlow went to the same district court seeking an injunction to prohibit the inspector from making a warrantless search on the ground that the OSHA inspection violated the Fourth Amendment.

This time the district court ruled in Barlow's favor. The district court held that the Fourth Amendment required a warrant for the type of search involved and that the authorization for warrantless inspections under the OSHA statute was unconstitutional. A permanent injunction against such searches or inspections was entered on the behalf of Barlow. The appeal by OSHA to the Supreme Court challenged the validity of that injunction.

Case 4.4

MARSHALL v. BARLOW'S, INC.

Supreme Court of the United States, 1978.
436 U.S. 307, 98 S.Ct. 1816, 56 L.Ed.2d 305.

WHITE, Justice delivered the opinion of the Court.

* * * *

The Warrant Clause of the Fourth Amendment protects commercial buildings as well as private homes. To hold otherwise would belie the origin of that Amendment, and the American colonial experience. * * *

* * * [U]nless some recognized exception to the warrant requirement applies, * * * a warrant [is required] to conduct the inspection sought in this case.

* * * Certain industries have such a history of government oversight that no reasonable expectation of privacy, could exist for a proprietor over the stock of such an enterprise. Liquor and firearms are industries of this type; when an entrepreneur embarks upon such a business, he has voluntarily chosen to subject himself to a full arsenal of governmental regulation.

* * * The element that distinguishes these enterprises form ordinary businesses is a long tradition of close government supervision, of which any person who chooses to enter such a business must already be aware. * * *

The clear import * * * is that the closely regulated industry * * * is the exception. * * *

* * * *

The critical fact in this case is that entry over Mr. Barlow's objection is being sought by a Government agent. Employees are not being prohibited from reporting OSHA violations. What they observe in their daily functions is undoubtedly beyond the employer's reasonable expectation of privacy. The Government inspector, however, is not an employee. Without a warrant he stands in no better position than a member of the public. What is observable by the public is observable, without a warrant, by the Government inspector as well. The owner of a business has not, by the necessary utilization of employees in his operation, thrown open the areas where employees alone are permitted to the warrantless scrutiny of Government agents. That an employee is free to report, and the Government is free to use, any evidence of noncompliance with OSHA that the employee observes furnishes no justification for federal agents to enter a place of business from which the public is restricted and to conduct their own warrantless search.

*   *   *   *

Whether the Secretary proceeds to secure a warrant or other process, with or without prior notice, his entitlement to inspect will not depend on his demonstrating probable cause to believe that conditions in violation of OSHA exist on the premises. Probable cause in the criminal law sense is not required. For purposes of an administrative search such as this, probable cause justifying the issuance of a warrant may be based not only on specific evidence of an existing violation but also on a showing that ''reasonable legislative or administrative standards for conducting an . . . inspection are satisfied with respect to a particular [establishment].''

A warrant showing that a specific business has been chosen for an OSHA search on the basis of a general administrative plan for the enforcement of the Act derived from neutral sources such as, for example, dispersion of employees in various types of industries across a given area, and the desired frequency of searches in any of the lesser divisions of the area, would protect an employer's Fourth Amendment rights. We doubt that the consumption of enforcement energies in the obtaining of such warrants will exceed manageable proportions.

*   *   *   *

*   *   * The authority to make warrantless searches devolves almost unbridled discretion upon executive and administrative officers, particularly those in the field, as to when to search and whom to search. A warrant, by contrast, would provide assurances from a neutral officer that the inspection is reasonable under the Constitution, is authorized by statute, and is pursuant to an administrative plan containing specific neutral criteria. Also, a warrant would then and there advise the owner of the scope and objects of the search, beyond which limits the inspector is not expected to proceed. These are important functions for a warrant to perform, functions which underlie the Court's prior decisions that the Warrant Clause applies to inspections for compliance with regulatory statutes. We conclude that the concerns expressed by the Secretary do not suffice to justify warrantless inspections under OSHA or vitiate the general constitutional requirement that for a search to be reasonable a warrant must be obtained.

*   *   *   *

DECISION AND REMEDY   *The permanent injunction was upheld. OSHA inspections conducted without warrants were held to be unconstitutional when the business to be inspected is not one that is otherwise regulated by close government supervision.*

Fifth Amendment Applications   Under the Fifth Amendment, a person cannot be forced to testify against himself or herself in a criminal case. The Supreme Court has held that a corporation is not a person within the meaning of the Constitution, and thus corporations are not eligible for Fifth Amendment protection.

Administrative agencies may require businesses to make and maintain records. Because corporations are not persons, the records that they must maintain are not included under the self-incrimination clause and, therefore, may be disclosed in criminal or civil cases. These types of corporate records become, in effect, quasi-public records. An agency has the right to inspect these records to ensure accuracy of the reports it receives on a periodic basis.

Although these records are quasi-public, the disclosure requirement is not tantamount to public disclosure. Businesses legitimately have secrets concerning the product or service sold; they may have secret marketing strategies or trade secrets, as well as sensitive personal records. Congress has provided protection in two ways. First, the enabling act may specifically prohibit the records from being made public and prohibit the agency's employees from disclosing the information. Second, in 1966 Congress passed the Freedom of Information Act. Although this act promotes access and availability of information to the public and individuals, certain information is restricted from disclosure. This act will be examined in detail in the next section. In short, business records are protected from public disclosure under certain restricted circumstances.

Congressional Statutes

When Congress creates an agency, its statutory scheme includes congressional limitations on that agency. Although certain general rules apply to all agencies, a person dealing with a specific agency must be aware of these congressional limitations. Some statutes amend the Administrative Procedure Act and thus affect all agencies, while other statutes apply only to one agency.

Freedom of Information Act The Freedom of Information Act (FOIA), is an amendment to the Administrative Procedure Act. All administrative agencies are subject to FOIA. FOIA makes all the information held by federal agencies available to

the public. Exemptions do exist if the information falls within certain categories.

Information may be disclosed under FOIA in one of three ways. First, the *Federal Register* publishes information, such as policy statements and procedural and substantive rules, from the agencies. Second, agencies must make available for public inspection and copying certain information that is not printed in the *Federal Register*. Reprints of the opinions of the administrative law judges, public statements, interpretive rules, staff manuals and directives are all sold to the public for a nominal fee. Third, if the information is not published under either of these methods and it is not exempt, each agency has established reasonable procedures for the public to follow when requesting a copy of that information.

The important exempt categories are those that contain information in the following areas: information relating to national defense or foreign policy; internal personnel rules; information protected by another statute that prohibits disclosure; business trade secrets and privileged or confidential business information; and any information that violates personal privacy. Even though certain information may be classified in one of the exempt categories, the agency is not automatically prohibited from disclosing that information. FOIA gives the agency discretion as to whether or not to disclose the information.

When an agency decides not to disclose information under FOIA, the agency must disclose its reasons to the requester. After exhausting the administrative remedies, the requester has the right to file a lawsuit in district court to force the agency to disclose the information. The agency has the burden of proof to support its action. The following case examines FOIA from a different perspective.

BACKGROUND AND FACTS *This case is known as a reverse Freedom of Information Act (FOIA) case. In this type of case, the submitter of information (usually a business) seeks to prevent the government from releasing the information to a third party in response to its FOIA request. The government must still follow the FOIA rules in determining whether to release the information.*

CNA Financial Corporation is an insurance company that does business with the federal government. As part of the contract, CNA had to report its affirmative action performance on an Equal Employment Opportunity

 Case 4.5

CNA FINANCIAL CORPORATION v. DONOVAN

United States Court of Appeals, District of Columbia Circuit, 1987.

830 F.2d 1132.

(EEO) form. In 1977 a group called Women Employed requested from the government the affirmative action programs, EEO forms, and government documents concerning CNA's compliance with the affirmative action requirements.

CNA objected to the disclosures under the Trade Secrets Act. CNA argued that the act qualified as a statute that authorized the withholding of information under the FOIA exemption. Claiming substantial competitive harm, CNA asserted that, if the information was released, the disclosure would facilitate the raiding of its employees, demoralize its employees, generate adverse publicity if the data were misconstrued, and reveal to competitors CNA's plans to enter, expand, or contract different markets and product lines.

The Office of Federal Contract Compliance Programs (OFCCP) hired an expert to evaluate the data submitted by CNA. After careful examination of the report and of other evidence that had been submitted, the OFCCP hearing officer determined that the Trade Secrets Act was not a withholding statute within the meaning of Exemption 4 of FOIA. The hearing officer ordered the information to be disclosed. The district court affirmed OFCCP's decision.

ROBINSON, Circuit Judge.

* * * *

FOIA is itself the product of a most thoughtful and deliberate weighing process, in which Congress considered the views of those who submit information, those who collect it, and those who desire it. * * * To the extent that commercial and financial data within the ambit of the Trade Secrets Act do not fall within one of the FOIA exemptions, * * * the decision has been made that on balance it ought to be unmasked in the interest of informing the public of the bases for governmental action. To the extent that such data as trade secrets and confidential financial information are excepted from mandatory disclosure by one or more of the exemptions that Congress has incorporated into FOIA, the Trade Secrets Act will bar a discretionary release unless, after notice and comment, an agency, possessing delegated power to do so, promulgates, a contrary rule having the force of law. Clearly, this resolution does not undermine the foundation of the Trade Secrets Act by throwing open the door to wholesale, haphazard revelation of private financial and business data in the possession of governmental agencies.

* * * *

CNA and OFCCP disagree on what material is within the purview of Exemption 4. The data that OFCCP proposes to release can be grouped into three principal types: statistics on the racial and sexual composition of the workforce within various CNA departments; goals developed for equal employment purposes; and "applicant flow information" showing the percentage, by race and sex, of applications hired from without and employees promoted from within.

CNA's objections and the responses thereto by OFCCP may also be arranged in three occasionally overlapping categories. First, OFCCP says that much of the information sought by CNA to be confined is already publicly available, and this assertion has not been contested before this court. To the extent that any data requested under FOIA are in the public domain, the submitter is unable to make any claim to confidentiality—a *sine qua non* of Exemption 4. We do not further consider CNA's arguments regarding these data.

Second, several of CNA's claims with respect to other information relate not to alleged competitive harm but rather to anticipated displeasure of its employees or to adverse public reaction. CNA has protested, for example, that release of information on the number of women and minorities hired might result in unfavorable publicity. It also fears that its employees may become "demoralized" following disclosure of data showing the percentage of individuals promoted. We have previously found such complaints unrelated to the policy behind Exemption 4 of protecting submitters from external injury. These proffered objections simply do not amount to "harm flowing from the affirmative use of proprietary information by competitors."

The remaining disagreements between CNA and OFCCP concern the long-range consequences of the release of the data at issue. CNA submitted affidavits predicting a number of harmful effects; OFCCP, while offering no independent evidence, has answered these contentions with its own predictions of the repercussions of disclosure. One noteworthy objection by CNA to revelation of applicant flow data is that it would enable competitors more easily to direct their recruiting efforts to the best sources of potential employees. OFCCP counters with the logical rejoinder that these data will not be of any particular help to competitors since the employee-source and employee-position categories are broad, and the applicant pool is a function of the labor market and beyond an individual competitor's control.

These and other similar contentions presented no more than two contradictory views of what likely would ensue upon release of information that CNA sought to protect. In each case, OFCCP retorted with reasonable and thorough prognoses of its own. We thus are confronted by the type of judgments and forecasts courts traditionally leave largely to agency expertise, with judicial review limited by the narrow standard sanctioned. After careful consideration of OFCCP's decision, we are satisfied that it cannot in any way be characterized as arbitrary, capricious, or an abuse of discretion. CNA's objections were answered fully, and OFCCP's explanations of anticipated effects were certainly no less plausible than those advanced by CNA. Each of OFCCP's explanations is well reasoned, logical and consistent, and predictive judgments are not capable of exact proof. We find OFCCP's application of Exemption 4 entirely rational, and therefore legally permissible.

The court of appeals affirmed the decision of the district court. The Trade Secrets Act does not qualify as a statute that authorizes the withholding of this type of information under the FOIA exemption. OFCCP presented a reasoned and detailed basis for its decision, and it was legally sufficient to be upheld after judicial review.

DECISION AND REMEDY

Privacy Act   The **Privacy Act** was a result of a 1974 amendment of the Administrative Procedure Act. The Privacy Act protects only individuals who are citizens or legal aliens. By statutory definition, corporations or other business entities are not covered.

Agencies accumulate tremendous amounts of information on individuals. If a person requests it, agencies are required to give the person all the information that it has on him or her. The information maintained must be correct, accurate, and current. If this information is stale, inaccurate, or

incomplete, the individual is able to make corrections. The Privacy Act does not require an agency to disclose the information it has on that individual under certain circumstances. For example, if a person is being investigated for a crime, the investigating agency does not have to disclose that information even if it is requested.

On the other hand, the agency is not allowed to disclose this information to others unless the conditions under the statute are met. For example, a newspaper requests information from an agency on a particular person. The agency cannot provide that information because it is protected under the Privacy Act; no exceptions to the act exist for newspapers.

Sunshine Act   The **Sunshine Act of 1976** also amended the Administrative Procedure Act. This act prohibits agencies from holding secret meetings. An agency must give notice of the time and place of the meeting and list the matters to be discussed. Not all meetings are open to the public. Even though the meeting is closed to the public, the meeting notice must post the fact that there will be a meeting and whether the meeting is open or closed. The Sunshine Act prevents secret, not closed, meetings.

If a person believes that the agency was in error in its decision to close the meeting, the person can sue the agency in district court. The court may grant an injunction against future violations of the Sunshine Act. The court may not, however, overturn the action taken by the agency behind closed doors solely because the Sunshine Act was violated. Any basis for overturning the agency act must be established on other legal grounds.

Regulatory Flexibility Act   In 1980 Congress again amended the Administrative Procedure Act. The **Regulatory Flexibility Act** takes into account the differences among the various businesses subject to regulation. A regulation may have a different effect on a small business than it has on a large corporation. The act requires a special regulatory flexibility agenda to be printed in the *Federal Register* twice a year, in April and October. An agency must publish a list of all rules that the agency is considering or may consider during the next few months. The rules listed are the ones likely to have a significant economic impact on a substantial number of small businesses.

Sunset Acts   **Sunset acts** are included in the statutes that create specific agencies. A sunset act sets an automatic expiration date for the agency in order to force regular legislative review. In the past, some administrative agencies have outlived their purpose or usefulness but have continued to exist because the agency's enabling act had not been repealed. If an agency is to continue, Congress must take affirmative action. When Congress

reviews an agency periodically, the agency is more likely to be responsive to the public will. At reviewing time, Congress can make known its concerns about the agency through manipulating its budget or by threatening to reorganize or dismantle the agency.

Judicial Review

Administrative decisions can be appealed to the courts because the judiciary has the power and the duty to interpret the law. The province of Congress is to formulate legislative policy, to mandate programs and projects, and to establish their relative priority for the nation. Once Congress has exercised its legislative power by creating a new administrative agency and giving it a mandate, then the agency is to administer the law, and the judiciary is to interpret and enforce the law.

In a judicial review of an agency's decision, the courts investigate first whether that agency has any authority for rulemaking. If the court finds that the agency has the authority, the court then determines whether the agency has exceeded its properly delegated authority. The first question focuses on whether the delegation from Congress was proper. The second question focuses on whether the exercise of that power by the agency was proper.

Congress delegated broad discretionary powers over a specialized subject matter to administrative agencies. As a result, a court gives **judicial deference** to agency decisions and does not reverse an agency action unless it finds the agency violated a condition set out by the Administrative Procedure Act.

Each agency has a series of procedures that a person must follow before an appeal may be made to the courts. The requirement that the appealing party must follow these procedures is called the **doctrine of exhaustion of remedies.** This doctrine is deeply rooted in history and provides a reasonable balance between a person's rights and the rights of the government.

Deregulation

The federal government has imposed restraints on agencies by limiting the number of ineffective or potentially harmful rules. In 1978 President Carter issued an order requiring agencies to determine the possible impact of various government regulations that effect the economy.

Although in office for only four years, President Carter's administration made dramatic strides toward deregulation. Congress passed many deregulatory acts that took effect after President Reagan took office. The deregulation has taken place mainly in the agencies responsible for economic regulation.

In 1981 President Reagan issued two executive orders that further limited administrative regulations. These executive orders had several purposes: to establish regulatory priorities, to increase the accountability of agency officials, to provide for presidential oversight of the regulatory process, to reduce the burdens of existing and future regulations, to minimize duplication and conflict of regulations, and to enhance public and congressional understanding of the regulatory objectives.

Each agency must submit to the Office of Management and Budget (OMB) each year a statement of its regulatory policies, goals, and objectives for the coming year, along with information concerning all significant regulatory action under way or planned. Each agency must prepare a regulatory impact analysis of major rules. These executive orders apply only to the agencies in the executive branch and not to independent agencies, but many independent agencies have chosen to comply voluntarily.

FACING A LEGAL ISSUE   Administrative Law: Facing Zoning Problems

You want to open a small video rental store that offers movies appealing to college students. You find a perfect location with a low monthly rent near the dormitories and other student housing.

Before signing the lease, however, your prospective landlord insists that you contact the local municipal zoning agency to make certain that this type of business activity is permitted.

Wanting to open the store as soon as possible, you go to the proper city office and discover that the zoning ordinance does not allow the rental of products, only the sale of products. You ask whether there are any exceptions to this ordinance. The zoning official states that you can either obtain a use permit or a variance to the zoning ordinance, or you can attempt to have city council change the zoning ordinance.

This venture is your first contact with administrative law. In order to obtain a variance or use permit, you must submit an application to the zoning board. An appointed official will grant or deny your application in a summary manner. If it is denied, you have a right to appeal his or her decision to a board of adjustment. Normally, the members of the board of adjustment are appointed by the elected officials, either the members of the city council or the mayor. If your request is denied by the board of adjustment, you can then take your appeal to the judicial system.

You may try another administrative route. You can file a petition for a zoning change with the city planning department. The department will make a recommendation to the planning and zoning commission. This body is also appointed by elected officials; however, unlike the board of adjustment, which has the power to make final administrative decision, the actions of the planning and zoning commission are simply advisory to the city council. Once a recommendation is made, it must be adopted by the city council, which acts in a legislative manner when deciding zoning issues.

You probably should file a petition for a change because the ordinance seems to be rather arbitrary in excluding rental businesses but allowing commercial sales. No doubt it was just an oversight when the ordinance was initially adopted, and it needs to be changed.

Summary

Administrative agencies handle two areas of public concern: economic regulation and public welfare. Economic regulation takes several forms. An agency may control entry into the marketplace through licensing procedures, setting rates, or setting standards. Public welfare includes the protection of the public as well as entitlement programs. Public welfare has two meanings; the broad meaning covers regulation that is for the benefit of the public at large, while the second meaning covers programs for lower-income people. Entitlement programs, such as Social Security, benefit those people who meet the programs' eligibility requirements.

Federal regulatory agencies have several features that allow them to deal with certain problems more effectively than the legislatures or the courts. First, an agency develops expertise in a particular area. Second, a regulatory agency consists of a very well-developed hierarchy that helps ensure continuity of personnel and experience. Third, an agency has more flexibility than the legislature.

When an agency is under the direct control of the president, it is known as a line agency. The members of the president's cabinet are heads of line agencies. Congress also has established independent agencies, which are freestanding from the president and from Congress. Government agencies are created by Congress to administer a quasi-business venture. Quasi-official agencies are also created by Congress but do not have the same authority as other agencies.

Administrative agencies engage in three prime areas of activity: they make rules, they acquire and act on information, and they judge cases. These activities are carried out through the quasi-legislative, quasi-executive, and quasi-judicial powers that an agency possesses. The Administrative Procedure Act (APA) standardized the procedures that agencies must use in exercising their powers. In addition, agencies must not violate a person's constitutional rights.

The APA has been amended several times. The Freedom of Information Act makes all the information held by federal agencies available to the public unless the information falls within one of the exempt categories. The important exempt categories are: information relating to national defense or foreign policy; internal personnel rules; information protected by another statute that prohibits disclosure; business trade secrets and privileged or confidential business information; and any information that violates personal privacy.

The Privacy Act protects U.S. citizens and legal aliens, but not corporations. A person is entitled to see the information that an agency has concerning him or her. The Sunshine Act prohibits agencies from holding secret, not closed, meetings. If the topics before the meeting do not qualify for a closed meeting, the meeting must be open.

The Regulatory Flexibility Act takes into account differences in the way a regulation affects a small business versus a large business. The rules that will affect small businesses must be published in the *Federal Register*.

The sunset acts are not part of the APA but are included in the statutes that create the agencies. A sunset act sets an automatic expiration date for the agency.

Actions taken by administrative agencies can be appealed to the courts. The courts investigate first whether the authority delegated by Congress to that agency is valid. If the court finds that the agency has the authority, the court then determines whether the agency has exceeded its properly delegated authority.

Because an agency is given broad discretionary powers over a specialized subject matter, a court will give judicial deference to agency decisions. A court will not reverse an agency action unless it finds that the agency violated a condition set out by the Administrative Procedure Act.

Deregulation has taken place since the late 1970s. Two executive orders limit administrative regulations of line agencies. Each agency must submit to the Office of Management and Budget a statement of the goals of the upcoming year and set out major planned programs. Each agency must also prepare a regulatory impact analysis of major rules.

Key Terms

administrative law **(74)**
Administrative Procedure Act (APA) of 1946 **(81)**
consent decree **(86)**
doctrine of exhaustion of remedies **(96)**
economic regulation **(74)**
enabling act **(78)**
entitlement programs **(74)**
formal rulemaking **(82)**
Freedom of Information Act (FOIA) of 1966 **(82)**

general policy statement **(78)**
government agency **(78)**
independent agency **(78)**
informal rulemaking **(82)**
interpretive rules **(82)**
judicial deference **(96)**
line agency **(78)**
order **(86)**
Privacy Act of 1974 **(95)**
procedural rules **(82)**
public welfare **(74)**
quasi-executive function **(81)**

quasi-judicial function **(81)**
quasi-legislative function **(81)**
quasi-official agency **(78)**
Regulatory Flexibility Act of 1980 **(96)**
substantive rules **(82)**
Sunshine Act of 1976 **(96)**
sunset acts **(96)**

Questions and Case Problems

1. An appellate court will affirm the findings of the administrative law judge if those findings are supported by "substantial evidence on the record." When an administrative agency conducts a quasi-judicial hearing, a record is made of all the evidence and testimony presented at the hearing. The Adolph Coors Company was accused by the Federal Trade Commission (FTC) of engaging in certain price-fixing agreements in violation of the Sherman Antitrust Act. After a hearing, the FTC concluded that Coors had in fact engaged in illegal price fixing. Substantial evidence was presented at the hearings in support of the findings. Coors also presented substantial evidence that it had never entered into any price-fixing arrangements. Should an appellate court uphold the FTC's findings? [Adolph Coors Co. v. Federal Trade Commission, 497 F.2d 1178 (10th Cir. 1974)]

2. An agency must provide notice and a hearing before it can deprive a party of his or her property or rights. New York state and New York City officials administered various federally assisted welfare programs. Some of those on welfare filed a complaint in court alleging that the state and city terminated, or were about to terminate, the aid without prior notice and a hearing, thereby denying the plaintiffs due process of law. The state and the city, however, adopted procedures, posted notice, and had a hearing *after* these suits were brought. Does the failure to provide a welfare recipient with a notice of termination before the aid is stopped violate procedural due process? [Goldberg v. Kelly, 397 U.S. 254, 90 S.Ct. 1011, 25 L.Ed.2d 287 (1970)]

3. Thompson Medical Company produced an over-the-counter analgesic medicine that was sold under the name Aspercreme. The product did not contain any aspirin. The Federal Trade Commission (FTC) brought action against Thompson, claiming that the name of the product was false and misleading. Thompson took the position that the Food and Drug Administration (FDA) was the agency entrusted with the authority to evaluate and regulate over-the-counter medicine and that the FDA had exclusive regulatory authority. Was Thompson correct in its position? [Thompson Medical Co. v. Federal Trade Commission, 791 F.2d 189 (D.C. Cir. 1986)]

4. Congress passed the Marine Mammal Protection Act (MMPA) to protect porpoises during commercial fishing operations. Captains of fishing boats are allowed to take porpoises only if the captains comply with certain conditions. The MMPA requires that captains allow government observers to board and accompany vessels on regular fishing trips either to do research or to observe and collect data on the fishing operations for enforcement proceedings by the National Marine Fisheries Service. The captains of two fishing vessels object. You are the judge. On what will you base your decision as to whether government scientific observers should be required aboard the fishing vessel to collect data and conduct research? These inspectors will collect data on the captain's fishing practices for later inclusion in any quasi-judicial proceeding against the captain if he or she has failed to follow the government regulations. Will your decision be different if the fishing boat is out for one day or for a six-month trip? [Balelo v. Baldrige, 724 F.2d 753 (9th Cir. 1984)]

5. Regulations were published under the Federal Food, Drug, and Cosmetic Act that established the standard for farina and enriched farina. Quaker Oats could not sell its product under either label because the product did not meet the regulations for farina or enriched farina. The product was not farina because it contained vitamin D, and the product was not enriched farina because it did not contain the minimum quantities of vitamin B-1, riboflavin, nicotinic acid, or iron. Quaker Oats sues the government. You are the hearing officer. Will you uphold the regulations? State your reasons. [Federal Security Administration v. Quaker Oats Co., 318 U.S. 218, 63 S.Ct. 589, 87 L.Ed. 724 (1943)]

6. Eldridge received disability benefits under the Social Security Act. He was informed that there was a determination that he no longer qualified and that his benefits were being stopped. After the benefits were terminated, he was allowed a hearing. Eldridge filed a lawsuit claiming that he had been denied due process. You are the judge. Give your decision and support it with your reasons. [Mathews v. Eldridge, 424 U.S. 319, 96 S.Ct. 893, 47 L.Ed.2d 18 (1976)]

Chapter 5   Alternative Dispute Resolution Procedures

All disputes (if unhappily any should arise) shall be decided by three impartial and intelligent men, known for their probity and good understanding, two to be chosen by the disputants, each having the choice of one, and the third by those two, which three men thus chosen shall, unfettered by law or legal constructions, declare their sense of the testator's intention, and such decision is, to all intents and purposes, to be binding on the parties as if it had been given in the Supreme Court of the United States.

—George Washington's last will and testament

OUTLINE

Introduction

Many lawsuits are unwieldy in terms of money and time, for both the litigants and the taxpayers. Money is expended by the litigants on attorneys' fees, court fees, and the development of evidence. The taxpayers, however, pay the actual cost since the litigants' fees do not cover the real cost of running the judicial system. The time from the filing of a lawsuit to the final disposition of the case is always uncertain and usually is measured in years. As a result, the memories of the witnesses fade and evidence may be destroyed or lost. As long as the litigation is in progress, the litigants will often harbor very negative feelings about both the opposition and the judicial system. Litigation is a stressful ordeal.

Many persons have arrived at the conclusion that less expensive and more expeditious methods must be found to settle disputes. Various advocates of **alternative dispute resolution** (ADR) **procedures** have different interests, but all have the same basic goal: a speedy and just determination of the dispute at a reasonable cost to both parties.

Advocates of Alternative Dispute Resolution Procedures

Who in society is advocating the use of alternative dispute resolution procedures and why?

Today the judiciary is one of the strong advocates of alternative dispute resolution procedures. Former Chief Justice of the United States Supreme Court Warren E. Burger advocates the development of "mechanisms that can produce an acceptable result in the shortest possible time, with the least possible expense and with a minimum of stress on the participants." He has spoken continuously on the topic for the past decade.

The judiciary recognizes that the average citizen does not have his or her rights protected when he or she must spend thousands of dollars and several years in litigation to reach a decision, especially for routine cases, such as automobile accident cases. More often than not, the case is settled literally in front of the courtroom door after considerable expense, frustration, and years in the judicial system.

The business sector is another strong proponent of alternative dispute resolution procedures. Businesspersons need expeditious justice at a reasonable cost, but they also need to be able to maintain a business relationship with the opponent while resolving a particular dispute. Most disputes between businesses involve a contractual problem. People in business accept the fact that disputes are inevitable. Even when the written contract was carefully drawn, problems will arise over the interpretation of a clause or over a disputed set of facts. Delays in manufacturing, disputes over the quality of merchandise, problems with the performance of the contract, and other such misunderstandings are bound to arise.

Once a dispute occurs, most businesspersons would like to resolve the dispute quickly, privately, inexpensively, and informally. Maintaining a business relationship while involved in litigation is very difficult, if not impossible. To preserve goodwill, most businesspersons are in favor of alternative dispute resolution procedures that will be fair, inexpensive, and quick, but that will also arrive at a just result.

The public has a great interest in reducing the caseload handled by the judiciary. Most cases in court are routine in nature and rarely involve great legal issues. Like businesspersons, the public wants fair, inexpensive, and quick procedures to settle routine legal problems.

The courts, however, have not always been supportive of alternative dispute resolution procedures. The court in the case on the next page gives the reasons why courts should reject attempts by disputing parties to use arbitration to resolve their disputes.

Comparisons Between Alternative Dispute Resolution Procedures and the Judicial System

The Institute for Civil Justice, established within The Rand Corporation, has developed data from its studies of the judicial system. The Institute for Civil Justice has performed one of the few research projects that critically examines the problems within the court system. With this data a comparison can be made between the judicial system and ADR procedures. Six factors that can be

BACKGROUND AND FACTS *Gates (the plaintiff) brought a lawsuit against Arizona Brewing Company (the defendant) to recover wages. The contract, which Gates alleged had been breached, was between Arizona Brewing and the International Union of United Brewers, Flour, Cereal, and Soft Drink Workers of America. Gates was a member of the union and thus covered by the contract. The contract stated that the employer and the union were to try to settle their differences. If the parties could not reach a settlement, the matter was to be settled by arbitration.*

No attempt was made by the plaintiff to submit the dispute between him and the defendant to arbitration. Gates alleged that the arbitration clause was void under the Arizona arbitration statutes. Defendant's position was that Gates could not bring a lawsuit until after arbitration had occurred.

 Case 5.1

GATES v. ARIZONA BREWING CO.
Supreme Court of Arizona, 1939.
54 Ariz. 266, 95 P.2d 49.

LOCKWOOD, Judge.
*   *   *   *

Broadly speaking, arbitration is a contractual proceeding, whereby the parties to any controversy or dispute, in order to obtain an inexpensive and speedy final disposition of the matter involved, select judges of their own choice and by consent submit their controversy to such judges for determination, in the place of the tribunals provided by the ordinary processes of law. There are two kinds of arbitration, one under the common law and the other by virtue of express statutes. Under the common law, the overwhelming weight of authority holds that an agreement that all disputes and contentions which may arise between the parties under a contract shall be settled by arbitration to the exclusion of the courts, is void as an attempt to oust the courts of jurisdiction. This rule is set forth in *Blodgett Co. v. Bebe Co.* in the following language: "*   *   * (A)n agreement between parties to a contract to arbitrate all disputes *   *   * is invalid and unenforceable, as constituting an attempt to oust the legally constituted courts of their jurisdiction and to set up private tribunals. *   *   * Judges *   *   * have ascribed the origin of the rule to the jealousy of courts in the matter of their power and jurisdiction. *   *   * Another and better ground assigned for it is that citizens ought not to be permitted or encouraged to deprive themselves of the protection of the courts by referring to the arbitrament of private persons or tribunals, in no way qualified by training or experience to pass upon them, questions affecting their legal rights. *   *   *"

While it is true that the right of arbitration has been greatly extended in recent years, this is practically universally done by statute. The legislature has the power to extend this right *   *   *.

Arizona *   *   * has provided a statutory method of arbitration. [This statute states as follows:] "*   *   * provisions of this act shall not apply to collective contracts between employers and *   *   * associations of employ[ees]. *   *   *"

*   *   * For this reason we hold that both under the common law and the statute, the (contract) clause cannot stand, and that plaintiff was not obliged to submit his controversy with defendant to arbitration before he brought this action.

The judgment of the trial court was reversed. The case was returned to the trial court with instructions to proceed with the trial. The Supreme Court of Arizona held that Gates could have his case decided by a trial court without going to arbitration first.

DECISION AND REMEDY

reviewed are money, time, privacy, formality, selection of the decision maker, and the forum.

Financial Costs

The first comparison is the cost in terms of money. Government expenditures vary widely in running the judicial system. The cost of a jury trial including judge, jury members, court reporter, bailiff, clerk, and secretary averages about $8,300 in California. In Los Angeles County the cost is high: $10,500 for a jury trial. Perhaps because of these costs, only about 1 percent of the civil lawsuits filed in all of California end up in a jury trial. In Florida the cost is much less, around $3,000 for a jury trial. At a daily cost of $2,700 to use a federal court, the cost of the average federal trial is more than $10,800.

What did the plaintiff win? The plaintiff did not win any money in 43 percent of the cases when the defendant disputed liability. The average award over the 20-year period was $84,000. However, the Rand study discovered that one-fourth of the jury awards were less than $8,000, and in one-half of the cases, the awards were less than $21,000. Only in 19 percent of the cases did the plaintiff equal or exceed the $84,000 average. Ten percent of the awards were over $181,000 and only 1 percent exceeded $1,000,000. The plaintiffs in the automobile accident cases received the smallest awards; over 50 percent were under $15,000. Thus, most of the money went to only a few plaintiffs.

Another way of stating these facts is that in one-fourth of the cases decided, the cost to the public of the trial was more than the amount recovered by the plaintiff. Not all types of lawsuits should be judged strictly by the cost, but in terms of the sheer numbers of cases filed on routine matters (such as automobile accident cases), there should be and can be a better method of resolving the dispute between the two parties. The amount in controversy in routine cases does not justify the public expense of the trial.

The costs of alternative dispute resolution procedures also have a wide range, but on the lower end of the cost scale. The court administrators in the federal district courts estimate that the average court-mandated arbitration proceeding costs only $47. The American Arbitration Association estimates the average cost of a private arbitration to be as low as $275. If the arbitration is private, the cost is paid by the disputing parties, not the taxpayers. Over 50,000 cases are arbitrated each year, and the number is increasing.

Time Costs

The second comparison is the cost factor measured in time. Extremes exist in the processing time, which is measured from the date a lawsuit is filed to the date of its final disposition. In Arizona, this time period is less than 12 months, but in Connecticut the courts were recently backlogged beyond a 5-year period, with over 60,000 tort cases alone waiting for trial. Half of these cases were pending before the courts in just four cities.

In Los Angeles County a 41-month delay exists from the time of filing to the time of final disposition. This time lag exists even though judicial arbitration is required. In Los Angeles County only 10 percent of the cases filed ever go to trial. Forty percent of the cases were disposed of by the court and 50 percent were either settled or dropped by the litigants. One federal district court lessened the waiting period from filing to final disposition from 14 months to less than 5 because of mandatory judicial arbitration.

Reasons for Time Lag Why is the time lag so long in a lawsuit? During a lawsuit a continuing debate exists between the attorney representing the plaintiff and the attorney representing the defendant. For example, in a personal injury case, the plaintiff's attorney argues that he or she has little reason to encourage delay. An injured plaintiff must receive and pay for medical care and is usually off work while recovering. A plaintiff's attorney receives compensation from the amount recovered on behalf of the client. It is in his or her best interest to dispose of the case quickly. But a practice has developed whereby, once the plaintiff's medical condition has stabilized and the attorneys have finished the discovery stage, the plaintiff's attorney will wait and see what the defense attorney will do.

Unless the judge forces the case to move along, it will stall at this stage until the plaintiff's attorney or the court sets the trial date. Even if the trial date is set early in the case, it will not have preference, because of all the other lawsuits (including criminal proceedings) ahead of it that must be tried. Most courts have a rule that a lawsuit must go to trial within a specific time period. As cases pile up, many are in danger of going beyond that time period; thus those cases have a preference on the trial calendar.

There is a tendency for both sides to polarize their positions as the case is being processed through the court system. As the case proceeds, the attorneys for the plaintiff and the defendant will evaluate the evidence. Quite often one attorney will make an offer to settle the case. The other attorney will consider the settlement offer and make a recommendation to the client. The party must weigh the settlement offer (i.e., money paid now) against the potential of winning or losing more in a trial at a later time.

Typically the first offer is rejected and a counteroffer is made. In between each offer there is usually a waiting period. Only when faced with the decision of actually getting ready for trial is a settlement seriously pursued, and even then attorneys usually wait to see if the judge will force early case preparation. A judge can force early case preparation by controlling the court calendar, refusing to allow continuances of the case, limiting discovery to a reasonable level, and by promoting pretrial settlement conferences.

ADR Time Periods   Statistics on the time it takes for alternative dispute resolution procedures are hard to find, because of the wide range of different procedures that may be used. The time spent in the court system, however, may be contrasted with the time spent in arbitration. In private arbitration, the average commercial case takes 145 days from the time of the filing until the arbitrator makes the decision.

California has two types of judicially mandated arbitration: volunteer and court-ordered. Those litigants who volunteer to have their lawsuit arbitrated have a decision within 7 months. Those litigants who are ordered by the court to have their case arbitrated wait 22 months for a decision. Thus in California either type of arbitration is faster than the judicial system.

Privacy Factor

A third comparison is the privacy factor. Civil court procedures are of public record. Anyone can observe many of the pretrial procedures and all of the trial. As a result, information that people or businesses would prefer to keep private are available for anyone to read. The disclosure factor becomes critical when a business must reveal trade secrets, budget planning, marketing strategies, or other sensitive information in court.

Most alternative dispute procedures are private and not open to the public. Nonjudicial procedures allow for confidentiality of most information, whereas judicial proceedings, by law, are rarely closed to the public.

Formality

A fourth comparison is the difference in formality. A judicial proceeding is very formal in nature. The judge wears a black robe, and his or her entry into the courtroom is announced in a formal manner by the bailiff. Only attorneys and the litigants are allowed beyond the railing that separates the public area from the formal courtroom area. Courtroom decorum has developed through the centuries and is strictly adhered to by judges. During the trial itself, court rules and the rules of evidence are closely followed. Although the rules have a definite purpose, the application often seems meaningless and confusing to the litigants.

Alternative dispute resolution procedures are informal in their setting. This allows the parties to be more relaxed, reducing stress from the level the parties would feel in a courtroom setting. Do not confuse an informal setting with a sloppy or inadequate presentation of material—as in a courtroom, the better prepared the parties are in presenting their cases, the better the chance of resolving the dispute in a manner acceptable to both sides.

Selection of the Decision Maker

A fifth comparison is the selection of the decision maker. In the judicial system the parties have very little control as to which judge is selected for their case. Most alternative dispute resolution procedures allow the participants to play a role in deciding who will be the decision maker. When people have a voice in choosing the decision maker, they usually are more ready to accept the decision.

Choice of Forum

A sixth comparison is the choice of the forum. The parties in a lawsuit have little control over where the case will be heard. The judicial system has limited the ability of the parties to "forum shop."

Arbitration will allow the disputing parties the opportunity to select a common forum in advance. This selection opportunity is particularly important when there are business arrangements between the parties in more than one state. Because the disputing parties are not subject to a court system, they can decide the best place to hold the arbitration hearing. The American Arbitration Association operates in all states and in foreign countries. As a result, the disputing parties are not restricted by the jurisdictional limits they would encounter in a particular court system.

Alternative Dispute Resolution Procedures

Before examining various alternative dispute resolution procedures, negotiations need to be studied. Negotiations are an integral part of the dispute resolution process, for both alternative dispute resolution procedures and judicial procedures.

Negotiation

Negotiation is the process where two or more persons meet to discuss their differences and attempt to arrive at a settlement acceptable to both. Negotiation is a technique used to resolve a dispute, not win an argument. Although reasonableness cannot be ensured by using negotiation, people can use it to engage in joint problem solving through cooperative behavior and arrive at a mutually acceptable agreement.

All parties should win in a successful negotiation. If only one party gains and the other loses completely, the loser has no vested interest in making sure that the agreement will work. In fact

it is human nature to try to sabotage a forced agreement. Negotiation is at the same time both a skill that can be learned and an art form to be practiced.

Negotiation is an integral part of all alternative dispute resolution procedures. It is not, within itself, an alternative dispute resolution procedure in any formal sense. No alternative dispute resolution procedure, however, could exist without negotiation. In fact, the act of filing a lawsuit may be a negotiating technique. Negotiation is by far the best dispute resolution technique, because the parties arrive at a solution that they design themselves.

Negotiation Skills   As important a skill as negotiation is, many persons are inexperienced at it. People generally have poorly developed negotiating skills. Bargaining or negotiating is rarely taught at primary or secondary schools and is not often found at the college or university level. In addition, the business level at which consumers purchase merchandise or services is not geared to constant negotiation. For example, the price of clothing at a department store is not subject to negotiation. The same is true of other items, such as food in a grocery store or restaurant, or a motel room for a night.

Negotiating skills are necessary in the business world. For example, a customer purchases merchandise, becomes dissatisfied with it, and desires to return it. The customer would like a full cash refund. The businessperson must decide whether to accept the merchandise back, and if the merchandise is returnable, whether credit towards the purchase of additional products from the store or a full refund will be offered. Both parties want different results, but will normally settle for something less than what they initially thought would be appropriate.

When Negotiation Occurs   Negotiation may occur at any stage of a dispute. This time period ranges from the moment the customer purchases the merchandise to the time immediately before the judge renders a decision if a lawsuit has resulted. In fact, sometimes negotiation of a settlement will occur even after a case has been tried and the judge has entered a judgment.

LEGAL HIGHLIGHT   Code of Ethics for Arbitrators

Arbitrators operate under a Code of Ethics. The persons who act as arbitrators undertake a serious responsibility to the public as well as to the parties involved. If the arbitrators do not discharge their duties in good faith and in a diligent manner, the whole system becomes suspect and the public could lose faith in arbitration. The American Arbitration Association has developed a Code of Ethics. There are seven canons.

First, the arbitrator will uphold the integrity and fairness of the arbitration process. Second, if the arbitrator has an interest or relationship that is likely to affect his or her impartiality or that might create an appearance of partiality or bias, it must be disclosed. Third, an arbitrator in communicating with the parties should avoid impropriety or the appearance of it. Fourth, the arbitrator should conduct the proceedings fairly and diligently. Fifth, the arbitrator should make decisions in a just, independent, and deliberate manner. Sixth, the arbitrator should be faithful to the relationship of trust and confidentiality inherent in that office. Finally, in a case where there is a board of arbitrators, each party may select an arbitrator. That arbitrator must ensure that he or she follows all the ethical considerations in this type of situation.

Most cases filed in any court system are settled through negotiation by the attorneys. Rarely do lawsuits end in a full trial where the judge or jury makes the decision. In other words, comparatively few cases are fully litigated. Good faith negotiation is a necessity—without it the judicial system would collapse if even one-fifth of the lawsuits filed ever went to trial.

Arbitration

Arbitration is a procedure where the parties to a dispute submit it to an impartial third person called an *arbitrator*. An arbitrator is a person who frequently specializes in an area, such as real estate or labor, and arbitrates disputes in that area. This person is selected by the parties to make a decision based upon evidence they both submit. The decision of the arbitrator is binding, similar to the judgment entered by a court.

American Arbitration Association   The **American Arbitration Association** (AAA) was founded in 1926 as a private, nonprofit organization. The AAA was an outgrowth of two earlier arbitration associations. Within both associations were two groups which held different philosophies con-

cerning arbitration. One group was comprised of business leaders and trade association executives. They viewed arbitration as a businessperson's court, much like the trade and guild courts of the Middle Ages.

The other group was comprised of attorneys who, although they believed in arbitration, also believed in the fundamental concepts of due process and fairness. As a result, when it was founded the AAA adopted as its purpose "to foster the study of arbitration in all of its aspects, to perfect its techniques under arbitration law, and to advance generally the science of arbitration for the prompt and economical settlement of disputes."

Besides the administration of arbitration, the AAA's other functions are education, promotion, and research into the uses of arbitration for settling all types of disputes. With the slogan of "Speed, Economy and Justice," the performance of the AAA has repeatedly shown that justice does result when there is speed and economy.

Federal Legislation   Congress passed the **Federal Arbitration Act** in 1925 and by doing so declared a federal policy favoring arbitration. The act withdraws from states the power to require a judicial forum for the resolution of disagreements if the parties have agreed by contract to solve the problem by arbitration. In the following case the Supreme Court upholds the intent of Congress to have parties abide by their contract that requires the arbitration of any subsequent disputes.

Case 5.2

SHEARSON/AMERICAN EXPRESS, INC. v. McMAHON

Supreme Court of the United States, 1987.
482 U.S. 220, 107 S.Ct. 2332,
96 L.Ed.2d 185.

BACKGROUND AND FACTS *McMahon and others were customers of Shearson/American Express, Inc. The customer agreements provided for arbitration of any controversy relating to their accounts. The customers filed suit in federal district court for violations of the Securities Exchange Act of 1934 and the Racketeer Influenced and Corrupt Organizations Act (RICO). Shearson/American Express, Inc. moved to have the case arbitrated. The trial court granted the motion to have the alleged Securities Exchange Act violations arbitrated, but denied the motion as to the RICO violations. The court of appeals upheld the trial court as to the RICO but reversed as to the Exchange Act claims. Shearson/American Express, Inc. appealed to the Supreme Court.*

O'CONNOR, Justice.

This case presents two questions regarding the enforceability of predispute arbitration agreements between brokerage firms and their customers. The first is whether a claim brought under § 10(b) of the Securities Exchange Act of 1934 (Exchange Act) must be sent to arbitration in accordance with the terms of an arbitration agreement. The second is whether a claim brought under the Racketeer Influenced and Corrupt Organizations Act (RICO) must be arbitrated in accordance with the terms of such an agreement.

*   *   *   *

The Federal Arbitration Act provides the starting point for answering the questions raised in this case. * * * The Arbitration Act * * * provid[es] that arbitration agreements "shall be valid, irrevocable, and enforceable, save upon such grounds as exist at law or in equity for the revocation of any contract." The Act also provid[es] that a court must stay [stop or delay] its proceedings if it is satisfied that an issue before it is arbitrable under the agreement, and it authorizes a federal district court to issue an order compelling arbitration if there has been a "failure, neglect, or refusal" to comply with the arbitration agreement.

The Arbitration Act thus establishes a "federal policy favoring arbitration."

*   *   *

The Arbitration Act * * * mandates enforcement of agreements to arbitrate statutory claims. Like any statutory directive, the Arbitration Act's mandate may be overridden by a contrary congressional command. The burden is on the party opposing arbitration, however, to show that Congress intended to preclude a waiver of judicial remedies for the statutory rights at issue. * * *

*   *   *   *

* * * Since the 1975 amendments to the Exchange Act, * * * the [Securities and Exchange] Commission (SEC) has had expansive power to ensure the adequacy of the arbitration procedures employed by the SROs [self-regulatory organizations]. No proposed rule change may take effect unless the SEC finds that the proposed rule is consistent with the requirements of the Exchange Act, and the Commission has the power, on its own initiative, to "abrogate, add to, and delete from" any SRO rule if it finds such changes necessary or appropriate to further the objectives of the Act. In short, the Commission has broad authority to oversee and to regulate the rules adopted by the SROs relating to customer disputes, including the power to mandate the adoption of any rules it deems necessary to ensure that arbitration procedures adequately protect statutory rights.

In the exercise of its regulatory authority, the SEC has specifically approved the arbitration procedures of the New York Stock Exchange, the American Stock Exchange, and the National Association of Securities Dealers, the organizations mentioned in the arbitration agreement at issue in this case. We conclude that where, as in this case, the prescribed procedures are subject to the Commission's authority, an arbitration agreement does not effect a waiver of the protections of the Act. * * *

* * * *

* * * Accordingly, we hold the McMahons' agreements to arbitrate Exchange Act claims "enforce[able] . . . in accord with the explicit provisions of the Arbitration Act." * * *

Unlike the Exchange Act, there is nothing in the text of the RICO statute that even arguably evinces congressional intent to exclude civil RICO claims from the dictates of the Arbitration Act. This silence in the text is matched by silence in the statute's legislative history. * * *

Because RICO's text and legislative history fail to reveal any intent to override the provisions of the Arbitration Act, the McMahons must argue that there is an irreconcilable conflict between arbitration and RICO's underlying purposes. Our decision in *Mitsubishi Motors Corp. v. Soler Chrysler-Plymouth Inc.*, however, already has addressed many of the grounds given by the McMahons to support this claim. In *Mitsubishi,* we held that nothing in the nature of the federal antitrust laws prohibits parties from agreeing to arbitrate antitrust claims arising out of international commercial transactions. Although the holding in *Mitsubishi* was limited to the international context, much of its reasoning is equally applicable here. Thus, for example, the McMahons have argued that RICO claims are too complex to be subject to arbitration. We determined in *Mitsubishi,* however, that "potential complexity should not suffice to ward off arbitration." Antitrust matters are every bit as complex as RICO claims, but we found that the "adaptability and access to expertise" characteristic of arbitration rebutted the view "that an arbitral tribunal could not properly handle an antitrust matter."

* * * *

The legislative history * * * reveals the same emphasis on the remedial role of the treble-damages provision. In introducing the treble-damages provision to the House Judiciary Committee, Representative Steiger stressed that "those who have been wronged by organized crime should at least be given access to a legal remedy." The policing function * * *, although important, was a secondary concern. * * *

* * * *

In sum, we find no basis for concluding that Congress intended to prevent enforcement of agreements to arbitrate RICO claims. The McMahons may effectively vindicate their RICO claim in an arbitral forum, and therefore there is no inherent conflict between arbitration and the purposes underlying [RICO]. Moreover, nothing in RICO's text or legislative history otherwise demonstrates congressional intent to make an exception to the Arbitration Act for RICO claims. Accordingly, the McMahons, "having made the bargain to arbitrate," will be held to their bargain. Their RICO claim is arbitrable under the terms of the Arbitration Act.

The federal law establishes a policy favoring arbitration. This policy is not reduced when a person raises a claim founded upon statutory rights. The Supreme Court held that when parties have an agreement to arbitrate, it includes statutory rights under the securities laws and for RICO violations. An arbitrator has the authority to grant punitive damages in the amount of three times the original damages for violations of RICO.

DECISION AND REMEDY

State Legislation   The **Uniform Arbitration Act** was drafted by the National Conference of Commissioners on Uniform State Laws in 1955. The American Bar Association has approved it. The act is designed to make legislation on arbitration more uniform throughout the country. Covering standards of procedure and rules to be used in the arbitration process, the act also provides for judicial enforcement of the agreements to arbitrate.

The stated purpose of the act is to "validate voluntary, written arbitration agreements, make the arbitration process effective, provide necessary safeguards, and provide an efficient procedure when judicial assistance is necessary." This act has been adopted in 30 states and the District of Columbia. See Exhibit 5–1. The states that have not yet adopted the act normally follow many of the procedures suggested by it.

Contractual Arbitration   Arbitration occurs in one or two settings: contractual or judicial. The **contractual agreement to arbitrate** may be reached before or after the dispute arises. The parties may include a future dispute arbitration clause in their initial contract, ensuring that they will submit any future disputes to arbitration. If a dispute arises, the party making the complaint serves the Demand for Arbitration notice upon the opposing party. See Exhibit 5–2.

Exhibit 5–1 Chart of States that Have Adopted the Uniform Arbitration Act

Alaska	Missouri
Arizona	Montana
Arkansas	Nevada
Colorado	New Mexico
Delaware	North Carolina
Dist. of Columbia	Oklahoma
Idaho	Pennsylvania
Illinois	South Carolina
Indiana	South Dakota
Iowa	Tennessee
Kansas	Texas
Maine	Utah
Maryland	Vermont
Massachusetts	Virginia
Michigan	Wyoming
Minnesota	

If the parties fail to include an arbitration clause in the contract, however, when a dispute arises they may then agree to submit the problem to arbitration. This agreement is called a Submission to Arbitration and is signed by both parties. See Exhibit 5–3.

The Agreement to Arbitrate   Two requirements exist for voluntary arbitration: first, the agreement must be entered voluntarily; and second, it must be in writing to be enforceable in a court. Initially this last requirement may seem like a contradiction, but, even though there is a written agreement to arbitrate, one of the parties may refuse to participate in the arbitration proceedings or may file a lawsuit, such as in the *Shearson* case. The other party may request the court to order the first party to arbitrate. An oral agreement to arbitrate will not suffice. The reason that the agreement is required to be in writing is that the parties are giving up a federal constitutionally guaranteed right. The Seventh Amendment preserves the right to a trial by jury for civil cases at common law exceeding $20.

The modern view is that arbitration is binding upon the parties once they have agreed to it. In other words, a legal action cannot be brought if the parties have agreed to submit a controversy to arbitration. The arbitration procedures must be utilized to the fullest extent prior to filing a court action. The only exception would be when both parties refuse to arbitrate after initially agreeing to it.

If one party refuses to arbitrate, the other party may file a lawsuit and seek a court order to compel arbitration. The only defense is that there was no written agreement to arbitrate. The court will order arbitration and stay any other proceedings if it finds there was an agreement to arbitrate. An arbitration agreement is a contractual obligation into which the parties have voluntarily entered. The terms will be enforced as long as they are not illegal or contrary to public policy. Although the court may now be ordering both parties to arbitrate, the initial contract clause to submit disputes to arbitration was agreed to voluntarily.

The following case illustrates the court's attitude towards arbitration in a domestic relations case. Although the court allowed the arbitrator's award to stand, it made sure that the state's interest in this matter was protected.

Exhibit 5–2 Sample Demand for Arbitration

COMMERCIAL ARBITRATION RULES

DEMAND FOR ARBITRATION

DATE: _____

TO: (Name) _____
(of party upon whom the demand is made)

(Address) _____

(City and State) _____ (ZIP Code) _____

(Telephone) _____

Named claimant, a party to an arbitration agreement contained in a written contract,

dated _____, providing for arbitration, hereby

demands arbitration thereunder.

(Attach arbitration clause or quote hereunder.)

NATURE OF DISPUTE:

CLAIM OR RELIEF SOUGHT: (amount, if any)

TYPE OF BUSINESS:

Claimant _____ Respondent _____

HEARING LOCALE REQUESTED: _____
(City and State)

You are hereby notified that copies of our arbitration agreement and of this demand are being filed with the American Arbitration Association at its _____ regional office, with the request that it commence the administration of the arbitration. Under Section 7 of the Commercial Arbitration Rules, you may file an answering statement within seven days after notice from the administrator.

Signed _____ _____ Title _____
(may be signed by attorney)

Name of Claimant _____

Home or Business Address of Claimant _____

City and State _____ ZIP Code _____

Telephone _____

Name of Attorney _____

Attorney's Address _____

City and State _____ ZIP Code _____

Telephone _____

To institute proceedings, please send three copies of this demand and the administrative fee, as provided in Section 48 of the rules, to the AAA. Send the original demand to the respondent.

Form C2-AAA–7/87

Exhibit 5–3 Sample Submission to Arbitration

American Arbitration Association

SUBMISSION TO ARBITRATION

Date:

The named Parties hereby submit the following dispute to arbitration under the COMMERCIAL ARBITRATION RULES of the American Arbitration Association:

Amount of money involved: ....

Place of Hearing: ....

We agree that we will abide by and perform any Award rendered hereunder and that a judgment may be entered upon the Award.

Name of Party ....

Telephone ....

Address ....

Signed by ....

Name of Party ....

Telephone ....

Address ....

Signed by ....

PLEASE FILE TWO COPIES
Consult counsel about valid execution

BACKGROUND AND FACTS *Susan and Roger Faherty were divorced. Prior to their divorce both parties, represented by attorneys, entered into a property settlement agreement. The agreement, which mandated that any financial dispute arising out of it must be arbitrated before any court action could be taken, was incorporated into the final divorce decree. The rules of the American Arbitration Association were to be used in any such arbitration and the arbitrator's decision would be binding on the parties.*

Roger fell behind in alimony and child support payments. Susan went to court to seek enforcement of the agreement and payment of arrearages. Roger made a motion to have the court compel arbitration, and the court issued such an order. The arbitration took seven months. The arbitrator's award fixed alimony arrearages at $37,648 and child support arrearages at $12,284. The arbitrator made no written findings of fact. Susan moved the court to confirm the award. Roger made a cross-motion and, although he originally petitioned the court to compel arbitration, now challenged the validity of the arbitration clause in alimony and child support matters. He contended that as a matter of public policy, these matters should not be permitted to be settled outside the courts.

 Case 5.3

FAHERTY v. FAHERTY
Supreme Court of New Jersey,
1984.
97 N.J. 99, 477 A.2d 1257.

GARIBALDI, J.

* * * *

[Court's discussion on arbitrating disputes over alimony]

* * * Since the parties may settle spousal support rights and obligations by contract there is no policy reason to prohibit their submitting disputes arising out of such contracts to binding arbitration. * * * Rather than frowning on arbitration of alimony disputes, public policy supports it. We recognize that in many cases arbitration of matrimonial disputes may offer an effective alternative method of dispute resolution. As commentators have noted, the advantages of arbitration of domestic disputes include reduced court congestion, the opportunity for resolution of sensitive matters in a private and informal forum, reduction of the trauma and anxiety of marital litigation, minimization of the intense polarization of parties that often occurs, and the ability to choose the arbitrator. In this sensitive and intensely private area of domestic disputes, arbitration expressly contracted for by the spouses is highly desirable. We accordingly hold today that under the laws of New Jersey, parties may bind themselves in separation agreements to arbitrate disputes over alimony. * * *

* * * *

[Court's discussion on arbitrating disputes over child support]

* * * [T]here has been a growing tendency to recognize arbitration in child support clauses. We do not agree with those who fear that by allowing parents to agree to arbitrate child support, we are interfering with the judicial protection of the best interests of the child. We see no valid reason why the arbitration process should not be available in the area of child support; the advantages of arbitration in domestic disputes outweigh any disadvantages.

Nevertheless, we recognize that the courts have a nondelegable, special supervisory function in the area of child support that may be exercised upon review of an arbitrator's award. We therefore hold that whenever the validity of an arbitration award affecting child support is questioned on the grounds that it does not provide adequate protection for the child, the trial court should conduct a special review of the award. This review should consist of a two-step analysis. First, as with all arbitration awards, the courts should review child support awards[.] * * * Second, the courts should conduct a *de novo* review unless it is clear on the face of the award that the award could not adversely affect the substantial best interests of the child.

* * * Thus, only an arbitrator's award that either reduced child support or refused a request for increased support could be subject to court review beyond the review provided by statute, because only such an award could adversely affect the interests of the child. * * *

* * * *

* * * [W]e note that the arbitrator made no written findings of fact. The AAA [American Arbitration Association] rules do not require such findings, but because alimony and child support are always subject to modification for changed circumstances, we suggest, but do not mandate, that the arbitrator in all future domestic dispute arbitrations make reasonably detailed findings of fact upon which she or he bases the arbitration award. Such findings will aid not only the court's review of the award but also will aid later arbitrators in determining requests for modification. * * *

DECISION AND REMEDY   *The court approved the arbitrator's award as having satisfied the statutory and public policy requirements. The state's interest in the welfare of the children was protected. Roger had to pay Susan the amounts awarded by the arbitrator.*

COMMENT   *Although the matters of child custody and visitation rights were not before the court, it noted that the development of a fair and workable mediation or arbitration process to resolve these issues would be more beneficial for children than the present system of courtroom confrontation. The court went on to state that the policy reasons for its holding with respect to child support may be equally applicable in child custody and visitation rights in any future cases.*

Judicial Arbitration **Judicial arbitration** is compulsory (court-mandated) arbitration. In some courts, after the parties have started a lawsuit they can volunteer to have their case arbitrated and the judge will issue an order to that effect. Even if the parties do not volunteer, they may be ordered by the judge to submit their case to arbitration. In some jurisdictions, cases under a certain amount, such as $50,000, must be arbitrated. The types of civil disputes required to be submitted to arbitration are those in which money damages are sought.

Even though the arbitration is court mandated, the parties still have a considerable amount of discretion as to who the arbitrator will be and how the case will proceed. The actual hearing is the same as if it were in contractual arbitration. No judge or jury is involved, and the arbitrator does not submit a written decision which sets out the reasons for the decision. Instead, only an award is issued which is similar to a judgment. In the hearing, the parties may use depositions, interrogatories, and certified documents to save the cost of a person testifying at the hearing. Because the time spent to resolve the case is shorter than if the case went to court, the attorneys' fees are usually less.

Although the arbitration award may be appealed, the appeal rate has been less than 2 percent during the 10-year period compulsory arbitration has been in effect in the federal court system. The rate is 8 percent for all the other decisions involving lawsuits that were not submitted to arbitration.

Differences   Nine differences exist between a contractual arbitration and a judicial arbitration. First, under the contract arrangement the proceedings are private, but they are public for a judicial arbitration. Second, under judicial arbitration full discovery rights are preserved, while discovery is usually not allowed under the contract arrangement. Third, subpoena power is fully preserved under the court arbitration, while none exists in the contract arrangement unless provided by statute. A subpoena is issued by a court, not an arbitrator.

Fourth, the rules of evidence apply in a judicial arbitration, but not in the contract arrangement. Fifth, the award is binding under the AAA arbitration rules, while in the judicial arbitration the award is binding only if it is not appealed. Sixth, the appeal rights are fully preserved in a judicial area, and if the appeal is granted the parties have a right to a trial in the court. Under the AAA arrangement the arbitrator's decision is binding and final. Appeals may be made on very limited grounds.

Seventh, in the judicial arbitration setting the arbitrator is usually an attorney with little or no experience in arbitration, selected at random from the legal community. Under the contractual arrangement, the arbitrator is selected because of subject matter expertise. Eighth, the cost to the client is less under the contract arrangement because no lawsuit has been filed. Under the judicial arrangement, the cost is more because the case is pending before the courts. The cost, however, is usually less than that of a full court trial. Ninth, the stress on the parties is greater under judicial arbitration because the case is already in the court system. The stress level is less under the contract arrangement because the arbitration has been mutually agreed to by both parties.

Arbitration Procedure   Just as a lawsuit has a series of steps to be followed, so does arbitration. Within this process exists a language peculiar to arbitration. Some of the procedure is similar to a

judicial proceeding while other parts are unique to arbitration.

Tribunal Administrator   The American Arbitration Association maintains offices around the country. The regional office has the responsibility of providing a **tribunal administrator**. This person manages the administrative matters and all communications between the parties and the **arbitrator**. The advantage is that the administrative burden of managing details and arrangements is not placed on the arbitrator, who may be located some distance from the parties and the place of the hearing. The arbitrator will not be in direct communication with either of the parties except at the hearing. This arrangement prevents the problem of one side making any arguments, presenting evidence, or making suggestions to the arbitrator without the other side having an opportunity to be heard.

Selection of the Arbitrator   If the parties have thought about arbitration, they will have determined the method of appointing arbitrators in the arbitration agreement. The arbitration agreement can specify the procedure in selecting arbitrators because it is a contractual arrangement. In the judicial system this control cannot be exercised in selecting a judge—usually the parties must accept any judge assigned to the case.

Generally the parties do not have the foresight to include the method of selecting the arbitrator in the contract. The American Arbitration Association has a simple system for selecting an arbitrator. Each party receives a prepared list of proposed arbitrators that has been specifically drawn for a controversy of the nature of their dispute. Every arbitrator on the list is technically qualified on the subject matter of the dispute to resolve it. Each party examines the list, crossing off the names of the arbitrators not wanted, and then lists the remaining names in order of preference.

The two lists are then compared by the tribunal administrator to determine which arbitrators are mutually acceptable and the order of preference. This process can be repeated until a mutually acceptable choice is selected. If the parties cannot agree upon an arbitrator, the AAA can appoint one. The arbitrator will not be one whose name was crossed out by either party. If this is a case where a lawsuit has been filed and the dispute is subject to compulsory arbitration, the court has the authority to appoint an arbitrator.

Preparation for the Hearing   The parties determine a mutually convenient day and time for the hearing. Written notice of the hearing must be given to each party. Each side will prepare for the hearing as it would for a trial. All documents and papers to be submitted into evidence will be assembled and placed in a logical order. Proper arrangements will be made if the arbitrator needs to visit a place for an on-the-spot investigation. Before the hearing all the witnesses should be interviewed. The case must be studied from the opposing party's viewpoint, so the opposition's evidence and arguments can be answered. If a transcript of the hearings is needed, arrangements will be made with the tribunal administrator for a stenographer to be present.

The Hearing   An arbitration proceeding is very similar in form to a trial, but it is not quite the adversarial proceeding that a trial is. A cooperative attitude is necessary for effective arbitration. Ordinary rules of courtesy and decorum are encouraged. Exaggeration, overemphasis, concealing of facts, and use of legal technicalities to disrupt or delay the hearing are not encouraged and may have an adverse effect on the arbitrator.

Each party presents his or her case to the arbitrator in an orderly and logical manner. Just as in a trial, each side starts out with a clear but concise opening statement. The complaining party usually starts first, and tells the arbitrator what remedy is sought. After the second party's opening statement, documents, depositions, and other materials are presented to the arbitrator by both parties. If there are witnesses, they are examined to help each party establish his or her case. Finally, each side makes a closing argument. The closing argument includes a summary of the evidence, a refutation of the points made by the other side, and an argument as to why the arbitrator should decide in favor of that person. At the conclusion of the closing arguments, the arbitrator will declare the hearing closed.

The arbitrator may hear and determine the controversy upon the evidence produced, even if a party failed to appear after being notified of the hearing. A party to the case may have an attorney present, but it is not required. Witnesses can be compelled to appear at an arbitration hearing through the use of subpoenas, but these subpoenas must be issued by a court.

The technical judicial rules of evidence are not followed in arbitration hearings. Often an arbitrator will hear evidence that would not be allowed in a courtroom—an arbitrator will listen to most evidence. This aspect of arbitration has been criticized. The technical rules of evidence used in court were developed to make certain there is a fair hearing. Evidence must not be based upon gossip, prejudices, or include irrelevant material. The arbitrator must be especially careful to consider only evidence that has a bearing on the case. The hearing can be adjourned to another time if the first meeting is not sufficient to hear all the evidence.

The Award   The arbitrator must make his or her decision within 30 days after the hearing. If there are two or more arbitrators on the case, the majority decision is the binding one. The parties may agree beforehand that only a unanimous decision will be binding. The arbitrator's decision is called the **award**. The award is based upon the facts presented at the hearing. The purpose is to dispose of the controversy in a final and complete manner. The arbitrator must rule on each claim that has been submitted for a decision.

Once the award is made, the arbitrator cannot change it. Only if the parties both agree to reopen the proceedings and restore power to the arbitrator can the award be changed. The award merely states the decision of the arbitrator with no written support for it. The award is final and binding upon the parties. If the arbitration was court ordered, the award is submitted to the court. Once the court accepts the award, it becomes the judgment of the court.

The Appeal   The following are the only grounds upon which the losing party may appeal the award in contractual arbitration:

1. The award was obtained by corruption, fraud, or other undue means.
2. Misconduct or partiality was exhibited by the arbitrator.

3. The arbitrator exceeded his or her powers.

4. There was a refusal to postpone the hearing or a refusal to hear evidence material to the controversy which substantially prejudiced the rights of one of the parties.

5. The parties did not have an arbitration agreement and the issue of whether to take the dispute to arbitration was not determined in a court action to compel arbitration.

If the court does find one of the above grounds applicable to the case, it orders either a rehearing in front of the same arbitrator or a new hearing with a different arbitrator. The court does have the right to modify the award in the event of an evident miscalculation of figures, an evident mistake in the description of any person or property referred to in the award, or if the matters determined by the arbitrator were not those submitted to arbitration or the award was not in the proper form. A court is not allowed to modify an award on any other grounds.

In judicial arbitration, either party may appeal to the court. Normally, no grounds are required for the appeal other than that the appealing party does not accept the decision of the arbitrator. The appeal is treated by the court as a completely new case, and a new trial will be ordered. In legal language, this is called a trial *de novo*. The arbitration is treated as if it never happened. The case proceeds as a lawsuit, as it normally would have without the arbitration hearing.

Arbitration does have certain inherent disadvantages when it is compared to a judicial proceeding. First, the arbitrator's background is probably not well known to a party when a case is first submitted to arbitration. All persons have their own bias or prejudice that may affect the outcome of a case, even when serving as an arbitrator and attempting to be neutral. Judges in lawsuits, however, also have biases and prejudices. But with formal judicial proceedings a record is maintained, and an appeal can be based upon a judge's prejudicial behavior, while normally a record is not maintained in an arbitration hearing. The bias or prejudice of a judge which wrongfully affects the outcome of a case can be reversed. The same cannot be said about a contractual arbitration proceeding.

Second, it has been argued that arbitrators tend to compromise in making awards, rather than making clear-cut decisions for either party. Therefore justice is also being compromised. Judicial decisions most often decide for or against one of the parties based on the merits of the case. Third, future parties lose the use of prior decisions as precedent. Written judicial opinions are one of the foundations of the development of American law.

The following case spells out the power of an arbitrator's award and how it may not be appealed.

BACKGROUND AND FACTS *Broadway Realty and Trust Company sold Hembree a home. The purchase contract had an arbitration clause requiring arbitration of any controversy or claim between the parties. The home had a defective roof. The case was arbitrated, and an award was given to Hembree based upon breach of implied warranty. The decision was appealed on the basis that (1) the arbitrator acted beyond his scope of authority and (2) the law of implied warranty should not have been applied. The trial court confirmed the award, and Broadway Realty appealed.*

 Case 5.4

HEMBREE v. BROADWAY REALTY AND TRUST COMPANY, INC.
Court of Appeals of Arizona, 1986.
151 Ariz. 418, 728 P.2d 288.

HATHAWAY, Chief Judge.
* * * *
I. SCOPE OF AUTHORITY
    * * * [T]he superior court will not confirm an arbitrator's award if the arbitrator exceeded his authority. An arbitrator's powers are defined by the agreement of the parties. The contract between appellees and appellants states that arbitration will be available for any controversy or claim ''arising out of or *relating to this contract.''* (Emphasis added) * * * [O]nce an implied warranty comes into existence by reason of the circumstances of the sale, the law conceives such

a warranty as being a term of the contract. Appellants argue that appellees' implied warranty claim does not arise out of or relate to "this contract." The gist of appellant's argument is that implied warranty can only apply to the sale of a home by a builder/vendor, and since appellant is a developer/vendor, the arbitration clause does not encompass this breach of implied warranty allegation. Appellants' argument, however, is legal rather than jurisdictional. The dispute between these parties relates to the sale of the home and the allegedly defective roof. In their lawsuit, appellees alleged a number of theories including implied warranty. Whether or not that theory was viable under these circumstances was a legal question for the arbitrator. The dispute, however, clearly arose out of and related to this contract for the sale of a home. Therefore, we find the arbitrator was within his authority in addressing the implied warranty claim.

II.   MISTAKE OF LAW

As stated above, appellants argue that parties who are not builders may not be held liable for breach of an implied warranty of habitability. It is settled case law that upon application to confirm an arbitration award, the superior court may not inquire as to whether errors of law were made by the arbitrator in reaching his decision. The power of this court is likewise severely circumscribed. Therefore this court may not review whether or not the arbitrator was correct in his application of the law. *   *   *

DECISION AND REMEDY   *The court upheld the award of the arbitrator. Although noting that the arbitrator might have been mistaken as to the legal issues on the implied warranty, the court held it could not inquire into errors of law made by an arbitrator.*

COMMENT   *Possibly one of the major reasons why some lawyers do not like arbitration is that an error of law cannot be appealed. An award from a trial judge who makes an error of law can be reversed on appeal. But arbitration allows the dispute to be expedited even though the award may be based upon wrong legal doctrine.*

Conciliation

Conciliation occurs whenever a third party successfully brings together the conflicting parties. A conciliator does not take an active part in the negotiations, but rather attempts to limit all parties' passions and negative rhetoric. Conciliation is a method to obtain a negotiated settlement from the parties.

Conciliation has not been used as extensively in this country as it has in other cultures. It is, however, used extensively in labor disputes, and is part of the federal labor law. Also, many states have statutory provisions relating to conciliation in divorce actions. When a divorce is filed, one of the parties may request a conciliation hearing, which is similar to marriage counselling.

Conciliation is not restricted only to divorce cases—judges use conciliation in many other types of litigated cases. As an example, when a judge holds a pretrial conference and attempts to bring the two parties together in a negotiated settlement, he or she is using conciliation.

The Better Business Bureau uses conciliation techniques when it handles complaints between businesses and customers. It attempts to bring the two parties together to reach a settlement of their differences.

Newspaper and radio and television stations may have a team devoted to resolving disputes involving its readers or listeners. Often a reader or listener will contact the media, informing them of the problem. A person from the media will then contact the business with whom the client has a dispute. Because the media have extensive resources and are very visible, reporters can often reach the person who has the power to resolve the dispute. Most businesses want to avoid bad publicity.

Mediation

The terms mediation and conciliation are used interchangably. However, mediation procedures are more involved than conciliation procedures. The mediation process is completely voluntary. The essence of mediation is compromise. In **mediation**, an impartial third person first persuades the parties to discuss their issues.

The American Arbitration Association has developed mediation rules. Early mediation intervention allows for a quick solution to the problem before the positions taken by the parties become polarized. Mediation is a first step that allows the parties to fall back to arbitration or even a lawsuit if they cannot work out their differences. Often the contract requires that money be deposited to cover the expenses of arbitration or litigation, if the dispute should reach that stage. Mediation does not require the setting aside of these funds, thus giving the parties another incentive to attempt to resolve their differences by this process.

If the parties cannot agree on the issues, the mediator will assist in clarifying them. The mediator will also make suggestions as to possible settlement parameters. Having no formal position, the mediator can be discharged at any time by either party. The mediator does not have the power to make a decision or to force the parties to accept any suggestions or recommendations. Only when the parties come to a final settlement of their differences is mediation successful.

Hybrid Mediation and Arbitration

commercial agreements today have a hybrid system of combining mediation and arbitration to resolve disputes. If a dispute arises, mediation is used first. The mediator will attempt to help the parties find their own solution to the problem. Meeting with the parties separately, the mediator suggests various solutions. The effect is to guide the parties to a resolution by building momentum in that direction. The resolution is an agreement mutually reached by the disputing parties.

The parties know that if they do not resolve their difference by mutual agreement, the next step is arbitration. The arbitrator's award is binding on both parties. It is, in effect, a forced solution.

Mediation is used in many different legal areas. Mediation and arbitration are used extensively in labor disputes. The Federal Mediation and Conciliation Service has experienced mediators available who serve in labor–management disputes. If direct negotiations between management and labor break down, the mediators are sent by the service to mediate the dispute.

The Magnuson-Moss Product Warranty Act of 1975 authorizes mediation when a dispute occurs between a consumer and a business over a malfunctioning consumer product. A business may establish a mediation procedure on its own to resolve disputes that customers may have: this procedure has been used by automobile manufacturers when customers have had disputes with dealerships, and a combination of mediation and arbitration is used extensively in the construction industry.

Fact Finding

Used in complex commercial disputes, **fact finding** is an investigative process whereby an independent third party will investigate the issues and make findings of fact. Courts use fact finders when confronted with a highly technical and involved fact situation requiring a high degree of expertise in a given area.

Frequently a fact finder's role is solely that of making a recommendation. Having an independent person determine certain facts assists in reaching many settlements. If nothing else, the conclusions reached by the fact finder give the parties an indication as to what might occur if the dispute were litigated in a judicial system. This indication by itself will assist the parties in reaching a negotiated settlement.

Mini-Trial

The **mini-trial** is a procedure recently utilized as an alternative dispute resolution mechanism. Its name possibly misstates its purpose and the pro-

LEGAL HIGHLIGHT	Cross-Cultural Conflict on the Texas Gulf Coast*

Since 1975, over 800,000 Southeast Asians have migrated to the United States. As of June 1987, an estimated 62,700 Southeast Asians had made their home in the state of Texas. A large number earn their living through fishing, shrimping, and/or crabbing in the Gulf of Mexico, making their homes in small coastal towns with names like Palacios, Seabrook, and Rockport, some with populations numbering around 4,000.

During the past decade, the Community Relations Services (CRS) has built a significant body of conflict resolution casework responding to tensions between Vietnamese fishermen, shrimpers, and crabbers and their white counterparts along the Texas Gulf Coast. More recently, CRS has been working to improve interaction between the Vietnamese fisherman and the institutions governing their livelihood.

Early on, tensions among whites arose as a result of Vietnameses violations of traditional Gulf Coast fishing customs. These unknowing violations of local customs often made complete sense in the Vietnamese cultural context. White reactions to these behavioral differences resulted in boat burnings, followed by a killing of a white by a Vietnamese, and serious but less violent tension on a number of different fronts.

The CRS interventions, aimed at building bridges between disputing parties, employed Asian individuals who were more acculturated to American society and/or more conversant in English as intermediaries. To decrease tension levels between white and Vietnamese groups

*The CRS work along the Texas Gulf Coast described in this case study was conducted by Efram Martinez, a conciliator working out of the Houston Field Office. This excerpt from CRS experience has been contributed by Barbara Huie, CRS program analyst, to provide examples of cross-cultural conflict and resolution. This excerpt first appeared in National Institute for Dispute Resolution, *Dispute Resolutions Forum* (September 1987).

and individuals, CRS met with each separately and was able to identify and clarify areas of key tension. Bringing the groups together, CRS assisted them to present their perceptions to each other. Some of the differences they discovered were:

One Side: White fishermen whose boats had broken down out on the water were incensed when Vietnamese fisherman smiled and waved as they passed by. The white Texans felt that they were being mocked and laughed at by foreigners.

And the Other: The "universal" sign for a fisherman in distress on the Gulf waters is for him to raise both arms in front of his body, fists closed, and to make a motion as if breaking a pencil. The Vietnamese thought that the white fishermen were waving to them, smiled and waved back.

One Side: White shrimpers along the Texas Gulf Coast were angered that groups of Vietnamese shrimpers would work their nets in the same area, overfishing the waters.

And the Other: When a white shrimper discovered a good harvesting spot, other white shrimpers would pass, leaving the lucky individual alone to reap the rewards of his labor. Vietnamese shrimpers on the other hand, upon discovering a good spot, would invite everyone else to the area to share in the good fortune.

One Side: White fishermen were irate that the federal government was subsidizing the success of the Vietnamese, helping them to buy newer and bigger boats.

And the Other: Vietnamese were borrowing money from family members, working together in large family units, and limiting living expenses in order to put more money back into their business. After buying

---

LEGAL HIGHLIGHT	Cross-Cultural Conflict on the Texas Gulf Coast

their first boat from Americans, Vietnamese fishermen learned how to construct their own—using the same pattern and through group efforts similar to the old American pioneer barn raisings.

Through this process of facilitated cross-cultural education, each of the disputing parties learned about the different priorities and values that guided the behavior of the other. They were better able to understand and to adapt to each other, decreasing tension-producing interactions.

Evidence of CRS success in the process of their party intervention were follow-on requests for assistance. For example, a series of requests from community leaders and a local Parks and Wildlife game warden led CRS to develop a seminar for the Vietnamese fishermen, which featured the following:

■ the Parks and Wildlife Regional Director provided an updated copy of the Texas fishing laws translated into Vietnamese,

■ the city's mayor presented a list of local customs allegedly violated by Vietnamese during the previous shrimping season which were the most irritating to Anglo shrimpers,
■ the local Parks and Wildlife game warden participated in the seminar and led the presentation on the current laws, and
■ an interpreter was present for the seminar and served as an intermediary in order to convey accurately both the words used and the nuances intended.

As part of a follow-through, CRS has focused on increasing the direct communication between Vietnamese and institutional representatives. For example, state agencies and local Vietnamese groups have begun to work together to build a network providing translations and dissemination of both emergency weather information and the changing regulations guiding sport and commercial fishing and shrimping.

---

cedures involved with it—a mini-trial is another voluntary procedure where all parties must agree to its use. The primary purpose in initiating a mini-trial is to resolve questions of fact and law in complex, commercial disputes. It may be used in addition to fact finding.

In a mini-trial, there is no judge. Instead, the parties agree on an advisor. Normally the advisor is a person who has had considerable experience with the subject matter that is the basis of the dispute. The parties determine the amount of authority that can be exercised by the advisor.

Upon being appointed, the advisor will establish an abbreviated discovery process. This process requires exchanging the documents, exhibits,

written arguments, and names of witnesses that will be used by the parties. Upon conclusion of the discovery phase the advisor will meet with the parties, issue rulings on discovery matters, and attempt to resolve questions of procedure.

When all parties know what facts actually exist, settlement of the case is facilitated. Many lawyers and judges believe that one major reason for trials is the lack of discovery. When the parties have full knowledge of what the facts are and what the case entails, the parties will be better able to reach settlement. Mini-trials attempt to expedite discovery of the facts.

Another advantage of the mini-trial is the confidentiality of its procedures. Many businesses do

During the mid-1970s many workers discovered they had asbestos-related diseases. These workers sued their employers, the asbestos manufacturers, for failing to protect them from diseases that the manufacturers knew could result if safety measures were not taken. Currently it is estimated that there are 25,000 asbestos suits pending in the various court systems throughout the United States. These actions are to recover for personal injuries and property damage.

Over a period of decades the various asbestos manufacturers had a variety of insurance coverage by different insurance carriers. Furthermore, these insurance carriers were insured by other insurance companies through a program called *reinsurance*. Reinsurance is a redistribution of liability to other insurance companies.

An interesting twist to the situation of the workers suing their employers is that the asbestos manufacturers are also engaged in lawsuits with their insurance carriers. The basic issue is which insurance carriers or reinsurance carriers will be liable and have to pay the employees if they win their cases.

In San Francisco, five asbestos manufacturers are in court against 50 insurance companies to determine who should pay the personal injury claims filed by the workers exposed to asbestos. More than 400 lawyers are involved with over $1.5 billion in insurance coverage in the dispute.

This is not the typical type of lawsuit but a declaratory action to determine the extent of each insurance company's liability. During the course of a single worker's lengthy employment, his or her employer may have coverage with several insurance companies. Moreover, by the time the disease is discovered, yet another insurance company may be involved.

The court trial is taking place in a former school auditorium that has been renovated just for this proceeding, at a cost to the taxpayers of $210,000. The litigation started in March 1985. In the meantime, however, the insurance companies developed a non-judicial method of resolving liability on particular claims by creating an Asbestos Claims Facility.

The Asbestos Claims Facility works in this fashion: a claimant, with or without an attorney, files a claim at the Facility. The claim is assigned to a claims agent who is responsible for the claim as long as it is in the Facility. The agent reviews the claim and offers a settlement. If the claimant does not like the settlement offer, negotiations will take place. If negotiations fail, the claim is submitted to either binding or nonbinding arbitration. The choice is up to the claimant.

If the claim is submitted to nonbinding arbitration, and the claimant still does not accept the award, he or she is free to sue. The lawsuit is against the Facility only, not the original manufacturer and the appropriate insurance carriers. As a result, each side is represented by only one legal team, since the Facility has its own legal counsel.

The Facility offers a blend of most of the alternative dispute mechanisms in order to resolve a very complex case. Because the Facility was developed after the case started, it is now estimated that it will take several years to settle all the claims.

not want to disclose information to the general public. The mini-trial provides a procedure to limit information from being made public.

Mini-trials have been used in cases of patent infringement, product liability, unfair competi-tion, and anti-trust violations. It is not considered an appropriate mechanism for cases involving constitutional law issues, or where there is a large number of multiple parties, when novel questions about the law need be answered.

Private Judge

A few states, particularly California, will allow the parties in a dispute to privately hire a judge, who is called a *referee*. Normally the referee is a person who has retired from the judiciary. The parties attempt to obtain a referee with expertise in the subject matter of the litigation. The referee is given the full powers of a judge, except the power to find someone in contempt of court.

When this procedure is utilized it is the same as a regular courtroom proceeding. The proceedings are in front of the referee, no jury is allowed, and all trial procedures and rules of evidence are followed. A record is maintained for appeal purposes. The formality of the proceedings and the judicial nature of this procedure set it apart from arbitration.

The advantage of a **private judge** is the fact that the parties are not controlled by the local court calendar. The case will be heard prior to cases filed earlier because it will not be heard by the judges in the local court system. This procedure allows expeditious treatment of the case before a referee who has both experience as a judge and special expertise in the subject matter.

The parties pay most, if not all, of the cost of this type of litigation. It can be expensive and is, therefore, available only to parties who can afford it. Because of this expense, the use of private judges has been criticized as creating a legal system for the wealthy that may result in a dual system of justice (i.e., one for the rich and one for the less advantaged). The wealthy are able to have their cases decided rather quickly in front of judges who have specialized experience and will devote full time to their cases, while the thousands of other parties to lawsuits must wait for months and often years before their cases are placed on the court calendar.

Recently, relatively low-cost alternative private courts have been created as a for-profit business. These business private courts allow both parties to decide on the date of the hearing, where the hearing will be held, who will be the presiding judge, and whether the judge's decision is binding. Each party is charged a filing fee, and a set fee for each half–day hearing session. Obviously, the longer the hearing, the more costly the procedure becomes.

FACING A
LEGAL ISSUE   **Arbitration of Disputes Involving "Lemons"**

You have purchased your first new automobile. On the way home it suddenly stops. This event is just the beginning of your nightmare. After 12 trips to the dealership in a six-week period, you come to the realization that you have a true lemon.

You could bring a judicial action against the manufacturer and dealer to compensate you for your loss. But you know this will be very expensive and it will take months or years to finally have your day in court. Because of this, the majority of states have enacted "lemon laws." These laws generally allow a purchaser to go through an alternative dispute resolution, such as arbitration, to resolve the purchaser's

problem. This is usually a modified arbitration procedure and if the vehicle meets the criteria for the "lemon" classification, the consumer is entitled to a replacement auto or an appropriate cash refund. If the consumer is not satisfied with the decision of the arbitrator, the consumer can take his or her case to court. The automobile manufacturer however, is bound by the decision. Many of these cases are handled through the local Better Business Bureau.

You should check your state law or contact your dealership to see if this procedure is available. Most regional offices of the manufacturer also can give you this information. In many states you are not bound by the arbitration, but the manufacturer is. You have nothing to lose in using this alternative dispute mechanism.

Summary

The judicial system is overburdened with litigation that results in long and expensive delays from the time of filing a complaint to the final conclusion of the case. The judiciary, businesspersons, and the public have a real interest in alternatives to formal court procedures. These alternative dispute resolution procedures include informal negotiation, arbitration, conciliation, and mediation.

Arbitration is very similar to a judicial trial because the arbitrator makes a decision, called an *award*, that is binding. The award can be made into a judgment by a court, if necessary. Arbitration is the only alternative to a judicial trial, where an independent third-party decision is binding upon the disputing parties.

Arbitration can be activated by either a statutory provision making it mandatory or by a contractual agreement. An arbitration hearing is con-

ducted more informally than a judicial trial. The parties limit the grounds of appeal when they contractually agree to arbitration. A judicial award is easier to appeal than an arbitration award, but the appeal results in a new trial.

Business problems have increased because of the complexity of our modern society. More formal complaints among businesses and between businesses and the general public occur. Alternative dispute resolution procedures have assisted in limiting the number of cases handled by the judiciary. These procedures save considerable expense and time between the litigants. In the future it is anticipated that alternative dispute resolution procedures will be used more extensively as there is greater acceptance by the legal system, by businesspersons, and by the public.

Key Terms

alternative dispute resolution procedures **(102)**
American Arbitration Association **(107)**
arbitration **(107)**
arbitrator **(115)**
award **(116)**

conciliation **(118)**
contractual agreement to arbitrate **(110)**
fact finding **(119)**
Federal Arbitration Act **(107)**
judicial arbitration **(114)**
mediation **(119)**

mini-trial **(118)**
negotiation **(106)**
private judge **(123)**
tribunal administrator **(115)**
Uniform Arbitration Act **(110)**

Questions and Case Problems

1. Do you think that mediation should be used before a civil case goes to trial? If so, should the judge trying the case be the mediator? What advantages and disadvantages do you see in such a situation?

2. With a few exceptions, parties arbitrate their disputes because they have agreed to do so. Even with an agreement to arbitrate, one of the parties frequently has a change of mind and decides not to arbitrate the dispute. Why do you think a person would want to avoid arbitration?

3. You are the president of a medium-sized company manufacturing air conditioners. Recently you have noticed a substantial increase in legal expenses due to legal actions being brought against your firm. Most, if not all, are being brought by former employees, customers, and suppliers of inventory. In all cases you believe the actions are not justified but you want to decrease the cost of formal litigation. What types of cases would you allow to be handled through alternative dispute resolution procedures? What types of cases would you not allow to be handled through alternative dispute resolution procedures?

4. The Southland Corporation is the owner and franchisor of 7-Eleven convenience stores. Within its franchise agreement there is an arbitration clause requiring arbitration for any controversy or claim arising out of it. California has a franchise statute that allows legal actions to be brought in the court. Some of the franchisees brought action against Southland Corporation based upon violations of the California franchise law, along with other claims for fraud, misrepresentation, and breach of contract. Southland moved to force arbitration. What should the court hold? [Southland Corp. v. Keating, 465 U.S. 1, 104 S.Ct. 852, 79 L.Ed.2d 1 (1984)]

5. Mr. Alexander lost his job. He argued that he had been discharged because of his race. He had his case arbitrated but lost because the arbitrator found that Mr. Alexander's discharge was for just cause. Mr. Alexander appealed to a federal court to have the arbitration award overturned. On appeal his employer argued that Mr. Alexander has waived his rights under federal law to have the case heard by a court. Do you think Mr. Alexander should have a new trial over the same issues and facts decided by the arbitrator? [Alexander v. Gardner-Denver Co., 415 U.S. 36, 94 S.Ct. 1011, 39 L.Ed.2d 147 (1974)]

6. Lamar Byrd sold his medical practice and invested $160,000 in securities through Dean Witter Reynolds, Inc. The value of his investments declined to about $60,000. Because of this, Byrd brought an action to recover his investment under the Securities Exchange Act of 1934 and also stated causes of action to recover under state law. There have been numerous decisions holding that actions under the Securities Exchange Act of 1934 could not be subject to arbitration because of federal statute. The question presented to the United States Supreme Court was whether arbitration of the state law claims had to occur prior to any action being taken concerning the alleged federal violations. What do you think was the result? Explain your answer. [Dean Witter Reynolds, Inc. v. Byrd, 470 U.S. 213, 105 S.Ct. 1238, 84 L.Ed.2d 158 (1985)]

Chapter 6   Legislative and Executive Process

The American constitution is the most wonderful work ever struck off at a given time by the brain and purpose of man.

William Gladstone (1809–1898)

OUTLINE

Introduction

Why is it important for businesspeople to study the legislative and executive branches of government? The decisions of Congress have a direct effect on the legal environment of business. Congress decides which bills will be passed. Once passed, these bills become statutes. Statutes have a substantial effect on the business world; for example, some statutes set tax rates. Congress also sets national policy through various legislative schemes.

The president also exerts great influence over the business environment. He or she sets the tone of the administration by the types of political appointees, by the openness of the administration to business leaders, and by deciding which laws will be vigorously enforced. She or he has the power to veto bills, while Congress has the right to overrule a veto.

Each state has a legislature and has a governor as its executive. For our purposes, we will examine only the federal legislature, Congress, and the federal executive branch, headed by the president. The same general concepts apply to state legislative and executive branches. State government is also very important to businesses, and its importance should not be underestimated by businesspeople.

The Legislature

During the four months the delegates met in 1787 to draw up the Constitution, a heated debate ensued on the design of the legislative branch. Finally, the delegates from Connecticut suggested a compromise. Congress would be made up of two branches: the House of Representatives would consist of candidates who would run in a popular and direct election every two years, and the size would be based on the population; the Senate would have two appointed members from each state for a six-year period, giving each state an equal vote.

Today, even though Senators are popularly elected, the basic reason for the Senate still exists; it acts as a cooling element to actions taken by the House. The Senate helps to protect the interests of the small states and is a balance to the acts of the House. Historically, the Senate has always been more conservative than the House.

Specific Powers and Limitations

Article I of the Constitution outlines the framework of Congress and its functions. Section 8 specifies particular powers of Congress. For example, Congress has the right to borrow money, to regulate commerce, to establish the laws on bankruptcies, to coin money, to provide punishment for counterfeiting, to establish post offices, to establish copyright and patent laws, to declare war, and to raise and support armies.

While Section 8 gives Congress specific rights, Section 9 sets out what Congress may not do. For example, Congress may not impose a tax on goods exported from any state, may not pass a bill of attainder or an *ex post facto* law, and may not grant any title of nobility.

Committees: How Congress Does Its Work

The legislative work of Congress is done by its committees. There are fifteen Senate and twenty-two House standing committees. A committee receives the bills that have been assigned to it. The committee can move the bill through the legislative process, can stall the bill, or can stop the bill from going any further. Without the committee's approval, a bill has virtually no chance of reaching the floor of the full House or Senate for consideration.

The House and Senate determine the jurisdiction of a committee and appropriate the money to operate the committee. A committee, however, has total control over the bills it receives. Special, select, or ad hoc committees are created by the House or Senate to perform specific investigations or to perform an oversight function. These committees generally cease to exist once the investigation is complete or when the need for the oversight has ended.

Members of Congress seek membership on committees in which they have a personal and professional interest and in which the interests of their constituents will best be served. Some committees are more powerful and influential than oth-

LEGAL HIGHLIGHT   Congressional Record

The Congressional Record *is the newspaper of Congress. Published are the bills, the meetings of the committees, and remarks made by members of Congress. In the remarks sections, members of Congress are able to comment on a variety of topics. Examples include recognition of young people who have earned Eagle Scout status and tributes to specific individuals or groups such as the Black Women Filmmakers; there are also eulogies and salutes to new citizens. Here are the remarks of the representative from Texas concerning truth in the Pizza Labeling Act.*

TRUTH IN LABELING FROZEN PIZZAS
HON. CHARLES W. STENHOLM

OF TEXAS

IN THE HOUSE OF REPRESENTATIVES

Friday, August 7, 1987

Mr. STENHOLM. Mr. Speaker, today I am introducing, along with many of my colleagues, a bill that amends the Federal Meat Inspection Act to require frozen pizza products containing imitation cheese and meat to be labeled to reflect the fact that imitation cheese is contained therein.

Specifically, this legislation would require frozen pizzas containing imitation cheese to note that fact in prominent letters contiguous to the product name. It would not force any pizza manufacturer to use real cheese; it would simply require that consumers be informed

through clear and prominent labeling when the frozen, meat-topped pizza they purchase contains imitation cheese.

Mr. Speaker, I would agree that a technical subject of this kind is usually dealt with in the proper regulatory process. However, the legislation is necessary because of a bureaucratic inconsistency on food labeling policy. Under current Department of Agriculture [USDA] policy, the "cheese" component of a meat-topped pizza need only contain 10 percent real cheese while up to 90 percent can be imitation cheese. But under the labeling requirements of the Food and Drug Administration [FDA], this blend of predominately imitation cheese would have to be clearly and prominently labeled because FDA, just like consumers, recognizes cheese as a "characterizing ingredient of pizza." Consequently, I believe this conflicting situation violates the accepted standard of identity or "characterizing" ingredient guidelines.

In summary, I believe this legislation will aid in eliminating the apparent consumer deception and Federal agency inconsistency which persists with this issue. Let me point out that I would welcome any suggestions for changes in the language I have used provided it would accomplish and fulfill my intent that imitation cheese content in frozen meat-topped pizzas be labeled in such a way that the typical consumer knows what he or she is buying.

---

ers. The House Ways and Means Committee and the Senate Finance Committee consider and recommend passage of tax legislation and thus are powerful committees. The House and Senate Budget Committees are also very important. These committees allow Congress to establish national priorities through the national budget.

How a Bill Moves Through Congress

Many sources of help are available to a member of Congress in the preparation of a bill, amendment, rider, or resolution. Some of these sources are: the Office of Legislative Counsel (House or

Senate); committee professional staff members; lobbyists; and experts in the executive branch.

Preparation of a Bill

A congressperson can start preparing a bill with any of a number of sources. Generally, the congressperson first seeks someone who has drafting expertise to assist in writing the initial drafts of the bill. The Office of Legislative Counsel is comprised of attorneys who are experts at drafting legislation and who know how to avoid the typical drafting pitfalls. They are generalists, however—not experts in a particular subject. The congressperson must rely on others for expert knowledge of the bill's subject matter.

The important committees have professional staffs that include lawyers. Among these lawyers are experts on the subject matters that are under the committee's jurisdiction. These people frequently help in the drafting process.

The number of lobbyists available for drafting legislation that is in their favor is endless. These representatives, moreover, have bountiful resources (including experts) on which they can call. Lobbyists have a good handle on how the proposed legislation will affect a particular industry and the general public. For example, if a bill concerns Social Security benefits, one lobbying group that would be involved is the American Association of Retired Persons. This association not only can help draft the bill but will also inform the legislator of the interests of the retired people that the association represents. Lobbyists are an important source of technical advice.

The executive branch of government has within it the majority of administrative agencies. Within those agencies resides a tremendous amount of expertise on a particular subject. This expertise can assist the legislative branch. The congressional committee that oversees several administrative agencies cannot match the resources available to each of those agencies. For example, the Senate Committee on Labor and Human Resources has only about 100 people in its employ and cannot match the level of information commanded by the Department of Labor (and, within that department, by the Bureau of Labor Statistics with its large legal staff) or by the Department of Health and Human Resources.

Introduction of the Bill

A member of either the House or the Senate may introduce a bill. For the sake of simplicity, we will follow the passage of a bill that starts in the House. After its introduction, the bill is referred to a committee by the parliamentarian and the leadership of the House. The chairperson of the committee and its staff members determine which subcommittee, if any, is best suited to handle the bill. The assignment of the bill is crucial because, if someone wants to kill the bill, he or she usually does it at the committee or subcommittee level.

Subcommittee The subcommittee is the place where the bill usually receives thorough consideration. A proper, public notice of the subcommittee hearing date is given. The notice is published in the *Congressional Record, Federal Register,* newspapers, and trade publications.

While holding public hearings, the subcommittee may request the attendance of certain people that it believes may have information or insights into the pending bill. For instance, if the bill affects a federal administrative agency, officials from that agency will be called as witnesses. Written letters and position papers are also accepted and considered by the members. Often these hearings are televised.

Full Committee After the hearings and reports are completed, the subcommittee votes on the bill. If the majority of the subcommittee approves, the bill goes to the full committee. The full committee may accept or reject the subcommittee recommendation. The bill may be returned to the subcommittee for further consideration. If the full committee approves, the bill is reported to the full House. House bills are first sent to the Rules Committee where debate time limits are set. Once the format for discussion is established, the bill moves to the House floor for action.

Floor of the House The House may have a full debate on the bill on the House floor, but more often members merely have their statements printed in the *Congressional Record.* The floor of the House (or Senate) is rarely occupied. The real work of Congress is done in the subcommittees and committees.

LEGAL HIGHLIGHT	**Where to Obtain Bills and Committee Reports and How to Reach Your Congressperson**

To obtain a bill or committee report, write or call:

> House Document Room
> H-226 Capitol
> Washington, D.C. 20515
>
> (202) 255-3456
>
> Senate Document Room
> B-004 SHOB
> Washington, D.C. 20510
>
> (202) 224-7860

You can write your representative by addressing your letter as follows:

> The Honorable _____
> United States House of Representatives
> Washington, D.C. 20515

Your senator can be reached by addressing your letter as follows:

> The Honorable _____
> United States Senate
> Washington, D.C. 20510

Each senator and representative has a local office in his or her district; this address is listed in the *Congressional Directory,* available at bookstores and in libraries.

Amendments may be offered to the bill on the floor of the House. If the amendment is approved, it becomes part of the bill. Riders may also be offered. A **rider** is an added provision to the bill, but rarely does the rider have anything to do with the bill on the floor. It is attached so that it may "ride" to approval on the strength of the bill. A rider may be attached to a bill that stands a good chance of being approved so that the rider will also be approved. A really repugnant rider also may be attached to a bill that is sure of approval in order to defeat that bill. In other words, no one wants the rider, and the House would rather not pass the whole bill than to pass the bill with the rider attached.

The Senate Process If the bill is passed by the House, it is sent over to the Senate. The Senate leadership assigns the bill to a committee, where in turn it is assigned to a subcommittee, if one exists. Once again, the process of committee approval takes place. By the time the bill is approved by the subcommittee, committee, and Senate, it

will, in all likelihood, not be exactly the same as the bill that was passed by the House.

Conference Conferees from the House and the Senate are selected to work out the differences between the two bills. Usually, this is an informal procedure, but the conferees do write a conference report. The bill will receive final approval and passage into law when both chambers approve the conference report.

If the versions are significantly different and neither chamber will yield to the language contained in the other's bill, a conference committee is established. This committee exists only to work out the differences of that particular bill. Usually, only significant legislation merits a conference committee. Because of the significance of the legislation and the interests involved, the most concentrated and toughest legislative work takes place at this level.

The conference committee meetings are not open to the public so that various options may be explored without the members having to make any public commitment to a particular position. Progress reports are given to the press. Usually the committee has a harsh schedule of meetings for several months before it agrees on a final version of the bill. The conference committee issues its report, which includes this final version. Just as with the more informal conference, approval and passage of the bill comes when both the House and the Senate approve the report of the conference committee.

President's Role   Once the bill has been passed by Congress, it is sent over to the president for his or her signature. Bills of major importance are signed in a ceremony held either in the Oval Office or in the Rose Garden. If the president exercises the power of the **executive veto**, which vetoes the bill, Congress can override this veto by a two-thirds vote.

When the president signs the bill or when a congressional vote overrides a veto, the bill becomes a statute. The statute receives a Public Law number, and it will be referred to either by this number or by a popular name. The number is made up of the number of the Congress and the number of bills signed to date by the president. For example, P.L. 90-321 refers to the Ninetieth Congress, and it was the bill number 321 signed into law by the president. The popular name of P.L. 90-321 is the Consumer Credit Protection Act.

The statute may cover several topics. The new statute will not be placed as a whole unit (as it was when it was in bill form) into the code book. The statute is divided and placed into the appropriate sections. For example, the Consumer Credit Protection Act was passed in 1968 as P.L. 90-321. The act as originally passed contained a section concerning crimes. That section was placed in the Crimes and Criminal Procedure Code, Title 18, and the rest of the statute was placed in the Commerce and Trade Code, Title 15.

The law in its original form is sent to the General Services Administration for permanent deposit as a document in the National Archives. Bills not passed by one Congress are not held over for consideration by the next Congress. Each Congress is held for a two-year period. The bill must be reintroduced by a member of Congress to be considered again. Most bills that are introduced are not considered by any committee at all; in other words, most bills die.

Legislative Veto

Congress has granted the executive branch the authority to carry out certain tasks, generally through administrative agencies. For decades, Congress has also exercised its final authority over those designated to carry out assigned tasks by either approving the actions of the executive branch or by expressing disapproval through a device called the **legislative veto**. For example, when Congress passed the Federal Trade Commission Authorization Act, it reserved the power to veto any Federal Trade Commission regulation.

The Supreme Court in 1983 examined the concept of the legislative veto when it was challenged on constitutional grounds in the following case. In this landmark decision, the Supreme Court held that the congressional veto provision in the act in question was unconstitutional.

Case 6.1

IMMIGRATION AND NATURALIZATION SERVICE v. CHADHA

Supreme Court of the United States, 1983. 462 U.S. 919, 103 S.Ct. 2764, 77 L.Ed.2d 317.

BACKGROUND AND FACTS   *The Immigration and Nationality Act delegated to the executive branch, through the Immigration and Naturalization Service, the authority to determine if an alien was subject to being deported. The act required that an alien be given a hearing before the Immigration Court. If an alien was ordered to be deported by the immigration judge, the act allowed the alien to apply to the attorney general for relief. The act delegated to the attorney general the discretionary authority to suspend the deportation of the alien. Congress reserved to itself the right for only one of its houses to invalidate the decision made by the executive branch to allow a particular deportable alien to remain in the United States.*

Chadha, age forty, was an East Indian who was born in Kenya and held a British passport. He was lawfully admitted to the United States in 1966 on a nonimmigrant student visa but stayed after the visa had expired. He could not go back to Great Britain because he was not a citizen and Britain had severely restricted applications for reentry. The British courts never ruled on Chadha's request for reentry. He could not return to Kenya because of the political turmoil that had occurred since he had left.

He was arrested and a deportation hearing was held. Chadha submitted evidence and the results of a character investigation. Based on this evidence, the immigration judge ordered that Chadha's deportation be suspended in July 1974. The attorney general also determined that Chadha should not be deported.

Congress had two years, while it was in session, to act on this decision. At the end of the second year, in December 1975, a resolution was passed by the House denying the granting of permanent residence in the United States to Chadha and six others. Why they were singled out from the 339 suspension cases pending before Congress was never disclosed. After the House passed the resolution, the deportation proceedings were reopened. Chadha was ordered to be deported in March 1977. Chadha appealed to the Ninth Circuit Court of Appeals, which upheld the congressional decision in a narrow ruling. He then appealed to the United States Supreme Court.

BURGER, Chief Justice, delivered the opinion of the Court.
* * * *

We turn now to the question whether action of one House of Congress under [the Act] violates strictures of the Constitution. We begin, of course, with the presumption that the challenged statute is valid. Its wisdom is not the concern of the courts; if a challenged action does not violate the Constitution, it must be sustained. * * *

By the same token, the fact that a given law or procedure is efficient, convenient, and useful in facilitating functions of government, standing alone, will not save it if it is contrary to the Constitution. Convenience and efficiency are not the primary objectives—or the hallmarks—of democratic government and our inquiry is sharpened rather than blunted by the fact that congressional veto provisions are appearing with increasing frequency in statutes which delegate authority to executive and independent agencies:

> "Since 1932, when the first veto provision was enacted into law, 295 congressional veto-type procedures have been inserted in 196 different statutes as follows: from 1932 to 1939, five statutes were affected; from 1940–1949, nineteen statutes; between 1950–1959, thirty-four statutes; and from 1960–1969, forty-nine. From the year 1970–1975, at least one hundred sixty-three such provisions were included in eighty-nine laws." Abourezk, The Congressional Veto: A Contemporary Response to Executive Encroachment on Legislative Prerogatives, 52 Ind.L.Rev. 323, 324 (1977).

* * * *

The records of the Constitutional Convention reveal that the requirement that all legislation be presented to the President before becoming law was uniformly accepted by the Framers. Presentment to the President and the Presidential veto were considered so imperative that the Draftsmen took special pains to assure that these requirements could not be circumvented. * * *

* * * *

The Constitution sought to divide the delegated powers of the new Federal Government into three defined categories, Legislative, Executive, and Judicial, to assure, as nearly as possible, that each Branch of government would confine itself to its assigned responsibility. The hydraulic pressure inherent within each of the separate Branches to exceed the outer limits of its power, even to accomplish desirable objectives, must be resisted.

* * * *

Finally, we see that when the Framers intended to authorize either House of Congress to act alone and outside of its prescribed bicameral legislative role, they narrowly and precisely defined the procedure for such action. There are four provisions in the Constitution, explicit and unambiguous, by which one House may act alone with the unreviewable force of law, not subject to the President's veto:

(a) The House of Representatives alone was given the power to initiate impeachments.

(b) The Senate alone was given the power to conduct trials following impeachment on charges initiated by the House and to convict following trial.

(c) The Senate alone was given final unreviewable power to approve or to disapprove Presidential appointments.

(d) The Senate alone was given unreviewable power to ratify treaties negotiated by the President.

Clearly, when the Draftsmen sought to confer special powers on one House, independent of the other House, or of the President, they did so in explicit, unambiguous terms. These carefully defined exceptions from presentment and bicameralism underscore the difference between the legislative functions of Congress and other unilateral but important and binding one-House acts provided for in the Constitution. These exceptions are narrow, explicit, and separately justified; none of them authorize the action challenged here. On the contrary, they provide further support for the conclusion that congressional authority is not to be implied and for the conclusion that the veto provided for in [the Act] is not authorized by the constitutional design of the powers of the Legislative Branch.

* * * *

We hold that the congressional veto provision in [the Act] is severable from the Act and that it is unconstitutional. * * *

DECISION AND REMEDY

The decision by Congress to deport Chadha was reversed. The Supreme Court found only part of the Immigration and Nationality Act unconstitutional—that is, the part that authorized one house of Congress, by resolution, to invalidate a decision of the executive branch.

COMMENT

The simple facts of this case—the decision to deport an illegal alien—resulted in a major decision by the United States Supreme Court. This decision overturned more legislation (more than 200 statutes containing legislative veto provisions) than all the decisions made by the Supreme Court since the doctrine of judicial review was adopted by the Court in Marbury v. Madison.[a]

Two current members of the United States Supreme Court played a role in this case. Justice Anthony Kennedy (then a justice on the Ninth Circuit Court of Appeals) wrote the opinion that was appealed to the Supreme

---

a. 1 Cranch 137 (1803). See Chapter 2 for the case.

Court. During that same time period, Justice Antonin Scalia, then a representative of the American Bar Association, was appearing before Congress in hearings held on the issue of the legislative veto. He testified against it.

Chadha became a citizen of the United States on April 10, 1984; his place in legal history is secure.

Lobbyists

Among the rights protected by the First Amendment is the right of people to lobby their government. Lobbying government officials has been recognized as a legitimate, constitutionally protected activity from the time of the adoption of the Constitution. Currently, 8,800 **lobbyists** are registered under the **Federal Regulation of Lobbying Act of 1942**. The true lobby population has been placed more realistically at around 20,000. Lawyers, public relations consultants, and specialists in government affairs are among those who have access to congresspeople and who may, in effect, lobby for or against legislation, but who are not registered.

Regulation of the Lobbyists' Activities

Congress chose to regulate lobbyists through disclosure laws rather than through a regulatory agency. The major relevant statute is the Federal Regulation of Lobbying Act of 1942, which requires lobbyists to register with the clerk of the House and the secretary of the Senate. Lobbyists must also file quarterly financial reports that are available to anyone to examine. The act does not directly control the lobbyists' activities.

Presidential Lobby

Most people do not think of the president as a lobbyist, but the president is actually the strongest and most influential lobbyist with Congress. The president can exert continuing pressure over long time periods. This pressure can come indirectly through the use of that old standby, the patronage system; in other words, the president can appoint people to various high-level government positions and can make some federal contract decisions. The president also has the ability to veto legislation.

The president can exert direct pressure on members of Congress either personally or through an effective staff. When the president is unable to convince Congress, he or she can appeal directly to the people by making an appearance on television or speaking on the radio. Congress does not have this option. Congress is made up of diverse members who represent a variety of philosophically different congressional districts. Thus, although the president can speak with one voice, Congress is rarely unanimous about anything. Even in the declaration of war that took the United States into World War II, there was one dissenting vote.

Effective use of television and radio allows the president to marshal public opinion. The strength of public opinion almost always convinces Congress to support the president's legislative request.

If Congress, however, does pass a bill of which the president does not approve, the president can always exercise the veto. The veto can also be used to dramatize the president's position on an issue; in other words, it tells Congress that the president is very serious about his or her position. When this happens, the president places the prestige of the office on the line, for there is always a chance that he or she will be embarrassed if Congress overrides the veto. For example, President Carter was the first president since Truman to have a veto overridden by a Congress that was controlled by his own party.

Political Action Committees

The difference between lobbyists and **political action committees** (**PACs**) is that lobbyists' activities are directed toward incumbent members of

LEGAL HIGHLIGHT   Golden Fleece Award

In March 1975, Senator Proxmire from Wisconsin initiated the "Golden Fleece of the Month Award" in order to publicize what he perceived as outrageous examples of fraud, waste, and abuse. The award was announced in speeches, newsletters, and press releases.

Proxmire chose Hutchinson, a research behavioral scientist, as the recipient of the award. Hutchinson received from various government sources $500,000 to measure aggression objectively by concentrating on animal behavior patterns, such as the animals' clenching of their jaws. This research was supported by both the National Aeronautics and Space Agency (NASA) and the Department of the Navy. Among other statements, Senator Proxmire wrote that "Dr. Hutchinson's studies should make the taxpayers as well as his

monkeys grind their teeth. In fact, the good doctor has made a fortune from his monkeys and in the process made a monkey out of the American taxpayer." Hutchinson sued.[a]

The Supreme Court held that Hutchinson had a right to sue. Senator Proxmire's speech would be covered by the immunity doctrine if the speech came on the floor of the Senate or in another legislative setting. The newsletters and the press releases were to inform those outside the legislative body, and they represented his single view and not the views of Congress. Therefore, Congressional member newsletters and press releases are not protected by the speech and debate clause immunity doctrine.

a.   Hutchinson v. Proxmire, 443 U.S. 111, 99 S.Ct. 2675, 61 L.Ed.2d 411 (1979).

Congress while the activities of political action committees are directed toward raising and spending money to elect lawmakers.

Political action committees have existed since the late 1940s. Real growth in the number and amount of influence exerted by PACs came in the late 1970s after the Watergate hearings documented the corruption of President Nixon's reelection committee. In the aftermath of those hearings, the 1974 amendments to the **Federal Election Campaign Act (FECA) of 1971** were passed. As a result, an individual can contribute up to $1,000 to a federal candidate in each separate election (primary, runoff, or general election). An individual cannot contribute more than $25,000 to all federal candidates in a year.

These restrictions severely inhibited the previously unrestrained donations of wealthy individuals, whether they were business executives or others who chose to become financially involved in the political process. The FECA amendments set the stage for the rise of the PACs. No federal statute defines a political action committee, but the FECA does define a nonparty political com-

mittee as any committee, club, association, or other group of members that has receipts or expenditures of at least $1,000 each year, or operates a separate fund to raise and disburse money in federal campaigns.

Today over 6,000 PACs are registered with the Federal Election Commission. Since the meteoric rise of PACs, a national debate has ensued on their merits. The proponents of PACs maintain that political committees are a practical way for individuals to exercise their constitutional right, since PACs offer a centralized and organized way for an individual to participate in the political process. The PACs have opened a way for an individual to support a particular philosophy or group interest. Because of the variety and number of PACs, no one PAC can become dominant; corporate PACs are balanced by labor PACs, for example. The concept and use of PACs are not really new; throughout history, Americans have formed associations to support causes and candidates.

Opponents contend that the PACs are a corrupting influence on the political process. PACs are another form of buying political influence because donations to a candidate's campaign do not come without strings attached. Both corporate and labor PACs are accused of soliciting contributions from employees or members through coercion. In addition, PACs are not really accountable to anyone. Although they must report their contributions and expenditures to the Federal Election Commission, the amount of disclosure is left to the PAC; thus, it is difficult to assess and compare various PACs, and opponents contend that PACs operate in an undemocratic and unaccountable manner.

Senator Robert Dole (R-Kansas) has expressed this concern about PACs:

> When these political action committees give money, they expect something in return other than good government. It is making it difficult to legislate. We may reach a point where everybody is buying something with PAC money. We cannot get anything done.

Legislative Immunity

The Constitution provides for **legislative immunity** from lawsuits for the members of Congress. The speech and debate clause of the Constitution allows congressional members to talk and debate freely. This clause protects them from being held accountable for the acts and utterances that are part of their legitimate legislative duties.

Whether legislative immunity applies is not based on public or private benefit or on political value, but strictly on whether the acts or speeches were legislative. The protection extends well beyond the bounds of the floor of Congress to hearings, reports, resolutions, and other acts that can be considered legislative.

The writers of the Constitution balanced the potential damage to a person from false statements about him or her that might be made by a legislator against the need for a legislator to be free to make any statement deemed necessary. A member of the legislature should not have to worry about being tied up in court defending what she or he has said while carrying out legislative duties. During colonial times, members of English Parliament had been arrested during speeches and debates; the drafters of the Constitution decided to protect legislators in this country from similar occurrences.

The following case emphasizes the right of a member of Congress to refuse to speak. This right is part of the speech and debate clause of the Constitution.

BACKGROUND AND FACTS *In November 1966, Adam Clayton Powell, Jr., was elected from New York to serve in the Ninetieth Congress. Pursuant to a House resolution, he was not permitted to take his seat. During the Eighty-Ninth Congress, to which he had also been elected, a report was filed concluding that he had deceived the House authorities concerning travel expenses. No formal action had been taken by the Eighty-Ninth Congress. When the Ninetieth Congress met to organize itself, Powell was asked to step aside. At a later hearing, he refused to answer any questions other than to state his qualifications. The House refused to swear him in. He filed suit. Among other issues, the Supreme Court addressed the speech and debate clause of the Constitution.*

Case 6.2
POWELL v. McCORMACK
Supreme Court of the United States, 1969.
395 U.S. 486, 89 S.Ct. 1944, 23 L.Ed.2d 491.

WARREN, Chief Justice, delivered the opinion of the Court.
* * * *

The Speech or Debate Clause, adopted by the Constitutional Convention without debate or opposition, finds its roots in the conflict between Parliament and the Crown culminating in the Glorious Revolution of 1688 and the English Bill of Rights of 1689. Drawing upon this history, we concluded . . . that the purpose of this clause was "to prevent intimidation [of legislators] by the executive and accountability before a possibly hostile judiciary." Although the clause sprang from a fear of seditious libel actions instituted by the Crown to punish unfavorable speeches made in Parliament, we have held that it would be a "narrow view" to confine the protection of the Speech or Debate Clause to words spoken in debate. Committee reports, resolutions, and the act of voting are equally covered, as are "things generally done in a session of the House by one of its members in relation to the business before it." Furthermore, the clause not only provides a defense on the merits but also protects a legislator from the burden of defending himself.

Our cases make it clear that the legislative immunity created by the Speech or Debate Clause performs an important function in representative government. It insures that legislators are free to represent the interests of their constituents without fear that they will be later called to task in the courts for that representation. * * *

DECISION AND REMEDY *The Supreme Court held that Adam Clayton Powell, Jr., had been duly elected by the voters of his congressional district and was not ineligible to serve under any other provision of the Constitution. The House action to prevent him from taking his seat was set aside and he was allowed to serve his district in the Ninetieth Congress.*

COMMENT *Adam Clayton Powell, Jr., was defeated in 1970 when he ran for reelection. He died in 1972.*

The Executive Branch

"The executive Power shall be vested in a President of the United States of America. He shall hold his Office during the Term of four Years * * *"; so starts Article II of the Constitution. The Constitution, however, is not very specific about other elements of the president's power. For instance, the framers of the Constitution did not define executive power, nor is it clear whether the section making the president the commander in chief of the armed forces conferred only a title or granted authority. Most of the powers of the president have evolved over the past 200 years as the Supreme Court has decided specific issues in cases brought before it. Many issues of presidential power and authority remain unresolved even to this day.

Specific Powers

The Constitution does list certain specific presidential powers and responsibilities. For example, the president is the commander in chief of the army and navy. The Constitution gives him or her the power to grant reprieves and pardons; the power to make treaties, dependent on ratification by two-thirds of the Senate; the power to appoint ambassadors, public ministers, consuls, judges of the Supreme Court, and other officers of the United States; and the power to fill any vacancies that might occur while the Senate is in recess (appointments made while the Senate is in recess are called recess appointments; these terms of office expire at the end of the next session of the Senate).

The president also must give Congress information on the state of the Union, recommend legislation, and receive ambassadors and other public ministers. He or she ensures that the laws are faithfully executed and commissions all the officers of the United States.

Finally, as mentioned before, the Constitution gives the president the right to veto congressional bills, and Congress, in turn, has the right to override a presidential veto. The framers of the Constitution had two purposes in mind when they decided to include this veto power. First, legislatures have a tendency to intrude on the rights of others and to take or give power to various branches of government depending on the responsiveness of that particular branch. With the veto power, the president can defend the prerogatives of the executive office. Second, the veto powers of the

LEGAL HIGHLIGHT   One Vote

The power of a single vote is illustrated in these examples where one person's vote was decisive:

■ Hitler won leadership of the German Nazi Party in 1923.
■ Congress saved the U.S. Army from instant collapse by voting on August 12, 1941, to extend the Selective Service Act of 1940 (about to lapse) for another eighteen months; this took place less than four months before the Japanese bombed Pearl Harbor.
■ Thomas Jefferson won the American presidency over Aaron Burr when the election was thrown into the House of Representatives.

■ John Quincy Adams became president in a deadlock between Adams and Andrew Jackson in 1824.
■ Rutherford B. Hayes became president over Samuel Tilden in 1876 by a single electoral vote.
■ Texas was admitted to the Union in 1845.
■ Andrew Johnson was not convicted at his impeachment trial.
■ The English language was chosen over German in 1775.
■ A Texas convention chose Lyndon B. Johnson over ex-Governor Coke Stephenson in a contested election in 1948 for a seat in the United States Senate.

---

president provide an additional check against the passing of improper laws.

Flowing from these specific powers are implied powers. An implied power is one that is necessary to carry out a specific power. For example, the president has the express power to commission all military officers, and thus he or she has the implied power to check the candidates' backgrounds in order to ensure that they meet the relevant criteria.

Inherent powers are also exercised by the president. These powers are probably the ones subjected most often to litigation. For example, the president does not have a clear mandate from the Constitution that he or she can exercise sole authority in foreign affairs. The Supreme Court in a series of cases has upheld the president's inherent right, on the basis of our very existence as a nation, to have sole authority in this area. The United States of America must speak with one voice when dealing with foreign governments, and that voice is the president's.

Informal Power

The president and vice president are the only two federal officials who are elected by all the people,

even though this takes place through the electoral college system. The president is thus the representative of all the people, while members of Congress represent local, not nationwide, constituencies. The president's popular mandate justifies his or her authority.

The president's ability to persuade Congress to pass or defeat certain bills and to set a national policy on particular issues is based on this popular mandate. If necessary, the president can go over the heads of members of Congress and can ask the people to urge their congressional representatives to vote on a bill in accordance with the president's wishes. President Reagan has used this method of pressuring Congress on numerous occasions and, because of his immense popularity, he has won congressional support in spite of great odds and predicted defeat by the media.

Executive Orders

Executive orders are another tool of the president's domestic authority. Three types of executive orders exist: orders that carry out his or her duty as chief executive in accordance with a specific authorization of Congress; orders that are administrative in nature, reflecting the president's position as head of the executive branch; and orders that are issued as commander in chief. These orders have been upheld by the Supreme Court.

For example, executive orders have been used since President Franklin Roosevelt's time to promote civil rights. On the other hand, President Roosevelt also used the executive order to transfer Japanese-Americans to relocation centers, an order upheld by two Supreme Court decisions. Similarly, it was by executive order that President Truman seized the steel industry. (See the next case, *Youngstown Sheet & Tube Co. v. Sawyer.*) The executive order can be a powerful tool.

Limitations of Power

The powers of the president are limited by the Constitution. The president is the head of only one of the three branches of government, and these three are in never-ending tension.

The following case discusses judicial review of the actions of the president when he seized the steel companies. It is a good example of the doctrine of separation of powers, and it illustrates a limitation placed on the powers of the president.

Case 6.3

YOUNGSTOWN SHEET & TUBE CO. v. SAWYER

Supreme Court of the United States, 1952.
343 U.S. 579, 72 S.Ct. 863, 96 L.Ed. 1153.

BACKGROUND AND FACTS   *In the latter part of 1951, a dispute arose between the steel companies and their employees over the terms and conditions that should be included in new collective bargaining agreements. Long-continued conferences failed to resolve the dispute, and the labor union, the United Steelworkers of America, gave notice of an intention to strike when the existing bargaining agreement expired. The Federal Mediation and Conciliation Service intervened in an effort to get the union and the management to agree. This effort failed.*

President Truman, a few hours before the strike was to begin, issued an executive order that directed the secretary of commerce, Mr. Sawyer, to take possession of the steel mills and to keep them running. The next morning the president sent a message to Congress reporting his action. Congress took no action in response. Although the companies, under protest, obeyed the secretary's orders, they filed a lawsuit against him. The district court held the executive order unconstitutional and the case was eventually appealed to the United States Supreme Court.

BLACK, Justice, delivered the opinion of the Court.
* * * *

We are asked to decide whether the President was acting within his constitutional power when he issued an order directing the Secretary of Commerce to take possession of and operate most of the Nation's steel mills. The mill owners argue that the President's order amounts to lawmaking, a legislative function which the Constitution has expressly confided to the Congress and not to the President. The Government's position is that the order was made on findings of the President that his action was necessary to avert a national catastrophe which would inevitably result from a stoppage of steel production, and that in meeting this grave emergency the President was acting within the aggregate of his constitutional powers as the Nation's Chief Executive and the Commander in Chief of the Armed Forces of the United States. * * *
* * * *

The President's power, if any, to issue the order must stem either from an act of Congress or from the Constitution itself. There is no statute that expressly authorizes the President to take possession of property as he did here. Nor is there any act of Congress to which our attention has been directed from which such a power can fairly be implied. * * *

* * * *

* * * [T]he use of the seizure technique to solve labor disputes in order to prevent work stoppages was not only unauthorized by any congressional enactment; prior to this controversy, Congress had refused to adopt that method of settling labor disputes. * * *

It is clear that if the President had authority to issue the order he did, it must be found in some provision of the Constitution. And it is not claimed that express constitutional language grants this power to the President. The contention is that presidential power should be implied from the aggregate of his powers under the Constitution. Particular reliance is placed on provisions in Article II which say that "the executive Power shall be vested in a President . . ."; that "he shall take Care that the Laws be faithfully executed"; and that he "shall be Commander in Chief of the Army and Navy of the United States."

The order cannot properly be sustained as an exercise of the President's military power as Commander in Chief of the Armed Forces. * * * Even though "theater of war" be an expanding concept, we cannot with faithfulness to our constitutional system hold that the Commander in Chief of the Armed Forces has the ultimate power as such to take possession of private property in order to keep labor disputes from stopping production. This is a job for the Nation's lawmakers, not for its military authorities.

Nor can the seizure order be sustained because of the several constitutional provisions that grant executive power to the President. In the framework of our Constitution, the President's power to see that the laws are faithfully executed refutes the idea that he is to be a lawmaker. * * *

* * * *

The Founders of this Nation entrusted the lawmaking power to the Congress alone in both good and bad times. * * *

The Supreme Court affirmed the district court's declaration that the orders of the president and the secretary were unconstitutional and therefore invalid.

DECISION AND REMEDY

The Youngstown *case is one of the few Supreme Court cases that discusses at length the powers of the president under the Constitution; thus, it is one of the important constitutional law cases. The significance of this case is that it establishes that the courts will review the actions of the president if those actions are challenged. This case arose after a period of twenty years during which presidential power had steadily expanded under President Roosevelt. President Truman believed that he had the authority to take over the steel mills. He thought it was necessary to ensure the continued supply of arms to the United Nations' troops, which included Americans, during the Korean Conflict, then in its second year.*

Many people were shocked at the president's action. Presidents had seized plants before, but never during peacetime and never in an industry as basic to the American economy as steel. President Truman's seizure of the steel mills triggered a classic constitutional and political crisis that raised fundamental questions about the limits of presidential power under

COMMENT

the Constitution. The importance of the Youngstown *precedent would be appreciated later when the Supreme Court reviewed the abuses of power in the Nixon administration. The Supreme Court in both cases reconfirmed the basic principle that everyone, including the president, is subject to the law.*

Executive Privilege

The Constitution is silent as to whether the president must supply information to or has the right to withhold information from either Congress or the courts. In fact, the phrase **executive privilege** was not used until 1958 during the Eisenhower administration; the concept, however, has been applied ever since George Washington's presidency.

Similar to the attorney-client privilege, the concept of executive privilege holds that the president has the right to keep certain communications a secret. The concept is based on public policy that seeks to protect the integrity of sources and the confidentiality of discussions within the executive branch. It allows those participating in the decision-making process to be free to express their opinions without fear of disclosure.

The president has not often used the executive privilege. If it is used, it arises, more often than not, when Congress is conducting an investigation. Usually Congress and the president reach an agreement prior to any court action as to which

documents will be disclosed. For example, during the Senate confirmation hearings of Chief Justice Rehnquist, President Reagan exerted executive privilege over memorandums written while Rehnquist had worked in the Department of Justice. Eventually, the Senate subcommittee was able to examine the documents it wanted, but only after representatives from both sides had agreed which documents were releasable.

In fact, Congress is reluctant to take an executive privilege dispute to court. First of all, if Congress loses its investigatory power might be permanently limited. (Remember that Congress, for decades, had used the legislative veto, only to have the Supreme Court decide that Congress did not have that right.) Congress also does not want the judicial branch to assume any larger role than is absolutely necessary in congressional investigations.

Surprisingly, the first case on the doctrine of executive privilege was *United States v. Nixon.* In this case, the Supreme Court recognized the validity of executive privilege but held that it is a qualified, rather than an absolute, right.

Case 6.4
UNITED STATES v. NIXON
Supreme Court of the United States, 1974.
418 U.S. 683, 94 S.Ct. 3090, 41 L.Ed.2d 1039.

BACKGROUND AND FACTS *Former government officials and presidential campaign officials of the Nixon presidency were being prosecuted for conspiracy to defraud the United States and to obstruct justice. The special prosecutor had a subpoena* duces tecum *issued directing President Nixon to produce tape recordings and documents relating to his conversations with aids and advisers. President Nixon moved to quash the subpoena.*

BURGER, Chief Justice, delivered the opinion of the Court.
* * * *

In the performance of assigned constitutional duties each branch of the Government must initially interpret the Constitution, and the interpretation of its powers by any branch is due great respect from the others. The President's counsel * * * reads the Constitution as providing an absolute privilege of confidentiality for all Presidential communications. Many decisions of this Court, however, have unequivocally reaffirmed the hold of *Marbury v. Madison* that ''[i]t is emphatically the province and duty of the judicial department to say what the law is.''

No holding of the Court has defined the scope of judicial power specifically relating to the enforcement of a subpoena for confidential Presidential communications for use in a criminal prosecution, but other exercises of power by the Executive Branch and the Legislative Branch have been found invalid as in conflict with the Constitution.

* * * *

* * * Neither the doctrine of separation of powers, nor the need for confidentiality of high-level communications, without more, can sustain an absolute, unqualified Presidential privilege of immunity from judicial process under all circumstances. The President's need for complete candor and objectivity from advisers calls for great deference from the courts. However, when the privilege depends solely on the broad, undifferentiated claim of public interest in the confidentiality of such conversations, a confrontation with other values arises. Absent a claim of need to protect military, diplomatic, or sensitive national security secrets, we find it difficult to accept the argument that even the very important interest in confidentiality of Presidential communications is significantly diminished by production of such material for *in camera* inspection with all the protection that a district court will be obliged to provide.

* * * *

Since we conclude that the legitimate needs of the judicial process may outweigh Presidential privilege, it is necessary to resolve those competing interests in a manner that preserves the essential functions of each branch. The right and indeed the duty to resolve that question does not free the Judiciary from according high respect to the representations made on behalf of the President.

* * * *

In this case we must weigh the importance of the general privilege of confidentiality of Presidential communications in performance of the President's responsibilities against the inroads of such a privilege on the fair administration of criminal justice. The interest in preserving confidentiality is weighty indeed and entitled to great respect. However, we cannot conclude that advisers will be moved to temper the candor of their remarks by the infrequent occasions of disclosure because of the possibility that such conversations will be called for in the context of a criminal prosecution.

* * * *

We conclude that when the ground for asserting privilege as to subpoenaed materials sought for use in criminal trial is based only on the generalized interest in confidentiality, it cannot prevail over the fundamental demands of due process of law in the fair administration of criminal justice. The generalized assertion of privilege must yield to the demonstrated, specific need for evidence in a pending criminal trial.

* * * *

* * * It is elementary that *in camera* inspection of evidence is always a procedure calling for scrupulous protection against any release or publication of material not found by the court, at that stage, probably admissible in evidence and relevant to the issues of the trial for which it is sought. That being true of an ordinary situation, it is obvious that the District Court has a very heavy responsibility to see to it that Presidential conversations, which are either not relevant or not admissible, are accorded that high degree of respect due the President of the United States. Mr. Chief Justice Marshall, sitting as a trial judge in the *United States v. Burr* case, was extraordinarily careful to point out that "[i]n no case of this kind would a court be required to proceed against the president as against an ordinary individual."

Marshall's statement cannot be read to mean in any sense that a President is above the law, but relates to the singularly unique role under Art. II of a President's communications and activities, related to the performance of duties under that Article. Moreover, a President's communications and activities encompass a vastly wider range of sensitive material than would be true of any "ordinary individual." It is therefore necessary in the public interest to afford Presidential confidentiality the greatest protection consistent with the fair administration of justice. * * * We have no doubt that the District Judge will at all times accord to Presidential records that high degree of deference suggested in *United States v. Burr,* and will discharge his responsibility to see to it that until released to the Special Prosecutor no *in camera* material is revealed to anyone. This burden applies with even greater force to excised material; once the decision is made to excise, the material is restored to its privileged status and should be returned under seal to its lawful custodian.

DECISION AND   *The district court and special prosecutor were allowed to examine the*
REMEDY   *president's tape recordings and documents, and pertinent information was*
      used in the pending trials.

COMMENT   *The case was decided unanimously with seven justices joining the chief*
      justice in the opinion. At that time, Chief Justice Rehnquist was an associate
      justice, having been appointed in 1972 to the Supreme Court by President
      Nixon. He did not participate in the decision because he had participated
      in the Watergate investigation while working at the Department of Justice.

      The decision, by virtue of its having been delivered by the chief justice
      and because of its unanimity, strongly affected President Nixon. Shortly
      after this decision, he resigned as president in August 1974.

Executive Immunity

Under the Constitution, the executive branch is immune from certain lawsuits. The framers decided wisely to provide **executive immunity** so that the executive branch would be able to carry out its official functions without worrying about whether its members would be personally liable for damages caused by its actions.

Based on public policy, the president is able to carry out the law faithfully and to exercise his or her executive power free from the fear of a lawsuit. Lawsuits are expensive, both in time and money. To have to defend the validity of each and every action in court would be disastrous. First, the courts do not have the information, knowledge, or expertise to second-guess constantly the executive branch's decisions. Second,

the executive branch would sink in a hopeless quagmire of cases and would essentially cease to function.

The Supreme Court has consistently held that officials in the executive branch of government are protected by executive immunity as long as they are within the boundaries of their duties. People in the executive branch lose the protection of executive immunity when they engage in criminal activity or commit what is known as a **constitutional tort** in civil law. A constitutional tort occurs when an executive branch official violates a constitutional right of a person. The president and all the officials in the executive branch are not above the law and are subject to the Constitution. The following case demonstrates the loss of executive immunity when members of the executive branch engage in illegal or unconstitutional acts.

BACKGROUND AND FACTS   *A. Ernest Fitzgerald worked for the United States Air Force as a civilian. Against the orders of his superiors in the air force, he testified, during congressional hearings, about the enormous cost overruns on the C-5, then the world's largest airplane. Known as a whistle-blower, Fitzgerald subsequently became involved in a number of lawsuits in order to retain his position.*

The record revealed that Secretary of the Air Force Seamans had called in Bryce Harlow, who was the presidential aide principally responsible for congressional relations, to inquire about likely congressional reaction to a draft reorganization plan that would cause Fitzgerald's dismissal. Although informed that this issue was a very sensitive item in Congress, the air force went ahead with the reorganization. Later that year, a public announcement was made of Fitzgerald's impending dismissal. Fitzgerald filed this lawsuit against Harlow and others for conspiring to violate his constitutional and statutory rights.

The district court denied Harlow's motion for summary judgment, and the court of appeals upheld the trial court. The Supreme Court granted certiorari *because it had never determined the executive immunity available to the senior aides and advisers of the president of the United States.*

Case 6.5
HARLOW v. FITZGERALD
Supreme Court of the United States, 1982.
457 U.S. 800, 102 S.Ct. 2727, 73 L.Ed.2d 396.

POWELL, Justice, delivered the opinion of the Court.
*   *   *   *

[O]ur decisions consistently have held that government officials are entitled to some form of immunity from suits for damages. As recognized at common law, public officers require this protection to shield them from undue interference with their duties and from potentially disabling threats of liability.

Our decisions have recognized immunity defenses of two kinds. For officials whose special functions or constitutional status requires complete protection from suit, we have recognized the defense of ''absolute immunity.'' The absolute immunity of legislators, in their legislative functions, *   *   * and of judges, in their judicial functions, *   *   * now is well settled. Our decisions also have extended absolute immunity to certain officials of the Executive Branch. These include prosecutors and similar officials, *   *   * executive officers engaged in adjudicative functions, *   *   * and the President of the United States[.] *   *   *

For executive officials in general, however, our cases make plain that qualified immunity represents the norm. In *Scheuer v. Rhodes*, we acknowledged that high officials require greater protection than those with less complex discretionary responsibilities. *   *   *

Petitioners argue that they are entitled to a blanket protection of absolute immunity as an incident of their offices as Presidential aides. In deciding this claim we do not write on an empty page. In *Butz v. Economou*, the Secretary of Agriculture—a Cabinet official directly accountable to the President—asserted a defense of absolute official immunity from suit for civil damages. We rejected his claim. *   *   * ''[T]he greater power of [high] officials,'' we reasoned, ''affords a greater potential for a regime of lawless conduct.'' Damages actions against high officials were therefore ''an important means of vindicating constitutional guarantees.''

Having decided in *Butz* that Members of the Cabinet ordinarily enjoy only qualified immunity from suit, we conclude today that it would be equally untenable to hold absolute immunity an incident of the office of every Presidential subordinate based in the White House. Members of the Cabinet are direct subordinates of the

President, frequently with greater responsibilities, both to the President and to the Nation, than White House staff. The considerations that supported our decision in *Butz* apply with equal force to this case. * * *
* * * *

Even if they cannot establish that their official functions require absolute immunity, petitioners assert that public policy at least mandates an application of the qualified immunity standard that would permit the defeat of insubstantial claims without resort to trial. We agree.

The resolution of immunity questions inherently requires a balance between the evils inevitable in any available alternative. In situations of abuse of office, an action for damages may offer the only realistic avenue for vindication of constitutional guarantees. * * * It is this recognition that has required the denial of absolute immunity to most public officers. * * *

Qualified or "good faith" immunity is an affirmative defense that must be pleaded by a defendant official. Decisions of this Court have established that the "good faith" defense has both an "objective" and a "subjective" aspect. The objective element involves a presumptive knowledge of and respect for "basic, unquestioned constitutional rights." The subjective component refers to "permissible intentions." Characteristically the Court has defined these elements by identifying the circumstances in which qualified immunity would *not* be available. Referring both to the objective and subjective elements, we have held that qualified immunity would be defeated if an official "*knew or reasonably should have known* that the action he took within his sphere of official responsibility would violate the constitutional rights of the [plaintiff], *or* if he took the action *with the malicious intention* to cause a deprivation of constitutional rights or other injury. * * *" (emphasis added).
* * * *

Consistently with the balance at which we aimed in *Butz,* we conclude today that bare allegations of malice should not suffice to subject government officials either to the costs of trial or to the burdens of broad-reaching discovery. We therefore hold that government officials performing discretionary functions, generally are shielded from liability for civil damages insofar as their conduct does not violate clearly established statutory or constitutional rights of which a reasonable person would have known.

In this case petitioners have asked us to hold that the respondent's pretrial showings were insufficient to survive their motion for summary judgment. We think it appropriate, however, to remand the case to the District Court for its reconsideration of this issue in light of this opinion. The trial court is more familiar with the record so far developed and also is better situated to make any such further findings as may be necessary.

DECISION AND   *The Supreme Court held that senior aides and advisers do not have immunity*
REMEDY   *if their conduct clearly violates the statutory or constitutional rights of which a reasonable person would have known. These executive branch officials are granted only qualified or good-faith immunity. Government officials, such as the president or prosecutors, whose special functions or constitutional status requires complete protection from lawsuits, are entitled to the defense of absolute immunity. The case was remanded back to the district court to review whether Fitzgerald's pretrial showings would give the court a sufficient basis to deny Harlow's motion for a summary judgment.*

Eventually, Fitzgerald was not dismissed, although he did not go back to **COMMENT**
his old position. He retired from government service in 1988.

Foreign Policy

The executive branch has the prerogative to conduct foreign affairs. Historically, the president has made foreign policy and has had the power and authority to negotiate with foreign powers. The Supreme Court has rarely limited presidential activities in foreign affairs.

The president and the Senate share the treaty-making power. The president negotiates and makes the treaty; the Senators ratify. In recent decades, it has been harder for the president to persuade the Senate to ratify treaties; thus, the president has turned to another foreign policy instrument known as the executive agreement, which does not require the consent of the Senate.

The Supreme Court has held that, while an executive agreement is not a treaty, it is an international compact and should be considered as the supreme law of the land.

Congressional Inquiry of a Pending Agency Case

Members of Congress regularly hear from their constituents about their problems with a particular agency. This type of inquiry is handled by a congressional caseworker, who asks the particular agency about the status of the constituent's case.

Even the most innocuous inquiry about the case means that the file is flagged "Congressional Inquiry." This ensures that the case is not treated capriciously. The status and, later, the disposition of the case are reported to the congressperson, and, of course, the status is reported with great dispatch, usually within ten days of the initial congressional request.

A member of Congress never inquires of a judge or an administrative law judge about the status of a case. The congressperson may ask a lawyer involved in a case as to its status, whether that case is currently before a court or an administrative agency. The lawyers are advocates before their own agency or in court, and they are authorized to answer inquiries concerning the case. Congresspeople are very much aware of the doctrine of separation of powers and thus refrain from any acts that might be interpreted as interfering with the operations of the other two branches of government.

FACING A LEGAL ISSUE   Haunting the Legislative Hallways

You have just leased a residence near your university for an entire year. All kinds of problems develop, from the sewer drains backing up to finding termites under the sink. You seek assistance from the landlord, but he turns a deaf ear to your problems. You next consult an attorney, who informs you that tenants in your state have no rights. You could move out, but you would still be liable for the rent under your state law. After considering your options, you decide that the law is not fair and that you are going to try to change it.

You talk to other tenants and form a tenants' group. As a group, you decide to talk and write to your state legislators, asking them to pass a tenants' rights bill. The group raises money and elects you as its legislative relations person. You are to spend the money to cover your costs, such as printing draft bills, buying gas, and parking. You decide that you will personally visit and write each legislator. You plan to haunt the legislative hallways and talk to any legislator willing to stop for a moment. You should register as a lobbyist, especially since there are funds involved. Without registering as a lobbyist, you run the risk of being convicted of a crime.

You should also find out if other lobbyists have similar views. If you are not initially successful, you might decide to form a political action committee in order to elect to the state legislature people who favor your point of view.

Summary

Businesspeople must know the operations of the executive and legislative branches of government. The decisions of these branches directly affect business, from taxes to regulations and at both the state and federal level.

The legislative branch of government is divided into the House and the Senate. Members of the House are elected for two years, while those in the Senate are elected for six years. Historically, the Senate has been more conservative than the House. Congress was given specific powers in Article I, Section 8, of the Constitution. Similarly, under Article I, Section 9, certain actions are prohibited to Congress, such as granting titles of nobility.

A bill is initiated when a problem comes to the attention of a congressperson, who is persuaded that a statute is needed to resolve the problem. The Office of Legislative Counsel, committee staff members, lobbyists, and experts in the executive branch are all available to help members of Congress draft a bill. A bill introduced to Congress is submitted to a committee for consideration.

The legislative work of Congress is done by its committees. They receive the bills introduced and can either act on them, stall them, or even stop them. The committee, in turn, sends the bill to a subcommittee for thorough consideration. Hearings are held and reports made. Once the subcommittee approves the bill, it is submitted to the committee and then to the full House or Senate. Any differences that exist between the bills passed by the House and by the Senate are finalized in a conference committee. The president can veto a bill, but the veto can be overridden by a two-thirds vote of both the House and the Senate.

At one time, the legislature held veto power over actions that the executive branch carried out under the authority delegated to it by Congress.

The Supreme Court, however, declared this overseeing of the executive branch by Congress to be unconstitutional.

Lobbyists play an important role in seeking to pass or attempting to stop legislation. Federal statutes attempt to regulate the actions of lobbyists through disclosure procedures. Lobbyists provide members of Congress with assistance in deciding which bills should be passed.

The number of political action committees (PACs) has increased over the past twenty years. The difference between lobbyists and political action committees is that lobbyists' activities are directed toward incumbent congresspeople, while the activities of political action committees are directed toward raising and spending money to elect lawmakers.

The Constitution grants members of Congress immunity from lawsuits. Members should not have to worry about being tied up in a civil action while they are serving their term.

The Constitution does not state very specifically what powers the executive branch has. It does make the president the commander in chief of the army and navy. It also gives him or her the power to grant reprieves and pardons; the power to make treaties, with ratification by two-thirds of the Senate; the power to appoint ambassadors, public ministers, consuls, judges of the Supreme Court, and other officers of the United States; and the power to fill any vacancies that might occur while the Senate is in recess. These terms expire at the end of the next Senate session.

The president can veto legislation and has inherent powers but is still limited by the Constitution in the actions she or he may take. Executive privilege is similar to the attorney-client privilege. The first Supreme Court case to discuss this issue was *United States v. Nixon*, which held that executive privilege could not be used to stop a criminal court case. Executive immunity prohibits civil suits from being brought against the president or the officials serving under him or her.

Key Terms

constitutional tort (**144**)
executive immunity (**144**)
executive order (**139**)
executive privilege (**142**)
executive veto (**132**)

Federal Election Campaign
 Act (FECA) of 1971 (**136**)
Federal Regulation of
 Lobbying Act of 1942 (**135**)
legislative immunity (**137**)

legislative veto (**132**)
lobbyist (**135**)
political action committee
 (PAC) (**135**)
rider (**131**)

Questions and Case Problems

1. Article I, Section 8 of the Constitution lists the powers of Congress. To the end of Section 8, the framers added the "necessary and proper clause," giving Congress power "To make all Laws which shall be necessary and proper for carrying into Execution the foregoing Powers, and all other Powers vested by this Constitution in the Government of the United States, or in any Department or Officer thereof." In *The Federalist* No. 44—one of a series of essays published in New York newspapers in 1787 and 1788 urging New York's ratification of the Constitution— James Madison wrote that "Without the substance of [the necessary and proper clause] the whole Constitution would be a dead letter." Why?

2. Can or should classification of a governmental function as "legislative" or "executive" determine what department or agency of government may perform that function? In what areas might legislative and executive authority overlap?

3. Are all subjects concerning which Congress might make laws removed from the possibility of the executive branch's action? If not, to what extent can, for example, the president act in an area in which Congress might have legislated but has not? Should the president interpret nonaction by Congress on an issue as an implied prohibition or an implied authorization for presidential action?

4. When both Congress and the president may reasonably claim authority to act in a certain matter, which should be recognized as the paramount power in (a) domestic affairs and (b) foreign affairs? Why?

5. Compare lawmaking by the legislative branch with lawmaking by the executive branch.

6. What functions does a political action committee perform?

7. Discuss the concepts of executive privilege, executive immunity, and legislative immunity.

8. Discuss the relationship among Congress, the executive branch, and the judicial branch.

9. Chastain and other attorneys were associated with the Memphis Area Legal Services (MALS). Since 1978 they had been involved in a dispute with the Juvenile Court of the City of Memphis and Shelby County. The juvenile court supervises the collection of child support payments from parents. MALS alleged that the procedures the juvenile court used to collect these payments violated the constitutional rights of indigent parents. In 1984 Chastain successfully argued in federal court that indigent parents under custodial interrogation for nonpayment of support are entitled to attorneys and that those responsible for illegal jailing could be held liable for damages.

Congressman Don Sundquist of Tennessee wrote a letter to the attorney general on official congressional stationery; in it, he expressed his concern that MALS might be obstructing the administration of the child support enforcement laws. The third paragraph turned directly to the activities of Chastain:

Also MALS seems to be employing at least one attorney, Wayne Chastain, to do nothing but harass Juvenile Court Judge Kenneth A. Turner and court referees Curtis S. Person, Jr., and William Ray Ingram. Mr. Chastain works in concert with two convicted felons, Paul A. Avarin and Richard E. Love. These individuals and Mrs. Alma Morris, the MALS client council chairperson, call frequent press conferences and stage street demonstrations against the Juvenile Court.

A copy of the letter along with a press release was distributed to the media in Memphis and appeared in the *Commercial Appeal,* a paper with a daily circulation of 200,000. Chastain sued Sundquist for defamation. Is Sundquist protected under the speech and debate clause? [Chastain v. Sundquist, 833 F.2d 311 (D.C. Cir. 1987)]

10. In response to the Iran hostage taking, President Carter, in an executive order, ordered all claims of American plaintiffs against Iranian defendants to be settled by binding arbitration before the Iran–United States Claims Tribunal. This executive order was ratified by President Reagan. Charles Main had filed a lawsuit in federal district court against the Iranian company of Khuzestan Water & Power Authority before the executive order was issued. Should the case continue in the federal court, or does the president have the authority through the executive order to have all cases pending removed from the federal court system to the tribunal? [Charles T. Main International, Inc. v. Khuzestan Water & Power Authority, 651 F.2d 800 (1st Cir. 1981)]

Chapter 7

Ethics and Corporate Social Responsibility

*There is one and only one social responsibility of business * * * to increase its profits. * * ***

Milton Friedman

If you want to read about Tammy Bakker, read Sinclair Lewis. If you want to read about insider trading, read Ida Tarbell.

Daniel Patrick Moynihan

OUTLINE

Introduction

Corporate business executives have a responsibility to their shareholders and employees to make decisions that help their business to make a profit. A company's bottom-line goal, after all, is to minimize costs and maximize profits. All business people also have a responsibility to the public and to themselves to behave ethically. How a business analyzes its goals, particularly its goal to make profits, can influence the decisions that are made and can have an impact on the business's ethical standards. When short-term profits are emphasized, the temptation may be greater to act unethically—although, certainly, just because a business makes substantial short-term profits does not mean that it has been unethical. Still, when a business considers profits over the long term rather than on an annual basis, ethical considerations and social responsible actions are enhanced.

For example, a business might fund scholarships at a university with the expectation that some of the recipients, on graduation, will actually become employees of the firm. The company might not see any profits from these scholarships for years. It has no guarantee that the recipients will become employees, yet it is for the long-term benefit of the business to give these scholarships. In this case, the business's decision makers are fulfilling both their responsibility to benefit the education community and at the same time enhancing the possible future profit making of the business; the fulfillment of these responsibilities constitutes ethical and social responsible behavior.

In this chapter, we will look at the concept of **ethics** and determine what comprises ethical conduct. We will examine how ethics relates to what is legal or illegal, and we will look at the different forms of ethical and social responsibility in the business world. Finally, we will discuss briefly the issue of ethics in the legal profession.

What Constitutes Ethical Conduct

Essentially, **ethical conduct** is conduct that, regardless of its arena, is fair, just, and socially desirable. Each of us has a different specific definition of what is ethical, since each person's definition of what is fair, right, and just depends on his or her unique cultural background, experiences, religious beliefs, and political beliefs. These and other factors help to form a person's conscience, which guides his or her behavior.

Despite these differences, all of us would readily agree that certain conduct is or is not ethical. In almost all cases, what is illegal is also unethical. Generally, the converse is true in our society, that is, what is legal is also considered to be ethical. Sometimes, however, conduct that is legal is considered unethical. For example, a business that locates itself in a developing country in order to avoid the many U.S. environmental and safety regulations or a U.S. corporation that sells in foreign countries drugs that have not been approved for sale in the U.S. is acting legally but may be considered to be acting unethically. There have been cases when a product that has been banned as a health hazard in the U.S. has been sold in other countries where there is no government ban; again, this would probably be considered unethical, but it is legal.

Many managers confuse legality and ethics, thinking that, if an act is legal (or, at least, not forbidden), it is also ethical. Although legality and ethics often coincide, they are not one and the same.

The law has developed through ratification of constitutions, through court cases, and through statutes passed by legislative bodies. This development of the law is a reactive process. For example, specific laws forbidding computer crimes were not written before the first crime was committed. They were written only after computer crime became rampant; legislatures then passed statutes defining this "new" type of crime. During the period when there were no specific laws forbidding theft by computer, were those thefts ethical? Of course not. Thus, the law is imperfect: There may be no law where there needs to be one, and, where there is a law, it may not always be obeyed or even enforced. The law cannot necessarily cure a particular problem in business behavior. For this reason, business people must make what is fair and just, as well as what is legal, a priority in deciding how to run a business.

Why Do Ethical Issues Arise?

For businesspersons, ethical issues arise because of competing interests in the business world among buyers, sellers, managers, nonmanagers, and others.

Ethical problems may arise when there is a conflict between the goals of different departments in the same company. Middle managers are often the ones who face ethical dilemmas, for they must be concerned with the needs and the reactions of upper management as well as with the needs and reactions of lower-level employees. For example, the issue of disclosing or not disclosing problems in product quality places a great deal of pressure on middle managers. Is it your ethical responsibility to disclose quality problems, even if the situation is clearly under someone else's control and that person is obviously content to ignore what you perceive to be unethical conduct?

Sometimes the problem becomes whether to be a ''whistle-blower'' or to keep quiet in order to hold onto a job. (A **whistle-blower** is one who informs public officials of an unsafe or illegal activity conducted covertly by a business.) This can be a major ethical dilemma, for keeping quiet compromises a person's own ethical standards and may require his or her participation in the unethical or illegal actions. Choosing the alternative, however, may lead to undesirable results: Employees who blow the whistle often find themselves disciplined or even fired by their employers.

As will be discussed in Chapter 15, the common law holds that an employee normally can be hired and discharged at-will by an employer. Except where limited by contract or statute, employers are free to determine the conditions and terms of employment and to conduct their affairs without judicial or administrative interference. Some states[1] have passed special laws with respect to workers and whistle-blowing, and federal legislation covers employees in certain areas. Many states, however, still uphold the common-law at-will doctrine; in such states, whistle-blowers have relatively little protection.

The case of *Geary v. United States Steel Corporation*[2] illustrates some of the possible consequences of such an ethical dilemma. George Geary was an employee-at-will of the United States Steel Corporation. He sold tubular products to the oil and gas industry. Geary believed that one of the company's new products, a tubular casing, had not been adequately tested and constituted a serious danger to anyone who used it. Even though Geary at all times performed his duties to the best of his abilities, he continued to express his reservations with respect to the company's new product. Geary alleged that, because of his outspokenness, he was summarily discharged without notice.

The Supreme Court of Pennsylvania held that Geary had no right of action against his employer for wrongful discharge. The court stated that Geary vigorously expressed his own point of view by bypassing his immediate superiors and taking his case to a vice-president of the company. It concluded that the most natural inference from the chain of events was that Geary had made a nuisance of himself; hence, the company had discharged him to preserve administrative order.

The court in *Geary* recognized the potential for abuse if it upheld a nonstatutory exception to the at-will discharge in this case. Legal action brought by a disgruntled employee against a company could severely disrupt the company's normal operations. There would also be substantial problems of establishing proof if a legal forum were created for this type of plaintiff. How does one prove that an employee has been discharged for one reason as opposed to another?

Clearly, there are conflicting interests in this area to which our laws must address themselves. On the one hand, laws must be structured in such a way as to discourage frivolous suits that unnecessarily disrupt business. On the other hand, our legal system should encourage individuals to acknowledge their ethical responsibilities since it is in the public interest for them to do so. How many working men or women, however, are willing to risk their jobs or, at best, to face subtle types of punishment in order to expose business behavior that they know is unethical, unsafe, or even il-

---

1. Including California, Connecticut, Maine, Michigan, and New York.

2. 456 Pa. 171, 319 A.2d 174 (1974).

legal? In the public's interest whistle-blowing should be encouraged, but the pressure on individuals to tolerate or ignore unethical behavior is often too great for them to overcome.

Changing Standards of Ethical Behavior

Law reflects societal values; thus, when values change, the law also changes. Since law develops in response to conditions in society, there is a time lag between any changes in society's values and the corresponding changes in the law. Before any change in the law can occur, someone must actually question whether the existing laws are fair and represent current values.

For example, only recently did the commercial bribery of foreign government officials become an ethical issue. It took several scandals involving large payoffs to bring this issue to the forefront. In response to these payoffs, which were prohibited in the United States, Congress felt compelled to pass a law making it illegal, under most circumstances, for any corporate official to offer bribes to foreign government officials for the purpose of obtaining business. This statute is known as the Foreign Corrupt Practices Act of 1977.[3] Corporate leaders have since complained that such legislation has kept U.S. businesses from competing on an equal footing with the corporations of other countries. They argue that other countries have no such law and that corporate officials (or government officials) of other countries feel no compunction about paying bribes in order to consummate business deals. On the other hand, Congress passed the law prohibiting these bribes because enough groups had concluded that this type of behavior was unethical. Throughout this book, we have seen and will see how the law has been changed when it was revealed to be in conflict with society's prevailing standards of fairness and justice. A changing society results in changing ethical and legal conduct.

---

3.   15 U.S.C. Sections 78dd-1, 78dd-2.

To Whom Are Business Ethics Owed?

A business corporation must take into consideration five basic groups of people when dealing with the ethical issues of its responsibilities. These groups are: (1) the shareholders, (2) the employees, (3) the customers, (4) the suppliers, and (5) the community or public at large. Emphasizing any one of these groups in making decisions sometimes has the ultimate effect of harming one or more of the other groups; thus, business managers must balance the interests of all five groups in order to make decisions that are ethical.

Shareholders and Ethics

As we have noted, one of the prime objectives of our capitalist society is for a business, over the long run, to maximize its profits. Without a profit, a business cannot survive. The owners, and the primary investors in a business corporation, are the shareholders. As an owner and investor the shareholder expects a monetary return from the activities of the corporation. This return basically comes from the profits made by the corporation. Therefore any decisions by the management of the corporation to increase employee wages and benefits, to lower the price or improve the quality and safety of the product for the consumer, or to contribute improvements for the well-being of the community, could mean lower profits.

Obviously shareholders expect that their interests will be fully protected by corporate management. This protection is expected by both majority and minority shareholders, and when shareholders believe corporate management has acted improperly, shareholders have the right to file a *shareholders' derivative suit* to correct any such mismanagement activity.

Corporate management, however, is given wide latitude under the application of the *business judgment rule* (discussed in more detail in Chapter 17) in setting aside shareholder demands, including the board of directors' right to refuse to pay dividends.

There can be numerous reasons for a board's decision to refuse to pay dividends to shareholders. It is obvious if those reasons are to improve the welfare of the corporation's employees and lower the cost to customers, an ethical conflict arises between these groups. The following case, decided in 1919, illustrates the court's dilemma in resolving the conflict between what is ethical behavior toward a shareholder versus what is ethical behavior toward an employee and customer.

BACKGROUND AND FACTS *Ford Motor Company was formed in 1903. Henry Ford, the president and majority shareholder, attempted to run the corporation as if it were a one-man operation. The business expanded rapidly and, in addition to regular quarterly dividends, often paid special dividends. Sales and profits were:*

Case 7.1
DODGE v. FORD MOTOR CO.
Supreme Court of Michigan, 1919.
204 Mich. 459, 170 N.W. 668.

1910   18,664 cars; $4,521,509 profit.
1911   34,466 cars; $6,275,031 profit.
1912   68,544 cars; $13,057,312 profit; $14,475,095 surplus.
1913   168,304 cars; $25,046,767 profit; $28,124,173 surplus.
1914   248,307 cars; $30,338,454 profit; $48,827,032 surplus.
1915   264,351 cars; $24,641,423 profit; $59,135,770 surplus.

By 1919, surplus above capital was $111,960,907.

Originally, the Ford car sold for more than $900. From time to time, the price was reduced, and in 1916 it sold for $440. For the year beginning August 1, 1916, the price was reduced again, to $360. In the interests of setting aside money for future investment and expansion, Ford Motor Company paid no special dividend after October 1915. The plaintiffs were minority stockholders, who owned one-tenth of the shares of the corporation. They petitioned the court to compel the directors to declare a dividend.

OSTRANDER, Chief Justice.
*   *   *   *
*   *   * [I]t is charged that notwithstanding the earnings for the fiscal year ending July 31, 1916, the Ford Motor Company has not since that date declared any special dividends:

"And the said Henry Ford, president of the company, has declared it to be the settled policy of the company not to pay in the future any special dividends, but to put back into the business for the future all of the earnings of the company, other than the regular dividend of five per cent (5%) monthly upon the authorized capital stock of the company—two million dollars ($2,000,000)."

This declaration of the future policy, it is charged in the bill, was published in the public press in the city of Detroit and throughout the United States in substantially the following language:

" 'My ambition,' declared Mr. Ford, 'is to employ still more men; to spread the benefits of this industrial system to the greatest possible number, to help them build up their lives and their homes. To do this, we are putting the greatest share of our profits back into the business.' "

It is charged further that the said Henry Ford stated to plaintiffs personally, in substance, that as all the stockholders had received back in dividends more than they had invested they were not entitled to receive anything additional to the regular dividend of 5 per cent a month, and that it was not his policy to have larger dividends declared in the future, and that the profits and earnings of the company would be put back into the business for the purpose of extending its operations and increasing the number of its employes, and that, inasmuch as the profits were to be represented by investment in plants and capital investment, the stockholders would have no right to complain. * * *

* * * *

"It is a well-recognized principle of law that the directors of a corporation, and they alone, have the power to declare a dividend of the earnings of the corporation, and to determine its amount. Courts of equity will not interfere in the management of the directors unless it is clearly made to appear that they are guilty of fraud or misappropriation of the corporate funds, or refuse to declare a dividend when the corporation has a surplus of net profits which it can, without detriment to its business, divide among its stockholders, and when a refusal to do so would amount to such an abuse of discretion as would constitute a fraud, or breach of that good faith which they are bound to exercise towards the stockholders."

* * * *

There is committed to the discretion of directors, a discretion to be exercised in good faith, the infinite details of business, including the wages which shall be paid to employes, the number of hours they shall work, the conditions under which labor shall be carried on, and the price for which products shall be offered to the public.

* * * [I]t is not within the lawful powers of a board of directors to shape and conduct the affairs of a corporation for the merely incidental benefit of share-holders and for the primary purpose of benefiting others, and no one will contend that, if the avowed purpose of the defendant directors was to sacrifice the interests of shareholders, it would not be the duty of the courts to interfere.

* * * *

Defendants say, and it is true, that a considerable cash balance must be at all times carried by such a concern. But, as has been stated, there was a large daily, weekly, monthly, receipt of cash. The output was practically continuous and was continuously, and within a few days, turned into cash. Moreover, the contemplated expenditures were not to be immediately made. The large sum appropriated for the smelter plant was payable over a considerable period of time. *So that, without going further, it would appear that, accepting and approving the plan of the directors, it was their duty to distribute on or near the 1st of August, 1916, a very large sum of money to stockholders.* [Emphasis added.]

In reaching this conclusion, we do not ignore, but recognize, the validity of the proposition that plaintiffs have from the beginning profited by, if they have not lately, officially, participated in, the general policy of expansion pursued by this corporation. We do not lose sight of the fact that it had been, upon an occasion, agreeable to the plaintiffs to increase the capital stock to $100,000,000 by a stock dividend of $98,000,000. These things go only to answer other contentions now made by plaintiffs, and do not and cannot operate to estop them to demand proper dividends upon the stock they own. It is obvious that an annual dividend of 60 per cent upon $2,000,000, or $1,200,000, is the equivalent of a very small dividend upon $100,000,000, or more.

DECISION AND REMEDY   *The defendant, Ford, was ordered by the court to declare a dividend.*

Employees and Ethics

What are a corporation's duties to its employees? The answer to this ethical question is not an easy one because of the trade-offs involved. To the extent that the corporation provides higher than competitive wages, better than "reasonable" working conditions, and other benefits, its costs per unit of production will be higher. This means that the price of the product will be higher. Who has a greater "right," the employee or the consumer? In addition, this presents a conflict between the shareholder and the employee. The more employees receive, presumably the less shareholders will receive. No easy solution to such conflicts is available.

An employer has the duty to the employee of providing adequate compensation and reimbursement and safe working conditions. Think about the ethical implications of the last point. To what extent does a businessperson have an ethical mandate to provide a safe working environment for employees? To what extent, for example, should a company use its own resources to eliminate health risks from some airborne by-product of production? Should individual employees, who are willing to work in spite of possible exposure to dangerous chemicals, bear such a responsibility, or should businesses be constrained by government to eliminate such risks?

To ensure that employers provide safe working conditions for their employees, government regulation of the workplace has increased dramatically in the last decade. Such government regulation, mostly carried out by the Occupational Safety and Health Administration (OSHA), was a result of inadequate action on the part of employers. Even so, not everyone agrees with OSHA's operating methods; some argue that there is such a thing as "too much" safety in the workplace, that the regulations may upset the balance between economic and ethical concerns. For many employers, the safer the workplace, the higher the cost related to labor in the production process. That higher cost is paid for by consumers in the form of higher prices, by stockholders in the form of lower profits, or by employees in the form of lower wages. Once again, there exists a conflict among the responsibilities of a business toward these groups of people.

Employers not only have an ethical and a legal duty to provide employees a safe working environment, but they must treat employees fairly in hiring, training, compensating, and dismissing them. To do otherwise is costly, as it invites an employee lawsuit. These suits have become more frequent in recent years, and to minimize losing in a lawsuit employers develop and maintain documented records on their employees. The extent and detail of these records creates a conflict between the potential legal liability of the employer and the employee's right of privacy. The environment of trust between employer and employee can easily become strained. Thus the employer has an ethical conflict: developing detailed records (sometimes through "spying") to protect the business from legal liability versus retaining the employee's privacy and trust. Such a dilemma was faced in the situation described in the Legal Highlight entitled "It Takes Guts."

Customers and Ethics

What is the nature of a corporation's duty to the consumer? This issue often dominates discussions of product quality, pricing, and advertising. The customer often believes that he or she has absolutely no effect on the pricing, quality, and nature of the products and services offered by today's giant corporations. Some consumers believe, therefore, that corporations should be heavily regulated by the government and the courts in order to ensure protection of the consumers' rights.

The critics of modern-day corporations assert that these corporations consider profit maximization to be basically their only duty. The supporters of these corporations, however, claim that it is impossible for the well-being of the consumer to be ignored. In fact, they assert that ultimate control of a corporation actually lies in the hands of the consumer. After all, the consumer freely chooses to buy or not to buy a corporation's product. Even in the absence of effective competition, the consumer can purchase a smaller quantity of the product being offered. Thus, it is in the corporation's best interest to attempt to satisfy the consumer.

Regardless of whether the consumer has the power to control a corporation or not, ethical ques-

LEGAL HIGHLIGHT	It Takes Guts

We have never seen a (business) form or manual that couldn't be reduced by 50 to 75 percent. But it does take guts to give up on the paper. Paper is a form of security, and something is lost when it's given up, something that must be replaced by mushy old trust (abetted by prior training and development). And it takes guts of another sort, as well: A friend runs a forty-person establishment. Someone is fired (for, it seems to us, just causes), and for a while it appeared that the separated employee might file a suit, which, though frivolous, would have been expensive and time-consuming to defend. One day her lawyer sat our friend down and took her

through the routine she must follow, he said, in order to avoid such eventualities in the future. It turned out that if she followed through exactly, she would have to accumulate an FBI-like dossier on each of her people. She refused flatly, because to do so would be in complete contradiction to the people-oriented philosophy behind her fine and spirited (and profitable) business. "I'd rather be sued and lose than become an undercover agent spying on our people" was her conclusion. And it took guts.

Source: Reprinted from Tom Peters and Nancy Austin, *A Passion for Excellence* (New York: Random House, 1985), p. 315.

tions remain. If corporate leaders know or suspect that certain of their products may have long-run deleterious effects on the consumer, shouldn't such corporate leaders have an ethical responsibility to inform the consumer? Eli Lilly, for example, failed to recognize an ethical responsibility that resulted in the death of an eighty-one-year-old woman who had taken Lilly's arthritis drug, Oraflex. Lilly had had Oraflex approved for sale in the United States without informing the Food and Drug Administration of thirty-two overseas deaths associated with the use of this drug. A $6 million judgment was entered against Lilly.

What ethical responsibility does a corporation have to citizens in other countries? If the Food and Drug Administration has prohibited the sale of a particular substance in the United States be-

cause it might have long-run carcinogenic effects, should the manufacturer sell it in those countries where it is still legal? This is an example of an ethical conflict between short-term profits for shareholders and concern for the well-being of customers. When such a conflict arises, ethical businesses consider the effects of their products on customers and do not consider only the short-range profit picture.

The following case represents a situation in which a corporation was more concerned about its short-term profit. No doubt it utilized what is commonly known as high-pressure sales techniques. In reviewing the case, you should ask yourself whether these sales practices best serve the long-term interests of the corporation.

Case 7.2

VOKES v. ARTHUR MURRAY, INC.
Court of Appeal of Florida, 1968.
212 So.2d 906.

BACKGROUND AND FACTS *Audrey E. Vokes, fifty-one years old, was a widow who wanted to become an accomplished dancer. On several occasions, an instructor and other salespersons for Arthur Murray told her that she had great dance potential and would reach her goal; in reality, the plaintiff had difficulty hearing the beat in the music. With continued assurance of her progress, she contracted for over $31,000 in dance lessons;*

at one time, she had over 1,200 unused hours of credit when she was induced to buy an additional 175 hours of instruction at a cost of $2,472.75 in order to obtain a free trip to Mexico. In total, she contracted for well over 2,000 hours of instruction. The lower court dismissed the case because the plaintiff failed to state in her complaint a proper cause of action. Vokes appealed.

PIERCE, Judge.

* * * *

The material allegations of the complaint must, of course, be accepted as true for the purpose of testing its legal sufficiency. Defendants contend that contracts can only be rescinded for fraud or misrepresentation when the alleged misrepresentation is as to a material fact, rather than an opinion, prediction or expectation, and that the statements and representations set forth at length in the complaint were in the category of "trade puffing", within its legal orbit.

It is true that "generally a misrepresentation, to be actionable, must be one of fact rather than of opinion." But this rule has significant qualifications, applicable here. It does not apply where there is a fiduciary relationship between the parties, or where there has been some article or trick employed by the representor, or where the parties do not in general deal at "arm's length" as we understand the phrase, or where the representee does not have equal opportunity to become apprised of the truth or falsity of the fact represented.

* * * *

It could be reasonably supposed here that defendants had "superior knowledge" as to whether plaintiff had "dance potential" and as to whether she was noticeably improving in the art of terpsichore. And it would be a reasonable inference from the undenied averments of the complaint that the flowery eulogiums heaped upon her by defendants as a prelude to her contracting for 1944 additional hours of instruction in order to attain the rank of the Bronze Standard, thence to the bracket of the Silver Standard, thence to the class of the Gold Bar Standard, and finally to the crowning plateau of a Life Member of the Studio, proceeded as much or more from the urge to "ring the cash register" as from any honest or realistic appraisal of her dancing prowess or a factual representation of her progress.

Even in contractual situations where a party to a transaction owes no duty to disclose facts within his knowledge or to answer inquiries respecting such facts, the law is if he undertakes to do so he must disclose the *whole truth*. From the face of the complaint, it should have been reasonably apparent to defendants that her vast outlay of cash for the many hundreds of additional hours of instruction was not justified by her slow and awkward progress, which she would have been made well aware of if they had spoken the "whole truth."

* * * *

[W]here parties are dealing on a contractual basis at arm's length with no inequities or inherently unfair practices employed, the Courts will in general "leave the parties where they find themselves." But in the case sub judice, from the allegations of the unanswered complaint, we cannot say that enough of the accompanying ingredients * * * were not present which otherwise would have barred the equitable arm of the Court to her. In our view, from the showing made in her complaint, plaintiff is entitled to her day in Court.

It accordingly follows that the order dismissing plaintiff's last amended complaint with prejudice should be and is reversed.

DECISION AND REMEDY   *The decision of the lower court was reversed. The appellate court held that the defendant owed a duty to the plaintiff to be truthful, even in expressions of opinion. A person cannot knowingly misrepresent his or her opinion in order to profit from misleading another.*

COMMENT   *This case illustrates how a court will handle an ethical problem in legal terms. The defendant took unfair advantage of the plaintiff. Our legal system attempts to control this type of overreaching by one party in relationship to another.*

Suppliers and Ethics

All businesses are dependent on suppliers in obtaining everything from major inventory purchases to paper clips. A business has an ethical responsibility to its current supplier when the business is considering obtaining supplies from a different source. Often such a decision is based on finances: For example, a business may have located a less expensive supplier, it may have decided to produce the item itself, or a different supplier may offer better service. This type of major change, however, may have an adverse effect on the former supplier and its employees. Often the former supplier has assisted the company when business was difficult, and many times these relationships have spanned a considerable period of time. To terminate them suddenly does not seem fair. On the other hand, is it fair for a new supplier who offers a better or less expensive product or who provides better service not to be able to increase his or her market share? Switching to a new supplier may lower expenses and thus increase profits for the shareholders and lower prices to customers, but you may be terminating economic relationships that have been built over years.

The Community and Ethics

Early common law absolutely prohibited a corporation from giving to charity. It was thought that this was a misuse of corporate funds. Shareholders could give to charity, but the corporation could not. The money being given away belonged to the shareholders, and they should each decide whether to give or not to give.

The law has changed, however, and now allows private corporations to give to charity. Corporate nonprofit activity is justified by social policy. The argument is that the wealth of the nation is no longer primarily in the hands of private individuals; instead, much of it belongs to corporations. In addition, because the costs of government have increased dramatically since the 1930s, taxation has increased accordingly, and the philanthropic abilities of private individuals have been diminished.

Despite criticisms of a lack of corporate social responsiveness, most major corporations do engage in philanthropic activities. Corporations routinely donate to hospitals, the arts, universities, and the like. Most major corporations employ one or more individuals to screen charitable requests and to determine which organizations should be the recipients of charitable contributions. B. Dalton Bookseller, for example, put up $3 million to launch a massive drive against functional illiteracy. Over the succeeding four years, this contribution will have helped support 50,000 volunteer literacy tutors. The Bank of America has created a $10 million revolving loan program in which funds are loaned to community development groups at a 3 percent interest rate.

The following case discusses the right of a corporation to make a charitable gift. As you read the case, you might consider whether you agree with the current legal thinking on this issue.

LEGAL HIGHLIGHT Have You Gotten Our Letter Yet?

A colleague, Pat Townsend, reports an example of Perdue Farms' response to a customer (remember, this is a three-quarter-billion-dollar company): "A friend of mine mentioned last week that he once bought a Perdue chicken that, he discovered after getting home, was all dry and nasty. He took it back to the store and got an immediate refund. Then he decided to write Frank [Perdue, president of Perdue Farms]—having seen him on TV—and tell him that he had bought one of his damn quality chickens and it was all dry and nasty. By return mail he got a letter from Frank that not only included profuse apologies and a certificate for a free chicken but also

enlisted his help to make sure it never happened again by asking a whole list of specific questions. Where did he buy it? When? Exactly what was wrong? What did he think had happened? What exactly did the store say when he returned it? Etc., etc. Two days later an executive of Perdue Chickens called to make sure he'd gotten the letter , to make sure that all was well, and to ask some more specific questions. My friend will never buy anything but Perdue Chicken."

Source: Reprinted from Tom Peters and Nancy Austin, *A Passion for Excellence* (New York: Random House, 1985), p. 85.

BACKGROUND AND FACTS *The board of directors of A. P. Smith Manufacturing Company passed a resolution to donate $1,500 to Princeton University. Barlow was an A. P. Smith shareholder who objected to this gift. The plaintiff brought the action to determine whether the gift was a legitimate use of corporate funds.*

Case 7.3
A. P. SMITH MANUFACTURING CO. v. BARLOW
Superior Court of New Jersey,
Chancery Division, 1953.
26 N.J. Super. 106,
97 A.2d 186.

STEIN, J.S.C.
* * * *
    * * * I cannot conceive of any greater benefit to corporations in this country than to build, and continue to build, respect for and adherence to a system of free enterprise and democratic government, the serious impairment of either of which may well spell the destruction of all corporate enterprise. Nothing that aids or promotes the growth and service of the American university or college in respect of the matters here discussed can possibly be anything short of direct benefit to every corporation in the land. The college-trained men and women are a ready reservoir from which industry may draw to satisfy its need for scientific or executive talent. It is no answer to say that a company is not so benefited unless such need is immediate. A long-range view must be taken of the matter. * * *
* * * *
    First as to [the plaintiff's contention that the contribution was] *ultra vires* [an act outside corporate authority]. It is settled law here and in England that a corporation or association possesses not only those powers which are expressly conferred upon it by its charter, franchise or articles of association, but also all incidental powers reasonably designed or required to give fuller or greater effect to the expressed powers. An expressed power to a company to sell its wares does not require that with it there be also expressed the right to advertise its merchandise

by the public press, radio, television, or any of the infinite variety of media of publicity and promotion. Such activity is a power present by necessary implication. So in respect of good-will. Anything that tends to promote with the public a company's good-will is a reasonable measure towards the corporate objective of earning profits. * * * It is to the credit and the glory of the common law that it has always had within itself the seed of change, keeping pace with the march of the years and the advance of thought. Wherever it has lagged it has been because of a conservatism which was hesitant to recognize the changing times and the need to revise the law's precedents. But always and eventually the common law caught up with the times and molded itself to the newer needs for the public good. An example of this occurred in England. Exactly 70 years ago the English Court of Chancery said, "Charity has no business to sit at boards of directors." Fifty years went by, with all the changes in industry that took place in that period, and the same court gave its judicial stamp of approval to a contribution of £100,000 voted by a chemical company to several English universities for "the furtherance of scientific education and research." * * *

* * * *

[The court quoted from an 1896 New York case:]

"As industrial conditions change, business methods must change with them, and acts become permissible which at an earlier period would not have been considered to be within corporate power."

DECISION AND   *The court held that giving to charity was a proper corporate right.*
REMEDY

A considerable number of corporations include moral and political considerations as part of their social responsibilities. In 1983 the Bank of America announced that future loans would be barred to the South African government and its governmental entities until concrete steps had been taken to dismantle the apartheid laws. Coca-Cola Corporation has established the National Hispanic Business Agenda—a major program to expand ties with the Hispanic community. This corporation has agreed to patronize more Hispanic firms, employ more Hispanic employees, and support Hispanic educational and job-training programs. These are but two examples of modern corporations seeking to follow an ethical course of social actions.

Legal Ethics

Some mention of **legal ethics** and the practice of law should be made in a course involving the legal environment of business. Although the legal profession is the butt of many jokes concerning ethical issues, most lawyers are ethical. Lawyers face legal ethical issues every day. The unanswered ethical issue, "Should a lawyer defend a criminal defendant the lawyer knows is guilty?", is just one example. Bar associations and the public frown upon the so-called "ambulance chasers." Yet persons who are injured usually need immediate legal counsel to protect or perserve their rights.

Courts are becoming increasingly irritated by the "frivolous" lawsuit. It is true a few lawyers will take cases knowing there is no chance of winning on the merits, leading the clients to believe otherwise.

Lawyers' fees are continuing to increase. The very nature of how lawyers charge creates ethical issues. Is the contingency fee (a fee based generally on a percentage—typically between 20 and 40 percent—of an award granted by a court) ethical? It may seem sensible that if the lawyer cannot get the client a judgment, the client does not owe the lawyer a fee, but it can cause ethical concerns. For example, if the judgment includes only med-

---

**LEGAL
HIGHLIGHT**   **Supplier As "Customer"**

It seems that one of the half-dozen traits that we hear exemplify Japanese management (in contrast to management in the United States) is the long-term, almost familial relations between suppliers and producers. But there's no Japanese magic about it; it can happen in the United States—and does in many of the best companies. . . .

Domino's Pizza Distribution Company (Domino's ingredients and equipment supplier) just say, "Thanks." They regularly stage Vendor Appreciation Days. A horde of Domino's people will descend on a Wisconsin cheese maker or a California olive grower and shower the supplier with attention. Distribution executive Jeff Smith can't imagine it any other way. "They're part of the family, aren't they," he says, with surprise that anyone could conceive of a different position on the issue. (Interestingly, family relations with vendors are an explicit part of Domino's Distribution statement of its mission. Now, that is rare. But why not?)

Source: Reprinted from Tom Peters and Nancy Austin, *A Passion for Excellence* (New York: Random House, 1985), pp. 19–21.

---

ical expenses, should the lawyer receive a percentage of this amount?

When a lawyer charges by the hour, law firms frequently divide the hour into segments. At $200–$300 per hour, this can add up. Some firms use fifteen-minute segments. Thus, if you consult with your lawyer for ten minutes, you are charged for fifteen. Is this ethical?

The American Bar Association drafted a code of ethics for attorneys. This code is in effect in almost every state. Attorneys must follow the code's standards of professional ethics, or they will not be allowed to practice law. It has been suggested that a similar approach might be applied to the business community—a separate code of ethics could be adopted by the states for different business endeavors. As with attorneys, if a business did not follow the ethical code, it would be unable to continue its operations in those states.

When Should You Blow the Whistle?

Ethics consist of a person's basic moral values. No doubt you have been tempted at times, either in school or in the workplace, to act in a manner contrary to your basic moral values.

In our society we have been taught not to inform against another person. This concept is instilled at an early age, when we are told not to "tattle" on another child, and it is reinforced throughout our lives. It raises many problems for employees and for the businesses that employ them, however. For example, assume that you are employed by a wholesaler who sells a large number of consumer goods from toys to small appliances. You have always been honest and fair in your dealings with your employer. You discover, however, that one of your fellow employees is stealing small quantities of items to use as Christmas gifts. What should you do? If you inform your employer about these thefts, are you not "tattling" on a fellow employee? If you do not inform the employer, are you not, morally speaking, as guilty as the dishonest employee? The legal system can give you direction here: In most states it is a crime not to disclose this type of situation. This means that either you inform your employer about it or you will face the possibility of being criminally prosecuted.

Summary

This chapter has addressed the subject of ethics. Because each individual has a different background and different values, there can be no one definition of ethical conduct. A person's ethics consist of his or her basic moral values as established by cultural background, experiences, religious and political beliefs, and ideas about what is fair. Most activity that is illegal is also unethical, but ethical conduct addresses broader issues than simply the question of what is legal.

Ethical issues arise because of competing interests in the business world among buyers, sellers, managers, nonmanagers, and others. Many times these issues arise over the question of how to make a profit in the short run versus how to maximize profits over a period of time.

What is considered ethical conduct does change over time. As society changes, so does society's concept of what is ethical.

Whistle-blowing is a major ethical dilemma confronted by employees. They must choose between condoning unethical, unsafe, and illegal activities and coming forth to blow the whistle on their employers. The first choice requires unethical conduct while the second choice may mean termination of employment.

Businesses are ethically responsible to competing interest groups. In particular, the following five groups occasionally have conflicting interests: the shareholders or owners of a business, its employees, customers, suppliers, and the community or public at large.

All attorneys are bound by rules of professional conduct. An attorney who does not follow these rules is subject to censure and disbarment. But even attorneys who operate within the rules face ethical issues and considerations daily.

Key Terms

ethical conduct **(152)**
ethics **(152)**

legal ethics **(162)**
whistle-blower **(153)**

Questions and Case Problems

1. Define ethics and distinguish between ethics, morals, and law.

2. Should businesses be concerned with ethics? In other words, should companies have social or ethical goals in addition to profit-making goals, and if so, who in the company should set these goals?

3. Should the decision about who sets a company's goals depend on the type of business conducted or on the current political and environmental climate?

4. Should ethics be solely a concern of top management, or should it be a shared concern of all employees, distributors, suppliers, and so on?

5. United States automobile manufacturers have recently been attempting to produce higher-quality cars. Did this result from an ethical concern of the companies? If so, why did this concern not exist before? Alternatively, is the attempt to produce higher-quality cars merely a result of Japanese competition, and will such an attempt cease if and when the Japanese competition disappears?

6. To what extent does competition in the marketplace obviate the need for standards of business ethics?

7. Can a human life be subjected to a cost-benefit analysis? For example, consider the following situation: A rule is proposed that will require all commercial airlines to use jets that have two additional emergency exit doors. Given the average number of airline crashes per year and the average number of individuals injured or killed in such crashes, it is estimated that the new safety standard will save an additional ten lives per year. Should the standard therefore be instituted? What if it costs $10 million? $50 million? $3 billion? To what extent, if any, is cost relevant where human life is concerned?

8. Should conservation of natural resources and other environmental considerations become ethical concerns to which businesses should address themselves?

9. Michael Hauck was a deckhand for Sabine Pilot Service, Inc. He was employed at will. One of his duties each day was to pump the bilges (the inner hulls) of one of his employer's boats into the waterways. Hauck had noticed a sign on the boat that stated it was illegal to empty the bilges into the water. He had also called the United States Coast Guard concerning this, and a Coast Guard officer had confirmed that it was indeed illegal. Hauck thereafter refused to perform this illegal act for his employer, and he was fired because of this refusal. Hauck brought an action against Sabine for wrongful discharge. Texas was an employment-at-will state, and the Texas courts had steadfastly refused to grant any exception to this doctrine. On what basis might the Texas court to which this case was appealed create an exception to the at-will doctrine? Discuss your answer. [Sabine Pilot Service, Inc. v. Hauck, 687 S.W.2d 733 (Tex. 1985)].

10. A husband whose wife's death by lung cancer was caused by her forty-year history of cigarette smoking sued the Liggett Group of tobacco producers for damages. The husband contended that the Liggett Group should be liable for damages under product liability laws because it not only manufactured and marketed a harmful product but also failed to stress adequately to consumers the harmful consequences of cigarette smoking. This and similar cases raise the question as to whether cigarette producers should be liable for the ultimate harm caused to consumers using their products, even though the consumers who use their products voluntarily assume the health risks associated with cigarette smoking. Should it make any difference that the manufacturer posted a health warning on the cigarette packages? What public policies must be weighed in answering this question? [Cipollone v. Liggett Group, Inc., 644 F.Supp. 283 (D.N.J. 1986)]

Chapter 8 White-Collar Criminal Law

Small crimes always precede great ones. Never have we seen timid innocence pass suddenly to extreme licentiousness.

Jean Baptiste Racine (1639–1699)

OUTLINE

Introduction

At first, the subject of criminal law may seem out of place in a discussion of the legal environment of business. Businesspeople, for the most part, are basically honest and truthful, and their integrity is beyond question. Certain business activities, however, once considered legal, are now deemed to be criminal. Both Congress and state legislatures have regulated specific corporate activities by passing criminal statutes.

For example, not until 1911 was there an attempt by a state to regulate the sale of securities through criminal statutes. Two decades later, the federal government passed the first federal statute, the Securities Act of 1933, which regulates the sale of new securities. Today, stockbrokers, accountants, lawyers, and others are being convicted of violating the securities laws.

Before discussing specific criminal acts, we need to emphasize the distinction between civil and criminal law. When a person brings an action against another for an alleged violation of the law, he or she is seeking legal redress through a civil case of a harm committed against himself or herself. If the plaintiff wins the lawsuit, he or she usually obtains a monetary award.

When there is a violation of criminal law, the government—no matter at what level: city, county, state, or federal—can prosecute the accused person. All criminal actions are brought in the name of the state—for example, *The United States of America v. John James Smith, Defendant.* The defendant must have violated a specific law for which a punishment is generally prescribed. The accused may be incarcerated, fined, or both. The harm here is not to a specific individual but to society as a whole.

The same wrongful act, at times, can be a crime and can also result in civil litigation. For example, a person who intentionally kills another is guilty of the crime of murder. He or she is also liable to the victim's estate for the civil tort of wrongful death. Two major differences exist between a criminal trial and a civil trial: First, the burden of proof is higher in the criminal case (**beyond a reasonable doubt**) than in the civil case (**preponderance of the evidence**). Second, the Fifth Amendment right against self-incrimination does not apply in a civil case. With the exception of these two issues, the procedures involved in a criminal action and a civil action are similar in many respects.

In this chapter we will discuss the classification of crimes and the elements of crimes in general. Then we will focus on criminal activity that has a direct application to the business world frequently referred to as white-collar crime.

Classification of Crimes

A crime is classified as a **felony, misdemeanor**, or **petty offense**, according to its seriousness. The definitions of these classifications vary greatly among the states and the federal government.

A felony is more serious than a misdemeanor or a petty offense and is punishable by imprisonment in a federal or state penitentiary for more than a year, by a fine, or even by death. The Model Penal Code makes the following four distinctions among felonies, based on their seriousness: Capital offenses are punishable by death; first-degree felonies are punishable by a maximum penalty of life imprisonment; second-degree felonies are punishable by a maximum of ten years' imprisonment; and third-degree felonies are punishable by up to five years' imprisonment. These classifications set the maximum penalties; an actual sentence is usually less.

A misdemeanor is a crime punishable by a fine or by confinement for up to a year. People convicted of a misdemeanor are incarcerated in a city or county jail instead of in the state penitentiary. Disorderly conduct and trespassing are common misdemeanors. Misdemeanors are tried in city or county courts, while felonies are tried in state or federal courts.

A petty offense is often not classified as a crime but as a civil offense. These offenses include many traffic violations or violations of building codes. Even for petty offenses, a guilty party can be put in jail for a few days, or fined, or both.

Crimes can also be classified according to their nature. For example, there are crimes against the person (murder, assault, rape), crimes against property (theft, burglary, arson), and crimes against

LEGAL HIGHLIGHT   White-Collar Crime

White-collar criminals receive less prison time than other criminals. During 1985, there were 10,733 convictions concerning white-collar crimes, such as fraud, embezzlement, and forgery. From 1980 to 1985, all other convictions increased 43 percent while white-collar crime increased 18 percent. Over 8,300 drug-law violators were in prison (an increase of 60 percent in five years), but only 350 embezzlers were behind bars.

Most white-collar crimes are prosecuted in federal courts. Of those sentenced, probation is granted to 40 percent of antitrust law violators, to 61 percent of those convicted of fraud, and to 70 percent of embezzlers. Those convicted of white-collar crimes are sentenced to twenty-nine months of imprisonment on the average versus fifty months for all other offenders.

Combined total take from burglary, robbery, and other property losses amounts to $4 billion White-collar crimes, such as computer crimes, failure to comply with regulations, insider trading, fraud, and misappropriated funds, cost the country, it is estimated, from $40 billion to $200 billion a year.

Source: U.S. Justice Department, *Report on White-Collar Crime*, October 1987.

the government (perjury, bribery). These classifications are used to group crimes within a statutory code. The criminal code is structured to punish acts, not classifications of people despite the popular use of such terms as ''white-collar crimes.''

Criminal Statutory Law

Originally, criminal acts were defined by the judiciary under common law and not by legislative statutes. Today, all crimes are based on statutes, but judges still use the original common-law definitions when interpreting these criminal statutes.

Every criminal statute prohibits certain behavior. The statute sets out the specific elements of the crime. The prosecutor must prove each element of the crime before a person can be convicted. Most crimes require an act of commission—that is, a person must *do* something in order to commit a crime. In some cases, an act of omission can be a crime, but only if the person has failed to carry out a legal duty. Failure to file a tax return is an example of an omission that is a crime.

Statutes in criminal law are narrowly interpreted by the courts. Courts take into consideration the statutory language, legislative history, and the purpose of the statute in order to determine what type of behavior is prohibited. In the following case, the United States Supreme Court interpreted a criminal statute passed by Congress.

BACKGROUND AND FACTS   *Dowling and others had an extensive bootleg record operation involving the manufacture and distribution by mail of recordings of vocal performances by Elvis Presley. In 1976 Dowling, an avid collector of Presley recordings, began to manufacture phonorecords of unreleased Presley recordings. He used material from a variety of sources, including studio outtakes, soundtracks from Presley motion pictures, and tapes of Presley concerts and television appearances. Dowling never obtained authorization from or paid royalties to the owners of the copyrights*

 Case 8.1

DOWLING v. UNITED STATES

Supreme Court of the United States, 1985.
473 U.S. 207, 105 S.Ct. 3127, 87 L.Ed.2d 152.

of the musical compositions. Dowling mailed several hundred packages per week and regularly spent $1,000 per week on postage.

The Federal Bureau of Investigation started investigating Dowling. Dowling was arrested and tried. He was convicted of one count of conspiracy to transport stolen property in interstate commerce, eight counts of interstate transportation of stolen property, three counts of mail fraud, and nine counts of copyright infringement. He appealed all the convictions except those for copyright infringement. The Supreme Court considered whether this activity, which did not involve Dowling stealing physical items, was covered by the National Stolen Property Act.

BLACKMUN, Justice.
* * * *

Federal crimes, of course, "are solely creatures of statute." Accordingly, when assessing the reach of a federal criminal statute, we must pay close heed to language, legislative history, and purpose in order strictly to determine the scope of the conduct the enactment forbids. Due respect for the prerogatives of Congress in defining federal crimes prompts restraint in this area, where we typically find a "narrow interpretation" appropriate. * * *

Applying that prudent rule of construction here, we examine at the outset the statutory language. [18 U.S.C. §2314] requires, first, that the defendant have transported "goods, wares, [or] merchandise" in interstate or foreign commerce; second, that those goods have a value of $5,000 or more"; and, third, that the defendant "kno[w] the same to have been stolen, converted or taken by fraud." * * * [Dowling] argues * * * that the goods shipped were not "stolen, converted or taken by fraud." * * * The Government argues, however, that the shipments come within the reach of § 2314 because the phonorecords physically embodied performances of musical compositions that Dowling had no legal right to distribute. According to the Government, the unauthorized use of the musical compositions rendered the phonorecords "stolen, converted or taken by fraud" within the meaning of the statute. We must determine, therefore, whether phonorecords that include the performance of copyrighted musical compositions for the use of which no authorization has been sought nor royalties paid are consequently "stolen, converted or taken by fraud" for purposes of § 2314. We conclude that they are not.

* * * [C]ases * * * prosecuted under § 2314 have always involved physical "goods, wares, [or] merchandise" that have themselves been "stolen, converted or taken by fraud." This basic element comports with the common-sense meaning of the statutory language: by requiring that the "goods, wares, [or] merchandise" be "the same" as those "stolen, converted or taken by fraud," the provision seems clearly to contemplate a physical identity between the items unlawfully obtained and those eventually transported, and hence some prior physical taking of the subject goods.
* * * *

* * * There is no dispute in this case that Dowling's unauthorized inclusion on his bootleg albums of performances of copyrighted compositions constituted infringement of those copyrights. It is less clear, however, that the taking that occurs when an infringer arrogates the use of another's protected work comfortably fits the terms associated with physical removal employed by § 2314. The infringer invades a statutorily defined province guaranteed to the copyright holder alone. But he does not assume physical control over the copyright; nor does he wholly deprive its owner of its use. While one may colloquially link infringement with some general notion of wrongful appropriation, infringement plainly implicates a more complex set of property interests than does run-of-the-mill theft, conversion, or fraud. As a result, it fits but awkwardly with the language Congress chose—''stolen, converted or taken by fraud''—to describe the sorts of goods whose interstate shipment § 2314 makes criminal. ''And, when interpreting a criminal statute that does not explicitly reach the conduct in question, we are reluctant to base an expansive reading on inferences drawn from subjective and variable 'understanding.' ''

* * * *

No more than other legislation do criminal statutes take on straightjackets upon enactment. In sanctioning the use of § 2314 in the manner urged by the Government here, the Courts of Appeals understandably have sought to utilize an existing and readily available tool to combat the increasingly serious problem of bootlegging, piracy, and copyright infringement. Nevertheless, the deliberation with which Congress over the last decade has addressed the problem of copyright infringement for profit, as well as the precision with which it has chosen to apply criminal penalties in this area, demonstrates anew the wisdom of leaving it to the legislature to define crime and prescribe penalties. Here, the language of § 2314 does not ''plainly and unmistakably'' cover petitioner Dowling's conduct. * * * In sum, Congress has not spoken with the requisite clarity. Invoking the ''time-honored interpretive guideline'' that '' 'ambiguity concerning the ambit of criminal statutes should be resolved in favor of lenity,' '' * * * we reverse the judgment of the Court of Appeals.

DECISION AND REMEDY

The Supreme Court narrowly interpreted the National Stolen Property Act. The phonorecords were made by Dowling; therefore, they were not physical items ''stolen, converted, or taken by fraud''; it was the nonphysical item of the copyright that was stolen. The statutory language required the item unlawfully obtained and the item unlawfully transported to be the same physical item. The Court in reviewing the history of the statute found that Congress did not intend to include copyright infringement under this act. Dowling's convictions were reversed.

COMMENT

Three of the justices dissented. They believed that the act was too narrowly interpreted and noted that it does not make any distinction between tangible and intangible property. As the dissenting opinion observed, Dowling ''could not have had any doubt that he was committing a theft as well as defrauding the copyright owner.'' He had no right to reproduce the copyrighted Elvis Presley performances, and it was that same property that Dowling transported across state lines. Dowling did steal the intangible copyrighted material, even if he could not physically carry it away.

As a result of this decision, Congress is considering amending the National Stolen Property Act to include intangible goods.

Constitutional Safeguards

The criminal justice system operates on the premise that it is far worse for an innocent person to be punished than for a guilty person to go free. A person is innocent until proved guilty, and guilt must be proved beyond a reasonable doubt. The procedures of the criminal legal system are designed to protect the rights of the individual and to preserve the presumption of innocence.

Criminal law brings the weighty force of the state, with all its resources, to bear against the individual, but safeguards are provided in the Bill of Rights for those accused of crimes. The United States Supreme Court has ruled that most of these safeguards apply not only in federal but also in state courts by virtue of the due process clause of the Fourteenth Amendment.

In past years, the Supreme Court has been active in interpreting these constitutional rights. The *Miranda v. Arizona*[1] case, for example, established the rule that a person who is arrested must be given his or her rights. The *Miranda* warnings include the right to remain silent because anything said can be used against the accused in court, the right to have a lawyer present, and, if the accused cannot pay for a lawyer, the right to have the state provide one.

Criminal Procedure

A criminal prosecution differs procedurally from a civil case in several respects. These differences reflect the desire to safeguard the rights of the individual against the state. Before a warrant for arrest can be issued, probable cause must exist for believing that the individual in question has committed a crime. Probable cause can be defined as involving a substantial likelihood that the individual has committed a crime. Note that probable cause involves a likelihood, not just a possibility. Arrests may sometimes be made without a warrant when there is no time to get one, but the action of the arresting officer is still judged by the standard of probable cause.

Individuals must be formally charged with having committed specific crimes before they can be brought to trial. This charge is called an **indictment** if issued by a grand jury or a **bill of information** if issued by a magistrate. Before a charge can be issued, the grand jury or the magistrate must determine that there is sufficient evidence to justify bringing the individual to trial.

At the trial, the accused person does not have to prove anything. The entire burden of proof is on the prosecution (the state). The prosecution must show that, based on all the evidence, the defendant's guilt is established beyond a reasonable doubt. A verdict of not guilty is not the same as a statement that the defendant is innocent. It merely means that not enough evidence was properly presented to the court to prove criminal guilt beyond a reasonable doubt.

Courts have complex rules about the types of evidence that may be presented and about how the evidence may be presented, especially in jury trials. These rules are designed to ensure that evidence in the trial is relevant, reliable, and not unfairly prejudicial to the defendant. The defense attorney will cross-examine the witnesses who present evidence against his or her client in an attempt to show that their evidence is not reliable. Of course, the state may also cross-examine any witnesses presented by the defendant.

Basic Elements of Criminal Responsibility

Common law developed the twin requirements of criminal intent (**mens rea**) and criminal conduct. Thinking about embezzling funds or about stealing a computer program may be morally wrong, but these thoughts in themselves are not criminal until they are translated into action. A person can be punished for attempting to commit a crime, but only if substantial steps toward the criminal objective have been taken.

In most cases, a wrongful mental state is required along with the wrongful act to establish criminal liability. In these cases, the mental state of the accused is important in determining the degree of wrongfulness of the crime. For example, the same criminal act that causes the death of another can be committed by different defendants with varying mental states. One person may kill in a cold-blooded manner with premeditation: This is murder in the first degree. A second person may kill in the heat of passion: This is voluntary manslaughter. A third person may kill as the result of negligence: This is involuntary manslaughter, as when someone dies as a result of extreme carelessness involving an automobile accident. In each of these situations, the law recognizes a different

---

1. 384 U.S. 436, 86 S.Ct. 1602, 16 L.Ed.2d 694 (1966).

LEGAL HIGHLIGHT   Film Recovery Systems, Inc.

Three managers of Film Recovery were convicted in 1985 of murder, and Film Recovery and its parent company, Metallic Marketing Systems, Inc., were found guilty of involuntary manslaughter and reckless conduct. An employee had died of acute cyanide poisoning while working at the plant.

The company reclaimed silver from exposed X-ray film. Workers stirred the cyanide solution in large, open vats, with wooden paddles. The cyanide would splash on the employees and enter their bodies through their pores; the workers also breathed the hydrogen cyanide gas and were frequently ill as a result of this exposure. The judge found that the managers knew of the substantial possibility of cyanide poisoning and of the failure to provide safe working conditions.

degree of wrongfulness, and the punishment differs accordingly. The greater the degree of *mens rea*, the more reprehensible the crime and thus the greater the punishment.

Categories of Criminal Intent

The Model Penal Code recognizes four categories of *mens rea*:

1. Purpose: What did the accused intend to be doing, or what was his or her conscious objective?
2. Knowlege: Did the accused act with knowledge of what he or she was doing, or did he or she act knowingly with respect to the result?
3. Recklessness: Did the accused act in such a wanton manner—that is, with knowledge and conscious disregard—that he or she created a considerable and unjustifiable risk to others?
4. Negligence: Did the accused act so negligently—that is, deviate so substantially from the standard of care a reasonable person would exercise under the circumstances—that he or she created a substantial and unnecessary risk to others?

Some statutes do not require any criminal intent, only criminal conduct. For example, a person shoots a rifle in the air to help the neighborhood celebrate the New Year. The person does not intend any harm, but his or her conduct, the shooting of a rifle, was in violation of a statute, and that conduct constitutes the crime.

Criminal statutes in recent years have targeted corporate behavior by not requiring any criminal intent, only criminal conduct by the corporation. These statutes avoid the problem found in the past—namely, that a corporation cannot form a mental intent and, therefore, cannot be guilty of a crime. The following case involves a statute that does not require *mens rea*.

BACKGROUND AND FACTS *The defendant was the president of Acme Markets, Inc. As a large national food chain, Acme employed 36,000 employees and had 874 retail outlets, twelve general warehouses, and four special warehouses. During 1970, the president received a letter from the Food and Drug Administration (FDA) concerning rodents in a Baltimore warehouse where his firm stored a considerable amount of food. The rodents caused the food to become adulterated and not fit for consumption. The vice-president in charge of the warehouse responded to the FDA letter.*

 Case 8.2

UNITED STATES v. PARK

Supreme Court of the United States, 1975.
421 U.S. 658, 95 S.Ct. 1903, 44 L.Ed.2d 489.

In 1971 and 1972, similar conditions were observed. The defendant did not have direct control over the Baltimore warehouse but was convicted on five counts of causing adulteration of food that had been in interstate commerce. He was fined $50 for each of the five convictions under the Federal Food, Drug, and Cosmetic Act.

BURGER, Chief Justice.
* * * *

The Act does not * * * make criminal liability turn on "awareness of some wrongdoing" or "conscious fraud." The duty imposed by Congress on responsible corporate agents is, we emphasize, one that requires the highest standard of foresight and vigilance, but the Act, in its criminal aspect, does not require that which is objectively impossible. The theory upon which responsible corporate agents are held criminally accountable for "causing" violations of the Act permits a claim that a defendant was "powerless" to prevent or correct the violation to "be raised defensively at a trial on the merits." If such a claim is made, the defendant has the burden of coming forward with evidence, but this does not alter the Government's ultimate burden of proving beyond a reasonable doubt the defendant's guilt, including his power, in light of the duty imposed by the Act, to prevent or correct the prohibited condition. Congress has seen fit to enforce the accountability of responsible corporate agents dealing with products which may affect the health of consumers by penal sanctions cast in rigorous terms, and the obligation of the courts is to give them effect so long as they do not violate the Constitution.
* * * *

Although we need not decide whether this testimony would have entitled respondent to an instruction as to his lack of power had he requested it, the testimony clearly created the "need" for rebuttal evidence. That evidence was not offered to show that respondent had a propensity to commit criminal acts[;] its purpose was to demonstrate that respondent was on notice that he could not rely on his system of delegation to subordinates to prevent and correct insanitary conditions at Acme's warehouses, and that he must have been aware of the deficiencies of this system before the Baltimore violations were discovered. The evidence was therefore relevant since it served to rebut respondent's defense that he had justifiably relied upon subordinates to handle sanitation matters.

DECISION AND   *Even though the defendant had no actual criminal intent, he was still*
REMEDY   *convicted of a crime. All that was required was the wrongful conduct of producing adulterated food that was in interstate commerce.*

The trend today is to hold corporations criminally responsible for the conduct of their employees. The proposed Model Penal Code recognizes that a corporation can be guilty of a criminal offense through the actions of its employees if one of three situations occurs: First, the legislative purpose of the statute in question is to impose criminal liability on corporations for the acts of its employees, and the offense is within the scope of the employment. Second, the corporation has a legal statutory duty to perform a specific function, and it fails to perform that function, such as

keeping accurate accounting records. Third, the criminal act has been authorized, requested, commanded, performed, or recklessly tolerated by the higher echelons of corporate management.

Crimes Affecting Business

Two categories of crimes that affect businesses directly are offenses against property and white-collar crimes.

LEGAL HIGHLIGHT   Ford

Ford designed the Pinto to meet the Volkswagen competition. A decision was made not to include an $11 safety improvement that would have lessened the likelihood of an automobile fire in case of collision. Injury and death lawsuits totaled more than $1 billion. Losing several lawsuits, Ford made headlines when a judgment was awarded against it of $128.5 million, later reduced to $2.5 million.[a] By

1980 Ford had spent more than $50 million on litigation and recalls involving the Pinto.

In 1980 Ford went on trial in Indiana for reckless homicide as a result of the deaths of three people. Ford was eventually acquitted after it had spent $1 million to defend itself.

a.   Grimshaw v. Ford Motor Company, 119 Cal. App. 3d 757, 175 Cal. Rptr. 348 (1981). See Chapter 12.

Offenses Against Property

Businesses are most often involved in crimes against property. In this section, we examine the following offenses against property: (1) burglary, (2) larceny, (3) robbery, (4) receiving stolen goods, (5) arson, (6) forgery, (7) obtaining goods by false pretenses, and (8) embezzlement.

Burglary   **Burglary** is defined as entering into the building of another with the intent to commit a felony. For example, Ace breaks into a warehouse and intends to steal a truckload of video tape recorders. Before he can load his truck, the burglar alarm goes off, and he flees the scene. Ace is guilty of burglary because he intended to commit the felony of theft. Aggravated burglary, which is defined as burglary with the use of a deadly weapon or burglary of a dwelling place, incurs a heavier penalty.

Larceny   The wrongful or fraudulent taking and carrying away by any person of the personal property of another is **larceny**. Generally, the person must also have had the intent to deprive the owner of her or his property permanently. Many business-related larcenies entail fraudulent conduct. The place from which physical property is taken is generally immaterial, although statutes usually prescribe a stiffer sentence for property taken from such buildings as banks or warehouses. Larceny

differs from robbery in that robbery involves force or fear, and larceny does not. Therefore, picking pockets is larceny, not robbery.

As society has become more complex, the question often arises as to what is property. In most states, the definition of the property that is subject to larceny statutes has been expanded. Stealing computer programs may constitute larceny even though the programs consist of magnetic impulses. Trade secrets can be subject to larceny statutes. Stealing the use of telephone wires by the device known as a blue box is subject to larceny statutes. The theft of natural gas or electricity is often covered by special larceny statutes.

Robbery   **Robbery** is defined as taking personal property of another from the other's person or in his or her presence by force or intimidation with the intent to permanently deprive the other of it. The use of force or fear is necessary for an act of theft to be considered a robbery. Thus, picking pockets is not robbery because the action is unknown to the victim. Typically, states have more severe penalties for aggravated robbery—robbery with the use of a deadly weapon. Liquor stores, all-night convenience stores, and banks are especially vulnerable to being robbed.

Receiving Stolen Goods   In the crime of **receiving stolen goods**, the recipient of the goods does not need to know the true identity of the owner or of the thief. All that is necessary is that the recipient knows or should have known that the goods were stolen. This knowledge implies an intent to deprive the owner of those goods.

Arson   The willful and malicious burning of a building (and, in some states, of personal property) owned by another is the crime of **arson**. Arson statutes apply to all kinds of buildings. If someone is killed as a result of arson, the act is felony murder.

Every state has a special statute that covers burning a building in order to collect insurance. If Akin owns an insured apartment building that is falling apart and burns it himself or pays someone else to set fire to it, Akin is guilty of arson to defraud insurers. Of course, the insurer need not pay the claim when insurance fraud has been proved.

Forgery   The fraudulent making or altering of any writing that changes the legal liability of another is **forgery**. If Smith signs Brown's name without authorization to the back of a check made out to Brown, Smith has committed forgery. Forgery also includes changing trademarks, falsifying

public records, counterfeiting, and the altering of any legal document.

Most states have a special statute, often called a credit card statute, to cover the illegal use of credit cards. Thus, the state attorney can prosecute a person who uses a forged credit card for violating either the forgery statute or the special credit card statute.

Obtaining Money or Goods by False Pretenses   The crime of **obtaining goods by false pretenses** consists of obtaining title to another's property by a knowing false statement of a past or existing fact with intent to defraud the other. Statutes covering such illegal activities vary widely from state to state. Almost all states have created a separate crime prohibiting the giving of a no-account or insufficient funds check with the intent to defraud.

Congress, in 1984, passed the **Trademark Counterfeiting Act**, which makes it a federal crime to deal in goods or services under a trademark that is a counterfeit. The federal **False Statement Act** makes it a crime to make a false statement intentionally to the United States government in order to obtain a monetary return. The following case emphasizes this point.

Case 8.3

UNITED STATES v. PETULLO

United States Court of Appeals, Seventh Circuit, 1983. 709 F.2d 1178.

BACKGROUND AND FACTS   *Defendants Petullo and Argentiere were convicted of conspiracy and of making false statements in violation of 18 U.S.C. Section 1001. In 1979, they devised a scheme for obtaining money by submitting false claims for snow removal work. The claims were submitted to the city of Chicago and not to a federal agency, but the defendants were charged with the federal crime because federal disaster relief funds were used to pay for snow removal. The defendants argued that the government failed to prove all of the necessary elements for a violation of the law.*

CUDAHY, Judge.
*   *   *   *

The federal false statement statute, 18 U.S.C. § 1001, imposes criminal penalties on one who (1) makes a statement that (2) was false, (3) was material, (4) was made knowingly and willfully, and (5) was made in a matter ''within the jurisdiction of any department or agency of the United States.''

Appellants focus on the last of these elements: whether the government proved beyond a reasonable doubt that the false vouchers for snow removal involved a matter within the jurisdiction of a department or agency of the United States. The issue arises because the vouchers were submitted not to a federal agency but to the

City of Chicago, which was using commingled federal, state and local funds to pay for snow removal work. Also, because the fraud was discovered fairly rapidly by the city, the false information contained in the vouchers apparently was not passed on to a federal government agency. * * *

* * * *

* * * Appellants assume that the actual receipt of funds is the critical event and argue that the evidence does not establish clearly that any federal funds were received until after they submitted their vouchers.

We think it follows from the purpose of section 1001 that at least in the emergency relief context it should be the *authorization* of federal assistance that triggers federal jurisdiction under the false statements statute. As explained by this court, ''[t]he term 'jurisdiction' merely incorporates Congress' intent that the statute apply whenever false statements would result in the perversion of the authorized functions of a federal department or agency.'' In the instant case, on January 16, 1979, President Carter authorized the Federal Disaster Assistance Administration (the ''FDAA'') to reimburse the City of Chicago for two-thirds of certain costs of snow removal work performed between January 16, 1979 and January 21, 1979. On January 20, 1979, the FDAA authorization was extended to January 25, 1979. In addition to the FDAA funds, in January 1979 the United States Department of Housing and Urban Development (''HUD'') authorized the city to use Community Development Block Grant funds for snow removal expenses. In effect, the city received a line of credit from the federal government which it knew would enable it to pay later for services that were needed immediately. Accordingly, federal funds were effectively (and, for all practical purposes, irrevocably) committed and ''spent'' once the authorization came through. Therefore, we think that at least in this context section 1001 jurisdiction may commence as early as the officially effective commitment of federal assistance. But we note that in the case before us the jury could have found that the federal funds had actually been received at the time of the offenses. An employee of the Federal Emergency Management Agency testified that $5,000,000 was disbursed to Chicago on February 2, 1979.

* * * *

The defendants' convictions were affirmed by the court of appeals. The actual transfer of money from the federal government to Chicago was not the element that triggered federal jurisdiction; it was the authorization of federal assistance that was the key element.

DECISION AND REMEDY

Embezzlement The fraudulent conversion of property or money of another by a person in lawful possession of that property is **embezzlement**. Typically, it involves an employee who fraudulently appropriates money. Banks and other businesses face this problem where corporate officers or accountants ''jimmy'' the books to cover up the fraudulent conversion of money for their own benefit. Embezzlement is not larceny because the wrongdoer does not physically take the property from the possession of another, and it is not robbery because there is no taking by use of force or fear.

Whether the accused takes the money from the victim or from a third person is immaterial. If, as the comptroller of a large corporation, Saunders pockets a certain number of checks from third parties that were given to her to deposit into the account of another company, she has committed embezzlement.

Often the owner of a property will give money to a contractor specifically to pay various people who have worked on the owner's building. The contractor who does not use the money for this purpose commits a special form of embezzlement called **misapplication of trust funds**. The funds

---

LEGAL HIGHLIGHT   E. F. Hutton & Co.[a]

From July 1980 to February 1982, E. F. Hutton and Company engaged in check kiting. This crime involves depositing a check drawn on one bank into an account held at another bank, usually one located across the country. The balance of the account is inflated by the amount of the deposit, which is as yet uncollected by the deposit bank from the bank on which the check is drawn. The party then has use of this money, which is known as the float, during the time it takes for the deposited check to make it back to the original bank and for the funds actually to be transferred. The party can invest the money during the two to seven days it takes the check to clear the banking system without really having any actual cash involved. The interest income can be considerable.

a.   E. F. Hutton was acquired in 1987 by Shearson Lehman Brothers, Inc. The company is now known as Shearson Lehman Hutton, Inc.

Over a period of two years, senior employees at Hutton wrote at least $4 billion in overdrafts, which created the float, thus cheating 400 banks out of millions of dollars. The Securities Exchange Commission estimates that Hutton earned $4 million on floats in 1980, $9 million in 1981, and $4.7 million in 1982 when the scheme was stopped. Approximately 15.8 percent of the $22 million increase in interest income was a result of the check-kiting scheme. Hutton pled guilty to 2,000 counts of mail and wire fraud and paid over $2.5 million in fines and settlements.

In a separate criminal action in 1988, Hutton pled guilty to concealing at least $532,000 from the Internal Revenue Service. The income came from a money-laundering scheme in which cash transactions of over $10,000 from 1981 to 1984 were not reported as required by federal disclosure rules. As a result, Hutton faced up to $1 million in fines.

---

are entrusted to the contractor for a specific purpose, and that trust is violated. The fact that the accused may intend eventually to replace the embezzled property does not constitute a sufficient defense.

White-Collar Crime

The concept of **white-collar crime** distinguishes those crimes that involve offenses for monetary gain from crimes committed by physical means, such as the crimes described earlier in this chapter. Crimes, however, cannot be easily pigeonholed; for example, forgery, obtaining goods by false pretenses, and embezzlement could also be called white-collar crimes. Today, over 30 percent of the criminal filings in federal district courts involve white-collar crimes.

White-collar crime consists of two categories: occupational and corporate. Occupational crime is committed by people through their work. Businesspeople, labor union leaders, politicians, and such professionals as medical doctors, lawyers, accountants, and stockbrokers may commit crimes in the course of doing their jobs. Insider trading, tax evasion, defrauding Medicare, check kiting, kickbacks, and bribes are a few examples of occupational crimes.

Corporate crime is committed by a complex organization. Because of its large size, the delegation of decisions, and the need to specialize a corporation can compete effectively in the marketplace; these elements also result in the ability of employees to disavow any personal responsibility for corporate decisions. The executives at higher levels can distance themselves from criminal responsibility by claiming ignorance of the illegal activities of lower-echelon employees. At the same time, the lower-echelon employees can also disclaim criminal liability. They may receive

---

LEGAL HIGHLIGHT   **Criminal Schemes**

Although all criminal acts have some cost to society, some types of criminal schemes involve millions of dollars. The following lists some examples of these illegal practices:

1. Charles Ponzi developed a loan-investment system that has become known as the Ponzi Scheme. He promised people who gave him money 50 percent interest on their money if he could keep it for thirty days and 100 percent if he could keep it for ninety days. By word of mouth, news of this fantastic investment spread, and people invested large sums of money. He paid the first people with the money coming in from the later investors. Eventually, he disappeared with most of the money. Today, similar scams exist as multilevel marketing schemes.

2. Glen W. Turner had a firm called Dare to Be Great. His company sold motivation self-improvement material by using another multilevel scheme. When a person sold one of Turner's courses, he or she kept some of the money and forwarded the rest up the pyramid, with each person at a higher level taking a cut. The seller would, in turn, work his or her way up the pyramid by recruiting others into the scheme; they would purchase the materials through him or her, and the recruiter would also take a cut when the new people had resold the materials. Money went to the top of the pyramid where people no longer had to recruit or to sell the courses through their own efforts. Turner was finally tried and convicted after earning millions of dollars.

3. The pigeon drop is a standard confidence game. One person will allegedly discover, in front of the victim (who is usually elderly), a billfold containing a large sum of money. The victim is told he or she can share the money, but he or she has to put up security. An accomplice offers to take the victim to the bank to withdraw money to be used as the security to show good faith. The victim gives the accomplice the money. The "lost" billfold is switched with one that has no money in it. The switched billfold is given to the victim to hold as an act of good faith by the two accomplices. They disappear leaving the victim with nothing.

4. C.O.D., in this scheme means collect on death, not delivery. Obituaries are watched to discover possible victims. The perpetrators approach a family member, stating that the decedent had ordered certain goods, such as a Bible. They convince the victim to purchase the unordered merchandise. In a variation on this scheme, fraudulent medical bills are sent to the estate in the hope that these bills will be paid along with the rest of the deceased's bills. This approach is effective when the obituary states that the person died after a lengthy illness.

5. The bank examiner scheme is successful because most people are honest and want to work with the authorities. A victim is contacted by telephone; the caller claims to be a bank examiner who suspects a bank teller of embezzling money. The caller requests that the victim go to the bank and remove a large sum of money. A very respectable-looking person then goes to the victim's residence, claims to be the bank examiner, gives the victim a receipt, takes the money, and disappears. In actuality, bank examiners never use laypeople in any type of investigation.

---

goals that they believe must be achieved by almost any means if they want to keep their jobs; since the decision on how to achieve the goals is made by various groups, no one person is responsible.

Each subgroup participates, and eventually an activity results that is criminal in nature and that has potentially dangerous ramifications in civil court if the harmed individuals also sue the corporation.

Since it is impossible to cover the range of what are considered to be white-collar crimes, the rest of this chapter will center on five areas: (1) computer crimes, (2) use of the mails to defraud, (3) RICO crimes, (4) bribery, (5) bankruptcy fraud, and (6) corporate crimes.

Computer Crimes Computers have been used by governments and businesses since the 1940s, but the real explosion of computers for government, business, and home use took place in the late 1970s through the 1980s. This growth will continue; by the 1990s, one in every forty persons will have a computer. **Computer crimes** are an unfortunate result of this widespread use.

Computers can be used to commit a wide range of crimes and can do so in record time, as little as three milliseconds. Detection is often difficult. Companies, and even the government, have discovered multimillion-dollar electronic thefts, but only after a significant amount of time has elapsed. These electronic thefts are made by causing a computer to write extra paychecks, transfer monies, or shave cents off interest accounts and place them into personal accounts.

The law involving computer crime is still in its formative state. To counter the rising computer crime activity, Congress passed the **Counterfeit Access Device and Computer Fraud and Abuse Act** in 1985 and the **Electronic Communications Privacy Act** in 1986. These statues make it a crime for anyone without proper authorization to seek entrance into other computer systems, including electronic mail, computer-to-computer data transmissions, remote computing services, and private video conferences; they also prohibit the establishment of bulletin boards that list the passwords of individuals or businesses. The acts apply to governmental computers, computers of federally insured institutions, cellular car telephones, and computer access that crosses state lines. The penalties vary but can be as much as ten years in prison plus a $100,000 fine.

The full extent of computer crime in business is not known. Firms victimized by computer crime rarely publicize the fact. They are afraid that their customers will then doubt the accuracy of their computer-generated material. Trials of apprehended perpetrators of computer crimes are rare. The affected business usually allows the case to be plea-bargained instead of going to trial. Sometimes, for fear of publicity, the business will not even report the crime and may be blackmailed into giving the person who committed the crime a reference for another job.

In the following case, the court adopted the modern view of computer theft.

Case 8.4

STATE v. McGRAW
Indiana Court of Appeals,
Second District, 1984.
459 N.E.2d 61.

BACKGROUND AND FACTS *McGraw was charged with unlawfully exerting control over the property of the city of Indianapolis through the unauthorized use of the city's computer. It was undisputed at the trial that McGraw used the computer to operate a business involving the sale of a dietary product known as NaturSlim. Employees had no authority to use the computers for private business. McGraw was convicted by the jury, but the trial judge dismissed the conviction because he thought that the use of the computer could not be theft.*

NEAL, Judge.
* * * *

No Indiana case under the modern theft statute exists which addresses this question. We view McGraw's arguments as derived from old common law concepts which do not control the much broader definition of property and theft contained in modern statutes. * * *
* * * *

The view that under modern theft statutes unauthorized use of computer services is theft is supported by the analysis of Michael Gemignani, J.D., Acting Chairman of the Computer Sciences section of Indiana University-Purdue University at Indianapolis, in his article on computer crime in 13 Indiana Law Review 681.

We deem McGraw's interpretation of the statutes overly restrictive. In short, he is arguing old common law precepts pertaining to larceny. In our view his contentions are inapposite to the plain meaning of the statutory sections involved herein.

Computer services, leased or owned, are a part of our market economy in huge dollar amounts. Like cable television, computer services are ". . . anything of value". Computer time is "services" for which money is paid. Such services may reasonably be regarded as valuable assets to the beneficiary. Thus, computer services are property within the meaning of the definition of property subject to theft. When a person "obtains" or "takes" those services, he has exerted control. * * * Taking without the other person's consent is unauthorized taking. Depriving the other person of any part of the services' use completes the offense.

Property must be shown to have a value, however slight, but the monetary value of property is of no concern, and the jury may under proper instructions infer some value. The theft statute comprehends a broad field of conduct, and does not limit the means or methods by which unauthorized control of property may be obtained. * * *
* * * *

The court of appeals reversed the trial court's order to dismiss the two counts of theft for the unauthorized use of computer services. The definition of property and theft is no longer restricted to the old common-law concept of larceny, which is the actual taking and carrying away of an item. The statute was worded broadly enough to include the theft of computer services.

DECISION AND REMEDY

Use of the Mails to Defraud **Use of the mails** (or telegrams) **to defraud** the public is a federal crime. Illegal use of the mails involves (1) mailing a writing for the purpose of executing a scheme to defraud and (2) an organized scheme to defraud by false pretenses. If, for example, Daniel Webster sends in a mail advertisement offering for sale a cure for baldness that he knows to be fraudulent, he can be prosecuted for use of the mails to defraud.

RICO Crimes Congress passed an amendment to the Organized Crime Control Act of 1970, known as the **Racketeer Influenced and Corrupt Organizations Act of 1970 (RICO)**. The policy behind the amendment was to control organized crime's investments in legitimate business and to force forfeiture of any profits made as a result of criminal activity. Any offenses that violate this statute are called **RICO crimes**. RICO has two major sections: criminal and civil. Many states have followed the federal example and have adopted what are known as Little RICOs, which are very similar to the federal statute.

Criminal RICO Criminal RICO requires that a person show a "pattern of racketeering activity," which is defined as two or more racketeering acts within ten years of each other. The federal statute lists specific federal and state crimes that constitute these acts, such as mail fraud, wire fraud, fraud in the sale of securities, bankruptcy fraud, extortion, interference with interstate commerce by violence or by threats of violence, interstate transportation of stolen property, arson, murder, gambling, robbery, and drug dealing.

More than thirty offenses are listed, and a conviction of any two within ten years can lead to a conviction under criminal RICO. A person convicted under this act can be fined $25,000, sentenced to twenty years in prison, and must forfeit to the federal government the property obtained through the criminal activity.

LEGAL HIGHLIGHT   Equity Funding

Equity Funding started operations in 1960, primarily selling mutual fund shares and life insurance policies. Listed on the New York Stock Exchange, it was audited by independent accounting firms and by government regulators. Still, for over a decade, it carried out complicated schemes of both insurance fraud and securities fraud. The Equity Funding scandal was broken by Ray Dirks, a financial analyst who was informed by a fired Equity employee. From 1964 to 1972, $143 million in fictitious income was reported. In one fraudulent maneuver, more than 64,000 insurance policies, of the 97,000 that Equity claimed on its reports to have issued, were bogus. Equity's fraud cost investors over $2 billion, making it to date the largest single company fraud.

Civil RICO   The unique aspects of this section are the civil remedies for its violation and the triple-damage awards. Treble damages equal the amount of the actual damages multiplied by three. The RICO civil action section has resulted in cases being filed against such firms as General Motors, Merrill Lynch, American Express, and Prudential Insurance Company of America. An American Bar Association task force found that, from 1976 to 1984, 270 civil RICO cases had been tried in federal district courts. Of the 270 cases, 40 percent involved securities fraud, 37 percent common-law fraud in a commercial or business setting, and only 9 percent allegations of a criminal activity generally associated with professional criminals.

The inclusion of acts of fraud and of securities violations under the RICO statutes accounts for the increase in civil RICO suits. These violations establish a pattern of racketeering. Most lawyers, when bringing civil actions, ignored this statute until the last few years. Now it is very common to include a RICO violation when bringing a civil action against a business. In the following case, the United States Supreme Court considerably broadened the effect of RICO. Injured parties now are not required to show a prior criminal conviction against the defendant before a civil lawsuit can be brought, and they do not need to show a distinct racketeering injury.

Case 8.5
SEDIMA S.P.R.L. v.
IMREX CO.
Supreme Court of the United States, 1985.
473 U.S. 479, 105 S.Ct. 3275,
87 L.Ed.2d 346.

BACKGROUND AND FACTS *The plaintiff, Sedima, and defendant, Imrex, entered into a joint-venture agreement to provide electronic components to Sedima after it had obtained orders from European customers. They were to split the net proceeds. Although $8 million in orders were processed, Sedima became convinced that Imrex was inflating the bill and cheating Sedima out of profits. Sedima filed suit claiming common-law actions for unjust enrichment, conversion, breach of contract, and constructive trust. In addition, it asserted RICO claims based on mail fraud and wire fraud because Imrex used the mails and wires allegedly to overbill Sedima.*

WHITE, Justice.
* * * *
RICO takes aim at ''racketeering activity,'' which it defines as any act ''chargeable'' under several generically described state criminal laws, any act ''indictable''

under numerous specific federal criminal provisions, including mail and wire fraud, and any "offense" involving bankruptcy or securities fraud or drug-related activities that is "punishable" under federal law. * * *

Congress provided criminal penalties of imprisonment, fines, and forfeiture for violation of these provisions. In addition, it set out a far-reaching civil enforcement scheme, including the following provision for private suits:

"Any person injured in his business or property by reason of a violation of section 1962 of this chapter may sue therefor in any appropriate United States district court and shall recover threefold the damages he sustains and the cost of the suit, including a reasonable attorney's fee." [§ 1964]

* * * *

The language of RICO gives no obvious indication that a civil action can proceed only after a criminal conviction. The word "conviction" does not appear in any relevant portion of the statute. To the contrary, the predicate acts involve conduct that is "chargeable" or "indictable," and "offense[s]" that are "punishable," under various criminal statutes. As defined in the statute, racketeering activity consists not of acts for which the defendant has been convicted, but of acts for which he could be. "[A] racketeering activity . . . must be an act in itself *subject to* criminal sanction" (emphasis added). Thus, a prior-conviction requirement cannot be found in the definition of "racketeering activity." * * *

* * * *

* * * [W]e note that a prior-conviction requirement would be inconsistent with Congress' underlying policy concerns. Such a rule would severely handicap potential plaintiffs. A guilty party may escape conviction for any number of reasons—not least among them the possibility that the Government itself may choose to pursue only civil remedies. Private attorney general provisions such as § 1964 are in part designed to fill prosecutorial gaps. This purpose would be largely defeated, and the need for treble damages as an incentive to litigate unjustified, if private suits could be maintained only against those already brought to justice.

In sum, we can find no support in the statute's history, its language, or considerations of policy for a requirement that a private treble-damages action under § 1964 can proceed only against a defendant who has already been criminally convicted. To the contrary, every indication is that no such requirement exists. Accordingly, the fact that Imrex and the individual defendants have not been convicted under RICO or the federal mail and wire fraud statutes does not bar Sedima's action.

* * * *

The United State Supreme Court held that a private party may win treble damages if the defendant has committed a RICO violation. The plaintiff does not have to establish that the defendant has been or could be criminally prosecuted and does not have to show a separate racketeering injury.

DECISION AND REMEDY

As a result of this Supreme Court decision, and the numbers of RICO civil suits, Congress has considered legislation to make RICO less broad.

COMMENT

Bribery Three types of actions called **bribery** are considered crimes: (1) bribery of foreign officials, (2) bribery of public officials, and (3) commercial bribery.

Bribery of Foreign Officials Until the 1970s, bribery of foreign officials to obtain business contracts was rarely, if ever, discussed. Indeed, payments in cash or in-kind benefits to government officials for such purposes were considered normal business practice. This is not to say that the practice was legal. In order to reduce the amount of bribes given to foreign government officials by representatives of American corporations, in 1977 Congress passed the **Foreign Corrupt Practices Act (FCPA)**.

The act is divided into two major parts. The first part applies to all American companies, their directors, officers, shareholders, employees, or agents. The act prohibits bribes (offering something of value in return for official action) to foreign government officials where the purpose is to obtain or retain business for the American company.

The second part applies to all businesses registered with the Securities and Exchange Commission (SEC), even if the business operates only in the United States. In fact, the second part does not have anything to do with bribery or foreign corrupt practices. This part of the FCPA is directed toward accountants and financial officers, because previous bribes were often concealed in corporate financial records. All registered companies are required to keep detailed records that "accurately and fairly" reflect the company's financial activities, and these companies must have an accounting system that provides "reasonable assurance" that all transactions entered into by the company are accounted for and are legal.

Any person in the company is prohibited from making false statements to accountants and no person can make any false entry in any record or account. Any violation of the act may result in a fine of up to $1 million and the incarceration of convicted officers or directors for up to a maximum of five years. Those officers and directors can also be fined up to $10,000, and the fine cannot be paid with company funds.

Bribery of Public Officials The attempt to influence a public official to act in a way that serves a private interest is a crime. As an element of this crime, intent, must be present and proved. The bribe offered can be anything that the recipient of the offer considers to be valuable. The act of bribery is committed when the bribe is offered or when the recipient accepts the bribe.

Commercial Bribery Kickbacks and payoffs from an individual working for one company to an individual working for another company are crimes. No public official need be involved. Such commercial bribes are typically given with the intent of obtaining proprietary information, covering up an inferior product, or securing new business. Industrial espionage sometimes involves this kind of activity—for example, a payoff of some type may be made to an employee in a competing firm in exchange for trade secrets and pricing schedules.

Bankruptcy Fraud Today, individuals or businesses can be relieved of oppressive debt under the federal Bankruptcy Reform Act of 1978 as amended. This act is discussed in more detail in Chapter 11. **Bankruptcy fraud** takes place when a person is involved in bankruptcy and is not honest with the bankruptcy court. The following are examples of white-collar crimes that can be perpetrated during a bankruptcy proceeding.

False Claims of Creditors Creditors are required to file their individual claims against a debtor who is in bankruptcy proceedings. A creditor who files a false claim commits a crime.

Transfer of Property Obviously, a debtor, knowing that he or she will be in bankruptcy proceedings, has an incentive to transfer assets to favored parties before or after the petition for bankruptcy is filed. For example, a company-owned automobile worth $15,000 can be sold at a bargain price of $1,000 to a trusted friend or relative. Closely related to the crime of fraudulent transfer of property is faudulent concealment of property. The number of ways in which debtors have fraudulently, but cleverly, concealed assets would require several books to outline.

Scam Bankruptcies The term "scam bankruptcy" has been used to indicate a swindle in which a bankruptcy is planned in advance. The perpetrators purchase a legitimate business that sells highly movable goods, such as jewelry or electronic home entertainment equipment. Numerous items are purchased on credit by the new owners. The creditors are paid off within a relatively short period of time.

This activity continues until the creditors are willing to offer larger and larger amounts of credit to the new owners. Finally, the new owners order a very large amount of merchandise on credit, sell it at whatever price is necessary to unload it quickly for cash, and then close down the business. Of course, the business is bankrupt. The amount that those creditors will recover, however, is typically very small, and the scam operators are nowhere to be found.

Corporate Crimes Criminal statutes do not have specific crimes that are called **corporate crimes**. The term is generic and covers many types of crimes that are related to corporations. Corporate criminal liability has been expanding over the last decade to include more than the traditional monetary crime. Statutes are now drafted in such a manner that corporations can be held criminally liable for their acts.

For example, a corporation may be held criminally liable for antitrust violations (such as price fixing), for failing to meet securities standards in the issuing of stock in the corporation, or for failing to meet statutory safety standards. Corporations may also fail to pay their taxes and be held criminally liable. In addition, the corporate officers and directors who were in a position to prevent the crime can be prosecuted and, if found guilty, can be fined and/or incarcerated.

Regulatory Offenses As discussed in detail in Chapter 4, Congress has passed statutes that regulate businesses. Among these statutes are: the Occupational Safety and Health Act, the Clean Water Act, the Clean Air Act, the Environmental Protection Act, the Securities Act of 1933, the Securities Exchange Act of 1934, the Sherman Antitrust Act, the Clayton Act, and the Food, Drug, and Cosmetic Act. These acts have created regulatory agencies that monitor business activi-

ties. If the agency finds that a business is in violation of a statute, the business may be criminally prosecuted by the Justice Department.

These same violations may be pursued through the use of administrative law courts. In fact, in the past decade, more violators have been assessed civil and administrative penalties than have been given criminally prosecuted. The burden of proof is less in an administrative court, no right to a jury exists, and settlements can be reached more easily. At the same time, administrative penalties may amount to more than $1 million a day. All of these factors make administrative law courts an attractive alternative in cases involving regulatory violations.

Breach of Fiduciary Duty The federal government can prosecute executives for breach of their fiduciary duty under the federal mail fraud statute. The government needs to prove that the executives failed to disclose material information that they had a duty to disclose and that the misleading information was sent to others through the mails.

Obstruction of Justice Executives may be prosecuted for destroying or hiding corporate records that they have a duty to turn over to a grand jury, to the court, or to the investigative agency. The crime of obstruction of justice is independent of any other criminal violation. Even if the corporation is not guilty of any other criminal act, it can be found guilty of obstruction of justice.

Conspiracy or Aiding and Abetting A corporation can be found criminally liable under several federal statutes if it aids, abets, counsels, commands, induces, procures, or conspires to commit a crime. Two distinct crimes exist: aiding and abetting, and conspiracy. Aiding and abetting does not require proof of an agreement to carry out a criminal act, while a conspiracy needs an agreement with others in order for this crime to have been committed.

FACING A LEGAL ISSUE Bad Checks

All states have a statute that makes it a crime to write a check when there are insufficient funds in the account or when the account is closed. Many times these crimes constitute a felony, and a defendant, if convicted, is sentenced to prison. Each year, businesses lose millions of dollars because of bad checks. The following are some of the ways a business might reduce these losses:

1. Most bad checks are written on new accounts. If the printed number of the check on the upper right-hand corner is low or is a handwritten number, this should signal that the check might not be good.
2. A business should never accept a postdated check, even though it is not illegal to postdate a check. To convict a person of writing bad checks requires proof that the defendant at the time of giving the check intended to defraud the business. When a merchant accepts a postdated check, she or he acknowledges that presently there is not enough money in the account to cover the check; in effect, the merchant is granting credit by accepting a postdated check. The check cannot be dishonored until the date on the check, which makes it very difficult to prove the fraudulent intent at the time that the check was written.
3. The person writing the check may write a figure different in numbers than in longhand on a check. If the figures do not match, a bank is

supposed to return the check to the business. Check processors, however, review hundreds of checks an hour and often look only at the numbers; they may not take time to verify that the words written out are a match. Generally, the figure written in words is the amount legally posted to the bank account. [UCC3-118(c)]
4. For identification of the check writer at trial, merchants, when accepting a check, should require picture identification, such as a driver's license, and should record the identifying driver's license number on the check.
5. Forged checks may be spotted in several ways. First, each geographic area has a specific two-digit federal reserve number that appears twice on the check: as the first two digits of the nine-digit series at the bottom and as the denominator of the fraction at the upper right. If these are not the same, the check is forged. A businessperson should know the federal reserve number for his or her area. Second, the nine-digit number has a special magnetic ink that has a dull finish. Third, checks should have one edge that is perforated. Most forgers use a regular paper cutter that leaves all four sides of the check smooth.
6. A businessperson should never threaten criminal prosecution after receiving a bad check. Making such a threat could result in the merchant being charged with extortion. The crook might go free, and the businessperson might end up serving time! If the businessperson believes a crime has taken place, he or she should report it to the police, or county or district attorney's office.

Summary

This chapter has stressed criminal law and how it relates to the business community. A wrongful act may be both a criminal and a civil wrong. When criminal conduct occurs, society is harmed. All criminal actions are brought in the name of the state—for example, *United States of America v.*

John Worthless. Many criminal acts also give rise to a private civil action by the injured party.

Crimes may be classified as felonies, misdemeanors, and petty offenses. A person convicted of a felony may serve a sentence of one year or more in a state or federal prison, be fined, or be put to death. A person convicted of a misdemeanor may serve time of less than one year in a local jail and/or be fined. If convicted of a petty offense, a person usually is fined.

Historically, most crimes require both criminal intent (*mens rea*) and criminal conduct. For murder, the *mens rea* is the intent to take life. Many modern crimes require only criminal conduct and not criminal intent, which allows corporations incapable of criminal ''intent'' to be convicted of crimes.

When a person is charged with a crime, the government must prove the defendant guilty beyond a reasonable doubt. The guarantees found in the Constitution protect individuals and businesses when accused of crimes.

We have discussed generally the requirements for some of the more important crimes, such as burglary, larceny, robbery, receiving stolen goods,

arson, forgery, obtaining goods or money by false pretenses, and embezzlement. This chapter emphasized white-collar crimes, including computer crimes, use of the mails to defraud, RICO crimes, bribery, bankruptcy fraud, and corporate crimes.

One of the most important additions to federal law was the passage of the Racketeer Influenced and Corrupt Organizations Act. This act has both criminal and civil provisions. A business that has committed more than two acts of racketeering in ten years may be criminally prosecuted and may be liable for treble damages to the injured party in a civil lawsuit. Racketeering acts consist of such criminal activity as mail fraud, wire fraud, fraud in the sale of securities, bankruptcy fraud, extortion, interference with interstate commerce, interstate transportation of stolen property, arson, murder, gambling, and robbery.

Key Terms

arson (**176**)
bankruptcy fraud (**184**)
beyond a reasonable doubt (**168**)
bill of information (**172**)
bribery (**183**)
burglary (**175**)
computer crimes (**180**)
corporate crimes (**185**)
Counterfeit Access Device and Computer Fraud and Abuse Act (**180**)
Electronic Communications Privacy Act (**180**)

embezzlement (**177**)
False Statement Act (**176**)
felony (**168**)
Foreign Corrupt Practices Act (FCPA) (**184**)
forgery (**176**)
indictment (**172**)
larceny (**175**)
mens rea (**172**)
misapplication of trust funds (**177**)
misdemeanor (**168**)
obtaining goods or money by false pretenses (**176**)

petty offense (**168**)
preponderance of the evidence (**168**)
Racketeer Influenced and Corrupt Organizations Act (RICO) (**181**)
receiving stolen goods (**175**)
RICO crimes (**181**)
robbery (**175**)
Trademark Counterfeiting Act (**176**)
use of the mails to defraud (**181**)
white-collar crime (**178**)

Questions and Case Problems

1. Civil trials and criminal trials follow essentially the same format. There are, however, several important differences. In criminal trials, the defendant must be proven guilty beyond a reasonable doubt, whereas, in civil trials, the defendant need only be proven guilty by a preponderance of the evidence. Can you see any reason for this difference? Explain

2. The following fact situations are similar (all involve the theft of Jean's television set); yet three different crimes are described. Identify the three crimes, noting the differences among them.

(a) While passing Jean's house one night, Sam sees a portable television set left unattended on Jean's lawn. Sam takes the television set, carries it home, and tells everyone he owns it.

(b) While passing Jean's house one night, Sam sees Jean outside with a portable television set. Holding Jean at gunpoint, Sam forces her to give up the set, and he runs away with it.

(c) While passing Jean's house one night, Sam sees a portable television set in a window. Sam breaks the front door lock, enters, and leaves with the set.

3. Two basic elements are needed for a person to be convicted of a crime. The first element is called criminal intent, and the second is called criminal conduct. Explain what these terms mean, and discuss how each is applied to the following:

(a) Murder

(b) Forgery

(c) Arson.

4. Fernando Banderas presented false claims to Banco del Ecuador for humanitarian aid that had never been rendered. When the fraud was discovered, Banco del Ecuador sued under RICO for treble damages. Fernando Banderas defended by arguing that he was not part of organized crime and that his fraud, if any, was of a lesser degree than that found in criminal law. Should he be successful in this defense? [Banderas v. Banco Central del Ecuador, 461 So.2d 265 (Fla.App. 1985)]

5. Joseph Russello was involved with committing arson on a building he owned. Prior to being charged and convicted, he had been able to collect the insurance on the building. What type of crime has Russello committed under these circumstances? [Russello v. United States, 464 U.S. 16, 104 S.Ct. 296, 78 L.Ed.2d 17 (1983)]

6. Faulknor was a seaman on the ship *Zemindar*. One night, while on duty, Faulknor went in search of the rum that he knew the ship was carrying. He found it and opened one of the kegs, but, because he was holding a match at the time, he inadvertently ignited the rum and set fire to the ship. At the trial, it was determined that, even though he had not intended to set fire to the rum, he had been engaged in the unlawful act of stealing it. Does Faulknor's theft of the rum make him criminally liable for setting fire to the ship? [Regina v. Faulknor, 13 Cox Crim. Cas. 550 (Ireland 1877)]

7. In 1965, Rybicki failed to pay all the income tax he owed the federal government. Attempts by the IRS to collect the tax proved fruitless. The IRS, therefore, through lawful means, obtained a tax lien on Rybicki's personal property, which included his truck. A tax lien can be placed by the IRS on all property owned by a delinquent taxpayer. In February 1967, Rybicki's wife, on hearing the truck's motor running awoke her sleeping husband. Wielding a shotgun, Rybicki went to his front door and told the two men who were attempting to take his truck to stop. Rybicki later claimed that he did not know that the two men were IRS agents. Subsequently, the federal government indicted Rybicki for obstructing justice. Can Rybicki be held criminally liable if he did not know that the men were IRS agents performing their duty? [United States v. Rybicki, 403 F.2d 599 (6th Cir. 1968)]

8. Lund was working on his doctoral dissertation in statistics at Virginia Polytechnic Institute in Blacksburg, Virginia. He was required to use the computer facilities at the university. His faculty adviser neglected to arrange for the use of the computer. Lund, nonetheless, went ahead and used it without obtaining proper authorization. At the trial, Lund was convicted of grand larceny for obtaining approximately $30,000 worth of computer services without authorization. Four faculty members testified that computer time ''probably would have been'' or ''would have been'' assigned to Lund if properly requested. Lund appealed his conviction. What was the result? [Lund v. Commonwealth, 217 Va. 688, 232 S.E.2d 745 (1977)]

UNIT II   BUSINESS AND PRIVATE LAW

Chapter 9   Contracts and Sales Law

An acre of performance is worth the whole world of promise.

J. B. Howell, *Familiar Letters, 1650*

OUTLINE

Introduction

Millions of contracts are entered into and performed daily. Few people go through even one day without making or acting on a contract. A **contract** is an agreement between two or more parties that can be enforced in a court of law or equity. In the legal environment of business, questions and disputes about contracts arise daily; answering those questions and resolving those disputes are the essence of contract law.

The legal framework provides the stability and the structure within which businesses can plan and carry out their contracts. When adverse business conditions occur, a businessperson cannot rely on the good faith that the other party to the contract will perform simply out of a sense of duty. The enforceability of contracts in courts of law and equity ensures the promised performance or entitles the person harmed to some form of relief.

Businesspeople need to have a working knowledge of contract law because the fundamental method of exchanging goods, services, property, and money is through contracts. It is the businessperson who negotiates and frequently drafts contracts. Contract law is a complicated topic that can be reviewed only briefly in a legal environment course.

In this chapter, we will look at the evolution of contract law, at the elements that make up a contract, at the Uniform Commercial Code and its effect on contract law, and at some unique contractual terms.

Evolution of Contract Law

Evidence exists that society has enforced the promises of individuals since the beginning of recorded time. The Code of Hammurabi, 1800 B.C., had specific provisions enforcing obligations. Shortly after the Norman invasion in 1066, the early courts of England established procedures to enforce promises. By the late 1700s, contract law had became an important part of the common law.

The common law that existed in 1776 in the United States was not well equipped to handle the disputes that began to arise as the business world evolved in the new country. By the end of the

nineteenth century, it was evident that statutes needed to replace, at least to some extent, the common law when it came to business transactions.

During the 1930s, businesspeople thought that Congress should pass legislation to handle all interstate commercial transactions. After considerable debate, Congress decided that it would be better for the individual states to adopt a uniform act that would apply to both interstate and intrastate transactions. Today, all the material provisions of the Uniform Commercial Code (UCC) have been adopted by forty-nine states (Louisiana has adopted only parts of the UCC).

Of the eleven articles that make up the UCC, only three have importance in this and the next two chapters. Article 2 (Sales), Article 3 (Commercial Paper), and Article 9 (Secured Transactions; Sales of Accounts and Chattel Paper) are the three articles used most frequently in contractual situations. Article 2 covers sales of goods, including basically anything that is a movable item. Statutes and court decisions cover contracts of the sale of real property—that is, land and anything permanently attached to it. In this chapter, we will cover the common law, statutes, and several provisions of Article 2, Sales. We will review Articles 3 and 9 in Chapter 10.

Contract Terms

A contract is an agreement between two or more parties to perform—or refrain from performing—some act now or in the future, and when valid, this agreement is enforceable in a court of law or equity. A contract is based on a promise, but not all promises are legally enforceable. A contract is developed by an offer and an acceptance of that offer.

An **offer** presents a promise that can be met with **acceptance** (a return promise) or with **rejection**. Every offer involves at least two parties. The **offeror** is the party making the offer. The offeror is promising to do—or not to do—an act. The **offeree** is the party to whom the offer is made and who has the power to accept or reject the offer. If the offeree accepts (by performing an act or by returning a promise), the contract is formed because promises have been exchanged. A rejection terminates the offer.

The offer stage is when negotiations occur. Negotiations may take years, as in the purchase of a large tract of land, or may be over quickly, as in the decision to purchase a soft drink.

Terms Used with Contracts

Contract law uses specific terms to describe different contractual situations. Three sets of terms describe the formation of the contract, the enforceability of the contract in a court of law, and the performance of the contract.

Formation   These terms define the various situations in which a contract is formed.

Unilateral and Bilateral Contracts   Whether the contract is unilateral or bilateral depends on what the offeror is requiring of the offeree to accept the offer. If the offeror makes a promise that requires the offeree to complete his or her performance of the contract with a return act (not with a promise), then the contract is called a **unilateral contract**. The person making the promise wants the other person to perform an act as an acceptance in return. An example is the reward situation; the promisor offers a cash amount for the return of a lost dog: *REWARD . . . for return of 2 year-old male basset hound. Responds to name Charlie.* The person offering the reward wants action, the return of Charlie, not promises.

A **bilateral contract** is created when the offeror wants the offeree to give her or his promise to perform. The offeree's return promise is the acceptance. A bilateral contract is a ''promise for a promise.'' Most contracts are bilateral. For example, Miguel offers to sell his residence for $100,000. When someone agrees (gives a return promise) to purchase Miguel's residence at that price, a bilateral contract is the result. In a sale of land, a statute (called the statute of frauds) requires that this type of contract must be in writing in order to be enforceable.

Express and Implied Contracts   In an **express contract**, the terms of the offer on acceptance are specially stated, whether orally or in writing. If the terms are not exactly set out but are implied,

a valid contract exists, but it is called an **implied-in-fact contract**. Implied contracts are created by the conduct of the parties. When individuals act as if there is a contract, even though no words have been spoken or written to that effect, the law will imply that there is one. For example, when a person visits the doctor's office to be treated for a cold, the person by her or his conduct is agreeing to pay for the doctor's services.

Quasi-Contracts   Occasionally a person will be unjustly enriched at the expense of another. No express contract exists, and no conduct has happened to imply a contract, yet it is unjust for the one individual to be enriched at the expense of the other. The law will imply a promise to pay. This type of conduct creates a contract by operation of law, an implied-in-law contract. More commonly called **quasi-contracts**, the parties did not make any promise by word or conduct, but the law will impose a promise on the party who benefited.

A quasi-contract is distinguishable from an implied-in-fact contract. An implied-in-fact contract is a true contract made between the parties and is enforceable in court. In contrast, only a court can declare that a quasi-contract exists, because it is a legal fiction. The court creates a quasi-contract (that is, a fictional contract) for reasons of social policy, i.e., to prevent a person from being enriched unjustly at the expense of another. Quasi-contracts are equitable, rather than contractual, in nature.

Here is an example of a quasi-contract. Joel is a salesman. He returns home at 10:00 A.M. to find a work crew ready to paint his house. He knows that they are supposed to be painting his neighbor's house. He does not say anything and leaves. When he returns to his house at 5:00 P.M., the house is painted. Under a quasi-contract, the painting company will be able to collect a reasonable amount for the paint job from Joel. He has received a benefit, and it would be unjust for him to retain that benefit without paying for it. Joel had a chance to stop the painting, and he failed to do so. Until he pays, he has been unjustly enriched at the expense of the paint company.

Formal and Informal Contracts   Statutes set out the provisions for a **formal contract**, requiring it

LEGAL HIGHLIGHT	The Tow Truck and the Implied-In-Fact Contract

In Maryland, Ron's car got stuck in the mud in a swampy area behind the local bait shop. He called a tow truck to haul the car out of the mud; then he went fishing. The tow truck came and got stuck in the mud. The driver called another tow truck, which promptly got stuck in the mud in front of the first tow truck. The two drivers called a third tow truck, which also got stuck.

A bulldozer was called in. It too got stuck in the mud. Next called was a construction company, which, with the help of four dump trucks, constructed a dirt road. With a solid base now in place, the bulldozer, the three tow trucks, and Ron's car were rescued from the mud. The bill was $4,740. Who pays? Ron says he will pay for one tow truck. The first tow truck driver says Ron told him to get the car out and that Ron's father would pay for it. Ron's father says, "No way."

As in many cases of this type, the dispute was settled out of court, and only the parties know how it ended. All in all, it is a muddled contract case.

to be in a special form to be valid. All formal contracts must be written but not all written contracts are classified as formal contracts. An example of a formal contract is a bail bond, which is a bond to obtain the release of someone from jail. Other examples are negotiable instruments and letters of credit. (See Chapter 10.) Most contracts do not require a specified form or formality for their validity, and therefore almost all contracts today are classified as **informal contracts** and can be oral or written.

Enforceability   The following terms describe the enforceability of a contract by a court.

Valid, Void, Voidable and Unenforceable Contracts   Most contracts are valid. A **valid contract** meets all the elements required for the contract to be enforced in a court. (These elements are discussed in detail in the next section.) A void contract, on the other hand, is a misnomer. Whenever a contract is rendered void, the law will not enforce the agreement. For example, if the purpose of the contract is illegal, it is a **void agreement**. In these cases, the word agreement is used because by definition a contract is a legal situation.

A **voidable contract** means that one party to the contract is bound, but the other party may disaffirm (or avoid) it. For example, a minor has the right to disaffirm most contracts—that is, he or she can avoid performing the contracts.

An **unenforceable contract** is one that started out as a valid contract, but, for some legal reason, it now cannot be enforced in court against the other party. Some statutes forbid the courts to enforce the contract. Consider this example: A person enters into a valid contract to buy a stereo set on credit. Later the person goes into bankruptcy, and the contract debt is discharged (forgiven) by the bankruptcy court. The valid contract has been converted into an unenforceable contract by the bankruptcy statute as applied by the bankruptcy court. Now the creditor cannot sue the debtor to collect the money owed on the contract.

Performance   The following terms describe the contract based on the performance status of each of the parties.

Executed or Executory Contracts   These terms can refer to one of two situations. First, they can refer to the status of the contract seen as a whole. An **executed contract** is a fully performed contract, while an **executory contract** is one that has not been performed. Second, these terms can refer to the state of performance by one party in relationship to the other. For example, Ann hands over a textbook to a friend with the understanding that she will receive twenty dollars for it. Ann's performance is fully executed while the friend's performance is executory. In this case, the contract is partially performed.

Exhibit 9–1 summarizes the contract terms covered here.

Elements of a Contract

All legally enforceable contracts must satisfy these requirements:

1. Offer: An offer (promise) must be made.
2. Acceptance: An acceptance to the offer must be given, whether by return promise or an act. (The offer and acceptance constitute mutual assent).

3. Consideration: Promises must be bargained for and exchanged, have legal value, and be sufficient to support the offer and acceptance.
4. Capacity: The parties must have the legal capacity to form a contract.
5. Legality: The subject matter of the contract must be legal.
6. Writing: Certain agreements must be in writing to be enforceable in court. (Not all contracts need to meet this requirement.)

Requirements of the Offer

An offer is a promise to do—or to refrain from doing—some specified thing now or in the future. Three elements are necessary for an offer to be effective: (1) There must be *objective intent* by the offeror to be bound by his or her offer; (2) the terms of the offer must be *reasonably definite;*

Exhibit 9–1 Contract Terms

Contract Formation	1. How offeree is required to respond (accept the offer) determines this classification of contract.
	    a. *Unilateral*—A promise for an act (completed act is acceptance).
	    b. *Bilateral*—A promise for a promise.
	
	2. The parties' manner of expression determines this classification of contract.
	    a. *Express*—Formed by words (oral, written, or both).
	    b. *Implied-in-Fact*—Formed by the conduct of the parties.
	
	3. A court decision determines this classification of contract.
	    a. *Quasi-Contract*—Imposed by law to prevent unjust enrichment.
	
	4. Form determines this classification of contract.
	    a. *Formal*—Required by law to be in special written form to be valid.
	    b. *Informal*—No special form. May be oral or written.

Enforceability	1. *Valid*—The contract has the necessary contractual elements of offer and acceptance, consideration, and parties with capacity, and it is made for a legal purpose. 2. *Voidable*—One party has the option of avoiding or enforcing the contractual obligation. 3. *Void*—No contract exists, or there is an agreement without legal obligations. 4. *Unenforceable*—A contract exists, but it cannot be enforced because of a legal defense.
Performance	1. *Executed*—A fully performed contract. 2. *Executory*—A contract not fully performed.

and (3) the offer must be *communicated* to the offeree. For a valid contract to exist, the first question to be answered is: Is there an offer?

Intention   An offeror must objectively intend to be bound by his or her offer. Objective intent is determined from the words and actions of the parties as interpreted by a reasonable person. The issue is whether the offeror intends to be bound

to his or her offer if the offeree accepts it. Offers made in obvious anger, jest, or excitement, do not meet the objective intent test. Since these offers are not effective, the offeree's acceptance does not create a valid contract.

In the following case, the court must decide whether a statement was a joke, as the officer of a corporation contended, or whether it met the objective intent test and was a valid offer.

Case 9.1

BARNES v. TREECE

Court of Appeals of the State of Washington, 1976.
15 Wash.App. 437,
549 P.2d 1152.

BACKGROUND AND FACTS   *Treece, the defendant, was a vice-president of Vend-A-Win, Inc., a corporation that was in the business of distributing punchboards (a gambling device). The Washington State Gambling Commission was investigating various aspects of gambling. Treece spoke before the commission on behalf of Vend-A-Win's application for a temporary license to distribute punchboards. During his appearance, which was televised, he stated, "I'll pay a hundred thousand dollars to anyone to find a crooked board. If they find it, I'll pay it." The statement brought laughter from the audience.*

Barnes, the plaintiff, watched a television news report of Treece's statement and also read a newspaper account. Barnes telephoned Treece, asking him if his statement was serious. Treece restated that he meant it and that the money was being held in escrow. Barnes was in possesssion of two crooked punchboards. Following Treece's instructions, Barnes brought one of the punchboards into Vend-A-Win's offices for inspection. He turned the other board over to the Washington State Gambling Commission.

Treece and Vend-A-Win each refused to pay Barnes. Barnes filed a lawsuit. The trial court held Treece personally liable for the $100,000. The case against Vend-A-Win was dismissed because the court found that Treece never inquired of Vend-A-Win whether he had the authority to bind the corporation on this matter, and Vend-A-Win did not have time to deny that Treece had this authority. The case was appealed. The issue was whether the statement was an offer for a unilateral contract.

CALLOW, Judge.
* * * *

The first issue is whether the statement of Treece was the manifestation of an offer which could be accepted to bind the offeror to performance of the promise. Treece contends that no contract was formed. He maintains that his statement was made in jest and lacks the necessary manifestation of a serious contractual intent.

When expressions are intended as a joke and are understood or would be understood by a reasonable person as being so intended, they cannot be construed as an offer and accepted to form a contract. However, if the jest is not apparent and a reasonable hearer would believe that an offer was being made, then the speaker risks the formation of a contract which was not intended. It is the objective manifestations of the offeror that count and not secret, unexpressed intentions. As stated in *Wesco Realty, Inc. v. Drewry:*

If a party's words or acts, judged by a reasonable standard, manifest an intention to agree in regard to the matter in question, that agreement is established, and it is immaterial what may be the real but unexpressed state of the party's mind on the subject.

The trial court found that there was an objective manifestation of mutual assent to form a contract. This was a matter to be evaluated by the trier of fact. The record includes substantial evidence of the required mutual assent to support the finding of the trial court. Although the original statement of Treece drew laughter from the audience, the subsequent statements, conduct, and the circumstances show an intent to lead any hearer to believe the statements were made seriously. There was testimony, though contradicted, that Treece specifically restated the offer over the telephone in response to an inquiry concerning whether the offer was serious. Treece, when given the opportunity to state that an offer was not intended, not only reaffirmed the offer but also asserted that $100,000 had been placed in escrow and directed Barnes to bring the punchboard to Seattle for inspection. The parties met, Barnes was given a receipt for the board, and he was told that the board would be taken to Chicago for inspection. In present day society it is known that gambling generates a great deal of income and that large sums are spent on its advertising and promotion. In that prevailing atmosphere, it was a credible statement that $100,000 would be paid to promote punchboards. The statements of the defendant and the surrounding circumstances reflect an objective manifestation of a contractual intent by Treece and support the finding of the trial court.

The trial court properly categorized Treece's promise of $100,000 as a valid offer for a unilateral contract. The offer made promised that a contract would result upon performance of the act requested. Performance of the act with the intent to accept the offer constituted acceptance. The trial judge entered a specific finding that Barnes performed the requested act of acceptance when he produced a rigged and fraudulent punchboard. We concur with the trial court's holding that a binding unilateral contract was formed between Barnes and Treece and uphold the conclusions of the trial court in that regard.

Barnes won a $100,000 judgment against Treece. Under other circumstances, Treece's statement might have been a joke, but Treece made the statement before an official state commission that was investigating a multi-million-dollar business, he knew that the statement was being reported on television and in the newspapers, and he repeated the statement over the telephone to Barnes. The court found the objective intent standard had been met. The statement was an offer calling for an action; thus, when Barnes produced the crooked boards, a unilateral contract resulted.

DECISION AND REMEDY

Definiteness   An offer must have reasonably definite terms. The parties must be able to determine what they must do in order to perform the contract. If a dispute arises, a court must be able to determine if the contract promises have been broken and, if so, to decide on an appropriate remedy.

Even prior to the adoption of the Uniform Commercial Code, the courts were reluctant to declare a contract invalid based on the indefiniteness of its terms if, during the trial, the evidence showed a clear intention by both parties to enter into the contract. The courts inserted reasonable terms wherever possible to resolve ambiguous or missing terms.

Article 2 of the UCC has liberalized the requirement of definiteness. Under the UCC, even though one or more of the contract's terms are left open, a contract for the sale of goods may be enforced by a court. If it is clear that the parties intended to make a contract and if a reasonably certain basis exists for giving an appropriate remedy, the court will supply the missing terms. [UCC 2-204(3)] The missing terms are provided in some of the following ways.

If no price is stated, the price is the reasonable price at the time the goods were delivered. [UCC 2-305(1)] If no place of delivery is specified, delivery is at the seller's place (not the buyer's) home or business. [UCC 2-308(a)] If the time for shipment or delivery is not provided, the deadline is a reasonable period after the contract is formed. [UCC 2-309] If the time for payment is not specified, payment is due at the time and place of delivery. [UCC 2-310(a)] This means that unless you have arranged to pay for the goods on credit, you must pay in cash (currency or check) at the time and place that the goods are delivered to you.

Communication   The third requirement for an effective offer is communication. A person cannot agree to a contract without knowing that the contract exists. Suppose Emerman advertises a reward of $100 for the return of her lost dog. Garcia, not knowing of the reward, finds the dog and returns it to Emerman. Garcia cannot recover the $100 in a court because he did not know it was offered, and, therefore, no contract existed to be enforced. Emerman may still give the reward to Garcia, but Emerman cannot be forced by a court to do so.

Exhibit 9–2 summarizes the requirements for an effective offer.

Termination of the Offer

An effective offer gives the offeree the power to transform that offer into a contract by accepting it. This power of acceptance, however, does not continue forever. An offer can be terminated either by an action of one of the parties or by the law. First, the offer can be ended in three ways by an action of one of the parties: (1) **revocation** of the offer *by the offeror,* (2) **rejection** of the offer *by the offeree,* or (3) **counteroffer** *by the offeree.* Second, an offer can be terminated by **operation of law** (lapse of time, destruction of the specific subject matter of the offer, death or incompetence of either party, and illegality of the offer). The question is: Is the offer still open?

Revocation of the Offer by the Offeror   Revocation is the withdrawal of the offer by the offeror. Even if the offeror promises to keep the offer open, he or she can inform the offeree of the revocation before the offeree accepts. Revocation may be achieved by expressly repudiating the offer (such as "I withdraw my previous offer of October 17") or by an act inconsistent with the existence of the offer (such as selling the item and the offeree knowing about the sale).

The offeree must be informed of the revocation before she or he accepts the offer. If the revocation comes after the offeree has accepted the offer, the revocation is not normally effective. A valid contract has already been formed because an acceptance is usually effective at the time it is made. The general rule followed by most states is that a revocation is effective only on actual receipt of the revocation by the offeree.

For example, an offer is made on April 1. When the offeree accepts the offer on April 3, a contract is formed. If the offeror sends a revocation on April 2 that is delivered to the offeree

---

Exhibit 9–2 Requirements for an Effective Offer

1. *Intent*—A serious, objective intention by the offeror to become bound by the offer.

2. *Definiteness*—The terms of the offer must be sufficiently definite to be ascertainable by the parties or by a court. Under the UCC, the court can supply missing terms if it is clear the parties intended to make a contract for the sale of goods and if a reasonably certain basis exists for giving an appropriate remedy. [UCC 2-204]
   a. No price: reasonable price at time of delivery [2-305]
   b. No delivery place: seller's place of business or if none, seller's home [2-308(a)]
   c. No time set to ship or deliver: reasonable time after contract formed [2-309]
   d. No time set for payment: money to be paid on delivery. [2-310(a)]

3. *Communication*—The offer must be communicated to the offeree.

on April 4, it is too late. But if the revocation had reached the offeree on April 2, the offer would have been terminated.

Although most offers are revocable, certain offers can be made irrevocable. Three types of irrevocable offers are: (1) those involved in option contracts, (2) firm offers under the UCC, and (3) those made irrevocable by virtue of promissory estoppel. The question is: Is this type of offer revocable?

Option Contract An **option contract** is a separate contract that takes away the offeror's right to revoke the offer for the period of time specified in the option. If an offeror promises to hold an offer open for a specific time period and the offeree pays for the promise, an option contract has been created. If no time is specified, a reasonable period of time is implied.

For example, Beverly plans to purchase twelve acres at a prime location. She needs time to determine if she can obtain financing. If she cannot obtain financing, she does not want to buy the property. Beverly pays the landowner $1,000 to give up his right to sell the land to someone else or withdraw the offer within a specified period of time, such as 180 days. An option contract has been created. During the 180 days, the landowner cannot revoke his offer to Beverly. At the end of the 180 days, the option expires. If she does not obtain financing, Beverly will not be obligated to purchase the land under this option contract.

Firm Offer Created by the UCC, a **firm offer** occurs when a **merchant** (a person who regularly deals in a particular type of goods) makes a written, signed offer to buy or sell goods and states in the offer words to the effect that it is not revocable. The merchant's offer is irrevocable without the payment of consideration by the offeree. [UCC 2-205] The offer remains open for the stated period of time; if no time is specified, the offer remains open for a reasonable period, but the period cannot exceed three months.

Promissory Estoppel Estoppel means to bar, to impede, or to stop. **Promissory estoppel** means that the promisor (the offeror) is prevented from revoking the offer. Increasingly, courts are refusing to allow an offeror to revoke an offer when the offeree has changed his or her position by relying on the offer. In such cases, revocation is considered unjust to the offeree.

For example, Dan (the offeree) owns a grocery business and the store. Big Chain (the offeror) offers him a manager's position in a new store that it plans to build, but Dan is told by Big Chain he will have to sell his business to be hired as manager. In reliance thereof, Dan sells his store; then Big Chain says that it no longer plans to build its store and thus does not plan to employ Dan. Had the offer not been made, Dan still would have his store and grocery business. Dan has a case based on promissory estoppel: Big Chain cannot revoke its offer because the offeree, relying on the offer, has changed his situation.

Rejection of the Offer by the Offeree An offeree may reject the offer, in which case the offer ends. A rejection, by conduct or by words, shows an intent not to accept the offer. Any other words or conduct by the offeree does not terminate the offer. Rejection is not effective as a termination of the offer until the offeror learns of the rejection.

For example, suppose Mary has made an offer to sell her used personal computer printer to Dan for $450. On May 1, Dan responds that the offer appears to be a little high, and asks if Mary would lower her price. Mary cannot treat these words as a rejection because Dan's words did not indicate an intent not to accept, but only make an inquiry whether Mary would modify her offer. Suppose further Mary refuses to modify her offer and on May 3 Dan mails to Mary a letter of rejection. Before Mary receives Dan's letter, Dan calls Mary and accepts her offer. Since Dan's rejection had not been received by Mary at the time of Dan's acceptance, Dan and Mary have a valid and enforceable contract.

Counteroffer by the Offeree A counteroffer is a rejection of the original offer and, at the same time, it constitutes a new offer. Any subsequent attempt to accept the expired offer by the offeree (now the offeror) will be construed as a new offer, giving the original offeror (now the offeree) the power of acceptance. Suppose Arnold offers to sell his computer to Dale for $1,000. Dale responds, "Your price is too high. I'll offer to purchase your computer for $650." Dale's response

Exhibit 9–3 The Dynamics of a Rejection and Counteroffer

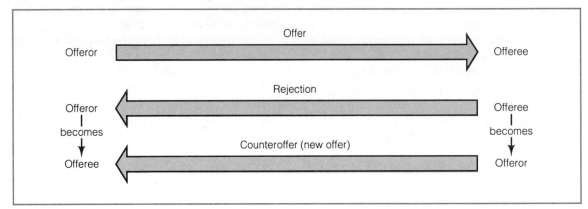

is termed a counteroffer, since it constituted a rejection and ended Arnold's offer to sell at $1,000 and at the same time created a new offer by Dale to purchase at $650. Exhibit 9–3 illustrates how the relationships of offeror and offeree change when a counteroffer is made.

Mirror-Image Rule   At common law, the **mirror-image rule** requires the offeree's acceptance to match the offeror's offer exactly; in other words, the acceptance must mirror the offer. Any change in, or addition to, the terms of the original offer automatically ends that offer and constitutes a counteroffer. The original offeror (now the offeree) can accept the terms of the counteroffer and thus create a valid contract.

UCC Rules on Acceptances and Exceptions
Slight variations in terms between the offer and the acceptance that violate the mirror-image rule have caused considerable problems in commercial transactions. In the business world, when goods are bought and sold, the buyer usually uses his or her standard *purchase order* form and the seller accepts on her or his standard *confirmation* form. Chances are high that the two forms will vary to some degree. For example, the confirmation form may contain a requirement that any disputes must be submitted to arbitration (see Chapter 5), while the purchase order form may be silent on this topic. Such a conflict is referred to as the "battle of the forms." Under the common law's mirror-

image rule, no contract results when different standardized forms are used.

If, however, a contract falls under the UCC's rules concerning the sale of goods, the contract is formed when the offeree "accepts" the offer, even though the terms of the acceptance (the confirmation form) modify or add to the terms of the original offer. [UCC 2-207(1)] If the contract is between merchants, the new terms become part of the contract automatically. For example, if the confirmation form requires disputes to be arbitrated, this new term becomes part of the contract, unless an exception exists.

The UCC has three *exceptions* to this rule: First, the offer can clearly require the acceptance to be the same as the offer with no variations. The purchase form can include a statement ("Acceptance to be on these terms only") that any additional terms in the confirmation order will not become part of the contract. Second, if the new or changed terms of the contract materially change the other party's duties, the new terms in the confirmation order will not be part of the contract. In our example, the issue is whether submitting disputes to arbitration materially alters the right of the offeror to go to a judicial court. If so, the arbitration clause addition does not become a part of the contract. Third, the offeror can read the new or changed terms and object to (reject) those terms within a reasonable period of time.

The UCC rule is different if one or both parties are *nonmerchants*. Then the contract is formed according to the terms of the offer, not according to the additional terms of the acceptance.

Termination of the Offer by Operation of Law The offeree's power to change an offer into a contract can be ended by operation of law. Four conditions can end the offer:

1. *Lapse of time*—in other words, either the time to accept the offer has expired or the offeree has failed to accept the offer within a reasonable time.
2. The *specific subject matter* of the offer is destroyed.
3. *Death or incompetence* of the offeror or offeree is established. Death or incompetence does not terminate, however, an irrevocable offer (such as an option).
4. After the offer is made, the legislature or court makes that type of offer *illegal*. For example, Congress passes a law making it illegal to sell computer chips to any Eastern-bloc countries. Any outstanding offers to sell computer chips to a firm in East Germany would now be ended by operation of law.

Exhibit 9–4 summarizes the ways in which an offer may be terminated.

Acceptance

Acceptance is a voluntary act by the offeree; it can be either words or conduct that shows assent (agreement) to the terms of an offer. The acceptance must be unequivocal and communicated to the offeror.

Except in certain special circumstances, only the person to whom the offer is made or that person's authorized agent can accept the offer and create a binding contract. Part of the offer identifies the offeree and is one of the conditions of the offer. For example, Jones offers to sell his motorcycle to Hanley. Hanley rejects the offer, but Hanley's friend, Smith, attempts to accept the offer. No contract is formed.

Silence as an Act of Acceptance Ordinarily, silence does not constitute acceptance, even if the offeror states, "By your silence and inaction you will be deemed to have accepted this offer." An offeree does not have the burden of performing some act in order to reject an offer unless the offeree has a "duty to speak" such as by agreement or where the offeree solicited the offer.

Book and record clubs have an agreement with their members that a book or record selection will be sent out automatically unless the member returns a card indicating that no selection is wanted in the upcoming month. Silence acts as an acceptance because the contract between the club and the member sets out silence as a method of acceptance. These clubs fall under the Federal Trade Commission's Negative Option Rule, which requires the clubs to give the members enough time

---

Exhibit 9–4 Termination of an Offer

1. *By acts of the parties:*
   a. Revocation—Unless the offer is irrevocable, it can be revoked at any time before acceptance without liability; not effective until *known* by the offeree. Irrevocable offers are: a merchant's firm offer [UCC 2-205], those made irrevocable by virtue of promissory estoppel, and those involved in option contracts.
   b. Rejection—Accomplished by words or actions that demonstrate a clear intent not to accept or consider the offer further; not effective until *known* by the offeror.
   c. Counteroffer—A rejection of the original offer and the making of a new offer.

2. *By operation of law:*
   a. Lapse of time—The offer terminates (a) at the end of the time period specified in the offer, or (b) if no time period is stated in the offer, at the end of a reasonable time period.
   b. Destruction of the specific subject matter of the offer—Automatically terminates the offer.
   c. Death or mental incompetence—Terminates the offer unless the offer is irrevocable.
   d. Illegality—Supervening illegality terminates the offer.

to respond if they do not want the monthly selection.

Communication of Acceptance Whether the offeror must be notified of the acceptance depends on the nature of the offer. In a unilateral contract, generally it is not necessary to notify the offeror because the act of acceptance is evident [see, however, UCC 2-206(2)]. The offer calls for the full performance of the act; therefore, acceptance is not completed until the act has been fully performed. For example, only when someone returns the lost dog for the reward in the example used previously to illustrate a unilateral contract is the contract complete.

In a bilateral contract, communication of acceptance is necessary because acceptance takes the form of a promise (not an act), and the contract is formed when the promise is made (rather than when the act is performed). Acceptance takes effect when *sent* if the offeree uses a method of communication authorized by the offeror. This method can be expressly stated by the offeror in the offer. If the offeror does not state any specific method of responding, such as by telegram, the rule is to mail the acceptance. It will be effective when mailed.

Under the UCC, an offer may be accepted in any manner and by any medium reasonable under the circumstances. [UCC 2-206(1)(a)] This is a practical rule for business transactions, and the acceptance is effective when sent; under these rules a contract can be formed even though the offeror never receives the message of acceptance.

The UCC also provides that an order to buy goods may be treated as either a bilateral or a unilateral offer. The offer can be accepted through a promise to ship or through actual shipment. [UCC 2-206(1)(b)] For example, Peters receives a telegram that he is to ship red shirts to Johnson. Peters can accept by either promptly shipping the red shirts or by sending a telegram to Johnson, saying that he is going to ship the goods. If the shipment will take a considerable amount of time, Peters would be wise to telegraph Johnson that the goods are in transit.

Exhibit 9–5 summarizes the requirements for acceptance of a contract.

Exhibit 9–5 Acceptance of a Contract

1. Can be made only by the offeree or the offeree's authorized agent.

2. Must be unequivocal.
   a. Mirror-image rule—Under common law, terms of acceptance must be same as terms of offer.
   b. UCC rule—A definite acceptance of an offer is not a counteroffer, even if new terms modify the terms of the original offer. [UCC 2-207] If either party is a nonmerchant, additional terms are proposals for addition to the contract, but not part of it. Between merchants the additional terms become a part of the contract—Exceptions:
      i. Offer limits acceptance to its terms.
      ii. New terms materially change offer.
      iii. New terms are rejected.

3. Acceptance of a bilateral offer can be communicated to the offeror by authorized mode of communication and is effective upon dispatch. Unless the mode of communication is expressly specified by the offeror, the following methods are impliedly authorized:
   a. The same mode used by the offeror, or a faster mode.
   b. By mail, when the two parties are at a distance.
   c. In acceptance of offers for the sale of goods, under the UCC, any medium that is reasonable under the circumstances.

4. Acceptance of an offer to buy goods for prompt shipment under the UCC:
   a. By prompt shipment of conforming goods.
   b. By prompt promise to ship.

To summarize, the offeror and the offeree must have a meeting of the minds, called **mutual assent**. In other words, the offer made by one person must be the offer accepted by another person; the terms of the offer must be the terms of the acceptance. Mutual assent means that both sides are contracting for the same item or service, for example.

In the following case, the court was confronted with the issue of whether the jury should have been instructed about the requirement for a meeting of the minds.

BACKGROUND AND FACTS   *The plaintiff, Flo-Products Company, gave a quote over the telephone of "fifteen thirty-six" for certain cylinders to be used in the defendant's dairy packaging machine. The defendant's maintenance supervisor testified that the oral quote was "fifteen thirty-six," which he thought was $15.36. The cylinders were shipped to the defendant billed at $1,536. The defendant refused to accept delivery because of the question as to price.*

Flo-Products sued Valley Farms. The trial court did not instruct the jury to consider whether the parties had ever had a meeting of the minds. The plaintiff won a judgment in the trial court. Valley Farms appealed because the jury was not given instructions concerning the "meeting of the minds" element.

 Case 9.2

FLO-PRODUCTS CO. v. VALLEY FARMS DAIRY CO.
Court of Appeals of Missouri, 1986.
718 S.W.2d 207.

DOWD, Judge.
*   *   *   *

*   *   * The jury was instructed *   *   * to find for plaintiff if they believe[d] plaintiff furnished the cylinders at defendant's request and that the charges for the cylinders were reasonable. Defendant requested the court to instruct the jury that "meeting of the minds" was a necessary element of plaintiff's case but the court refused the instruction.

Defendant alleges the trial court erred: in refusing to give defendant's requested instruction on "meeting of the minds."

*   *   * "Meeting of the minds" is a necessary element to the making of a contract *   *   * [A] "meeting of the minds" as to price was a controverted issue. For a verdict-directing instruction in favor of plaintiff to be acceptable, it must require the jury to find all the necessary elements of plaintiff's case except for uncontroverted facts. It is reversible error for an instruction to assume or ignore a controverted fact.

The discrepancy in the parties' understanding of the price term remained a controverted fact throughout the trial. Plaintiff Flo-Products Co. chose to submit its case to the jury[.] *   *   * [T]he jury [is required] to find for plaintiff if they believe: 1) Defendant requested plaintiff to furnish the goods, 2) Plaintiff furnished the goods to defendant, and 3) Plaintiff's charges were reasonable. Instructing the jury *   *   * under these circumstances resulted in a directed verdict for plaintiff without the only controverted issue of the case ever being before the jury.

The trial court erred in not giving the jury an instruction on the requirement that the parties must have a meeting of the minds to have a valid contract. The discrepancy in the parties' understanding of the price remained the contested issue throughout the trial, yet the jury never made a decision on these contested facts. The trial court's judgment was reversed, and the case was remanded to the trial court.

DECISION AND REMEDY

Genuiness of Mutual Assent

Factual disputes occur when it seems as if there was a meeting of the minds but in reality the parties did not reach an understanding. No genuine assent exists as to the terms of the contract when there is **fraud**, **misrepresentation**, certain forms of **mistake**, **duress**, or **undue influence**. These situations are defenses a party to the contract can use to show why he or she should not be ordered by a court to perform the contract.

Fraud and Misrepresentation When fraud occurs, the contract is voidable by the injured party. The five requirements that establish fraud are: (1) a misrepresentation of a material fact exists; (2) the contract is made with the knowledge by the guilty party that the material fact is false; (3) the guilty party has the intent to deceive; (4) the innocent party has justifiably relied on the misrepresentation; and (5) the innocent party has suffered damages.

Fraud is difficult to prove because the knowledge and wrongful intent of the other party must be established. Because of the difficulty in proving fraud, many injured parties sue for misrepresentation instead. To establish a claim for misrepresentation, one need not prove intent to deceive. Obviously, this makes misrepresentation much easier to prove.

Mistake, Duress, and Undue Influence Mistakes occur in two forms: A **unilateral mistake** is made by only one of the contracting parties while a **mutual mistake** is made by both of them.

Unilateral Mistake A unilateral mistake does not affect the contract, which is still valid and enforceable, unless the mistake is so obvious that the other party should have known it was a mistake.

For example: Jean runs a retail camera store. Jim, a salesperson for a printing company, obtains an order from Jean for return address labels. Jean was busy at the time she filled out the form and wrote "4,000 m.m." Jim returns to the office with this order, elated that he has a sale for 4 billion labels. Neither he nor his company has ever had such a large order. In fact, a special press run has to be made, and delivery must be made by a freight

company rather than by the usual method of sending the labels through the mails. Jean refuses delivery because she wanted only 4,000 labels. In this case, Jim should have known there was a mistake. He could have easily telephoned Jean to recheck before going to all the trouble and expense of having these labels printed.

On the other hand, had Jean filled out the form for "4,900" labels (with intent to only order 4,000), her unilateral mistake would fall on her, and she would be held liable for the purchase of 4,900 address labels. The mistake would not have been so obvious, and thus, Jim would not have known of it.

Mutual Mistake No contract is formed when there is a mutual mistake in a couple of circumstances: (1) when the parties are in disagreement as to the identity of the subject matter of the contract or (2) when they are mistaken as to the existence of the subject matter. If one of these two events occurs, there is no meeting of the minds, and a court will not find a binding contract. If a court finds that a mutual mistake has occurred as to the value of the subject matter of the contract, the contract generally will be fully enforceable against both parties. For example, Gary contracts to sell Kathy a painting for $5,000. Both believe the artist of the painting is Rory. They now learn that the artist is Lori. Since the mutual mistake went to the identity of the subject matter, there is no meeting of the minds and neither can enforce the contract. Had the mistake been as to the value—not the artist—of the painting, the contract is fully enforceable.

Duress Duress occurs when one of the parties is forced into the contract by fear. The courts allow the party who was under duress to rescind the contract. For example, if Piranha Loan Company threatens to harm Chang unless he signs over to Piranha his $10,000 car in order to secure a $100 loan, Piranha is guilty of using duress.

Duress may involve the threat of physical harm or economic harm, such as the loss of a job. The threatened act must be wrongful or illegal. In a lawsuit, the party who was under duress (whose freewill was overcome) can choose to carry out the contract or to avoid the entire transaction.

Undue Influence Undue influence arises from special kinds of relationships in which one party can greatly influence another party, thus overcoming that party's free will. Minors and elderly people are often under the influence of close relatives. If Shady influences an elderly person who is under his legal care to enter into a contract that benefits Shady, undue influence has been exerted.

Undue influence can arise from a number of fiduciary (that is, founded on trust) or confidential relationships: attorney-client, doctor-patient, guardian-ward, parent-child, husband-wife, or trustee-beneficiary. The essential feature of undue influence is that the party being taken advantage of does not, in reality, exercise free will when entering into the contract. A contract made when one person is unduly influenced lacks genuine assent and is voidable.

Exhibit 9–6 summarizes the defenses a party to a contract can use to show that mutual assent was not obtained.

Consideration

The third requirement of a legally enforceable agreement is consideration. Consideration is broken into two elements: (1) Something of **legal value** must be given in exchange for a promise, and (2) the promises must be **bargained for and exchanged**. The "something of legal value" may consist of a return promise or a performance.

Requirements of Consideration In order to create a binding contract, the elements of consideration must not only exist but must also be legally sufficient. To be legally sufficient, consideration for a promise must be legally detrimental to the promisee—the one receiving the promise—or legally beneficial to the promisor—the one making the promise. In every bilateral contract, each party (offeror and offeree) is treated as both a promisor and a promisee. **Legal detriment** or **legal benefit** is not synonymous with actual economic detriment or benefit.

Exhibit 9–6 Problems of Assent

Mistake	1. *Mutual*—When both parties' mistake goes to a material fact, such as identity, either party can avoid the contract. If the mistake goes to value or quality, either party can enforce the contract.
	2. *Unilateral*—Generally, the mistaken party is bound by the contract *unless* the other party knows or should have known of the mistake.
Misrepresentation	1. *Fraud*—When fraud occurs, usually the innocent party can enforce or avoid the contract. The five elements necessary to establish fraud are: a. Misrepresentation of a material fact exists. b. Contract is made with knowledge that fact is false. c. Contract is made with the intent to deceive. d. Innocent party justifiably relies on the misrepresentation. e. Innocent party is damaged.
	2. *Other*—Intent to deceive need not be shown. Usually, the innocent party can rescind the contract but cannot seek damages.
Influence/Coercion	1. *Undue influence*—Arises from special relationships, such as fiduciary or confidential relationships, in which one party's free will has been overcome by the undue influence exerted by the other party. Usually, the contract is voidable.
	2. *Duress*—Defined as forcing a party to enter a contract under fear induced by a threat; for example, the threat of violence or economic pressure. The party forced to enter the contract can rescind the contract.

Note the change in language from offeror and offeree to promisor and promisee. The former two words describe the parties during the formation of contract stage; once the parties have exchanged promises, they are called the promisor and promisee.

Legal detriment occurs when a person does or promises to do something that he or she did not have a prior legal duty to do. Conversely, legal benefit occurs when a person obtains something that he or she had no prior legal right to obtain.

For example, Fine Gravel Company owns and mines a gravel pit. The land owned by Fine Gravel is adjacent to a school, but the actual mining takes place on the land furthest from the school. The school is one mile away from that mining site. Years later, Fine Gravel decides to mine within a few hundred yards of the school. It also plans to build a road for its trucks next to the school fence. The school board objects because of the danger to the children and the noise that will be produced. The school board offers $150,000 to Fine Gravel Company to refrain from building the road and from mining near the school. The gravel company agrees. The consideration flowing from the gravel company is the promise to refrain from an act that it is legally entitled to do—that is, to earn a living by mining gravel. The consideration flowing from the school board to Fine Gravel is the promise to pay a sum of money that it is not otherwise legally required to pay.

In the following case, one of the classics of contract law, the court found that refraining from certain behavior at the request of another was sufficient consideration to support a promise to pay a sum of money.

Case 9.3
HAMER v. SIDWAY
Court of Appeals of New York,
Second Division, 1891.
124 N.Y. 538, 27 N.E. 256.

BACKGROUND AND FACTS *William E. Story, Sr., was the uncle of William E. Story II. In the presence of family members and guests at a family gathering, Story, Sr., promised to pay his nephew $5,000 if he would refrain from drinking, using tobacco, swearing, and playing cards or billiards for money until he became twenty-one.*

The nephew agreed and fully performed his part of the bargain. When he reached age twenty-one, he wrote his uncle that he had kept his part of the agreement and was entitled to $5,000. The uncle replied that he was pleased with his nephew's performance and that he was keeping the nephew's money in the bank to earn interest. The nephew agreed that his uncle should keep the money according to the terms and conditions of the letter.

The uncle died about twelve years later without having paid his nephew any part of the $5,000 and interest. Sidway, the executor of the uncle's estate (the defendant in this action), did not want to pay the $5,000 and interest to the nephew, claiming that the nephew had not given valid consideration for the promise. In the meantime, the nephew sold his interest (his right to collect the $5,000 if the court ruled in his favor) to Hamer. Hamer sued Sidway to collect the $5,000. The court disagreed with the executor and reviewed the doctrine of detriment-benefit as valid consideration under the law.

PARKER, Justice.

* * * The defendant contends that the contract was without consideration to support it, and therefore invalid. He asserts that the promisee, by refraining from the use of liquor and tobacco, was not harmed, but benefited; that which he did was best for him to do, independently of his uncle's promise,—and insists that it follows that, unless the promisor was benefited, the contract was without consideration,—a contention which, if well founded, would seem to leave open for controversy in many cases whether that which the promisee did or omitted to do was in fact of such benefit to him as to leave no consideration to support the enforcement of the promisor's agreement. Such a rule could not be tolerated, and is without foundation in the law. The exchequer chamber [a type of court] in 1875 defined "consideration" as follows: "A valuable consideration, in the sense of the law, may consist either in some right, interest, profit, or benefit accruing to the one party, or some forbearance, detriment, loss, or responsibility given, suffered, or undertaken by the other." Courts "will not ask whether the thing which forms the consideration does in fact benefit the promisee or a third party, or is of any substantial value to any one. It is enough that something is promised, done, forborne, or suffered by the party to whom the promise is made as consideration for the promise made to him. In general a waiver of any legal right at the request of another party is a sufficient consideration for a promise." * * * Now, applying this rule to the facts before us, the promisee used tobacco, occasionally drank liquor, and he had a legal right to do so. That right he abandoned for a period of years upon the strength of the promise of the testator that for such forbearance he would give him $5,000. We need not speculate on the effort which may have been required to give up the use of those stimulants. It is sufficient that he restricted his lawful freedom of action within certain prescribed limits upon the faith of his uncle's agreement, and now, having fully performed the conditions imposed, it is of no moment whether such performance actually proved a benefit to the promisor, and the court will not inquire into it; but, were it a proper subject of inquiry, we see nothing in this record that would permit a determination that the uncle was not benefited in a legal sense. * * *

The court ruled that the nephew had provided legally sufficient consideration by giving up smoking, drinking, swearing, and playing cards or billiards for money until he became twenty-one, and, therefore, he was entitled to the money promised him.

DECISION AND REMEDY

The Hamer v. Sidway *case is a good illustration of the distinction between a benefit to the promisor and a detriment to the promisee. Here the court did not inquire as to whether a benefit flowed to the promisor, but required only that there was a legally sufficient detriment to the promisee.*

COMMENTS

Adequacy of Consideration Adequacy of consideration refers to the fairness of the bargain. A court will not normally question the adequacy of the consideration if it is legally sufficient. If a person buys an item at too high a price, he or she may have buyer's remorse, but the court will not set the contract aside unless a reason, such as fraud or mistake, exists.

Exhibit 9–7 summarizes the legal elements of consideration.

Contractual Capacity

Contractual capacity—that is, the competence (or legal ability) of the parties—is the fourth require-

ment for a valid contract. Full competence exists when both parties have full legal capacity to enter into a contract and to have the contract enforced against them. No competence exists when a party has been judged by a court to be mentally incompetent; such a person has no legal capacity to form a contract, and any contract into which he or she enters is void.

Limited competence exists when one or both parties are minors, are intoxicated, or are mentally incompetent but not yet officially judged to be mentally incompetent by a court. These parties have full and legal capacity to enter into a contract, but, if they want, they can avoid liability under the contract. This type of contract is said to be

In San Francisco, Bill, a certified public accountant, asked Ann to join him in attending the opera and to have dinner afterward. The date was made three months in advance. Late on the afternoon of the date, Ann called Bill to tell him that she would have to break the date because her old boyfriend was in town. Because it was late in the afternoon, Bill was unable to find anyone else to accompany him.

He sued Ann for breach of contract and asked for the following damages:

■ The cost of one ticket to the opera
■ One-half of the cost of the mileage to purchase and pick up the ticket in advance
■ The cost of his time to find someone else to take her place.

The small-claims court dismissed the case, stating that a promise to go on a date was not a legally enforceable contract.

voidable. We will emphasize the contracts of minors here because this is the area that involves the most litigation.

Minors   The **age of majority** (when a person is no longer a minor) for contractual purposes varies from state to state. For the sake of discussion in this text, the most commonly adopted age will be used: eighteen years. The general rule of law is that a minor can enter into any contract that an adult can enter into, provided that the contract is not one prohibited by law. For example, in most states a person must be twenty-one years old to purchase any alcoholic beverages.

Although minors can enter into contracts, they also have the right to **disaffirm** (or avoid) their liabilities under the contracts, subject to certain exceptions. A minor may disaffirm the contract any time prior to age eighteen or during a reasonable period of time thereafter. If, however, by the time the minor becomes an adult, he or she has failed to disaffirm an executed contract, the contract is ratified. **Ratification** is the act of accepting and giving legal force to any contract that the minor had a right to disaffirm. Only after minors reach adulthood can they ratify contracts made when they were minors.

A contract to purchase necessaries (that is, goods or services needed for the sustenance of the minor such as food, clothing or shelter) may not be totally disaffirmed by a minor. The rule applicable to contracts for the purchase of necessaries is that the minor is liable to the other contracting party for the *reasonable value* of the

Exhibit 9–7 Consideration

Elements of Consideration	1. *Legal value*—not economic value.
	   a. Legal detriment—to promisee who promises to do (or refrain from doing). No prior legal duty to perform or (refrain from doing).
	   b. Legal benefit—to promisor.
	
	2. *Bargained For and Legally Sufficient*—The promisee's performance or promises to perform must be given in exchange for the promisor's promise. Adequacy of consideration relates to "how much" consideration is given and whether a fair bargain was reached. Courts will inquire into the adequacy of consideration (if the consideration is legally sufficient) only when fraud, undue influence, or duress may be involved.

property or services *actually used*. This imposes a quasi-contractual liability on the minor for purchases needed to fulfill the basic needs of the minor where no parent or guardian is *willing* and *able* to furnish or provide the required necessity.

When disaffirmance occurs, the adult must also give back to the minor whatever she or he has received as a result of the contract. If the property itself cannot be returned, the adult must pay the minor its equivalent value.

Under the UCC, dealing with the sale of goods, a minor cannot recover the goods transferred by the adult purchaser to a third party who is a bona fide purchaser (a good-faith purchaser for value). The buyer needs to know that the items he or she buys in good faith will not be taken as the result of a dispute between the seller and a minor from whom the seller purchased the item. For example, Minor owns a car at age sixteen. He sells the car to Al Adult. Al drives the car for six months and then sells it to Susan. Minor now decides he wants the car back. He could disaffirm the contract with Al, but Minor cannot recover the car from Susan.

When disaffirmance occurs, the minor is required to give back whatever he or she has received and still possesses as a result of the contract. Under the majority view, the minor's duty of restoration is only to return the goods (or other consideration). If this condition is met, the minor is not liable for depreciation or nonwillful damage to the goods. In the following case, for example, a minor was not liable for damages to an automobile.

BACKGROUND AND FACTS *Halbman, the plaintiff, contracted with Lemke, the defendant, to purchase a 1968 Oldsmobile for $1,250, of which Halbman paid $1,100 to Lemke. Halbman was a minor when he purchased the vehicle. A connecting rod broke, and Halbman took it to a garage for repairs. He did not pay the repair bill. The mechanic, therefore, placed a lien (called an artisan's lien) on the car for his repairs. This lien was foreclosed, and the engine was sold to another person to pay for the repairs. The car was towed to Halbman's residence.*

Halbman disaffirmed the contract. He contacted Lemke to come get the car and to return the $1,100. Lemke claimed he did not have a legal obligation to take back the car. Eventually the car was vandalized, making it unsalvageable. Halbman sued Lemke for the return of his $1,100. The trial court entered a judgment for Halbman. Lemke appealed.

Case 9.4

HALBMAN v. LEMKE

Supreme Court of Wisconsin, 1980.
99 Wis.2d 241,
298 N.W.2d 562.

CALLOW, Justice.
* * * *

The sole issue before us is whether a minor, having disaffirmed a contract for the purchase of an item which is not a necessity and having tendered the property back to the vendor, must make restitution to the vendor for damage to the property prior to the disaffirmance. Lemke argues that he should be entitled to recover for the damage to the vehicle up to the time of disaffirmance, which he claims equals the amount of the repair bill.

Neither party challenges the absolute right of a minor to disaffirm a contract for the purchase of items which are not necessities. That right, variously known as the doctrine of incapacity or the "infancy doctrine," is one of the oldest and most venerable of our common law traditions. Although the origins of the doctrine are somewhat obscure, it is generally recognized that its purpose is the protection of minors from foolishly squandering their wealth through improvident contracts with crafty adults who would take advantage of them in the marketplace. Thus it is settled law in this state that a contract of a minor for items which are not necessities is void or voidable at the minor's option.

Once there has been a disaffirmance, however, as in this case between a minor vendee and an adult vendor, unresolved problems arise regarding the rights and responsibilities of the parties relative to the disposition of the consideration exchanged on the contract. As a general rule a minor who disaffirms a contract is entitled to recover all consideration he has conferred incident to the transaction. In return the minor is expected to restore as much of the consideration as, at the time of disaffirmance, remains in the minor's possession.

The minor's right to disaffirm is not contingent upon the return of the property, however, as disaffirmance is permitted even where such return cannot be made.

* * * In this case we have a situation where the property cannot be returned to the vendor in its entirety because it has been damaged and therefore diminished in value, and the vendor seeks to recover the depreciation. Although this court has been cognizant of this issue on previous occasions, we have not heretofore resolved it.

The law regarding the rights and responsibilities of the parties relative to the consideration exchanged on a disaffirmed contract is characterized by confusion, inconsistency, and a general lack of uniformity as jurisdictions attempt to reach a fair application of the infancy doctrine in today's marketplace. * * *
* * * *

The principal problem is the use of the word "restitution." * * * When the contract is disaffirmed, title to that part of the purchased property which is retained by the minor revests in the vendor; it no longer belongs to the minor. The rationale for the rule is plain: a minor who disaffirms a purchase and recovers his purchase price should not also be permitted to profit by retaining the property purchased. The infancy doctrine is designed to protect the minor, sometimes at the expense of an innocent vendor, but it is not to be used to bilk merchants out of property as well as proceeds of the sale. Consequently, it is clear that, when the minor no longer possesses the property which was the subject matter of the contract, the rule requiring the return of property does not apply. The minor will not be required to give up what he does not have. We conclude that the word "restitution" * * * is limited to the return of the property to the vendor.

Here Lemke seeks restitution of the value of the depreciation by virtue of the damage to the vehicle prior to disaffirmance. Such a recovery would require Halbman to return more than that remaining in his possession. It seeks compensatory value for that which he cannot return. Where there is misrepresentation by a minor or willful destruction of property, the vendor may be able to recover damages in tort. But absent these factors, as in the present case, we believe that to require a disaffirming minor to make restitution for diminished value is, in effect, to bind the minor to a part of the obligation which by law he is privileged to avoid.

DECISION AND REMEDY

The trial court's decision was affirmed. The court did not require restitution by the minor in order for him to recover what he had paid. When Halbman disaffirmed the contract, the title went back to Lemke; thus, when the automobile was vandalized, the automobile was owned by Lemke. Because Lemke failed to remove the automobile from Halbman's yard when first called by Halbman, it was rendered unsalvageable. Naturally, Halbman cannot now make actual restitution; Halbman did, however, attempt to make restoration, and the law will not make him return what he no longer has—especially in this case, when it was not his fault.

LEGAL HIGHLIGHT

"Blue" Sabbath

As a result of the Puritan spirit, nearly all contracts were at one time considered to be illegal if made on Sunday. Eventually the types of contracts that could or could not be made on Sunday became a hodgepodge. Called blue laws, the restrictions have eased significantly over the years. Court challenges have struck down the blue laws in Virginia, North Carolina, Tennessee, Mississippi, Arkansas, and, as recently as in 1984, in Louisiana. That last court decision came in time for tourists to be able to buy souvenirs anywhere in Louisiana, without being restricted on Sundays to the 1984 World's Fair or the French Quarter in New Orleans.

In the past, the hodgepodge of restrictions included the following:

■ You could go to the grocery store and buy such "necessities" as *Playboy* (deemed literature) but not meat (not deemed necessary to survive the day).
■ You could buy a house, but not any furniture.
■ You could buy a battery, but not a car.
■ In South Carolina, you could go to a movie only in the eight largest cities, but not in the rural areas.

Only one blue law is still enforced in almost every state: Liquor still cannot be sold on Sunday mornings.

Legality

The fifth requirement for a valid contract is legality; the contract must be for the performance of a legal act. An agreement is illegal if either its formation or its performance is criminal, tortious, or otherwise opposed to public policy. The reasoning for this is quite simple: If a civil court requires a person to perform a contract that involves the commission of an illegal act, a criminal court could punish that person for committing a crime as a result of a civil court order. This is not only illogical and contrary to common sense but it is also against public policy for the courts to be a party to a crime.

The general effect of an illegal agreement is that it is void, and the court leaves the parties where they are found. Neither party has rights against the other when the agreement has an illegal purpose.

Writing

Certain valid contracts, by statute, must be in writing to be legally enforceable by a court. This stat-

ute is called the Statute Against the Perpetuation of Fraud, or the **Statute of Frauds** for short. The writing must be signed by the person against whom it is being enforced. Good business practice requires a written contract.

The statute of frauds varies from state to state. The major types of business contracts required to be in writing are:

1. Contracts involving interests in land, such as leases and sales.
2. Contracts that, by their terms, cannot be performed within one year from the date that the contract was formed.
3. **Collateral contracts**, such as promises to pay the debt or perform the duties of someone else.
4. Contracts for the sale of goods priced at $500 or more.

The statute of frauds allows other methods to substitute for a written contract. For example, the UCC requires that contracts involving the sale of goods for the price of $500 or more must be in writing and signed by the party against whom enforcement is sought. [UCC 2-201] But if the

Exhibit 9–8 Contracts Covered by the Statute of Frauds

Contracts to Guarantee the Debt of Another	*Application*—Applies only to express contracts made between the guarantor and the creditor, whose terms make the guarantor secondarily liable for the debt of another.
Contracts Involving an Interest in Realty	*Application*—Applies to any contract for an interest in realty, such as sale or lease.
Contracts Whose Terms Cannot Be Performed Within One Year	*Application*—Applies only to contracts objectively impossible to perform fully within one year from the date of the contract's formation.

Contracts for the Sale of Goods Priced at $500 or More	1. *Application*—Applies only to the sale of goods whose purchase price (excluding taxes) is $500 or more. [UCC 2-201(1)]
	
	2. *Exceptions:*
	  a. Between merchants, where one sends a written confirmation and the recipient does not object in writing within ten days.
	  b. Admission under oath of an oral contract.
	  c. Partial performance by buyer's payment or possession, at least to the extent paid or quantity possessed. [UCC 2-201(2)(3)]

Exception to Contracts Otherwise Unenforceable Under the Statute of Frauds	*Memorandum*—Written evidence of an oral contract signed by the party against whom enforcement is sought. Generally, the writing must name the parties and identify the subject matter of the contract. In the sale of goods, the quantity must be stated. In the sale of realty usually need land description and price.

signed writing is insufficient because it omits or incorrectly states a term, the UCC provides that the contract is still valid. (In any case, however, a contract is not enforceable under the UCC for any amount of goods greater than that stated in the writing.) If there is an oral agreement between merchants and if one of them sends the other a written confirmation, the confirmation is the written evidence of the oral contract. The receiver has ten days to give her or his written objection; if this is not sent, the terms of the oral contract are enforceable and are presumed to be those contained in the written confirmation. The contract is binding on both parties even though not signed.

The UCC allows oral contracts to be enforced up to the amount to which the parties admit in any court action. Also, the UCC allows courts to enforce oral contracts up to the amount of payment that has been made or up to the quantity of the goods already received and accepted by the buyer. Any other parts of the oral contract remain unenforceable.

Exhibit 9–8 summarizes the contracts covered by the statute of frauds.

The following case discusses whether an oral contract was primarily for the sale of goods or of services. The UCC is concerned with the sale of goods and not services.

COLORADO CARPET INSTALLATION v. PALERMO

Supreme Court of Colorado, 1983.
668 P.2d 1384.

BACKGROUND AND FACTS *Colorado Carpet Installation filed this lawsuit to collect on an alleged oral contract in which the Palermos (husband and wife) agreed to pay $4,775.75 for the purchase and installation of carpeting, other flooring materials, and bathroom tile. The Palermos denied that they ever ordered anything beyond the tile for the bathroom.*

QUINN, Justice.

* * * *

We address the court of appeals' determination that the contract was one for the sale of goods, rather than for the performance of labor or services. We conclude that the agreement in question involved a contract for the sale of goods[.] * * *

* * * The Uniform Commercial Code defines ''goods'' to mean ''all things * * * which are movable at the time of identification to the contract for sale other than the money in which the price is to be paid, investment securities . . . and things in action.'' * * * A ''sale,'' by statutory definition, ''consists in the passing of title from the seller to the buyer for a price[.]'' * * *

In this case the subject of the contract involved ''goods'' because the carpeting and other materials were movable at the time that Colorado Carpet procured them for installation pursuant to the agreement. Since the agreement contemplated that title to the carpeting and other materials would pass to the Palermos, it constituted a ''contract for sale.'' The scope of the contract, however, included not only the sale of goods but also the performance of labor or service. Thus, we must determine whether such a mixed contract qualified as a contract for the sale of goods or, instead, constituted a contract for labor or service outside the scope of [the U.C.C.].

The performance of some labor or service frequently plays a role in sales transactions. ''Goods,'' however, are not the less ''goods'' merely because labor or service may be essential to their ultimate use by the purchaser. The mere furnishing of some labor or service, in our view, should not determine the ultimate character of a contract for purposes * * * of the Uniform Commercial Code. Rather, the controlling criterion should be the primary purpose of the contract— that is, whether the circumstances underlying the formation of the agreement and the performance reasonably expected of the parties demonstrates the primary purpose of the contract as the sale of goods or, in contrast, the sale of labor or service. * * *

[The] ''primary purpose'' test, we believe, is designed to promote one of the expressed statutory policies of the Uniform Commercial Code—''[t]o simplify, clarify, and modernize the law governing commercial transactions.'' * * * Useful factors to consider in determining whether ''goods'' or ''service'' predominates include the following: the contractual language used by the parties[;] whether the agreement involves one overall price that includes both goods and labor or, instead, calls for separate and discrete billings for goods on the one hand and labor on the other[;] the ratio that the cost of goods bears to the overall contract price[;] and the nature and reasonableness of the purchaser's contractual expectations of acquiring a property interest in goods * * *.

Considering the contract under these guidelines, we are satisfied that, as a matter of law, its primary purpose was the sale of goods and not the sale of labor or service. The language in Colorado Carpet's proposal referred to the parties as ''seller'' and ''customer.'' In addition, the agreement called for an overall contract price that included both the cost of goods and labor, and, as the trial evidence established, the charge for labor was slight in relation to the total contractual price. Finally, the carpeting and other materials were movable when Colorado Carpet procured them for the purpose of selling them to the Palermos. The fact that these materials might later be installed in the Palermo home and assume the character of fixtures does not undermine the primary purpose of the contract as one for a sale of goods. * * *

The court found that this contract was for the sale of goods, not services. The oral agreement was not enforceable because the statute of frauds requires a written contract for the sale of goods priced at $500 or more.

DECISION AND REMEDY

Other Contractual Problems

After all the requirements of a valid contract have been met, other problems may arise. First, third parties may have rights based on the contract even though they did not participate in its original formation. Second, if a contract dispute arises, the parties need to know the available remedies.

Third-Party Rights

Sometimes people not directly connected with the initial contract become involved in it. Third parties can acquire an interest in a contract by assuming the rights or duties arising from it. An original party to a contract can transfer his or her rights or duties to a third person (that is, someone who was not an original party) after the original contract has been made.

Each party to the contract has rights and duties. One party has the right to the performance that the other party has promised; the other party has a duty to perform it. The transfer of duties to another person is called a **delegation**. When a party to a contract transfers her or his rights to a third person, it is known as an **assignment**, and the original party is known as the **assignor**. The third party who takes the assignment is known as the **assignee**. The assignee steps into the shoes of the original party to the contract. If the other party to the contract has a defense to the contract, the defense may also be used against the assignee.

For example, Nancy contracts to purchase a computer for $4,000. She is going to pay Computer Company $200 a month. Computer Company (the assignor) assigns the right to receive the $4,000 to Finance Company (the assignee). Nancy is now required to pay the $200 a month to Finance Company until she has paid the $4,000 and the contract ends. If the computer fails to work or Nancy has a good defense, such as fraud, against the contract with Computer Company, that defense may also be used against the assignee, Finance Company.

A contractual duty can be delegated to someone else to perform unless the duty of performance is personal and must be performed by the original party. For example, Vic has a house for sale. Alex wants to buy the house. He can assume the **mortgage** (the amount owed) that Vic has on the house. Vic is under a duty to pay, but his duty can be delegated to Alex if Alex is financially qualified. Now Alex is primarily liable on the mortgage, but Vic still is liable if Alex fails to pay. A person who owes a duty is not relieved of the duty if he delegates it to someone else to perform. If the performance is personal in nature, such as a contract with a surgeon to perform a heart transplant, the surgeon has no right to delegate this duty to a third person, even another surgeon, without the consent of the patient.

Exhibit 9–9 summarizes third-party rights.

Remedies and Damages

Breach of contract is the failure to perform what a party to a contract is under an absolute duty to perform—in other words, to do what he or she promised to do. Once a party fails to perform or performs inadequately, the other party (the nonbreaching party) can choose one or more of several remedies. A **remedy**, in contract law, is the relief provided for an innocent party when the other party has breached the contract. A remedy enforces a right or gives redress to an injury. Strictly speaking, the remedy is not a part of a lawsuit; it is the end result of the lawsuit.

The most common remedies available to a nonbreaching party are the equitable remedies of rescission and restitution, specific performance of the contract, and reformation of the contract, and the legal remedy of money damages.

Equitable Remedies Rescission of the contract means that the parties are restored to their original positions before the contract was made. Recission is available when fraud, a mistake, duress, or failure of consideration occurs. If the contract is rescinded, each party must return any money or items that he or she received from the other party under the contract. Giving back the items is called **restitution**. Restitution prevents unjust enrichment.

Specific performance of a contract is not allowed very often. If money damages would be an inadequate remedy and a contract involves land or a piece of unique personal property, the court may grant the equitable remedy of specific per-

Exhibit 9–9 **Third-Party Rights**

Assignment	An assignment is the transfer of *rights* under a contract to a third party whereby the rights of the assignor (the person making the assignment) may be extinguished, and the assignee (the person to whom the rights are assigned) has a right to demand performance from the other original party to the contract. Generally all rights are assignable except where the law prohibits such, the contract prohibits assignment, or where the assignment would materially alter or increase the duties of the original party to the contract.
Delegation	A delegation is the transfer of *duties* under a contract to a third party whereby the delegate (the third party) assumes the obligation of performing the contractural duties previously held by the delegator (the one making the delegation). Generally duties cannot be delegated because most duties are personal or their delegation is prohibited by contract.

formance by ordering each party to perform the specific promises in the contract. Specific performance can be ordered for contracts relating to unique goods and real estate, but not for those relating to personal services.

Reformation of the contract occurs when the contract needs to be rewritten (reformed) because of errors in the written document. The court orders the contract to be reformed in accordance with the true intentions of the parties.

Legal Remedies   Nonbreaching parties most often seek the legal remedy of money damages. The two most common damages sought in a contract case are **compensatory damages** and **consequential damages**.

Compensatory Damages   Compensatory damages make up for the money lost by the injured party because the other party has breached the contract. The damages place the party, as nearly as possible, where he or she would have been if the contract had been performed.

Consequential Damages   Consequential damages, on the other hand, are foreseeable damages that result when a party breaches the contract. The damages arise, not directly out of the contract, but as a consequence of it.

For example, TV Systems Manufacturer contracts to sell for $40,000 four wide-screen television sets with full Dolby sound to Stereo Systems. The delivery date is December 1. Stereo Systems plans immediately to resell the television

sets and to make a profit of $15,000. TV Systems Manufacturer is aware of Stereo Systems' resell plans. On November 25, TV calls up Stereo Systems to say that the television sets will not be delivered and that the contract has been canceled. Stereo Systems purchases from another manufacturer equivalent televisions for $50,000. Stereo Systems can sue TV for compensatory damages in the amount of $10,000—the difference between the open market price, $50,000, and the contract price, $40,000 (plus any costs incurred because of the breach). In addition, Stereo Systems is entitled to any foreseeable loss it can prove, which in this illustration would be lost profits.

Exhibit 9–10 summarizes the remedies available for a breach of contract.

Discharge

A contract is usually discharged because it has been fully performed, but contracts can also be discharged in other ways.

Discharge by Agreement   If the contract has not been fully performed, the parties may agree to discharge the contract. An understanding of the enforceability of agreements that settle claims or discharge debts is important in the business world. The following agreements are the most frequent transactions: (1) accord and satisfaction, (2) covenant (agreement) not to sue, and (3) novation.

Accord and Satisfaction   The concept of **accord and satisfaction** involves a debtor's offer to settle

Exhibit 9–10 **Remedies for Breach of Contract**

LEGAL REMEDY	
Damages	A legal remedy designed to compensate the nonbreaching party for the loss of the bargain. By awarding money damages, the court tries to place the parties in the position they would have occupied had the contract been fully performed. The nonbreaching party frequently has a duty to *mitigate* (lessen or reduce) the damages incurred as a result of the contract's breach. There are two broad categories of damages: 1. *Compensatory Damages*—Compensate the nonbreaching party for injuries actually sustained and proved to have arisen directly from the loss of the bargain resulting from the breach of contract. 2. *Consequential Damages*—Damages resulting from special circumstances beyond the contract itself; they flow only from the consequences of a breach. For a party to recover consequential damages, the damages must be the foreseeable result of a breach of contract, and the breaching party must have known at the time the contract was formed that special circumstances existed and that the nonbreaching party would incur additional loss upon breach of the contract. Also called *special* damages.
EQUITABLE REMEDIES	
Rescission and Restitution	1. *Rescission*—An action to cancel the contract and return the parties to the positions they occupied prior to the transaction. Available when fraud, a mistake, duress, or failure of consideration is present. 2. *Restitution*—When a contract is rescinded, both parties must make restitution to each other by returning goods, property, or money previously conveyed. Restitution prevents the unjust enrichment of the defendant.
Specific Performance	An equitable remedy calling for the performance of the act promised in the contract. Only available in special situations—such as contracts for the sale of unique goods or land, and where monetary damages would be an inadequate remedy. Specific performance is not available as a remedy in breached contracts for personal services.
Reformation	An equitable remedy allowing a contract to be "reformed" or rewritten to reflect the parties' true intentions. Available when an agreement is imperfectly expressed in writing.

a debt he or she owes by a performance different from that originally agreed on and a creditor's acceptance of the offer. The accord is the agreement in which one of the parties agrees to perform—and the other party agrees to accept in satisfaction of a claim—an act either as originally agreed (when an accord is made, the original obligation is merely suspended) or different from that provided for in the original contract. Satisfaction takes place when the accord has been executed—that is, when the agreed performance has been completed. At that point, the accord and satisfaction are concluded and the debtor's obligation is discharged.

Covenant Not to Sue A **covenant not to sue** is a contract between the two parties agreeing that one person will give up his or her right to sue, usually in return for a settlement. For example, Brian is involved in an automobile accident because of Kay's negligence. Kay offers Brian $500 if he will release her from any further liability

Exhibit 9–11 **Discharge of a Contract by Agreement**

1. *Accord and satisfaction*—The agreement by one party to a contract to give or perform, and the other party to accept, something different from that which is purportedly owed in satisfaction of a contractual claim; the agreement is the accord, and the execution of the agreement is the satisfaction.

2. *Covenant not to sue*—An agreement not to sue on a present, valid claim.

3. *Novation*—A valid contract that substitutes a new party for one of the original parties thereby discharging the original contract.

resulting from the accident. Brian believes that the damages to his car will not exceed $400 and agrees to the release by signing a covenant not to sue. Later Brian discovers that the damage to his car is $600. Can Brian collect the balance of $100? The answer is no; Brian is limited to the $500 by the covenant not to sue. He no longer has the right to file a negligence lawsuit.

Novation A **novation** is a contract entered into by the parties whereby one party is substituted for another party; that is, one party is completely discharged from the contract, and another is substituted. The discharged party is no longer liable under the original contract.

Exhibit 9–11 summarizes the ways in which a contract can be discharged by agreement.

Discharge by Operation of Law A contract may also be discharged by operation of law. Alteration of the contract, running of the time prescribed in

a statute of limitations, a discharge decree in bankruptcy, or objective impossibility of performance due to the death of one of the parties or the destruction of the specific subject matter of the contract can cause a contract to be discharged.

If the terms of the contract have been altered unilaterally by one party without the knowledge of the other party, the contract may be discharged because there was no meeting of the minds on the part of the contract changed. If a contract has been breached, the harmed party must file his or her lawsuit during a certain time period prescribed in a statute of limitations. If the time period during which the harmed party could have sued has passed, the contract is discharged. In addition, if one of the parties goes into bankruptcy and receives a discharge from the court, or he or she dies or becomes mentally incompetent, and that person's performance is essential to completion of the contract, the contract ends.

Making Sure You Are Insured

A common problem confronted by businesses involves consumer complaints about the provided product or service. For example, you go to Jim Onest Insurance Agency to purchase automobile liability insurance coverage. Mr. Onest obtains all the necessary information to bind your vehicle for coverage and records this information in his computer. You pay the initial premium and leave his office. Shortly after you leave, a power failure causes all the information contained in the computer to be lost.

As you are driving down the street, you overlook a stop sign and collide with a vehicle that had the right of way. No personal injuries are sustained, but extensive property damage does occur to the other vehicle. You contact Mr. Onest to inform him of the accident. He attempts to verify coverage but cannot do so because the information in the computer has been lost. He forgets about your check and informs you that there is no coverage.

This simple example illustrates all of the aspects of contract law. When you went to the insurance agency, you made an offer to purchase insurance, which was accepted. Legal consideration was present because the promises were bargained for and exchanged, and each party received a legal benefit and suffered a legal detriment. Lack of capacity or having an illegal contract is not at issue here. In most states, this type of contract does not have to be in writing to be enforceable. You have proof of this contract in your canceled check. By not recognizing your contract, Mr. Onest has breached it.

You should have done several things, however, in order to protect yourself. While you were in his office, you should have asked for the name of the company that was insuring you, obtained the policy number, and requested a receipt instead of relying on your check as your receipt.

If you filed a lawsuit, you would seek compensatory damages amounting to the cost of repairs to the other vehicle. In most states, you could also recover your attorney's fees and court costs. On the other hand, if you had obtained the specifics of who, what, when, where, and how much before you left the office, this lawsuit could have been avoided.

Summary

This chapter has emphasized basic contract law. The Industrial Revolution resulted in the production of more goods, which in turn gave rise to an increased number of commercial disputes. In response, commercial law was developed. The Uniform Commercial Code has eleven articles of which Article 2, Sales, is the important article for contract law.

Contracts are divided into three elements: formation, enforceability, and performance. The following terms describe the types of formation of a contract: formal and informal contracts, unilateral and bilateral contracts, express and implied-in-fact contracts, and quasi-contracts (implied-in-law)

contracts. Enforceability of a contract is described as valid, void, voidable, or unenforceable. The performance status of the contract is either executed or executory.

To have a valid and enforceable contract, the parties must ensure that the following items are present:

1. Offer: An offer must be made.
2. Acceptance: An acceptance must be given by return promise or by an act.
3. Consideration: Promises must be bargained for and exchanged, have legal value, and be legally sufficient to support the offer and acceptance.

4. Capacity: The parties must have the capacity to form a contract.

5. Legality: The subject matter of the contract must be legal.

6. Writing: Certain agreements must be in writing to be enforceable.

An offer and an acceptance represent the concept of mutual assent or a meeting of the minds. To have a valid offer: (1) the offeror must have an objective intent to contract, (2) the terms must be reasonably definite (the UCC liberalizes this rule), and (3) the terms must be communicated. An offer may be terminated by revocation, rejection (including a counteroffer), and by operation of law.

Acceptance is a voluntary act by which the offeree agrees to the terms of the offer. Silence normally does not constitute acceptance. The UCC includes specific rules as to when an acceptance is valid for a contract for the sale of goods. Sometimes there is an appearance of a meeting of the minds because an offer and an acceptance have been made, but, in reality, mutual consent has not been given because of fraud, mistake, duress, or undue influence.

Legal consideration has two elements: bargained for and exchanged promises and the giving of something of legal value and sufficiency (that is, a legal benefit to the promisor or a legal detriment to the promisee). The courts normally are not concerned with the adequacy of consideration, only with the sufficiency.

The parties must have the capacity to contract. Minors and most mentally incompetent people can enter into contracts, but these contracts are voidable. A minor is liable for necessary items, but only to the extent of the reasonable value of the property or services actually used. When disaffirmance occurs, a minor must give back whatever she or he can return that was obtained under the contract. If a court has determined a person to be mentally incompetent, that person's contracts made thereafter are void.

A valid contract must have a legal object or subject matter. The general rule is that an illegal agreement is void. The law requires certain contracts to be in writing to be enforceable, but the law also allows other ways to prove a contract than by a written document.

Contractual rights and duties can be transferred to a third person through assignment of the rights or delegation of the duties.

Whenever a party breaches his or her contractual commitments, he or she is liable for the damages caused. The injured party has a right to the legal remedy of recovering money damages or to the equitable remedies of rescission and restitution, specific performance, or reformation.

Contracts can be discharged by acts or agreement of the parties (such as performance, accord and satisfaction, covenant not to sue, or novation) or by operation of the law (such as unilateral alteration of a written contract, passing of the period prescribed in a statute of limitations, discharge in bankruptcy, or objective impossibility of performance due to death or insanity of a party or the destruction of the specific subject matter of the contract).

Key Terms

acceptance (**192**)
accord and satisfaction (**215**)
age of majority (**208**)
assignee (**214**)
assignment (**214**)
assignor (**214**)
bargained for and exchanged (**205**)
bilateral contract (**193**)
breach of contract (**214**)
capacity (**195**)

collateral contracts (**211**)
compensatory damages (**215**)
consequential damages (**215**)
consideration (**195**)
contract (**192**)
counteroffer (**198**)
covenant not to sue (**216**)
delegation (**214**)
disaffirm (**208**)
duress (**204**)
executed contract (**194**)

executory contract (**194**)
express contract (**193**)
firm offer (**199**)
formal contract (**193**)
fraud (**204**)
implied-in-fact contract (**193**)
informal contract (**194**)
legal benefit (**205**)
legal detriment (**205**)
legality (**195**)
legal value (**205**)

merchant **(199)**	operation of law **(198)**	restitution **(214)**
misrepresentation **(204)**	option contract **(199)**	Statute of Frauds **(211)**
mirror-image rule **(200)**	promissory estoppel **(199)**	undue influence **(204)**
mortgage **(214)**	quasi-contract **(193)**	unenforceable contract **(194)**
mutual assent **(203)**	ratification **(208)**	unilateral contract **(193)**
mutual mistake **(204)**	reformation **(215)**	unilateral mistake **(204)**
novation **(217)**	rejection **(192)**	valid contract **(194)**
offer **(192)**	rejection **(198)**	void agreement **(194)**
offeree **(192)**	remedy **(214)**	voidable contract **(194)**
offeror **(192)**	revocation **(198)**	

Questions and Case Problems

1. James is confined to his bed. He calls a friend who lives across the street and offers to sell her his watch next week for $100. If his friend wants to accept, she is to put a red piece of paper in her front window. The next morning, she places a red piece of paper in her front window. Is this contract bilateral or unilateral? Explain.

 2. Six Industries, Inc., is a general contractor for the construction of an insurance building. Six Industries entered into a subcontract with Kirk Williams Company for heating and air-conditioning the building. As a standard practice on projects of this size, the contract between the parties was changed by formal written change orders on several occasions. Near completion of the building, Six Industries submitted two last change orders. Kirk Williams refused to sign or complete the change orders because it claimed that Six Industries had delayed the project to the detriment of Kirk Williams. Six Industries issued a check to Kirk Williams for $14,850.04. On the check, the following language appeared: "Endorsement and/or negotiation of the check constitutes a full and complete release of Six Industries, Inc., and acknowledges full payment of all monies due." Kirk Williams received the check in the normal course of business and deposited it. Is there an accord and satisfaction through the cashing of the check? Explain. [Kirk Williams Co. v. Six Industries, Inc., 11 Ohio. App. 3d 152, 463 N.E.2d 1266 (1983)]

 3. The Olivers were planning to sell off some of their ranch land and mentioned this fact to Southworth, a neighbor. Southworth expressed interest in purchasing the property and later notified the Olivers that he had the money available to buy it. The Olivers told Southworth they would let him know shortly about the details concerning the sale. The Olivers later sent a letter to Southworth—and (unknown to Southworth) to several other neighbors—giving information about the sale, including the price, the location of the property, and the amount of acreage involved. When Southworth received the letter, he sent a letter to the Olivers "accepting" their offer. The Olivers stated that the information letter had not been intended as an "offer" but merely as a starting point for negotiations. Southworth

brought suit against the Olivers to enforce the "contract." Did a contract exist? [Southworth v. Oliver, 284 Or. 361, 587 P.2d 994 (1978)]

 4. In 1982, Webster Street Partnership, Ltd. (Webster) entered into a lease agreement with Matthew Sheridan and Pat Wilwerding. Webster was aware that both Sheridan and Wilwerding were minors. Both tenants were living away from home, apparently with the understanding that they could return home at any time. Sheridan and Wilwerding paid the first month's rent, but then failed to pay the rent for the next month and vacated the apartment. Webster sued them for breach of contract. They claimed that the lease agreement was voidable since they were minors. Who will win, and why? [Webster Sreet Partnership, Ltd. v. Sheridan, 220 Neb. 9, 368 N.W.2d 439 (1985)]

 5. James owned timber that he desired to sell. Notices were sent to numerous potential buyers for bids (offers) for the timber. Eames responded by submitting the highest bid (offer), but James refused to go through with the transaction and Eames sued. What are the legal arguments for James and Eames? [Eames v. James, 452 So.2d 384 (La.App. 1984)]

 6. Vrgora, a general contractor, entered into a contract with the Los Angeles Unified School District (LAUSD) to construct an automotive service shed and a specifically enclosed room outfitted with an electronic vehicle performance tester. The contract called for damages of $100 per day if the project was not completed within 250 days. Vrgora was responsible for purchasing and installing the tester. A dispute between the manufacturer of the tester and Vrgora arose. The tester was finally delivered over six months later. As a result, Vrgora completed the project several months late. LAUSD now wants Vrgora to pay $20,700 in damages for failing to complete the contract within 250 days. Who should win and why? [Vrgora v. Los Angeles Unified School District, 152 Cal. App. 3d 1178, 200 Cal. Rptr. 130 (1984)]

 7. Laemmar was an employee of J. Walter Thompson Company. During the years of his employment, he purchased shares of common stock from the company. Laemmar's stock was to be subject to repurchase by the company if Laemmar's employment was terminated for any reason. The officers and directors of the company decided to increase their control and demanded that Laemmar and several other employees sell their stock back to the company or lose their jobs. Although Laemmar did not want to sell his stock, he did so in order to keep his job. The officers and directors never made any physical threats or suggestions of physical harm to Laemmar. Later, Laemmar instituted a lawsuit to rescind his sale of the stock on the basis of duress. Can Laemmar rescind? Explain. [Laemmar v. J. Walter Thompson Co., 435 F.2d 680 (7th Cir. 1970)]

 8. Alchem, an Israeli corporation, manufactures and sells lightweight, small-sized, halogenated aerosol fire extinguishers. Alchem entered into a contract with Gerard that made Gerard its exclusive distributor outside of Israel. A condition in the contract required the approval of the Underwriters Laboratories (UL). A UL approval in the United States is an indication of safety, quality control, and reliability, and is required by almost all purchasers. Approval by the UL is essential if the product is to be marketed in the United States, but it means very little, if anything, outside the United States. UL approval takes a long time, ranging from a minimum of three years to a maximum of fifteen years. After seven years, Alchem still had not obtained UL approval. Naturally, Gerard did not sell any extinguishers in the United States. Alchem, however, did sell some fire extinguishers in territories to which it had given exclusive dealership to Gerard. Alchem and Gerard ended up in a lawsuit. Alchem argued that Gerard could have sold the product outside the United States and, by not doing so, it had acted in bad faith. Gerard argued that it did not have a duty to sell any products prior to UL approval. Which company is correct? Was there a mutual mistake? Please explain your answer. [Gerard v. Almouli, 746 F.2d 936 (2d Cir. 1984)]

Chapter 10 **Commercial Paper and Secured Transactions**

We promise according to our hopes, we perform according to our selfishness and our fears.

François de la Rochefoucauld (1613–1680)

OUTLINE

Introduction

Contracts are essential for the existence of a market economy. Many contracts are completed simply by the exchange of an item for money; for example, you purchase a textbook and pay the cashier. Other contracts, especially those involving large sums of money, are not completed so quickly. For example, people generally do not purchase automobiles with cash. How does the buyer (debtor) purchase expensive goods or real estate, and how does the seller (creditor) protect himself, herself, or itself to ensure that the money it has loaned is paid back?

The answer is found in two concepts that the law has developed over the centuries: **commercial paper** and **secured transactions**.

Commercial paper has a very long history, going back to the age of Hammurabi, around 2100 B.C. In Europe, starting in the thirteenth century, traveling merchants used some form of commercial paper due to the problems of transporting and guarding gold and silver. In the early 1700s, the English Parliament adopted the first commercial paper statutes; these, in turn, have led to the present law of commercial paper. Today, in the United States, the law of commercial paper is found in the Uniform Commercial Code (UCC), Article 3. Under Article 3 of the UCC, commercial paper consists of negotiable instruments (signed writings that contain an unconditional promise or order to pay an exact sum of money either on demand or at a specified time in the future) in the form of drafts, checks, notes, or certificates of deposits.

Secured transactions are nearly as old as commercial paper; they date back to Roman times. A secured transaction has two parts: First, a debtor and a creditor have a contract in which the debtor agrees to repay the creditor the money he or she has lent the debtor or to repay the credit extended to the debtor. Second, the debtor promises the creditor that he or she can take specific property (personal or real) that belongs to the debtor if the debtor fails to repay the debt. If the debtor is in default the creditor can then repossess and sell the property, and use the proceeds to pay the debt. The law of secured transactions is found in the Uniform Commercial Code, Article 9.

In this chapter, we will review some of the more important provisions of the law concerning commercial paper, the banking system, and secured transactions. Each of these areas is very complex and can only be reviewed briefly in a legal environment textbook.

Functions of Commercial Paper

Commercial paper has the dual purposes of substituting for currency and serving as a credit device.

A Substitute for Money

The financial system does not have enough currency to meet all the needs of society. For centuries commercial paper has been used, as it still is today, as a substitute for money. Seldom does anyone in our society actually use money to purchase an automobile, a residence, a business, or any other large purchase. Commercial paper is used because it is convenient and safe.

A Credit Device

Commercial paper is one method by which credit is extended to debtors. For example, Ed Foster wants to purchase an automobile but needs to borrow money to finance the purchase. When Ed borrows money from a financial institution, the Anywhere Bank of Iowa, he signs a type of commercial paper called a **promissory note**. In it, Ed promises to repay the money he owes. See Exhibit 10–1 for a sample note.

Parties to Commercial Paper

Who the parties to commercial paper are may seem confusing at first because two types of commercial paper exist. One type (which involves a promise to pay) has two parties to the instrument (either a note or a certificate of deposit) while the other type (which involves an order to pay) has three parties (either a check or a draft).

Exhibit 10–1 **A Sample Note**

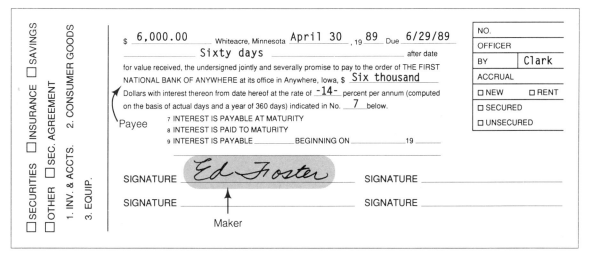

Makers and Payees

The first type of commercial paper (called a "promise to pay") has two parties: the **maker** and the **payee**. A maker is the person who signs and issues an instrument with a *promise* to pay a certain sum of money to a payee. To **issue** means to deliver the instrument involved for the first time. The maker's signature must appear on the face of the commercial paper if the maker is to be liable. The payee is the person to whom an instrument is made payable. The maker is usually the debtor to the payee.

For example, Gary Ross goes to Citizen's Bank, where he has an account, to purchase a **certificate of deposit** (**CD**). Ross is lending the bank his money, and he expects to earn interest on it. Ross is considering the purchase of one of three lake lots within the next six months and may need the CD as a down payment. Therefore Ross wants the CD payable to **bearer** (person who has physical possession of the instrument). Citizen's Bank signs the certificate of deposit as a maker and issues the CD to Ross payable to bearer. See Exhibit 10–2 for a sample certificate of deposit.

Drawers, Drawees, and Payees

The second type of commercial paper (called an "order to pay") has three parties: **drawers, draw-ees**, and payees. One party (the drawer) creates an instrument that *orders* another party (the drawee) to pay money, usually to a third party (the payee). The payee can be either a specific person or anyone who is the bearer of the instrument. The drawee is a debtor of the drawer.

A **draft** (historically referred to as a bill of exchange) is an instrument drawn on a drawee (not necessarily a bank) which orders the drawee to pay money, usually to a third party. In the business world, a trade acceptance is a form of a draft frequently used in the payment for the sale of goods.

For example, Travis Lake Fabrics sells $50,000 worth of fabric to Quilts Plus, Inc. each fall on terms requiring payment to be made in ninety days. One year Travis Lake needs cash, so it draws a *trade acceptance* that orders Quilts Plus to pay $50,000 to the order of Travis Lake Fabrics ninety days hence. Travis Lake presents the paper to Quilts Plus. Quilts Plus *accepts* by signing the face of the paper and returns it to Travis Lake Fabrics. Quilts Plus' acceptance creates an enforceable promise to pay the instrument when it comes due in ninety days. Travis Lake can sell the trade acceptance in the commercial money market more easily than it can assign the $50,000 account receivable. Trade acceptances are the standard credit instruments in sales transactions. See Exhibit 10–3 for a sample trade acceptance.

Exhibit 10–2 A Sample Small Certificate of Deposit

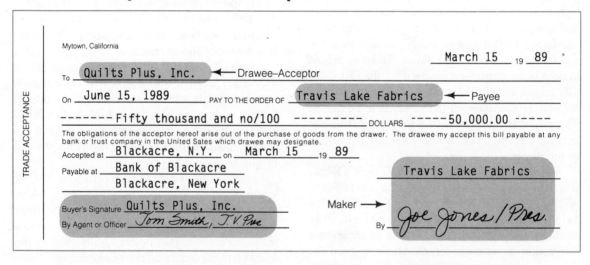

Exhibit 10–3 A Sample Time Draft—Trade Acceptance

A **check** is the most commonly used three-party instrument. For example, Marilyn Hicks has a checking account at the First National Bank of Anytown. She plans to pay for her new automobile by check. She signs the check as the drawer and issues it to Car Company, the payee. On the face of the check, she orders the drawee, First National Bank, to pay the amount written on the face of the check to the payee, Car Company. See Exhibit 10–4 for a sample check.

Indorsers and Indorsees

If commercial paper is to be used as a substitute for currency, a method to transfer an order instrument from the payee to a third person must exist. This method of transfer is simple. The payee indorses (signs) the instrument on the back and delivers it to another person. The payee is the **indorser**, and the person who receives the instrument is the **indorsee**. Thus, indorsement means

Exhibit 10–4 A Sample Check

to sign on the back of the instrument for the purpose of transferring the ownership. The various types of indorsements will be explored later in this chapter.

For example, Marie Holland, a medical doctor, receives a check for $125 from a patient. Marie wants to purchase some software for her computer from Positive Logic Computer Company. She indorses (signs her name) on the back of the check and delivers it to Positive Logic. Marie is both the payee on the check and the indorser on the back of the check. Positive Logic is the indorsee and is entitled to the $125. Positive Logic can then indorse the check to someone else and become an indorser as well.

Bearers

A bearer is any person who has physical possession of an instrument that either is payable to anyone without designation or is indorsed in blank. The maker or drawer controls whether the instrument will have a named payee or whether a bearer is entitled to payment. Often the instrument will be made out as "payable to bearer," which means that any person who physically has possession of the commercial paper is entitled to the payment. At other times, a maker or a drawer will not name a payee but will make the commercial paper out to "Cash." Again, whoever has possession is entitled to the payment.

An instrument can also become a bearer instrument through the action of the indorser. When the payee indorses the instrument on the back, as Marie did in the example above, this indorsement is called a **blank indorsement**. This type of indorsement makes the instrument payable to any bearer because the indorser, Marie, did not name another payee in her indorsement, although she had the right to do so. See Exhibit 10–5 for a sample blank indorsement.

Exhibit 10–5 A Sample Blank Indorsement

Marie Holland

Holders and Holders in Due Course

Commercial paper can be held by one of two designees: the **holder** or the **holder in due course** (**HDC**). Legally the two have very different rights.

Holder   A holder is a person who possesses a commercial paper "drawn, issued, or indorsed to him or his order or to bearer or in blank." [UCC 1-201(20)] A holder is one of two people: First, the holder may be the original payee. Second, if the payee has transferred the commercial paper to another, that person (also called the transferee) is a holder and has the status of an assignee of a contract right. As an assignee the holder obtains only those rights that his or her predecessor-transferor had in the instrument. If there is a conflicting, superior claim or defense to the instrument, an ordinary holder is not able to collect payment.

The holder is usually the owner of the commercial paper but not necessarily. For example, Valdez takes a check made payable to him. He indorses the check on the back in blank, anticipating that he will deposit the check in his bank in the afternoon. He misplaces the check, and someone steals it. The thief is a holder under the law; even though, obviously, he or she is not the owner, the thief can legally transfer the check (a bearer instrument because of Valdez's blank indorsement) to another person and that person can collect the money. This third person now becomes the holder.

Holder in Due Course   A holder in due course is a special-status transferee of negotiable commercial paper. An HDC has a very special and protected standing within the law. If a holder has acquired the instrument in a manner that meets the UCC requirements, the holder transforms his or her position from that of ordinary holder to that of holder in due course. An HDC is *normally* immune to any defenses (excuses) asserted by the drawer or maker against paying the instrument.

The reason that an HDC is protected by the law is that commercial paper is used as a substitute for currency. If people are going to accept commercial paper as a substitute, they must have some protection. The law, therefore, does not allow the drawer or maker many reasons for not paying the instrument that he or she signed.

In order to become an HDC, a holder of a negotiable instrument must meet three requirements. The holder must take the instrument (1) for value, (2) in good faith, and (3) without notice that it is overdue or is defective. [UCC 3-302]

The underlying requirement of due-course status is, of course, that a person must first be an ordinary holder of that instrument.

Value   An HDC must give value for the instrument. [UCC 303] A person who receives an instrument as a gift or who inherits the instrument has not met the requirement of value. In these situations, the person remains an ordinary holder and does not possess the rights of an HDC. The concept of value in the law of negotiable instruments is not the same as the concept of consideration in the law of contracts. For example, under contract law a promise to pay a debt the person already owes is not consideration, but a holder taking an instrument in payment of a prior debt has given value. Likewise, an executory promise (a promise to perform or pay in the future) is valid consideration to support a contract, but does not constitute value to qualify a holder as an HDC. Therefore, a holder takes the instrument for value only to the extent the consideration has been actually performed or paid. For example, Lori makes out a check for $500 payable to Rory on Sunday. Rory is in the need of funds but cannot cash the check until Monday. Rory negotiates the check to Gary who pays Rory $200 in cash and promises Rory he will pay the balance on Friday when he gets his paycheck. Gary has only given value in the amount of $200 and can only qualify as an HDC for that amount.

Good Faith   An HDC must take the instrument in good faith. [UCC 3-302(1)(b)] The purchaser-holder must act honestly in the process of acquiring the instrument. "Good faith" is defined as honesty in fact in the conduct of the transaction concerned. [UCC 1-201(19)] The good-faith requirement applies only to the holder; whether the transferor acted in good faith is immaterial. Thus, a person who in good faith takes a negotiable instrument from a thief can be an HDC.

Without Notice   HDC protection is not given to a person who acquires an instrument knowing, or having reason to know, that it is defective in any one of the following ways: It is overdue, it has been dishonored, there is a defense against it, or there is another claim to it. [UCC 3-302(1)(c)] Before taking the instrument, a person should examine it to see if there is anything wrong with it (any erasures or words crossed out) and to see if the time for payment has passed. The following case emphasizes this issue.

BACKGROUND AND FACTS *Chalfont Industries was a manufacturer of an automotive product. Kutner Buick was an automobile dealer. Chalfont Industries and Kutner Buick maintained a close relationship: Kutner Buick was wholly owned by Jules Kutner, and Chalfont Industries was wholly owned by Jules's son, Jerome. From December 1981 to February 1982, Chalfont negotiated with Sturart Crawford concerning the possible purchase of a distributorship. During the negotiations, Chalfont made a number of false representations to Crawford relating to the product and the distributorship. Chalfont drafted a contract and sent the draft to Crawford. Crawford's attorney redrafted the contract.*

Crawford went to Chalfont's office to sign the redrafted contract. Crawford presented the contract and wrote a check in the amount of $42,023 to Chalfont. One of Chalfont's employees took the contract and check into Jerome's office for him to sign, while Crawford was made to wait in the outer office. The employee came out and gave Crawford the signed contract, but that contract was not the one Crawford had presented; it was, rather, a substitute one. Immediately after Crawford left Chalfont's offices, Jerome indorsed and delivered the check to Kutner Buick, which immediately deposited the check.

On discovering the fraud, Crawford successfully stopped payment on the check. When the check was presented to Crawford's bank for payment out of Crawford's account, the bank refused to pay because of the stop-payment order. Crawford's bank sent the check back to Kutner Buick's bank, which withdrew the amount out of Kutner Buick's account; thus, Kutner Buick was out of pocket $42,023.

Crawford reentered negotiations with Chalfont. Finally, Crawford had a cashier's check drawn in the amount of $50,023. He mailed the check to Chalfont. Later, however, Crawford had misgivings after Chalfont's national sales manager called and warned Crawford to stop payment on his check. Crawford instructed his lawyer to try to stop payment while he went to Chalfont's office to intercept the check. Crawford's attorney went to court and obtained a restraining order that prohibited the bank from paying the check.

Crawford waited for two days in Chalfont's offices after Chalfont's employee told him that he could have the check on arrival. He was told the check had not arrived. In fact, the check had been received, and Chalfont already had indorsed and delivered it to Kutner Buick. Kutner Buick deposited the check into its bank account.

Crawford's bank was caught in a legal bind. The bank could not refuse to pay a cashier's check, but it could not disobey the judicial restraining order that prohibited payment. The bank did not pay the check, but filed an interpleader naming Chalfont, Kutner Buick, and Crawford as defendants. (An interpleader means that the bank has paid the money to the court

Case 10.1
BANKERS TRUST COMPANY OF WESTERN NEW YORK v. CRAWFORD
United States Court of Appeals, Third Circuit, 1986.
781 F.2d 39.

and is asking the court to decide who is entitled to the money.) The trial court ordered the bank to pay the check to Kutner Buick.

ROSENN, Judge.

* * * *

Crawford * * * argues that Kutner Buick was under a "duty to inquire" into the transactional circumstances surrounding the receipt of the check and, because it failed to do so, did not take the check in good faith. * * *

In Pennsylvania, a holder in due course is a person "who takes the instrument: (1) for value; (2) in good faith; and (3) without notice that it is overdue or has been dishonored or of any defense or claim to it on the part of any person." * * * A holder in due course takes an instrument free of all defenses except for fraud in factum and such illegality as would render the obligation of the party a nullity. * * * Therefore, if Kutner Buick was a holder in due course, it is not subject to defenses arising from the underlying transaction, and properly received the check proceeds regardless of any defenses Crawford has against Chalfont.

* * * *

Crawford * * * argues, as he did in the trial court, that Kutner Buick was not a holder in due course because it did not take the check in good faith. In order to have taken in good faith, Crawford maintains, Kutner Buick had a duty to inquire into the circumstances surrounding transfer of the check. The district court held that the proper test for determining good faith is to ascertain whether the transferee exhibited willful dishonesty or actual knowledge, and that the evidence did not demonstrate that Kutner Buick was guilty of either.

* * * *

* * * In this case * * * the district court made three insurmountable findings of fact that are supported by the record and are not clearly erroneous.

There is no evidence that Jules Kutner or any employee of Kutner Buick knew or had reason to know of Crawford's attempt to stop or reclaim the cashier's check.

There is no evidence that Jules Kutner or any employee of Kutner Buick knew or had reason to know of the occurrence of substance of any conversations between Crawford and employees of Chalfont.

There is no evidence that the failure of Jules Kutner or any employee of Kutner Buick to make any inquiries about the cashier's check stemmed from any desire to evade knowledge of Crawford's efforts to stop the check.

These findings contrast sharply with the facts of *Norman v. World Wide Distributors, Inc.,* also cited by appellant. In *Norman,* the appellate court found that the transferee of the note had been previously purchasing similar notes from the seller and its suspicions had been aroused sufficiently concerning the honesty of the underlying transaction as to prompt a call to the maker of the note in question "whether they were satisfied with the transaction." Moreover, the court concluded that the frequency with which the transferors changed their operating name—three times in one year—and the sale of the note made payable three days after the date of its execution to the transferee at a substantial discount were circumstances that imposed a duty upon the transferee of the note to have inquired further into the sales operation of the seller of the notes. Thus, in *Norman,* there were circumstances in the negotiation of the note itself, as well as other strong circumstances, suggesting irregularities in the underlying transaction for the note.

Thus, it appears from an analysis of the foregoing case that Pennsylvania consistently follows the common law rule adopted by * * * the Uniform Commercial Code that there is no affirmative duty of inquiry on the part of one taking a negotiable instrument, and there is no constructive notice from the circumstances of the transaction, unless the circumstances are so strong that if ignored they will be deemed to establish bad faith on the part of the transferee.

The close relationship between the father and son, the unusual financial transactions between Kutner Buick and Chalfont, the extensive loans and guarantees of the father personally and of Kutner Buick and the advance of the bankruptcy filing fee, may raise questions as to how much Kutner Buick knew of the frauds practiced by Chalfont. The district court, however, found no evidence from the circumstances of the negotiation of the Crawford cashiers check or from the face of the instrument as would impose an affirmative duty on Kutner Buick to inquire into the underlying transaction. Kutner Buick apparently received the cashier's check in substitution for the check of February 10 on which Crawford had stopped payment. We have carefully reviewed the record and we can find nothing in the circumstances pertaining to the actual negotiation of the Crawford check or from the face of the check to put Kutner Buick on notice of any infirmity in the underlying transaction to suggest an affirmative duty of inquiry by Kutner Buick.

Although the detestable fraud practiced upon Crawford by Chalfont commands a searching inquiry into the validity of the negotiation of the check, we are confronted by very broad principles of public policy that support the circulation and credit of negotiable instruments. We are constrained to conclude that under Pennsylvania law Kutner Buick accepted the cashier's check as a holder in due course.

DECISION AND REMEDY

The court affirmed the judgment of the trial court. Crawford was a victim of Chalfont's fraud. Crawford could not collect the amount of the check from Chalfont because Chalfont filed for bankruptcy, nor can Crawford collect the amount from Kutner Buick because it is a holder in due course. Crawford is out the money.

COMMENT

The court upheld the law of negotiable instruments and, by doing so, upheld the policy behind it. If negotiable instruments are to be treated as substitutes for money, even in a case such as this one where a hardship is imposed on one party, the public's faith in the use of negotiable instruments must be maintained.

Types of Commercial Paper

Four types of instruments (commercial paper) are set out in UCC 3-104: certificates of deposit, notes, drafts, and checks. All of these instruments fall into one of two categories: **promises to pay** or **orders to pay**.

Generally, instruments classified as promises to pay are two-party instruments, such as notes and certificates of deposit, and they are used as credit devices. Instruments that are classified as orders to pay are three-party instruments and are used in lieu of cash, such as checks and drafts.

Promises to Pay

The two most common types of promises to pay are promissory notes and certificates of deposit.

Promissory Notes The promissory note is a written promise to pay (other than a certificate of deposit) made between two parties. [UCC 3-104(2)(d)] One party is the maker of the promise to pay and the other is the payee, the one to whom the promise is made. A promissory note, commonly referred to as a *note,* can be made payable at a definite time or on demand. Notes are commonly used by banks and by other financial institutions to document a loan of money.

Various types of credit transactions use notes. Often the name of the type of loan appears in the name of the note. For example, a promissory note to repay money lent to purchase real property is called a **mortgage note**. A mortgage is a separate document by which the debtor agrees to repay the money lent on the note; if he or she fails to repay, the creditor can take the property, sell it, and use the proceeds to pay what is owed on the mortgage note. Although the note is not the mortgage, it lets others know that payment on it is secured (or backed up) by a mortgage.

Similarly, a **collateral note** indicates that money was lent to a debtor to purchase personal property. The item purchased, such as an automobile, is used to secure the repayment; that is, the automobile serves as collateral (hence the name of the note) to secure repayment of the loan. An **installment note** means that the note is payable by installments, such as when you pay for a stereo set over a twenty-four-month period. The names of these contracts overlap frequently. For example, if the stereo was given as collateral to secure repayment over the twenty-four months, the contract may be called a "collateral installment note."

Certificate of Deposit   A certificate of deposit (CD) is an acknowledgment by a bank of the receipt of money with an agreement to repay it. [UCC 3-104(2)(c)] Certificates of deposit pay interest, and are either negotiable or nonnegotiable instruments. Most large CDs ($100,000 or more) are negotiable. Their negotiability allows them to be sold, to be used to pay debts, or to serve as security (collateral) for a loan.

Orders to Pay

When an instrument is an order to pay, three parties are on the document. The drawer creates an instrument that orders the drawee to pay money, usually to a third party who is either a specific payee or a bearer. The drawer can make the instrument payable to himself or herself—for example, you can make a check out to yourself. The drawer "orders" the instrument to be paid by the drawee. The drawer does not "make" a promise to pay, which is the language used in instruments that have only two parties. The two most common orders to pay are drafts and checks.

Drafts   A draft is an unconditional written order. [UCC 3-104(2)(a)] The draft represents a debt owed by the drawee to the drawer. The debt has been made either by agreement or through a debtor-creditor relationship. Two types of drafts are recognized: **time drafts** and **sight drafts**. A time draft is a draft that is payable at a definite future

time. See Exhibit 10–3 for a sample time draft. A sight (or demand) draft is payable on sight. When the holder presents for payment a sight draft, such as a share draft used by a credit union, the draft is paid. Insurance companies use sight drafts to pay claims.

Checks   A check is drawn on a bank or financial institution, ordering it to pay a sum of money on demand. [UCC 3-104(2)(b)] The person who writes the check is called the drawer and is a depositor in the bank on which the check is drawn. The person to whom the check is payable is the payee. The bank on which the check is drawn is the drawee. If Dominic writes a check on his checking account to pay for his boat, he is the drawer, his bank is the drawee, and the boat seller is the payee.

Requirements for a Negotiable Instrument

Commercial paper is either **negotiable** or nonnegotiable. Both the form and content determine whether the instrument is negotiable. In order for an instrument to be negotiable, according to UCC 3-104(1), it must:

1. Be in writing
2. Be signed by the maker or drawer
3. Be an unconditional promise or order to pay
4. Be stated in a specific sum of money
5. Be payable on demand or at a definite time
6. Be payable to order or to bearer.

In Writing

Negotiable instruments must be written and they must be written on something that has permanence and on something that is portable so it can be freely transferred. It is impossible to transfer to a third party an oral promise with its danger of fraud and with the difficulty of determining liability. Having the negotiable instrument in writing makes it possible for it to be used as a substitute for currency.

Signed by the Maker or the Drawer

For an instrument to be negotiable, it must be signed by the maker of a note or certificate of deposit or by the drawer of a check or draft. [UCC 3-104(1)(a)] Extreme latitude is granted in determining what constitutes a signature. The word ''signed'' includes any symbol used by the party with the intention of authenticating the instrument. Various symbols can be used in lieu of the traditional written signature. Initials, an ''X,'' a thumbprint, or anything else will suffice if it is intended to be a signature.

Unconditional Promise or Order to Pay

The terms of payment must be included in the writing on the face of a negotiable instrument. The party who is holding the instrument must be able to look only at the instrument and determine what the terms are. These terms cannot be conditioned on an event or agreement. [UCC 3-104(1)(b)] The instrument cannot be controlled by events beyond the instrument itself. [UCC 3-105] If conditional promises had to be investigated by the holder, the use of these documents as a substitute for money would be dramatically reduced.

For an instrument to be negotiable, it must contain an express order or promise to pay a specific sum of money. A mere acknowledgment of the debt, which might logically imply a promise, is not sufficient. For example, the traditional note (IOU) is only an acknowledgment of indebtedness. The IOU is a written instrument, but it is not a negotiable one.

To Pay a Specific Sum of Money

A specific sum of money must be stated—at least in such a manner that the debtor can calculate the amount he or she must pay. [UCC 3-106] If the instrument's value were stated in terms of goods or services, it would be too difficult to ascertain the market value. For example, if the value in a ten year promissory note was stated in computer chips, what value does a sixty-four-bit chip have today as compared to its value in ten years?

Payable on Demand or at a Definite Time

A negotiable instrument must be payable on demand or at a definite time. [UCC 3-104(1)(c)] Clearly, the maker or drawee must know when he or she is required to pay. With an interest-bearing instrument, one must know the exact interval during which the interest will accrue in order to determine the present value of the instrument.

The very nature of the instrument may indicate that it is payable on demand. [UCC 3-108] For example, a check, by definition, is payable on demand. [UCC 3-104(2)(b)] Negotiable time drafts, on the other hand, are payable at a definite time that is specified on the face of the instrument. [UCC 3-109] The maker or drawee is under no obligation to pay until the specified time has arrived or elapsed.

Payable to Order or to Bearer

Because one function of a negotiable instrument is to substitute for money, freedom to transfer the instrument is an essential requirement. A negotiable instrument requires that it be ''payable to order or to bearer.'' [UCC 3-104(1)(d)] These words acknowledge that another person, unknown at the time that the instrument is issued and thus not the immediate payee, may eventually be the owner. These words or their equivalents must be present on both the three-party order-to-pay instruments and the two-party promise-to-pay instruments. If these words are not present, the instrument is nonnegotiable, and, therefore, it is only assignable and would be governed by contract law.

An instrument that states ''payable to order'' and that names a *specific payee* (named with certainty) is often referred to as **order paper**. [UCC 3-110] When no specific payee is designated so that essentially the instrument is payable to any person, the paper is called **bearer paper**. [UCC 3-111]

Assignment or Negotiation

Once issued, a negotiable instrument can be transferred by assignment or by negotiation. The critical distinction is this: Contract rights are *assigned* to a third party who has the status of an assignee and who has no better rights than the transferor-assignor, while a negotiable instrument is *negotiated* to a third person who if he or she has the status of an HDC and can have better rights than the transferor. Again, because negotiable instruments are used as substitutes for currency, a person who accepts an instrument wants to be reasonably certain that he or she can collect on it free from any defenses that may be asserted against the holder of a normal contract assignment.

Assignment

Assignment is a transfer of rights under a contract. Recall from Chapter 9 that, under general contract principles, a transfer by assignment from an assignor (the original party to the contract) to an assignee (the person buying the contract right) gives the assignee only those rights that the assignor has possessed. Any defenses to the contract that can be raised against the assignor can also be raised against the assignee. Nonnegotiable commercial paper cannot be negotiated but can be assigned. Furthermore, when a transfer fails to qualify as a negotiation, it becomes an assignment.

Negotiation

Negotiation is the transfer of a negotiable instrument in a manner such that the transferee becomes a holder. [UCC 3-202(1)] The holder, at the very least, receives the rights of the previous possessor. [UCC 3-201(1)] Unlike an assignment, a transfer by negotiation makes it possible for a holder to become a holder in due course and to receive more rights in the instrument than the prior possessor. [UCC 3-305] Two methods of negotiating an instrument exist that allow the receiver to become qualified as a holder or as an HDC.

Negotiating Order Paper   Order paper initially names a specific payee who is then able to indorse the instrument.

Two steps are required to negotiate (transfer) order paper: indorsement and delivery. For example, the Transco Company issues a payroll check "to the order of Wang." Wang takes the check to the supermarket, signs her name on the back (a blank indorsement), gives it to the cashier (a delivery), and receives cash. Wang has negotiated the check (an order instrument) by a blank indorsement and delivery to the supermarket. [UCC 3-202(1)] The supermarket is now an HDC because it took the check for value, in good faith, and without notice of any problems with the check.

Negotiating Bearer Paper   Bearer paper is negotiated by delivery alone. No indorsement is necessary. [UCC 3-202(1)] In an actual situation, the bank may require a person cashing a check indorsed in blank (now a bearer instrument) to sign the back of the check, but, technically, the signature on the back is not required for negotiation. The bank may require it for purposes of identification and verification that this person received the money. [UCC 3-505] The use of bearer paper involves more risk through loss or theft than does the use of order paper.

Assume Bob Brown writes a check "payable to cash" and hands it (a delivery) to Mary Maack. Brown has negotiated the check (bearer paper) to Maack by delivery alone. Maack places the check in her wallet, which is subsequently stolen. The thief has possession of the check. At this point, negotiation has not occurred, because delivery must be voluntary on the part of the transferor. If the thief "delivers" the check to an innocent party, negotiation will have occurred. All rights to the check will be passed absolutely to that party, and Maack will lose all rights to recover the proceeds of the check from that party. [UCC 3-305] Of course, she can recover her money from the thief, if the thief can be found.

Converting Order to Bearer Paper and Vice Versa   The method used for negotiation depends on the character of the instrument at the time the negotiation takes place. Once the payee has negotiated the instrument to a holder, the indorsement on the back determines whether the instrument is now order or bearer paper. For example, a check originally payable to "Cash" is bearer paper and is negotiated by delivery. If the check is subsequently indorsed "Pay to Jones," it now must be negotiated as order paper (by indorsement and delivery) because it now names a specific payee. [UCC 3-204(1)] Bearer paper may be converted to order paper if the back of the paper has a **special indorsement** (payable to a specific person), such as "pay to Wang. [signed] Joe Jones. See Exhibit 10–6 for a sample special indorsement. An instrument originally payable to the order of a named payee (order paper) and indorsed in blank (the payee signs only her or his name) becomes a bearer instrument. [UCC 3-204(2)]

Exhibit 10–6 A Sample Special Indorsement

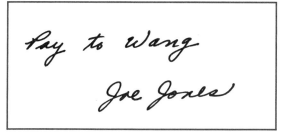

The following case discusses the difference between an assignment of a contract and the negotiation of an instrument. You will see that the transfer of an instrument that is not negotiable makes the new holder subject to all the defenses that the maker may have against the original payee.

BACKGROUND AND FACTS *A promissory note and purchase money mortgage (a lien taken by the seller or lender of the realty to secure the unpaid purchase price) were executed by the appellant, Holly Hill Acres, as maker in favor of Rogers and Blythe as payees. Subsequently, Rogers and Blythe pledged the promissory note and mortgage in question to the appellee, Charter Bank of Gainesville, to secure their own note. Charter Bank took the note and mortgage either under an assignment-of-a-contract theory or under the negotiation theory if the note was a negotiable instrument. Ultimately, both Rogers and Blythe and Holly Hill Acres defaulted (failed to pay) on their notes.*

Charter Bank sued both Rogers and Blythe and Holly Hill to recover payment on the promissory note executed by Holly Hill Acres. Charter Bank alleged that the note was a negotiable instrument and that the bank was a holder in due course. As a holder in due course, the bank claimed that it was entitled to collect on the note from Holly Hill Acres despite any underlying disputes between Rogers and Blythe and Holly Hill Acres.

Holly Hill Acres answered the complaint by alleging that Rogers and Blythe had defrauded it and that the note was not a negotiable instrument because the note incorporated by reference the terms of the purchase money mortgage. If the note was not negotiable, any defenses that Holly Hill had against Rogers and Blythe were also available against any assignee of Rogers and Blythe, such as Charter Bank.

The trial court ruled in a summary judgment that the note was negotiable and allowed the bank to recover. Holly Hill Acres appealed the decision.

Case 10.2
HOLLY HILL ACRES, LTD. v. CHARTER BANK OF GAINESVILLE
District Court of Appeal, Florida, 1975.
314 So.2d 209.

SCHEB, Judge.
* * * *
* * * The note * * * contains the following stipulation:
This note with interest is secured by a mortgage on real estate, of even date herewith, made by the maker hereof in favor of the said payee, and shall be construed and enforced according to the laws of the State of Florida. *The terms of said mortgage are by this reference made a part hereof.* (Emphasis supplied.)
* * * *

The note having incorporated the terms of the purchase money mortgage was not negotiable. The appellee Bank was not a holder in due course, therefore, the appellant was entitled to raise against the appellee any defenses which could be raised between the appellant and Rogers and Blythe. Since appellant asserted an affirmative defense of fraud, it was incumbent on the appellee to establish the nonexistence of any genuine issue of any material fact or the legal insufficiency of appellant's affirmative defense. Having failed to do so, appellee was not entitled to a judgment as a matter of law; hence, we reverse.

The note, incorporating by reference the terms of the mortgage, did not contain the unconditional promise to pay required by [UCC 3-104(1)(b)]. Rather, the note falls within the scope of [UCC 3-105(2)(a)]. * * *

* * * Mere reference to a note being secured by mortgage is a common commercial practice and such reference in itself does not impede the negotiability of the note. There is, however, a significant difference in a note stating that it is "secured by a mortgage" from one which provides, "the terms of said mortgage are by this reference made a part hereof." In the former instance the note merely refers to a separate agreement which does not impede its negotiability, while in the latter instance the note is rendered non-negotiable. * * *

As a general rule the assignee of a mortgage securing a non-negotiable note, even though a bona fide purchaser for value, takes subject to all defenses available as against the mortgagee. * * *

DECISION AND REMEDY *The appellate court ruled that the note was conditional on its face. A holder of the note had to look at the mortgage to determine all the terms of the note. As a result, the note was nonnegotiable, and Charter Bank was not a holder in due course. The court set aside the summary judgment and ordered a new trial. At the new trial, Holly Hill can assert the affirmative defense of fraud on the contract, note, and mortgage against both the bank and Rogers and Blythe.*

Defenses

Defenses by a party to avoid payment fall into two general categories: **real defenses** and **personal defense**. Real defenses are used to avoid payment to all holders of a negotiable instrument including an HDC. [UCC 3-305(2)] Personal defenses are used to avoid payment to an ordinary holder of a negotiable instrument. [UCC 3-306]

Real Defenses

Real (or universal) defenses are valid against all holders, including HDCs or holders who take an instrument through an HDC. (A holder who does not qualify as an HDC but who derives his or her title through an HDC acquires the rights and privileges of an HDC. [UCC 3-201] This is sometimes referred to as the "shelter principle.") The following are some of these defenses.

Forgery Forgery of a maker's or a drawer's signature cannot bind the person whose name is used unless that person ratifies the signature. [UCC 3-401 and 3-404(1)]

Fraud in Execution A person may be deceived into signing a negotiable instrument, as when a person believes that she or he is signing something other than a negotiable instrument (for example, a receipt). This is called fraud in execution. For instance, a consumer unfamiliar with the English language signs a paper presented by a salesperson as a request for an estimate. In fact, it is a promissory note. Even if the note is negotiated to an HDC, the consumer may have a valid defense based on the real defense of fraud in execution. This defense cannot be used if a reasonable person would or should not have been deceived as to the character of the instrument being signed.

Alteration An alteration is material if it changes the contract terms between any two parties in any way. Examples of material alterations are: changing the number or relations of the parties, completing the instrument in an unauthorized manner, or adding to or removing something from the writing after it has been signed. [UCC 3-407(1)] Material alteration is a complete defense against an ordinary holder but is at best only a partial defense against an HDC. A holder cannot recover anything on an instrument if it has been materially altered. [UCC 3-407(2)] If the original terms have been altered, such as the amount payable, the HDC can collect the original amount from the maker or drawer. If the instrument was incomplete and later completed in an unauthorized manner, alteration cannot be used as a defense as against an HDC, and the HDC can enforce the instrument as completed. [UCC 3-407(3)]

Bankruptcy When a debt represented by a negotiable instrument has been discharged (forgiven) in bankruptcy, that discharge is an absolute defense against paying the instrument to either a holder or an HDC. The purpose of bankruptcy is to settle and forgive all of the insolvent party's debts. [UCC 3-305(2)(d)]

Operation of Law When illegal conduct renders an instrument void, no payment can be made to either a holder or an HDC. If a person is declared mentally incompetent by state proceedings, any instrument issued by that person thereafter is null and void. The instrument is void from the beginning (time of issue) and unenforceable by any holder or an HDC. [UCC 3-305(2)(a)]

When a person signs and issues a negotiable instrument under such extreme duress as an immediate threat of force or violence (for example, at gunpoint), the instrument is void and unenforceable by any holder or HDC. [UCC 3-305(2)(a)]

Personal Defenses

All other defenses that are valid in a contract setting, such as breach of contract, breach of warranty, misrepresentation, mistake, undue influence, and duress, are considered personal defenses. These defenses are not valid against an HDC; only against an ordinary holder.

To illustrate: Penny owns a bar and wants to install a big-screen television for the patrons. Penny agrees to purchase from an acquaintance a big-screen television for $2,800. Slick, knowing his statements to be false, tells Penny that the television is only six months old and is in good working order. In addition, he tells Penny that he owns the television free and clear of all claims. Penny pays Slick $500 in cash and issues a negotiable promissory note for the balance. As it turns out, Slick still owes the original seller $500 on the purchase of the television, and the television is subject to a filed security interest (lien). In addition, the television is three years old. Penny can refuse to pay the note if it is held by an ordinary holder; but, if Slick has negotiated the note to an HDC, Penny must pay the HDC. Of course, Penny can then sue Slick. (Penny cannot use the FTC rule described in the next section because she owns a bar and therefore does not qualify as a consumer.)

Federal Limitations on Holder-in-Due-Course Rights

A Federal Trade Commission (FTC) rule has severely limited the preferential position enjoyed by an HDC in a **consumer credit transaction**. Payment by check is not a credit transaction for purposes of this FTC rule.

Prior to the FTC rule, the law giving preferential treatment to an HDC worked a severe hardship on consumers. For example, Ron, a consumer, buys a new wide-screen television from Shady TV Dealers for $2,500. Ron signs a promissory note to pay for the television; the payee is Shady TV Dealers. Shady turns around and sells the note (negotiates it) at a discounted amount to Better Bank. The bank, having paid value, taken the note in good faith, and taken it without notice of any problems with the note, qualifies as an HDC. Ron discovers the television is defective and will never work properly. This is a personal defense and naturally, he does not want to pay for it. The note, however, is now held by the bank, an HDC. Ron is forced to pay the bank on the note. The defenses Ron has on the contract for the purchase of the defective television are valid only against Shady TV Dealers, not the bank.

Now, under the FTC rule, this type of note is given as a part of a consumer credit **contract**. The note must contain a warning to any holder who may qualify as an HDC. It states that the holder of the note is subject to all contract defenses that the original purchaser may have against the original seller. In other words, in a consumer credit contract, even personal defenses are valid against an HDC. Ron can now use the defenses he has against both Shady TV Dealers and Better Bank.

Indorsements

As previously discussed, indorsements are required whenever the instrument being negotiated is classified as order paper. An indorsement is the signature of the person, known as the indorser, and is used to transfer ownership of the instrument to someone else. The indorsement may or may not include additional words or statements limiting liability, and it is written on the back of the instrument itself. The indorsement should be identical to the name that appears on the instrument. The payee or indorsee whose name is misspelled can indorse with the misspelled name, the correct name or both. [UCC 3-203]

Categories

Four categories of indorsements are recognized: blank, special, **qualified**, and **restrictive**.

Blank and Special Indorsements—Signature and Transfer Warranty Liability   Unless a blank or special indorser can claim a valid defense against the holder demanding payment, the indorser may be held liable by the holder on the instrument either on the basis of his or her signature (guaranty of payment) or on breach of warranties made on transfer of the instrument.

For signature liability, the blank and special indorser have what is called *secondary* liability. What this means is that their signature liability is dependent upon the instrument being properly presented to the person with the responsibility of paying it, that the instrument has been dishonored, and that the secondary party received timely notice of dishonor. [UCC 3-414]

Proper presentment requires the holder to present the instrument to the party responsible for its payment (for example a note to the maker), in a

proper manner (for example a check at the drawee bank or at the holder's bank to go through a clearing house), and on or before the instrument is due. [UCC 3-503, 3-504] Most improper presentments are the result of the holder's failure to present the instrument within a proper time. Time instruments must be presented on or before due date, and demand instruments (other than domestic checks) within a reasonable period after date or issue. For domestic checks, to hold blank and special indorsers liable on their signatures, the holder must present the check within seven days of the indorser's indorsement. [UCC 3-503(2)]

Dishonor usually occurs when the party responsible for payment fails to do so upon presentment. There are some actions that this party can require of the holder, and the holder's failure to comply relieves the party responsible to pay from constituting a dishonor of the instrument. [UCC 3-505]

Once dishonored, the holder is required to give notice (in any reasonable manner) to any secondary party the holder wishes to hold on signature liability. This notice must be given by a bank before midnight of the next banking day after receipt. For those other than a bank, the notice must be given before midnight of the third business day. Written notice is effective when sent even though it is not received. [UCC 3-308]

Should the holder fail to make proper presentment, or give the blank or special indorser proper notice of dishonor, the indorser is *completely discharged* from contract signature liability. [UCC 3-502]

In addition to possible signature liability of the blank and special indorser, these indorsers, if they receive consideration from the transferee, make five transfer warranties. [UCC 3-417(2)] These warranties flow to all subsequent holders of the instrument. The five warranties are:

1. The transferor has good title to the instrument or is otherwise authorized to obtain payment or acceptance on behalf of one who does have good title.
2. All signatures are genuine or authorized.
3. The instrument has not been materially altered.
4. No defense of any party is good against the transferor.

5. The transferor has no knowledge of any insolvency proceedings against the maker, the acceptor, or the drawer of an unaccepted instrument.

Therefore should any of these warranties be breached at the time of the indorser's transfer, a subsequent holder can hold the indorser liable. This action is independent of presentment, and notice of dishonor (signature liability). Thus a holder could sue for breach of warranty even if the instrument was improperly presented.

Nonindorsers also transfer an instrument and as such make the same transfer warranties as a blank or special indorser. There is one exception to the extent of liability, however: these warranties only flow to the nonindorsers' immediate transferee, not to all subsequent holders.

Qualified Indorsement Generally, an indorser, merely by indorsing, promises to pay the holder, or any subsequent indorser, the amount of the instrument in the event that the drawee (on behalf of the drawer) or maker defaults on the payment. [UCC 3-414(1)] A **qualified indorsement** is used by an indorser to disclaim or limit this liability on the instrument. This form of indorsement commonly includes the notation ''without recourse.''

Blank and special indorsements are unqualified indorsements; that is, the blank or special indorser is guaranteeing payment of the instrument in addition to transferring title to it. The qualified indorser is not guaranteeing any payment, but the qualified indorsement still transfers title to the indorsee or holder, and an instrument bearing a qualified indorsement can be further negotiated. See Exhibit 10–7 for a sample blank qualified indorsement.

Exhibit 10–7 A Sample Qualified Blank Indorsement

A qualified indorser, who receives consideration, also makes transfer warranties. These warranties are the same as those made by a blank or special indorser (with one exception), and these warranties also flow to all subsequent holders. The one exception is that a qualified indorser warrants only that he or she has no *knowledge* of a defense good against the transferor, rather than the broad warranty that there are no defenses. [UCC 3-417(2)(3)]

Restrictive Indorsement The **restrictive indorsement** requires future indorsees or holder to comply with certain instructions regarding the funds involved.

Other types of restrictive indorsements are: conditional indorsements (Pay to Rosemary Porter on condition of her delivery of her blue truck at 100 Green Street by August 7, 1989), prohibiting indorsements (Pay to Regina Heise only), and trust indorsements (Pay to Katherine Burns in trust for David Burns). [UCC 3-205] As a general rule restrictive indorsements do not prevent the further transfer or negotiation of the instrument. [UCC 3-206(1)] A common type of restrictive indorsement is one that makes the indorsee (almost always a bank) a collecting agent of the indorser. For example, ''For Deposit Only'' is a very common indorsement (see Exhibit 10–8). This type of indorsement has the effect of locking the instrument into the bank collection process. A restrictive indorser cannot be held liable unless the restriction (instruction) has been met.

Exhibit 10–8 A Sample Restrictive Indorsement

Signature Liability of Makers, Acceptors, and Drawers

Makers and acceptors (an acceptor is a drawee who by signature has agreed to pay the drawer's instrument or by a bank's certification of a check) are *primarily* liable on the instrument. [UCC 3-413(1)] This means that the maker or acceptor is absolutely required to pay the face amount of the instrument (assuming there is no valid defense) at the time he or she signs is. There is no requirement for the holder to make proper presentment or give the maker or acceptor any notice.

A drawer is a party *secondarily* liable (much the same as a blank or general indorser). [UCC 3-413(2)] Thus to hold the drawer absolutely liable on his or her signature requires the holder to make proper presentment (for example for a domestic check within thirty days of date or issue) and to give the drawer proper notice of dishonor. There is one difference, however, in the liability of the drawer if the holder fails to make a proper presentment or give proper notice of dishonor and the drawee is a bank. The drawer is excused from liability only if the drawee bank is insolvent, and such insolvency caused the drawer to suffer a loss. [UCC 3-502(1)(b)]

Discharge

Discharge from liability on an instrument can come from payment, cancellation, or material alteration. If the drawer or maker pays the instrument, it is discharged. [UCC 3-603] The payee or holder may cancel the instrument by intentionally marking it paid or by destroying it. [UCC 3-605] If the instrument has been materially altered as previously discussed, liability on the instrument may be totally, partially, or not at all discharged. [UCC 3-407]

Checks and the Banking System

Checks are the most common kind of commercial paper regulated by the Uniform Commercial Code. Checks, credit cards, and charge accounts are rapidly replacing currency as a means of payment in almost all transactions for goods and services. Approximately 57 billion personal and commercial checks are written each year in the United States. Checks are more than a daily convenience; "checkbook money" is an integral part of the economic system. A check is a credit instrument treated as if it were cash.

The Bank-Customer Relationship

Modern bank deposit and collection procedures are governed by Article 4 of the UCC. This article governs the relationship of banks with one another as they process checks for payment, and it establishes a framework for deposit and checking agreements between a bank and its customers.

The extent to which any party is either liable or not liable on a check is established according to the provisions of Article 3 of the UCC. A check can fall within the scope of Article 3 as a negotiable instrument and yet be subject to the provisions of Article 4 while it is in the course of collection. In the case of a conflict between Articles 3 and 4, Article 4 controls. [UCC 4-102(1)]

Duties of the Bank

A commercial bank serves its customers primarily in two ways:

1. By honoring checks for the withdrawal of funds deposited in the customer's account
2. By accepting deposits in United States currency and collecting checks written to or indorsed to its customers that are drawn on other banks.

Honoring Checks When a commercial bank provides checking services, it agrees to honor the checks written by its customers if sufficient funds are available in the account to pay each check. When a drawee bank wrongfully fails to honor a check, it is liable to its customer, not the holder of the check, for damages resulting from its refusal to pay. The bank has a contract with the customer, not the holder of the check. [UCC 4-402]

The bank may agree with the customer to accept overdrafts. An overdraft charges the customer's account for the amount of the check, even though the account contains insufficient funds to cover the check. [UCC 4-401(1)] Once a bank makes special arrangements with a customer to accept overdrafts on an account, the bank may be liable to the customer for damages caused by any wrongful dishonoring of overdrafts. Today, overdrafts are treated as loans to the customer, and interest is often charged from the day the overdraft is paid until funds are deposited to cover the overdraft.

The following case discusses the contractual relationship between a bank and its customers and the bank's right to pay an overdraft on a closed account.

BACKGROUND AND FACTS *MJZ maintained its corporate checking account at the Gulfstream First Bank & Trust. MJZ closed its account on April 2, 1980. Unbeknownst to MJZ, the bank had a policy of continuing to honor checks on closed accounts for thirty days after closure. The bank followed this practice as a convenience to customers who might otherwise be embarrassed by bounced checks.*

Late in April, two checks signed prior to the closing were presented to the bank for payment. The bank paid both checks and looked to MJZ for reimbursement. When MJZ refused the bank sued MJZ to recover the amount paid by the bank. The trial court ruled in the bank's favor.

Case 10.3
MJZ CORPORATION v. GULFSTREAM FIRST BANK & TRUST
District Court of Appeal, Florida, 1982.
420 So.2d 396.

HURLEY, Judge.

* * * *

We begin our analysis by noting that the relationship between a bank and its depositing customer is contractual. The delivery of money to a bank implies an "agreement on the part of the bank that the deposit will be paid out on the order of the depositor or returned to him upon demand." Deposits are either general or special. A general deposit is credited to the depositor to be drawn upon by him in the usual course of banking business. Absent some agreement demonstrating otherwise, a bank deposit is presumed to be general. The contractual relationship established between bank and depositor is one of debtor to creditor.

In the instant case, there was no proof that the MJZ corporate account was anything but a general account. Thus, a contractual debtor/creditor relationship existed between the corporation and the bank. When Mr. Zappone closed the account, the remaining funds were 'returned to him upon demand.' This terminated the contractual relationship between the corporation and the bank; the corporation ceased to be the bank's customer. We find the bank's reliance on the Uniform Commercial Code to be unavailing. The Code speaks to the duties and obligations of viable banking relationships. It provides no support for the bank's post-termination action in this case. In short, the bank had no authority to create an overdraft on a closed account. It acted as a volunteer and now is without legal basis to recoup its loss from its former customer.

At this juncture, we must caution against an overly broad reading of this decision. We do not hold that banks cannot maintain a thirty day 'open account after closure' policy. Rather, we hold that such a policy, without notice to the customer, cannot bind the customer. Furthermore, in the absence of any special agreement known to the customer, closure of an account terminates the contractual relationship. General principles of law, not the provisions of the Uniform Commercial Code, govern the legal relationships thereafter.

The appellate court reversed the trial court's judgment. The court found that the bank had no authority to create an overdraft on a closed account; therefore, the bank had no legal basis for recouping its loss from MJZ.

DECISION AND REMEDY

Honoring Stop-Payment Orders Only a customer can order his or her bank to pay a check, and only a customer can order the payment of the check to be stopped. This right does not extend to holders (such as, payees or indorsees) because the drawee bank's contract is only with its customer-drawers. A **stop-payment order** can be given orally, usually by phone, and it is binding on the bank for fourteen calendar days unless confirmed in writing. A written stop-payment order is effective for six months, unless renewed in writing. [UCC 4-403(2)] When the customer uses her or his bank guarantee card in writing a check, the customer gives up the right to stop payment on that check.

The bank must be given a reasonable time to permit the bank to put the stop-payment order in effect. Until such time, the bank is not liable to its customer if the bank honors the check. If the drawee bank pays a check after the customer has instituted a proper stop-payment order, the bank is liable for the actual loss suffered by the customer-drawer because of the wrongful payment. This amount might be much less than the amount of the check. For example, JoAnn orders six plants priced at $50 each from Frank's Greenhouse. JoAnn pays Frank $300 in advance. Frank delivers only five plants and tells JoAnn it will be six months before the other plant will be delivered. JoAnn immediately stops payment on her $300 check. Inadvertently the bank honors the $300 check over her stop-payment order. JoAnn can only establish a loss of $50 having received five plants and the bank is liable for only that amount.

The bank has a duty to inform its customers of the requirements for a stop-payment order. This issue is presented in the next case.

Case 10.4
STAFF SERVICE ASSOCIATES, INC. v. MIDLANTIC NATIONAL BANK

Superior Court of New Jersey, Law Division, Essex County, 1985.
207 N.J.Super. 237,
504 A.2d 148.

BACKGROUND AND FACTS *Staff Services Associates, Inc. (Staff Service), the plaintiff, had a checking account with the Midlantic National Bank, the defendant. Staff Service issued a check in the amount of $4,117.12 on July 2, 1982. On July 7, 1982, Staff Service executed a stop-payment order, but incorrectly wrote the amount of the check as $4,117.72. The employee acknowledged that he had read the statement on the bottom of the stop-payment order, which stated:*

IMPORTANT: The information on this Stop Payment Order must be correct, including the exact amount of the check to the penny, or the bank will not be able to stop payment and this Stop Payment Order will be void.

The computer could not stop payment on the check unless the exact amount was indicated, but it could honor a stop payment if other information was not correct. The check was paid by the bank. Staff Service filed this lawsuit, and the bank filed a motion for a summary judgment. The trial court refused to grant the bank a summary judgment, and the bank appealed.

HIGGINS CASS, J.S.C.
* * * *

* * * Staff Service's representative did not know that Midlantic utilized a computer to effect stop payment of a check. In addition, Midlantic never informed Staff Service that the exact amount of the check is necessary for the computer to pull the check. It chose a computerized system which searches for stopped checks by amount alone. By electing this system Midlantic assumed the risk that it would not be able to stop payment of a check despite the customer's accurate description of the account number, the payee's name, the number and date of the check and a *de minimis* error in the check amount. Midlantic should not be permitted to relieve itself of this risk unless it calls attention to its computerized system and the necessity for the exact check amount to meet computer requirements.

The court is not persuaded by the clause in the stop payment order which states that Midlantic cannot stop payment unless the information provided by the customer is correct, including the exact amount of the check to the penny. Indeed this clause is inaccurate since, as Midlantic's representative explained in his certification, ''if the amount of the check is correct, the check will be stopped, although a discrepancy may exist in the remaining elements of the stop payment order, unless and until the customer instructs otherwise.'' Consequently, notwithstanding the clause, it appears that a check will be stopped even if all the information on the stop payment order is incorrect except the check amount.

Implicated also is the question of how said clause is affected by [the U.C.C.] which provides that bank and its customers may vary by agreement the effect of the provisions of article 4, but that

> (N)o agreement can disclaim a bank's responsibility for its own lack of good faith or failure to exercise ordinary care or can limit the measure of damages for such lack or failure; but the parties may be agreement determine the standards by which such responsibility is to be measured if such standards are not manifestly unreasonable.

Did the bank exercise good faith in the placement of a clause on the stop payment order which did not focus on the single critical item which it required? Moreover, in these circumstances, it is manifestly unreasonable to measure a bank's responsibility by a term not brought to the customer's attention with such specificity as to permit him to give the bank notice ''in such manner as to afford the bank a reasonable opportunity to act.''

Therefore, the court holds that a bank has a reasonable opportunity to stop payment on a check when a customer accurately describes the check in all respects except for a single digit error in the check amount. The result would be different only if the bank specifically informed the customer that its computer requires the exact check amount for stop payment.

The Uniform Commercial Code must be liberally construed and applied to promote its underlying purposes. The purpose of [the U.C.C.] is expressed in comment 2 following the section:

> The position taken by this section is that stopping payment is a service which depositors expect and are entitled to receive from banks notwithstanding its difficulty, inconvenience and expense. The inevitable occasional losses through failure to stop should be borne by the banks as a cost of the business of banking.

Accordingly, defendant's motion for summary judgment is denied.

The appellate court denied the motion by the bank for a summary judgment because the facts were contested. The court held that, if the bank is not to be held liable for an improperly filled out stop payment, it must show the court that it specifically notified the customer that the exact amount of the check is necessary for the computer to pull the check and stop payment.

DECISION AND REMEDY

Paying on a Forged Signature of the Drawer A forged drawer signature on a check has no legal effect. [UCC 3-404(1)] Banks require signature cards from each customer who opens a checking account. The bank is responsible for determining whether the signature on a customer's check is genuine. The general rule is that the bank must recredit the customer's account when it pays on a forged signature unless the customer's negligence substantially contributed to the making of the forgery, or the customer breached his or her duty to discover and report the forgery to the bank.

Customer Duties

When the customer's negligence substantially contributes to a forgery, the bank is not obliged to recredit the customer's account for the amount of the check. [UCC 3-406] Further, a customer has a duty to examine his or her monthly statements and canceled checks promptly, and if there is a series of forgeries, report any forged signatures within fourteen days. [UCC 4-406(1)] Failure to examine and report or any carelessness by the customer that results in a loss to the bank makes the customer liable for the loss. [UCC 4-406(1), (2)(a)(b)]

Electronic Funds Transfer Systems

The present basis of the payment-collection process is the check, but banks are finding it increasingly difficult to cope with these billions of pieces of paper. New systems known as **electronic funds transfer systems** (EFTs)[1] promise to rid banks of the burden of transferring money by moving mountains of paper.

An EFT system has:

1. Teller machines: Located conveniently and connected on-line to the bank's computers, these machines receive payments on loans, receive deposits for or dispense cash from checking or savings accounts, and make credit card advances.
2. Point-of-sale systems: Located in the merchant's store and connected on-line to the bank's computers, a point-of-sale system immediately debits the customer's checking account and transfers the funds to the merchant's account.
3. Automatic payments and direct deposits: Advance authorization allows regular electronic transfers of funds from an account (for the automatic payment of bills) or into an account (for a direct deposit).
4. Telecommunications systems: A customer can order by telephone or through the use of a computer the transfer of money to and from her accounts or for payment of a bill.
5. Automatic clearinghouses: Entries are made in the form of electronic signals; no checks are used. Clearinghouses are used by businesspeople for recurrent payments, such as payroll, social security, or pension funds.

This new technology, however, has aroused some serious consumer concerns. With the speed of the transmissions, it is difficult to issue stop-payment orders. Precisely because the transmissions are electronic, fewer paper records are available. These systems allow more opportunities for an unauthorized person to tamper with an account, and there is a resulting decrease in privacy. The time between the writing of a check and its deduction from an account (the float time) is lost.

A Bank's Liability in EFTs

Federal rules such as the Electronic Fund Transfer Act (EFTA) govern electronic funds transfer accounts that are operated by telephone or by the presentation of a debit card to merchants when making purchases. The information concerning the consumer's rights under federal law must be given to every customer who opens an EFT account.

A monthly statement must be made for every month in which there is an electronic transfer of funds; otherwise, statements must be made every quarter. The statement must show the amount and date of the transfer, the names of the retailers involved, the location or identification of the terminal, the fees, and an address and telephone number for inquiries and error notices. The bank must furnish receipts for transactions made through computer terminals, but it is not obliged to do so for telephone transfers. The customer has the duty to reconcile his or her receipts against the statements.

Secured Transactions

The concept of a secured transaction is as basic to modern business practice as the concept of credit. Few purchasers (manufacturers, wholesalers, retailers, or consumers) have the resources to pay cash for major goods being purchased. Lenders

---

1. The terms electronic funds transfer system (EFT) and electronic transfer of funds system (ETF) are used interchangeably in business.

LEGAL
HIGHLIGHT   Consumers, Paper, and Electronic Banking

Visionaries in the 1960s foresaw a paperless, checkless society by the mid 1980s. All-electronic business would prevail. What has happened instead is that:

■ The average person writes twenty-five checks per month, a rate that has steadily increased.

■ By the early 1990s, over 62 billion checks a year will be written.

■ Consumers pay their bills:

  ■ First with checks (almost 90 percent of the time)

  ■ Second with credit cards (over 50 percent of the time)

  ■ Third and trailing far behind, alas, the debit card is used less than 5 percent of the time.

What went wrong? Consumers are a suspicious lot. They fear the computer. They know that a computer can mess up their bank accounts thoroughly. They fear the loss of security if the computer breaks down. Worse, they lose the float time that occurs between the time the check is written and the time the amount is actually debited from their account, sometimes days.

Who is happy? Check manufacturers, printers of paper charge slips, and, of course, printers of monthly statements, otherwise known as bills.

---

are reluctant to lend money to a debtor based solely on the debtor's promise to repay the debt. The simple fact is that sellers and lenders want to minimize the risk of loss because of nonpayment. The seller will not sell goods or lend money unless the promise of payment is somehow guaranteed.

To minimize the risk of loss, the creditor often requires the debtor to provide some type of security. When this security takes the form of personal property or real property that is owned by the debtor or in which the debtor has a legal interest, the transaction becomes known as a secured transaction, more commonly called a lien.

Business today cannot exist without secured transactions. Secured creditors are generally not subject to state exemption laws that exist to protect debtors. Secured creditors under federal bankruptcy laws have a favored position over unsecured creditors should the debtor become bankrupt.

The underlying philosophy of secured transaction laws deals with two major concerns of the creditor should the debtor default on the obligation: First, the debt will be satisfied from specific property (collateral) of the debtor. Second, the creditor's debt will have priority over the claims of other creditors to and purchasers of that specific collateral.

Article 9 of the UCC applies to any transaction that is intended to create a security interest in *personal property*. Transactions involving real property are excluded from Article 9. [UCC 9-104]

Exhibit 10–9 shows a sample security agreement.

Creating a Security Interest

In order for a creditor to become a secured party, the creditor must have a security interest in the collateral of the debtor. Three requirements must be met before a creditor has an enforceable security interest. First, unless the creditor has possession of the collateral, there must be a written security agreement signed by the debtor. Second, the creditor must give something of value to the debtor. Normally, the value given by a secured

Exhibit 10–9 A Sample Security Agreement

Date

| Name | No. and Street | City | County | State |

(hereinafter called "Debtor") hereby grants to _____

Name

| No. and Street | City | County | State |

(hereinafter called "Secured Party") a security interest in the following property (hereinafter called the "Collateral"): ____

_____

to secure payment and performance of obligations identified or set out as follows (hereinafter called the "Obligations"):

_____

   Default in payment or performance of any of the Obligations or default under any agreement evidencing any of the Obligations is a default under this agreement. Upon such default Secured Party may declare all Obligations immediately due and payable and shall have the remedies of a secured party under the _____ Uniform Commercial Code.
   Signed in (duplicate) triplicate.

Debtor
By _____

Secured Party
By _____

---

party is in the form of a direct loan, or it involves a commitment to sell goods on credit.

Third, the debtor must have rights in the property used as collateral; that is, the debtor must have some ownership interest or right to obtain possession of that collateral. The debtor's rights can represent either a current or a future legal interest in the collateral. For example, a retail seller-debtor can give a secured party a security interest not only in existing inventory owned by the retailer but also in future inventory to be acquired by the retailer.

Once these requirements are met, the creditor's rights are said to "attach to" the collateral. Attachment means that the creditor has an enforceable security interest against the debtor. The attachment of the security interest establishes the rights and liabilities of the debtor and creditor. [UCC 9-203]

Exhibit 10–10 diagrams the relationship established between creditor and debtor in a secured transaction.

Perfection

Even though the creditor's security interest has attached to the debtor's property, the secured creditor must take steps in order to protect his or her claim to the collateral over claims that third parties may have to the same property. Often a creditor can protect himself or herself by filing the required forms in the appropriate public office. The third parties may be other secured creditors, general creditors, trustees in bankruptcy, or purchasers of the collateral.

There are three methods of perfection:

1. Upon attachment: If there is a purchase-money security interest in consumer goods (goods used or brought primarily for personal, family or household purposes), perfection occurs automatically upon creation of the security interest without a filing or the secured party taking possession.

2. Upon possession: A secured party's possession of a debtor's collateral is notice of a possible lien

Exhibit 10–10 **Security Transaction Concept and Terminology**

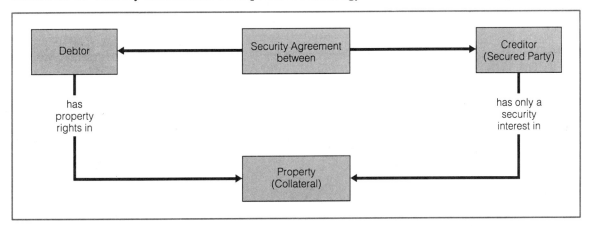

and thus perfection. Negotiable instruments can only be perfected by possession.

3. Upon filing: The most common method is for the secured party to file with an appropriate government official a *financing statement*. [UCC 9-402]

As a general rule, first in time of perfection or purchase is first in priority right to the collateral. There is one group of purchasers who will prevail regardless of a secured party's perfection and even if the purchaser knows of the secured party's interest at the time of purchase. Those are any purchasers who purchase goods in the ordinary course of business. [UCC 9-307(1)]

For example, Last Bank has a perfected security interest in the inventory of Gary's retail TV store. Joan purchases one of the TV's from Gary subject to Last Bank's perfected security interest. Joan takes the TV set free of Last Bank's security interest (if Gary goes into default, Last Bank cannot repossess the TV from Joan), even if Joan knew of it at the time of sale.

Default

Article 9 of the UCC defines the rights, duties, and remedies in case a debtor defaults on a secured loan. When a debtor defaults, a secured creditor can protect his or her claim to the collateral and enforce his or her security interest by a court judg-

ment, by foreclosure, or by any available judicial process. [UCC 9-501]

Secured Party's Remedies A secured party's remedies can be divided into two basic categories. First, a secured party can forego his or her security interest and proceed to a court judgment on the debt. Once the secured party has the judgment, he or she can use it to take other assets of the debtor to satisfy the judgment debt. This procedure is used when the value of the secured collateral has been greatly reduced below the amount of the debt, such as a wrecked automobile, and the debtor has other assets available to satisfy the debt. [UCC 9-501(1)]

Second, a secured party can take possession, called repossession, of the collateral covered by the security agreement. [UCC 9-503] On repossession, the secured party can retain the collateral covered by the security agreement for satisfaction of the debt [UCC 9-505(2)] or can resell the goods and apply the proceeds toward the debt. The sale must be conducted in a commercially reasonable manner. [UCC 9-504]

The creditor's rights and remedies under the UCC are cumulative; therefore, if a creditor is unsuccessful in enforcing his or her rights by one method, another method can be pursued. The UCC does not require the creditor to choose between remedies—that is, between a lawsuit to obtain a judgment and repossession of the collateral.

LEGAL HIGHLIGHT   A Tale of Woe!

After the Wall Street stock market crash on October 19, 1987, many stockbrokers found themselves without a job. Arthur, a former stockbroker, owned two cars and owed money on both. Hoping to cut back on his expenses now that he was unemployed, he decided to turn one car over to the bank, an act called voluntary repossession. Just as many people do, Arthur believed that he did not now owe the unpaid amount of the loan.

This belief is wrong. Not only does Arthur lose his car but he also still owes the difference between the debt still to be repaid and what the bank receives when it sells his car.

Arthur originally purchased the car for $30,000, paid $5,000 down, and financed the remaining $25,000. Over the past year, he has paid the balance of the principle down to $20,000. The blue book value is $17,000.

If the bank is able to sell the car for the $20,000 plus costs of resale, Arthur will owe nothing. If the bank sells it for more, Arthur receives the surplus. Unfortunately, most cars in this type of situation are sold for less than the amount still owed the bank. If the bank is able to get $13,000, Arthur will still owe the deficiency of $5,000.

If Arthur fails to pay the $5,000, the bank can to go court and obtain a deficiency judgment (that is, a judgment for the amount still deficient to have the contract paid in full).

The secured party has the right to take peaceful possession of the collateral on default. As long as there is no breach of the peace, the secured party can simply repossess the collateral. Otherwise, the secured party must resort to the judicial process. [UCC 9-503]

What constitutes a breach of the peace is of prime importance to both parties, for such an act can open the secured party (the party repossessing) to tort liability. The UCC does not define breach of the peace; the parties must look to the state laws to determine it.

In most states the secured party must be able to obtain the collateral without breaking and entering, committing assault or battery, or trespassing.

Generally, the creditor or the creditor's agent cannot enter a debtor's home, garage, or place of business without permission. For example, say that an automobile is the collateral on a defaulted loan. If the repossessing party walks onto the debtor's premises, proceeds up the driveway, enters the vehicle without entering the garage, and drives off, this probably will not amount to a breach of the peace. In some states, however, an action for wrongful trespass could be the basis for the debtor to file a breach-of-the-peace lawsuit. Thus, most car repossessions occur when the car is parked on a street or in a parking lot.

Proceeds from the Disposition of Collateral   If the secured party sells the collateral upon the debtor's default, proceeds from the sale of the collateral are applied in the following order. First, reasonable expenses stemming from the retaking, holding, or preparing for sale are paid. These expenses can include reasonable attorneys' fees and legal expenses. Second, satisfaction of the balance of the debt owed to the secured party is made. Third, subordinate security interests whose written demands have been received prior to the completion of distribution of the proceeds are paid. Subordinate security interests are for loans that are second or third liens on the property.

For example, Bill buys an expensive antique automobile, one that is known to appreciate in value, and signs a security agreement. He has the car nearly paid off, but has to use the car (equity) as collateral for a loan to start a small business. Unfortunately, the business fails, and Bill defaults on the original car loan and on the second (business) loan. When the creditor repossesses the car and sells it, first the costs of the whole process of repossession are paid, then the original loan balance is paid, and finally the second (business) loan balance is paid assuming the business loan secured party gave written notice. [UCC 9-504(1)]

If there is any surplus, it is paid to the debtor. If the loan balances are not paid, the creditor may go to court and obtain a deficiency judgment. The following case represents a creditor seeking to collect on a deficiency judgment.

BACKGROUND AND FACTS *The plaintiff, Poti Holding Company, a secured creditor, sold Piggott, the defendant, a wire-insulating machine. Poti Holding in return took a collateral note—that is, a promissory note that was secured with a lien on the wire-insulating machine (the collateral). Piggott defaulted on paying the note. Poti Holding repossessed and sold the machinery. The proceeds from the sale did not cover the amount owed on the note. Poti Holding sued Piggott for a deficiency judgment on a promissory note.*

The trial court appointed a special master to determine whether the sale of the machine was commercially reasonable. A special master investigates the facts and makes findings for the court. The lower court found for the defendant because the plaintiff had not proved that the sale was conducted in a commercially reasonable manner.

Case 10.5
POTI HOLDING COMPANY, INC. v. PIGGOTT
Appeals Court, Massachusetts, 1983.
15 Mass.App.Ct. 275,
444 N.E.2d 1311.

DREBEN, Justice.
* * * *

After sale or disposition of the collateral held by a secured party, the debtor, unless otherwise agreed, ''is liable for any deficiency.'' The defendant argues, however, that a creditor who missteps in conducting a sale automatically loses his right to a deficiency judgment.

In concluding that the plaintiff had not sustained its burden of proving that the sale had been conducted in a commercially reasonable manner, the master did not find that the plaintiff had engaged in sharp or unconscionable practices. Rather, he relied on the plaintiff's failure to submit evidence on a number of matters such as: the normal commercial practices in disposing of collateral of this type; the experience of the auctioneer in auctioning this kind of machinery; the areas of circulation of the newspapers in which the advertisements were placed; and whether there were experienced brokers available to sell goods of this type. He also noted that although the plaintiff had placed advertisements in the Boston Herald American, the Wall Street Journal and a local newspaper, and had notified between 210 and 235 parties, including the defendant, it had only notified two of the nine or more companies in the high temperature wire business in the eastern United States, and had not advertised in any publication of the wire industry. These findings underscore the lack of precision in the meaning of the term ''commercially reasonable;'' its determination depends on the particular facts in each case.

* * * *

We think more consistent with Massachusetts law and the provisions for remedies in the Uniform Commercial Code are those authorities which provide for a balancing of equities between the parties and allow the ''remedy and the recovery . . . [to] be adjusted to the particular situation.''

Although we have found no case in the Supreme Judicial Court or this court on the precise issue before us, our cases frown on forfeitures and penalties. In addition, where violations of the Code are not involved, wrongdoings of a creditor do not normally preclude a deficiency. * * *

The Code does not require automatic forfeiture. Specific remedies are provided * * * against a secured creditor who, among other misdeeds, fails to sell collateral in a commercially reasonable manner. A debtor may restrain an improper sale and also "has a right to recover from the secured party any loss caused by [the] failure to comply" with the Code. There is no mention of a forfeiture of the right to a deficiency and, in addition, the Code remedies are to be "liberally administered to the end that the aggrieved party may be put in as good a position as if the other party had fully performed but neither consequential or special nor penal damages may be had except as specifically provided in this chapter or by other rule of law."

In view of the specific remedies provided, the reluctance of Massachusetts to impose forfeitures, and the explicit statement in [the UCC] against penalties, "[w]e are unwilling to assume that the Legislature intended to effect such a forfeiture of private contractual rights."

DECISION AND REMEDY *The appellate court reversed the trial court. Poti Holding could recover the deficiency. The courts do not like forfeitures or penalties. In this case, the term "commercially reasonable manner" does not have a precise meaning. Since the statute does not authorize a forfeiture—that is, forfeiting the right to sue for a deficiency judgment by failing to sell an item in a commercially reasonable manner—the court would not allow a forfeiture under the facts in this case.*

Termination

When a debt is paid, the secured party must send a termination statement to the debtor or must file such a statement in the same place where the original financing statement is located. The termination statement shows that the debt has been paid. If the secured party fails to file such a termination statement or fails to send it within ten days after proper demand or for a consumer debt paid the secured party failed to file a termination within thirty days, the secured party may be liable to the debtor for $100. Additionally, the secured party is liable for any loss caused to the debtor for failing to file the appropriate release-of-debt documents.

The Problem of Postdating a Check

On Wednesday, Sally sees an advertisement to join a health club, stating "today only for one-half price." After work, she stops by to check out the club. A salesman shows her all the club features and reminds her of the one-half price sale. Payday is Monday, five days away, but she wants to get the bargain rate. The salesman agrees to accept a postdated check and assures her that the check will not be deposited until Monday.

Arriving home on Tuesday after work, she received a notice from her bank that her account is overdrawn. Two minutes later, she has a call from the health club concerning her bounced check. On Wednesday, she checks with the bank and finds out that the postdated check was deposited on the previous Thursday. The health club is threatening criminal action. Has Sally committed a crime?

Most people believe that postdating or antedating a check is illegal. No date is required on a check to make it negotiable because it is a demand instrument; thus, to postdate or antedate a check is not illegal. The act of postdating or antedating the check becomes illegal when the drawer intends to defraud the payee by not having the money in his or her account. It is difficult to prove fraud under these circumstances, however. As you may remember from Chapter 9, to prove fraud you must prove an objective intent to deceive at the time of the act. Intent is difficult to prove with a postdated check.

In Sally's case, the district attorney will not prosecute because it was clear on the face of the check that the funds were not available until Monday. If Sally can show that the money (her paycheck) was in the account on Monday, the district attorney cannot show intent to deceive.

Many payees, such as the health club, will require a date to be inserted on the check. Under UCC 4-404 a check is "stale" if it is not presented to the bank for payment within six months after the date on the check. Thus, after six months, the bank is not obligated to pay the check but can do so in good faith. Wanting to make sure that the bank will pay the check, the payee may require the date to be filled in.

A check is a credit instrument (conditional on being honored) even though banks treat it as a cash instrument. A merchant accepting a check may have signed up for a bank's guarantee protection program and may have paid the bank a fee for the service. In this case, if the customer's bank account does not have enough cash to honor the check, the bank, not the merchant, is responsible for collecting the amount from the customer. The merchant does not even know that the check has bounced if he or she has signed up for the guarantee program. A merchant who has not signed up for a bank's guarantee protection program may require a person writing a check to produce a bank guarantee card in an attempt to limit losses caused by bad checks.

The lessons Sally learned include:

- Never write a postdated check.
- Never rely on the oral assurances of a salesperson.

Summary

Commercial paper serves two purposes: as a substitute for cash and as a credit device. The UCC recognizes four basic types of commercial paper: drafts, checks, notes, and certificates of deposit.

These instruments, in turn, fall into one of two categories: orders to pay or promises to pay. In order for these instruments to be negotiable, six requirements must be met. A negotiable instrument must be: (1) in writing, (2) signed by the maker or drawer, (3) contain an unconditional promise or order to pay, (4) stated in a specific sum of money, (5) payable on demand or at a definite time, (6) payable to order or to bearer.

A distinction exists between an assignment and a negotiation. An assignment of a contract right does not transfer to the assignee any greater rights in the contract than the original party had. If an instrument is negotiated, the holder of the instrument may have greater rights than the original party. Such a holder is known as a holder in due course. Only those defenses known as real defenses (defenses that apply to the document itself) may be asserted against a holder in due course and will preclude payment of the instrument to the HDC.

The relationship between a bank and its customers is governed by the UCC. The bank has a duty to pay checks drawn on a customer's account and to accept deposits. The customer has a duty to check her or his statements every month and to check for forged signatures. The banking system is being revolutionized by electronic funds transfer systems, which include teller machines, point-of-sale systems, and automated clearinghouses. Federal laws govern many aspects of electronic funds transfers.

When a merchant extends credit, he or she wants to make sure that the debt is secured by some type of collateral. If the seller extends credit for the purchase of an item or if the debtor borrows money to purchase an item and the debt is secured by the item purchased, this transaction is called a purchase money security interest. The creditor's security interest must be valid against the debtor's right to the item and must have priority over any claims by third parties.

Key Terms

bearer (**225**)
bearer paper (**233**)
blank indorsement (**227**)
certificate of deposit (CD) (**225**)
check (**226**)
collateral note (**232**)
commercial paper (**224**)
consumer credit contract (**237**)
contract (**237**)
draft (**225**)
drawees (**225**)
drawers (**225**)

electronic funds transfer systems (**244**)
holder (**227**)
holder in due course (HDC) (**227**)
indorsee (**226**)
indorser (**226**)
installment note (**232**)
issue (**225**)
maker (**225**)
mortgage note (**231**)
negotiable (**232**)
order paper (**233**)

orders to pay (**231**)
payee (**225**)
personal defenses (**236**)
promises to pay (**231**)
promissory note (**224**)
qualified indorsement (**238**)
real defenses (**236**)
restrictive indorsement (**238**)
secured transactions (**224**)
sight drafts (**232**)
special indorsement (**234**)
stop-payment order (**242**)
time drafts (**232**)

Questions and Case Problems

1. The following note is written by Gloria Natale on the back of an envelope: "I, Gloria Natale, promise to pay to Perry Wilson or bearer $1,000 on demand." Is this note a negotiable instrument? Please discuss fully.

2. A check is drawn by Jeff for $500 and made payable to the order of Kelley. Jeff turns the check over to Kelley. Kelley owes her landlord $500 in rent and transfers the check to her landlord with the following indorsement: "For rent paid. [Signed] Kelley." Kelley's landlord has contracted to have Eric repair the electrical wiring in sev-

eral apartments. Eric insists on immediate payment. The landlord transfers the check to Eric without indorsement. Later, in order to pay for the electrical supplies at Supply Store, Eric transfers the check with the following indorsement: "Pay to Supply Store, without recourse [Signed] Eric." Supply sends the check to its bank indorsed "For deposit only. [Signed] Supply Store."

a. Classify each of these indorsements.

b. Was the transfer from Kelley's landlord to Eric without indorsement an assignment or a negotiation? Explain.

3. Mansfield issues a ninety-day negotiable promissory note payable to the order of Eastwood. The amount of the note is left blank until the price of the diamond Mansfield plans to buy from Eastwood is determined. Mansfield orally authorizes Eastwood to fill in the blank, but the amount is not to exceed $10,000. Eastwood, without authority, fills in the note in the amount of $200,000 and thirty days later sells the note to the First National Bank for $16,000. Eastwood does not buy the diamond and leaves the state. First National Bank had no knowledge that the instrument was incomplete when issued or that Eastwood had no authority to complete the instrument in an amount over $10,000. Does the bank qualify as a holder in due course and, if so, for what amount? Explain fully.

4. On June 1, Jesse draws a check payable to George for $2,000 to reroof his house by July 1. George indorses the check in blank to Ronald on June 15 as payment for a debt he owed (value). Ronald, on July 5, negotiates the check to Peter, without indorsement, as payment for fireworks that he bought for the July 4 celebration. George never reroofs the house and Jesse stops payment on the check on July 3. Peter attempts to cash the check. Jesse claims that his defense—that George never performed the agreed-on services (reroofing the house)—is valid against Peter. Peter claims that the check must be honored. Who is right? Explain fully.

5. James Balkus died. Discovered among his personal assets were several deposit slips from a local bank with a handwritten statement that they were payable to the order of his sister. Each deposit slip was dated and signed by James. His estate administrator and his sister both claimed these sums. Are these deposit slips negotiable instruments? Explain. [Matter of Estate of Balkus, 128 Wis.2d 246, 381 N.W.2d 593 (1985)]

6. Roberts executed a promissory note that was made payable to the order of Baines. Baines gave this note to Duxbury along with a separate document stating that he was transferring it to Duxbury. Roberts refused to pay the note to Duxbury because it had not been indorsed. What rights does Duxbury have, if any? Is he a holder of the note or a holder in due course? Explain. [Duxbury v. Roberts, 388 Mass. 385, 446 N.E.2d 401 (1983)]

7. Money Mart cashed a paycheck for an employee of Epicycle. Epicycle had placed a stop payment on this check because of claims it had against the employee. Was Money Mart required to verify the validity of this check before cashing it? [Money Mart Check Cashing Center, Inc. v. Epicycle Corp., 667 P.2d 1372 (Colo. 1983)]

8. Wade purchased a Ford automobile that was financed by Ford Motor Credit. Wade fell behind in her monthly payments. The vehicle was repossessed by an agent of Ford Motor Credit. Wade testified that she heard a car burning rubber, looked out, and saw her vehicle was missing. No other confrontation occurred. Wade claims that this repossession was a breach of the peace and was wrongful. She sought damages from Ford Motor Credit while Ford Motor Credit sought $2,900 as a deficiency. Was this repossession wrongful? Was Ford Motor Credit entitled to a deficiency judgment? [Wade v. Ford Motor Credit Co., 8 Kan.App.2d 737, 668 P.2d 183 (1983)]

9. SCCI, Inc., employed Susan Wolf as a secretary and bookkeeper. She forged and collected on more than ninety checks drawn on SCCI, Inc.'s bank. SCCI, Inc., claimed that the bank owed it the money that the bank had wrongfully paid to others on the forged checks. After making this claim, SCCI, Inc., accepted a promissory note from Susan Wolf in satisfaction for all sums owed. The bank took the position that this note discharged any liability that it owed SCCI, Inc. Was the bank correct? Please explain your answer. [SCCI, Inc. v. United States National Bank of Oregon, 78 Or.App. 176, 714 P.2d 1113 (1986)]

Chapter 11 Rights of Consumers, Debtors, and Creditors

Creditors have better memories than debtors; they are a superstitious sect, great observers of set days and times.

Benjamin Franklin

OUTLINE

Introduction

Purchase on credit is the foundation of our business community. In the last forty years, we have converted from a cash to a credit society. Credit card use by consumers has led this transformation. Consumer credit has increased from $2.5 billion at the end of World War II to $500 billion by 1989. Major consumer products, such as automobiles, stereos, televisions, and furniture, are almost always purchased on credit. Consumer credit rests on two assumptions: the debtor's willingness to pay and the debtor's ability to pay.

By the mid 1960s, the tremendous increase in credit had unfortunately also led to a rise in the abuse of consumers. Consumers were not informed sufficiently in order to shop comparatively for interest rates, they were misled into signing installment contracts, debt collectors were harassing them, they were denied access to their credit reports, and, worst of all, if the computer said they owed a bill, the poor consumer had no one with whom to talk. Consumers were not adequately protected by state law.

The United States Congress became concerned and, in 1968, adopted the **Consumer Credit Protection Act**, which has been amended several times. These amendments are known by their popular names. In this chapter, we will review the following acts:

1. **Consumer Credit Cost Disclosure Act**, commonly known as the **Truth-in-Lending Act (TILA)**
2. **Fair Credit Billing Act**
3. **Fair Credit Reporting Act**
4. **Equal Credit Opportunity Act**
5. **Fair Debt Collection Practices Act**

The Electronic Fund Transfer Act is also part of the Consumer Credit Protection Act and is discussed in Chapter 10. To finish the chapter, we will discuss the rights of creditors and review some of the bankruptcy laws.

Consumer Credit Protection Act

The Consumer Credit Protection Act (CCPA) is the primary source of federal law covering credit transactions, and numerous federal agencies enforce the CCPA. Individual consumers can also use the act to protect their rights when a business does not fully comply with the CCPA's provisions; the legal consequences vary for each provision violated, but both criminal and civil sanctions exist if a business fails to comply.

Consumer Credit Cost Disclosure: Truth-in-Lending Act

During hearings in 1968, Congress discovered that financial institutions were using a variety of ways to state rates of interest and the total dollar cost of a loan. Rates of interest were based on recognized, but varying, financial methods of calculation. No uniform method of stating an interest rate existed. Congress heard considerable debate as to whether charges for insurance, credit reports, discount points, and other items should be classified as interest charges. Prior to 1968, a consumer could not shop for credit because of the difficulties in comparing one lending institution's charges with another.

To resolve this problem, Congress passed Title I of the Consumer Credit Protection Act. Title I is commonly known as the Truth-in-Lending Act (TILA). The TILA deals with deceptive credit practices and requires notice and disclosure to prevent sellers and creditors from taking unfair advantage of consumers. Through disclosure, the purchaser can more easily compare the credit terms that are available. The act applies to most consumer credit transactions.

Disclosure Requirements of the TILA   The disclosure requirements apply to credit transactions in which a finance charge is imposed or in which payment is to be made in more than four installments. The most important information that a lender must disclose includes: (1) the cash price; (2) the down payment or trade-in allowance, if any; (3) the unpaid cash price (the cash price minus the down payment) that is to be financed; (4) the **finance charge** (the total amount of interest and other charges such as filing fees and insurance premiums); and (5) the **annual percentage rate** (the true rate of interest charged on a yearly basis) by which the finance charge is calculated.

The creditor must also tell the debtor the date that the finance charge starts; the number, amounts, and due dates of payments; the late-payment charges; and if there is a prepayment penalty. A prepayment penalty is an amount that the debtor must pay if he or she wants to pay off the debt early. In the past, the prepayment penalty often was a substantial amount of the debt. For example, say that Harris borrowed $5,000 and that over time he has paid back $4,000. He now wants to pay the remaining $1,000 in order to complete the loan payments. The prepayment penalty, however, might be $2,000; in other words, he would have to pay a total of $3,000 in order to pay off the loan early. Today, many states do not allow prepayment penalties.

The provisions of the Truth-in-Lending Act apply to both sales and leases of personal and real property. Two key terms summarize the disclosure philosophy of the act: finance charge and annual percentage rate. Armed with this information, the consumer can now comparison shop for a loan or credit.

The Federal Reserve Board issues the administrative rules that implement the TILA. Known as Regulation Z, these rules include model forms for businesses to follow. The forms, if used correctly by a business, are in full compliance with the statute. Examples are found in Exhibits 11–1 and 11–2.

Creditors Subject to the TILA   The Truth-in-Lending Act does not apply to everyone. It applies to businesses that, in the ordinary course of their operations, lend money, sell on credit, or arrange for the extension of credit to consumers. For this reason, sales or loans made between two consumers do not come under the act. Only debtors who are individuals (natural persons) are protected by this law; corporations or other legal entities (including governmental agencies) are not.

Transactions involving purchases of property (real or personal) for personal, family, household, or agricultural use come under the terms and provisions of the act if the amount being financed is less than $25,000. Transactions covered by the act typically include retail and installment sales, installment loans, car loans, home improvement loans, and certain real estate loans. Real estate loans of more than $25,000 on a debtor's residence are not covered by the act.

Penalties   A creditor who fails to comply with the disclosure requirements may be liable to the consumer for any actual damages plus twice the amount of the finance charge, plus attorneys' fees. In no event may damages exceed $1,000, however. The consumer has one year from the date of the violation to bring suit against a creditor who has failed to provide the disclosure statement. A person who willfully and knowingly violates these provisions is liable criminally and may be fined $5,000 and/or imprisoned for up to one year. In addition, the debtor is entitled to rescind the transaction at anytime up to three years from the date of consummation of the transaction.

Other Provisions of the CCPA

Over the years, other statutes have been adopted that add to the CCPA's initial provisions. These provisions cover, in particular, real estate improvements, credit card usage, credit billing errors, equal credit opportunities, and rules governing collection of debt practices.

Real Estate   Often when a creditor forms a contract to improve a consumer's residence, the consumer will, in turn, give the creditor a security interest in the residence to secure payment for the improvement. Under the TILA, each consumer has the right to rescind the transaction by midnight of the third business day following the signing of the transaction even if all disclosure provisions of the TILA have been followed. A consumer must be given notice of this right to rescind along with the material disclosures of annual percentage rate, the finance charge, the amount financed, the total payments, and the payment schedule.

For example, Sandy wants to have a pool built. She signs a contract with Pool Company to have the pool built in return for $4,000. Sandy does not have $4,000, so she signs a note to repay the $4,000 and gives Pool Company a security interest in her home. If she fails to pay the note, Pool Company will still have its interest in the $4,000 secured under its contract. The company may be able to force the sale of the house to recover the $4,000. To have this right, however, the security contract must clearly state Sandy's right to rescind

Exhibit 11–1 Sample Credit Sale Contract Supplied by the Federal Reserve Board

Big Wheel Auto   Alice Green

ANNUAL PERCENTAGE RATE The cost of your credit as a yearly rate.	FINANCE CHARGE The dollar amount the credit will cost you.	Amount Financed The amount of credit provided to you or on your behalf.	Total of Payments The amount you will have paid after you have made all payments as scheduled.	Total Sale Price The total cost of your purchase on credit, including your downpayment of $ *1500 –*
14.84 %	$1496.80	$6107.50	$7604.30	$9129.30

You have the right to receive at this time an itemization of the Amount Financed.

☐ I want an itemization.   ☒ I do not want an itemization.

Your payment schedule will be:

Number of Payments	Amount of Payments	When Payments Are Due
36	$211.23	Monthly beginning 6-1-81

Insurance

Credit life insurance and credit disability insurance are not required to obtain credit, and will not be provided unless you sign and agree to pay the additional cost.

Type	Premium	Signature	
Credit Life	$120 –	I want credit life insurance.	*alice Green* Signature
Credit Disability		I want credit disability insurance.	Signature
Credit Life and Disability		I want credit life and disability insurance.	Signature

Security: You are giving a security interest in:

☒ the goods being purchased.

☐ _____.

Filing fees $ 12.50   **Non-filing insurance $** _____

Late Charge: If a payment is late, you will be charged $10.

Prepayment: If you pay off early, you

☐ may ☐ will not   have to pay a penalty.

☒ may ☐ will not   be entitled to a refund of part of the finance charge.

See your contract documents for any additional information about nonpayment, default, any required repayment in full before the scheduled date, and prepayment refunds and penalties.

I have received a copy of this statement.

alice Green   5-1-81

Signature   Date

_____

e means an estimate

Source: 12 *Code of Federal Regulations*, Section 226, Appendix H-10

Exhibit 11–2 Sample Installment Loan Contract Supplied by the Federal Reserve Board

---

Friendly Bank & Trust Co.

700 East Street

Little Creek, USA

Lisa Stone
22-4859-22
300 Maple Avenue
Little Creek, USA

ANNUAL PERCENTAGE RATE The cost of your credit as a yearly rate.	FINANCE CHARGE The dollar amount the credit will cost you.	Amount Financed The amount of credit provided to you or on your behalf.	Total of Payments The amount you will have paid after you have made all payments as scheduled.
12 %	$675.31	$5000-	$5675.31

You have the right to receive at this time an itemization of the Amount Financed.

☐ I want an itemization.　　☐ I do not want an itemization.

Your payment schedule will be:

Number of Payments	Amount of Payments	When Payments Are Due
1	$262.03 e	6/1/81
23	$235.36	Monthly beginning 7/1/81

Late Charge: If a payment is late, you will be charged $5 or 10% of the payment, whichever is less.

Prepayment: If you pay off early, you ☒ may　☐ will not　have to pay a penalty.

Required Deposit: The annual percentage rate does not take into account your required deposit.

See your contract documents for any additional information about nonpayment, default, any required repayment in full before the scheduled date, and prepayment refunds and penalties.

---

e means an estimate

Source: 12 *Code of Federal Regulations*, Section 226, Appendix H-11

---

the contract, must include all disclosure requirements, and Sandy must be notified of her right to rescind the contract within three days, and she must not have rescinded it.

If the consumer rescinds the transaction, the security interest in the residence is void, and no finance charge may be charged. The creditor must return any money or property that was received, and the consumer must give back whatever she or he has received. If this is impracticable, she or he must give back the reasonable value of what has been received.

Two exceptions to the three-day right of rescission have primary importance. The first exception involves an emergency situation in which the customer needs to have her or his home repaired immediately, as in the case of damage resulting from a fire or storm.

The second major exception is when a consumer purchases a house and grants the lender a first lien (mortgage).

The following case illustrates the need for businesses to comply with the requirements of the Truth-in-Lending Act.

Case 11.1
COLE v. LOVETT

United States District Court,
Southern District, Mississippi,
1987.
672 F.Supp. 947.

BACKGROUND AND FACTS   *In November 1982, plaintiffs Norman and Judy Cole were visited by two salesmen, Stepp and Smith, from Capitol Roofing, who were selling siding for homes. After a sales pitch, it was estimated that the cost to cover the Coles' house would be $4,900. Before the salesmen left, the Coles had signed a number of documents, including a work order, a home improvement retail installment contract, a security agreement and disclosure statement, a loan application, a notice of right to cancel, and a deed of trust.*

The only document the Coles really saw was the work order; they only saw the signature block on the other papers. The salesmen misrepresented to the Coles the real nature of the paperwork that they were signing. They were told they had signed a work order, credit application, and insurance papers.

Shortly after the salesmen left, the Coles decided that they wanted to hold off on the work order so they could ask for estimates from other companies. Mrs. Cole called Capitol Roofing the next morning and told the salesman that they had decided to wait. She was told that the papers had been processed, the workers would be out at the end of the week, and there was nothing she could do. She went to work and, when she returned, she found the crew installing the siding. She did not tell them to leave because she thought that she and her husband were bound by the contract.

The contract was assigned by Capitol Roofing to United Companies Mortgage (UCM). The Coles had continuing problems with the siding. After repeated unsuccessful calls by Mrs. Cole to Capitol Roofing, the problems were not remedied. After eleven payments, the Coles became frustrated and discontinued payment to UCM. They retained an attorney, who, by letter, informed both Capitol Roofing and UCM that the Coles were exercising their right of rescission under the Truth-in-Lending Act. After receiving no answer, the Coles filed this lawsuit seeking rescission, and UCM counter-claimed, alleging the Coles' default under the contract.

LEE, Judge.
*   *   *   *

[Court's discussion of security interest]

    The first violation which plaintiffs contend entitles them to rescind the transaction under TILA is the failure of Capitol Roofing to disclose the security interest that was being acquired in their home. Under TILA, the right to rescind is available in any "credit transaction in which a security interest is or will be retained or acquired in the consumer's principal dwelling." The testimony of the parties regarding the deed of trust signed by the Coles was in direct contradiction. Stepp testified that he explained to the Coles that they were granting a security interest in their home, and further said that either he or Smith completed the relevant portions of the deed of trust, with the exception of the property description, before the Coles signed the document. *   *   * According to Stepp, both the Coles knew they were granting a second mortgage on their home. Plaintiffs, on the other hand, testified that neither Smith nor Stepp informed them that their home would be security for the siding contract. Neither of them recalled having signed a deed of trust. The disclosure statement signed by the Coles did not mention a deed of trust but contained the following language:

Security: Buyers are giving a security interest in:

___ the goods or property being purchased.

 X land located at *P.O. Box D'Lo, MS.*

[The TILA] requires the creditor to disclose "the fact that the creditor has or will acquire a security interest in the property purchased as part of the transaction, or in other property identified by item or type." * * * [B]oth Norman and Judy Cole denied any knowledge of the existence of a deed of trust against their home and stated affirmatively that they did not learn of the deed of trust until approximately a year later when they applied for credit to make interior improvements on their home and the deed of trust was discovered in the land records. * * * The court credits the testimony of the Coles and is of the opinion that Capitol Roofing did not disclose to them the fact that a security interest was being acquired in their home. Therefore, * * * this constituted a material violation of TILA and Regulation Z, * * * and plaintiffs are entitled to rescind.

[Court's discussion of notice to rescind]

The plaintiffs next charge that Capitol Roofing failed to furnish them with notice of their right to rescind as required by TILA. TILA and Regulation Z expressly require the creditor in a consumer credit transaction, in which a security interest is being conveyed in the property used by the consumers as their principal dwelling, to provide each consumer who own[s] an interest in the property two copies of a notice of the right to rescind. At trial, Stepp testified that he verbally informed the Coles of their right to rescind the transaction and gave them each two copies of a notice of right to cancel form which contained the required information. Capitol Roofing introduced a document entitled "notice of right to cancel" with an acknowledgement of receipt of form signed by both plaintiffs and dated November 9, 1982. However, the Coles claimed that they had never seen the notice of right to cancel and that, despite their having signed the acknowledgement portion of the document, neither of them ever received copies of the notice form. Moreover, both testified that Stepp never explained the right of rescission and, in fact, after her discussion with Stepp on November 10, Judy Cole was under the impression that she and her husband were bound by having signed the contract. The effect of the Coles' signatures on the acknowledgment * * * "does no more than create a rebuttable presumption of delivery thereof." As it appears from the testimony that the Coles were unaware of any right of rescission and did not learn of their right until much later upon consulting with an attorney, the court is of the opinion that the Coles have effectively rebutted the presumption of delivery. The court finds that plaintiffs were not informed of their right to rescind and that, notwithstanding their signing an acknowledgement of receipt of forms, they never received copies of the notice. The failure by Capitol Roofing to provide each of the plaintiffs with the required notice constituted a violation of TILA and entitled them to rescind the transaction. As they were never given proper notice of their right to rescind, they timely exercised this right, having notified defendants of their rescission within three years following consummation of the transaction.

* * * *

As a result of Capitol Roofing's violations of TILA, plaintiffs were entitled to rescind the transaction. After the Coles served notice on defendants of their election to cancel the transaction, defendants were required to "return to the [Coles] any money or property given as earnest money, down payment, or otherwise, and [were required to] take any action necessary or appropriate to reflect the termination of any security interest created under the transaction." Plaintiffs' attempt at cancellation was met with total inaction by defendants. Consequently, the Coles are entitled to the cancellation of the finance charges in their transaction, and to have the security interest in their home voided.

DECISION AND   *The district court found that Capitol Roofing had violated the Truth-in-*
REMEDY   *Lending Act. First, the Coles were not informed that they were granting*
Capitol Roofing a security interest in their home.

Second, the Coles were not furnished with notice of their right to rescind the contract. Since Capitol Roofing had not complied with the TILA, the Coles had three years to rescind the contract. The Coles notified Capitol Roofing in a timely manner of their problems and of their decision to rescind the contract. Capital Roofing failed to demand possession of the siding within a reasonable time after the Coles had canceled the contract. The end results were that the Coles retained the siding free of any further payment, the finance charges were canceled, and the security interest in the Coles' house was released.

Credit Cards   The TILA has specific provisions that cover the issuance and use of credit cards. First, an initial credit card cannot be sent to an individual or a business unless it is requested. Any unauthorized use of such a card cannot be charged to the named cardholder. Renewal credit cards can be sent without a specific request. Second, if a credit card is lost or stolen, fifty dollars is the limit of the cardholder's liability for the unauthorized use of the card. The fifty-dollar limit is for each card, so if a consumer loses ten cards, the actual loss to the consumer could be $500.

Fair Credit Billing Act   Even with computers, errors are made on charge accounts. It can be an unnerving experience to try to get these errors corrected. An amendment to the TILA, the Fair Credit Billing Act, requires creditors to correct errors promptly and without damage to a person's credit rating.

A person who believes his or her statement is in error must notify the creditor in writing with a statement explaining the perceived error. The customer must pay the *undisputed* amount while waiting for an answer from the business on the amount in question. Within thirty days the creditor must acknowledge the inquiry, and within ninety days either the account must be corrected or an explanation must be given as to why the creditor believes the account is correct. During this time, the

creditor is not allowed to give an unfavorable credit report or to attempt to collect the amount in dispute.

Fair Credit Reporting Act   At one time, consumers did not have access to the contents of credit and investigative reports kept on them by others, and they could not control the use of these reports. Inaccuracies, once reported, were almost impossible to uncover, much less to correct.

In 1970, Congress enacted the Fair Credit Reporting Act as a part of the Consumer Credit Protection Act. Consumers are entitled, on request, to be informed of the nature and scope of a credit investigation, the kind of information that is being compiled, and the names of people who will be receiving the report.

Any inaccurate or misleading material must be reinvestigated and, if not verified, removed from the file. If there is a dispute about the accuracy of certain parts of the report, consumers have the right to include in the file their own 100-word statement describing their position with regard to disputed matters. The law also provides for updating information. Information over seven years old must be deleted, and information regarding any bankruptcy more than ten years old must be removed.

A consumer credit reporting agency that fails to comply with the terms of the act can be held

---

LEGAL HIGHLIGHT   **Earth Calling Computer, Earth Calling Computer, Do You Read Me?**

When Congress was considering passing the Fair Credit Billing Act, the members of Congress heard horror stories such as the following about computers that sent bills to consumers:

■ A woman in Yonkers, New York, bought furniture from Gimbels. One piece arrived damaged beyond repair and was returned. The replacement piece did not match and was returned. The third piece had not arrived after five months. Payment was made for the delivered pieces, but not for the undelivered piece. The woman was in constant contact with the Gimbels credit department, but apparently no one talked to the computer. It billed her for one year, then turned the unpaid bill over to a debt collection agency. The letter to her read, "The good things of life are obtainable by many people through their recorded credit reputation." In frustration, she wrote to the debt collection agency, three Gimbels executives, the attorney general for New York, the Federal Trade Commission, Consumers Union, Senator Proxmire, and the New York State Consumer Protection Board. She had replies from all except the debt collection agency and Gimbels.

■ BankAmericard sent an unsolicited credit card to a man in the Bronx, New York. He never received the card because it was stolen, but that did not stop the computer from sending him the bill, plus interest, plus late-payment charges, despite his repeated efforts to inform the computer that these charges were not his.
■ A couple from Monaghan, New York, ordered furniture from Macy's. They owed $1,217, but the furniture delivered was not what they had ordered. It was sent back twice. After ten months, the correct furniture was finally delivered, and the couple paid what was owed. They were in contact with Macy's during this period, but no one told the computer. It billed them for finance charges for the ten months, plus 6 percent sales tax, although the sales tax in that area was only 3 percent. Finally, they wrote the chairman of the board of Macy's. He expressed concern, but within three days an attorney for Macy's wrote them, giving them five days to pay up or be taken to court. They contacted the New York State Consumer Protection Board, which resolved the problem. In the meantime, they could not buy a house because of this "unpaid" bill.

---

liable for actual damages, for punitive damages, and for attorneys' fees and court costs.

The following case involves a credit reporting agency and one of its reports.

BACKGROUND AND FACTS *Plaintiff Roseman resigned his job as an insurance agent for the John Hancock Insurance Company after an audit revealed shortages in his account. A credit report, prepared by Retail Credit Company, Inc., contained the following information:*

> *We have handled [sic] at the home office in Boston and find that Mr. Roseman was employed as a debit agent [for John Hancock]. He resigned due to discovery of discrepancies in his accounts amounting to $314.84. This was all repaid by Mr. Roseman. His production in 1970, 1971, and 1972 was above average and in 1973 and 1974 it was below*

 Case 11.2

ROSEMAN v. RETAIL CREDIT CO.

United States District Court, Eastern District, Pennsylvania, 1977.
428 F.Supp. 643.

average. This was the extent of the information available from John Hancock due to strict company policy.

When Roseman learned that this information was on file, he requested that the credit reporting agency reinvestigate. A second inquiry by the agency confirmed the truth of the initial report. Roseman then sued the defendant to have this information removed from his file and for damages.

BRODERICK, Judge.

This is an action for damages under the Fair Credit Reporting Act. Plaintiff, Seymour Roseman, alleges that defendant, Retail Credit Co., Inc. violated the Act in failing to: (1) take reasonable steps to assure the accuracy of its original credit report and subsequent reinvestigation; (2) inform the plaintiff that he had the right to have a statement of his version of the dispute included as a part of his consumer report; and (3) disclose the sources of its information in preparing the reports.* * *
* * * *

The purpose of the Act is to protect consumers from having inaccurate information circulated concerning them. In this case the defendant's reports were accurate and therefore complied with the purpose of the Act. Since, on the basis of the record in this case, we have found that defendant's reports were accurate, the Act was not violated.

Plaintiff also contends that defendant violated the Act by failing to inform the plaintiff that the Act gives a consumer the right to have a statement of his version of the dispute included as part of the consumer report. The Act provides that a consumer may, in those situations where the completeness or accuracy of the report is disputed, prepare and file a brief statement setting forth the nature of the dispute. While it is clearly the better practice for the consumer reporting agency to inform the consumer of his right to file such a statement, the Act does not place an affirmative duty on the reporting agency to so advise the consumer.

Plaintiff's final contention is that defendant violated the Act in failing to disclose the sources of its information used in the reports. This contention merits little discussion since we find that the reports on their face disclose that the information was obtained from John Hancock.

DECISION AND REMEDY   *The judgment was for the defendant, Retail Credit Company, Inc. No violation of the Fair Credit Reporting Act occurred because the reports were accurate.*

Equal Credit Opportunity Act In 1974, Congress enacted the Equal Credit Opportunity Act as part of the Consumer Credit Protection Act. The Equal Credit Opportunity Act forbids certain forms of discrimination. Credit cannot be denied on the basis of race, color, religion, national origin, sex, marital status, age (providing the applicant has the income to repay), or a person's income being derived from public assistance. To discriminate against a person by denying him or her credit on any of these bases is illegal. The civil liabilities for violation of this act include actual damages as well as punitive damages up to $10,000, plus attorneys' fees and court costs.

Fair Debt Collection Practices Act In 1977 Congress passed the Fair Debt Collection Practices Act, which is another section of the Consumer Credit Protection Act. This act applies to anyone who is in the *business* of consumer debt

---

LEGAL HIGHLIGHT **Gossip, Gossip, Gossip**

What type of information was placed in people's credit files prior to the passage of the Fair Credit Reporting Act? Here are a few examples:

■ A man who applied for automobile insurance was denied. He later found this statement in his file: "Subject's son is a hippie type."

■ A woman's application for automobile insurance was denied. In her file was a notation that she was a topless dancer who was divorced.

■ A man who applied for life insurance was denied. In his record was a statement based on hearsay that his former boss had "suspected him of taking money from the till." No charges had ever been filed.

■ Another man was fortunate. In his file was found this statement: "We learn of no connection with any Peace movement or other serversice [sic] type organization. He is regarded as a normal loyal american [sic]."

■ A man who applied for life insurance was denied. In his file was a false statement that he kept "unsavory company." The second statement, over fifteen years old, was that he had destroyed property. The truth was that he had accidentally broken a neighbor's plate glass window while playing softball. When he went to the credit bureau and told his story, the credit bureau agreed to correct his file for a fee. The fee to check out his story was ten

dollars an hour, with a fifteen-hour minimum, payable in advance.

■ A man in Atlanta, had immigrated to the United States from his native Hungary. He arrived in the United States penniless and knowing little English. Twelve years later he had a thriving business. When he went to borrow money, however, he was denied credit again and again. Finally he found that his record noted that he had been involved in a $200 lawsuit, had bad debts, had gone bankrupt, and had skipped town. In fact he had a business, had lived in the same house for twelve years, was not involved in a $200 lawsuit, had no bad debts, and had never filed for bankruptcy.

After two personal visits to the credit reporting bureau and letters to the Justice Department, the Federal Trade Commission, President Nixon, and his hometown newspaper—and with lawyers talking directly to the credit reporting bureau—he still had not cleared the false information from his file. This problem began in 1966. He was finally told that the incorrect information had been expunged from his file in March 1972, but, when he applied for credit cards from Standard Oil and Sears in May 1972, credit was denied. Both companies cited the same source of their negative information: the credit reporting agency that he had been fighting for years.

---

collection for others (collection agencies). Even without federal statutory provisions, however, it is not legal to invade a person's privacy or intentionally to cause emotional distress.

For example, under the Fair Debt Collection Practices Act, Ace, a debt collector, cannot contact Dan, a debtor, before 8 A.M. or after 9 P.M. Repeatedly calling Dan on the telephone is prohibited. Dan cannot be reached at his place of

employment if his employer has a policy against debt collectors contacting employees at work. Ace can contact a third party one time for Dan's address, but cannot tell the third party that a debt is owed. Dan can tell (write) Ace to stop communicating with him. If Dan has an attorney, and Ace knows it, subsequent communications must be made with Dan's attorney. On postcards or envelopes that Ace uses, the return address cannot

---

LEGAL HIGHLIGHT   **Women and the Credit Revolution**

The Equal Credit Opportunity Act was passed in 1974. Until this act was adopted, most single working women could not obtain credit or buy homes or automobiles in their own names without a cosigner.

A woman whose marriage had ended either in divorce or by the death of her husband also found it impossible to obtain credit. A married couple's credit was kept in the name of the husband, even though the wife may have been the only person working. When the marriage was over, the woman had no credit rating. She would discover that no financial institution would grant her a loan, credit cards, or a bank card. Worse, although an ex-husband's good credit rating did not follow her, the bad credit rating of an ex-husband did. The following are further examples:

■ A woman received $250,000 in a divorce settlement. From 1970 to 1972 she repeatedly applied for a bank card with a $500 limit; she was denied credit because she was divorced.

■ In 1973, a married woman attorney who had a ten-year law practice was denied a department store credit card in her own name.

■ In 1969, a widow of six years found it easier to get a credit card in her deceased husband's name than in her own name.

Congress heard many similar stories. Recognizing that women had become a stable part of the nation's work force, Congress passed the Equal Credit Opportunity Act.

As a side note, prior to this law, both single women and single men found it nearly impossible to purchase a house. Single people were deemed unstable by financial institutions. Today, over one-fourth of all houses, condominiums, and townhouses are sold to single people.

---

indicate that Ace is a debt collector. Ace cannot threaten to use physical violence and cannot threaten to harm Dan's reputation or his property. Use of obscene or profane language is forbidden.

Ace cannot imply that he is collecting the debt under the authority of the government and cannot use a badge or uniform. Ace cannot misrepresent that nonpayment of the debt will result in Dan's arrest or imprisonment. The threats of the seizure, garnishment, attachment, or sale of any of Dan's property or his wages is forbidden unless Ace intends to file a lawsuit against Dan and informs Dan of the remedies that Ace may use to collect if Ace wins the suit.

If a provision of the act is violated, the collection agency must pay actual damages, plus additional damages up to $1,000 and attorneys' fees. The following case illustrates two ways in which a debt collection agency can violate the act.

Case 11.3
KIMBER v. FEDERAL FINANCIAL CORP.
United States District Court,
Middle District, Alabama, 1987.
668 F.Supp. 1480.

BACKGROUND AND FACTS *In 1976, W. T. Grant Stores assigned its accounts receivable (debts owed to Grant) to Federal Financial Corporation (FFC), a debt collection agency. In 1985, FFC filed a lawsuit against Kimber to collect a debt she owed. In an independent lawsuit, plaintiff Kimber sued FFC for violations of the Fair Debt Collection Practices Act.*
Kimber alleged that FFC had sued her for a debt while knowing that it was not entitled to recover because the time limitation imposed by the

statute of limitations had passed. FFC, therefore, had sued her on stale debts, or, in the language of the court, the debts were "time-barred." Kimber also alleged that FFC had attempted to collect a debt against her by falsely claiming it could win the lawsuit, although FFC knew the debt was time-barred; thus, FFC's conduct was false and deceptive.

THOMPSON, Judge.

* * * *

* * * To help ensure the most complete protection possible, determinations as to whether conduct violates the Act are made in keeping with the standard of the "least sophisticated consumer." Thus, in applying the law to this case, the court must decide whether FFC's actions were unfair or unconscionable, or whether the least sophisticated of consumers would have been deceived, misled, or harassed by such practices.

* * * *

[Court's discussion of time-barred debts]

The court agrees with Kimber that a debt collector's filing of a lawsuit on a debt that appears to be time-barred, without the debt collector having first determined after a reasonable inquiry that that limitations period has been or should be tolled, is an unfair and unconscionable means of collecting the debt. * * * [T]ime-barred lawsuits are * * * unjust and unfair as a matter of public policy, and this is no less true in the consumer context. As with any defendant sued on a stale claim, the passage of time not only dulls the consumer's memory of the circumstances and validity of the debt, but heightens the probability that she will no longer have personal records detailing the status of the debt. Indeed, the unfairness of such conduct is particularly clear in the consumer context where courts have imposed a heightened standard of care—that sufficient to protect the least sophisticated consumer. Because few unsophisticated consumers would be aware that a statute of limitations could be used to defend against lawsuits based on stale debts, such consumers would unwittingly acquiesce to such lawsuits. And, even if the consumer realizes that she can use time as a defense, she will more than likely still give in rather than fight the lawsuit because she must still expend energy and resources and subject herself to the embarrassment of going into court to present the defense; this is particularly true in light of the costs of attorneys today.

* * * *

The court must therefore conclude that FFC violated [the Act] when it filed suit against Kimber. There is no question that the debt FFC sought from Kimber was barred as stale. * * *

[Court's discussion of misrepresentation]

Kimber argues next that FFC made false, deceptive and misleading representations in violation of the Fair Debt Collection Practices Act by threatening to sue her on a claim the corporation knew was barred. * * *

* * * *

* * * She alleges that by threatening her with a lawsuit which the corporation knew or reasonably should have known was time-barred, the corporation falsely represented the legal status of her debt, misled her as to what action might be legally taken against her, and deceptively used this threat in attempting to collect on her alleged debt. In so doing, Kimber argues, FFC preyed upon the ignorance of an unsophisticated consumer. Threats to sue communicated through an attorney would only naturally represent to the least sophisticated consumer that a lawsuit was viable, even when in fact it was not, Kimber contends.

FFC answers that since it was clearly possible to *file* a lawsuit against Kimber—whether or not it was possible to *win* one—there was no deception as to the legal status of the debt, nor any false threat of legal action used to coerce payment. FFC asserts that ordinary statutes of limitations bar only the remedy, not the underlying right.

Whether it is true that a statute of limitations defense does not erase the right underlying a lawsuit but rather prevents success on a claim is immaterial, for the court cannot agree with FFC that this legal principle, even if true, lends approval to the practice of threatening and undertaking lawsuits for which the statute of limitations has clearly run and for which there is no evidence that would warrant tolling. The dispositive fact is that a debt collector could not legally prevail in such lawsuit, and for the debt collector to represent otherwise is fraudulent.
* * * *

Here, it is obvious to the court that by employing the tactics it did, FFC played upon and benefitted from the probability of creating a deception. Honest disclosure of the legal unenforceability of the collection action due to the time lapsed since the debt was incurred would have foiled FFC's efforts to collect on the debt. So instead, the corporation implicitly misrepresented to Kimber the status of the debt, and thereby misled her as to the viability of legal action to collect. As such, FFC's conduct was false and deceptive[.] * * *

DECISION AND REMEDY   *The court found that FFC had violated the act when it filed a lawsuit against Kimber because the lawsuit had not been filed within the time limits established by the statute of limitations. The court also found that FFC had misrepresented its ability to win a lawsuit in a false and deceptive manner. The case, however, was sent back to the trial court on another issue.*

Other Consumer-Oriented Laws

At the federal and state levels, a variety of consumer protection laws exist. These laws regulate a range of activities from the operation of dance studios and health clubs to used automobile sales and even the sale of funerals. We will review three major laws here.

Uniform Consumer Credit Code

In 1968, the National Conference of Commissioners on the Uniform State Laws promulgated the **Uniform Consumer Credit Code** (UCCC). The UCCC has been controversial, and only a few states have adopted it. It is a comprehensive body of rules governing the most important aspects of consumer credit. Sections of the UCCC, for example, focus on truth in lending, door-to-door sales, referral sales, and maximum credit interest rate ceilings.

The UCCC is also concerned with creditor remedies, including deficiency judgments and gar-

nishments (proceedings where property, money, or wages controlled by a third person are transferred to the court to satisfy a judgment). The UCCC applies to most types of sales, including real estate. It also covers installment loans, retail installment sales, and **usury** (charging more than the maximum rate of interest allowed by state law).

Real Estate Settlement Procedures Act

The **Real Estate Settlement Procedures Act** (RESPA) was passed by Congress in 1974. It governs the purchase of a house and the borrowing of money to pay for it. RESPA requires that all closing costs be specifically outlined before a person buys a home.

After a person applies for a mortgage loan, the lender must, within three business days, send a booklet, prepared by the United States Department of Housing and Urban Development, that outlines the applicant's rights and explains settlement procedures and costs. The lender must give an estimate of most of the settlement costs within that three-day period. If the loan is approved, the lender must provide a truth-in-lending statement that shows the annual percentage rate on the mortgage loan.

State Usury Laws

Usury laws are over 2,500 years old. Typically, usury laws prescribe a maximum rate of interest, such as 10 percent, and a lender cannot charge a person a rate of interest above that maximum amount. Usury is the charging of an interest rate above the maximum amount allowed by statute. Many states, during the inflationary period of the late 1970s, abolished their usury laws or increased the maximum rates a creditor could legally charge.

Usury laws apply to cash loans made to individuals and do not include any protection for businesses. Because only cash loans are covered by usury laws, interest charged on credit cards is not covered, unless a cash advance is made. States have adopted laws that specifically cover the maximum interest charge on credit cards, setting maximum limits on the rate of interest that credit card issuers can charge their customers. Many times the maximum interest rate that can be charged for the use of credit cards is different from the maximum interest rate for cash loans.

Creditors' Rights

A creditor has the right to payment. When the debtor does not fulfill his or her obligation to make timely payments, state laws establish procedures by which a creditor can secure payment of the debt or recovery of the goods for which the debt was incurred.

Writ of Execution

A debt must be past due in order for a creditor to commence legal action against a debtor. If the creditor is successful, the court awards the creditor a judgment against the debtor (usually for the amount of the debt plus any interest and legal costs incurred in obtaining the judgment). If the debtor still does not or cannot pay the judgment, the creditor is entitled to go back to the court and obtain a **writ of execution**.

A writ of execution is an order, issued by a judge or the clerk of the court, directing the sheriff to seize and sell any of the debtor's *nonexempt* real or personal property that is within the court's geographic jurisdiction (usually the county in which the courthouse is located). The proceeds of the sale are used to pay off the judgment and the costs of the sale itself. This procedure is known as a **judicial sale**. Any excess is paid to the debtor.

At any time before the sale takes place, the debtor can pay the judgment and redeem the nonexempt property. **Exempt property** is property that, according to a statute, can be kept by the debtor and is protected from the creditor; such property may include the debtor's home, furniture, and other essentials for living.

Attachment

Attachment is the court-ordered seizure and taking into custody of property that is in controversy over a debt. Attachment rights are created by state statutes. Attachment is normally a prejudgment remedy. It occurs either at the time of or immediately after the commencement of a lawsuit but before the entry of a final judgment. By statute, the restrictions and requirements concerning a creditor's right to attachment before judgment are very specific. The due process clause of the Fourteenth Amendment to the Constitution limits a court's power to authorize seizure of a debtor's property without notice to the debtor or a hearing on the facts.

In order to use attachment as a remedy, the creditor must follow certain procedures. He or she must file with the court an affidavit stating that the debtor is in default and stating the statutory grounds under which attachment is sought. A bond must be posted by the creditor to cover court costs, the value of the loss of the use of the goods as suffered by the debtor, and the value of the property attached. When the court is satisfied that all the requirements have been met, it issues a writ of attachment. This writ is similar to a writ of execution in that it directs the sheriff or other officer to seize nonexempt property. If the creditor prevails at trial, the seized property can be sold to satisfy the judgment.

Garnishment

A **garnishment** is a statutory procedure in which a debtor's property, currently in another's possession, is applied to the payment of that person's debts. An example might be the wages owed to a debtor by his or her employer; a writ of garnishment for these wages is issued by the court and addressed to the employer requiring that a portion of the employee's paycheck be paid to the creditor.

Garnishments are regulated by federal and state law. Before the federal law was passed, many states allowed the creditor to garnish (that is, to take) the debtor's entire paycheck. The lack of laws protecting debtors encouraged lenders to extend credit to people who could not afford the payments. But many employers fired the employee if his or her paycheck was garnished.

Congress determined that debtors needed some limited protection. The federal law sets out the maximum amounts that can be garnished. State laws frequently set even lower limits on the amounts that can be garnished. Now the employee has at least some of his or her paycheck to take home. One exception is that there is no maximum amount when a judgment has been won by the government stating that the debtor owes taxes. In this case, the government can garnish the entire paycheck until all the taxes owed are paid. An employer cannot discharge an employee for garnishment of the employee's paycheck. If the debtor is fired, the employer may be fined $1,000, imprisoned for one year, or both.

Even without federal or state statutes, the United States Supreme Court has declared that a consumer has a right to a hearing before wages can be garnished. The following case established this right.

Case 11.4

SNIADACH v. FAMILY FINANCE CORP.

Supreme Court of the United States, 1969.
395 U.S. 337, 89 S.Ct. 1820, 23 L.Ed.2d 349.

BACKGROUND AND FACTS *Family Finance Corporation attempted under Wisconsin law to garnish the wages of Mrs. Sniadach after she failed to make timely payments on a loan. No trial or hearing was ever held to determine that Mrs. Sniadach had defaulted on the debt or that the garnishment was otherwise authorized. Her only notice was served on her at the same time that her wages were garnished.*

Mrs. Sniadach contended that the finance company's failure to give her notice that the wages would be seized violated her right to due process. Both the trial court and the Wisconsin Supreme Court upheld the procedure allowed by Wisconsin law to garnish wages without prior notice to the consumer. Mrs. Sniadach took her case to the United States Supreme Court.

DOUGLAS, Justice.

Respondents instituted a garnishment action against petitioner as defendant and Miller Harris Instrument Co., her employer, as garnishee. The complaint alleged a claim of $420 on a promissory note. * * *
* * * * *
* * * She * * * claims that the Wisconsin garnishment procedure violates that due process required by the Fourteenth Amendment, in that notice and an opportunity to be heard are not given before the *in rem* seizure of the wages. What happens in Wisconsin is that the clerk of the court issues the summons at the request of the creditor's lawyer; and it is the latter who by serving the garnishee sets in motion the machinery whereby the wages are frozen. They may, it is true, be unfrozen if the trial of the main suit is ever held and the wage earner wins on the merits. But in the interim the wage earner is deprived of his enjoyment of earned wages without any opportunity to be heard and to tender any defense he may have, whether it be fraud or otherwise.

Such summary procedure may well meet the requirements of due process in extraordinary situations. But in the present case, no situation requiring special protection to a state or creditor interest is presented by the facts; nor is the Wisconsin statute narrowly drawn to meet any such unusual condition. Petitioner was a resident of this Wisconsin community and *in personam* jurisdiction was readily obtainable.

* * * In this case, the sole question is whether there has been a taking of property without that procedural due process that is required by the Fourteenth Amendment. We have dealt over and over again with the question of what constitutes "the right to be heard" within the meaning of procedural due process. * * * [W]e said that the right to be heard "has little reality or worth unless one is informed that the matter is pending and can choose for himself whether to appear or default, acquiesce or contest." * * *

A prejudgment garnishment of the Wisconsin type is a taking which may impose tremendous hardship on wage earners with families to support. Until a recent Act of Congress which forbids discharge of employees on the ground that their wages have been garnished, garnishment often meant loss of a job. Over and beyond that was the great drain on family income. As stated by Congressman Reuss:

> The idea of wage garnishment in advance of judgment, of trustee process, of wage attachment, or whatever it is called is a most inhuman doctrine. It compels the wage earner, trying to keep his family together, to be driven below the poverty level.

* * * *

The result is that a prejudgment garnishment of the Wisconsin type may as a practical matter drive a wage-earning family to the wall. Where the taking of one's property is so obvious, it needs no extended argument to conclude that absent notice and a prior hearing this prejudgment garnishment procedure violates the fundamental principles of due process.

The court ruled that the Wisconsin statute was unconstitutional. As a result of this decision, today a court must determine that a valid debt exists before wages can be garnished, and there must be proper notice and a hearing available to the debtor before garnishment can take place.

DECISION AND REMEDY

Mortgage Foreclosure on Real Property

In Chapter 10, we reviewed how a secured party (a creditor) repossesses personal property. The basic format is the same for repossessing real property, but some differences do exist. Various methods exist to create a lien on real estate. For this discussion, we will group all of them under the term mortgage.

Creation of the Mortgage A real estate mortgage is a lien against the realty to secure payment of a loan given usually to secure the purchase of real property. For example, Jane wants to purchase a house. After entering into a purchase agreement (contract) to buy a house, she arranges with a lender to borrow money over a thirty-year period at a 9 percent interest rate. She must sign a note with the lender in which she, the debtor-borrower, agrees to pay back the money in monthly installments to the creditor-lender over the next thirty years. At this point, the unsecured note is the only evidence of the debt, and if Jane were to default on the note, all the creditor could do would be to sue her in court on the note.

What the creditor wants is something to back up the note; that is, the creditor wants a secured note. In real estate, the note is secured by a lien against the home, known as a mortgage. Jane, the debtor-borrower, creates a mortgage on the real estate; thus, she is called the **mortgagor**. This creator-lender is the beneficiary of the mortgage and is called the **mortgagee**. Once the mortgage is created to back up (secure) the note, the note is usually called a mortgage note.

Default and Foreclosure   Let's say that Jane now defaults. The real estate mortgage agreement provides that, if the mortgagor (debtor-borrower) defaults in making the payments, the mortgagee (creditor-lender) can declare that the entire mortgage debt is due immediately. The mortgagee can obtain payment in full by a lawsuit called a foreclosure.

In this suit, the real estate that is covered by the mortgage is usually sold at a court-ordered sale (a judicial sale) under the authority of a writ of execution. If the proceeds of the sale are sufficient to cover both the costs of the foreclosure and the mortgaged debt, any surplus is paid to the debtor. Jane is entitled to this money since she is the owner of the property. The creditor holds only a lien against her property; thus, the creditor is entitled to have only the lien paid back and is not entitled to make a profit. All the creditor can collect is the amount of the unpaid debt.

Deficiency Judgment   If, on the other hand, the sale proceeds are insufficient to cover the foreclosure costs and the mortgaged debt, the mortgagee can seek to recover the difference from Jane (the mortgagor) by obtaining a deficiency judgment in most states. A deficiency judgment represents the deficiency amount—that is, the difference between the mortgaged debt and costs of foreclosure and the amount actually received from the proceeds of the foreclosure sale.

A deficiency judgment is normally obtained in a separate legal action that is filed after the foreclosure, because the creditor does not know until after the sale if there is a surplus or a deficiency. The creditor can recover the deficiency judgment from other property owned by the debtor. Only nonexempt property (property that is subject to execution or garnishment) can be used to satisfy the deficiency judgment. In many states, the creditor cannot obtain a deficiency judgment at all against a debtor when the foreclosure involves the debtor's residence.

From the time of default until the time of the foreclosure sale, Jane can redeem her property by paying the full amount of the debt, plus any in-terest and other costs that have accrued. In some states, Jane may even be able to redeem her property within a statutory period after the judicial sale.

Protection for the Debtor

In most states, certain types of real and personal property are exempt from levy of execution or attachment. Probably the most familiar of these exemptions is the **homestead exemption**. Each state permits the debtor to retain the family home, either in its entirety or up to a specified dollar amount, free from unsecured creditors or trustees in bankruptcy claims. The purpose is to ensure that the debtor will retain or be able to obtain some form of shelter.

For example, Daniels owes Carey $40,000. The debt is the subject of a lawsuit, and the court awards Carey a judgment of $40,000 against Daniels. At some time before, during, or in some states even after the judgment, Daniels can file a homestead exemption. Daniels's home is valued at $50,000. To satisfy the judgment debt, Daniels's family home is sold at public auction for $45,000. Assume that the state law allows a homestead exemption of $25,000. The proceeds of the sale are distributed as follows:

1. Daniels is paid $25,000 as his homestead exemption.
2. Carey is paid $20,000 toward the judgment debt.
3. A $20,000 debt is still owed.

Carey now obtains a deficiency judgment for $20,000. This deficiency judgment can be satisfied from any other nonexempt property (personal or real) that Daniels may have, if allowed by state law.

Personal property that is most often exempt from satisfaction of judgment debts includes:

1. Household furniture, such as beds, dining tables and chairs, usually up to a specified dollar amount;
2. Clothing and certain personal possessions, such as family pictures, books, tools, and Bibles; and
3. A vehicle for transportation (at least up to a specified dollar amount).

Bankruptcies and Reorganizations

The United States Constitution, Article I, Section 8, provides that "the Congress shall have Power . . . To establish . . . uniform Laws on the subject of Bankruptcies throughout the United States." Congress has adopted a series of bankruptcy statutes; the latest are the Bankruptcy Reform Acts of 1978, 1984, and 1986. Federal law governs bankruptcy proceedings. Bankruptcy courts are special federal courts, and the bankruptcy judges are appointed for fourteen-year terms by the United States Courts of Appeals.

Goals of Bankruptcy

Bankruptcy law is designed to accomplish two main goals. The first is to provide relief and protection (a fresh start) to debtors who are deeply in debt and cannot recover financially without help. The second major goal of bankruptcy is to provide a fair means of distributing a debtor's assets among all creditors. Although the bankruptcy acts are federal law, state laws on secured transactions, liens, judgments, and exemptions play a role in federal bankruptcy proceedings.

The Bankruptcy Reform Acts of 1978, 1984, and 1986

The Bankruptcy Reform Acts of 1978, 1984, and 1986 are contained in Title 11 of the United States Code and have several chapters. Chapters 1, 3, and 5 include general definitions and provisions governing the case administration, the creditors, the debtor, and the estate. These three chapters apply generally to all bankruptcies. Several chapters set forth different types of bankruptcy relief. Chapter 7 provides for liquidations. Chapter 9 governs the adjustment of debts of a municipality. Chapter 11 allows for reorganizations, of individual and business debtors. Chapter 12 provides for bankruptcy relief of family farmers, and Chapter 13 provides for the adjustment of debts of individuals with regular income. The following sections deal with Chapter 7, Liquidations; Chapter 11, Reorganizations; Chapter 13, Adjustment of Debts of Individuals; and Chapter 12, Adjustment of Debts of Family Farmers.

The 1986 act created the position of U.S. Trustee in each federal judicial district. U.S. Trustees monitor the administrative side of bankruptcies.

Chapter 7: Liquidations   The most familiar type of bankruptcy proceedings is often referred to as a **straight bankruptcy**. Put simply, a debtor in a straight bankruptcy lists his or her debts and turns his or her assets over to a trustee. The trustee sells the assets and distributes the proceeds to creditors. Most of the balance of the debts are then discharged (extinguished), and the debtor is relieved from the obligation to pay these debts.

Any person—defined here to include individuals, partnerships, and corporations—may be a debtor under Chapter 7. "Corporation" as used here includes unincorporated companies and associations; it also covers labor unions. Chapter 7 does not apply to railroads, insurance companies, banks, savings and loan associations, and governmental units. Other chapters of the Bankruptcy Act or other federal and state statutes apply to them.

Bankruptcy Procedure   A straight bankruptcy is started by the filing of a petition on the official forms of the bankruptcy court. The debtor can file a voluntary petition, or unsecured creditors whose aggregate claims equal $5,000 or more can involuntary petition the debtor into bankruptcy. The petition contains a list of both secured and unsecured creditors, their addresses, and the amount of debt owed to each; a statement of the financial affairs of the debtor; and a list of all property owned by the debtor, including property claimed by the debtor to be exempt. The official forms must be completed accurately, sworn to under oath, and signed by the debtor. To conceal assets or knowingly supply false information on these schedules is a federal crime and can be grounds for denying the debtor a discharge in bankruptcy.

The filing of a petition operates as an **automatic stay** that stops or suspends all civil litigation against the debtor. In other words, creditors cannot start or continue legal actions against the debtor to recover claims they have against him or her, nor can creditors take any action to repossess property in the hands of the debtor. All actions against the debtor must now go through the bankruptcy court.

Trustees   A court-appointed trustee is to be distinguished from a U.S. Trustee. The U.S. Trustee is an administrative position within the bankruptcy court. A regular trustee (interim or permanent) is appointed by the court to represent the creditors.

The court appoints an interim trustee to preside over the debtor's property until the first meeting of creditors. At this first meeting, a permanent trustee is elected. The trustee's principal duty is to collect the debtor's property, reduce it to money, and close up the estate as soon as possible, keeping in mind the best interests of all parties. Trustees are entitled to compensation for services rendered plus reimbursement for expenses.

A trustee steps into the shoes of the debtor, and the trustee has specific powers of avoidance. Any reason that a debtor can use to obtain return of his or her property can be used by the trustee as well. These grounds include fraud, duress, incapacity, and mutual mistake. For example, Ben sells his boat to Frank. Frank gives Ben a check, knowing that there are insufficient funds in the bank account to cover the check. Frank has committed fraud. Ben has the right to cancel the contract and to recover the boat from Frank. If Ben has filed for bankruptcy, the trustee for Ben can exercise the same right to recover the boat from Frank. The trustee's power of avoidance includes setting aside preferences (payments made by the debtor to a creditor while insolvent) and setting aside certain statutory liens, such as a landlord's lien.

Exemptions   An individual debtor is entitled to exempt certain property from bankruptcy. An individual debtor can choose between the exemptions provided under the state law or under the federal law, if the state law allows this choice. The following lists some of the property that is exempt under federal law:

1. Equity interest in a debtor's residence up to $7,500;
2. One motor vehicle up to $1,200;
3. Household furnishings and apparel up to $4,000 with no one item being worth more than $200;
4. Jewelry up to $500;
5. Professional books or tools of no more than $750;
6. Life insurance contracts;
7. Professionally prescribed health aids;
8. Miscellaneous property up to $400;

9. Social security, profit sharing, disability, alimony, and other funds for the support of the debtor or of his or her dependents; and
10. Amounts paid to the debtor under a crime victims law, wrongful death award, and up to $7,500 not including pain and suffering for a personal injury.

Property Distribution   The trustee, after reducing the debtor's available estate to money, is obligated to pay the debts of those unsecured creditors who appropriately file claims. Bankruptcy law establishes an order of priority for certain classes of debts owed these unsecured creditors. Each class must be fully paid before the next class on the list is entitled to any proceeds. If there are insufficient proceeds to pay a class, the proceeds are prorated among the creditors of that class and all classes lower in priority receive nothing. If all classes are fully paid and there is a remaining balance, it goes to the debtor.

Examples of the order of priority among classes of unsecured creditors is as follows:

1. All bankruptcy costs have top priority.
2. Claims for unpaid wages, salaries, or commissions due employees earned within ninety days of the bankruptcy petition limited to $2,000 per employee.
3. Claims for funds prepaid by creditors to the debtor for goods or services not delivered by the debtor up to $900 for each claim.
4. Certain taxes (and penalties) owed to government entities.

All of these creditors and others must be paid before any unsecured general creditor is entitled to any proceeds from the debtor's estate.

Nondischargeable Debts   From the debtor's point of view, the primary purpose of a Chapter 7 liquidation is to obtain a fresh start through the **discharge** of debts. There are circumstances, however, in which a debt will not be discharged.

Debts that are not dischargeable include claims for back taxes accruing within three years prior to bankruptcy; claims against property or money obtained by the debtor under false representations; claims for alimony and child support; claims for certain student loans; and judgments or consent decrees awarded against a debtor for liability incurred as a result of the debtor's operation of a motor vehicle while legally intoxicated. Discharges are granted only to "individuals" as debtors; not to corporations or partnerships. The latter may use Chapter 11 or, where appropriate, Chapter 12 bankruptcy proceedings.

Reaffirmation   Under previous bankruptcy acts, it was very common for a creditor to convince the debtor to **reaffirm** (renew) his or her debts. For example, a finance company would offer a debtor a loan of $1,000 if he or she would reaffirm the debt that had been owed to the finance company but that had been discharged by bankruptcy. Creditors knew that the debtor could not file for bankruptcy again for six more years. Reaffirmation tended to defeat one of the purposes of bankruptcy: to give a debtor a fresh start.

As a result, Congress has restricted the procedure of reaffirmations. Since 1984, to be enforceable, reaffirmation agreements must be made before a debtor is granted a discharge. The agreement must be filed with the court. The debtor must be counseled by his or her attorney, and a declaration must be filed stating that the debtor knows the consequences of the voluntary agreement and that it does not impose a hardship on the debtor or on his or her dependents. If the debtor is not represented by an attorney, court approval is required except for the debtor's real property. Here the court must find that the agreement presents no undue hardship and that it is in the best interests of the debtor.

The debtor has the ability to rescind the agreement at any time prior to discharge or within sixty days of the filing of the agreement, whichever is later. This rescission period must be stated clearly and conspicuously in the reaffirmation agreement.

Chapter 11: Reorganizations   Chapter 11 reorganization is used most commonly by a corporate debtor. Essentially, in a reorganization the creditors and the debtor formulate a plan under which the debtor pays a portion of his or her debts and is discharged of the remainder. The debtor is allowed to continue in business. Although this type of bankruptcy is commonly a corporate reorganization, debtors who are eligible for Chapter 7 relief and railroads are also eligible for Chapter 11 relief. Proceedings may be initiated by either a voluntary or involuntary petition.

The same principles that govern the filing of a Chapter 7 petition apply to Chapter 11 proceedings and to the court's entry of the order for relief. The automatic stay and adequate protection provisions previously discussed are applicable in reorganizations.

The debtor generally continues to operate his or her business as a "debtor in possession." The court may appoint a trustee to operate the debtor's business if gross mismanagement of the business is shown or if it is in the best interests of the debtor.

The debtor files a Chapter 11 plan that must be "fair and equitable." Classes of claims, such as secured and unsecured creditors, under the plan must be designated, and each claim within a particular class must be provided the same treatment. Once the plan has been developed, it is submitted to each class of creditors for acceptance. Acceptance of a plan is required by each class.

The plan must be in the best interests of the creditors. On confirmation, the debtor is given a Chapter 11 discharge for all claims not protected under the plan. Those debts protected by the plan are paid in part according to the plan, but the remainder of those debts is also discharged.

The following case examines whether unsecured creditors can have a fund established for them when the fund was not part of the reorganization plan.

BACKGROUND AND FACTS   *A. H. Robins Company is a pharmaceutical firm. From 1971 to 1974, it sold the Dalkon Shield intrauterine device (IUD) to physicians and clinics. Over 2.2 million women were fitted with the Dalkon Shield. From the start, Robins received complaints. Eventually more than 12,000 women filed lawsuits. They sought damages for debilitating pain, severe bleeding, perforated uteri, unplanned pregnancies, spontaneous miscarriages, septic abortions, chronic pelvic inflammatory dis-*

Case 11.5
OFFICIAL COMMITTEE OF EQUITY SECURITY HOLDERS v. MABEY
United States Court of Appeals, Fourth Circuit, 1987.
832 F.2d 299.

ease, and for being rendered sterile. Over twenty women died. Although Robins won the initial lawsuits, as more information was disclosed about Robins's negligence in designing, testing, and marketing the Dalkon Shield, more women won their lawsuits, some receiving judgments of over $1 million.

Robins, in 1985, filed a petition for relief under Chapter 11. The United States District Court for the Eastern District of Virginia, where Robins's headquarters are located, took jurisdiction over certain aspects of the bankruptcy, including all the lawsuits filed by the women. The district court ordered a notice of claim to be advertised worldwide so that any woman who had a Dalkon Shield claim against Robins could file a claim with the court. The court expected less than 30,000 notices of claims to be filed; over 325,000 notices of claims were actually filed. Of these claims, only 180,000 filed the notices in a timely manner and returned the court questionnaire.

At the time that this aspect of the case arose, Robins was challenging the validity and amount of the claims. None of the claims had been estimated for a value amount, thus none had been allowed by the district court as a payable claim. Additionally, the final reorganization plan had not been filed. In the meantime, the Official Committee of Equity Securities Holders (The Equity Committee) had been appointed by the district court to represent Robins's public shareholders. Common stock for the Robins Company is traded on the New York Stock Exchange, with more than 20 million shares outstanding.

In August 1986, the district court appointed Mabey as an examiner to evaluate a plan of reorganization. He, together with Robins, the Dalkon Shield Claimants' Committee, and the future claimants' representative created the concept of an emergency treatment fund that would provide payment for surgery or cash payments to qualified women. In May 1987, the district court ordered Robins to establish the fund and to fund it with $15 million. The Equity Committee appealed this order.

CHAPMAN, Judge.
* * * *

The May 21, 1987 order of the district court approving the Emergency Treatment Fund makes no mention of its authority to establish such a fund prior to the allowance of the claims of the women who would benefit from the fund, and prior to the confirmation of a plan of reorganization of Robins. However, in its order denying The Equity Committee's Motion for a Stay Pending Appeal of the May 21, 1987 order, the district court relied upon the "expansive equity power" of the court. [The court stated that it:]

> * * * recognizes that the establishment of an emergency treatment fund is unusual and, indeed, may be unprecedented. Nevertheless, the Code provides the Court * * * with an expansive equity power to 'issue any order, process or judgment that is necessary or appropriate to carry out the provisions of this title.' The dire circumstances of this case required the Court to invoke its power under Section 105(a) and take those steps needed to treat these claimants equitably. *See also Midlantic Nat'l Bank v. New Jersey Dept. of Envt'l Protection.*

We have searched *Midlantic* without finding any reference to the equitable powers and we find such decision has no relevance to the issues presently before

us. While equitable powers are quite important in the general bankruptcy scheme, and while such powers may encourage courts to be innovative, and even original, these equitable powers are not a license for a court to disregard the clear language and meaning of the bankruptcy statutes and rules. * * *
* * * *

The Bankruptcy Code does not permit a distribution to unsecured creditors in a Chapter 11 proceeding except under and pursuant to a plan of reorganization that has been properly presented and approved. * * * The clear language of * * * the Bankruptcy Rules * * * does not authorize the payment in part or in full, or the advance of monies to or for the benefit of unsecured claimants prior to the approval of the plan of reorganization. The creation of the Emergency Treatment Program has no authority to support it in the Bankruptcy Code and violates the clear policy of Chapter 11 reorganizations by allowing piecemeal, pre-confirmation payments to certain unsecured creditors. Such action also violates [the] Bankruptcy Rule which allows distribution to creditors only after the allowance of claims and the confirmation of a plan.

The creation of the emergency treatment fund was premature. The fund was created prior to the district court allowing the claims for payment and prior to the confirmation of Robins's plan for reorganization. The district court order was in violation of the Bankruptcy Code, and the district court had no other basis of authority to create the fund.	**DECISION AND REMEDY**

Chapter 13: Adjustment of Debts of an Individual with Regular Income

The former Bankruptcy Act provided for the formulation of wage-earner plans as a means of allowing wage earners to pay off their debts free from the harassment of creditors. Under these plans, the wage earner avoided the stigma of being adjudicated a "bankrupt." Today, Chapter 13 of the Bankruptcy Code provides for "Adjustment of Debts of an Individual with Regular Income."

Who May File   Individuals (not partnerships or corporations) with regular income who owe unsecured debts of less than $100,000 and secured debts of less than $350,000 may take advantage of Chapter 13. The act includes individual business proprietors and individuals on welfare, social security, fixed pension, or investment income. Many small-business debtors have the choice of filing a plan under either Chapter 11 or Chapter 13.

Several advantages come with filing a Chapter 13 plan, among them the fact that it is less expensive and less complicated than a Chapter 11 proceeding or a Chapter 7 liquidation. A Chapter 13 case can only be initiated by the voluntary filing of a petition by the debtor. Any eligible debtor, who is presently in a Chapter 7 or Chapter 11 bankruptcy proceeding, can convert to a Chapter 13 case.

Bankruptcy Proceedings   When a debtor files a Chapter 13 petition, the automatic stay previously discussed takes effect.

The debtor may propose a plan that provides for either full payment or partial payment of the debts. A Chapter 13 plan must provide for the turnover of future earnings or income of the debtor to the trustee as is necessary to carry out the plan. Full payment of all claims entitled to priority must be included in the plan. The full payment is made by paying smaller amounts over a longer time period than would have been allowed under the original creditor-debtor agreement. Each claim within a particular class must be treated equally; each secured debt, for example, must be paid in the same method as all other secured debts. The time for payment under the plan may not exceed three years unless the court approves an extension. The plan with extension may not exceed five years.

The plan must be confirmed by the court as long as all of the debtor's projected disposable income will be applied to making payments. Disposable income is all income less amounts needed to support the debtor (and dependents) and/or those needed to meet ordinary expenses to continue operation of a business.

The debtor is required to make "timely payments." Payments must begin under the proposed plan within thirty days after the plan has been filed. Failure of the debtor to make timely payments or to commence payments within the thirty-day period will allow the court to convert the case to a Chapter 7 liquidation or to dismiss the petition.

After completion of all payments under a Chapter 13 plan, the court grants a discharge of all debts provided for by the plan. Taxes, alimony, and child support debts cannot be discharged. Because there are fewer nondischargeable debts under Chapter 13, the discharge is even greater than that provided for in a Chapter 7 liquidation.

Even if the debtor does not complete the plan, a hardship discharge may be granted if the failure to complete the plan was due to circumstances beyond the debtor's control and if the property distributed by the plan was greater than would have been paid in a Chapter 7 liquidation. For example, if the debtor is seriously injured in an accident and is permanently disabled, the debtor's income would be severely reduced, and he or she would be unable to complete the plan. In such a case, a discharge of the remaining debts may be granted.

Chapter 12: Adjustment of Debts of a Family Farmer with Regular Annual Income On No-

vember 27, 1986, the Family Farmer Bankruptcy Act became law. The new law defines a family farmer as one whose gross income is at least 50 percent farm-dependent and whose debts are at least 80 percent farm-related. The total debt must not exceed $1,500,000. A partnership or closely held corporation (at least 50 percent owned by the "farm family") can also take advantage of this law.

A Chapter 12 filing is very similar in procedure to a Chapter 13 filing. The farmer debtor must file a plan not later than ninety days after the order of relief. The filing of the petition acts as an automatic stay against creditors and co-obligor actions against the estate.

The content and confirmation of the plan is basically the same as a Chapter 13 filing. The plan can be modified by the farmer-debtor but, except for cause, must be confirmed or denied within forty-five days of the filing of the plan. The plan must provide for payment of secured debts at the value of the collateral. If the secured debt exceeds the value of the collateral, the remaining debt is unsecured. For unsecured debtors, the plan must be confirmed if either the value of the property to be distributed under the plan equals the amount of the claim, or if the plan provides that all of the debtor-farmer's disposable income received in a three-year period (longer by court approval) will be applied to making payments.

Disposable income is all income received less amounts needed to support the farmer-debtor and family and continue the farming operation. Completion of payments under the plan is discharge of all debts provided for by the plan.

The Proper Way to Grant Credit

You are a manager of a medium-sized manufacturing firm that sells predominantly to retail consumers. Your average sale to a customer is $2,500, which makes it necessary for your firm to grant credit. Most of your consumers do not pay cash for your products.

No problems arise when your customers pay in accordance with your agreement, and normally your customers do pay on time. You, however, must plan ahead to give your company the best position possible under federal and state laws in the event that a customer does not pay.

First, before granting credit, you should obtain a detailed credit application that lists all the consumer's assets and liabilities. Included on this form are the names and addresses of creditors and relatives. The information about the relatives may help you find out what assets are available for attachment, execution, or garnishment, and may help you locate the debtor if he or she moves. You can ask for, but cannot require a social security number, although this information is helpful for identification purposes, especially when the consumer has a common name such as Brown, Smith, or Jones. With this application, you can verify credit with reporting agencies or with the creditors listed.

If you will be receiving more than four payments, you must comply with the truth-in-lending laws. Using the forms suggested by the Federal Reserve Board saves the time needed to draft forms and will prevent you from running afoul of the law. If you sell your product door to door, you must give the consumer a cooling-off period of three business days before you can regard the sale as irrevocable.

If you are selling personal property (goods), you must decide whether to secure your interest under the Uniform Commercial Code, Article 9. This procedure is covered in Chapter 10.

Remember that you must have a written security agreement if the consumer-debtor has possession of the product. To protect your company's right fully, you must file a financing statement with the appropriate public office.

If an account becomes delinquent, what can your firm do to collect the monies owed? You should review the provisions of the Fair Debt Collection Practices Act. Keep in mind, first, that the collection agency you hire cannot harass or invade the right of privacy of an individual, and, second, there cannot be the threat of physical harm. Never threaten criminal prosecution, even if the debtor has committed a criminal act such as giving a bad check or committing fraud on the credit application. Such threatening could be considered duress in a civil action, and the threats themselves could result in you being charged with the crime of extortion.

Your firm should have a written policy as to the sequence of events that occur when it is confronted with a bad debt. Remember that, if the consumer contests the bill, you must investigate and respond to his or her inquiry.

At times your firm will have to write off a debt as uncollectable and take a tax loss if that is allowed. The old saying that "you can't get blood out of a turnip" has application today. If the consumer has lost his or her job, is in prison, is disabled, or has suffered some other catastrophe, your firm should take the loss as soon as possible. In fact, if you do not have some losses on credit sales, it would indicate that your credit policies are too rigid. Your firm might be able to increase sales by relaxing those policies.

Lastly, you should be aware of the possibility of the debtor filing for bankruptcy. Having knowledge of the bankruptcy chapters available to the debtor and the ramifications for you as creditor under each chapter is important in establishing your credit policy.

Summary

This chapter has emphasized three areas of the law: consumer laws, creditors' rights, and bankruptcy.

The Consumer Credit Protection Act has five sections that apply directly to businesses and consumers. These sections may be summarized briefly as follows:

1. Truth-in-Lending Act: This statute requires the disclosure of the price owed, the finance charges, and the annual percentage rate of interest for the privilege of paying off the debt over a period of time. It also allows a three-day cooling-off period for credit transactions involving liens on residences (except first liens). The Federal Reserve Board has prepared forms that allow businesses to comply with this act. Under this act, a consumer cannot normally incur more than fifty dollars' liability on a stolen or lost credit card for its unauthorized use.

2. The Fair Credit Reporting Act establishes certain rights for consumers. First, only information from the last seven years may be maintained, and information regarding bankruptcies over ten years old must be deleted from the record. The consumer can obtain the information contained in his or her credit records. In the event that the debtor contests this information, the reporting agency must investigate and correct misinformation and/or allow the debtor to file his or her explanation. Reports can only be used for legitimate credit or insurance purposes.

3. The Equal Credit Opportunity Act prohibits the creditor from discriminating against credit applicants based on race, color, religion, national origin, sex, marital status, age, or the receipt of income through public assistance.

4. The Fair Debt Collection Practices Act was adopted to protect consumers from overzealous collection agencies. Debt collectors must refrain from certain practices that would cause an invasion of privacy of the debtor and refrain from the intentional infliction of emotional distress, or duress.

5. The Fair Credit Billing Act was enacted to assist a debtor to correct a billing error. The law allows any debtor who believes a billing statement is in error to notify the creditor in writing explaining the error. The debtor does not have to pay the disputed amount at that time. The creditor must acknowledge receipt of the error inquiry and within ninety days correct the account or inform the debtor by explanation that the account is correct.

Creditors use three judicial methods to try to collect on judgments owed them: writ of attachment, writ of execution, and writ of garnishment. Writs of attachment and execution are directed against nonexempt property in the possession of the debtor, while a writ of garnishment is directed against the debtor's property that is in the possession of a third party.

Chapters 7, 11, 12, and 13 of the Bankruptcy Code are of major importance to businesses. Chapter 11 provides for reorganization, while Chapter 7 allows a discharge of most debts. Chapters 12 and 13 permit family farmers and individuals to readjust their debts with a pay-out plan over a three- to five-year period. Some debts are not dischargeable by bankruptcy. In addition, there are certain assets that are exempt from bankruptcy by law; thus, the debtor may keep these assets.

Key Terms

annual percentage rate (**256**)
attachment (**269**)
automatic stay (**273**)
bankruptcy law (**273**)
Consumer Credit Cost
    Disclosure Act (**256**)

Consumer Credit Protection
    Act (**256**)
discharge (**274**)
Equal Credit Opportunity Act
    (**256**)
exempt property (**269**)

Fair Credit Billing Act (**256**)
Fair Credit Reporting Act (**256**)
Fair Debt Collection Practices
    Act (**256**)
finance charge (**256**)
garnishment (**270**)

homestead exemption (**272**)
judicial sale (**269**)
mortgagee (**272**)
mortgagor (**271**)
reaffirm (**275**)

Real Estate Settlement
   Procedures Act (**268**)
straight bankruptcy (**273**)
Truth-in-Lending Act (TILA)
   (**256**)

Uniform Consumer Credit
   Code (**268**)
usury (**268**)
writ of execution (**269**)

Questions and Case Problems

1. The East Bank was a secured party on a loan of $5,000 that it made to Sally. Sally later got into financial difficulty, and creditors other than the East Bank petitioned her into Chapter 7 involuntary bankruptcy. The value of the secured collateral had substantially decreased in value; on sale, the debt to East Bank was reduced only to $2,500. Sally's estate consisted of $100,000 in exempt assets and $2,000 in nonexempt assets. After the bankruptcy costs and back wages to Sally's employees were paid, nothing was left for unsecured creditors. Sally received a discharge in bankruptcy. Six years later she decided to go back into business. By selling a few exempt assets and getting a small loan, she would be able to buy a small but profitable restaurant. She went to East Bank for the loan. East Bank claimed that the balance of its secured debt was not discharged in bankruptcy. Sally agreed and signed an agreement to pay East Bank the $2,500, as the bank was not a party to the petitioning of Sally into bankruptcy. Because of this, East Bank made the new unsecured loan to Sally.

    a. Discuss East Bank's claim that the balance of its secured debt was not discharged in bankruptcy.

    b. Discuss the legal effect of Sally's agreement to pay East Bank $2,500 after the discharge in bankruptcy.

    c. If, one year later, Sally went into voluntary bankruptcy, what effect would the bankruptcy proceedings have on the new unsecured loan?

2. Green receives two new credit cards on May 1. One was solicited from the King Department Store, and the other was unsolicited from the Flyways Airline. During the month of May, Green makes numerous credit card purchases from King, but she does not use the Flyways Airline card. On May 31, a burglar breaks into Green's home and, along with other items, steals both credit cards. Green notifies the King Department Store of the theft on June 2, but she fails to notify Flyways Airline. Using the King credit card, the burglar makes a $500 purchase on June 1 and a $200 purchase on June 3. The burglar then charges a vacation flight on the Flyways Airline card for $1,000 on June 5. Green receives the bills for these charges and refuses to pay them. Discuss Green's liability in these situations.

3. Prior to filing for bankruptcy, Bray was making loan payments to his company's credit union through payroll deductions. Bray's employer continued to deduct the loan payments from Bray's paychecks after being notified of

the bankruptcy petition. Is this a violation of the Bankruptcy Code? [In re Bray, 17 B.R. 152 (Bkrtcy. N.D.Ga. 1982)]

4. Does conversion of nonexempt property to exempt property on the eve of a bankruptcy constitute a fraudulent conveyance? (For example, purchasing a home could convert $7,500 in cash to $7,500 in exempt property.) [Wudrick v. Clements, 451 F.2d 988 (9th Cir. 1971)]

5. John Yee earned more than $16,000 in his position with CBS. Prior to working for CBS he obtained a degree in accountancy from Bernard M. Baruch College of the City University of New York. He obtained this degree through the assistance of the National Student Direct Loan, to which he owed $2,583. His other debts totaled $10,790, and he had no assets. John Yee filed a Chapter 13 plan wherein he proposed to pay a total of $918 over thirty-six months on all of his loans. Do you think the court should accept this plan? Was it made in good faith? [In re Yee, 7 B.R. 747 (Bkrtcy. E.D.N.Y. 1980)]

6. Harold Grey signed an installment contract as payment for membership in European Health Spas Club, Inc. The disclosure documents that accompanied the installment loan contract were printed in regular type, with the exception of the following words, which were printed in capital letters: "FINANCE CHARGE," "ANNUAL PERCENTAGE RATE," and "MEMBER ACKNOWLEDGES THAT HE HAS READ AND RECEIVED A FILLED-IN SIGNED COPY OF THIS AGREEMENT." In addition, at the top of the disclosure statement, the words "NOTICE TO BUYER" were printed. Under federal truth-in-lending regulations, the words "finance charge" and "annual percentage rate" must be printed conspicuously in the truth-in-lending disclosure statements; otherwise, the creditor is deemed in violation of the act. Has the requirement of conspicuousness been met? [Grey v. European Health Spas, Inc., 428 F.Supp. 841 (D.Conn. 1977)]

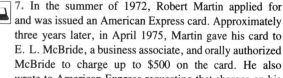 **7.** In the summer of 1972, Robert Martin applied for and was issued an American Express card. Approximately three years later, in April 1975, Martin gave his card to E. L. McBride, a business associate, and orally authorized McBride to charge up to $500 on the card. He also wrote to American Express requesting that charges on his account be limited to $1,000. In June 1975, however,

Martin received a statement from American Express indicating that the amount owed on his card account was approximately $5,300. Under the Truth-in-Lending Act, for how much will Martin be liable to American Express? [Martin v. American Express, Inc., 361 So.2d 597 (Ala.App. 1978)]

 8. Johns-Manville Corporation was a highly successful business that was listed as a Fortune 500 company. Over 16,000 lawsuits had been brought as a result of one of its products—asbestos. Johns-Manville sought the protection of the federal court by filing a Chapter 11 petition in bankruptcy. People who filed lawsuits argued to the court that Johns-Manville was perpetrating a fraud by exaggerating the economic distress of these lawsuits and that it was not insolvent. Was Johns-Manville correct in filing for protection under Chapter 11 of the bankruptcy law? [In re Johns-Manville Corporation, 36 B.R. 727 (Bkrtcy. S.D.N.Y. 1984)]

Chapter 12 Torts and Product Liability

I am charmed with many points of the Turkish law; when proved the authors of any notorious falsehood, they are burned on the forehead with a hot iron.

Lady Montague

OUTLINE

Introduction

Tort is a French word for wrong. Society recognizes an interest in one's personal physical safety and in the prevention of damage to property. Tort law provides remedies for those acts that cause harm. Society also recognizes other more intangible interests in such things as personal privacy, family relations, reputation, and dignity; tort law provides a remedy for the invasion of these protected interests, too.

Tort law is a part of the civil law. Injured parties may file civil lawsuits hoping to be compensated for their injuries. An act that is a tort can also be a crime; thus, criminal law and tort law overlap. For example, Cal drives an automobile while under the influence of alcohol. He runs a red light and has an accident that wrecks Tex's automobile and injures the driver. Cal has committed a crime, driving under the influence of alcohol, and has committed a tort, negligent driving.

Some tort actions result solely in civil lawsuits; there is no criminal prosecution. The burden of proof in a criminal action is higher (beyond a reasonable doubt) than the burden of proof in a civil tort case (by a preponderance of the evidence). (Preponderance means that the greater weight of the evidence was presented by the plaintiff and was more convincing than the evidence presented by the defendant.) Thus, a person might be found innocent of a crime, but still be liable to an injured party in a civil lawsuit.

In this chapter we will examine those situations where the law imposes liability on a person or a business through tort law.

Types of Torts

Torts are traditionally divided into three categories. **Intentional torts**, as the name implies, are injuries caused by intentional acts. For example, when a movie star hits a photographer, this is the intentional tort of assault and battery. **Negligence** consists of harm caused by careless acts or failure to perform a legal duty. Most automobile accidents are the result of negligence.

Strict or **absolute liability** requires someone to compensate the injured party without regard to fault; generally, this liability is imposed by law. For example, in most states, a business that manufactures a defective product would be strictly liable for any injuries or damages caused by that product.

Intentional Torts

An intentional tort arises from an act that the defendant consciously performs. He or she either intends to harm another or knows with substantial certainty that injury to another could result. The intent to perform the act is the important element. The actual nature of the damage ultimately caused is irrelevant in determining whether there was intent.

For example, if Sean intentionally pushes Lil and she falls to the ground and breaks her arm, it does not matter that Sean never intended to break Lil's arm. Sean did intend to push Lil, and that in itself is a tortious act of assault and battery; Sean is liable for the consequences, including injury to Lil's arm. If the push were accidental, no intentional tort would exist, but liability might be imposed for negligent conduct.

Intentional torts are subdivided into two categories: wrongs against the person and wrongs against property.

Wrongs Against the Person

Intentional torts against a person include assault and battery, false imprisonment, infliction of mental distress, defamation (including disparagement of goods, slander of title, and defamation by computer) and fraud or deceit. In any of these torts, if the person suffers an injury it is often referred to as a personal injury or PI.

Assault and Battery   An intentional act (that is not excused or privileged on grounds of self defense or defense of others) that creates in another person a reasonable apprehension or fear of harm is an *assault,* and if there is physical contact injuring that person, a *battery.*

For example, Foster threatens to hit Heise with a baseball bat during an argument. The threat is an assault, and if Foster strikes Heise, a battery has occurred.

Physical injury does not have to occur. An unwelcome kiss, or escorting a person out of your apartment by holding his or her arms, can constitute assault and battery.

False Imprisonment   **False imprisonment**, frequently associated with false arrest, is the intentional confinement or restraint of a person without justification and interferes with the person's ability to move about freely and without restraint. Physical barriers, physical restraint, or threats of physical force can be used to confine someone. It is essential that the person being restrained not comply with the restraint willingly. On the other hand, a person is under no duty to risk personal harm in trying to escape.

The loss to business from shoplifting is estimated to exceed $10 billion a year. Almost all states have adopted **merchant protection legislation** that allows a merchant to detain any suspected shoplifter, provided that there is reasonable cause for suspicion and provided that the confinement is carried out in a reasonable way. The merchants are given statutory protection from being sued successfully and are an exception to the common law. The following case provides a good discussion of whether a merchant's actions in a particular situation were reasonable.

BACKGROUND AND FACTS   *Mrs. Gathers, a schoolteacher and the plaintiff in this case, went to Harris Teeter Supermarket, the defendant, to purchase a particular brand of cigarettes and some other items. Mrs. Gathers searched the cigarette displays at each cash register. Unable to find the particular brand, she went to the rack containing cartons of cigarettes. She found one package of this brand, picked it up, examined it, and replaced it on the shelf because it was crushed. She picked up the other items in the store, went to the checkout stand, purchased the items, and left.*

During this time, she was observed by Ackerman, who was on duty as a police officer. Ackerman's second job was as a security officer for another Harris Teeter store. On his normal break from his duties as a police officer, he had gone to the office of Harris Teeter's assistant manager, Steven Marks.

There he observed Mrs. Gathers through the glass wall of the office. With Marks's full knowledge of what he was about to do, Ackerman asked the cashier if Mrs. Gathers had purchased any cigarettes. She said no. Ackerman then detained Mrs. Gathers outside the store and asked her to return inside with him.

After he had detained Mrs. Gathers, he interrogated her in the glass-walled office (with Marks's permission) in full view of the store's customers. Mrs. Gathers was not given her Miranda *warnings.[1] She was not allowed to call her husband or her attorney. Her three requests that he check the cigarette display rack were refused. Ackerman told her she would be searched.*

Case 12.1
GATHERS v. HARRIS TEETER SUPERMARKET
Court of Appeals of South Carolina, 1984.
282 S.C. 220, 317 S.E.2d 748.

---

1. Miranda v. Arizona, 384 U.S. 436, 86 S.Ct. 1602, 16 L.Ed.2d 694 (1966). The *Miranda* warnings are:

     1. You have a right to remain silent.
     2. If you say anything, it may be used against you in a court of law.
     3. You have a right to an attorney.
     4. If you cannot afford an attorney, one will be appointed for you.

She was subjected to a pat-down body search, including the breast and groin areas by a female store employee, not a female police officer. Ackerman searched her grocery bag, pocketbook, and raincoat. The searches did not produce any stolen goods. She was then told she was free to go.

She sued for slander, assault and battery, and false imprisonment. She won a $20,000 judgment. Harris Teeter appealed. The trial court found that Ackerman was an agent of Harris Teeter. Although he was employed as a police officer and in uniform at the time, he was off duty and taking a coffee break. He specifically told Marks he was about to catch a shoplifter, and Marks was aware of what he was going to do.

In its review of the case, the appellate court examined the merchant protection statute, Section 16-13-140 of the 1976 South Carolina Code of Laws. The court had to decide whether Ackerman was acting as a police officer or as an agent of Teeters. If he were acting as an agent of Teeters, the question was whether Ackerman's action violated the merchant protection statute in such a manner that Teeters lost the protection of the statute.

SHAW, Judge.
* * * *

Section 16-13-140 [of the South Carolina Code of Laws] reads

In any action brought by reason of having been delayed by a merchant or merchant's employee or agent on or near the premises of a mercantile establishment for the purpose of investigation concerning the ownership of any merchandise, it shall be a defense to such action if: (1) the person was delayed in a reasonable manner and for a reasonable time to permit such investigation, and (2) reasonable cause existed to believe that the person delayed had committed the crime of shoplifting.

In *Faulkenberry v. Spring Mills, Inc.,* the S.C. Supreme Court stated that probable cause is now a defense under Section 16-13-140 to actions arising from a merchant's delay of suspected shoplifters. Probable cause is defined as a good faith belief that a person is guilty of a crime when this belief rests on such grounds as would induce an ordinarily prudent and cautious man, under the circumstances, to believe likewise. The issue of probable cause is essentially a question of fact and ordinarily for the determination of the jury.

The trial judge properly submitted the issues of probable cause and reasonable delay to the jury. As there is evidence which supports the jury's findings, we are bound to uphold them. In *Faulkenberry,* the good faith belief of guilt resulted from two reports from an eyewitness that the plaintiff was seen placing cloth in her purse. Here, Ackerman admitted that he never saw Mrs. Gathers put anything in her pockets. In *Faulkenberry,* the restraint was for only about twenty minutes, and the investigation consisted solely of requests that the plaintiff open her purse. These requests were refused and no further searches were attempted. Here, Mrs. Gathers was delayed for about one hour and subject to a full pat-down body search. We cannot say as a matter of law that probable cause existed or that Mrs. Gathers' delay was reasonable.

Harris Teeter claims that Mrs. Gathers consented to all of the actions taken against her. It is true that no one can enforce a right arising out of a transaction which he has voluntarily assented to. This rule applies to intentional acts which would otherwise be tortious. Where the evidence as to whether consent was given is conflicting, ambiguous, or inconsistent, it becomes a question of fact for the jury.

Mrs. Gathers allowed the search by [the store employee] but only because she was in a custodial situation, did not know her rights, and was afraid that she would be taken to jail if she refused. From this evidence, the jury could have reasonably concluded that the consent was a product of duress or coercion, express or implied, and not voluntarily given. Again, we cannot say as a matter of law that Mrs. Gathers consented to the search.

Harris Teeter takes exception to the jury charges made by the trial judge. Initially, the store claims that the defense of probable cause was not charged to the causes of action for slander and assault and battery. This argument is without merit. Prior to charging the law on false imprisonment, the trial judge listed all of the defenses Harris Teeter has raised, including probable cause. The trial judge then stated, ''And so as not to have to repeat it each time, I'll cover it all in the next cause of action, each of those defenses.'' He then later instructed the jury on probable cause.

* * * *

Mrs. Gathers prayed for actual damages of $300,000 and was awarded $20,000. The proper amounts to be rendered as actual or punitive damages are left almost entirely to the jury and trial judge. An appellate court cannot reduce a verdict and will only strike down a verdict *in toto* in those rare cases where the amount is so shockingly excessive as to indicate it was the result of passion, partiality, prejudice, or corruption.

We see no evidence of passion, partiality, prejudice or corruption.

The trial court's judgment was affirmed. Sending the issue of probable cause to detain Mrs. Gathers to the jury was proper. The judgment of $20,000 was not so shockingly excessive as to indicate that it was the result of passion, partiality, prejudice, or corruption, and, therefore, it was not struck down.

DECISION AND REMEDY

Infliction of Mental Distress People have a right to be free from mental distress. The tort of **infliction of mental distress** is defined as an intentional act that amounts to extreme and outrageous conduct resulting in severe emotional distress. For example, a creditor telephones Paul every hour during the night attempting to collect a debt. As a result, Paul suffers intense mental anxiety. The courts have found such acts by the creditor to be extreme and outrageous conduct that exceeds the bounds of decency accepted by society. The person committing these acts may be liable in a tort action. These acts are also in violation of the Fair Debt Collection Practices Act, which is described in Chapter 11.

Defamation **Defamation** of character involves wrongfully hurting a person's good reputation. The law imposes a general duty on all people to refrain from making false, defamatory statements about others. Breaching this duty verbally involves the tort of **slander**; breaching it in writing involves the tort of **libel**.

The basis of the tort is the publication of a statement or statements that hold an individual up to contempt, ridicule, or hatred. Publication means that the defamatory statements are made to or within the hearing of people other than the defamed party. If Thompson writes Andrews a private letter accusing him of embezzling funds, that letter does not constitute libel. If Peters calls Gordon dishonest, unattractive, and incompetent when no one else is around, that act does not constitute slander. In neither case was the message communicated to a third party.

A person who is sued for defamation may assert several defenses. First, truth is normally a complete defense against a defamation charge.

LEGAL HIGHLIGHT   Can the Dead Be Defamed?

Errol Flynn was a flamboyant movie star of the 1940s and 1950s. In the book, *Errol Flynn: The Untold Story,* Charles Higham described the popular celebrity as a homosexual and Nazi spy. His family was outraged and brought a civil lawsuit against the publisher.*

Both the trial court and the court of appeals held that, no matter how egregious or disturbing the material, California law does not allow the surviving family members, who were not defamed, to bring a lawsuit. A California law that made libel tending to blacken the memory of one who is dead a crime had been declared unconstitutional by a California court in 1976. Essentially, at least in California, the

surviving family members cannot sue to protect their beloved deceased from any defamation.

The family, however, can prevent others from making economic gains from the use of the name or likeness of the deceased person whose fame and, occasionally, earning power continue after death. Many families have formed corporations that have the right to all the mascots, logos, likenesses, licensing and distribution rights, and even trademarks associated with their deceased relatives.

*Flynn v. Higham, 149 Cal. App. 3d 677, 197 Cal. Rptr. 145 (1983).

Second, under the defense of **privilege of immunity**, even if the statement is false, no action can be brought against the speaker. Privileged communications are of two types: absolute and qualified.

In general, these privileges are granted where there is some important and overriding social value in sanctioning a person's conduct even though the conduct may result in defamation.

Absolute privilege applies to judicial and legislative proceedings, but only when it is relevant to the activities of either governmental body. For example, statements made by an elected representative on the floor of Congress are absolutely privileged communications. These same statements, if made in a different arena, such as a newsletter or a press conference, are not so privileged. **Qualified privilege** is a common-law concept based on the philosophy that a person's right to know or to speak is of equal importance to another person's right not to be defamed. If the communication has a qualified privilege, the plaintiff must show that the privilege was abused in order to recover.

An example of a qualified privilege is found in letters of recommendation and in written eval-

uations of employees. Generally, if the communicated statements are made in good faith and the publication is limited to those who have a legitimate interest in the communication, the statement falls within the qualified privilege.

Disparagement of Goods, Slander of Title, and Defamation by Computer   These three torts involve defamation and directly involve business. A false statement made about a person's product is a tort called **disparagement of goods**. For example, a salesperson might lie about a competitor's product.

Defaming the title (proof of ownership) that a person has to his or her property may prevent a person from being able to sell the property. This tort is called **slander of title**.

Erroneous information from a computer about a person's credit standing or business reputation can impair that person's ability to obtain further credit. If the company that owns the computer information fails to correct the information in a timely manner, it may be liable to the victim. This tort is called **defamation by computer**. The company is also responsible, under the Fair Credit

Reporting Act discussed in Chapter 11, for making sure that the information is correct.

Fraud or Deceit   The tort of **fraud** or **deceit** involves: (1) a misrepresentation of material facts, (2) made with the intent to deceive or with reckless disregard as to the truthfulness of the facts, (3) made with the knowledge that they are false, (4) justifiable reliance on these facts by the victim, and (5) damages. Sometimes failure to disclose material facts is a form of deceit. For example, the owner of a house knows that the roof has started to leak even though it is not evident. The house is for sale. The owner must inform any potential buyer of this latent (hidden) defect. If he or she fails to disclose this fact to any potential buyer, he or she may be held liable for any damages that the buyer suffers in the future as a result of the leaky roof.

Wrongs Against Property

Torts that are wrongs against property include trespass, conversion, and nuisance. In these types of torts, the property is said to be damaged.

Trespass to Land   Anytime a person enters upon another's land, or causes something to enter onto the land, or to remain there without consent or privilege, a tort of trespass to land has been committed.

Once established as a trespasser, certain rights, duties, and privileges flow to both the owner and the trespasser. Some of these are:

1. A trespasser is liable for any damage he or she causes to the property.
2. A trespasser can be removed from the premises by use of *reasonable force* without being liable for assault and battery.
3. The trespasser generally assumes the risks of the premises (that is, a trespasser cannot complain of personal injuries that occur as a result of the condition of the premises). This rule does not permit the owner to lay traps, and even may require a warning of dangers to be found on the property, such as guard dogs. Under the "attractive nuisance doctrine," young children do not assume the

risks of premises if it is the condition of the premises that attracts them to it (such as a swimming pool, large sand piles on construction sites, and the like).

Conversion   Whenever personal property is taken from its rightful owner or possessor and placed in the service of another, the tort of **conversion** occurs. Conversion is the civil side of those crimes relating to stealing. A store clerk who steals merchandise from the store commits a crime of theft and the tort of conversion at the same time. Of course, when conversion occurs, the lesser offense of trespass to personal property usually occurs as well.

If the initial taking of the property were unlawful, there is trespass. The retention of that property is conversion. Even if the initial taking of the property were permitted by the owner, failure to return the property may be conversion.

Nuisance   It is possible to commit a tort through the unreasonable use of your own property. A **nuisance** is an improper activity (which may involve the use of your own property) that interferes with another's enjoyment or use of his or her property. Nuisances can be either public or private. This topic is discussed in more detail in Chapter 23.

A **public nuisance** disturbs or interferes with the public and is generally a crime. A **private nuisance** interferes with the property interest of a limited number of individuals and is a tort. Reasonable limitations are placed on the use of property; such limitations prevent the owner from unreasonably interfering with the health and comfort of neighbors or with their right to enjoy their own private property.

For example, Rick cannot keep chickens in his townhouse because this would constitute a nuisance, even if there were no city ordinances prohibiting such activity. Hal cannot set up a speaker system in his backyard and play rock-and-roll music or symphonic music at such a volume that his neighbors are disturbed. This may also be a crime (public nuisance) as a typical city ordinance specifies that no sound exceeding 100 decibels shall be audible within 100 feet of one's property between the hours of 11 P.M. and 7 A.M.

Negligence

Intentional torts involve a particular mental state. In negligence, however, the actor neither intends to bring about the consequences of the act nor believes that the consequences will occur. The actor's conduct merely creates the risk of such consequences. Without the creation of a risk, there can be no negligence. Moreover, the risk must be foreseeable; that is, it must be such that a reasonable person would anticipate it and guard against it.

Many of the actions discussed in the section on intentional torts would constitute negligence if they were committed carelessly but without intent. For instance, carelessly bumping into someone who then falls and breaks an arm constitutes negligence. Likewise, carelessly (as opposed to intentionally) flooding someone's land constitutes negligence. In a sense, negligence describes a *way* of committing a tort rather than constituting a distinct *category* of torts.

Negligence occurs when a person is injured or his or her property is damaged because someone else's conduct falls below the required duty of care. Three elements are involved: (1) breach (failure) of duty of care, (2) injury, and (3) causation. Various defenses may be available to the person accused of negligence.

Breach of Duty of Care

The first element of negligence can be broken into a two-part question:

1. Is there a duty of care?
2. Did the defendant's action breach (fail to live up to) that duty?

Tort law recognizes several standards for the duty of care depending on the particular fact situation. First, the standard of care may be measured by an **objective standard** of reasonableness—the "reasonable person" standard. In determining whether a tort has been committed, the courts ask: How would a reasonable person have acted in the same or similar circumstances?

The reasonable person standard is objective. It is not necessarily how a particular person would act, but it is society's judgment as reflected by a jury as to how people should act in the same situation. If the reasonable person existed, he or she would be careful, conscientious, even-tempered, and honest. This hypothetical reasonable person is frequently used in discussions of law.

Many types of businesses are held to a higher standard of care than that of reasonableness. In the following case, the court reviews the standard of care based on a reasonably prudent motel operator.

Case 12.2

KVERAGAS v. SCOTTISH INNS, INC.
United States Court of Appeals, Sixth Circuit, 1984.
733 F.2d 409.

BACKGROUND AND FACTS   *Charles and Esther Kveragas, the plaintiffs, rented a motel room at the Scottish Inns in Knoxville, Tennessee. That night three intruders kicked open the door, shot Charles, injured Esther, and robbed them of $3,000. The Kveragases filed a lawsuit alleging that the motel owners and operators failed to make adequate provisions for the safety of the motel guests.*

The evidence at trial showed that the room was equipped with a hollow-core door that fit poorly into the door frame. The only door lock was that incorporated into the handle, described as a grade three lock, although a security chain was provided. The plaintiffs had both locked and chained the door. A single kick, however, was the only force applied to the door, and all that was necessary to open it.

Evidence showed that dead-bolt locks and other security devices were easily available and in use throughout the motel industry. Dead-bolt locks are considerably stronger than the type of lock employed at this motel. Evidence also showed that a dead-bolt lock could withstand the force that was applied to the door.

The trial court directed the jury to return a verdict for the defendants, which the jury did, on the grounds that the motel owners and operators had no duty to protect their guests from sudden criminal acts. The plaintiffs appealed.

MERRITT, Judge.

*   *   *   *

The common law has long recognized the special legal relationship between innkeepers and registered guests. Historically, innkeepers operated under an extreme standard of liability, approaching that of an insurer against all dangers save acts of God. The Supreme Court of New York long ago offered an explanation for the emergence of the innkeeper's special responsibility:

> This rigorous rule had its origin in the feudal conditions which were the outgrowth of the Middle Ages. In those days there was little safety outside of castles and fortified towns for the wayfaring traveler, who, exposed on his journey to the depredations of bandits and brigands, had little protection when he sought at night temporary refuge at the wayside inns, established and conducted for his entertainment and convenience. Exposed as he was to robbery and violence, he was compelled to repose confidence, when stopping on his pilgrimages over night, in landlords who were not exempt from temptation; and hence there grew up the salutary principles that a host owed to his guest the duty, not only of hospitality, but also of protection.

Although castles and fortified towns are no longer part of our landscape, bandits and brigands remain. The common law has responded to these cultural changes by lessening, but not removing, the innkeeper's liability for criminal acts committed by third parties. *   *   *

*   *   *   *

[In *Zang v. Leonard,* the] *Zang* court *   *   * set out the standard of care which we believe the Tennessee Supreme Court would apply in cases such as the instant one: the duty placed on innkeepers to protect registered guests from the misconduct of third persons is a duty of due care under all the circumstances. Put differently, the "reasonable person" standard, the cornerstone of common law tort jurisprudence, is the standard that applies to innkeepers in the protection of their guests, just as it governs countless other relationships.

The *Zang* court did not leave the application of the general due care standard to the unfettered discretion of the jury, and neither do we. The *Zang* court addressed the factors which a jury should consider in assessing due care:

> The measure of the liability of the possessor of land to invitees is due care under all the circumstances including the nature and use of the land, the nature of the invitation, the nature of the relationship with the invitee, the opportunity of the possessor and the invitee to know and avoid existing or probable dangers, and any and all other factors which would challenge the attention of the possessor and/or invitee to the probability of danger to the invitee and produce the precautions which a reasonably prudent person would instigate under the same or similar circumstances.

Under the *Zang* rule, the first responsibility of the factfinder is to determine "what, if any, protective measures would have been employed by a reasonably prudent motel operator under the same circumstances" which the factfinder finds existed at the time of the injury. The finding of fact as to the protective measures which a reasonably prudent motel operator would have employed is to be based on a comprehensive study of *all* relevant conditions. The *Zang* court listed some of the appropriate considerations: whether the motel is advertised as an unusual establishment which offers better than ordinary facilities; whether the location of the motel is such as to be convenient to criminals; and whether prior assaults or other criminal acts have occurred on the premises.

* * * *

Once the factfinder determines what, if any, protective measures would have been employed by a reasonably prudent motel operator under the same circumstances, the fact-finder next should determine "whether the actions of the responsible defendants conform to the actions of a reasonably prudent motel operator" as found by the factfinder. If the factfinder determines that the responsible defendants did not comply with this standard of care, then it should find the defendants' negligent; otherwise, it should find them not negligent.

* * * *

Turning now to the facts of the case, * * * we conclude that under the *Zang* rule plaintiffs have presented sufficient proof to survive a motion for a directed verdict. The evidence that the assailants gained entry to the room by kicking open the door, that the door fit poorly and had a grade three lock with no deadbolt lock; that other types of doors and locks were available and in use in the motel industry which could withstand the force applied to the door in this case; this evidence, together with the inferences that arise therefrom, is sufficient to permit a jury to find that a reasonably prudent motel operator would, under the circumstances of this case, have employed a more substantial door and lock; that the responsible defendants failed to adopt these protective measures; and that if the protective measures had been adopted the assailants would not have been able to gain entry into the plaintiffs' room. These facts, if found by the jury, are sufficient to establish a cause of action under the *Zang* standard. Hence, it was error to direct a verdict for the defendants.

DECISION AND REMEDY   *The appellate court reversed the judgment of the trial court and remanded the case to the trial court for a new trial. At the new trial, the jury would decide the standard of care for a reasonably prudent motel operator under these circumstances.*

A second standard of care may be imposed by a statute. Everyone driving a vehicle has a **statutory duty** not to proceed through an intersection when the traffic light is red. Reasonableness is not involved under this standard of care. For example, a person receives a traffic ticket for running a red light. He may tell the judge that at 3:00 A.M. he was rushing his pregnant wife to the hospital, that he stopped at the red light, that he looked both ways and determined that no cross traffic was coming from either direction, and that he then proceeded through the signal. The judge in his or her wisdom may dismiss the ticket. If the driver had hit someone in the intersection, reasonableness as to his action would not be used as the standard of care. The statutory duty to stop at the red light is the standard of care.

Injury

The plaintiff must suffer some loss, harm, wrong, or invasion of a protected interest in order to recover damages for a negligent act. The reason for the requirement of injury is obvious. Without an injury of some kind, the defendant is not required to give the plaintiff compensation. Compensation is paid in an effort to make the plaintiff "whole" again. Essentially, the purpose of the tort of negligence is to compensate the victim for legally recognized injuries resulting from acts of the wrongdoer; its intent is not to punish those acts.

Causation

Causation is the last element necessary to prove negligence. If a person breaches her or his duty of care, that breach must cause harm, and the person's negligent act must be closely linked with the harm for the person to be liable. The courts have imposed limits on the amount of a person's liability, however, if the negligent act is not wholly responsible for the harm that results.

In deciding whether there is causation, the court must address two questions:

First, is there *causation in fact*? Did the injury occur because of the defendant's act, or would it have occurred anyway? Causation in fact can usually be determined by the *but for* test: but for the wrongful act, the injury would not have occurred. If Carl carelessly leaves a campfire burning and the fire burns down the forest, causation in fact exists. The forest would not have burned but for Carl's negligent act; therefore, Carl is liable for the damages he caused.

If Carl carelessly leaves a campfire burning, but it burns out, and lightning causes a fire that burns down the forest, there is no causation in fact. In both examples, there is a wrongful act (Carl leaving the campfire burning), and there is damage, but, in the second example, no causal connection exists between the act and the damage and thus Carl is not liable.

The second question is: Was the act the **proximate cause** of the injury? How far should a de-

fendant's liability extend for a wrongful act that was a *substantial* factor in causing injury? For example, Carl's fire not only burns down the forest but also sets off an explosion in a nearby ammunition plant that levels the entire plant, destroys the marshmallow factory located next door, and severely damages houses and businesses in the nearby community. Should Carl be liable to the ammunition plant owners, the marshmallow plant owners, and the people harmed in the nearby community?

The limitations on a person's liability are the issue when the courts consider proximate cause. Proximate cause is a question of public policy; the courts must ask whether the connection between an act and an injury is strong enough to justify imposing liability.

The courts use **foreseeability** as the test for proximate cause. If the consequences of the harm done or the victim of the harm were unforeseeable, there is no proximate cause. Carl was negligent, but how far does his liability go? Is this the chain of events that a reasonable person would usually guard against? In the next case, the court reviews the issue of foreseeability.

BACKGROUND AND FACTS *Charles Bigbee, the plaintiff, was in a telephone booth on Century Boulevard. Looking up, he saw an automobile coming toward him and realized that it was going to hit the telephone booth. He attempted to flee, but the door to the booth jammed, trapping Bigbee inside. The evidence at the trial showed that the driver of the automobile was intoxicated. Evidence also showed that the telephone booth had been demolished by an automobile twenty months before.*

Bigbee sued the driver and the companies that served the driver alcoholic beverages. The case was settled as to those defendants. Bigbee also sued Pacific Telephone and Telegraph Company for negligence and strict liability for the design, location, installation, and maintenance of the telephone booths. Pacific Telephone was granted a summary judgment that, in effect, dismissed the case. Bigbee appealed.

Case 12.3
BIGBEE v. PACIFIC TELEPHONE AND TELEGRAPH CO.
Supreme Court of California, 1983.
34 Cal.3d 49, 665 P.2d 947, 192 Cal.Rptr. 857.

BIRD, Chief Justice.
*   *   *   *

[The] defendants contend that their duty to use due care in the location, installation, and maintenance of telephone booths does not extend to the risk encountered by plaintiff and that neither their alleged negligence in carrying out these activities nor any defect in the booth was a proximate cause of plaintiff's injuries. These contentions present the same issue in different guises. Each involves this question—was the risk that a car might crash into the phone booth and injure plaintiff reasonably foreseeable in this case?

Ordinarily, foreseeability is a question of fact for the jury. It may be decided as a question of law only if, "under the undisputed facts there is no room for a reasonable difference of opinion." Accordingly, this court must decide whether foreseeability remains a triable issue in this case.

If any triable issue of fact exists, it is error for a trial court to grant a party's motion for summary judgment.

* * * *

Turning to the merits of this case, the question presented is a relatively simple one. Is there room for a reasonable difference of opinion as to whether the risk that a car might crash into the phone booth and injure an individual inside was reasonably foreseeable under the circumstances set forth above?

In pursuing this inquiry, it is well to remember that "foreseeability is not to be measured by what is more probable than not, but includes whatever is likely enough in the setting of modern life that a reasonably thoughtful [person] would take account of it in guiding practical conduct." One may be held accountable for creating even " 'the risk of a slight possibility of injury if a reasonably prudent [person] would not do so.' " Moreover, it is settled that what is required to be foreseeable is the general character of the event or harm—e.g., being struck by a car while standing in a phone booth—not its precise nature or manner of occurrence.

Here, defendants placed a telephone booth, which was difficult to exit, in a parking lot 15 feet from the side of a major thoroughfare and near a driveway. Under these circumstances, this court cannot conclude as a matter of law that it was unforeseeable that the booth might be struck by a car and cause serious injury to a person trapped within. A jury could reasonably conclude that this risk was foreseeable. This is particularly true where, as here, there is evidence that a booth at this same location had previously been struck.

Indeed, in light of the circumstances of modern life, it seems evident that a jury could reasonably find that defendants should have foreseen the possibility of the very accident which actually occurred here. Swift traffic on a major thoroughfare late at night is to be expected. Regrettably, so too are intoxicated drivers. Moreover, it is not uncommon for speeding and/or intoxicated drivers to lose control of their cars and crash into poles, buildings or whatever else may be standing alongside the road they travel—no matter how straight and level that road may be.

* * * *

It is of no consequence that the harm to plaintiff came about through the negligent or reckless acts of Roberts. "If the likelihood that a third person may act in a particular manner is the hazard or one of the hazards which makes the actor negligent, such an act whether innocent, negligent, intentionally tortious, or criminal does not prevent the actor from being liable for harm caused thereby." Here, the risk that a car might hit the telephone booth could be found to constitute one of the hazards to which plaintiff was exposed.

* * * *

Since the foreseeability of harm to plaintiff remains a triable issue of fact, the judgment is reversed and the case is remanded to the trial court for further proceedings consistent with the views expressed in this opinion.

DECISION AND   *Bigbee was entitled to have a trial. The Supreme Court of California held*
REMEDY   *that there was a substantial fact issue as to the foreseeability of risk for*

the user of the telephone booth. The booth was difficult to exit, placed in a parking lot fifteen feet from the side of a major thoroughfare, near a driveway, and the booth had been struck before. The court's decision only gives Bigbee a right to have a trial.

Defenses to Negligence

Defenses to negligence are: (1) superseding intervening forces, (2) assumption of risk, and (3) contributory and comparative negligence. A superseding or intervening force may break the causal connection between a wrongful act and injury to another. If so, it cancels out the wrongful act.

For example, Jed takes his automobile to a mechanic to have his brakes repaired. After repair of the brakes, on replacing the tires, the mechanic fails to tighten two bolts. Jed is driving along when he hears a terrible rattle coming from the automobile. As he is stopping his car along the shoulder of the freeway, the wheel comes off. Just then a drunk driver comes along, hits the car, and injures Jed. The drunk driver is an intervening force and may break the connection between the mechanic's wrongful act and the damage to Jed and his automobile that resulted from the accident.

A plaintiff who voluntarily enters into a risky situation, knowing the risk involved, will not be allowed to recover. This defense is called **assumption of risk**. For example, a driver who enters a race knows that there is a risk of being killed or injured in a crash. The driver has assumed the risk of injury. Knowledge of the risk and voluntary assumption of that risk are the two requirements for this defense.

All individuals are expected to exercise a reasonable degree of care in looking out for themselves. In some jurisdictions, recovery for injury resulting from negligence is prevented when the injured person has failed to exercise such care over himself or herself. The defense of **contributory negligence** is available where both parties have been negligent, and their combined negligence has contributed to cause the injury. When one party sues the other in tort for damages from negligence, the defendant can claim contributory negligence, which is a complete defense under common-law rules.

The modern legal trend, however, is toward narrowing the scope of this defense. Instead of allowing contributory negligence to negate a cause of action completely, an increasing number of states allow recovery based on the doctrine of **comparative negligence**. This doctrine enables computation of both the plaintiff's and the defendant's negligence. The plaintiff's damages are reduced by a percentage that represents the degree of his or her contributing fault.

For example, Mario is driving his automobile. Although it is equipped with safety belts, he is not wearing his. Mario is approaching an intersection with a green light. Peter turns left in front of Mario's automobile. The cars collide, and Mario is thrown from his automobile and severely injured.

Subsequently, Mario files a lawsuit against Peter alleging negligence. Peter defends by using the comparative negligence theory. Through expert witnesses, Peter can show that Mario would have been injured in the automobile accident even if he had been wearing his safety belt, but his injuries would have been significantly less than the injuries he did sustain by not wearing his safety belt. Mario may not recover for the full extent of his injuries. His failure to wear safety belts was an act of negligence which contributed to the extent of his injuries. Several states have now adopted this view because the data demonstrate that the frequency and severity of injuries are lessened when motorists wear seat belts.

Strict Liability

The final category of torts is called strict liability, or liability without fault. Negligent torts involve an act that departs from a standard of care and causes an injury. Under the doctrine of strict liability, liability for injury is imposed for reasons other than fault.

When a person engages in abnormally dangerous activities, that person will be liable under strict liability if any harm occurs to others. Abnormally dangerous activities have three characteristics:

1. The activity involves potential harm of a serious nature to persons or to property.
2. The activity involves a high degree of risk that cannot be completely guarded against by exercising reasonable care.
3. The activity is not commonly performed in the community.

Strict liability is applied because of the extreme risk of the activity. Few defenses exist. Although an activity such as blasting with dynamite is performed with all reasonable care, there is still a risk of injury to innocent persons. Thus, unless a person voluntarily and with knowledge enters a posted work site in which blasting is occurring, the dynamiter is liable for any damage to property or injury to a person caused by the blasting.

Because of the risk of harm, public policy requires that the person engaged in the activity must be held liable for injuries caused by the activity. Although fault does not exist, responsibility is imposed because of the nature of the activity. It is reasonable to require the person engaged in the activity to carry insurance or otherwise be prepared to compensate anyone who suffers harm.

In the past, strict liability was thought to apply basically to ultrahazardous activities, such as blasting. In the next case, the court applies strict liability for a hidden defect in a common everyday item, a shower door made of untempered glass. The courts are expanding the application of strict liability. In this case, the court is faced with deciding who will be responsible when two innocent parties are involved: the landlord who did not have any actual knowledge of the hidden defect or the tenant who did not have knowledge or control over the type of glass in the shower door.

Case 12.4
BECKER v. IRM CORP.
Supreme Court of California,
1985.
38 Cal.3d 454,
698 P.2d 116,
213 Cal.Rptr. 213.

BACKGROUND AND FACTS *George Becker, plaintiff, rented an apartment from IRM Corporation (IRM), the defendant. The apartment complex was built in 1962 and 1963 and sold to IRM in 1974. The shower doors in the apartments were of untempered frosted glass. No visible difference exists between tempered and untempered glass. In 1978 when Becker was taking a shower, he slipped and fell against the shower door, breaking the glass and severely lacerating his arm. He sued IRM in strict liability and in negligence, asserting that it was liable for a latent defect. Undisputed evidence showed that the risk of serious injury is reduced if the shower door is of tempered glass rather than untempered glass.*

The trial court granted the defendant's motion for a summary judgment that it was not liable to a tenant for a latent defect of the rented premises absent concealment of a known danger or an expressed contractual or statutory duty to repair.

BROUSSARD, Justice.
* * * *

In *Greenman v. Yuba Power Products, Inc.* we established the rule: ''A manufacturer is strictly liable in tort when an article he places on the market, knowing that it is to be used without inspection for defects, proves to have a defect that causes injury to a human being. Recognized first in the case of unwholesome food products, such liability has now been extended to a variety of other products that create as great or greater hazards if defective.'' The court recognized that the cases imposing strict liability had ''usually been based on the theory of an express or implied warranty running from the manufacturer to the plaintiff.'' The justification for departing from warranty theory and for establishing a doctrine of strict liability in tort was the recognition that the liability was imposed by law and the refusal to permit the manufacturer to define the scope of its own liability for defective products.

* * * *

Greenman also noted that the purpose of strict liability in tort is ''to insure that the costs of injuries resulting from defective products are borne by the manufacturers that put such products on the market rather than by the injured persons who are powerless to protect themselves.''

We follow a stream of commerce approach to strict liability in tort and extend liability to all those who are part of the ''overall producing and marketing enterprise that should bear the cost of injuries from defective products.'' The doctrine of strict liability in tort has been applied not only to manufacturers but to the various links in the commercial marketing chain including a retailer, a wholesale-retail distributor, personal property lessors and bailors, and a licensor of personalty. In holding that strict liability in tort was applicable to lessors and bailors in *Price v. Shell Oil Co.,* it was pointed out that strict liability does not apply to isolated transactions such as the sale of a single lot.

* * * *

A similar development appears with respect to the landlord-tenant relationship.

* * *

* * * *

We are satisfied that the rationale of the foregoing cases, establishing the duties of a landlord and the doctrine of strict liability in tort, requires us to conclude that a landlord engaged in the business of leasing dwellings is strictly liable in tort for injuries resulting from a latent defect in the premises when the defect existed at the time the premises were let to the tenant. It is clear that landlords are part of the ''overall producing and marketing enterprise'' that makes housing accommodations available to renters. A landlord, like defendant owning numerous units, is not engaged in isolated acts within the enterprise but plays a substantial role. The fact that the enterprise is one involving real estate may not immunize the landlord. Our courts have long recognized that contracts relating to realty may give rise to implied warranties.

Absent disclosure of defects, the landlord in renting the premises makes an implied representation that the premises are fit for use as a dwelling and the representation is ordinarily indispensable to the lease. The tenant purchasing housing for a limited period is in no position to inspect for latent defects in the increasingly complex modern apartment buildings or to bear the expense of repair whereas the landlord is in a much better position to inspect for and repair latent defects. The tenant's ability to inspect is ordinarily substantially less than that of a purchaser of the property.

* * * *

Landlords are an integral part of the enterprise of producing and marketing rental housing. * * * They have more than a random or accidental role in the marketing enterprise. In addition, landlords have a continuing relationship to the property following the renting in contrast to the used machinery dealer who sells. As we have seen, in renting property the landlord * * * makes representations of habitability and safety.

* * * *

We conclude that the absence of a continuing business relationship between builder and landlord does not preclude application of strict liability in tort for latent defects existing at the time of the lease because landlords are an integral part of the enterprise and they should bear the cost of injuries resulting from such defects rather than the injured persons who are powerless to protect themselves.

DECISION AND   *The Supreme Court of California decided that IRM could be held strictly*
REMEDY   *liable for injuries resulting from latent defects on its premises. The landlord*
had a duty to exercise due care in inspecting for dangerous conditions in
connection with the purchase of rental premises. The fact that the landlord
was not aware of the dangerous condition did not necessarily preclude
liability. The trial court's judgment was reversed.

Other applications of the strict liability principle are found in the workers' compensation acts and in the area of product liability. Product liability is discussed at the end of this chapter. In workers' compensation and product liability, the liability is borne by either the employer or the manufacturer as a matter of public policy. Such liability is based on two factors:

1. The employer and manufacturer are better able to bear the cost of injury than the injured person because they can spread it out to society through an increase in the cost of goods and services. For example, a toy manufacturer would normally sell a toy to a million customers for twenty dollars. The price can be raised to twenty-one dollars (an increase of 5 percent) in order to pay for the liability claim ($1 million) of one customer.
2. The employer and manufacturer are making a profit from their activities and, therefore, as a matter of public policy, should bear the cost of injury as an operating expense.

Specific Torts Related to Business

Some torts that have a direct application to the business environment are:

1. Wrongful interference with a contractual or business relationship;
2. Infringement of trademarks, trade names, patents, and copyrights; and
3. Theft of trade secrets.

Wrongful Interference with a Contractual or Business Relationship

The application of tort law relating to intentional **interference with a contractual or business re-**

lationship has increased greatly in recent years. In such a case, the plaintiff must prove that the defendant intentionally induced the breach of a valid contractual or business relationship, not merely that the defendant reaped the benefits of the broken relationship.

For example, Alicia has a one-year requirements contract to deliver to Eat-Rite Restaurants all the doughnuts Eat-Rite requires for its breakfast menu. Frank's Doughnut Hole had unsuccessfully bid for the contract earlier. Frank offers Eat-Rite a special price, much lower than Alicia's, if Eat-Rite will change suppliers immediately, and further offers to pay for any costs Eat-Rite incurs in making the change. Eat-Rite breaks its contract with Alicia.

This is clearly a wrongful interference with a contractual relationship. Suppose however Frank merely advertises a special price, and further states it will beat any valid price offered by a competitor. Eat-Rite reads the advertisement, breaks its contract with Alicia, and contracts with Frank's Doughnut Hole. Although Frank will reap the benefits of Eat-Rite's breach of contract with Alicia, Frank will not be liable for the tort of wrongful interference with a contractual relationship.

The best-known case of wrongful interference is *Texaco v. Pennzoil*.[2] The trial jury found that Texaco wrongfully interfered with a planned merger (the contract) between Pennzoil and Getty Oil Company. The jury found that the three elements required for a wrongful interference with a contract relationship were present, as follows.

1. A *valid contract* existed between Pennzoil and Getty.
2. Texaco *knew* that this contract existed.

---

2.   729 S.W.2d 768 (Tex.Ct.App. 1987).

3. Texaco *intentionally induced* the breach of the contract by Getty resulting in an economic or pecuniary gain.

The trial judgment was the largest in United States history—$7.53 billion in actual damages and $3 billion in punitive damages.[3]

Infringement of Trademarks, Trade Names, Patents, and Copyrights

A **trademark** is a distinctive mark, motto, device, or implement that a manufacturer stamps, prints, or otherwise affixes to the goods it produces. For example, WordPerfect, a software word-processing program, is a trademark owned by Word-Perfect Corporation. The trademark allows goods to be identified on the market; it vouches for their origin. At common law, the person who uses a trademark is protected. Clearly, if a person uses the trademark of another, consumers will be misled into believing that the goods were made by someone else. The law seeks to avoid this kind of confusion.

A **service mark** is similar to a trademark but is used to distinguish the services of one person from those of another. For example, each airline has a particular mark or symbol associated with its name. Titles or character names used in radio and television are frequently registered as service marks.

Once a trademark or service mark has been registered, a firm is entitled to the exclusive use of it for marketing purposes. Whenever that trademark or service mark is copied to a substantial degree or used in its entirety by another, intentionally or unintentionally, the trademark or service mark has been infringed. The trademark need not be registered with the state or with the federal government in order to obtain protection from the tort of trademark infringement, but registration does furnish proof of the date of inception of its use.

A **patent** is a grant from the government that conveys and secures to an inventor the exclusive

right to make, use, and sell an invention for a period of seventeen years. Patents for a lesser period are given for designs, as opposed to inventions. For either a regular patent or a design patent, the applicant must demonstrate to the satisfaction of the United States Patent Office that the invention, discovery, or design is genuine, novel, useful, and not obvious in the light of the technology of the time. A patent holder gives notice to all that an article or design is patented by placing on it the word ''Patent'' or the abbreviation ''Pat.,'' plus the patent number.

If a firm uses a device that is substantially similar to someone else's patented device, the tort of patent infringement exists. Patent infringement may exist even though not all features or parts of an invention are copied.

A **copyright** is a right granted by statute to the author or originator of certain literary or artistic productions. Works created after January 1, 1978, are automatically given statutory copyright protection for the life of the author plus fifty years. Note that it is not possible to copyright an idea. What is copyrightable is the particular way in which an idea is expressed. Recent legislation permits the copyright of computer programs.

Whenever the form of expression of an idea is copied, an infringement of copyright has occurred. The production does not have to be exactly the same as the original, nor does it have to reproduce the original in its entirety. If a substantial part of the original is reproduced, a copyright infringement exists. Limited copying is permitted under the ''fair use'' doctrine, such as copying a page of this text for classroom use.

Theft of Trade Secrets

Some processors or items of information that are not patented or are not patentable are nevertheless protected by law against appropriation by a competitor. Businesses that have trade secrets generally protect themselves by having all employees who use the process or information agree in their contracts never to divulge it. If a salesperson tries to solicit the company's customers for noncompany business or if an employee copies the employer's unique method of manufacture, he or she

---

3. The case was settled in 1988 for $3 billion. The day of the payment, Texaco completed its reorganization and emerged from twelve months in bankruptcy proceedings.

has appropriated a trade secret and has also broken a contract—two separate wrongs.

When confidential data are stolen through industrial espionage, as when a business taps into a competitor's computer, this constitutes a **theft of trade secrets** without any contractual violations, and the wrong is actionable in itself.

Product Liability

We have been discussing different forms of liability based on tort law. Increasingly, the courts are combining tort law and contract law when the lawsuit involves products that malfunction and cause injuries. Consumers buy beer, medicine, microwave ovens, hair dryers, sporting goods, automobile tires, and thousands of other items with the complete faith that the product is properly designed and manufactured for its intended use, is safe for consumption, and is correctly labeled. In 1987, the National Safety Council, however, reported that 23,000 people died from defective products (other than automobiles) placed on the market by American businesses. Additionally, defective products were responsible for 3 million disabling injuries, and 20 million people suffered some lesser form of injury.

How should the losses from injury and death due to defective products be allocated? The distribution of these losses and of what is called "economic loss"—the loss suffered because a product did not perform as expected—makes up an area of the law called **product liability**. It does not fit squarely into any one body of law.

Common-law rules of torts and contracts once set the parameters of product safety, but the common-law standards applicable to product liability vary greatly from state to state. The Uniform Commercial Code helps the courts to give some degree of uniformity when determining potential liability for products through warranty law.

Historical Development

A long-established rule holds that the seller of goods has a duty to exercise the care of a reasonable person in ensuring that the goods do not harm the buyer. In the past, this rule was enforced by using negligence as a basis for liability. Even in applying negligence principles, however, earlier courts required privity of contract in product liability cases. The privity requirement meant that the injured party who sued in negligence also had to prove that there was a contract—that is, that he or she had bought the defective item from the defendant.

This same requirement was found in contract and warranty law. A warranty is a legally binding guarantee. Contract, warranty, and tort laws were insufficient by themselves to protect the consumer completely from unsafe products. Because of the requirement of privity, the ultimate consumer frequently was not covered. The courts eventually resorted to the law of torts, specifically negligence and later strict liability principles, and abandoned the privity requirement. Yet negligence, too, proved to be inadequate because the manufacturer could avoid liability by proving that he or she had exercised reasonable care in producing the goods.

In the absence of a legal theory that fully compensated victims of defective products, a new theory developed. To deal with the dilemma of the injured but uncompensated victim, the common law extended the theories of contracts and torts, finally blending them to develop a cohesive restraint. This new doctrine, known as product liability, permits an injured plaintiff to recover, even though the manufacturer exercised reasonable care. This legal hybrid emerged from theories of negligence, strict liability, and warranty.

Product Liability Based on Negligence

As previously discussed, negligence is defined as failure to use that degree of care that a reasonable, prudent person would have used under similar circumstances. The manufacturer of a product must exercise due care to make that product safe to be used as it was intended. Due care must be exercised in designing the product, in selecting the materials, in using the appropriate production process, in assembling and testing the product, and in placing adequate warnings on the label of dangers of which an ordinary person might not be aware. The duty of care extends to the inspection and testing of purchased products that are used in the final product sold by the manufacturer.

The defendant-manufacturer can prove it used due care in the manufacture of its product as an appropriate defense against a negligence suit. A major problem of the plaintiff is to tie the defendant-manufacturer's failure to exercise due care to the plaintiff's injury. Numerous events, involving different people, take place between the time a product is manufactured and the time the plaintiff uses the product. If any of these events can be shown to have caused or contributed to the injury, the manufacturer will claim no liability on the basis of this intervening cause. Other defenses may also be used, but their application varies from state to state.

Two defenses discussed earlier in this chapter are contributory negligence and, where recognized, assumption of risk. For example, when a person plugs an electric cord into an outlet, plugs the other end into the plug-in of an electric lawn mower that has a bare metal pushbar, and tries to mow wet grass, he or she may be electrocuted. The bare metal pushbar may be a negligent design, but mowing a wet lawn may be contributory negligence.

Likewise, any time a plaintiff misuses a product, the manufacturer will claim that the plaintiff contributed to the cause of the injuries. The defense is that the plaintiff's negligence offsets the negligence of the manufacturer.

Product Liability Based on Strict Liability

In early English history, people were liable for the results of their act regardless of their intentions or their exercise of reasonable care. A person whose conduct resulted in the injury of another was held liable for damages, even if he or she had not intended to injure anyone and had exercised reasonable care. This approach was abandoned around 1800 in favor of the fault approach (negligence), in which the act became a tort only if it was wrongful or blameworthy in some respect.

Dissatisfaction with the warranty and tort theories in product liability cases led to a return to the English doctrine of strict liability. Modern strict liability (or product liability as it is commonly characterized) states basically that the purchaser of a product who is injured has a cause of action against the manufacturer simply by showing: (1) that the product was defective, (2) that the defect made the product unreasonably dangerous, and (3) that the defect was the proximate cause of the injury.

Requirements of Strict Product Liability The difference between negligence and strict liability is that negligence evaluates the conduct of a supplier, processor, or manufacturer, while strict liability focuses entirely on the condition of the product. The five basic requirements of strict product liability are:

1. The defendant must sell the product in a defective condition.
2. The defendant must be engaged in the business of selling that product.
3. The product must be unreasonably dangerous to the user or consumer because of its defective condition.
4. The defective condition must be the proximate cause of the injury or damage.
5. The goods must not have been substantially changed from the time the product was sold to the time the injury was sustained.

In any action against a manufacturer or seller, the plaintiff does not have to show why or in what manner the product became defective. The plaintiff does, however, have to show that, at the time the injury was sustained, the condition of the product was essentially the same as it was when it left the hands of the defendant-manufacturer. In addition, all states have extended strict liability's protection to "bystanders." Thus the injured party does not have to be a consumer or user of the product. In the following case, the court reviews the use of an expert witness to show management's attitude toward safety and the use of documentary evidence to show that management knew the product was unsafe but decided not to correct the defect because of cost considerations.

Case 12.5
GRIMSHAW v. FORD MOTOR CO.

Court of Appeal of California,
Fourth District, 1981.
119 Cal.App.3d 757,
174 Cal.Rptr. 348.

BACKGROUND AND FACTS   *In November 1971, the Grays purchased a new 1972 Pinto hatchback. The Grays had trouble with the car from the beginning. The car was returned for repairs a number of times, including excessive gas and oil consumption, downshifting of the automatic transmission, lack of power, and stalling. The stalling and excessive fuel consumption were caused by a heavy carburetor float.*

On May 28, 1972, Mrs. Gray and thirteen-year-old Richard Grimshaw set out on a trip in the Pinto, which was then six months old and had 3,000 miles on it. Getting on the freeway, Mrs. Gray was driving at sixty miles per hour. As she approached a major exit ramp where the traffic was congested, she moved from the outer fast lane to the middle lane of the freeway. Shortly after this lane change, the Pinto suddenly stalled and coasted to a halt in the middle lane. It was later established that the carburetor float had become so saturated with gasoline that it suddenly sank, opening the float chamber and causing the engine to flood and stall. The Pinto erupted into flames when it was rear-ended by a car proceeding in the same direction. Mrs. Gray suffered fatal burns, and Grimshaw suffered severe and permanently disfiguring burns on his face and entire body.

Grimshaw and the heirs of Mrs. Gray, the plaintiffs, sued Ford Motor Company, the defendant. Following a six-month jury trial, verdicts were returned in favor of the plaintiffs. The Gray family was awarded $559,680 in compensatory damages. Grimshaw was awarded $2,516,000 in compensatory damages and $125 million in punitive damages. The trial court reduced the punitive damages to $3.5 million. Ford appealed the judgment on seven major grounds.

TAMURA, Acting Presiding Justice.
*   *   *   *

Ford seeks reversal of the judgment as a whole *   *   *.

In the ensuing analysis (ad nauseam) of Ford's wideranging assault on the judgment, we have concluded that Ford has failed to demonstrate that any errors or irregularities occurred during the trial which resulted in a miscarriage of justice requiring reversal.

*   *   *   *

[Court's discussion of expert witness who was a former Ford employee]

A party offering an expert witness is entitled to examine him ''as to his qualifications and experience so that the full weight to be accorded his testimony will become apparent.'' Such examination ''should not be limited by narrow and stringent rules.'' It was therefore within the court's discretion to permit plaintiffs to elicit from Mr. Copp testimony as to when he left Ford and why. Evidence as to why he left Ford was part of the background information concerning the witness' professional experience which would assist the fact finder in determining the weight to be given to his testimony. While the evidence may also have tended to enhance the witness' credibility, the purpose of permitting a party producing an expert to question him as to his educational background, training, and experience in his area of expertise is not only to establish ''the competency of the witness to the satisfaction of the court, but also for the purpose of making plain the strength of the witness's [sic] grounds of knowledge and the reason for trusting his belief.'' Therefore, the fact that the evidence may have enhanced the witness' credibility did not render it inadmissible.

* * * *

* * * The fact that Ford fired a high ranking engineering executive for advocating automotive safety was indicative of Ford management's attitude towards safety in automobile production and was thus relevant to the issue of malice. It had a tendency in reason to prove that Ford's failure to correct the Pinto's fuel system design defects, despite knowledge of their existence, was deliberate and calculated. Ford's argument that firing Mr. Copp in 1976 for speaking out on safety does not reasonably tend to show that Ford disregarded safety in designing the Pinto some five years earlier lacks merit. The evidence was not that Mr. Copp first took his stand on safety in 1976; he testified that he had been outspoken on auto safety during all the many years he worked for Ford.

Ford complains that since Mr. Copp was permitted to testify to the circumstances surrounding his termination, Ford was compelled to cross-examine him to show that the reason for his dismissal was unexplained absences from work and unsatisfactory work performance; that if the court had not permitted Mr. Copp to give his version of the reason for termination, Ford would have had little or no reason to examine him about his retirement and plaintiffs would not have been able to adduce rehabilitation testimony highly prejudicial to Ford. The record discloses that Mr. Copp testified only briefly concerning the circumstances of his early retirement from Ford but that on cross-examination Ford engaged in extensive questioning to show that the reason for his termination was not his safety views but unsatisfactory work and absenteeism. Plaintiffs thereafter introduced rehabilitating testimony. Mr. Copp was permitted to testify to his campaign for automotive safety during his entire period of employment with Ford, including a conversation he had with Henry Ford II on the subject, his testimony before a United States Senate Committee concerning the Chevrolet Corvair's unsafe design and his role in exposing Ford's conduct in connection with the emission control program. Ford argues that but for the court's erroneous initial ruling and its consequent cross-examination on the reason for Mr. Copp's retirement, the damaging rehabilitation evidence would not have come in. Since we find no error in the court's initial ruling and since Ford has not advanced any independent reason why the rehabilitating evidence should have been excluded, Ford's complaint concerning the prejudicial nature of that evidence must be rejected.

* * * *

[Court's discussion of documentary evidence]

Ford contends that the court erroneously admitted irrelevant documentary evidence highly prejudicial to Ford. We find the contention to be without merit.

(1) *Exhibit No. 125:*

Exhibit No. 125 was a report presented at a Ford production review meeting in April 1971, recommending action to be taken in anticipation of the promulgation of federal standards on fuel system integrity. The report recommended * * * deferral from 1974 to 1976 of the adoption of ''flak suits'' or ''bladders'' in all Ford cars, including the Pinto, in order to realize a savings of $20.9 million. The report stated that the cost of the flak suit or bladder would be $4 to $8 per car. The meeting at which the report was presented was chaired by Vice President Harold MacDonald and attended by Vice President Robert Alexander and occurred sometime before the 1972 Pinto was placed on the market. A reasonable inference may be drawn from the evidence that despite management's knowledge that the Pinto's fuel system could be made safe at a cost of but $4 to $8 per car, it decided to defer corrective measures to save money and enhance profits. The evidence was thus highly relevant and properly received.

* * * *

(2) *Exhibits Nos. 95 and 122:*

Ford urges that a report (Exhibit No. 95) and a motion picture depicting Ford's crash test No. 1616 (Exhibit No. 122) should have been excluded because they were irrelevant and highly prejudicial to Ford in that they showed that in a 21.5-mile-per-hour crash of a 1971 Pinto prototype into a fixed barrier the filler neck of the fuel tank separated allowing fluid to spill from the tank, whereas no such filler neck separation occurred in the Gray vehicle. Under the test for ascertaining relevancy of evidence to which we have previously alluded, we find no abuse of discretion in the court's ruling. Not only did the filler neck separation show the vulnerability of the Pinto fuel system in a 21.5-mile-per-hour fixed barrier test, but crash test No. 1616, as Ford conceded, resulted in a puncture of the fuel tank from the exposed bolt heads on the differential housing. Thus, the exhibits showed the defect in the Pinto's gas tank location and design, the hazard created by the protrusions on the differential housing, and, in addition, they served as evidence of Ford's awareness of those defects. Exhibits Nos. 95 and 122 were properly received in evidence.

*   *   *   *

Ford contends that Grimshaw's counsel committed prejudicial misconduct in referring to Ford's executives meeting in the "glass house" and deciding to approve the Pinto's fuel tank design with knowledge that it was unsafe and would result in the loss of many lives. Ford argues that although there was evidence that the corporate headquarters of Ford was referred to as the "glass house" there was no evidence of management meetings held there in connection with the Pinto design. The record contains substantial evidence from which it reasonably may be inferred that Ford's management knew that the Pinto was unsafe but nevertheless decided not to alleviate the problem because of cost considerations, and thus that those decisions were made in Ford's corporate headquarters.

DECISION AND REMEDY *The court of appeals, in a forty-one-page opinion, found against Ford on every issue on appeal. The trial court's judgment was affirmed.*

Defenses to Strict Product Liability The traditional defense of contributory fault has frequently been rejected in strict tort liability actions even though it remains a defense in a negligence action. In principle, negligence and contributory negligence are immaterial in any action based on the theory of strict liability in tort. After all, strict liability assumes that the danger presented was foreseeable by the manufacturer of the product.

The exclusion of the defense of contributory fault has forced courts to utilize assumption of risk as a defense in product liability suits. Assumption of risk can be used as a defense in an action based on strict liability in tort. The defendant must show: (1) that the plaintiff voluntarily proceeded while recognizing the risk; (2) that the plaintiff knew and appreciated the risk created by the defect; and (3) that the plaintiff's decision to undertake the known risk was unreasonable.

Most courts have not limited the application of the strict liability doctrine to cases in which only personal injuries have occurred. Thus, when a defective product causes only property damage, the seller also may be liable under the theory of strict liability.

Product Liability Based on Warranty

Warranty liability is applied in product liability cases. The concept of warranty is based on the seller's assurance to the buyer that goods will meet certain standards. If the goods fail to meet those standards, the warranty is breached and the defendant will be liable. The UCC designates several types of warranties that can arise: express warranties [UCC 2-313], implied warranties of merchantability [UCC 2-314], and implied warranties of fitness for a particular purpose [UCC 2-315].

LEGAL HIGHLIGHT   **Mass Torts**

Often the media talks about mass torts. Just what is a mass tort? In this type of tort, an act has harmed a number of plaintiffs, with the numbers sometimes in the hundreds or even thousands. Some recent examples of mass disaster litigation include the following cases:

■ In 1981, the skywalks in the Hyatt Regency Hotel in Kansas City collapsed. The federal court certified two class-action suits. Over 100 people were killed, and hundreds were injured.
■ A. H. Robins manufactured the Dalkon Shield, an IUD product from 1971 to 1974. Between 1974 and 1986 over 12,000 women

filed damage suits. Robins went into bankruptcy court in 1986. Currently, 130,000 claims are pending against Robins.
■ In 1979, a fire swept through the lobby of the MGM Grand Hotel in Las Vegas, Nevada. The final settlement was in excess of $205 million.
■ In 1982, an Air Florida flight crashed after takeoff from National Airport in Washington, D.C. Seventy-eight people were killed.
■ In 1976, the Teton Dam collapsed. Eleven people were killed, and the surrounding communities suffered a loss of over $1 billion.

Express Warranties   A seller can create an **express warranty** by making representations concerning the quality, condition, description, or performance potential of the goods. Express warranties arise when a seller suggests that:

1. The goods will conform to the seller's affirmation of fact or promise. (Such affirmations or promises are usually made during the bargaining process through such statements as "these drill bits will easily penetrate stainless steel without dulling.")
2. The goods will conform to a description of them. (For example, the description states "Crate contains one 150-horsepower diesel engine," or the contract calls for delivery of a "camel's hair coat.")
3. The goods will conform to a sample or model.

For any express warranty to be created, the seller's affirmation or promise must become part of the basis of the bargain. If the seller merely makes a statement that relates to the value or worth of the goods or makes a statement of opinion or recommendation about the goods, the seller is not creating an express warranty. For example, a seller claims, "This is the best used car to come along

in years; it has four new tires and a 350-horsepower engine just rebuilt this year." The seller has stated several facts that create a warranty: The automobile has an engine; it is a 350-horsepower engine; the engine was rebuilt this year; there are four tires on the automobile; the tires are new.

The seller's opinion that it is "the best used car to come along in years" is known as "puffing" and creates no warranty. Puffing is the expression of an opinion by a seller that is not made as a representation of fact. A statement relating to the value of the goods, such as "it's worth a fortune" or "anywhere else you'd pay $10,000 for it," will not normally create a warranty.

Implied Warranties   Implied warranties are created by law from the facts of the case and are not expressly stated by the parties.

An **implied warranty of merchantability** automatically arises in every sale of goods made by a merchant who deals in goods of that kind. A retailer of ski equipment makes an implied warranty of merchantability every time the retailer sells a pair of skis, but a neighbor selling skis at a garage sale does not.

Goods that are merchantable must be reasonably fit for the ordinary purposes for which such goods are used. They must be of at least average, fair, or medium-grade quality. The quality must be comparable to the quality of similar goods on the market. In addition, the goods, to be merchantable, must be adequately packaged and labeled, and they must conform to their labels.

Some examples of nonmerchantable goods include: light bulbs that explode when switched on, pajamas that burst into flames on slight contact with a stove burner, high heels that break off during normal use, or shotgun shells that explode prematurely.

The implied warranty of merchantability also imposes liability on the merchant for the safe performance of the product; it makes no difference whether the merchant knew of or could have discovered a defect that makes the product unsafe. Merchants, however, are not absolute insurers against all accidents arising in connection with the goods. For example, a bar of soap will not be unmerchantable merely because a user can slip and fall by stepping on it.

The **implied warranty of fitness for a particular purpose** arises when any seller (merchant or nonmerchant) knows the particular purpose for which a buyer will use the goods and knows that the buyer is relying on the seller's skill and judgment to select suitable goods. A "particular purpose of the buyer" differs from the "ordinary purpose for which goods are used" (merchantability). Goods can be merchantable but still not fit for the buyer's particular purpose. For example, house paints suitable for outside wooden siding are not suitable for painting over stucco walls.

A contract can include both a warranty of merchantability and a warranty of fitness for a particular purpose, which relates to a specific use or to a special situation in which a buyer intends to use the goods. For example, a merchant-seller recommends a particular pair of shoes, knowing that a customer is looking for mountain climbing shoes. The buyer purchases the shoes relying on the seller's judgment. If the shoes are found to be not only improperly made but also suitable only for walking, not for mountain climbing, the seller has breached both the warranty of fitness for a particular purpose and the warranty of merchantability.

Exhibit 12–1 summarizes the three types of warranty covered by the Uniform Commercial Code.

Exhibit 12–1 Three Warranties under the UCC

TYPE	HOW CREATED
Express Warranty UCC 2-313	As part of a sale or bargain— 1. An affirmation of fact or promise. 2. A sale by description. 3. A sample shown as conforming to bulk.
Warranty of Merchantability UCC 2-314	1. Where the seller is a merchant and 2. Deals in goods of the kind.
Warranty of Fitness for a Particular Purpose UCC 2-315	1. The buyer's particular purpose or use must expressly or impliedly be known by the seller, and 2. The buyer must purchase in reliance on the seller's selection.

Disclaimers or Defenses Against Implied Warranty Liability

The Uniform Commercial Code permits a seller to disclaim implied warranties or to have certain defenses against implied warranty liability. Some of these disclaimers or defenses are as follows:

1. The seller (manufacturer) can specifically disclaim either or both implied warranties. To specifically disclaim *any* implied warranty of fitness, the disclaimer must be in writing and conspicuous. The Code gives an example—"There are no warranties which extend beyond the description on the face hereof." To specifically disclaim the implied warranty of merchantability, the disclaimer can be oral or written, but must "mention merchantability," and if in writing such must be conspicuous. [UCC 2-316(2)]
2. The seller can disclaim both implied warranties by selling the goods with expressions such as "with all faults" or sold "as is." [UCC 2-316(3)(a)]

3. A defense may be available to the seller if the buyer actually examines the goods. The defense is that the buyer cannot complain of any defect he or she found or should have found. [UCC 2-316(3)(b)]

4. Implied warranties can also be excluded or modified by usage of trade or previous course of performance or dealings between the parties. [UCC 2-316(3)(c)]

Because of the availability of these defenses and disclaimers, implied warranties may have limited importance to a buyer in seeking recovery under the warranty theory of product liability.

Magnuson-Moss Warranty Act The **Magnuson-Moss Warranty Act** of 1975 is designed to prevent deception in warranties by making them easier to understand. The Magnuson-Moss Warranty Act is enforced mainly by the Federal Trade Commission (FTC). To some degree, the Magnuson-Moss Warranty Act modifies the UCC warranty rules where consumer sales transactions are involved. The UCC remains the primary statute of warranty rules for commercial (business-to-business) transactions.

No seller is required to give a written warranty for consumer goods, but, if a seller chooses to make an express written warranty and the cost of the consumer goods is more than ten dollars, the warranty must be labeled as ''full'' or ''limited.'' In addition, if the cost of the goods is more than fifteen dollars (FTC regulation), the warrantor is required to make certain disclosures fully and conspicuously in a single document in ''readily understood language.'' These disclosures include the names and addresses of the warrantor(s), what specifically is warranted, procedures for enforcement of the warranty, any limitations on warranty relief, and the fact that the buyer has legal rights.

Although a **full warranty** may not cover every aspect of the consumer product sold, what it covers ensures some type of buyer satisfaction in case the product is defective. Full warranty requires free repair or replacement of any defective part; if it cannot be repaired within a reasonable time, the consumer has the choice of either a refund or a replacement without charge. The full warranty frequently does not have a time limit on it.

The warrantor need not perform warranty services if the problem with the product was caused by damage to the product or by unreasonable use by the consumer. A **limited warranty** arises when the written warranty fails to meet one of the minimum requirements for a full warranty.

Implied warranties do not arise under the Magnuson-Moss Warranty Act, only under the UCC provisions. Where an express warranty is made in a sales contract, however, the Magnuson-Moss Warranty Act prevents sellers from disclaiming or modifying the implied warranties of merchantability and fitness for a particular purpose. Sellers can impose a time limit on the duration of an implied warranty, but such a time limit has to correspond to the duration of the express warranty.

FACING A LEGAL ISSUE   **When a Retailer Becomes Liable**

You are the chief executive officer (CEO) for a chain of stores that sells retail toys and hobby supplies. Your segment of the market is directed toward older children and adults. Your firm does not manufacture products but rather purchases inventory directly from manufacturers located throughout the world.

Recently, one of your competitors lost a case and was held liable for $1.5 million involving a miniature radio-controlled automobile kit. The customer had bought a kit; it exploded because of a short-circuit and caused the customer to suffer severe eye damage.

Your firm sells the same type of product, and you become concerned that your firm might be confronted with a similar case. You wonder what legal theories might be used in this type of case or similar ones. You contact your attorney for general information about product liability.

To your surprise, she lists several different legal theories that could be used. If you are a retailer, you may be liable to the consumer even though you did not manufacture or package the product.

First, a plaintiff may bring action based on a breach of express warranty because the product must conform to the description on the box or to the model that you use for demonstration purposes.

Second, a plaintiff may rely on the theory of breach of the implied warranties of merchantability and of fitness for a particular purpose.

Third, a plaintiff may base his or her action on the legal theory of strict liability. This theory applies whenever a product is unreasonably dangerous and causes an injury.

An action for negligence might be brought, but normally this will be used against the manufacturer.

Fraud might also exist if you intended to deceive the customer about a material fact. The deception must be made with the knowledge of

its falsity and must be relied on by the customer to his or her injury.

How can you limit your potential liability? Obviously, one way would be through the use of liability insurance. The cost of insurance, however, has greatly increased during the last few years. Your firm has decided to be a self-insured organization. This means that your firm has no insurance to protect itself from legal action and has decided to assume this potential liability.

What else can you do to give the maximum protection to your firm in the absence of insurance coverage? Two possible legal routes might be used.

First, you could obtain from each customer a signed written statement that would disclaim any liability for your firm. This approach might be applicable to a small service business such as a Go-Kart Track. As a practical matter, this is not an acceptable business practice for most retail concerns. The disclaimer of liability also does not prevent a consumer who was not the original purchaser from filing a lawsuit.

The second procedure is to use the Uniform Commercial Code. The retailer is allowed to bring into the lawsuit the manufacturer, if the lawsuit is brought for breach of warranty. The manufacturer must either defend the lawsuit or be bound by the court decision. The practical effect is that the manufacturer is ultimately held liable.

Note, however, that this provision applies only to warranties and not to strict product liability. Remember, too, that your firm purchases inventory from international sources. It is not possible to enforce a judgment against a manufacturer outside of the United States on inventory bought from Asia, South America, or other parts of the world.

In other words, in your type of business, no foolproof method exists to protect your firm from lawsuits brought by consumers based on malfunctioning products. Even though insurance rates are high, insurance may be the only reliable method of protecting your firm. The cost of this protection will have to be passed on to the consumer in the form of higher prices.

Summary

This chapter has introduced the subjects of tort and product liability. Three general forms of tort were examined. First, intentional torts are injuries caused by intentional acts. Second, negligence is a tort theory under which careless acts can result in liability. Third, strict liability is imposed by law without regard for fault.

Intentional torts can be caused by wrongs against the person, such as false imprisonment, intentional infliction of mental distress, defamation (including slander of title and disparagement of goods), invasion of the right of privacy, and fraud. Intentional torts can also be wrongs against property, such as trespass to real and personal property, conversion, and nuisance. All of these actions are based on the concept that the person or property was intentionally harmed.

The concept underlying negligence is that the defendant did not intend to harm another, but, through his or her carelessness, a person was injured or there was property damage.

The first element of negligence is a breach of duty of care. This duty is the objective standard of care that each of us owes one another. The duty of care is breached when someone fails to act as a reasonable and prudent person would act when confronted with similar circumstances or fails to act in accordance with the duties as defined by statutes. The second requirement for negligence is that there is an injury or damage. The last requirement is causation—in other words, did the breach of the duty of care cause the damages?

A limiting factor to liability on a negligence theory is the doctrine of foreseeability—could the defendant foresee the injury or damages to persons in the plaintiff's position when he or she breached the duty of care? Defenses to negligence include superseding intervening forces, assumption of risk, and contributory negligence.

Strict or absolute liability is based on the idea that certain dangerous activities automatically create liability if there are damages or injuries. The law imposes this liability because of public policy.

Certain torts apply only in a business situation. For example, a business cannot wrongfully interfere with contractual or business relationships. A business cannot infringe on another's trademark, trade name, patent or copyright, nor may a business use another's trade secrets.

Product liability causes specific legal problems for a business. Several legal doctrines apply when a product malfunctions. Negligence can be used, although, when this doctrine is used, there is the difficulty of establishing at what point the breach of the duty of care occurred. Under certain conditions, strict liability has been used in product cases. Warranty liability has been applied by many successful plaintiffs. Three types of warranties are: (1) express warranty, (2) implied warranty of merchantability, and (3) implied warranty of fitness for a particular purpose.

Key Terms

absolute privilege (**288**)
assumption of risk (**295**)
causation (**292**)
comparative negligence (**295**)
contributory negligence (**295**)
conversion (**289**)
copyright (**299**)
defamation (**287**)
defamation by computer (**288**)

disparagement of goods (**288**)
express warranty (**305**)
false imprisonment (**285**)
foreseeability (**293**)
fraud or deceit (**289**)
full warranty (**307**)
implied warranty of fitness for a particular purpose (**306**)
implied warranty of

merchantability (**305**)
infliction of mental distress (**287**)
intentional tort (**284**)
interference with a contractual or business relationship (**298**)
libel (**287**)
limited warranty (**307**)

Magnuson-Moss Warranty
 Act (**307**)
merchant protection
 legislation (**285**)
negligence (**284**)
nuisance (**289**)
objective standard (**290**)
patent (**299**)

private nuisance (**289**)
privilege of immunity (**288**)
product liability (**300**)
proximate cause (**293**)
public nuisance (**289**)
qualified privilege (**288**)
service mark (**299**)
slander (**287**)

slander of title (**288**)
statutory duty (**292**)
strict (or absolute) liability
 (**284**)
theft of trade secrets (**300**)
tort (**284**)
trademark (**299**)

Questions and Case Problems

1. Kerly is standing on a street corner waiting for a ride to work. Beyer has just purchased a new car manufactured by Able Motors. Beyer is driving down the street when suddenly the steering mechanism breaks, causing Beyer to run over Kerly. Kerly suffers permanent injuries. Beyer's total income per year has never exceeded $15,000. Kerly files suit against Able under the theory of strict liability in tort. Able pleads no liability because: (1) due care was used in the manufacture of the car, and (2) Able is not the manufacturer of the steering mechanism (Smith is). What is the outcome of Kerly's lawsuit?

2. Baxter manufactures electric hair dryers. Garza purchases a Baxter dryer from her local Ace Drug Store. Green, a friend and guest in Garza's home, has taken a shower and wants to dry her hair. Garza tells Green to use the new Baxter hair dryer. As Green plugs in the dryer, sparks fly out from the motor and continue to do so as she operates it. Despite this, Green begins drying her hair. Suddenly, the entire dryer ignites into flames, severely burning Green's scalp. Green sues Baxter on the basis of the torts of negligence and strict liability. Baxter denies liability, particularly since Green did not purchase the dryer. Discuss the validity of Green's actions and any defense claimed by Baxter.

3. Beech Aircraft Corporation manufactured airplanes. Some of the parts could be installed backwards, which would cause a plane to crash. George Nesselrode was a passenger in a plane that did crash; everyone on board was killed. The crash was caused by the reverse installation of parts. His estate brought an action against Beech Aircraft. Beech Aircraft argued that they were not at fault because they had not installed the parts. Were they correct? [Nesselrode v. Executive Beechcraft, Inc., 707 S.W.2d 371 (Mo. 1986)]

4. K-Mart sold a rifle to William Knuck, who was a heavy user of marijuana and was under indictment for a felony. Federal law prohibits the sale of any firearm to such a person. K-Mart was supposed to ask the question about

marijuana use or felony indictments prior to the sale. This was not accomplished. William Knuck's brother, a heroin addict and alcoholic, took the rifle while drunk and assaulted his estranged wife and a police officer. The police officer brought a negligence action against K-Mart, who defended on the grounds of intervening circumstances. Was K-Mart successful? [K-Mart Enterprises v. Keller, 439 So.2d 283 (Fla. Dist. Ct. App. 1983)]

5. A truck belonging to Barberton Glass Company contained many sheets of glass. Due to improper loading, one of the sheets fell off the truck. Elliot Schultz was some distance behind the truck when this occurred. He suffered no physical injury but brought suit on the basis of emotional distress. Was he successful? [Schultz v. Barberton Glass Co., 4 Ohio St.3d 131, 447 N.E.2d 109 (1983)]

6. Ford Motor Company manufactured and distributed the Ford Cortina, which had only a cardboard shield separating the fuel tank from the passenger compartment. Nanda suffered severe disabling burns when the gas tank in his car exploded on being struck in the rear by another car. In a strict liability action by Nanda against Ford Motor Company, Nanda argued that the absence of a fire wall or metal shield between the fuel tank and passenger compartment constituted an unreasonably dangerous defect in the product and that his injuries were caused by this defect. What was the result? [Nanda v. Ford Motor Co., 509 F.2d 213 (7th Cir. 1974)]

7. A two-year-old child lost his leg when he became entangled in a grain auger on his grandfather's farm. The auger had a safety guard that prevented any item larger than four and five-eighths inches from coming into contact with the machine's moving parts. The child's foot was smaller than the openings in the safety guard. Was such an injury reasonably foreseeable? [Richelman v. Kewanee Machinery & Conveyor Co., 59 Ill.App.3d 578, 375 N.E.2d 885, 16 Ill.Dec. 778 (1978)]

8. Larry Colvin, an ironworker, was setting a steel truss on a concrete column while in a squatting position. He reached above his head to pull himself up and grabbed an I-beam, known as a purlin, which was eight or ten feet long and was not yet welded into place. The purlin failed to support Colvin's weight, and he fell. The plans for the building called for the purlins to be over forty feet long, but only seven were that length. The remaining purlins were substantially shorter and were welded together to serve their purpose as spacers between the trusses and the roof. The purlins were supplied by Red Steel Company. Explain whether Red Steel is strictly liable for Colvin's injury due to the short length of the purlins. [Colvin v. Robert E. McKee, Inc., 671 S.W.2d 556 (Tex.Civ.App.—Dallas 1984)]

 9. Only recently has it become known that smoking may cause cancer. Edwin Green died of lung cancer after smoking for many years. His widow brought an action against the American Tobacco Company for damages resulting from his death. The basis for her action was strict liability and breach of the implied warranty of merchantability. Would she be successful on these two theories? [Green v. American Tobacco Co., 409 F.2d 1166 (5th Cir. 1969)]

Chapter 13   Consumer Protection

Caveat emptor: *Let the buyer beware*.

Latin maxim

OUTLINE

Introduction

In earlier chapters we have seen how the law attempts to protect the interests of consumers. Certain business practices have been outlawed after they have been determined by courts, administrative agencies, or legislatures to be unfair or deceptive. In this chapter we will discuss laws that attempt to control unfair and deceptive trade practices, to prevent misleading advertising, and to encourage the development of safe products.

Consumer protection statutes promote both safety and fair dealing. They try to prevent injury to a person's body or damage to his or her property or economic well-being. Although some statutes provide a specific remedy if the consumer suffers an injury, the aim of consumer protection is to eliminate the harm itself, and many of these statutes do not have remedies for injured consumers. Redress for injuries suffered usually involves another area of the law, such as contract or tort law (covered in Chapters 9 and 12).

Costs are associated with consumer protection: Businesses bear the cost of complying with government regulation; these costs in turn, are passed on to consumers in the form of higher prices for goods and services.

For every consumer protection statute, society poses three questions:

1. From what harm does the statute protect consumers?
2. Whom does the statute protect?
3. What is the cost of this protection?

Exhibit 13–1 lists statutes and regulations designed to protect consumers. Complete coverage of all of them would be impossible in a book of this length. This chapter will familiarize you with the nature and existence of some of the important statutes. Chapter 11, on credit regulation, explores the most significant legislation applicable to consumer financing.

Federal Trade Commission

Consumer protection, as we know it today, originated with the **Wheeler-Lea Act** of 1938. The 1938 law amended the **Federal Trade Commis-**sion Act, which was originally passed in 1914 to supplement such statutes as the Sherman Antitrust Act. The Wheeler-Lea amendment gave the Federal Trade Commission Act a dual focus: to regulate anticompetitive business behavior and to provide consumer protection. Prior to 1938, courts aided only a few purchasers who sued sellers of defective goods by finding that the seller had breached a contract, had breached a warranty, or had violated a duty to the purchaser. As pointed out in Chapter 12, these claims are often difficult to prove.

The Wheeler-Lea amendment, through its prohibition of "**unfair or deceptive acts or practices**," enabled the Federal Trade Commission (FTC) to focus its attention on direct protection of the consumer. The FTC was also given the authority to monitor deceptive advertising practices. The amendment eliminated the need for the FTC to prove an anticompetitive effect before a practice could be stopped. The definitions of "unfair" and "deceptive" are left to the FTC. In general, any practice that would tend to mislead consumers is unfair or deceptive.

As a result of this amendment, the FTC has two bureaus: the Bureau of Competition and the Bureau of Consumer Protection. The antitrust activities of the FTC are handled by the Bureau of Competition. The Bureau of Consumer Protection monitors advertising and labeling practices, investigates complaints, and prosecutes cases involving alleged unfair practices. Exhibit 13–2 shows the organizational structure of the FTC.

Trade Regulation Rules

As an administrative agency, the FTC is able to adopt trade regulation rules. A **trade regulation rule** is a statement by the agency that has general applicability, and the effect of the rule is to implement the law, policy, or practice of the agency. In other words, a rule has the force of law.

An FTC trade regulation rule applies to an entire industry rather than to a particular seller. The commission has the authority to focus on an industry and can formulate standards to which all businesses within that industry must conform. In the past, the FTC has investigated household detergents, appliances, office copiers, the title insurance business, the funeral business, and car

Exhibit 13–1 Consumer Protection Statutes and Regulations

DATE	POPULAR NAME	PURPOSE
ADVERTISING		
1938	Wheeler-Lea Act	Amends Federal Trade Commission Act (1914); prohibits deceptive and unfair trade practices
1950	Oleomargarine Tax Repeal Act	Prohibits advertising that oleomargarine is a dairy product
1969	Public Health Cigarette Smoking Act	Prohibits advertising of cigarettes on television
1973	FTC Rules of Negative Options	Regulates advertisements for book and record clubs
INSPECTION AND CERTIFICATION		
1906	Meat Inspection Act	Provides for inspection of meat
1967	Wholesome Meat Act	Amends Meat Inspection Act
1938	Food, Drug, and Cosmetic Act	Provides for inspection and regulation of food, drugs, and cosmetics
1958	Food Additive (Delaney) Amendment to Food, Drug, and Cosmetic Act	Requires that food additives not cause cancer and be safe
1966	Hazardous Substances Act	Regulates hazardous substances
1968	Poultry Inspection Act	Provides for inspection of poultry
1969	Child Protection and Toy Safety Act	Amends Hazardous Substances Act; bans toys that pose electrical, mechanical, or thermal hazards
1972	Odometer Act	Regulates odometers
1976	Medical Device Amendments	Requires premarket clearance of medical devices
LABELING		
1939	Wool Products Labeling Act	Requires accurate labeling of wool products
1951	Fur Products Labeling Act	Prohibits misbranding of fur products
1958	Textile Fiber Products Identification Act	Requires accurate labeling of textiles
1960	Hazardous Substances Labeling Act	Requires accurate labeling of hazardous substances
1966	Fair Packaging and Labeling Act	Requires accurate names, quantities, and weights
1966	Child Protection Act	Requires childproof devices and special labeling
1966	Cigarette Labeling and Advertising Act	Requires labels warning of possible health hazards
SALES AND WARRANTIES		
1968	Interstate Land Sales	Requires full disclosure in interstate land sales
1973	FTC Rule on Door-to-Door Sales	Regulates door-to-door sales contracts
1975	Magnuson-Moss Warranty Act	Regulates warranties
1976	Real Estate Settlements Procedures Act	Requires disclosure of home-buying costs
1980	FTC Rule on Vocational and Correspondence Schools	Regulates contracts with these types of schools

Exhibit 13–2 Federal Trade Commission

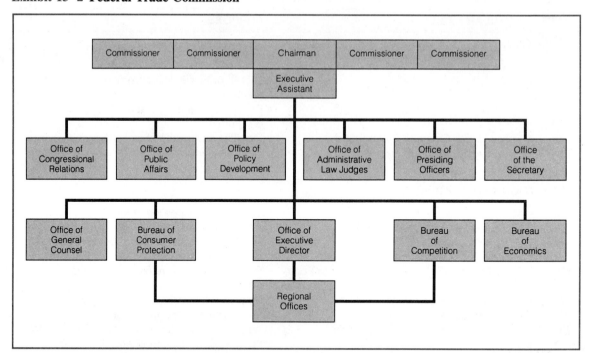

Source: Office of the Federal Register, *United States Government Manual, 1987–1988* (Washington, D.C.: U.S. Government Printing Office, 1987), p. 569.

rental agencies. Other investigations include such industries as transportation, health care facilities, nursing homes, agriculture, and energy.

The FTC can bring an action against an alleged wrongdoer either in its administrative law court or in federal court. The FTC tries first to force a seller to stop an unfair or deceptive practice. Most cases are settled by a **consent decree**. The seller consents to an order restraining the activity that the FTC has found unfair or deceptive. This agreement is then finalized in the form of a consent decree. The FTC may also force a defendant-seller to compensate injured buyers when the seller has violated an FTC rule or order.

The FTC can also seek to obtain a **cease and desist order**. This ruling, issued by the administrative law court, orders the defendant to cease its activities and desist from committing those activities in the future. This type of order forces the seller to correct its business operations. The FTC can also obtain court injunctions to restrain or prohibit a particular practice. Fines for violations may amount to $10,000 per day. Any person or

firm subject to an FTC order or rule may seek review of the FTC's action in a United States court of appeals.

Additional remedies and forceful orders that the FTC can issue include affirmative disclosure orders, corrective advertising orders, and multiple product orders. By issuing an **affirmative disclosure order**, the FTC requires the defendant to place in future advertisements affirmative disclaimers in order to remedy the past, deceptive advertisements. For example, the FTC required the J. B. Williams Company to state in its future advertisements for Geritol that it would not be of any benefit to the great majority of people who suffer from tiredness. Geritol had advertised that it was effective for any illness that had tiredness as a symptom. The advertising was deceptive according to the FTC because tiredness is a symptom of many illnesses including cancer and diabetes, for which Geritol had no effect.

A **corrective advertising order** is very similar in nature to affirmative disclaimers, but it takes the remedy one step further. This order requires the defendant to place in the advertisements a statement to the effect that its past advertisements were false. The FTC can order the words "contrary to prior advertising" to be placed in future advertisements if the defendant has engaged in egregious and intentional deception. A corrective advertising order is one of the issues at stake in *Warner-Lambert Co. v. FTC* (Case 13.3), found later in this chapter.

Generally, if the FTC finds deceptive advertising, it will require the firm to refrain from making any further deceptive advertisements. In cases where a firm sells multiple products, such an order may have little effect. If the FTC finds not only deceptive advertising but also a history of false advertising, the FTC has the power to issue a **multiple product** (or multiproduct) **order**. This order requires all future advertisements for all of the firm's products (or for all of the products in a certain category) to be accurate, not just advertisements for the product that was originally falsely advertised. In the following case, the court of appeals reviews the power of the FTC to issue a multiple product order.

BACKGROUND AND FACTS *Sears, Roebuck and Company directly petitioned the court of appeals after Sears was issued an order by the Federal Trade Commission. The case questioned the validity of a multiple product order that was the result of the use by Sears of certain alleged unfair and deceptive advertising practices to sell one of the products in a product group.*

In the early 1970s, Sears had formulated a plan to increase sales of its top-of-the-line Lady Kenmore dishwasher. The plan did not call for reengineering of the dishwasher or for any other mechanical improvement. Rather, the plan fostered a change of image for the Lady Kenmore, or, in sales jargon, Sears sought to "reposition" the machine in the marketplace. The objective was to change the consumer image from a "price" brand to a superior product at a reasonable price. The machine was to move from market leadership to market dominance as the market share increased.

Sears knew that a machine that actually performed the entire job of washing dishes, eliminating the need to prerinse and prescrape dishes, would attract new customers and command a premium price. It also knew that a machine's ability to clean dishes on the upper rack as thoroughly as those on the bottom rack would be a further attraction for new customers.

Based on this knowledge, Sears prepared advertisements claiming that the Lady Kenmore "completely eliminated" the need for prescraping and prerinsing and characterizing the machine as the "freedom maker." Advertisements for the Lady Kenmore appeared in print and on television throughout the country over a four-year period at a cost to Sears of roughly $8 million. During the first three years, Lady Kenmore unit sales rose 300 percent. The value of the company's total dishwasher sales rose from $73,470,000 in 1971 to $94,500,000 in 1973.

The "no scraping, no prerinsing" claim was not true. Sears had no reasonable basis for asserting the claim, and the owner's manual that customers received after they had purchased the dishwasher contradicted the claim. A 1973 survey conducted for Sears found that more than half of recent Lady Kenmore purchasers disagreed with the proposition that the Lady Kenmore did not require prerinsing.

The FTC began an investigation of the advertisements in 1975. In 1977 the FTC issued a complaint, charging Sears and its advertising agency, J.

 Case 13.1

SEARS, ROEBUCK AND CO. v. FEDERAL TRADE COMMISSION
United States Court of Appeals, Ninth Circuit, 1982.
676 F.2d 385.

Walter Thompson Company, with disseminating deceptive and unfair advertisements. After an extensive administrative hearing, the administrative law judge held Sears liable for deceptive and false advertising. The remedy ordered was that Sears was not to make any performance claims for any major home appliances without first possessing a reasonable basis consisting of competent and reliable tests. Sears was to keep records for three years.

REINHARDT, Judge.
* * * *

A judgment regarding "reasonable relation" in multi-product order cases "depends upon the specific circumstances of the case." "[T]he ultimate question is the likelihood of the petitioner committing the sort of unfair practices [the order] prohibit[s][.]" We answer that question by first examining the specific circumstances present in a particular case. Then, giving due deference to the Commission's expertise and judgment, we determine whether there is a "reasonable relation" between those circumstances and the concern regarding future violations manifested by the Commission's order.

Where a fair assessment of an advertiser's conduct shows a ready willingness to flout the law, sufficient cause for concern regarding further, additional violations exists. Two factors or elements frequently influence our decision—the deliberateness and seriousness of the present violation, and the violator's past record with respect to unfair advertising practices. Other circumstances may be weighed, including the adaptability or transferability of the unfair practice to other products. The weight given a particular factor or element will vary. The more egregious the facts with respect to a particular element, the less important it is that another negative factor be present. In the final analysis, we look to the circumstances as a whole and not to the presence or absence of any single factor.
* * * *

* * * Sears states that advertisements concerning the other covered products, e.g., microwave ovens and trash compactors, are *never* related to those promoting dishwashers since dishwashers do not perform work similar to the work performed by the microwave ovens or trash compactors, and that, therefore, an order covering these functionally unrelated machines is inherently unreasonable. This argument misses the fundamental point that the Commission is concerned not with how machines work, but with how machines are sold. Thus, the correct question is not whether the machines function in similar ways but whether the machines could be sold with similar techniques. * * *
* * * *

* * * Under [the specific] circumstances, Sears' advertising campaign demonstrates "blatant and utter disregard" for the law. The Commission also considered petitioner's compliance record and concluded that it was "a wash." We see no reason to find otherwise.

Sears' advertisements were no accident or "isolated instance." Rather, they were part of an advertising strategy, with attendant slogans, adopted without regard to the actual performance of the advertised machines. As the Commission pointed out, the covered machines are major ticket items generally purchased infrequently by any particular person. For that reason, their profitability does not depend on repeat purchases as is the case with frequently purchased, low-cost items. A selling strategy based on this purchasing fact, *e.g.,* the making of false and unsubstantiated performance claims as to a major ticket item, would be effective for a considerable period of time, with great benefit to the merchant but at great cost to consumers. This selling strategy could readily be transferred to the marketing of other machines in the home appliance category.

The prevention of "transfers" of unfair trade practices is a fundamental goal of the Commission's remedial work. Justice Brandeis, a draftsman of the 1914 legislation which created the Commission, made this point in *Federal Trade Comm'n v. Gratz[.]* Objecting to the Court's attempt to narrow the Commission's remedial authority, he expressed a view which has since become law:

The purpose of Congress [in creating the Commission] was to prevent any unfair method which may have been used by any concern in competition from becoming its general practice. It was only by stopping its use before it became general practice, that the apprehended effect of an unfair method . . . could be averted.

It is not only pretermitting a "general practice" which is important here, however. The "transfer" to any other single major home appliance could well cause substantial damage to consumers prior to the time that the Commission could again investigate the facts and obtain the evidence necessary to prove that a similar violation had occurred. By that time, it would be too late to protect the large number of consumers who, in reliance on the truthfulness of the advertised claims, had purchased a major home appliance which they expected to perform the advertised work for many years. This danger is particularly acute where national brands, like Sears' major home appliances, are involved and the advertising campaigns are both widespread and intensive.

In addition, if we were to deny "transfer prevention" authority to the Commission under these circumstances, unscrupulous merchandisers (and we do not imply that Sears falls in that category) might be encouraged to transfer unlawful but successful advertising techniques from product to product, leaving the Commission the job of instituting separate proceedings to secure new orders for each unlawfully advertised product. Because so drastic a limitation on the Commission's enforcement procedure would conflict with the Congressional intent described by Justice Brandeis, would consume enormous resources, and would afford no particular protection to lawful advertisements and little protection to consumers, the Commission need not wait until a "transfer" occurs before issuing multiproduct orders in cases like the one before us. It may issue and enforce such orders to avert an "apprehended effect."

To prevent the false and unsubstantiated performance claims strategy from being used in connection with another major home appliance or from becoming Sears' general practice with respect to such appliances, the Commission deemed a broad order necessary. A judgment of this nature depends on detailed knowledge of the major home appliances business and its related advertising techniques. "[D]eceptive advertising cases necessarily require 'inference and pragmatic judgment.' " This sort of knowledge of the commercial world and the ability to make the type of judgment required lie in the realm of the Commission's greatest expertise.

We note one other important fact. * * * [T]he order before us is not an all-products order. It is a limited order that applies only to 14 major ticket items. These 14 items constitute a small proportion of the total number of products sold by Sears.

In light of the flagrant and egregious nature of the violation found and the other circumstances present here, and giving the Commission's conclusions the required "great weight," we find no basis for substituting our judgment for the Commission's regarding the necessity for this multi-product order. We hold that the multi-product order is reasonably related to the petitioner's conduct, that a multi-product order is appropriate, and that the inclusion of the "performance claims" provision in that order is supported by the record before us and does not render the order overbroad.

DECISION AND REMEDY

The court of appeals upheld the validity of the FTC's multiproduct order covering all of the major home appliances from Sears, including clothes washers, clothes dryers, disposals, trash compactors, refrigerators, freez-

ers, ranges, stoves, ovens, and stereophonic consoles. As the court pointed out, the FTC's fundamental goal is to prevent the "transfer" of unfair trade practices from one product to another. Congress created the FTC to stop unfair practices before they became a general practice; thus, the FTC has the power to issue multiproduct orders.

Exemptions to FTC Regulation

The major exemptions to FTC trade regulation activities are those firms or industries that are regulated by local, state, or other federal authorities. For example, public utilities are regulated by state authorities; thus, few public utilities have been subjected to the FTC's authority.

Industries directly regulated by federal agencies are also outside the scope of FTC investigations. For example, the securities markets are regulated by the Securities and Exchange Commission. Some exceptions exist where both the FTC and another federal agency have the power from Congress to investigate the same industry. For example, the FTC enforces some credit protection statutes even though the Federal Reserve Board, the Federal Home Loan Bank Board, and other federal agencies regulate credit. Another example is where both the FTC and the Food and Drug Administration regulate labeling of food and drugs.

These agencies have interagency agreements that set out the specific duties of each agency and indicate which one will have primary investigation and enforcement powers. Thus, only one federal agency will handle the aspects of any given case, rather than two or more federal agencies competing against each other and wasting resources by repeating the same investigation and enforcement procedures.

Deceptive Advertising

Through its focus on advertising, the FTC can intervene before there is an injury to consumers. If an advertiser challenges an FTC administrative court ruling in a judicial court, the FTC needs only to prove that the advertisement could deceive consumers, not that it actually did so. Evidence of consumer understanding of the claims made in the advertisement is usually not offered.

In 1983, the FTC adopted a policy statement that set out the guidelines as to what constitutes deceptive advertising. First, the advertising must contain a representation, omission, or practice. Second, the act or omission must be found likely to mislead consumers acting reasonably under the circumstances. Third, the representation, omission, or practice must be material (or significant). The act or practice must be likely to mislead; an actual deception need not occur.

Advertisements are most frequently challenged based on one of the following:

1. False statements or claims.
2. Failure to disclose important facts.
3. Statements that are less than the whole truth.
4. Unsupported claims.

False Statements or Claims

Misrepresentations about the quality, composition, origin, character, or availability of products are illegal. An explicit false statement or claim is unnecessary. An advertisement that creates a false impression is deceptive; no verbal or written statement is required. For example, a cosmetic company advertises a "rejuvenescence cream" that would rejuvenate and restore youth or the appearance of youth to the skin. Unfortunately, virtually nothing is known to medical science that could bring about a restoration of youthfulness to the skin. This type of advertising is false and deceptive.

Failure to Disclose Important Facts

Silence may be considered deceptive when it represents a failure to disclose important facts. Some facts known to the seller are so important that these facts should be communicated to prospective buyers. While the FTC does not require that every negative fact about a product must be revealed, instances exist when the FTC will force an advertiser either to include additional information or to stop its advertising program. Even if state law permits a practice (that is, a certain type of advertising or certain wording used in advertising), an FTC ruling will preempt the state's determination of legality. In the following case, the FTC required the disclosure of certain facts within the advertisements.

BACKGROUND AND FACTS *The defendants (petitioners) operated a weight loss clinic in California. The FTC issued a cease and desist order prohibiting their continued use of an advertisement that failed to indicate that a drug used by the clinic was new and had not been approved for such use by the Food and Drug Administration (FDA).*

The clinics utilized the Simeon method of weight reduction. After an initial physical examination by a licensed physician, patients were put on a four- or six-week treatment program, which generally included a 500-calorie-per-day diet, daily medical counseling, and daily injections of human chorionic gonadotropin (HCG)—a prescription drug derived from the urine of pregnant women. The FDA declared that HCG was a new drug and approved it for some uses, but not for the treatment of obesity because it found that there was no substantial evidence that HCG was safe or effective for such use.

As one of the principal means of promoting the business of their weight reduction clinics, the petitioners placed advertisements in newspapers, magazines, and other media. These advertisements represented that the treatment program the clinics utilized was safe, effective, and medically approved. The advertisements did not mention HCG or that the injection of a drug would be part of the treatment program.

The clinics were registered under the Health Plan Act that had been passed by the California legislature. The act required the clinics' advertisements to be reviewed by the state attorney general's office prior to dissemination.

The FTC commenced administrative proceedings against the clinics. The advertisements were challenged as deceptive, unfair, and false because they failed to disclose that the treatments offered involved injections of HCG and that HCG was not approved by the FDA as safe and effective for use in weight control.

Case 13.2
SIMEON MANAGEMENT CORP. v. FEDERAL TRADE COMMISSION
United States Court of Appeals, Ninth Circuit, 1978.
579 F.2d 1137.

BURNS, Judge.
* * * *

Petitioners * * * contend that we should set aside the cease and desist order because, after reviewing the advertisements pursuant to the Knox-Mills Health Plan Act, the California Attorney General did not disapprove of their nature and contents. Petitioners argue that this failure to disapprove constitutes a prima facie determination that the advertisements are representative, fair and legal. They also argue that FTC regulation of their advertisements impermissibly interferes with the state regulation.

These contentions lack merit. Whether a state official has approved the advertisements or not is irrelevant to the operation of the federal regulatory scheme set forth in the [Federal Trade Commission Act (FTCA)]. That scheme does not impermissibly intrude upon state regulation.

Petitioners contend that the FTC has no jurisdiction to encroach upon the confidential relationship between a physician and patient. They argue that, because HCG is administered by or under the supervision of a physician as part of the weight reduction program, the Commission has no jurisdiction to regulate the advertising used in promoting the clinics.

This contention also lacks merit. The Commission's order does not pretend to affect the right of a physician to prescribe or administer HCG for his or her patients as part of a course of weight reduction treatments. The order prevents petitioners from advertising their clinics and weight reduction program in a way which fails to disclose that the FDA has not approved HCG for such use and that there is no substantial evidence that HCG is effective in the treatment of obesity. The order in no way impinges upon the traditional physician-patient relationship.

*   *   *   *

The Commission found that (1) some consumers will reasonably believe that the government exercises control over the promotion and use of prescription drugs; (2) this belief is intensified by the advertisements' representations that the weight loss treatments are safe, effective and medically approved; and (3) the representations may therefore reasonably lead consumers into the mistaken belief that the claims of safety and effectiveness are based, not on the advertiser's own opinion, but on a determination by the FDA. It further found that, in view of the public's belief that the government strictly regulates drugs, the fact that the treatments involve administration of a drug lacking FDA approval for such use may materially affect a consumer's decision to undergo the treatment. Accordingly, the Commission declared that the failure to disclose that the weight reduction treatments involve injection of a drug lacking FDA approval for such use renders the advertisements deceptive and thus in violation of § 5 of the FTCA.

*   *   *   *

The need for the courts to defer to the Commission's judgment results in part from the statutory scheme and in part from the weight of accumulated agency expertise. The generality of the § 5 proscriptions "necessarily gives the Commission an influential role in interpreting § 5 and in applying it to the facts of particular cases arising out of unprecedented situations." Determining whether a particular advertisement is deceptive requires a familiarity with the expectations and beliefs of the public, especially where the alleged deception results from an omission of information instead of a statement. The Commission has been engaged in making such determinations since 1938, when its jurisdiction was extended to include the prevention of unfair or deceptive acts or practices in commerce. As a result, the Commission has accumulated extensive experience and is therefore generally in a better position than the courts to determine when a practice is deceptive within the meaning of the FTCA.

*   *   *   *

Once the Commission has found an advertisement to be deceptive, it is authorized, within the bounds of reason, to infer that the deceptive information would be a material factor in the consumer's decision to buy. The Commission found that the fact that the advertised treatments involve administration of a drug lacking FDA approval for such use might materially affect the consumer's decision to obtain such treatments. Again, in view of the extent of governmental regulation in this area, we cannot say that this determination is unreasonable.

*   *   *   *

For the foregoing reasons, we hold that the Commission's determination that the petitioners' advertisements are deceptive in violation of § 5 of the FTCA is supported by substantial evidence on the record as a whole and is not arbitrary, capricious, an abuse of discretion or otherwise not in accordance with law.

The Commission is authorized, and indeed required, to prevent such deceptive advertising by issuing a cease and desist order.

The court of appeals upheld the FTC order preventing the petitioners' use of the advertisements because they were deceptive and in violation of Section 5 of the Federal Trade Commission Act.

DECISION AND REMEDY

This case did not stop the use of HCG for possible weight reduction, but it did require more disclosures by providers of this product to the consumer.

COMMENT

Statements That Are Less Than the Whole Truth

This form of deception, stating less than the whole truth, is the counterpart to failing to disclose important facts. Instead of omitting a material fact, the advertiser uses true statements out of context or in a way that is deliberately misleading. A product that is "guaranteed for life" usually means for the life of the consumer, not for the life of the product. The FTC restrained the Parker Pen Company from making such guarantees after Parker revealed that it was referring to the life of its pens.

Ocean Spray Cranberry Juice was required by a consent order to explain in future advertisements its statement that "Cranberry Juice Cocktail has more food energy than orange juice or tomato juice." Ocean Spray was using "food energy" not to mean vitamins or minerals, but calories. Beechnut advertised its baby apple juice as being made from apples. Two officers of the company went to prison when it was discovered there were no apples or juice from apples in its product.

Unsupported Claims

Reasonable, scientific evidence is required to substantiate advertising claims; otherwise the advertisement is making unsupported claims. If a product is claimed to be faster or safer than similar products, sufficient testing must prove the validity of the claim. Certain statements are merely considered puffing and are not deceptive advertising. "Puffing" means an affirmative expression of opinion by the seller of goods. For example, a manufacturer's statement that his or her product is "the best" would not be regarded as a product claim but merely as puffing. On the other hand, a statement that a product lasts three times longer than comparable products must be supported by reasonable evidence. During the 1950s, one of the major cigarette companies advertised that their cigarettes were "just what the doctor ordered." Today this advertisement would be a violation of the law.

The next case demonstrates the requirement that a product must live up to the claims made about it.

BACKGROUND AND FACTS *Warner-Lambert manufactures Listerine mouthwash. The Federal Trade Commission issued a cease and desist order to prevent Warner-Lambert from advertising that Listerine prevented, cured, or alleviated the common cold. The FTC also required the seller to undertake corrective advertising by including in future advertisements the information that, "contrary to prior advertising," Listerine would not help prevent colds or sore throats or lessen their severity. Warner-Lambert petitioned the court of appeals for review of the FTC order.*

Case 13.3
WARNER-LAMBERT CO. v. FEDERAL TRADE COMMISSION
United States Court of Appeals, District of Columbia Circuit, 1977.
562 F.2d 749.

WRIGHT, Judge.
* * * *

The order under review represents the culmination of a proceeding begun in 1972, when the FTC issued a complaint charging petitioner with violation of Section

5(a)(1) of the Federal Trade Commission Act by misrepresenting the efficacy of Listerine against the common cold.

Listerine has been on the market since 1879. Its formula has never changed. Ever since its introduction it has been represented as being beneficial in certain respects for colds, cold symptoms, and sore throats. Direct advertising to the consumer, including the cold claims as well as others, began in 1921.

* * * *

The first issue on appeal is whether the Commission's conclusion that Listerine is not beneficial for colds or sore throats is supported by the evidence. The Commission's findings must be sustained if they are supported by substantial evidence on the record viewed as a whole. We conclude that they are.

* * * *

First, the Commission found that the ingredients of Listerine are not present in sufficient quantities to have any therapeutic effect. This was the testimony of two leading pharmacologists called by Commission counsel. The Commission was justified in concluding that the testimony of Listerine's experts was not sufficiently persuasive to counter this testimony.

Second, the Commission found that in the process of gargling it is impossible for Listerine to reach the critical areas of the body in medically significant concentration. The liquid is confined to the mouth chamber. Such vapors as might reach the nasal passage would not be in therapeutic concentration. Petitioner did not offer any evidence that vapors reached the affected areas in significant concentration.

Third, the Commission found that even if significant quantities of the active ingredients of Listerine were to reach the critical sites where cold viruses enter and infect the body, they could not interfere with the activities of the virus because they could not penetrate the tissue cells.

* * * *

Petitioner contends that even if its advertising claims in the past were false, the portion of the Commission's order requiring "corrective advertising" exceeds the Commission's statutory power. The argument is based upon a literal reading of Section 5 of the Federal Trade Commission Act which authorizes the Commission to issue "cease and desist" orders against violators and does not expressly mention any other remedies. The Commission's position, on the other hand, is that the affirmative disclosure that Listerine will not prevent colds or lessen their severity is absolutely necessary to give effect to the prospective cease and desist order; a hundred years of false cold claims have built up a large reservoir of erroneous consumer belief which would persist, unless corrected, long after petitioner ceased making the claims.

* * * *

Having established that the Commission does have the power to order corrective advertising in appropriate cases, it remains to [be] consider[ed] whether use of the remedy against Listerine is warranted and equitable. We have concluded that part 3 of the order should be modified to delete the phrase "Contrary to prior advertising." With that modification, we approve the order.

* * * *

We turn next to the specific disclosure required: "Contrary to prior advertising, Listerine will not help prevent colds or sore throats or lessen their severity." Petitioner is ordered to include this statement in every future advertisement for Listerine for a defined period. In printed advertisements it must be displayed in type size at least as large as that in which the principal portion of the text of the advertisement appears and it must be separated from the text so that it can be readily noticed. In television commercials the disclosure must be presented simultaneously in both audio and visual portions. During the audio portion of the disclosure in television and radio advertisements, no other sounds, including music, may occur.

These specifications are well calculated to assure that the disclosure will reach the public. It will necessarily attract the notice of readers, viewers, and listeners, and be plainly conveyed. Given these safeguards, we believe the preamble ''Contrary to prior advertising'' is not necessary. It can serve only two purposes: either to attract attention that a correction follows or to humiliate the advertiser. The Commission claims only the first purpose for it, and this we think is obviated by the other terms of the order. The second purpose, if it were intended, might be called for in an egregious case of deliberate deception, but this is not one. While we do not decide whether petitioner proffered its cold claims in good faith or bad, the record compiled could support a finding of good faith. On these facts, the confessional preamble to the disclosure is not warranted.

DECISION AND REMEDY *The court of appeals upheld the FTC order prohibiting the advertising of Listerine as a cure for colds but modified the corrective advertising that the FTC sought.*

COMMENT *Warner-Lambert, in the next $10 million of advertising of Listerine, placed the statement that ''Listerine will not help prevent colds or sore throats or lessen their severity.''*

Other Deceptive Practices

Every year complaints flow into the Federal Trade Commission office. By categorizing the complaints, the FTC can determine if a pattern of behavior has developed. Once a pattern of deception evolves, the FTC may issue rules to curb this practice. The following are a few of the more important regulations that the FTC has developed in order to protect the public.

Bait and Switch

In some cases, the Federal Trade Commission has promulgated specific rules to govern advertising.

One of its more important rules is called ''Guides on Bait Advertising.'' It is designed to prohibit bait-and-switch advertisements that specify a very low price for a particular item. The low price is the bait to lure the consumer into the store. The salesperson then tries to switch the consumer to some other more expensive item. According to the FTC guidelines, bait advertising occurs if the seller refuses to show the advertised item, fails to have adequate quantities of it available, fails to promise or deliver the advertised item within a reasonable time, or discourages employees from selling the item.

The following case illustrates an application of this FTC rule.

BACKGROUND AND FACTS *All-State Industries, a producer of residential aluminum siding, storm windows, and other products, used a bait-and-switch sales technique in selling its products. The ''ADV'' lower-cost grade of aluminum was featured in the company's advertisements, but salespeople, following the training manual, attempted actually to sell the ''PRO'' grade after contacting the customers. The Federal Trade Commission found this practice to be ''unfair and deceptive'' under Section 5(b) of the FTC Act, and the FTC issued a cease and desist order. All-State Industries appealed.*

 Case 13.4

ALL-STATE INDUSTRIES OF NORTH CAROLINA, INC. v. FEDERAL TRADE COMMISSION

United States Court of Appeals, Fourth Circuit, 1970.
423 F.2d 423.

BRYAN, Judge.

* * * *

* * * From the Hearing Examiner's findings of fact, the following account unfolds of how they vend their products. These are of two grades. The "ADV" is the cheaper. It is extensively advertised, primarily through mailouts to people whose names and addresses are culled from telephone directories. "PRO," the other grade, is of a higher quality and not so widely publicized.

Respondents' sales technique, or "pitch," is devised to create, first, a demand for the "ADV" product. Through inflated promotion it is presented as a "special offer" with "limited time" prices. But the Examiner found the "ADV" is actually priced uniformly and without time limit. He held as untrue All-State's claim that they deal directly from their factory with the output "100% guaranteed."

Inquiries or "leads" are answered by a supposed "sales manager." He attempts to pressure the prospect into signing a contract, a note and a deed, committing him to the purchase of "ADV" articles but leaving blank the monetary obligation. As soon as the contract is executed, the salesperson brings out a sample of the "ADV" and points out deficiencies in it, "whether real or imaginary." The "PRO" is then shown in contrast, to the detriment of the "ADV." Whenever possible the "PRO" is then sold "at the highest price obtainable from the individual customer." The salesmen have incentives to substitute the "PRO"—they receive no commission on "ADV" but only on "PRO" sales.

This "bait and switch" artifice, the Examiner discovered, was fully set forth in the sale force's training manual and was employed generally. He also reported that All-State's agents utilized "gimmicks whereby the original prices quoted for respondents' products can be reduced." For example, the representative would promise a potential buyer a special discount, even below the quoted sale price, if the latter would allow the use of his home for demonstration or display purposes. Rarely, however, would a patron's home be so utilized. It was found as a bare inducement to overcome "sales resistance at a higher price" and provide "some apparently reasonable basis for the reduction in price."

DECISION AND   *The cease and desist order was enforced against All-State Industries as*
REMEDY   *well as against each of All-State's sales agents.*

Deceptive Comparisons

Deceptive comparative advertising is subject to the **Lanham Act** of 1946. This statute prohibits false descriptions about products or services when people are likely to be damaged by these deceptive comparative advertisements. An inaccurate comparative advertisement is one in which the defendant makes false statements about either the quality or the price of its own product as compared to the competitors'.

The FTC has ruled that several forms of pricing are deceptive. Stating the price of goods in a way that causes consumers to believe they are getting a bargain or a good deal when in fact they are not is unlawful. If the seller compares the current sales price to a higher regular price, the goods must actually have been offered by that seller at the higher price in the recent past. It is deceptive to compare the retail price of goods to a "manufacturer's list price" that is not the usual and customary retail price in the area.

The FTC has issued guidelines for the offer of "free" merchandise. If goods are offered "two for the price of one" or "buy one, get one free," the price charged for the two items must not exceed the regular price for the same single item.

The seller cannot immediately recover the cost of the free item by marking up the regular price of the item to be purchased or by substituting inferior merchandise.

In the case that follows, Vidal Sassoon, Inc., charged Bristol-Myers Company with inaccurate comparative advertising for a shampoo product that competed with Sassoon's.

BACKGROUND AND FACTS *In the spring of 1980, Bristol-Myers Company (Bristol), the defendant, decided to wage an aggressive, new advertising campaign on behalf of its shampoo product, "Body on Tap," so named because of its high beer content. In June 1980, Bristol began to broadcast on national television a commercial using Cristina Ferrare, a well-known model. In the advertisement she claimed that, "in shampoo tests with over 900 women like me, Body on Tap got higher ratings than Prell for body. Higher than Flex for conditioning. Higher than Sassoon for strong, healthy-looking hair." Prell, Flex, and Sassoon are shampoo competitors of Body on Tap.*

Bristol had had tests conducted by an independent market research firm, Marketing Information Systems, Inc. (MISI). In fact, 900 women, after trying both or all shampoos, did not make a product-to-product comparison between Body on Tap and its competitors. Rather, groups of 200 women tested one shampoo and rated it. Bristol instructed the marketing agency to have the women who tested Sassoon use it contrary to Sassoon's own instructions. Bristol also allowed the women during the testing period to use other brands while they were testing Sassoon. The propriety of this type of testing for the purpose of comparative advertising claims is in doubt.

At trial, Sassoon submitted, along with other evidence, a consumer perception study by ASI Market Research, Inc. (ASI). This study showed that viewers thought that the 900 women had tested two or more brands. Sassoon sued and was granted a preliminary injunction for a violation of Section 43(a) of the Lanham Act. Bristol appealed the injunction.

Case 13.5
VIDAL SASSOON, INC. v. BRISTOL-MYERS CO.
United States Court of Appeals, Second Circuit, 1981.
661 F.2d 272.

KAUFMAN, Judge.
* * * *

Bristol asserts that the misrepresentations alleged by Sassoon are only misstatements concerning the test results and the manner in which the tests were conducted, not the "inherent quality," of Body on Tap. Misleading statements regarding consumer test methodology, Bristol argues, do not fall within § 43(a). We agree that Bristol has not in so many words falsely described the quality of Body on Tap. It has not, to give a hypothetical example, baldly stated that the shampoo smells like roses when it in fact does not. The inaccuracies alleged concern the number and age of the women in the tests, how the comparisons were made, and how the results were tabulated. After a careful review of cases interpreting the Lanham Act and its legislative history, however, we are persuaded that § 43(a) does prohibit the misrepresentations alleged here.
* * * *

One of the principal purposes of the 1946 revisions of the Lanham Act was "[t]o modernize the trade-mark statutes so that they will conform to legitimate present-day business practice." We are therefore reluctant to accord the language of § 43(a) a cramped construction, lest rapid advances in advertising and marketing methods outpace technical revisions in statutory language and finally defeat the clear purpose of Congress in protecting the consumer. The language of § 43(a) is indeed very broad: "Any person who shall . . . use *in connection with* any goods or services . . . any false description or representation . . . shall be liable" (emphasis supplied). Certainly the alleged untruths concerning the MISI tests were at least "in connection with" Body on Tap, and, as the ASI study reveals, they quite probably created the impression that Body on Tap was superior. Judge Stewart could appropriately find, moreover, that this view was probably false because, if the qualitative rating categories were combined in a different manner, there would be no significant statistical difference between Sassoon and Body on Tap. While we recognize that § 43(a) encompasses only misrepresentations with reference to the " 'inherent quality or characteristic' " of defendant's product, we are nevertheless convinced that Judge Stewart was correct in concluding that Sassoon would probably succeed in showing that the intent and total effect of the advertisements were to lead consumers into believing that Body on Tap was competitively superior, surely a representation regarding its "inherent quality."

In a case like this, where many of the qualities of a product (such as "body") are not susceptible to objective measurement, it is difficult to see how the manufacturer can advertise its product's "quality" more effectively than through the dissemination of the results of consumer preference studies. In such instances, the medium of the consumer test truly becomes the message of inherent superiority. We do not hold that every misrepresentation concerning consumer test results or methodology can result in liability pursuant to § 43(a). But where depictions of consumer test results or methodology are so significantly misleading that the reasonably intelligent consumer would be deceived about the product's inherent quality or characteristics, an action under § 43(a) may lie.

Finally, we believe that Sassoon made an adequate showing of the possibility of irreparable injury. Although the likelihood of injury and causation cannot be presumed, Judge Stewart properly concluded that Sassoon had offered "proof providing a reasonable basis for the belief that . . . [it] is likely to be damaged as a result of the false advertising." Sassoon and Body on Tap compete in the same market, and it is quite likely that the apparently effective suggestions of competitive superiority, if repeatedly communicated to consumers, would eventually result in loss of sales to Sassoon. Although Sassoon offered no evidence of actual sales loss directly traceable to the alleged misrepresentations, proof of diversion of sales is not required for an injunction to issue pursuant to § 43(a). * * *

DECISION AND   *The injunction was upheld by the court of appeals. Bristol's own "Shampoo*
REMEDY   *Tracking Study" revealed that awareness and purchases of Body of Tap*
                     among women ages eighteen to thirty-four increased significantly shortly
                     after the commencement of the "Ferrare–900 Women" advertising campaign. Sassoon did not have to suffer actual irreparable injury from the
                     advertisements; it only had to show the likelihood of injury in order to be
                     entitled to the preliminary injunction. Bristol's advertisements were removed from television and the print media.

Deceptive Testimonials and Endorsements

From its inception, the FTC has proceeded with vigor against deceptive testimonials and endorse-

ments used to promote products. This advertising technique is intended to make consumers believe that someone other than the seller believes in the benefits of the product. Film stars and athletes

LEGAL HIGHLIGHT   Singing the Refund Blues

The singer Pat Boone appeared in many commercials endorsing Acne-Statin, advertised for the treatment of acne. Boone promoted the product on television and in printed advertisements, telling the public that all of his daughters had used Acne-Statin. Many people relied on his endorsement and purchased the product. When the product did not work as advertised, complaints were filed with the FTC.

An investigation revealed that, in fact, not all of Boone's daughters had used the product and, therefore, that these advertisements were unfair and deceptive. The FTC required Boone to contribute to a fund for making refunds to those purchasers who had relied on his endorsement.

Source: In the Matter of Cooga Mooga, Inc., 92 F.T.C. 310 (1978).

---

often endorse products. FTC guidelines require that the endorsements reflect the celebrity's honest opinion about the product. The endorser must be a user of the product.

If an advertisement represents that the endorser has superior expertise in making a judgment about the product, the endorser must have experience or training that qualifies her or him as an expert. If an advertisement represents that the person making the endorsement is a doctor, the endorser must have a medical degree. Some advertisements contain dramatizations of scenes involving purported doctors or scientists. Since the public recognizes that these people are actors, these advertisements have not been held to be endorsements.

Other Consumer Protection Laws

Over the years, Congress has passed laws that provide protection to consumers from abhorrent business practices. The following subsections examine the more significant of these statutes.

Fair Packaging and Labeling Act

The number of products that are prepackaged has increased significantly since 1950. The packaging often prevents the consumer from inspecting the product, so the label becomes the only source of information about the contents of the package. The **Fair Packaging and Labeling Act** (FPLA) was enacted by Congress in 1966, and it gave the De-

partment of Commerce the authority to deal with this problem.

The FPLA applies to those who package or label any consumer commodity. The primary focus is on items sold in supermarkets. Four provisions of the FPLA are mandatory:

1. The label must contain the name and address of the manufacturer, packer, or distributor.
2. The net quantity must be indicated on the front panel.
3. The quantity must be listed in a specific manner.
4. If the quantity is stated as a specified number of servings, the size of each serving must be indicated.

These mandatory provisions enable the purchaser to compare competing products. The Department of Commerce, the Federal Trade Commission, and the Food and Drug Administration all promulgate rules under the FPLA.

Other federal statutes also apply to packaging and labeling. These acts include the Wool Products Labeling Act (1939), the Fur Products Labeling Act (1951), the Cigarette Labeling and Advertising Act (1966), and the Flammable Fabrics Act (1967).

Magnuson-Moss Warranty Act

Dissatisfaction with automobile warranties led Congress to pass the Magnuson-Moss Warranty Act of 1975. This act, also discussed in Chapter

12, establishes standards for consumer warranties. The Magnuson-Moss Warranty Act requires that every warranty disclosure contain certain information that is necessary for a consumer to determine the extent of the warranty and the method of enforcing it. If a warrantor refuses to honor the warranty, the consumer can bring a legal action in either a state or a federal court. The government may also bring a court action to prevent a manufacturer from continuing to issue deceptive warranties or for failing to comply with the act.

Food, Drug, and Cosmetic Act

The purpose of the Food and Drug Administration (FDA) is to protect the public from harm caused by food, drugs, cosmetics, therapeutic items, household substances, pesticides, poisons, and other consumer items. The FDA is part of the Department of Health and Human Services. Through its rule-making authority, the FDA attempts to ensure that food is safe, pure, and wholesome, that drugs and therapeutic items are safe and effective, that cosmetics are harmless, and that consumers are not exposed to excessive risks of injury.

The **Food, Drug, and Cosmetic Act** of 1938 prohibits the adulteration or misbranding of various items. The FDA informs the public through press releases about products that pose an imminent danger to health or products that grossly deceive the consumer. Recent warnings have involved soup, fish, cranberries, and baby food.

Although numerous amendments to the act have been passed, none has been more important than the 1962 Drug Amendment. The amendment was adopted after a drug called thalidomide had been sold extensively in Europe. This drug caused numerous birth defects. The 1962 Drug Amendment requires the Food and Drug Administration to follow certain procedures in approving new prescription drugs for marketing.

The FDA has been severely criticized throughout its history. Many people contend that the agency takes too long to approve new drug applications, keeping the benefits of new scientific discoveries from the consumer for unreasonable periods of time. Others complain that FDA procedures are not only time consuming but also ineffective in protecting the consumer from harm.

The FDA can impose fines on those who violate its regulations, and violations of the Food, Drug, and Cosmetic Act can result in imprisonment. In addition, civil lawsuits for damages are frequently brought by plaintiffs who allege that they have suffered harm from an adulterated or misbranded product. These plaintiffs generally introduce evidence that the defendant has violated an FDA rule or regulation.

Despite many criticisms of the FDA's procedures, the courts defer to FDA determinations in most cases. In the following case, the Supreme Court upheld the FDA's authority to regulate drugs given to terminally ill patients.

Case 13.6

UNITED STATES v. RUTHERFORD

Supreme Court of the United States, 1979.
442 U.S. 544, 99 S.Ct. 2470.

BACKGROUND AND FACTS *Terminally ill cancer patients brought this action to enjoin the government from interfering with the interstate shipment and sale of Laetrile, a drug not approved for distribution under the Food, Drug, and Cosmetic Act. The district court concluded that Commissioner Rutherford of the Food and Drug Administration had infringed constitutionally protected privacy interests by denying cancer patients access to Laetrile. The court of appeals held that the act's safety and effectiveness standards have no reasonable application to terminally ill cancer patients. The case was appealed to the Supreme Court.*

MARSHALL, Justice.
* * * *

In the Court of Appeals' view, an implied exemption from the Act was justified because the safety and effectiveness standards set forth in §201 (p)(1) could have "no reasonable application" to terminally ill patients. We disagree. Under our constitutional framework, federal courts do not sit as councils of revision, empowered to rewrite legislation in accord with their own conceptions of prudent public policy. Only when a literal construction of a statute yields results so manifestly unreasonable that they could not fairly be attributed to congressional design will an exception to statutory language be judicially implied. Here, however, we have no license to depart from the plain language of the Act, for Congress could reasonably have intended to shield terminal patients from ineffectual or unsafe drugs.

A drug is effective within the meaning of §201 (p)(1) if there is general recognition among experts, founded on substantial evidence, that the drug in fact produces the results claimed for it under prescribed conditions. Contrary to the Court of Appeals' apparent assumption, effectiveness does not necessarily denote capacity to cure. In the treatment of any illness, terminal or otherwise, a drug is effective if it fulfills, by objective indices, its sponsor's claims of prolonged life, improved physical condition, or reduced pain.

So too, the concept of safety under §201 (p)(1) is not without meaning for terminal patients. Few if any drugs are completely safe in the sense that they may be taken by all persons in all circumstances without risk. Thus, the Commissioner generally considers a drug safe when the expected therapeutic gain justifies the risk entailed by its use. For the terminally ill, as for anyone else, a drug is unsafe if its potential for inflicting death or physical injury is not offset by the possibility of therapeutic benefit. Indeed, the Court of Appeals implicitly acknowledged that safety considerations have relevance for terminal cancer patients by restricting authorized use of Laetrile to intravenous injections for persons under a doctor's supervision.

Moreover, there is a special sense in which the relationship between drug effectiveness and safety has meaning in the context of incurable illnesses. An otherwise harmless drug can be dangerous to any patient if it does not produce its purported therapeutic effect. But if an individual suffering from a potentially fatal disease rejects conventional therapy in favor of a drug with no demonstrable curative properties, the consequences can be irreversible. For this reason, even before the 1962 Amendments incorporated an efficacy standard into new drug application procedures, the FDA considered effectiveness when reviewing the safety of drugs used to treat terminal illness. The FDA's practice also reflects the recognition, amply supported by expert medical testimony in this case, that with diseases such as cancer it is often impossible to identify a patient as terminally ill except in retrospect. Cancers vary considerably in behavior and in responsiveness to different forms of therapy. Even critically ill individuals may have unexpected remissions and may respond to conventional treatment. Thus, as the Commissioner concluded, to exempt from the Act drugs with no proved effectiveness in the treatment of cancer "would lead to needless deaths and suffering among . . . patients characterized as 'terminal' who could actually be helped by legitimate therapy."

It bears emphasis that although the Court of Appeals' ruling was limited to Laetrile, its reasoning cannot be so readily confined. To accept the proposition that the safety and efficacy standards of the Act have no relevance for terminal patients is to deny the Commissioner's authority over all drugs, however toxic or ineffectual, for such individuals. If history is any guide, this new market would not be long overlooked. Since the turn of the century, resourceful entrepreneurs have advertised a wide variety of purportedly simple and painless cures for cancer, including liniments of turpentine, mustard, oil, eggs, and ammonia; peat moss; arrangements of colored floodlamps; pastes made from glycerine and limburger cheese; mineral tablets; and "Fountain of Youth" mixtures of spices, oil, and suet. In citing these examples, we do not, of course, intend to deprecate the sincerity of Laetrile's current proponents, or to imply any opinion on whether that drug may ultimately prove safe and effective for cancer treatment. But this historical experience does suggest why Congress could reasonably have determined to protect the terminally ill, no less than other patients, from the vast range of self-styled panaceas that inventive minds can devise.

DECISION AND REMEDY   *The Supreme Court determined that Laetrile was a new drug that could not be distributed in the United States without FDA approval because the Food, Drug, and Cosmetic Act applies to drugs administered to terminally ill patients.*

COMMENT   *A moral dilemma is developing as a result of the acquired immune deficiency syndrome (AIDS) crisis. Once a person has developed AIDS, the long-term prognosis is death, usually within one to three years after diagnosis. The pressure by various groups to make experimental drugs more widely available to these dying patients is becoming more intense. The FDA, on the other hand, is concerned with the fact that an experimental drug may cause death faster than the disease does. The* Rutherford *case only begins to touch on the ethical and moral issues involved in governmental monitoring and control of experimental drugs for terminally ill patients.*

Postal Fraud Statutes

Consumers purchase billions of dollars' worth of products through the mail each year. Two federal statutes prohibit mail fraud; one is criminal in nature and the other civil. The criminal statute provides for imprisonment and fines.

The civil statute allows the postmaster general to return all mail addressed to or mailed by a promoter who has made a false representation. This procedure of intercepting the fraudulent seller's mail is a very effective weapon in combating deceptive practices. In more serious cases, the postmaster can also confiscate the mail instead of returning it. The postal regulations also require unordered merchandise to have a clear and conspicuous statement that the merchandise is a free sample. No action can be taken to persuade the consumer to pay for the merchandise later.

Mail-Order Houses

Mail-order houses, a growing industry, have annual sales exceeding $80 billion. Consumers buying from mail-order houses have typically been given less protection than those who purchase items in stores. Many mail-order houses are in a different state from the purchaser, thus making it more costly for the customer who seeks redress for grievances. The FTC and the postal service share enforcement of the laws concerning mail-order houses.

Negative option plans used by book, record, videotape, and compact disc clubs are regulated. Such plans require the member to return a card if he or she does not wish the merchandise to be sent. A negative option plan must disclose all its terms, must send the notice of intent to send the product in enough time for the member to accept or reject, and must include a rejection form for use by the club member.

An FTC rule requires the mail-order house to ship the merchandise promptly. If the business is unable to ship the goods within thirty days, the buyer must be notified of his or her option either to cancel the order and receive a refund or to accept further delay of the shipment.

Interstate Land Sales Full Disclosure Act

During the 1950s and early 1960s, many older people invested their life savings in real estate, particularly in Florida and in the Southwest. Much of this land was marketed through advertisements in magazines and newspapers, through mail and telephone solicitations, and by personal contact in booths set up near convention facilities. The purchasers rarely saw the parcel of land prior to signing the purchase contract and paying for the land. Later they discovered that the land they had purchased was under water or was years away from being ready for development.

The **Interstate Lands Sales Full Disclosure Act**, passed in 1968 and administered by the Department of Housing and Urban Development (HUD), is intended to decrease the opportunities for fraud and deception that are inherent in these "sight unseen" sales. The Office of Interstate Land Sales Registration within HUD now regulates the sale of undeveloped land for homesites. Regulations require developers to disclose fully their financial condition, and these rules also govern advertising and sales practices.

The act is similar to the Securities Act of 1933. Developers must file a registration statement with the agency before commencing sales. If the Office of Interstate Land Sales Registration determines that the disclosure is adequate, the developer can solicit sales. If the disclosure is inadequate, the developer must file additional information in order to gain approval.

Purchasers must receive a copy of the property report before they sign a contract. The act applies to both sales and leases of property in subdivisions and to condominium units that will not be completed within two years of the date of purchase. Congress used its power under the interstate commerce clause to pass this legislation. If the developer fails to follow the statute, the purchaser may be entitled to a full refund.

Consumer Product Safety Act

The **Consumer Product Safety Act** was passed in 1972 to protect consumers from unreasonable risk of injury from hazardous products. The act is administered by the Consumer Product Safety Commission (CPSC). The CPSC has sweeping powers to regulate the production and sale of potentially hazardous consumer products. Consumer product safety legislation began earlier with a variety of statutes that sought to improve the safety standards in selected industries.

The act is very comprehensive. The CPSC is charged with regulating "any article, or component part thereof produced or distributed for sale to a consumer for use in or around a permanent or temporary household or residence, a school, in recreation or otherwise, or for the personal use, consumption or employment of a consumer." The authority to administer earlier consumer-oriented protection statutes was transferred to the CPSC. These acts include the Refrigerator Safety Act (1956), the Flammable Fabrics Act (1967), the Child Protection and Toy Safety Act (1969), the Poison Prevention Packaging Act (1970), and the Hazardous Substances Act (1966).

Congress has charged the CPSC to conduct research on product safety and to maintain a clearinghouse that collects, investigates, analyzes, and disseminates injury data relating to the causes and the possible prevention of death, injury, and illness associated with consumer products.

The commission has the authority to establish construction standards as well as performance standards for the finished product and to issue adequate warnings of danger. If the CPSC can isolate a consumer product that is extremely hazardous to consumers, the commission has the authority to ban the product from sale.

Door-to-Door Sales

Door-to-door sales are singled out for special treatment in the laws of most states and by FTC regulation. This type of business has a lengthy history of using high-pressure tactics (such as staying in the prospective customer's house all night) and other systematic consumer abuse (such as sending encyclopedias with blank or missing pages). The special treatment also stems in part from the nature of the sales transaction. A door-to-door seller has a captive audience because individuals are in their own home and are hesitant to ask people to leave.

Since repeat purchases are not as likely with door-to-door sales as they are in stores, the seller has little incentive to establish goodwill with the purchaser. Furthermore, the seller is unlikely to present alternative products and their prices. Thus, a number of states and the FTC have rules that permit the buyers of goods sold door to door to

When the television program "Battlestar Galactica" was broadcast in the early 1980s, Mattel, Inc., had the contract to manufacture the "Battlestar Galactica" toy. Unfortunately, after the toy was placed on the store shelves, it became apparent that small children could swallow or inhale the missiles. Mattel recalled the toys by sending 20,000 letters to store outlets, by mailing 1,400 mailgrams, and by placing advertisements in numerous newspapers, urging consumers to return these toys. Fortunately, no child died before the recall was completed. The CPSC became involved with this situation under the Child Protection and Toy Safety Act of 1969.

cancel their contracts within a specified period of time, usually three days after the sale.

In addition, a Federal Trade Commission regulation makes it a violation for door-to-door sellers to fail to give consumers a notice of their right to cancel the sale within three days. This rule applies in addition to whatever rules are mandated by state statute so that consumers are given the most favorable benefits of the FTC rule and of their own state laws. Finally, the FTC rule requires that the notification be given in the same language in which the sale was negotiated.

Miscellaneous Consumer Protection Statutes

A variety of other consumer protection statutes exist that we are not able to examine in depth here. Various states have statutes that prohibit unfair or deceptive acts or practices (UDAP statutes). These state laws provide private remedies to fight the wide range of abuses of the consumer. Every state has at least one UDAP statute. Most of these statutes were adopted during the period from the mid-1960s to the mid-1970s. The following consumer areas are regulated by the FTC or another federal agency and/or by the states' UDAP statutes.

Statutes cover subject matters ranging from automobiles to funeral homes. For example, the federal Odometer Act prohibits odometers from being rolled back. The FTC Used Car Rule governs the sales of used cars. State laws regulate towing company charges (based on abuses in the past). Many other federal and state laws regulate such areas as mobile home sales, private vocational schools, insurance sales, solar energy equipment, hearing aids, and carpet sales.

These statutes and regulations only hint at the volume of consumer protection in force today from both the federal and the state governments. As a direct result of the abuse of consumers by a few businesses, all businesses and consumers are now paying the price for this protection.

FACING A LEGAL ISSUE   Operating a Mail-Order Business

After much consideration, you decide to start a new business. You believe that it should initially be the type of business that will have limited overhead. After reviewing numerous business opportunities, you decide to operate a mail-order business. You can operate it from your home during your spare time, thus limiting overhead expense.

The big expense in the mail-order business is advertising through magazines, catalogues, and brochures. You learn that, to be successful, you need repeat sales from satisfied customers based on your promotional materials. You also need to offer products that are not readily available in local stores. You decide to offer a line of "how-to" books that describe how to construct different pieces of furniture, how to refinish furniture, and how to make general household repairs. You prepare your advertisements to be placed in magazines and newspapers of general interest, such as *Better Homes & Gardens, Reader's Digest,* and the *National Enquirer.* You also prepare a small catalogue offering thirty-two different books or plans.

If you do not think that your business has any major involvement with federal or state laws, you are wrong. First, you must be in compliance with the regulations of the United States Postal Service. You cannot advertise in a fraudulent manner by misrepresenting your products. If you do, the postal service will return your customers' mail, and the Department of Justice may bring criminal charges against you. You cannot make claims that you cannot prove. For example, if you use testimonials from customers, they must be from real customers, and you must be able to prove

this to the postal service authorities should they inquire. If you offer a money-back guarantee, any customer who is dissatisfied with your product must be given a full and prompt refund.

The actual mailing of your product is another problem. The postal service offers a book rate that is considerably lower than the first-class postal rate. At the book rate, however, you cannot include with the book any advertisements for your other products. The book offered must be a book and not merely plans for the construction of certain products. If you fail to follow the postal service rules, your mailing will be returned to you or, worse, confiscated.

The rules of the Federal Trade Commission also must be followed. Your promotional material is not completely honest if false claims are made, if important facts are not disclosed, if the whole truth is not stated, or if unsupported claims are made. The FTC and the postal service cooperate in their investigations if fraudulent materials are involved.

If you had decided to sell other products through the mail, you would be required to comply with the regulations of other administrative agencies. For example, you would have to comply with the Fair Packaging and Labeling Act if your product had a label. The label must disclose at least the minimum required information. If you sell cosmetics through the mail, you will have to comply with the regulations of the Food, Drug, and Cosmetic Act.

As you can see, a simple business operated from your home can involve compliance with many federal laws and regulations. Some states have similar legal provisions. These laws are intended to protect the consumers, even though the laws may be troublesome and costly for business.

Summary

This chapter has emphasized the importance of consumer law and the protection of the consumer from both financial and bodily harm. Costs are associated with this protection, and these costs are eventually paid by the consumer in the form of higher prices.

The Federal Trade Commission has the primary duty to prohibit "unfair or deceptive acts or practices." The Bureau of Consumer Protection carries out this responsibility by obtaining consent decrees or cease and desist orders and by issuing trade regulations that apply to entire industries.

The FTC regulates advertising that either makes false statements or claims, fails to disclose important facts, does not relate the whole truth, or makes unsupported claims. The FTC also has rules against bait-and-switch advertisements. These advertisements entice a consumer to respond by offering an alleged bargain; then attempts to switch the consumer to a more expensive product.

Other statutes that protect consumers include the Fair Packaging and Labeling Act, which requires certain information to be disclosed on any package that does not allow the consumer to inspect the product. The Food, Drug, and Cosmetic Act ensures that goods are safe, pure, and wholesome and that pharmaceutical products are therapeutic and not experimental. The United States Postal Service has the power to return or confiscate any mail that makes a false representation. The Interstate Land Sales Full Disclosure Act controls the sale of unimproved lots through interstate commerce. Finally, the Consumer Product Safety Act ensures the safety of products that are sold to the public.

Key Terms

affirmative disclosure order **(316)**

cease and desist order **(316)**

consent decree **(316)**

Consumer Product Safety Act **(333)**

corrective advertising order **(316)**

Fair Packaging and Labeling Act **(329)**

Federal Trade Commission Act **(314)**

Food, Drug, and Cosmetic Act **(330)**

Interstate Land Sales Full Disclosure Act **(333)**

Lanham Act **(326)**

multiple product order **(317)**

trade regulation rule **(314)**

unfair or deceptive acts or practices **(314)**

Wheeler-Lea Act **(314)**

Questions and Case Problems

1. Harry's Home-Sweet-Home Rocking Chair Company advertised in the newspaper a special sale price of $159 on machine-caned rocking chairs. In the advertisement was a drawing of a natural wood rocking chair with a caned back and seat. The average person would not be able to tell from the drawing whether the rocking chair was machine-caned or hand-caned. Hand-caned rocking chairs were selling for $259. John and Joanne Wolf went to Harry's because they had seen the advertisement for the machine-caned rocking chair and were very interested in purchasing one. The Wolfs arrived the morning that the sale began. Harry said the only machine-caned rocking chairs he had were painted lime green and were priced at $159. He immediately turned the Wolfs' attention to the hand-caned rocking chairs, praising their workmanship, and pointing out that, for the extra $100, the hand-caned chair was a better value. The Wolfs, preferring the natural wood, machine-caned rocking chair for $159 as pictured in the advertisement, said they would like to order one, but Harry told them that this was not possible. Discuss fully whether Harry has violated any consumer protection laws.

2. Joyce made toys at home. She began a new line of homemade dolls. These stuffed dolls were especially appealing because they had real glass marbles for eyes. Young Samantha received one of these marble-eyed dolls for her birthday. Samantha was captivated by the shiny marble eyes. Unfortunately, after a month of use, the glue holding the marbles on the face of the doll disintegrated to the point that Samantha was able to pull the marbles off, put one in her mouth, choke on it, and then swallow it. She was rushed to the hospital where her stomach was pumped. Can Joyce, as the manufacturer, be regulated by a federal agency? If so, which agency would regulate and under what act? What will the agency be able to do to regulate the marble-eyed dolls?

3. Monty advertises a fuel-saving device for automobile engines. The advertisement claims that the device is "an important unique invention," that "every car needs one," and that a typical driver will realize a significant improvement in fuel economy. Jane buys the device and installs it on her automobile. After six months, she checks her maintenance records, and she finds that she has not realized any savings in fuel economy. Discuss fully any rights that Jane may have under consumer protection laws.

4. IRONMED advertises that it can cure "tired blood." One television advertisement states, "If you often have a tired and run-down feeling and if you take vitamins and still feel worn out, remember your trouble may be due to iron-poor blood. Vitamins alone can't build up your iron-poor blood. But IRONMED can. Just two tablets daily contain seven vitamins, plus twice the iron in a whole pound of calves' livers. IRONMED starts strengthening your iron-poor blood in twenty-four hours."

Ron begins to take IRONMED daily. After six months, he feels the same—worn out and tired. Ron hears that most people feel tired not as a result of iron deficiency anemia but for a variety of other reasons that only medical tests can detect. Discuss fully the rights Ron has under consumer protection laws. Is there any federal agency that regulates IRONMED's actions? If so, discuss fully.

5. Baby Food, Inc., makes and sells a baby formula from which it has removed all the salt. Ann feeds her baby the infant formula, but she notices that the baby is sick and weak after being on the formula for a while. Although she takes the baby to a pediatrician, the baby dies in six weeks from a lack of salt. Ann checks the label on the formula and sees that one of the ingredients is salt.

Later she learns through a magazine article that Baby Food, Inc., had removed the salt from the infant formula two years before her baby was born. The American Academy of Pediatrics Committee on Nutrition has found that salt is absolutely necessary for a baby's nutrition. Discuss fully the rights Ann may have under consumer protection laws. Is there any federal agency that regulates Baby Food's actions? If so, discuss fully.

6. At one time, *Reader's Digest* used large bulk mailings that contained simulated checks for readers to win big prizes. The FTC thought that this practice was deceptive, and *Reader's Digest* accepted a consent decree. Years later, *Reader's Digest* used simulated cash-convertible bonds and travel checks in the same type of promotion. The federal district court found that *Reader's Digest* had violated the consent decree by mailing more than 17 million of these items. The court assessed a $1,750,000 fine. Was this the proper method of determining damages, or were there only two violations? If the latter, what might have been the penalty? [United States v. Reader's Digest Association, Inc., 662 F.2d 955 (3d Cir. 1981)].

7. In the past, it was common for used automobile dealers to turn back the odometers on used cars. The federal Odometer Act allows the entry of a judgment for $1,500 for each occurrence. The attorney general of Ohio brought action against Hughes Motors. The defense was based on the grounds that (1) the attorney general did not have standing without joining consumers and (2) there could not be a judgment entered unless there was proof of actual loss. Was the defendant successful in its legal position? [Celebrezze v. Hughes, 18 Ohio 3d 71, 479 N.E.2d 886 (1985)].

8. Cliffdale Associates, Inc., sold through the mail a gas valve that was designed to allow greater air flow into an automobile engine; in theory, this would increase gas mileage. The defendant advertised this product as an "amazing automobile discovery" and "the most significant automotive breakthrough in the last ten years." The FTC instituted a proceeding to stop these sales on the theory that these claims were deceptive. Was this puffing, or were these claims deceptive? [In re Cliffdale Associates, Inc., 48 Antitrust and Trade Reg. Rep. (BNA) 703 (1984)].

9. The Consumer Product Safety Commission proposed safety standards that mandated placing a warning on swimming pool slides. It was shown that there was one chance in 10 million that a spinal injury could occur when using a pool slide. Would you consider a warning standard reasonably necessary and that the use of a pool slide constitutes an "unreasonable risk" of bodily harm? [Aqua Slide N Dive Corp. v. Consumer Product Safety Commission, 569 F.2d 831 (1978)].

10. American Home Products sold one of its products under the trade name Anacin. The company promoted Anacin by claiming that it consisted of a unique painkilling formula far superior to that of similar products. In reality Anacin was only aspirin. The FTC issued a cease and desist order after finding this claim to be deceptive. American Home Products appealed the decision. Was this trade puffing, or was it deceptive advertising? [American Home Products Corp. v. FTC, 695 F.2d 681 (1982)].

Chapter 14 Property Law and Computer Law

Property, or the dominion of man over external objects, has its origin from the Creator, as his gift to mankind.

William Blackstone,
Commentaries: Book II, 1765

OUTLINE

Introduction

In our culture, individual rights and property rights are so interwoven with one another that any discussion of one must include both. We place a premium on individual rights, but property rights are also protected whenever they do not conflict with individual rights.

If property rights were not recognized, we could not have the economic system that exists today. Our business community could not exist without the concept of property rights and the law that protects these rights. Business organizations own or control property that, with the addition of labor, produces a final product or service. The end result of any successful business is a profit based on the sale of these products or services. Property rights are the foundation of our free enterprise system.

Property rights are specifically recognized and protected by the Constitution. The Fifth Amendment provides that ''[n]o person shall be * * * deprived of life, liberty, or property, without due process of law; nor shall private property be taken for public use, without just compensation.'' Similar language is found in the Fourteenth Amendment: ''No State shall * * * deprive any person of life, liberty, or property, without due process of law * * *.''

Property use is regulated under the **police power** of government. This power is the inherent power of any government or sovereign to govern itself. In our country, police power is controlled and limited by the above constitutional provisions.

It is important to study the distinction between real property and personal property because different laws apply to each category. In particular, the law of taxation and the methods of property transfer will vary depending on whether property is personal or real. Thus, in this chapter we will study: (1) the classifications of property, (2) property rights and ownership title, (3) how we acquire ownership over personal property, (4) bailments, (5) real property, and (6) property law as it affects computers.

Classifications of Property

Property is divided into these classifications: real or personal, tangible or intangible, and fixtures.

Real and Personal Property

Real property (sometimes called real estate or realty) means the land surface, the air space, those materials that are underneath the surface, and those items that are permanently attached to the land. Everything else is **personal property**.

The same article may at different times be both real and personal property. For example, a growing tree would be considered real property. When it is cut down and turned into lumber, the tree becomes personal property. The tree becomes real property again when it is transformed into the framing of a house. In other words, if an item is not land or permanently attached to land, it is personal property.

Tangible and Intangible Property

All property is classified as being either tangible or intangible. **Tangible property** is visible and has physical existence, such as land, cattle, buildings, sheep, automobiles, or computers. **Intangible property** has an invisible value, such as annuities, checks, copyrights, patents, common stock, debts, or bonds. The value of any of these properties is invisible and is represented by a piece of paper stating that it is a bond, copyright, and so forth. The rights these pieces of paper represent are recognized by the law.

Fixtures

Certain personal property can become so closely associated with the real property to which it is attached that the law views it as real property. Such property is known as a **fixture**—a thing affixed to realty. Personal property becomes a fixture when the personal property is attached to the realty by roots, embedded in it, or permanently attached by means of cement, plaster, bolts, nails, or screws. Gravity can even be the method of attachment if the item is large enough; a two-ton statue, for example, qualifies as a fixture. The fixture can be physically attached to real property, can be attached to another fixture, or can even be without any actual physical attachment to the land as long as the owner intends the property to be a fixture.

Fixtures are included in the sale of land unless the sales contract provides otherwise. The sale of a house includes the land and the house and garage on it, as well as the cabinets, plumbing, and windows. Since these items are permanently affixed to the property, they are considered a part of it. Unless otherwise agreed, the curtains and throw rugs are not included. Items such as drapes, metal storage units, and window-unit air-conditioners are difficult to classify. A contract for the sale of a house or commercial realty should indicate which items are included in the sale.

In order to determine whether a certain item is a fixture, we must examine the intention of the party who placed it on the property. If the facts indicate that the person intended the item to be a fixture, it will be treated as a fixture. The following case emphasizes some of the problems surrounding fixtures. While reading the case, try to decide whether you agree with the court in its determinations of what is real and what is personal property.

BACKGROUND AND FACTS *Plaintiff Lawrence Paul purchased an elegant residence from the First National Bank of Cincinnati, the defendant. The bank was the executor of Augustine Long's estate. Before possession was given to Paul, the Long children removed certain light fixtures and other items that might be classified as fixtures. The bank as executor had a duty to preserve the property.*

Case 14.1
PAUL v. FIRST NATIONAL BANK OF CINCINNATI
Common Pleas Court of Ohio, 1976.
52 Ohio Misc. 77,
369 N.E.2d 488.

BLACK, Judge.
* * * *

The converted items must be considered in two groups, as follows:

(1) 4 Handmade lighting fixtures around swimming pool
Lighting fixture in living quarters of apartment over stable
2 Lighting fixtures removed from chapel
3 Metal cranes
4 Garden statues.
(2) Ornamental housing over well
Mercury statue
Walnut organ bench

In the court's judgment, group (1) are legally classified as ''fixtures,'' and group (2) are ''appurtenances,'' under the intent and meaning of the purchase contract. This conclusion is based on three considerations: the law of fixtures, the intent and meaning of the purchase contract, and the intent and meaning of the testamentary gift to the children.

Under the terms of the will the Long children were given ''all household furnishings, appliances, decorations and equipment.'' These items are disposed of before the real estate ''passes'' to the Executor as a part of the residue. The Executor can sell only what is left after this bequest to the children. They were not given all the decedent's tangible personal property; only the listed items. A reasonable interpretation of the will leads this court to the conclusion that none of the items in groups (1) or (2) passed to the children by the will. Only the ''stair carpeting'' and the stove passed to them. * * *

In *Masheter v. Boehm,* the [Ohio] Supreme Court designated, in paragraph two of the syllabus, six ''facts'' to be considered in determining whether an item is a fixture:

(1) The nature of the property;
(2) The manner in which the property is annexed to the realty;
(3) The purpose for which the annexation is made;

(4) The intention of the annexing party to make the property a part of the realty;

(5) The degree of difficulty and extent of any loss involved in removing the property from the realty; and

(6) The damage to the severed property which such removal would cause.

As the [Ohio] Supreme Court ruled, the expression of "a comprehensive and generally applicable rule of law" about fixtures has bedevilled the courts for years and is complicated by the need for different definitions in those situations where the relationship between the parties is different. That case dealt with eminent domain (what comprises the "real estate" which was appropriated?), while the instant case deals with a buyer and a seller, and the distributees under a will. Nevertheless, the six considerations listed in *Masheter v. Boehm* are pertinent and applicable in the interpretation of "all fixtures relating to said real estate" in paragraph II of Exhibit "A" of the purchase contract.

* * * *

The three metal cranes and the four garden statues also meet five of the six criteria, in the judgment of the court. The "nature" of these items is that they were a part of the total elegance of Long Acres. They are not the type of fixture which would be commonly found on other lawns or in other gardens, but they are an integral part of this sumptuous country estate. * * *

Group (2), being the ornamental well housing, the Mercury statue and the organ bench, were not attached in a permanent way. However, interpreting the contract from its four corners, in the light of all the facts and circumstances in evidence, the Court concludes that these items were "appurtenances" to the real estate, both in contemplation of law and in interpretation of this word as used in the purchase contract.

The word "appurtenance" means more than rights of way or other incorporeal rights: it includes an article adapted to the use of the property to which it is connected and which is intended to be a permanent accession to the freehold.

All three items in group (2) form a part of the character of Long Acres and enhance the style of its elegance. They are appurtenant to Long Acres in the sense that they are necessarily connected with the use and enjoyment of this country estate. They are incidental to the total value of this estate. The source of that value is not only the grand design but also all of the details whereby that design is executed: the location of the house on the property, the sweep of the driveway as it approaches the porte cochere, the spread-out location of the barns and other outbuildings, the majesty of the formal gardens, the spaciousness of the lawns on every side, and all the details of the exterior and interior of the mansion itself.

* * * *

The term "stair carpeting" is a misnomer. This was a small oriental rug of a size commonly called a "throw rug." It was tacked down to the short set of stairs from the Great Hall to the music room, but that was to keep it from slipping and causing injury. It was a floor rug adapted to this location on what the court considers a temporary basis. It was a "furnishing" which was given to the children by the will; and it was listed as a chattel in the probate inventory and was so disposed of in settling the probate estate.

DECISION AND REMEDY
The court held certain items to be fixtures based on the six-point test recited in the case. Other items were labeled by the court as appurtenances, which meant they were, likewise, real estate. Some items did pass in the will to the children as personal property. This case emphasizes the importance of knowing the definitions of fixture, real property, and personal property.

Property Rights and Ownership Title

Property can be viewed as a bundle of rights. These rights include:

1. The right of possession
2. The right of disposition by sale, by gift, by leasing, and by will.

More than one person can hold the same bundle of rights at one time. You may own, with another person, either personal or real property in one of the four types of concurrent ownerships:

1. Tenancy in common
2. Joint tenancy with right of survivorship, commonly called joint tenancy
3. Tenancy by the entirety
4. Community property.

Tenancy in Common

Tenancy in common is co-ownership in which two or more persons own an undivided fractional interest in the property, but, on one tenant's death, that interest passes to his or her heirs. For example, brother and sister, Michael and Laura, own a farm as tenants in common. Should Michael die before Laura, one-half of the farm would become the property of Michael's heirs. If Michael sold his interest to Patricia before he died, Patricia and Laura would be co-owners as tenants in common. If Patricia died, her interest in the property would pass to her heirs, and they in turn would own the property with Laura as tenants in common.

Joint Tenancy with Right of Survivorship

In a **joint tenancy with right of survivorship**, two or more people own an undivided interest in either personal or real property. If a joint tenant dies, his or her interest is transferred to the remaining joint tenants, not to his or her heirs. If Michael and Laura are joint tenants and Michael dies before Laura, the entire farm becomes the property of Laura. Michael's heirs receive absolutely no interest in the real estate. If, prior to Michael's death, he sells his interest to Patricia, Patricia and Laura become tenants in common.

Michael's sale terminates the joint tenancy. Joint tenancy with right of survivorship can be terminated any time by gift or by sale before the joint tenant's death.

Tenancy by the Entirety

Tenancy by the entirety is less common today than it used to be. Only a husband and wife can own property in tenancy by the entirety. Typically, it is created by a husband and wife purchasing property. It is distinguished from joint tenancy with right of survivorship because neither spouse can transfer separately his or her interest during his or her life without the consent of the other. The two must sell the property together. A divorce will end a tenancy by the entirety and, depending on the state in which the property is located, will usually turn the estate into a tenancy in common.

Community Property

This type of ownership applies only in Arizona, California, Idaho, Louisiana, Nevada, New Mexico, Texas, Washington, and Wisconsin. The **community property** laws apply only to the property of married couples. Each spouse owns an undivided one-half interest in most property acquired during the marriage. Under this type of ownership, when a spouse dies, he or she can give his or her one-half community property interest to someone other than the other spouse through a last will and testament. The deceased cannot deprive the other spouse of his or her own one-half interest.

Several exceptions do exist. Property acquired prior to the marriage or property obtained by gift or inheritance during the marriage is not usually classified as community property, but rather as "separate property."

Real Property

Real property consists of land, buildings, plants, trees, subsurface and air rights, and fixtures. Whereas personal property is movable, real property is immovable.

Air and Subsurface Rights

The owner of real property has relatively exclusive rights to the air space. Until fifty years ago, the right to use air space was not significant. Today, cases involving air rights present questions such as the right of air space for high-rise buildings, the right of individuals and governments to seed clouds and produce artificial rain, and the right of commercial and private airplanes to fly over property. Flights over private land do not normally violate the property owners' rights unless the flights are low and frequent, causing a direct interference with the enjoyment and use of the land.

In many states, the owner of the surface of a piece of land is not the owner of the subsurface; hence, the land ownership may be separated. Subsurface rights can be extremely valuable, as these rights include the ownership of minerals and, in most states, oil and natural gas. Water rights are also extremely valuable, especially in the West. When the ownership is separated into surface and subsurface rights, each owner can pass title to what he or she owns without the consent of the other.

Significant limitations on either air rights or subsurface rights normally are indicated on the deed transferring title at the time of purchase.

Ownership Interest in Real Property: Estates in Land

Ownership of property is an abstract concept that does not exist independently of the legal system. No one can actually possess or hold a piece of land, the air above, the earth below, and all the water contained on it. The legal system therefore recognizes certain rights and duties that constitute the ownership interest in real property. Rights of ownership in real property are called estates and are classified according to their nature, interest, and extent. Interests in real property are divided into two classifications: freehold estates and non-freehold estates.

Freehold Estates   A **freehold estate** is one in which the owner has the right to the land for an undetermined time period. The two classes of freehold estates are estates in fee and life estates.

Estates in Fee   The three major categories of estates in fee are: **fee simple absolute** (the title to the land is held by the owner with virtually no limitations); **fee simple defeasible** (the title to the land is taken away automatically from the owner under certain conditions); and **fee simple subject to a condition subsequent** (the title to the land may be taken away by the original owners if a specified event occurs).

A fee simple absolute (generally called a fee simple) encompasses the greatest aggregation of rights, privileges, and power possible. The owner of a fee simple absolute has the right to use the land for whatever purpose he or she sees fit, subject to two restrictions. First, laws prevent the owner from unreasonably interfering with another person's land. Second, the owner is subject to applicable zoning, building, and other regulations. A person can own a fee simple absolute for an indefinite period of time, but he or she can dispose of it by deed, by will, by gift, or by sale.

The owner of a fee simple defeasible or of a fee simple subject to a condition subsequent has less rights than the owner of a fee simple absolute. With a fee simple defeasible or a fee simple subject to a condition subsequent, the right of ownership can be taken away if specific conditions set out in the deed either occur or fail to occur.

For example, a conveyance from Lincoln "to Tex and his heirs as long as the land is used for a church" creates a fee simple defeasible. In this type of conveyance, Lincoln retains a partial ownership interest. As long as the specified condition occurs (the land is used for a church), Tex has all other ownership rights. If the specified condition does not occur (the land ceases to be used for a church), the land reverts (returns) to the original owner, Lincoln, or, if he is not alive, to his heirs. The interest that Lincoln retains is called a *future interest* since, *if* it arises, it will arise in the future.

In the following case, a conveyance was made for a courthouse and jail. The deed included the phrase "and shall be used for no other purpose." The Arizona Supreme Court had to interpret these words of conveyance in reaching its decision.

BACKGROUND AND FACTS *The plaintiff's father deeded in 1898 certain property to the County of Navajo, Territory of Arizona, under a deed that stated the following:*

> *The title to which said foregoing described tract or lot of land shall vest in said County of Navajo, Territory of Arizona at any time, said county shall or may begin the erection [sic] of a courthouse and jail for use of said county, on said tract or lot of land and shall be used for no other purpose.*

The property ceased to be used as the county courthouse in 1976. The plaintiff brought this action to obtain the real estate, arguing that, since the property was not used as a county courthouse, the land reverted to her, as the only heir of her father.

KLEINSCHMIDT, Judge.
* * * *

The deed did not grant a fee simple determinable [defeasible]. A fee simple determinable is created by any limitation in a conveyance which creates an estate in fee simple and then provides that the estate shall automatically expire upon occurrence of a stated event. Such an intent is usually manifested by a limitation which contains the words "until," "so long as," or "during." The conveyance must express the intent of the grantor that the estate will automatically expire upon the happening of an event and a mere statement as to the purpose of the grant is not sufficient.
* * * *

A fee simple subject to a condition subsequent is created by an effective conveyance in fee simple which provides that upon the occurrence of a stated event the grantor or his successor shall have the power to terminate the estate created. The reversion is not automatic but depends upon a decision on the part of the grantor to re-enter. The instrument of conveyance must manifest the conditional nature of the deed and must contain some provision demonstrating the grantor's power to re-enter and terminate. Since forfeitures are not favored the intent must be clear.
* * * *

* * * The deed "grants," "sells," and "conveys" in return for consideration recited and speaks of title vesting in the county when construction of the courthouse is begun. * * * Everything in the record, including the grantor's disclaimer of any remainder interest in the land at the time he was going through bankruptcy, points to an outright conveyance of the fee * * *.

The court found that the conveyance to Navajo County, Arizona, was not a fee simple subject to a condition subsequent nor a fee simple defeasible but an outright conveyance of the fee (that is, a fee simple absolute).

In order to create a fee simple defeasible, the words used in the deed must be conditional words. The magic words are "until," "so long as," and "during." In this case, if the deed had contained one of these words, the property would have automatically reverted back to the plaintiff. The deed could have read as follows:

Case 14.2
LACER v. NAVAJO COUNTY
Arizona Supreme Court, 1983.
141 Ariz. 396, 687 P.2d 404.

DECISION AND REMEDY

COMMENT

The title to which said foregoing described tract or lot of land shall vest in said County of Navajo, Territory of Arizona at any time, said county shall or may begin the erection [sic] of a courthouse and jail for use of said county, on said tract or lot of land and so long as the said county shall use the tract or lot of land for no other purpose, then title shall remain vested in said county.

Similarly, to create a fee simple subject to a condition subsequent, the deed must clearly state its conditional nature and contain a provision demonstrating the grantor's power to take the land away from the current owner by doing something affirmative to regain it. The deed could have read as follows:

The title to the said foregoing described tract or lot of land shall vest in said County of Navajo, Territory of Arizona, but if the tract or lot of land shall be used for any purpose other than that of a county courthouse and jail, the grantor or his heirs shall have the right to reenter and repossess the land.

The law does not favor forfeitures and requires that the original owner's intent be made very clear and be written in very specific language.

Life Estates   A **life estate** is one in which the duration is measured by the life of one or more human beings. A life estate may be created, for example, by a conveyance of the land by the owner to another to occupy and use the land during his or her lifetime. The person holding a life estate does not own the land. The person granting the life estate has designated someone else (or the owner himself or herself) as owner of the land who holds the land in fee simple absolute after the life tenant. During the life estate, however, the life tenant has the same rights as a fee simple owner except that he or she must preserve the value of the land for the holder of the future interest.

Nonfreehold Estates   A **nonfreehold estate** occurs when a person has the right to possess real estate but does not own the property. This type of estate is generally treated as a personal interest and not as an interest in real property. Nonfreehold estates are commonly called leases or tenancies. Leases are classified as: (1) tenancy for years, (2) tenancy from period to period, or (3) tenancy at will.

Another tenancy is called tenancy by sufferance, but it is not actually an estate, as we will see shortly.

Landlord-Tenant Relationship   Before looking at these types of tenancies, we need to define the landlord-tenant relationship. Most owners of real property do not use that property themselves. Instead, others, called **tenants**, occupy and use the property under a **lease**. A lease is a contract by which the **landlord**—the owner—grants the tenant an exclusive right to use and possess the land, usually for a specific period of time. The tenant is under an obligation to pay rent and to return the premises in good condition at the end of the lease period.

The landlord has a duty to ensure that the tenant is able to possess the property at the time the lease period begins. Thus, the landlord must not have rented the premises to others or allow others to occupy and remain on the premises. The tenant, while in possession, is entitled to possess the premises in peace and without disturbance. Whether the landlord is under an obligation to maintain and repair the premises is usually deter-

---

LEGAL
HIGHLIGHT   **Whose House Is This?**

Edna Snowden of Sunset Beach, California, thought life estates were wonderful. She was the beneficiary of one.

In 1928, Edna moved in with Mrs. Mary Jane McKinley as live-in housekeeper and companion. When Mrs. McKinley died in 1946, her two sons inserted a clause into the deed that gave Edna a life estate. She was to live in the house rent free, and the owners were to

maintain all the utilities and provide whatever work was necessary to keep the place livable at no cost to her. She was sixty-eight years old at that time. When she died in the early 1980s, over 100 years old, she had outlived the two sons and six more owners. The last owner, a schoolteacher, was the first owner to be able to live in the house in almost forty years.

---

mined by the lease. In absence of agreement generally the tenant is liable for maintenance and normal repairs and the landlord for major repairs and improvements.

Types of Tenancies   A tenancy for years, tenancy from period to period, and tenancy at will involve the transfer of the right to possession from the landlord (lessor) to a tenant (lessee) for a specified period of time. In every lease, the tenant has a qualified right to exclusive possession (qualified by the right of the landlord to enter the premises for limited purposes, such as emergency repairs). The tenant can make appropriate use of the land—for example, to grow crops—but cannot injure the land by such activities as cutting down timber for sale or pumping gas or oil.

A **tenancy for years** is created by express contract (which can sometimes be oral) in which the property is leased for a specified period of time. For example, signing a one-year lease to rent an apartment creates a tenancy for years. At the end of the period specified in the lease, the lease ends (without notice) and the right to possession of the apartment returns to the lessor.

A **tenancy from period to period** is created by a lease that does not specify how long it is to last but does specify that rent is to be paid at certain intervals. This type of tenancy is automatically renewed for another rental period unless *properly* terminated.

Suppose a landlord rents an apartment to a tenant "for as long as both agree." In such a case, the tenant receives a leasehold estate known as a **tenancy at will**. At common law, either party can terminate the tenancy without notice. This type of estate usually arises when a tenant who has been under a tenancy for years retains possession, with the landlord's consent, after the termination date of that tenancy. Sometimes no rent is paid, but the tenant acknowledges that the landlord does own the property. Quite often this tenancy is converted to a tenancy from period to period, which then is automatically renewed and proper notice of termination is required.

A **tenancy by sufferance** is not a true tenancy; it is the mere possession of land without right. A tenancy by sufferance is not an estate, since it is created by a tenant wrongfully retaining possession of property. Whenever a tenancy for years, tenancy from period to period, or tenancy at will ends and the tenant retains possession of the premises without the owner's permission, a tenancy by sufferance is created. The tenant is subject to immediate eviction.

Exhibit 14–1 summarizes the forms of ownership described in this section.

Transfer of Ownership

A number of methods exist by which the ownership of real property can pass from one person

Exhibit 14–1 **Forms of Ownership of Real Property**

FORMS OF OWNERSHIP	TYPES AND DEFINITIONS

Freehold Estate (Held indefinitely)	1. Estate in Fee—
	  a. Fee Simple Absolute—Most complete form of ownership.
	  b. Fee Simple Defeasible—Ownership ends automatically if specified condition occurs or fails to occur; land reverts to original owner.
	  c. Fee Simple Subject to a Condition Subsequent—Ownership may end if the specified condition occurs or fails to occur; ownership continues in the current owner; original owner must take affirmative action to reacquire the land.

Nonfreehold Estates (Possessory interests held for a specified period of time)	1. Tenancy for Years—Lasts for periods of time stated by express contract. 2. Tenancy from Period to Period—Period determined by frequency of rent payments; automatically renewed unless proper notice is given. 3. Tenancy at Will—For as long as both parties agree; no notice of termination required. 4. Tenancy by Sufferance—Possession of land without legal right.
Concurrent Ownership (Jointly held ownership)	1. Tenancy in Common—Each tenant owns an undivided fractional share of the property. Such interests can be conveyed without consent, and, upon death, pass to tenant's heirs. 2. Joint Tenancy (with right of survivorship)—Each tenant owns an undivided share of the property. Such interest can be conveyed without consent, converting the interest to tenancy in common. Upon death, interest passes to surviving joint tenant, not heirs. 3. Tenancy by the Entirety—A joint tenancy with right of survivorship between husband and wife. 4. Community Property—Most property acquired during marriage by either or both spouses is owned equally by each spouse.

to another. These methods include: (1) inheritance or will, (2) eminent domain, (3) adverse possession, and (4) conveyance by deed (which includes transfer by sale and by gift).

Transfer by Inheritance or Will Property that is transferred on an owner's death is passed to the beneficiaries or heirs either by will or by inheritance. When the owner of land dies with a will, the land passes according to the terms of the will. When the owner dies without a will, the land passes according to state statutes that set out who will inherit the property. Joint tenancy with right of survivorship overrides any will provisions.

Eminent Domain Even where ownership in real property is fee simple absolute, a superior ownership may limit that fee simple absolute. Called

eminent domain, it is the power of the government to condemn land in order to convert it to public use. The government has a right to acquire real property in the manner authorized by the Constitution and by the laws of the state whenever the public interest requires it.

For example, when a new public highway is to be built, the government must decide where to build it and how much land to condemn. The power of eminent domain is generally invoked through condemnation proceedings. After the government determines that a particular parcel of land is necessary for public use, it brings a judicial proceeding to obtain title to the land. Then, in another proceeding, the court further determines the fair value of the land, which is usually approximately equal to its market value. Under the Fifth Amendment, private property may not be taken for public use without just compensation.

In the following case, the United States Supreme Court had to decide whether an ordinance temporarily restricting the use of land was a taking of property that required compensation to be paid by Los Angeles County, California.

BACKGROUND AND FACTS   *First English Evangelical Lutheran Church operated a retreat and recreational area for handicapped children. In 1978, a flood destroyed the buildings. Afterward, the County of Los Angeles adopted an ordinance prohibiting any construction of buildings within the area. Shortly after passage of this ordinance, the church filed an action claiming damages in inverse condemnation. Inverse condemnation is an indirect taking of property by the government without compensation. The trial court granted a motion to dismiss that was upheld by the California Court of Appeals. The United States Supreme Court took jurisdiction of the case.*

Case 14.3
FIRST ENGLISH EVANGELICAL LUTHERAN CHURCH v. COUNTY OF LOS ANGELES
Supreme Court of the United States, 1987.
482 U.S. ___, 107 S.Ct. 2378, 96 L.Ed.2d 250.

REHNQUIST, Chief Justice.
*   *   *   *

Consideration of the compensation question must begin with direct reference to the language of the Fifth Amendment, which provides in relevant part that ''private property [shall not] be taken for public use, without just compensation.'' As its language indicates, and as the Court has frequently noted, this provision does not prohibit the taking of private property, but instead places a condition on the exercise of that power. This basic understanding of the Amendment makes clear that it is designated not to limit the governmental interference with property rights per se, but rather to secure *compensation* in the event of otherwise proper interference amounting to a taking. Thus, government action that works a taking of property rights necessarily implicates the ''constitutional obligation to pay just compensation.''

We have recognized that a landowner is entitled to bring an action in inverse condemnation as a result of '' 'the self-executing character of the constitutional provision with respect to compensation. . . .' '' [It] has been established at least since *Jacobs v. United States* that claims for just compensation are grounded in the Constitution itself:

''The suits were based on the right to recover just compensation for property taken by the United States for public use in the exercise of its power of eminent domain. *That right was guaranteed by the Constitution.* The fact that condemnation proceedings were not instituted and that the right was asserted in suits by the owners did not change the essential nature of the claim. The form of the remedy did not qualify the right. It rested upon the Fifth Amendment. Statutory recognition was not necessary. A promise to pay was not necessary. Such a promise was implied because of the duty imposed by the Amendment. *The suits were thus founded upon the Constitution of the United States.*'' (Emphasis added.)

Jacobs, moreover, does not stand alone, for the Court has frequently repeated the view that, in the event of a taking, the compensation remedy is required by the Constitution.
*   *   *   *

*   *   * While the typical taking occurs when the government acts to condemn property in the exercise of its power of eminent domain, the entire doctrine of inverse condemnation is predicated on the proposition that a taking may occur without such formal proceedings. * * *

* * * *

* * * It is axiomatic that the Fifth Amendment's just compensation provision is "designed to bar Government from forcing some people alone to bear public burdens which, in all fairness and justice, should be borne by the public as a whole." In the present case the interim ordinance was adopted by the county of Los Angeles in January 1979, and became effective immediately. Appellant filed suit within a month after the effective date of the ordinance and yet when the Supreme Court of California denied a hearing in the case on October 17, 1985, the merits of appellant's claim had yet to be determined. The United States has been required to pay compensation for leasehold interests of shorter duration than this. The value of a leasehold interest in property for a period of years may be substantial, and the burden on the property owner in extinguishing such an interest for a period of years may be great indeed. Where this burden results from governmental action that amounted to a taking, the Just Compensation Clause of the Fifth Amendment requires that the government pay the landowner for the value of the use of the land during this period. Invalidation of the ordinance or its successor ordinance after this period of time, though converting the taking into a "temporary" one, is not a sufficient remedy to meet the demands of the Just Compensation Clause.

* * * *

Nothing we say today is intended to abrogate the principle that the decision to exercise the power of eminent domain is a legislative function, " 'for Congress and Congress alone to determine.' " Once a court determines that a taking has occurred, the government retains the whole range of options already available— amendment of the regulation, withdrawal of the invalidated regulation, or exercise of eminent domain. We hold that where the government's activities have already worked a taking of all use of property, no subsequent action by the government can relieve it of the duty to provide compensation for the period during which the taking was effective.

* * * We realize that even our present holding will undoubtedly lessen to some extent the freedom and flexibility of land-use planners and governing bodies of municipal corporations when enacting land-use regulations. But such consequences necessarily flow from any decision upholding a claim of constitutional right; many of the provisions of the Constitution are designed to limit the flexibility and freedom of governmental authorities and the Just Compensation Clause of the Fifth Amendment is one of them. As Justice Holmes aptly noted more than 50 years ago, "a strong public desire to improve the public condition is not enough to warrant achieving the desire by a shorter cut than the constitutional way of paying for the change."

Here we must assume that the Los Angeles County ordinance denied appellant all use of its property for a considerable period of years, and we hold that invalidation of the ordinance without payment of fair value for the use of the property during this period of time would be a constitutionally insufficient remedy. The judgment of the California Court of Appeals is therefore reversed, and the case is remanded for further proceedings not inconsistent with this opinion.

DECISION AND REMEDY   *The United States Supreme Court held that, under the Fifth Amendment, where the government has denied the owner all use of its property, even if only temporarily, a taking has occurred for which compensation must be paid by the government.*

Adverse Possession **Adverse possession** is a means of obtaining title to land without a deed being delivered. Essentially, one person must possess the property of another in an open, hostile, notorious manner and for an uninterrupted statutory period of time (ranging from three to thirty years, with ten years being most common). Called an adverse possessor, that person acquires title to the land and cannot be removed from the land by the original owner.

For example, Bill and Karen find an unoccupied house in the woods. They decide to occupy the house, find the owner, and buy it. After six months, they cannot find the owner, and since the land has two years of back taxes owed they assume the owner has abandoned the property. Bill and Karen pay the back taxes, and for ten years live on the property, fence in the property, remove trespassers, pay taxes and utilities, have mail and other items delivered to it, and invite community guests to the house. Suddenly, the recorded title owner, Jerry Foster, appears and demands that Bill and Karen vacate the premises. If Bill and Karen have possessed the property continuously for the required statutory period (assume ten years), they will be able to successfully claim title by adverse possession. Their possession was open, it was exclusive as to others (hostile), and they were living on the premises without the permission of Jerry Foster.

The adverse possessor must file a **quiet title** action in court in order to have the title placed in his or her name. A quiet title action is just what the name implies: an action that will decide who has title to the property, thus settling a dispute over the title and placing the title in the name of the true owner. The adverse possessor is vested with a perfect title just as if there had been a conveyance by deed.

Conveyance by Deed   Possession and title to land are generally passed from person to person by means of a **deed**—the written instrument of conveyance of real property. A deed is signed by an owner of property in order to transfer title to it to another person. Deeds must meet certain requirements, such as being delivered from the grantor to the grantee, and containing a full description of the property and, in some states, an acknowl-

edgement of the grantor's signature by a notary public.

Several types of deeds are used today. The first is a **general warranty deed**. This type of deed gives the buyer the most protection against defects in the title to the land. The seller is warranting first, that he or she has the right and power to convey the title to the land; second, that no liens or interests exist, or if there are liens or interests, that they are listed and/or known to the buyer (liens and interests include mortgages, tax liens, mechanic's liens, and easements); third, that the buyer will have "quiet enjoyment" of the property—in other words, that no one will come in with a better title than the seller to force the buyer from the property.

A second type of deed is the **special warranty deed**. The seller warrants only that he or she has not previously done anything to lessen the value of the real estate. The third type of deed is called the **quitclaim deed** and conveys less than other types of deeds. This deed conveys to the buyer whatever interest the grantor (who is not necessarily the seller) has, if any. For example, a piece of realty is held in the name of the husband. The husband and wife have separated. A prospective buyer of the property may want a warranty deed from the seller husband and a quitclaim deed from the wife. By paying a nominal amount of money, the wife will sign a quitclaim deed transferring any interest she may have in the property, including any homestead rights.

Recording Statutes   Every state has a **recording statute**. The purpose of these statutes is to provide prospective buyers with a way to check the history of the property and to determine what outstanding interests, liens, judgments, or taxes have been placed against the title to the property. Recording a deed (or a lien) gives notice to the world that a certain person is now the owner of a particular parcel of real estate and notice that a "cloud" may be on the title.

Anything recorded against the property can act as a cloud on its title for persons interested in purchasing or lending money on it. For example, by recording your deed you are placing everyone on notice as to who the true owner is. Thus, in the case of recorded deeds, former owners are prevented from fraudulently conveying the land to other purchasers, and in the case of recorded liens, owners are prevented from selling their land without paying what is owed to creditors who have a lien on the property.

Nonpossessory Interests

Some interests in land do not include any rights of possession. One important nonpossessory interest is an **easement**. An easement is the right to make limited use of another person's real property without actually possessing it. Often an easement is called a "right-of-way." The right to drive across another's property and the right to place water and sewage pipes, electrical or telephone wires, or cables on another's property are examples of easements. Easements can be created by deed, will, contract, or law.

Land-Use Control

Land-use control deals with the limitations placed on property owners. Some limitations arise by agreement, such as covenants running with the land; others are imposed by the government, such as zoning.

Covenants Running with the Land   A **covenant running with the land** is an agreement under which a landowner either acquires certain rights or is under certain obligations merely because he or she owns the land that is subject to the covenant.

   For example, Juanita is the owner of the 2,000-acre El Mirage Ranch. A large reservoir is located in the western part of the ranch. Juanita wants to convey the land with the reservoir to the town of Pumpkin Center. Before she does, she constructs an irrigation canal that connects the reservoir with 100 acres that she uses as farmland.

   When Juanita conveys the reservoir to Pumpkin Center, she enters into an agreement with the town. The agreement, also contained in the deed, states: "Pumpkin Center, its heirs and assigns, promises not to remove more than one hundred thousand (100,000) gallons of water per day from the El Mirage Ranch reservoir." Juanita has created a covenant running with the land under which Pumpkin Center and all future owners of the reservoir are limited as to the amount of water they can draw from the reservoir.

Zoning   **Zoning** occurs when the state or local government imposes restrictions on the use of the land. The purpose of zoning is to have an orderly development of land area by controlling land use. Although private individuals can control the land use of property they own or sell, state and local governments have far greater resources and enforcement powers to control the development and use of land.

   Zoning is based on the police powers of the state. The government may advance the public health, safety, and welfare through zoning laws. For example, one area of a town may be zoned for single-family houses, while another area may be zoned for light industrial use.

Acquiring Ownership of Personal Property

The ownership of personal property can be acquired in a variety of ways. Rights can be acquired by possession, purchase, production, gift, will or inheritance, accession, and confusion.

Possession

Possession is exactly what the word implies: If you have possession, you normally have ownership. A familiar adage is "Possession is nine-tenths of the law." In reality, this concept of ownership is limited in its application. Possession is important in the following situations: wildlife, lost or mislaid property, and abandoned property. One example of acquiring ownership by possession is the capture of wild animals. Wild animals belong to no one in their natural state, and the first person to take possession of a wild animal normally owns it. The killing of a wild animal amounts to assuming ownership of it. A commercial fishing captain, for example, acquires ownership over fish caught in the open seas.

Mislaid and Lost Property   Property that has been placed somewhere by the owner voluntarily and then inadvertently forgotten is **mislaid property**. Whenever mislaid property is found, the finder does not obtain title to or possession of the goods. Instead, the owner of the place where the property was mislaid becomes the caretaker of the property because it is highly likely that the true owner will return. Suppose you leave your textbook under your chair after class. The textbook is mislaid property, and if a school employee finds it, the school is entrusted with the duty of reasonable care for the goods.

Property that is not voluntarily left and forgotten is **lost property**. A finder of lost property can claim title to the property against everyone in the whole world, except the true owner. If the true owner demands that the lost property be returned, the finder must do so. If a third party attempts to take possession of lost property from a finder, the third party cannot assert a better title than the finder.

Abandoned Property Property that has been discarded by the true owner with no intention of claiming title to it is **abandoned property**; for example, garbage qualifies as abandoned property. Someone who finds abandoned property acquires title to it, and such title is good against everyone in the whole world, including the original owner. The owner of lost property who eventually gives up any further attempt to find the lost property is frequently held to have abandoned the property.

Purchase

Purchase is one of the most common means of acquiring and transferring ownership of personal property. The purchase or sale of personal property (called goods) is covered in Chapter 9.

Production

Production—the fruits of labor—is another means of acquiring ownership of personal property. Nearly everyone in the United States today is involved in some sort of production. For example, writers, inventors, and manufacturers all produce personal property and thereby acquire title to it. If you are employed to produce an item, however, your employer will own the item.

Gifts

A **gift** is another fairly common means of both acquiring and transferring ownership of personal property. A gift is essentially a voluntary transfer of property ownership. It is not supported by legally sufficient consideration to make a contract since the very essence of a gift is giving without consideration. A gift must be transferred or delivered in the present rather than in the future, and the donor must intend to make a gift.

For example, suppose that your aunt, the donor, tells you, the donee, that she is going to give you a new Mercedes-Benz for your next birthday. This is simply a promise to make a gift. It is not considered a gift until the Mercedes-Benz is delivered to you. Once the gift has been unconditionally delivered, it is irrevocable.

Will or Inheritance

The law in our society requires that, on the death of a person, title to the decedent's property must vest (deliver full possession) in someone. The decedent can direct the passage of property after his or her death through the legal instrument known as a will, subject to certain limitations imposed by the state. If the person dies without a will, he or she is said to have died intestate, and state law determines the distribution of his or her property among next of kin. If no kin can be found, the property escheats (title is transferred) to the state.

In addition, a person can transfer property through a trust. The owner (settlor) of the property transfers legal title to a trustee, who has a duty imposed by law to hold the property for the use or benefit of another (the beneficiary).

Accession

Accession means addition or increase, or coming into possession of a right. In property law, accession refers to someone's adding value to a piece of personal property (owned by another) by either labor or materials. Generally no dispute exists about who owns the improved property after accession has occurred, especially when the accession is accomplished with the owner's consent.

For example, Michio takes his Corvette to Corvette Customizing Garage. Michio wants a unique bumper placed on his Corvette. Michio simply pays the customizer for the value of the labor for improving his automobile, and he retains title to the Corvette with the unique bumper.

Confusion

Confusion occurs when you mix property of the same type, otherwise known as **fungible goods**. Fungible goods are identical goods (the equivalent of other like units) by nature or usage of trade. For example, a farmer takes his or her wheat crop to the grain elevator. Once the wheat is mixed with other farmers' wheat of like grade and quality, there is a change in ownership. The farmers become owners of the grain as tenants in common. The farmer now owns a percentage of the wheat in the grain elevator. Because the goods are fungible, there is no way or reason to separate the farmer's original grain from the other farmers' grain. Thus, title can pass without the grain being removed from the grain elevator.

Bailments

Virtually every individual and business is affected by the law of bailments at one time or another (and sometimes even on a daily basis). When individuals deal with bailments, whether they realize it or not, they are subject to the obligations and duties that arise from the bailment relationship. A **bailment** is formed by the delivery of personal property, without transfer of title, by one person, called a **bailor**, to another, called a **bailee**, usually under an agreement for a particular purpose (for example, loan, storage, repair, or transportation). On completion of the purpose, the bailee is obligated to return the bailed property to the bailor or a third person, or to dispose of it as directed.

Most bailments are created by agreement but not necessarily by contract, because in many bailments not all of the elements of a contract, such as mutual assent or consideration, are present. For example, if you mislay your copy of *Legal Environment of Business,* its finder and subsequent possessor is a bailee, but not by contract, because there is not mutual assent. Similarly, if you loan your copy of *Legal Environment of Business* to a friend so that your friend can read tomorrow's assignment, a bailment is created, but not by contract, because there is no consideration. On the other hand, many commercial bailments, such as

the delivery of your suit or dress to the cleaners for dry cleaning, are based on contract.

A bailment is distinguished from a sale or a gift in that, in a bailment, possession is transferred without passage of title or without intent to transfer title. In a sale or gift, on the other hand, title is transferred from the seller or donor to the buyer or donee.

Once a bailment is created, the bailee has certain duties and rights concerning the bailed property. Exhibit 14–2 summarizes these rights and duties.

Computer Law

A distinction must be made between **software** and **hardware** when discussing computer law. By software, we mean the programming involved with a computer system. The two basic kinds of software are system programs, which coordinate the operation of the computer, and application programs, which solve particular user problems, such as word-processing programs or spread-sheet programs. Some authorities believe that software encompasses the programming plus the advice, assistance, and counseling in loading a machine for a certain program.

The hardware is the equipment itself. In most cases, the general principles of contract, sales, and leasing law will suffice when discussing hardware. The unique aspect of computer law really involves software. In particular, it becomes necessary to discuss the creation and protection of programs, the transfer of programs, and the use of them. Unless otherwise stated, the following discussion covers only software.

Contract Law Versus the Sale of Goods

As noted in Chapter 9, the Uniform Commercial Code has been adopted in part by all jurisdictions. Article 2 of the UCC applies to the sale of goods. The question is whether there is a sale of goods or a sale of service when there is a sale of a computer program. The importance of this determination is that Article 2 gives very specific rights and obligations to both the buyer and seller. If Article 2 does not apply, the doctrine of basic contract law will apply. Article 2 is more protec-

Exhibit 14–2 Rights and Duties of a Bailee

BAILEE	BASIC RULES
Rights	1. A bailee has the right to be compensated or reimbursed for keeping bailed property. This right is based in contract or quasi-contract. 2. Unpaid compensation or reimbursement entitles the bailee to a lien (usually possessory) on the bailed property and the right of foreclosure. 3. A bailee has the right to limit his or her liability. An ordinary bailee can limit risk or monetary amount or both, provided proper notice is given and the limitation is not against public policy. In special bailments, limitations on types of risk are usually not allowed, but limitations on the monetary amount at risk are permitted by regulation. 4. The right of possession allows actions against third persons who damage or convert the bailed property, and allows actions against the bailor for wrongful breach of the bailment. 5. The right to an insurable interest in the bailed property allows the bailee to insure and recover under the insurance policy for loss or damage to the property.
Duties	1. A bailee must exercise reasonable care over property entrusted to him or her. A common carrier (special bailee) is held to a standard of care based on *strict liability* unless the bailed property is lost or destroyed due to: (a) an act of God, (b) an act of a public enemy, (c) an act of a governmental authority, (d) an act of a shipper, or (e) the inherent nature of the goods. 2. Bailed goods in a bailee's possession must be returned to the bailor, or disposed of according to bailor's directions. 3. A bailee cannot use or profit from bailed goods except by agreement or in situations where the use is implied to further the bailment purpose.

tive of the buyer, while common law tends to give more protection to the seller, such as under the doctrine of caveat emptor (let the buyer beware).

The courts have uniformly held that, when software is sold with or given with the sale of hardware, a sale of goods occurs. Thus, Article 2 of the UCC applies. The problem occurs when only software is sold. The courts tend to treat it as a sale of goods when the software is purchased from a store because it is sold under a sales contract, but what happens when a program is written for a specific use, not for common usage? Is this a sale of goods or the provision of a service?

The cases are divided on this issue. Logic dictates that this transaction would be considered a sale of a specialty good. After all, there is a transfer of a tape or disk. Under the law, the definition of goods is very broad and should encompass the sale of software. Some cases hold, however, that it is a transaction involving service and not a sale of goods. In those jurisdictions, the general principles of contract law will be applied, and the protection given to buyers by Article 2 of the UCC will not be applicable.

Another problem arises with the application of Article 2 to the transfer of computer programs. Many of the statutory provisions cover the sale of goods but not other transactions in goods. A large segment of the computer software business involves transfer by either a lease or a license but not by a sale.

In general, three legal theories exist that grant the UCC Article 2 protection to licenses and leases. First, the transaction is treated as a sale if the lease allows the user to purchase the program or hardware. Second, a theory known as the third-party beneficiary doctrine applies when a financing company purchases the items and then leases the program to the user. Under this doctrine, the user can utilize the same legal rights as the purchaser. Third, the courts can extend the coverage of Article 2 to leases or licenses.

In a few years, the need to extend Article 2 by theory to leases will disappear in most states. The Permanent Editorial Board of the UCC has approved a codification of the law with respect to leases of goods. This codification, entitled Article 2A of the UCC is substantially similar in content to the present Article 2 (except, of course, that it relates to leases expressly). It is presently being considered for adoption by a number of states. Thus, Article 2 (Article 2 and Article 2A) of the UCC will cover both the sales and leases of goods.

Software Warranties

If we assume that the UCC applies to the transfer (sale or lease) of software, specific warranties apply. In particular, the UCC grants express warranties, the implied warranty of merchantability, and the implied warranty of fitness for a particular purpose. These warranties are covered in Chapter 12. All of them give the buyer-user specific rights that are not available from the common law.

Unconscionability Doctrine

Unconscionability is a term that was not used in any statutory form until the UCC was drafted; thus, it is a relatively new provision of the law. The concept underlying this term derives from the equity courts. **Unconscionability** occurs when a clause in a contract, or the entire contract, is so unjust as to be considered one-sided in light of the general commercial background, the bargaining strength of the parties, and the needs of a particular trade. On concluding that a clause or contract is unconscionable, a court will declare it void.

This doctrine has had direct application to computer law. Society is beginning to utilize computers throughout business operations. Every day new procedures are developed to produce products or goods more efficiently. Programmers are the key to facilitating these changes through the use of the computer. One small mistake by a programmer can result in an entire plant being inoperative, raising the possibility of thousands or even millions of dollars in damages. Many firms involved in writing programs include language in their contracts that excludes any and all liability for extensive damages.

For example, assume the following clause has been inserted in a contract limiting computer program liability:

> The programmer will make every effort to provide an accurate program, but assumes no liability for any events arising out of its use. Replacement of the disk for a period of thirty days will be the sole liability of the programmer. There are no other express warranties and all implied warranties of merchantability or of fitness for a particular purpose shall be of no greater duration than for said thirty days.

Is this clause unconscionable?

Let's assume that a programmer—a recent college graduate with no assets—includes this clause in a contract for a programming job with a Fortune 500 firm. A mistake in the programming forces the closing of a factory employing 500 people and causes $1 million in damages. The factory's owner sues, arguing that the clause is unconscionable. Under the circumstances, however, the court may conclude that the firm acted ineptly in signing the contract, that the clause is not unconscionable, and that the firm should stand the loss.

It is difficult to state with any certainty whether a court may find a contract clause unconscionable. The following case reviews a contract clause concerning which state should have jurisdiction (called a forum selection clause) over this contract for computers. Notice how the court balances the interest of the small business person with no experience in computers with that of the large corporation that drafted the contract.

Case 14.4
HORNING v. SYCOM
United States District Court, Eastern District of Kentucky, 1983.
556 F.Supp. 819.

BACKGROUND AND FACTS *The plaintiffs are Dr. Charles Horning, a solo practitioner dentist located in Florence, Kentucky, and his wife Sandra, who manages the office. The defendants are the members of a limited partnership (Sycom), seller of computer hardware, with its principal place of business in Wisconsin; Tandy Corporation, a manufacturer of computer hardware, with its principal place of business in Texas; and E. F.*

Hutton Credit Corporation, holder of leasing documents used to finance the plaintiffs' acquisition of a computer system from Sycom, with its principal place of business in Delaware.

The defendants filed a motion to transfer the case. The defendants' position was that the contract had selected the forum, Wisconsin; therefore, the case should be moved to Wisconsin. The district court had to decide whether to transfer the case to Wisconsin in accordance with the contract terms or to retain the case in Kentucky.

BERTLESMAN, Judge.

* * * *

On January 28, 1981, Sycom's local sales representative, Dennis McDonough, whose office is in Cincinnati, and its Eastern Regional Manager, Jerry Conca, whose office is in New York, visited Dr. Horning in his office in Florence and attempted to interest him in installing Sycom's Micro-System Data Plan. Apparently, the plaintiffs were persuaded. After further meetings at their office, on February 25, 1981, McDonough sent them a letter relating that, for a total investment of $16,779, at $348 a month for 84 months, they could obtain a Tandy computer, Sycom's software, and maintenance and assistance in the use of the system from Sycom. On March 4, 1981, Dr. Horning signed a "purchase agreement" within which Sycom promised to license its computer software to Dr. Horning and he promised to buy the hardware.

The plaintiffs' purpose in having the system installed was to assist them in compiling accurate financial data, tax records and patient information. The plaintiffs claim that, from the date of installation, the system never worked properly. Nevertheless, they continued making lease-purchase payments for 10 months, paying approximately one-quarter of the total cost, around $4,000. It is alleged that during this time, the system was not performing as it should have; that the plaintiffs were not being effectively schooled in its use; that Sycom was made aware of this state of affairs; and that Sycom acknowledged that a "communication gap" existed and promised to remedy it. At one point, apparently, when six weeks had elapsed and Sycom had not responded to a service call to its Cincinnati office, the plaintiffs paid an independent computer consultant some $2500 to come in and identify the problems in the system.

Around January of 1982, the plaintiffs ceased making monthly payments on the system. They obtained an attorney and, on April 16, 1982, met with a Sycom representative to discuss solving the problems in the system. When this did not work, in a letter dated July 19, 1982, they asked for rescission of the contract and repayment of the money they had expended. In November of 1982, plaintiffs filed suit in Boone Circuit Court, alleging breach of contract, breach of UCC warranties, negligence and fraud against Sycom and the other defendants. The action was removed to this court. E. F. Hutton has counterclaimed against plaintiffs and cross-claimed against Tandy and Sycom.

Defendants' motion is based on a forum selection clause in the form sales contract, which provides:

"(a) this Agreement shall be governed by the laws of the Sate of Wisconsin and the exclusive jurisdiction for any legal proceeding regarding this Purchase Agreement shall be the State of Wisconsin."

The court has carefully reviewed the file and the memoranda of the parties and finds that this matter may be disposed of without great difficulty.

* * * *

* * * [T]his court finds that Kentucky has adopted the position of the American Law Institute, as stated in Sec. 80, *Restatement 2d, Conflict of Laws*. That section of the *Restatement* reads:

"The parties' agreement as to the place of the action cannot oust a state of judicial jurisdiction but such an agreement will be given effect unless it is unfair or unreasonable."

* * * *

* * * The plaintiff, a solo dental practitioner, would be seriously inconvenienced by being required to litigate this matter in Wisconsin, whereas the defendant would not be inconvenienced by being required to litigate here. While the court cannot say that the defendant has engaged in overreaching, it does regard the clause as bordering on unconscionability as applied to the sale of an important piece of office machinery to a small businessman for the substantial purchase price involved. In the opinion of the court, there was a disparity of bargaining power with regard to the particular clause of the contract in question. The forum selection clause is only one of many clauses in the form contract that together represent the best job of boiler-plating since the building of the Monitor.

DECISION AND REMEDY   *The court held that the case could not be transferred. The court found the forum selection clause unconscionable in this particular contract with a small business. The plaintiff did not have any say in the drafting of the contract. Courts are reluctant to enforce a contract term solely because it is a contract term when it inflicts undue hardship on one party—in this case, Dr. and Mrs. Horning. The court believed that the plaintiff should be protected in this situation.*

When a court determines that a contract or a clause within the contract is unconscionable, UCC Section 2-302 allows a court to: (1) refuse to enforce the contract, (2) enforce the remainder of the contract without the unconscionable clause, or (3) limit the application of the clause to avoid an unconscionable result.

Under this third provision, a court might remove a clause limiting or disclaiming warranty rights inserted by a programmer and in its place apply the warranties of merchantibility and/or fitness for a particular purpose (see Chapter 12). Similarly, if a user places a provision in a standard contract making the programmer liable for anything that might occur, a court may also remove or restrict this provision under the authority granted by the UCC.

Protection of Property Rights in Computer Programs

The real success of computers is based not necessarily on the hardware itself but on how the hardware is utilized. This utilization requires the proper development of the software. When someone creates a new software program, the law provides methods by which he or she can obtain a proprietary interest in it. This protection is granted through patents, trademarks, copyrights, and the doctrine of trade secrets. These topics are discussed briefly in Chapter 12 and in detail in Chapter 16. The following case examines some of the problems concerning software and its protection.

BACKGROUND AND FACTS *Apple Computer, Inc., the plaintiff, is one of the leading manufacturers of personal computers and computer programs. Apple had sold over 400,000 Apple II computers, distributed over 150 programs (of which fourteen were the subject of the lawsuit), employed approximately 3,000 people, and had annual sales of $335 million for fiscal year 1981.*

Franklin Computer Corporation employed about seventy-five people and manufactured the ACE 100 personal computer that could use the Apple software. Fewer than 1,000 ACE 100 computers had been sold. Franklin's copying of Apple's operating system was the reason this action was filed. Franklin did not dispute that it had copied the Apple programs. Apple made a motion for a preliminary injunction to enjoin Franklin from infringing the copyrights on Apple's computer programs. The motion was denied because the district court found that the object code, as distinguished from the source code, may not be the proper subject of a copyright.

Two footnotes from the case have been retained in this edited version because the information contained in them adds to the understanding of the case. The original footnote numbers, numbers 3 and 7, from the case have been retained.

Case 14.5
APPLE COMPUTER, INC. v. FRANKLIN COMPUTER CORP.

United States Court of Appeals, Third Circuit, 1983.
714 F.2d 1240.

SLOVITER, Judge.

* * * *

There are three levels of computer language in which computer programs may be written. High level language, such as the commonly used BASIC or FORTRAN, uses English words and symbols, and is relatively easy to learn and understand (e.g., "GO TO 40" tells the computer to skip intervening steps and go to the step at line 40). A somewhat lower level language is assembly language, which consists of alphanumeric labels (e.g., "ADC" means "add with carry"). Statements in high level language, and apparently also statements in assembly language, are referred to as written in "source code." The third, or lowest level computer language, is machine language, a binary language using two symbols, 0 and 1, to indicate an open or closed switch (e.g., "01101001" means, to the Apple, add two numbers and save the result). Statements in machine language are referred to as written in "object code."

The CPU [central processing unit] can only follow instructions written in object code. However, programs are usually written in source code which is more intelligible to humans. Programs written in source code can be converted or translated by a "compiler" program into object code for use by the computer. Programs are generally distributed only in their object code version stored on a memory device.

A computer program can be stored or fixed on a variety of memory devices, two of which are of particular relevance for this case. The ROM (Read Only Memory) is an internal permanent memory device consisting of a semi-conductor "chip" which is incorporated into the circuitry of the computer. A program in object code is embedded on a ROM before it is incorporated in the computer. Information stored on a ROM can only be read, not erased or rewritten.[3] The ACE 100 apparently contains EPROMS (Erasable Programmable Read Only Memory) on which the stored information can be erased and the chip reprogrammed, but the district court found that for purposes of this proceeding, the difference between ROMs and EPROMs is inconsequential. The other device used for storing the programs at issue is a diskette or "floppy disk," an auxiliary memory device consisting of a flexible magnetic disk resembling a phonograph record, which can be inserted into the computer and from which data or instructions can be read.

Computer programs can be categorized by function as either application programs or operating system programs. Application programs usually perform a specific task for the computer user, such as word processing, checkbook balancing, or playing a game. In contrast, operating system programs generally manage the internal functions of the computer or facilitate use of application programs. The parties agree that the fourteen computer programs at issue in this suit are operating system programs.

* * * *

[Court's discussion of the copyrightability of a computer program expressed in object code]

The 1980 amendments [to the Copyright Act] added a definition of a computer program:

A "computer program" is a set of statements or instructions to be used directly or indirectly in a computer in order to bring about a certain result.

* * * *

We considered the issue of copyright protection for a computer program in *Williams Electronics, Inc. v. Artic International, Inc.,* and concluded that "the copyrightability of computer programs is firmly established after the 1980 amendment to the Copyright Act." * * *

The district court here questioned whether copyright was to be limited to works "designed to be 'read' by a human reader [as distinguished from] read by an expert with a microscope and patience." * * *

Under the statute, copyright extends to works in any tangible means of expression *"from which they can be perceived,* reproduced, or otherwise communicated, either directly or *with the aid of a machine or device."* ([E]mphasis added). Further, the definition of "computer program" adopted by Congress in the 1980 amendments is "sets of statements or instructions to be used *directly or indirectly* in a computer in order to bring about a certain result." ([E]mphasis added). As source code instructions must be translated into object code before the computer can act upon them, only instructions expressed in object code can be used "directly" by the computer. * * *

The defendant in *Williams* had also argued that a copyrightable work "must be intelligible to human beings and must be intended as a medium of communication to human beings." We reiterate the statement we made in *Williams* when we rejected that argument: "[t]he answer to defendant's contention is in the words of the statute itself."

The district court also expressed uncertainty as to whether a computer program in object code could be classified as a "literary work." [7] However, the category of "literary works," one of the seven copyrightable categories, is not confined to literature in the nature of Hemingway's *For Whom the Bell Tolls.* The definition of "literary works" in section 101 includes expression not only in words but also "numbers, or other . . . numerical symbols or indicia," thereby expanding the common usage of "literary works." * * * Thus a computer program, whether in object code or source code, is a "literary work" and is protected from unauthorized copying, whether from its object or source code version.

* * * *

[Court's discussion of copyrightability of a computer program embedded on a ROM]

Just as the district court's suggestion of a distinction between source code and object code was rejected by our opinion in *Williams* issued three days after the district court opinion, so also was its suggestion that embodiment of a computer program on a ROM, as distinguished from in a traditional writing, detracts from its copyrightability. In *Williams* we rejected the argument that ''a computer program is not infringed when the program is loaded into electronic memory devices (ROMs) and used to control the activity of machines.'' Defendant there had argued that there can be no copyright protection for the ROMs because they are utilitarian objects or machine parts. We held that the statutory requirement of ''fixation,'' the manner in which the issue arises, is satisfied through the embodiment of the expression in the ROM devices. Therefore we reaffirm that a computer program in object code embedded in a ROM chip is an appropriate subject of copyright.

3.   In contrast to the permanent memory devices a RAM (Random Access Memory) is a chip on which volatile internal memory is stored which is erased when the computer's power is turned off.

7.   The district court stated that a programmer working directly in object code appears to think more as a mathematician or engineer, that the process of constructing a chip is less a work of authorship than the product of engineering knowledge, and that it may be more apt to describe an encoded ROM as a pictorial three-dimensional object than as a literary work. The district court's remarks relied in part on a quotation about ''microcode''; Apple introduced testimony that none of the works in suit contain ''microcode.'' Moreover, Apple does not seek to protect the ROM's architecture but only the program encoded upon it.

The court found that Franklin's argument that computer operating systems were not copyrightable was not valid. In fact, the court found that Congress intended computer software programs to be protected by copyright laws.   **DECISION AND REMEDY**

The Ever-Developing Field

In an ever-changing society, the concept of personal property is expanding to take into account new types of such property. Often after a new type of property is developed, the courts and legislature must resolve problems that arise from it. For example, it is now a crime to make illegal duplicate tapes of records, audio tape recordings, video tape recordings, and computer programs. The next question will be: Is the law broad enough to cover illegal duplicates of compact discs? Then, is it broad enough to cover the developing problems of personal property in outer space, in space laboratories, or during long-term space flights?

FACING A LEGAL ISSUE   Protecting Real Property

You decide to purchase a specific parcel of real property. It consists of several vacant buildings located in a suburban area on twenty acres of land. Because the property is rather isolated, numerous illegal intrusions into the buildings have been made by transients in order to stay a night or two and by youths for parties. These individuals have caused considerable damage to the buildings.

You are considering several alternatives to deal with these occurrences, namely: (1) placing guard dogs on the premises, (2) hiring a night watchperson, (3) setting up shotguns that would be triggered by a person touching a string close to the floor, or (4) simply letting these people use the premises until you find a tenant to lease the property.

You check with an attorney to find out which alternative is best. You are told that the first alternative is not allowed. Many states, including yours, have adopted laws that the owner of a dog is liable for any bites caused when the owner knows the dog is vicious. The second alternative is possible: The use of a night watchperson is proper as long as he or she does not use a firearm against trespassers. No one has the right to shoot mere trespassers.

Before a person can use deadly force, a clear danger to the person or another person must exist.

The third alternative is the worst choice and should not be considered. The owner of the property who sets up this type of gun arrangement is liable for criminal and civil charges if anyone is injured. According to longtime English and American laws, no one has the right to protect property by this method.

The fourth alternative is not the best solution either. If a person, even though a trespasser, is injured on your property by falling into a hole or tripping on debris, you may be liable. As the owner of the property, you have certain legal duties toward them. Many states require that you act as a reasonable and prudent person would under the same or similar circumstances. Other states require you to make the premises reasonably safe once you are aware that other people are using them.

What should you do? First, make sure you have sufficient liability insurance covering the property. Second, you should post ''No Trespassing'' signs. Third, you should board up the buildings, making them very difficult for anyone to enter. Fourth, you should inform the police department about the situation and have them watch the premises. These alternatives are the safest ones that an owner of real estate may exercise.

Summary

Property rights are of prime importance to our society. In fact, property rights are protected by the United States Constitution.

These classifications of property are recognized: real or personal, tangible or intangible, and fixtures. All property constitutes either real estate or personal property. Tangible property has physical existence, while intangible property consists of rights. Fixtures are items that are installed in real estate and that become part of the land.

A person may own real property with another person. These joint forms of ownership are tenancy in common, joint tenancy with right of survivorship, tenancy by the entirety, and community property. To own an interest in either tenancy by the entirety or community property, the joint owners must be husband and wife.

The seven ways to obtain ownership of personal property are by possession, purchase, production, gift, will or inheritance, accession, and confusion.

Bailments concern the transfer of possession of personal property without transfer of title from the ''owner'' to another person. The bailment can be based on a contract, or it can be gratuitous.

Different interests in real property are found in freehold and nonfreehold estates. A freehold estate provides a person ownership for an indefinite period. Among freehold estates are the fee simple absolute, fee simple defeasible, fee simple subject to a condition subsequent, and life estates. The nonfreehold estates are leases that govern possessory rights to real property in the relationship between a landlord and a tenant.

Eminent domain is the right of the government to take a person's property. The government must pay just compensation to the owner, even if the taking is temporary. The government may control an owner's use of real property through zoning laws.

Transferring an interest in real property occurs by deed, by will, by operation of law, or by adverse possession. Adverse possession means obtaining title to land (without a deed) by the adverse use of real property for a specified period of time.

Computer law is a unique branch of the law that has just recently started to develop. An important question in computer law is whether there is a sale of goods or of service when a computer program is transferred.

Under recent legislative changes adopted by the United States Congress, the law of patents, copyrights, and trade secrets now applies to computer hardware and software.

Key Terms

abandoned property (**353**)
accession (**353**)
adverse possession (**351**)
bailee (**354**)
bailment (**354**)
bailor (**354**)
community property (**343**)
confusion (**354**)
covenant running with land (**352**)
deed (**351**)
easement (**352**)
eminent domain (**348**)

fee simple absolute (**344**)
fee simple defeasible (**344**)
fee simple subject to a condition subsequent (**344**)
fixture (**340**)
freehold estate (**344**)
fungible goods (**354**)
general warranty deed (**351**)
gift (**353**)
hardware (**354**)
intangible property (**340**)
joint tenancy with right of survivorship (**343**)

landlord (**346**)
lease (**346**)
life estate (**346**)
lost property (**353**)
mislaid property (**352**)
nonfreehold estate (**346**)
personal property (**340**)
police power (**340**)
production (**353**)
purchase (**353**)
quiet title (**351**)
quitclaim deed (**351**)
real property (**340**)

recording statute (**351**)
software (**354**)
special warranty deed (**351**)
tangible property (**340**)
tenancy at will (**347**)

tenancy by sufferance (**347**)
tenancy by the entirety (**343**)
tenancy for years (**347**)
tenancy from period to period
(**347**)

tenancy in common (**343**)
tenants (**346**)
unconscionability (**356**)
zoning (**352**)

Questions and Case Problems

1. Sally goes into Meyer's Department Store to do some Christmas shopping. She becomes engrossed in looking over a number of silk blouses when she suddenly realizes she has a dinner engagement. She hastily departs from the store, inadvertently leaving her purse on a sales counter. Julie, a sales clerk at the store, notices the purse on the counter but leaves it there, expecting Sally to return for it. Later, when Sally returns, the purse is gone. Sally files an action against Meyer's Department Store for the loss of her purse. Discuss the probable outcome of her suit.

2. Goodman contracts to lease an apartment near the campus from landlord Lopez for one year, with the monthly rent due and payable on the first of each month. At the end of the year, Goodman does not vacate the apartment, and Lopez does not object. Goodman continues to pay the rent on the first day of the month, and it is accepted by Lopez. Six months later, Lopez informs Goodman that the apartment has been leased to Green and that Goodman must vacate the premises by the end of the week. Goodman refuses to leave, and Lopez threatens eviction proceedings. Discuss the rights of the parties under these circumstances.

3. Bill Heise is a janitor for the First Mercantile Department Store. While walking to work, Bill discovers an expensive watch lying on the curb. Later that day, while Bill is cleaning the aisles of the store, he discovers a wallet containing $500 but no identification. Bill turns over the wallet to his superior, Joe Frances. Bill gives the watch to his son Gordon. Two weeks later, Martin Avery, the owner of the watch, discovers that Bill found the watch and demands it back from Gordon. Bill decides now to claim the wallet with its $500, but Joe refuses to turn it over, saying that Bill is not the true owner and that the money is really the property of the store. Discuss who is entitled to the watch and who is entitled to the wallet containing $500.

4. Harold was a wanderer until twenty-two years ago. At that time, he decided to settle down on a vacant three-acre piece of land, which he did not own. People in the area indicated to him that they had no idea who owned it. Harold built a house on the land, got married, and raised three children while living there. He fenced the land, placed a gate with a sign, "Harold's Homestead," above it, and had trespassers removed. Harold is now confronted by Joe

Moonfeld, who has a deed in his name as owner of the property. Moonfeld orders Harold and his family off the property, claiming his own title ownership. Discuss who has best "title" to the property.

5. Lee owns and operates a service station. Walter's car needs some minor repairs. Walter takes his car to Lee's station. Lee tells Walter that he will be unable to do work until the next day and that Walter can either bring the car back at that time or leave it overnight. Walter leaves the car with Lee. The next afternoon Walter comes to pick up his car. Lee presents Walter with a bill for $220 and refuses to return the car until he has been paid. On inspecting the car, Walter discovers that the mileage indicator shows 150 more miles on the car than when he brought it in. Lee claims that he was allowed by law to let one of his employees road test the car by taking it home and driving it during the previous evening. Under bailment law discuss Walter's and Lee's legal rights under these circumstances.

6. The owners of the Seven Palms Motor Inn decided that their motel was in need of renovation. Accordingly, they ordered a large quantity of bedspreads, curtain rods, and drapes from Sears, Roebuck and Company. Thereafter, Seven Palms Motor Inn failed to pay its bill, which amounted to approximately $8,000, including installation. Under Missouri law, a supplier of fixtures can establish a lien on the land and the building to which the fixtures become attached. Sears sought to establish such a lien to make it easier to recover the debt that Seven Palms owed it. Which, if any, of the above-named items will Sears be able to argue are fixtures? [Sears, Roebuck & Co. v. Seven Palms Motor Inn, Inc., 530 S.W.2d 695 (Mo. 1975)]

7. A mortgage was placed on a parcel of land. Afterward, a grain storage facility was constructed. It consisted of a number of steel structures bolted into concrete slabs that were partially embedded into the ground and that included fifty to sixty feet of underground tubing. Air was electronically pumped through the tubing in order to move grain from the dryer to several storage bins. To remove these structures would take about two weeks. The owner of the facility defaulted on the mortgage, leading the mortgage creditor to file an action to regain the property. The mortgage creditor argued that this facility was a fixture and should remain on the land. Do you agree? Please explain your answer fully. [Metropolitan Life Insurance Co. v. Reeves, 223 Neb. 299, 389 N.W.2d 295 (1986)]

8. Paul was the owner of real estate located in Putnam County, Florida. In 1982, while Paul was living with Lucille, he executed a deed conveying the property to himself and Lucille as joint tenants with right of survivorship. In 1985, Paul and Lucille stopped living together, and three months later Lucille conveyed her interest in the property to her daughter, Sandra. What type of interest does Sandra possess in the property, and why? [Foucart v. Paul, 516 So.2d 1035 (Fla.Dist.Ct.App. 1987)]

9. Danny Smith and his brother discovered a sixteen-foot boat lying beside a roadway in Alabama. Danny Smith informed the police, who immediately impounded the boat and stored it in a city warehouse. Although Smith acquiesced to the police action, he told the police that if the true owner did not claim the boat he wanted it. When the true owner did not come forward, the police department refused to relinquish the boat to Smith and instead told Smith that it planned to auction it to the highest bidder on behalf of the city. Smith sued for custody of the boat. Since Smith never physically held the boat but rather allowed the police to take possession, should Smith succeed in his claim to title as finder? Could Smith defeat a claim if the true owner sought to retake the boat? [Smith v. Purvis, 474 So.2d 1131 (Ala.Civ.App. 1985)]

Chapter 15   Agency and Employment Law

Employment gives health, sobriety, and morals. Constant employment and well-paid labor produce, in a country like ours, general prosperity, content, and cheerfulness.

Daniel Webster (1782–1852)

OUTLINE

Introduction

Agency law is important because its rules permeate the entire legal system. Agency law defines the relationship between two parties in which one of them, called the **agent**, agrees to represent or act for the other, called the **principal**. The principal has the right to control the agent's conduct in matters entrusted to the agent.

The actual rules are relatively simple and straightforward, although the application of the rules to a specific problem is not always easy. Both agency law and its counterpart, employment law, have evolved over the centuries, but the basic concepts have not really changed that much. In this chapter we will discuss agency law and regulation of the employment relationship.

Background

The forerunners of agency law were the legal principles developed during Roman times that related to the ownership of slaves. Even in ancient times, an owner was financially liable for the torts of his or her slaves. The reasoning was that, if a person was able to increase his or her wealth through the services of slaves, he or she should be responsible for the slaves' acts.

The concept adopted by the Romans continued to develop through the Middle Ages. Eventually a body of law governing the relationship of master and servant evolved. A master could be held liable for the servants' acts that were committed within the scope of their employment. A servant could not make contracts on behalf of the master. The normal liability of a master was, therefore, limited to tort law. For example, the master would be held liable if a servant negligently harnessed a carriage and this resulted in damages or injuries to another person. Today the same concept is applied to the employer-employee relationship. The employer is responsible for the harm caused by the torts of his or her employees who were acting within the scope of their employment.

The Industrial Revolution started in the mid 1700s and ended in the mid 1800s; it created the need for many contractual relationships. The owners of new industrial plants had to enter into many contracts at any given time in order to keep the plant operating. The owner had to purchase raw materials in volume from several sources and also had to sell the manufactured products over a wide territory to many people. No longer would the majority of contracts be between the individual who produced an item and another individual who would purchase the item.

People who owned industrial plants began to delegate the responsibility to enter into these contracts to individuals known as agents. By using agents, the owner (or principal) could conduct multiple business operations simultaneously in various locations. In addition, the owner of the industrial plant incurred liability on the contracts made on his or her behalf by the agents. Thus, the concept of agency law developed.

The underlying concept of the employer-employee and principal-agent legal relationship is summarized by a Latin phrase, *qui facit per alium facit per se,* which means "he who acts through another acts through himself." This phrase summarizes the theory that has been the foundation of agency law from Roman times through today: If a person increases business profits through the use of other people, he or she should be liable for the actions of those people.

Formation of the Agency Relationship

Generally, no formalities are required to create an agency. The agency relationship can arise by one of several methods: agreement, ratification, or estoppel.

Agency by Agreement

Agency is a consensual relationship. The agency relationship is based on some affirmative indication that the principal agrees to have the agent act on behalf of the principal and that the agent agrees to act for the principal. Most agency relationships are created in this manner.

Many agency relationships are based on express agreements that are oral. Good business practice, however, dictates that the agreement should be in writing. Because the agency rela-

---

LEGAL HIGHLIGHT — Power of Attorney

A power of attorney is given by a principal to an agent in a written document that is usually notarized. Like all agency relationships, a power of attorney can be special—permitting the agent to perform specific acts only—or it can be general—permitting the agent to transact all business dealings for the principal.

A power of attorney appoints a person to be "an attorney-in-fact." This is a very powerful document because, under a general power of attorney, the attorney-in-fact can do almost anything in the principal's name. The attorney-in-fact, for example, can drive the principal into bankruptcy by misusing the power of attorney.

Powers of attorney can be revoked at any time. Powers of attorney are also revoked on the death of the principal or when a principal becomes mentally incompetent. Many states now have statutes that allow a power of attorney to continue even though the principal is mentally incompetent.

---

tionship is a contractual one, contract rules apply, including the Statute of Frauds (see Chapter 9). This statute requires certain types of contracts to be in writing if they are to be enforceable in a court. For example, the sale of any interest in real estate must be in writing. Thus, real estate listing agreements between the seller and the real estate broker are required to be in writing.

Agency by Ratification

On occasion, a person who is not in fact an agent or who is acting outside the scope of his or her authority as an agent may make a contract on behalf of a purported principal. No authority from the principal, either express or implied, is present when the unauthorized contract or act is made. If the principal approves or affirms that contract by word or by action, an agency relationship is created by ratification. Ratification is a question of intent, and intent can be expressed by either words or conduct.

Ratification binds the principal to the agent's acts and treats the agent's acts or contracts as if they had been authorized by the principal from the beginning. Thus, the principal must be aware of all material facts; otherwise, the ratification is not effective. The principal's ratification can be either express or implied from the words or conduct of the principal. The creation of the agency by ratification "relates back" to the time of the unauthorized act. By his or her acceptance, the principal acknowledges all the advantages and disadvantages of this agency and that this contract started at the time of the unauthorized act.

The following case looks at whether silence on the part of a purported principal can be construed as ratification.

BACKGROUND AND FACTS *In 1974, Mrs. Crawford executed a power of attorney naming her daughter, Mrs. Howe, as her agent. Mrs. Howe and her husband operated a dairy farm. Mrs. Crawford took no part in the management of the dairy business and received no benefits from it.*

In 1980, the Howes experienced severe financial difficulties in the operation of their farm, and they needed to refinance their debt. A few days before the new loan closed, Mrs. Howe advised the attorney handling the transaction that she would like to sign the loan instruments as agent for

Case 15.1
FIRST NATIONAL BANK OF SHREVEPORT v. CRAWFORD
Court of Appeal of Louisiana, 1984.
455 So.2d 1209.

her mother under the 1974 power of attorney so that her mother would not have to come to town for the closing. The attorney examined the power of attorney, approved it, and the loan papers were prepared. Mrs. Howe acted as an agent for Mrs. Crawford in this matter without her knowledge or consent. Mrs. Crawford testified at the trial that she knew nothing about the loan transaction. Mrs. Howe testified that she told her mother something about it sometime, approximately a month after the loan was closed, but her testimony as to what she told her mother was very vague and indefinite.

Mr. and Mrs. Howe were unable to pay the debt and went into bankruptcy. The bank sued Mrs. Crawford to collect the loan, alleging that Mrs. Crawford had ratified the agreement. The trial court entered a judgment for Mrs. Crawford.

HALL, Judge.
* * * *

The bank argues that Mrs. Crawford, by her silence and inaction after being informed of the bank transaction, ratified the action of her agent in executing the note and mortgage, and is bound thereby regardless of the agent's original authority.

The concept of ratification by a principal of an agent's unauthorized acts is recognized in two articles of the Civil Code:

[1] "The attorney can not go beyond the limits of his procuration; whatever he does exceeding his power is null and void with regard to the principal, unless ratified by the latter, and the attorney is alone bound by it in his individual capacity."

[2] "The principal is bound to execute the engagements contracted by the attorney, comformably to the power confided to him.

"For anything further he is not bound, except in so far as he has expressly ratified it."

The applicable principles are well expressed in *Bamber Contractors v. Morrison Engineering:*

"Ratification, in the law of agency, is the adoption by one person of an act done on his behalf by another without authority. Ratification amounts to a substitute for prior authority. The burden of proving ratification is on the party asserting it and to find ratification of an unauthorized act, the facts must indicate a clear and absolute intent to ratify the act, and no intent will be inferred when the alleged ratification can be explained otherwise. Ratification will occur when the principal, knowing of the contract, does not repudiate it but accepts its benefits."

The bank did not prove by a preponderance of the evidence that Mrs. Crawford knew and understood what her agent had done in this case. Mrs. Crawford denied knowing anything about the transaction until this suit was filed. Mrs. Howe's testimony was vague and indefinite as to what she told her mother about the transaction and when she told her. A clear intent to ratify the [loan] * * * cannot be inferred from the facts of this case. Ratification was not established.

DECISION AND REMEDY

The court of appeal affirmed the trial court's judgment for Mrs. Crawford. Ratification must be proved by the plaintiff; there must be a clear and absolute intent to ratify the unauthorized act. Under these circumstances, where Mrs. Crawford's knowledge of the loan had not been proved, mere silence did not amount to ratification.

Agency by Estoppel

When a principal leads a third person to believe that another person is her or his agent and the third person deals with the supposed agent, the principal cannot deny the agency relationship. In other words, the principal is not allowed to claim that no agency relationship exists. In these situations, the principal's actions create the appearance of an agency that does not in fact exist.

For example, Kona is in the insurance business and hires McGant as an agent to solicit and sell insurance. Kona advertises to the general public that McGant is his agent. After a period of time, Kona discovers that McGant is keeping some of the premiums paid in cash. Obviously, McGant is dishonest and probably has committed a criminal act. McGant is fired immediately, but he still has the appearance, through the advertisements, of being Kona's agent. If McGant should contract with an innocent third party after he was fired, Kona will be estopped from denying that McGant was Kona's agent. Kona has represented McGant to the public as his agent, and an innocent purchaser has relied on this representation. Kona is, therefore, not allowed to claim a lack of an agency relationship. To avoid possible future liability, Kona might publish notice that McGant is no longer Kona's agent.

Kinds of Agency Relationships

Three types of agency relationships exist:

1. Principal-agent, including professional agents.
2. Employer-employee.
3. Employer's or principal's relationship with an independent contractor.

The legal principles developed under either employer-employee law or agency law have similar applications. Moreover, a person can be both an employee and an agent at the same time. For example, a business may employ a person fulltime to analyze the real estate market and that person could also have the authority to negotiate the price of and to purchase or sell specific pieces of land. Because these two areas can easily be intertwined,

a clear application of separate legal principles is not always possible.

Relationship Between the Principal and Agent

A principal cannot be everywhere to transact his or her own business. The agent acts on behalf of and instead of the principal to negotiate, conduct, and contract business with third persons. The agent has **derivative authority**—that is, he or she derives the authority to carry out the principal's business from the principal and not from his or her own acts. The principal is liable to the third party for the acts of the agent based on that contract.

Say that Staid Corporation, for example, hires Fast Freddy, a booking agent, to negotiate and contract with the Hot Rockers, the latest hot rock-and-roll group, for a series of appearances and television commercials endorsing Staid's products. Contracts made by Fast Freddy, the agent, within his authority are binding and legally enforceable by Staid Corporation, the principal. The Hot Rockers, the third party, may also enforce the contract against Staid Corporation. If Fast Freddy had no authority to represent Staid Corporation, he cannot on his own bind Staid to a contract with the Hot Rockers. The authority must come from the principal. A principal cannot be held liable for acts of another unless the principal hires an agent or otherwise satisfies or acts in such a way as to create an agency relationship.

Scope of Agent's Authority A principal's liability in a contract with a third party arises from the authority given the agent to enter legally binding contracts on the principal's behalf. An agent's authority to act stems from one of the following sources:

1. Actual authority
   a. Express (or specific)
   b. Implied
2. Apparent authority.

Even if an agent contracts outside the scope of his or her authority, the principal may still be liable by ratifying the contract, as discussed earlier in this chapter.

Actual Authority   An agent who acts on behalf of the principal either by agreement or by operation of law will have **actual authority**. Actual authority can be either express or implied.

Express authority offers the agent specific instructions on matters germane to the agency. Express authority can be granted orally or in writing. A principal who writes out express instructions that establish the agent's authority is engaging in good business practice. A well-drafted instrument allows both the principal and the agent to be clear about their relationship.

Even in the best instruments giving an agent express authority, however, many of the agent's responsibilities are not covered. These responsibilities are part of the agent's **implied authority**. Often implied authority is conferred by virtue of the customary practices of that particular agency. Implied authority may be inferred from the position the agent occupies. For example, in a department store, the manager of the men's clothing section has the implied authority to discount a shirt that has a spot on it.

Implied authority can also be claimed for an act that is reasonably necessary in order for the agent to carry out what he or she has been expressly authorized to do. For example, Cherri is employed by Dolly's Clothing to manage one of its stores. Dolly's Clothing has not expressly stated Cherri's authority to contract with third persons, but the authority to manage a business implies the authority to do what is reasonably required in order to operate the business. Thus, Cherri's implied authority includes the ability to make contracts with employees, buy merchandise and equipment, and advertise the products sold in the store.

Apparent Authority   A principal, by either word or action, makes a third party reasonably believe that a particular person has the authority to act on the principal's behalf. If the third party relies on the appearance of authority that the principal has given that person, the person is said to be an agent by **apparent authority**. The principal is stopped from saying the person did not have any authority to act on the principal's behalf, even though the agent has no express or implied authority.

Apparent authority is often considered to be *title authority*—that is, the authority exists by virtue of the person's business title—general manager, assistant manager, sales manager, and so on. It also depends on the size and scope of the business. For example, not all radio station managers have the authority to promote other station personnel. In a small station, the owner may retain the right to promote personnel, while in larger stations, the general manager may have that authority.

The following case discusses the creation of an agency relationship based on the concept of apparent authority.

Case 15.2
FUNK v. HANCOCK
Court of Appeals of Ohio,
1985.
26 Ohio App.3d 107,
498 N.E.2d 490.

BACKGROUND AND FACTS   *In June 1982, Donald R. Funk, Jr., was brought to the emergency room at Fayette County Memorial Hospital by his mother for treatment of an injury to his left forearm. Following a preliminary examination by the emergency room physician, Donald's injury was diagnosed as a fracture of the left forearm. Dr. Thomas Hancock was, thereafter, called in for consultation. After examining the injury, Dr. Hancock placed the arm in a cast. No surgical intervention was performed even though the arm had a puncture wound.*

After being discharged from the hospital, Donald began to experience discomfort in his left arm, and it was subsequently determined that the arm had become infected in the area of the puncture wound. As a result, surgery was performed on the arm to relieve swelling and restore normal blood flow. Later, a portion of Donald's left arm was amputated.

In May 1983, Donald and his parents, Donald R. Funk, Sr., and Judy Funk, filed suit in the Fayette County Court of Common Pleas against Dr.

Hancock and Fayette Memorial Hospital. The complaint alleged that the defendant, Hancock, had committed medical malpractice as a result of "improper casting of a compound fracture without debridement and appropriate follow-up observation and care." The plaintiff's position was that Dr. Hancock was the agent of the hospital and that, therefore, the hospital was liable for his acts. The lower court granted the hospital's motion for a summary judgment, and the plaintiffs appealed.

PER CURIAM [By the whole court. This phrase distinguishes an opinion of all judges in a multijudge panel from an opinion of any single judge.]
* * * *

Appellants in essence argue that since the emergency and follow-up care provided to Donald Funk, Jr. was rendered by a staff physician who was "on call" at the hospital emergency room, and since neither the patient nor his parents requested the services of the particular physician and the physician only became involved due to his relationship with the hospital, any negligence on the part of the physician may be imputed to the hospital on the basis of actual agency, joint venture or agency by estoppel [apparent authority].
* * * *

* * * An "agency relationship" is a consensual fiduciary relationship between two persons where the agent has the power to bind the principal by his actions, and the principal has the right to control the actions of the agent. Agency by estoppel or apparent authority occurs when a person dealing with an agent acting outside the scope of his or her authority reasonably believes the agent's conduct to be within the scope of authority due to conduct by the principal; in this situation, the principal is estopped from denying that the agent's actions were within the scope of authority. The agency by estoppel argument appears to have particular application to the case now before us, and we therefore direct our attention fully upon it without discounting the more remote possibility that an actual agency relationship might be proved to exist as between Dr. Hancock and the hospital.
* * * *

* * * [Prior] decisions reflect the * * * underlying philosophy: agency by estoppel is applicable to cases involving physicians practicing in hospital emergency rooms, and if a hospital's actions are such that emergency room patrons are encouraged to rely on a presumed agency relationship between a treating physician and the hospital, the hospital may in fact be estopped from denying such relationship.

Turning to the record before us, we find that there is evidence pertaining to the issue of agency by estoppel which, if construed in a manner most favorable to appellants, raises an issue of material fact upon which reasonable minds could differ. The record discloses that Judy Funk, Donald Funk, Jr.'s mother, stated in an affidavit that when she took her son to the Fayette County Memorial Hospital emergency room on the date of his injury she "believed, based upon all of the circumstances, that the physician provided [Dr. Hancock] was working for the hospital at their request." The record further indicates that the hospital, not Mrs. Funk or her son, contacted Dr. Hancock and requested that he treat Donald, and that Dr. Hancock had staff privileges at the hospital and was on its board of directors. Certainly this evidence raises sufficient questions about Dr. Hancock's relationship with the hospital, including the Funks' perception of such relationship[.] * * *

DECISION AND REMEDY

The appellate court reversed the trial court's granting of a summary judgment because an issue of fact was in dispute. In other words, the appellate court decided that the plaintiffs should have a chance at trial to show how and why Dr. Hancock appeared to be an agent of the hospital. If the trial court finds that the hospital held out Dr. Hancock as its agent to innocent third parties, such as the plaintiffs, the hospital will not be able to deny the agency relationship. The hospital would then be liable for Dr. Hancock's negligent acts.

COMMENT   *The contract between a hospital and the physician's group that supplies physicians for the emergency room often includes a provision that states that, if the hospital is found liable and is required to pay for injuries to a plaintiff, the physician's group will reimburse the hospital. Such reimbursement is usually covered by insurance.*

Cases that are returned to a trial court are often settled out of court. Thus, the public has no way of knowing who ultimately won, whether the hospital was ordered to pay the Funks, or what the award was, if any.

Professional Agents   A **professional agent** is in a business that handles contracts in a particular field. Professional agents are often licensed by the state government to represent principals in contracts in those fields. Examples of professional agents are insurance agents, real estate brokers, travel agents, attorneys, and entertainment agents.

For example, real estate brokers are licensed to represent a person who wants to sell his or her real estate. The real estate broker, then, is the professional agent; the "real estate agent" is actually a subagent of the real estate broker and cannot represent anyone except through his or her employer, the real estate broker. You must learn the lines of authority in a particular business in order to determine what each person is authorized to do.

Relationship Between the Employer and Employee

The law defines an employee as one employed by the employer to perform services; the employee's conduct is controlled by the employer. Agency law also applies to the employer-employee relationship. The rules governing the employer-employee relationship arose out of the impact of the Industrial Revolution and, more recently, social legislation. We examine the impact of social legislation in Chapters 21 and 22.

The employer-employee relationship is included in this chapter because frequently an employee is also an agent for his or her employer-principal. For example, Ruby is employed by a large department store as a clerk in the jewelry section. When she is stocking or straightening inventory, she is an employee. When Ruby sells a bracelet, she is an agent who is contracting with a customer on behalf of her employer, who is also the principal. On the other hand, a person employed as an electrician in the department store is strictly an employee and does not have any authority to transact business on behalf of the employer. The employer is liable, however, for any torts that the electrician commits on the job.

Independent Contractors

An **independent contractor** is not an employee but may be an agent. A person who hires an independent contractor is said to have "employed" the independent contractor. Thus, when the term "employment" is used in connection with an independent contractor, it is not used in the legal context of employer-employee. The employer of an independent contractor does not have control over the all details of the performance of the independent contractor. Because the employer does not control the independent contractor, the employer is not normally responsible for the torts of the independent contractor.

LEGAL HIGHLIGHT

Whose Agent Are You, Anyway?

Television advertisements for insurance may leave you with the impression that the insurance agent is your (the customer's) agent. Legally this is not true. The agent represents the insurance company, not you. The company is the principal, and the insurance agent is an agent of the insurance company, not your agent. The agent is paid by the insurance company, not by you.

The same is true of travel agents. The travel agent is selling a travel package to you, the third party, on behalf of his or her principal, such as a hotel or airlines. The travel agent represents and is paid by the hotel or airline, not by you. If you have a travel agent make reservations at a hotel and something goes wrong, and if, as you are standing at the counter, the clerk tells you that "your travel agent" made a mistake, you might gently inform the clerk that the travel agent is the hotel's agent, not yours. As the principal, the hotel is responsible for the acts of its agent.

Restatement, Second, Agency, Section 2, defines an independent contractor as:

> * * * a person who contracts with another to do something for him but who is not controlled by the other nor subject to the other's right to control with respect to his physical conduct in the performance of the undertaking. He may or may not be an agent.

The courts review many elements to determine whether a relationship is one of employer-employee or of employer and independent contractor. Some factors considered by the courts are:

1. The extent of control exercised by the employer over the details of the work;
2. The type of job, business, or occupation involved and the amount of skill required to perform the job;
3. Who supplies the tools or equipment;
4. The length of employment;
5. The method of payment; and
6. The tax return filed by both parties.

The construction industry is a good example of an employer–independent contractor relationship. Say that an owner of raw land wants to build an office building. She or he hires a general contractor who is responsible for building the office complex. The general contractor in turn hires subcontractors, such as electrical subcontractors or plumbing subcontractors, who are responsible for specific portions of the building. The general contractor is an independent contractor, and the property owner does not control the acts of this professional. The property owner does not have any contractual relationship with the subcontractors who are hired by the general contractor, and thus the owner is not responsible for the acts of the subcontractors. Today there is a whole area of the law governing the construction industry, but these general concepts are still applicable.

If the property owner in this example hires a real estate broker to negotiate a sale of the property, the owner not only has contracted with an independent contractor (the real estate broker) but also has established an agency relationship for the specific purpose of finding a third party who will enter into a contract to purchase the property.

A person retaining the services of an independent contractor is normally not responsible for his or her acts because of the lack of control over the independent contractor. An employer is responsible for the acts of an independent contractor, however, if the independent contractor is performing one of the employer's duties, as established by law. For example, a department store cannot avoid its liability if it has hired an independent security agency to supply security and a security officer makes an illegal arrest for shoplifting. The store, along with the security agency, is liable for the victim. An employer is also liable for acts of independent contractors if the activity involves ultrahazardous conduct, such as handling explosives.

Exhibit 15–1 summarizes the types of agency relationships recognized by law. Throughout the rest of this chapter, we will use the terms "principal" and "agent" to include the terms "employer" and "employee," unless otherwise stated.

The following case discusses the employer-employee relationship versus the relationship between an employer and an independent contractor.

Case 15.3
BARTHOLOMEW v.
CNG PRODUCING CO.
United States Court of Appeals,
Fifth Circuit, 1987.
832 F.2d 326.

BACKGROUND AND FACTS *Robert Bartholomew, the plaintiff, was injured on October 30, 1984, while working on an offshore production platform on the outer continental shelf off the Louisiana coast. He was employed by Booker Drilling Company. Booker was working as an independent contractor for the defendant, CNG Producing Company (CNG), which owned the platform.*

CNG reserved the right to inspect the work being performed. Bartholomew and others were putting pipe in the wellhole when he slipped because of a wet and muddy floor. The fall resulted in serious injuries. The district court awarded a $325,000 judgment for Bartholomew against CNG.

JOHNSON, Judge.
* * * *

The Bartholomews brought this negligence suit against CNG, asserting that CNG was negligent (1) in ordering Bartholomew's employer, Booker, to engage in an unsafe work practice and (2) in contracting with Booker for an inadequate number of floor hands to operate the equipment safely. In defense, CNG argues that as a principal which exercised no operational control over its independent contractor, Booker, CNG was insulated from liability in this case. Because we find that some evidence exists to support a finding by the jury that CNG expressly authorized an unsafe work practice on the platform, we reject CNG's arguments and affirm the district court's judgment without addressing the claim that CNG was negligent in failing to contract for adequate personnel.

It is well established that a principal is not liable for the activities of an independent contractor committed in the course of performing its duties under the contract. However, two notable exceptions exist to this general rule. First, a principal may not escape liability arising out of ultrahazardous activities which are contracted out to an independent contractor. Second, and of importance to the instant case, a principal is liable for the acts of an independent contractor if he exercises operational control over those acts or expressly or impliedly authorizes an unsafe practice.

Where an available safe method, which includes the taking of adequate precautions, will render it at least ordinarily safe, and the work is done in an unsafe manner, the employer will be liable if he has expressly or impliedly authorized the particular manner which will render the work unsafe, and not otherwise.
* * * *

Bartholomew testified at trial that the company man, J. T. Madison, expressly told the driller, Perry Gill, not to wash the rig floor until after the operation was completed. Bartholomew also testified that the driller was fearful for his job. As a floor hand, Bartholomew took his orders directly from the driller. Bartholomew's testimony was not directly contradicted by any of CNG's witnesses. In fact, the Booker tool pusher testified that he had heard of some company men ordering the driller to speed up the operations and not to wash down the rig. Emmett Farrar, the other company man for CNG, who was independently employed, testified that he did not know whether or not Madison had ever issued such an order to the driller. Thus, the question was one of Bartholomew's credibility. The jury was entitled to make that credibility determination and did so. On the record before us, we conclude that some evidence supported a finding by the jury that CNG, through its representative on the rig, J. T. Madison, expressly authorized the unsafe practice of failing to wash down the rig floor which eventually caused Bartholomew's accident.

It is submitted by CNG that because Madison possibly gave him order not to wash down the floor two days prior to the accident, CNG was not exercising operational control at the time of the accident and therefore was not liable. Without determining who the company man was at the time of the accident, we conclude that whether Madison was on duty at the time of the accident or whether he gave the order two days prior to the accident is not dispositive. An employee does not stop obeying his employer's orders merely because the employer is no longer present. It is not unrealistic to expect the driller, as well as the floor hands, to continue to conduct operations without washing down the floor, in light of Madison's previous order to do so. Since there was some evidence to support a finding by the jury that CNG expressly authorized an unsafe work practice, we affirm the district court's judgment.

DECISION AND REMEDY

The decision of the district court was affirmed. The court of appeals concluded that some evidence existed to support the trial court's judgment that CNG had expressly authorized unsafe practices by telling the rigger not to wash down the rigging floor until after operations were completed. The principal (CNG, the employer of Booker, the independent contractor) is liable for damages sustained by an employee (Bartholomew) of the independent contractor when the principal-employer expressly authorizes unsafe working conditions.

Exhibit 15–1 **Legal Relationships in Agency Law**

TYPES OF LEGAL RELATIONSHIPS	DEFINITIONS
Principal-Agent	An agent acts on behalf of and instead of the principal, using a certain degree of his or her own discretion.
Employer-Employee	An employee's physical conduct is controlled or subject to control by an employer. An employee can also be an agent.
Principal– or Employer– Independent Contractor	The contractor is not an employee, and the employer or principal has no control over the details of physical performance. Except for professional agencies, the contractor is usually not an agent.

Duties of Agents and Principals

Once the principal-agent relationship has been created, both parties have duties that govern their conduct. The principal-agent relationship is **fiduciary**—that is, it is one based on trust. In it, each party owes the other the duty to act with the utmost good faith. Neither party may keep from the other information that has any bearing on their agency relationship.

The Agent's Duty to the Principal

The duties that an agent owes to a principal are set out in the agency agreement or arise by operation of law. The duties are also implied from the agency relationship itself and exist between the principal and the agent whether or not the identity of the principal is disclosed to a third party. Generally, the agent owes the principal the following five duties: performance, notification, loyalty, obedience, and accounting.

The Duty of Performance   An implied condition in every agency contract is the agent's agreement to use reasonable diligence and skill in performing the work. When an agent fails to perform the work in this way, liability for breach of contract will occur. In addition, the principal may be liable to a third party for any negligent act of the agent that occurs within the context of the contract.

For example, a principal hires a real estate broker to sell her house. A potential buyer asks how many square feet the house has. The real estate broker negligently answers 2,700 square feet because he is too lazy to look up the precise footage and he thinks he is good at guessing. When the buyer finds out that the actual amount is 2,500 square feet, the principal is liable for the agent's negligent conduct because it is within the context of the contract. Of course, the agent is in turn liable to the principal if the buyer successfully collects money for damages against the principal.

The degree of skill or care required of an agent is usually that expected of a reasonable person under similar circumstances. Although this standard is usually interpreted to mean "ordinary care," if an agent has presented herself or himself as possessing special skills (such as those of an accountant or an attorney), the agent is expected to exercise the skill claimed. Even if the agent is not paid, she or he must exercise the same degree of skill or care as a paid agent. Failure to do so constitutes a breach of the agent's duty. When an agent performs carelessly or negligently, the agent can also be liable in tort.

The Duty of Notification   A maxim in agency law is that "all the agent knows, the principal knows." This refers to the duty of notification. The agent is required to notify the principal of all matters that come to his or her attention concerning the subject matter of the agency. The common law has adopted the **legal fiction** that knowledge to the agent is the same as knowledge to the principal. A legal fiction is an assumption in law; regardless of what actually happened, the law treats this assumption as if it had occurred. Thus, even if the agent has not told the principal something he or she should have, the law will assume that the principal knew what the agent knew and will hold the principal liable. (The principal can sue the agent for failing to fulfill the duty of notification.)

The Duty of Loyalty   Loyalty is one of the most fundamental duties in a fiduciary relationship. Basically stated, the agent has the duty to act solely for the benefit of his or her principal and not in the interest of the agent or a third party. Under common law, this fiduciary duty is owed only in one direction: from the agent to the principal. For example, International Business Machines (IBM) has the right to appoint two sales agents to the same territory—unless IBM has specifically contracted with one agent for an exclusive territory. On the other hand, the IBM sales agent does not have the right to represent more than one computer manufacturer.

Numerous obligations result from this duty. First, the agent has a duty not to represent two principals in the same transaction unless both principals know of the dual capacity and consent to it. For example, a real estate broker cannot represent both the seller and the buyer in the sale of a house. After all, the seller wants to sell at the highest price, and the buyer wants to buy at the lowest price. The real estate broker's commission is a percentage based on the sale price and is paid out of the proceeds due the seller; thus, ordinarily it is the seller who lists the house with a real estate broker.

Often a buyer also seeks the assistance of a real estate broker, however. Although the buyer may at first believe that this broker is representing him or her, in fact it is the seller who pays the broker's commission. In most states, the ethical code of the state real estate association requires that the broker inform the buyer of this conflict. Once both the buyer and the seller have full knowledge of the role of the real estate broker, they can authorize him or her to proceed with the representation.

Another concept states that an agent cannot have any dealings with himself or herself that involve his or her principal. An agent employed by a principal to purchase property cannot buy that property for himself or herself and then turn around and sell the property to the principal.

On the other hand, an agent employed to sell property cannot purchase the property without the principal's consent. In short, the agent's loyalty must be undivided. The agent's actions must be strictly for the benefit of the principal and must not result in any secret profit for the agent.

The Duty of Obedience   When an agent is acting on behalf of the principal, the agent has a duty to obey all lawful and clearly stated instructions of the principal. The agent violates this duty whenever he or she deviates from those instructions. If the circumstances merit it—for example, during emergency situations when the principal cannot be consulted—the agent may deviate from such instructions without violating this duty. Whenever instructions are not clearly stated, the agent can fulfill the duty of obedience by acting in good faith and in a reasonable manner under the circumstances.

The Duty of Accounting   The agent has a duty to the principal to keep and make available an accounting of all property and money received and paid out on behalf of the principal. The principal is entitled to receive all gifts from third persons collected by the agent. For example, an airline gives the agent a gift for qualifying as a frequent flyer. The agent accumulated the mileage while traveling on business for the principal. The gift received by the agent belongs to the principal.

Commingling of personal and agency funds is not allowed. The agent has a duty to maintain separate accounts, one for her or his own personal funds and another for the principal's funds. Whenever a licensed professional, such as an attorney, real estate broker, or insurance agent, violates the duty to account, she or he may be subject to disciplinary proceedings by the appropriate regulatory institution. These proceedings are in addition to the agent's liability to the principal for failure to account.

The following case is an example of the legal problems that arise when an agent breaches various duties owed to the principal.

BACKGROUND AND FACTS   *Donnie Douglas, the plaintiff, was hired as an agent by Aztec Petroleum Corporation, the defendant, to obtain oil leases in Anderson County, Texas. Douglas was to receive $5,000 along with a small royalty interest in the leases obtained. On February 23, 1980, Aztec sent Douglas a $5,000 payment in advance and two checks in the amount of $124,180 to pay for the leases. Douglas obtained most of the leases; when the checks arrived from Aztec, however, he put checks in his personal account and went on a spending spree. He purchased two cars, a boat, and paid for numerous personal expenses.*

Douglas sent Aztec a photocopy of each check, but he altered the payee to show that a lessor had received the money he had spent on the personal items. Aztec later sent Douglas $343,557. He kept $42,000 as cash for himself. When he made a final accounting to Aztec, Douglas sent bogus receipts to show that the cash went to the lessors. He forged all the signatures on the receipts.

Case 15.4
DOUGLAS v. AZTEC PETROLEUM CORP.
Court of Appeals of Texas, 1985.
695 S.W.2d 312.

Douglas filed this lawsuit to enforce the agreement claiming he was owed the royalty interest. Aztec filed a counterclaim seeking damages for falsification of records, forgery, theft, conversion, and embezzlement. The trial court denied Douglas's claim and awarded Aztec $107,000 actual damages and $100,000 exemplary damages. Douglas appealed.

BLASS, Justice.

* * * *

It is uncontroverted that Douglas was Aztec's agent. An agency is a fiduciary relationship. The law requires more of a fiduciary than arms-length marketplace ethics. He owes his principal loyalty and good faith; integrity of the strictest kind; fair, honest dealing; and the duty not to conceal matters which might influence his actions to his principal's prejudice. He is obligated to exercise a high degree of care to conserve his principal's money and to pay it only to those entitled to receive it. He must keep his principal's funds as a separate and identifiable account. The agent must make an accounting to his principal of any money that has come into his possession because of his agency. A fiduciary has no right to make merchandise of the confidence reposed in him.

Douglas' own testimony is a startling catalogue of violations of almost every fiduciary duty. It is undisputed that a substantial portion of the funds advanced did not go for the purposes stated in the agreement, the purchase of oil leases. Douglas admits spending large sums on two new cars, a boat, and other personal expenses almost immediately after getting Aztec's money. He admits failing to account honestly. He confesses forging receipts and altering checks to "plug in" whatever figures were necessary to add up to the $343,000 entrusted to him and to conceal the diversion of his principal's money. As justification he urges a secret kickback agreement with Aztec's president. As we have said previously, an estoppel cannot arise from such facts.

DECISION AND REMEDY   *The court of appeals upheld the decision of the trial court. The facts clearly showed that Aztec had conclusively proved that Douglas had breached his fiduciary duty.*

An agent has a fiduciary relationship with his principal. An agent owes his principal loyalty and good faith, fair and honest dealings, and has the duty not to conceal matters and to keep the principal's funds separate and in an identifiable account.

Principal's Duties to the Agent

The principal's duties to the agent are: compensation, reimbursement and indemnification, co-operation, and safe working conditions. These duties may be set out in a contract, or the duties may be implied by law.

The Duty of Compensation   The principal must pay for his or her agent's services unless it is a **gratuitous agency** relationship. Such a relation-ship occurs when the agent performs services without any compensation. Even though the agent may not be paid, she or he still owes the principal the duties of care and loyalty as discussed in the previous section.

The principal and agent must agree to compensate the agent for her or his services before the agent is entitled to remuneration. When the amount of compensation is agreed on by the parties, the principal owes the duty to compensate the agent on completion of the specified activities.

If no amount is agreed on, the principal owes the agent the customary compensation for such services. For example, in the auction of horses, the auctioneer normally takes a 10 percent commission. If no amount is established either by custom or by law, the principal owes the agent the reasonable value of her or his services.

The Duty of Reimbursement and Indemnification When an agent enters into a contract with a third party to purchase something, it is the principal who has the ultimate duty to pay the third party, not the agent. The principal may use one of several methods to pay the third party. The principal may arrange with the third party to pay her or him directly, the principal may advance the funds to the agent to pay the third party, or the agent may pay the third party out of his or her own pocket. In the last case, the principal then has the duty to reimburse the agent for expenses that the agent has incurred while performing his or her job for the principal. Thus, if an agent pays for other necessary expenses in the course of reasonable performance of agency duties, the principal has the duty to reimburse the agent.

The principal has an overlapping duty to indemnify the agent for any losses that the agent suffers while performing her or his duties for the principal. For example, if the agent loses money while performing a contract, the principal must compensate the agent for those losses.

Agents cannot recover for expenses or losses incurred by their own misconduct or negligence. For example, if an agent has the principal's money on hand to pay a bill on time but negligently fails to pay it, the late penalty must be paid by the agent, and the principal does not have a duty to reimburse the agent.

The Duty of Cooperation A principal has a duty both to cooperate with and to assist an agent in performing his or her duties. The principal must do nothing to prevent such performance. For example, a seller hires a real estate broker to sell a house. The broker finds a buyer who is willing, able, and ready to buy the house. The seller-principal must cooperate with the agent, must sign the papers in a timely manner, and must not do anything that would cause the buyer not to proceed with the purchase.

The Duty to Provide Safe Working Conditions The common law requires the principal to provide safe premises, equipment, and conditions for all agents and employees. The principal has a duty to inspect working conditions and to warn agents and employees about any unsafe areas. If the agent is also an employee (as in the case of a department store clerk, for example), the employer's liability is frequently covered by workers' compensation insurance, which is the primary remedy for an employee's injury on the job.

Liability of Principals and Agents to Third Parties

Once the principal-agent relationship is created, attention often focuses on the rights of third persons who deal with the agent. Both the agent and the principal may become liable to a third person based either on contract or tort law.

Principal's and Agent's Liability for Contracts

Principals are classified as disclosed, partially disclosed, or undisclosed. A **disclosed principal** is a principal whose identity is known by the third party at the time the contract is made by the agent. A **partially disclosed principal** is a principal whose identity is not known by the third party, but the third party knows that the agent is acting for a principal at the time the contract is made. An **undisclosed principal** is a principal whose identity is totally unknown by the third party, and the third party has no knowledge that the agent is acting in an agency capacity at the time the contract is made.

Liability of Disclosed Principals If an agent acts within the scope of her or his authority, a disclosed principal is liable to a third party for a contract made by the agent. In these situations, an agent has no contractual liability for the nonperformance of the principal or of the third party.

Liability of Partially Disclosed and Undisclosed Principals In most states, if the principal is partially disclosed, the principal and agent are both treated as parties to the contract, and the third party can hold either liable if the contract is not performed.

The third party is deemed to be dealing directly with the agent personally if neither the fact of agency nor the identity of the principal is disclosed. Thus, for an undisclosed principal, the agent is liable as a party on the contract.

For example, Disney Company decides to build another amusement park. Research shows that, in a specific prime tourist area, the needs for the new park will be met if Disney can purchase five parcels of land. Disney, however, knows that if word gets out that it plans to purchase land, the price of the land will be higher. Disney hires five different agents to make the five different land purchases. Naturally, Disney is the undisclosed principal. The five agents make the respective purchases over the period of a year. Each agent has purchased the land in his or her own name, and the sellers have relied on the respective agent's credit and reputation and not on that of Disney.

On the other hand, since each agent has acted within the scope of his or her authority, the undisclosed principal, Disney, is fully bound to perform just as if it had been fully disclosed to each seller at the time the purchase contract was made. Moreover, Disney, even though an undisclosed principal, can enforce the contract against each seller.

Warranties of the Agent

Occasionally the agent will lack authority for an action or will exceed the scope of her or his authority. When this situation occurs, the agent, not the principal, is liable to the third party. The agent's liability to the third party is based on a breach of **implied warranty of authority**, not on breach of the contract itself.

The agent can breach the implied warranty of authority by committing an intentional breach of the warranty or by a good-faith mistake. The agent is liable if the third party relied on the agent's status. On the other hand, when the third party knows at the time the contract is made that the agent is mistaken or if the agent indicates to the third party uncertainty about the extent of his or her authority, the agent is not personally liable for breach of warranty. In these situations, the third party knew something was amiss and should have checked further about the agent's authority.

Tort Liability

An agent or employee is liable for his or her own torts and crimes. A principal or employer becomes liable for the negligent torts of the person hired if the torts are committed within the scope of the agency or the scope of employment. This liability is known as the doctrine of *respondeat superior*.

The principal or employer is rarely liable in common law for the intentional torts of the employed person. In some states, however, a statute may exist that places liability on the employer or principal. In the following discussion, most references will be made to the employer-employee context, but the same rules apply to the principal-agent relationship. Three areas will be examined: negligence and the doctrine of *respondeat superior*, misrepresentation, and strict liability.

Negligence and the Doctrine of *Respondeat Superior* The theory of liability based on the **doctrine of** *respondeat superior* imposes strict liability on the employer. Liability is imposed without regard to the personal fault of the employer for negligent torts committed by an employee in the course of employment. For example, an employee works for a construction company and part of his or her job is to drive the company pickup truck from one job site to another. One day the employee has a traffic accident by negligently turning left in front of an oncoming automobile. The employee is liable because he or she was negligent, but the company is also liable under the doctrine of *respondeat superior*.

Also, an employer who knows or should know that an employee has a propensity for committing tortious acts is liable for the employee's acts even if they would not ordinarily be considered within the scope of employment.

When an employee goes on a frolic of his or her own—that is, departs from the employer's business to take care of personal affairs—is the employer liable? It depends. If the employee's activity is a substantial departure akin to an utter abandonment of the employer's business, the employer is not liable.

For example, Clint, a traveling salesperson, is driving his employer's automobile to call on a customer for a possible sales order. On the way to the customer's place of business, Clint deviates one block from his usual route to mail a letter at the post office. As Clint approaches the post office, Clint negligently runs into a parked vehicle owned by Doug. Clint's departure from the employer's business to take care of a personal affair is not substantial. Clint is still within the scope of his employment, and his employer is liable to Doug.

If Clint decided to pick up a few friends for cocktails in another city and in the process negligently ran the vehicle into Doug, Doug normally could not hold Clint's employer liable; only Clint would be liable in this case.

The court considers the following general factors in determining whether an agent's particular tort occurred within the course or scope of employment:

1. Was the act authorized by the employer?
2. What was the time, place, and purpose of the act?

3. Was the act one commonly performed by employees on behalf of their employers?
4. What was the extent to which the employer's interest was advanced by the act?
5. What was the extent to which the private interests of the employee were involved?
6. Did the employer furnish the means or instrumentality (for example, a truck or a machine) that caused the injury?
7. Did the employer have reason to know that the employee would do the act in question, and had the employee ever done it before?
8. Did the act involve the commission of a serious crime?

The following case is a classic in employer-employee law. Although it is over 150 years old, the legal principle it represents is still applicable today.

BACKGROUND AND FACTS   *The plaintiff was walking across Bishopsgatestreet when he was knocked down by a cart driven negligently by an employee of the defendant. The plaintiff suffered a fractured leg and multiple injuries. The plaintiff took the position that the defendant was liable for his injuries because the defendant's employee was driving the cart that caused the injuries. The defendant argued that his cart was never driven in the neighborhood in which the plaintiff was injured. Moreover, it was suggested that the defendant's employee had gone out of his way for his own purposes and might have taken the cart at a time when it was not wanted for business purposes to pay a visit to some friends.*

Case 15.5
JOEL v. MORISON
Court of Exchequer, England, 1834.
6 Carrington & Payne Reports 501.

PARKE, Judge.
*   *   *   *

His Lordship afterwards, in summing up, said—This is an action to recover damages for an injury sustained by the plaintiff, in consequence of the negligence of the defendant's servant. There is no doubt that the plaintiff has suffered the injury, and there is no doubt that the driver of the cart was guilty of negligence, and there is no doubt also that the master, if that person was driving the cart on his master's business, is responsible. If the servants, being on their master's business, took a detour to call upon a friend, the master will be responsible. If you think the servants lent the cart to a person who was driving without the defendant's knowledge, he will not be responsible. Or, if you think that the young man who was driving took the cart surreptitiously, and was not at the time employed on his master's business, the defendant will not be liable. The master is only liable where the servant is acting in the course of his employment. If he was going out of his way, against his master's implied commands, when driving on his master's business, he will make his master liable; but if he was going on a frolic of his own, without being at all on his master's business, the master will not be liable. As to the damages, the master *   *   * [although not himself] guilty of any offence, *   *   * is only responsible in law, therefore the amount should be reasonable.

DECISION AND   *The jury found that the employee was pursuing his employer's business,*
REMEDY   *thus holding the employer liable for the harm done to the plaintiff. The plaintiff was awarded damages of £30 (about $50). In this case, the employer was held liable for the acts of his employee.*

Misrepresentation   Whenever a third person sustains losses because of the agent's misrepresentation, the principal is exposed to tort liability. The key to a principal's liability is whether the agent was actually or apparently authorized to make representations and whether such representations were made within the scope of the agency.

When a principal has placed an agent in a position to defraud a third party, the principal is liable for the agent's fraudulent acts. For example, Harmon is a loan officer for State Employees Credit Union. In the ordinary course of her job, Harmon approves and services loans and has access to the credit records of all customers. Harmon calls Lopez, a member of the credit union who has an outstanding loan. Harmon falsely represents to Lopez that the credit union believes that Lopez is about to default on his loan and will call in the loan (meaning that Lopez must pay the loan in full) unless he provides additional collateral such as stocks and bonds. Lopez gives Harmon numerous stock certificates that Harmon keeps in her own possession. She later uses them to make personal investments, and she loses money on all these investments. The credit union is liable to Lopez for losses sustained on the stocks, even though the credit union had no direct role or knowledge of the fraudulent scheme.

The principal (the credit union) placed the agent (Harmon) in a position that conveys to third persons (such as Lopez) the impression that Harmon had the authority to make statements and perform acts consistent with the ordinary duties of the position. When an agent appears to be acting within the scope of the authority that the position of agency confers but is actually taking advantage of a third party, the principal who placed the agent in that position is liable. For example, if a security guard had told Lopez that the credit union required additional security for a loan, Lopez would not be justified in relying on that person's authority to make that representation. Lopez could reasonably expect, however, that the loan officer was telling the truth.

Intentional Torts   The employer may be liable for intentional torts of the employee committed within the scope of employment. In this area, the employer's liability is very limited. For example, an employer may be liable in some states for an employee's intentional torts, such as assault and battery or false imprisonment, committed while acting within the time and work space of his or her employment and while he or she is trying to further the employer's business.

For example, Duffy's Tavern employs Vicious Vic as a bouncer, knowing that he has a history of arrests for assault and battery. While he is working one night within the scope of his employment, he viciously attacks a patron who "looks at him funny." Duffy's Tavern will bear the responsibility for Vicious Vic's assault and battery because it knew he had a propensity for committing such acts and because he committed this tort during the normal course of his job.

Termination of the Agency Relationship

An agency can be terminated either by an act of the parties or by operation of law. Once the relationship between the principal and agent has ended, the agent no longer has the right to bind the principal. The principal must notify third persons when the agency has been ended in order to stop an agent's apparent authority.

Termination by Act of the Parties

Often the agency agreement sets out the time period during which the agency relationship will exist. The agency ends when that time expires. If no definite time is stated, the agency continues for a reasonable time and can be terminated at will by either party. A reasonable time depends on the circumstances and the nature of the agency relationship.

An agent can be employed to accomplish a particular objective, such as the purchase of a computer system for a business. In this case, the agency relationship automatically ends after the computer system has been purchased.

Parties can cancel (rescind) a contract by mutually agreeing to terminate the contractual relationship. For example, Leslie no longer wants Cisco to be her agent, and Cisco does not want to work for Leslie any longer. Either Leslie or Cisco can communicate with the other the intent to end the relationship. Agreement to terminate the agency relationship effectively relieves each party of the rights, duties, and powers inherent in the relationship.

Termination by Operation of Law

The general rule is that death or insanity of either the principal or the agent automatically and immediately terminates the ordinary agency relationship. Knowledge of the death is not required. For example, Cassie sends Marcia to Mexico to purchase a rare coin. Before Marcia makes the purchase, Cassie dies. Marcia's status as an agent ends at the moment of death, even though Marcia does not know that Cassie has died.

An exception to this rule applies to banks. UCC 4-405 allows banks to honor checks up to ten days after the death of their customers. A bank cannot honor payment of notes or drafts after death, however.

When the specific subject matter of an agency is destroyed or lost, the agency terminates. For example, Priscilla employs Mark to sell her house. Prior to any sale, the house is destroyed by a hurricane. Mark's agency and authority to sell Priscilla's house are both ended. In addition, when it is impossible for the agent to perform the agency's responsibilities lawfully because of war or because of a change in the law, the agency is terminated.

When an event occurs that has such an unusual effect on the subject matter of the agency that the agent can reasonably infer that the principal will not want the agency to continue, the agency terminates. Priscilla hires Aaron to sell a tract of land for $1 million. Subsequently, Aaron learns that the soil is contaminated with toxic substances, and the land is now worth $50,000. The agency and Aaron's authority to sell the land for $1 million are both terminated.

Notice Required for Termination

When an agency terminates by operation of law because of death, insanity, or some other unforeseen circumstance, no duty exists to notify third persons. If, however, the parties themselves have terminated the agency, the principal has the duty to inform any third parties who knew of the existence of the agency that it has been terminated.

The principal is expected to notify directly any third person whom the principal knows has dealt with the agent. For third persons who have heard about the agency but have not dealt with the agent, constructive notice is sufficient. In other words, a notice should be published in a newspaper within the general area or in commercial journals for technical employees, stating that the agent is no longer employed by the principal. Until notice is given, the agent retains apparent authority for a reasonable length of time.

Regulation of the Employer-Employee Relationship

Many statutory provisions adopted at both the federal and the state levels control the employer-employee relationship. A body of common law, however, also exists that has direct application to this relationship.

Employment Contracts

Employer-employee relationships are generally created by a contract. The contract basically gives the employer the right to control the employee's conduct, workplace, work habits, and the benefits enjoyed within the scope of the employee's employment.

An employment contract is a mutual agreement between the employer and the employee. Basic contract rules apply. The parties can include any contract terms they desire, as long as these terms are not in violation of a statute or against public policy. For example, a contract today for an hourly wage of $1.00 is in violation of the Fair Labor Standards Act and is illegal.

In some employment contracts, an employee agrees that, should she or he ever leave her or his employment for whatever reason, she or he will not accept employment with a competitor. This clause in the employment contract is called a *covenant not to compete*. If the scope of the prohibition is reasonable in geographic area and duration, the covenant is generally enforceable.

Modern View on Termination of Employees

If termination of the employment breaches the employment contract, the employee can seek damages, but most employment situations are created without a written employment contract and are called "employment at will." In this case, a person can be terminated at any time and has no course of action against the employer.

This situation has led to abuses by employers. In some states, specific statutes have been passed to protect an employee from an arbitrary termination after she or he has been employed for a specified period of time. Specific grounds must be set out before a person can be fired.

Other states without statutory provisions have attempted through the courts to create certain rights for employees. For example, an employee manual given to all employees has been interpreted to be the employment contract in the absence of a contract. If an employer establishes certain procedures in the manual, these procedures must be followed before an employee can be fired, or the employer will be held liable for breach of contract.

In addition, an employer cannot terminate an employee for failing to follow instructions that would force the employee to break the law. In the following case, the court grants damages for termination of employment because the plaintiff refused to break the law.

Case 15.6
WAGENSELLER v. SCOTTSDALE MEMORIAL HOSPITAL
Arizona Supreme Court, 1985.
147 Ariz. 370, 710 P.2d 1025.

BACKGROUND AND FACTS *Wagenseller was employed by the Scottsdale Memorial Hospital from March 1975 until November 1979. Her supervisor was Kay Smith. She was promoted over the years and received very favorable comments from Smith in her reviews until May 1979.*

In May, both Smith and Wagenseller joined a group of personnel from other hospitals for an eight-day camping and rafting trip down the Colorado River. Smith and others during the trip engaged in public urination, heavy drinking, "grouping up" with other rafters, staging a parody of the song "Moon River" that concluded with members of the group "mooning" the audience, and other similar activities. The "Moon River" skit was allegedly performed twice at the hospital after the trip. Wagenseller refused to participate in any of these activities. After the trip, the relationship between her and Smith deteriorated, and finally Wagenseller was terminated. Wagenseller was an at-will employee.

The trial court entered a summary judgment in favor of the hospital. The appellate court affirmed in part and reversed in part that decision. Wagenseller then appealed to the Arizona Supreme Court.

FELDMAN, Justice.
     *   *   * The issues we address are:
     1. Is an employer's right to terminate an at-will employee limited by any rules which, if breached, give rise to a cause of action for wrongful termination?

2. If "public policy" or some other doctrine does form the basis for such an action, how is it determined?

3. Did the trial court err * * * when it determined as a matter of law that the terms of Scottsdale Memorial Hospital's personnel policy manual were not part of the employment contract?

* * * *

As early as 1562, the English common law presumed that an employment contract containing an annual salary provision or computation was for a one-year term. Originally designed for the protection of seasonal farm workers, the English rule expanded over the years to protect factory workers as well. Workers were well protected under this rule, for the one-year presumption was not easy to overcome. English courts held an employer liable for breaching the employment contract if he terminated an employee at any time during the year without "reasonable cause to do so." To uphold an employer's discharge of an employee without a showing of "good cause," the courts required a clear expression of a contrary intent as evidenced either on the face of the contract or by a clearly defined custom of the industry.

In the early nineteenth century, American courts borrowed the English rule. The legal rationale embodied in the rule was consistent with the nature of the predominant master-servant employment relationship at the time because it reflected the master's duty to make provision for the general well-being of his servants. In addition, the master was under a duty to employ the servant for a term, either a specified or implied time of service, and could not terminate him strictly at will. The late nineteenth century, however, brought the Industrial Revolution; with it came the decline of the master-servant relationship and the rise of the more impersonal employer-employee relationship. In apparent response to the economic changes sweeping the country, American courts abandoned the English rule and adopted the employment-at-will doctrine. This new doctrine gave the employer freedom to terminate an at-will employee for any reason, good or bad.

* * * *

The trend has been to modify the at-will rule by creating exceptions to its operation. Three general exceptions have developed. The most widely accepted approach is the "public policy" exception, which permits recovery upon a finding that the employer's conduct undermined some important public policy. The second exception, based on contract, requires proof of an implied-in-fact promise of employment for a specific duration, as found in the circumstances surrounding the employment relationship, including assurances of job security in company personnel manuals or memoranda. Under the third approach, courts have found in the employment contract an implied-in-law covenant of "good faith and fair dealing" and have held employers liable in both contract and tort for breach of that covenant.

* * *

* * * *

We therefore adopt the public policy exception to the at-will termination rule. We hold that an employer may fire for good cause or for no cause. He may not fire for bad cause—that which violates public policy. * * *

* * * *

In the case before us, Wagenseller refused to participate in activities which arguably would have violated our indecent exposure statute. She claims that she was fired because of this refusal. * * *

While this statute may not embody a policy which "strikes at the heart of a citizen's social right, duties and responsibilities" as clearly and forcefully as a statute prohibiting perjury, we believe that it was enacted to preserve and protect the commonly recognized sense of public privacy and decency. The statute does, therefore, recognize bodily privacy as a "citizen's social right." * * *

* * * *

* * * Arizona is among the jurisdictions that have recognized the implied-in-fact contract term as an exception to the at-will rule. In *Leikvold v. Valley View Community Hospital,* * * * this court held that a personnel manual can become part of an employment contract and remanded the cause for a jury determination as to whether the particular manual given to Leikvold had become part of her employment contract with Valley View.

* * * *

* * * Employers are certainly free to issue no personnel manual at all or to issue a personnel manual that clearly and conspicuously tells their employees that the manual is not part of the employment contract and that their jobs are terminable at the will of the employer with or without reason. Such actions, either not issuing a personnel manual or issuing one with clear language of limitation, instill no reasonable expectations of job security and do not give employees any reason to rely on representations in the manual. However, if an employer does choose to issue a policy statement, in a manual or otherwise, and, by its language or by the employer's actions, encourages reliance thereon, the employer cannot be free to only selectively abide by it. Having announced a policy, the employer may not treat it as illusory.

DECISION AND REMEDY

The Arizona Supreme Court adopted the "public policy" exception to the at-will termination rule. The court found that Scottsdale Memorial Hospital possibly had illegally terminated the plaintiff because she refused to participate in conduct that would have been a violation of law. Because of this possibility, Wagenseller was entitled to a jury trial in which she could try to show that her termination was caused by her refusal to perform some act contrary to public policy. An issue also existed as to whether the employee manual could form the basis of an employment contract when there is no other written contract. The court held that she had a right to have this issue tried before a jury.

Government Regulation of Employment Law

Employment law today has many aspects that are controlled by government regulation. Federal and state laws govern the relationship between management and labor. Discrimination on the basis of sex, race, national origin, religious beliefs, and other invidious classifications are forbidden by statutes. We examine the government's role in employment law in Chapters 21 and 22.

FACING A LEGAL ISSUE   Do You Have to Pull the Trigger?

You are hired at Lucky Lasso, Inc., a restaurant with a western theme, to work as a waiter. The hours are long and the pay is minimal. The restaurant is not attracting enough customers. Your boss and the owner of the restaurant decide to obtain more visibility by having their employees present a show that requires the use of guns. Your boss instructs you to inflate a huge balloon that, when inflated, looks like a dog. Assume both of these actions are illegal under state and local law: The use of guns in public is a felony, and the use of the balloon constitutes an advertising sign in violation of the local zoning laws.

At first, you and your coworkers decide not to participate, but you are informed that any employee who refuses to take part will be fired. You need the job, so you agree to participate. During one show, live ammunition is used accidentally instead of the usual blanks. A spectator is shot. He falls over and knocks a candle off the table, igniting a bale of hay and causing a fire that destroys the building next door. The local newspapers and television news programs decide to emphasize the show and accident. The police arrest all employees who were onstage during the show for assault with a deadly weapon.

Because of the publicity, the restaurant prospers. Your employer retains a lawyer for all of the employees, but you are all found guilty of a reduced charge. Having never been arrested before, you do not want a repeat conviction on your record. You decide not to take part in future performances and are fired. Shortly afterward, you are sued by the spectator with a civil complaint for his injuries, which add up to

$150,000 in medical and hospital bills and $300,000 for pain and suffering. You are also sued by the owner of the destroyed building for damages in the amount of $250,000.

The above facts are ones with which an employee could be confronted. An employer can create a situation where the employee is required to commit a crime for which, if apprehended, he or she could be prosecuted and found guilty. In addition, the employee can be held liable in a civil lawsuit. Following your employer's directions is not a legal defense in criminal or civil lawsuits, and it does not matter whether you were instructed to violate the law in the manner described in this example, to violate the antitrust laws, to pay off corrupt officials, or to commit any other crime. Similarly, you are liable for civil damages as a result of your own torts whether your employer is liable or not.

In this case, because the injuries and damages were caused by a gun, you would probably be liable under strict liability rules. In other words, you would be held liable if you were the one who pulled the trigger, despite the fact that you did not intend to harm anyone. Liability insurance would not be applicable because the use of guns and other ultrahazardous activities are normally excluded from coverage.

Based on the facts in this case and the case of *Wagenseller v. Scottsdale Memorial Hospital,* you would have a valid claim for future wages because of your illegal termination. Even though you were an at-will employee, the modern trend is to allow recovery when an employee relationship is terminated because the employee refused to follow instructions that would constitute violations of the state law.

Summary

This chapter emphasizes the private relationship of the employment sphere. This body of law has its origins in the legal principles concerning the ownership of slaves. During the Middle Ages, the principles were expanded to cover the master-servant relationship. With the Industrial Revolution, the law developed the concepts of principal and agent. The distinction between employer-employee and principal-agent is that an employee does not enter into contracts on behalf of his or her employer while an agent does on behalf of his or her principal. A person can be both an employee and an agent. Basically, the same rules apply whether it is an employer-employee or principal-agent relationship.

The concept underlying these relationships is summarized by this phrase: ''He [or she] who acts through another acts through himself [or herself].'' The theory is that, if a company increases its business through the use of employees, the company should be responsible for the acts of those employees. The company, however, should not be liable if it cannot control the acts of an individual, unless the company has a legal duty to ensure such control. The general rule is that a company is not liable for acts of independent contractors unless the company has delegated one of its own legal duties to that contractor.

An agency relationship can be created by agreement, by ratification, or by estoppel. The most common means is by agreement. Ratification occurs when an agent who has no authority acts in the name of a principal or when an agent exceeds his or her limited authority, and the principal lets the action stand. Apparent authority applies when an agent is terminated but continues to act for the former principal.

The agent owes certain duties to the principal. The agent must not act in a negligent manner, must notify the principal of important facts, owes a high degree of loyalty and obedience, and must account to the principal for all property that is in the control of the agent. The principal owes a duty to compensate the agent, to reimburse the agent for expenditures incurred in the performance of the agency, to cooperate with the agent, and to provide safe working conditions.

Both the principal and agent can be held liable to third persons. An agent has either express or apparent authority. A principal is liable for any torts or contracts concluded within this authority. An agent is normally not responsible for contracts unless she or he has exceeded the authority granted or is acting for a partially disclosed or an undisclosed principal. An agent is always responsible for her or his own torts, even if the principal is also liable under the doctrine of *respondeat superior*.

An agency relationship may be terminated when the date stated in the employment contract is reached, when the purpose is achieved, by mutual agreement or whenever either party decides to terminate, by death or insanity of either party, by impossibility or illegality, and by bankruptcy of the principal. On termination, notice should be given to anyone dealing with the agency, and a notice of termination should be published to inform anyone who has never dealt with the agency.

Most employment involves employment at will. Historically, an employer could terminate an employee for any reason. This doctrine has changed. The law now gives employees some rights; in particular, a person cannot fire an employee for refusing to violate the law.

Key Terms

actual authority **372**
agency law **368**
agent **368**
apparent authority **372**
derivative authority **371**
disclosed principal **381**
doctrine of *respondeat
    superior* **382**

express authority **372**
fiduciary **378**
gratuitous agency **380**
implied authority **372**
implied warranty of authority
    382
independent contractor **374**

legal fiction **378**
partially disclosed principal
    381
principal **368**
professional agent **374**
undisclosed principal **381**

Questions and Case Problems

1. Roy makes deliveries for a local pizza restaurant. Roy drives the company car with the restaurant's telephone number printed on the side. One day, after a delivery but while still on duty, Roy picks up three of his friends who need a ride into the next town. Figuring that the restaurant is so busy that he won't be missed, he agrees to take them. While in the next town, Roy accidentally backs into Mr. Phillip's truck, putting a small dent in the truck's bumper. Because it is such a small dent and because Roy needs to get back to work, he leaves without writing a note to the truck's owner. When he arrives back at work, Tony, the owner of the restaurant, is waiting for him. Mr. Phillips had been watching his truck from a window in his apartment; he saw the accident and the telephone number on the side of the car. When he called the telephone number, he reached Tony. Who is responsible for the cost of fixing Mr. Phillip's bumper? Discuss fully.

2. Able is hired by Peters as a traveling salesperson. Able not only solicits orders but also delivers the goods and collects payments from his customers. Able places all payments in his private checking account and at the end of each month withdraws sufficient cash from his bank to cover the payments made. Peters is totally unaware of this procedure. Because of a slowdown in the economy, Peters tells all his salespeople to offer 20 percent discounts on orders. Able solicits orders, but he offers only 15 percent discounts, pocketing the extra 5 percent paid by customers. Able has not lost any orders by this practice, and he is rated one of Peters's top salespeople. Peters now learns of Able's actions. Discuss fully Peters's rights in this matter.

3. Paula owes Adam $1,000, and the debt is due and payable. Paula does not have the cash to pay the debt, but she has some stereo equipment valued at $1,800. Paula gives Adam the authority to sell the stereo equipment to satisfy the debt, with any surplus being paid back to Paula. Later Paula and Adam have a severe disagreement over another matter, and Paula sends a letter to Adam terminating his authority and agency to sell the stereo equipment. In spite of this letter, Adam contracts to sell the equipment to Francis for $1,200. Francis pays Adam, but Paula refuses to turn over the stereo equipment to Francis or to accept the $200 from Adam. Paula claims that, at the time the contract with Francis was made, no agency existed. Discuss fully Paula's contention.

4. Mark is a pilot for the Big Canyon Tour Company. He flies passengers into the canyon to photograph the view. Over the past few years, he has been honored with all but one of Big Canyon's employee awards for outstanding service. The state legislature has passed a law that prohibits all aircraft from flying below the rim of the canyon. Wayne, the owner of Big Canyon Tour Company, has told all the pilots to ignore the new law because the quality of the view available without flying below the rim of the canyon is poor. Mark has refused to break this law even though he has been threatened with losing his job if he does not follow company orders. Mark, an at-will employee, is fired. Is Mark entitled to damages of any kind? Discuss fully.

5. Anne is an agent for Fish Galore, Inc. She has express authority to solicit orders and receive payments in advance of shipment. She is well known as an agent in the region. Seafood Quality has been a regular customer of hers for five years, has usually made large orders, and has always paid Anne in advance to get the discount offered by Fish Galore. Fish Galore learns that Anne has incurred large gambling debts and has recently used some of the customers' payments to pay off these debts. When Anne cannot reimburse Fish Galore, she is fired. Fish Galore hires a new agent and publishes in the regional newspapers that the new agent will be covering the territory. Desperately in need of cash, Anne solicits a large order from Seafood Quality and receives payment. Then she calls on a new customer, Catfish Heaven, who also gives Anne an order and payment. Anne absconds with the money. Fish Galore refuses to honor either order. Seafood Quality and Catfish Heaven claim Fish Galore is in breach of contract. Discuss fully their claims.

6. Michael Smith leased a car from the Marshall Berwick Leasing Company. In the lease was an insurance policy that included an uninsured motorist liability limit of $10,000. This insurance, although not mentioned by name, was actually with the American Auto Insurance Company (AAIC). This master policy had been issued to Berwick so that it could offer coverage to long-term automobile lessees. Later, Smith, as a pedestrian, was hit by a car that was driven by an uninsured motorist. After it was determined that no actual authority existed to bind American Auto Insurance Company, Smith claimed benefits under AAIC's policy, stating that AAIC was an apparent agent. Considering the fact that there was no representation made to Smith by AAIC with respect to Berwick's authority to act as its agent, can Smith establish apparent authority to collect $10,000? Discuss fully. [Smith v. American Auto Insurance Co., 498 So.2d 448 (Fla.App. 1986)]

7. Roy Haven brought a medical malpractice action against his surgeon, Dr. Judson Randolph and the hospital where his surgery had been performed. Haven claimed that the doctor's negligence had caused him to suffer paralysis as a result of minor surgery. Haven also wished to hold the hospital responsible as Randolph's principal. Randolph was not employed by the hospital, and any services that the hospital provided were at Randolph's direction. Would

Randolph be deemed an agent of the hospital? Discuss fully. [Haven v. Randolph, 342 F.Supp. 538 (D.D.C. 1972)]

8. During the course of the administration of the estate of Baldwin M. Baldwin, it became necessary to sell a vast apartment complex owned by the estate, known as Baldwin Hills Village. Lemby, a real estate broker doing business as Skyline Realty, was commissioned to make the sale. A number of prospective purchasers were contacted, and they were present at the private sale of Baldwin Hills Village. On a number of prior occasions, Lemby had indicated to the executors of Baldwin's estate that he was interested in purchasing the property. At the private sale, Lemby outbid all others and bought Baldwin Hills Village. Lemby then sought his commission on the sale from the Baldwin estate. Will anything in agency law prevent Lemby from recovering? Discuss fully. [In re Estate of Baldwin, 34 Cal.App. 3d 596, 110 Cal.Rptr. 189 (1973)]

9. Hohenberg Brothers was a Memphis-based cotton merchandiser, and Killebrew was a Mississippi cotton farmer. Both parties were represented by D. T. Syle, Jr., a cotton agent. In February 1973, Killebrew signed and delivered to Syle a one-page purchase and sales agreement form covering the sale of Killebrew's 1973 cotton crop. All of the blanks in this document were completed, except for the name and signature of the purchaser, who was still unknown. On March 2, Syle secured an oral commitment that Hohenberg would purchase Killebrew's crop at the prices set forth in the one-page contract. Hohenberg immediately sent Syle its standard three-page purchase and sales agreement, the terms of which were identical to Killebrew's one-page document. Syle signed Killebrew's name and returned it to Hohenberg. Has Syle acted beyond the scope of his agency in signing Killebrew's name? Discuss fully. [Hohenberg Brothers Co. v. Killebrew, 505 F.2d 643 (5th Cir. 1974)]

10. Alaska Mack Trucks of Fairbanks is a dealer and franchisee of Mack, Inc., of Allentown, Pennsylvania. As part of the franchise agreement, Mack allowed Alaska Mack to use the name "Mack"; Alaska Mack was listed in the telephone directory under the heading "MACK TRUCKS"; the Mack bulldog was displayed on the Alaska Mack building; and the Mack logo was on Alaska Mack's posters, printed Mack brochures, and promotional materials. Further, a distributorship agreement existed between Alaska Mack and Mack, Inc.; Mack provided training for the distributorship's employees; Mack engaged in national advertising programs and in joint advertising with the distributor; and Mack established sales quotas and required reports as to the use of the vehicles sold.

The city of Delta Junction, Alaska, entered into a contract with Alaska Mack Trucks for a fire truck. The truck was modified by Alaska Mack to carry a 5,000-gallon tank on it. After delivery, the truck exceeded the specifications for total gross weight, and it was dangerous to drive. The city brought action against Alaska Mack and Mack, Inc. Did Alaska Mack have apparent authority to act as an agent for Mack, Inc., and did the act of modifying the truck exceed the possible limits of any apparent authority? Discuss fully. [City of Delta Junction v. Mack Trucks, Inc., 670 P.2d 1128 (Alaska 1983)]

UNIT III BUSINESS FORMATION

Chapter 16 Business Enterprises: Sole Proprietorships and Partnerships

It is a socialist idea that making profits is a vice. I consider the real vice is making losses.

Sir Winston Churchill (1874–1965)

OUTLINE

Introduction

Many people consider owning a business at some point in their lives. A common belief is that, when people are in business for themselves, they set their own hours, are their own boss, and make a comfortable living. Although this belief has some validity, the sad truth is that most small businesses fail.

Many reasons exist for the large number of failures among small businesses. They include lack of planning, of financing, of effective marketing strategies, of good management structures, and of consideration of the legal issues. If a business employs fewer than twenty employees, there is almost a 91 percent chance of failure in the first ten years.

This chapter will examine three different forms of businesses: **sole proprietorships, partnerships**, and **limited partnerships**. This chapter also includes a discussion of the Bulk Sales Act.

A sole proprietorship is a business owned by one person. A partnership is a business that is run for profit in which two or more people have an undivided (and sometimes unequal) ownership interest. In a limited partnership two or more people own the business, and at least one person, called the **general partner**, has unlimited liability, while the **limited partner(s)** have limited liability. This type of business entity is often used as an investment vehicle and for tax benefits.

Comparing Business Enterprises

Knowing the different forms of business entities can help you make the proper decisions when starting a business. The four entities most often considered are a sole proprietorship, a general partnership, a limited partnership, and a corporation. A corporation is by far the most complex of any business entity. Corporations are discussed in detail in Chapter 17.

In deciding which form to adopt, you should take into consideration the following factors, among many others:

- Difficulty of forming the organization
- Liability

- Tax considerations
- Continuity of existence and ability to transfer ownership
- Management and control
- Financing and licenses

Each of these factors has legal as well as business ramifications. Decisions on each of these issues help determine which business form best suits the needs of the owners, since each type of business organization has its own advantages and disadvantages.

Difficulty of Forming the Organization

Some business organizations are easier to create than others. A sole proprietorship is the easiest because a person merely starts doing business. The person may have to obtain a business license from the city or county before starting, but no legal formalities are demanded by the state. If the person is going to use a business name other than his or her own, he or she may be required to file a fictitious name. A **fictitious name filing** consists of filing with the state a simple form that gives the proprietor's real name and address and the name under which business will be conducted. This notifies the public that a particular person is participating in this business.

A partnership is similarly easy to form. Two or more people simply conduct a business for profit. A person may even be in a partnership without realizing it. Again, besides obtaining a business license or filing for the use of a fictitious name, no legal formalities are required. All states, however, have legal requirements that must be met before a limited partnership or a corporation can do business. Although a limited partnership is created initially by agreement, to form a limited partnership the parties must execute a certificate of limited partnership, and the certificate must be filed in the appropriate state office (in most states with the secretary of state).

Liability

A businessperson may be financially liable to a variety of people, such as customers, guests on the property, and at times even trespassers. Financial liability may stem from a negligent act of the businessperson, such as failure to keep the business premises free of hazards, or from a product liability case (discussed in Chapter 12). Sole proprietors and general partners have unlimited liability. This means that, if the sole proprietor or partnership (or partner) is successfully sued, the person who has obtained a judgment may seek to have the judgment paid out of the assets of the business *and* out of the personal assets of the sole proprietor or general partner.

Personal liability is limited in the case of a limited partner or an owner of a corporation. A limited partner, for example, is liable generally to the extent of his or her investment in the limited partnership. With a corporation, the owners are the shareholders, and their liability generally is limited to their investment in the shares.

Tax Considerations

The federal and state tax laws must be considered in deciding on a type of business organization, and the income tax law is usually the most important. No tax advantages are available to a business operated as a sole proprietorship. Because it is not a legal entity separate from the owner, it does not file any tax returns. The sole proprietor reports and pays taxes on the income earned.

Partnerships and limited partnerships are not subject to income tax. Each must file with the government an informational return. The income or deductions are passed from the partnership to the individual partner, who is subject to income tax laws.

A corporation is taxed as an entity on its income. In addition, stockholders who are paid dividends are subject to individual income tax laws. Depending on the current tax laws and the amount of income involved, the income tax rates for individuals may be higher or lower than the tax rates for corporations (called C corporations in the federal tax laws). Federal tax laws currently allow corporations that meet specific guidelines to qualify for various tax breaks. These are called S corporations, and they are discussed in more detail in Chapter 17. Some states have more favorable tax laws for businesses than other states.

Continuity of Existence and Ability to Transfer Ownership

A sole proprietorship usually exists as long as the owner is able to work. Once the person becomes incapacitated or dies, the business ends, and any sale of the business normally takes place only after a probate case has been opened in court. Even if the person is alive and well, the business may be hard to sell for any number of reasons, including whether there is a market for this type of business. Often only the assets of the business are salable. If the sale includes inventory, the Bulk Sales Act provisions of the Uniform Commercial Code discussed later in this chapter must be followed.

A partnership is dissolved whenever a new partner is added or a current partner dies or otherwise leaves the business. Although the partnership is technically dissolved, the business may continue under the new partnership formed by the change in personnel. Selling a partnership interest may be difficult, again depending on the market. The same holds true for a limited partnership.

Corporate ownership is usually sold by the selling of the owner's shares of stock. If a corporation's shares are listed on a major stock exchange, the transfer of the shares is relatively easy because a structured market exists. For a corporation that does not have its shares sold on a stock exchange, selling the stock may be difficult or nearly impossible. In this situation, people are often willing to buy the physical assets of the corporation but not an ownership interest in the corporation. A purchaser may be reluctant to buy an ownership interest because of an outstanding liability that the corporation may have. For example, an employee is at fault in an accident with a company automobile in January 1989. The corporation is sold in July 1989. A lawsuit is filed against the corporation in December 1989. The corporation is found liable in an amount that bankrupts it. If the person had purchased only the corporation's assets, he or she would not be liable for the harm caused by the automobile accident.

Management and Control

A sole proprietor has total management and control over his or her business. With a partnership arrangement, in absence of agreement, each partner has as much management and control as the other partners. Thus, each partner has one vote in management matters regardless of the proportionate size of his or her interest in the partnership. This can lead to major problems if the partners do not agree on the same business strategy. In a limited partnership, the general partners have the responsibility of management and control.

In a corporation, the shareholders elect a board of directors, who in turn hire officers to manage the activities of the corporation. Therefore the shareholders, through the election of the board of directors, control and manage the corporation.

Financing

A sole proprietor obtains loans based on her or his personal worth, which includes the assets of the business. The same may be true of general partnerships unless the partnership has a lengthy business record; then the loans may be made on the strength of the partnership's assets and business abilities, rather than on the creditworthiness of the individual partners. Since a limited partner's liability is generally limited to his or her capital investment in the partnership, loans are made more on the basis of the value of the limited partnership assets.

Corporations raise money by selling shares. A corporation may also obtain loans based on the strength of its assets and business record. A lending institution, however, that is dealing with a new corporation or one with few shareholders may require the individual shareholders or officers to be personally liable for the corporate loans in case the corporation fails. For example, a ten-year-old

corporation is owned by a family. The bank may require each shareholder to guarantee personally the corporation's $15 million operating line of credit.

Licenses

A businessperson must consider which licenses are needed in order to conduct business. Almost all states require some type of sales or use tax license, since a business is required to collect taxes to be remitted to the state from its customers. In addition, many businesses are subject to specific regulations. For example, licenses are required for insurance agents, real estate brokers, contractors, exterminators, sellers of regulated products such as alcohol, guns, or explosives, and operators of such businesses as pawnshops, funeral homes, nursing homes, day-care centers, and food preparation businesses. Most regulated businesses must obtain a specific license.

The importance of having a license cannot be overemphasized, especially when the purpose of the licensing statute is to regulate and not to raise revenues. Any contract entered into by an unlicensed individual whose business is required to have a license may be void if the purpose of the statute is to regulate the business or profession. In addition, if an individual should conduct business without a license under these circumstances, it may result in criminal prosecution and civil liability, including the inability to collect amounts owed on contracts that the business has completed.

The following case reviews the reasons why a license is required and what happens when a person fails to obtain one.

Case 16.1
GROSS v. BAYSHORE LAND CO.
Supreme Court of Alaska, 1985.
710 P.2d 1007.

BACKGROUND AND FACTS *Bayshore is a corporation in the business of subdividing land and selling lots, primarily to builders. Gross is a self-employed general contractor in the business of building houses. Gross had used the name Creative Builders, Inc., for many years.*

Gross entered into a contract with Bayshore Land Company to purchase nine lots. Part of the contract required Gross to construct houses on them. Gross did not hold a contractor's license at the time of entering into the contract, but had held one prior to that time. Bayshore required payment of one-half of the money down, with the other half being due once the homes were completed and sold. Gross obtained a loan commitment from the Alaska Bank of Commerce in order to purchase the lots, on the condition that the bank would have a first lien on the property and Bayshore would have a second lien interest.

Bayshore refused to be a second lien holder. It sent a letter to Gross canceling the Gross contract prior to the closing of the nine lots—that is, before the title to the nine lots was put in Gross's name. Gross filed a lawsuit against Bayshore for breach of contract. Among other defenses that Bayshore used, it claimed that Gross had failed to comply with the Alaskan registration requirements and that therefore the contract was void.

The trial court found for Bayshore on other grounds. Gross appealed to the state supreme court. There, Bayshore argued that, even if Bayshore was not correct in any of its other arguments, Gross was barred from filing a lawsuit since he had failed to comply with Alaska's Construction Contractors Registration Act.

BURKE, Justice.
* * * *

A person acting in the capacity of a contractor who is unregistered at the time of contracting is barred from bringing an action in state court for breach of contract. A critical issue in this case is whether the trial court erred in holding * * * that registration as a contractor was not required.
* * * *

A contractor who has not registered at all, not filed the required surety bond, nor obtained insurance has not substantially complied with the registration requirements of [the statute]. The burden of compliance is solely the responsibility of the unlicensed contractor.
* * * *

Gross has not substantially complied with the construction contractor's registration requirements because Gross' failure to register at all prevented the public from ascertaining his status. In fact, state records available to the public at the time of the contract's formation would have shown that Gross had not been registered since 1978, and that Creative Builders was involuntarily dissolved in September 1980. Gross' registration did not lapse for a short period. * * * On the contrary, Gross has not been registered since 1978. Two months before signing the contract, Gross filed and then withdrew his application for registration. Consequently, he was well aware of his non-registered status at the time of contract formation.
* * *

* * * The purchase agreement is a contract for which registration is required. Bayshore is within the class the legislature intended to protect under the contractor's licensing act. Gross was therefore required to register as a contractor. Gross did not substantially comply with the registration requirements because he did not afford the public or Bayshore the same protection which strict compliance would offer.

The trial court's judgment was affirmed. The purchase agreement was a contract for which registration was required. Bayshore was within the class of businesses that the legislature intended to protect under the contractor's licensing act. Gross was, therefore, required to register as a contractor before he could bring a lawsuit.

DECISION AND REMEDY

COMMENT   *In most states, a person must have a contractor's license to construct residential homes. The lack of a license may result in the contractor not being able to bring a lawsuit for any breach of contract committed by others.*

Location

The location of the new business is an important decision regardless of the form you adopt. There are numerous legal restrictions which may determine your choice of location. When reviewing a prospective location, an owner should consider the visibility of the business, including signs that promote it. Many local ordinances control the size, location, and type of signs that can be used. The owner must make certain that the zoning regulations allow his or her type of business, along with the appropriate signs, to be established in a particular location. Obtaining **use permits** and/or **variances** from local governmental bodies may be required. A use permit grants permission to operate a given type of business, while a variance allows an exception to the zoning laws. Chapter 14 discussed other legal issues concerning property that are relevant to businesses.

Partnerships

All but two states have officially adopted the major provisons of the **Uniform Partnership Act** (UPA). If a partnership agreement exists but is silent on certain matters, the UPA supplies the missing provisions. Most sections of the UPA have no application when the partners have made provisions in the agreement addressing that particular area.

A partnership is defined as "an association of two or more persons to carry on as co-owners a business for profit." [UPA Section 6] A partnership agreement is a contract. Although most partnerships are formed pursuant to a partnership agreement among the parties, a partnership may also arise as a result of the conduct of the parties. A sharing of profits from a business, for example, raises a presumption of a partnership. [UPA Section 7(4)] In addition, if the conduct of the parties leads third parties to believe that a partnership

exists, then a partnership may be found to exist legally. This is known as a **partnership by estoppel**. [UPA Section 16]

There is no law that requires a partnership agreement to be in writing. If two or more people decide to operate a business as co-owners for profit, that is all that is required in order for a court to find that a partnership exists. Even though it is not legally required, however, a written document should be prepared whenever the partnership form of business organization is used. Partners are in a very close relationship that is not unlike a marriage; both relationships are based on trust, confidence, and mutual reliance. Misunderstandings, frustrating situations, and disagreements are bound to occur. Through a written partnership agreement, many of these problems can be resolved before they have a chance to escalate.

The statute of frauds (discussed in Chapter 9) requires the agreement to be in writing if the partnership is to last more than one year. Without a written agreement, the partnership is at will, which means that it can be dissolved by a partner at any time.

A partnership is treated as a legal entity for certain purposes. For example, partnership property can be held and transferred in the partnership name. [UPA Section 8] In some states partners can be sued jointly (but as individuals) by a suit filed against the partnership. In most situations, however, the partnership is treated as an "aggregate" of individuals. Thus, property can be held and transferred in the name of an individual partner [UPA Section 10], partners can individually be sued [UPA Section 15], and partners have unlimited individual liability.

Capital Requirements and Funding of a Partnership

A partnership is generally funded through the capital contributions of each partner. The partnership may also be able to obtain credit and loans based

LEGAL HIGHLIGHT
The Uniform Partnership Act of 1914

The National Conference of Commissioners on Uniform State Laws (NCC) first discussed the desirability of a uniform act on partnership law in 1902 at their annual meeting. The Committee on Commercial Law was instructed at that time to oversee the preparation of a draft on partnership law, and during the following decade a number of drafts were prepared.

A major problem for the drafters of the act was determining which theory of partnership should be employed. Under common law, the partnership was interpreted as an *aggregate* of individuals associated in business—this was the theory commonly used in most of the states. An alternate theory regarded the partnership as an *entity*. In order to make the best determination, the committee invited to a 1910 conference in Philadelphia "all the teachers of, and writers on, partnerships, besides several other lawyers known to have made a special study of the subject"— something which, needless to say, would be inconceivable today! At the conclusion of this meeting, the assembled experts recommended that the act be based on the aggregate, or

common-law, theory. Thus, the committee requested that the partnership act be drafted on this basis.

At the 1914 meeting of the NCC, the eighth and final draft of the act was reported to the conference, which passed a resolution recommending the act for adoption by the legislatures of all the states. Thus, after a decade of drafting and deliberation, the Uniform Partnership Act (UPA) became a reality.

The UPA contains forty-five sections and is divided into seven parts. Its laws are applied by the courts whenever a partner or a partnership is involved in a dispute in an area not covered by the express agreement of the partners. All of the law affecting partnerships is not contained in the UPA; it therefore provides that the law of agency and the law of estoppel be followed where applicable, and it further states that, in situations not covered by the act, common law and equity will govern.

The first state to adopt the UPA was Pennsylvania, which did so in 1914; other states followed, and today all of the states except Georgia and Louisiana have adopted the UPA.

on the creditworthiness of all of the partners, plus the creditworthiness of the business itself. In addition, the partners may make loans to the partnership.

Partnership Management and Control

Each partner has an equal right to manage and control the partnership [UPA Section 18(e)] and to use partnership property for an appropriate purpose. [UPA Section 25(2)(a)] These rights can be altered by an agreement among the partners. Each partner is an agent for the partnership and for every other partner. [UPA Section 9] Thus, each partner is in a fiduciary relationship with the other part-

ners, and this relationship imposes a responsibility on each partner to act in good faith for the benefit of the partnership and to consider the mutual welfare of all partners in partnership activities. For example, unless an agreement states otherwise, a partner cannot engage in outside activities that involve the partnership's time.

The partners are not generally entitled to compensation for their management of the partnership's business. [UPA Section 18(f)] The profit of the business is their compensation. In the absence of an agreement, profits are shared equally and losses are shared in the same proportion as profits, or, if an agreement exists, they are shared in the proportion that this agreement sets out. [UPA

Section 18(a)] The amount of capital contributions by the partners has no application in the sharing of profits and losses unless a contrary agreement has been made.

Although the partners may agree to delegate day-to-day management responsibilities to one or more of the partners, generally each partner has one vote in management matters regardless of his or her capital contribution, and a majority vote is usually required for such partnership decisions. [UPA Section 18(b)] The unanimous consent of all the partners, however, is required in matters significantly altering the nature of the partnership business or property. Other actions requiring the consent of all of the partners include: an act by a partner that makes it impossible to carry on the business of the partnership in the usual way; the disposition of the goodwill of the business; and the submission of a partnership dispute to arbitration. [UPA Section 9(3)]

Any act of any partner that apparently carries on the business of the partnership in the usual way binds the partnership to that act. This principle does not apply if the partner has in fact no authority and if the person with whom the partner is dealing knows that there is no authority. [UPA Section 9(1)]

Liability of Partners

Each partner is liable for the entire amount of the partnership's debts. A partner is liable for any act by another partner, even if the act is wrongful, that results in liability for the partnership. [UPA Section 13] This is because, when a partner acts, he or she acts as an agent for the partnership. Such liability can result from either a contract or a tort. [UPA Section 15] A partner is not liable for other partners' debts that are not connected with the business.

In satisfying their claims based on partnership liabilities, creditors can look to the assets of the individual partners after the partnership assets have been exhausted. If a person joins an existing partnership, her or his capital contribution is subject to the claims of prior creditors, but she or he is not personally liable for the prior debts of the partnership. [UPA Section 17] The new partner is personally liable for debts incurred after she or he joins the partnership, just as an original partner would be.

Duration and Termination of the Partnership

A partnership has indefinite duration unless the partnership agreement states a specific time period. The members of the partnership may change, but no person can become a partner without the consent of all of the existing partners, unless the partnership agreement states otherwise. [UPA Section 18(g)]

Ending a partnership is a three-step process: **dissolution**, **winding up**, and **termination**. A new partner, a transfer of a partner's interest in the partnership, a partner's decision to withdraw, or unanimous consent by all the partners will dissolve the original partnership. A partnership is also dissolved: if the business of the partnership becomes unlawful; if the business can only be carried on at a loss or if it becomes bankrupt; if a partner dies, becomes mentally ill, or becomes bankrupt; or if a court orders a dissolution. [UPA Sections 31 and 32]

Dissolution does not mean that the business is automatically terminated. [UPA Section 30] Depending on the circumstances, the business may continue, but it is considered a new entity. When a partnership dissolves, each partner is a co-owner with the other partners of the partnership property.

When dissolution occurs and a new partnership is not going to be formed, then winding up of the business takes place. All the partners must be notified. At this point, the partners can no longer create any new liabilities on behalf of the partnership. The only authority they have is to complete the transactions begun but not yet finished at the time of the dissolution and to wind up the business. [UPA Section 35] Winding up includes collecting and preserving partnership assets, paying debts, and accounting to each partner for the value of her or his partnership interest.

Both creditors of the partnership and creditors of the individual partners can make claims on the partnership's assets. In general, partnership creditors have priority on the partnership assets, and individual creditors have priority on the personal assets of the partners.

When the business has been wound up, it is then terminated. The assets, if any, are distributed in the following order:

1. Debts owed to creditors other than partners;
2. Debts owed to partners for loans made to the partnership;
3. Debts owed to partners for capital; and

4. Debts owed to partners as profits. [UPA Section 40]

The following case discusses some of the problems that can arise when a partnership is dissolved. Notice that the business continued after dissolution.

BACKGROUND AND FACTS *Lange was a partner in a business known as Pool Boys that installed swimming pools. Art Lange and Bert Bartlett had worked together installing pools for several years on a part-time basis. In 1972, they verbally agreed to form the partnership ''Pool Boys'' and began operating the business full time. This arrangement continued until April of 1975 when Lange told Bartlett that he no longer wanted to participate in the partnership.*

Bartlett eventually offered Lange $3,000 in payment for Lange's share of the partnership; Lange refused this offer. Neither Bartlett or Lange obtained an accounting nor was Lange paid any money. Subsequently, in 1978, Lange sued to recover his interest in the partnership, claiming he was entitled to one-half of both the assets and the profits from the business subsequent to April 1975. The trial court entered a judgment that gave him only one-half of the assets. Lange appealed, asserting that he was also entitled to one-half of the profits. The judge in the trial court had seemed confused about whether a windup had occurred, first deciding that it had, then changing his mind and holding that there was a continuation of the business.

Case 16.2
LANGE v. BARTLETT
Court of Appeals of Wisconsin, 1984.
121 Wis.2d 599,
360 N.W.2d 702.

BROWN, Presiding Judge.
* * * *

Before discussing the trial court's decision after trial, it is important for a clear understanding of this case to review the basic tenets of partnership law.

When a partner dies or retires, the partnership is dissolved. However, the partnership is not terminated upon dissolution; it continues until the wind-up of the partnership affairs are completed.

It is at this juncture, the point of dissolution, that the retiring partner makes an election. He can either force the business to ''wind-up'' and take his part of the proceeds, sharing in profits and losses after dissolution, or he can permit the business to continue and claim as a creditor the value of his interest at dissolution. The determination of whether the retiring partner consented to or acquiesced in the continuation of the business is a question of fact.

Thus, the first task for a trial court faced with making a settlement of a former partner's account after dissolution is to determine what election the retiring partner made at the point of dissolution. Every partnership dissolution causes a wind-up rather than a continuation unless the outgoing partner ''consents'' to a continuation. Distinguishing in the first instance whether a wind-up or a continuation is at hand is critical simply because the settlement of the former partner's account differs depending on whether it is a wind-up or a continuation.

For instance, if a trial court determines that a business was engaged in a wind-up, the former partner receives the value of his or her interest at the date of liquidation or final settlement. *   * * In other words, the outgoing partner shares in both profits *and losses* until termination. The former partner, therefore, does not take as a creditor. The outgoing partner gets a share of the profits, if any, only after all of the other creditors have been paid and only until termination. Termination is the point in time when all of the partnership affairs are wound up.

Continuation, however, effects a totally different settlement of the former partner's account. The outgoing partner can agree, at the time of dissolution, that the business will be continued. If the outgoing partner elects to allow the business to continue, then that partner has a second election—to receive either interest or profits from the date of dissolution—in addition to the value of his or her interest in the partnership. This "second election" can be made only by the former partner; it cannot be made by either the continuing partner or the trial court. The profits garnered from continuation are different from the profits at wind-up simply because, in a continuation, the outgoing partner is not responsible for the debts of the continuing partnership. The outgoing partner, instead, takes as a creditor.

* * * *

Having analyzed the basic law, we now turn to the trial court's decision, which we hold is inconsistent with these tenets. The trial court found that a wind-up had taken place rather than a continuation. It then determined the worth of the assets at the date of dissolution and divided the value of those assets equally between the two parties. Instead of determining the value of the assets at the time of dissolution, it should have determined profits and losses from the date of dissolution to the date of the hearing. This would assume that the assets have been sold as part of the wind-up and the income derived therefrom added to the amount to be divided or that the trial court place a market value on the assets as if sold. It did not, and this alone is error.

Moreover, the trial court's decision is inconsistent with an earlier decision it made following a pretrial motion by Lange. At the conclusion of that earlier hearing, the trial court held that a continuation had taken place, not a wind-up.

* * * *

Finally, we reach a contention by Bartlett which is found to be a common complaint in partnership dissolution in our research of cases across the country. Bartlett strenuously argues that the business has greatly expanded since Lange left in 1975. He claims it is not the intent of the statutes to allow Lange to reap profits from aspects of the business which were not operating at the time of the partnership dissolution. Bartlett is incorrect. [The statute] states that the retiring partner may opt, in lieu of interest, for "profits attributable *to the use of his right in the property of the dissolved partnership.* *   * *" (Emphasis added.) This figure may differ from year to year depending upon Bartlett's use of partnership property. Lange's partnership property includes not only the tangible assets but also any goodwill in the "Pool Boys" name and reputation prior to dissolution that would have contributed to the success of Bartlett's sauna, spa and hot tub business.

However, we understand Bartlett's concerns, and they can be addressed by compensating Bartlett for his efforts. Although authorities are not in accord regarding the problem of compensation to continuing partners in the absence of a specific agreement, we feel the better reasoned view is that one who continues a partnership business after dissolution and contributes substantial labor and management services is entitled to compensation for that effort.

We conclude that regardless of the expended effort on behalf of Bartlett, Lange is still entitled to a share of the partnership profit from the day of dissolution. However, a court can take into account the substantial labor and management services made by the continuing partner and deduct that amount before arriving at the figure of what profit is due the former partner.

The trial court's judgment was reversed, and the case was remanded for a new trial. Whenever a partner withdraws from a partnership, a determination must be made as to whether the partnership is in the stage of winding up with the expectation of termination or whether it is being continued. This is a question of fact to be determined based on the conduct of all partners.

DECISION AND REMEDY

When a person is involved with a partnership that is dissolved because one partner is leaving, the partner winding up the partnership should insist on an accounting and a determination as to what the retiring partner's interest is worth. Otherwise, the remaining partner or partners are left open to great liability. If the business fails, the remaining partners will have to pay the retiring partner his or her investment. If the business is a success after the partner leaves, the retiring partner must be paid a share of the profits even though he or she did not take part in making the business a success.

COMMENTS

Limited Partnerships

A limited partnership is used when one or more partners want to manage the day-to-day activities of the business while the other partners merely want to make an investment in it. The investing partners find a limited partnership attractive for two reasons: A limited partnership limits the liability of its limited partners, and tax advantages exist. Although the 1986 Tax Reform Act curtailed many of these tax benefits, enough incentives still exist—especially in certain industries, such as oil and lumber—to make limited partnerships an inviting investment.

A limited partnership must have at least one general partner and one or more limited partners. The limited partners, as such, are not bound by the obligations of the partnership and cannot have any day-to-day management responsibilities. The general partner or partners have total responsibility for management of the partnership and unlimited liability for all of its debts.

A limited partnership is a statutory creation and must comply with all statutory requirements to be formed. Failure to comply may change the limited partnership into a general partnership. The **Uniform Limited Partnership Act** (ULPA) of 1916 and the **Revised Uniform Limited Partnership Act** (RULPA) of 1976 contain the current law on limited partnerships. The original ULPA was updated in the RULPA to resolve current problems with limited partnerships. All states, except Louisiana, have adopted either the ULPA or the RULPA.

The ULPA and the RULPA require the limited partnership to file a certificate (see Exhibit 16–1) that becomes part of the public record. The certificate is similar to the articles of incorporation for a corporation. A partnership certificate contains basic information, such as the name, location, and business of the partnership; the name and residence of each partner, general or limited; the term for which the partnership will exist; and the amount of cash and property contributed by each limited partner.

In addition to the certificate of limited partnership, the partners often enter into a more detailed partnership agreement that is not filed as part of the public record but that covers such items as the share of the profits to which each partner is entitled.

Limited partnership interests are considered to be securities (like stock certificates or corporate bonds). First, there is money paid from one person (the limited partner) to another (the general partner). Second, the money is invested in a common enterprise from which the investor is led to expect profits. Third, the profits arise primarily from the efforts of people other than the investor. Thus, the issuance, sale, and transfer of a limited partner's interest are subject to federal and state securities laws (discussed in detail in Chapter 18).

Exhibit 16–1 Sample Certificate of Limited Partnership

CERTIFICATE OF LIMITED PARTNERSHIP

The undersigned, desiring to form a Limited Partnership under the Uniform Limited Partnership Act of the State of _____ , make this certificate for that purpose.

§ 1. **Name.** The name of the Partnership shall be "_____ _____ ".

§ 2. **Purpose.** The purpose of the Partnership shall be to [*describe*].

§ 3. **Location.** The location of the Partnership's principal place of business is _____County, _____ .

§ 4. **Members and Designation.** The names and places of residence of the members, and their designation as General or Limited Partners are:

_____	[*Address*]	General Partner
_____	[*Address*]	General Partner
_____	[*Address*]	Limited Partner
_____	[*Address*]	Limited Partner

§ 5. **Term.** The term for which the Partnership is to exist is indefinite.

§ 6. **Initial Contributions of Limited Partners.** The amount of cash and a description of the agreed value of the other property contributed by each Limited Partner are:

[*Name*]	[*Describe*]
[*Name*]	[*Describe*]

§ 7. **Subsequent Contributions of Limited Partners.** Each Limited Partner may (but shall not be obliged to) make such additional contributions to the capital of the Partnership as may from time to time be agreed upon by the General Partners.

§ 8. **Profit Shares of Limited Partners.** The share of the profits which each Limited Partner shall receive by reason of his contribution is:

[*Name*]	_____ %
[*Name*]	_____ %

Signed _____ , 19____

_____

_____

_____

_____

Signed and sworn before me, the undersigned authority, this _____ _____ , 19____ .

Notary Public

_____County, _____

Sources of Funding for Limited Partnerships

The general and the limited partners contribute to the capital of the limited partnership and may also make loans to it. The partnership agreement may provide for additional contributions and voluntary or involuntary assessments of the partners after formation of the partnership. Since the liability of the limited partners is restricted to the amount of their contributions, the ability of the partnership to obtain loans from third parties will be based on the partnership's assets and the creditworthiness of the general partner or partners, who have unlimited liability.

Liability in Limited Partnerships

A limited partnership must have at least one general partner who has unlimited liability. Most states now allow the general partner to be a corporation, as well as a natural person.

Generally speaking, the limited partners' liability is limited to their capital contributions. This includes the amount of capital that limited partners have pledged to contribute but that they have not yet actually paid.

Limited partners can lose their limited liability if they participate in the management and control of the partnership's business. Certain state statutes specify that the right of a limited partner to demand that the general partner be expelled from the partnership will not be considered as taking part in the control of the business.

Partnership agreements also commonly provide for a majority (in interest) of the limited partners to be able to elect a successor general partner, amend certain provisions of the partnership agreement, dissolve the partnership, and consent to the disposal of all or substantially all of the assets of the partnership. The ULPA is not clear about whether such powers may cause the limited partners, under certain circumstances, to be deemed general partners with a resulting loss of limited liability. These powers are specifically allowed under the RULPA and exercise thereof does not constitute general partner liability.

The following case examines the question of whether the limited partners had lost their limited liability status. This case was decided under the ULPA.

BACKGROUND AND FACTS *In January 1967, Diversified Properties was organized as a real estate limited partnership with Weil as the only general partner. That status remained until May 1968, when the partnership was hard pressed for cash. At a partnership meeting, Weil offered to discontinue his salary and close up the partnership office in order to save $75,000. Weil's proposal was accepted, and, at the next partnership meeting two weeks later, two of the limited partners were selected to manage the properties on a commission basis; the partnership books and records were transferred to a third limited partner's office. Weil went to work for a real estate company as its vice-president.*

From then on, the partners were involved in refinancing and meeting further capital demands. All partners hoped to keep the partnership afloat. Weil's name appeared on various obligations that in fact had been assigned to the partnership. Creditors turned to Weil for payment. The limited partners did not put forth any more money to meet the creditors' demands.

Weil brought a lawsuit seeking to have the court declare the limited partners as general partners because of their participation in management activities. Weil wanted to spread the liability to all the limited partners.

Case 16.3
WEIL v. DIVERSIFIED PROPERTIES
United States District Court, District of Columbia, 1970.
319 F.Supp. 778.

GESELL, Judge.

* * * *

Cases relating to whether or not limited partners have taken part in control of the business and are thus to be treated as general partners involve claims by creditors against the partners. No case has been found where a general partner has invoked Section 7 of the [ULPA] against his own limited partners. The purpose of Section 7 is to protect creditors:

The Act proceeds on the assumption that no public policy requires a person who contributes to the capital of a business, acquires an interest in its profits, and some degree of control over the conduct of the business to become bound for the obligations of the business, provided creditors have no reason to believe that when their credits were extended that such persons were so bound.

* * * *

Even if a general partner might hold his limited partners to account as general partners under certain circumstances, Weil cannot do so on the facts of this case. Weil considers himself still a general partner and recognizes that the written partnership agreement by its terms is a bona fide limited partnership under the Code. As between themselves, partners may make any agreement they wish which is not barred by prohibitory provisions of statutes, by common law, or by considerations of public policy. Whatever may be the obligations of the limited partners as against creditors or third parties, Weil may not prevail against them if they have not breached the terms of the agreement. Having entered into the partnership agreement with advice of counsel, an agreement made largely for his own benefit in a field where he was especially experienced, he is bound by its terms. Accordingly, the initial inquiry must be to determine whether the limited partners have in any way violated the terms of the written agreement.

* * * *

Thus it is apparent that the partners contemplated the general partner would receive a substantial salary and have the day-to-day management of the properties. For reasons already suggested, this expectation was altered by events which resulted in the general partner foregoing his salary and turning over immediate day-to-day responsibility to [the limited partners,] who were employed on a commission basis. After May 1, 1969, the partnership operation became a matter of salvaging what could be salvaged in the enterprise as it then existed. This naturally involved refinancing and sale of properties and other matters not in the normal course of day-to-day business. As to these nonroutine matters, the limited partners by the very terms of their agreement had a majority vote, and were certainly authorized to comment upon them. Weil believes he should have had exclusive say as to how and what bills were to be paid with any money available beyond immediate operating needs, but under the prevailing conditions this clearly was not a normal day-to-day business question; it involved the very ability of the enterprise to survive. Moreover, the funds coming in were far from sufficient to meet current obligations, and no partnership account was being accumulated.

Weil has not by a preponderance of the evidence established any violation by the limited partners of terms of the agreement with him, which at the very most is all that Weil can complain of in his effort to have the limited partners declared general partners. Since the partnership agreement was not violated by the limited partners, Weil has no cause of action and his request for the appointment of a receiver and an accounting will be denied. The provisions of the Limited Partnership Act are primarily designed to protect creditors. So long as the provisions of the agreement were followed, no partner can complain.

DECISION AND REMEDY *The district court dismissed Weil's complaint. A general partner can bring action against limited partners if, in violation of the partnership agreement,* *a limited partner interferes with the management of the partnership. In this case, however, the general partner gave up his duties and turned them over to the limited partners. The court held that the actions of the limited partners in attempting to salvage the business and continue its operations did not constitute taking control of the business within the meaning of the statute.*

Control of the Limited Partnership

The control and management of the limited partnership is vested in the hands of the general partner. Thus, control does not necessarily follow ownership interest, as it does in a corporation. A general partner may have a very small ownership interest, but retains the right to control the entity. Unless there is an agreement to the contrary, the general partner will have absolute discretion as to when distributions of profits are made.

The general partner has all of the rights and powers and is subject to all of the restrictions and liabilities of a partner in a general partnership. The general partner does not have authority to act in a manner that contravenes the partnership certificate.

A limited partner has the same rights as any general partner to access partnership books and records; to have an accounting of the partnership business; to have a dissolution and winding up of the partnership by court order; to receive the share of profits or compensation stipulated in the partnership certificate; and to have a return of his or her contribution on dissolution and distribution of the partnership assets, subject to the rights of creditors.

Exhibit 16–2 illustrates the basic comparisons of general partnerships and limited partnerships under both the ULPA and the RUPLA.

Tax Consequences for a Limited Partnership

The taxation of a limited partnership is the same as that of a general partnership. The partnership makes an informational filing, reporting the allocation of profits and losses and other tax items to the various partners. Individual partners, limited and general, report on their own tax returns their allocated profits or losses. The partnership itself is not a taxable entity, and profits and losses pass through to the individual partners.

Since limited partnerships have been used extensively as tax shelters, their tax status as partnerships has often been challenged by the Internal Revenue Service. For federal income tax purposes, the Internal Revenue Service regulations provide that a limited partnership will be classified as a "partnership" rather than as "an association taxable as a corporation," as long as it does not possess more corporate than noncorporate characteristics.

The characteristics which, according to the regulations, distinguish a corporation from a partnership are the following: continuity of life, limited liability, free transferability of interest, and centralization of management. If an entity lacks any two of these corporate characteristics, it will be classified as a partnership rather than as a corporation for tax purposes.

Since all limited partnerships have the characteristic of centralized management in the hands of the general partner or partners, a limited partnership agreement will often impose restrictions on transferability of interest in order to avoid the corporate characteristic of free transferability.

In addition, to avoid the corporate characteristic of limited liability, a general partner must have sufficient net worth so that the theoretical unlimited liability of the general partner is not in reality limited by a lack of assets. An individual general partner must have substantial assets and must not be acting as a "dummy" agent of the limited partners. The regulations do not provide any clear-cut guidance as to what constitutes substantial assets. As previously pointed out, even with the changes involved in the 1986 Tax Reform Act, definite tax advantages are still authorized for specific business ventures, and these advantages can provide great tax savings.

Exhibit 16–2 **Basic Comparison of Partnerships**

CHARACTERISTIC	GENERAL PARTNERSHIP	LIMITED PARTNERSHIP	REVISED LIMITED PARTNERSHIP
Creation	By agreement of two or more persons to carry on a business as co-owners for profit.	By agreement of two or more persons, under the laws of the state, having one or more general partners and one or more limited partners to carry on a business as co-owners for profit. Filing of certificate in appropriate state office is required.	Same as limited partnership, except filing of certificate with Secretary of State is required.
Sharing of profits and losses	By agreement, or in absence thereof, profits are shared equally by partners and losses are shared in same ratio as profits.	Profits are shared as required in certificate agreement, and losses shared likewise, except limited partners share losses only up to their capital contribution.	Same as limited partnership, except in absence of provision in certificate agreement, profits and losses are shared on basis of percentages of capital contributions.
Liability	Unlimited personal liability of all partners.	Unlimited personal liability of all general partners; limited partners only to extent of capital contributions.	Same as limited partnership.
Capital contribution	No minimal or mandatory amount; set by agreement.	Set by agreement; may be cash, property, or any obligation except services.	Same as limited partnership; contribution of services is allowed.
Management	By agreement, or in absence thereof, all partners have an equal voice.	General partners by agreement, or else each has an equal voice. Limited partners have no voice, or else subject to liability as general partners.	Same as limited partnership, except limited partner involved in partnership management is liable as a general partner *only* if third party has knowledge of such involvement. Limited partner may act as agent or employee of partnership, and vote on amending certificate or sale or dissolution of partnership.
Duration	By agreement, or can be dissolved by action of partner (withdrawal), operation of law (death or bankruptcy), or court decree.	By agreement in certificate, or by withdrawal, death, or insanity of general partner in absence of right of other general partners to continue the partnership. Death of a limited partner, unless he or she is only remaining limited partner, does not terminate partnership.	Same as limited partnership, except it enlarges class of activities by general partner that result in termination.

Exhibit 16–2 Basic Comparison of Partnerships—*continued*

CHARACTERISTIC	GENERAL PARTNERSHIP	LIMITED PARTNERSHIP	REVISED LIMITED PARTNERSHIP
Priorities (order) upon liquidation	1. Outside creditors. 2. Partner creditors. 3. Capital contribution of partners. 4. Profits of partners.	1. Outside creditors. Limited partner creditors. 2. Profits to limited partners. 3. Limited partner capital contributions. 4. General partner creditors. 5. Profits to general partners. 6. Capital contributions to general partners.	1. Outside creditors. Partner creditors. 2. Amounts before withdrawal to which partners are entitled. 3. Capital contributions—limited and general partners. 4. Profits—limited and general partners.

Bulk Transfers: Buying a Going Business

When a person decides to go into business, he or she will often purchase an existing business. If the business being purchased sells merchandise (not just services), the bulk transfer provisions of the Uniform Commercial Code, Article 6, usually apply. A **bulk transfer** is defined as any transfer of a major part of the material, supplies, merchandise, or other inventory not made in the ordinary course of the transferor's business. [UCC 6-102]

No problems exist if all the creditors of the seller are paid in full at the time that the business is transferred to the buyer. The problems occur when the seller's creditors are not paid. The creditors have certain rights against the buyer if the bulk transfer provisions are not followed.

The following requirements must be met to protect the buyer from the former creditors of the seller:

1. The seller (transferor) must furnish to the transferee a sworn list of the person's existing creditors. This list must include those whose claims are disputed, stating names, business addresses, and amounts due. [UCC 6-104(1)(a)]
2. The buyer and the seller must prepare a schedule of the property transferred. [UCC 6-104(1)(b)]
3. The buyer must preserve the list of creditors and the schedule of property for six months. She

or he must permit inspections by any creditor of the seller or file the list and the schedule of property in a designated public office. [UCC 6-104(1)(c)]
4. Notice of the proposed bulk transfer must be given (usually by the buyer) to each creditor of the seller at least ten days before the buyer takes possession of the goods or makes payments for them, whichever happens first. [UCC 6-105]

If all four of these steps are taken, the bulk transfer complies with the statutory requirements. The buyer acquires title to the goods free of all claims of the creditors of the seller.

The specific requirements of the contents of the notice to the creditors are:

1. A statement that a bulk transfer is about to be made;
2. The names and business addresses of the seller in bulk and buyer in bulk; and
3. Information about whether the debts of the seller in bulk are to be paid in full as a result of the bulk transfer and, if so, the addresses to which creditors should send their bills. [UCC 6-107(1)]

Whenever the debts of the transferor in bulk are not to be paid in full as they fall due, the notice to creditors must also state such things as the location and general description of the property to be transferred, the address where the schedule of property and list of creditors may be inspected, and whether the transfer is for new consideration or payment for a preexisting debt. [UCC 6-107(2)]

When the requirements of Article 6 are not complied with, goods in the possession of the transferee continue to be subject to the claims of the unpaid creditors of the seller for a period of six months. If the transfer was concealed, however, actions may be brought (including levy on the goods) for up to six months after discovery of the transfer. [UCC 6-111] Nonetheless, a bona fide purchaser of these goods from the transferee who pays value in good faith, not knowing that the goods are still subject to the claims of the transferor's creditors, acquires the goods free of any claim of those creditors.

If a creditor did not receive notice because of the fault of the seller—for example, the creditor

was not on the seller's list—the seller is liable to the buyer for any loss incurred by the buyer. If the creditor did not receive notice because of the buyer's fault, and the creditor satisfied his or her claim from the property that was transferred, the buyer can only recover from the seller the amount of the debt that the seller owed to that creditor (this is the quasi-contractual theory).

In the following case, the court was faced with a bulk transfer of the assets of a business but without any notice to a creditor being given. The issue before the court was whether the six-month period began with the date of the transfer of possession of the assets to the buyer or with the date of the creditor's discovery of the transfer.

Case 16.4
COLUMBIAN ROPE CO. v. RINEK CORDAGE CO.

Pennsylvania Superior Court, 1983.
314 Pa.Super. 585, 461 A.2d 312.

BACKGROUND AND FACTS   *The plaintiff, Columbian Rope Company, extended credit to the defendants, Rinek Cordage Company and its president, Jerome Brose. The defendants confronted serious financial problems and owed the plaintiff $22,683.48. Rinek Cordage Company also owed Rinek Rope Company $17,588.55. Rinek Cordage and Rinek Rope operated out of the same address, both used the Rinek name, and Brose was not conscientious in maintaining the corporate identity of each company. Rinek Cordage Company transferred its entire inventory to Rinek Rope Company; thus, the debt of $17,588.55 was canceled.*

This transaction, on April 1, 1974, constituted a bulk sales transfer. The complaint by Columbian Rope Company was not filed until November 12, 1976, but this was within six months of its discovery of the transfer. The lower court dismissed the action based on the six-month statute of limitations.

HOFFMAN, Judge.

Appellant, a creditor, contends that the lower court erred in denying its claim against Jerome Brose, the former president of a debtor corporation, and against Rinek Rope Co. [Rope], which received the debtor's remaining assets in a bulk transfer. We find the claim against Brose was properly denied. However, because the bulk transfer to Rope was "concealed," * * * the six-month statute of limitations did not begin running until appellant discovered the bulk transfer. Accordingly, we reverse the lower court's order dismissing appellant's claim against Rope, and remand for findings of fact as to whether appellant commenced its action within six months of discovering the bulk transfer.
* * * *

Appellant contends that Rope's complete failure to give notice of the bulk transfer constituted a concealment of the bulk transfer, and thus the statute of limitations did not begin to run against it until its discovery of the transfer. We agree. The Uniform Commercial Code, Article 6, concerning bulk transfers, * * * is designed to remedy the "major bulk sales risk" of the merchant, owing debts, who sells away virtually all his stock in trade and disappears leaving his creditors unpaid. The statute's basic mechanism is to require the prospective transferee to give advance notice to the transferor's creditors of the impending bulk sale. The transferee must also take steps to insure that the proceeds are applied to the benefit of the transferor's creditors. The prior notice affords the creditors an opportunity to participate in structuring the transfer or commence legal action against their debtor, the transferor, before the assets are sold away. To promote compliance, the statute establishes three alternative time limitations for creditor actions against the transferee. First, if the transferee gives the statutory notice and otherwise complies with the statute, the bulk transfer will be "effective" against any creditor of the tranferor. The complying transferee will be shielded immediately upon the transfer from the creditors' actions. Creditors will therefore be required to act expeditiously against their debtor, the transferor, within the ten or more days between the statutory notice and the transfer or they will effectively lose their opportunity to collect their debt. Second, if the transferee does not give the required notice, the transfer will be "ineffective" against the transferor's creditors, who may then commence actions for the transferor's debts against the transferee within the six months following the transfer. Third, if the transferee's failure to give notice is not simply non-compliance with the statute but amounts to "concealment" of the bulk transfer, the transferee is subject to actions by the transferor's creditors commenced within six months of when the creditor discovers the concealed bulk transfer. The question we face here is whether a completely undisclosed bulk transfer should be treated as "concealed" for purposes of the U.C.C.'s statute of limitations.

Case law is divided upon what constitutes concealment of a bulk transfer. No prior Pennsylvania appellate decision has interpreted this statutory term. Some courts have required "active" or "affirmative" concealment. Others have held that "*complete* failure to comply with the notice provisions of [U.C.C.] Article 6 . . . was tantamount to a concealment of a transfer of assets * * *." We find that the complete failure to give notice of the impending bulk transfer is not merely noncompliance, but "concealment."
* * * *

Applying these principles, the record reveals that the bulk transfer here was wholly undisclosed, and thus concealed. No notice, formal or informal, was sent to Cordage's two outstanding creditors, apparently because Rope's and Cordage's officers did not think it necessary. The circumstances in no way revealed to creditors that the transfer had occurred. Both transferor and transferee operated out of the same business address, with Cordage owning the premises and Rope leasing space. Both used the "Rinek" name. Even after the transfer, Cordage's president was not scrupulous in differentiating between the two entities. Letter from Jerome Brose to Michael Hole, April 25, 1974 ("I have completed refinancing of the *Rinek* real estate" (emphasis added)). Moreover, although Rope had existed separately since 1971, and used stationery showing its own name—Rinek Cordage forms with "Cordage" blacked-out and "Rope" rubber-stamped above—such a precaution did not reveal the fact of the bulk transfer on April 1, 1974. Accordingly, even though the record contains no proof of deceptive intent, the bulk transfer was effectively "concealed" from creditors by the complete nondisclosure. We thus reverse the lower court's dismissal of the action against Rope, and remand for findings of fact to determine whether appellant commenced action within six months of its discovering the bulk transfer.

The court found that, because the transfer was concealed until a creditor discovered that a bulk transfer had occurred, the six-month statute of lim- **DECISION AND REMEDY** *itations had not begun. The complete failure to comply with the bulk transfer provisions, including the failure to give the creditor notice, constituted concealment. Therefore, the innocent creditor was not precluded from exercising its rights upon the passage of six months from the date the buyer took possession.*

Drafting a Partnership Agreement

You and a friend decide to go into partnership to sell a new product. The following are some of the considerations to be included in your written partnership agreement:

1. Names and addresses of the general partners and the designation of partnership status
2. Name of the partnership and address of the principal place of business
3. Character of the business
4. Duration of the partnership
5. Contributions of the partners
   a. Form of contribution
   b. Interest on contribution
   c. Additional contribution requirements
6. Assets of the partnership
   a. Identification of the assets
   b. Valuation of the assets
   c. Control of the assets and accountability for them
   d. Distribution of the assets
7. Duties of the partners
8. Distribution of profits and losses
9. Compensation, benefits, and expenses of the partners
10. Policy and management of the business
11. Accounting practices and procedures
12. Liability and insurance requirements
13. Indemnity clause (to compensate for loss or to reimburse expenses)

14. Changes in the partners by withdrawal, retirement, death, mental illness, bankruptcy, or admission of additional partners
15. Sale or assignment of the partnership interest
16. Arbitration provisions
17. Amendment provisions
18. Dissolution, winding up, and termination of the partnership
19. Date of the agreement
20. Signatures of the partners.

With a well-drafted agreement, you should also be able to answer these questions, which frequently arise:

1. What happens if one of you does not spend the necessary amount of time in the business—for example, what happens if your partner goes to Europe for a six-month vacation?
2. What happens if one of you should become disabled or die?
3. How will the profits and losses be shared?
4. What happens if the business requires additional capital?
5. How much time should each partner spend doing partnership business?
6. Who should sign the checks and make the deposits?
7. What happens if one partner decides to leave the partnership? How does the partnership end?

Summary

Four principal forms of business organization exist: sole proprietorship, general partnership, limited partnership, and corporation. Concerns in selecting a type of business entity include the difficulty in forming it, limited liability, tax considerations, continuity of existence, transferability, and management.

The sole proprietorship is the most informal business organization. The sole owner of a business has unlimited liability, and the business may cease to operate on the death or incapacity of the owner. No tax advantages exist for this form of ownership, but it does give maximum control of the business to the owner.

The general partnership allows people to join together to operate a business. No formal requirements exist for its organization. If a partner should die, become incapacitated, or otherwise leave the partnership, a dissolution of the partnership will occur. Assuming a dissolution occurs, the remaining partners should buy out the withdrawing partner's interest as soon as possible. Just as with a sole proprietorship, there are no real tax advantages to a partnership. In the absence of an agreement among the partners, most business decisions are based on majority vote and not the amount of capital contribution.

The limited partnership must be organized in accordance with statutory provisions. All limited partnerships must have at least one general partner and one limited partner. The general partner manages the operation of the business. If a limited partner takes an active role in managing, that limited partner assumes unlimited liability for the debts of the business. Otherwise, a limited partner's only liability is his or her capital contribution. The death of a limited partner will not cause a dissolution of the partnership. In the past, there have been major tax advantages for a limited partnership; the Tax Reform Act of 1986 greatly reduces these advantages.

Corporations are the fourth form of business organization; they are covered in the next chapter.

When a person purchases a going business, compliance with the bulk sales provisions of the Uniform Commercial Code may be required. Any purchase of a business that sells merchandise must comply with the act.

Key Terms

bulk transfer **411**	partnerships **396**	Uniform Partnership Act **400**
dissolution **402**	Revised Uniform Limited	use permits **400**
fictitious name filing **396**	Partnership Act **405**	variances **400**
general partner **396**	sole proprietorships **396**	winding up **402**
limited partners **396**	termination **402**	
limited partnerships **396**	Uniform Limited Partnership	
partnership by estoppel **400**	Act **405**	

Questions and Case Problems

1. Suppose Lisa, Amy, and Mary are college graduates, and Lisa has come up with an idea for a new product that she believes could make the three of them very wealthy. Her idea is to manufacture beer dispensers for home use, and her goal is to market them to consumers throughout the Midwest. Lisa's personal experience qualifies her to be both first line supervisor and general manager of the new firm. Amy is a born salesperson. Mary has little interest in sales or management but would like to invest a large sum of money that she has inherited from her aunt. What should Lisa, Amy, and Mary consider in deciding which form of business organization to adopt?

2. Assume that Mary, in problem 1, is willing to put her inherited money into the business but that she does not want any further liability should the beer dispenser man- ufacturing business fail. The bank is willing to lend capital at a 14 percent interest rate, but it will do so only if certain restrictions are placed on management decisions. This is not satisfactory to Amy or Lisa, and the two decide to bring Mary into the business. Under these circumstances, discuss the types of business organizations best suited to meet the needs of Mary.

3. The limited liability aspect of the corporation or limited partnership is one of the most important reasons that firms choose to organize as corporations or limited partnerships rather than as general partnerships or sole proprietorships. Limited liability means that, if a corporation or limited partnership is not able to meet its obligations with corporate or partnership assets, creditors will not be allowed to look to the owners (stockholders) of the corporation or the limited partners to satisfy their claims. Assume that Lisa and Amy (from problem 1) do not have a wealthy friend like Mary who wants to go into business with them and that, therefore, they must borrow money to start their business. Lisa and Amy decide to incorporate. What do you think a lender will ask them when they seek a loan? What effect does this have on the "advantage" of limited liability under corporations?

4. Able, Baker, and Carlton have formed a twenty-year partnership to purchase land, develop it, manage it, and then sell the property. The partnership agreement calls for the partners to devote full time to the business. Assume one of the following events takes place:

a. After two years, Baker and Carlton agree that the working hours of the partnership will be from 8:00 A.M. to 6:00 P.M., rather than the previously established schedule of 9:00 A.M. to 5:00 P.M. Able refuses to come to work before 9:00 A.M. and quits promptly at 5:00 P.M.

b. After two years, Able quits the partnership.

c. After two years, Able becomes insolvent.

d. After two years, Able dies.

Discuss fully which of the above acts constitutes a dissolution and whether there is any ensuing liability for Able.

5. Rosemary and George have formed a partnership. At the time of formation, Rosemary's capital contribution was $10,000, and George's was $15,000. Later Rosemary made a $10,000 loan to the partnership when it needed working capital. The partnership agreement provides that profits are to be shared, with 40 percent for Rosemary and 60 percent for George. The partnership is dissolved by George's death. At the end of the dissolution and winding up of the partnership, the partnership's assets are $50,000, and the partnership's general creditor debts are $8,000. Discuss fully how the assets will be distributed.

6. Able and Baker form a limited partnership with Able as the general partner and Baker as the limited partner. Baker puts up $15,000, and Able contributes some office equipment that he owns. A certificate of limited partnership is properly filed, and business is begun. One month later Able becomes ill. Instead of hiring someone to manage the business, Baker takes over complete management himself. While Baker is in control, he makes a contract with Thomas involving a large sum of money. Able returns to work. Because of other commitments, the Thomas contract is breached. Thomas contends that he can hold Able and Baker personally liable if his judgment cannot be satisfied out of the assets of the limited partnership. Discuss this contention.

7. The Sports Factory, Inc., executed a lease with Ridley Park Associates, a limited partnership, to operate a health and racketball club. William Chanoff was the general partner of Ridley Park Associates. Over several months, Ridley Park failed to meet the original agreement with Sports Factory, Inc., including the failure to alter the architectural plans for the racquetball courts and the failure to acquire the zoning changes needed for the operation of a health spa. Sports Factory brought a cause of action for breach of their agreement with Ridley Park. Who was liable? [Sports Factory, Inc. v. Chanoff, 586 F.Supp. 342 (E.D.Pa.1984)]

8. Oddo and Ries entered into a partnership agreement in March 1978 to create and publish a book describing how to restore F-100 pickup trucks. Oddo was to write the book, and Ries was to provide the capital. Oddo supplied Ries with the manuscript, but Ries was dissatisfied and hired someone else to revise the manuscript. Ries published the book containing substantial amounts of Oddo's work. Did Ries's actions constitute a dissolution of the partnership, and can Oddo require Ries to account formally for the profits on the book? [Oddo v. Ries, 743 F.2d 630 (9th Cir. 1984)]

9. In April 1970, Harber, Pittman, and Calvert entered into an oral agreement to build and sell 235 houses. Following their agreement, Harber withdrew $6,000 in partnership funds and purchased three lots on which houses were to be built. The lots were purchased in his name, and, after the homes were constructed, title was also in his name. When Harber sells the houses (at a profit), can he retain the proceeds for himself? Did the partnership fail because the agreement was not in writing? [Davis v. Pioneer Bank & Trust Co., 272 So.2d 430 (La. Ct. App. 1973)]

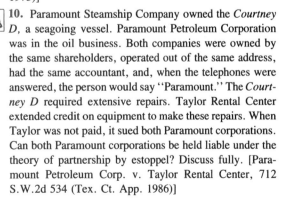 **10.** Paramount Steamship Company owned the *Courtney D*, a seagoing vessel. Paramount Petroleum Corporation was in the oil business. Both companies were owned by the same shareholders, operated out of the same address, had the same accountant, and, when the telephones were answered, the person would say "Paramount." The *Courtney D* required extensive repairs. Taylor Rental Center extended credit on equipment to make these repairs. When Taylor was not paid, it sued both Paramount corporations. Can both Paramount corporations be held liable under the theory of partnership by estoppel? Discuss fully. [Paramount Petroleum Corp. v. Taylor Rental Center, 712 S.W.2d 534 (Tex. Ct. App. 1986)]

Chapter 17 Corporate Law and Franchising Law

A corporation is an artificial being, invisible, intangible, and existing only in contemplation of law.

Chief Justice John Marshall
Dartmouth College v. Woodward,
17 U.S. (4 Wheat.) 518, 4 L.Ed. 629 (1819).

OUTLINE

Introduction

The corporate form of organization is the most important type of business organization in the United States. Corporations are the most formal kind of business organization, but they offer many advantages over other types of business entities.

A **corporation** is a separate legal entity that is owned by shareholders. Although many exceptions exist, corporations, generally speaking, are characterized by centralized management, continuity of existence, limited liability of the shareholders, and freely transferable shares.

The corporate organizational structure is well suited to a public offering of securities and a listing on a stock exchange. Any publicly offered securities are subject to federal and/or state securities laws, which are discussed in detail in Chapter 18.

Ease of Formation

Corporations are formed under state law. While the Model Business Corporation Act is adopted or followed by a majority of states, the state corporate codes are not entirely uniform. **Incorporators** are the people who start the corporation. They have a choice of states in which to charter their corporation. Most states allow a business to incorporate in one state but to locate its principal place of business elsewhere, as long as the corporation maintains a registered office in the state where it is incorporated.

Incorporators look for favorable state corporate and tax codes and also consider the state's case law interpreting its corporate code. The more developed the state's law, the more certain the corporation can be about the legal consequences of its actions.

Incorporators frequently hire a **promoter**, who makes contacts for and takes preliminary steps in organizing the corporation. Unless a promoter specifically limits his or her liability in the contract by requiring parties to look to the corporation yet to be formed, the promoter has personal liability for all pre-incorporation contracts. These contracts can include the purchase or lease of land, contracts to construct buildings, purchase of equipment and inventory, and even financing agreements with third parties. Even after the corporation is formed, the promoter remains personally liable until the corporation, through its board of directors, assumes responsibility for the contracts through novation.

Articles of Incorporation

The creation of a corporation requires a formal public filing. As part of the initial incorporation process, the incorporators must file **articles of incorporation** with a designated state office, usually the office of the secretary of state. The articles provide basic information about the corporation and are the primary source of authority for its future operations. The articles of incorporation are analogous to a constitution for the corporation.

While specific requirements vary somewhat from state to state, basically the articles of incorporation include:

1. The name of the corporation;
2. The purpose of the corporation, which may be stated in a general way in order to include all lawful business;
3. The duration of the corporation, which is almost always perpetual;
4. The date and time of the commencement of corporate existence, which usually starts with the filing of the articles with the secretary of state or which may be set by statute;
5. The number of shares that the corporation has the authority to issue, which often includes a list of the various classes of shares and their rights and limitations and any minimum capital invested to start business;
6. The address of the corporation's registered office and the name of its registered agent in the state;
7. The number of members on, and where required the names and addresses of, the first board of directors and the name and address of each incorporator; and
8. The right (if such is desired) for shareholders to have preemptive rights (the rights of existing shareholders to purchase newly issued stock to maintain their position of control and financial interest in the corporation).

In many states only one incorporator is required, and the incorporator may be a natural person, a corporation, a partnership, a limited partnership, or an association. The corporation's name must include the word "corporation," "incorporated," "company," "limited," or an abbreviation of one of these words.

Exhibit 17–1 shows sample articles of incorporation.

Bylaws

After the charter has been issued and the corporation has been formed, the incorporator(s) elect the board of directors, and the initial board meets and, among other things, adopts the corporation's **bylaws**. In many states the board of directors may consist of only one person. The bylaws cannot conflict with the state corporate code or the articles of incorporation.

If the articles of incorporation are considered equivalent to a constitution, the bylaws are equivalent to statutes. Just as the constitution (articles of incorporation) is the basic governing document and is hard to change, statutes (bylaws) carry out the guidelines of the constitution and are easier to change.

The bylaws set forth the internal rules of management for the corporation, typically including what constitutes a quorum (minimum number of members who must be present at a meeting in order to take valid actions), voting requirements

Exhibit 17–1 Sample Articles of Incorporation

ARTICLE ONE: Name
The name of the corporation is Private Investigators, Inc.

ARTICLE TWO: Time Period
The period of its duration is perpetual.

ARTICLE THREE: Purpose
This corporation is organized for the purpose of transacting any or all lawful business for which corporations may be incorporated under the laws of the State of Nevada, including private investigations.

ARTICLE FOUR: Shares
The aggregate number of shares that the corporation shall have authority to issue is 1,000 of the par value of $10 dollars each (or without par value).

ARTICLE FIVE: Capital
The amount of stated capital is $10,000.

ARTICLE SIX: Address
The address of the corporation's registered office is 1 Avenida de Estrellas, Hot Desert, Nevada, and the name of its registered agent at such address is Ron Kilgore.

ARTICLE SEVEN: Directors
The number of initial directors is one and the name and address of the director is Ron Kilgore, 1 Avenida de Estrellas, Hot Desert, Nevada.

ARTICLE EIGHT: Incorporator
The name and address of the incorporator is Ron Kilgore, 1 Avenida de Estrellas, Hot Desert, Nevada.

(signed) _____
                                    (Incorporator)
Sworn to before me on _____ by the above named incorporator.
                            (date)

_____
Notary Public, Thornhill County, Nevada
My Commission expires _____, 19_____.   (Notary Seal)

LEGAL HIGHLIGHT

The Model Business Corporation Act and The Revised Model Business Corporation Act

The Model Business Corporation Act (MBCA) is a codification of modern corporation law. A "model" statute is created with the understanding that it may need amendments or changes in order to reflect local interests, needs, or problems, but it is presented for various jurisdictions to draw upon in forming their decisions concerning corporate law.

The MBCA was first published in its complete form in 1933 by the Committee on Corporate Laws of the American Bar Association. It was patterned after the Illinois Business Corporation Act of 1933. The act was drafted, in part, in response to the tumultuous history of corporations in the United States prior to that time. While the corporate form of business organization is common today, it was rare until after the Civil War. Until the late 1800s, the corporate privilege was granted sparingly, and only when the grant seemed necessary to procure some specific benefit for the community.

The reason the corporate form was limited was because people feared that the sheer size of a corporate enterprise, along with its concentration of economic power and its separation of ownership from control, would have disastrous effects on the economic life of the community. It was believed that corporations could easily swallow up individual businesspersons and could virtually enslave labor and thus dominate the state. Even when the use of the corporate structure was eventually permitted for more general business purposes, the states placed severe restrictions on the size and scope of its use. The states also limited the scope of the business corporation's powers and activities, established a maximum duration for corporate franchises, and required state residence as a prerequisite to incorporation.

Because of the growing interest in the corporate form of business by the turn of the century, however, a number of states removed these safeguards from their incorporation statutes in order to capture the significant revenue to be obtained by granting corporate charters. For example, a New York corporation would be permitted to incorporate under the more permissive laws of New Jersey and yet continue to operate principally in New York. The consequent rivalry between states vying for revenues and control incident to domestic incorporation created notable inconsistencies in corporate law among the states and substantial confusion in the courts.[1] The need for some kind of uniformity in corporate law was evident—a need filled by the Model Business Corporation Act (MBCA). Since 1933 the act has undergone several changes and was last revised and renumbered in 1969.

The Revised Model Business Corporation Act (RMBCA), as approved in June of 1984, was drafted as a convenient guide for revision of state business corporation acts. It was designed for use by both publicly held and closely held corporations and includes provisions for the rights and duties of shareholders, management, and directors. Already a number of states have amended their corporation laws, to a limited degree, based on the RMBCA.

Neither the revised and renumbered 1969 act nor the 1984 act has been totally adopted by any state in its current form. The 1969 act, however, has been influential in the codification of corporate statutes in more than thirty-seven states and in the District of Columbia. It should be kept in mind that there is considerable variation among the state statutes based on the MBCA; therefore, those individual statutes should be relied upon rather than the MBCA.

1. The intense competition among the states to attract corporate charters is vividly described by Justice Brandeis in Louis K. Liggett Co. v. Lee, 288 U.S. 517, 548–564, 53 S.Ct. 483, 490–496, 77 L.Ed.929 (1933).

for shareholders and directors, the requirements for election of the directors and officers and the terms for which they will serve, the duties of the officers, and similar provisions.

Source of Funding

A corporation can raise money in several different ways. The two most common ways are: (1) to sell a part ownership in the corporation by issuing **equity securities** and (2) to borrow money by issuing **debt securities**.

A corporation commonly acquires funds by accepting offers to buy an interest in it. The corporation gives pieces of paper—stock—representing that ownership interest to the purchaser. This ownership interest in a corporation, represented by stock, is known as an equity security.

A corporation may also raise money by borrowing it. Often a corporation will issue **bonds** (which represent a long-term secured debt) or **debentures** (which represent an unsecured debt), and these are known as debt securities. Each represents a debt of the corporation.

Equity Securities versus Debt Securities

Differences exist between equity securities (shares in the corporation) and debt securities (evidence of borrowed money). With an equity security, if the value of the shares increases, the holder of the shares is able to profit from the increased valuation as an owner of the corporation. If the value of the shares decreases, the shareholder loses the equity and may even lose her or his entire investment.

A debt security is treated like any loan. With a debt security, the holder knows that he or she will receive interest paid at a specific rate, such as 10 percent, on the loan. It is immaterial whether the value of the equity security increases or decreases in value. If the corporation is dissolved, the debt holders always have a higher priority for repayment than the equity holders when the assets are divided up.

Common Stock

The owners of **common stock** generally have voting rights in the election of directors, in the amendment of articles and bylaws, and in other major corporate matters. Common stock is an equity security. The shareholder also has a right to a share of the corporation's profits, proportionate to the number of shares owned, if a dividend is declared by the board of directors. Common stock generally does not have a fixed dividend rate and does not carry with it any inherent right to have a dividend declared, even when the corporation is profitable.

On dissolution and liquidation of a corporation, the shareholders have a right to a proportionate share of the assets after the creditors' claims have been satisfied. Unless stock is redeemed (repurchased) by the corporation, the shares have an indefinite duration.

Preferred Stock

Although **preferred stock** is generally considered an equity security, from an investment standpoint it also bears certain similarities to a debt security. Preferred stock offers various designated preferences that are set by the articles of incorporation. Generally, preferred stock carries a preference in payment of dividends before dividends are paid to common stock holders and often pays dividends at a fixed rate. Also upon corporate dissolution and liquidation of assets, preferred shareholders often have priority over common shareholders. If the corporation is not profitable and preferred dividends cannot be paid, some preferred stock carries the right to accumulate the unpaid dividend. This means that, if, in the future, a dividend is declared, the preferred stockholder must receive the previous unpaid dividend before any payment of dividends is made to the common stockholders. These shares are called **cumulative preferred stock**.

Preferred stockholders may or may not have voting rights on corporate issues. Most often voting rights are reserved strictly for common stockholders. On liquidation, the debt securities and other debts of the corporation are paid first, then depending on provisions in the articles of incorporation the value of the preferred stock may be paid to its holder before any payments are made to holders of common stock. Preferred stock dividends paid by the corporation are not deductible as an interest expense (treated as an equity security) for corporate income tax purposes.

There are numerous types and definitions of stock. Exhibit 17–2 is illustrative.

Debt

Different forms of debt exist, including bonds and debentures. A bond is a long-term commitment, and repayment to the creditor is secured by property. A debenture is unsecured by any property; the loan is made to the corporation based on its ability to repay the debt. A bond or debenture does not carry with it any right to control the management of the corporation and usually does not offer any voting rights on other matters.

Bonds and debentures earn interest at a fixed rate that is payable regardless of the corporation's profitability. The bonds or debentures mature at a specified date when the principal must be paid. Generally, bond and debenture holders have first claim against the assets of the corporation on its liquidation.

Liability

The corporate form of business entity is favored because liability is limited for shareholders, directors, and officers. Liability may stem from creditors' claims or from a judgment against the

Exhibit 17–2 Types and Definitions of Stock

TYPES	DEFINITIONS
Common Stock	Voting shares that represent ownership interests in a corporation with lowest priorities with respect to payment of dividends and distribution of assets upon the corporation's dissolution.
Preferred Stock	Shares of stock that have priority over common stock shares as to payment of dividends and distribution of assets upon corporate dissolution. Dividend payments are usually a fixed percentage of the face value of the share.
Cumulative Preferred Stock	Preferred stock for which required dividends not paid in a given year must be paid in a subsequent year before any common stock dividends are paid.
Participating Preferred Stock	Preferred stock entitling owner to receive dividends from funds available after preferred shareholders receive required agreed dividends, and common shareholders receive dividends.
Convertible Preferred Stock	Preferred stock giving holders the option to convert their shares into a specified number of common shares either in the issuing corporation or, sometimes, in another corporation.
Redeemable or Callable Preferred Stock	Preferred shares issued with the express condition that the issuing corporation has the right to repurchase the shares as specified.
Authorized Shares	Shares allowed to be issued by the articles of incorporation.
Issued Shares	Shares that are actually transferred to shareholders.
Outstanding Shares	Authorized and issued shares still held by shareholders.
Treasury Shares	Shares that are authorized and issued, but are not outstanding (reacquired by the corporation).
No Par Value Shares	Shares issued with no stated value. The price is usually fixed by the board of directors or shareholders.
Par Value Shares	Shares issued and priced at a stated value per share.

LEGAL HIGHLIGHT   Some Costs of Businesses

Starting a business is not cheap. Consider the following costs, but remember that these are only the basic ones:

1. Lawyers' fees—Fees can range from a minimum of $250 to $25,000 or more if the business is a corporation that must meet securities law requirements in its issue of stock.
2. Filing fees—The fees for filing the incorporation papers can range from a few dollars to several hundred dollars. Often businesses other than corporations (such as limited partnerships) also must pay fees associated with the filing of appropriate forms in various state or federal offices.

Once a business has been established, the ongoing costs are significant. A few of these costs include:

1. Unemployment insurance taxes—Payment of state unemployment insurance taxes for all employees is mandatory in all states.
2. Employer's contribution to social security—Payment of the nonrefundable employer's contribution to the federal social security

system for all employees is mandatory. A self-employed person must pay the equivalent of the employer's plus the employee's contributions to social security.
3. Annual legal and accounting fees—Businesses must keep accurate books both for tax purposes and as a good business practice. The books should be audited by an accountant (CPA). Audit costs can range from several hundred dollars to thousands of dollars. Various forms must be filed on a monthly, quarterly, and annual basis. Corporate records and minute books must be maintained, usually by an accountant or a lawyer. Annual fees for such services can run into many hundreds or thousands of dollars.
4. Insurance plans—Some states require a business to provide a health plan for all its employees.
5. Retirement plans—Although no state requires a business to provide retirement plans for its employees, if such a plan is adopted, the business must comply with the federal and state requirements.

---

corporation. The limit on liability offered by a corporation is not, however, absolute.

Liability of Shareholders

If a creditor has a claim against the corporation, the claim must be satisfied from corporate assets. As a general rule, the shareholder has limited liability to the extent of her or his investment in the corporation; in other words, the shareholder can lose the amount she or he had invested in stock, but her or his personal assets are insulated from the liabilities of the corporation.

In some circumstances, especially with smaller corporations, when the corporation obtains a loan or enters into a contract, the creditor may require,

in addition to the corporation's liability, a personal guarantee from the shareholders or officers. This means, of course, that the guarantor will have his or her personal assets at risk if the corporation does not meet its obligations.

In some circumstances, a court may **pierce the corporate veil** (ignore the corporate structure) and look to the shareholders' personal assets to satisfy corporate obligations. The corporate veil may be pierced for a number of reasons. First, the shareholder may have ignored the existence of the corporation by failing to comply with the corporate formalities, such as holding meetings of the board of directors or keeping corporate minutes. Second, the shareholder may have commingled personal and corporate assets. Thus the corporation may be regarded as merely the alter-ego (cannot distinguish between the shareholder and the corporation) of the shareholder. Third, the shareholder may have undercapitalized the corporation to such an extent that creditors are unable to collect against the corporation. Fourth, he or she may have put in money as loans rather than capital taking security interest in the corporate assets. Finally, any evidence that the corporation was used to perpetuate a fraud, to circumvent the law, or to accomplish some illegal objective may lead a court to disregard the corporate existence.

In the following case, the court had to decide whether to disregard the corporate entity (pierce the corporate veil) and hold the shareholder personally liable.

Case 17.1
AMFAC FOODS, INC. v. INTERNATIONAL SYSTEMS & CONTROLS CORP. AND FLODIN, INC.
Supreme Court of Oregon, 1982.
294 Or. 94, 654 P.2d 1092.

BACKGROUND AND FACTS *The plaintiff, Amfac Foods, Inc. (Amfac), is a food-processing firm that manufactures potato products. Through another party, Amfac entered into a contract with Flodin, Inc., to build and install certain machinery. Flodin is solely owned by International Systems and Control Corporation (ISC). Flodin had limited assets, but its parent corporation was financially secure. The equipment supplied was not constructed properly. Amfac brought this action to hold ISC liable for breach of contract. Amfac won a jury verdict in the trial court, and that decision was upheld by the court of appeals. ISC then petitioned the supreme court of Oregon to review the case.*

PETERSON, Justice.
* * * This case involves the question whether a corporate shareholder, by exercising control over the affairs of a corporation of which it is the sole shareholder, may lose the limitation of liability which corporate shareholders normally enjoy and become liable to creditors of the corporation.
* * * *

Limited shareholder liability was extended to corporate shareholders to encourage risk capital investments. * * *

The corporate form was not intended to be a device by which persons could engage in business without obligation or risk. The privilege of limited liability of the shareholders of a business corporation carries with it the obligation to conduct business as a corporation, and abuse of the privilege may create personal liability for the act of the corporation.

It soon became apparent that the benefits of limited shareholder liability could lead to corporate abuses. The turn of the century saw the rise of numerous claims against corporate shareholders by creditors of insolvent corporations. A body of common law was created, denying shareholder limited liability when the corporation was being used for an improper purpose. * * *
* * * *

The disregard of a legally established corporate entity is an extraordinary remedy which exists as a last resort, where there is no other adequate and available remedy to repair the plaintiff's injury. Inasmuch as it is an extraordinary remedy, the doctrine is limited by conditions and limitations which are inapplicable to other remedies. Accordingly, when a plaintiff seeks to impose liability upon a stockholder of a defaulting corporation, the plaintiff and the court must be careful to keep the theories of recovery scrupulously segregated.

The statements of the exceptions have taken many forms. Courts' opinions often described results more than rules, saying that the shareholder would be held liable "to prevent injustice," "to prevent fraud," to prevent "evasion of just responsibility," to prevent the "distortion or hiding of the truth," to prevent a public wrong, to protect the rights of innocent parties where recognition of corporate separateness would result in "a manifest absurdity," or to prevent the avoidance of a legal obligation or duty.

* * * *

Analysis of the opinions reveals that in many cases shareholder immunity was upheld even though the defendant was the sole owner of the stock and controlled the day-to-day operations of the company. Though control is an element in the formula, we are convinced that if one does not look beyond the element of control (adding "domination" to "control" does not aid the analysis), hopeless confusion will be the result of an inductive effort to derive a legal rule which can be applied to attain predictable results.

* * * *

We state the exception to the rule as follows: When a plaintiff seeks to collect a corporate debt from a shareholder by virtue of the shareholder's control over the debtor corporation rather than on some other theory, the plaintiff must allege and prove not only that the debtor corporation was under the actual control of the shareholder but also that the plaintiff's inability to collect from the corporation resulted from some form of improper conduct on the part of the shareholder. This causation requirement has two implications. The shareholder's alleged control over the corporation must not be only potential but must actually have been exercised in a manner either causing the plaintiff to enter the transaction with the corporation or causing the corporation's default on the transaction or a resulting obligation. Likewise, the shareholder's conduct must have been improper either in relation to the plaintiff's entering the transaction or in preventing or interfering with the corporation's performance or ability to perform its obligations toward the plaintiff.

Conduct which has been held to be "improper" under the foregoing rule has included:

Inadequate capitalization: It has been held that gross undercapitalization of the debtor corporation, by itself, may suffice to hold the shareholder liable to a creditor who is unable to collect against the corporation because it was inadequately capitalized.

Milking: Shareholders have been held liable for a corporation's debt because they have milked a corporation by payment of excessive dividends.

Misrepresentation, commingling and holding out: Misrepresentations which may not be sufficient to constitute fraud would support a recovery against a shareholder on a misrepresentation theory. In some number of cases, shareholders have been held liable for corporate debts because of misrepresentations by the shareholder to the creditor, or because the respective enterprises were not held out to the public as separate enterprises.

Violation of Statute: In a number of cases involving regulations, courts have enjoined conduct of parent corporations which, in order to evade federal or state regulation, were doing business by means of wholly-owned subsidiaries.

The foregoing examples are just that, examples. This case is being remanded for a new trial. The plaintiff will have the opportunity to plead and prove the specific acts of ISC which are claimed to result in its loss of shareholder immunity. This case was tried on the "injustice" theory referred to above, and the evidence in the record of the specific instances of shareholder misconduct apart from proof of an agency relationship is not notably specific or in detail. Setting forth the precise evidence upon which the plaintiff relied to prove its case against ISC would only add to the length of the opinion and we see no need to do so. * * *

DECISION AND REMEDY   *The supreme court of Oregon reversed the decision of the court of appeals and remanded the case to the trial court to be retried.*

COMMENTS   *It is unusual for a shareholder to be liable for the debts of a corporation. This case listed factors to be considered by a court when it is asked to pierce the corporate veil in order to hold the shareholder liable. The opinion emphasizes that control by the shareholder alone will not result in personal liability. The plaintiff must show that it cannot collect from the debtor corporation because of improper conduct by the shareholder. A causal relationship between any shareholder misconduct and the fact that the creditor's claim cannot be paid must exist.*

Liability of Directors and Officers

The **directors** and **officers** of a corporation are fiduciaries of the corporation and of its shareholders. A fiduciary relationship is based on trust and confidence. Directors are elected by the shareholders to the **board of directors**. The board of directors is responsible for the overall policy and management of the corporation. The board of directors (and in rare instances the shareholders) hire officers to implement the management policy and oversee the daily operations of the corporation.

Directors and officers are required to perform their duties in good faith and in a manner that they reasonably believe to be in the best interest of the corporation. While the officers and directors of the corporation are not guarantors of its success, they cannot ignore their obligation to perform their duties. In performing their duties, they are entitled to rely on information presented by officers or employees of the corporation whom they reasonably believe to be reliable and competent in the matters presented. Directors of corporations that must register with the Securities and Exchange Commission (SEC) have a greater exposure to liability because they are ultimately responsible for compliance with the SEC rules.

Directors may not rely on information provided by officers and employees if the directors have knowledge or expertise that would make such a reliance unwarranted. Directors are required to be diligent in seeking information. They must act with the care that a reasonably prudent person in a comparable position would use under similar circumstances. If they perform their duties as directors in compliance with this standard, they will have no liability based simply on their being, or having been, directors of the corporation.

While the law imposes on directors and officers a duty to deal honestly and in good faith in steering the corporation, it gives them wide latitude in making valid business decisions. The law will not hold directors and officers liable for honest errors in business decisions if these decisions have been made with the correct motives and in good faith. This is referred to as the **business judgment rule**. The decisions must be within the powers of the corporation, and the resulting actions must be exercised with due care. The test of the decisions is objective: The directors and officers must exercise the same degree of care that reasonably prudent people use in the conduct of their own business affairs to avoid personal liability.

Directors must act in the best interests of the corporation as a whole, rather than on behalf of any individual or group of shareholders. Because they are fiduciaries, the directors and officers of a corporation may not usurp business opportunities that legitimately belong to the company itself. When a business opportunity would be of interest to the company, the directors or officers, in good faith, may take advantage of the opportunity only if the company is unable to and only if the directors or officers are not in direct competition with the company.

In the following case, the court reviewed a situation in which officers, directors, and shareholders attempted to secure advantages for themselves at the expense of the corporation.

BACKGROUND AND FACTS *The defendants, Morad and Thomson, were officers, directors, and shareholders of Bio-Lab, Inc. Bio-Lab had one additional shareholder: the plaintiff, Coupounas. While serving as officers and directors of Bio-Lab, the defendants had incorporated and operated a competing business, Med-Lab, Inc.*

The plaintiff brought a derivative suit on behalf of Bio-Lab against the defendants and Med-Lab, alleging that, in opening the competing business, they had usurped a corporate opportunity of Bio-Lab. (A derivative lawsuit is brought by a shareholder to enforce a cause of action that the corporation has against a third party when the corporation has not brought the lawsuit itself.)

The trial court held Med-Lab and its stockholders liable for usurping the corporate opportunity and ordered them to offer 30 percent of the stock to Coupounas. The trial court also imposed a constructive trust on the defendants to run Med-Lab for the benefit of Coupounas and Bio-Lab. The defendants appealed.

 Case 17.2

MORAD v. COUPOUNAS

Supreme Court of Alabama, 1978.
361 So.2d 6.

FAULKNER, Justice.

* * * *

* * * "It is well settled that directors and other governing members of a corporation are so far agents of the corporation that in their dealings respecting corporate interests, they are subject to the rules which apply generally to persons standing in fiduciary relations and which forbid such persons to secure an advantage for themselves which fidelity to the trust reposed in them would carry to others whose interests they ought to represent."

* * * *

"[I]n general the legal restrictions which rest upon such officers in their acquisitions are generally limited to property wherein the corporation has an interest already existing, or in which it has an expectancy growing out of an existing right, or to cases where the officers' interference will in some degree balk the corporation in effecting the purposes of its creation." * * *

* * * "[I]f there is presented to a corporate officer or director a business opportunity which the corporation is financially able to undertake, is, from its nature, in the line of corporation's business and is of practical advantage to it, is one in which the corporation has an interest or a reasonable expectancy, and, by embracing the opportunity, the self-interest of the officer or director will be brought into conflict with that of his corporation, the law will not permit him to seize the opportunity for himself." * * * "[N]umerous factors are to be weighed, including the manner in which the offer was communicated to the officer; the good faith of the officer; the use of corporate assets to acquire the opportunity; the financial ability of the corporation to acquire the opportunity; the degree of disclosure made to the corporation; the action taken by the corporation with reference thereto; and the need or interest of the corporation in the opportunity. These, as well as numerous other factors, are weighed in a given case. The presence or absence of any single factor is not determinative of the issue of corporate opportunity." * * *

* * * *

* * * [T]estimony revealed that $44,000 had been required to establish Med-Lab. At the end of 1974 Bio-Lab had only $24,300 available for this purpose. But, Raburn [a certified public accountant, familiar with the books of both Med-Lab and Bio-Lab] also testified that in 1974 Bio-Lab had paid a "rather high" dividend of $20,000. His testimony indicated that the payment of dividends is often restricted when a corporation wishes to expand. Thus, if the dividend had not been paid, Bio-Lab clearly should have had the financial ability to expand * * * with or without a loan. In light of this testimony the trial court's finding that defendants improperly formed Med-Lab to the detriment of Bio-Lab is clearly supportable and will not be disturbed by this Court on appeal.

DECISION AND REMEDY *The Alabama supreme court affirmed the trial court's decision to impose a contructive trust on Med-Lab, but reserved the order requiring the defendants to offer 30 percent of Med-Lab's stock to Coupounas. The court pointed out that Coupounas and the defendants were not getting along prior to Med-Lab being formed; therefore, the court should not force individuals into business arrangements they clearly do not want.*

COMMENTS *Directors and officers of a corporation are expected to act with undivided loyalty. This rule restricts them from competing with the corporation, and, at the very least, it requires fiduciaries to allow the corporation to take advantage of business opportunities.*

Control

In theory, one of the characteristics of a corporation is centralized management. Directors set policy for the corporation and hire the officers to run the corporation on a day-to-day basis. An officer can also be a director of the corporation. The usual officers are the president, at least one vice-president, the secretary, and the treasurer. Under the MBCA a person may have more than one office but cannot serve as both president and secretary. Corporate officers can be removed by the board of directors at any time with or without cause (without shareholder approval). A wrongful dismissal could result in breach of contract liability, however.

Shareholders' Rights

The shareholders elect the directors and have voting rights on major corporate matters, such as amending the articles of incorporation or bylaws, deciding to merge or consolidate with another corporation, opting to sell all or substantially all of the corporate assets, or dissolving the corporation.

Controlling, or majority, shareholders also have a fiduciary duty to the corporation and to minority shareholders when transferring their shares, a duty similar to that of officers and directors. While a controlling shareholder is free to dispose of his or her stock and to receive a premium price for the ability to control, the controlling shareholder may not sell control of the corporation if a reasonably prudent person would foresee the possibility of mismanagement by the purchaser.

Generally, in the absence of extraordinary circumstances, such as fraud or detriment to the corporation, courts have held that directors, officers, and controlling shareholders are free to buy and sell their shares without including or even making disclosures to minority shareholders. Minority shareholders can receive some protection through bylaws or restrictions stamped on the stock certificate. This protection may include requiring a majority shareholder or officer or director to give notice of sale or purchase to minority shareholders, or providing the right of first refusal (to be discussed later) to the minority shareholders or the corporation to purchase the shares being sold.

Close Corporation Control

A **close corporation** has its shares closely held by members of a family or by relatively few persons. Close corporations are often referred to as *closed, closely held, family,* or *privately held* cor-

---

LEGAL HIGHLIGHT   Voting Techniques

Once a quorum is present, a majority vote of the shares represented at the meeting is usually required to pass resolutions and elect members of the board of directors. Most states permit or require shareholders to elect directors by cumulative voting, a method designed to allow minority shareholders representation on the board of directors. Cumulative voting operates in the following way: The number of members of the board to be elected is multiplied by the number of voting shares held by the shareholder. The result equals the number of votes a shareholder has, and this total can be cast for one or more nominees for director. All nominees running for the elective board seats to be filled stand for election at the same time. Where cumulative voting is not required either by statute or under the articles of incorporation, the entire board can be elected by a majority of shares at a shareholders' meeting.

For example, say that a corporation has 10,000 shares issued and outstanding. The minority shareholders hold only 3,000 shares, and the majority shareholders hold the other 7,000. Three members of the board are to be elected. The majority shareholders' nominees are Anne, Betty, and Charlene. The minority shareholders' nominee is Diane. Can Diane be elected by the minority shareholders?

If cumulative voting is allowed, the answer is yes. The minority shareholders have 9,000 votes among them (the number of directors to be elected (3) times the number of shares (3,000) equals the number of votes (9,000). All of these votes can be cast to elect Diane. The majority shareholders have 21,000 votes (3 times 7,000 equals 21,000), but these votes have to be distributed among their three nominees. Under the principle of cumulative voting, no matter how the majority shareholders cast their 21,000 votes, they will not be able to elect all three directors if the minority shareholders cast all of their 9,000 votes for Diane.

---

porations. The members know each other personally, and, because the number of shareholders is so small, frequently no trading market exists for these shares. In practice, these corporations operate more like a partnership.

In a close corporation, the question of who controls the business is very important. It is often said that a person should always try to obtain 51 percent ownership, accept 50 percent, but never accept 49 percent or less common-stock ownership. In a close corporation, the board of directors can be one person. That person controls the corporation because the board of directors appoints officers and establishes the budget, including the amount to be paid in salaries and the types of fringe benefits.

Directors' Control

The board of directors is authorized to exercise all of the corporate powers, to manage the business, and to set the policy of the corporation. The directors' responsibilities include the declaration and payment of dividends to shareholders. The board also fixes the compensation of the officers and directors.

In larger corporations, the directors will often select an executive committee from among the board members to handle management decisions between meetings of the board. Often officers are also directors of the corporation and sit on many of the executive committees created by the board of directors. The board of directors delegates much of the responsibility for day-to-day management to the officers.

Major policy, financial, and contract decisions involving the management of a corporation cannot be delegated by the board of directors to the officers of the corporation. The following case discusses this issue.

Case 17.3

BOSTON ATHLETIC ASSOCIATION v. INTERNATIONAL MARATHONS, INC.

Supreme Judicial Court of Massachusetts, 1984. 392 Mass. 356, 467 N.E.2d 58.

BACKGROUND AND FACTS *Boston Athletic Association (BAA), the plaintiff, was responsible for organizing the Boston Marathon. This activity was the principal business of the corporation. The president was William T. Cloney. In the past Cloney had negotiated all sponsorship and broadcast coverage contracts, but the BAA had never engaged an independent promoter for the Marathon. At the April 27, 1981, meeting of the board of directors, Cloney was granted the authority to negotiate and execute agreements to promote the Marathon. No mention was made of hiring an exclusive promoter.*

Without the knowledge of the board of directors, Cloney entered into a contract with the defendant, International Marathons, Inc., (IMI) in September 1981. The contract purported to designate IMI as the exclusive promoter of the Boston Marathon. The exclusive promoter arrangement was accomplished through the transfer by the BAA to IMI of "all right, title, and interest to the exclusive use of the Boston Marathon and BAA Marathon logo(s)."

The majority of the members of the board did not learn of the agreement until February 1982. A lawsuit was brought by BAA to declare the contract void based on improper delegation of authority by its board of directors. The trial court declared the agreement void and unenforceable, and IMI appealed.

LYNCH, Justice.
* * * *
* * *Whether the board intended by its vote of April 27, 1981, to confer upon Cloney the authority to enter into the sponsorship agreement with IMI, that contract is void. The board of directors of a corporation cannot delegate total control of the corporation to an individual officer. Neither can it delegate authority which is so broad that it enables the officer to bind the corporation to extraordinary commitments or significantly to encumber the principal asset or function of the corporation.

The contract seriously encumbers the manner in which the BAA may conduct the Marathon. The BAA is obliged to produce the race in its traditional form and to pay the entire bill. But it is not entitled to "present" the race. That right, as well as the right to use the name and logo of the BAA, belongs to IMI or its assignee. The BAA may not use its own logo in any way "inconsistent" with IMI's rights pursuant to the contract. The right to enter into sponsorship agreements belongs exclusively to IMI, although the BAA can reasonably withhold its approval. The BAA may not make independent agreements without written permission from IMI. Finally, the contract between IMI and the BAA is automatically renewable at the option of IMI. Under the plain language of the agreement, there is no way for the BAA to end the relationship.

In return for carrying out its obligations under the contract, the BAA is to be paid a $400,000 fee. Any revenues in excess of $400,000 are directly payable to IMI, and there is no limit to the number of sponsors who may be solicited or to the amount of money which may be raised. The annual fee is to be paid prior to the actual running of the race, but if the Marathon should not be run for some reason, the fee is to be returned to IMI.

According to the traditional principles of corporate governance, the board of governors of the BAA does not have the power to delegate to an individual officer authority to enter into a contract which so totally encumbers the most significant purpose of the BAA, the presentation of the Marathon. The by-laws of the BAA indicate that its organization and operation are, in all material respects, the same as those of a Massachusetts business corporation. Principles of corporate governance with respect to the power of the board of governors to delegate authority to individual officers are applicable to profit and nonprofit corporations alike. In fact, the powers of an officer of a charitable corporation to bind the corporation without specific ratification by the board of governors or directors are more strictly construed than would be similar powers of an officer of a business corporation. The validity of the board's purported delegation of authority to Cloney must be analyzed in this context.

Corporate officers are generally empowered, by delegation of authority of the board of directors, with general managerial functions. They are responsible for the day to day operation of the corporation. Courts are usually flexible and accommodating in allowing boards to delegate authority as necessary or expedient. But certain powers cannot be delegated generally. Certain transactions require specific authorization by the board in order to be valid. For example, in *Stoneman v. Fox Film Corp.*, the court found that the president, although authorized to act as a general manager on behalf of a film company, was not authorized to commit the company to the purchase of a theatre, an extraordinary transaction which involved a large financial commitment. The court indicated that delegation of authority to conduct such business was a ''course of conduct manifestly . . . unusual and extraordinary in the management of a corporation.'' It was an abdication of ''the entire control'' of the corporation and ''[t]he functions of directors may not be abdicated.''

* * * *

In light of these principles, it is clear that if the delegation to Cloney was so broad as to enable him to commit the BAA to an extraordinary contract which encumbered substantially all its assets, the board would have delegated away control of the very essence of the BAA's corporate existence. * * *

* * * *

For the foregoing reasons, the board of governors of the BAA was not empowered to delegate to Cloney the right to make this contract with IMI.

DECISION AND REMEDY

The reviewing court upheld the lower court's decisions declaring the agreement void and unenforceable. A board of directors cannot delegate total control of the corporation to an individual officer. Neither can it delegate authority that is so broad that it enables the officer to bind the corporation to extraordinary commitments or to encumber the principal assets or function of the corporation.

Transferability of Interest

Another characteristic of corporations is the free transferability of shares. The law generally recognizes the right of an owner to transfer property unless there are valid restrictions on its transferability. Some restrictions are imposed by securities laws if the shares are registered with the Securities and Exchange Commission or if, for example, insiders, such as directors, officers, or controlling shareholders of the corporation who may have access to inside information, trade their securities on the basis of this information. Other restrictions may be imposed by contract, articles of incorporation, or bylaws.

Restrictions for Close Corporations

Within a close corporation, the need to provide restrictions on the transfer of common shares is greater than in other types of corporations. The interpersonal relationship of the principal shareholders of the close corporation is very intense; in many close corporations, a person spends more time with fellow shareholders than with his or her own family. This commitment requires mutual respect, trust, and understanding among the shareholders. The possibility is always present that one of the principal shareholders may die, may obtain a divorce, or may decide to leave the corporation or retire from the business. Without restrictions on the transferability of shares, a remaining shareholder might find himself or herself in business with the former associate's ex-spouse, heirs, or even some stranger. The shareholder may find it impossible to work with and to be closely associated with these new parties.

One method of restricting transfer of shares in a close corporation is providing for the option of *right of first refusal* when any member's shares are being transferred. The articles of incorporation or bylaws normally will provide that the shares to be transferred must first be offered for sale to the remaining shareholders and often to the corporation itself. These shareholders or the corporation have the first right to either buy the shares, or the right to refuse to buy the shares. It is extremely important that there be a procedure established to determine the price of the stock and that the corporation or remaining shareholders have the capability to buy the shares. For example, the articles of incorporation, the bylaws, or a shareholder agreement could give the corporation or remaining shareholders a right to purchase the stock upon the death of a shareholder with the value of the shares to be determined by an independent appraiser. Funds for the purchase of the stock on the death of the shareholder could be provided by a life insurance policy taken out and paid for by the corporation on the shareholder's life.

Notice of Restrictions

Any restrictions on transferability (including right of first refusal) must be placed on the stock certificate, but they should also at least be contained in the bylaws; in some states, they must be included in the articles of incorporation. The common law does not like restrictions on transferability; because of this, the restrictions must be written in very specific language and follow the state law exactly.

The following case illustrates common-law attitude in a situation where the heirs of shareholders wanted the stock transferred to them.

Case 17.4 **GLENN v. SEAVIEW COUNTRY CLUB** Superior Court of New Jersey, Chancery Division, 1977. 154 N.J.Super 69, 380 A.2d 1175.	**BACKGROUND AND FACTS** *When originally formed, Seaview Country Club sold shares in its business. A restriction against the sale of shares was placed on the certificates. One of the original investors died, and the plaintiffs were the heirs. They wanted the decedent's shares transferred to them. The corporation refused because of the restriction against selling the shares. The heirs took the position that the restriction allowed the shares to be transferred to them because this was not a sale. The following is the trial court's decision.*

GRUCCIO, Judge.

* * * *

The certificates of stock in question were issued on April 18, 1942, subject to certain restrictions on transfer. The restriction is set forth in an addendum printed on the certificate which states:

> This certificate can be sold, assigned, transferred, pledged to, [or] otherwise disposed of, provided that the stockholder holding the certificate shall be first obliged to offer the stock represented by this certificate for sale to this company, and this company shall have the right and option to purchase the same before said stock is offered for sale to some third party by any stockholder of the company.

The restriction placed upon the certificate is not the same restriction contained in defendant's certificate of incorporation, as amended and filed on April 2, 1942. This amendment included a resolution of the board of directors, adopted January 18, 1942, and reads as follows:

> Be it resolved that it is for the best interests of this company that the Certificate of Incorporation be amended so that the total and sole authorized stock of this company shall be 190 shares of par value of $500 each with the restriction that the stockholder holding said stock of this company shall be first obliged to offer said stock for sale to this company and this company shall have the first right and option to purchase the same before said stock is *offered for sale to some third party* by any stockholder of this company. * * * [Emphasis supplied]

Plaintiffs submit that the amendment authorizes only restrictions on the *sale* of defendant's stock to some third party. It is plaintiffs' position that since the transfers involved here are testamentary in nature, not sales, these transfers are not within the scope of the restriction.

Defendant contends that the transfers are not governed by the N.J. Business Corporations Act because the restrictive agreement was placed upon the stock 27 years before the statute was enacted and the statute should not be given retrospective application. At common law our courts were less amenable to restrictions on transfers than under the statute. The restriction upon transfer which defendants here assert is essentially a right of first refusal which has been upheld in this State as the first step in an agreement of sale.

* * * *

The language on the stock certificates indicate that any stockholder may sell, transfer, assign, pledge or otherwise dispose of his share, *provided* he offers it for sale to the corporation prior to offering it for sale to some third person. The language of the restriction is clear and its meaning is unambiguous. It does not use the broad term ''transfer'' to describe the stockholder's action which triggers the company's right of first refusal. Rather, the language refers to offering the share for sale. The same is true of the Amended Certificate of Incorporation, which states that by resolution of the board of directors the corporation has first right and option to purchase a stockholder's shares ''before said stock is offered for *sale* to some third party by any stockholder of this company.'' (Emphasis supplied.) Additionally, the minutes of the board meeting held December 6, 1941, when the amendment to the certificate of incorporation was adopted indicate that the discussion regarding the stock restriction centered around a right of first refusal prior to the sale of a stock certificate.

In the light of the fact that all the evidence before me reflects an intent by the corporation to restrict the sale of stock to third parties, it remains to be determined whether the testamentary transfer proposed here is within the scope of the term ''sale'' which appears on the stock certificates, the amended certificate of incorporation and the minutes of the board meeting as intended by the parties. It is clear to this court that the term ''sale'' is a narrower term than the term ''transfer'' and is included within that term. The stock certificate itself lists ''sale'' as one of several terms to describe the disposition of the stock, i.e., the certificate may be ''*sold, assigned, transferred, pledged or otherwise disposed of * * *.*'' It is significant that of all the assorted terms chosen to describe the disposition of the stock, only the terms ''offer * * * for sale'' is included in the provision which creates the right of first refusal.

* * * *

* * * Any attempt to validly place a restriction upon the testamentary disposition of stock, the provision in the certificate of incorporation, bylaws or written agreement among shareholders which creates the right of first refusal or other restriction, must be couched in language which clearly and explicitly makes the restriction applicable to disposition by will. Only in this fashion will the provision stand a chance of survival to legal challenge.

* * * *

Accordingly, I order defendant Seaview Country Club to transfer the shares of stock on the books of the corporation in accordance with the direction of the wills of the deceased stockholders.

DECISION AND REMEDY   *The restriction did not allow for a transfer by a sale of the stock, but, because this transfer was not a sale, the court required the stock to be turned over to the heirs. This emphasizes that courts will strictly construe and limit any restriction on the transferability of shares.*

Taxes

The corporation, as a separate entity, is also a separate taxpayer. The corporation pays taxes on its earnings in the year earned. When the earnings are distributed to the shareholders as dividends, the shareholders are also taxed. Unlike a partnership, however, the shareholders are not taxed until they actually receive the distribution in the form of dividends. Losses are also deducted by the corporation; they offset corporate income rather than passing through to the shareholders to be deducted from their income for tax purposes.

One means of avoiding the double taxation where the shareholders are also officers or employees of the corporation is by paying salaries to them rather than dividends. The salaries will be a deduction for the corporation and are therefore not taxed at the corporate level. This deduction may be disallowed, however, by the Internal Revenue Service (IRS) if the salaries are held to be excessive or unreasonable.

Avoidance of Taxes

Shareholders also can avoid double taxation by means of their capital structure as well. Rather than contributing all of their money to the capital of the corporation, a portion of it is given as a loan. The interest on the loan is a deductible item for the corporation and therefore is not taxable. Again, the IRS pays close attention to undercapitalization of corporations. Generally, a debt-to-equity ratio greater than three to one may be challenged by the IRS. This type of undercapitalization also endangers the limited liability of shareholders.

As long as the corporation's earnings are not distributed to the shareholders as dividends, no tax is paid by the shareholder. Often the corporation will accumulate earnings rather than distributing them. The IRS, however, has rules that will impose a tax on the corporation for excessive accumulated earnings. The IRS rules encourage the distribution of earnings to shareholders rather than the retention of those earnings that are not needed for the business.

S Corporation

The label **S Corporation** refers to the tax status of a corporation and not to a type of corporation. S Corporation refers to the IRS statutes that set out the qualifications for and the advantages of meeting the S Corporation requirements. S Corporation is a voluntary tax status for a close corporation. In other words, the shareholders must elect to adopt the S Corporation status.

This status allows the corporation to be taxed as a partnership (yet retain the advantages of a corporation such as limited liability) and to have all losses and gains passed through to the individual shareholders without taxation at the corporate level. In an S Corporation, the profit is passed through to the shareholders for tax purposes regardless of whether it is actually distributed to them in the form of dividends.

To qualify, an S Corporation may not have more than thirty-five shareholders, and no more than 25 percent of its income may be earned from passive investments such as rentals, interest, royalties, and dividends. An S Corporation is allowed to have only one class of stock. Only domestic corporations can qualify for this status. Many technical requirements must be met for a corporation to become an S Corporation, and the IRS may retroactively revoke the S Corporation status if these conditions are not met. If the shareholders want to maintain the S Corporation status, the shareholders' agreement must provide that their shares can be transferred only to qualified shareholders (corporations, partnerships, and many trusts cannot be shareholders).

Duration

Unless otherwise specified in the articles of incorporation, a corporation has perpetual existence. In theory, the death of a shareholder, officer, or director has no effect on the corporate entity. As a practical matter, in many close corporations, the death of the major shareholder, who is also a director or an officer, effectively brings an end to the business, if not the corporation. In such instances, the estate of the deceased shareholder may attempt to find a buyer for the corporation's shares who will continue the operation. If a buyer cannot be found, the corporation may have to be dissolved.

Dissolution

Under most state statutes, a corporation may be dissolved following adoption by the board and a majority of the shareholders of a resolution called the **articles of dissolution**. The corporation may then either proceed with its own liquidation of the business and its assets, or it may apply to the court to supervise the liquidation. The court has the power to appoint a receiver who, with the powers and duties specified by the court, will proceed to liquidate the assets and the business.

After the business and assets have been liquidated, all the liabilities of the corporation are paid. If there are any remaining assets, they will be distributed to shareholders according to their respective rights and interests. Finally, the articles of dissolution are filed with the state and the existence of the corporation ceases. In most states, for a period of years following the filing of the articles of dissolution, claims that existed prior to the dissolution may be made against the corporation and its directors, officers, or shareholders.

The dissolution of a corporation does not extinguish its debts or terminate its contracts. Under some circumstances, a corporation may be held liable for failure to perform a contract if the corporation has been dissolved voluntarily.

Dissolution can also occur by means other than the voluntary filing of the resolution for articles of dissolution. For example, any of the following may result in dissolution:

1. An act of the legislature in the state of incorporation (such as making the activities of the corporation illegal).
2. Expiration of the time of existence specified in the charter or statute without a renewal.
3. By a court decree through an action brought by the state attorney general when the actions of the corporation justify dissolution (such as pro-

curement of the charter by fraud, abuse of corporate powers, abandonment of operations, and continued violation of criminal statutes).

4. By merger (a legal combination of two or more corporations by which one corporation is absorbed into the surviving corporation thus dissolving the other corporation).

5. By consolidation (a combination of two or more corporations by which the corporations are joined to form a new corporation, dissolving the original corporations).

Franchising

The Federal Trade Commission defines a **franchise** as an arrangement between a **franchisor**, who is the owner of a trademark, a trade name, or a copyright, and another person known as the **franchisee**. The franchisor licenses the franchisee (the holder of the franchise) to use the trademark, trade name, or copyright in marketing the goods or services under specified conditions or limitations. Most franchisees are corporations, but ownership is not limited to the corporate form.

The franchise system has also been described as an organization composed of distributive units established and administered by a supplier as a means of expanding and controlling the market for its products. Each franchise dealer is a legally independent but economically dependent unit of the integrated business system. The individual franchisee operates as an independent business, yet it obtains the advantages of affiliation with the regional or national organization, which supplies the products, advertising, and other services.

The use of franchises has expanded rapidly in recent years. Between 1910 and 1940, franchising was used primarily in the automobile industry, sports, and the soft-drink bottling industry. Now franchises account for about 25 percent of all retail sales and more than 13 percent of the gross national product in the United States. The franchise pattern of business development is a particularly appealing form of capitalist enterprise, as it enables groups of individuals with small amounts of capital to become entrepreneurs.

Types of Franchises

The three types of franchises are: **distributorship**, **business format**, and **manufacturing** or **processing plant**.

1. Distributorship—A manufacturing concern (the franchisor) licenses a dealer (the franchisee) to sell its product. The franchise outlets serve merely as conduits through which the trademarked goods of the franchisor flow. The trademark in a distributorship franchise represents the end product marketed by the system. Often, a distributorship covers an exclusive territory. Two diverse examples of this type of franchise are an automobile dealership and a Baskin-Robbins Ice Cream Company franchisee.

2. Business format—This franchise is the typical chain-style business. The franchisor merely provides the trademark, and the franchisee is responsible for the manufacture and sale of the end product. The franchisee operates under the franchisor's trade name and is identified as a member of a select group of dealers that engages in the franchisor's business. The franchisee is generally required to follow standardized methods of operations. Often the franchisor requires that minimum prices and quality standards be maintained. Examples of this type of franchise are McDonald's and most other fast-food chains.

3. Manufacturing or processing plant—The franchisor transfers to the franchisee the essential ingredients or formula to make a particular product. The franchisee then markets it either wholesale or retail in accordance with the franchisor's standards. Examples of this type of franchise are Coca-Cola and other soft-drink corporations.

The Law of Franchising

The growth in franchise operations has outdistanced the law of franchising. No solid body of franchise law has been developed. Because of the absence of law precisely addressed to franchising, the courts tend to apply general common-law principles and federal or state statutes when appropriate. Although the franchise agreement itself is a contract, the franchise relationship has characteristics associated with agency law and employment law, as well as ordinary contract law.

Disclosure Protection   A franchise purchaser can suffer substantial losses if the franchisor has not provided complete information regarding the franchisor-franchisee relationship, as well as the details of the contract under which the business will be operated.

Only a few of the states that have enacted legislation concerning franchising have included disclosure provisions. California was the first state to enact a franchise disclosure law, and it has served as a model for other disclosure statutes. The California Franchise Investment Law sets out twenty-two items that must be disclosed in a registration filed with the state. Some of the items of disclosure include:

1. The name and business address of the franchisor;
2. The business experience of any people affiliated with the franchisor;
3. Whether any person associated with the franchisor has been convicted of a felony;
4. A recent financial statement;
5. A typical franchise agreement;
6. A statement of all fees that the franchisee is required to pay; and
7. Other information that the commissioner of corporations may reasonably require.

When misrepresentation permeates the initial sale of a franchise operation, the common-law remedy of fraud does not provide adequate relief. In most cases, the franchisee has already paid the franchise purchase price and may also have incurred substantial losses in the initial operating phases of the business. The elements of fraud are exceedingly difficult to prove. The franchisee has a great burden to show that the franchisor's original offer was fraudulent.

The FTC Franchise Rule of 1978 was promulgated in response to widespread evidence of deception and unfair practices in connection with the sale of franchises and business opportunity ventures. This rule requires that, within a specified time, franchisors and franchise brokers must fur-

nish the information that prospective franchisees need in order to make an informed decision about entering into a franchise relationship. The rule sets forth the circumstances under which a franchisor or broker can make claims about the projected sales income or profits of existing or potential outlets. The rule also imposes requirements that concern the establishment and termination of the franchise relationship.

The Franchise Agreement

The relationship between the franchisor and the franchisee is defined by a contract. Each franchise relationship and each industry have their own characteristics, so it is difficult to describe the broad range of details that a franchising contract may include. The following sections, however, will define the essential characteristics of the franchise relationship.

Payment for Franchise   The franchisee ordinarily pays an initial fee or lump-sum price for the franchise license (the privilege of being granted a franchise). This fee is separate from the various products that the franchisee purchases from or through the franchisor. In some industries, the franchisor relies heavily on the initial sale of the franchise in order to realize a profit. In other industries, the continued dealing between the parties brings profit to both.

In most situations, the franchisor will receive a stated percentage of the annual sales or annual volume of business done by the franchisee. The franchise agreement may also require the franchisee to pay a percentage of advertising costs and certain administrative expenses incurred throughout the franchise arrangement.

Location and Business Organization   Typically, the franchisor will determine the territory to be served. The franchise agreement can specify whether the premises for the business must be leased or purchased outright. In some cases, construction of a building is necessary to meet the terms of the franchise agreement.

In addition, the agreement will specify whether the franchisor supplies equipment and furnishings for the premises or whether this is the responsibility of the franchisee. When the franchise is a service operation such as a motel, the contract often provides that the franchisor will establish certain standards for the facility and will make inspections to ensure that the standards are being maintained in order to protect the franchise name and reputation.

The business organization of the franchisee is of great concern to the franchisor. Depending on the terms of the franchise agreement, the franchisor may specify particular requirements for the form and capital structure of the business. The franchise agreement can provide that certain standards of operation, such as sales quotas, quality considerations, or record keeping, must be met by the franchisee.

Furthermore, a franchisor may want to retain stringent control over the training of personnel involved in the operation and over administrative aspects of the business. Although the day-to-day operation of the franchise business is normally left up to the franchisee, the franchise agreement can provide for whatever amount of supervision and control the parties desire.

One area of franchises that causes a great deal of conflict is the *territorial exclusivity* of the franchise. Many franchise agreements, while they do define the territory allotted to a particular franchise, specifically state that the franchise is nonexclusive. Nonexclusivity allows the franchisor to establish multiple franchises in the same territory. The following case illustrates a situation where the franchise agreement did not guarantee exclusivity in a specific territory.

Case 17.5

IMPERIAL MOTORS, INC. v. CHRYSLER CORP.

United States District Court, District of Massachusetts, 1983.
559 F.Supp. 1312.

BACKGROUND AND FACTS   *In early 1976, the plaintiff, Imperial Motors, Inc., and Flynn, who owned the dealership, entered into direct dealer agreements for Chrysler and Plymouth dealerships with the defendant, Chrysler Corporation. The direct dealer agreements explicitly provided that Imperial would not have the exclusive right to purchase for resale defendant's cars in a four-town area of South Carolina. The Chrysler district manager, however, orally told Flynn that Imperial's Chrysler-Plymouth dealership would be the only one in these four towns.*

In August of 1976, Chrysler allowed another Chrysler-Plymouth dealer, Carroll Motors, to move into a new showroom seven miles from Imperial's location. Imperial claimed that Chrysler had violated the Automobile Dealers' Day in Court Act (a federal statute governing written franchise agreements between auto manufacturers and auto dealers) by approving the relocation of Carroll Motors. Chrysler moved for summary judgment contending that the plaintiff had not established a cause of action for the lawsuit.

ZOBEL, Judge.
*   *   *   *

Defendant's motion for summary judgment is proper as to that part of plaintiffs' claim which alleges that defendant's approval of Carroll's relocation was a violation of the [Automobile Dealers' Day in Court Act]. The Act covers only those actions of a franchisor which amount to a "failure . . . to act in good faith in performing or complying with any of the terms or provisions of the franchise, or in terminating, cancelling, or not renewing the franchise with a dealer." Good faith is narrowly defined as "the duty of each party . . . to act in a fair and equitable manner toward each other so as to guaranty the one party freedom from coercion, intimidation or threats of coercion or intimidation by the other party. The failure to abide by the terms of a franchise agreement cannot by itself constitute a violation of the act. Moreover, the Act explicitly defines a franchise as a "written agreement"; accordingly, oral promises are not part of a franchise agreement and cannot form the basis of a claim of bad faith.

Chrysler's motion for summary judgment was granted. The court held that granting a franchise to Carroll in the same area as Imperial was not a violation of the franchise agreement or of the Automobile Dealers' Day in Court Act because the promise was oral, not written.

DECISION AND REMEDY

The franchisee in this case was left unprotected by the franchise agreement as far as territorial exclusivity was concerned. The same denial of relief resulted under the Unfair Trade Practices Act when a Ford automobile dealer (with a nonexclusive franchise agreement) filed suit after Ford Motor Company had granted another Ford dealership in close proximity to his own. [See McLaughlin Ford, Inc. v. Ford Motor Company, *192 Conn. 558, 473 A.2d 1185 (1985)].*

COMMENTS

Price and Quality Controls   Franchises provide the franchisor with an outlet for the firm's goods and services. Depending on the nature of the business, the franchisor may require the franchisee to purchase products from the franchisor at an established price. Of course, a franchisor cannot set the prices at which the franchisee will resell the goods, as this is a violation of state or federal antitrust laws. A franchisor can suggest retail prices but cannot insist on them.

Although a franchisor can require franchisees to purchase supplies from it, requiring a franchisee to purchase *exclusively* from the franchisor may violate state or federal antitrust laws. The implications of antitrust violations on territorial restrictions, restrictions on products sold, resale price fixing, and price discrimination is discussed in Chapter 19.

As a general rule, no question exists as to the validity of a provision permitting the franchisor to enforce certain quality standards. Since the franchisor has a legitimate interest in maintaining the quality of the product or service in order to protect its name and reputation, it can exercise greater control in this area than would otherwise be tolerated.

Termination of the Franchise Arrangement

The duration of the franchise is a matter to be determined between the parties. Generally, a franchise will start out for a short period, such as a year, so that the franchisee and the franchisor can determine whether they want to stay in business with one another. The franchise agreement will usually specify that termination must be for cause, such as death or disability of the franchisee, insolvency of the franchisee, breach of the franchise agreement, or failure to meet specified sales quotas. Most franchise contracts provide that notice of termination must be given.

Much franchise litigation has arisen over termination provisions. Since the franchise agreement is normally a "form" contract prepared by the franchisor and since the bargaining power of the franchisee is rarely equal to that of the franchisor, the termination provisions of contracts are generally more favorable to the franchisor. The lack of statutory law and case law in this area affects the franchisee most keenly. Franchisees in automobile dealerships and gasoline stations have some statutory protection under the Automobile Dealers' Day in Court and Petroleum Marketing Practices Acts.

The franchisee normally invests a substantial amount of time and money in the franchise operation to make it successful. Despite this fact, the franchisee may receive little or nothing for the business on termination. The franchisor owns the trademark and hence the business.

Franchisee's Relationship to Franchisor: Agent or Independent Contractor?

The mere licensing of a trade name does not create an agency relationship. The courts have determined that certain other factors in the franchisor-franchisee relationship may indicate the existence of an agency relationship:

1. The terms of the agreement create an agency relationship.
2. The franchisor exercises a high degree of control over the franchisee's activities.
3. A third person looking at the relationship between the franchisor and the franchisee would reasonably believe that there is an agency relationship.
4. The franchisor derives an especially great benefit from the franchisee's activities. The greater the benefit, the more likely an agency relationship will be found.

If these factors show a very close relationship between the franchisor and the franchisee, their relationship will be deemed to be that of an employer-employee or principal-agent in dealings with third parties. If the factors show a high degree of independence between the franchisee and franchisor, the franchisee will be deemed an independent contractor.

The characterization of the relationship has tax implications and implications for the regulatory treatment of the business organization. In addition, if an agency relationship is found, the franchisor is liable for the franchisee's improper actions or injuries to third parties both in tort and in contract.

Choosing the Best Form
of Business Organization

A friend has developed a new oil filter for use in internal combustion engines that enables the engine to use the same oil up to ten times as long as is currently possible. She believes there is a market for such a product, but, being totally unfamiliar with business matters, she comes to you for advice.

After reviewing the materials she has developed to explain the product, you believe that the project is worth pursuing. The two of you would like to begin a business to produce and sell the product.

Good business practice would suggest that you consult an attorney before proceeding with your plans. A good business lawyer can discuss with you your goals, alternative courses of action to meet those goals, and the probable consequences of each alternative.

To take maximum advantage of the time spent with your attorney, you should prepare certain information. What assets will be part of the business? In whose name are those assets held now? You may be transferring real property to the business, or your friend may be transferring patent or other rights, and you will need to discuss the tax consequences of those transfers.

Each of you will also want to collect information on your individual financial and tax statuses that may enter into the decision as to what form of business entity is appropriate for you. How much money will you need to bring

to your business in order to carry it through the first year? You should have some idea of how you will raise this money. Can you and your friend provide it personally from your savings or through a bank loan, or will you bring in other equity investors?

If you bring in other investors, the questions of liability and control of the business will become more complex. Even if you and your friend provide all of the capital, however, the issues of liability and of control of day-to-day operations and long-term policy are critical and will be an important element in choosing the form of business entity.

You must also consider how freely ownership interests in your business can be transferred. Your friend may have implicit trust in your business judgment, but would she want to be in business with your heirs if you should die? Would you want to proceed if she were to sell her interest in the business to a stranger without her technical skills? Perhaps both of you will want the option to buy the other's interest in the business in case of death, or you may want a right of first refusal if one of you decides to transfer your interest during your lifetime.

Obviously, the answers to all of these questions have an impact on what form of business organization you should use. By considering these questions in advance and bringing with you cash-flow projections, as well as tax and other relevant information, your attorney will be better able to assist you in starting your business.

Summary

A corporation is the most formal type of business entity. The first step in formalizing a corporation is to file articles of incorporation with the appropriate state agency. Among the items included in this document are the name, address, and general purpose of the corporation, its duration, the number and class of shares, the number of directors, and the names of the incorporators. In some states, as few as one person can file articles of incorporation.

The next step is the adoption of bylaws. The bylaws control the internal operation of the business. In addition, any business must have funds with which to operate. Funds are obtained by issuing securities. The two broad classes of securities are equity securities and debt securities.

The most frequently used equity security is common stock. This form of security generally offers voting rights in the election of the board of directors and other major corporate matters. Common stock does not have a fixed dividend rate. On dissolution, the shareholders have a right to a proportionate share of the assets after payment of all other parties.

Closely akin to common stock is preferred stock. It is considered an equity security, but it bears great similarity to a debt obligation. Normally, preferred shareholders have a preference for dividends that are paid at a fixed rate. During dissolution, preferred stock is paid ahead of common stock but after corporate debt obligations.

Debt financing is used by all businesses. The most common long-term debt is represented by a bond or debenture. These debts will pay a fixed interest rate whether or not the corporation is profitable. On dissolution, debt securities are paid ahead of equity securities. Generally, in the absence of a personal guarantee, shareholders are immune from liability for the debts of the corporation. If the corporation is not properly conducted, however, the courts may allow a piercing of the corporate veil in order to hold shareholders liable.

As long as directors and officers do not breach their fiduciary duties, they are likewise not personally liable for the debts of the corporation. They can, however, be held liable for mismanagement in carrying out their responsibilities. They are protected from legal actions based on losses brought about by their making honest errors in business decisions (the business judgment rule).

The shareholders own the corporation. They elect the board of directors. The board of directors sets corporate policy and appoints the officers. Like the incorporators, the board of directors, in some states, can include as few as one person. All corporations must have officers, which include a president, at least one vice-president, a secretary, and a treasurer. The same person may occupy several positions except for president and secretary.

A corporation can limit the transferability of securities. These restrictions must be reasonable, and the limitations must be known (placed on the security) to the holder and prospective purchaser.

Whenever a business decision is made, its effects on taxes must be considered. This is especially true when selecting a corporate form of organization. Special tax advantages occur if S Corporation status is selected instead of the normal tax status of a corporation. All losses and profits are passed through the corporation to the shareholders if a corporation elects to be taxed under the S Corporation provisions of the Internal Revenue Code.

The law of franchising is developing through cases and through state and federal statutes. A franchise exists when there is a contract in which one party owns a trademark, trade name, or copyright and he or she allows another party to use this right under specified conditions or limitations. Three different types of franchises have been developed: (1) distributorship, (2) business format, and (3) manufacturing or processing plant.

The franchise agreement establishes the rights of the franchisor and franchisee. Among the items included in this document may be the payments required, the location of the business, pricing and quality control provisions, and how the franchise may be terminated.

The franchise industry is facing increasing controls from both the state and federal governments. This is due in part to prior negative conduct on the part of franchisors. Among these controls are the Federal Trade Commission's disclosure rules, which specify information that must be given to all franchisees before they sign franchise agreements. This information enables franchisees to analyze the potential business success of the venture.

Key Terms

Questions and Case Problems

1. Acme, Inc., has a board of directors consisting of three members (Able, Baker, and Carter) and approximately 500 shareholders. At a regular meeting of the board, the board selects Green as president of the corporation by a two-to-one vote, with Able dissenting. The minutes of the meeting do not register Able's dissenting vote. Later, when an audit occurs, it is discovered that Green is a former convict and has embezzled $500,000 from Acme, Inc. This loss is not covered by insurance. The corporation wants to hold directors Able, Baker, and Carter liable. Able claims no liability. Discuss the personal liability of the directors of the corporation.

2. Blake is interested in becoming a service station dealer. He contacts Esco Oil Corporation and obtains a franchise contract in which Esco agrees to furnish Blake all gasoline, oil, and related products necessary to run the service station. In addition, Esco provides Blake with Esco signs and promotional materials. A sign reading ''Blake's Esco Service'' is provided for the front of the station. In return for supplying all the necessary products, promotional materials, signs, and other services, Esco is to receive a percentage of receipts on all products sold. Esco advertises that it stands behind its dealers. The relationship between Blake and Esco is challenged. Discuss whether the association is strictly a franchisor-franchisee relationship or whether it is a principal-agent (employer-employee) relationship.

3. Carter Corporation has issued and has outstanding 100,000 shares of common stock. Four stockholders own 60,000 of these shares, and for the past six years they have nominated a slate of people for membership on the board, all of whom get elected. John and twenty other shareholders, owning 20,000 shares, are dissatisfied with corporate management and want a representative on the board who shares their views. Explain under what cir-

cumstances John and the minority shareholders can elect their representative to the board.

4. Pointer formed a corporation with $1,000 capital and later loaned over $400,000 to the corporation. Six days after the loan, he was notified that Tigrett had filed suit against his corporation, and Pointer transferred corporate assets amounting to $400,000 to himself as repayment of the loans. Pointer then transferred these assets to another corporation, of which he was the sole shareholder. The second corporation took over all the business and duties of the original corporation. At the time that Pointer undertook these transfers, Tigrett had not obtained a judgment against the corporation and so was not one of its creditors. By the time Tigrett was awarded a judgment against the original corporation, it had no assets. Is there any way for Tigrett to collect the amount of her judgment? [Tigrett v. Pointer, 580 S.W.2d 375 (Tex.Civ.App. 1978)]

5. Klinicki and Lundgren formed Berlinair, a closely held Oregon corporation, to provide air transportation out of West Germany. Klinicki, who owned 33 percent of the company stock, was the vice-president and a director. Lundgren and his family owned 66 percent of Berlinair, and Berlinair's attorney owned the last 1 percent of stock. One of the goals of Berlinair was to obtain the contract with BFR, a West German consortium of travel agents, to provide BFR with air charter service. Later Lundgren learned that the BFR contract might become available. Lundgren then incorporated Air Berlin Charter Company, of which he was the sole owner, and bid for the BFR contract. Lundgren won the BFR contract for Air Berlin while using Berlinair working time, staff, money, and facilities without the knowledge of Klinicki. When Klinicki learned of the BFR contract, he filed a derivative suit, as a minority stockholder, against Lundgren and Air Berlin for usurping a corporate opportunity. Should Klinicki re-

cover against Air Berlin? If so, what should Klinicki be awarded as damages? [Klinicki v. Lundgren, 67 Or.App. 160, 678 P.2d 1250 (1984)]

6. Salem Tent & Awning Company was a corporation in the business of renting awnings and tents. Dusty Schmidt came into the office to rent seven tents to use as covers for his Christmas trees during the four weeks before Christmas. Although Dusty and another owned Western Oregon Christmas Trees, Inc., he signed the prepared invoice without indicating that he was part owner of this corporation or that the tents were for the business. The invoice stated: "Renter is Responsible for Damages." Dusty gave Salem Tent a $2,000 down-payment check on which was printed "Western Oregon Christmas Trees." No indication was made that a corporation existed. Dusty received the tents and began to use them. A sudden storm destroyed several of the tents. When Dusty refused to pay for the damaged tents, Salem Tent sued for damages. Are both Western Oregon Christmas Trees, Inc., and Dusty Schmidt liable for this loss, or is just one of them liable? [Salem Tent & Awning Co. v. Schmidt, 79 Or.App. 475, 719 P.2d 899 (1986)]

7. Atlantic Properties, Inc., had only four shareholders, each of whom owned 25 percent of the capital stock. The bylaws required an 80 percent affirmative vote of the shareholders on all actions taken by the corporation. This provision had the effect of giving any of the four original shareholders a veto in corporate decisions. One shareholder refused for seven years to vote for any dividends, although he was warned that his actions might expose the corporation to Internal Revenue Service penalties for unreasonable accumulation of corporate earnings and profits. The Internal Revenue Service did impose such penalties on the corporation. Can the dissenting shareholder be held personally liable for these penalties? [Smith v. Atlantic Properties, Inc., 12 Mass.App.Ct. 201, 422 N.E.2d 798 (1981)]

8. Harvey's is a group of New York corporations. Five of these corporations entered into an agreement with Flynt Distributing Company for Flynt to distribute their magazines. Following this agreement, Harvey failed to pay Flynt or to ship their magazines to Flynt, causing Flynt injury. Two of Harvey's shareholders converted the assets of the five corporations to their own use, which left the corporations undercapitalized. Discuss if this conduct amounts to an abuse of corporate business, allowing Flynt to pierce the corporate veil. [Flynt Distributing Co. v. Harvey, 734 F.2d 1389 (9th Cir. 1984)]

9. Pacific Development, Inc., was incorporated in the District of Columbia for the purpose of international brokerage consulting. Pacific's founder, president, and sole shareholder was Tongsun Park, a South Korean who was on close terms with South Korea's president, Park Chung Hee. The government alleged that Park's main purpose was to influence Congress to give economic and military aid to South Korea. The IRS assessed $4.5 million in back taxes against Park in 1977. It then seized the assets of Pacific Development, Inc., claiming that the company was a mere alter ego of Park. Valley Finance, Inc., was another of Park's wholly owned corporations. It had loaned money to Pacific Valley Finance, and it held a second deed of trust on the real property that the IRS had seized. Both Pacific Development and Valley Finance attempted to obtain the return of Pacific Development's assets. The plaintiffs claimed that the IRS had improperly pierced the corporate veil of Pacific. Discuss whether you agree with the plaintiffs. [Valley Finance, Inc. v. United States, 629 F.2d 162 (D.C. Cir. 1980)]

UNIT IV BUSINESS AND GOVERNMENT REGULATION

Chapter 18 Securities Regulation

They [corporations] cannot commit treason, nor be outlawed nor excommunicated for they have no soul.

Sir Edward Coke,
Case of Sutton's Hospital (1625)

OUTLINE

Introduction

This chapter covers the regulation of transactions involving securities. Only in this century did any governmental body consider establishing statutory or administrative laws to regulate this area of business. The first such law was adopted in 1911 by the state of Kansas. This statute and subsequent state legislation regulated the sale of securities within the state (intrastate transactions). To pass the initial legislation, a member of the Kansas legislature claimed that promoters were so shrewd that they could sell anyone a "piece of the blue sky itself." Since then, statutes that regulate the sales of securities within a state have been known as **blue sky laws**.

This chapter defines securities and looks in detail at the major laws that regulate these transactions.

What Is a Security?

Securities are created by the issuing party; they can be issued in unlimited amounts, at relatively little cost, because securities are nothing more than pieces of paper that represent a financial interest. Securities are not used or consumed; rather, they are a type of currency, traded in what is called the "secondary market." Securities in the secondary market are bought and sold by people who normally are not the issuers of the security.

Securities are more vulnerable to price fluctuation than other types of investments, such as automobiles or real estate, because the value of a security may rise or fall on the basis of information concerning the entity; true, false, and misleading information all influence the stock price. This distinctive feature of securities makes it very easy for individuals or brokerage firms to misrepresent the value of an investment. Securities laws attempt to protect investors in two ways: by mandating disclosure and by prohibiting fraud.

What constitutes a security? Stocks and bonds are two types of securities. The definition of a security, set out in the Securities Act of 1933, is very broad, and the exact definition is not clear. The courts have interpreted this language expansively. In addition to the traditional stocks and bonds, investment contracts have been found to

be securities. An investment contract is defined as: (1) an investment of money or other consideration, (2) in a common enterprise, (3) with the investor expecting a profit, and (4) the profit is derived primarily through the efforts of a promoter or a third party other than the investor.

To meet the criteria of an investment contract, the investor must turn money over to another individual for investment purposes, and the capital must be pooled with the capital of other investors so that each individual owns an undivided interest in the whole. The investor does not have any day-to-day control over the enterprise. The owner of a security is passive. An officer or employee who owns stock in his or her company is always considered to be a passive investor.

Securities laws have been applied to various transactions that have not traditionally been thought of as securities. Examples of these transactions include the sale of interest in land involving orange groves and pecan groves, the sale of limited partnership interests, and investments in mink and chinchilla farms. The possibility that a business venture may be termed a security must be considered in every transaction, as the legal ramifications of engaging in the buying and selling of securities are far reaching.

Major Securities Laws

The devastating effects of the Great Depression led Congress to hold hearings. These investigations tried to search out the causes of the collapse of the financial system in 1929 so that legislation could be adopted to prevent another such disaster. Some of the laws eventually adopted were specifically aimed at the regulation of financial markets. Some of the statutes regulated practices, while others regulated specific industries. As a result of congressional action at that time and over the intervening decades, two major pieces of legislation, along with their amendments, were adopted to regulate securities, and to control insider trading of securities.

Securities Act of 1933

The first statute enacted by Congress was the **Securities Act of 1933**, which is often referred to

LEGAL HIGHLIGHT	**Earthworms and Salvador Dali Are Securities?**

Earthworms and Securities

Allen J. Gross solicited buyer-investors to raise earthworms. In a newsletter, Gross promised that he would give any buyer growing instructions that would ensure a profitable farm, that the time required would be similar to that of raising a garden, that the earthworms double in quantity every 60 days, and that he would buy back all baitsize worms produced for $2.25 per pound. Gross told Smith that success was guaranteed because Gross agreed to repurchase Smith's production.

In reality, worms multiply at a maximum of eight rather than 64 times per year. The price of $2.25 per pound was ten times greater than the true market conditions. The only way for Smith to make a profit was to sell the worms for $2.25. This qualified as a "common enterprise" since the fortune of the Smiths was interwoven with and dependent on the efforts and success of Gross. The efforts of those other than the investor were undeniably significant: Smith was promised that the effort necessary to raise worms was minimal, and the promised income could only occur if Gross purchased the worms. As a result, the court

found the sale of the earthworm farms to be an investment security. [*Smith v. Gross,* 604 F.2d 639 (9th Cir. 1979)]

Salvador Dali and Securities

Some art galleries have been selling fake Salvador Dali prints to customers for several years. Some of these sales are boiler-room operations where the seller places calls to people, telling them that they can own an affordable Dali print. The print, purchased by the seller for $25 to $50, is sold to the victim for $1,500 to $2,500. The only problem is that the print is really a reproduction and not a genuine limited-edition lithograph. The "fake" Dali prints are prints, but are neither authorized nor supervised reproductions by Dali of his own works.

Although each victim is overcharged a relatively small sum, the total amount is staggering. In New York, a boiler-room operation was convicted of deceiving investors out of $1.3 million. Because the owners of this operation had sold the Dali prints to victims over the telephone as investments, they were convicted of securities fraud.

as the "Truth in Securities" law. Full and truthful disclosure is required by companies issuing securities. The securities must be registered before they are offered or sold to the public. The 1933 act was designed to protect the investing public through full disclosure of information about the securities. The act also forbids fraud and deceit in the distribution of the securities, even those that are not required to be registered.

Securities Exchange Act of 1934

A year later, Congress adopted the **Securities Exchange Act of 1934**. Divided into six major parts, this statute created the **Securities and Exchange**

Commission (SEC). Second, it requires that all national securities exchanges, such as the New York Stock Exchange and the American Exchange, and all broker-dealers who have interstate operations be registered with the SEC. Third, in order to monitor the activities of the various securities markets, the SEC is required to maintain surveillance of them, which it does now through the use of computers.

Fourth, like the 1933 act, the 1934 act establishes a registration and disclosure requirement that applies to corporations whose securities are listed on any national securities exchange and that covers the exchange of these securities. A fifth section regulates the solicitation of proxies (written authorization given by a shareholder to a third party to vote the shareholder's stock). Finally, insider trading is prohibited under two sections of the statute: Section 16 and Section 10(b).

The Securities and Exchange Commission is an independent regulatory agency. Congress delegated to the SEC administrative rule-making powers and the responsibility for administering all federal securities law. The SEC is composed of five members who serve staggered five-year terms. They are appointed by the president, but no more than three members may be from the same political party.

The Securities Investor Protection Act of 1970

A series of stock brokerage houses failed in the 1960s, leading Congress to amend the 1934 act to protect the consumer. The amendment created the **Securities Investor Protection Corporation** (SIPC). This corporation manages a fund that protects investors from the financial harm caused when stock brokerage houses fail. The fund is similar to the fund administered by the Federal Deposit Insurance Corporation (FDIC), which protects depositors in banks.

Foreign Corrupt Practices Act

The **Foreign Corrupt Practices Act** (FCPA) of 1977 also amended the 1934 act. Although part of the FCPA applies to corporations doing business in other countries, the rest of the act applies to all corporations registered with the SEC, whether or not they are engaged in foreign business.

This act requires, for the first time, public corporations to keep and maintain records that accurately reflect their financial activities. All corporations reporting to the SEC under the 1934 act must comply, even if they only operated in the United States and have no international business relations. Further, the FCPA requires all corporations reporting under the 1934 act to have an internal accounting system in order to ensure accurate records.

This act attempts to prevent the concealment of illegal activities. The type of illegal actions that Congress discovered in its hearings ranged from

the purchasing of castles in Ireland for top management to the paying of millions to foreign officials in order to ensure lucrative contracts. These millions of dollars in payment were not disclosed to the shareholders or to the SEC. Some of the activities were criminal acts even prior to the adoption of the FCPA.

Insider Trading Sanctions Act of 1984

The **Insider Trading Sanctions Act** (ITSA) of 1984 gives additional power to the SEC for violations of insider trading. The SEC is allowed to recover up to three times the profit made in these situations. Any recovery goes to the government and not to the parties who may have been injured by such activity. In 1988, this act was amended (by the Insider Trading and Securities Fraud Enforcement Act). The amendment enlarged the scope of persons who would have civil liability under the act, gave the SEC authority to reward informants in insider-trading cases, gave the SEC rulemaking authority to require specific policies and procedures to prevent insider trading, and increased criminal penalties (increased maximum jail terms from five to ten years, and criminal fines for individuals from $100,000 to $1 million and for corporations and partnerships from $500,000 to $2.5 million). The amendment also provided for the award of treble damages against securities firms for failing to maintain a proper system of supervision to prevent and detect insider trading violations by employees.

The Securities Act of 1933

The Securities Act of 1933 was designed to prohibit various forms of fraud and to stabilize the securities industry by requiring that all essential information concerning the issuing of securities be made available to the investing public. The 1933 act is basically a disclosure requirement for new issues of securities.

Requirements of the Registration Statement

Corporations issuing a security unless exempt must file a registration statement with the SEC. The security must be registered before it is offered to the public. Additionally, investors must be provided with a **prospectus**, which is the document that is utilized to sell the security. In principle, the registration statement and prospectus supply sufficient information to enable unsophisticated investors to evaluate the financial risk involved.

The registration statement must be signed by the corporation's principal executive officer, principal accounting officer, principal financial officer, and at least a majority of the members of the board of directors. Signing the registration statement makes a person potentially liable if there are any errors or material omissions in it.

The SEC does not attempt to determine whether an investment is a good one. The only thing demanded is that sufficient information be available to a potential investor so that he or she can make an intelligent decision.

Requirements of the Registering Corporation

Before filing the registration statement and prospectus with the SEC, the corporation is allowed to obtain an underwriter who will monitor distribution of the new issue. A twenty-day waiting period after registration is mandated before any sale can take place. This period may be extended by the SEC, or the registration statement may require amendments that start the twenty-day period over again. During this period, oral offers between interested investors and the issuing corporation concerning the purchase and sale of the proposed securities may take place, but the securities cannot be legally bought or sold.

During the waiting period, written advertising is allowed in the form of a **tombstone advertisement**. This advertisement is so named because the format resembles a tombstone and is outlined in black. Such advertisements simply tell the investor where and how to obtain a prospectus. Normally, any other type of advertising is prohibited.

At this time, a **red herring prospectus** may be distributed. It gets its name from the red legend printed across it, stating that the registration has been filed but has not become effective. The red legend indicates that the prospectus is still preliminary and not yet approved by the SEC.

Misrepresentations in Registering with the SEC

A registration statement that contains material untruths or omissions makes the issuer (such as a corporation) liable for violation of the securities laws. In addition, all individuals who signed, were named, or participated in drafting the registration statement are liable. Several defenses are available to those who sign a false statement. For example, the defendants will not be held liable if there is proof that the plaintiff knew the statement was untrue. Also, a defendant who exercised ''due diligence'' in verifying the truth of the statement may also escape liability for false statements made to the SEC. The **due diligence defense** is available to all defendants except the issuer.

In the following case, the court found that the registration statement contained material false statements of fact and material omissions and the court imposed liability on the individuals who were involved in the issuance of new securities.

BACKGROUND AND FACTS   *This lawsuit was brought by purchasers of BarChris debentures under Section 11 of the Securities Act of 1933. The plaintiffs alleged that the registration statement filed with the Securities and Exchange Commission, which became effective on May 16, 1961, contained material false statements and material omissions.*

The defendants fell into three categories: (1) the people who signed the registration statement, (2) the underwriters (consisting of eight investment banking firms), and (3) BarChris's auditors—Peat, Marwick, Mitchell & Co. Included in the group of defendants who signed the registration statement were: (1) BarChris's nine directors, (2) BarChris's controller, (3) one

Case 18.1
ESCOTT v. BARCHRIS CONSTRUCTION CORP.
United States District Court, Southern District of New York, 1968.
283 F.Supp. 643.

of BarChris's attorneys, (4) two investment bankers who were later named as directors of the BarChris Corporation, and (5) numerous other people participating in the preparation of the registration statement.

BarChris grew out of a business started in 1946 as a bowling-alley building company. The introduction of automatic pin-setting machines in 1952 sparked rapid growth in the bowling industry. BarChris benefited from this increased interest in bowling, and its construction operations expanded rapidly. It was estimated that in 1960 BarChris installed approximately 3 percent of all bowling lanes built in the United States. BarChris's sales increased dramatically between 1956 and 1960, and the company was recognized as a significant factor in the bowling construction industry.

BarChris was in constant need of cash to finance its operations, a need that grew more and more pressing as the operations expanded. In 1959, BarChris sold over a half-million shares of its common stock to the public. By early 1961 it needed additional working capital, and this time it decided to sell debentures.

BarChris filed a registration statement of the debentures with the SEC and received the proceeds of the financing. Nevertheless, it experienced increasing financial difficulties, which in time became insurmountable. By early 1962, it was painfully apparent that BarChris was beginning to fail. In October BarChris filed a petition for an arrangement under the Bankruptcy Act, and it defaulted on the interest due on the debentures in November.

The plaintiffs challenged the accuracy of the debenture registration statement and charged that the text of the prospectus—including many of the figures—was false and that material information had been omitted. The federal district court reviewed all of the figures and statements included in the prospectus.

McLEAN, Judge.

* * * *

The action is brought under Section 11 of the Securities Act of 1933. Plaintiffs allege that the registration statement [and the prospectus included in it] with respect to these debentures filed with the Securities and Exchange Commission, which became effective on May 16, 1961, contained material false statements and material omissions.
* * * *
* * * On the main issue of liability, the questions to be decided are (1) did the registration statement contain false statements of fact, or did it omit to state facts which should have been stated in order to prevent it from being misleading; (2) if so, were the facts which were falsely stated or omitted ''material'' within the meaning of the Act. * * *
* * * *

It is a prerequisite to liability under Section 11 of the Act that the fact which is falsely stated in a registration statement, or the fact that it is omitted when it should have been stated to avoid misleading, be ''material.'' The regulations of the Securities and Exchange Commission pertaining to the registration of securities define the word as follows:

''The term 'material,' when used to qualify a requirement for the furnishing of information as to any subject, limits the information required to those matters as to which an average prudent investor ought reasonably to be informed before purchasing the security registered.''

What are ''matters as to which an average prudent investor ought reasonably to be informed''? It seems obvious that they are matters which such an investor needs to know before he can make an intelligent, informed decision whether or not to buy the security.

Early in the history of the Act, a definition of materiality was given in Matter of Charles A. Howard, which is still valid today. A material fact was there defined as:

''* * * a fact which if it had been correctly stated or disclosed would have deterred or tended to deter the average prudent investor from purchasing the securities in question.''

The average prudent investor is not concerned with minor inaccuracies or with errors as to matters which are of no interest to him. The facts which tend to deter him from purchasing a security are facts which have an important bearing upon the nature or condition of the issuing corporation or its business.

Judged by this test, there is no doubt that many of the misstatements and omissions in this prospectus were material. This is true of all of them which relate to the state of affairs in 1961, i.e., the overstatement of sales and gross profit for the first quarter, the understatement of contingent liabilities as of April 30, the overstatement of orders on hand and the failure to disclose the true facts with respect to officers' loans, customers' delinquencies, application of proceeds and the prospective operation of several alleys.

BarChris Corporation itself, all the signers of the registration statement for the debentures, the underwriters, and the corporation's auditors were held liable.

DECISION AND REMEDY

Exemptions

A corporation can avoid the high cost and complicated procedures associated with registration by taking advantage of certain exemptions to the registration requirement. Two general types of exemptions are allowed: **exempt transactions** and **exempt securities**.

Exempt Transactions   The three exempt transactions allowed by the 1933 act are: **small offering exemptions**, **intrastate offering exemptions**, and **private offering exemptions**. These exemptions are available only for the current transaction and do not cover future transactions. The next transaction must either be registered or must be exempt from registration in its own right.

Small Offering Exemptions   The SEC rules outline three different types of small offering exemptions. These offerings by an issuer are not large enough for the federal government to reg-

ulate: (1) certain types of bank loans, (2) privately negotiated sales of securities to large institutional investors, and (3) business-venture promotions by a few closely related persons.

Regulation D of the 1933 act creates the distinction between an **accredited investor** and an **unaccredited investor**. The accredited investor is not likely to need government protection in making its investment determinations. An accredited investor is one of the following:

1. An institutional investor, such as an insurance company, bank, credit union, or pension fund.
2. The seller's directors and officers.
3. An individual investor with an annual income of over $200,000 for three consecutive years.
4. An individual with a net worth of over $1 million.
5. An individual who buys at least $150,000 worth of securities, provided that the purchase price does not exceed 20 percent of the person's net worth.

An unaccredited investor does not meet these requirements. Regulation D has three sections covering exemptions, some of which are concerned with unaccredited investors.

Under Regulation D, Rule 504, a seller may offer up to $500,000 in securities during any twelve-month period if no general solicitation or advertising is used. Although registration is not required, a notice must be filed with the SEC. Resale of these issues is restricted. This exemption is for small businesses who are not reporting to the SEC under the Securities Exchange Act of 1934.

Under Rule 505 of Regulation D, the seller may sell up to $5 million in securities during any twelve-month period if there are no more than thirty-five unaccredited investors. These transactions are exempt if no general solicitation or advertising is used. The number of accredited investors is unlimited. If the sale involves any unaccredited investors, all investors must be given material information about the offering company, its business, and the securities before the sale. The issuer is not required to believe that each unaccredited investor "has such knowledge and experience in financial and business matters that he is capable of evaluating the merits and the risks of the prospective investment." A notice must be filed with the SEC. This exemption applies to corporations even if they are covered by the 1934 act.

Under rule 506 of Regulation D, businesses, including the ones covered by the 1934 act, may offer an unlimited amount of securities if the securities are not generally solicited or advertised. An unlimited number of accredited investors can participate but there can be no more than thirty-five unaccredited investors and the seller must determine that each unaccredited investor has enough knowledge and experience in financial and business matters to be able to evaluate the merits and the risks of the prospective investment. If there are any unaccredited investors, the issuer must provide to all purchasers material information about itself, its business, and the securities before the sale. A notice must be filed with the SEC.

Thus, Rule 506 differs from Rule 505 in that it requires material information to be given to unaccredited investors, and it requires the seller to verify that the unaccredited investor has sufficient knowledge or experience to evaluate the risks and merits of the issue.

Under SEC Regulation A, a seller is allowed to sell up to $1.5 million in a one-year period with a simplified registration process. No limit is placed on the number of purchasers, and disclosure is not required if the offering is under $100,000. Any offering above $100,000 must have an offering circular that discloses material information regarding the investment. The circular must be filed with the SEC ten days prior to the sale of the securities.

Intrastate Offering Exemptions The federal government allows each state to regulate securities offerings that are within its boundaries. An intrastate offering must be made only to resident investors in one state by a seller that resides within that state. The seller must have its principal office located in the state, have 80 percent of its assets and 80 percent of its gross revenues in the state, and 80 percent of the proceeds of the offering must be used within the state. One effect of an offer to an out-of-state resident would be the cancellation of this exemption.

Private Offering Exemptions The federal government is not interested in offerings that are privately made, since the protection of the public is the goal of the 1933 act. A private offering can be made to no more than thirty-five non-accredited investors who have experience in business and financial matters or have the advice of such a person. The investor must have access to all the information needed to make an informed investment decision. This exemption was developed by case law. It has not been determined whether Rule 506 has preempted this exemption.

Exempt Securities In addition to the exempt transactions, some types of securities are exempt from registration under the 1933 act. These include securities issued by governments (state and federal), banks, savings and loan associations, charitable organizations, and common carriers that are regulated by other federal laws. Securities distributed as stock dividends or in stock splits are also exempt.

The Securities Exchange Act of 1934

The primary purposes of the Securities Exchange Act are to ensure the integrity of stock and securities sold through national stock exchanges and over-the-counter markets, to inform the investing public of the financial condition of a business and to protect the public from fraudulent activity. The act provides for the regulation and registration of security exchanges, brokers, dealers, and national securities associations, such as the National Association of Securities Dealers (NASD). It regulates the markets in which securities are traded by maintaining a continuous disclosure system for all corporations with securities on the securities exchanges and for those companies that have assets in excess of $5 million and 500 or more shareholders. The SEC is allowed by the 1934 act to engage in market surveillance in order to regulate such undesirable market practices as fraud, market manipulation, and misrepresentation.

Proxy Requirement

The act regulates proxy solicitation for voting. A **proxy** is a written authorization to cast a shareholder's vote. A person can solicit proxies from a number of shareholders in an attempt to concentrate voting power. The SEC reviews the procedures used in obtaining proxies, and the SEC's rules require that proposed proxy material be filed in advance for examination. In any solicitation there must be clear disclosures on all matters which stockholders are to vote on and the stockholder must be afforded the right to vote a simple yes or no on each matter.

Forms That Must Be Filed

Publicly held corporations are required to update their registration periodically with annual and quarterly reports. The annual report, Form 10-K, is filed at the end of the fiscal period, and it must include audited financial statements, the present status of the business, and its securities holdings.

Form 10-Q is the quarterly report that reflects any financial changes that have occurred since the last reporting period. In addition, any time a material event occurs, such as a change in control or bankruptcy, Form 8-K must be filed. The legal definition of a material event is any occurrence that a reasonably prudent investor would want to know about in order to reevaluate his or her investment.

Insider Trading and Fraud

One of the most important parts of the 1934 act relates to **insider trading**. Because of their positions, corporate directors, officers, and key employees often obtain advance inside information that can affect the future market value of the corporate stock. Obviously, their positions can give them a trading advantage over the general public and shareholders. Another important part of the 1934 act is to promote investor protection by prohibition of fraud. Several provisions of the 1934 act deal with insider trading and prohibition of fraud—specifically **Section 16** and **Section 10(b)**, together with SEC **Rule 10b-5**.

Section 16   Section 16 covers directors, officers, and owners of more than 10 percent of the shares of any one class of stock of a company registered under the 1934 act. These people are designated as "insiders," and they must file reports of their holdings and transactions with the SEC.

If these people make a purchase and sale or sale and purchase of stock within a six-month period that results in a profit, that profit is illegal and may be forfeited to the issuer of the stock. Called an "illegal short-swing profit," liability is *automatic* because Congress decided not to require the SEC to prove that the person had used insider information for personal gain. For stock owned longer than six months, it must be proved that these people made a profit based on insider information. If the case is proved, they can be forced to return the illegal profit to the corporation.

Section 10(b) and Rule 10b-5   One of the basic tools employed by the SEC to provide and promote investor protection is the prohibition of fraud. The most widely applied section is Section 10(b) of the 1934 act, along with SEC Rule 10b-5. Section 10(b) makes it unlawful "to use or employ, in connection with the purchase or sale of any

LEGAL HIGHLIGHT   **Crime and Punishment**

Starting in the mid 1980s, federal prosecutors acting mainly on tips unearthed some of the largest insider trading scandals in American history. Americans and Wall Street were shocked by the numerous revelations of insider trading that have resulted in the prosecution of some of the most successful traders. The following is a partial list of these people and their activities and ages at the time of sentencing.

PAUL THAYER, 65. *History:* Thayer was a corporate director with a number of major corporations. During the time he served on those boards, he leaked inside information to his girlfriend and a stockbroker, who, in turn, earned $3 million from the tips. Thayer did not make any money. The SEC brought civil and criminal charges. He pleaded guilty to obstructing justice by lying to the SEC.

Sentence: In May 1985, Thayer was sentenced to four years in prison and fined $5,000. He also paid the government $550,000 as a fine for the profits earned by others through his tips.

DENNIS B. LEVINE, 34. *History:* Levine was an investment banker who worked on Wall Street. Through his contacts, he set up an information network of Wall Street sources at investment banks and law firms. He traded on insider information through an offshore bank account from which he earned $12.6 million on stock trades. He pleaded guilty to insider trading, perjury, and tax violations. He was given a lighter sentence in view of his cooperation with authorities, which led SEC investigators to Ivan Boesky and others.

Sentence: In February 1987, Levine was sentenced to two years in prison and fined $362,000. He has repaid $11.6 million.

ROBERT M. WILKIS, 37. *History:* Wilkis was an investment banker who gave Levine confidential information. He also traded through offshore banks, where he earned more than $3 million. He pleaded guilty to insider trading and tax evasion.

Sentence: In February 1987, Wilkis was sentenced to one year and a day in prison to be followed by five years' probation. He has repaid $2.5 million.

ILAN K. REICH, 32. *History:* Reich is a lawyer who gave Levine information about his law firm's corporate clients who were planning major corporate moves. He stopped giving Levine information on two occasions. Despite this, Levine set aside $300,000 for Reich, who never claimed the money. He pleaded guilty to charges of securities fraud.

Sentence: In January 1987, Reich was sentenced to one year and a day in prison and five years' probation. He has paid $485,000 to the SEC.

ANDREW SOLOMON, 27. *History:* Solomon was an investment analyst who received tips from a law-firm contact. He passed the information on to his superiors at the arbitrage firm where he worked. (*Arbitrage* is the simultaneous buying and selling of currencies or securities at different values in order to profit from price differences.) Solomon apparently earned no personal profit but hoped to advance his career. He pleaded guilty and cooperated in the government's investigation.

Sentence: In November 1986, Solomon was sentenced to one year's probation and 250 hours of community service and fined $10,000.

IVAN BOESKY. *History:* Boesky was known as Mr. Arbitrage on Wall Street. He is by far the biggest investor to be caught trading with insider information. Much of his information came from Dennis Levine. After cooperating with the SEC, he pleaded guilty to one felony count.

Sentence: In November 1987, Boesky was sentenced to three years in prison. He had previously paid the government $50 million in illegal profits, had paid $50 million in civil penalties, and had agreed to withdraw permanently from the securities business.

Source: *Business Week,* June 15, 1987, p. 85.

security . . . any manipulative or deceptive device or contrivance, in contravention of such rules and regulations as the [SEC] may prescribe . . . ." Rule 10b-5 makes it "unlawful for any person, directly or indirectly, by use of any means or instrumentality of interstate commerce, or of the mails, or of any facility of any national securities exchange to defraud or mislead anyone in the purchase or sale of any security."

The antifraud rule applies to the purchase or sale of any security, regardless of how small or large the amount of the transaction is or of whether it is a public or private offering. The exemptions discussed earlier apply only to registration, not to the antifraud provisions. Therefore, the rule covers virtually every transaction involving a security. Furthermore, the act does not specify what constitutes an offense of fraud or misrepresentation. As a result, the SEC rules and the courts have broadly defined this offense and the criteria for a violation of Rule 10b-5. Violations generally fit into two categories: insider trading cases, and claims arising out of corporate misstatements or omissions (such as knowingly inflating earning projections, or manipulating of financial records to show profits rather than a real loss) and fraud

and manipulation by brokers and dealers in the trading of stock.

Disclosure Under Rule 10b-5 Any material omission or misrepresentation of material facts in connection with the purchase or sale of a security may violate Section 10(b) and Rule 10b-5. The key to liability is whether the insider's information is material.

Some examples of material facts calling for a disclosure under the rule have been: a new ore discovery, fraudulent trading in the company stock by a broker-dealer, a dividend change (whether up or down), a contract for the sale of corporate assets, a new discovery (of a process or a product), a significant change in the firm's financial condition, or a takeover bid by another firm or individual.

The Supreme Court in the following case expressly adopts the standard of materiality applicable to Section 10(b) and Rule 10b-5. According to this standard, an omitted fact is material if there is a substantial likelihood that its disclosure would have been considered significant by a reasonable investor. This case is a private class-action lawsuit; the SEC was not involved in this case.

BACKGROUND AND FACTS *Basic Incorporated was a publicly traded company primarily engaged in manufacturing chemical refractories for the steel industry. Combustion Engineering, Inc., was a company that produced alumina-based refractories. Combustion was interested in acquiring Basic. In 1976, representatives from the two companies conferred concerning the possibility of a merger. During 1977 and 1978, Basic made three public statements denying that it was engaged in merger negotiations (October 21, 1977, September 25, 1978, and November 6, 1978).*

On December 18, 1978, Basic asked the New York Stock Exchange to suspend trading in its shares and issued a release stating that it had been "approached" by another company concerning a merger. On December 19, Basic's board of directors endorsed Combustion's offer and the following day announced its approval of Combustion's offer for all outstanding shares.

The plaintiffs were former Basic shareholders who had sold their stock after Basic's first public statement of October 21, 1977, and before the suspension of trading on December 18, 1978. The class action against Basic and its directors asserted that the defendants had issued three false or misleading public statements that violated Section 10(b) and Rule 10b-5. The shareholders were harmed by selling Basic shares at artificially depressed prices in a market affected by Basic's misleading statements.

Case 18.2
BASIC INC. v. LEVINSON
Supreme Court of the United States, 1988.
485 U.S. ___, 108 S.Ct. 978, 99 L.Ed.2d 194.

The district court found that the alleged misstatements were immaterial and granted a summary judgment in favor of Basic. The court of appeals reversed the summary judgment and found that information concerning otherwise insignificant developments becomes material solely because of an affirmative denial of the existence of these developments. The United States Supreme Court granted certiorari.

BLACKMUN, Justice.

* * * *

The application of [the] materiality standard to preliminary merger discussions is not self-evident. Where the impact of the corporate development on the target's fortune is certain and clear, the * * * materiality definition admits straightforward application. Where, on the other hand, the event is contingent or speculative in nature, it is difficult to ascertain whether the ''reasonable investor'' would have considered the omitted information significant at the time. Merger negotiations, because of the ever-present possibility that the contemplated transaction will not be effectuated, fall into the latter category.

* * * *

We * * * find no valid justification for artificially excluding from the definition of materiality information concerning merger discussions, which would otherwise be considered significant to the trading decision of a reasonable investor, merely because agreement-in-principle as to price and structure has not yet been reached by the parties or their representatives.

* * * *

Whether merger discussions in any particular case are material therefore depends on the facts. Generally, in order to assess the probability that the event will occur, a factfinder will need to look to indicia of interest in the transaction at the highest corporate levels. Without attempting to catalog all such possible factors, we note by way of example that board resolutions, instructions to investment bankers, and actual negotiations between principals or their intermediaries may serve as indicia of interest. To assess the magnitude of the transaction to the issuer of the securities allegedly manipulated, a factfinder will need to consider such facts as the size of the two corporate entities and of the potential premiums over market value. No particular event or factor short of closing the transaction need be either necessary or sufficient by itself to render merger discussions material.

* * * *

* * * The courts below accepted a presumption * * * that persons who had traded Basic shares had done so in reliance on the integrity of the price set by the market, but because of petitioners' material misrepresentations that price had been fraudulently depressed. Requiring a plaintiff to show a speculative state of facts, i.e., how he would have acted if omitted material information had been disclosed, or if the misrepresentation had not been made, would place an unnecessarily unrealistic evidentiary burden on the Rule 10b-5 plaintiff who has traded on an impersonal market.

* * * The presumption of reliance employed in this case is consistent with, and, by facilitating Rule 10b-5 litigation, supports, the congressional policy embodied in the 1934 Act. * * *

DECISION AND REMEDY   *The United States Supreme Court reversed the judgment of the court of appeals and sent the case back to the district court for further proceedings. Materiality depends on the facts in each particular case, and, therefore,* *the decision whether a violation of Rule 10b-5 has occurred must be made on a case-by-case basis. The statements must be misleading as to a material fact.*

Timing of Disclosure Under Rule 10b-5 Courts have struggled with the problem of when information becomes public knowledge. Clearly, when inside information becomes public knowledge, all insiders should be allowed to trade without disclosure. The courts have suggested that insiders should refrain from trading for a reasonable waiting period when the news is not readily translatable into investment action. Presumably, this time period gives the news time to filter down and to be evaluated by the investing public. What constitutes a reasonable waiting period is not at all clear.

The following is one of the landmark cases interpreting Section 10(b) and Rule 10b-5. The SEC sued Texas Gulf Sulphur for issuing a misleading press release. The release underestimated the magnitude and value of a mineral discovery. The SEC also sued several of Texas Gulf Sulphur's directors, officers, and employees under Rule 10b-5 after these people had purchased large amounts of the corporate stock prior to the announcement of the corporation's rich ore discovery.

BACKGROUND AND FACTS *Texas Gulf Sulphur Co. (TGS) drilled a hole on November 12, 1963, near Timmins, Ontario. It appeared to yield a core with exceedingly high mineral content. Since TGS did not own the mineral rights in the surrounding regions, it maintained secrecy about the results of the core sample. Evasive tactics were undertaken to camouflage the drill site, and a second hole was drilled. TGS completed an extensive land acquisition program and then began drilling this lucrative site. Rumors began to spread, and, by early April 1964, a "tremendous staking rush [was] going on."*

On April 11, 1964, an unauthorized report of the extraordinary mineral find hit the papers. On April 12, TGS issued a press release that played down the discovery and stated that it was too early to tell whether the ore finding would be significant. Charles Fogarty, executive vice-president of TGS, had already purchased 1,700 shares of stock during the month of November 1963 and an additional 300 shares in December. In March 1964 he bought 400 shares, and in April he bought 300 shares. Other TGS officials had also purchased stock. They had accepted stock options on February 20, 1964.

The Securities and Exchange Commission filed suit against TGS and several of its officers, directors, and employees to prevent TGS's continued violation of the Securities Exchange Act of 1934 and to compel the individual defendants to rescind the securities transactions they had made. The complaint alleged that, on the basis of material inside information concerning the results of TGS's drilling, the defendants either personally or through agents had purchased TGS stock, while the information concerning the drill site remained undisclosed to the investing public. The SEC further charged that certain of the defendants (tippers) had divulged information to certain

Case 18.3
SECURITIES AND EXCHANGE COMMISSION v. TEXAS GULF SULPHUR CO.
United States Court of Appeals, Second Circuit, 1968.
401 F.2d 833.

others (tippees) for their use in purchasing TGS stock before the information was disclosed to the public or to other sellers. In addition, certain defendants had accepted options to purchase TGS stock without disclosing material information about the progress of the drilling to either the stock option committee or the TGS board of directors. Finally, the complaint charged that TGS had issued a deceptive press release on April 22, 1964.

The deceptive press release should be the focus in reading the following case. The trial court judge held that the issuance of the press release was lawful because it was not issued for the purpose of benefiting the corporation, and there was no evidence that any insider had used the information in the press release to personal advantage. Thus it was not "misleading or deceptive on the basis of the facts then known." The trial court went on to find that most of the defendants had not violated Rule 10b-5. The case was appealed.

WATERMAN, Judge.
*   *   *   *

I. THE INDIVIDUAL DEFENDANTS
*   *   *   *

In each case, *   *   * whether facts are material within Rule 10b-5 when the facts relate to a particular event and are undisclosed by those persons who are knowledgeable thereof will depend at any given time upon a balancing of both the indicated probability that the event will occur and the anticipated magnitude of the event in light of the totality of the company activity. Here, *   *   * knowledge of the possibility, which surely was more than marginal, of the existence of a mine of the vast magnitude indicated by the remarkably rich drill core located rather close to the surface (suggesting mineability by the less expensive openpit method) within the confines of a large anomaly (suggesting an extensive region of mineralization) might well have affected the price of TGS stock and would certainly have been an important fact to a reasonable, if speculative, investor in deciding whether he should buy, sell, or hold. After all, this first drill core was "unusually good and *   *   * excited the interest and speculation of those who knew about it."
*   *   *   *

Finally, a major factor in determining whether the *   *   * discovery was a material fact is the importance attached to the drilling results by those who knew about it. In view of other unrelated recent developments favorably affecting TGS, participation by an informed person in a regular stock-purchase program, or even sporadic trading by an informed person, might lend only nominal support to the inference of the materiality of the *   *   * discovery; nevertheless, the timing by those who knew of it of their stock purchases and their purchases of short-term calls—purchases in some cases by individuals who had never before purchased calls or even TGS stock—virtually compels the inference that the insiders were influenced by the drilling results. *   *   *
*   *   *   *

We hold, therefore, that all transactions in TGS stock or calls by individuals apprised of the drilling results *   *   * were made in violation of Rule 10b-5. Inasmuch as the visual evaluation of that drill core (a generally reliable estimate though less accurate then a chemical assay) constituted material information, those advised of the results of the visual evaluation as well as those informed of the chemical assay traded in violation of law. *   *   *
*   *   *   *

II. THE CORPORATE DEFENDANT

*   *   *   *

At 3:00 P.M. on April 12, 1964, evidently believing it desirable to comment upon the rumors concerning the Timmins project, TGS issued the press release quoted in pertinent part [as follows:

[Recent drilling on one property near Timmins has led to preliminary indications that more drilling would be required for proper evaluation of this prospect. The drilling done to date has not been conclusive, but the statements made by many outside quarters are unreliable and include information and figures that are not available to TGS.

[The work done to date has not been sufficient to reach definite conclusions and any statement as to size and grade of ore would be premature and possibly misleading. When we have progressed to the point where reasonable and logical conclusions can be made, TGS will issue a definite statement to its stockholders and to the public in order to clarify the Timmins project.]

*   *   *   *

*   *   * It does not appear to be unfair to impose upon corporate management a duty to ascertain the truth of any statements the corporation releases to its shareholders or to the investing public at large. Accordingly, we hold that Rule 10b-5 is violated whenever assertions are made, as here, in a manner reasonably calculated to influence the investing public, e.g., by means of the financial media, if such assertions are false or misleading or are so incomplete as to mislead irrespective of whether the issuance of the release was motivated by corporate officials for ulterior purposes. It seems clear, however, that if corporate management demonstrates that it was diligent in ascertaining that the information it published was the whole truth and that such diligently obtained information was disseminated in good faith, Rule 10b-5 would not have been violated.

*   *   *   *

We conclude, then, that, having established that the release was issued in a manner reasonably calculated to affect the market price of TGS stock and to influence the investing public, we must remand to the district court to decide whether the release was misleading to the reasonable investor and if found to be misleading, whether the court in its discretion should issue the injunction the SEC seeks.

DECISION AND REMEDY

The appellate court's judgment was favorable to the SEC. The information contained in the press release was material, and the transaction in stock by the insiders who knew of it had violated Rule 10b-5. Thus, the options of the individual defendants were rescinded. However, the questions of whether the press release was misleading and what remedies should be imposed were remanded to the trial court for decision. A trial court is bound to apply the law as enunciated by the court of appeals in making this type of decision.

COMMENTS

Texas Gulf Sulphur Company was not only sued by the SEC but numerous civil actions for damages were also brought against it by plaintiff-investors who had sold their TGS stock as a result of the deceptively gloomy press release regarding the corporation's mineral exploration. All these suits were settled in 1972. In a federal lawsuit filed against TGS some two years after the initial case, a court of appeals held that investors who had sold stock relying on the representations in the press release could recover damages from the corporation and the officers who had drafted the release. The court went on to state that the proper measure of damages was the difference between the selling price and the price at which the investors could have reinvested within a reasonable period of time after they became aware of TGS's curative press release announcing the 25-million-ton strike.

After TGS issued its curative press release, the court held that a diligent and reasonable investor would have become informed of it within four days, and investors who had sold their stock more than four days after the second press release was issued could not recover under the Securities Exchange Act on the basis of reliance on the earlier, deceptive release.

Scienter *Requirement Under Rule 10b-5*   The elements of a Section 10(b) and Rule 10b-5 violation are the use of a manipulative or deceptive device in connection with the purchase or sale of a security, where a material fact has been misrepresented or omitted. In addition, the act must have been committed with *scienter* (guilty knowledge that is greater than simple negligence). The additional requirement of *scienter* limited the broad application of Section 10(b) after the *Texas Gulf Sulphur* case. The first case to establish this criterion was the following one.

Case 18.4
ERNST & ERNST v. HOCHFELDER
Supreme Court of the United States, 1976.
425 U.S. 185, 96 S.Ct. 1375, 47 L.Ed.2d 668.

BACKGROUND AND FACTS   *Ernst & Ernst, a Chicago accounting firm, was retained by First Securities Company, a brokerage firm, to audit its books. In addition to the auditing, Ernst & Ernst prepared and filed the necessary reports of First Securities with the SEC. The president of First Securities, Leston B. Nay, manipulated a fraudulent scheme of investment in which Hochfelder and several others invested their money. The scheme involved interest rates on low-risk escrow accounts. These accounts never existed, and, for over twenty years, Hochfelder continued unknowingly to place money into the nonexistent account.*

Nay took the money for his own use. The escrow accounts never appeared in Ernst & Ernst's audits. Nay committed suicide and left information describing the fraud. Hochfelder then filed a complaint against Ernst & Ernst for aiding and abetting Nay's fraud. The district court granted Ernst & Ernst a summary judgment, the court of appeals reversed the decision, and the United States Supreme Court reviewed the issue.

POWELL, Justice.

The issue in this case is whether an action for civil damages may lie under Section 10(b) of the Securities Exchange Act of 1934, and Securities and Exchange Commission Rule 10b-5, in the absence of an allegation of intent to deceive, manipulate, or defraud on the part of the defendant.

Petitioner, Ernst & Ernst, is an accounting firm. From 1946 through 1967 it was retained by First Securities Company of Chicago (First Securities), a small brokerage firm and member of the Midwest Stock Exchange and of the National Association of Securities Dealers, to perform periodic audits of the firm's books and records. In connection with these audits Ernst & Ernst prepared for filing with the Securities and Exchange Commission (Commission) the annual reports required of First Securities. It also prepared for First Securities responses to the financial questionnaires of the Midwest Stock Exchange (Exchange).

Respondents were customers of First Securities who invested in a fraudulent securities scheme perpetrated by Leston B. Nay, president of the firm and owner of 92 percent of its stock. Nay induced the respondents to invest funds in "escrow" accounts that he represented would yield a high rate of return. Respondents did so from 1942 through 1966, with the majority of the transactions occuring in the 1950s. In fact, there were no escrow accounts as Nay converted respondents' funds to his own use immediately upon receipt.

This fraud came to light in 1968 when Nay committed suicide, leaving a note that described First Securities as bankrupt and the escrow accounts as "spurious." Respondents subsequently filed this action for damages against Ernst & Ernst * * *. As revealed through discovery, respondents' cause of action rested on a theory of negligent nonfeasance. The premise was that Ernst & Ernst had failed to utilize "appropriate auditing procedures" in its audits of First Securities, thereby failing to discover internal practices of the firm said to prevent an effective audit. The practice principally relied on Nay's rule that only he could open mail addressed to him at First Securities or addressed to First Securities to his attention, even if it arrived in his absence. Respondents contended that if Ernst & Ernst had conducted a proper audit, it would have discovered this "mail rule." The existence of the rule then would have been disclosed in reports to the Exchange and to the Commission by Ernst & Ernst as an irregular procedure that prevented an effective audit. This would have led to an investigation of Nay that would have revealed the fraudulent scheme. Respondents specifically disclaimed the existence of fraud or intentional misconduct on the part of Ernst & Ernst.
* * * *

We granted *certiorari* to resolve the question whether a private cause of action for damages will lie under Sec. 10(b) and Rule 10b-5 in the absence of any allegation of "scienter"—intent to deceive, manipulate, or defraud. We conclude that it will not and therefore we reverse.
* * * *

Section 10 of the 1934 Act makes it "unlawful for any person . . . [t]o use or employ, in connection with the purchase or sale of any security . . . any manipulative or deceptive device or contrivance in contravention of such rules and regulations as the Commission may prescribe as necessary or appropriate in the public interest or for the protection of investors." * * *

Although Sec. 10(b) does not by its terms create an express civil remedy for its violation, and there is no indication that Congress, or the Commission when adopting Rule 10b-5, contemplated such a remedy, the existence of a private cause of action for violations of the statute and the Rule is now well established. * * *

Section 10(b) makes unlawful the use or employment of "any manipulative or deceptive device or contrivance" in contravention of Commission rules. The words "manipulative or deceptive" used in conjunction with "device or contrivance" strongly suggest that Sec. 10(b) was intended to proscribe knowing or intentional misconduct.
* * * *

* * * When a statute speaks so specifically in terms of manipulation and deception, and of implementing devices and contrivances—the commonly understood terminology of intentional wrongdoing—and when its history reflects no more expansive intent, we are quite unwilling to extend the scope of the statute to negligent conduct.

DECISION AND   *The United States Supreme Court reversed the court of appeals and held*
REMEDY   *that, in the absence of* scienter, *no cause of action for fraud exists under*
Section 10(b).

COMMENTS   Scienter *is generally defined as a mental state embracing the intent to*
deceive, manipulate, or defraud. The more difficult question is whether
recklessness is enough to satisfy the scienter *requirement. In certain areas*
of the law, recklessness is considered a form of intentional conduct if the
conduct is so careless as to evince a total disregard for the welfare of
others and will create liability.

Persons Who Have a Duty Under Rule 10b-5   The
SEC will prosecute insiders who, based on nonpublic information, trade a security to their financial benefit. The reasoning behind this rule is that
an insider should not use nonpublic information
to his or her gain because such actions are unfair
to the individual investors who are not privy to
such information and have no equal means of acquiring the information. Thus, the courts and the
SEC prohibit insiders from trading unless information is first disclosed to the general public.

Insider trading rules cover not only corporate
officers, directors, and majority shareholders but
also generally anyone having access to or receiving information of a nonpublic nature from an
insider on which trading is based. Those people
to whom the material information is given are
known as **tippees**.

The following case involved a printer who obtained information through his job about future
takeover bids. He was not an employee or otherwise connected with the corporations but did have
advance knowledge through his position. The
question was: Did he have a duty under Section
10(b)?

Case 18.5
**CHIARELLA v. UNITED
STATES**
Supreme Court of the United
States, 1980.
445 U.S. 222, 100 S.Ct. 1108,
63 L.Ed.2d 348.

BACKGROUND AND FACTS   *Chiarella was a printer who worked in a*
New York composing room. He handled announcements of corporate take-
over bids. Even though the documents that were delivered to the printer
concealed the identity of the target corporations by blank spaces and false
names, Chiarella was able to deduce the names of the target companies
from other information contained in the documents. Without disclosing his
knowledge, he purchased stock in the target companies and sold the shares
immediately after the takeover attempts were made public. He realized a
gain of slightly more than $30,000 in the course of fourteen months.

The SEC began an investigation of his trading activities. In May 1977,
Chiarella entered into a consent decree with the SEC in which he agreed
to return his profits to the sellers of the shares. In 1978, a trial court
convicted him on seventeen counts of violating Section 10(b) of the Securities
Exchange Act of 1934 and SEC Rule 10b-5. The court of appeals affirmed
that conviction. The United States Supreme Court granted certiorari.

POWELL, Justice.
* * * *

In this case, the petitioner was convicted of violating § 10(b) although he was
not a corporate insider and he received no confidential information from the target

company. Moreover, the ''market information'' upon which he relied did not concern the earning power or operations of the target company, but only the plans of the acquiring company. Petitioner's use of that information was not a fraud under § 10(b) unless he was subject to an affirmative duty to disclose it before trading. In this case, the jury instructions failed to specify any such duty. In effect, the trial court instructed the jury that petitioner owed a duty to everyone; to all sellers, indeed, to the market as a whole. The jury simply was told to decide whether petitioner used material, nonpublic information at a time when ''he knew other people trading in the securities market did not have access to the same information.''

The Court of Appeals affirmed the conviction by holding that ''*[a]nyone*—corporate insider or not—who regularly receives material nonpublic information may not use that information to trade in securities without incurring an affirmative duty to disclose.'' Although the court said that its test would include only persons who regularly receive material, nonpublic information, its rationale for that limitation is unrelated to the existence of a duty to disclose. The Court of Appeals, like the trial court, failed to identify a relationship between petitioner and the sellers that could give rise to a duty. Its decision thus rested solely upon its belief that the federal securities laws have ''created a system providing equal access to information necessary for reasoned and intelligent investment decisions.'' The use by anyone of material information not generally available is fraudulent, this theory suggests, because such information gives certain buyers or sellers an unfair advantage over less informed buyers and sellers.

* * * *

This reasoning suffers from two defects. First not every instance of financial unfairness constitutes fraudulent activity under § 10(b). Second, the element required to make silence fraudulent—a duty to disclose—is absent in this case. No duty could arise from petitioner's relationship with the sellers of the target company's securities, for petitioner had no prior dealings with them. He was not their agent, he was not a fiduciary, he was not a person in whom the sellers had placed their trust and confidence. He was, in fact, a complete stranger who dealt with the sellers only through impersonal market transactions.

We cannot affirm petitioner's conviction without recognizing a general duty between all participants in market transactions to forego actions based on material, nonpublic information. Formulation of such a broad duty, which departs radically from the established doctrine that duty arises from a specific relationship between two parties, should not be undertaken absent some explicit evidence of congressional intent.

DECISION AND REMEDY

The United States Supreme Court reversed Chiarella's conviction. Chiarella could not be convicted for failure to disclose his knowledge to the public. He was under no duty to disclose this knowledge because he had no prior dealings with the companies. A duty to disclose under the statute does not arise from mere possession of nonpublic market information.

COMMENTS

Since the Chiarella *case, federal courts have made a number of decisions affecting tippees' liability under Rule 10b-5. In* Dirks v. SEC,[1] *the Supreme Court held that a tippee's liability is derivative only. Thus, unless an insider breaches a fiduciary duty in making a disclosure, a tippee is not liable. The Court made clear, however, that insider trading rules apply to lawyers, accountants, and investment bankers that a corporation hires. In* SEC v. Lund[2], *the court imposed liability on a ''temporary insider''—that is, a person who receives confidential information in order to make a legitimate decision as to whether to act on it. (For example, a temporary insider would be one who receives confidential information when considering whether to enter into a joint corporate venture with the party disclosing the information.) Also, in* United States v. Newman,[3] *it was held that any tippee who misappropriates or steals inside information is liable.*

1. 463 U.S. 646, 103 S.Ct. 3255, 77 L.Ed.2d 911 (1983).
2. 570 F.Supp. 1397 (C.D. Cal. 1978).
3. 664 F.2d 12 (2d Cir. 1981).

State Securities Laws

All states have their own corporate securities laws that regulate the offer and sale of securities within individual state borders. Since the adoption of the 1933 and 1934 acts, the state and federal governments have regulated securities concurrently. Indeed, both acts specifically allow state securities laws. Certain features are common to all state blue sky laws. For example, they all have antifraud provisions, many of which are patterned after the federal law, and most state corporate securities laws regulate securities brokers and dealers.

Typically, these laws provide for the registration or qualification of securities offered or issued for sale within the state. Unless an applicable exemption from registration is found, issuers must register or qualify their stock with the appropriate state official, often called a corporations commissioner.

A difference in philosophy exists among the state statutes. Many statutes are similar to the Securities Act of 1933 and mandate certain disclosures before the registration is effective; they may also require a permit to sell the securities. Other statutes have fairness standards that a corporation must meet in order to offer or sell stock in the state. A few states require a merit registration, whereby the states review the registration for its merits and are not restricted to reviewing the registration for disclosures only. The Uniform Securities Act (adopted in part by several states) was drafted to be acceptable to states with differing regulatory philosophies.

FACING A LEGAL ISSUE   Making a Public Offering

You have decided to go into business for yourself. You are interested in types of businesses requiring considerable initial capital for buildings and equipment. You have tried to raise this capital from family members, local banks, and other local financial institutions, as well as from the Small Business Administration, but without success.

A classmate of yours has joined the investment banking firm of Smart, Tight, and Moresight. In the past, this firm has been very conservative, only involving itself with extremely profitable corporations. Recently, however, they have promoted a person to partner whose financial philosophy is to assist new ventures that will offer the investment firm greater profits but higher risks. Your friend works for this new partner.

One day you meet your friend for lunch. You explain your predicament in not being able to raise capital and ask for any suggestions. Your friend recommends that you seek capital in the form of equity funds from the open market. This will require a public offering.

You must be concerned with both federal and state regulatory laws. The first thing you must remember when going public is that all material facts must be disclosed and presented in an honest format. The problem lies in deciding what is material. A material fact that is omitted can result in liability just as much as misstating a fact within a disclosure statement can. It is better to err on the side of giving more information than necessary than to neglect to disclose something that is material.

Normally, audited financial statements and an attorney's opinion letter must be filed with the registration statement. To obtain this information can be expensive and time consuming. You must bear the costs because you are the issuer. Your investment banking friend may assist you by overseeing the information, but such a firm normally does not advance funds to allow you to obtain this information. Going public also requires intensive work with your investment banker (the underwriter), lawyers, and accountants. All three advisers will make comments that will require changes to your prospectus. This procedure can take months, before you can file your legal documents with the appropriate governmental agency.

Because you do not have a financial record, you might be better off concentrating your efforts on locating a small corporation that has gone public. These types of firms have already become duly registered with state and federal authorities, and they already have a history of financial transactions. You can obtain control of one of these firms by purchasing a controlling interest of its common stock or through some form of merger or consolidation.

As you can see from this simple example, it is difficult and time consuming to start a business venture by yourself when you seek funding from the general public. If you take this approach, you will need the backing of good professional individuals along with a lot of perseverance.

Summary

This chapter has emphasized the regulation of securities both by federal and state authorities. A security can be something other than a stock or bond. It is any financial transaction in which an investor exchanges money for an interest in a common enterprise with the expectation of making a profit through the endeavors of the promoter or third party. Two primary federal statutes have been adopted—the Securities Act of 1933 and the Securities Exchange Act of 1934.

The 1933 act regulates new issues of securities and requires, prior to issuance, a full disclosure of all material facts. This information is presented in a prospectus, which is based on the registration statement. The registration statement is filed with the SEC and must be signed by the corporation's principal executive officer, principal accounting officer, and financial officer and by a majority of the members of the board of directors. Any person signing the registration statement is personally liable if there has not been a full and truthful disclosure of all material facts. Certain transactions and securities are exempt from the registration requirements of the 1933 act.

The Securities Exchange Act of 1934 regulates securities that are traded on national exchanges and ones extensively traded over the counter. In addition, this statute established the Securities and Exchange Commission.

Both acts prohibit fraud in the issuance of securities and in disclosure of information available to the investing public.

Under Rule 10b-5 no individual may generally take advantage of insider information whether a situation involves new securities or ones actively traded. Most insiders are either directors, officers, key employees, or owners of 10 percent or more of the common stock. Rule 10b-5 applies, however, to both insiders and tippees. Any profits realized from inside information will belong to the corporation and substantial criminal penalties can be assessed.

Key Terms

accredited investor **455**
blue sky laws **450**
due diligence defense **453**
exempt securities **455**
exempt transactions **455**
Foreign Corrupt Practices Act **452**
insider trading **457**
Insider Trading Sanctions Act **452**
intrastate offering exemptions **455**

private offering exemptions **455**
prospectus **453**
proxy **457**
red herring prospectus **453**
Rule 10b-5 **457**
scienter **464**
Section 10(b) **457**
Section 16 **457**
Securities Act of 1933 **450**

Securities and Exchange Commission **451**
Securities Exchange Act of 1934 **451**
Securities Investor Protection Corporation **452**
small offering exemptions **455**
tippees **466**
tombstone advertisement **453**
unaccredited investor **455**

Questions and Case Problems

1. Maresh, an experienced geologist, owned certain oil and gas leases covering land in Nebraska. To raise money for the drilling of a test well, he undertook to sell fractional interests in the leases. He approached Garfield, a man with whom he had done business in the past. Garfield had mentioned that he would be interested in investing in some of Maresh's future oil ventures. Garfield had wide business experience in the stock market and in oil stocks. He felt that the investment in Maresh's gas leases could be lucrative. Based on Garfield's promise to wire the money promptly, Maresh began drilling. Soon after, when Maresh realized that the land was dry, Garfield claimed that he could rescind the agreement to invest since the in-

vestment offered by Maresh was a security within the meaning of the Securities Act of 1933, and it had not been registered. Did Maresh offer a security within the meaning of the 1933 act? [Garfield v. Strain, 320 F.2d 116 (10th Cir. 1963)]

2. The Howey Company owned large tracts of citrus acreage in Lake County, Florida. For several years, it planted about 500 acres annually, keeping half of the groves itself and offering the other half to the public to help finance additional development. Howey-in-the-Hills Service, Inc., was a service company engaged in cultivating and developing these groves, including the harvesting and marketing of the crops. Each prospective customer was offered both

a land sales contract and a service contract, after being told that it was not feasible to invest in a grove unless service arrangements were made. Of the acreage sold by Howey, 85 percent was sold with a service contract with Howey-in-the-Hills Service, Inc. Must Howey register the sales of these parcels of citrus groves with the Securities and Exchange Commission? [Securities and Exchange Comm'n v. W. J. Howey Co., 328 U.S. 293, 66 S.Ct. 1100, 90 L.Ed. 1244 (1946)]

3. Children's Hospital offered and sold a number of 8 percent mortgage bonds in order to raise enough money to begin operation. Its promoters solicited purchasers mainly through the mails and through local newspaper advertisements. Children's Hospital was to be a nonprofit medical organization established mainly to serve the needs of children in the local community. The promoters, however, expected to earn large profits from organizing the hospital. Must the promoters of Children's Hospital register the sale of the mortgage bonds with the Securities and Exchange Commission? [Securities and Exchange Comm'n v. Children's Hospital, 214 F.Supp. 883 (D. Ariz. 1963)]

4. On September 1, 1971, the Ecological Science Corporation issued a press release stating, in part, that it had renegotiated the terms of approximately $14 million in loans from its prime lender and that, under the renegotiated agreement, $4 million was due on demand and the remainder on a specified date. The press release, however, failed to mention that, on the same date as the renegotiated loan agreement, an insurance and annuity association had refused to provide the corporation with the $4 million loan that it had planned to use to repay the demand loan. Moreover, while discussing its European prospects in the press release, Ecological Science Corporation failed to mention the proposed transfer of voting control among its European subsidiaries. Has Ecological Science Corporation violated any of the provisions of the Securities Exchange Act of 1934? [Securities and Exchange Comm'n v. Koenig, 469 F.2d 198 (2d Cir. 1972)]

5. Emerson Electric Company owned 13.2 percent of Dodge Manufacturing Company's stock. Within six months of the purchase of this stock, Emerson sold enough shares to a broker to reduce its holding to 9.96 percent of its former Dodge holdings. One week later (but still less than six months after Emerson's initial purchase), Emerson sold its remaining shares of Dodge stock. The sole purpose of Emerson's initial sale of just over 3 percent of its Dodge stock was to avoid liability under Section 16 of the Securities Exchange Act of 1934, which prohibits short-swing trading. Assuming Emerson made no profit on the initial sale of stock but made substantial profits when it sold the remaining 9.96 percent of Dodge stock, must it return the profits it made on the sale? [Reliance Electric Co. v. Emerson Electric Co., 404 U.S. 418, 92 S.Ct. 596, 30 L.Ed.2d 575 (1972)]

6. American Breeding Herds (ABH) offered a cattle-breeding plan for which Ronnett contracted to buy thirty-six Charolais cows at $3,000 per head and a one-quarter interest in a Charolais bull at $5,000, totaling $113,000. The ABH agreement described itself as a "tax shelter program . . . unlike the purchase of securities such as stocks and bonds." Ronnett entered into the agreement after receiving investment advice from Shannon, an investment counselor. The cows were tagged and sent to an ABH-approved breeding ranch. Ronnett signed a maintenance agreement and paid a monthly maintenance fee. Was the ABH plan a security, and should it have been registered under the securities law? [Ronnett v. American Breeding Herds, Inc., 124 Ill.App.3d 842, 464 N.E.2d 1201, 80 Ill.Dec. 218 (1984)]

7. Dirks advised institutional investors as to the financial merits of different insurance companies. A former officer of Equity Funding of America told Dirks that Equity Funding had fraudulently overstated many assets in its financial reports. While investigating this information, Dirks openly discussed the matter with reporters and a number of his clients. He did not own any shares. Some of his clients sold their stock based on information received from Dirks. The stock fell from about twenty-six dollars a share to fifteen dollars a share in two weeks. Dirks was censured by the SEC, contending that he was an insider or a tippee of an insider. Was the SEC correct to censure Dirks? Discuss fully. [Dirks v. Securities and Exchange Comm'n, 463 U.S. 646, 103 S.Ct. 3255, 77 L.Ed.2d 911 (1983)]

8. Adams devised a plan to sell "rabbit kits." For $7,200 per kit, a person would receive twelve female and two male rabbits that should produce 720 breeding females within a year. Part of the sales promotion was that Adams would be available for consultation. Also, Adams requested all buyers to join an association that would purchase all of the buyers' pelts. Membership in the association was not part of the "rabbit kit." The association was controlled by Adams. The state of Florida claimed that Adams was selling an unlicensed security. Was Adams selling securities that should have been registered? Discuss fully. [Adams v. State, 443 So.2d 1003 (Fla. Dist. Ct. App. 1983)]

 9. MAI was in the business of financing computer installations through sale and lease-back agreements. In this type of agreement, MAI would purchase the computer and lease it back to the original owner. As part of the lease, MAI was required to maintain and repair the computers. MAI did not have the facilities or capacity to perform maintenance services. MAI entered into a contract with IBM to service the machines. Subsequently, MAI learned that IBM would substantially increase its maintenance charges, and the monthly net earnings of MAI would decrease by 75 percent. When this information became public, the price of MAI stock fell from $28 to $11. Prior to this information becoming public, two officers of MAI had sold their stock. A lawsuit was filed against them by the shareholders on behalf of the corporation claiming the two officers' actions violated Rule 10b-5 and Section 10(b) of the Securities Exchange Act. Are the two officers liable to the corporation for profits resulting from the sale? Discuss fully. [Diamond v. Oreamuno, 24 N.Y.2d 494, 248 N.E.2d 910, 301 N.Y.S.2d 78 (1969)]

Chapter 19   Antitrust Law: Statutes and Exemptions

The Sherman Act does not announce a new principle of law, but applies old and well recognized principles of the common law.

Senator John Sherman
1890

OUTLINE

Introduction

A trust is a legal entity in which a trustee holds title to property for the benefit of another. The trustee manages the property, and the beneficiaries of the trust are entitled to the income from the property. Most trusts are legal, and their use flourishes today, particularly in estate planning.

In the past, this form of organization was used to restrain trade. After the Civil War, trusts were used by groups of corporations to eliminate competition. Corporations that were engaged in the same type of business transferred their stock to a trustee and received trust certificates. The trustee made decisions that fixed prices, controlled production, and determined the control of exclusive geographical markets for the entire industry. Corporations participating in a trust no longer competed with each other. The trusts wielded such power that corporations outside the trusts were unable to affect the market.

States attempting to control such monopolistic restraints in trade behavior enacted statutes to outlaw the use of trusts. That is why all laws that regulate economic competition are referred to as **antitrust laws**. The purpose is to prevent monopolists from controlling the economy through restraints. In 1887, the federal government recognized that monopolies were a national problem and passed the **Interstate Commerce Act** and then enacted the **Sherman Antitrust Act** in 1890. These laws and subsequent ones prohibited anticompetitive behavior and are based on the belief that competition lowers prices, encourages innovation, and provides for equitable distributions of wealth between producers and consumers.

This chapter discusses the major antitrust statutes that are enforced by the Department of Justice and the Federal Trade Commission. Particular emphasis will be given to arrangements that create monopolies. The next chapter focuses on various contractual and business actions, examines current trends in the antitrust laws, and discusses possible defenses to claims of antitrust conduct.

Trusts and Common Law in the United States

American common law protected every person's freedom to enter a market and his or her rights to trade, but the common law was inadequate to deal with the giant corporations and trusts that developed in the latter half of the nineteenth century. The power of the railroads, for example, exceeded the power of the courts to deal with them. The railroads refused to serve sparsely populated areas, charged high rates to some shippers, and offered rebates to others. Several states regulated railroad rates and service to overcome these problems, but state regulation could not solve interstate trade abuses.

In the second half of the nineteenth century, the Standard Oil Company and other trusts gained control of several major industries—oil, cotton, whiskey, sugar, and linseed oil. Their activity constituted a monopoly in each geographical area. For example, there were situations where Standard Oil would sell kerosene at a price below its own costs in order to drive competitors out of business. Once its monopoly position was assured, Standard Oil would raise prices to recoup the losses and reap monopoly profits.

Similar activity was found in other business areas. The public became concerned that the trusts were controlling an increasing number of industries and using unfair methods to gain this control. Congress had to find a way to destroy the trusts without destroying free enterprise.

The 1890 Sherman Antitrust Act was the response, and its purpose was to promote competition within the United States economy. The author of the legislation, Senator John Sherman, argued that the Sherman Act did not announce a new principal of law, but simply applied old and well-recognized principles of the common law. The common law, however, was never very clear on the issues of trusts and competition. The statute was adopted to placate, among others, those who favored small, locally owned businesses and farmers, who were forced to pay high prices for equipment due to anticompetitive agreements. The Sherman Act was an attempt by Congress to make the federal courts create a common body of federal antitrust law.

Sherman Antitrust Act

Sections 1 and 2 contain the main provisions of the Sherman Act. They are:

LEGAL HIGHLIGHT   **Antitrust Common Law in England**

One of the earliest recorded cases about trade restraints in the common law involved a man named John Dyer.[1] Dyer had agreed not to "use his art of a dyer's craft within the town * * * for half a year." Dyer breached the agreement by going back into business within the six-month period. The court held that the agreement was in restraint of trade according to the common law. At that time, restraint of trade was defined as the failure to promote "fair" commercial activity.

The same issue has arisen on numerous occasions. A celebrated case occurred in 1711 when a man named Mitchell leased a baking shop for five years, subject to the condition that the lessor, Reynolds, who was also a baker, would not practice the baking art in the immediate area for the term of the lease. Mitchell was actually buying the use of a baking shop *and* the trade that went with it. Reynolds went back into the bakery business before the five years were over. The court ruled in favor of Reynolds.[2]

This particular case is celebrated because the court's opinion systematically classified trade restraints into those that were good and those that were bad. Lord Parker, who rendered the opinion, distinguished between general and particular restraints, the former

being invalid and the latter valid. These distinctions are still followed today in American law. Basically, his reasoning went as follows.

A general restraint is defined as a restraint used to eliminate competition. This type of restraint is illegal. On the other hand, some types of particular restraints are allowed. These partial, or ancillary, restraints, as they are known, are generally upheld if the restriction is limited in time and place. Partial restraints, however, fall under the rule of reason, which means that the court will determine whether the restraint in question is reasonable. Today, as will be discussed in this chapter, the rule of reason plays an important role in antitrust litigation in the United States.

Partial restraints can be enforced if found to be reasonable in two types of situations: in employment situations and in the sales of businesses. For example, if Webber purchases a hardware business, he will not want the seller to open a hardware business in the same general locality. Part of his purchase will include goodwill on the part of the seller. Webber can enforce the covenant not to compete for a reasonable length of time and within a reasonable geographic area. In other words, antitrust laws do not forbid all restraints of trade, only certain activities.

1. *Dyer's Case,* Y. B. Pasch. 2 Hen. V, f. 5, pl. 26 (1414).

2. *Mitchell v. Reynolds,* 1 P. Wms. 181, 24 Eng. Rep. 347 (1711).

Sec. 1: Every contract, combination in the form of trust or otherwise, or conspiracy, in restraint of trade or commerce among the several States, or with foreign nations, is hereby declared to be illegal [and is a felony punishable by fine and/or imprisonment]. * * *

Sec. 2: Every person who shall monopolize, or attempt to monopolize, or combine or conspire with any other person or persons, to monopolize any part of the trade or commerce among the several

States, or with foreign nations, shall be deemed guilty of a felony [and is similarly punishable]. * * *

Sections 1 and 2 Compared

These two provisions are relatively vague and cover different commercial activity. Congress left it to the courts to determine what constituted a violation of this act. The courts have continued to consider the meaning of these two provisions through the intervening decades.

These two main sections are quite different from each other. Section 1 requires action by two or more people, since a person cannot combine or conspire alone. Thus, the essence of the illegal activity is the act of joining together. Section 2 applies to both an individual person and to several people because it states, ''[e]very person who * * *.'' Thus, conduct by one person can result in a violation of Section 2. The cases brought to court under Section 1 of the Sherman Act differ from those brought under Section 2. Section 1 cases are often concerned with finding an agreement (written, oral, or based on conduct) that leads to a restraint of trade.

Section 2 cases deal with the structure of a monopoly that exists in the marketplace. Thus, Section 1 focuses on agreements that are restrictive—that is, agreements that have a wrongful purpose—while Section 2 looks at the misuse of monopoly power in the marketplace. Both sections seek to curtail commercial practices that result in undesired pricing, collusion, and other restraints of trade. Any case brought under Section 2, however, must be one in which the threshold or necessary amount of monopoly power already exists.

The Sherman Act does not regulate how a business should act. The statute sets out how a business should not act. In this sense, the statute is proscriptive rather than prescriptive. It is the basis for policing rather than regulating business conduct.

The Rule of Reason

The most important early case involved Standard Oil Company of New Jersey. The Supreme Court found the oil company guilty of violations of both Sections 1 and 2. Having determined that Congress could not have intended a literal interpretation of every restraint of trade in Section 1, the Court used a standard of reasonableness to analyze the conduct of the oil company.

The **rule of reason** is still used to determine which anticompetitive acts violate the antitrust laws. The rule requires a court to review all the circumstances of a case in order to decide whether the defendant's practice was an unreasonable restraint on competition. Certain conduct is conclusively presumed to be unreasonable; as we will discuss later, this means that the conduct is illegal *per se* and is not subject to the rule of reason. When reading the following case, try to determine when the rule of reason should be applied.

Case 19.1

STANDARD OIL CO. OF NEW JERSEY v. UNITED STATES

Supreme Court of the United States, 1911.
221 U.S. 1, 31 S.Ct. 502, 55 L.Ed. 619.

BACKGROUND AND FACTS   *Standard Oil Company of New Jersey and thirty-three other corporations, John D. Rockefeller, William Rockefeller, and five other individual defendants were the appellants in this case. They attempted to reverse a decree holding that they were conspiring ''to restrain the trade and commerce in petroleum, commonly called 'crude oil,' in refined oil, and in the other products of petroleum, among several States and Territories of the United States and the District of Columbia and with foreign nations, and to monopolize the said commerce.'' The conspiracy was alleged to have been formed around 1870 by three of the individual defendants—John D. Rockefeller, William Rockefeller, and Henry M. Flagler.*

The government charged that the individual defendants organized the Standard Oil Corporation of Ohio and soon afterward became participants in an illegal plan to acquire substantially all of the oil refineries located in Cleveland, Ohio. Therefore, the government charged the original owners of the company with being in an illegal combination for the restraint and monopolization of all interstate commerce in petroleum products.

In addition, the government charged that there was a trust agreement in which the stock of over forty corporations, including Standard Oil of Ohio, was held for the benefit of the members of the combination. The court voided the trust agreement because it was in restraint of trade, and the trust was ordered dissolved. It is questionable whether the trust was actually dissolved as required by the decree, because the stock held by the trust was apparently shifted around, and control of the companies was preserved in the same hands.

In the third phase of its case, the government charged that the individual defendants operated a holding company through Standard Oil Company of New Jersey. This company acquired the majority of stock in various other corporations engaging in the purchasing, transporting, refining, shipping, and selling of oil in the United States, the District of Columbia, and foreign nations. In short, the government attacked the Standard Oil Trust, the Standard Oil Company, and the Standard Oil Company of New Jersey because the net effect of these organizations was to create a monopoly and restrain trade. The government sought an injunction to prevent the defendants from continuing their control over the subsidiary corporations.

WHITE, Chief Justice.

* * * *

Let us consider the language of the first and second sections, guided by the principle that where words are employed in a statute which had at the time a well-known meaning at common law or in the law of this country they are presumed to have been used in that sense unless the context compels to the contrary.

As to the first section, the words to be interpreted are: ''Every contract, combination in the form of trust or otherwise, or conspiracy in restraint of trade or commerce * * * is hereby declared to be illegal.'' As there is no room for dispute that the statute was intended to formulate a rule for the regulation of interstate and foreign commerce, the question is, What was the rule which it adopted?

In view of the common law and the law in this country as to restraint of trade, which we have reviewed, and the illuminating effect which that history must have under the rule to which we have referred, we think it results:

a. That the context manifests that the statute was drawn in the light of the existing practical conception of the law of restraint of trade, because it groups as within that class, not only contracts which were in restraint of trade in the subjective sense, but all contracts or acts which theoretically were attempts to monopolize, yet which in practice had come to be considered as in restraint of trade in a broad sense.

b. That in view of the many new forms of contracts and combinations which were being evolved from existing economic conditions, it was deemed essential by an all-embracing enumeration to make sure that no form of contract or combination by which an undue restraint of interstate or foreign commerce was brought about could save such restraint from condemnation. The statute under this view evidenced the intent not to restrain the right to make and enforce contracts, whether resulting from combination or otherwise, which did not unduly restrain interstate or foreign commerce, but to protect that commerce from being restrained by methods, whether old or new, which could constitute an inference that is an undue restraint.

c. And as the contracts or acts embraced in the provision were not expressly defined, since the enumeration addressed itself simply to classes of acts, those classes being broad enough to embrace every conceivable contract or combination which could be made concerning trade or commerce or the subjects of such commerce, and thus caused any act done by any of the enumerated methods anywhere in the whole field of human activity to be illegal if in restraint of trade, it inevitably follows that the provision necessarily called for the exercise of judgment which required that some standard should be resorted to for the purpose of determining whether the prohibitions contained in the statute had or had not in any given case been violated. Thus not specifying but indubitably contemplating and requiring a standard, it follows that it was intended that the standard of reason which had been applied at the common law and in this country in dealing with subjects of the character embraced by the statute, was intended to be the measure used for the purpose of determining whether in a given case a particular act had or had not brought about the wrong against which the statute provided.

*   *   *   *

*   *   * The merely generic enumeration which the statute makes of the acts to which it refers, and the absence of any definition of restraint of trade as used in the statute, leaves room for but one conclusion, which is, that it was expressly designed not to unduly limit the application of the act by precise definition, but, while clearly fixing a standard, that is, by defining the ulterior boundaries which could not be transgressed with impunity, to leave it to be determined by the light of reason, guided by the principles of law and the duty to apply and enforce the public policy embodied in the statute, in every given case whether any particular act or contract was within the contemplation of the statute.

*   *   *   *

Recurring to the acts done by the individuals or corporations who were mainly instrumental in bringing about the expansion of the New Jersey corporation during the period prior to the formation of the trust agreements of 1879 and 1882, including those agreements, not for the purpose of weighing the substantial merit of the numerous charges of wrongdoing made during such period, but solely as an aid for discovering intent and purpose, we think no disinterested mind can survey the period in question without being irresistibly driven to the conclusion that the very genius for commercial development and organization which it would seem was manifested from the beginning soon begot an intent and purpose to exclude others which was frequently manifested by acts and dealings wholly inconsistent with the theory that they were made with the single conception of advancing the development of business power by usual methods, but which on the contrary necessarily involved the intent to drive others from the field and to exclude them from their right to trade and thus accomplish the mastery which was the end in view. The exercise of the power which resulted from that organization fortifies the foregoing conclusions, since the development which came, the acquisition here and there which ensued of every efficient means by which competition could have been asserted, the slow but resistless methods which followed by which means of transportation were absorbed and brought under control, the system of marketing which was adopted by which the country was divided into districts and the trade in each district in oil was turned over to a designated corporation within the combination and all others were excluded, all lead the mind up to a conviction of a purpose and intent which we think is so certain as practically to cause the subject not to be within the domain of reasonable contention.

DECISION AND REMEDY   *The Supreme Court agreed with the lower court and affirmed the decree. Standard Oil was forbidden to engage in any future combinations in violation of the Sherman Antitrust Act. In addition, the decree attempted to neutralize the effect of the monopoly that Standard Oil had created by* *commanding the dissolution of the combination (the trust) and causing the New Jersey corporation to divest itself of the numerous shares of stock that it controlled.*

The Court in *Standard Oil* reasoned that Congress had intended the Sherman Act to apply only to unreasonable restraints on trade that would achieve monopolization. This is what is meant by the rule of reason. The Court rejected the idea that the act should reach every restraint, regardless of its reasonableness. If the Court had not interpreted the act in this way, every conceivable business practice would have violated the Sherman Act.

Two doctrines are used in deciding Sherman Act cases: the rule of reason and *per se* illegality.

Per Se Rule

Certain types of restrictive agreements are deemed to be inherently anticompetitive and are always an unreasonable restraint on trade. These agreements are subject to the ***per se* rule** (no evidence beyond the fact that the agreement existed is re-

quired to prove the illegality), because these agreements are violations of the Sherman Act and are considered inherently evil. Price-fixing is one of the practices to which courts apply the *per se* standard rather than the rule of reason. Price-fixing occurs when competitors conspire to fix the price of an item or service.

The following case, decided in 1940, established the principle that price-fixing agreements are unlawful *per se*. *Standard Oil Co. of New Jersey v. United States* is the classic case on the rule of reason, and *United States v. Socony-Vacuum Oil Co.* is the classic case on the *per se* doctrine.[1]

---

1. Saconey-Vacuum Oil Company was one of the companies in the Standard Oil Trust. Socony-Vacuum Oil Company and Standard Oil of New York are now Mobil Oil Company.

BACKGROUND AND FACTS *During the Great Depression, more oil was refined into gasoline than consumers demanded at the then-current market price. The major oil refiners had ample storage facilities and the capacity to distribute gasoline to retailers. Smaller, independent refiners lacked storage facilities and sold their gasoline at distressed prices on the spot market for immediate delivery to retailers. Prices on the spot market affected prices throughout the industry, and the glut of gasoline available in the spot market drove prices down.*

The major oil companies embarked on a program of purchasing and storing the "distressed oil." Each major company agreed to buy from a particular independent. Although it appeared that the bidding and buying were based on the market price, the major companies through their bidding established a floor for gasoline prices that enabled them to prevent prices on the spot market from falling any lower.

Case 19.2
UNITED STATES v. SOCONY-VACUUM OIL CO.
Supreme Court of the United States, 1940.
310 U.S. 150, 60 S.Ct. 811, 84 L.Ed 1129.

DOUGLAS, Justice.
* * * *

The elimination of the so-called competitive evils is no legal justification for such buying programs. The elimination of such conditions was sought primarily for its effect on the price structures. Fairer competitive prices, it is claimed, resulted when distress gasoline was removed from the market. But such defense is typical of the protestations usually made in price-fixing cases. Ruinous competition, financial disaster, evils of price cutting and the like appear throughout our history as ostensible justifications for price-fixing. If the so-called competitive abuses were to be appraised here, the reasonableness of prices would necessarily become an issue in every price-fixing case. In that event the Sherman Act would soon be emasculated; its philosophy would be supplanted by one which is wholly alien to a system of free competition; it would not be the charter of freedom which its framers intended.

The reasonableness of prices has no constancy due to the dynamic quality of business facts underlying price structures. Those who fixed reasonable prices today would perpetuate unreasonable prices tomorrow, since those prices would not be subject to continuous administrative supervision and readjustment in light of changed conditions. Those who controlled the prices would control or effectively dominate the market. And those who were in that strategic position would have it in their power to destroy or drastically impair the competitive system. But the thrust of the rule is deeper and reaches more than monopoly power. Any combination which tampers with price structures is engaged in an unlawful activity. Even though the members of the price-fixing group were in no position to control the market, to the extent that they raised, lowered, or stabilized prices they would be directly interfering with the free play of market forces. The Act places all such schemes beyond the pale and protects that vital part of our economy against any degree of interference. Congress has not left with us the determination of whether or not particular price-fixing schemes are wise or unwise, healthy or destructive. It has not permitted the age-old cry of ruinous competition and competitive evils to be a defense to price-fixing conspiracies. It has no more allowed genuine or fancied competitive abuses as a legal justification for such schemes than it has the good intentions of the members of the combination. If such a shift is to be made, it must be done by Congress. Certainly Congress has not left us with any such choice. Nor has the Act created or authorized the creation of any special exception in favor of the oil industry. Whatever may be its peculiar problems and characteristics, the Sherman Act, so far as price-fixing agreements are concerned, establishes one uniform rule applicable to all industries alike. There was accordingly no error in the refusal to charge that in order to convict the jury must find that the resultant prices were raised and maintained at "high, arbitrary and noncompetitive levels." The charge in the indictment to that effect was surplusage.

*   *   *   *

Under the Sherman Act a combination formed for the purpose and with the effect of raising, depressing, fixing, pegging, or stabilizing the price of a commodity in interstate or foreign commerce is illegal *per se*. Where the machinery for price-fixing is an agreement on the prices to be charged or paid for the commodity in the interstate or foreign channels of trade, the power to fix prices exists if the combination has control of a substantial part of the commerce in that commodity. Where the means for price-fixing are purchases or sales of the commodity in a market operation or, as here, purchases of a part of the supply of the commodity for the purpose of keeping it from having a depressive effect on the markets, such power may be found to exist though the combination does not control a substantial part of the commodity. In such a case that power may be established if as a result of market conditions, the resources available to the combinations, the timing and the strategic placement of orders and the like, effective means are at hand to accomplish the desired objective. But there may be effective influence over the market though the group in question does not control it. Price-fixing agreements may have utility to members of the group though the power possessed or exerted falls far short of domination and control. Monopoly power is not the only power which the Act strikes down, as we have said. Proof that a combination was formed for the purpose of fixing prices and that it caused them to be fixed or contributed to that result is proof of the completion of a price-fixing conspiracy under § 1 of the Act. *   *   *

The Supreme Court affirmed the judgment of the trial court. Each corporation was fined $5,000; each individual, $1,000. It was held that it is illegal to try to fix prices even though the prices seem to be reasonable. Any attempt to fix prices is an illegal per se *violation of the Sherman Act.*

DECISION AND REMEDY

In addition to the price-fixing agreements that violate Section 1 of the Sherman Act, two other types of agreements are *per se* illegal: horizontal market divisions and group boycotts.

Horizontal Market Divisions   Dividing a market for the sale of a specific product among competitors is a *per se* violation. Market division can be accomplished in many ways, all of which are illegal. Competitors cannot allocate among themselves exclusive territories, products, or customers. Even though such agreements might seem reasonable, they eliminate competition. Whether price-fixing and other restraints on trade are part of the plan to divide a market is irrelevant.

These activities among competitors are referred to as horizontal restraints when the competitors are on the same basic level of business operation—for example, retailers, manufacturers, or producers. The parties involved may be sellers of the same brand, suppressing intrabrand competition, or of different brands, suppressing interbrand competition. Franchise agreements seem to be the only exception, but they are subject to the rule of reason.

In the next case, supermarket owners entered into a joint venture to create their own house brand. Having their own brand names enabled the independent grocers to compete with the national supermarket chains. As part of the agreement, each participant received an exclusive territory in which to sell the new brand-name products—a violation of the Sherman Act.

BACKGROUND AND FACTS   *The United States sought an injunction against the cooperative association, Topco. Topco is a cooperative association of approximately twenty-five small and medium-sized regional supermarket chains that operate independently. No grocery business is operated under the Topco name. Its basic function is to act as a purchasing agent for its members and to provide products to them under the brand name of Topco.*

The government charged that Topco's scheme of dividing markets among its members operated to prohibit competition in Topco-brand products. Topco contended that it needed the territorial divisions in order to maintain its private label program. The district court applied a rule of reason and upheld the restrictive practices as reasonable and procompetitive. The United States appealed directly to the Supreme Court.

Case 19.3
UNITED STATES v. TOPCO ASSOCIATES, INC.
Supreme Court of the United States, 1972
405 U.S. 596, 92 S.Ct. 1126, 31 L.Ed.2d 515.

MARSHALL, Justice.
*   *   *   *
While the Court has utilized the ''rule of reason'' in evaluating the legality of most restraints alleged to be violative of the Sherman Act, it has also developed

the doctrine that certain business relationships are *per se* violations of the Act without regard to a consideration of their reasonableness. * * *

It is only after considerable experience with certain business relationships that courts classify them as *per se* violations of the Sherman Act. One of the classic examples of a *per se* violation of Section 1 is an agreement between competitors at the same level of the market structure to allocate territories in order to minimize competition. Such concerted action is usually termed a "horizontal" restraint, in contradistinction to combinations of persons at different levels of the market structures; e.g., manufacturers and distributors, which are termed "vertical" restraints. This Court has reiterated time and time again that "[h]orizontal territorial limitations * * * are naked restraints of trade with no purpose except stifling of competition."

We think that it is clear that the restraint in this case is a horizontal one, and, therefore, a *per se* violation of Section 1. The District Court failed to make any determination as to whether there were *per se* horizontal territorial restraints in this case and simply applied a rule of reason in reaching its conclusion that the restraints were not illegal. * * *
* * * *

Whether or not we would decide this case the same way under the rule of reason used by the District Court is irrelevant to the issue before us. The fact is that courts are of limited utility in examining difficult economic problems. Our inability to weigh, in any meaningful sense, destruction of competition in one sector of the economy against promotion of competition in another sector is one important reason we have formulated *per se* rules.

In applying these rigid rules, the Court has consistently rejected the notion that naked restraints of trade are to be tolerated because they are well intended or because they are allegedly developed to increase competition.

Antitrust laws in general, and the Sherman Act in particular, are the Magna Carta of free enterprise. They are as important to the preservation of economic freedom and our free-enterprise system as the Bill of Rights is to the protection of our fundamental personal freedoms. And the freedom guaranteed each and every business, no matter how small, is the freedom to compete—to assert with vigor, imagination, devotion, and ingenuity whatever economic muscle it can muster. Implicit in such freedom is the notion that it cannot be foreclosed with respect to one sector of the economy because certain private citizens or groups believe that such foreclosure might promote greater competition in a more important sector of the economy.

DECISION AND *The Supreme Court struck down Topco's territorial restrictions, thus al-*
REMEDY *lowing Topco's members to sell their products wherever they chose. The Court found this horizontal restraint to be illegal* per se *and a violation of Section 1 of the Sherman Act.*

Group Boycotts Concerted refusals to deal, usually called boycotts, are a *per se* offense. A boycott generally involves two different levels of business operation rather than competitors on the same basic level. Traders on one level coerce traders on another level not to deal with certain parties. For example, a group of wholesalers may refuse to buy from a supplier who sells to a particular wholesaler. Or the group of wholesalers may refuse to sell to retailers who buy from a specified wholesaler. The group undertaking the boycott seeks to protect itself from competition by depriving the excluded party of trade relationships. The boycotting group threatens to stop dealing with any business that sells to or buys from a business that is not a group member.

Concerted refusals to deal violate the Sherman Act only when their purpose is to drive out competitors or to prevent their entry into business. For example, boycotts to prevent the sale of copies of designer clothing and the boycott by car dealers to prevent General Motors from selling cars to discount outlets were *per se* violations of the antitrust laws. A boycott by the National Organization for Women of states that did not ratify the Equal Rights Amendment did not violate the Sherman Act. Since the purpose was to influence legislation rather than to enhance the organization's position among competitors, the boycott was held to be outside the scope of the antitrust laws. Further, these activities were protected by the First Amendment to the Constitution.

Clayton Act

In 1914 Congress attempted to strengthen federal antitrust laws by adopting the **Clayton Act**, which was aimed at specific monopolistic practices. The important sections of the Clayton Act are Sections 2, 3, 7, and 8.

Section 2, as originally passed, was very weak. Thus, Congress passed the Robinson-Patman Act, which strengthened Section 2, and today that Section is known as the Robinson-Patman Act. The objective of Section 2 is to promote economic equality in the purchasing and selling of goods. In other words, Section 2 deals with price discrimination. The Robinson-Patman Act does not apply to services.

A seller of goods cannot obtain an unfair advantage over its competitors by giving a better price (and thus discriminating) between different buyers of like goods where the effect will be to lessen competition substantially or where it may create a monopoly. For example, Flour Mill offers flour to all the big bakeries in the state at a lower price than it sells flour to small bakeries. Big bakeries all purchase from Flour Mill. Competitors of Flour Mill are either driven out of business or end up with a smaller share of the market because they sell only to the smaller bakeries.

The reverse is also prohibited: Buyers cannot use their economic power to obtain better prices

from the seller in order to gain an economic advantage over their competitors.

Section 3 prohibits exclusive dealing agreements and tying arrangements. Under an exclusive dealing agreement, the seller of goods requires the buyer to promise not to handle products of any competitors of the seller. Tying arrangements are prohibited by a court decision that interpreted Section 3. Under a tying arrangement, the buyer must purchase one item in order to purchase the tied product. The item required to be purchased might not even be wanted by the buyer. Tying arrangements and exclusive dealing contracts are also violations of Section 2 of the Sherman Act.

For example, Fast-Food Franchise requires its franchisees to purchase from it not only its secret recipe mix but also all paper products, such as paper boxes, paper bags, and paper napkins. The franchisee cannot purchase any paper products elsewhere; otherwise it will lose the franchise. This requirement is an illegal tying arrangement under Section 3, since the franchisee must purchase the paper products in order to buy the tied product, the secret recipe mix. Paper products have nothing to do with Fast-Food Franchise and can be purchased at lower prices from others. On the other hand, remember that franchise agreements may allocate geographical areas. Thus, these provisions are subject to the rule of reason.

Section 7 was also weak; in 1950, Congress passed the Celler-Kefauver Act, which strengthened and expanded this section. Corporations are prohibited from merging with another corporation if the merger may lessen competition or tend to create a monopoly. Corporate mergers are legally tested under this section.

Section 8 prohibits interlocking directorships. A person cannot be a director of two or more competing businesses where one of them has assets exceeding $1 million.

The Sherman Act proscribed activities that eliminated competition or resulted in monopoly power, but it did not reach activities that merely *reduced* competition or *could* lead to monopoly power. The Clayton Act declares these specific activities to be illegal, even though these practices might not constitute the contract, combination, or conspiracy in restraint of trade necessary for a Sherman Act violation. Actual monopolization is unnecessary under the Clayton Act as is any attempt to monopolize. The act does not require that an injury to competition be demonstrated; therefore, the burden of proof for violations of the Clayton Act is less than for violations of the Sherman Act. In short, the Clayton Act reaches practices before a monopoly is actually created.

Federal Trade Commission Act

In 1914 Congress also passed the Federal Trade Commission Act, which created the Federal Trade Commission (FTC), a bipartisan, independent administrative agency headed by five commissioners. No more than three commissioners can be from the same political party. The act gives the FTC broad powers to prevent "unfair methods of competition in commerce and unfair or deceptive acts or practices in commerce." The Magnuson-Moss Act of 1975, which amended the Federal Trade Commission Act, broadened the commission's powers.

The FTC has the authority to conduct investigations relating to alleged violations of antitrust statutes. In addition, the FTC makes reports and recommendations to Congress regarding legislation. More important, the FTC can promulgate interpretive rules and general statements of policy with respect to unfair or deceptive acts or practices. The FTC can also adopt trade regulation rules that define particular unfair or deceptive acts or practices, including requirements whose purpose is to prevent such acts or practices. The FTC has no power to enforce the Sherman Act, but it does have authority to bring civil actions under the Clayton Act, and it enforces the Federal Trade Commission Act.

Exhibit 19–1 lists the major antitrust laws and gives a brief summary of each.

Exemptions from Antitrust Laws

Congress's attention to the antitrust laws since passing the Clayton Act has focused primarily on creating exceptions from the coverage of the Sherman Act. The Norris-LaGuardia Act of 1932 and the National Labor Relations Act of 1935 protected unions from antitrust legislation. Today, unions can lawfully engage in actions that are

normally prohibited as long as they act in their own self-interest and do not conspire or combine with nonlabor groups to accomplish their goals.

Likewise, agricultural organizations are made exempt from the Sherman Antitrust Act by the Clayton Act, as well as by the Capper-Volstead Act (1922), by the Cooperative Marketing Act (1926), and by certain provisions of the Robinson-Patman Act. Although most commercial sport activities are subject to the antitrust laws, there is an exception. Baseball remains untouched by the antitrust laws. The U.S. Supreme Court held that baseball was not to be commerce in the Sherman Act's original contemplation and is thus not commerce today. Baseball's exemption is anomalous, especially since no other professional sport receives such treatment.

Professionals and their organizations, such as lawyers and doctors, are no longer exempt from antitrust enforcement. They cannot establish minimum- or maximum-fee schedules or prohibit competitive bidding in any way. The traditional incantations about the maintenance of high quality no longer shield professionals from the antitrust laws.

The **McCarran-Ferguson Act**, enacted in 1945, exempted from the antitrust laws all activities that are in the business of insurance. The primary element of the insurance business is the spreading and underwriting of policyholder risk. Thus, strict insurance activities are exempted from the antitrust laws by the McCarran-Ferguson Act. An agreement between an insurance company and pharmacies setting the profit margin in prescription drugs, however, is subject to the antitrust laws.

Sometimes a decision to exempt certain activities from antitrust actions is made in the belief that certain goals can be better achieved through cartelization—that is, a banding together of competing firms. For example, the Webb-Pomerene Act exempts acts or agreements made in the course of export trade by associations of producers formed solely for the purpose of engaging in export trade. Cartelization promotes an increased national investment in the covered activities, thereby aiding the nation's balance of payments.

The **Noerr-Pennington Doctrine** was derived from two United States Supreme Court cases. Basically, the Court held that "the Sherman Act does

Exhibit 19-1 **Major Antitrust Statutes**

STATUTES LIMITING COMBINATIONS	STATUTES LIMITING CONTRACTUAL AND BUSINESS ACTIONS
Sherman Act (1890) Section 2* prohibits monopolies and attempts or conspiracies to monopolize. **Clayton Act** (1914) Section 7 prohibits mergers when the effect may be to lessen competition substantially or to create a monopoly. Amended (1950)—Celler-Kefauver Act clarified application of Section 7 to acquisition of assets. **Clayton Act** (1914) Section 8 prohibits interlocking directorates.	**Sherman Act** (1890) Section 1* prohibits combinations and conspiracies in restraint of trade, including vertical and horizontal price-fixing, group boycotts, division of markets, and other practices. **Clayton Act** (1914) Section 2 prohibits price discriminations, substantially lessening sellers' competition (primary violations). Amended (1936)—Robinson-Patman Act prohibits price discriminations, substantially lessening buyers' competition (secondary violation). **Clayton Act** (1914) Section 3 prohibits exclusive dealing and tying arrangements where the effect may be to lessen competition substantially. **Federal Trade Commission Act** (1914) Section 5† prohibits unfair methods of competition; it established and defined powers of FTC. Amended (1938)—Wheeler-Lea Act prohibits unfair trade practices and false advertising. Amended (1976)—Hart-Scott-Rodino Act increases merger-reporting requirements.

*Amended in 1974 and 1976 to increase penalties and broaden enforcement.
†Amended in 1973 and 1975 to increase penalties and grant industry-wide rule-making power.

not prohibit two or more persons from associating together in an attempt to persuade the legislature or the executive to take particular action with respect to a law that would produce a restraint or a monopoly." In other words, businesses are allowed to work with congresspeople in order to pass appropriate but favorable laws.

In general, actions taken by state, local, and other public jurisdictions are exempt from antitrust laws. In 1978 it was held, however, that this doc-

trine of "state action unity" does not exempt all government entities from federal antitrust laws. Thus, unauthorized anticompetitive practices by state bodies are subject to antitrust laws. Recently the United States Supreme Court has reversed itself slightly, which has resulted in an enlargement of this exemption. The following case emphasizes the state action exemption in dealing with an ordinance that established rents on residential property.

BACKGROUND AND FACTS   *The city of Berkeley, California, passed an ordinance controlling rent ceilings on residential property. The plaintiffs were landlords and sought an injunction to stop the enforcement of the ordinance.*

 Case 19.4

ALEXANDRA FISHER v. CITY OF BERKELEY, CALIFORNIA

Supreme Court of the United States, 1986.
475 U.S. 260, 106 S.Ct. 1045, 89 L.Ed.2d 206.

MARSHALL, Justice.

The question presented here is whether a rent control ordinance enacted by a municipality pursuant to popular initiative is unconstitutional because pre-empted by the Sherman Act.

* * * *

Recognizing that the function of government may often be to tamper with free markets, correcting their failures and aiding their victims, this Court noted in *Rice v. Norman Williams Co.*, that a "state statute is not pre-empted by the federal antitrust laws simply because the state scheme may have an anticompetitive effect." We have therefore held that a state statute should be struck down on pre-emption grounds "only if it mandates or authorizes conduct that necessarily constitutes a violation of the antitrust laws in all cases, or if it places irresistible pressure on a private party to violate the antitrust laws in order to comply with the statute."

* * * *

Recognizing this concerted action requirement, appellants argue that the Ordinance "forms a combination between [the City of Berkeley and its officials], on the one hand, and the property owners on the other. It also creates a horizontal combination among the landlords." In so arguing, appellants misconstrue the concerted action requirement of Section 1. A restraint imposed unilaterally by government does not become concerted action simply because it has a coercive effect upon parties who must obey the law. The ordinary relationship between the government and those who must obey its regulatory commands whether they wish to or not is not enough to establish a conspiracy. Similarly, the mere fact that all competing property owners must comply with the same provisons of the Ordinance is not enough to establish a conspiracy among landlords. Under Berkeley's Ordinance, control over the maximum rent levels of every affected residential unit has been unilaterally removed from the owners of those properties and given to the Rent Stabilization Board. While the Board may choose to respond to an individual landlord's petition for a special adjustment of a particular rent ceiling, it may decide not to. There is no meeting of the minds here. The owners of residential property in Berkeley have no more freedom to resist the city's rent controls than they do to violate any other local ordinance enforced by substantial sanctions.

DECISION AND REMEDY   *The United States Supreme Court upheld the right of the city of Berkeley to control rents on residential property. In doing so, the Court held that no violation of the Sherman Act had occurred because there had been no concerted action.*

Enforcement of Antitrust Laws

Enforcement of the various antitrust laws is handled by the Federal Trade Commission, Department of Justice, and private parties. All three, however, do not have the right to enforce all the laws. The Department of Justice is the only federal department authorized to bring criminal charges, and only the Sherman Act has criminal provisions.

Enforcement by the Federal Trade Commission

The Federal Trade Commission has the authority to enforce the FTC Act, the Sherman Act, and the Clayton Act under civil charges. Neither the Justice Department nor any private party has the right to enforce the Federal Trade Commission Act. When the Federal Trade Commission has jurisdiction, the usual procedure is for the FTC to issue a cease and desist order (an order to stop certain activities or practices), prohibiting the individual or corporation from further violating the law. If the cease and desist order is ignored, the Justice Department seeks to impose criminal sanctions.

The FTC investigates business conduct and holds administrative hearings. A cease and desist order issued by the FTC may be appealed; it is then reviewed by an appellate court. Businesses that violate an FTC cease and desist order are subject to fines of up to $10,000 per day for each day of continued violation.

The Federal Trade Commission Act overlaps with a number of other antitrust statutes, including the Sherman Act, the Clayton Act, and other laws designed to reduce unfair methods of competition. The FTC initiates investigations and issues cease and desist orders particularly for violations of the Clayton Act, as amended by the Robinson-Patman Act, and for other acts.

Enforcement by Private Parties

Private parties can also sue for up to three times their damages and for other remedies. They may bring action under either the Sherman or Clayton Acts but not under the Federal Trade Commission Act. The courts have determined that the test of ability to sue depends on the directness of the injury suffered by the purported plaintiff. Thus, a person wishing to sue under the Sherman Act must prove: (1) that the antitrust violation either directly caused or was at least a substantial factor in causing the injury that was suffered and (2) that the unlawful actions of the purported defendant affected business activities of the plaintiff that were protected by the antitrust laws.

The plaintiffs in the following case alleged a price-fixing agreement among attorneys and sought damages for the injury they suffered.

BACKGROUND AND FACTS *When Mr. and Mrs. Goldfarb contracted to purchase a home in Fairfax County, Virginia, they were unable to find a lawyer who would examine the title for less than the fee prescribed in a minimum-fee schedule published by the Fairfax County Bar Association and enforced by the Virginia State Bar. The Goldfarbs brought this action seeking injunctive relief and damages. They alleged that the minimum-fee schedule and its enforcement mechanism, as applied to fees for legal services relating to residential real estate transactions, constituted price-fixing in violation of Section 1 of the Sherman Act.*

Case 19.5
**GOLDFARB v.
VIRGINIA STATE BAR**
Supreme Court of the United States, 1975.
421 U.S. 773, 95 S.Ct. 2004, 44 L.Ed.2d 572.

BURGER, Chief Justice.
* * * *

Our inquiry can be divided into * * * steps: did respondents engage in price fixing? If so, are their activities in interstate commerce or do they affect interstate commerce? If so, are the activities exempt from the Sherman Act because they involve a "learned profession?" * * *
* * * *

A purely advisory fee schedule issued to provide guidelines, or an exchange of price information without a showing of an actual restraint on trade, would present us with a different question. The record here, however, reveals a situation quite different from what would occur under a purely advisory fee schedule. Here a fixed, rigid price floor arose from respondents' activities: every lawyer who responded to petitioners' inquiries adhered to the fee schedule, and no lawyer asked for additional information in order to set an individualized fee. * * * The fee schedule was enforced through the prospect of professional discipline from the State Bar, and the desire of attorneys to comply with announced professional norms; the motivation to conform was reinforced by the assurance that other lawyers would not compete by underbidding. This is not merely a case of an agreement that may be inferred from an exchange of price information, for here a naked agreement was clearly shown, and the effect on prices is plain.

Moreover, in terms of restraining competition and harming consumers like petitioners the price-fixing activities found here are unusually damaging. A title examination is indispensable in the process of financing a real estate purchase, and since only an attorney licensed to practice in Virginia may legally examine a title, consumers could not turn to alternative sources for the necessary service. All attorneys, of course, were practicing under the constraint of the fee schedule. * * * On this record respondents' activities constitute a classic illustration of price fixing.

The County Bar argues, as the Court of Appeals held, that any effect on interstate commerce caused by the fee schedule's restraint on legal services was incidental and remote. In its view the legal services, which are performed wholly intrastate, are essentially local in nature and therefore a restraint with respect to them can never substantially affect interstate commerce. * * *

These arguments misconceive the nature of the transactions at issue and the place legal services play in those transactions. As the District Court found, "a significant portion of funds furnished for the purchasing of homes in Fairfax County comes from without the State of Virginia," and "significant amounts of loans on Fairfax County real estate are guaranteed by the United States Veterans Administration and Department of Housing and Urban Development, both headquartered in the District of Columbia." Thus in this class action the transactions which create the need for the particular legal services in question frequently are interstate transactions. * * *

* * * *

The County Bar argues that Congress never intended to include the learned professions within the terms "trade or commerce" in Sec. 1 of the Sherman Act, and therefore the sale of professional services is exempt from the Act. No explicit exemption or legislative history is provided to support this contention; rather, the existence of state regulation seems to be its primary basis. Also, the County Bar maintains that competition is inconsistent with the practice of a profession because enhancing profit is not the goal of professional activities; the goal is to provide services necessary to the community. * * *

In arguing that learned professions are not "trade or commerce" the County Bar seeks a total exclusion from antitrust regulation. Whether state regulation is active or dormant, real or theoretical, lawyers would be able to adopt anticompetitive practices with impunity. We cannot find support for the proposition that Congress intended any such sweeping exclusion. The nature of an occupation, standing alone, does not provide sanctuary from the Sherman Act, nor is the public-service aspect of professional practice controlling in determining whether Sec. 1 includes professions. Congress intended to strike as broadly as it could in Sec. 1 of the Sherman Act, and to read into it so wide an exemption as that urged on us would be at odds with that purpose.

The language of Sec. 1 of the Sherman Act, of course, contains no exception. * * * And our cases have repeatedly established that there is a heavy presumption against implicit exemptions. * * * Indeed, our cases have specifically included the sale of services within Sec. 1. Whatever else it may be, the examination of a land title is a service; the exchange of such a service for money is "commerce" in the most common usage of that word. * * * In the modern world it cannot be denied that the activities of lawyers play an important part in commercial intercourse, and that anticompetitive activities by lawyers may exert a restraint on commerce.

DECISION AND REMEDY   *The minimum-fee schedule violated the Sherman Act. The case was remanded to the district court for issuance of an injunction against the legal associations and for determination of the damages suffered by the Goldfarbs.*

After this case, the cost of title examination fell from around $500 to under **COMMENT**
$50. Across the country, minimum-fee schedules set by state bar associations were abandoned.

Enforcement by the Department of Justice

Any person violating either Section 1 or 2 of the Sherman Act is subject to criminal prosecution for a felony by the Department of Justice. Currently, on conviction, a person can be fined up to $100,000, imprisoned for three years, or both. A corporation can be fined $1 million.

The Department of Justice can simultaneously institute civil proceedings to restrain the conduct that is in violation of the act. The various remedies that the Justice Department has asked the court to impose include: confiscation of goods in interstate commerce; divestiture, dissolution, and divorcements; and the demand that a company give up one of its operating functions. A group of meat packers, for example, can be forced to divorce themselves from controlling or owning butcher shops.

The Antitrust Division of the Department of Justice settles most cases before the trial stage. These out-of-court settlements, however, must receive court approval. In order to gain approval, the court must find that the settlement is in the national interest. Because the issues in antitrust cases are extremely complex and sometimes take years to litigate, settlements reduce the cost of enforcement. Probably one of the best examples of such a settlement is the recent divestiture and breakup of American Telephone and Telegraph.

A high percentage of these cases are settled through the use of *nolo contendere* pleas in criminal cases and consent decrees in civil cases. A *nolo contendere* plea does not admit guilt, but a court may treat the plea as if the defendant had pleaded guilty and may impose the same penalty as for a guilty plea. With a consent decree, the defendant allows the court to impose remedial measures aimed at correcting the anticompetitive effects of the defendant's actions. Such remedial measures include ordering the defendant to divest itself of the stock of another company, to cancel a contract, to refrain from a particular type of conduct, or to dissolve itself and go out of business.

FACING A LEGAL ISSUE **Price Fixing**

You know how to use video cameras, so, to finance your college education and to assist in your education, you decide to offer the local real estate agents a service of going around to residences that are for sale and videotaping them from both the outside and the inside. Then the realtor can show these tapes to a prospective buyer in the comfort of his or her office. This service will save many hours both for the salesperson and the buyer.

You decide to charge $25 per house. After several months, you are making enough money to continue your college education. Several other students, however, see your success and decide to open similar businesses. This competition forces your fee down to $10 per house. You decide that this is ruinous competition, and you contact your competitors. They feel likewise, and all of you agree to set your prices at $22 per house. If any of you violates this charge, they must pay other competitors $500 each. You put this agreement into writing, and everyone signs it. About a month later, after you have increased your prices, it is discovered that one of your competitors has violated the agreement by charging only $20 per house.

You and your competitors have entered into a price-fixing agreement that may be in violation of Section 1 of the Sherman Act. If this is true, the contract you entered into is not enforceable, and you cannot collect the $500. The only defense would be that it does not involve interstate commerce and/or that it would be subject to the rule of reason. However, the courts have held that a price-fixing agreement is conclusively presumed to be a *per se* violation of the Sherman Act. The real question, then, is whether interstate commerce is involved. A court would probably find that it is involved. This is particularly true if you and your competitors are going into different states in competition with one another. Many states have statutes similar to the federal laws; thus, this conduct might be a violation of state law even if it does not involve interstate commerce.

Summary

This chapter has introduced you to antitrust law. Even in early common law, the court of England found certain agreements that restricted competition to be illegal. This basic theory has been carried forward through the federal laws adopted in the United States.

The major antitrust statutory provisons are found in the Sherman Act. The first provision of this law makes it illegal to enter into any contract, combination, or conspiracy in restraint of trade or commerce. The second section makes it illegal to monopolize or attempt to monopolize any trade or commerce. Any criminal violation of this act may result in a felony conviction and a prison sentence of up to three years, plus liability for three times the damages incurred. Further, goods shipped in intrastate commerce may be seized, and the federal government can obtain an order to stop the illegal conduct.

The major defense to this act is that the conduct is subject to the rule of reason. Certain conduct, however, is conclusively presumed to be in violation of this act and not subject to the rule of reason. For example, any agreement to fix prices or to have a group boycott is illegal *per se* if it involves interstate commerce.

The second major act to be adopted that involves antitrust law is the Clayton Act. This statute makes illegal certain specified actions such as price discrimination, exclusive dealing and tying arrangements, certain types of mergers, and interlocking directorates.

The Federal Trade Commission Act is the third major legislation. Establishing the Federal Trade Commission, the FTC Act authorizes the FTC to investigate and to issue cease and desist orders when it finds unfair or deceptive acts or practices, including antitrust violations.

A number of exemptions to the antitrust laws exist: labor unions, agriculture organizations, baseball, insurance, certain foreign trade groups, and certain activities conducted by individual states. In enforcing antitrust laws, the Department of Justice is the only one that can bring criminal cases. The Federal Trade Commission may issue cease and desist orders, and private persons may bring action for three times the actual damages.

Key Terms

antitrust laws **474**
Clayton Act **483**
Interstate Commerce Act **474**
McCarran-Ferguson Act **484**

Noerr-Pennington Doctrine **484**
nolo contendere **489**

per se rule **479**
rule of reason **476**
Sherman Antitrust Act **474**

Questions and Case Problems

1. The Fuller Corporation, the leading manufacturer of electric transformers, and five other major manufacturers of electric transformers, agree to a five-year price-maintenance maximum increase of 10 percent per year over their current prices. Green Interstate, an electric cooperative that purchases large quantities of transformers on competitive bidding, has purchased over $500,000 worth of transformers from Fuller over a three-year period. Green learns of the price-maintenance agreement. The Department of Justice has filed no action against Fuller and the five other manufacturers. Discuss fully whether Green can bring a private action against Fuller.

2. Assume the following events take place. Discuss which antitrust law has been primarily violated, if any.

(a) Acme, Inc., and Jimenez Corporation are interstate competitors selling similar appliances principally in the states of Wisconsin, Illinois, Minnesota, and Iowa. Acme and Jimenez agree that Acme will no longer sell in Wisconsin and Minnesota, and Jimenez will no longer sell in Iowa and Illinois.

(b) The partnership of Montoya and Marsh is engaged in the oil well-head service industry in the states of New Mexico and Colorado. They presently have about 40 percent of the market for this service. The firm of West, Williams, and Wilson, Inc., is engaged in competition with the Montoya-Marsh partnership in the same geographic area. The West corporation has approximately 35 percent of the market. Montoya and Marsh acquire the stock and assets of West.

3. Mickey's Appliance Store is a new retail seller of appliances in Sunwest City. Mickey's innovative sales techniques and financing have caused a substantial loss of sales from the appliance department of Luckluster Department Store. Luckluster is a large department store and is part of a large chain with substantial buying power. Luckluster tells a number of appliance manufacturers that, if they continue to sell to Mickey's, Luckluster will discontinue its large volume of purchases from these manufacturers. The manufacturers immediately stop selling appliances to Mickey's. Mickey's files suit against Luckluster and the manufacturers, claiming that their actions constitute an antitrust violation. Luckluster and the manufacturers can prove that Mickey's is a small retailer with a small portion of the market, and, since the relevant market was not substantially affected, they claim they are not guilty of restraint of trade. Discuss fully whether there is an antitrust violation.

4. Meister Brau, Inc., was engaged in the business of brewing beers, malts, and ales. It acquired the Berger Meister Beer Company through a purchase of the latter's common stock. Berger Meister sold the beer it brewed through distributors who operated as individual businesses separate from Berger Meister. Soon after Meister Brau acquired Berger Meister, it terminated some of Berger Meister's distributors. The distributors handled the products of a number of other breweries, but they complained that the reduced sales volume that would result from their being terminated by Meister Brau would drive them out

of business. The distributors thus brought suit against Meister Brau, alleging that its agreement with its new subsidiary, Berger Meister, to terminate the distributors constituted a conspiracy in restraint of trade in violation of Section 1 of the Sherman Act. The distributors alleged that the terminations would reduce competition in a market that was already tending toward concentration. Has Meister Brau violated Section 1 of the Sherman Act? [Ricchetti v. Meister Brau, Inc., 431 F.2d 1211 (9th Cir. 1970)]

5. On August 5, 1969, at a hearing held before the Arizona Corporation Commission, the Arizona Water Company, a private corporation, sought and was granted the right to deliver water in a specified geographic area. Subsequently, the state of Arizona issued the company a "certificate of convenience and necessity," which confirmed the company's exclusive right to sell water in the specified area. In light of antitrust laws that prohibit the exercise of monopoly powers, should Arizona Water Company be granted this exclusive right? Under what conditions should the state of Arizona be allowed to withdraw the "certificate of convenience and necessity" that it awarded Arizona Water Company? [Fernandez v. Arizona Water Co., 21 Ariz.App. 107, 516 P.2d 49 (1974)]

6. American Oil Company was a producer and distributor of oil, gas, and related products. Olson was engaged in bulk distribution and retail sales of oil products. Early in 1967, American decided to acquire control of Olson's bulk distribution operations, and it purchased substantially all of Olson's assets. Thereafter, American hired Lawrence McMullin to assume control of the Olson operation for American. Under the agreement, McMullin was to take charge of the Olson plant and was to be paid on a com-

mission basis in lieu of salary for the bulk petroleum sales that he procured. In addition, the contract between American and McMullin imposed certain territorial limitations and price restrictions on sales by the operations that McMullin was to control. Could the agreement between McMullin and American Oil imposing price restrictions and territorial controls on the operations of which McMullin took charge constitute a violation of Section 1 of the Sherman Antitrust Act? Explain. [American Oil Co. v. McMullin, 508 F.2d 1345 (10th Cir. 1975)]

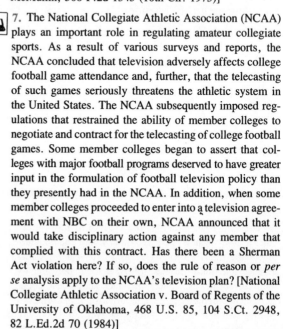 7. The National Collegiate Athletic Association (NCAA) plays an important role in regulating amateur collegiate sports. As a result of various surveys and reports, the NCAA concluded that television adversely affects college football game attendance and, further, that the telecasting of such games seriously threatens the athletic system in the United States. The NCAA subsequently imposed regulations that restrained the ability of member colleges to negotiate and contract for the telecasting of college football games. Some member colleges began to assert that colleges with major football programs deserved to have greater input in the formulation of football television policy than they presently had in the NCAA. In addition, when some member colleges proceeded to enter into a television agreement with NBC on their own, NCAA announced that it would take disciplinary action against any member that complied with this contract. Has there been a Sherman Act violation here? If so, does the rule of reason or *per se* analysis apply to the NCAA's television plan? [National Collegiate Athletic Association v. Board of Regents of the University of Oklahoma, 468 U.S. 85, 104 S.Ct. 2948, 82 L.Ed.2d 70 (1984)]

Chapter 20 Antitrust Law: Enforcement and Trends

Every agreement concerning trade, every regulation of trade, restrains. To bind, to restrain, is of their very essence. The true test of legality is whether the restraint imposed is such as merely regulates and perhaps thereby promotes competition or whether it is such as may suppress or even destroy competition.

Justice Brandeis,
Board of Trade of the City of Chicago v. United States,
246 U.S. 231, 38 S.Ct. 242, 62 L.Ed. 683 (1918)

OUTLINE

Introduction

In the last seventy-five years antitrust statutes and court decisions have modified and narrowed the range of acceptable business competitive behavior. Certain types of restraints have been found valid, but many other types of behavior are now illegal. Wrongful behavior often involves potential violations of more than one statute.

This chapter discusses the activities that are illegal and that involve either horizontal or vertical restraints. It then looks at how the courts decide when a given corporation has monopoly power and when the courts will allow a merger of companies that would tend to create a monopoly. We also look at restrictions on discrimination in price, or promotional material. Finally, the last part of this chapter discusses the defenses to which these doctrines are subject.

Horizontal and Vertical Restraints

Antitrust and trade regulation enforcement falls generally into two categories: that dealing with **horizontal restraints** of trade and that dealing with **vertical restraints**. Horizontal restraints involve two or more firms at the same level in an industry, while vertical restraints affect various levels of production, distribution, and marketing within an industry. A third category of possible restraints involves conglomerates in which unrelated and diversified businesses are acquired by a firm.

The probability of a costly prison sentence or the payment of damages deters businesspeople from openly entering into agreements or conspiracies to fix prices, boycott competitors, or perform other unlawful activities. Often, therefore, the courts must determine whether the parties acted *in concert* on the basis of an implicit agreement to perform such unlawful activities. Sometimes these implicit agreements are difficult to detect.

Horizontal Restraints

The courts must infer the purpose of implicit agreements, combinations, and contracts to determine whether they violate the antitrust laws. In the following case, which involved horizontal restraint of trade, the United States Supreme Court held that the state of mind of the defendants had to be considered in addition to the effect of the alleged illegal business practice in deciding whether the businesses had acted in concert.

Case 20.1

UNITED STATES v. UNITED STATES GYPSUM CO.

Supreme Court of the United States, 1978.
438 U.S. 422, 98 S.Ct. 2864, 57 L.Ed.2d 845.

BACKGROUND AND FACTS   *The United States government indicted and convicted several major gypsum-board manufacturers and their officers for violations of Section 1 of the Sherman Act by allegedly engaging in a price-fixing conspiracy. The conspiracy involved interseller price verification—that is, the practice of telephoning a competing manufacturer to determine the price currently offered on gypsum board to a specific customer.*

The defendants argued that the purpose of the price information exchanges was to enable them to take advantage of the defense of "meeting competition," contained in Section 2(b) of the Clayton Act as amended by the Robinson-Patman Act. This act permits a seller to rebut a prima facie price discrimination charge by showing that a lower price to a purchaser was made in good faith to meet a competitor's equally low price.

BURGER, Chief Justice.
* * * *
Beginning in 1966, the Justice Department, as well as the Federal Trade Commission, became involved in investigations into possible antitrust violations in the

gypsum board industry. In 1971, a grand jury was empaneled and the investigation continued for an additional 28 months. In late 1973, an indictment was filed in the United States District Court for the Western District of Pennsylvania charging six major manufacturers and various of their corporate officials with violations of Section 1 of the Sherman Act.

* * * The indictment proceeded to specify some 13 types of actions taken by conspirators ''[i]n formulating and effectuating'' the combination and conspiracy, the most relevant of which, for our purposes, is specification (h) which alleged that the conspirators

> ''telephoned or otherwise contacted one another to exchange and discuss current and future published or market prices and published or standard terms and conditions of sale and to ascertain alleged deviations therefrom.''

* * * *

* * * The jury was instructed that if it found interseller verification had the effect of raising, fixing, maintaining, or stabilizing the price of gypsum board, then such verification could be considered as evidence of an agreement to so affect prices. They were further charged, and it is this point which gives rise to our present concern, that ''if the effect of the exchanges of pricing information was to raise, fix, maintain, and stabilize prices, then the parties to them are presumed, *as a matter of law,* to have intended that result.''

* * * *

We agree with the Court of Appeals that an effect on prices, without more, will not support a criminal conviction under the Sherman Act, but we do not base that conclusion on the existence of any conflict between the requirements of the Robinson-Patman and the Sherman Acts. Rather, we hold that a defendant's state of mind or intent is an element of a criminal antitrust offense which must be established by evidence and inferences drawn therefrom and cannot be taken from the trier of fact through reliance on a legal presumption of wrongful intent from proof of an effect on prices. * * *

The United States Supreme Court affirmed the court of appeals decision reversing the trial court's finding that the gypsum-board manufacturers were guilty of price conspiracy without proof of intent. In order to find people guilty of this crime, a court must find that the defendants had an intent to fix prices. No intent was found by the Court in this case.

DECISION AND REMEDY

Illegal Concerted Action by Trade Associations Businesspeople in certain types of associations must be careful not to engage in actions that might be considered in violation of the antitrust laws.

For example, competitors often organize into **trade associations** in order to pursue common interests. These associations disseminate information, represent the members' business interests before governmental bodies, initiate joint adver-tising campaigns, and attempt to police their own industry. These exchanges of information among related businesses pose special antitrust problems. Trade association activities are, by their very nature, joint actions, and they are subject to the antitrust laws. In the following case, the United States Supreme Court had to decide whether certain actions of a trade association constituted violations of these laws.

Case 20.2
AMERICAN SOCIETY OF MECHANICAL ENGINEERS, INC. v. HYDROLEVEL CORP.
Supreme Court of the United States, 1982.
456 U.S. 556, 102 S.Ct. 1935, 72 L.Ed.2d 330.

BACKGROUND AND FACTS *The petitioner, the American Society of Mechanical Engineers, Inc. (ASME) is a nonprofit corporation with over 90,000 members. It promulgates engineering codes mainly through the work of volunteers from all fields of mechanical engineering. These codes are incorporated into federal, state, and local laws. Two of ASME's volunteer workers, James and Hardin, issued an advisory opinion on ASME's letterhead, stating that a product manufactured by the respondent, Hydrolevel, was unsafe. James, who worked for a company that competes with Hydrolevel, used this fraudulent letter to discourage customers from dealing with the respondent.*

On learning of the letter, Hydrolevel urged ASME to issue a correction that would explain that the Hydrolevel product conformed to ASME's safety codes. ASME, unaware of James's motives in issuing the letter, declined to refute the dishonest statements. Hydrolevel sued ASME for violations of Sections 1 and 2 of the Sherman Act. Both the district court and the court of appeals ruled in favor of Hydrolevel. The jury awarded Hydrolevel $7.5 million in damages. ASME petitioned the Supreme Court.

BLACKMUN, Justice.
* * * *

* * * ASME contends it should not bear the risk of loss for antitrust violations committed by its agents acting with apparent authority because it is a nonprofit organization, not a business seeking profit. But it is beyond debate that nonprofit organizations can be held liable under the antitrust laws. Although ASME may not operate for profit, it does derive benefits from its codes, including the fees the Society receives for its code-related publications and services, the prestige the codes bring to the Society, the influence they permit ASME to wield, and the aid the standards provide the profession of mechanical engineering. Since the antitrust violation in this case could not have occurred without ASME's codes and ASME's method of administering them, it is not unfitting that ASME be liable for the damages arising from that violation. Furthermore, as shown above, ASME is in the best position to take precautions that will prevent future antitrust violations. Thus, the fact that ASME is a nonprofit organization does not weaken the force of the antitrust and agency principles that indicate that ASME should be liable for Hydrolevel's antitrust injuries.
* * * *

We need not delineate today the outer boundaries of the antitrust liability of standard-setting organizations for the actions of their agents committed with apparent authority. There is no doubt here that Hardin acted within his apparent authority when he answered an inquiry about ASME's Boiler and Pressure Vessel Code as the chairman of the relevant ASME subcommittee. And in this case, we do not face a challenge to a good-faith interpretation of an ASME code reasonably supported by health or safety considerations. We have no difficulty in finding that this set of facts falls well within the scope of ASME's liability on an apparent authority theory.

When ASME's agents act in its name, they are able to affect the lives of large numbers of people and the competitive fortunes of businesses throughout the country. By holding ASME liable under the antitrust laws for the antitrust violations of its agents committed with apparent authority, we recognize the important role of ASME and its agents to speak for them. We thus make it less likely that competitive challengers like Hydrolevel will be hindered by agents of organizations like ASME in the future.

* * * *

The verdict against ASME was affirmed. The court held that a trade association can be held liable for acts of its agents that decrease competition. Trade associations are subject to the antitrust laws. To hold otherwise would allow businesses to commit anticompetitive acts through their trade associations. The amount of the damages was appealed separately and was not determined by this opinion.

DECISION AND REMEDY

Illegal Concerted Action by Professional Associations For many years, professionals were thought to be outside the scope of the antitrust laws because their activities did not involve trade or commerce. This is not so today. The impact that professional services have on the economy has been used to impose antitrust liability on **professional associations**. For example, in *Goldfarb v. Virginia State Bar* (cited in Chapter 19), an association of lawyers violated the Sherman Act by setting minimum fees.

In the next case, two medical societies were alleged to have engaged in an illegal conspiracy to establish maximum-fee schedules.

BACKGROUND AND FACTS *The Maricopa Foundation for Medical Care and the Pima Foundation for Medical Care are nonprofit Arizona corporations composed of doctors engaged in private practice. The foundations offer an alternative to the usual health insurance plan. Instead of the patient being reimbursed by insurance for a portion of his or her medical expenses, insurers agreed to pay the charges, up to a scheduled amount for the doctors participating in the foundations, and the doctors agreed to accept those amounts as full payment for their services.*

The doctors in the foundations established the schedules of maximum fees, revised them periodically, and agreed to use the fee schedules when treating patients insured by a foundation-endorsed plan. The state of Arizona alleged that these activities violated Section 1 of the Sherman Act.

 Case 20.3

ARIZONA v. MARICOPA COUNTY MEDICAL SOCIETY

Supreme Court of the United States, 1982.
457 U.S. 332, 102 S.Ct. 2466, 73 L.Ed.2d 48.

STEVENS, Justice.
* * * *

Our decisions foreclose the argument that the agreements at issue escape *per se* condemnation because they are horizontal and fix maximum prices. [Two prior cases] place horizontal agreements to fix maximum prices on the same legal—even if not economic—footing as agreements to fix a minimum or uniform price. The *per se* rule "is grounded on faith in price competition as a market force [and not] on a policy of low selling prices at the price of eliminating competition." In this case the rule is violated by a price restraint that tends to provide the same economic rewards to all practitioners regardless of their skill, their experience, their training, or their willingness to employ innovating and difficult procedures in individual cases. Such a restraint also may discourage entry into the market and may deter experimentation and new developments by individual entrepreneurs. It may be a masquerade for an agreement to fix uniform prices, or it may in the future take on that character.

Nor does the fact that doctors—rather than nonprofessionals—are the parties to the price-fixing agreements support the respondents' position. In *Goldfarb v. Virginia State Bar* we stated that the "public service aspect, and other features of the professions, may require that a particular practice, which could properly be viewed as a violation of the Sherman Act in another context, be treated differently." The price fixing agreements in this case, however, are not premised on public service or ethical norms. The respondents do not argue, as did the defendants in *Goldfarb* and *Professional Engineers,* that the quality of the professional service that their members provide is enhanced by the price restraint. The respondents' claim for relief from the *per se* rule is simply that the doctors' agreement not to charge certain insureds more than a fixed price facilitates the successful marketing of an attractive insurance plan. But the claim that the price restraint will make it easier for customers to pay does not distinguish the medical profession from any other provider of goods or services.

* * * *

The respondents' principal argument is that the *per se* rule is inapplicable because their agreements are alleged to have procompetitive justifications. The argument indicates a misunderstanding of the *per se* concept. The anticompetitive potential inherent in all price fixing agreements justifies their facial invalidation even if procompetitive justifications are offered for some. Those claims of enhanced competition are so unlikely to prove significant in any particular case that we adhere to the rule of law that is justified in its general application. Even when the respondents are given every benefit of the doubt, the limited record in this case is not inconsistent with the presumption that the respondents' agreements will not significantly enhance competition.

* * * *

Our adherence to the *per se* rule is grounded not only on economic prediction, judicial convenience, and business certainty, but also on a recognition of the respective roles of the Judiciary and the Congress in regulating the economy. Given its generality, our enforcement of the Sherman Act has required the Court to provide much of its substantive content. By articulating the rules of law with some clarity and by adhering to rules that are justified in their general application, however, we enhance the legislative prerogative to amend the law. The respondents' arguments against application of the *per se* rule in this case therefore are better directed to the legislature. Congress may consider the exception that we are not free to read into the statute.

DECISION AND REMEDY *The Supreme Court held that the maximum-fee schedules were* per se *illegal. The Court rejected the foundations' arguments that the fee arrangement was procompetitive.*

Other Concerted Horizontal Restraints There are other types of horizontal restraints which violate antitrust laws. One type is the **joint refusals to deal**. Sellers of goods and services generally have the right to select customers, provided that such a selection is not based on a customer's re- ligious beliefs, color, sex or national origin. When two or more sellers act in concert to refuse to sell to a particular buyer or class of buyers, however, the courts have generally found such acts unlawful under either the Sherman Act or the Clayton Act, or both.

Another type of horizontal restraint is **territorial and customer divisions**. It is a Section 1 violation of the Sherman Act for competitors to divide up territories or customers. For example, manufacturers A, B, and C compete against each other in the states of Kansas, Nebraska, and Iowa. By agreement, A sells products only in Kansas, B sells only in Nebraska, and C sells only in Iowa. This concerted action reduces costs and allows all three (assuming there is no other competition) to raise the price of the goods sold in their respective states.

The same violation would take place if A, B, and C had simply agreed that A would sell only to institutional purchasers (school districts, universities, state agencies and departments, cities, etc.) in the three states, B only to wholesalers, and C only to retailers.

Vertical Restraints

Trade practices involving firms at different levels of the production and distribution processes may violate the antitrust laws. When they do, they are referred to as vertical restraints of trade. Vertical relationships are more complex than horizontal ones, and they vary to such a degree that it is sometimes difficult even to do define the typical vertical arrangement. The most common vertical restraints are discussed here.

Resale Price Maintenance   When a seller and a buyer agree to the price at which the buyer must resell the product, it is a *per se* violation of Section 1 of the Sherman Act. Some commentators believe that even **resale price maintenance agreements** should not be subject to a *per se* rule, since restraints that are *per se* illegal in horizontal actions are not always as detrimental to competition in a vertical context.

At one time, federal law allowed sellers to establish resale prices if the products were sold under a trademark. This practice was known as *fair trade* and was allowed under the Miller-Tydings Act of 1937. A state had to pass local legislation to allow this practice. In 1975, the Consumer Goods Pricing Act was passed, which repealed the state's right to pass fair-trade laws.

Fair-trade laws went against the procompetitive nature of the antitrust laws and are now illegal.

Restrictions in the Distribution Process   The methods by which manufacturers market their products vary greatly. A manufacturer may sell directly to retailers or to wholesale distributors, who in turn sell to retailers. The manufacturer may enter into franchise agreements that permit retailers to present themselves to the public as dealers of the manufacturer's product. The manufacturer may even own the retail outlets where its products are sold.

Regardless of the arrangement selected, both the manufacturer and the retailer are seeking maximum profits. Some of the methods that increase profits violate the antitrust laws; others do not. The manufacturer will often impose territorial restrictions on each of its retailers in order to prevent the retailers from competing with each other. This creates a sales advantage for each retailer, since the desired product cannot be purchased anywhere else in the immediate area. Thus, selling goods of the same make under territorial restrictions results in less competition.

The manufacturer or distributor may also require the retailer not to sell the products of competing firms. This is an **exclusive dealing contract**. Conversely, individual firms can refuse to sell their products to certain buyers. As long as it is an individual decision and not a concerted refusal to deal (a boycott) by a group of firms, such action is legal.

Manufacturers may attempt to prohibit wholesalers or retailers from reselling the products to certain classes of buyers, such as competing retailers; therefore, these actions constitute consumer restrictions. Territorial and customer restrictions are lawful unless their use unreasonably restricts trade.

In the following case, a seller terminated a dealership which continuously sold the seller's product below the suggested retail price recommended by the seller. Another competing dealership had complained to the seller, and the terminated dealership claimed the termination was an illegal vertical restraint.

Case 20.4
**BUSINESS
ELECTRONICS CORP.
v. SHARP
ELECTRONICS**

Supreme Court of the United
States, 1988.
___U.S. ___, 108 S.Ct. 1515,
99 L.Ed.2d 808.

BACKGROUND AND FACTS *Business Electronics Corporation and another retailer (Hartwell) were authorized by Sharp Electronics to sell its electronic calculators in the Houston, Texas, area. Business Electronics continuously reduced its prices below those suggested by Sharp Electronics, thus underselling Hartwell on the same products. In response to Hartwell's complaints regarding Business Electronics Corporation's selling prices, Sharp Electronics terminated its dealership with Business Electronics.*

Business Electronics brought suit, alleging that Sharp and Hartwell had conspired to terminate the dealership and that such conspiracy resulted in a vertical restraint of trade which was illegal per se *under Section 1 of the Sherman Act. the federal district court found for Business Electronics, but the United States Court of Appeals reversed the finding. The United States Supreme Court granted* certiorari.

SCALIA, Justice.
* * * *
    Section 1 of the Sherman Act provides that "every contract, combination in the form of trust or otherwise, or conspiracy, in restraint of trade or commerce among the several States, or with foreign nations, is declared to be illegal." Since the earliest decisions of this Court interpreting this provision, we have recognized that it was intended to prohibit only unreasonable restraints of trade. Ordinarily, whether particular concerted action violates Section 1 of the Sherman Act is determined through case-by-case application of the so-called rule of reason—that is, the factfinder weighs all of the circumstances of a case in deciding whether a restrictive practice should be prohibited as imposing an unreasonable restraint on competition." Certain categories of agreements, however, have been held to *per se* illegal, dispensing with the need for case-by-case evaluation. We have said that *per se* rules are appropriate only for "conduct that is manifestly anticompetitive," that is, conduct "that would always or almost always tend to restrict competition and decrease output[.]" * * *
    Although vertical agreements or resale prices have been illegal *per se* since *Dr. Miles Medical Co. v. John D. Park & Sons Co.,* we have recognized that the scope of *per se* illegality should be narrow in the context of vertical restraints. In *Continental T. V., Inc., v. GTE Sylvania Inc.,* we refused to extend *per se* illegality to vertical nonprice restraints, specifically to a manufacturer's termination of one dealer pursuant to an exclusive territory agreement with another. We noted that especially in the vertical restraint context "departure from the rule-of-reason standard must be based on demonstrable economic effect rather than . . . upon formalistic line drawing." We concluded that vertical nonprice restraints had not been shown to have such a "pernicious effect on competition" and to be so "lacking in . . . redeeming value" as to justify *per se* illegality. Rather, we found, they had real potential to stimulate interbrand competition, "the primary concern of antitrust law."
* * * *
    Our approach to the question presented in the present case is guided by the premises of *GTE Sylvania:* that there is a presumption in favor of a rule-of-reason standard; that departure from that standard must be justified by demonstrable economic effect, such as the facilitation of cartelizing, rather than formalistic distinctions; that interbrand competition is the primary concern of the antitrust laws; and that rules in this are should be formulated with a view towards protecting the doctrine of *GTE Sylvania.* These premises lead us to conclude that the line drawn by the Fifth Circuit is the most appropriate one.

There has been no showing here that an agreement between a manufacturer and a dealer to terminate a "price cutter," without a further agreement on the price or price levels to be charged by the remaining dealer, almost always tends to restrict competition and reduce output. Any assistance to cartelizing that such an agreement might provide cannot be distinguished from the sort of minimal assistance that might be provided by vertical nonprice agreements like the exclusive territory agreement in *GTE Sylvania*, and is insufficient to justify a *per se* rule. * * * * * * *

In sum, economic analysis supports the view, and no precedent opposes it, that a vertical restraint is not illegal *per se* unless it includes some agreement on price or price levels. * * *

The United States Supreme Court affirmed the court of appeals which had reversed the trial court's holding that Sharp Electronics and Hartwell had violated Section 1 of the Sherman Act under the per se *rule. The court rejected the* per se *rule in favor of the rule of reason for a case where a business dealership is terminated because it did not follow the suggested pricing of the manufacturer.*

DECISION AND REMEDY

Tying Arrangements Tie-ins exist when a seller refuses to sell a product (the tying product) unless the buyer also purchases another product (the tied product). *Tying arrangements* (as discussed in Chapter 19) enable the holder of a legal monopoly in one market (such as copying machines) to gain a monopoly in another market (photocopy paper).

Under both Section 1 of the Sherman Act and Section 3 of the Clayton Act, such arrangements may be illegal if they affect a substantial amount of trade or commerce. Under the Sherman Act, both goods *and* services are covered, while the Clayton Act covers only goods. Tying arrangements were once treated as *per se* illegal, but recently courts have required the seller to have economic power in the market for the tying product in order for such dealings to be illegal.

Exclusive Dealing Contracts Section 3 of the Clayton Act prohibits exclusive dealing contracts when their effect is "to substantially lessen competition or tend to create a monopoly." In an exclusive dealing contract, the seller requires the buyer not to purchase the products of competing sellers. This type of agreement limits the outlets available to competing sellers for the distribution of products, thus reducing interbrand competition.

Requirements Contracts Just as an exclusive dealing contract limits a buyer to dealing with only one seller, **requirements contracts** reduce buyers' and sellers' freedom of choice. These arrangements provide either that the buyer will purchase all of his or her requirements of a particular product for a specific time from the seller or that the seller will supply all of the product the buyer requests. The purpose of requirements contracts does not always involve economic power in the relevant market. These arrangements allow the participants some certainty in future planning. Accordingly, the courts employ the rule of reason to analyze requirements contracts.

All of these types of agreements involve vertical control, which might be used to hinder competition. In such cases, the court must decide whether an activity constitutes concerted illegal action. Recently the courts have tended to use the rule of reason rather than *per se* illegality when confronted with issues of vertical restraint.

Structural Analysis of Monopoly Power

Courts are not always concerned with concerted activity among competitors; they may be confronted with an alleged monopoly, for example. Courts must decide when a firm has **monopoly power** as antitrust statutes do not define the term monopoly. Consequently, a judicial review is concerned with whether the firm has **market power**. Is the power of the firm so great that it can force its decisions on others? The courts must also ask whether the firm has obtained monopoly power with the wrongful intent of acquiring that power.

Although various methods for assessing market power could be used, courts today employ the structural analysis advanced by Judge Learned Hand in the following case. Stated simply, the structural analysis of market power involves the following two steps:

1. Define the market in which the firm's power should be evaluated;
2. Measure the extent of the firm's share of that market.

Structural analysis involves more than identifying the firms within a market and comparing their sales. Structural analysis is not exact; it is a tool used by the courts to support the inference that monopoly power exists. After defining the **relevant product market** and the **relevant geographic market**, the court compares the sales of the firms within these markets. In addition to the firm's market share, the court considers any barriers to entry that may exist and whether acceptable substitutes are available for the firm's product. The following case illustrates how the courts analyze whether a firm has an illegal monopoly.

Case 20.5
UNITED STATES v.
ALUMINUM COMPANY
OF AMERICA (ALCOA)
United States Court of Appeals,
Second Circuit, 1945.
148 F.2d 416.

BACKGROUND AND FACTS *The United States charged Aluminum Company of America (Alcoa) with monopolizing interstate and foreign commerce in the manufacture and sale of "virgin" aluminum ingot. Alcoa was the sole producer of virgin ingot in the United States, and the government contended that that fact alone made Alcoa an unlawful monopoly. Alcoa contended that it was subject to competition from imported virgin ingot and from "secondary" ingot (recycled aluminum) and therefore did not have monopoly power. The district court found that Alcoa had a 33 percent of the market, which included both the secondary material that had been salvaged from scrap and the new ingot. The lower court found for Alcoa. The court of appeals computed the market share differently and found that Alcoa had 90 percent of the virgin ingot market.*

HAND, Judge.
* * * *

From 1902 onward until 1928 "Alcoa" was making ingot in Canada through a wholly owned subsidiary; so much of this as it imported into the United States it is proper to include with what it produced here. In the year 1912, the sum of these two items represented nearly ninety-one percent of the total amount of "virgin" ingot available for sale in this country. * * * The effect of such a proportion of the production upon the market we reserve for the time being, for it will be necessary first to consider the nature and uses of "secondary" ingot, the name by which the industry knows ingot made from aluminum scrap. * * *

There are various ways of computing "Alcoa's" control of the aluminum market—as distinct from its production—depending upon what one regards as competing in that market. The judge figured its share—during the years 1929–1938, inclusive—as only about thirty-three percent; to do so he included "secondary," and excluded that part of "Alcoa's" own production which it fabricated and did not therefore sell as ingot. If on the other hand, "Alcoa's" total production, fabricated and sold, be included, and balanced against the sum of imported "virgin" and "secondary," its share of the market was in the neighborhood of 64% for that

period. The percentage we have already mentioned—over 90—results only if we both include all ''Alcoa's'' production and exclude ''secondary.'' That percentage is enough to constitute a monopoly; it is doubtful whether sixty or sixty-four percent would be enough; and certainly thirty-three percent is not. Hence it is necessary to settle what we shall treat as competing in the ingot market. That part of its production which ''Alcoa'' itself fabricates, does not of course ever reach the market as ingot. * * * [T]he ingot fabricated by ''Alcoa,'' necessarily had a direct effect upon the ingot market. All ingot—with trifling exceptions—is used to fabricate intermediate, or end, products; and therefore all intermediate, or end, products which ''Alcoa'' fabricates and sells, pro tanto reduce the demand for ingot itself. The situation is the same, though reversed, as in *Standard Oil Co. v. United States,* where the court answered the defendants' argument that they had no control over the crude oil by saying that ''as substantial power over the crude product was the inevitable result of the absolute control which existed over the refined product, the monopolization of the one carried with it the power to control the other.'' We cannot therefore agree that the computation of the percentage of ''Alcoa's'' control over the ingot market should not include the whole of its ingot production.
* * * *

We conclude therefore that ''Alcoa's'' control over the ingot market must be reckoned at over ninety percent, that being the proportion which its production bears to imported ''virgin'' ingot. If the fraction which it did not supply were the product of domestic manufacture, there could be no doubt that this percentage gave it a monopoly—lawful or unlawful, as the case might be. The producer of so large a proportion of the supply has complete control within certain limits. * * *
* * * *

We disregard any question of ''intent.'' Relatively early in the history of the Act—1935—[Justice] Holmes in *Swift & Co. v. United States,* explained this aspect of the Act [Sherman] in a passage often quoted. Although the primary evil was monopoly, the Act also covered preliminary steps, which, if continued, would lead to it. These may do no harm of themselves; but, if they are initial moves in a plan or scheme which, carried out, will result in monopoly, they are dangerous and the law will nip them in the bud. For this reason conduct falling short of monopoly, is not illegal unless it is part of a plan to monopolize, or to gain such other control of a market as is equally forbidden. To make it so, the plaintiff must prove what in the criminal law is known as a ''specific intent''; an intent which goes beyond the mere intent to do the act. By far the greatest part of the fabulous record piled up in the case at bar, was concerned with proving such an intent. The plaintiff was seeking to show that many transactions, neutral on their face, were not in fact necessary to the development of ''Alcoa's'' business, and had no motive except to exclude others and perpetuate its hold upon the ingot market. Upon that effort success depended in case the plaintiff failed to satisfy the court that it was unnecessary under Section 2 to convict ''Alcoa'' of practices unlawful of themselves. The plaintiff has so satisfied us, and the issue of intent ceases to have any importance; no intent is relevant except that which is relevant to any liability, criminal or civil: i.e. an intent to bring about the forbidden act. * * * In order to fall within Section 2, the monopolist must have both the power to monopolize, and the intent to monopolize. To read the passage as demanding any ''specific,'' intent, makes nonsense of it, for no monopolist monopolizes unconscious of what he is doing. So here, ''Alcoa'' meant to keep, and did keep, that complete and exclusive hold upon the ingot market with which it started. That was to ''monopolize'' that market, however innocently it otherwise proceeded. So far as the judgment held that it was not within Section 2 it must be reversed.
* * * *

DECISION AND **REMEDY**	*The court of appeals found Alcoa had monopolized the aluminum industry by having 90 percent share of the virgin ingot market along with having an intent to acquire a monopoly of this market.*

Defining the Relevant Market

One of the most important questions facing the courts in monopoly cases is: What is the relevant market for measuring monopoly power? Over time, the courts have narrowed the definition of the relevant market by considering more information about the characteristics of the product, its substitutes, and the geographic area where the product is sold. Because the market share is extremely sensitive to the definition of relevant market, both sides in these cases take considerable care in assembling and presenting evidence to help determine the market.

The importance of determining the market share was well illustrated in the *Alcoa* decision. If the relevant market consisted only of those who bought virgin ingot, Alcoa was the sole producer at that time. The secondary market was not considered because it would not exist except for the sale of virgin ingot. Another definition of the relevant market included those who bought secondary aluminum, which is an almost perfect substitute for virgin ingot; this definition significantly broadened the relevant market and lowered the measure of Alcoa's share. And, when the market was further broadened to include fabricated and secondary aluminum, the measure of Alcoa's share fell roughly to 33 percent of the aluminum production market.

Product Market Substitutes are available for most products. If General Motors raised the prices for its cars significantly, consumers would purchase more Fords or other brands. If the question

arose as to whether General Motors' Cadillac division had monopoly power, courts would have to determine the relevant product market. Should all cars sold in the United States be included in the computation of Cadillac's market share? Should only luxury cars be included? Do Japanese imports compete with Cadillacs for sales? Although General Motors is the sole producer of Cadillacs, it will not have monopoly power as long as there are substitute products, since market forces will keep the price of Cadillacs competitive with the price of substitute products.

Courts determine the relevant product market by defining the products that can be substituted for the product that is alleged to be dominating the market to the exclusion of competitors. In some cases, the product market will be extremely wide. Including all cars sold in the United States makes Cadillac's market share relatively small. Measuring Cadillac sales against the combined sales of cars and trucks decreases Cadillac's share even further. If only luxury cars are considered, Cadillac has a larger share of the market. Whenever monopoly power is alleged, courts must decide which products offer competition to the dominant product.

The method of determining the relevant product market is discussed in the next case. The existence of a wide variety of substitute products will always make it extremely unlikely that any producer can achieve monopoly power because, if the price of the leading product is raised, consumers will switch to the less expensive substitutes.

Case 20.6 **UNITED STATES v. E. I.** **du PONT de NEMOURS** **& CO.** Supreme Court of the United States, 1956. 351 U.S. 377, 76 S.Ct. 994, 100 L.Ed. 1264.	**BACKGROUND AND FACTS** *The United States government charged du Pont with monopolizing the cellophane market in violation of Section 2 of the Sherman Act. Although du Pont produced almost 75 percent of the cellophane sold in the United States, cellophane constituted less than 20 percent of all flexible packaging materials sold in the United States.* *The trial court found the relevant market to be the market for flexible packaging materials and that competition from other materials in that market prevented du Pont from possessing monopoly power. The trial court*

dismissed the government's complaint, and the government appealed directly to the United States Supreme Court.

REED, Justice.
* * * *

The Government asserts that cellophane and other wrapping materials are neither substantially fungible nor like priced. For these reasons, it argues that the market for other wrappings is distinct from the market for cellophane and that the competition afforded cellophane by other wrappings is not strong enough to be considered in determining whether du Pont has monopoly powers. Market delimitation is necessary under du Pont's theory to determine whether an alleged monopolist violates § 2. The ultimate consideration in such a determination is whether the defendants control the price and competition in the market for such part of trade or commerce as they are charged with monopolizing. Every manufacturer is the sole producer of the particular commodity it makes but its control in the above sense of the relevant market depends upon the availability of alternative commodities for buyers; i.e., whether there is a cross-elasticity of demand between cellophane and the other wrappings. This interchangeability is largely gauged by the purchase of competing products for similar uses considering the price, characteristics and adaptability of the competing commodities. The court below found that the flexible wrappings afforded such alternative. This court must determine whether the trial court erred in its estimate of the competition afforded cellophane by other materials.
* * * *

The Relevant Market. When a product is controlled by one interest, without substitutes available in the market, there is monopoly power. Because most products have possible substitutes, we cannot give "that infinite range" to the definition of substitutes. Nor is it a proper interpretation of the Sherman Act to require that products be fungible to be considered in the relevant market. The Government argues:

"We do not here urge that in *no* circumstances may competition of substitutes negative possession of monopolistic power over trade in a product. The decisions make it clear at the least that the courts will not consider substitutes other than those which are substantially fungible with the monopolized product and sell at substantially the same price."

But where there are market alternatives that buyers may readily use for their purposes, illegal monopoly does not exist merely because the product said to be monopolized differs from others. If it were not so, only physically identical products would be a part of the market. To accept the Government's argument, we would have to conclude that the manufacturers of plain as well as moistureproof cellophane were monopolists, and so with films such as Pliofilm, foil, glassine, polyethylene, and Saran, for each of these wrapping materials is distinguishable. These were all exhibits in the case. New wrappings appear, generally similar to cellophane; is each a monopoly? What is called for is an appraisal of the "cross-elasticity" of demand in the trade. The varying circumstances of each case determine the result. In considering what is the relevant market for determining the control of price and competition, no more definite rule can be declared than that commodities reasonably interchangeable by consumers for the same purposes make up that "part of the trade or commerce," monopolization of which may be illegal. As respects flexible packaging materials, the market geographically is nationwide.
* * * *

An element for consideration as to cross-elasticity of demand between products is the responsiveness of the sales of one product to price changes of the other. If a slight decrease in the price of cellophane causes a considerable number of customers of other flexible wrappings to switch to cellophane, it would be an indication that a high cross-elasticity of demand exists between them; that the products compete in the same market. The court below held that the "[g]reat sensitivity of customers in the flexible packaging markets to price or quality changes" prevented du Pont from possessing monopoly control over price. The record sustains these findings.

We conclude that cellophane's interchangeability with the other materials mentioned suffices to make it a part of this flexible packaging material market.

* * * *

The "market" which one must study to determine when a producer has monopoly power will vary with the part of commerce under consideration. The tests are constant. That market is composed of products that have reasonable interchangeability for the purposes for which they are produced—price, use and qualities considered. While the application of the tests remains uncertain, it seems to us that du Pont should not be found to monopolize cellophane when that product has the competition and interchangeability with other wrappings that this record shows.

* * * *

**DECISION AND
REMEDY**   *The United States Supreme Court affirmed the trial court's dismissal of the government's complaint. Since the relevant product market included all flexible packaging materials, not just cellophane, du Pont did not possess monopoly power.*

Geographic Market   The relevant geographic market is usually less difficult to determine than the relevant product market. If sellers within an area can raise prices or reduce the supply of products without quantities of lower-priced goods quickly flowing into the area, the sellers have a separate geographic market for their products.

Geographic markets may be local, regional, or national. The mobility of both competing sellers and of purchasers must be considered. The courts consider whether a buyer can easily go outside the immediate area to purchase the goods at a lower price or whether a seller in another geographic area can easily ship goods into the area. Because consumers are willing to travel greater distances to make major purchases than to buy everyday necessities, the geographic market will be defined more broadly for sales of automobiles than for sales of milk. Car dealers within a three-county area may be direct competitors; car dealers in different states are probably not in the same geographic market unless they are adjacent to state lines, such as in Kansas City, Missouri, and Kansas City, Kansas.

Determining the Market Share

After defining the relevant product and geographic markets, the court can determine the percentage of the market held by any one firm. This percentage is the firm's market share—the comparison of one firm's position to the positions of all other firms with which it competes. Monopoly power is a matter of degree. In the *Alcoa* case, 90 percent of the relevant market was sufficient for the court to conclude that Alcoa was a monopoly.

Courts have found there was no monopoly where the firms have controlled less than 65 percent of their relevant markets. The court in *Alcoa* said that two-thirds of the relevant market would be a questionable case, but one-third of the market would not be a monopoly situation. What the courts actually attempt to determine is whether a firm has such substantial power that it can engage in actions not associated with natural growth to exclude competitors and control prices. Market share is the measurement used to make that determination objectively.

Mergers

A **merger** is the combination of two or more businesses into one. Mergers, whether horizontal or vertical, result in one business gaining greater control of the market. Accordingly, the antitrust laws apply to mergers and are used to prevent consol-

apply to mergers and are used to prevent consolidations that would substantially lessen competition.

Section 7 of the Clayton Act is the principal statute that applies to horizontal and vertical mergers. It prohibits one "person" (corporations, partnerships, sale proprietorship, etc.) from acquiring another if the merger would tend to lessen competition substantially or to create a monopoly.

Horizontal Mergers

Section 7 of the Clayton Act was enacted because Congress feared that concentration by merger or consolidation would potentially facilitate collusion among sellers in the market and that such collusion would be difficult to detect. In general, the FTC and the Antitrust Division of the Justice Department determine the legality of **horizontal mergers** by looking at the degree of concentration or market shares of merging firms.

If a merger facilitates horizontal collusion without increasing production or marketing efficiencies, it will be declared unlawful. Mergers will be permitted when they enhance consumer welfare by increasing efficiency, as long as they do not increase the probability of horizontal collusion. Mergers that facilitate collusion *and* increase efficiency must be evaluated according to the relative magnitude of these two facts.

Vertical Mergers

Vertical mergers occur when a company at one stage of distribution acquires a company at a higher or lower stage of distribution. Thus, the acquisition of a tire plant by an automobile manufacturer would constitute a backward vertical integration, while acquisition of a car-renting agency would constitute a forward vertical integration. The government's approach to vertical mergers depends on a number of factors, including definition of the relevant product and geographic markets as well as the characteristics identified as impeding competition.

The government will attack any vertical merger that keeps competitors of either party from a segment of the market that otherwise would be open to them. The law's current theory of injury to competition in vertical mergers is contained in the concept of foreclosure. For example, a manufacturer can acquire a retailer and force the new retail subsidiary to sell the manufacturer's product. This acquisition would foreclose rival manufacturers from the market. The FTC has found that "foreclosure manifests a particularly anticompetitive character when it occurs as part of a trend toward forward integration in a concentrated market."

The following is probably one of the most important cases involving a vertical merger. The court emphasized the issue of whether the sharing of the customer market would be hindered by the merger.

BACKGROUND AND FACTS *The United States government brought a lawsuit to enjoin the merger of two corporations Brown Shoe Co., Inc. and G. R. Kinney Company, Inc. The government alleged that the effects of the merger might substantially lessen competition or tend to create a monopoly in the production, distribution, and sale of shoes in violation of Section 7 of the Clayton Act.*

The district court found that the merger would increase concentration in the shoe industry, both in manufacturing and retailing, eliminate one of the corporations as a substantial competitor in the retail field, and establish a manufacturer-retailer relationship. This new relationship would deprive all but the top firms in the industry of a fair opportunity to compete, and, therefore, it probably would result in a further substantial lessening of competition and an increased tendency toward monopoly. The shoe companies appealed to the United States Supreme Court.

Case 20.7
BROWN SHOE CO. v. UNITED STATES
Supreme Court of the United States, 1962.
370 U.S. 294, 82 S.Ct. 1502, 8 L.Ed.2d 510.

WARREN, Chief Justice.
* * * *

Economic arrangements between companies standing in a supplier-customer relationship are characterized as "vertical." The primary vice of a vertical merger or other arrangement tying a customer to a supplier is that by foreclosing the competitors of either party from a segment of the market otherwise open to them, the arrangement may be as a "clog on competition," which "deprive[s] * * * rivals of a fair opportunity to compete." Every extended vertical arrangement by its very nature, for at least a time, denies to competitors of the supplier the opportunity to compete for part or all of the trade of the customer-party to the vertical arrangement. However, the Clayton Act does not render unlawful all such vertical arrangements, but forbids only those whose effect "may be substantially to lessen competition, or to tend to create a monopoly" "in any line of commerce in any section of the country." Thus, as we have previously noted,

> "[d]etermination of the relevant market is a necessary predicate to a finding of a violation of the Clayton Act because the threatened monopoly must be one which will substantially lessen competition 'within the area of effective competition.' Substantiality can be determined only in terms of the market affected."

The "area of effective competition" must be determined by reference to a product market (the "line of commerce") and a geographic market (the "section of the country").
* * * *

Once the area of effective competition affected by a vertical arrangement has been defined, an analysis must be made to determine if the effect of the arrangement "may be substantially to lessen competition, or to tend to create a monopoly" in this market.

Since the diminution of the vigor of competition which may stem from a vertical arrangement results primarily from a foreclosure of a share of the market otherwise open to competitors, an important consideration in determining whether the effect of a vertical arrangement "may be substantially to lessen competition, or to tend to create a monopoly" is the size of the share of the market foreclosed. However, this factor will seldom be determinative. If the share of the market foreclosed is so large that it approaches monopoly proportions, the Clayton Act will, of course, have been violated; but the arrangement will also have run afoul of the Sherman Act. And the legislative history of Section 7 indicates clearly that the tests for measuring the legality of any particular economic arrangement under the Clayton Act are to be less stringent than those used in applying the Sherman Act. On the other hand, foreclosure of a *de minimis* share of the market will not tend "substantially to lessen competition."

Between these extremes, in cases such as the one before us, in which the foreclosure is neither of monopoly nor *de minimis* proportions, the percentage of the market foreclosed by the vertical arrangement cannot itself be decisive. In such cases, it becomes necessary to undertake an examination of various economic and historical factors in order to determine whether the arrangement under review is of the type Congress sought to proscribe.
* * * *

The present merger involved neither small companies nor failing companies. In 1955, the date of this merger, Brown was the fourth largest manufacturer in the shoe industry with sales of approximately 25 million pairs of shoes and assets of over \$72,000,000 while Kinney had sales of about 8 million pairs of shoes and assets of about \$18,000,000. Not only was Brown one of the leading manufacturers of men's, women's, and children's shoes, but Kinney, with over 350 retail outlets, owned and operated the largest independent chain of family shoe stores in the Nation. Thus, in this industry, no merger between a manufacturer and an independent retailer could involve a larger potential market foreclosure. Moreover, it is apparent both from past behavior of Brown and from a testimony of Brown's President, that Brown would use its ownership of Kinney to force Brown shoes into Kinney stores. Thus, in operation this vertical arrangement would be quite analogous to one involving a tying clause.

Another important factor to consider is the trend toward concentration in the industry. It is true, of course, that the statute prohibits a given merger only if the effect of *that* merger may be substantially to lessen competition. But the very wording of Section 7 requires a prognosis of the probable *future* effect of the merger.

The existence of a trend toward vertical integration, which the District Court found, is well substantiated by the record. Moreover, the court found a tendency of the acquiring manufacturers to become increasingly important sources of supply for their acquired outlets. The necessary corollary of these trends is the foreclosure of independent manufacturers from markets otherwise open to them. And because these trends are not the product of accident but are rather the result of deliberate policies of Brown and other leading shoe manufacturers, account must be taken of these facts in order to predict the probable future consequences of this merger. It is against this background of continuing concentration that the present merger must be viewed.

Brown argues, however, that the shoe industry is at present composed of a larger number of manufacturers and retailers, and that the industry is dynamically competitive. But remaining vigor cannot immunize a merger if the trend in the industry is toward oligopoly. It is the probable effect of the merger upon the future as well as the present which the Clayton Act commands the courts and the Commission to examine.

Moreover, as we have remarked above, not only must we consider the probable effects of the merger upon the economics of the particular markets affected but also we must consider its probable effects upon the economic way of life sought to be preserved by Congress. Congress was desirous of preventing the formation of further oligopolies with their attendant adverse effects upon local control of industry and upon small business. Where an industry was composed of numerous independent units, Congress appeared anxious to preserve this structure. The Senate Report, quoting with approval from the Federal Trade Commission's 1948 report on the merger movement, states explicitly that amended Section 7 is addressed to the following problem:

"Under the Sherman Act, an acquisition is unlawful if it creates a monopoly or constitutes an attempt to monopolize. Imminent monopoly may appear when one large concern acquires another, but it is unlikely to be perceived in a small acquisition by a large enterprise. As a large concern grows through a series of such small acquisitions, its accretions of power are individually so minute as to make it difficult to use the Sherman Act test against them. * * *

"Where several large enterprises are extending their power by successive small acquisitions, the cumulative effect of their purchases may be to convert an industry from one of intense competition among many enterprises to one in which three or four large concerns produce the entire supply."

The District Court's findings, and the facts, convince us that the shoe industry is being subjected to just such a cumulative series of vertical mergers which, if left unchecked, will be likely "substantially to lessen competition."

We reach this conclusion because the trend toward vertical integration in the shoe industry, when combined with Brown's avowed policy of forcing its own shoes upon its retail subsidiaries, may foreclose competition from a substantial share of the markets for men's, women's, and children's shoes, without producing any countervailing competitive, economic, or social advantages.

* * * *

DECISION AND REMEDY	*Brown and Kinney had merged before this case reached the United States Supreme Court. The Court required Brown Shoe Company to divest itself of all of Kinney's stock and assets. Before the merger, Brown was the third largest seller of shoes by dollar volume, and Kinney was the eighth largest. In no municipal market did the combined sales exceed 57 percent. Yet this merger was still held to violate the antitrust laws.*

Conglomerate Mergers

A **conglomerate merger** is the consolidation of two or more firms dealing in unrelated products and operating in markets not horizontally or vertically linked. For example, a firm that operates motion picture theaters acquires a firm that manufactures automobile parts. Sometimes the products of the merged firms are complementary, and a merger permits the marketing of additional products at very little expense.

The Department of Justice Guidelines

The Department of Justice (and the FTC) has guidelines that determine whether a proposed merger should be consummated. The guidelines look at the concentration of the relevant market and the increase in concentration resulting from the merger. The department also looks at nonmarket considerations, such as how easy an entry is into the type of business and the competitive strength of the merged firms. In determining this, the department uses a statistical formula called the Herfindahl-Hirschman Index. After considering the other factors and implementing this index, the department will determine whether a merger is likely to be challenged. (The index is featured in the Legal Highlight.)

Price Discrimination

Section 2(a) of the Clayton Act, as amended by the Robinson-Patman Act, makes it illegal for any seller to discriminate in the prices charged for *goods* of the same quality to different purchasers. Sales at differing prices must have an anticompetitive effect for there to be a violation of the act. The courts view any two sales at different prices among competitors as a discrimination under Robinson-Patman.

Section 2(a) of the Clayton Act fortifies Section 2 of the Sherman Act by making **price discrimination** unlawful even when the firm engaging in it does not have and is not seeking monopoly power.

To have a violation of the Robinson-Patman Act, the seller must be engaged in interstate commerce, sell goods of like grade and quality to different purchasers resulting in one suffering a competitive injury.

The three defenses to price discrimination under Section 2 of the Clayton Act are: **meeting competition, cost justification**, and **changing market conditions**.

The Meeting-Competition Defense

The statutory provisons of the Clayton Act allow the reduction of a price made "in good faith to meet an equally low price of a competitor." The meeting-competition defense allows a business to sell at a lower price to some customers if it is really necessary to meet a competitor's price. But this price must be lowered in order to meet but not to beat a competitive price. The lowering cannot be made with intent to drive the competitor out of business. Also, the lower price must be for goods of similar quality to those of the competitor. Finally, the lower price to these customers must be temporary so as not to result in a competitive injury to other customers of the seller. As long as these three conditions are met, a business may sell at a lower price to certain customers to meet competition.

The Cost-Justification Defense

It may be less expensive to manufacture and sell a thousand units of an item instead of ten units. A due allowance in pricing is permitted for these savings due to a particular customer's purchase. The seller must carry the burden of proof when using a cost-justification defense. A large-volume

---

LEGAL HIGHLIGHT — Herfindahl-Hirschman Index

In June 1984, the Justice Department modified merger guidelines that had originally been issued in 1982. These guidelines are based on what is called the Herfindahl-Hirschman Index (HHI). The underlying theme of the guidelines is that mergers should not be permitted to create or enhance market power or to facilitate its exercise. A market is defined as "a product or group of products and a geographic area in which it is sold such that a hypothetical, profit-maximizing firm, not subject to price regulation, that was the only present and future seller of those products in that area would impose a 'small but significant and nontransitory' increase in price above prevailing or likely future levels."

The Justice Department basically asks whether the merger will tend to create a monopoly. The department determines the answer through the use of the index. If the index is less than 1,000 points, the merger normally will not be questioned. If the index is between 1,000 and 1,800 points, it likewise will not be challenged if the index increases by 100 or less after the merger. The same is true above 1,800 if the index increases by 50 points or less. If it is 1,800 and above and increases more than 50 points after the merger, it will be challenged in most circumstances.

The index is obtained by squaring the market shares and then adding all industry shares together. The Justice Department does not like decimals so they are multiplied by 100. The following is an example:

FIRM	MARKET SHARE	MARKET SHARE × 100	MARKET SHARE SQUARED
A	.30	30	900
B	.10	10	100
C	.40	40	1600
D	.05	5	25
E	.15	15	225
The Herfindahl-Hirschman Index:			2850

Based on guidelines, a proposed merger of any two firms among those listed would not be allowed. For example if D and E were to merge, the new market share would be (5 + 15) 20. This, squared, would result in a market share of 400. Since the market share of D and E before merger would be 250 (25 + 225), the difference of (400 − 250) 150 would be greater than 50 points on a HHI index that exceeds 1,800. This merger would be challenged.

---

purchase by itself does not mean that the seller can give that purchaser a lower price. The seller must prove that it obtains savings from such a large purchase, such as lower transportation costs, and then the seller can pass these savings on to a buyer who orders a carload, planeload, and the like. Actual evidence of these savings must be shown. It is sometimes very difficult to determine the proper allocation of overhead and other expenses in order to demonstrate these savings.

The Changing-Market-Conditions Defense

The changing-market-conditions defense to price discrimination allows a business to discontinue a product or product line, have fire or bankruptcy sales, and the like. In doing so, the business may sell the product at a reduced price. This defense allows a business to discount prices on seasonal goods or goods that will deteriorate.

Defenses To Alleged Antitrust Violations

Several defenses have been upheld by the courts for businesses confronted with allegations of creating an illegal monopoly or conspiring to restrain trade. The subsections that follow describe some defenses that the courts have accepted.

The *Colgate* Doctrine

The ***Colgate* doctrine** comes from *United States v. Colgate & Co.*[2] The United States Supreme Court allowed Colgate to refuse unilaterally to deal with retailers who did not follow its suggested retail prices. This refusal to deal was a vertical restraint. The Court emphasized that a firm can deal with whom ever it desires.

The Standing Defense

The **standing defense** is used when the plaintiffs do not have the standing to institute the action. To be able to bring an action, the plaintiff must have suffered a direct antitrust injury. For example, in *Illinois Brick Co. v. State of Illinois,*[3] the United States Supreme Court held that the state of Illinois did not have the standing to bring an action based on an alleged price-fixing agreement among the suppliers of brick to the state for public buildings. Illinois did not purchase the bricks directly. It hired a general contractor to build the buildings. The general contractor hired subcontractors who, in turn, had purchased the bricks from the suppliers. The Court reasoned that the state was an indirect purchaser. The argument that the cost of the buildings was higher as a result of antitrust violations that were passed through to

2.   250 U.S. 300, 39 S.Ct. 465, 63 L.Ed. 992 (1919).
3.   431 U.S. 720, 97 S.Ct. 2061, 52 L.Ed.2d 707 (1977).

Illinois was too remote and was not adopted. It was the Court's position that the proper party to bring the case would have been the subcontractor who had purchased the brick. In short, the state of Illinois lacked proper standing.

The Thrust-Upon Defense

A business that has a monopoly can use the **thrust-upon defense** by showing that the monopoly itself was thrust upon it. Such a monopoly might have been created by the production of a superior product, by better business practices, or by events, such as owning the only restaurant in an area where all the other restaurants have closed as a result of economic conditions. For this defense, there must exist no wrongful intent to create the monopoly.

The Failing-Company and Inadequate-Resources Defenses

The courts have allowed a merger, even if it violates antitrust guidelines when a company is confronting complete failure and there are no other prospective purchasers. This is known as the **failing-company defense**. Closely akin to this doctrine is the **inadequate-resources defense**. If a company does not have the financial resources to be a competitor, the courts will allow a merger with another competing company, even though the result violates antitrust guidelines.

FACING A LEGAL ISSUE   Avoiding Antitrust Violations

You are the marketing director of a firm that has just patented a revolutionary product similar to plastic but with the strength of steel, the breathing ability of leather, the smoothness of silk, and the flexibility of rubber. Your business goal is to maximize profits, but not to run afoul of the antitrust laws.

In preparing a detailed marketing plan to reach your goal, you have one large benefit granted by federal law. Assuming that your product is patentable, you will have an automatic exemption to the antitrust laws in the event that your product creates a monopoly. This does not mean that other antitrust aspects can be ignored. For example, you cannot sell this product at a different price to different competing distributors, unless you obtain cost savings in filling large orders. Also, you cannot require the distributors to sell at a given price unless you have retained title to the product. These are several examples of how a business must be concerned with antitrust violations even when the law grants them the right to create a monopoly.

Summary

This chapter has emphasized certain activities that constitute violations of the antitrust laws. These violations normally occur when there is an attempt to control prices or distribution on a horizontal or a vertical basis. The problem for the courts lies in defining illegal concerted action in the controlling of prices and distribution of products. The courts must find an intent by the defendants to participate in this illegal concerted action.

Certain activities of organizations or of the members of these organizations may constitute violations of the law. When a trade association or professional organization attempts to set prices or to discourage the use of certain products, it will be found in violation of the antitrust laws.

Any agreement to maintain prices among competitors is an illegal *per se* violation of the antitrust laws and is known as a horizontal restraint of trade. The same rule applies to vertical restraints, although some courts are tending to view these cases not as being illegal *per se* but as being subject to the rule of reason. This is particularly true when the vertical restraint consists of controlling distribution through territorial restrictions, tying arrangements, exclusive dealing contracts, or requirements contracts.

The courts have had difficulty in determining when a firm has monopoly power. To do so, the courts first define the relevant product and geographic markets. If the court limits either the product line or the geographic market, the court tends to find a monopoly. This has particular application to mergers, whether they are horizontal, vertical, or conglomerate. Whether a merger will be allowed is largely determined by the Department of Justice and FTC guidelines.

Several defenses to possible violations of the antitrust laws can be used. Among them are the defenses of meeting competition, cost justification, and changing market conditions; the *Colgate* doctrine; the lack of standing to sue; the thrust-upon defense; the failing-company doctrine; and the inadequate-resources doctrine.

Key Terms

changing-market-conditions
defense **510**
Colgate doctrine **512**
conglomerate merger **510**
cost-justification defense **510**
exclusive dealing contract
failing-company defense **512**
horizontal merger **507**
horizontal restraint **494**
inadequate-resources defense
512

joint refusals to deal **498**
market power **502**
meeting-competition defense
510
merger **506**
monopoly power **501**
price discrimination **510**
professional association **497**
relevant geographic market
502
relevant product market **502**

requirements contract **501**
resale price maintenance
agreement **499**
standing defense **512**
territorial and customer
division **499**
thrust-upon defense **512**
trade association **495**
vertical merger **507**
vertical restraint **494**

Questions and Case Problems

1. Discuss fully whether each of the following situations is in violation of the Sherman Act:

a. Genovese Foods, Inc., is the leading seller of frozen Italian foods in the northeastern United States. The various retail outlets that sell Genovese products are in close competition, and customers are very price conscious. Genovese has conditioned its sales to retailers on the agreement that the retailer will not sell below a minimum price or above a maximum price. Except for these limits, the retailer is allowed to set any price the retailer feels appropriate.

b. Zimmermann, Inc., Hicks, Inc., and Micro, Inc., are competitors in the manufacture and sale of microwave ovens sold primarily on the West Coast. As a patriotic gesture and to assist the unemployed, the three competitors agree to lower their prices on all microwave models by 20 percent for a three-month period, which includes July Fourth and Labor Day.

c. Best Beer, Inc., sells beer to distributors all over the United States. Best Beer sends to each of its distributors a recommended price list, explaining that past records indicate that beer sold at these prices should ensure the distributor a reasonable rate of return. The price list clearly states that the sale of the beer by Best Beer, Inc., to the distributor is not conditioned on the distributor reselling the beer at the recommended price, and the distributor is free to set the price.

2. Innovative Appliance Store is a new retail seller of appliances in Sunwest City. Innovative's different sales techniques and financing have caused a substantial loss of sales for the appliance department of Depressed Department Store. Depressed is a large department store and is part of a large chain with substantial buying power. Depressed told a number of appliance manufacturers that, if they continued to sell to Innovator, Depressed would dis-

continue its large volume of purchases from these manufacturers. The manufacturers immediately stopped selling appliances to Innovator. Innovator files suit against Depressed and the manufacturers, claiming their actions constitute an antitrust violation. Depressed and the manufacturers can prove that Innovator is a small retailer with a small portion of the market, and, since the relevant market was not substantially affected, they claim they are not guilty of restraint of trade. Discuss fully whether there is an antitrust violation.

3. Fast Photo, Inc., is a manufacturer of photographic film. At the present time, Fast Photo has approximately 50 percent of the market. Fast Photo launches a campaign in which, when a customer purchases Fast Photo film, the purchase price includes photo processing by Fast Photo, Inc. Fast Photo claims that its film processing is specially designed to improve the quality of the finished photos when using Fast Photo's film. Discuss fully whether Fast Photo's combination of purchase and film processing is an antitrust violation.

4. Brock Brewery, Inc., is a regional producer and seller of Suds Beer. In its five-state area, Brock has 15 percent of the beer market. Barrel Tap, Inc., is a corporation that has exclusive beer-sales-concession taverns in all major airports in a twenty-state area. Barrel Tap purchases beer from Brock, Miller, and Anheuser-Busch, Inc. Brock acquires the stock and assets of Barrel Tap, Inc. What type of merger is this? Discuss fully whether this merger is in violation of the Clayton Act, Section 7.

5. The plaintiff, Spray-Rite, was an authorized distributor of Monsanto herbicides from 1957 to 1968, and the defendant, Monsanto Company, manufactures chemical products, including agricultural herbicides. In October 1968, Monsanto declined to renew Spray-Rite's distributorship. Spray-Rite subsequently brought an action against Monsanto under Section 1 of the Sherman Act. In its complaint, Spray-Rite alleged that Monsanto and some of its distributors had conspired to fix the resale price of Monsanto herbicides. Monsanto contended, however, that Spray-Rite's distributorship had been terminated because of its failure to hire trained sales personnel and to promote sales to dealers adequately.

The court of appeals concluded that proof of Spray-Rite's termination subsequent to competitor complaints is sufficient to support an inference of concerted action. Can price-fixing be inferred from the fact that a manufacturer terminated a price-cutting distributor in response to complaints from other distributors? What is the standard of proof necessary to establish a vertical price-fixing conspiracy in violation of Section 1 of the Sherman Act? [Monsanto Co. v. Spray-Rite Service Corp., 465 U.S. 752, 104 S.Ct. 1464, 79 L.Ed.2d 775 (1984); rehearing denied 466 U.S. 994, 104 S.Ct. 2378, 80 L.Ed.2d 850 (1984)]

6. The plaintiff, Edwin G. Hyde, a certified anesthesiologist, applied for a position on the medical staff of the defendant, East Jefferson Parish Hospital. Because the hospital had entered into a contract in which all anesthesiological services required by the hospital's patients were to be performed by a professional medical corporation, it denied the plaintiff's application. The plaintiff subsequently brought an action, alleging that the contract violated Section 1 of the Sherman Act. Does this contract provision constitute a *per se* violation of Section 1 of the Sherman Act, since every patient undergoing surgery at Jefferson Hospital must use the services of one firm of anesthesiologists? (Remember that tying arrangements are subject to the *per se* rule.) [Jefferson Parish Hospital District No. 2 v. Hyde, 466 U.S. 2, 104 S.Ct. 1551, 80 L.Ed.2d 2 (1984) remanded to Hyde v. Jefferson Parish Hosp. Dist. No. 2, 764 F.2d 1139 (5th Cir. 1985)]

7. Febco, Inc., manufactured lawn and turf equipment. The Colorado Pump and Supply Company was a wholesale distributor of such equipment in the Colorado area. An important item that Colorado Pump distributed was a control device for sprinkling systems. Although Febco manufactured one of the better sprinkler controls, a number of other manufacturers competed in the field with competitively priced and satisfactory substitutes for the Febco controllers. In an agreement between Febco and Colorado

Pump under which Colorado Pump was given the right to distribute Febco products, Colorado Pump was required to stock a complete line of Febco products. Industry data proved that, in this line of goods, it was important for distributors to protect the "goodwill" of manufacturers by carrying a complete line of a manufacturer's goods or none at all. Does the requirement by Febco that Colorado Pump stock an entire line of Febco products constitute an illegal tying arrangement? [Colorado Pump and Supply Co. v. Febco, Inc., 472 F.2d 637 (10th Cir. 1973)]

8. In 1972, the Federal Maritime Commission approved an agreement under which the world's two largest containership operators, Sea-Land Service, Inc., and United States Lines, Inc., would become subsidiaries of the same corporate parent, R. J. Reynolds Tobacco Company. The commission approved the acquisition agreement on the condition that the subsidiaries would remain independent companies in competition with each other. The Federal Maritime Commission, however, does not have the power to immunize companies from the antitrust laws. Knowing this, do you think the agreement violates any of the antitrust statutes discussed in this chapter? [American Mail Line Limited v. Federal Maritime Comm'n, 503 F.2d 157 (D.C. Cir. 1974)]

9. Sylvania sold its televisions directly to franchised retailers. Sylvania limited the number of franchises granted for any given area and required each franchise to sell the Sylvania products from only the locations of the franchise. A franchise did not constitute an exclusive territory, and Sylvania retained sole discretion to increase the number of retailers in an area, depending on the success or failure of existing retailers in developing their market.

Continental T.V., a Sylvania franchisee, withheld all payments owed for Sylvania products after a dispute over additional locations sought by Continental. John P. Maguire & Company, the finance company that handled the credit arrangements between Sylvania and its franchisees, sued Continental T.V. for payment and for return of secured merchandise (the televisions). In turn, Continental T.V. claimed that Sylvania had violated Section 1 of the Sherman Act by entering into and by enforcing franchise agreements that allowed the sale of Sylvania products only in specified locations. Was this a violation of the Sherman Act? [Continental T.V., Inc., v. GTE Sylvania, Inc., 433 U.S. 36, 97 S.Ct. 2549, 53 L.Ed.2d 568 (1977)]

Chapter 21 Legislative Control over Labor and Labor Relations

Labor disgraces no man; unfortunately you occasionally find men disgrace labor.

Ulysses S. Grant

Speech at Midland International Arbitration Union,
Birmingham, England (1877)

OUTLINE

Introduction

In the past, the freedom to contract, as applied to employment, gave rise to perceived inequities in the employer-employee relationship and resulted in such abuses as child labor camps, dangerous working conditions, and worker discrimination. These abuses produced two major responses in the United States. First, the federal government passed national legislation that covered working standards, discrimination, and safety. Second, the workers began to unionize in an attempt to gain a more powerful position in bargaining with management.

The earliest attempts by Congress to set employment standards were ruled unconstitutional on grounds that the laws infringed on an individual's right to contract. Over time, though, the courts began to limit the employers' power in employment contracts and to recognize Congress's constitutional power to regulate employment practices under the commerce clause.

Today, unions make up less than 20 percent of the American work force; governmental employees, both federal and state, comprise 15 percent; and 65 percent of all American workers are employed at will, or without a written contract. Regardless of the contractual category of the worker, the employer must meet certain minimum standards with reference to pay, hours, and working conditions. This chapter discusses the legislation that protects employees; then it looks at the rights of employees to form unions and describes what unions can and cannot accomplish.

Fair Labor Standards Act

The **Fair Labor Standards Act (FLSA)** of 1938 established a minimum wage, overtime standards, record-keeping requirements, and child labor prohibitions. The act affects more than 70 million full-time and part-time workers. These fundamental standards are applicable to people employed in private industry, government, and unions. In addition, the FLSA spells out the administrative procedures for enforcing and complying with these standards.

Who Is Covered?

The FLSA is an extensive statute that was enacted based on the commerce clause of Article I of the Constitution. Generally, the FLSA applies to employees: (1) who are engaged in commerce, (2) who are engaged in the production of goods to be placed in commerce, or (3) who are employed in an enterprise engaged in commerce.

The first two types of coverage involve the "employee test," which looks at the nature of the employee's work, not the nature of the business. In the third category, the controlling factor is the nature of the business. If the enterprise is covered, all the employees are covered, regardless of the relationship between their duties and commerce.

The FLSA explains which actions by an employer constitute a punishable violation of the statute and the rules promulgated under it. Understanding the meaning of "employer" for purposes of the act is key to determining which actions will be considered violations.

The FLSA's definition of the term "employer" is extremely broad: An employer "includes any person acting directly or indirectly in the interest of an employer in relation to an employee." An individual, such as a corporate officer, who actively participates in the running of a business, including the employment practices of the business, is an employer within the meaning of the statute. Such an individual will be personally liable, with the corporation, for any violations of the act and, therefore, will be liable for the payment of any fines under the act.

An employer who violates the FLSA is liable in a civil action to the employee, who may recover from the employer unpaid wages, overtime compensation, liquidated damages, and reasonable attorneys' fees. The statute also empowers a court to issue an injunction restraining further violations. The employer may be criminally prosecuted by the federal government and, if found guilty, may be punished by a fine of up to $10,000 for the first offense and a fine of up to $10,000 plus imprisonment for up to six months for subsequent violations.

Exempt Employees

Because of the nature of certain industries, it would be impossible to operate some businesses under the FLSA. In order to accommodate these businesses, Congress allowed exemptions to the act. Each exemption is narrowly defined by the statute.

The employer asserting the exemption must meet each element of the statutory requirement for exemption. Some of the classes of industries whose workers are exempt from the FLSA include agriculture, commercial fishing, some retail service businesses, and domestic services. In addition, many white-collar positions are not included under the act, because it is believed that these individuals are able to protect themselves from the employer abuses that the FLSA prohibits.

Wage and Hour Requirements

Both state and federal statutes govern the minimum-wage and maximum-hour requirements for workers. For the most part, state laws are congruent with the FLSA. Since most businesses are subject to the federal act, the FLSA is the most important guarantee of proper treatment for employees.

Wages The minimum wage was initially twenty-five cents an hour in 1938. Periodically, this amount has been increased. In 1981, the minimum wage was raised to $3.35 an hour. By the time you read this text, it may have been increased further. The increases in the minimum wage over the years are shown in Exhibit 21–1.

The FLSA provides for an exception to the minimum wage in the case of tipped employees. The statute defines tipped employees as those who customarily and regularly receive more than thirty

Exhibit 21–1 Federal Minimum-Wage Chart

YEAR	MINIMUM WAGE
1938	$ .25
1945	.40
1950	.75
1960	1.15
1965	1.25
1970	1.60
1975	2.10
1980	3.10
1981 to present	3.35

dollars a month in tips. In such a case, the employer may consider the tips as part of the wages, but the wage credit (tips) must not exceed 40 percent of the minimum wage.

Hours An employee must be paid for all hours worked in a week; however, what constitutes working time is not completely clear. Generally, the hours worked—those for which an individual must be paid at least the minimum wage and which must be included when computing total hours worked in order to determine overtime hours—encompass all the time that an employee is actually at work or is required to be on duty and that the employee is not free to use for his or her own purposes.

For example, all police officers are regularly required to be at work twenty minutes ahead of the hour (say, 8:00) in order to change into their uniforms and be in formation by 8:00. The officers must be paid for those twenty minutes in addition to their eight-hour shifts.

The calculation and payment of overtime wages can be confusing and is usually the source of many employee-employer misunderstandings. Violations of FLSA's requirement for overtime wages can easily happen because the formulas for determining overtime pay are complex and appear at times to be unfair and illogical.

The FLSA stipulates that, when an employee has worked in excess of forty hours for one work week, that employee must be paid no less than one and one-half times her or his regular hourly rate for any hours worked in excess of forty. Overtime is not one and one-half times minimum wage but one and one-half times the employee's regular wages. In calculating hours, each work week is a separate unit; hours may not be carried to the next week or averaged over two or more weeks. A person working four ten-hour days in one week has no right to overtime.

Certain compensation, such as commissions and incentive bonuses, must be included in the calculation of overtime pay as compensation at the regular rate; however, there are several forms of nonstandard payment that may be excluded from the calculation of the regular rate. These exceptions include travel expenses, bonuses that are completely at the discretion of the employer, payment for vacations, and some other forms of wages.

It can be very confusing for businesses to comply with these laws. The following case helps to demonstrate some of the basic principles and difficulties involved in wage and hour determinations, specifically those concerning overtime pay.

Case 21.1

MUMBOWER v. CALLICOTT

United States Court of Appeals, Eighth Circuit, 1975. 526 F.2d 1183.

BACKGROUND AND FACTS   *Lorraine Mumbower was a switchboard operator for an answering service that was owned by Callicott. She had worked for the prior owner of the company. Her hours changed after Callicott purchased the business. She brought an action against Callicott and others, who were her employers, for violation of FLSA concerning maximum hours and overtime pay provisions. The lower court ruled in favor of her employer, Callicott, and Mumbower appealed.*

GIBSON, Chief Judge.

*   *   *   *

At the time of the purchase by Callicott, plaintiff agreed to operate the switchboard by herself for $80 per week, maintaining the same hours as before, 8:00 a.m. to 6:00 p.m., six days per week, with one hour for lunch. Up to the time of her discharge in August, 1973, her hours gradually decreased and pay increased.

Plaintiff had her own key to the premises and served as her own supervisor. The fifty-line, single-operator switchboard was located in a six foot square, windowless room. Callicott occupied a nearby office. Plaintiff testified that Callicott determined the hours the switchboard was to be open. However, no employment records were maintained. She testified that she arrived early on a regular basis and usually received a call from Callicott at 7:30 a.m. with instructions for the day. He requested her to perform duties such as admitting the janitor, opening the mail, posting checks, maintaining a record of accounts in Callicott's office, obtaining the appointment book of a customer, Dr. Walter, from his nearby office to take the day's appointments, reviewing customers' daily itineraries, and meeting with customers who picked up their packages and messages. These duties she performed regularly between 7:30 a.m. and 8:00 a.m. with Callicott's knowledge and "tacit" approval before the switchboard opened. Callicott specifically approved the special routine for Dr. Walter.

Plaintiff also testified that she was instructed by Callicott to remain on duty after the switchboard officially closed to transmit daily messages to customers calling in. Her hours thus extended fifteen to thirty minutes beyond the official closing time. During this time she would also empty trash, lock the office and turn off lights. Callicott occasionally called to remind her of these and other duties. She further testified that she had complained of her inability to take lunch periods because no one was available to replace her. Over the years she worked through occasional illnesses and eventually in July, 1972, was hospitalized for fatigue for several weeks. During her hospital stay she was replaced by another operator whom she had trained in advance. After her discharge in August, 1973, she was replaced by two part-time operators, each working half days.

*   *   *   *

Section 7(a) of the FLSA requires an employee to be paid overtime compensation for hours worked in excess of forty per week "at a rate not less than one and one-half times the *regular rate* at which he is employed." (Emphasis added.) This provision has been uniformly interpreted to require the fifty percent overtime premium to be added to the actual wage paid, not to the statutory minimum wage for hours up to forty, with the "intended effect" of requiring extra pay for overtime even for employees whose hourly wages exceed the statutory minimum. This principle applies to employees hired on a weekly as well as an hourly basis.

If the parties wish to modify the statutory rule by contracting for a "regular rate" of pay greater than the minimum wage, they may do so provided the employee is paid time and one-half the regular rate for hours over forty per week.

* * * *

The term "work" is not defined in the FLSA, but it is settled that duties performed by an employee before and after scheduled hours, even if not requested, must be compensated if the employer "knows or has reason to believe" the employee is continuing to work, and the duties are an "integral and indispensable part" of the employee's principal work activity. Plaintiff contends that she regularly performed morning duties before officially opening the board and afternoon duties after scheduled closing, and that such extra work was knowingly permitted by the managing partner. If so, she is entitled to be compensated therefore at her regular rate. The employer who wishes no such work to be done has a duty to see it is not performed. He cannot accept the benefits without including the extra hours in the employee's weekly total for purposes of overtime compensation. If the employer has the power and desire to prevent such work, he must make every effort to do so.

A similar rule applies to meal periods during which an employee is not completely relieved of duty. Plaintiff testified without contradiction that she was not relieved during lunch periods. Defendants Barks and Schaefer conceded that fact during oral argument in this court. The record also indicates that two of the defendants were informed that no replacement operator was available and that plaintiff wished to be relieved, but none was provided. The nature of the answering service business requires noon hour coverage and plaintiff apparently continued to operate the switchboard in a conscientious effort to avoid losing customers, not because she was ordered to do so. Such extra work for the employer's benefit and with his tacit approval must be included in determining whether overtime compensation is statutorily required.

The trial court ruling was reversed. On remand, the lower court had to recalculate the overtime compensation so that it was consistent with Section 7(a) of the FLSA.	**DECISION AND REMEDY**

Investigation and Enforcement Procedures The FLSA delegates to the secretary of labor the power to examine the records of employers to see if there have been violations committed under the act. The Wage and Hour Division (WHD) of the Department of Labor has the primary responsibility for enforcing and administering the FLSA. The WHD has officers throughout the United States who conduct investigations and gather data on wages, hours, and other employment conditions.

The FLSA provides several methods for recovering unpaid wages. The methods include: supervision by the WHD of the employer's payment of back wages; court action by the secretary of labor to collect unpaid wages; a lawsuit by the employee for unpaid wages and for attorneys' fees; and an injunction obtained by the secretary of labor to restrain employers from further violation of the FLSA.

Child Labor Laws

The provisions of the FLSA that govern child labor are simple, yet the penalties for violating these standards are severe and should not be ignored by the private businessperson. The child labor laws are part of public policy; they are intended to ensure that each minor has the opportunity to attend school, and they prohibit the employment of children in hazardous jobs or under working con-

LEGAL HIGHLIGHT
Exemptions and Requirements Under the Minimum-Wage and Overtime Laws

Certain employees are exempt from both the minimum-wage and overtime provisions. These exemptions include:

1. Executive, administrative, and professional employees, including teachers in elementary or secondary schools;
2. Employees of individually owned and operated small retail or service establishments and family-owned stores, if the annual gross income is under $350,000;
3. Employees of seasonal amusement or recreational businesses;
4. Employees of small newspapers that have a circulation of less than 4,000;
5. Switchboard operators of small telephone companies with less than 750 stations;
6. Sailors employed on foreign vessels;
7. Employees engaged in fishing operations;
8. Certain farm workers; and

9. Casual babysitters and people employed as companions to the elderly or infirm.

Employers subject to both minimum-wage and overtime provisions must have on file for each employee the following items:

1. Personal information, including name, home address, occupation, sex, and birth date;
2. Hour and day when the work week begins;
3. Total hours worked each work week and workday;
4. Total daily or weekly straight-time earnings;
5. Regular hourly pay rate for any week when overtime is worked;
6. Total overtime pay for the work week;
7. Deductions from or additions to wages;
8. Total wages paid each pay period; and
9. Date of payment and pay period covered.

ditions that are dangerous to their health or well-being.

An individual who is over seventeen years of age does not fall under the child labor provisions of the statute. Minors between the ages of sixteen and seventeen are allowed to be employed, but there are restrictions. Certain industries are considered to be dangerous and, therefore, off limits for sixteen- and seventeen-year-olds. In addition, children between fourteen and fifteen years of age may be employed only in specially approved jobs; these jobs include retail stores, restaurants, and service stations.

Children under the age of fourteen are prohibited from working except in certain occupations, such as agricultural employment, and are subject to FLSA regulations requiring school obligations. Young actors, actresses, and performers are also exempt, when certain conditions are met, from the FLSA prohibitions against child labor.

Retirement and Income Security

Federal and state governments participate in programs of insurance to cover the financial impact on employees of retirement, disability, death, hospitalization, and unemployment. The key federal law in this area is the **Social Security Act** of 1935.

Social Security

Social security is more formally known as **Old Age, Survivors, and Disability Insurance (OASDI)**. Both employers and employees must contribute under the **Federal Insurance Contributions Act (FICA)** to help fund social security. The employee's contribution is a percentage of his or her annual wage base (the annual wage base is the maximum amount of an employee's wages that are subject to the tax). In 1988, for example, the annual wage base was a maximum of $45,000.

```
┌──────────────────────────────────────────────────────────────┐
│  LEGAL                                                         │
│  HIGHLIGHT          Checking on Your Social Security Account   │
└──────────────────────────────────────────────────────────────┘
```

Before any social security benefits can be paid, you must have credit for a certain amount of work. Measured in "quarters of coverage," you can earn a maximum of four quarters a year (obviously, three months per quarter). If your job is covered by the Social Security Act, you have an individual lifetime earnings record established at the Social Security Administration headquarters in Baltimore, Maryland. Your earnings are reported under your name and social security number. You should check on your social security account every three years to ensure that your record is properly credited.

How do you check on your record? You can send a letter to the Social Security Administration. Or an easier method is to obtain a form entitled "Request for Statement of Earnings" from your local Social Security Administration office, fill it out, and send it in. Within six weeks, a summary of your account will be returned. It will list the last three years individually. If there is a mistake, you can correct it immediately (yes, by sending in *another* form along with your W-2 forms). Otherwise, if the mistake is left in your record, your social security check at retirement may be reduced because your account does not accurately reflect the amount of money you have really earned. Even if there is a mistake, however, your checks will not be reduced if you are receiving the minimum amount allowed to be collected.

The employee had to pay 7.51 percent and so, too, did the employer, up to a maximum of $6,759 per employee.

Social security benefits are fixed by statute, but they increase automatically with increases in the cost of living of 3 percent or more between specified periods.

A health insurance program, **Medicare**, is administered by the Social Security Administration to people sixty-five years of age and older and for those under sixty-five who are disabled. It has two parts, one pertaining to hospital costs and the other to nonhospital medical costs, such as doctors' office visits. People who have Medicare hospital insurance can obtain additional federal medical insurance if they pay small monthly premiums that increase as the cost of medical care increases.

Private Retirement Plans

Significant legislation now regulates retirement plans set up by employers. These plans are used to supplement social security benefits. The major piece of legislation of this type is the **Employee** **Retirement Income Security Act (ERISA)** of 1974. ERISA covers the financing, vesting, and administration of pension plans for workers in private business and industry. The Department of Labor, through the Pension Benefit Guaranty Corporation and the Labor Management Services Administration, and the treasury department enforce ERISA's provisions.

Unemployment Compensation

Unemployment insurance is funded by employers who pay into the fund; the proceeds are paid out to qualified unemployed workers. The major piece of federal legislation concerning unemployment is the **Federal Unemployment Tax Act (FUTA)**, which became law in 1954. This act established a state system that provides **unemployment compensation** to eligible individuals—those who worked a certain minimum number of weeks, earned wages in a certain amount, and are involuntarily out of work. The cost of administering the unemployment insurance program is paid by the federal government out of part of the tax collected.

LEGAL
HIGHLIGHT   **All for the Want of a Penny**

The Place: Yuma, Arizona
The Time: 1987
The Parties: Immaculate Conception
               Church and the
               Internal Revenue Service

The Immaculate Conception Church underpaid
its quarterly federal employment withholding tax
for twenty-nine employees by one penny. Once

the error was discovered, the church sent a
check in the amount of one cent to the Internal
Revenue Service, but it was too late. The
church was assessed $453.60 worth of
penalties—in other words, a 45,360 percent
penalty. The Internal Revenue Service waived
the penalty several months later when the
matter was brought to its attention.

This is not a welfare program. The unemployed
person does not have to show a need to receive
benefits; the decision to grant or deny benefits is
based on whether the individual is willing and able
to work.

Other Statutes for
Employee Protection

Numerous state statutes are designed to protect
employees and their families from the risk of accidental injury, death, or disease resulting from
their employment. This section covers state workers' compensation laws and the Occupational Safety
and Health Act of 1970.

State Workers' Compensation Acts

Workers' compensation laws are usually administered by a state agency that has quasi-judicial
powers. All rulings of these agencies are subject
to review by the courts. These laws are not based
on federal law.

The right to recover under workers' compensation laws is given to the injured employee without regard to the existence of negligence or fault
of the employer. Rather, the right to recovery is
predicated on the employment relationship and the
fact that the injury arose out of the employment.

Basically, employers are under a system of strict
liability. This is similar to the strict liability used
in product liability cases, which we discuss in
Chapter 12. Few, if any, defenses exist for them.

The simple, two-pronged test for determining
whether an employee can receive workers' compensation consists of these questions:

1. Was the injury accidental?
2. Did the injury arise out of and in the course
of employment?

Intentionally inflicted self-injuries are not considered accidental and are not covered. In the past,
heart attacks or other medical problems arising
out of preexisting disease or physical conditions
were not covered, but recently the courts have
started to treat these medical problems as covered
under the act. Some states have limited by legislation the legal recovery possible when an employee has a heart attack on the job.

The following case discusses the question of
injuries caused by asbestos that was used in the
work environment. The major question presented
is whether an employee can seek workers' compensation while filing a separate lawsuit. The lawsuit alleged that the employer was liable for the
injuries because the employer did fully inform the
employee of the dangers of asbestos and did not
protect the employee from those dangers.

BACKGROUND AND FACTS *Reba Rudkin, the real plaintiff in this case, brought this action against Johns-Manville, his employer for twenty-nine years. The defendant had been in the business of manufacturing asbestos for many years. Rudkin alleged in his complaint that, as a result of his exposure to asbestos, he developed pneumonoconiosis, lung cancer, and other asbestos-related illnesses.*

Rudkin also alleged that Johns-Manville had known since 1924 that long exposure to asbestos or the ingestion of that substance is dangerous to health, yet it had concealed this knowledge from the plaintiff and had advised him that it was safe to work in close proximity to asbestos. It failed to provide him with adequate protective devices, and it did not operate the plant in accordance with state and federal regulations governing dust levels.

Johns-Manville filed an answer alleging that the action was barred. It requested the trial court to take judicial notice of an application filed by the plaintiff seeking workers' compensation benefits for disability caused by "[e]xposure to asbestos." The defendant moved for judgment on the pleadings. The trial court denied the motion. The defendant appealed to the California Supreme Court.

 Case 21.2

JOHNS-MANVILLE PRODUCTS CORP. v. CONTRA COSTA SUPERIOR COURT

Supreme Court of California, 1980.
27 Cal.3d 465,
612 P.2d 948,
165 Cal.Rptr. 858.

MOSK, Justice.

[T]he Labor Code provides that an employer is liable for injuries to its employees arising out of and in the course of employment, and *   *   * declares that where the conditions of workers' compensation exist, the right to recover such compensation is the exclusive remedy against an employer for injury or death of an employee. The issue to be decided in this proceeding is whether an employee is barred by these provisions from prosecuting an action at law against his employer for the intentional torts of fraud and conspiracy in knowingly ordering the employee to work in an unsafe environment, concealing the risk from him, and, after the employee had contracted an industrial disease, deliberately failing to notify the state, the employee, or doctors retained to treat him, of the disease and its connection with the employment, thereby aggravating the consequences of the disease.

We conclude that while the workers' compensation law bars the employee's action at law for his initial injury, a cause of action may exist for aggravation of the disease because of the employer's fraudulent concealment of the condition and its cause.

*   *   *   *

Prior to 1917, the law allowed an employee a choice of remedies if an injury was caused by an employer's gross negligence or willful misconduct. He could either claim workers' compensation benefits or maintain an action at law for damages. In that year, however, this provision was deleted and a new section added specifying a one-half increase in compensation in the event of serious and willful misconduct by the employer. This history, contends defendant, demonstrates that the right to seek additional compensation for injuries caused by the serious and willful misconduct of the employer was intended by the Legislature as a substitute for the right to seek damages in an action at law for such conduct.

We find the historical background cited by defendant to be persuasive. The clear implication is that the addition in 1917 of the "exclusive remedy" limitation and the provision for a penalty for the willful misconduct of the employer was a substitute for the previous right of an employee to bring an action at law.

*   *   *   *

Thus, if the complaint alleged only that plaintiff contracted the disease because defendant knew and concealed from him that his health was endangered by asbestos in the work environment, failed to supply adequate protective devices to avoid disease, and violated governmental regulations relating to dust levels at the plant, plaintiff's only remedy would be to prosecute his claim under the workers' compensation law.

But where the employer is charged with intentional misconduct which goes beyond his failure to assure that the tools or substances used by the employee or the physical environment of a workplace are safe, some cases have held that the employer may be subject to common law liability. A physical assault by the employer upon the employee has been held to justify an action at law against the employer. In *Ramey v. General Petroleum Corporation*, it was held that an action for fraud could be maintained against an employer who made misrepresentations regarding the employee's right to medical care and conspired with a third party to conceal from the employee that his injuries, which occurred while he was working, were caused by the third party against whom he had recourse. And in *Unruh v. Truck Insurance Exchange*, we allowed an action at law against an insurer for assault, battery, and intentional infliction of emotional distress, based upon its deceitful conduct in investigating a workers' compensation claim.

* * * *

We conclude the policy of exclusivity of worker's compensation as a remedy for injuries in the employment would not be seriously undermined by holding defendant liable for the aggravation of this plaintiff's injuries, since we cannot believe that many employers will aggravate the effects of an industrial injury by not only deliberately concealing its existence but also its connection with the employment. Nor can we believe that the Legislature in enacting the workers' compensation law intended to insulate such flagrant conduct from tort liability. Finally, although plaintiff filed an application for workers' compensation and may receive an award in that proceeding, double recovery may be avoided by allowing the employer a set-off in the event plaintiff is awarded compensation for the aggravation of his injury in that proceeding and in the present case as well.

DECISION AND REMEDY   *Johns-Manville could not escape civil liability if the trial court should determine that the plaintiff's allegations were correct. The plaintiff was entitled to both workers' compensation benefits and additional damages if his employer had intentionally concealed the danger of asbestos. To avoid a double recovery, however, the court could offset the amount of workers' compensation benefits awarded to compensate the plaintiff for the aggravation of his injury against any damages awarded for the same purpose.*

Health and Safety Protection

The main federal legislation for employee health and safety protection is the **Occupational Safety and Health Act** of 1970. This act was passed to ensure safe and healthful working conditions for practically every employee in the country. The act created the **Occupational Safety and Health Administration (OSHA),** the Occupational Safety and Health Review Commission, and the National Institute for Occupational Safety and Health. OSHA promulgates and enforces workers' safety and health standards, as well as conducting inspections and investigations, requiring employers to keep detailed records of worker injuries and illnesses, and conducting research.

In most instances, an employee will make a written complaint requesting an OSHA inspection. OSHA will generally protect the identity of the complaining employee. As an added protection, OSHA prohibits the discharge of, or any discrimination against, an employee who, by submitting a formal complaint against an employer, exercises his or her rights under the statute. The act stipulates that an employee who believes that she or he has been discriminated against for bringing possible violations to the attention of OSHA may, within thirty days, file a complaint with the secretary of labor. The secretary will conduct an investigation and, if appropriate, seek relief for the employee in federal court. The next case is an example of such an occurrence.

BACKGROUND AND FACTS *Whirlpool has a plant that produces appliances. Within the plant, the machines are transported on conveyors. In order to protect the employees below the conveyor belt from appliances that occasionally fall, Whirlpool installed high guard screens. As part of their routine duties, maintenance employees were required to remove fallen parts from the screens. In order to do so, the workers had to walk on the screens. Starting in 1973, Whirlpool began replacing the screen material with heavier gauge mesh. Several workers had fallen through the old screen, and, on June 28, 1974, a maintenance employee had fallen to his death through the mesh in a section where stronger gauge mesh had not yet been installed.*

Subsequently, Whirlpool made some repairs and issued a general order to clean the screens without walking on them. Two weeks after the death, two employees asked for the local OSHA officer's phone number. The next night they were ordered onto the screens; they refused. As a result, the employees were not allowed to work their shift and were issued written reprimands that were placed in their files.

The secretary of labor filed suit against Whirlpool for suspending and reprimanding the employees in violation of rules promulgated under OSHA by the Department of Labor. The secretary sought to have the employees' reprimands expunged from their records and to recover the pay lost due to the disciplinary action. The trial court denied the request. The appellate court reversed and granted relief to the employees. Whirlpool appealed to the United States Supreme Court, challenging the regulation promulgated by the secretary of labor.

Case 21.3
WHIRLPOOL CORP. v. MARSHALL
Supreme Court of the United States, 1980.
445 U.S. 1, 100 S.Ct. 883, 63 L.Ed.2d 154.

STEWART, Justice.

The Occupational Safety and Health Act of 1970 (Act) prohibits an employer from discharging or discriminating against any employee who exercises "any right afforded by" the Act. The Secretary of Labor (Secretary) has promulgated a regulation providing that, among the rights that the Act so protects, is the right of an employee to choose not to perform his assigned task because of a reasonable apprehension of death or serious injury coupled with a reasonable belief that no less drastic alternative is available. The question presented in the case before us is whether this regulation is consistent with the Act.

* * * *

The regulation clearly conforms to the fundamental objective of the Act—to prevent occupational deaths and serious injuries. The Act, in its preamble, declares that its purpose and policy is "to assure so far as possible every working man and woman in the Nation safe and healthful working conditions and to *preserve* our human resources . . . .'' (Emphasis added.)

To accomplish this basic purpose, the legislation's remedial orientation is prophylactic in nature. The Act does not wait for an employee to die or become injured. It authorizes the promulgation of health and safety standards and the issuance of citations in the hope that these will act to prevent deaths or injuries from ever occurring. It would seem anomalous to construe an Act so directed and constructed as prohibiting an employee, with no other reasonable alternative, the freedom to withdraw from a workplace environment that he reasonably believes is highly dangerous.

Moreover, the Secretary's regulation can be viewed as an appropriate aid to the full effectuation of the Act's ''general duty'' clause. That clause provides that ''[e]ach employer * * * shall furnish to each of his employees employment and a place of employment which are free from recognized hazards that are causing or are likely to cause death or serious physical harm to his employees.'' As the legislative history of this provision reflects, it was intended itself to deter the occurrence of occupational deaths and serious injuries by placing on employers a mandatory obligation independent of the specific health and safety standards to be promulgated by the Secretary. Since OSHA inspectors cannot be present around the clock in every workplace, the Secretary's regulation ensures that employees will in all circumstances enjoy the rights afforded them by the ''general duty'' clause.

The regulation thus on its face appears to further the overriding purpose of the Act, and rationally to complement its remedial scheme. In the absence of some contrary indication in the legislative history, the Secretary's regulation must, therefore, be upheld, particularly when it is remembered that safety legislation is to be liberally construed to effectuate the congressional purpose. * * *

DECISION AND REMEDY *The Supreme Court held that the secretary's regulation must be upheld. The regulation was made in accordance with the congressional statutory scheme. Employees may refuse to perform work under certain circumstances when confronted with hazardous job conditions.*

Unions and Collective Bargaining

Government regulation of employment and labor relations is very much present in our society. Businesses must operate within the confines established by these regulating statutes. Over the years, legislation has greatly affected the rights and liabilities of employees, as well as employers.

Until the early 1930s, laws at the federal and state levels generally favored management. Collective activities such as unions were discouraged, sometimes forcibly, by employers. Early legislation and agencies protecting the rights of employees, such as the National War Labor Board that operated during World War I, were often temporary. In addition, the legislation was frequently restricted to a particular industry, such as the Railway Labor Act of 1926, which required railroads and their employees to attempt to make employment agreements through representatives chosen by each side. Beginning in 1932, however, a number of statutes were enacted that greatly increased employees' rights to join unions and to engage in collective bargaining.

Norris-LaGuardia Act

Congress protected peaceful strikes, picketing, and boycotts in 1932 with the **Norris-LaGuardia Act**. The statute restricted the power of federal courts to issue injunctions against unions engaged in peaceful strikes. In effect, the act declared a national policy permitting employees to organize.

National Labor Relations Act

The **National Labor Relations Act (Wagner Act)** of 1935 established the rights of employees to engage in collective bargaining and to strike. The Wagner Act created the **National Labor Relations Board (NLRB)** to oversee elections and to prevent employers from engaging in unfair and illegal antiunion activities and unfair labor practices.

The act defined a number of practices by employers as unfair to labor:

1. Interference with the efforts of employees to form, join, or assist labor organizations;
2. An employer's domination of a labor organization or contribution of financial or other support to it;
3. Discrimination in the hiring or awarding of tenure to employees based on union affiliation;
4. Discrimination against employees for filing charges under the act or giving testimony under the act; and
5. Refusal to bargain collectively with the duly designated representative of the employees.

Until this act was passed, an employer could refuse to bargain with a union. Now, an employer is required to recognize the union as a bargaining power if the employees so decide by a neutral election.

The **Labor-Management Relations Act (Taft-Hartley Act)** of 1947 amended the Wagner Act. This act contains provisions protecting employers as well as employees. The act was bitterly opposed by organized labor groups because it provided a detailed list of unfair labor activities that unions as well as management are now forbidden to practice. Moreover, a free speech amendment allowed employers to propagandize against unions prior to any National Labor Relations Board election.

Both the Wagner and the Taft-Hartley acts affected certain types of businesses known as closed shops and union shops. A **closed shop** is a firm that requires union membership from its workers

as a condition of employment. Closed shops were made illegal under the Taft-Hartley Act because they put the unions in charge of hiring, rather than the employers.

A **union shop** does not require membership as a prerequisite for employment but can, and usually does, require that workers join the union after a specified amount of time on the job. In an **agency shop**, membership in a union is not a prerequisite to be hired, and workers are not required to join the union after they have been hired. Workers, however, can be required to pay initiation fees and union dues, the theory being that these people are enjoying the benefits of the union.

The Taft-Hartley Act allowed individual states to pass their own **right-to-work laws**. A right-to-work law makes it illegal for union membership to be required for continued employment in any establishment. Thus, union shops are technically illegal in states with right-to-work laws.

One of the most controversial aspects of the Taft-Hartley Act was the eighty-day cooling-off period. This provision allows federal courts to issue injunctions against strikes that would create a national emergency. The president of the United States can obtain such a court injunction that will last eighty days. For example, President Eisenhower applied the eighty-day injunction to striking steelworkers in 1959, President Nixon applied it to striking longshoremen in 1971, and President Carter applied it to striking coal miners in 1978.

Labor-Management Reporting and Disclosure Act of 1959

The **Labor-Management Reporting and Disclosure Act (Landrum-Griffin Act)** of 1959 instituted an employee bill of rights as well as reporting requirements for union activities. This act regulates internal union business, such as union elections. Elections of officers must be regularly scheduled, and secret ballots must be used. Ex-convicts and members of the Communist party are precluded form holding union office. Union officials are accountable for union property and for union funds. Members have the right to attend and to participate in union meetings, to nominate officers, and to vote in most union proceedings.

The National Labor Relations Board

The National Labor Relations Board enforces all of these statutes. The NLRB consists of five members who are appointed by the president with the advice and consent of the Senate. The board members have staggered five-year terms and may be removed only for neglect of duty or malfeasance.

The board has the usual administrative powers and is charged with supervising secret elections in which the employees determine whether a union will represent them in collective bargaining. The board then certifies the union selected by the majority of employees as the collective bargaining agent. Charged with preventing and remedying unfair labor practices, the board hears and rules on charges of unfair labor practices from unions and employers.

The Taft-Hartley Act transferred the investigative and prosecutorial roles of the board to a general counsel who is also appointed by the president with the advice and consent of the Senate. The general counsel supervises the NLRB's 31 regional offices and is responsible for the conduct of union representative elections. Individual charges of unfair labor or antiunion practices are filed with one of the NLRB's regional offices. The regional director may, at her or his discretion, file a complaint after investigating the charges.

Complaints filed by regional directors are heard initially by administrative law judges who have delegated authority from the NLRB. If appealed, the administrative law judge's decision serves as a recommendation to the board. Board decisions may be appealed to the court of appeals and from there to the Supreme Court of the United States.

Remedies

The NLRB has broad discretionary authority to fashion appropriate remedies whenever it finds unfair labor practices. The courts have held that the board's orders will not be overturned unless it can be shown that the remedies ordered cannot fairly be said to effectuate the policies of the NLRA, as amended.

The board may issue cease and desist orders and may also require a person to take an action designed to carry out the purposes of the act. The board may order reinstatement of an employee who is wrongfully discharged, along with the payment of back wages and the restoration of seniority. When union election results are contested, the board may order new elections if unfair labor practices are deemed to have influenced the outcome, or it may, in certain instances, require an employer to bargain with the appropriate union without holding a new election.

The Collective Bargaining Agreement

The NLRA requires both employers and the unions who represent their employees to bargain in good faith. This obligation requires the employer and union to meet at reasonable times and to confer in good faith with respect to wages, hours, and other terms and conditions of employment. The obligation to bargain in good faith does not require the parties to come to an agreement. But the purpose behind the statute is to encourage parties to negotiate enforceable contracts. The following case involves the enforceability of a collective bargaining agreement that contained a no-strike provision.

Case 21.4
JACKSONVILLE v. INTERNATIONAL LONGSHOREMEN ASSOCIATION

Supreme Court of the United States, 1982.
457 U.S. 702,
102 S.Ct. 2672,
72 L.Ed.2d 327.

BACKGROUND AND FACTS *President Carter announced an embargo of certain goods that were to be shipped to the Soviet Union because of its intervention in Afghanistan. The respondent, the International Longshoremen's Association, announced that its members would not handle any cargo bound to or coming from the Soviet Union. When an affiliated local union refused to load any goods, including goods not contained in the presidential embargo, bound for the Soviet Union, the petitioners, Jacksonville, brought suit in federal district court against the international union pursuant to the Labor-Management Relations Act.*

Jacksonville alleged that the union's work stoppage violated the terms of a collective bargaining agreement that contained a no-strike clause and a provision requiring arbitration of disputes. The court ordered the union to arbitrate the question of whether the work stoppage violated the collective bargaining agreement, and it granted a preliminary injunction pending arbitration. The court reasoned that the political motivation behind the work stoppage rendered inapplicable the Norris-LaGuardia Act. This act prohibits injunctions against strikes "in any case involving or growing out of any labor dispute." The trial court decided this was not a labor dispute.

The court of appeals affirmed the district court's order insofar as it required arbitration, but it disagreed with the conclusion that the Norris-LaGuardia Act was not applicable.

MARSHALL, Justice.

In this case, we consider the power of a federal court to enjoin a politically motivated work stoppage in an action brought by an employer pursuant to § 301(a) of the Labor Management Relations Act (LMRA) to enforce a union's obligations under a collective-bargaining agreement. We first address whether the broad anti-injunction provisions of the Norris-LaGuardia Act apply to politically motivated work stoppages. Finding these provisions applicable, we then consider whether the work stoppage may be enjoined under the rationale of *Boys Markets, Inc. v. Retail Clerks,* pending an arbitrator's decision on whether the strike violates the collective-bargaining agreement.

* * * *

Section 4 of the Norris-LaGuardia Act provides in part:

"No court of the United States shall have jurisdiction to issue any restraining order or temporary or permanent injunction in any case involving or growing out of any labor dispute to prohibit any person or persons participating or interested in such dispute * * * from doing, whether singly or in concert, any of the following acts:

"(a) Ceasing or refusing to perform any work or to remain in any relation of employment."

Congress adopted this broad prohibition to remedy the growing tendency of federal courts to enjoin strikes by narrowly construing the Clayton Act's labor exemption from the Sherman Act's prohibition against conspiracies to restrain trade. This Court has consistently given the anti-injunction provisions of the Norris-LaGuardia Act a broad interpretation, recognizing exceptions only in limited situations where necessary to accommodate the Act to specific federal legislation or paramount congressional policy.

At the outset, we must determine whether this is a "case involving or growing out of any labor dispute" within the meaning of § 4 of the Norris-LaGuardia Act. Section 13(c) of the Act broadly defines the term "labor dispute" to include "any controversy concerning terms or conditions of employment."

* * * *

The language of the Norris-LaGuardia Act does not except labor disputes having their genesis in political protests. Nor is there any basis in the statutory language for the argument that the Act requires that *each* dispute relevant to the case be a labor dispute. The Act merely requires that the case involve "any" labor dispute. Therefore, the plain terms of § 4(a) and § 13 of the Norris-LaGuardia Act deprive the federal courts of the power to enjoin the Union's work stoppage in this * * * action, without regard to whether the Union also has a nonlabor dispute with another entity.

* * * *

The attempts by the Solicitor General and the Employer to characterize the underlying dispute as arbitrable do not withstand analysis. The "underlying" disputes concerning the management-rights clause or the work-conditions clause simply did not trigger the work stoppage. To the contrary, the applicability of these clauses to the dispute, if any, was triggered by the work stoppage itself. Consideration of whether the strike intruded on the management-rights clause or was permitted by the work-conditions clause may inform the arbitrator's ultimate decision on whether the strike violates the no-strike clause. Indeed, the question whether striking over a nonarbitrable issue violates other provisions of the collective-bargaining agreement may itself be an arbitrable dispute. The fact remains, however, that the strike itself was not over an arbitrable dispute and therefore may not be enjoined pending the arbitrator's ruling on the legality of the strike under the collective-bargaining agreement.

*   *   *   *

In conclusion, we hold that an employer's *   *   * action to enforce the provisions of a collective-bargaining agreement allegedly violated by a union's work stoppage involves a "labor dispute" within the meaning of the Norris-LaGuardia Act, without regard to the motivation underlying the union's decision not to provide labor. Under our decision in *Boys Markets* *   *   * when the underlying dispute is not arbitrable, the employer may not obtain injunctive relief pending the arbitrator's ruling on the legality of the strike under the collective-bargaining agreement.

DECISION AND REMEDY

The Supreme Court held that the parties still had to arbitrate to reach a conclusion, even though the dispute giving rise to the strike was not arbitrable. An injunction cannot be issued, even though this involved a political and not an economic issue.

Duty of Fair Representation

Both in negotiating and in administering a collective bargaining agreement, a union has an implied duty of fair representation for the employees it represents. A union must act fairly, impartially, and in good faith. The right to determine eligibility for its own membership remains with the union, but it is, nevertheless, obligated in collective bargaining to represent nonunion or minority union members without hostile discrimination and fairly, impartially, and in good faith.

The union has the power to exercise its discretion in contract negotiations in order to draw reasonable distinctions among groups of employees based on differences relevant to the authorized purposes of the contract, such as differences in seniority, type of work performed, competence, and skill. A relationship stills exist between federal labor statutory provisions and contract law as interpreted under state law. The following is a case in which a labor union sought to impose fines against union members who did not participate in a strike.

Case 21.5
LOCAL 165, INTERNATIONAL BROTHERHOOD OF ELECTRIC WORKERS v. BRADLEY
Illinois Court of Appeals, First District, 1986.
149 Ill.App.3d 193,
499 N.E.2d 577.

BACKGROUND AND FACTS *The plaintiff, Local 165, a labor union, went on strike against Illinois Bell Telephone Company. A labor picket line was established, which the defendants ignored. The defendants were employees of Illinois Bell Telephone Company and members of the union. The union gave notice to the defendants that a union trial board would conduct a hearing in order to determine the charges against them—namely, that they had crossed the picket line. The defendants failed to attend their hearings.*

At the hearing conducted by the union, the trial board found the defendants guilty, assessed $1,357 in fines against them, and barred them *from membership meetings for five years. When the defendants failed to pay, a suit was filed in small-claims court, and a judgment was entered against the defendants.*

SCARIANO, Justice.

* * * *

* * * [T]he law is well-settled in Illinois that the constitution and bylaws of labor unions are contracts binding upon the union and its members. * * * [T]here is no question but that a suit such as this, to collect union fines, can be filed in Illinois circuit courts.

Defendants had a right to appeal the decision of the local union's trial board, but they did not do so. * * * [This] suit [is] brought by a union to collect union fines by obtaining a money judgment in our courts that is enforceable by the full coercive power of this state.

* * * [T]he union is free to file such a suit, but it must abide by the same principles of contract law that would apply to any other litigant. * * * We find no Federal or state law principle that defendants' failure to appear and defend before the union's trial board, or to appeal within the union, prevents this court from determining whether the prerequisites for a contract action have been met. Consequently, we proceed to consider the merits of defendants' arguments.

[Court's discussion of the union's disciplinary actions]

* * * [T]he Illinois Supreme Court has recognized our courts' power to consider the basic fairness of disciplinary actions by voluntary unincorporated associations and the Labor Management Reporting & Disclosure Act of 1959 (LMRDA) provides:

"Nothing contained in this subchapter * * * shall limit the rights and remedies of any member of a labor organization under any State or Federal law before any court or other tribunal, or under the constitution and bylaws of any labor organization."

We need not decide the extent of court review, under Illinois law, of the adequacy of proof before a union trial board pursuant to the reasonableness inquiry recognized in *N.L.R.B. v. Allis-Chalmers Manufacturing Co.* * * * Defendants themselves filed records of the trial board proceedings. One record indicates that union member Dewey Viars stated that Bradley showed up for work and crossed the picket line on Monday, Tuesday, Wednesday, and Friday of the first week, all of the following week and the first few days of the third week of the strike. This covers the entire period of the strike, except for Thursday, August 11, 1983. However, John Cheeseman indicated that he saw Bradley cross the picket line August 8 through August 12. As to Stankoskey, James Leamy's written charge that he "crossed the picket line and worked throughout the strike" was read into the record, and Leamy stated that he had nothing to add. This covers the entire period for which Stankoskey was fined. In their affidavits in the circuit court, defendants did not deny that they worked every day during the strike. Thus, the record shows that plaintiff was entitled to judgment as a matter of law, under even the most stringent standards of proof, on the claim that defendants worked throughout the strike.

[Court's discussion of the union's trial board procedures]

Defendants next argue that there is a material issue of fact as to whether Local 165's trial board procedures constituted a fair hearing under the Labor Management Reporting and Disclosure Act. [T]he Act provides:

"No member of any labor organization may be fined, suspended, expelled or otherwise disciplined except for nonpayment of dues by such organization or by any officer thereof unless such member has been (A) served with written specific charges; (B) given a reasonable time to prepare his defense; (C) afforded a full and fair hearing.''

Statutes in existence at the time a contract is entered are considered as much a part of the contract as if they were expressly incorporated, and the contracting parties are deemed to accept these laws as part of the agreement. * * *

[This action is] brought by a union to collect fines for breach of its constitution and bylaws. This court has an obligation to construe contracts if possible so that they do not violate Federal law. * * * Nonetheless, * * * the LMRDA is not authority for broad-ranging judicial review of union actions and the requirements of the section are satisfied if there is *some* evidence to support the charges. This requirement was clearly satisfied for every day for which a fine was levied.

In addition, it has been held that a disciplinary sanction may be void under * * * the LMRDA if based upon facts and allegations not within the scope of the written charges on which the hearing was to have been held.

Similarly, it has been held, as a matter of Illinois law, that to enforce a disciplinary fine in state court, a union must furnish the disciplined member with advance notice of the charges and the union trial date. The record shows that notice was sent to Bradley a week before he was to appear before the union trial board and notice was delivered to Stankoskey 10 days before he was to appear. Both notices contained copies of the complaint filed against defendants by John Cheeseman charging them with violating Article 17, Section 1(17) by crossing a picket line August 8 through August 23. For example, Cheeseman's written complaint, which was mailed to Bradley, asserts that ''Brother Bradley crossed the I.B.E.W. picket line at approximately 8 A.M. on 8/8/83, and worked throughout the strike.'' Thus, Bradley was put on notice that he would have to face charges that he worked every day of the strike. Stankoskey received a similar notice. Both notices also provided:

> ''You may bring witnesses to give evidence in your behalf. You will be afforded the opportunity at the hearing to present any relevant evidence and to cross-examine any witnesses you may desire. You may, if you desire have an *IBEW member* act as your counsel.'' (Emphasis in the original.)

As previously noted, defendants failed to attend their hearings.

DECISION AND REMEDY   *The Illinois court found that an employee may be fined by the union of which he or she is a member. These fines can be enforced by the courts.*

FACING A LEGAL ISSUE **Unfair Labor Practices**

Although you have asked your employees not to discuss their salaries with each other, you learn that one of your employees has not only been talking about what he makes but has also been encouraging others to do so.

You have called the employee into your office. "Listen, Mark," you begin, "you knew when I hired you what the rule was. All you're going to do is cause jealousy by comparing salaries. I can justify the differences in various employees' pay, but, if I have to explain to a worker why he is not as good as the next, he's not going to believe it anyway and it's just going to hurt morale."

But Mark tells you, "We have no way of knowing if you're treating us fairly unless we talk about what we all make. The secrecy only benefits you by keeping us from being able to negotiate with you to pay all of us what you should."

Your immediate response may be to fire this employee. After all, he understood when he was hired that you expected employees to refrain from comparing salaries, and he implicitly agreed to this when he accepted the job. Federal labor laws, however, may prohibit you from firing him.

Section 7 of the National Labor Relations Act safeguards the right of employees to engage in concerted activities "for the purpose of collective bargaining or other mutual aid or protection." While most cases under Section 7 involve strikes or other activities by unions, the language of the section protects not only union activities but also activities of all workers. The comparing of salaries by your workers could be viewed as their gathering information in order to obtain more equitable pay scales. Thus, although your employees are not organized as a union, their discussions could be construed to fall under the protection of Section 7, and your firing of the employee could be an unfair labor practice.

Even if Mark's attempts to instigate salary discussions with the other employees had been unsuccessful, his own activities would still be protected, and, as long as he does not engage in threats or violence, he may not be fired. You could fire Mark if he were insubordinate, disloyal, or disobedient, as long as these behaviors were not part of a protected concerted activity.

Summary

This chapter has covered statutory regulation of labor and labor unions. We have seen that federal law has had a significant impact in both areas.

The Fair Labor Standards Act establishes a minimum wage of (currently) $3.35 per hour, overtime provisions requiring time and a half pay for any work over forty hours per week, certain record-keeping requirements, and child labor protection. Some employees are exempt under this act, but the great majority of American businesses are bound by its terms. The act is enforced by the Wage and Hour Division of the Department of Labor.

Federal acts govern other labor-related concerns. Social security provisions include old age, survivors, and disability insurance and Medicare. Unemployment compensation is handled through both federal and state funding. State workers' compensation laws cover employees injured while on the job. For an injury to be covered by these laws, the only questions asked are whether the injury was accidental and whether it arose in the course of employment.

Federal law also attempts to ensure safe and healthful working conditions for practically every employee in the country through the Occupational Safety and Health Act.

Employees have the right to organize unions and to participate in collective bargaining. These rights are protected by federal statutory provisions. The National Labor Relations Act of 1935 is the cornerstone of protection for the labor movement. This act has been amended several times to reflect changing attitudes toward the labor movement.

Certain activities are illegal under the NLRA. It outlaws the closed shop in which a person must be a union member in order to be employed. A union shop requires a person to join a union after employment has started. An agency shop requires a person to pay initiation fees and dues, but the person is not required to join the union. These agreements are legal in the absence of a state right-to-work law.

The National Labor Relations Board (NLRB) was established by the 1935 act. It is charged with supervising union elections and with determining when an unfair labor practice has occurred. Both unions and employers have certain specified rights when there is an election, and each has a duty to bargain in good faith with the other.

Key Terms

agency shop **529**
closed shop **529**
Employee Retirement Income
   Security Act (ERISA) **523**
Fair Labor Standards Act
   (FLSA) **518**
Federal Insurance
   Contributions Act (FICA)
   522
Federal Unemployment Tax
   Act (FUTA) **523**
Labor-Management Relations
   Act (Taft-Hartley Act) **529**

Labor-Management Reporting
   and Disclosure Act
   (Landrum-Griffin Act) **529**
Medicare **523**
National Labor Relations Act
   (Wagner Act) **529**
National Labor Relations
   Board (NLRB) **529**
Norris-LaGuardia Act **528**
Occupational Safety and
   Health Act **526**
Occupational Safety and

Health Administration
   (OSHA) **526**
Old Age, Survivors, and
   Disability Insurance
   (OASDI) **522**
right-to-work laws **529**
Social Security Act **522**
unemployment compensation
   523
union shop **529**
workers' compensation laws
   524

Questions and Case Problems

1. Workers' compensation statutes cover the injuries, disease, or death of employees while at work. Professor Able is employed by a private university in California. He is attending a professional meeting. Prior to traveling, he requested permission and travel money to attend the meeting. He was granted permission, but was not granted the travel money. After the meeting, but three hours prior to his airplane trip to return home, he visited a cathedral that is noted for its beauty. When he emerged from the cathedral, he stumbled down the stairs and injured himself. He was taken by ambulance to the hospital where he was seen by the emergency room physician. He was treated and

released in time to catch the return flight. Are his injuries covered by workers' compensation? Did the injuries occur while at work?

2. Hamburger Joint is a nationwide franchised fast-food outlet. The management is very interested in teenage unemployment. Consequently, it creates a program for hiring teens. The program would hire fifty people in each age bracket. The fourteen-year-olds would be janitors, the fifteen-year-olds would work at the counter taking orders, the sixteen-year-olds would learn to cook the various foods, and the seventeen-year-olds would drive the company vehicles and deliver the food orders. Do you see any violations of the child labor laws in this program?

3. Joseph owns an interstate business engaged in manufacturing and selling boats. Joseph has 500 nonunion employees. Representatives of these employees approach Joseph seeking a four-day, ten-hours-per-day work week. Joseph is concerned that this proposal will require him to pay his employees time and a half after eight hours per day. Discuss fully which federal act concerns Joseph and whether the proposal will require Joseph to pay time and a half.

4. Yeshiva University is a private university. The faculty association, acting as a bargaining agent for the full-time faculty members, filed a petition with the NLRB. The university opposed this on the basis that faculty members are managerial personnel and are not under the jurisdiction of the NLRB. Do you think college professors are managers or workers? [NLRB v. Yeshiva University, 444 U.S. 672, 100 S.Ct. 856, 63 L.Ed.2d 115 (1979)]

5. Gary Segler was employed by Caterpillar Tractor Company. About twenty-five feet from his work was a large industrial oven that had a conveyor system going through it. Molds for parts were placed on the conveyor belt and sent through the oven. One day the conveyor belt was not operating, and Segler placed a pie inside the oven. As he was retrieving it, the conveyor system started functioning, which resulted in a mold striking him, causing serious injuries. The corporation took the position that the injuries were not work related and therefore Segler was not covered by workers' compensation. Were they correct? [Segler v. Industrial Commission, 81 Ill.2d 125, 406 N.E.2d 542 (1980)]

6. Jiffy June Farms had properly paid overtime to its employees. It entered into a collective bargaining agreement that purportedly exempted it from paying time and a half for overtime but that increased basic wages considerably. The lower court found that this was a willful vi-

olation of the FLSA. Do you agree? [Coleman v. Jiffy June Farms, 458 F.2d 1139 (5th Cir. 1972)]

7. Sure-Tan, Inc.'s employees were organized by a union. Afterward, the president of Sure-Tan, Inc. sent a letter to the Immigration and Naturalization Service (INS) asking it to check to see if there were any illegal aliens working for Sure-Tan. The INS investigated and found five Mexican nationals without work visas. They were deported. The union claimed that this was an unfair labor practice and that it amounted to members being terminated due to union activity. What do you think was the United States Supreme Court's position concerning these facts? [Sure-Tan, Inc. v. NLRB, 467 U.S. 883, 104 S.Ct. 2803, 81 L.Ed.2d 732 (1984)]

8. James Brown was a union member and worked for City Disposal Systems, Inc. He was ordered to drive a truck that he thought had faulty brakes. Because of this, he refused to drive and was discharged. He filed an unfair labor practice charge that challenged his dismissal. What was the result? [NLRB v. City Disposal Systems, Inc., 465 U.S. 822, 104 S.Ct. 1505, 79 L.Ed.2d 839 (1984)]

9. At an REA shipping terminal, a conveyor belt was inoperative because an electrical circuit had shorted out. The manager called a licensed electrical contractor. When the contractor arrived, REA's maintenance supervisor was in the circuit breaker room. The floor was wet, and the maintenance supervisor was using sawdust to try to soak up the water. While the licensed electrical contractor was attempting to fix the short circuit, standing on the wet floor, he was electrocuted. Simultaneously, REA's maintenance supervisor, who was standing on a wooden platform, was burned and knocked unconscious. OSHA wanted to fine REA Express $1,000 for failure to furnish a place of employment free from recognized hazards. What was the result? [REA Express, Inc. v. Brennan, 495 F.2d 822 (2d Cir. 1974)]

Chapter 22   Employment Law and Equal Opportunity

Laborin' man an' laborin' woman
Hev one glory an' one shame;
Ev'y thin' thet's done inhuman
Injers all on 'em the same.

A Fable for Critics

OUTLINE

Introduction

At common law, both employment and membership in labor unions were considered private contractual matters. Little or no protection was provided against arbitrary and discriminatory actions on the part of employers or of officers of labor unions. Not until the National Labor Relations Act of 1935 did employees obtain some protection against discrimination. Under the act, employers are prohibited from discriminating against employees or applicants because of union or organizational activity. Within a decade after the act, the United States Supreme Court prohibited certain forms of racial discrimination by unions.

This chapter looks first at the federal laws that prohibit discrimination and then discusses affirmative action plans.

The Civil Rights Act of 1964—Title VII

Title VII of the **Civil Rights Act** of 1964 prohibits discrimination in all areas of employment on the basis of race, color, religion, or national origin or on the basis of sex, including pregnancy, childbirth, or abortion. Title VII does not prohibit discrimination based on physical disability or age because these areas are covered by other federal statutory provisions. Title VII coverage extends to state and local governments as well as to specified federal employers.

Limitations of Title VII

Title VII is limited to employers with at least fifteen workers, labor unions with at least fifteen members, and employment agencies that obtain workers for an employer covered by the law. In order for Title VII to apply, the activities of the employer, labor union, or employment agency must be part of or must affect interstate commerce, which is interpreted very broadly.

Noncovered Employment Situations

Title VII exempts religious associations and religious educational institutions from the prohibition against discrimination on the basis of religion. Whenever these organizations are employers, they are prohibited from discriminating on the basis of sex, race, or national origin. Congress has exempted itself not only from Title VII but also from all of the Civil Rights Act of 1964. Except for specified federal employers, the federal government is exempt from Title VII, since it is prohibited from discriminating on the basis of race, color, religion, sex, and national origin under other acts and executive orders. Indian tribes and departments of the District of Columbia are also exempt.

Theories of Discrimination Under Title VII

Two basic but not mutually exclusive theories of discrimination are covered under Title VII: **disparate impact** and **disparate treatment**. Often both disparate treatment and disparate impact claims are combined in the same case.

Disparate Impact Sometimes employment practices may appear neutral on the surface, but they nonetheless adversely affect a protected class. This is the nature of disparate impact discrimination cases. With such cases, statistics on the impact of the practice or device on a protected class are not only relevant but are also often the only way to establish a *prima facie* case that the practice has a disproportionately adverse effect on a protected class. In the following case, the Supreme Court reviews an employment practice that appeared neutral but that in fact had a disparate impact on black employees.

Case 22.1
GRIGGS v. DUKE POWER CO.
Supreme Court of the United States, 1971.
401 U.S. 424, 91 S.Ct. 849, 28 L.Ed.2d 158.

BACKGROUND AND FACTS *Thirteen black employees of Duke Power Company brought this class action suit against their employer. Prior to July 2, 1965, the effective date of the Civil Rights Act of 1964, the company had hired blacks in only one of its five departments, the Labor Department; there, the highest-paying jobs paid less than the lowest-paying jobs in the other departments in which only whites were employed. In 1955 the company* *had instituted a policy of requiring a high school diploma for initial assignment to any department except labor. When the company abandoned its policy of restricting blacks to the Labor Department in 1965, completion of high school was made a prerequisite for transfer from labor to any other department.*

In 1965, the company added a further requirement for new employees in all departments other than labor—satisfactory scores on two professionally prepared aptitude tests. Completion of high school alone continued to render employees eligible for transfer to the more desirable departments if they had been employed by Duke Power prior to the time the testing requirement was instituted. Employees who lacked a high school education could qualify for transfer to other departments by passing the two aptitude tests.

The district court found that the company had followed a policy of overt racial discrimination prior to enactment of the Civil Rights Act of 1964 but that its discriminatory conduct had ceased. The court of appeals concluded that there was no showing of a discriminatory purpose in the adoption of the diploma and test requirements and, therefore, no violation of the Civil Rights Act. The Supreme Court then reviewed the case to determine whether such requirements were unlawful under Title VII if they were not shown to be job related.

BURGER, Justice.

The objective of Congress in the enactment of Title VII is plain from the language of the statute. It was to achieve equality of employment opportunities and remove barriers that have operated in the past to favor an identifiable group of white employees over other employees. Under the Act, practices, procedures, or tests neutral on their face, and even neutral in terms of intent, cannot be maintained if they operate to "freeze" the status quo of prior discriminatory employment practices.

The Court of Appeals' opinion, and the pretrial dissent, agreed that, on the record in the present case, "whites register far better on the Company's alternative requirements" than Negroes. This consequence would appear to be directly traceable to race. Basic intelligence must have the means of articulation to manifest itself fairly in a testing process. Because they are Negroes, petitioners have long received inferior education in segregated schools and this Court expressly recognized these differences in *Gaston County v. United States*. There, because of the inferior education received by Negroes in North Carolina, this Court barred the institution of a literacy test for voter registration on the ground that the test would abridge the right to vote indirectly on account of race. Congress did not intend by Title VII, however, to guarantee a job to every person regardless of qualifications. In short, the Act does not command that any person be hired simply because he was formerly the subject of discrimination, or because he is a member of a minority group. Discriminatory preference for any group, minority or majority, is precisely and only what Congress has proscribed. What is required by Congress is the removal of artificial, arbitrary, and unnecessary barriers to employment when the barriers operate invidiously to discriminate on the basis of racial or other impermissible classification.

Congress has now provided that tests or criteria for employment or promotion may not provide equality of opportunity merely in the sense of the fabled offer of milk to the stork and the fox. On the contrary, Congress has now required that the posture and condition of the job-seeker be taken into account. It has—to resort again to the fable—provided that the vessel in which the milk is proffered be one all seekers can use. The Act proscribes not only overt discrimination but also practices that are fair in form, but discriminatory in operation. The touchstone is business necessity. If an employment practice which operates to exclude Negroes cannot be shown to be related to job performance, the practice is prohibited.

DECISION AND REMEDY   *The judgment of the court of appeals was reversed. The Supreme Court held that diploma and test requirements had to be job related. Duke Power must prove that the test and degree requirements were necessary for the job.*

Disparate Treatment   The simplest form of discrimination involves the treatment of a member of one class that differs from the treatment of other employees or other applicants. When the plaintiff-employee has established a *prima facie* case of discrimination, the defendant-employer has the burden of articulating some legitimate, nondiscriminatory reason for the employee's rejection.

If the defendant is successful in rebutting the *prima facie* case, the plaintiff, in the third stage of a disparate treatment case, must prove that the reason articulated by the employer is not legitimate but is rather a pretext to cover up discrimination. As we see in the next case, the United States Supreme Court has set out the steps for establishing a *prima facie* case of disparate treatment under Title VII.

Case 22.2

McDONNELL DOUGLAS CORP. v. GREEN

Supreme Court of the United States, 1973.
411 U.S. 792, 93 S.Ct. 1817, 36 L.Ed.2d 668.

BACKGROUND AND FACTS   *Respondent Green, the plaintiff in this case, worked for the petitioner, McDonnell Douglas Corporation, as a mechanic and laboratory technician for eight years before he was laid off in the course of a general reduction in McDonnell Douglas's work force. Green, a black man, protested that his discharge was racially motivated and that the petitioner's hiring practices were racially discriminatory.*

As part of this protest, Green and other members of the Congress on Racial Equality stalled their cars on the main roads leading to the petitioner's plant in order to block access to the plant during the morning shift change. On another occasion, a padlock was placed on the door of a building to prevent the petitioner's employees from leaving. The extent of Green's involvement in the lock-in was unclear.

After these events, McDonnell Douglas advertised for mechanics and Green applied for reemployment. McDonnell Douglas refused to rehire the respondent because of his participation in the "stall-in" and the lock-in. The respondent filed a complaint with the Equal Employment Opportunity Commission claiming that the petitioner had refused to rehire him because of his race and his involvement in the civil rights movement.

The respondent alleged that the petitioner's action violated section 703(a)(1) of the Civil Rights Act of 1964, which prohibits racial discrimination in any employment decision, and section 704(a), which forbids discrimination against applicants or employees for attempting to protest discriminatory conditions of employment.

The court of appeals ruled that unlawful protests were not protected activities under section 704(a), but ordered the case remanded to the lower court for a trial of Green's claim that McDonnell Douglas's refusal to rehire him was racially discriminatory. The Supreme Court reviewed the case to clarify the standards governing actions based on employment discrimination.

POWELL, Justice.

* * * *

We agree with the Court of Appeals that absence of a Commission finding of reasonable cause cannot bar suit under an appropriate section of Title VII and that the District Judge erred in dismissing respondent's claim of racial discrimination under sec. 703(a)(1).

* * * *

The critical issue before us concerns the order and allocation of proof in a private, non-class action challenging employment discrimination. The language of Title VII makes plain the purpose of Congress to assure equality of employment opportunities and to eliminate those discriminatory practices and devices which have fostered racially stratified job environments to the disadvantage of minority citizens.

* * * *

The complainant in a Title VII trial must carry the initial burden under the statute of establishing a *prima facie* case of racial discrimination. This may be done by showing (i) that he belongs to a racial minority; (ii) that he applied and was qualified for a job for which the employer was seeking applicants; (iii) that, despite his qualifications, he was rejected; and (iv) that, after his rejection, the position remained open and the employer continued to seek applicants from persons of complainant's qualifications. In the instant case, we agree with the Court of Appeals that respondent proved a *prima facie* case. Petitioner sought mechanics, respondent's trade, and continued to do so after respondent's rejection. Petitioner, moreover, does not dispute respondent's qualifications and acknowledges that his past work performance in petitioner's employ was ''satisfactory.''

The burden then must shift to the employer to articulate some legitimate, nondiscriminatory reason for the employee's rejection. We need not attempt in the instant case to detail every matter which fairly could be recognized as a reasonable basis for a refusal to hire. Here petitioner has assigned respondent's participation in unlawful conduct against it as the cause for his rejection. We think that this suffices to discharge petitioner's burden of proof at this stage and to meet respondent's *prima facie* case of discrimination.

The Court of Appeals intimated, however, that petitioner's stated reason for refusing to rehire respondent was a ''subjective'' rather than objective criterion which ''carr[ies] little weight in rebutting charges of discrimination.'' This was among the statements which caused the dissenting judge to read the opinion as taking ''the position that such unlawful acts as Green committed against McDonnell would not legally entitle McDonnell to refuse to hire him, even though no racial motivation was involved   *   *   *.'' Regardless of whether this was the intended import of the opinion, we think the court below seriously underestimated the rebuttal weight to which petitioner's reasons were entitled. Respondent admittedly had taken part in a carefully planned ''stall-in,'' designed to tie up access to egress from petitioner's plant at a peak traffic hour. Nothing in Title VII compels an employer to absolve and rehire one who had seized and forcibly retained an employer's factory buildings in an illegal sit-down strike.

* * * *

Petitioner's reason for rejection thus suffices to meet the *prima facie* case, but the inquiry must not end here. While Title VII does not, without more, compel rehiring of respondent, neither does it permit petitioner to use respondent's conduct as a pretext for the sort of discrimination prohibited by sec. 703(a)(1). On remand, respondent must, as the Court of Appeals recognized, be afforded a fair opportunity to show that petitioner's stated reason for respondent's rejection was in fact pretext. Especially relevant to such a showing would be evidence that white employees involved in acts against petitioner of comparable seriousness to the ''stall-in'' were nevertheless retained or rehired. Petitioner may justifiably refuse to rehire one who was engaged in unlawful, disruptive acts against it, but only if this criterion is applied alike to members of all races.

Other evidence that may be relevant to any showing of pretext includes facts as to the petitioner's treatment of respondent during his prior term of employment; petitioner's reaction, if any, to respondent's legitimate civil rights activities; and petitioner's general policy and practices with respect to minority employment. On the latter point, statistics as to petitioner's employment policy and practice may be helpful to a determination of whether petitioner's refusal to rehire respondent in this case conformed to a general pattern of discrimination against blacks.

* * * *

In sum, respondent should have been allowed to pursue his claim under sec. 703(a)(1). If the evidence on retrial is substantially in accord with that before us in this case, we think that respondent carried his burden of establishing a *prima facie* case of racial discrimination and that petitioner successfully rebutted that case. But this does not end the matter. On retrial, respondent must be afforded a fair opportunity to demonstrate that petitioner's assigned reason for refusing to re-employ was a pretext or discriminatory in its application. If the District Judge so finds, he must order a prompt and appropriate remedy. In the absence of such a finding, petitioner's refusal to rehire must stand.

DECISION AND REMEDY *Green's case was returned to the trial court. Green would have the opportunity to show that McDonnell Douglas Corporation's reason for refusing to rehire him was merely a pretext for discrimination in his case.*

COMMENTS *The order and allocation of proof set out in this case apply to a private individual's action challenging employment discrimination. The requirements for establishing a* prima facie *case omit any reference to the employer's intent and are nonsubjective elements of proof. Note also that the court mentions nothing in its first-stage requirements for a* prima facie *case about evidence of systematic discrimination by the employer, such as statistics concerning the composition of the employer's work force.*

To reiterate, the court requires in the first stage of such a case that the plaintiff show: (1)) that he or she belongs to a protected class; (2) that he or she applied for, and was qualified for, a job for which the employer was seeking applicants; (3) that despite the plaintiff's qualification for the job, he or she was rejected; and (4) that, after the plaintiff's rejection, the position remained open and the employer continued to seek applicants among people of the plaintiff's qualifications.

Patterns of Resistance

The government can bring suit through the **Equal Employment Opportunity Commission (EEOC)** against an employer when a pattern of discrimination is evident. These cases can be brought by the EEOC on the basis of disparate treatment or disparate impact. The government in these "pattern and practice" cases nonetheless bears the initial burden of establishing a *prima facie* case of discrimination. More than the mere occurrence of isolated or accidental or sporadic discriminatory acts must be proved.

The government must show that a protected class is suffering from discrimination because of a company's standard operating procedure. For example, the government can make out a *prima facie* case by showing large statistical disparities between the racial composition of the general work force and that of the more specialized employment positions. Then the government can strengthen its case by presenting evidence of specific instances of discrimination.

Specific Applications of Title VII

Employees' grievances about various types of discrimination represent important concerns. Title VII has been applied to cases involving sex discrimination, sexual harassment, pregnancy discrimination, pension and life insurance, and discrimination based on religion, national origin, or race.

Sex Discrimination Discrimination based on sex is prohibited under Title VII. Title VII, however, does not prohibit discrimination based on sexual or affectional preferences, nor does it protect transsexuals. Since its enactment, Title VII has been used to strike down protective state legislation, such as laws that prevented women from undertaking jobs deemed too dangerous or strenuous by the state. In reality, such "protective" state legislation often prevented women from obtaining higher-paying jobs. Under EEOC guidelines, state statutes may not be used as a defense to a charge of illegal sex discrimination.

Sex-plus discrimination has been made illegal by Title VII. This discrimination involves discrimination based on sex, plus an additional element. For example, women with preschool-age children have been refused employment. Now it is illegal for an employer to refuse to hire these women if the employer accepts men with pre-school-age children. An employer may not require that female employees be single if male employees may be married. EEOC guidelines forbid advertising jobs in publications as male or female, unless sex is a bona fide occupational qualification for the particular job.

Sexual Harassment By the late 1970s, the federal courts began ruling that sexual harassment constituted illegal sex discrimination under Title VII. Today, under EEOC guidelines, all unwelcome sexual advances, requests, or other physical or verbal conduct of a sexual nature are illegal sexual harassment if submission is a condition of employment or a basis of pay, promotion, or of other employment decisions. If this unwanted conduct interferes with an employee's job performance or creates an intimidating, hostile, or offensive environment, the conduct is illegal. The employer under some restricted circumstances also may be held liable for illegal sexual harassment perpetrated by supervisors in the company.

Pregnancy Discrimination Title VII was amended in 1978 by the **Pregnancy Discrimination Act**. This act redefined sex discrimination to include discrimination based on pregnancy, childbirth, or related medical conditions. Based on this amendment, health and disability insurance plans must cover pregnancy, childbirth, or related medical conditions in the same way that they cover any other temporary disability.

An employer must provide leaves of absence for pregnant women on the same terms and conditions as those provided to any other worker for any other temporary disability. A woman who is pregnant cannot be forced to take a maternity leave for any specified period of time. As long as she is capable of performing her duties, she must be allowed to work. The 1978 amendment applies both to married and unmarried women and to any aspect of employment.

Pension and Life Insurance Because women have a longer life expectancy than men, virtually all pension and annuity plans required either that women pay a higher annual amount to receive the same yearly retirement benefits or that women pay the same annual amount but retire with fewer annual benefits. Today, employers are required to treat employees as individuals rather than as a class of men or of women. Even though women as a class do live longer than men, many women do not live as long as the average man, and many men outlive the average woman.

Discrimination Based on Religion Pursuant to Title VII, employers must make reasonable accommodations to an employee's or a prospective employee's religious practices, beliefs, or observances, as long as the employer is able to do so without undue hardship in the conduct of her or his business. The following case shows what a court may consider in determining undue hardship for a business that is confronted with an employee who desires a certain day off.

Case 22.3
PROTOS v. VOLKSWAGEN OF AMERICA
United States Court of Appeals, Third Circuit, 1986.
797 F.2d 129.

BACKGROUND AND FACTS *Angeline Protos was employed by Volkswagen of American, Inc. She was terminated when she refused to work on Saturdays because of her religious beliefs. She brought this action under Title VII of the Civil Rights Act.*

ADAMS, Judge.

Under Title VII of the Civil Rights Act of 1964, employers are required to make reasonable accommodation for the religious practices of their employees. In this case, the district court ruled that Volkswagen had violated the statute by refusing to accommodate the request of an assembly line employee to be excused from overtime work on Saturday, her Sabbath. This appeal requires us to consider whether the trial judge erred in determining that accommodation of the request would not cause the company undue hardship.

Angeline S. Protos is a member of the Worldwide Church of God. Under the tenets of that church, the Sabbath lasts from sunset Friday to sunset Saturday. Work is prohibited during this time, and failure to observe the Sabbath is cause for excommunication.

* * * *

The principal issue before the district court was the degree of hardship that accommodating Protos's request for Saturdays off would have imposed on Volkswagen. Finding that "defendant suffered no economic loss" because of Protos's absence, and that the "efficiency, production, quality and morale" of her segment of the Trim Department and the entire assembly line remained intact without her, the district court ruled that Volkswagen could have accommodated her "without undue hardship and at no cost." Thus, the company was held to have violated the statute.

Section 703(a)(1) of the Civil Rights Act of 1964, Title VII, makes it an unlawful employment practice to "discharge * * *, or otherwise to discriminate against any individual with respect to his compensation, terms, conditions or privileges of employment, because of such individual's race, color, religion, sex, or national origin." Section 701(j) of the Act, added by Congress in a 1972 amendment, elaborated on this provision by defining religion:

> The term 'religion' includes all aspects of religious observance and practice, as well as belief, unless an employer demonstrates that he is unable to reasonably accommodate an employee's or prospective employee's religious observance or practice without undue hardship on the conduct of the employer's business.

* * * *

* * * [S]everal courts of appeals have set forth guidelines to use in evaluating a religious accommodation case: those guidelines are modeled after the shifting burdens of proof employed in race and gender discrimination suits under Title VII. A plaintiff must first establish a *prima facie* case, by showing: ''(1) he or she has a bona fide religious belief that conflicts with an employment requirement; (2) he or she informed the employer of this belief; (3) he or she was disciplined for failure to comply with the conflicting employment requirement.''

Once a plaintiff establishes a *prima facie* case, the burden then shifts to the employer to produce evidence showing that it cannot reasonably accommodate the worker without incurring undue hardship.

In the case at hand, the district judge followed these guidelines in considering the evidence. His determination that Protos established a *prima facie* case is not disputed on appeal. Volkswagen agrees that Protos's religious beliefs are sincere, and it is clear that her religion forbade her to work on Saturdays. It is also evident that she informed her employer of her beliefs and was disciplined for failure to work on Saturdays.

Thus, the primary issue is whether the district court erred in determining that the company would not have to incur even a ''*de minimis* cost'' to accommodate Protos. * * *

Here, the question of hardship was vigorously disputed at trial. The evidence showed that Volkswagen regularly maintained, along with employees assigned to specific posts on the assembly line, a crew of roving absentee relief operators (ARO) to be deployed as substitutes for absent employees. Protos introduced witnesses who testified that her job was easily learned, and that the line operated as efficiently when an ARO served in her stead as when she performed the job. Volkswagen's witnesses, by contrast, testified that the line operated with diminished efficiency in Protos's absence.

The court resolved this conflict in favor of Protos, finding that ''plaintiff's witnesses were more credible than the witnesses presented by the defendant,'' and that ''the efficiency, production, quality and morale of trim 15 and the entire assembly line remained intact during her absence.'' While Volkswagen argues that plant-wide absenteeism was especially high on Saturdays, and that Protos's absence therefore was felt more than it would otherwise have been, evidence supporting this contention was presented to the district court, and rejected as unpersuasive. * * * *

To summarize, we hold that the district court did not err in ruling that Volkswagen could have accommodated Protos without ''undue hardship,'' and that Title VII's religious accommodation requirement does not violate the Establishment Clause.

DECISION AND REMEDY

The court found that Protos had been discriminated against based on her religious views. In doing so, the court stated that the following three factors must be established to have a prima facie *case: (1) The employee has a bona fide religious belief that conflicts with an employment requirement; (2) he or she informed the employer of this belief; (3) he or she was disciplined for failure to comply with the conflicting employment requirement. Once a plaintiff has established a* prima facie *case, the burden then shifts to the employer to produce evidence showing that the company cannot reasonably accommodate the worker without incurring undue hardship.*

Discrimination Based on National Origin While prohibiting discrimination because of national origin, Title VII does not define the term. By case law, national origin refers to the country where a person is born or from which his or her ancestors came. In 1980, the EEOC issued guidelines that defined national origin discrimination to include denial of equal employment opportunity because of an individual's, or his or her ancestors', place of origin, or because an individual has the physical, cultural, or linguistic characteristics of a national origin group.

The question of discrimination against aliens is a thorny one, but Title VII does not prohibit discrimination against aliens. Such discrimination may, however, violate the Civil Rights Act of 1866 (discussed in the next subsection), or it may violate a union's duty of fair representation. The Civil Rights Act of 1866 made it illegal to discriminate, contractually or otherwise, based on race.

Title VII's prohibition of national origin discrimination forbids a foreign corporation doing business in the United States from discriminating in favor of its own nationals. This prohibition is waived if such discrimination is permitted specifically by a treaty.

Discrimination Based on Race Discrimination in employment on the basis of race has existed in this country for over 300 years. Over the last 100 years, serious attempts have been made to live up to the words in the Declaration of Independence "We hold these truths to be self-evident, that all Men are created equal. * * *" The Civil Rights Acts of 1866, 1870, 1875, and 1964, along with the Thirteenth, Fourteenth, and Fifteenth Amendments (called the Civil War Amendments) to the Constitution, have been applied to outlaw racial discrimination. Congress has not only forbidden racial discrimination by the government but has also directly legislated that private individuals cannot violate the constitutional rights of other individuals.

Today, Title VII is the cornerstone of employment discrimination law. **Affirmative action** is used to give work opportunities to those who have been deprived of employment based on race or other nonwork-related criteria. Affirmative action consists of a set of programs, some of which

are required by court decrees, some by national and state legislation, and some by administrative regulation.

Title VII's protection has always applied to nonwhite classes. Recent court decisions have concluded that Title VII prohibits racial discrimination against the white class (called **reverse discrimination**) based on the same standards applicable to nonwhites.

The Administration and Enforcement of Title VII

The Equal Employment Opportunity Commission is a five-member administrative agency created by the 1964 Civil Rights Act to administer Title VII. Members are appointed by the president with the advice and consent of the Senate. No more than three members may be of the same political party. Each serves a five-year term.

The EEOC can issue interpretive guidelines and regulations that do not, however, have the force of law. Rather, they give notice of the commission's enforcement policy. The EEOC also has been charged with investigatory powers. It has broad authority to require the production of documentary evidence, to hold hearings, and to subpoena and examine witnesses under oath. The EEOC may also require the covered parties to keep statistics and records of employment and employment practices.

When an aggrieved person files charges or when the commission members determine that a pattern or practice of illegal discrimination exists, the commission can litigate. Nonetheless, the commission must have the opportunity to attempt conciliation between the parties prior to filing the suit.

EEOC Procedures Any person claiming to be aggrieved may file a charge of discrimination with the EEOC. A member of the EEOC or others acting on behalf of an aggrieved person may likewise file a charge. Generally speaking, the charge must be filed within 180 days after the discriminatory action. Whenever a state or local fair employment practices agency exists, the commission will defer to it for sixty days. If, at the end of sixty days, the dispute has not been resolved, then the EEOC will take over.

Within ten days of the filing of a charge with the EEOC (or within ten days of the EEOC taking over), the agency must notify the employer. Once notified, the employer is prohibited from retaliation against the charging employee. Once the employer has been notified, the EEOC investigates the charge. If it finds reasonable cause to believe that Title VII has been violated, it will attempt to resolve the dispute by informal means.

Even when both the EEOC and the company are willing to accept a settlement, if the charging party does not accept it, his or her right to go to court to seek more favorable results cannot be prejudiced. If, on the other hand, the EEOC does not find reasonable cause to believe a violation has occurred, it will notify the charging party and inform him or her of the right to pursue the matter in court. When informal means do not result in a settlement, the EEOC may bring an action thirty days after the charge is filed.

Statutory Defenses Title VII's prohibitions against discrimination are subject to three main statutory exceptions:

1. Bona fide occupational qualifications (BFOQs);

2. Bona fide seniority or merit systems; and
3. Professionally developed ability tests.

Bona Fide Occupational Qualifications This defense allows discrimination in hiring and referrals where sex, religion, or national origin (but not race) is a "bona fide occupational qualification reasonably necessary to the normal operation of that particular business." Such a defense has been very narrowly interpreted by the courts. For example, the BFOQ defense is allowed in situations where sex or national origin is inherently part of the qualification for the job, such as for a wet nurse, or is necessary for authenticity, such as for actors or actresses.

The burden is on the defendant to establish a BFOQ defense. To do so, the defendant must show that the alleged discrimination is a business necessity. Customer preference does not make a particular sex, religion, or national origin a BFOQ.

Bona Fide Seniority Systems It is not unlawful for there to be differences in the terms, conditions, or privileges of employment based on a bona fide seniority (or merit) system. The differences, how-

ever, cannot be the result of an intent to discriminate. Most collective bargaining agreements include detailed seniority systems. Indeed, such
seniority systems are one of the most important
aspects of collective bargaining agreements.

In order for the seniority system to qualify as
an exception to Title VII, the system must be bona
fide. Four factors are necessary for a seniority
system to be bona fide:

1. The system must apply equally to all persons.
2. The seniority units (that is, occupational
groupings for purposes of hiring, promoting, and
terminating) must follow industry practices, and
the units must constitute separate collective bargaining units.
3. The seniority system must not have its genesis
in racial discrimination.
4. The system must be maintained free from any
illegal racial purpose.

Professionally   Developed   Ability   Tests
Employers may give and act on the results of any
professionally developed ability test. An ability
test, its administration, and the actions based on
the results must not be intended to discriminate in
any prohibited way. The employer must meet
the burden of proving that the particular test is job
related if the test has the effect of eliminating a
disproportionate number of members of a protected class. Job relation ordinarily must be proved
by validation studies meeting professional
standards.

The Equal Employment Opportunity Commission has adopted general guidelines for the use
of tests and has specified standards for validation.
Under these guidelines, the selection rate for
members of protected classes must be at least 80
percent of that for the group of applicants with
the highest selection rate.

Equal Pay Act

The **Equal Pay Act of 1963** was enacted as an
amendment to the Fair Labor Standards Act of
1938. The act is administered by the Equal Employment Opportunity Commission, and it concerns only sex-based discrimination and questions

of pay. Basically, it prohibits discrimination in
wages paid for equal work on jobs that require
equal skills, effort, and responsibility and that are
performed under similar conditions. Job content
rather than job description controls in all cases.

For the equal pay requirements to apply, the
act requires that male and female employees must
work at the same establishment. Thus, employees
of the same employer working at different establishments are not covered by the act. The courts,
however, are moving away from the physical separation test when attempting to determine what is
a single establishment. Rather, they are looking
more at questions of central authority and movement of employees. The less centralized the authority over a physically separate job location and
the less movement of employees there is between
it and other locations, the greater is the likelihood
of finding a single establishment.

When equal pay claims arise, the issue is not
the equivalence of the employees' skills and training. The issue is whether the jobs performed by
the two employees are substantially equal or not.
Small differences in job content do not justify
higher pay for one sex. The courts look to primary
duties involved in the two jobs. For example, a
barber and a beautician are considered to do essentially equal work. So, too, are a tailor and a
seamstress.

Enforcement

The government or private parties may bring suit
under the Equal Pay Act. If, however, the government sues on behalf of a particular employee,
that employee's right to sue is cut off unless, of
course, the employee has already brought suit. All
suits must be commenced within two years of the
violation or three years if the violation is willful.
Each payday is a new violation. No employer may
retaliate against an employee bringing suit or in
any other way attempting to enforce her or his
rights under the act.

Employers may not reduce the wages of men
in order to be in compliance with the act; rather,
the wages of women must be increased. Back pay
for up to two years (three years if the violation is
willful) is available to the successful employee.
Liquidated damages equal to the amount of back

LEGAL HIGHLIGHT   **What's in a Name?**

The National Organization for Women threatened in October 1982 to file charges against a local police department in Palm Beach County, Florida. The patrol cars were emblazoned with the word "patrolman," and the local group believed that this discouraged women from applying for police jobs.

Such concern with language may seem at first to be misplaced. But language is an important barometer of the society that uses it. For example, if a language contains phrases like "lady lawyer" or "woman doctor," you can be sure that women are new to these fields in that society. Language also directs and limits what we can think about. When you hear the word "fireman" or "policeman," it is hard to think of a woman in uniform. But a firefighter or police officer is something any youngster could grow up to be.

Under Title VII, employers may not use advertisements that indicate, through language or otherwise, any preference in hiring for a particular race, color, religion, sex, or national origin (except when a BFOQ exists). Similarly, the Age Discrimination in Employment Act forbids want ads that imply that older workers need not apply. An advertisement for a "girl Friday" or for an "ambitious young salesman," for example, might be unacceptable on both counts.

Are prospective applicants really deterred by these language cues and other indications, such as listing certain help-wanted ads under sex-segregated columns that are headed "Jobs—Male Interest"? Some studies show this to be the case. In one study,* fifty-two women were asked to rate their willingness to apply for each of thirty-two jobs. When the jobs were separated and labeled by sex, less than half of the women were as likely to apply for "male-interest" as for "female-interest" jobs. When the same ads were listed alphabetically with no reference to sex, more than 80 percent of the women preferred the "male-interest" jobs—not a surprising result in at least one respect: these jobs averaged higher pay.

*Testimony of Sandra L. Bem and Daryl J. Bem, then of the Department of Psychology at Carnegie-Mellon University, reproduced in Hearings on Section 805 of H.R. 16098, pp. 892–894, Special Subcommittee on Education of the House Committee on Education and Labor, July 31, 1970.

---

pay will be awarded as a penalty unless there were reasonable grounds for the employer to form a good-faith belief that he or she was actually acting lawfully. A successful plaintiff may also recover attorneys' fees.

Exceptions

Specific exceptions are provided in the Equal Pay Act. Whenever pay differentials are based on seniority systems, merit systems, piecework, production bonus systems, or on any considerations other than sex, they are allowed. These systems must be created in good faith and not created with the intention of specifically avoiding the act.

Bona fide training programs may justify pay discrimination. As with the seniority or merit system, the training program must be formal, communicated to employees, and have an articulated training goal. If, however, women employees are excluded from a training program, payment of a premium to male trainees is not defensible.

For example, shift differentials or bonuses paid because of job training would not violate the act as long as the jobs or bonuses were available to both males and females. The issue as to shift differentials is confronted in the following case.

Case 22.4
CORNING GLASS WORKS v. BRENNAN
Supreme Court of the United States, 1974.
417 U.S. 188, 94 S.Ct. 2223, 41 L.Ed.2d 1.

BACKGROUND AND FACTS *Corning Glass Works, the petitioner, paid a higher base wage to male night shift inspectors than it paid to female inspectors performing the same tasks on the day shift. In two suits arising under the Equal Pay Act, two separate courts of appeals reached different conclusions as to whether Corning's actions violated the principle of equal pay for equal work regardless of sex. The Supreme Court resolved the conflict between the two appellate court decisions.*

MARSHALL, Justice.

* * * *

Congress' purpose in enacting the Equal Pay Act was to remedy what was perceived to be a serious and endemic problem of employment discrimination in private industry—the fact that the wage structure of "many segments of American industry has been based on an ancient but outmoded belief that a man, because of his role in society, should be paid more than a woman even though his duties are the same."

* * * *

The Act also establishes four exceptions—three specific and one a general catchall provision—where different payment to employees of opposite sexes "is made pursuant to (i) a seniority system; (ii) a merit system; (iii) a system which measures earnings by quantity or quality of production; or (iv) a differential based on any other factor other than sex." Again, while the Act is silent on this question, its structure and history also suggest that once the Secretary has carried his burden of showing that the employer pays workers of one sex more than workers of the opposite sex for equal work, the burden shifts to the employer to show that the differential is justified under one of the Act's four exceptions. All of the many lower courts that have considered this question have so held, and this view is consistent with the general rule that the application of an exemption under the Fair Labor Standards Act is a matter of affirmative defense on which the employer has the burden of proof.

The contentions of the parties in this case reflect the Act's underlying framework. Corning argues that the Secretary has failed to prove that Corning ever violated the Act because day shift work is not "performed under similar working conditions" as night shift work. The Secretary maintains that day shift and night shift work are performed under "similar working conditions" within the meaning of the Act. Although the Secretary recognizes that higher wages may be paid for night shift work, the Secretary contends that such a shift differential would be based upon a "factor other than sex" within the catchall exception to the Act and that Corning has failed to carry its burden of proof that its higher base wage for male night inspectors was in fact based on any factor other than sex.

* * * *

While a layman might well assume that time of day worked reflects one aspect of a job's "working conditions," the term has a different and much more specific meaning in the language of industrial relations. As Corning's own representative testified at the hearings, the element of working conditions encompasses two subfactors: "surroundings" and "hazards." "Surroundings" measures the elements, such as toxic chemicals or fumes, regularly encountered by a worker, their intensity, and their frequency. "Hazards" takes into account the physical hazards regularly encountered, their frequency, and the severity of injury they can cause. This definition of "working conditions" is not only manifested in Corning's own job evaluation plans but is also well accepted across a wide range of American industry.

Nowhere in any of these definitions is time of day worked mentioned as a relevant criterion. The fact of the matter is that the concept of "working conditions," as used in the specialized language of job evaluation systems, simply does not encompass shift differentials. Indeed, while Corning now argues that night inspection work is not equal to day inspection work, all of its own job evaluation plans, including the one now in effect, have consistently treated them as equal in all respects including working conditions.

* * * *

We agree with Judge Friendly that "In light of this apparent congressional understanding, we cannot hold that Corning, by allowing some—or even many—women to move into the higher paid night jobs, achieved full compliance with the Act. Corning's action still left the inspectors on the day shift—virtually all women—earning a lower base wage than the night shift inspectors because of a differential initially based on sex and still not justified by any other consideration; in effect, Corning was still taking advantage of the availability of female labor to fill its day shift at a differentially low wage rate not justified by any factor other than sex."

The Supreme Court ruled that Corning had discriminated against female employees through the use of different base wages for night and day workers. The company's attempt to show that the wage differential was based on a neutral factor other than sex was unsuccessful. The wage differential operated to perpetuate the company's prior illegal practice of paying women less than men for equal work.

DECISION AND REMEDY

Comparable Worth

The concept of **comparable worth**, or pay equity, is that women should receive equal pay not just for equal work but also for work of comparable skill, effort, and responsibility. This notion is based on the idea that, because some work is traditionally "women's work," it has been undervalued and underpaid. Indeed, four out of five women hold jobs that are largely "women's work"—for example, secretary (95 percent female), telephone operator (94 percent female), and nurse (96 percent female).

In 1980, eight city nurses in Denver brought suit against the city for paying its tree trimmers, painters, and tire servicemen more than its nurses. Describing the comparable pay idea as "pregnant with the possibility of disrupting the entire economic system," the trial court ruled against the nurses' claim, and the appellate court upheld this decision. In the following case, Oregon jail matrons had better luck.

BACKGROUND AND FACTS *Four women who were employed to guard female prisoners brought this action against the county of Washington, Oregon. The women claimed that they were paid unequal wages for work substantially equal to that performed by male guards. The female guards attributed the pay differential to intentional sex discrimination. The lower courts found that the jobs of the female guards were not substantially equal to the jobs of the male guards because the male guards supervised ten times as many prisoners per guard as the female guards did.*

The women sought Supreme Court review only of the question whether the pay discrepancy was attributable to intentional sex discrimination.

Case 22.5
COUNTY OF WASHINGTON v. GUNTHER
Supreme Court of the United States, 1981.
452 U.S. 161, 101 S.Ct. 2242, 68 L.Ed.2d 751.

BRENNAN, Justice.

* * * *

We emphasize at the outset the narrowness of the question before us in this case. Respondents' claim is not based on the controversial concept of "comparable worth," under which plaintiffs might claim increased compensation on the basis of a comparison of the intrinsic worth or difficulty of their job with that of other jobs in the same organization or community. Rather, respondents seek to prove, by direct evidence, that their wages were depressed because of intentional sex discrimination, consisting of setting the wage scale for female guards, but not for male guards, at a level lower than its own survey of outside markets and the worth of the jobs warranted. The narrow question in this case is whether such a claim is precluded by the last sentence of Title VII, called the "Bennett Amendment."

Title VII makes it an unlawful employment practice of an employer "to discriminate against any individual with respect to his compensation, terms, conditions, or privileges of employment, because of such individual's * * * sex. * * *" The Bennett Amendment to Title VII, however, provides:

"It shall not be an unlawful employment practice under this subchapter for any employer to differentiate upon the basis of sex in determining the amount of the wages or compensation paid or to be paid to employees of such employer if such differentiation is authorized by the provisions of section 206(d) of title 29."

To discover what practices are exempted from Title VII's prohibitions by the Bennett Amendment, we must turn to the Equal Pay Act which provides in relevant part:

"No employer having employees subject to any provision of this section shall discriminate, within any establishment in which such employees are employed, between employees on the basis of sex by paying wages to employees in such establishment at a rate less than the rate at which he pays wages to employees of the opposite sex in such establishment for equal work on jobs the performance of which requires equal skill, effort, and responsibility, and which are performed under similar working conditions, except where such payment is made pursuant to (i) a seniority system; (ii) a merit system; (iii) a system which measures earnings by quantity or quality of production; or (iv) a differential based on any other factor than sex."

On its face, the Equal Pay Act contains three restrictions pertinent to this case. First, its coverage is limited to those employers subject to the Fair Labor Standards Act. Thus, the Act does not apply, for example, to certain businesses engaged in retail sales, fishing, agriculture, and newspaper publishing. Second, the Act is restricted to cases involving "equal work on jobs the performance of which requires equal skill, effort, and responsibility, and which are performed under similar working conditions." Third, the Act's four affirmative defenses exempt any wage differentials attributable to seniority, merit, quantity or quality of production, or "any other factor other than sex."

Our interpretation of the Bennett Amendment draws additional support from the remedial purposes of Title VII and the Equal Pay Act. Title VII makes it unlawful for an employer "to fail or refuse to hire or to discharge any individual, or otherwise to discriminate against any individual with respect to his compensation, terms, conditions, or privileges of employment" because of such individual's sex. As Congress itself has indicated, a "broad approach" to the definition of equal employment opportunity is essential to overcoming and undoing the effect of discrimination. We must therefore avoid interpretations of Title VII that deprive victims of discrimination of a remedy, without clear congressional mandate.

Under petitioner's reading of the Bennett Amendment, only those sex-based wage discrimination claims that satisfy the "equal work" standard of the Equal Pay Act could be brought under Title VII. In practical terms, this means that a woman who is discriminatorily underpaid could obtain no relief—no matter how egregious the discrimination might be—unless her employer also employed a man in an equal job in the same establishment, at a higher rate of pay. Thus, if an employer hired a woman for a unique position in the company and then admitted that her salary would have been higher had she been male, the woman would be unable to obtain legal redress under petitioners' interpretation. Similarly, if an employer used a transparently sex-biased system for wage determination, women holding jobs not equal to those held by men would be denied the right to prove that the system is a pretext for discrimination.

* * * *

Petitioner's reading is thus flatly inconsistent with our past interpretations of Title VII as ''prohibit[ing] all practices in whatever form which create inequality in employment opportunity due to discrimination on the basis of race, religion, sex, or national origin.'' As we said in *Los Angeles Dept. of Water & Power v. Manhart,* ''In forbidding employers to discriminate against individuals because of their sex, Congress intended to strike at the entire spectrum of disparate treatment of men and women resulting from sex stereotypes.'' We must therefore reject petitioners' interpretation of the Bennett Amendment.

DECISION AND REMEDY

The Supreme Court held that suits challenging sex-based wage discrimination under Title VII do not require the plaintiff to prove that she had performed equal work to that of males. The female guards could pursue their claim against the county despite the earlier court rulings that the women's work was not equal to that of the higher-paid male guards.

COMMENTS

The question of equal pay for comparable work will clearly be a critical one for employment discrimination cases in the 1990s. For example, the AFL-CIO filed a friend-of-the-court brief for the female jail matrons in County of Washington. *The American Federation of State, County, and Municipal Employees has also backed the pay equity issue. These groups and others will continue to press this important concept in the courts.*

Affirmative Action

Affirmative action can be defined as the remedial step taken to improve work opportunities for women, for racial and ethnic minority men, and for other people considered to have been deprived of job opportunities in the past.

Great attention has been paid to establishing goals under numerous affirmative action programs. No less important, however, are the identification and elimination of artificial barriers to equal employment. In addition, a work-force analysis may be undertaken to determine if women and protected minority men are being discriminated against, and goals and timetables may be

developed to correct any substantial disparities. Note that these goals and timetables are not quotas. If an employer makes a good-faith effort to meet goals and timetables, the requirements of affirmative action are met.

It is the employer's responsibility to publicize the existence of affirmative action programs, both internally and externally. Supervisors and managers must be advised of the company's policy and of their responsibilities in implementing it. Recruitment sources must also be advised of the company policy. The company must take active steps to expand its traditional recruitment sources to include those sources likely to result in a higher flow of protected minority and female applicants.

Finally, the employer must establish a procedure for monitoring the success of the program.

Affirmative action has been criticized as causing reverse discrimination. A person with better qualifications will be denied a job opportunity when a less qualified individual from a protected class is hired or promoted. The person with the lesser qualification must be minimally qualified for the job opportunity. This issue of reverse discrimination has now been decided by the United States Supreme Court in the following case.

Case 22.6
JOHNSON v.
TRANSPORTATION
AGENCY
Supreme Court of the United States, 1987.
480 U.S. 616, 107 S.Ct. 1442, 94 L.Ed.2d 615.

BACKGROUND AND FACTS   *The Santa Clara County Transportation Agency voluntarily adopted an affirmative action plan for hiring and promoting minorities and women in 1978. The plan provided that, in making promotions to jobs that had been traditionally segregated, the person's sex could be considered. The plan set short-range goals and annually adjusted these goals so that they could serve as a realistic guide for actual employment decisions. The long-term goal was to have a work force whose composition reflected the proportion of minorities and women in the local area's general work force.*

In 1979, the agency announced a vacancy for a road dispatcher. Twelve employees applied for the promotion, including Joyce, a woman, and Johnson, a man. Both were deemed qualified for the job after their applications had been reviewed by two panels. Johnson was tied for second, while Joyce was ranked next lower by two points. At the time, the agency had never employed a woman as a road dispatcher. Johnson was recommended to be promoted by a panel who reviewed both records.

The agency's affirmative action coordinator had the responsibility of keeping the director of the agency informed of opportunities for the agency to accomplish its objectives under the plan. The coordinator recommended that Joyce be hired for the job after he had also reviewed both applications with their respective qualifications, test scores, expertise, and background and had taken affirmative action matters into consideration.

The director accepted the recommendation of the coordinator and promoted Joyce. He considered the two-point difference in her ranking to be insignificant as he looked at the whole picture.

Johnson filed a complaint with the Equal Employment Opportunity Commission. He received a right-to-sue letter from the EEOC. The district court held for Johnson, but that decision was overturned by the Ninth Circuit Court of Appeals.

BRENNAN, Justice.
* * * *

As a preliminary matter, we note that petitioner bears the burden of establishing the invalidity of the Agency's Plan. Only last term in *Wygant v. Jackson Board of Education*, we held that ''[t]he ultimate burden remains with the employees to demonstrate the unconstitutionality of an affirmative-action program,'' and we see no basis for a different ruling regarding a plan's alleged violation of Title VII. * * * Once a plaintiff establishes a *prima facie* case that race or sex has been taken into account in an employer's employment decision, the burden shifts to the employer to articulate a nondiscriminatory rationale for its decision. The existence of an affirmative action plan provides such a rationale. If such a plan is articulated as the basis for the employer's decision, the burden shifts to the plaintiff to prove that the employer's justification is pretextual and the plan is invalid.

The first issue is therefore whether consideration of the sex of applicants for skilled craft jobs was justified by the existence of a "manifest imbalance" that reflected underrepresentation of women in "traditionally segregated job categories." In determining whether an imbalance exists that would justify taking sex or race into account, a comparison of the percentage of minorities or women in the employer's work force with the percentage in the area labor market or general population is appropriate in analyzing jobs that require no special expertise.

Where a job requires special training, however, the comparison should be with those in the labor force who possess the relevant qualifications. The requirement that the "manifest imbalance" relate to a "traditionally segregated job category" provides assurance both that sex or race will be taken into account in a manner consistent with Title VII's purpose of eliminating the effects of employment discrimination, and that the interests of those employees not benefitting from the plan will not be unduly infringed.

It is clear that the decision to hire Joyce was made pursuant to an Agency plan that directed that sex or race be taken into account for the purpose of remedying underrepresentation. The Agency Plan acknowledged the "limited opportunities that have existed in the past" for women to find employment in certain job classifications "where women have not been traditionally employed in significant numbers." As a result, observed the Plan, women were concentrated in traditionally female jobs in the Agency, and represented a lower percentage in other job classifications than would be expected if such traditional segregation had not occurred.

* * * *

We next consider whether the Agency Plan unnecessarily trammeled the rights of male employees or created an absolute bar to their advancement. In contrast to the plan in [another case] which provided that 50% of the positions in the craft training program were exclusively for blacks, and to the consent decree upheld last term in *Firefighters v. Cleveland,* which required the promotion of specific numbers of minorities, the Plan sets aside no positions for women. The Plan expressly states that "[t]he 'goals' established for each Division should not be construed as 'quotas' that must be met." Rather, the Plan merely authorizes that consideration be given to affirmative action concerns when evaluating qualified applicants. As the Agency Director testified, the sex of Joyce was but one of numerous factors he took into account in arriving at his decision. The Plan thus resembles the "Harvard Plan" which considers race along with other criteria in determining admission to the college. "In such an admission program, race or ethnic background may be deemed a 'plus' in a particular applicant's file, yet it does not insulate the individual from comparison with all other candidates for the available seats." Similarly, the Agency Plan requires women to compete with all other qualified applicants. No persons are automatically excluded from consideration; all are able to have their qualifications weighed against those of other applicants.

In addition, petitioner had no absolute entitlement to the road dispatcher position. Seven of the applicants were classified as qualified and eligible, and the Agency Director was authorized to promote any of the seven. Thus, denial of the promotion unsettled no legitimate firmly rooted expectation on the part of the petitioner. Furthermore, while the petitioner in this case was denied a promotion, he retained his employment with the Agency, at the same salary and with the same seniority, and remained eligible for other promotions.

* * * *

We therefore hold that the Agency appropriately took into account as one factor the sex of Diane Joyce in determining that she should be promoted to the road dispatcher position. The decision to do so was made pursuant to an affirmative action plan that represents a moderate, flexible, case-by-case approach to effecting a gradual improvement in the representation of minorities and women in the Agency's work force. Such a plan is fully consistent with Title VII, for it embodies the contribution that voluntary employer action can make in eliminating the vestiges of discrimination in the workplace.

DECISION AND   *The judgment of the court of appeals was affirmed. The agency had ap-*
REMEDY   *propriately taken into account Joyce's sex as one factor in determining that she should be promoted. The Supreme Court found that the agency's plan was moderate and flexible and that it provided a case-by-case approach to reaching the long-term goal of improvement in the representation of minorities and women in the agency's work force.*

Privacy Rights of Employees

In 1928, the United States Supreme Court established the right of privacy. Justice Louis D. Brandeis wrote that it is "the right to be let alone—the most comprehensive of rights and the right most valued by civilized man." The Court based this right on the Fourth Amendment's proscriptions against illegal searches and seizures by the government.

Today, this right is being used to oppose the utilization of drug and Acquired Immune Deficiency Syndrome (AIDS) testing. The right is also being used in reference to the distribution of information contained in an employee's record of employment.

Drug and AIDS Testing

At the present time, no federal or state statutory provisions exist covering preemployment drug testing. It has been recognized that an employer has a right to test an employee if the employer thinks the employee is under the influence of alcohol or drugs. The real problem lies in the area of random drug testing. Currently, the few courts that have considered this area have generally found that the random testing does violate an individual's reasonable and legitimate expectation of privacy because of the personal information that can be obtained from a person's body fluids.

For example, in *McDowell v. Hunter,*[1] the court held that a public employee with the Iowa Department of Corrections could not be forced to submit to blood, urine, or breath testing in the absence of a suspicion that the employee was under the influence of some drug or alcohol.

Testing for AIDS raises the question of whether Title VII would be applicable. This act prohibits discrimination in employment against people with a handicap. Some states have similar statutory provisions. The few courts that have considered this problem have found that these statutory provisions do protect an employee with AIDS. If this trend continues, it means that a business could be held liable either for not hiring or for terminating an employee with AIDS. Congress is currently considering legislation in this area.

Employee Records

Two legal theories apply to the use and distribution of information contained in an employee's personnel file: defamation and invasion of the right to privacy. A defamation case is founded on an employer communicating harmful information about a current or prior employee. Most of these communications are granted a limited privilege. As long as an employer is communicating with a prospective new employer, there is no major problem unless it can be proved that the first employer's comments are made with malice. To limit a claim that the information was released with the intent of harming a former employee, only the basic employment history should be disclosed. This information would be limited to job title, dates of employment, and ending salary.

If, on the other hand, an employer communicates to current employees that the terminated employee was fired on the basis of moral or other reasons, this can give rise to legal problems. These statements could go beyond the limited privilege that the law grants. Further, this can be considered an invasion of the right to privacy even if what is disclosed is true.

---

1.   612 F.Supp. 1122 (S.D. Iowa 1985).

FACING A LEGAL ISSUE   Discriminatory Questions

One of the more important business procedures is the hiring of new employees. Before an individual is hired, most businesses have standard employment applications or questions. Some of the information sought may be considered discriminatory in nature. Questions that can be discriminatory sometimes take forms like these:

1. • What was your maiden name?
2. How old are your children? How old is your youngest child?
3. What is your birth date?
4. Have you ever declared bankruptcy?
5. Are you married? (Single? Divorced? Separated? Widowed?)
6. (A more subtle form of the same question): Is there anyone in your life who strongly influences your decisions?
7. Who will care for your children while you are working?
8. How long have you lived at your present address?
9. What is your father's name?
10. Have you ever had your wages garnished?
11. Where do you bank? Do you have any loans outstanding?
12. Do you own or rent your home?
13. Were you ever arrested?
14. What religious group do you belong to? What is the name of your priest? (Rabbi? Minister?)
15. Where does your husband (wife, father, mother) work?
16. How did you learn to speak Spanish (German, Russian, and so on)?
17. List for me all the societies, clubs, and lodges you belong to.

Thinking through these questions before they come up will help an applicant to handle them in the best way. They may never come up. If they do, though, there are options. Answering militantly ("I'll see you in court for asking me that, mister!") is a no-win choice. Answering something like "Legally I do not have to provide you that information" is not the best option either.

Try to answer so as to: (1) courteously deflect that line of questioning, (2) give the interviewer some useful, helpful information, and (3) not put him or her in the wrong. Suppose the interviewer has asked, "How will you have your children cared for while you work?" One way to answer is "If you'll show how this question is related to my ability to do a good job for you, I'll be glad to answer." Or, applicants can say child care is all taken care of and then refer to their record of low absenteeism in their current job, despite family responsibilities.

Another way is to try to think why the interviewer is asking that question—why he or she is worried about how you will have your children cared for—and *restate the question behind the question*. You might say, "If by asking me that question you really mean, 'Will I be on the job every day, on time, and ready to give my full attention and energy to the job?,' the answer is most definitely 'Yes.'"

A third option is a little riskier but sometimes effective. *If* the rapport up until that question has been pleasant and *If* you are pretty sure you are not talking to an ogre, you might be able to laugh pleasantly a little and say, "I'll bet you didn't really mean to ask me that question, did you?"

Most often, interviewers will back away from the "don't-ask" questions if the applicants show in a low-key and courteous way that they want to answer only questions directly related to their qualifications for the job. If the interviewer does not back away, then the applicant might reconsider whether he or she really wants to work for this type of organization. Worse than not being hired is being hired by an organization where you would be unhappy.

Before the interview, then, think through all the possible questions, good and bad, that you might be asked, and determine how you will respond. Update your research on the company, too, because the third part of the interview usually consists of the interviewer's question:

"Now what questions do you have that I can answer?"

Adapted from J. W. Gilsdorf, *Business Correspondence for Today* (John Wiley & Sons, in press).

Summary

This chapter has emphasized laws that seek to prevent discrimination in employment. The major federal statutory provisons are Title VII of the Civil Rights Act of 1964 and the Equal Pay Act of 1963. There are also other acts that have attempted to restrict discrimination in the workplace based on age or physical disabilities.

Title VII prohibits discrimination for employment based on race, sex, color, religion, or national origin. It covers employers with fifteen or more employees, labor unions with fifteen or more members, and employment agencies. Certain exemptions are based on religious or ethnic grounds.

Two basic legal theories underlie actions based on Title VII: the disparate treatment theory, which involves treatment of any individual that differs from treatment of other employees based on his or her background or sex, and the disparate impact theory, in which, although on the surface a certain practice is not discriminatory, its effect is to discriminate against a protected class. Under either theory, the employer can be found liable.

Under Title VII, sex discrimination is illegal, but this does not cover discrimination based on sexual preference. It does, however, cover sexual harassment and discrimination based on sex in pension and life insurance plans.

The Equal Employment Opportunity Commission (EEOC) is charged with the enforcement of Title VII. A person files a charge with the EEOC, which then attempts to settle, through conciliation procedures, the potential dispute. The employer has three statutory defenses to any action under Title VII: (1) bona fide occupational qualifications (BFOQs), (2) bona fide seniority or merit system, and (3) professionally developed ability tests.

The other major federal statutory provision is the Equal Pay Act of 1963, which is also administered by the EEOC. It prohibits discrimination in wages paid for equal work on jobs that require equal skills, effort, and responsibility and that are performed under similar conditions. Some exemptions to the act allow different payment because of the job situation, such as shift differentials. Many actions have been brought under the legal theory of comparable worth or pay equity. This theory is that women and minorities should receive equal pay not just for equal work but also for work of comparable skill, effort, and responsibility.

Affirmative action is the process of improving work opportunities for women and others who have in the past been discriminated against. The idea behind affirmative action plans is that, if a member of a protected class has the necessary requirements for an employment position, that individual should be given the job over a person who is not a member of a protected class. Although it might seem that a person is being discriminated against because he or she is not within the protected class, the United States Supreme Court has approved these plans.

Key Terms

affirmative action **544**
bona fide occupational
    qualifications (BFOQs)
    549
bona fide seniority or merit
    systems **549**
Civil Rights Act, Title VII **540**

comparable worth **553**
disparate impact **540**
disparate treatment **540**
Equal Employment
    Opportunity Commission
    (EEOC) **545**
Equal Pay Act of 1963 **550**

Pregnancy Discrimination Act
    545
professionally developed
    ability tests **549**
reverse discrimination **548**

Questions and Case Problems

1. Discuss fully which of the following constitutes a violation of the 1964 Civil Rights Act, Title VII, as amended.

a. Causeway, Inc., is a consulting firm and has ten employees. These employees travel on consulting jobs in seven states. Causeway has an employment record of hiring only white males.

b. Filmtex, Inc., is making a film about Africa. Filmtex needs to employ approximately 100 extras for this picture. Filmtex advertises in all major newspapers in Southern California for the hiring of these extras. The ad states that only black people need apply.

c. Green Belt is a major processor of cheese sold throughout the United States. Green employs 100 employees at its principal processing plant. The plant is located in Windward City, whose population is 50 percent white, 25 percent black, and the balance Hispanic, Asian, and so on. Green requires a high school diploma as a condition of employment on its cleanup crew. Three-fourths of the white population complete high school, as compared to only one-fourth of the minority population. Green has an all-white cleaning crew.

2. Donnell was a black General Motors (GM) employee in St. Louis who applied for admission into a GM skilled-trade apprenticeship program that was established jointly by the company and the United Auto Workers (UAW). He was rejected because he did not meet the requirement that all applicants must have completed high school. He brought action under Title VII of the Civil Rights Act against both GM and the UAW, claiming that the requirement was discriminatory against blacks as well as unjustified as a business necessity. What was the result? [Donnell v. General Motors Corp., 576 F.2d 1292 (8th Cir. 1978)]

3. The state of Connecticut required the passing of a written examination before a person could be considered for a supervisor position. Those taking the tests had a 79 percent passing rate for whites and a 34 percent passing rate for blacks. The state of Connecticut showed, however, that more blacks than whites were promoted from the

eligibility list. The state argued that this "bottom line" was a defense to the discrimination suit. Was this a valid defense? [Connecticut v. Teal, 457 U.S. 440, 102 S.Ct. 2525, 72 L.Ed.2d 130 (1982)]

4. The city of Memphis, Tennessee, implemented an affirmative action plan. In 1981 the city was confronted by severe deficits and had to lay off a considerable number of employees. The city announced that it would follow the last-hired first-fired rule. This was contrary to the city's affirmative action plan and would cause a large number of blacks to be terminated. The district court ordered the city to modify the layoff plan so that it would not affect adversely so many blacks. The case was appealed to the United States Supreme Court. The issue presented was whether a seniority plan that was not intentionally discriminatory would be upheld when the effect was to lay off large numbers of blacks. What do you think the court held? [Firefighters Local Union No. 1784 v. Stotts, 467 U.S. 561, 104 S.Ct. 2576, 81 L.Ed.2d 483 (1984)]

5. Elizabeth Hishon was employed as an associate attorney for a large law firm in Atlanta, Georgia. The firm had more than 100 lawyers but had never made a woman a partner in the firm. The district court held that Title VII was not applicable to the selection of partners in a law firm. Do you think that district court was correct? [Hishon v. King & Spalding, 467 U.S. 69, 104 S.Ct. 2229, 81 L.Ed.2d 59 (1984)]

6. Western Airlines required all of its pilots to retire at age sixty. This rule was implemented because the Federal Aviation Administration (FAA) had regulations that required retirement at age sixty. Criswell was physically fit and wanted to continue flying past the age of sixty. When he was required to retire, he instituted action. Was this age requirement a valid BFOQ? [Western Airlines v. Criswell, 472 U.S. 400, 105 S.Ct. 80, 86 L.Ed.2d 321 (1985)]

7. Mantolete was an epileptic who applied for employment with her local post office. She was not hired because the post office was afraid she would have a seizure on the job while operating certain equipment. She brought action based on the theory that she was discriminated against solely by reason of her handicap. Was she successful? [Mantolete v. Bolger, 767 F.2d 1416 (9th Cir. 1985)]

8. Three former drug addicts desired employment positions with the city of Philadelphia. They were refused because of their prior drug habits. They brought action, arguing that drug addiction was a handicap under the Rehabilitation Act of 1974. What did the court hold? [Davis v. Bucher, 451 F.Supp. 791 (E.D. Pa. 1978)]

9. Five employees who were both white and black were terminated by Omni Georgia and replaced by five people of Korean origin. The supervisor who terminated the employees was of Japanese origin. Action was brought by the five terminated employees based on violation of Title VII. Was the law violated? [Bullard v. Omni Georgia, 640 F.2d 632 (5th Cir. 1981)]

10. Hasselman was required to wear a "revealing and provocative" uniform while working as a lobby attendant in a large office complex. She was subjected to repeated sexual harassment by different people. Finally, she refused to war the uniform and was terminated. Was her termination a violation of Title VII? [EEOC v. Sage Realty Corp., 507 F.Supp. 599 (S.D.N.Y. 1981)]

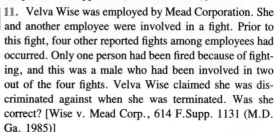

11. Velva Wise was employed by Mead Corporation. She and another employee were involved in a fight. Prior to this fight, four other reported fights among employees had occurred. Only one person had been fired because of fighting, and this was a male who had been involved in two out of the four fights. Velva Wise claimed she was discriminated against when she was terminated. Was she correct? [Wise v. Mead Corp., 614 F.Supp. 1131 (M.D. Ga. 1985)]

Chapter 23 **Environmental Law**

To waste, to destroy, our natural resources, to skin and exhaust the land instead of using it so as to increase its usefulness, will result in undermining in the days of our children the very prosperity which we ought by right to hand down to them amplified and developed.

President Theodore Roosevelt,
Message to Congress,
December 3, 1907

OUTLINE

Introduction

The traditional belief that air, water, and land will absorb all waste products without being harmed has been refuted by a considerable body of evidence. Acid rain has destroyed 200 lakes in the New York Adirondack Mountains, killed the fish, destroyed the majority of aquatic vegetation, and jeopardized the friendly relationship between the United States and Canada.

As society has become more urbanized, concern about the degradation of the environment has heightened. These forces, plus general economic growth, greater wealth, and the proliferation of synthetic products that resist decomposition, have caused policy makers and individuals to seek methods to reduce or prevent pollution.

These concerns have given rise to the field of environmental law, or the law of planetary housekeeping. Focusing on protecting nature and restraining the people whose activities upset the earth and its delicate life-sustaining ecosystems, environmental law concerns itself with the regulation of the land, air, water and human environment.

The price for such protection is high, but the price of not doing anything is higher. Every year billions of dollars are spent complying with environmental protection standards imposed by the government. A large burden to bear, it is often so costly that certain business operations may not be viable. The tension between the implementation of standards that will ensure the quality of our environment and the added expense of forcing businesses to adopt ecologically and environmentally sound practices is one that the government, the courts, society, and businesspeople must face.

This chapter covers how we have handled pollution problems in the past and how state and local governments have an effect on regulating the environment. The chapter emphasizes relatively recent federal legislation that covers such items as clean air, water, noise, and toxic substances. Most of these federal laws are implemented by administrative agencies through regulations and prosecutions.

Historical Background

Concerns about the environment are not new. The English Parliament passed a number of laws that regulated the burning of soft coal in medieval England. Moreover, in the United States through the common-law doctrine of **nuisance**, property owners historically were given relief from pollution in situations where the individual could identify a distinct harm to himself or herself separate from that affecting the general public. A nuisance occurs when a person used his or her property in such a manner as to affect adversely the neighbor's property. Thus, if a factory polluted the air and killed a farmer's crops, the farmer could recover damages from the factory.

Needless to say, nuisance suits that granted specific relief for individuals were inadequate when the harm from pollution could not be identified as affecting groups separate from the public at large. Under the common law, citizens were denied access to the courts unless specific harm could be shown. Thus, a group of citizens who wanted to stop a new development that would cause significant water pollution would be denied access to the courts on the ground that the harm to them did not differ from the harm borne by the general public. In these types of cases, only a public authority could sue for **public nuisance**.

Another common-law cause of action is trespass. This action is defined as the intentional or unintentional passing over another's land uninvited, regardless of whether any physical damage is done. Traditionally, to successfully bring an action under trespass, the landowner had to prove a direct physical invasion of the land, such as dumping dirt or debris on the property. In today's world, trespass occurs many times in a more subtle fashion—for example, through radiation pollution or through permeation by a harmful invisible gas. These types of invasions may hurt plant life or destroy animals, and recovery for such losses is possible under the doctrine of trespass. Today, courts often merge nuisance and trespass, requiring both invasion and harm that exceed the social good.

In addition to the torts of nuisance and trespass, injured parties may file a common-law negligence action. The basis for the allegation of negligence is the business's failure to use reasonable care toward the individual whose injury was foreseeable and was caused by the company. Failure to use pollution controls may give rise to an action for negligence when contamination of the air produces respiratory illnesses in employees and neighboring residents.

Most recently, courts have allowed injured parties to recover under the theory of strict liability in tort. Businesses that engage in ultrahazardous activities, such as blasting operations or transporting radioactive materials, are liable for injuries these activities cause even if the utmost care was exercised. With strict liability, the injured party does not need to prove that the damages resulted from the fault (failure to use care) of the party.

Historically the common law also limited relief from pollution in situations where the harm was caused by two or more independent sources. For example, if a number of firms were polluting the air, a harmed individual could sue any individual firm; however, until early in the twentieth century, the plaintiff was not able to sue all of the factories simultaneously. Thus, specific proof of damages in individual actions was often impossible.

These difficulties in seeking relief in pollution cases, coupled with the fact that tort theory initially only allowed for money damages and thus was not effective in preventing environmental harms, ultimately gave rise to the federal and state legislation that today regulates and controls activities affecting the environment.

Regulation By State Government

State government has some authority in regulating the environment. As just noted, private tort actions take place under state laws. More recent legislation has been passed to permit direct state or local governmental control of the environment. Many states have statutes against polluting the air, water, and the general environment.

These laws range from restricting the amount of emissions from motor vehicles, requiring environmental impact statements for developments above a certain size or amount, and restricting the disposal of toxic material. These laws also vary from one state to another because each state has its own unique problems. State environmental laws will influence decisions made by a business. Many of these state statutes have been passed under pressure from the federal government.

Several states have attempted to regulate dumping of bottles and cans through the use of what are commonly called "bottle bills." The following case illustrates the implementation of one of the first statutes of this kind of regulation.

BACKGROUND AND FACTS *The state of Oregon adopted a law prohibiting the use of nonreturnable containers for beer and carbonated beverages. The law also prohibited the sale of metal beverage containers that used detachable pull-top opening devices. The American Can Company instituted an action against the Oregon Liquor Control Commission attacking the validity of the statute claiming violation of equal protection and due process clauses of the Fourteenth Amendment and the Commerce Clause of the United States Constitution. The trial court upheld the law, and American Can Company appealed.*

 Case 23.1

AMERICAN CAN CO. v. OREGON LIQUOR CONTROL COMMISSION

Court of Appeals, Oregon, 1973.
15 Or.App. 618, 517 P.2d 691.

TANZER, Judge.
*   *   *   *

The primary legislative purpose of the bottle bill is to cause bottlers of carbonated soft drinks and brewers to package their products for distribution in Oregon in returnable, multiple-use deposit bottles toward the goals of reducing litter and solid waste in Oregon and reducing the injuries to people and animals due to discarded "pull tops."
*   *   *   *

One of the plaintiffs' main objectives at trial was to show that the bottle bill would have an effect not only upon manufacturers of bottles and cans, but also upon an entire distribution chain including brewers, soft drink bottlers and canners, beer wholesalers, retailers and, ultimately, consumers. The evidence in this regard demonstrated that the consumption of malt beverages and soft drinks had increased greatly in the United States in recent years, and that a large part of this increase could be attributed to the use of convenient "one-way" packages, including both cans and non-returnable bottles. Plaintiffs assert that non-returnable containers are essential to the existence of national and regional beer markets and that non-returnable containers are also essential to the continued existence of soft drink enterprises. The non-returnable containers were shown to have provided economies in the packaging and distribution of soft drinks and beer by eliminating the cost of shipping the containers both ways, thus causing an increase in feasible shipping distances and enlarging the market each manufacturer could cover. Among the effects of the bottle bill, plaintiffs' witnesses predicted, would be a substantial reduction in Oregon sales of soft drinks packaged outside Oregon, and impairment of the ability of distant brewers to compete in the Oregon market. The bottle bill would necessitate substantial changes in the structure of the industries involved in the manufacturing and merchandising of beer and soft drinks.

*   *   *   *

The Oregon legislature was persuaded that the economic benefit to the beverage industry brought with it deleterious consequences to the environment and additional cost to the public. The aggravation of the problems of litter in public places and solid waste disposal and the attendant economic and esthetic burden to the public outweighed the narrower economic benefit to the industry. Thus the legislature enacted the bottle bill over the articulate opposition of the industries represented by plaintiffs.

As with every change of circumstances in the market place, there are gainers and there are losers. Just as there were gainers and losers, with plaintiffs apparently among the gainers, when the industry adapted to the development of non-returnable containers, there will be new gainers and losers as they adapt to the ban. The economic losses complained of by plaintiffs in this case are essentially the consequences of readjustment of the beverage manufacturing and distribution systems to the older technology in order to compete in the Oregon market.

*   *   *   *

*   *   * [T]he introduction of any new circumstance affecting competition will cause economic winners and economic losers throughout the industry as it readjusts to that new circumstance. The evidence is that plaintiffs expect to be among the losers, unless, of course, they are able to make marketing adjustments.

Economic loss restricted to certain elements of the beverage industry must be viewed in relation to the broader loss to the general public of the state of Oregon which the legislature sought, by enactment of the bottle bill, to avoid. The availability of land and revenues for solid waste disposal, the cost of litter collection on our highways and in our public parks, the depletion of mineral and energy resources, the injuries to humans and animals caused by discarded pull tops, and the esthetic blight on our landscape, are all economic, safety and esthetic burdens of great consequences which must be borne by every member of the public. The legislature attached higher significance to the cost to the public than they did to the cost to the beverage industry and we have no cause to disturb that legislative determination.

The bottle bill is not discriminatory against interstate commerce and is not intended to operate to give Oregon industry a competitive advantage against outside firms. The ban on pull tops and the deposit-and-return return provisions apply equally to all distributors and manufacturers whether Oregon-based or from out of state. According to plaintiffs' testimony, the economic burden of the industry's adjustment to the change will be shared by Oregon businesses as well as non-Oregon businesses. * * *

* * * *

Plaintiffs' * * * constitutional challenges having failed, we hold the bottle bill to be a valid exercise of Oregon's police power. In doing so, we acknowledge having had the benefit of an able analysis by the trial court.

The appellate court affirmed the trial court's ruling that Oregon had legitimately exercised its state police power in passing laws concerning solid waste disposal. The additional cost to the beverage industry was recognized, but the court would not accept it as a justification for overturning a legislative enactment. Hence, the bottle bill was upheld.	**DECISION AND REMEDY**

Regulation by Local Government

County and municipal local governments have control over certain aspects of the environment. As discussed in Chapter 14, zoning laws adopted by local governments control the usage of land. Many communities have adopted ordinances controlling the appearance of buildings. Both usage and appearance regulations have a direct impact on the local government.

Local governments can also do other things that affect the environment. For example, waste or garbage removal has traditionally been a local governmental obligation. What is done with the garbage can have long-lasting effects on a community. Ordinances covering outdoor signs and billboards, antinoise laws that prohibit noise from being heard off the premises of a business, and the control of local parks and streets all affect the local environment. These types of ordinances have a direct application to both large and small businesses.

Regulation by Federal Government

Beginning in 1970, Congress passed a number of federal statutes directing administrative agencies to study the effects of pollution on the environment. The **National Environmental Policy Act** (NEPA) of 1969 mandated that an **environmental impact statement** (EIS) be prepared for every major federal action that significantly affects the quality of the environment. The EIS analyzes the impact on the environment that a particular federal project or project federally funded will have. The federal government has since passed a number of other laws to protect environmental quality.

Environmental Protection Agency

The **Environmental Protection Agency** (EPA) was created in 1970 to assemble various agencies responsible for environmental protection. Primarily an administrative organization, it employs approximately 10,000 individuals who carry out the directives of the numerous and complex federal regulations that affect the environment. Exhibit 23–1 shows the organizational structure of the EPA.

Environmental Impact Statement

One of the important responsibilities of the EPA is to ensure that all proposed federal action that significantly affects the environment is analyzed in an environmental impact statement. This statement has become an instrument for private citizens, consumer interests, businesses, and federal agencies to help shape the final outcome of regulatory actions. Even if an agency's analysis concludes that the impact statement is unnecessary,

---

LEGAL HIGHLIGHT   Solar Energy

In England the courts developed a doctrine known as "ancient lights," which held that owners of homes had a right to obtain light through their windows. The owners of neighboring property could not build too close to existing homes, since this would restrict the light. This doctrine was not generally accepted in the United States. For example, it is universally held in the United States that no one has the natural right to light or air from, or a view over, adjoining property. It has only been through case law (such as prohibiting a neighbor from erecting a "spite fence"), zoning laws, and land covenants that restrictions have been placed on a person's use and right to build on one's property.

The attitude of our courts is beginning to change, however. Recently, the Supreme Court of Wisconsin was confronted with a solar energy issue. Glenn Prah owned a home with solar heating. The defendant, Richard Maretti, started to build a residence close enough to Prah's home that it would restrict the amount of sunlight on the plaintiff's solar collectors. Maretti was in full compliance with the zoning and building codes. The court found Maretti's actions constituted a possible private nuisance and granted Prah a temporary injunction.[1]

1. Prah v. Maretti, 108 Wis.2d 223, 321 N.W.2d 182 (1982).

---

a statement supporting this conclusion must be filed.

The EIS must contain: (1) the environmental impact of the proposed action, (2) any adverse effects to the environment along with alternative actions that might be taken, and (3) what irreversible effects the action might create.

Private Litigation

Private parties continue to recover damages or obtain injunctions for environmental harms under a combination of statutory and common-law provisions. The Clean Air Act amendments of 1972, the Clean Water Act of 1972, and the Noise Control Act of 1972, for example, authorized private lawsuits for violations of air, water, and noise pollution standards. Furthermore, some courts have held that organizations can have legal standing in representing their members' interests even if there is no direct organizational interest in the dispute.

On the other hand, some federal statutes give the government exclusive rights to lawsuits for violations of environmental protection regula-tions. For example, the Environmental Protection Agency has the exclusive right to bring suits for violations of the Federal Water Pollution Control Act.

Air Pollution

Federal involvement with air pollution goes back to the 1950s when Congress authorized funds for air pollution research. The federal government passed the **Clean Air Act** in 1963, which focused on multistate air pollution and provided assistance to states for implementation. Various amendments, particularly in 1970 and 1977, strengthened the government's authority to regulate the quality of the air. Taken together, these acts provide the regulatory basis for promulgating standards to control pollution, primarily that arising from automobile and stationary sources.

The Environmental Protection Agency sets national air quality standards for major pollutants throughout the United States. The 1977 amendments to the Clean Air Act establish multilevel standards. For example, they attempt to prevent

Exhibit 23–1 **Environmental Protection Agency**

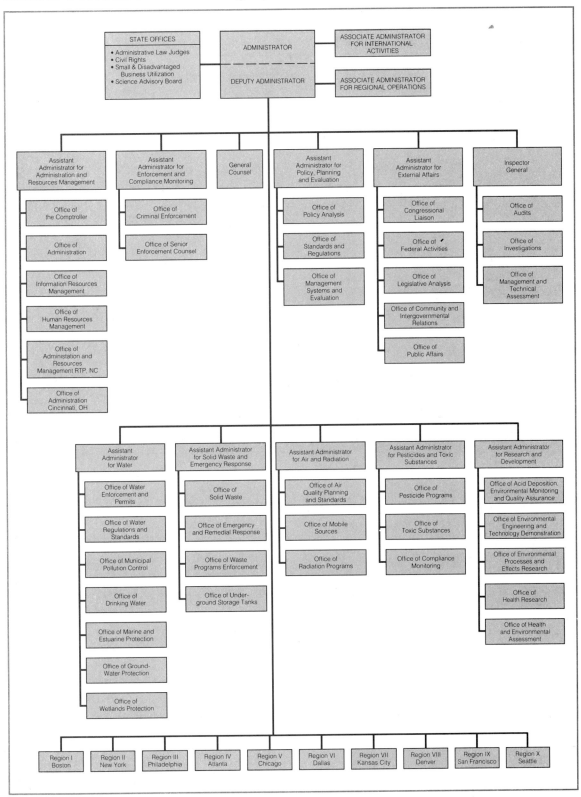

Source: U.S. Government Manual, 1987/1988.

LEGAL HIGHLIGHT — Environmental Control Statutes

Statutes That Regulate Governmental Activities

- *Federal Government*
  - National Environmental Policy Act of 1969
- *State Government*
  - Environmental legislation that governs states' activities on a state-by-state basis

Federal Statutes That Regulate Business Activities

- Clean Air Act of 1963, as amended in 1967, 1970, 1972, and 1977
- Federal Water Pollution Control Act of 1948 as amended in 1965, and as amended by the Clean Water Act of 1972, as amended in 1977 and 1987
- Marine Protection, Research, and Sanctuaries Act of 1972
- Safe Drinking Water Act of 1974, as amended in 1986.
- Federal Insecticide, Fungicide, and Rodenticide Act of 1947, as amended in 1972
- Federal Environmental Pesticide Control Act of 1972
- Solid Wastes Disposal Act of 1965, as amended in 1970 and as amended by the Resource Conservation and Recovery Act of 1976, as amended in 1984
- Comprehensive Environmental Response, Compensation, and Liability Act of 1980
- Toxic Substances Control Act of 1976
- Noise Control Act of 1972
- Rivers and Harbors Act of 1886 as amended in 1890 and 1899

Regulation Through the Lawsuits Brought by Private Persons and by the Government

- Public and private nuisance lawsuits
- Strict liability lawsuits
- Negligence lawsuits
- Trespass
- Enforcement procedures granted to private persons by various statutes

the deterioration of air quality even in areas where the existing quality exceeds that required by federal law. These air quality standards cover carbon monoxide, nitrogen dioxide, hydrocarbons, sulfur dioxide, and other harmful materials. General guidelines set out the requirements for protecting vegetation, climate, visibility, and certain economic conditions. The Department of Health and Human Services has divided the country into atmospheric areas for the purpose of preparing these controls, and each area is required to institute a plan for meeting the standards.

The ramifications of complying with standards set under the Clean Air Act can at times be very far-reaching, affecting the lives and businesses of an entire community. The next case is an example.

Case 23.2

McCOY-ELKHORN COAL CORP. v. ENVIRONMENTAL PROTECTION AGENCY

United States Court of Appeals, Sixth Circuit, 1980. 622 F.2d 260.

BACKGROUND AND FACTS   *The 1970 Clean Air Act set a 1975 deadline for the attainment of primary national ambient air quality standards (NAAQSs). Amendments to the act required states to design a state implementation plan in order to achieve the primary NAAQSs set by the EPA. If a state failed to implement a state plan, the EPA would promulgate one for it.*

Ohio was without a plan for sulfur dioxide, so the EPA formulated one for Ohio. To comply with the sulfur dioxide standards of the state plan formulated by the EPA, Ohio industries could either burn low-sulfur fuel or use high-sulfur fuel with flue gas desulfurization—that is, pollution control equipment, or scrubbers. Faced with this choice, Ohio Edison and other utilities chose low-sulfur fuel that they had to bring in from other regions of the country, such as Kentucky, rather than using locally made high-sulfur fuel with the scrubbers.

This decision caused problems under Section 125 of the Clean Air Act of 1977. Section 125 authorizes the president to prohibit a major fuel-burning factory or utility from using fuels other than locally available coal in order to comply with a state implementation plan if requirements buying distant fuel will result in local economic disruption or unemployment. In response to Ohio Edison's decision to buy Kentucky low-sulfur coal, the EPA (after receiving letters from Ohio labor union officials) proposed invoking Section 125 to require Ohio utilities to burn locally available high-sulfur coal (using the scrubbers).

Without waiting for a final EPA determination or order of prohibition, McCoy-Elkhorn Coal Corporation, a Kentucky producer of low-sulfur coal, filed a suit against the EPA, alleging that Section 125 violated the commerce clause of the Constitution and the due process clause of the Fifth Amendment. The federal district court upheld the constitutionality of Section 125 of the Clean Air Act, and McCoy-Elkhorn appealed.

JONES, Judge.

* * * *

Appellants contend that Section 125 violates the Commerce Clause by creating a discriminatory trade barrier around a state or states. Though recognizing the broad power of Congress to place restrictions or conditions on interstate commerce, appellants argue that Congress cannot contravene the principle of free trade among the states which is embodied in the Commerce Clause. Appellants would have us apply to Congress the limitations imposed by the Commerce Clause on the states.

It cannot be disputed that the Commerce Clause establishes a free flow of trade among the states. While the Commerce Clause prohibits a state from enacting legislation which discriminates against the trade of other states, no decision has applied to Congress the prohibition on the states against discriminatory legislation.

Since *Gibbons v. Ogden* it has been held uniformly that the plenary power of Congress to regulate commerce is restricted only by express limitations found in other provisions of the Constitution. Therefore, our review of Congressional legislation under the Commerce Clause itself is limited to whether the regulated activity is in the stream of interstate commerce and whether the means adopted by Congress to regulate commerce are appropriate for the purpose of the legislation. We cannot substitute our views on the wisdom of the legislation for those held by Congress.

It is beyond question that the sale of coal or other energy sources is in the stream of interstate commerce. Therefore, Congress clearly has the power to regulate coal purchases. It is inconsequential for purposes of the Commerce Clause that the Act may be applied only to one region of the country at any given time and that a region may include only one state. The Commerce Clause does not require nationally uniform regulation.

In Section 125 Congress has chosen a means of regulation that has harsh effects on the purchasers of coal and on coal companies. Congress possesses the power to prohibit goods from interstate commerce because of their detrimental effect on the economy, to establish quotas on production, to set quotas on sales, and to prohibit certain forms of business operations or corporate structure. The purpose of Section 125 is to give relief to areas suffering from significant economic disruption caused by environmental regulations. Section 125(b) would accord relief to the areas hurt by high unemployment. Though Congress could have chosen other less stringent means, restrictions imposed on purchasing companies are appropriate for the purpose of the legislation. It does not matter that some coal producers will be harmed by the use of Section 125. The balance of benefit and harm is a policy judgment confined to the discretion of Congress. Section 125 merely removes an unnatural benefit to McCoy-Elkhorn and Ohio Edison which was created by prior legislation and regulation. Therefore, we hold that Section 125 withstands attack under the Commerce Clause.

* * * *

DECISION AND REMEDY   *The judgment of the district court was affirmed. Section 125 of the Clean Air Act did not violate McCoy-Elkhorn's right to due process, nor did it violate the commerce clause of the Constitution.*

Regulations governing air pollution from automobiles and other mobile sources specify pollution standards and time schedules. For example, the 1970 Clean Air Act required a reduction of 90 percent in the amount of carbon monoxide and hydrocarbons emitted from automobiles by 1975. Carbon monoxide, a colorless, odorless gas, can reduce mental performance and result in death if inhaled in sufficient quantities. Hydrocarbons are unburned fuel, one of the principal ingredients that generate smog. Similar regulations for aircraft are administered by the Federal Aviation Administration. In addition, the act requires that manufacturers of automobiles reduce carbon monoxide emissions to certain levels, as illustrated by the following case.

Case 23.3
CHRYSLER CORP. v.
ENVIRONMENTAL
PROTECTION AGENCY
United States Court of Appeals,
District of Columbia Circuit,
1980.
631 F.2d 865.

BACKGROUND AND FACTS   *The Clean Air Act required automobiles to have carbon monoxide emissions of 3.4 grams per mile by 1975. If this was technologically unfeasible, the EPA agreed to postpone the 3.4 standard and designate an interim standard. The EPA did postpone imposition of the new standard and established a carbon monoxide emission requirement of 15 grams per mile for the 1975 model year. Chrysler, in trying to meet the 15-gram standards, equipped its 1975 model cars with catalytic converters. The converter oxidized emissions, dropping carbon monoxide levels. The oxygen supply was controlled by the carburetor idle.*

Some states, such as California, had higher standards, and cars destined for those states were equipped with air pumps to ensure that they met those standards. The Chrysler line, minus the air pumps, successfully passed EPA testing and was released to the public. Shortly after distribution, the EPA received reports from several state inspection stations that the 1975 Chryslers were failing to meet the 15-gram-per-mile carbon monoxide level. The EPA then conducted some of its own tests.

Pursuant to the Clean Air Act, an administrative law judge for the EPA ordered Chrysler to the recall and repair of 208,000 cars, which included all 1975 vehicles equipped with 360- and 400-cubic-inch-displacement (CID) engines. Chrysler appealed to the administrator of the EPA, who upheld

*the administrative law judge. The administrator determined that a sub-
stantial number of vehicles in the recall class failed to conform to the
applicable carbon monoxide emission standards when in actual use, even
though they had been "properly maintained and used." The administrator
ordered Chrysler to submit a plan for remedying the nonconformity. Chrysler appealed the EPA's decision.*

WRIGHT, Chief Judge.

* * * *

Chrysler has sold approximately 208,000 vehicles in the recall class, all equipped
with catalytic converters designed to reduce carbon monoxide emissions to within
federal standards. Not long after these vehicles had been sold, however, EPA
discovered that many of them were failing to meet the standards. After extensive
tests EPA determined that excessive emissions were primarily caused by misad-
justment of the carburetor idle mixture of the vehicles. The Agency gathered evidence that the misadjustments were the inevitable result of certain defects in the
design of the emission control system of the recall class, and later initiated an
administrative proceeding to require Chrysler to recall the vehicles and correct this
design. An initial hearing before an Administrative Law Judge (ALJ) resulted in a
recall order against Chrysler, which the company appealed to the Administrator.
The Administrator determined first, that as a matter of law a manufacturer must
be held responsible in a recall action for nonconformities primarily caused by design
defects, provided the manufacturer foresaw or should have foreseen the consequences of the defects but failed to take available steps to obviate them, and second,
on the evidence, that Chrysler's recall class must be recalled under this standard.
Chrysler disputes both of these positions. On the legal issue Chrysler argues that
since the nonconforming vehicles in the recall class were misadjusted, they were
not "properly maintained" within the meaning of the Act and thus should not be
recalled. On the factual issue Chrysler asserts that the Administrator's conclusions
were not supported by substantial evidence in the record. Because we agree with
the Administrator's interpretation of [the Act] and determine that there was substantial evidence to support his findings of a violation, we affirm.

* * * *

To reduce carbon monoxide emissions and bring its vehicles into conformity
with the interim federal standards Chrysler, like the other American auto manufacturers, installed catalytic converters in its 1975 model year vehicles. A catalytic
converter can reduce carbon monoxide emissions by 60–80 percent by promoting
a chemical reaction among the carbon monoxide, hydrocarbons and oxygen. This
reaction produces two harmless byproducts, carbon dioxide and water.

An adequate supply of oxygen in the exhaust system is essential to effective
operation of the catalytic converter. Unless there is enough oxygen to oxidize all
the emissions, the catalytic converter will begin to work poorly and at some point
cease to operate altogether. There are two major methods of supplying enough
oxygen: installation of an air pump to introduce additional oxygen into the system,
and precise adjustment of the carburetor idle to ensure that sufficient oxygen is
mixed with the fuel. The principal disadvantage of air pumps is that they increase
the cost of the system by about $50 per car; they also decrease gasoline mileage
and may in some cases inhibit proper oxidation of the emissions. On the other
hand, Chrysler engineers recognized that air pumps generally decrease emissions
more effectively than does the carburetor idle adjustment system. It was for just
that reason that Chrysler used air pumps in its 1975 model year vehicles subject
to the more stringent emission standards of California. Nevertheless, Chrysler did
not use air pumps in the recall class vehicles it sold in other states, because Chrysler

engineers thought them unnecessary to achieving compliance with federal standards. Instead, Chrysler decided to rely on the carburetor adjustment method to ensure an adequate supply of oxygen to the catalytic converter.

*   *   *   *

Unfortunately, the idle adjustment method has apparently not worked as well in practice as in theory. EPA researchers have linked the poor emission control performance of the recall class in actual use to certain characteristics of the carburetor idle adjustment process that make precise adjustment difficult and undesirable to owners and mechanics. *   *   *

*   *   *   *

*   *   * [The ALJ] reached a two-step conclusion: first, that idle misadjustments are characteristic of "properly maintained" vehicles, and second, that idle misadjustments have caused "a substantial number" of vehicles in the recall class to violate the carbon monoxide emission standards. Therefore, he found Chrysler liable to a recall action under the Act.

*   *   *   *

*   *   * The recall order recognizes no duty of Chrysler other than that imposed by the Act: to design and construct vehicles that would satisfy emission standards in actual use, when properly maintained, for five years or 50,000 miles. Chrysler was aware of this statutory duty, and of the consequences that would attach in the event of its failure to comply. According to the order under review, Chrysler chose to employ cheaper and less effective emission control equipment, in the face of evidence that misadjustments serious enough to cause widespread nonconformities were likely. Chrysler thus took a gamble that the idle adjustment method of providing sufficient oxygen to the catalytic converter would work, or that EPA would be unable to prove its case for a recall. The statute demands that Chrysler bear the consequences of its decision.

*   *   *   *

DECISION AND   *The EPA recall was upheld. Chrysler had to alter its cars to conform with*
REMEDY   *the designated carbon monoxide levels.*

Water Pollution

Federal regulations governing the pollution of water can be traced back over a century to the **Rivers and Harbors Act** of 1886 as amended in 1890 and in 1899. These regulations required a permit for discharging or depositing refuse in navigable waterways. The courts have even determined that hot water can be considered refuse because it affects the fish and aquatic plant life.

Clean Water Regulation

The most important and comprehensive legislation plan to eliminate pollution in our waters took place in 1972. The 1972 **Clean Water Act** established

these goals: (1) to make waters safe for swimming, (2) to protect fish and wildlife, and (3) to eliminate the discharge of pollutants into the water. Specific time schedules dating from the 1972 act were extended by amendment in 1977 and 1987. Regulations for the most part specify that businesses and governments install the best available technology.

The act requires both municipal and industrial dischargers to apply for permits before they discharge wastes into the nation's navigable waters. Finally, the act establishes legal standing for citizens (or organizations) whose interests have been affected by parties who violate EPA or state standards and orders. Both injunctive relief and damages can be sought through claims under the act.

Other Regulations

In 1972, through the **Marine Protection, Research, and Sanctuaries Act**, Congress established a system of permits that regulates the discharge and introduction of materials into coastal waters and continuous marine areas. The **Safe Drinking Water Act** of 1974 established additional regulations governing drinking water standards. The rules, which are similar to those of the Clean Water Act, provide that states assume the primary responsibility for complying with national standards. The federal government assumes responsibility where states fail to institute or enforce drinking water standards. In most cases, explicit penalties are imposed on parties that pollute the water. The polluting party can also be required to clean up pollution or to pay the cost of doing so, as is illustrated by the following case.

BACKGROUND AND FACTS   *In this action, the defendants were a number of oil companies, including Atlantic Richfield Company (Arco) and Gulf Oil Company. The defendants were assessed monetary penalties that included paying for the cost of cleaning up oil discharges. Arco argued that the imposition of such penalties in an accidental oil spill when the reporting and cleaning requirements had been satisfied constituted a criminal action. The court had to determine whether these penalties denied due process.*

Two cases were consolidated and heard by the district court simultaneously. In one case, Arco was the defendant; in the other, Gulf Oil Company was the defendant.

Case 23.4
UNITED STATES v. ATLANTIC RICHFIELD CO.
United States District Court, Eastern District of Pennsylvania, 1977.
429 F.Supp. 830.

BECKER, Judge.

These cases raise issues concerning the proper construction and the constitutionality of the ''civil penalty'' provision of the oil and hazardous substance sections of the Federal Water Pollution Control Act Amendments of 1972. The constructional issues boil down to whether Congress intended to impose the civil penalty on persons who spill oil accidentally, report such spill to the appropriate authorities, and clean it up at their own expense (hereinafter ''accidental, reporting self-cleaners''). * * *
* * * *

Turning now to the operative facts, we note that the stipulations as to the relevant events in each of the cases before us track essentially the same pattern. In each case either Arco or Gulf owned or operated a vessel or facility from which oil was discharged in harmful quantity into the navigable waters of the United States. The discharges were ''accidental'' or ''unintentional,'' but, perforce, they violated the prohibition on discharge of (b)(3); hence, without more, they subjected the owners (defendants) to liability for the civil penalty under (b)(6). However, the appropriate defendant (or its agent) promptly reported each spill and cleaned it up within the limits of technological feasibility and to the satisfaction of the Coast Guard. Despite defendants' compliance with their reporting and clean up duties, the Coast Guard, following the prescribed administrative procedure, assessed a civil penalty in each case. Upon defendants' refusal to pay, the government sued.
* * * *

The first prong of defendants' argument goes as follows: The stipulated facts would not survive a motion to dismiss for failure to state a claim under the common law of negligence; i.e., although the facts reveal ''accidental'' spills, they do not reveal a basis for inferring that defendants caused the spills through a lack of due care; but "negligence" is the lowest level of "fault" recognized by our law; i.e., non-negligent conduct is reasonable conduct; therefore, if the spills were not negligent, we can infer that there was no reasonable means for defendants to prevent the spills.

We find that defendants' argument makes more sense when translated into simple economic terms. A rational owner of an oil facility, recognizing his potential liabilities for clean ups (and for damages under common law damage remedies which sec.1321 [of the act] leaves untouched), will attempt to minimize the costs of spills. To accomplish this he will calculate the marginal costs of preventing spills and of potential liabilities. He will thereupon engage in prevention to the point where the marginal cost of prevention equals his marginal liability for spills. Because that point defines *reasonable* spill prevention, a reasonable person will spend money for just that much prevention and no more. To spend less would be negligent. To spend more would be wasteful or inefficient.

On this basis we can make some sense of defendants' argument that (b)(6) serves no regulatory purpose when applied to "faultless" spillers. But defendants move from the claim that they were "faultless" to the claim that no regulatory purpose would be served by imposing a (b)(6) penalty, an argument we reject because it proceeds from a faulty premise. While it is true that the stipulated facts about the spills themselves would not be sufficient to support an action in negligence, this is not such an action, but rather an action to enforce a penalty.

The elements of this statutory action are only that defendant violated (b)(3) and that the Coast Guard following the appropriate procedure assessed the (b)(6) penalty. The statute does not make "fault" an element of the cause of action, but rather a factor in the administrative penalty setting procedure. This is proper because there is no principle of law which requires that civil regulability through imposition of penalty be predicated upon a finding of fault. Moreover, a number of factors support civil regulability here in the absence of fault. First, as we explain more fully in our discussion of the Constitutional issues, the principal goal of (b)(6) is to *deter* spills. Second, the Congressional purpose here was to impose a standard of conduct higher than that related just to economic efficiency. Additionally, the Congress obviously believed: (a) that no clean up effort could be complete because, after discharge, it is impossible to guarantee against residual harm from quantities of oil too small or too well dispersed to be detectable; and (b) that even the transitory pollution of waters was deleterious to the environment.

* * * *

In view of the foregoing analysis we must reject defendant's contention that, as applied to accidental, reporting, self-cleaners, (b)(6) is really criminal rather than civil because, (1) the statutory language is not ambiguous; and (2) even where defendants are not at fault, the penalty does not act only as a punishment but serves the ends of civil regulation.

* * * *

DECISION AND REMEDY *The district court held that the penalties provided under the Federal Water Pollution Control Act Amendments of 1972 (Clean Water Act) were civil, not criminal, penalties. Therefore, the government could continue to assess and collect them against Atlantic Richfield, Gulf, and other oil companies for accidental oil spills.*

Noise Pollution

In 1972, Congress prescribed standards and regulations for the control of aircraft noise, including sonic booms, and the control of emissions of railroad and motor vehicles involved in interstate commerce. The **Noise Control Act** of 1972 established the goal of creating an environment free from noise that is injurious to the health and welfare of the public. The courts have ruled that local control of noise is preempted when state regulations conflict with those established by federal statutes.

Regulations promulgated by the Noise Control Act are administered by the Federal Aviation Administration, the Environmental Protection Agency, and the Department of Transportation. The EPA, for example, is authorized to establish noise emission levels for equipment, motors, and engines. It also reviews production processes, verifies reports for compliance with the law, conducts audit tests, and makes inspections of manufacturers' records.

Toxic Substances

The **Toxic Substances Control Act** was passed in 1976 to regulate chemicals and chemical compounds that are known to be toxic and to institute investigation of any possible harmful effects from new chemical compounds. The regulations authorize the Environmental Protection Agency to require that manufacturers, processors, and other organizations planning to use chemicals first determine their effect on human health and the environment. The EPA also has the authority to regulate substances that potentially create a hazard or an unreasonable risk of injury.

Pesticide and Herbicide Control

The use of chemical pesticides to kill insects and weeds has significantly increased agricultural productivity. On the other hand, there is a growing body of evidence that residuals from these chemicals have not been absorbed by the environment. In some cases, buildups of residuals have killed animals, and some potential long-term effects detrimental to the public have also been identified.

The original regulations governing pesticides were established by the **Federal Insecticide, Fungicide, and Rodenticide Act** of 1947, as amended in 1972 by the **Federal Environmental Pesticide Control Act**. The Environmental Protection Agency has been given the authority to control the introduction of pesticides into the environment.

Pesticides must be: (1) registered before they can be sold, (2) certified and used only for approved applications, and (3) used in amounts that meet established limits when they are applied to crops that provide food for animals or people. The EPA also has the right to inspect manufacturing establishments. In some situations, the supply of pesticides is controlled to keep hazardous chemicals off the market. Those substances that are identified as harmful are subject to suspension and cancellation of registration.

Waste Disposal

Waste disposal can occur on land, in the water, or in the air; thus, regulations protecting these resources from pollution also apply to waste disposal. In 1965 Congress passed the **Solid Wastes Disposal Act**, an act designed to reduce solid waste disposal by encouraging the recycling of waste and the reuse of materials by society. The act also provides for pilot projects in waste disposal utilizing modern technology. For example, the development and use of technology that converts garbage into useful products have been greatly encouraged by the solid waste programs of the Environmental Protection Agency.

The EPA also carries out the provisions of the **Resource Conservation and Recovery Act** of 1976, as amended in 1984 which governs EPA studies and recommendations on solid waste disposal, ranging from glass and plastic waste to airport landfill. The EPA is primarily concerned with issuing federal facility permits and reviewing the state permit system for the use of certain equip-

LEGAL HIGHLIGHT	Superfund

In 1980, the federal government established a superfund ($5 billion) to assist in the cleanup of certain toxic dump sites. This fund is handled through the Environmental Protection Agency. Initially, there were 600 separate locations that were considered critical. It is estimated that this number will increase to 2,000 sites.

It takes approximately three to five years from the time the EPA identifies a site until the site cleanup is complete. Each site must be chemically analyzed to determine what is contained in the dump. Then a decision must be made as to whether to treat the waste at the site or to transport it. Each year the EPA tackles about 150 new locations.

In the future, this should not be a problem. Today regulations ban waste disposal unless that waste has been treated. The EPA has a criminal enforcement program. Businesspeople are now going to prison if they are convicted of illegal dumping.

---

ment. It conducts on-site inspections of hazardous waste generators and cites violators. The Solid Waste Disposal Act gives each state the power to enact its own hazardous waste standards.

Federal statutes also attempt to generate state and local community initiative for solving solid waste disposal problems by providing monies and expert guidance for state and local studies. A number of states, influenced by the Solid Wastes Disposal Act as amended in 1970 have sought to reduce the problem of solid waste disposal by requiring recycling or the reuse of various products.

In 1980, Congress passed the **Comprehensive Environmental Response, Compensation, and Liability Act**, commonly known as the Superfund. This act provides that when a release or threatened release from a hazardous waste site occurs, the EPA may clean up the site to correct the problem. The government may then recover its cleanup costs from (1) the person who generated the wastes disposed at the site; (2) the person who transported wastes to the site; (3) the person who owned or operated the site at the time of the waste disposal; or (4) the current owner and operator of the site. Many companies may thus be liable for their past actions in waste disposal.

Moreover, Superfund mandates a harsh standard of liability. Strict liability applies by statute. In addition, liability among multiple defendants may be held to be joint and several. *Joint and*

several liability means that a company that is responsible for only a fraction of the waste may nonetheless be liable for all of the cleanup costs. Available defenses under Superfund are few. The Superfund is the subject of Legal Highlight.

Judicial Limits

In the first half of the 1970s, federal and state legislators enacted many statutes that regulate environmental quality. Judicial interpretations of these statutes have generally given broad discretionary powers to the administrative agencies that carry out their directives. Beginning in the mid 1970s, however, the courts began to place stricter limits on administrative discretion. Recent court decisions that impose a **cost-benefit standard** on administrative decisions are likely to limit discretion in the environmental area as well. Under the cost-benefit standard, courts will consider the cost of an action and compare it with the benefit that may result from the action.

Generally, the economic and technological infeasibility and/or cost-benefit considerations are not defenses in and of themselves to the charge of noncompliance with these acts. They are only factors courts *may* consider. For example, in *Union Electric Co. v. Environmental Protection Agency,*[1]

1.　427 U.S. 246, 96 S.Ct. 2518, 49 L.Ed.2d 474 (1976).

the utility claimed it would cost $500 million to comply with the Clean Air Act and that this sum could not be obtained through financial markets. The United States Supreme Court turned down this argument and held that the clean air regulations are of "technology-forcing character and are expressly designed to force regulated sources to develop pollution control devices that might at the time appear to be economically or technologically infeasible."

The conflict between the cost of maintaining the quality of our environment and the economic benefit of technological advances is frequently a consideration behind judicial rulings on environmental questions, as the next case clearly indicates.

BACKGROUND AND FACTS   *The Endangered Species Act of 1973 authorizes the secretary of the interior to declare a species "endangered." The secretary listed a small fish, popularly known as the snail darter, as an endangered species under this act. The snail darter lived in a portion of the Little Tennessee River in which the Tellico Dam was under construction. More than 100 million dollars had already been expended.*

The secretary ordered all federal agencies to take action to ensure that the critical habitat of the snail darter was not modified or destroyed. An association of scientists, a conservation group, and citizens of the Little Tennessee Valley brought this suit to enjoin completion of the dam, claiming that impoundment of the waters would violate the act by causing the snail darter's extinction.

Case 23.5
TENNESSEE VALLEY AUTHORITY v. HILL
Supreme Court of the United States, 1978.
437 U.S. 153, 98 S.Ct. 2279, 57 L.Ed.2d 117.

BURGER, Chief Justice.

* * * *

We begin with the premise that operation of the Tellico Dam will either eradicate the known population of snail darters or destroy their critical habitat. Petitioner does not now seriously dispute this fact. In any event, under the Act, the Secretary of the Interior is vested with exclusive authority to determine whether a species such as the snail darter is "endangered" or "threatened" and to ascertain the factors which have led to such a precarious existence. Congress has authorized— indeed commanded—the Secretary to "issue such regulations as he deems necessary and advisable to provide for the conservation of such species." As we have seen, the Secretary promulgated regulations which declared the snail darter an endangered species whose critical habitat would be destroyed by creation of the Tellico Reservoir. Doubtless petitioner would prefer not to have these regulations on the books, but there is no suggestion that the Secretary exceeded his authority or abused his discretion in issuing the regulations. Indeed, no judicial review of the Secretary's determinations has ever been sought and hence the validity of his actions are not open to review in this Court.

Starting from the above premise, two questions are presented: (a) would TVA [Tennessee Valley Authority] be in violation of the Act if it completed and operated the Tellico Dam as planned? (b) if TVA's actions would offend the Act, is an injunction the appropriate remedy for the violation? For the reasons stated hereinafter, we hold that both questions must be answered in the affirmative.

It may seem curious to some that the survival of a relatively small number of three-inch fish among all the countless millions of species extant would require the permanent halting of a virtually completed dam for which Congress has expended more than $100 million. The paradox is not minimized by the fact that Congress continued to appropriate large sums of public money for the project, even after congressional appropriations committees were apprised of its apparent impact upon the survival of the snail darter. We conclude, however, that the explicit provisions of the Endangered Species Act require precisely that result.

One would be hard pressed to find a statutory provision whose terms were any plainer than those of the Endangered Species Act. Its very words affirmatively command all federal agencies "to insure that actions *authorized, funded, or carried out* by them do not *jeopardize* the continued existence" of an endangered species or "result in the destruction or modification of habitat of such species. . . ." (Emphasis added.) This language admits of no exception. Nonetheless, petitioner urges, as do the dissenters, that the Act cannot reasonably be interpreted as applying to a federal project which was well under way when Congress passed the Endangered Species Act of 1973. To sustain that position, however, we would be forced to ignore the ordinary meaning of plain language. It has not been shown, for example, how TVA can close the gates of the Tellico Dam without "carrying out" an action that has been "authorized" and "funded" by a federal agency. Nor can we understand how such action will "insure" that the snail darter's habitat is not disrupted. Accepting the Secretary's determinations, as we must, it is clear that TVA's proposed operation of the dam will have precisely the opposite effect, namely the *eradication* of an endangered species.

* * * *

Concededly, this view of the Act will produce results requiring the sacrifice of the anticipated benefits of the project and of many millions of dollars in public funds. But examination of the language, history, and structure of the legislation under review here indicates beyond doubt that Congress intended endangered species to be afforded the highest of priorities.

* * * *

* * * Our system of government is, after all, a tripartite one, with each branch having certain defined functions delegated to it by the Constitution. While "[i]t is emphatically the province and duty of the judicial department to say what the law is," it is equally—and emphatically—the exclusive province of the Congress not only to formulate legislative policies and mandate programs and projects, but also to establish their relative priority for the Nation. Once Congress, exercising its delegated powers, has decided the order of priorities in a given area, it is for the Executive to administer the laws and for the courts to enforce them when enforcement is sought.

Here we are urged to view the Endangered Species Act "reasonably," and hence shape a remedy "that accords with some modicum of common sense and the public weal." But is that our function? We have no expert knowledge on the subject of endangered species, much less do we have a mandate from the people to strike a balance of equities on the side of the Tellico Dam. Congress has spoken in the plainest of words, making it abundantly clear that the balance has been struck in favor of affording endangered species the highest of priorities, thereby adopting a policy which it described as "institutionalized caution."

* * * *

DECISION AND REMEDY   *The United States Supreme Court enforced the Endangered Species Act by enjoining completion of the Tellico Dam.*

COMMENTS   *Scientists found that snail darters could live in another area of the Little Tennessee River that would be unaffected by the dam. The snail darters were moved at government expense, making it possible to complete the Tellico Dam.*

FACING A LEGAL ISSUE — Complying with Environmental Regulations

You have been living in campus housing since coming to college. Your dorm room is infested with bugs, including those insidious little things called cockroaches. You have tried all kinds of sprays and have had very limited success. Your roommate is a senior in biochemistry. One night, while working on a special class project, your roommate accidentally spills some material and a strong vapor results. Suddenly bugs start coming out from under the baseboards and from other places where they have been hiding, and they die. You take the substance to other residential units with the same result. Your roommate has no interest in business but recognizes that you do. You decide to go into business together, with your roommate overseeing the quality of the product and you managing all the business aspects.

As a good business practitioner, you must become very familiar with federal statutes and state statutes that are directed toward protecting the environment. The Toxic Substances Control Act has direct application to your situation. Before you can market this new product, you must submit considerable data to the Environmental Protection Agency. You must also comply with the Federal Insecticide, Fungicide, and Rodenticide Act. Remember that, before pesticides may be sold, they must be: (1) registered with the EPA, (2) certified and used for only approved applications, and (3) used only in amounts that meet established limits when they are applied to any crops that are for human or animal consumption. As you can see, besides the normal problems of establishing a new business, you must face the additional problems of compliance with federal and state statutes for environmental protection.

Summary

This chapter has discussed the private and public regulation of various activities in an attempt to protect our environment. The private regulations focus on the tort theories of nuisance, trespass, negligence, and strict liability. Most of these private actions face legal defenses that hinder a private party from successfully restricting activity that has or might harm the environment.

The local government has a direct effect on the environment through the adoption of statutes or ordinances covering such areas as zoning, building design, and noise.

Because of the problems associated with private actions and because of limited control at the local level, legislative bodies have passed legislation for the protection of the environment. On both the state and federal levels, administrative

agencies play an important role in implementing this legislation. In particular, the Environment Protection Agency (EPA) was created by the federal government to monitor numerous federal statutes for environmental protection. One of the effective tools that this agency uses is the environmental impact statement (EIS). Most projects using federal funds must prepare an EIS in order to ascertain the project's effect on the environment. Many states have similar statutory provisons for projects they fund or that affect their environments.

Numerous federal statutes have been adopted for specific problem areas. The Clear Air Act promotes standards for pollution control. Included in this act is an attempt to reduce by 90 percent the amount of carbon monoxide and hydrocarbons emitted from automobiles. The Rivers and Harbors Act, Federal Water Pollution Control Act, and the Clean Water Act were adopted to clean up our rivers, lakes, and ocean beaches.

Even noise control has been attempted through regulations covering airplanes and sonic booms, as well as railroad and motor vehicles and the amount of noise they may emit. Toxic substances and pesticides are also controlled by the EPA. Waste disposal is covered by the Solid Wastes Disposal Act, which attempts to reduce solid waste disposal by encouraging the recycling of waste

and the reuse of materials. The federal government has even provided funds under the Comprehensive Environmental Response, Compensation, and Liability Act (Superfund) to clean up dangerous hazardous waste disposal sites.

The courts have attempted to balance the adverse effect of certain activities on the environment and on society with the cost of rectifying these problems. The courts recently have tended to interpret legislation in the light of whether benefits bear a reasonable relationship to the standards' demonstrably high costs.

Key Terms

Clean Air Act **568**
Clean Water Act **574**
Comprehensive Environmental
    Response, Compensation,
    and Liability Act **578**
cost-benefit standard **578**
environmental impact
    statement **562**
Environmental Protection
    Agency **567**

Federal Environmental
    Pesticide Control Act **577**
Federal Insecticide,
    Fungicide, and
    Rodenticide Act **577**
Marine Protection, Research,
    and Sanctuaries Act **575**
National Environmental
    Policy Act **567**
Noise Control Act **577**

nuisance **564**
public nuisance **564**
Resource Conservation and
    Recovery Act **577**
Rivers and Harbors Act **574**
Safe Drinking Water Act **575**
Solid Wastes Disposal Act
    577
Toxic Substances Control Act
    577

Questions and Case Problems

1. Oakhill is a development-home building corporation that primarily develops retirement communities. Washington Feeds owns several feedlots in Buckeye. Oakhill purchased 20,000 acres of farmland in the same area and began building and selling homes on this acreage. In the meantime, Washington Feeds continued to expand its feedlot business, and eventually only 500 feet separated the two operations. Because of the odor and flies from the feedlots, Oakhill found it difficult to sell the homes in its development. Oakhill wants to enjoin Washington Feeds from operating its feedlots in the vicinity of the retirement home development. Under what theory would Oakhill file this action? Discuss fully.

2. Flylight, Inc., is a manufacturer of a new 250-seat passenger airplane that is fuel efficient and that travels at a cruising speed of 900 miles per hour. The plane would only be cost effective for flights of 1,000 miles or more. Traveling at 900 miles per hour creates a sonic boom lasting for no more than five seconds. The sound measured during the five-second period exceeds aircraft noise levels

established by the EPA. Discuss fully whether Flylight, Inc., aircraft can be banned from flying over the United States.

3. Glassworks, Inc., is a processor of a soft drink called "Double Cola." Glassworks, Inc., only uses returnable bottles and uses a special acid to clean its bottles for further beverage processing. The acid is diluted by water and then allowed to pass into a navigable stream. Glassworks, Inc., also crushes its broken bottles and throws the crushed glass into the stream. Discuss fully any federal environmental laws that Glassworks has violated.

4. The Government Services Administration (GSA) entered into an agreement with a private individual under which the individual was to construct a building to GSA's specifications and lease it to the GSA. Under the contemplated lease provision, GSA would have use of the entire building for a five-year (renewable) period. As many as 2,300 government employees would be assigned to the building, and most would commute by automobile. The cost of the lease was approximately $11 million. GSA proceeded with its plans for the building without preparing any environmental impact statement. Was a statement necessary? [S.W. Neighborhood Assembly v. Eckard, 445 F.Supp. 1195 (D.D.C. 1978)]

5. Citizens Against Toxic Sprays, Inc., was an organization established to challenge the use of toxic sprays in places where they could be harmful to humans, animals, or vegetation. The group sought to enjoin the United States Forest Service from using the herbicide TCDD because of its hazardous effect on people who breathed it. TCDD was used only in national forests, not in any residential areas. Citizens Against Toxic Sprays alleged that some of its members were affected by the use of TCDD in two of the national forests because they lived near them, worked in them, or used them for recreational activities. Does Citizens Against Toxic Sprays have the standing to sue the United States Forest Service? [Citizens Against Toxic Sprays, Inc. v. Bergland, 428 F.Supp. 908 (D.C. Or. 1977)]

6. Virginia Dalsis, the owner of a small store in the city of Olean, New York, brought a suit to enjoin the construction of a mall because of its projected size. Dalsis alleged that the large size of the shopping center would have an adverse environmental effect on the downtown area, causing economic blight and deterioration of the section in which her business was located. Dalsis, however, did not bring the suit until three months after construction of the shopping mall had begun, even though she was aware of the mall's potential size almost a year before construction started. Should Dalsis be allowed to enjoin the construction of the shopping mall under the National Environmental Policy Act? [Dalsis v. Hills, 424 F.Supp. 784 (W.D.N.Y. 1976)]

7. Judy Godwin began construction of her home. About the same time, Exxon began construction of a "separation" plant 700 feet north of the homesite. The residence and plant were completed about the same time. The plant emitted noise, vibration and sulfurous odors around the clock. These caused Godwin headaches, and, because of the odor, she would not bring her friends to her residence. What legal theories could she use against Exxon? What result would be obtained under them? [Exxon Corp., U.S.A. v. Dunn, 474 So.2d 1269 (Fla.Dist.Ct.App. 1985)]

8. Interpretation of the language in environmental statutes is very important. Section 505(a) of the Clean Water Act authorizes private citizens to commence a civil action for injunctive relief and/or the imposition of civil penalties in federal district court against any person "alleged to be in violation" of the conditions of a National Pollutant Discharge Elimination System (NPDES) permit. Between 1981 and 1984, Smithfield repeatedly violated the conditions of its NPDES permit by exceeding authorized effluent limitations. Because of the installation of new equipment, Smithfield's last reported violation occurred in May 1984. Nevertheless, in June 1984, having given notice of their intent to sue to the Environmental Protection Agency and to state authorities, as required by Section 505(b) of the act, Chesapeake Bay Foundation filed a Section 505(a) suit alleging that Smithfield "has violated . . . [and] will continue to violate its NPDES permit." Smithfield filed a motion to dismiss, alleging that the federal statute required that he be in violation of the act at the time the action was filed. What was the result? [Gwaltney of Smithfield v. Chesapeake Bay Foundation, ___U.S. ___, 108 S.Ct. 376, 98 L.Ed.2d 306 (1987)]

Chapter 24 International Business Law

The manufacturer who waits in the woods for the world to beat a path to his door is a great optimist. But the manufacturer who shows his "mousetraps" to the world keeps the smoke coming out of his chimney.

O.B. Winters

OUTLINE

Introduction

Since World War II, business has become increasingly multinational in character. It is not uncommon, for example, for a United States corporation to have investments or manufacturing plants in a foreign country or for a foreign corporation to have operations in the United States. Because the exchange of goods, services, and ideas on a global level is now a common phenomenon, it is important for the businessperson to have some familiarity with the laws pertaining to these international business transactions.

International law consists of a body of laws that are considered to be legally binding among otherwise independent nations. Although no sovereign nation can be compelled, against its will, to obey a law external to itself, nations can and do voluntarily agree to be governed in certain respects by international law for the purpose of facilitating international trade and commerce as well as civilized discourse. A nation's laws fundamentally control the relationship between the international business activities (conducted within its borders or conducted by the nation's businesses outside its borders) and the international agreements that the nation has signed.

This chapter explores the sources of international law, the legal principles and doctrines that guide judicial decisions in disputes involving a foreign element, the doctrine of sovereign immunity, antitrust laws, and the documents that facilitate international business transactions. The chapter concludes with a brief discussion of the proliferation of common markets in the postwar world and of their function in protecting the commercial interests of less-powerful nations in a world dominated by superpowers.

Sources of International Law

Businesses engaged in international commerce are regulated by international, regional, and national laws. International law has evolved in three ways: through international customs, through agreements that have the force of law, and through international organizations and conferences. Agreements or treaties are developed either by the nations themselves gathering together or by international agencies to which various nations belong.

International Customs

International customs have evolved among nations in their relations with one another. The International Court of Justice defines international custom as "evidence of a general practice accepted as law." Customary law serves as an independent form of law. The application of this definition, however, is subject to challenge on a case-by-case basis. The courts must decide, for example, when a particular custom has evolved into a general practice constituting a law.

Treaties

Treaties among foreign nations provide another source of international law. A **treaty** is an agreement or contract between two or more nations that must be authorized and ratified by the supreme power of each nation. Under Article II, Section 2, of the United States Constitution, the president has the power "by and with the Advice and Consent of the Senate, to make Treaties, provided two-thirds of the Senators present concur." A treaty usually results from a long series of meetings, sometimes lasting years, during which the various nations negotiate and finally reach an agreement that, if signed and ratified, becomes enforceable.

International Organizations and Conferences

International organizations and conferences further contribute to what is known as international law. These organizations adopt resolutions, declarations, and other types of standards that often require a particular behavior of nations. The General Assembly of the United Nations, for example, has adopted numerous resolutions and declarations that embody principles of international law. Disputes with respect to these resolutions and declarations may be brought before the United Nations International Court of Justice. In general, however, the court only has jurisdiction over legal disputes if the nations voluntarily submit to it.

**LEGAL
HIGHLIGHT**

**Multilateral International Organizations in
Which the U.S. Participates**

The United States is party to both multilateral
and bilateral organizations. The bilateral
organizations involve only two parties, the
United States and one other country—
generally, either Canada or Mexico. The United
States belongs to well over 100 multilateral
international organizations. Through the United
Nations alone, the United States belongs to
over twenty such organizations. Other
multilateral organizations have been formed for
peacekeeping purposes or are inter-American
organizations, regional organizations, or other
miscellaneous international organizations.
Participation in multilateral organizations results
from the provisions of treaties, other
international agreements, congressional
legislation, or executive arrangements. Some of
the organizations to which the United States
belongs are:

- International Monetary Fund
- Customs Cooperation Council
- General Agreement on Tariffs and Trade
- Hague Conference on Private International
Law
- International Bureau of the Permanent Court
of Arbitration
- International Bureau for the Publication of
Customs Tariffs
- International Bureau of Weights and
Measures
- International Coffee Organization
- International Institute for Cotton
- International Jute Organization
- International Office of Vine and Wine
- International Sugar Organization
- International Whaling Commission
- International Wheat Council

The United States belongs to various regional
organizations based, just as the name suggests,
on regional interests. Often smaller nations are
better able to exert their influence when they work
as a group on international problems; the Inter-
American Development Bank is an example. Other
regional organizations are not based on a geographical region but rather on a common problem
or the need for a common policy—for example,
the Organization of Petroleum Exporting Countries (OPEC).

Conflicts between International and National Law

National law is law that pertains to a particular
nation. National laws play a prominent role in
international business. Any firm doing business in
more than one country must contend with overlapping or conflicting national laws. Import laws,
export laws, quotas, and tax laws are but a few

of the types of national laws that have an impact
on international business. These laws are subject
to abrupt and constant change. For example, when
the Union of Soviet Socialist Republics (USSR)
invaded Afghanistan, President Carter stopped all
agricultural exports from the United States to the
USSR by executive order. All contracts in progress were unexpectedly ended.

Naturally, the laws of each nation differ from
those of others, since each country's legal system
reflects the country's cultural, historical, economic, and political background. Consequently,
it is not uncommon for a country's national law
to come into conflict with international law. The
two important principles that guide the settlement
of such conflicts are the act of state doctrine and
the principle of comity.

The Act of State Doctrine

The **act of state doctrine** is a judicially created
doctrine that provides that the judicial branch of

one country will not examine the validity of public acts committed by a recognized foreign government within its own territory. This doctrine is based on the theory that the judicial branch should not decide the validity of foreign acts when to do so would disturb the harmony of relations with that foreign nation.

In the following case, the United States Supreme Court examined the act of state doctrine in the context of an **expropriation** by the Cuban government. An expropriation occurs when a government seizes privately owned goods or a privately owned business for a proper public purpose, and it awards just compensation. A **confiscation**, on the other hand, occurs when there is a taking without a proper public purpose or an award of just compensation.

Case 24.1

BANCO NACIONAL DE CUBA v. SABBATINO

Supreme Court of the United States, 1964.
376 U.S. 398, 84 S.Ct. 923,
11 L.Ed.2d 804.

BACKGROUND AND FACTS   *The respondent, Sabbatino, an American commodity broker, had contracted with a Cuban corporation, largely owned by United States residents, to buy Cuban sugar. When the Cuban government expropriated the corporation's property and rights, the broker entered into a new contract to make payment for the sugar to the petitioner, a Cuban state-owned business, Banco Nacional de Cuba. Banco delivered the bills of lading and sight draft to Sabbatino, who accepted the documents and received payment for the sugar from its customer but then refused to deliver the proceeds to Banco's agent.*

Banco subsequently filed an action in the federal district court for the Southern District of New York, alleging under New York law conversion of the bills of lading, and seeking recovery of the proceeds from the respondent-broker.

The district court concluded that the corporation's property interest in the sugar was subject to Cuba's territorial jurisdiction and acknowledged the act of state doctrine which precludes judicial inquiry in the United States respecting the public acts of a recognized foreign sovereign power committed within its own territory. Nevertheless, the court held the taking was invalid under international law in three separate aspects: it was motivated by a retaliatory and not a public purpose; it discriminated against American nationals; and it failed to provide adequate compensation. A summary judgment against petitioner was granted. The court of appeals affirmed the decision and the United States Supreme Court granted certiorari.

HARLAN, Justice.
*   *   *   *

On July 6, 1960, the Congress of the United States amended the Sugar Act of 1948 to permit a presidentially directed reduction of the sugar quota for Cuba. On the same day President Eisenhower exercised the granted power. The day of the congressional enactment, the Cuban Council of Ministers adopted "Law No. 851," which characterized this reduction of the Cuban sugar quota as an act of "aggression, for political purposes" on the part of the United States, justifying the taking of countermeasures by Cuba. The law gave the Cuban President and Prime Minister discretionary power to nationalize by forced expropriation property or enterprises in which American nationals had an interest. Although a system of compensation was formally provided, the possibility of payment under it may well be deemed illusory. *   *   *
*   *   *   *

In these circumstances the question whether the rights acquired by Cuba are enforceable in our courts depends * * * upon the act of state doctrine * * *
* * * *

We do not believe that this doctrine is compelled either by the inherent nature of sovereign authority, as some of the earlier decisions seem to imply, or by some principle of international law. * * *
* * * *

If the act of state doctrine is a principle of decision binding on federal and state courts alike but compelled by neither international law nor the Constitution, its continuing vitality depends on its capacity to reflect the proper distribution of functions between the judicial and political branches of the Government on matters bearing upon foreign affairs. * * *
* * * *

When we consider the prospect of the courts characterizing foreign expropriations, however justifiably, as invalid under international law and ineffective to pass title, the wisdom of the precedents is confirmed. * * *
* * * *

* * * Following an expropriation of any significance, the Executive engages in diplomacy aimed to assure that United States citizens who are harmed are compensated fairly. * * * Judicial determinations of invalidity of title can, on the other hand, have only an occasional impact * * *. Such decisions would, if the acts involved were declared invalid, often be likely to give offense to the expropriating country; since the concept of territorial sovereignty is so deep seated, any state may resent the refusal of the courts of another sovereign to accord validity to acts within its territorial borders. * * *
* * * *

However offensive to the public policy of this country and its constituent States an expropriation of this kind may be, we conclude that both the national interest and progress toward the goal of establishing the rule of law among nations are best served by maintaining intact the act of state doctrine in this realm of its application.

DECISION AND REMEDY

The United States Supreme Court reversed the judgment of the court of appeals and remanded the case to the district court for proceedings consistent with this opinion. The Court concluded that the act of state doctrine reflects the desirability of presuming the validity of public acts committed by a foreign sovereign power in its own territory, and, thus, New York law regarding the tort of conversion may not be applied to foreign expropriations. The presumed validity of an expropriation is unaffected by the fact that the expropriation may constitute conversion or breach of contract under New York law.

COMMENTS

The judiciary's abstention in such matters reflects the notion of sovereign immunity (discussed later in this chapter) and the act of state doctrine. Each government is sovereign within its own borders, and the notion of comity (discussed next) commands that every sovereign nation that voluntarily recognizes the sovereignty of another nation is also bound to respect that nation's sovereign powers.

The Principle of Comity

The **principle of comity** may also arise when national and international laws conflict. Comity is defined as a deference by which one nation gives effect to the laws and judicial decrees of another nation. This recognition is based primarily on respect.

An extraterritorial effect is one that exists beyond the country's border. When this takes place, the court must decide whether principles of comity should be applied. The following case is illustrative.

Case 24.2
ALLIED BANK INTERNATIONAL v. BANCO CREDITO AGRICOLA DE CARTAGO
United States Court of Appeals, Second Circuit, 1985.
757 F.2d 516.

BACKGROUND AND FACTS *Allied Bank International is the agent for a syndicate of thirty-nine creditor banks. Defendants-appellees are three Costa Rican banks that are wholly owned by the Republic of Costa Rica and subject to the direct control of the Central Bank of Costa Rica (Central Bank). Allied brought this action in February 1982 to recover on promissory notes issued by the Costa Rican banks. The notes, which were in default, were payable in United States dollars in New York City. The parties' agreements acknowledged that the obligations were registered with Central Bank which was supposed to provide the necessary dollars for payment.*

The defaults were due solely to actions of the Costa Rican government. In July 1981, in response to escalating national economic problems, Central Bank issued regulations which essentially suspended all external debt payments. In November 1981, the government issued an executive decree which conditioned all payments of external debt on express approval from Central Bank. Central Bank subsequently refused to authorize any foreign debt payments in United States dollars, thus precluding payment on the notes here at issue. In accordance with the provisions of the agreements, Allied accelerated the debt and sued for the full amount of principal and interest outstanding.

Allied moved for summary judgment. The sole defense raised by appellees in response was the act of state doctrine.

The district court denied the motion. Reasoning that a judicial determination contrary to the Costa Rican directives could embarrass the United States government in its relations with the Costa Rican government, the court held that the act of state doctrine barred entry of summary judgment for Allied. Allied appealed.

MESKILL, Judge.
* * * *

The act of state doctrine operates to confer presumptive validity on certain acts of foreign sovereigns by rendering non-justiciable claims that challenge such acts. The judicially created doctrine is not jurisdictional; it is "a rule of decision under which an act meeting the definition . . . is binding on the court." The applicability of the doctrine is purely a matter of federal law.

The classic statement of the doctrine was delivered in *Underhill v. Hernandez:*
Every sovereign State is bound to respect the independence of every other sovereign State, and the courts of one country will not sit in judgment on the acts of the government of another done within its own territory. Redress of grievances by reason of such acts must be obtained through the means open to be availed of by sovereign powers as between themselves.

The modern formulation derives from the Supreme Court's opinion in *Banco Nacional de Cuba v. Sabbatino*:

[R]ather than laying down or reaffirming an inflexible and all-encompassing rule in this case, we decide only that the Judicial Branch will not examine the validity of a taking of property within its own territory by a foreign sovereign government, extant and recognized by this country at the time of suit, in the absence of a treaty or other unambiguous agreement regarding controlling legal principles, even if the complaint alleges that the taking violates customary international law.

It has always been clear that ''[t]he act of state doctrine does not . . . bar inquiry by the courts into the validity of extraterritorial takings.'' * * *
* * * *

The extraterritorial limitation, an inevitable conjunct of the foreign policy concerns underlying the doctrine, dictates that our decision herein depends on the situs of the property at the time of the purported taking. The property, of course, is Allied's right to receive repayment from the Costa Rican banks in accordance with the agreements. The act of state doctrine is applicable to this dispute only if, when the decrees were promulgated, the situs of the debts was in Costa Rica. Because we conclude that the situs of the property was in the United States, the doctrine is not applicable.
* * * *

[W]hile Costa Rica has a legitimate concern in overseeing the debt situation of state-owned banks and in maintaining a stable economy, its interest in the contracts at issue is essentially limited to the extent to which it can unilaterally alter the payment terms. Costa Rica's potential jurisdiction over the debt is not sufficient to locate the debt there for the purposes of act of state doctrine analysis.

* * * Consequently, this was not ''a taking of property within its own territory by [Costa Rica].'' The act of state doctrine is, therefore, inapplicable.

Acts of foreign governments purporting to have extraterritorial effect—and consequently, by definition, falling outside the scope of the act of state doctrine—should be recognized by the courts only if they are consistent with the law and policy of the United States. * * *

The Costa Rican government's unilateral attempt to repudiate private, commercial obligations is inconsistent with the orderly resolution of international debt problems. It is similarly contrary to the interests of the United States, a major source of private international credit. The government has procedures for resolving intergovernmental financial difficulties. * * *
* * * *

The Costa Rican directives are inconsistent with the law and policy of the United States. We refuse, therefore, to hold that the directives excuse the obligations of the Costa Rican banks. * * *

DECISION AND REMEDY

The court of appeals reversed the district court's denial of Allied's motion for summary judgment. In applying the principles of comity, the court concluded that acts of foreign governments having extraterritorial effect should be recognized by courts only when they are consistent with the laws and policy of the United States. Since the Costa Rican government had attempted to repudiate private, commercial obligations, the court held that such repudiation was inconsistent with the law and policy of the United States. Even though the Costa Rican government was experiencing international debt problems, the court recognized the fact that the United States government has procedures for resolving these types of difficulties.

The Doctrine of Sovereign Immunity

When certain conditions are satisfied, the **doctrine of sovereign immunity** immunizes foreign nations from the jurisdiction of the United States. In 1976, Congress codified the law of sovereign immunity in the **Foreign Sovereign Immunities Act (FSIA)**. The FSIA also modified the law of sovereign immunity in certain respects by expanding the rights that plaintiff creditors have against foreign nations.

The FSIA exclusively governs the circumstances in which an action may be brought against a foreign nation in the United States. Attachment of a foreign nation's property is also covered by this act. One of the primary purposes of the FSIA is to have federal courts, rather than the Department of State, determine claims of foreign sovereign immunity. It was thought that a determi-

nation of such an immunity by the courts would increase the degree of certainty in the law of sovereign immunity.

In the following case, a shipowner brought a lawsuit against Argentina. The ship was damaged in an attack by the Argentine Air Force during the Falklands War.[1] The trial court considered the application of the Foreign Sovereign Immunities Act to this situation.

---

1. For over a century, Argentina had claimed that the Falkland Islands were within its territory. The Falkland Islands, however, had been ruled by Great Britain for more than 200 years. In 1982, Argentina invaded the Falklands to assert its territorial claims. Great Britain sent troops to defend the islands. After several months of armed conflict, Argentina withdrew its troops from the Falklands, thus leaving Great Britain in control. The Argentinians call the Falkland Islands the Malvinas.

Case 24.3
AMERADA HESS SHIPPING CORP. v. ARGENTINE REPUBLIC
United States District Court, Southern District of New York, 1986.
638 F.Supp. 73.

BACKGROUND AND FACTS   *United Carriers, a Liberian corporation, owned the* Hercules, *a crude oil tanker. Amerada Hess Shipping Corp. chartered the* Hercules. *Because of its width, the tanker could not make passage through the Panama Canal; it had to sail around the southern tip of South America. On April 2, 1982, the war over the Falklands began between Argentina and Great Britain. Liberia was a neutral nation. While sailing north, the* Hercules *was diverted from its course when the Argentine navy requested that the tanker aid in the search for survivors of the* General Belgado, *an Argentine cruiser sunk by a British submarine. The* Hercules *was released after the task was completed.*

On its return trip south and while outside the war zone, without provocation or warning, Argentine military aircraft began to bomb the Hercules *three separate times on June 8. The tanker was left with an undetonated bomb and was so disabled that it was scuttled off the coast.*

Amerada Hess was unable to find an Argentine lawyer who would pursue its claim for the loss of the Hercules *in the Argentine Republic's courts. Amerada Hess and United Carriers sought relief in United States District Court. Argentina filed a motion to dismiss under the Foreign Sovereign Immunities Act.*

CARTER, Judge.
*   *   *   *

Foreign sovereign immunity has a venerable history in this country's courts, dating back at least to Chief Justice Marshall's decision in *The Schooner Exchange v. M'Faddon.* The doctrine developed over the next century and a half in a world of broadened state activity and burgeoning international trade. By the middle of this century, two aspects of foreign sovereign immunity that deserve mention had evolved. The first was substantive: the doctrine of ''restrictive'' immunity, which accords a foreign sovereign immunity for its public acts but not for its commercial, or quasi-private, activities. The second was procedural: usually, but not always, foreign nations would seek immunity from the State Department which would submit ''suggestions of immunity'' to the courts where it determined that immunity was appropriate. Political pressures exerted by foreign nations not infrequently affected the State Department's determination, leading to lack of uniformity and clarity in the doctrine. In 1976, Congress sought to codify the restrictive doctrine of foreign sovereign immunity and to place responsibility for making determinations of immunity squarely within the judiciary. Congress was emphatic that the FSIA be the sole means of assessing claims of immunity. That interest is apparent from the structure of the FSIA, which unequivocally states that:

> Subject to existing international agreements to which the United States is a party at the time of the enactment of this Act a foreign state shall be immune from the jurisdiction of the courts of the United States and of the States except as provided in sections 1605 to 1607 of this chapter.

A foreign state is subject to jurisdiction in the courts of this nation if, and only if, an FSIA exception empowers the court to hear the case. The legislative history strengthens this reading. The House report states that the FSIA ''sets forth sole and exclusive standards to be used in resolving questions of sovereign immunity raised by foreign states before Federal and State courts in the United States. It is intended to preempt any other State or Federal law (excluding applicable international agreements) for according immunity to foreign sovereigns, their political subdivisions, their agencies, and their instrumentalities.'' Almost without exception, courts interpreting the FSIA have assumed that the FSIA is the exclusive source of jurisdiction over foreign sovereigns.

Plaintiffs' claims undeniably fall outside of the exceptions of blanket foreign sovereign immunity provided by the FSIA. The only provision for tort claims, where the foreign sovereign has not waived immunity, requires that the ''damage to or loss of property'' occur ''in the United States.'' Interpretation of similar language in terms of the commercial activity exception in § 1605(a)(2) has been breathtakingly broad. Yet even the breadth is of no avail to these Liberian plaintiffs, who can claim no loss whatsoever occurring in the United States. * * *
* * * *

Plaintiffs next argue that foreign sovereign immunity is not absolute or requisite, and that the Argentine Republic's refusal to repay the plaintiffs is so manifest a violation of its obligation under international law that this country has a right to refuse it immunity. Let us assume that this argument is valid as a matter of international law. Nonetheless, that act does not empower this court to create an ad hoc exception to a Congressional statute in order to hear this case. Federal courts, it bears mentioning at this juncture, are courts of limited jurisdiction. Perhaps Congress could empower federal courts to hear cases such as this; the court, however, is constrained by Congress's failure to do so.

Amerada Hess and United's claim were not covered by exceptions to the Foreign Sovereign Immunities Act because the loss of the tanker did not occur in the United States. Argentina was not included in the class of defendants who could be sued under the Foreign Sovereign Immunities Act. The court could not find any basis for jurisdiction and granted Argentina's motion to dismiss. In other words, Amerada Hess and United could not recover for its loss through the United States courts.

DECISION AND REMEDY

Section 1605 of the FSIA Section 1605 of the Foreign Sovereign Immunities Act sets forth the major exceptions to the jurisdictional immunity of a foreign state (country). A foreign state is not immune from the jurisdiction of the courts of the United States when the foreign state has waived its immunity or when the action is based on a commercial activity carried on in the United States by the foreign state.

Issues frequently arise as to the entities that fall within the category of ''foreign state.'' The question of what is a commercial activity has also been the subject of dispute. Under Section 1603 of the FSIA, a foreign state is defined to include both a political subdivision of a foreign state and an instrumentality of a foreign state. A commercial activity is defined to mean a commercial activity that is carried on by the foreign state having substantial contact with the United States.

In the following case, the United States court of appeals examined the question as to whether the act of state doctrine precludes a court from exercising jurisdiction over a case when a Mexican bank is carrying on commercial activities in Ohio with an American citizen.

Case 24.4
RIEDEL v. BANCAM, S.A.
United States Court of Appeals, Sixth Circuit, 1986.
792 F.2d 587.

BACKGROUND AND FACTS *In January 1981, Riedel, a resident of the state of Ohio, purchased a certificate of deposit in the amount of $100,000 with the predecessor of Bancam, called Bamesa. In January 1982, Bamesa and another Mexican bank merged, forming Bancam. Riedel renewed the original certificate four times. Neither Bamesa nor Bancam registered the certificates of deposit with the Securities and Exchange Commission or the Ohio Division of Securities as an investment security. Banks within the United States do not normally have to register their certificates of deposits with the SEC or with state security agencies.*

In August 1982, the government of Mexico required the Mexican banks to pay principal and interest on dollar-denominated certificates of deposit in pesos, at a rate of exchange substantially below the financial market exchange rate. In September 1982, the government of Mexico nationalized all privately owned Mexican banks, including Bancam. At maturity of the certificate of deposit, Bancam sent Riedel a check in repayment of his certificate in the amount of 7,434,000 pesos. Riedel could only convert the pesos into $53,276.63.

In January 1984, Riedel brought this action, alleging breach of contract and violations of federal and Ohio securities laws. Bancam filed a motion to dismiss on several grounds. First, the Foreign Sovereign Immunities Act of 1976 precluded the district court from asserting personal or subject matter jurisdiction over the action. Second, Bancam argued that the act of state doctrine and the articles of agreement of the International Monetary Fund required dismissal for failure to state a claim because Riedel based his lawsuit solely on the government of Mexico's actions in issuing and enforcing currency exchange rules that required banks to repay dollar-denominated certificates of deposit in pesos. Finally, Bancam contended that the complaint failed to state a cause of action because the certificates of deposit were not securities. (Two other grounds were involved, but are not pertinent here.)

KENNEDY, Judge.
* * * *

Bancam argues that the ''act of state doctrine'' precluded the District Court from addressing Riedel's claims. The ''act of state doctrine'' precludes courts in this country from questioning the validity and effect of a sovereign act of a foreign nation performed in its own territory. * * * Under the "act of state doctrine," courts exercise jurisdiction but prudentially "decline to decide the merits of the case if in doing so we would need to judge the validity of the public acts of a sovereign state performed within its own territory."

In *Callejo v. Bancomer, S.A.* the Fifth Circuit concluded that the "act of state doctrine" precluded the court from inquiring into the validity of Mexico's currency exchange control regulations. * * *

* * * [W]e hold that the "act of state doctrine" precludes the District Court from addressing Riedel's breach of contract claim. Accordingly, we affirm the portion of the District Court's order denying Riedel's motion for a new trial on the breach of contract claim. The "act of state doctrine," however, does not bar the Ohio securities law claim. Riedel bases that claim on Bancam's failure to register the certificate of deposit with the Ohio Division of Securities and not on Bancam's failure to repay dollars at the certificate's maturity.
* * * *

* * * Riedel argues that the certificates of deposit that Bancam issued are "securities" under ORC [Ohio Revised Code] § 1707.01(B). Bancam argues that Riedel did not state a claim under the Ohio securities laws because certificates of deposit are not "securities" under Ohio law.

* * * ORC § 1707.07 requires registration by description, qualification, or coordination before a person may sell "securities" in Ohio. ORC § 1707.02(C), however, creates the following exemption from the registration provisions of ORC §§ 1707.08-1707.11:

> Any security issued by and representing an interest in or an obligation of a state or nationally chartered bank or credit union, or a governmental corporation or agency created by or under the laws of the United States or of Canada is exempt, if it is under the supervision of or subject to regulation by the government or state under whose laws it was organized.

* * * Since Bancam was not "incorporated or organized under the laws of the United States or of any state thereof, or of Canada or of any province thereof," Bancam is not a "nationally chartered bank" under ORC § 1707.02(C). Consequently, Bancam does not qualify for the ORC § 1707.02(C) exemption. We reject Bancam's contention that the certificates of deposit are not "securities" under ORC § 1707.01(B). Accordingly, we reverse the portion of the District Court's order denying Riedel's motion for a new trial on the Ohio securities law claim.

Since the District Court may have had subject matter jurisdiction, we remand the Ohio securities law claim for further proceedings consistent with this opinion. We also note that even if the District Court concludes that it has subject matter jurisdiction, Bancam has also argued that the District Court does not have personal jurisdiction. Assuming that the District Court decides that it has subject matter jurisdiction under the FSIA, the District Court will also have to make findings of fact to determine whether Bancam has sufficient "contacts" with the United States to satisfy due process. Furthermore, Bancam alleges that Ohio securities law does not apply because the circumstances giving rise to this action occurred in Mexico. Bancam claims that "[a]ny contact with Ohio was merely incidental as a result of Riedel's residence in Ohio." Accordingly, the District Court may have to decide whether Ohio securities law applies in the circumstances of this case. Finally, assuming that Ohio securities law required Bancam to register the certificates of deposit with the Ohio Division of Securities, the District Court must determine whether such a requirement impermissibly burdens foreign commerce because Congress has not required the registration of certificates of deposit sold by Mexican banks since certificates of deposit are not "securities" under the federal securities laws. Consequently, we remand the Ohio securities law claim to the District Court.

DECISION AND *The case was remanded to the district court for further decisions. The court*
REMEDY *of appeals found that, although the act of state doctrine barred Riedel's*
breach of contract claim, it did not bar his Ohio securities claim, and the
district court might have subject-matter jurisdiction over Riedel's claim.

Transacting Business Internationally

Businesses involved in international transactions have a number of decisions to make before they begin. First, will the business be involved in exporting, importing, or licensing? These three business arrangements are the least complex legally, and in many cases a firm can engage in them without a substantial capital investment. Second, will the company decide to make that business investment in a foreign country? An investment may be made in one of two ways, either by joint venture or by direct investment.

Exporting, Importing, and Licensing

Exporting is the selling of goods manufactured in and exported from (sent from) the domestic country to the foreign country. **Importing** is the opposite; it is the buying of goods manufactured in a foreign country that are then imported to (sent to) the domestic country. **Licensing** gives a business the right to use, lease, sell, or distribute goods or services in a foreign market.

The United States Constitution has a very specific sentence on exports: "No Tax or Duty shall be laid on Articles exported from any State." [Article I, Section 9, (5)] In 1868, the United States Supreme Court interpreted "exported" to mean exported to a foreign country and not to a sister state. Although no tax may be levied, Congress is able to legislate control over exports to foreign countries through various statutes. For example, Congress may set an export quota on grain being sold overseas.

The Department of Commerce is the primary government agency that assists businesses with exporting problems. The department prints publications, brochures, and pamphlets that guide firms through the bureaucratic paperwork; the department also holds meetings and posts exhibits on exporting. In addition, it will assist a company in

finding an import specialist in the country in which the firm will be shipping the goods and doing business.

Federal Tax Legislation to Assist Exports Congress has passed several statutes to help businesses engaged in exporting. The Revenue Act of 1971 gives tax benefits when a firm markets its products overseas through a **foreign sales corporation**. The benefit consists of a tax exemption on the business's income that is produced from the exports. The foreign sales corporation must be located outside the United States, although it may be based in a United States possession, such as Puerto Rico. If it is located in a foreign country, that country must be party to an information exchange agreement with the United States.

Export Trading Company Act The **Export Trading Company Act** of 1982 came about because of legal difficulties concerning the conduct of international business that violated federal antitrust laws. This act allows a person, partnership, corporation or any association to file an application for a certificate of antitrust immunity, which is based on an information statement regarding the company's business plans. Once the certificate is granted and as long as the company follows its business plan, the company will be immune from antitrust prosecution by the Justice Department as discussed in Chapters 19 and 20.

The act also allows United States banks to invest in and make loans to export trading companies. An export trading company is formed by exporting firms joining together to export a line of goods to foreign countries. The export trading company concept is modeled after those found in Japan.

Export-Import Bank The **Export-Import Bank** (**Eximbank**) provides financial assistance to exporting and importing firms. The primary assistance consists of the credit guarantees that Eximbank gives to commercial banks. The banks, in turn, make direct loans to exporting companies based on the guarantees provided by Eximbank.

Export Administration Act The **Export Administration Act** enacted in 1979 provides for the issuance of three types of licenses: a general license, a validated license, and a qualified license. The general license authorizes the exporter (license holder) to export goods without any further documentation or approval. The validated license authorizes the exporter to export a specific product. The qualified license authorizes the exporter to make multiple exports to only certain countries. A business determines if a license is necessary by contacting the Department of Commerce. This act attempts to control the exporting of technical data and items that would contribute to the military potential of another country. There are other federal acts which control exports. For example, export control provisions are found in the Atomic Energy Act of 1954 and the Nuclear Non-Proliferation Act of 1978.

Import Restrictions When a product is exported from one country, it must be imported to another country. The importing country may want to impose restrictions on imports. A country's power to restrict imports may be limited if the country belongs to the **General Agreement on Tariffs and Trade (GATT)** or the **International Monetary Fund (IMF)**.

Some of the types of restrictions that a nation may impose are prohibitions, quotas, tariffs, and licensing.

Prohibition Restrictions All nations have prohibitions on the import of goods that the country perceives to be harmful to it. For example, the **Trading with the Enemy Act of 1917** restricts imports from nations that have been designated as enemies to the United States. Other laws prohibit the importation of cocaine, which is an illegal drug, or of an agricultural product that poses a danger to domestic crops or animals. For example, diseased cattle may not be imported to the United States.

Quotas A **quota** places limits on the goods to be imported. For example, the United States at one time had a quota on the number of automobiles that could be imported from Japan. Other items that are subject to quotas are silicon chips and high-tech electronic machines.

Tariffs A **tariff** is a tax placed on imported goods. There is no equivalent tax on the same goods if they are produced domestically. A tariff generally is based on one of two formulas: an *ad valorem* basis or a flat-rate basis. An *ad valorem* tariff taxes a percentage of the value of the imported goods. A flat-rate tariff taxes a unit item, such as barrels of oil, or is based on weight, such as a tariff assessed on a tonnage basis.

Licensing A license is granted by a nation that gives a specific firm the right to conduct business within the boundaries of that nation. Property rights that require licensing may be based on statutory or nonstatutory sources. Property based on statutory sources include patents, copyrights, trademarks, trade names, or trade secrets. An example of property based on a nonstatutory source is technical data. Currently, a franchise type of license agreement is popular and enables firms to expand overseas. Examples include the International Hilton Hotel chain, McDonald's, and Coca-Cola.

Investing

If a business wants to make a more substantial foreign commitment, it will make an investment either through a joint venture or a direct investment. A **joint venture** is when two or more businesses join together to conduct business. An international joint venture works the same way as a domestic joint venture. A firm may contribute capital, management expertise, marketing expertise, or raw material. Of course, the firm is subject not only to the international laws but also to the laws of the nation where the business is being conducted. For example, the General Motors–Toyota agreement to produce automobiles in California is a joint venture.

If a corporation considers investing directly in a foreign country, the firm must consider many factors. The nation's political and economic stability is the first consideration. Other items to be reviewed are the investment laws, tax laws, antitrust laws, labor laws, worker safety laws, legal system, and corporation laws.

Methods of Transacting Business Contracts

Whether a company is in the importing or exporting business, is conducting business through a license arrangement, is engaging in a joint venture, or is making a direct investment in a foreign country, a fundamental need exists for a contract. As with all commercial contracts, the transnational (international) business contract should be in writing.

Parties to a transnational business contract should be aware of the three basic legal and economic systems. The common-law system, developed in England, was spread throughout the world by the English colonial system and is today found throughout the English-speaking countries, including the United States, Canada, Australia, and New Zealand. The court system and the legislature are the major sources of common law. Private ownership of business is predominant, and there is immense freedom to make and tailor contracts to a particular situation.

The civil law system is the legal system found in Western Europe. Much of the law is derived from the code passed by the legislature, while the judiciary plays a more subservient role. The economic system is a combination of businesses being owned both by private ownership and by government ownership. The freedom to contract is more restricted through the legislative code.

The third system is the socialistic system found in Eastern Europe and the Union of Soviet Socialist Republics. In this system, the judiciary is subservient to the government. The government owns all or most of the businesses, as opposed to predominantly private ownership under the other two systems. Under this system, there is very little freedom to contract in the sense of that found under the common-law system. Because of these major differences in the legal and economic systems, parties should agree in advance as to what law will be applied in the event of a dispute or breach of contract.

The United Nations Convention on Contracts for the International Sale of Goods was approved in 1980 but has been ratified by relatively few nations. These countries include the United States, France, Italy, Austria, Finland, Mexico, Switzerland, and the People's Republic of China. The convention deals with the international sale of goods and is similar in nature to the Uniform Commercial Code.

Provisions within a Contract

Contracts should be negotiated first with all the details understood. The contract should be drafted by attorneys familiar with the business involved and with international law. The drafts should be reviewed before reducing the contract to final form. Some contract provisions that should be considered in the formation of any international contract are covered in the following subsections.

Choice of Law   The parties can write into the contract a choice-of-law clause. A **choice-of-law clause** designates the forum in which adjudication will take place and what substantive law will be applied in the event of any disputes. The "forum" indicates where legal action shall be brought if a dispute should occur.

An arbitration clause may also be included in the contract. When providing for arbitration, the contract must specify the forum, governing law, and expertise of and method of selecting the arbitrator.

Many countries recognize the validity of choice-of-law and arbitration clauses and will enforce them in their courts. It is of critical importance, however, that, before entering into a transnational business contract, both parties must be familiar with the laws of the foreign country involved.

Official-Language Clause   The contract should also contain a clause that designates the official language to be used in interpreting the terms of the contract. This clause promotes a clear and precise understanding of the terms of the contract by each of the parties.

For example, in a sale of goods contract, the basic contract of sale should include a legal definition of terms, the price and manner of payment, and a provision specifying the acceptable currency for payment. A *force majeure* clause, which protects the parties from forces beyond their control such as acts of God, is also advisable.

Risk-of-Loss Clause   Transacting international business involves peculiar risks since buyers and

---

LEGAL HIGHLIGHT   **The Life Cycle of a Letter of Credit**

Although the letter of credit appears quite complex at first, it is not difficult to understand. It merely involves the exchange of documents (and money) through intermediaries. The following steps depict the letter-of-credit procurement cycle.

Step 1: The buyer and seller agree upon the terms of sale. The sales contract dictates that a letter of credit is to be used to finance the transaction.

Step 2: The buyer completes an application for a letter of credit and forwards it to his or her bank which will issue the letter of credit.

Step 3: The issuing buyer's bank then forwards the letter of credit to a correspondent bank in the seller's country.

Step 4: The correspondent bank relays the letter of credit to the seller.

Step 5: Having received assurance of payment, the seller makes the necessary shipping arrangements.

Step 6: The seller prepares the documents required under the letter of credit and delivers them to the correspondent bank.

Step 7: The correspondent bank negotiates the documents. If it finds them in order, it sends them to the issuing bank and pays the seller in accordance with the terms of the letter of credit.

Step 8: The issuing bank, having received the documents, examines them. If they are in order, the issuing bank will charge the buyer's account and send the documents on to the buyer or his or her customs broker. The issuing bank also will reimburse the correspondent bank.

Step 9: The buyer or broker receives the documents and picks up the merchandise from the shipper (carrier).

Source: National Association of Purchasing Management.

---

sellers are often separated by thousands of miles. Sellers want to avoid delivering goods for which they might not be paid. Buyers do not want to pay the sellers until there is evidence that the goods have been shipped. Specific clauses can dictate the exact moment risk of loss passes from the seller to the buyer. In addition, to limit the risks of nonpayment for goods shipped or for payment for goods not shipped, the parties frequently use letters of credit to facilitate international business transactions.

Letter of Credit

In a **letter-of-credit transaction**, at least three separate and distinct contracts are involved. The first contract is between the account party (buyer) and the beneficiary (seller). The second contract is between the issuer (bank) and the account party

(buyer). Finally, a letter of credit involves a contract between the issuer and the beneficiary. Given the fact that each contract is separate and distinct, the issuer's obligations under the letter of credit do not concern the underlying contract between the buyer and the seller. Rather, it is the issuer's duty to ascertain whether the documents presented by the beneficiary (seller) comply with the terms of the letter of credit.

In a simple letter-of-credit transaction, the issuer (a bank) agrees to issue a letter of credit and to ascertain the occurrence of certain acts by the beneficiary (seller). In return, the account party (buyer) promises to reimburse the issuer for the amount paid to the beneficiary. The issuer sends the letter of credit to a correspondent bank in the seller's country. The correspondent bank will expedite payment under the letter of credit.

Under a letter of credit, the issuer is bound to

pay the beneficiary (seller) through the correspondent bank when the beneficiary has complied with the terms and conditions of the letter of credit. The beneficiary looks to the issuer, not to the account party (buyer), when it presents the documents required by the letter of credit. Typically, the letter of credit will require that the beneficiary deliver a bill of lading to prove that shipment has been made. Letters of credit assure beneficiaries (sellers) of payment, while at the same time they assure account parties (buyers) that payment will not be made until the beneficiaries have complied with the terms and conditions of the letter of credit. See the Legal Highlight entitled "The Life Cycle of a Letter of Credit" for a letter of credit cycle.

The basic principle behind letters of credit is that payment is made against the documents presented by the beneficiary and not against the facts that the documents purport to reflect. Thus, in a letter-of-credit transaction, the issuer does not police the underlying contract: Again, a letter of credit is independent of the underlying contract between the buyer and the seller. By eliminating

the banks' (issuers') inquiry into whether the actual conditions have been satisfied, the costs of letters of credit are greatly reduced. Moreover, the use of a letter of credit protects both buyers and sellers.

If the documents presented by the beneficiary comply with the terms of the letter of credit, the issuer (bank) must honor the letter. Sometimes, however, it is difficult to determine exactly what a letter of credit requires. The courts are divided as to whether strict compliance or substantial compliance with the terms of a letter of credit is required. Traditionally, courts have required strict compliance with the terms of a letter of credit.

Letters of credit are used also in domestic transactions, such as in real estate transactions. The same rules governing letters of credit apply to both international and domestic transactions. In the following case, the district court discusses the fact that Illinois law has moved away from the traditional standard of strict compliance to one of reasonable compliance.

Case 24.5
CROCKER COMMERCIAL SERVICES v. COUNTRYSIDE BANK
United States District Court, Northern District of Illinois, 1981.
538 F.Supp. 1360.

BACKGROUND AND FACTS *On January 17, 1980, Crocker United Factors, Inc., changed its corporate name to Crocker Commercial Services, Inc. Approximately two weeks later, Countryside Bank issued a letter of credit to Crocker. The letter of credit stated that the drafts must be accompanied by invoices issued to Everyone's Effort, Inc., by Crocker Commercial Services before Countryside Bank would pay the drafts. When Crocker presented the draft for payment, however, the invoices reflected the name of Crocker United Factors, Inc. and payment was refused. Both Crocker and Countryside Bank filed cross-motions for summary judgment. Crocker wanted payment based on the letter of credit. Countryside Bank wanted the case dismissed because the invoices did not conform to the requirements of the letter of credit.*

SHADUR, Judge.
* * * *

This time of year invariably brings forth a spate of dramas in which the hardhearted banker is the villain, sometimes regenerate (Scrooge in Dickens' *Christmas Carol*), sometimes unregenerate (as in Frank Capra's *It's a Wonderful Life*). By chance this is the second occasion during the past two weeks in which the Court has had to deal with the unregenerate type—which tries to extricate itself from an unquestioned obligation by the kind of hypertechnical argument that has often tended to give the term "banker" pejorative connotations.

Illinois law however rejects Bank's position. Last year's decision in *First Arlington National Bank v. Stathis* * * * turned away from the "traditional standard'' of strict compliance to confirm that reasonable compliance with a letter of credit entitles beneficiary to payment.

Under a fair application of the *First Arlington* reasonable compliance doctrine, Crocker is clearly entitled to payment:

> Its certification conformed precisely to the Letter of Credit by referring to ''Crocker Commercial Services.'' Although it gratuitously enclosed documents that referred to ''Crocker United Factors, Inc.,'' and though that disparity might possibly have relieved Bank of responsibility had it been a real discrepancy, the fact is that no discrepancy existed. * * * Because the same corporation was involved, the change in corporate name does not negate ''reasonable compliance.'' * * *

There is another and self-sufficient ground that, though not mentioned by either party, also defeats Bank's nit-picking position. Bank's conduct may fairly be viewed as creating either a waiver or an estoppel, for it stood by silently and permitted the Letter of Credit to run out, even though an identification of the claimed deficiencies would have enabled Crocker to cure them.

* * * *

For that reason the failure to make timely objection is a waiver of any curable flaws in the beneficiary's demand. Had Bank voiced its objections to Crocker at any time through January 20, Crocker could have cured the hypertechnical language difficulties now relied upon by Bank. It is only equitable to apply the doctrine of waiver—if the time sequence permits—to bar Bank's purported defenses.

* * * *

Accordingly, alternate grounds of waiver or estoppel serve to support summary judgment in Crocker's favor. It should be stressed that this holding is independent of the doctrine of ''reasonable compliance,'' which alone requires the same result.

The district court granted Crocker's motion of summary judgment. It concluded that no genuine issue of material fact existed.	**DECISION AND REMEDY**

United States Antitrust Laws in a Transnational Setting

United States antitrust laws (discussed in Chapters 19 and 20) have a wide application. They may subject persons in foreign nations to their provisions as well as protect foreign consumers and competitors from antitrust-violation acts committed by U.S. citizens. Consequently, foreign persons, a term that by definition includes foreign governments, may sue under U.S. antitrust laws in U.S. courts.

Section 1 of the Sherman Act provides for the extraterritorial effect of the U.S. antitrust laws. (See Appendix D.) The United States is a major proponent of free competition in the global economy, and thus any conspiracy that has a substantial effect on U.S. commerce is within the reach of the Sherman Act. The act of violation may even occur outside the United States, and foreign governments as well as persons can be sued in violation of U.S. antitrust laws. Yet before U.S. courts will exercise jurisdiction and apply antitrust laws, it must be shown that the alleged violation had a *substantial effect* on U.S. commerce. U.S. jurisdiction is automatically invoked, however, when a *per se* violation occurs.

Substantial Effect on U.S. Commerce for Antitrust Violation

A *per se* violation may consist of resale price-fixing and tying, or tie-in, contracts. If a domestic firm, for example, joins a foreign cartel to control the production, price, or distribution of goods, and this cartel has a substantial restraining effect on U.S. commerce, a *per se* violation may exist. Hence, both the domestic firm and the foreign cartel have the potential to be sued in violation of the U.S. antitrust laws. Likewise, if foreign firms doing business in the United States enter into a price-fixing or other anticompetitive agreement to control a portion of U.S. markets, a *per se* violation may exist.

The United States has amended the Sherman Act and the Federal Trade Commission Act in their application to unfair methods of competition, when such methods or conduct involve U.S. export trade or commerce with foreign nations. The acts are not limited, however, where there is a "direct, substantial, and reasonably foreseeable effect" upon U.S. domestic commerce that results in a claim for damages.

A case that came before the U.S. Supreme Court in 1986 is illustrative. In *Matsushita Electric Industrial Co. v. Zenith Radio Corp.*,[2] several U.S. manufacturers of television sets alleged that Matsushita and other Japanese firms "illegally conspired to drive American firms from the consumer electronic products market" by means of a "scheme to raise, fix and maintain artificially *high* prices for television receivers sold by [Matsushita and others] in Japan and, at the same time, to fix and maintain *low* prices for television receivers exported to and sold in the United States." The alleged conspiracy began, according to Zenith, in 1953. The American firms claimed that the Japanese were engaged in a "predatory pricing" arrangement whereby the losses sustained by selling at such low prices in the United States were offset by monopoly profits obtained in Japan. Once the Japanese gained control over an overwhelming portion of the American market for electronic products, their monopoly power would enable them to recover their losses by charging artificially high prices in America as well.

In his opinion, Justice Powell found the allegation to be "implausible" and one "that simply makes no economic sense." Citing numerous authorities on predatory pricing, he argued that the risk of suffering real, immediate losses in the present in the mere hope of not only establishing monopoly power, but maintaining it for a sufficiently long period to recoup the losses at some point in the distant future, was one rarely, if ever, taken

by any firm. For a cartel, or alliance of firms, to undertake such a risk was even more unlikely. The difficulties involved in allocating losses and future profits among a group of firms and in ensuring that none of them cheated on the others—which would be especially tempting given the uncertainty of the future monopoly profits—were unlikely to be overcome.

Justice Powell further contended that the "alleged predatory scheme makes sense only if petitioners can recoup their losses. In light of the large number of firms involved here, petitioners can achieve this only by engaging in some form of price-fixing *after* they have succeeded in driving competitors from the market. Such price-fixing would, of course, be an independent violation of Section 1 of the Sherman Act." Thus, even if the cartel could overcome the difficulties mentioned above by consistently pricing below cost, the existence of antitrust legislation in the United States would still make it extremely difficult, if not impossible, to realize their goal of monopoly profits.

Finally, and perhaps most persuasively, Justice Powell noted a relevant fact: In 1953 the two leading television producers in the United States, RCA and Zenith, controlled approximately 40 percent of that market. During the twenty years during which the Japanese were implementing their alleged plan, that percentage remained approximately constant and had not changed significantly. "The alleged conspiracy's failure to achieve its ends in the two decades of its asserted operation," stated the Court, "is strong evidence that the conspiracy does not in fact exist." To claim such a conspiracy exists simply "makes no practical sense."

Justice Powell clearly indicated to both potential future litigants and to the courts that "cutting price in order to increase business often is the very essence of competition." To infer otherwise in cases such as this one can be "especially costly, because they chill the very conduct the antitrust laws are designed to protect."

Common Markets

After World War II, many smaller nations believed that their status in the evolving global econ-

---

2.   475 U.S. 574, 106 S.Ct. 1348, 89 L.Ed.2d 538 (1986).

omy was threatened by the dominant world powers. To gain economic recognition, they organized and integrated their economies into cohesive groups called **common markets**. An example of one such organization is the European Common Market.

The European Economic Community

Created by the European Economic Community (EEC), the European Common Market presently includes twelve Western European nations. These countries have eliminated public tariffs and private, restrictive agreements among themselves. The EEC promotes free trade and competition within its own common market in order to protect itself from competition outside the European Common Market.

The EEC came into existence in 1957 with the signing of the Treaty of Rome. Currently, Belgium, France, West Germany, Greece, Denmark, Ireland, Italy, the United Kingdom, Luxembourg, the Netherlands, Spain, and Portugal are members of the EEC. In addition to establishing common tariffs for outside nations and eliminating tariffs among EEC members, the treaty further promotes the free movement of workers, goods, and capital among the member nations.

The following often-cited case illustrates the EEC's regulation of the free movement of workers between the member countries.

BACKGROUND AND FACTS *In 1968 a government minister in the House of Commons stated that the government considered the practice of Scientology to be socially harmful. Thus, pursuant to government policy, foreign nationals intending to work or study at Scientology establishments were not allowed to enter the United Kingdom. The Home Office announced that the policy would be continued and would apply to members of the European Economic Community.*

In 1973 the plaintiff, a Dutch national, was offered employment as a secretary in the Church of Scientology at East Grinstead, Sussex. She was subsequently refused entry into the United Kingdom by an immigration officer. The plaintiff then brought an action against the Home Office, declaring that under the EEC treaty, she should be allowed to enter the United Kingdom. She alleged that refusal had been based solely on the grounds of public policy and that such a refusal was unlawful.

Case 24.6
VAN DUYN v. HOME OFFICE
Court of Justice of the European Communities, 1974.
Case No. 41/74.

SORENSEN, Drafting Judge.
* * * *

The question raises the problem of whether a Member State is entitled, on grounds of public policy, to prevent a national of another Member State from taking gainful employment within its territory with a body or organization, it being the case that no similar restriction is placed upon its own nationals.

In this connection, the Treaty, while enshrining the principle of freedom of movement for workers without any discrimination on grounds of nationality, admits, in Article 48(3), limitations justified on grounds of public policy, public security or public health to the rights deriving from this principle. Under the terms of the provisions cited above, the right to accept offers of employment actually made the right to move freely within the territory of Member States for this purpose, and the right to stay in a Member State for the purpose of employment are, among others, all subject to such limitations. Consequently, the effect of such limitations, when they apply, is that leave to enter the territory of a Member State and the right to reside there may be refused to a national of another Member State.

Furthermore, it is a principle of international law, which the EEC treaty cannot be assumed to disregard in the relations between Member States, that a State is precluded from refusing its own nationals the right of entry or residence.

It follows that a Member State, for reasons of public policy, can, where it deems necessary, refuse a national of another Member State the benefit of the principle of freedom of movement for workers in a case where such a national proposes to take up a particular offer of employment even though the Member State does not place a similar restriction upon its own nationals.

Accordingly, * * * Article 48 of the EEC Treaty and Article 3(1) of Directive 64/221 are to be interpreted as meaning that a Member State, in imposing restrictions justified on grounds of public policy, is entitled to take into account, as a matter of personal conduct of the individual concerned, the fact that the individual is associated with some body or organization the activities of which the Member State considers socially harmful but which are not unlawful in that State, despite the fact that no restriction is placed upon nationals of the said Member State who wish to take similar employment with these same bodies or organizations.

DECISION AND REMEDY *The Court of Justice determined that a Member State (nation) may exclude persons from entry into its country on the basis of public policy regardless of the Treaty of Rome, which promotes the free movement of workers among the member nations. Thus, the plaintiff was not wrongly denied entry into Great Britain.*

COMMENTS *A European Economic Community provision has limited the freedom-of-movement provision by allowing the exclusion of persons on the basis of public policy, public safety, and public health.*

Other Common Markets

Although the European Common Market is the most well known, there are many other economic cooperatives whose members are countries in close proximity to each other. The Central American states formed the Central American Common Market (CACM); the Caribbean states formed the Caribbean Community (CARICOM); and the French-speaking African states formed the Union Douanière at Economique de l'Afrique Centrale (UDEAC).

Common markets and international economic organizations represent one way to facilitate international business and trade. A basic problem in the international business setting, however, is the fact that both individual nations and groups of nations are at odds over the extent to which free competition on a global level is desirable. The more industrialized and technically advanced nations tend to monopolize certain technological interests by protective measures, such as patents, copyrights, licensing, and registration requirements. It is often the very technology that these countries seek to withhold that the less-developed countries most desire and need for their future development and growth.

FACING A LEGAL ISSUE

Many people would like to acquire one of those special automobiles manufactured by Rolls Royce, Mercedes Benz, Porsche, BMW and other prestigious companies. The cost of these vehicles is very high. This is particularly true if you make your purchase through a dealer who is authorized to sell the vehicles within the United States.

Considerable sums of money can be saved in a variety of ways. One is to take a trip to Europe and purchase a vehicle there. The current import tax on a vehicle is 2.5 percent of what you pay overseas. You might be able to negotiate a good price for the automobile and thus save on both original price and import duty. Or you can bypass the authorized dealers and purchase the automobile in what is commonly called the "grey market" through an unauthorized dealer here. This market offers both new and used vehicles.

Two major problems exist, however, with either approach. First, you must recognize that federal law requires certain equipment on all vehicles, such as antipollution devices, steel reinforcement in the doors, and side lights. The European countries do not have these requirements. It costs an estimated $5,000 to equip a European automobile to meet United States standards.

When a vehicle is imported to the United States, a bond of three times the value must be posted to guarantee that it will meet all federal standards. The owner has ninety days to bring the vehicle up to those standards, but he or she can obtain a thirty-day extension. If the automobile does not meet the standards within 120 days, it must be either exported or destroyed, and the bond is forfeited. Each time the vehicle is tested by the federal government, it costs $1,000. As you can see, importing and testing can be very expensive. Automobiles manufactured prior to 1968 do not have to have this equipment.

The second problem involves the possibility of purchasing a stolen vehicle. There have been cases where a vehicle has been stolen in Europe, then imported and sold through the grey market in the United States. Months later, the United States Custom Service office of enforcement has contacted the new owner and repossessed the vehicle on behalf of the European owner. This does not occur frequently, but it does occur.

After considering these factors, you may decide just to purchase this type of vehicle from an authorized United States dealer.

Summary

The growth in international business relations has led in turn to the development of international law. International law consists of a body of laws that are considered to be legally binding among otherwise independent nations. This legal area has developed through two methods: international customs, and agreements that have the force of law. International customs consist of the relationship that nations have developed over years with one another on particular legal matters. Agreements are reached either by nations acting independently, as in the signing of treaties or through international organizations and conferences.

Several important doctrines exist that help resolve the inevitable differences among laws. The act of state doctrine provides that the court system of one country will not examine the validity of public acts committed by a recognized foreign government within its own territory. The principle of comity is where the courts of one country give deference to the effect of the laws and judicial decrees of another nation. The doctrine of sovereign immunity prevents the United States from having jurisdiction over a foreign nation. Congress has passed the Foreign Sovereign Immunities Act to establish clearer guidelines in this area.

Businesses can transact business internationally by exporting (sending products to another country), importing (buying goods made in another country), or licensing, which permits a business the right to use, lease, sell, or distribute goods in a foreign country. A business can also invest in another country either by joint venture or by direct investments.

International sales contracts should be carefully drawn and reviewed. The parties should consider including clauses on choice of language, choice of law, and arbitration of disputes. The parties should also know about letters of credit, antitrust laws, labor and safety laws, tax laws, investment laws, and corporation laws.

Over the years, nations have joined together to protect their political and economic interests through organizations such as the European Economic Community, Central American Common Market, Caribbean Community, and Union Douanière et Economique de l'Afrique Centrale.

Key Terms

act of state doctrine **(587)**
choice-of-law clause **(598)**
common markets **(603)**
confiscation **(588)**
doctrine of sovereign
  immunity **(592)**
Export Administration Act
  (597)
Export Trading Company Act
  (596)
Export-Import Bank
  (Eximbank) **(596)**

exporting **(596)**
expropriation **(588)**
foreign sales corporation
  (596)
Foreign Sovereign Immunities
  Act (FSIA) **(592)**
General Agreement on Tariffs
  and Trade (GATT) **(597)**
importing **(596)**
international customs **(586)**
international law **(586)**
International Monetary Fund

(IMF) **(597)**
joint venture **(597)**
letter-of-credit transaction
  (599)
licensing **(596)**
national law **(587)**
principle of comity **(590)**
quota **(597)**
tariff **(597)**
Trading with the Enemy Act
  (597)
treaty **(586)**

Questions and Case Problems

1. Suppose that Arnold Roth, a United States wholesaler, enters into an agreement to purchase widgets from Manufacturers, Inc., a Columbian manufacturer. Roth further secures an irrevocable letter of credit from Sunnydays Bank, a U.S. bank. When Manufacturers, Inc., placed the sixty crates of widgets on board a steamship, it received in return the invoices required under the letter of credit. The invoices are being forwarded to Sunnydays Bank for payment. The purchaser, Arnold Roth, subsequently learns that Manufacturers, Inc. has filled the sixty crates with rubbish, not widgets. Given the fact that an issuer's obligation under a letter of credit is independent of the underlying contract between the buyer and seller, will the issuer be required to pay the letter of credit? (See UCC 5-114(2)(a).)

2. XYZ, Inc. desires to import goods from Nigeria. It wants to make certain that the goods are the ones desired

and that they are received in good condition. Nigeria desires to be paid if the goods are shipped. Describe what procedures should be followed.

3. Verlinden B. V. entered into a contract for the purchase of 240,000 metric tons of cement by the Federal Republic of Nigeria. Verlinden B. V., a Dutch corporation, subsequently sued the Central Bank of Nigeria and alleged that the Central Bank's actions constituted an anticipatory breach. May a United States federal court exercise subject-matter jurisdiction over an action brought by a foreign corporation against a foreign sovereign under the Foreign Sovereign Immunities Act of 1976? Discuss. [Verlinden B. V. v. Central Bank of Nigeria, 461 U.S. 480, 103 S.Ct. 1962, 76 L.Ed.2d 81 (1983)]

4. A letter of credit was issued by North Carolina National Bank for its customer, Adastra Knittiny Hills, Inc. The credit was to cover Adastra's purchases of acrylic yarn from Courtaulds, an Alabama corporation, the beneficiary. Under the letter of credit, Courtaulds was to present a draft accompanied by a commercial invoice stating that it covers 100 percent acrylic yarn. When Courtaulds presented the draft, the accompanying invoices stated that the goods were ''Imported Acrylic Yarn.'' The packing lists, however, disclosed that the packages contained 100 percent acrylic yarn. The bank refused to honor the draft claiming the invoices did not meet the requirements of the letter of credit. Should the bank be liable to Courtaulds for the amount of the draft? Discuss. [Courtaulds North America, Inc. v. North Carolina National Bank, 528 F.2d 802 (4th Cir. 1975)]

5. Section 1610(d)(1) of the Foreign Sovereign Immunities Act (FSIA) provides that the property of a foreign state that is used for a commercial activity in the United States shall not be immune from attachment prior to the entry of a judgment if the foreign state has ''explicitly waived its immunity from attachment prior to judgment.'' Banco Nacional, an instrumentality of the government of Costa Rica, entered into a written agreement with Libra Bank Ltd., the plaintiffs. In the agreement, Banco Nacional stated that it did not have ''any right of immunity from suit with respect to the Borrower's obligations'' under this particular agreement. Discuss whether Banco Nacional, the defendant, ''explicitly'' waived its immunity from prejudgment attachment as required by Section 1610(d)(1) of the FSIA? [Libra Bank Ltd. v. Banco Nacional de Costa Rica, 676 F.2d 47 (2d Cir. 1982)]

6. Harris Corporation, the plaintiff, entered into a contract with the defendant, National Iranian Radio and Television (NIRT), to manufacture and deliver 144 FM broadcast transmitters to Teheran, Iran. Due to the revolution in Iran, the plaintiff was unable to complete delivery of the transmitters. NIRT attempted to collect on a letter of credit that had been set up to guarantee performance. The plaintiff subsequently brought an action against the defendant seeking to enjoin receipt of payment on the letter of credit. Bank Melli Iran, the issuer, was also made a defendant. Both defendants alleged that the district court lacked jurisdiction over them under the Foreign Sovereign Immunities Act (FSIA). From 1969 to 1982, Melli maintained an office in New York City where it carried out significant business transactions. Moreover, NIRT entered into this contract that required performance by Harris in the United States and also required the training of NIRT personnel in the United States. Discuss whether this action falls under the FSIA. [Harris Corp. v. National Iranian Radio, Etc., 691 F.2d 1344 (11th Cir. 1982)]

7. Charles T. Main International brought an action to recover assets that had been lost due to the overthrow of the Shah in Iran. To obtain the release of hostages, President Carter had signed an agreement to submit all claims by either Iran or United States to binding arbitration. The plaintiff wanted to recover from Iran assets that had been frozen in the United States. Main claims the president's agreement freezing Iranian assets exceeded the president's authority and violated its constitutional rights as a taking of its property without just compensation. What result occurred? [Charles T. Main International v. Khuzestan Water and Power Authority, 651 F.2d 800 (1st Cir. 1981)]

8. Mitsubishi and Soler Chrysler-Plymouth entered a contract that required binding arbitration. A dispute occurred, and Mitsubishi wanted to arbitrate it. Soler Chrysler-Plymouth claimed that Mitsubishi had violated the antitrust laws of the United States, which made the parties' contract illegal and thus was not subject to arbitration. Who prevailed in this case? [Mitsubishi Motor Corp. v. Soler Chrysler-Plymouth, 473 U.S. 614, 105 S.Ct. 3346, 87 L.Ed. 2d 444 (1985)]

9. Nigeria contracted for the purchase of millions of tons of cement from Texas Trading and Milling Corp. and others. It overbought, resulting in the country's docks becoming clogged. Unable to accept the cement, Nigeria repudiated many of its cement contracts. Legal action was instituted by Texas Trading in the United States. Nigeria claimed its sovereign immunity under the Foreign Sovereign Immunities Act. Discuss the result. [Texas Trading and Milling Corp. v. Federal Republic of Nigeria, 647 F.2d 300 (2d Cir. 1981)]

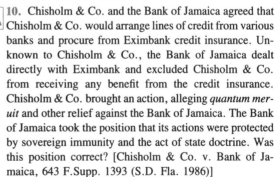 10. Chisholm & Co. and the Bank of Jamaica agreed that Chisholm & Co. would arrange lines of credit from various banks and procure from Eximbank credit insurance. Unknown to Chisholm & Co., the Bank of Jamaica dealt directly with Eximbank and excluded Chisholm & Co. from receiving any benefit from the credit insurance. Chisholm & Co. brought an action, alleging *quantum meruit* and other relief against the Bank of Jamaica. The Bank of Jamaica took the position that its actions were protected by sovereign immunity and the act of state doctrine. Was this position correct? [Chisholm & Co. v. Bank of Jamaica, 643 F.Supp. 1393 (S.D. Fla. 1986)]

Appendix A The Constitution of the United States of America

PREAMBLE

We the People of the United States, in Order to form a more perfect Union, establish Justice, insure domestic Tranquility, provide for the common defence, promote the general Welfare, and secure the Blessings of Liberty to ourselves and our Posterity, do ordain and establish this Constitution for the United States of America.

ARTICLE I

Section 1. All legislative Powers herein granted shall be vested in a Congress of the United States, which shall consist of a Senate and House of Representatives.

Section 2. The House of Representatives shall be composed of Members chosen every second Year by the People of the several States, and the Electors in each State shall have the Qualifications requisite for Electors of the most numerous Branch of the State Legislature.

No Person shall be a Representative who shall not have attained to the Age of twenty five Years, and been seven Years a Citizen of the United States, and who shall not, when elected, be an Inhabitant of that State in which he shall be chosen.

Representatives and direct Taxes shall be apportioned among the several States which may be included within this Union, according to their respective Numbers, which shall be determined by adding to the whole Number of free Persons, including those bound to Service for a Term of Years, and excluding Indians not taxed, three fifths of all other Persons. The actual Enumeration shall be made within three Years after the first Meeting of the Congress of the United States, and within every subsequent Term of ten Years, in such Manner as they shall by Law direct. The Number of Representatives shall not exceed one for every thirty Thousand, but each State shall have at Least one Representative; and until such enumeration shall be made, the State of New Hampshire shall be entitled to chuse three, Massachusetts eight, Rhode Island and Providence Plantations one, Connecticut five, New York six, New Jersey four, Pennsylvania eight, Delaware one, Maryland six, Virginia ten, North Carolina five, South Carolina five, and Georgia three.

When vacancies happen in the Representation from any State, the Executive Authority thereof shall issue Writs of Election to fill such Vacancies.

The House of Representatives shall chuse their Speaker and other Officers; and shall have the sole Power of Impeachment.

Section 3. The Senate of the United States shall be composed of two Senators from each State, chosen by the Legislature thereof, for six Years; and each Senator shall have one Vote.

Immediately after they shall be assembled in Consequence of the first Election, they shall be divided as equally as may be into three Classes. The Seats of the Senators of the first Class shall be vacated at the Expiration of the second Year, of the second Class at the Expiration of the fourth Year, and of the third Class at the Expiration of the sixth Year, so that one third may be chosen every second Year; and if Vacancies happen by Resignation, or otherwise, during the Recess of the Legislature of any State, the Executive thereof may make temporary Appointments until the next Meeting of the Legislature, which shall then fill such Vacancies.

No Person shall be a Senator who shall not have attained to the Age of thirty Years, and been nine Years a Citizen of the United States, and who shall not, when elected, be an Inhabitant of that State for which he shall be chosen.

The Vice President of the United States shall be President of the Senate, but shall have no Vote, unless they be equally divided.

The Senate shall chuse their other Officers, and also a President pro tempore, in the Absence of the Vice President, or when he shall exercise the Office of President of the United States.

The Senate shall have the sole Power to try all Impeachments. When sitting for that Purpose, they shall be on Oath or Affirmation. When the President of the United States is tried, the Chief Justice shall preside: And no Person shall be convicted without the Concurrence of two thirds of the Members present.

Judgment in Cases of Impeachment shall not extend further than to removal from Office, and disqualification to hold and enjoy any Office of honor, Trust, or Profit under the United States: but the Party convicted shall nevertheless be liable and subject to Indictment, Trial, Judgment, and Punishment, according to Law.

Section 4.   The Times, Places and Manner of holding Elections for Senators and Representatives, shall be prescribed in each State by the Legislature thereof; but the Congress may at any time by Law make or alter such Regulations, except as to the Places of chusing Senators.

The Congress shall assemble at least once in every Year, and such Meeting shall be on the first Monday in December, unless they shall by Law appoint a different Day.

Section 5.   Each House shall be the Judge of the Elections, Returns, and Qualifications of its own Members, and a Majority of each shall constitute a Quorum to do Business; but a smaller Number may adjourn from day to day, and may be authorized to compel the Attendance of absent Members, in such Manner, and under such Penalties as each House may provide.

Each House may determine the Rules of its Proceedings, punish its Members for disorderly Behavior, and, with the Concurrence of two thirds, expel a Member.

Each House shall keep a Journal of its Proceedings, and from time to time publish the same, excepting such Parts as may in their Judgment require Secrecy; and the Yeas and Nays of the Members of either House on any question shall, at the Desire of one fifth of those Present, be entered on the Journal.

Neither House, during the Session of Congress, shall, without the Consent of the other, adjourn for more than three days, nor to any other Place than that in which the two Houses shall be sitting.

Section 6.   The Senators and Representatives shall receive a Compensation for their Services, to be ascertained by Law, and paid out of the Treasury of the United States. They shall in all Cases, except Treason, Felony and Breach of the Peace, be privileged from Arrest during their Attendance at the Session of their respective Houses, and in going to and returning from the same; and for any Speech or Debate in either House, they shall not be questioned in any other Place.

No Senator or Representative shall, during the Time for which he was elected, be appointed to any civil Office under the Authority of the United States, which shall have been created, or the Emoluments whereof shall have been increased during such time; and no Person holding any Office under the United States, shall be a Member of either House during his Continuance in Office.

Section 7.   All Bills for raising Revenue shall originate in the House of Representatives; but the Senate may propose or concur with Amendments as on other Bills.

Every Bill which shall have passed the House of Representatives and the Senate, shall, before it become a Law, be presented to the President of the United States; If he approve he shall sign it, but if not he shall return it, with his Objections to the House in which it shall have originated, who shall enter the Objections at large on their Journal, and proceed to reconsider it. If after such Reconsideration two thirds of that House shall agree to pass the Bill, it shall be sent together with the Objections, to the other House, by which it shall likewise be reconsidered, and if approved by two thirds of that House, it shall become a Law. But in all such Cases the Votes of both Houses shall be determined by Yeas and Nays, and the Names of the Persons voting for and against the Bill shall be entered on the Journal of each House respectively. If any Bill shall not be returned by the President within ten Days (Sundays excepted) after it shall have been presented to him, the Same shall be a Law, in like Manner as if he had signed it, unless the Congress by their Adjournment prevent its Return in which Case it shall not be a Law.

Every Order, Resolution, or Vote, to which the Concurrence of the Senate and House of Representatives may be necessary (except on a question of Adjournment) shall be presented to the President of the United States; and before the Same shall take Effect, shall be approved by him, or being disapproved by him, shall be repassed by two thirds of the Senate and House of Representatives, according to the Rules and Limitations prescribed in the Case of a Bill.

Section 8.   The Congress shall have Power To lay and collect Taxes, Duties, Imposts and Excises, to pay the Debts and provide for the common Defence and general Welfare of the United States; but all Duties, Imposts and Excises shall be uniform throughout the United States;

To borrow Money on the credit of the United States;

To regulate Commerce with foreign Nations, and among the several States, and with the Indian Tribes;

To establish an uniform Rule of Naturalization, and uniform Laws on the subject of Bankruptcies throughout the United States;

To coin Money, regulate the Value thereof, and of foreign Coin, and fix the Standard of Weights and Measures;

To provide for the Punishment of counterfeiting the Securities and current Coin of the United States;

To establish Post Offices and post Roads;

To promote the Progress of Science and useful Arts, by securing for limited Times to Authors and Inventors the exclusive Right to their respective Writings and Discoveries;

To constitute Tribunals inferior to the supreme Court;

To define and punish Piracies and Felonies committed on the high Seas, and Offenses against the Law of Nations;

To declare War, grant Letters of Marque and Reprisal, and make Rules concerning Captures on Land and Water;

To raise and support Armies, but no Appropriation of Money to that Use shall be for a longer Term than two Years;

To provide and maintain a Navy;

To make Rules for the Government and Regulation of the land and naval Forces;

To provide for calling forth the Militia to execute the Laws of the Union, suppress Insurrections and repel Invasions;

To provide for organizing, arming, and disciplining, the Militia, and for governing such Part of them as may be employed in the Service of the United States, reserving to the States respectively, the Appointment of the Officers, and the Authority of training the Militia according to the discipline prescribed by Congress;

To exercise exclusive Legislation in all Cases whatsoever, over such District (not exceeding ten Miles square) as may, by Cession of particular States, and the Acceptance of Congress, become the Seat of the Government of the United States, and to exercise like Authority over all Places purchased by the Consent of the Legislature of the State in which the Same shall be, for the Erection of Forts, Magazines, Arsenals, dock-Yards, and other needful Buildings;—And

To make all Laws which shall be necessary and proper for carrying into Execution the foregoing Powers, and all other Powers vested by this Constitution in the Government of the United States, or in any Department or Officer thereof.

Section 9. The Migration or Importation of such Persons as any of the States now existing shall think proper to admit, shall not be prohibited by the Congress prior to the Year one thousand eight hundred and eight, but a Tax or duty may be imposed on such Importation, not exceeding ten dollars for each Person.

The privilege of the Writ of Habeas Corpus shall not be suspended, unless when in Cases of Rebellion or Invasion the public Safety may require it.

No Bill of Attainder or ex post facto Law shall be passed.

No Capitation, or other direct, Tax shall be laid, unless in Proportion to the Census or Enumeration herein before directed to be taken.

No Tax or Duty shall be laid on Articles exported from any State.

No Preference shall be given by any Regulation of Commerce or Revenue to the Ports of one State over those of another: nor shall Vessels bound to, or from, one State be obliged to enter, clear, or pay Duties in another.

No Money shall be drawn from the Treasury, but in Consequence of Appropriations made by Law; and a regular Statement and Account of the Receipts and Expenditures of all public Money shall be published from time to time.

No Title of Nobility shall be granted by the United States: And no Person holding any Office of Profit or Trust under them, shall, without the Consent of the Congress, accept of any present, Emolument, Office, or Title, of any kind whatever, from any King, Prince, or foreign State.

Section 10. No State shall enter into any Treaty, Alliance, or Confederation; grant Letters of Marque and Reprisal; coin Money; emit Bills of Credit; make any Thing but gold and silver Coin a Tender in Payment of Debts; pass any Bill of Attainder, ex post facto Law, or Law impairing the Obligation of Contracts, or grant any Title of Nobility.

No State shall, without the Consent of the Congress, lay any Imposts or Duties on Imports or Exports, except what may be absolutely necessary for executing it's inspection Laws: and the net Produce of all Duties and Imposts, laid by any State on Imports or Exports, shall be for the Use of the Treasury of the United States; and all such Laws shall be subject to the Revision and Controul of the Congress.

No State shall, without the Consent of Congress, lay any Duty of Tonnage, keep Troops, or Ships of War in time of Peace, enter into any Agreement or Compact with another State, or with a foreign Power, or engage in War, unless actually invaded, or in such imminent Danger as will not admit of delay.

ARTICLE II

Section 1. The executive Power shall be vested in a President of the United States of America. He shall hold his Office during the Term of four Years, and, together with the Vice President, chosen for the same Term, be elected, as follows:

Each State shall appoint, in such Manner as the Legislature thereof may direct, a Number of Electors, equal to the whole Number of Senators and Representatives to which the State may be entitled in the Congress; but no Senator or Representative, or Person holding an Office of Trust or Profit under the United States, shall be appointed an Elector.

The Electors shall meet in their respective States, and vote by Ballot for two Persons, of whom one at least shall not be an Inhabitant of the same State with themselves. And they shall make a List of all the Persons voted for, and of the Number of Votes for each; which List they shall sign and certify, and transmit sealed to the Seat of the Government of the United States, directed to the President of the Senate. The President of the Senate shall, in the Presence of the Senate and House of Representatives, open all the Certificates, and the Votes shall then be counted. The Person having the greatest Number of Votes shall be the President, if such Number be a Majority of the whole Number of Electors appointed; and if there be more than one who have such Majority, and have an equal Number of Votes, then the House of Representatives shall immediately chuse by Ballot one of them for President; and if no Person have a Majority, then from the five highest on the List the said House shall in like Manner chuse the President. But in chusing the President, the Votes shall be taken by States, the Representation from each State having one Vote; A quorum for this Purpose shall consist of a Member or Members from two thirds of the States, and a Majority of all the States shall be necessary to a Choice. In every Case, after the Choice of the President, the Person having the greater Number of Votes of the Electors shall be the Vice President. But if there should remain two or more who have equal Votes, the Senate shall chuse from them by Ballot the Vice President.

The Congress may determine the Time of chusing the Electors, and the Day on which they shall give their Votes; which Day shall be the same throughout the United States.

No person except a natural born Citizen, or a Citizen of the United States, at the time of the Adoption of this Constitution, shall be eligible to the Office of President; neither shall any Person be eligible to that Office who shall not have attained to the Age of thirty five Years, and been fourteen Years a Resident within the United States.

In Case of the Removal of the President from Office, or of his Death, Resignation or Inability to discharge the Powers and Duties of the said Office, the same shall devolve on the Vice President, and the Congress may by Law provide for the Case of Removal, Death, Resignation or Inability, both of the President and Vice President, declaring what Officer shall then act as President, and such Officer shall act accordingly, until the Disability be removed, or a President shall be elected.

The President shall, at stated Times, receive for his Services, a Compensation, which shall neither be increased nor diminished during the Period for which he shall have been elected, and he shall not receive within that Period any other Emolument from the United States, or any of them.

Before he enter on the Execution of his Office, he shall take the following Oath or Affirmation: ''I do solemnly swear (or affirm) that I will faithfully execute the Office of President of the United States, and will to the best of my Ability, preserve, protect and defend the Constitution of the United States.''

Section 2.   The President shall be Commander in Chief of the Army and Navy of the United States, and of the Militia of the several States, when called into the actual Service of the United States; he may require the Opinion,

in writing, of the principal Officer in each of the executive Departments, upon any Subject relating to the Duties of their respective Offices, and he shall have Power to grant Reprieves and Pardons for Offenses against the United States, except in Cases of Impeachment.

He shall have Power, by and with the Advice and Consent of the Senate to make Treaties, provided two thirds of the Senators present concur; and he shall nominate, and by and with the Advice and Consent of the Senate, shall appoint Ambassadors, other public Ministers and Consuls, Judges of the supreme Court, and all other Officers of the United States, whose Appointments are not herein otherwise provided for, and which shall be established by Law; but the Congress may by Law vest the Appointment of such inferior Officers, as they think proper, in the President alone, in the Courts of Law, or in the Heads of Departments.

The President shall have Power to fill up all Vacancies that may happen during the Recess of the Senate, by granting Commissions which shall expire at the End of their next Session.

Section 3.   He shall from time to time give to the Congress Information of the State of the Union, and recommend to their Consideration such Measures as he shall judge necessary and expedient; he may, on extraordinary Occasions, convene both Houses, or either of them, and in Case of Disagreement between them, with Respect to the Time of Adjournment, he may adjourn them to such Time as he shall think proper; he shall receive Ambassadors and other public Ministers; he shall take Care that the Laws be faithfully executed, and shall Commission all the Officers of the United States.

Section 4.   The President, Vice President and all civil Officers of the United States, shall be removed from Office on Impeachment for, and Conviction of, Treason, Bribery, or other high Crimes and Misdemeanors.

ARTICLE III

Section 1.   The judicial Power of the United States, shall be vested in one supreme Court, and in such inferior Courts as the Congress may from time to time ordain and establish. The Judges, both of the supreme and inferior Courts, shall hold their Offices during good Behaviour, and shall, at stated Times, receive for their Services a Compensation, which shall not be diminished during their Continuance in Office.

Section 2.   The judicial Power shall extend to all Cases, in Law and Equity, arising under this Constitution, the Laws of the United States, and Treaties made, or which shall be made, under their Authority;—to all Cases affecting Ambassadors, other public Ministers and Consuls;—to all Cases of admiralty and maritime Jurisdiction;—to Controversies to which the United States shall be a Party;—to Controversies between two or more States;—

between a State and Citizens of another State;—between Citizens of different States;—between Citizens of the same State claiming Lands under Grants of different States, and between a State, or the Citizens thereof, and foreign States, Citizens or Subjects.

In all Cases affecting Ambassadors, other public Ministers and Consuls, and those in which a State shall be a Party, the supreme Court shall have original Jurisdiction. In all the other Cases before mentioned, the supreme Court shall have appellate Jurisdiction, both as to Law and Fact, with such Exceptions, and under such Regulations as the Congress shall make.

The Trial of all Crimes, except in Cases of Impeachment, shall be by Jury; and such Trial shall be held in the State where the said Crimes shall have been committed; but when not committed within any State, the Trial shall be at such Place or Places as the Congress may by Law have directed.

Section 3. Treason against the United States, shall consist only in levying War against them, or, in adhering to their Enemies, giving them Aid and Comfort. No Person shall be convicted of Treason unless on the Testimony of two Witnesses to the same overt Act, or on Confession in open Court.

The Congress shall have Power to declare the Punishment of Treason, but no Attainder of Treason shall work Corruption of Blood, or Forfeiture except during the Life of the Person attainted.

ARTICLE IV

Section 1. Full Faith and Credit shall be given in each State to the public Acts, Records, and judicial Proceedings of every other State. And the Congress may by general Laws prescribe the Manner in which such Acts, Records and Proceedings shall be proved, and the Effect thereof.

Section 2. The Citizens of each State shall be entitled to all Privileges and Immunities of Citizens in the several States.

A Person charged in any State with Treason, Felony, or other Crime, who shall flee from Justice, and be found in another State, shall on Demand of the executive Authority of the State from which he fled, be delivered up, to be removed to the State having Jurisdiction of the Crime.

No Person held to Service or Labour in one State, under the Laws thereof, escaping into another, shall, in Consequence of any Law or Regulation therein, be discharged from such Service or Labour, but shall be delivered up on Claim of the Party to whom such Service or Labour may be due.

Section 3. New States may be admitted by the Congress into this Union; but no new State shall be formed or erected within the Jurisdiction of any other State; nor any State be formed by the Junction of two or more States,

or Parts of States, without the Consent of the Legislatures of the States concerned as well as of the Congress.

The Congress shall have Power to dispose of and make all needful Rules and Regulations respecting the Territory or other Property belonging to the United States; and nothing in this Constitution shall be so construed as to Prejudice any Claims of the United States, or of any particular State.

Section 4. The United States shall guarantee to every State in this Union a Republican Form of Government, and shall protect each of them against Invasion; and on Application of the Legislature, or of the Executive (when the Legislature cannot be convened) against domestic Violence.

ARTICLE V

The Congress, whenever two thirds of both Houses shall deem it necessary, shall propose Amendments to this Constitution, or, on the Application of the Legislatures of two thirds of the several States, shall call a Convention for proposing Amendments, which, in either Case, shall be valid to all Intents and Purposes, as part of this Constitution, when ratified by the Legislatures of three fourths of the several States, or by Conventions in three fourths thereof, as the one or the other Mode of Ratification may be proposed by the Congress; Provided that no Amendment which may be made prior to the Year One thousand eight hundred and eight shall in any Manner affect the first and fourth Clauses in the Ninth Section of the first Article; and that no State, without its Consent, shall be deprived of its equal Suffrage in the Senate.

ARTICLE VI

All Debts contracted and Engagements entered into, before the Adoption of this Constitution shall be as valid against the United States under this Constitution, as under the Confederation.

This Constitution, and the Laws of the United States which shall be made in Pursuance thereof; and all Treaties made, or which shall be made, under the Authority of the United States, shall be the supreme Law of the Land; and the Judges in every State shall be bound thereby, any Thing in the Constitution or Laws of any State to the Contrary notwithstanding.

The Senators and Representatives before mentioned, and the Members of the several State Legislatures, and all executive and judicial Officers, both of the United States and of the several States, shall be bound by Oath or Affirmation, to support this Constitution; but no religious Test shall ever be required as a Qualification to any Office or public Trust under the United States.

ARTICLE VII

The Ratification of the Conventions of nine States shall be sufficient for the Establishment of this Constitution between the States so ratifying the Same.

AMENDMENT I [1791]

Congress shall make no law respecting an establishment of religion, or prohibiting the free exercise thereof; or abridging the freedom of speech, or of the press; or the right of the people peaceably to assembly, and to petition the Government for a redress of grievances.

AMENDMENT II [1791]

A well regulated Militia, being necessary to the security of a free State, the right of the people to keep and bear Arms, shall not be infringed.

AMENDMENT III [1791]

No Soldier shall, in time of peace be quartered in any house, without the consent of the Owner, nor in time of war, but in a manner to be prescribed by law.

Amendment IV [1791]

The right of the people to be secure in their persons, houses, papers, and effects, against unreasonable searches and seizures, shall not be violated, and no Warrants shall issue, but upon probable cause, supported by Oath or affirmation, and particularly describing the place to be searched, and the persons or things to be seized.

AMENDMENT V [1791]

No person shall be held to answer for a capital, or otherwise infamous crime, unless on a presentment or indictment of a Grand Jury, except in cases arising in the land or naval forces, or in the Militia, when in actual service in time of War or public danger; nor shall any person be subject for the same offence to be twice put in jeopardy of life or limb; nor shall be compelled in any criminal case to be a witness against himself, nor be deprived of life, liberty, or property, without due process of law; nor shall private property be taken for public use, without just compensation.

AMENDMENT VI [1791]

In all criminal prosecutions, the accused shall enjoy the right to a speedy and public trial, by an impartial jury of the State and district wherein the crime shall have been committed, which district shall have been previously ascertained by law, and to be informed of the nature and cause of the accusation; to be confronted with the witnesses against him; to have compulsory process for obtaining witnesses in his favor, and to have the Assistance of Counsel for his defence.

AMENDMENT VII [1791]

In Suits at common law, where the value in controversy shall exceed twenty dollars, the right of trial by jury shall be preserved, and no fact tried by jury, shall be otherwise re-examined in any Court of the United States, than according to the rules of the common law.

AMENDMENT VIII [1791]

Excessive bail shall not be required, nor excessive fines imposed, nor cruel and unusual punishments inflicted.

AMENDMENT IX [1791]

The enumeration in the Constitution, of certain rights, shall not be construed to deny or disparage others retained by the people.

AMENDMENT X [1791]

The powers not delegated to the United States by the Constitution, nor prohibited by it to the States, are reserved to the States respectively, or to the people.

AMENDMENT XI [1798]

The Judicial power of the United States shall not be construed to extend to any suit in law or equity, commenced or prosecuted against one of the United States by Citizens of another State, or by Citizens or Subjects of any Foreign State.

AMENDMENT XII [1804]

The Electors shall meet in their respective states, and vote by ballot for President and Vice-President, one of whom, at least, shall not be an inhabitant of the same state with themselves; they shall name in their ballots the person voted for as President, and in distinct ballots the person voted for as Vice-President, and they shall make distinct lists of all persons voted for as President, and of all persons voted for as Vice-President, and of the number of votes for each, which lists they shall sign and certify, and transmit sealed to the seat of the government of the United States, directed to the President of the Senate;—The President of the Senate shall, in the presence of the Senate and House of Representatives, open all the certificates and the votes shall then be counted;—The person having the greatest number of votes for President, shall be the President, if such number be a majority of the whole number of Electors appointed; and if no person have such majority, then from the persons having the highest numbers not exceeding three on the list of those voted for as President, the House of Representatives shall choose immediately, by ballot, the President. But in choosing the President, the votes shall be taken by states, the representation from each state having one vote; a quorum for this purpose shall consist of a member or members from two-thirds of the states, and a majority of all states shall be necessary to a choice. And if the House of Representatives shall not choose a President whenever the right of choice shall devolve upon them, before the fourth day of March next following, then the Vice-President shall act as President, as in the case of the death or other constitutional disability of the President.—The person having the greatest number of votes as Vice-President, shall be the Vice-President, if such number be a majority of the whole number of Electors appointed, and if no person have a majority, then from the two highest numbers on the list, the Senate shall choose the Vice-President; a quorum for the purpose shall consist of two-thirds of the whole number of Senators, and a majority of the whole number shall be necessary to a choice. But no person constitutionally ineligible to the office of President shall be eligible to that of Vice-President of the United States.

AMENDMENT XIII [1865]

Section 1. Neither slavery nor involuntary servitude, except as a punishment for crime whereof the party shall have been duly convicted, shall exist within the United States, or any place subject to their jurisdiction.

Section 2. Congress shall have power to enforce this article by appropriate legislation.

AMENDMENT XIV [1868]

Section 1. All persons born or naturalized in the United States, and subject to the jurisdiction thereof, are citizens of the United States and of the State wherein they reside. No State shall make or enforce any law which shall abridge the privileges or immunities of citizens of the United States; nor shall any State deprive any person of life, liberty, or property, without due process of law; nor deny to any person within its jurisdiction the equal protection of the laws.

Section 2. Representatives shall be apportioned among the several States according to their respective numbers, counting the whole number of persons in each State, excluding Indians not taxed. But when the right to vote at any election for the choice of electors for President and Vice President of the United States, Representatives in Congress, the Executive and Judicial officers of a State, or the members of the Legislature thereof, is denied to any of the male inhabitants of such State, being twenty-one years of age, and citizens of the United States, or in any way abridged, except for participation in rebellion, or other crime, the basis of representation therein shall be reduced in the proportion which the number of such male citizens shall bear to the whole number of male citizens twenty-one years of age in such State.

Section 3. No person shall be a Senator or Representative in Congress, or elector of President and Vice President, or hold any office, civil or military, under the United States, or under any State, who having previously taken an oath, as a member of Congress, or as an officer of the United States, or as a member of any State legislature, or as an executive or judicial officer of any State, to support the Constitution of the United States, shall have engaged in insurrection or rebellion against the same, or given aid or comfort to the enemies thereof. But Congress may by a vote of two-thirds of each House, remove such disability.

Section 4. The validity of the public debt of the United States, authorized by law, including debts incurred for payment of pensions and bounties for services in suppressing insurrection or rebellion, shall not be questioned. But neither the United States nor any State shall assume or pay any debt or obligation incurred in aid of insurrection or rebellion against the United States, or any claim for the loss or emancipation of any slave; but all such debts, obligations and claims shall be held illegal and void.

Section 5. The Congress shall have power to enforce, by appropriate legislation, the provisions of this article.

AMENDMENT XV [1870]

Section 1. The right of citizens of the United States to vote shall not be denied or abridged by the United States or by any State on account of race, color, or previous condition of servitude.

Section 2. The Congress shall have power to enforce this article by appropriate legislation.

AMENDMENT XVI [1913]

The Congress shall have power to lay and collect taxes on incomes, from whatever source derived, without apportionment among the several States, and without regard to any census or enumeration.

AMENDMENT XVII [1913]

[1] The Senate of the United States shall be composed of two Senators from each State, elected by the people thereof, for six years; and each Senator shall have one vote. The electors in each State shall have the qualifications requisite for electors of the most numerous branch of the State legislatures.

[2] When vacancies happen in the representation of any State in the Senate, the executive authority of such State shall issue writs of election to fill such vacancies: *Provided*, That the legislature of any State may empower the executive thereof to make temporary appointments until the people fill the vacancies by election as the legislature may direct.

[3] This amendment shall not be so construed as to affect the election or term of any Senator chosen before it becomes valid as part of the Constitution.

AMENDMENT XVIII [1919]

Section 1. After one year from the ratification of this article the manufacture, sale, or transportation of intoxicating liquors within, the importation thereof into, or the exportation thereof from the United States and all territory subject to the jurisdiction thereof for beverage purposes is hereby prohibited.

Section 2. The Congress and the several States shall have concurrent power to enforce this article by appropriate legislation.

Section 3. This article shall be inoperative unless it shall have been ratified as an amendment to the Constitution by the legislatures of the several States, as provided in the Constitution, within seven years from the date of the submission hereof to the States by the Congress.

AMENDMENT XIX [1920]

[1] The right of citizens of the United States to vote shall not be denied or abridged by the United States or by any State on account of sex.

[2] Congress shall have power to enforce this article by appropriate legislation.

AMENDMENT XX [1933]

Section 1. The terms of the President and Vice President shall end at noon on the 20th day of January, and the terms of Senators and Representatives at noon on the 3d day of January, of the years in which such terms would have ended if this article had not been ratified; and the terms of their successors shall then begin.

Section 2. The Congress shall assemble at least once in every year, and such meeting shall begin at noon on the 3d day of January, unless they shall by law appoint a different day.

Section 3. If, at the time fixed for the beginning of the term of the President, the President elect shall have died, the Vice President elect shall become President. If the President shall not have been chosen before the time fixed for the beginning of his term, or if the President elect shall have failed to qualify, then the Vice President elect shall act as President until a President shall have qualified; and the Congress may by law provide for the case wherein neither a President elect nor a Vice President elect shall have qualified, declaring who shall then act as President, or the manner in which one who is to act shall be selected, and such person shall act accordingly until a President or Vice President shall have qualified.

Section 4. The Congress may by law provide for the case of the death of any of the persons from whom the House of Representatives may choose a President whenever the right of choice shall have devolved upon them, and for the case of the death of any of the persons from whom the Senate may choose a Vice President whenever the right of choice shall have devolved upon them.

Section 5. Sections 1 and 2 shall take effect on the 15th day of October following the ratification of this article.

Section 6. This article shall be inoperative unless it shall have been ratified as an amendment to the Constitution by the legislatures of three-fourths of the several States within seven years from the date of its submission.

AMENDMENT XXI [1933]

Section 1. The eighteenth article of amendment to the Constitution of the United States is hereby repealed.

Section 2. The transportation or importation into any State, Territory, or possession of the United States for delivery or use therein of intoxicating liquors, in violation of the laws thereof, is hereby prohibited.

Section 3. This article shall be inoperative unless it shall have been ratified as an amendment to the Constitution by conventions in the several States, as provided in the Constitution, within seven years from the date of the submission hereof to the States by the Congress.

AMENDMENT XXII [1951]

Section 1. No person shall be elected to the office of the President more than twice, and no person who has held the office of President, or acted as President, for more than two years of a term to which some other person was elected President shall be elected to the office of President more than once. But this Article shall not apply to any person holding the office of President when this Article was proposed by the Congress, and shall not prevent any person who may be holding the office of President, or acting as President, during the term within which this Article becomes operative from holding the office of President or acting as President during the remainder of such term.

Section 2. This article shall be inoperative unless it shall have been ratified as an amendment to the Constitution by the legislatures of three-fourths of the several States within seven years from the date of its submission to the States by the Congress.

AMENDMENT XXIII [1961]

Section 1. The District constituting the seat of Government of the United States shall appoint in such manner as the Congress may direct:

A number of electors of President and Vice President equal to the whole number of Senators and Representatives in Congress to which the District would be entitled if it were a State, but in no event more than the least populous state; they shall be in addition to those appointed by the states, but they shall be considered, for the purposes of the election of President and Vice President, to be electors appointed by a state; and they shall meet in the District and perform such duties as provided by the twelfth article of amendment.

Section 2. The Congress shall have power to enforce this article by appropriate legislation.

AMENDMENT XXIV [1964]

Section 1. The right of citizens of the United States to vote in any primary or other election for President or Vice President, for electors for President or Vice President, or for Senator or Representative in Congress, shall not be denied or abridged by the United States, or any State by reason of failure to pay any poll tax or other tax.

Section 2. The Congress shall have power to enforce this article by appropriate legislation.

AMENDMENT XXV [1967]

Section 1. In case of the removal of the President from office or of his death or resignation, the Vice President shall become President.

Section 2. Whenever there is a vacancy in the office of the Vice President, the President shall nominate a Vice President who shall take office upon confirmation by a majority vote of both Houses of Congress.

Section 3. Whenever the President transmits to the President pro tempore of the Senate and the Speaker of the House of Representatives his written declaration that he is unable to discharge the powers and duties of his office, and until he transmits to them a written declaration to the contrary, such powers and duties shall be discharged by the Vice President as Acting President.

Section 4. Whenever the Vice President and a majority of either the principal officers of the executive departments or of such other body as Congress may by law provide, transmit to the President pro tempore of the Senate and the Speaker of the House of Representatives their written declaration that the President is unable to discharge the powers and duties of his office, the Vice President shall immediately assume the powers and duties of the office as Acting President.

Thereafter, when the President transmits to the President pro tempore of the Senate and the Speaker of the House of Representatives his written declaration that no inability exists, he shall resume the powers and duties of his office unless the Vice President and a majority of either the principal officers of the executive department or of such other body as Congress may by law provide, transmit within four days to the President pro tempore of the Senate and the Speaker of the House of Representatives their written declaration and the President is unable to discharge the powers and duties of his office. Thereupon Congress shall decide the issue, assembling within forty-eight hours for that purpose if not in session. If the Congress, within twenty-one days after receipt of the latter written declaration, or, if Congress is not in session, within twenty-one days after Congress is required to assemble, determines by two-thirds vote of both Houses that the President is unable to discharge the powers and duties of his office, the Vice President shall continue to discharge the same as Acting President; otherwise, the President shall resume the powers and duties of his office.

AMENDMENT XXVI [1971]

Section 1. The right of citizens of the United States, who are eighteen years of age or older, to vote shall not be denied or abridged by the United States or by any State on account of age.

Section 2. The Congress shall have power to enforce this article by appropriate legislation.

Appendix B The Uniform Commercial Code (Excerpts)

Article 1
GENERAL PROVISIONS

§ 1—203. **Obligation of Good Faith.**

Every contract or duty within this Act imposes an obligation of good faith in its performance or enforcement.

§ 1—205. **Course of Dealing and Usage of Trade.**

(1) A course of dealing is a sequence of previous conduct between the parties to a particular transaction which is fairly to be regarded as establishing a common basis of understanding for interpreting their expressions and other conduct.

(2) A usage of trade is any practice or method of dealing having such regularity of observance in a place, vocation or trade as to justify an expectation that it will be observed with respect to the transaction in question. The existence and scope of such a usage are to be proved as facts. If it is established that such a usage is embodied in a written trade code or similar writing the interpretation of the writing is for the court.

(3) A course of dealing between parties and any usage of trade in the vocation or trade in which they are engaged or of which they are or should be aware give particular meaning to and supplement or qualify terms of an agreement.

(4) The express terms of an agreement and an applicable course of dealing or usage of trade shall be construed wherever reasonable as consistent with each other; but when such construction is unreasonable express terms control both course of dealing and usage of trade and course of dealing controls usage trade.

(5) An applicable usage of trade in the place where any part of performance is to occur shall be used in interpreting the agreement as to that part of the performance.

(6) Evidence of a relevant usage of trade offered by one party is not admissible unless and until he has given the other party such notice as the court finds sufficient to prevent unfair surprise to the latter.

Article 2
SALES

§ 2—201. **Formal Requirements; Statute of Frauds.**

(1) Except as otherwise provided in this section a contract for the sale of goods for the price of $500 or more is not enforceable by way of action or defense unless there is some writing sufficient to indicate that a contract for sale has been made between the parties and signed by the party against whom enforcement is sought or by his authorized agent or broker. A writing is not insufficient because it omits or incorrectly states a term agreed upon but the contract is not enforceable under this paragraph beyond the quantity of goods shown in such writing.

(2) Between merchants if within a reasonable time a writing in confirmation of the contract and sufficient against the sender is received and the party receiving it has reason to know its contents, its satisfies the requirements of subsection (1) against such party unless written notice of objection to its contents is given within ten days after it is received.

(3) A contract which does not satisfy the requirements of subsection (1) but which is valid in other respects is enforceable

(a) if the goods are to be specially manufactured for the buyer and are not suitable for sale to others in the ordinary course of the seller's business and the seller, before notice of repudiation is received and under circumstances which reasonably indicate that the goods are for the buyer, has made either a substantial beginning of their manufacture or commitments for their procurement; or

(b) if the party against whom enforcement is sought admits in his pleading, testimony or otherwise in court that a contract for sale was made, but the contract is not enforceable under this provision beyond the quantity of goods admitted; or

(c) with respect to goods for which payment has been made and accepted or which have been received and accepted (Sec. 2—606).

§ 2—204. Formation in General.

(1) A contract for sale of goods may be made in any manner sufficent to show agreement, including conduct by both parties which recognizes the existence of such a contract.

(2) An agreement sufficient to constitute a contract for sale may be found even though the moment of its making is undetermined.

(3) Even though one or more terms are left open a contract for sale does not fail for indefiniteness if the parties have intended to make a contract and there is a reasonably certain basis for giving an appropriate remedy.

§ 2—205. Firm Offers.

An offer by a merchant to buy or sell goods in a signed writing which by its terms gives assurance that it will be held open is not revocable, for lack of consideration, during the time stated or if no time is stated for a reasonable time, but in no event may such period of irrevocability exceed three months; but any such term of assurance on a form supplied by the offeree must be separately signed by the offeror.

§ 2—206. Offer and Acceptance in Formation of Contract.

(1) Unless other unambiguously indicated by the language or circumstances

(a) an offer to make a contract shall be construed as inviting acceptance in any manner and by any medium reasonable in the circumstances;

(b) an order or other offer to buy goods for prompt or current shipment shall be construed as inviting acceptance either by a prompt promise to ship or by the prompt or current shipment of conforming or non-conforming goods, but such a shipment of non-conforming goods does not constitute an acceptance if the seller seasonably notifies the buyer that the shipment is offered only as an accommodation to the buyer.

(2) Where the beginning of a requested performance is a reasonable mode of acceptance an offeror who is not notified of acceptance within a reasonable time may treat the offer as having lapsed before acceptance.

§ 2—207. Additional Terms in Acceptance or Confirmation.

(1) A definite and seasonable expression of acceptance or a written confirmation which is sent within a reasonable time operates as an acceptance even though it states terms additional to or different from those offered or agreed upon, unless acceptance is expressly made conditional on assent to the additional or different terms.

(2) The additional terms are to be construed as proposals for addition to the contract. Between merchants such terms become part of the contract unless:

(a) the offer expressly limits acceptance to the terms of the offer;

(b) they materially alter it; or

(c) notification of objection to them has already been given or is given within a reasonable time after notice of them is received.

(3) Conduct by both parties which recognizes the existence of a contract is sufficient to establish a contract for sale although the writings of the parties do not otherwise establish a contract. In such case the terms of the particular contract consist of those terms on which the writings of the parties agree, together with any supplementary terms incorporated under any other provisions of this Act.

§ 2—209. Modification, Rescission and Waiver.

(1) An agreement modifying a contract within this Article needs no consideration to be binding.

(2) A signed agreement which excludes modification or rescission except by a signed writing cannot be otherwise modified or rescinded, but except as between merchants such a requirement on a form supplied by the merchant must be separately signed by the other party.

(3) The requirements of the statute of frauds section of this Article (Section 2—201) must be satisfied if the contract as modified is within its provisions.

(4) Although an attempt at modification or rescission does not satisfy the requirements of subsection (2) or (3) it can operate as a waiver.

(5) A party who has made a waiver affecting an executory portion of the contract may retract the waiver by reasonable notification received by the other party that strict performance will be required of any term waived, unless the retraction would be unjust in view of a material change of position in reliance on the waiver.

§ 2—302. Unconscionable Contract or Clause.

(1) If the court as a matter of law finds the contract or any clause of the contract to have been unconscionable at the time it was made the court may refuse to enforce the contract, or it may enforce the remainder of the contract without the unconscionable clause, or it may so limit the application of any unconscionable clause as to avoid any unconscionable result.

(2) When it is claimed or appears to the court that the contract or any clause thereof may be unconscionable the parties shall be afforded a reasonable opportunity to present evidence as to its commercial setting, purpose and effect to aid the court in making the determination.

§ 2—305. **Open Price Term.**

(1) The parties if they so intend can conclude a contract for sale even though the price is not settled. In such a case the price is a reasonable price at the time for delivery if

    (a) nothing is said as to price; or

    (b) the price is left to be agreed by the parties and they fail to agree; or

    (c) the price is to be fixed in terms of some agreed market or other standard as set or recorded by a third person or agency and it is not so set or recorded.

(2) A price to be fixed by the seller or by the buyer means a price for him to fix in good faith.

(3) When a price left to be fixed otherwise than by agreement of the parties fails to be fixed through fault of one party the other may at his option treat the contract as cancelled or himself fix a reasonable price.

(4) Where, however, the parties intend not to be bound unless the price be fixed or agreed and it is not fixed or agreed there is no contract. In such a case the buyer must return any goods already received or if unable so to do must pay their reasonable value at the time of delivery and the seller must return any portion of the price paid on account.

§ 2—306. **Output, Requirements and Exclusive Dealings.**

(1) A term which measures the quantity by the output of the seller or the requirements of the buyer means such actual output or requirements as may occur in good faith, except that no quantity unreasonably disproportionate to any stated estimate or in the absence of a stated estimate to any normal or otherwise comparable prior output or requirements may be tendered or demanded.

(2) A lawful agreement by either the seller or the buyer for exclusive dealing in the kind of goods concerned imposes unless otherwise agreed an obligation by the seller to use best efforts to supply the goods and by the buyer to use best efforts to promote their sale.

§ 2—307. **Delivery in Single Lot or Several Lots.**

Unless otherwise agreed all goods called for by a contract for sale must be tendered in a single delivery and payment is due only on such tender but where the circumstances give either party the right to make or demand delivery in lots the price if it can be apportioned may be demanded for each lot.

§ 2—308. **Absence of Specified Place for Delivery.**

Unless otherwise agreed

(a) the place for delivery of goods is the seller's place of business or if he has none his residence; but

(b) in a contract for sale of identified goods which to the knowledge of the parties at the time of contracting are in some other place, that place is the place for their delivery; and

(c) documents of title may be delivered through customary banking channels.

§ 2—309. **Absence of Specific Time Provisions; Notice of Termination.**

(1) The time for shipment or delivery or any other action under a contract if not provided in this Article or agreed upon shall be a reasonable time.

(2) Where the contract provides for successive performances but is indefinite in duration it is valid for a reasonable time but unless otherwise agreed may be terminated at any time by either party.

(3) Termination of a contract by one party except on the happening of an agreed event requires that reasonable notification be received by the other party and an agreement dispensing with notification is invalid if its operation would be unconscionable.

§ 2—312. **Warranty of Title and Against Infringement; Buyer's Obligation Against Infringement.**

(1) Subject to subsection (2) there is in a contract for sale a warranty by the seller that

    (a) the title conveyed shall be good, and its transfer rightful; and

    (b) the goods shall be delivered free from any security interest or other lien or encumbrance of which the buyer at the time of contracting has no knowledge.

(2) A warranty under subsection (1) will be excluded or modified only by specific language or by circumstances which give the buyer reason to know that the person selling does not claim title in himself or that he is purporting to sell only such right or title as he or a third person may have.

(3) Unless otherwise agreed a seller who is a merchant regularly dealing in goods of the kind warrants that the goods shall be delivered free of the rightful claim of any third person by way of infringement or the like but a buyer who furnishes specifications to the seller must hold the seller harmless against any such claim which arises out of compliance with the specifications.

§ 2—313. **Express Warranties by Affirmation, Promise, Description, Sample.**

(1) Express warranties by the seller are created as follows:

    (a) Any affirmation of fact or promise made by the seller to the buyer which relates to the goods and becomes part of the basis of the bargain creates an express warranty that the goods shall conform to the affirmation or promise.

(b) Any description of the goods which is made part of the basis of the bargain creates an express warranty that the goods shall conform to the description.

(c) Any sample or model which is made part of the basis of the bargain creates an express warranty that the whole of the goods shall conform to the sample or model.

(2) It is not necessary to the creation of an express warranty that the seller use formal words such as "warrant" or "guarantee" or that he have a specific intention to make a warranty, but an affirmation merely of the value of the goods or a statement purporting to be merely the seller's opinion or commendation of the goods does not create a warranty.

§ 2—314. **Implied Warranty: Merchantability; Usage of Trade.**

(1) Unless excluded or modified (Section 2—316), a warranty that the goods shall be merchantable is implied in a contract for their sale if the seller is a merchant with respect to goods of that kind. Under this section the serving for value of food or drink to be consumed either on the premises or elsewhere is a sale.

(2) Goods to be merchantable must be at least such as

(a) pass without objection in the trade under the contract description; and

(b) in the case of fungible goods, are of fair average quality within the description; and

(c) are fit for the ordinary purposes for which such goods are used; and

(d) run, within the variations permitted by the agreement, of even kind, quality and quantity within each unit and among all units involved; and

(e) are adequately contained, packaged, and labeled as the agreement may require; and

(f) conform to the promises or affirmations of fact made on the container or label if any.

(3) Unless excluded or modified (Section 2—316) other implied warranties may arise from course of dealing or usage of trade.

§ 2—315. **Implied Warranty: Fitness for Particular Purpose.**

Where the seller at the time of contracting has reason to know any particular purpose for which the goods are required and that the buyer is relying on the seller's skill or judgment to select or furnish suitable goods, there is unless excluded or modified under the next section an implied warranty that the goods shall be fit for such purpose.

§ 2—316. **Exclusion or Modification of Warranties.**

(1) Words or conduct relevant to the creation of an express warranty and words or conduct tending to negate or limit warranty shall be construed wherever reasonable as consistent with each other; but subject to the provisions of this Article on parol or extrinsic evidence (Section 2—202) negation or limitation is inoperative to the extent that such construction is unreasonable.

(2) Subject to subsection (3), to exclude or modify the implied warranty of merchantability or any part of it the language must mention merchantability and in case of a writing must be conspicuous, and to exclude or modify any implied warranty of fitness the exclusion must be by a writing and conspicuous. Language to exclude all implied warranties of fitness is sufficient if it states, for example, that "There are no warranties which extend beyond the description on the face hereof."

(3) Notwithstanding subsection (2)

(a) unless the circumstances indicate otherwise, all implied warranties are excluded by expressions like "as is", "with all faults" or other language which in common understanding calls the buyer's attention to the exclusion of warranties and makes plain that there is no implied warranty; and

(b) when the buyer before entering into the contract has examined the goods or the sample or model as fully as he desired or has refused to examine the goods there is no implied warranty with regard to defects which an examination ought in the circumstances to have revealed to him; and

(c) an implied warranty can also be excluded or modified by course of dealing or course of performance or usage of trade.

(4) Remedies for breach of warranty can be limited in accordance with the provisions of this Article on liquidation or limitation of damages and on contractual modification of remedy (Sections 2—718 and 2—719).

§ 2—317. **Cumulation and Conflict of Warranties Express or Implied.**

Warranties whether express or implied shall be construed as consistent with each other and as cumulative, but if such construction is unreasonable the intention of the parties shall determine which warranty is dominant. In ascertaining that intention the following rules apply:

(a) Exact or technical specifications displace an inconsistent sample or model or general language of description.

(b) A sample from an existing bulk displaces inconsistent general language of description.

(c) Express warranties displace inconsistent implied warranties other than an implied warranty of fitness for a particular purpose.

§ 2—318. **Third Party Beneficiaries of Warranties Express or Implied.**

Note: If this Act is introduced in the Congress of the United States this section should be omitted. (States to select one alternative.)

Alternative A

A seller's warranty whether express or implied extends to any natural person who is in the family or household of his buyer or who is a guest in his home if it is reasonable to expect that such person may use, consume or be affected by the goods and who is injured in person by breach of the warranty. A seller may not exclude or limit the operation of this section.

Alternative B

A seller's warranty whether express or implied extends to any natural person who may reasonably be expected to use, consume or be affected by the goods and who is injured in person by breach of the warranty. A seller may not exclude or limit the operation of this section.

Alternative C

A seller's warranty whether express or implied extends to any person who may reasonably be expected to use, consume or be affected by the goods and who is injured by breach of the warranty. A seller may not exclude or limit the operation of this section with respect to injury to the person of an individual to whom the warranty extends. As amended 1966.

§ 2—319. **F.O.B. and F.A.S. Terms.**

(1) Unless otherwise agreed the term F.O.B. (which means ''free on board'') at a named place, even though used only in connection with the stated price, is a delivery term under which

    (a) when the term is F.O.B. the place of shipment, the seller must at that place ship the goods in the manner provided in this Article (Section 2—504) and bear the expense and risk of putting them into the possession of the carrier; or

    (b) when the term is F.O.B. the place of destination, the seller must at his own expense and risk transport the goods to that place and there tender delivery of them in the manner provided in this Article (Section 2—503);

    (c) when under either (a) or (b) the term is also F.O.B. vessel, car or other vehicle, the seller must in addition at his own expense and risk load the goods on board. If the term is F.O.B. vessel the buyer must name the vessel and in an appropriate case the seller must comply with the provisions of this Article on the form of bill of lading (Section 2—323).

(2) Unless otherwise agreed the term F.A.S. vessel (which means ''free alongside'') at a named port, even though used only in connection with the stated price, is a delivery term under which the seller must

    (a) at his own expense and risk deliver the goods alongside the vessel in the manner usual in that port or on a dock designated and provided by the buyer; and

    (b) obtain and tender a receipt for the goods in exchange for which the carrier is under a duty to issue a bill of lading.

(3) Unless otherwise agreed in any case falling within subsection (1)(a) or (c) or subsection (2) the buyer must seasonably give any needed instructions for making delivery, including when the term is F.A.S. or F.O.B. the loading berth of the vessel and in an appropriate case its name and sailing date. The seller may treat the failure of needed instructions as a failure of cooperation under this Article (Section 2—311). He may also at his option move the goods in any reasonable manner preparatory to delivery or shipment.

(4) Under the term F.O.B. vessel or F.A.S. unless otherwise agreed the buyer must make payment against tender of the required documents and the seller may not tender nor the buyer demand delivery of the goods in substitution for the documents.

§ 2—320. **C.I.F. and C. & F. Terms.**

(1) The term C.I.F. means that the price includes in a lump sum the cost of the goods and the insurance and freight to the named destination. The term C. & F. or C.F. means that the price so includes cost and freight to the named destination.

(2) Unless otherwise agreed and even though used only in connection with the stated price and destination, the term C.I.F. destination or its equivalent requires the seller at his own expense and risk to

    (a) put the goods into the possession of a carrier at the port for shipment and obtain a negotiable bill or bills of lading covering the entire transportation to the named destination; and

    (b) load the goods and obtain a receipt from the carrier (which may be contained in the bill of lading) showing that the freight has been paid or provided for; and

    (c) obtain a policy or certificate of insurance, including any war risk insurance, of a kind and on terms then current at the port of shipment in the usual amount, in the currency of the contract, shown to cover the same goods covered by the bill of lading and providing for payment of loss to the order of the buyer or for the account of whom it may concern; but the seller may add to the price the amount of the premium for any such war risk insurance; and

    (d) prepare an invoice of the goods and procure any other documents required to effect shipment or to comply with the contract; and

(e) forward and tender with commercial promptness all the documents in due form and with any indorsement necessary to perfect the buyer's rights.

(3) Unless otherwise agreed the term C. & F. or its equivalent has the same effect and imposes upon the seller the same obligations and risks as a C.I.F. term except the obligation as to insurance.

(4) Under the term C.I.F. or C. & F. unless otherwise agreed the buyer must make payment against tender of the required documents and the seller may not tender nor the buyer demand delivery of the goods in substitution for the documents.

§ 2—326. **Sale on Approval and Sale or Return; Consignment Sales and Rights of Creditors.**

(1) Unless otherwise agreed, if delivered goods may be returned by the buyer even though they conform to the contract, the transaction is

(a) a "sale on approval" if the goods are delivered primarily for use, and

(b) a "sale or return" if the goods are delivered primarily for resale.

(2) Except as provided in subsection (3), goods held on approval are not subject to the claims of the buyer's creditors until acceptance; goods held on sale or return are subject to such claims while in the buyer's possession.

(3) Where goods are delivered to a person for sale and such person maintains a place of business at which he deals in goods of the kind involved, under a name other than the name of the person making delivery, then with respect to claims of creditors of the person conducting the business the goods are deemed to be on sale or return. The provisions of this subsection are applicable even though an agreement purports to reserve title to the person making delivery until payment or resale or uses such words as "on consignment" or "on memorandum". However, this subsection is not applicable if the person making delivery

(a) complies with an applicable law providing for a consignor's interest or the like to be evidenced by a sign, or

(b) establishes that the person conducting the business is generally known by his creditors to be substantially engaged in selling the goods of others, or

(c) complies with the filing provisions of the Article on Secured Transactions (Article 9).

(4) Any "or return" term of a contract for sale is to be treated as a separate contract for sale within the statute of frauds section of this Article (Section 2—201) and as contradicting the sale aspect of the contract within the provisions of this Article on parol or extrinsic evidence (Section 2—202).

§ 2—328. **Sale by Auction.**

(1) In a sale by auction if goods are put up in lots each lot is the subject of a separate sale.

(2) A sale by auction is complete when the auctioneer so announces by the fall of the hammer or in other customary manner. Where a bid is made while the hammer is falling in acceptance of a prior bid the auctioneer may in his discretion reopen the bidding or declare the goods sold under the bid on which the hammer was falling.

(3) Such a sale is with reserve unless the goods are in explicit terms put up without reserve. In an auction with reserve the auctioneer may withdraw the goods at any time until he announces completion of the sale. In an auction without reserve, after the auctioneer calls for bids on an article or lot, that article or lot cannot be withdrawn unless no bid is made within a reasonable time. In either case a bidder may retract his bid until the auctioneer's announcement of completion of the sale, but a bidder's retraction does not revive any previous bid.

(4) If the auctioneer knowingly receives a bid on the seller's behalf or the seller makes or procures such as bid, and notice has not been given that liberty for such bidding is reserved, the buyer may at his option avoid the sale or take the goods at the price of the last good faith bid prior to the completion of the sale. This subsection shall not apply to any bid at a forced sale.

Article 3
COMMERCIAL PAPER

§ 3—104. **Form of Negotiable Instruments; "Draft"; "Check"; "Certificate of Deposit"; "Note".**

(1) Any writing to be a negotiable instrument within this Article must

(a) be signed by the maker or drawer; and

(b) contain an unconditional promise or order to pay a sum certain in money and no other promise, order, obligation or power given by the maker or drawer except as authorized by this Article; and

(c) be payable on demand or at a definite time; and

(d) be payable to order or to bearer.

(2) A writing which complies with the requirements of this section is

(a) a "draft" ("bill of exchange") if it is an order;

(b) a "check" if it is a draft drawn on a bank and payable on demand;

(c) a "certificate of deposit" if it is an acknowledgment by a bank receipt of money with an engagement to repay it;

(d) a ''note'' if it is a promise other than a certificate of deposit.

(3) As used in other Articles of this Act, and as the context may require, the terms ''draft'', ''check'', ''certificate of deposit'' and ''note'' may refer to instruments which are not negotiable within this Article as well as to instruments which are so negotiable.

§ 3—105. **When Promise or Order Unconditional.**

(1) A promise or order otherwise unconditional is not made conditional by the fact that the instrument

    (a) is subject to implied or constructive conditions; or

    (b) states its consideration, whether performed or promised, or the transaction which gave rise to the instrument, or that the promise or order is made or the instrument matures in accordance with or ''as per'' such transaction; or

    (c) refers to or states that it arises out of a separate agreement or refers to a separate agreement for rights as to prepayment or acceleration; or

    (d) states that it is drawn under a letter of credit; or

    (e) states that it is secured, whether by mortgage, reservation of title or otherwise; or

    (f) indicates a particular account to be debited or any other fund or source from which reimbursement is expected; or

    (g) is limited to payment out of a particular fund or the proceeds of a particular source, if the instrument is issued by a government or governmental agency or unit; or

    (h) is limited to payment out of the entire assets of a partnership, unincorporated association, trust or estate by or on behalf of which the instrument is issued.

(2) A promise or order is not unconditional if the instrument

    (a) states that it is subject to or governed by any other agreement; or

    (b) states that it is to be paid only out of a particular fund or source except as provided in this section.

§ 3—106. **Sum Certain.**

(1) The sum payable is a sum certain even though it is to be paid

    (a) with stated interest or by stated installments; or

    (b) with stated different rates of interest before and after default or a specified date; or

    (c) with a stated discount or addition if paid before or after the date fixed for payment; or

    (d) with exchange or less exchange, whether at a fixed rate or at the current rate; or

    (e) with costs of collection or an attorney's fee or both upon default.

(2) Nothing in this section shall validate any term which is otherwise illegal.

§ 3—107. **Money.**

(1) An instrument is payable in money if the medium of exchange in which it is payable is money at the time the instrument is made. An instrument payable in ''currency'' or ''current funds'' is payable in money.

(2) A promise or order to pay a sum stated in a foreign currency is for a sum certain in money and, unless a different medium of payment is specified in the instrument, may be satisfied by payment of that number of dollars which the stated foreign currency will purchase at the buying sight rate for that currency on the day on which the instrument is payable or, if payable on demand, on the day of demand. If such an instrument specifies a foreign currency as the medium of payment the instrument is payable in that currency.

§ 3—108. **Payable on Demand.**

Instruments payable on demand include those payable at sight or on presentation and those in which no time for payment is stated.

§ 3—109. **Definite Time.**

(1) An instrument is payable at a definite time if by its terms it is payable

    (a) on or before a stated date or at a fixed period after a stated date; or

    (b) at a fixed period after sight; or

    (c) at a definite time subject to any acceleration; or

    (d) at a definite time subject to extension at the option of the holder, or to extension to a further definite time at the option of the maker or acceptor or automatically upon or after a specified act or event.

(2) An instrument which by its terms is otherwise payable only upon an act or event uncertain as to time of occurrence is not payable at a definite time even though the act or event has occurred.

§ 3—110. **Payable to Order.**

(1) An instrument is payable to order when by its terms it is payable to the order or assigns of any person therein specified with reasonable certainty, or to him or his order, or when it is conspicuously designated on its face as ''exchange'' or the like and names a payee. It may be payable to the order of

    (a) the maker or drawer; or

    (b) the drawee; or

    (c) a payee who is not maker, drawer or drawee; or

(d) two or more payees together or in the alternative; or

(e) an estate, trust or fund, in which case it is payable to the order of the representative of such estate, trust or fund or his successors; or

(f) an office, or an officer by his title as such in which case it is payable to the principal but the incumbent of the office or his successors may act as if he or they were the holder; or

(g) a partnership or unincorporated association, in which case it is payable to the partnership or association and may be indorsed or transferred by any person thereto authorized.

(2) An instrument not payable to order is not made so payable by such words as "payable upon return of this instrument properly indorsed."

(3) An instrument made payable both to order and to bearer is payable to order unless the bearer words are handwritten or typewritten.

§ 3—111. Payable to Bearer.

An instrument is payable to bearer when by its terms it is payable to

(a) bearer or the order of bearer; or

(b) a specified person or bearer; or

(c) "cash" or the order of "cash", or any other indication which does not purport to designate a specific payee.

§ 3—112. Terms and Omissions Not Affecting Negotiability.

(1) The negotiability of an instrument is not affected by

(a) the omission of a statement of any consideration or of the place where the instrument is drawn or payable; or

(b) a statement that collateral has been given to secure obligations either on the instrument or otherwise of an obligor on the instrument or that in case of default on those obligations the holder may realize on or dispose of the collateral; or

(c) a promise or power to maintain or protect collateral or to give additional collateral; or

(d) a term authorizing a confession of judgment on the instrument if it is not paid when due; or

(e) a term purporting to waive the benefit of any law intended for the advantage or protection of any obligor; or

(f) a term in a draft providing that the payee by indorsing or cashing it acknowledges full satisfaction of an obligation of the drawer; or

(g) a statement in a draft drawn in a set of parts (Section 3—801) to the effect that the order is effective only if no other part has been honored.

(2) Nothing in this section shall validate any term which is otherwise illegal.

§ 3—113. Seal.

An instrument otherwise negotiable is within this Article even though it is under a seal.

§ 3—114. Date, Antedating, Postdating.

(1) The negotiability of an instrument is not affected by the fact that it is undated, antedated or postdated.

(2) Where an instrument is antedated or postdated the time when it is payable is determined by the stated date if the instrument is payable on demand or at a fixed period after date.

(3) Where the instrument or any signature thereon is dated, the date is presumed to be correct.

§ 3—115. Incomplete Instruments.

(1) When a paper whose contents at the time of signing show that it is intended to become an instrument is signed while still incomplete in any necessary respect it cannot be enforced until completed, but when it is completed in accordance with authority given it is effective as completed.

(2) If the completion is unauthorized the rules as to material alteration apply (Section 3—407), even though the paper was not delivered by the maker or drawer; but the burden of establishing that any completion is unauthorized is on the party so asserting.

§ 3—116. Instruments Payable to Two or More Persons.

An instrument payable to the order of two or more persons

(a) if in the alternative is payable to any one of them and may be negotiated, discharged or enforced by any of them who has possession of it;

(b) if not in the alternative is payable to all of them and may be negotiated, discharged or enforced only by all of them.

§ 3—118. Ambiguous Terms and Rules of Construction.

The following rules apply to every instrument:

(a) Where there is doubt whether the instrument is a draft or a note the holder may treat it as either. A draft drawn on the drawer is effective as a note.

(b) Handwritten terms control typewritten and printed terms, and typewritten control printed.

(c) Words control figures except that if the words are ambiguous figures control.

(d) Unless otherwise specified a provision for interest means interest at the judgment rate at the place of payment from the date of the instrument, or if it is undated from the date of issue.

(e) Unless the instrument otherwise specifies two or more persons who sign as maker, acceptor or drawer or indorser and as a part of the same transaction are jointly and severally liable even though the instrument contains such words as "I promise to pay."

(f) Unless otherwise specified consent to extension authorizes a single extension for not longer than the original period. A consent to extension, expressed in the instrument, is binding on secondary parties and accommodation makers. A holder may not exercise his option to extend an instrument over the objection of a maker or acceptor or other party who in accordance with Section 3—604 tenders full payment when the instrument is due.

§ 3—201. **Transfer: Right to Indorsement.**

(1) Transfer of an instrument vests in the transferee such rights as the transferor has therein, except that a transferee who has himself been a party to any fraud or illegality affecting the instrument or who as a prior holder had notice of a defense or claim against it cannot improve his position by taking from a later holder in due course.

(2) A transfer of a security interest in an instrument vests the foregoing rights in the transferee to the extent of the interest transferred.

(3) Unless otherwise agreed any transfer for value of an instrument not then payable to bearer gives the transferee the specifically enforceable right to have the unqualified indorsement of the transferor. Negotiation takes effect only when the indorsement is made and until that time there is no presumption that the transferee is the owner.

§ 3—202. **Negotiation.**

(1) Negotiation is the transfer of an instrument in such form that the transferee becomes a holder. If the instrument is payable to order it is negotiated by delivery with any necessary indorsement; if payable to bearer it is negotiated by delivery.

(2) An indorsement must be written by or on behalf of the holder and on the instrument or on a paper so firmly affixed thereto as to become a part thereof.

(3) An indorsement is effective for negotiation only when it conveys the entire instrument or any unpaid residue. If it purports to be of less it operates only as a partial assignment.

(4) Words of assignment, condition, waiver, guaranty, limitation or disclaimer of liability and the like accompanying an indorsement do not affect its character as an indorsement.

§ 3—203. **Wrong or Misspelled Name.**

Where an instrument is made payable to a person under a misspelled name or one other than his own he may indorse in that name or his own or both; but signature in both names may be required by a person paying or giving value for the instrument.

§ 3—204. **Special Indorsement; Blank Indorsement.**

(1) A special indorsement specifies the person to whom or to whose order it makes the instrument payable. Any instrument specially indorsed becomes payable to the order of the special indorsee and may be further negotiated only by his indorsement.

(2) An indorsement in blank specifies no particular indorsee and may consist of a mere signature. An instrument payable to order and indorsed in blank becomes payable to bearer and may be negotiated by delivery alone until specially indorsed.

(3) The holder may convert a blank indorsement into a special indorsement by writing over the signature of the indorser in blank any contract consistent with the character of the indorsement.

§ 3—205. **Restrictive Indorsements.**

An indorsement is restrictive which either

(a) is conditional; or

(b) purports to prohibit further transfer of the instrument; or

(c) includes the words "for collection", "for deposit", "pay any bank", or like terms signifying a purpose of deposit or collection; or

(d) otherwise states that it is for the benefit or use of the indorser or of another person.

§ 3—206. **Effect of Restrictive Indorsement.**

(1) No restrictive indorsement prevents further transfer or negotiation of the instrument.

(2) An intermediary bank, or a payor bank which is not the depositary bank, is neither given notice nor otherwise affected by a restrictive indorsement of any person except the bank's immediate transferor or the person presenting for payment.

(3) Except for an intermediary bank, any transferee under an indorsement which is conditional or includes the words "for collection", "for deposit", "pay any bank", or like terms (subparagraphs (a) and (c) of Section 3—205) must pay or apply any value given by him for or on the security of the instrument consistently with the indorsement and to the extent that he does so he becomes a holder for value. In addition such transferee is a holder in due course if he otherwise complies with the requirements of Section 3—302 on what constitutes a holder in due course.

(4) The first taker under an indorsement for the benefit of the indorser or another person (subparagraph (d) of Section 3—205) must pay or apply any value given by him for or

on the security of the instrument consistently with the indorsement and to the extent that he does so he becomes a holder for value. In addition such taker is a holder in due course if he otherwise complies with the requirements of Section 3—302 on what constitutes a holder in due course. A later holder for value is neither given notice nor otherwise affected by such restrictive indorsement unless he has knowledge that a fiduciary or other person has negotiated the instrument in any transaction for his own benefit or otherwise in breach of duty (subsection (2) of Section 3—304).

§ 3—207. Negotiation Effective Although It May Be Rescinded.

(1) Negotiation is effective to transfer the instrument although the negotiation is

(a) made by an infant, a corporation exceeding its powers, or any other person without capacity; or

(b) obtained by fraud, duress or mistake of any kind; or

(c) part of an illegal transaction; or

(d) made in breach of duty.

(2) Except as against a subsequent holder in due course such negotiation is in an appropriate case subject to rescission, the declaration of a constructive trust or any other remedy permitted by law.

§ 3—208. Reacquisition.

Where an instrument is returned to or reacquired by a prior party he may cancel any indorsement which is not necessary to his title and reissue or further negotiate the instrument, but any intervening party is discharged as against the reacquiring party and subsequent holders not in due course and if his indorsement has been cancelled is discharged as against subsequent holders in due course as well.

§ 3—301. Rights of a Holder.

The holder of an instrument whether or not he is the owner may transfer or negotiate it and, except as otherwise provided in Section 3—603 on payment or satisfaction, discharge it or enforce payment in his own name.

§ 3—302. Holder in Due Course

(1) A holder in due course is a holder who takes the instrument

(a) for value; and

(b) in good faith; and

(c) without notice that it is overdue or has been dishonored or of any defense against or claim to it on the part of any person.

(2) A payee may be a holder in due course.

(3) A holder does not become a holder in due course of an instrument:

(a) by purchase of it at judicial sale or by taking it under legal process; or

(b) by acquiring it in taking over an estate; or

(c) by purchasing it as part of a bulk transaction not in regular course of business of the transferor.

(4) A purchaser of a limited interest can be a holder in due course only to the extent of the interest purchased.

§ 3—305. Rights of a Holder in Due Course.

To the extent that a holder is a holder in due course he takes the instrument free from

(1) all claims to it on the part of any person; and

(2) all defenses of any party to the instrument with whom the holder has not dealt except

(a) infancy, to the extent that it is a defense to a simple contract; and

(b) such other incapacity, or duress, or illegality of the transaction, as renders the obligation of the party a nullity; and

(c) such misrepresentation as has induced the party to sign the instrument with neither knowledge nor reasonable opportunity to obtain knowledge of its character or its essential terms; and

(d) discharge in insolvency proceedings; and

(e) any other discharge of which the holder has notice when he takes the instrument.

§ 3—306. Rights of One Not Holder in Due Course.

Unless he has the rights of a holder in due course any person takes the instrument subject to

(a) all valid claims to it on the part of any person; and

(b) all defenses of any party which would be available in an action on a simple contract; and

(c) the defenses of want or failure of consideration, non-performance of any condition precedent, non-delivery, or delivery for a special purpose (Section 3—408); and

(d) the defense that he or a person through whom he holds the instrument acquired it by theft, or that payment or satisfaction to such holder would be inconsistent with the terms of a restrictive indorsement. The claim of any third person to the instrument is not otherwise available as a defense to any party liable thereon unless the third person himself defends the action for such party.

Part 4 Liability of Parties

§ 3—401. Signature.

(1) No person is liable on an instrument unless his signature appears thereon.

(2) A signature is made by use of any name, including any trade or assumed name, upon an instrument, or by any word or mark used in lieu of a written signature.

§ 3—404. Unauthorized Signatures.

(1) Any unauthorized signature is wholly inoperative as that of the person whose name is signed unless he ratifies it or is precluded from denying it; but it operates as the signature of the unauthorized signer in favor of any person who in good faith pays the instrument or takes it for value.

(2) Any unauthorized signature may be ratified for all purposes of this Article. Such ratification does not of itself affect any rights of the person ratifying against the actual signer.

§ 3—405. Impostors; Signature in Name of Payee.

(1) An indorsement by any person in the name of a named payee is effective if

(a) an impostor by use of the mails or otherwise has induced the maker or drawer to issue the instrument to him or his confederate in the name of the payee; or

(b) a person signing as or on behalf of a maker or drawer intends the payee to have no interest in the instrument; or

(c) an agent or employee of the maker or drawer has supplied him with the name of the payee intending the latter to have no such interest.

(2) Nothing in this section shall affect the criminal or civil liability of the person so indorsing.

§ 3—407. Alteration.

(1) Any alteration of an instrument is material which changes the contract of any party thereto in any respect, including any such change in

(a) the number or relations of the parties; or

(b) an incomplete instrument, by completing it otherwise than as authorized; or

(c) the writing as signed, by adding to it or by removing any part of it.

(2) As against any person other than a subsequent holder in due course

(a) alteration by the holder which is both fraudulent and material discharges any party whose contract is thereby changed unless that party assents or is precluded from asserting the defense;

(b) no other alteration discharges any party and the instrument may be enforced according to its original tenor, or as to incomplete instruments according to the authority given.

(3) A subsequent holder in due course may in all cases enforce the instrument according to its original tenor, and when an incomplete instrument has been completed, he may enforce it as completed.

§ 3—414. Contract of Indorser; Order of Liability.

(1) Unless the indorsement otherwise specifies (as by such words as "without recourse") every indorser engages that upon dishonor and any necessary notice of dishonor and protest he will pay the instrument according to its tenor at the time of his indorsement to the holder or to any subsequent indorser who takes it up, even though the indorser who takes it up was not obligated to do so.

(2) Unless they otherwise agree indorsers are liable to one another in the order in which they indorse, which is presumed to be the order in which their signatures appear on the instrument.

§ 3—417. Warranties on Presentment and Transfer.

(1) Any person who obtains payment or acceptance and any prior transferor warrants to a person who in good faith pays or accepts that

(a) he has a good title to the instrument or is authorized to obtain payment or acceptance on behalf of one who has a good title; and

(b) he has no knowledge that the signature of the maker or drawer is unauthorized, except that this warranty is not given by a holder in due course acting in good faith

(i) to a maker with respect to the maker's own signature; or

(ii) to a drawer with respect to the drawer's own signature, whether or not the drawer is also the drawee; or

(iii) to an acceptor of a draft if the holder in due course took the draft after the acceptance or obtained the acceptance without knowledge that the drawer's signature was unauthorized; and

(c) the instrument has not been materially altered, except that this warranty is not given by a holder in due course acting in good faith

(i) to the maker of a note; or

(ii) to the drawer of a draft whether or not the drawer is also the drawee; or

(iii) to the acceptor of a draft with respect to an alteration made prior to the acceptance if the holder in due course took the draft after the acceptance, even though the acceptance provided "payable as originally drawn" or equivalent terms; or

(iv) to the acceptor of a draft with respect to an alteration made after the acceptance.

(2) Any person who transfers an instrument and receives consideration warrants to his transferee and if the transfer

is by indorsement to any subsequent holder who takes the instrument in good faith that

(a) he has a good title to the instrument or is authorized to obtain payment or acceptance on behalf of one who has a good title and the transfer is otherwise rightful; and

(b) all signatures are genuine or authorized; and

(c) the instrument has not been materially altered; and

(d) no defense of any party is good against him; and

(e) he has no knowledge of any insolvency proceeding instituted with respect to the maker or acceptor or the drawer of an unaccepted instrument.

(3) By transferring "without recourse" the transferor limits the obligation stated in subsection (2) (d) to a warranty that he has no knowledge of such a defense.

(4) A selling agent or broker who does not disclose the fact that he is acting only as such gives the warranties provided in this section, but if he makes such disclosure warrants only his good faith and authority.

§ 3—502. **Unexcused Delay; Discharge.**

(1) Where without excuse any necessary presentment or notice of dishonor is delayed beyond the time when it is due

(a) any indorser is discharged; and

(b) any drawer or the acceptor of a draft payable at a bank or the maker of a note payable at a bank who because the drawee or payor bank becomes insolvent during the delay is deprived of funds maintained with the drawee or payor bank to cover the instrument may discharge his liability by written assignment to the holder of his rights against the drawee or payor bank in respect of such funds, but such drawer, acceptor or maker is not otherwise discharged.

(2) Where without excuse a necessary protest is delayed beyond the time when it is due any drawer or indorser is discharged.

§ 3—503. **Time of Presentment.**

(1) Unless a different time is expressed in the instrument the time for any presentment is determined as follows:

(a) where an instrument is payable at or a fixed period after a stated date any presentment for acceptance must be made on or before the date it is payable;

(b) where an instrument is payable after sight it must either be presented for acceptance or negotiated within a reasonable time after date or issue whichever is later;

(c) where an instrument shows the date on which it is payable presentment for payment is due on that date;

(d) where an instrument is accelerated presentment for payment is due within a reasonable time after the acceleration;

(e) with respect to the liability of any secondary party presentment for acceptance or payment of any other instrument is due within a reasonable time after such party becomes liable thereon.

(2) A reasonable time for presentment is determined by the nature of the instrument, any usage of banking or trade and the facts of the particular case. In the case of an uncertified check which is drawn and payable within the United States and which is not a draft drawn by a bank the following are presumed to be reasonable periods within which to present for payment or to initiate bank collection:

(a) with respect to the liability of the drawer, thirty days after date or issue whichever is later; and

(b) with respect to the liability of an indorser, seven days after his indorsement.

(3) Where any presentment is due on a day which is not a full business day for either the person making presentment or the party to pay or accept, presentment is due on the next following day which is a full business day for both parties.

(4) Presentment to be sufficient must be made at a reasonable hour, and if at a bank during its banking day.

§ 3—504. **How Presentment Made.**

(1) Presentment is a demand for acceptance or payment made upon the maker, acceptor, drawee or other payor by or on behalf of the holder.

(2) Presentment may be made

(a) by mail, in which event the time of presentment is determined by the time of receipt of the mail; or

(b) through a clearing house; or

(c) at the place of acceptance or payment specified in the instrument or if there be none at the place of business or residence of the party to accept or pay. If neither the party to accept or pay nor anyone authorized to act for him is present or accessible at such place presentment is excused.

(3) It may be made

(a) to any one of two or more makers, acceptors, drawees or other payors; or

(b) to any person who has authority to make or refuse the acceptance or payment.

(4) A draft accepted or a note made payable at a bank in the United States must be presented at such bank.

(5) In the cases described in Section 4—210 presentment may be made in the manner and with the result stated in that section.

§ 3—505. **Rights of Party to Whom Presentment Is Made.**

(1) The party to whom presentment is made may without dishonor require

(a) exhibition of the instrument; and

(b) reasonable identification of the person making presentment and evidence of his authority to make it if made for another; and

(c) that the instrument be produced for acceptance or payment at a place specified in it, or if there be none at any place reasonable in the circumstances; and

(d) a signed receipt on the instrument for any partial or full payment and its surrender upon full payment.

(2) Failure to comply with any such requirement invalidates the presentment but the person presenting has a reasonable time in which to comply and the time for acceptance or payment runs from the time of compliance.

§ 3—603. Payment or Satisfaction.

(1) The liability of any party is discharged to the extent of his payment or satisfaction to the holder even though it is made with knowledge of a claim of another person to the instrument unless prior to such payment or satisfaction the person making the claim either supplies indemnity deemed adequate by the party seeking the discharge or enjoins payment or satisfaction by order of a court of competent jurisdiction in an action in which the adverse claimant and the holder are parties. This subsection does not, however, result in the discharge of the liability

(a) of a party who in bad faith pays or satisfies a holder who acquired the instrument by theft or who (unless having the rights of a holder in due course) holds through one who so acquired it; or

(b) of a party (other than an intermediary bank or a payor bank which is not a depositary bank) who pays or satisfies the holder of an instrument which has been restrictively indorsed in a manner not consistent with the terms of such restrictive indorsement.

(2) Payment or satisfaction may be made with the consent of the holder by any person including a stranger to the instrument. Surrender of the instrument to such a person gives him the rights of a transferee (Section 3—201).

§ 3—605. Cancellation and Renunciation.

(1) The holder of an instrument may even without consideration discharge any party

(a) in any manner apparent on the face of the instrument or the indorsement, as by intentionally cancelling the instrument or the party's signature by destruction or mutilation, or by striking out the party's signature; or

(b) by renouncing his rights by a writing signed and delivered or by surrender of the instrument to the party to be discharged.

(2) Neither cancellation nor renunciation without surrender of the instrument affects the title thereto.

Article 4
BANK DEPOSITS AND COLLECTIONS

§ 4—401. When Bank May Charge Customer's Account.

(1) As against its customer, a bank may charge against his account any item which is otherwise properly payable from that account even though the charge creates an overdraft.

(2) A bank which in good faith makes payment to a holder may charge the indicated account of its customer according to

(a) the original tenor of his altered item; or

(b) the tenor of his completed item, even though the bank knows the item has been completed unless the bank has notice that the completion was improper.

§ 4—402. Bank's Liability to Customer for Wrongful Dishonor.

A payor bank is liable to its customer for damages proximately caused by the wrongful dishonor of an item. When the dishonor occurs through mistake liability is limited to actual damages proved. If so proximately caused and proved damages may include damages for an arrest or prosecution of the customer or other consequential damages. Whether any consequential damages are proximately caused by the wrongful dishonor is a question of fact to be determined in each case.

§ 4—403. Customer's Right to Stop Payment; Burden of Proof of Loss.

(1) A customer may by order to his bank stop payment of any item payable for his account but the order must be received at such time and in such manner as to afford the bank a reasonable opportunity to act on it prior to any action by the bank with respect to the item described in Section 4—303.

(2) An oral order is binding upon the bank only for fourteen calendar days unless confirmed in writing within that period. A written order is effective for only six months unless renewed in writing.

(3) The burden of establishing the fact and amount of loss resulting from the payment of an item contrary to a binding stop payment order is on the customer.

§ 4—404. Bank Not Obligated to Pay Check More Than Six Months Old.

A bank is under no obligation to a customer having a checking account to pay a check, other than a certified check, which is presented more than six months after its date, but it may charge its customer's account for a payment made thereafter in good faith.

§ 4—405. Death or Incompetence of Customer.

(1) A payor or collecting bank's authority to accept, pay or collect an item or to account for proceeds of its collection if otherwise effective is not rendered ineffective by incompetence of a customer of either bank existing at the time the item is issued or its collection is undertaken if the bank does not know of an adjudication of incompetence. Neither death nor incompetence of a customer revokes such authority to accept, pay, collect or account until the bank knows of the fact of death or of an adjudication of incompetence and has reasonable opportunity to act on it.

(2) Even with knowledge a bank may for 10 days after the date of death pay or certify checks drawn on or prior to that date unless ordered to stop payment by a person claiming an interest in the account.

§ 4—406. Customer's Duty to Discover and Report Unauthorized Signature or Alteration.

(1) When a bank sends to its customer a statement of account accompanied by items paid in good faith in support of the debit entries or holds the statement and items pursuant to a request or instructions of its customer or otherwise in a reasonable manner makes the statement and items available to the customer, the customer must exercise reasonable care and promptness to examine the statement and items to discover his unauthorized signature or any alteration on an item and must notify the bank promptly after discovery thereof.

(2) If the bank establishes that the customer failed with respect to an item to comply with the duties imposed on the customer by subsection (1) the customer is precluded from asserting against the bank

(a) his unauthorized signature or any alteration on the item if the bank also establishes that it suffered a loss by reason of such failure; and

(b) an unauthorized signature or alteration by the same wrongdoer on any other item paid in good faith by the bank after the first item and statement was available to the customer for a reasonable period not exceeding fourteen calendar days and before the bank receives notification from the customer of any such unauthorized signature or alteration.

(3) The preclusion under subsection (2) does not apply if the customer establishes lack of ordinary care on the part of the bank in paying the item(s).

(4) Without regard to care or lack of care of either the customer or the bank a customer who does not within one year from the time the statement and items are made available to the customer (subsection (1)) discover and report his unauthorized signature or any alteration on the face or back of the item or does not within three years from that time discover and report any unauthorized indorsement is precluded from asserting against the bank such unauthorized signature or indorsement or such alteration.

(5) If under this section a payor bank has a valid defense against a claim of a customer upon or resulting from payment of an item and waives or fails upon request to assert the defense the bank may not assert against any collecting bank or other prior party presenting or transferring the item a claim based upon the unauthorized signature or alteration giving rise to the customer's claim.

Article 6
BULK TRANSFERS

§ 6—102. "Bulk Transfers"; Transfers of Equipment; Enterprises Subject to This Article; Bulk Transfers Subject to This Article.

(1) A "bulk transfer" is any transfer in bulk and not in the ordinary course of the transferor's business of a major part of the materials, supplies, merchandise or other inventory (Section 9—109) of an enterprise subject to this Article.

(2) A transfer of a substantial part of the equipment (Section 9—109) of such an enterprise is a bulk transfer if it is made in connection with a bulk transfer of inventory, but not otherwise.

(3) The enterprises subject to this Article are all those whose principal business is the sale of merchandise from stock, including those who manufacture what they sell.

(4) Except as limited by the following section all bulk transfers of goods located within this state are subject to this Article.

§ 6—104. Schedule of Property, List of Creditors.

(1) Except as provided with respect to auction sales (Section 6—108), a bulk transfer subject to this Article is ineffective against any creditor of the transferor unless:

(a) The transferee requires the transferor to furnish a list of his existing creditors prepared as stated in this section; and

(b) The parties prepare a schedule of the property transferred sufficient to identify it; and

(c) The transferee preserves the list and schedule for six months next following the transfer and permits inspection of either or both and copying therefrom at all reasonable hours by any creditor of the transferor, or files the list and schedule in (a public office to be here identified).

(2) The list of creditors must be signed and sworn to or affirmed by the transferor or his agent. It must contain the

names and business addresses of all creditors of the transferor, with the amounts when known, and also the names of all persons who are known to the transferor to assert claims against him even though such claims are disputed. If the transferor is the obligor of an outstanding issue of bonds, debentures or the like as to which there is an indenture trustee, the list of creditors need include only the name and address of the indenture trustee and the aggregate outstanding principal amount of the issue.

(3) Responsibility for the completeness and accuracy of the list of creditors rests on the transferor, and the transfer is not rendered ineffective by errors or omissions therein unless the transferee is shown to have had knowledge.

§ 6—105. **Notice to Creditors.**

In addition to the requirements of the preceding section, any bulk transfer subject to this Article except one made by auction sale (Section 6—108) is ineffective against any creditor of the transferor unless at least ten days before he takes possession of the goods or pays for them, whichever happens first, the transferee gives notice of the transfer in the manner and to the persons hereafter provided (Section 6—107).

§ 6—107. **The Notice.**

(1) The notice to creditors (Section 6—105) shall state:

(a) that a bulk transfer is about to be made; and

(b) the names and business addresses of the transferor and transferee, and all other business names and addresses used by the transferor within three years last past so far as known to the transferee; and

(c) whether or not all the debts of the transferor are to be paid in full as they fall due as a result of the transaction, and if so, the address to which creditors should send their bills.

(2) If the debts of the transferor are not to be paid in full as they fall due or if the transferee is in doubt on that point then the notice shall state further:

(a) the location and general description of the property to be transferred and the estimated total of the transferor's debts;

(b) the address where the schedule of property and list of creditors (Section 6—104) may be inspected;

(c) whether the transfer is to pay existing debts and if so the amount of such debts and to whom owing;

(d) whether the transfer is for new consideration and if so the amount of such consideration and the time and place of payment; [and]

[(e) if for new consideration the time and place where creditors of the transferor are to file their claims.]

(3) The notice in any case shall be delivered personally or sent by registered or certified mail to all the persons shown on the list of creditors furnished by the transferor (Section 6—104) and to all other persons who are known to the transferee to hold or assert claims against the transferor.

§ 6—111. **Limitation of Actions and Levies.**

No action under this Article shall be brought nor levy made more than six months after the date on which the transferee took possession of the goods unless the transfer has been concealed. If the transfer has been concealed, actions may be brought or levies made within six months after its discovery.

Article 9
SECURED TRANSACTIONS; SALES OF ACCOUNTS AND CHATTEL PAPER

§ 9—201. **General Validity of Security Agreement.**

Except as otherwise provided by this Act a security agreement is effective according to its terms between the parties, against purchasers of the collateral and against creditors. Nothing in this Article validates any charge or practice illegal under any statute or regulation thereunder governing usury, small loans, retail installment sales, or the like, or extends the application of any such statute or regulation to any transaction not otherwise subject thereto.

§ 9—203. **Attachment and Enforceability of Security Interest; Proceeds; Formal Requisites**

(1) Subject to the provisions of Section 4—208 on the security interest of a collecting bank, Section 8—321 on security interests in securities and Section 9—113 on a security interest arising under the Article on Sales, a security interest is not enforceable against the debtor or third parties with respect to the collateral and does not attach unless:

(a) the collateral is in the possession of the secured party pursuant to agreement, or the debtor has signed a security agreement which contains a description of the collateral and in addition, when the security interest covers crops growing or to be grown or timber to be cut, a description of the land concerned;

(b) value has been given; and

(c) the debtor has rights in the collateral.

(2) A security interest attaches when it becomes enforceable against the debtor with respect to the collateral. Attachment occurs as soon as all of the events specified in subsection (1) have taken place unless explicit agreement postpones the time of attaching.

(3) Unless otherwise agreed a security agreement gives the secured party the rights to proceeds provided by Section 9—306.

§ 9—204. After-Acquired Property; Future Advances.

(1) Except as provided in subsection (2), a security agreement may provide that any or all obligations covered by the security agreement are to be secured by after-acquired collateral.

(2) No security interest attaches under an after-acquired property clause to consumer goods other than accessions (Section 9—314) when given as additional security unless the debtor acquires rights in them within ten days after the secured party gives value.

(3) Obligations covered by a security agreement may include future advances or other value whether or not the advances or value are given pursuant to commitment (subsection (1) of Section 9—105).

§ 9—302. When Filing Is Required to Perfect Security Interest; Security Interests to Which Filing Provisions of This Article Do Not Apply

(1) A financing statement must be filed to perfect all security interests except the following:

(a) a security interest in collateral in possession of the secured party under Section 9—305;

(b) a security interest temporarily perfected in instruments or documents without delivery under Section 9—304 or in proceeds for a 10 day period under Section 9—306;

(c) a security interest created by an assignment of a beneficial interest in a trust or a decedent's estate;

(d) a purchase money security interest in consumer goods; but filing is required for a motor vehicle required to be registered; and fixture filing is required for priority over conflicting interests in fixtures to the extent provided in Section 9—313;

(e) an assignment of accounts which does not alone or in conjunction with other assignments to the same assignee transfer a significant part of the outstanding accounts of the assignor;

(f) a security interest of a collecting bank (Section 4—208) or in securities (Section 8—321) or arising under the Article on Sales (see Section 9—113) or covered in subsection (3) of this section;

(g) an assignment for the benefit of all the creditors of the transferor, and subsequent transfers by the assignee thereunder.

(2) If a secured party assigns a perfected security interest, no filing under this Article is required in order to continue the perfected status of the security interest against creditors of and transferees from the original debtor.

(3) The filing of a financing statement otherwise required by this Article is not necessary or effective to perfect a security interest in property subject to

(a) a statute or treaty of the United States which provides for a national or international registration or a national or international certificate of title or which specifies a place of filing different from that specified in this Article for filing of the security interest; or

(b) the following statutes of this state; [list any certificate of title statute covering automobiles, trailers, mobile homes, boats, farm tractors, or the like, and any central filing statute.]; but during any period in which collateral is inventory held for sale by a person who is in the business of selling goods of that kind, the filing provisions of this Article (Part 4) apply to a security interest in that collateral created by him as debtor; or

(c) a certificate of title statute of another jurisdiction under the law of which indication of a security interest on the certificate is required as a condition of perfection (subsection (2) of Section 9—103).

(4) Compliance with a statute or treaty described in subsection (3) is equivalent to the filing of a financing statement under this Article, and a security interest in property subject to the statute or treaty can be perfected only by compliance therewith except as provided in Section 9—103 on multiple state transactions. Duration and renewal of perfection of a security interest perfected by compliance with the statute or treaty are governed by the provisions of the statute or treaty; in other respects the security interest is subject to this Article.

Amended in 1972 and 1977.

§ 9—307. Protection of Buyers of Goods.

(1) A buyer in ordinary course of business (subsection (9) of Section 1—201) other than a person buying farm products from a person engaged in farming operations takes free of a security interest created by his seller even though the security interest is perfected and even though the buyer knows of its existence [subject to the Food Security Act of 1985 (7 U.S.C. Section 1631)].

(2) In the case of consumer goods, a buyer takes free of a security interest even though perfected if he buys without knowledge of the security interest, for value and for his own personal, family or household purposes unless prior to the purchase the secured party has filed a financing statement covering such goods.

(3) A buyer other than a buyer in ordinary course of business (subsection (1) of this section) takes free of a security interest to the extent that it secures future advances made after the secured party acquires knowledge of the purchase, or more than 45 days after the purchase, whichever first occurs, unless made pursuant to a commitment entered into without knowledge of the purchase and before the expiration of the 45 day period.

§ 9—312. **Priorities Among Conflicting Security Interests in the Same Collateral**

(1) The rules of priority stated in other sections of this Part and in the following sections shall govern when applicable: Section 4—208 with respect to the security interests of collecting banks in items being collected, accompanying documents and proceeds; Section 9—103 on security interests related to other jurisdictions; Section 9—114 on consignments.

(2) A perfected security interest in crops for new value given to enable the debtor to produce the crops during the production season and given not more than three months before the crops become growing crops by planting or otherwise takes priority over an earlier perfected security interest to the extent that such earlier interest secures obligations due more than six months before the crops become growing crops by planting or otherwise, even though the person giving new value had knowledge of the earlier security interest.

(3) A perfected purchase money security interest in inventory has priority over a conflicting security interest in the same inventory and also has priority in identifiable cash proceeds received on or before the delivery of the inventory to a buyer if

(a) the purchase money security interest is perfected at the time the debtor receives possession of the inventory; and

(b) the purchase money secured party gives notification in writing to the holder of the conflicting security interest if the holder had filed a financing statement covering the same types of inventory (i) before the date of the filing made by the purchase money secured party, or (ii) before the beginning of the 21 day period where the purchase money security interest is temporarily perfected without filing or possession (subsection (5) of Section 9—304); and

(c) the holder of the conflicting security interest receives the notification within five years before the debtor receives possession of the inventory; and

(d) the notification states that the person giving the notice has or expects to acquire a purchase money security interest in inventory of the debtor, describing such inventory by item or type.

(4) A purchase money security interest in collateral other than inventory has priority over a conflicting security interest in the same collateral or its proceeds if the purchase money security interest is perfected at the time the debtor receives possession of the collateral or within ten days thereafter.

(5) In all cases not governed by other rules stated in this section (including cases of purchase money security interests which do not qualify for the special priorities set forth in subsections (3) and (4) of this section), priority between conflicting security interests in the same collateral shall be determined according to the following rules:

(a) Conflicting security interests rank according to priority in time of filing or perfection. Priority dates from the time a filing is first made covering the collateral or the time the security interest is first perfected, whichever is earlier, provided that there is no period thereafter when there is neither filing nor perfection.

(b) So long as conflicting security interests are unperfected, the first to attach has priority.

(6) For the purposes of subsection (5) a date of filing or perfection as to collateral is also a date of filing or perfection as to proceeds.

(7) If future advances are made while a security interest is perfected by filing, the taking of possession, or under Section 8—321 on securities, the security interest has the same priority for the purposes of subsection (5) with respect to the future advances as it does with respect to the first advance. If a commitment is made before or while the security interest is so perfected, the security interest has the same priority with respect to advances made pursuant thereto. In other cases a perfected security interest has priority from the date the advance is made.

Amended in 1972 and 1977.

§ 9—402. **Formal Requisites of Financing Statement; Amendments; Mortgage as Financing Statement.**

(1) A financing statement is sufficient if it gives the names of the debtor and the secured party, is signed by the debtor, gives an address of the secured party from which information concerning the security interest may be obtained, gives a mailing address of the debtor and contains a statement indicating the types, or describing the items, of collateral. A financing statement may be filed before a security agreement is made or a security interest otherwise attaches. When the financing statement covers crops growing or to be grown, the statement must also contain a description of the real estate concerned. When the financing statement covers timber to be cut or covers minerals or the like (including oil and gas) or accounts subject to subsection (5) of Section 9—103, or when the financing statement is filed as a fixture filing (Section 9—313) and the collateral is goods which are or are to become fixtures, the statement must also comply with subsection (5). A copy of the security agreement is sufficient as a financing statement if it contains the above information and is signed by the debtor. A carbon, photographic or other reproduction of a security agreement or a financing statement is sufficient as a financing statement if the security agreement so provides or if the original has been filed in this state.

(2) A financing statement which otherwise complies with subsection (1) is sufficient when it is signed by the secured party instead of the debtor if it is filed to perfect a security interest in

(a) collateral already subject to a security interest in another jurisdiction when it is brought into this state, or when the debtor's location is changed to this state. Such a financing statement must state that the collateral was brought into this state or that the debtor's location was changed to this state under such circumstances; or

(b) proceeds under Section 9—306 if the security interest in the original collateral was perfected. Such a financing statement must describe the original collateral; or

(c) collateral as to which the filing has lapsed; or

(d) collateral acquired after a change of name, identity or corporate structure of the debtor (subsection (7)).

(3) A form substantially as follows is sufficient to comply with subsection (1):

Name of debtor (or assignor) . . . .
Address . . . .
Name of secured party (or assignee) . . . .
Address . . . .
1. This financing statement covers the following types (or items) of property:
    (Describe) . . . .
2. (If collateral is crops) The above described crops are growing or are to be grown on:
    (Describe Real Estate) . . . .
3. (If applicable) The above goods are to become fixtures on *
*Where appropriate substitute either "The above timber is standing on . . . ." or "The above minerals or the like (including oil and gas) or accounts will be financed at the wellhead or minehead of the well or mine located on . . . ."
    (Describe Real Estate) . . . .
and this financing statement is to be filed [for record] in the real estate records. (If the debtor does not have an interest of record) The name of a record owner is

. . . .
4. (If products of collateral are claimed) Products of the collateral are also covered.

(use . . . .
whichever   Signature of Debtor (or Assignor)

is . . . .
applicable)   Signature of Secured Party
             (or Assignee)

(4) A financing statement may be amended by filing a writing signed by both the debtor and the secured party. An amendment does not extend the period of effectiveness of a financing statement. If any amendment adds collateral, it is effective as to the added collateral only from the filing date of the amendment. In this Article, unless the context otherwise requires, the term "financing statement" means the original financing statement and any amendments.

(5) A financing statement covering timber to be cut or covering minerals or the like (including oil and gas) or accounts subject to subsection (5) of Section 9—103, or a financing statement filed as a fixture filing (Section 9—313) where the debtor is not a transmitting utility, must show that it covers this type of collateral, must recite that it is to be filed [for record] in the real estate records, and the financing statement must contain a description of the real estate [sufficient if it were contained in a mortgage of the real estate to give constructive notice of the mortgage under the law of this state]. If the debtor does not have an interest of record in the real estate, the financing statement must show the name of a record owner.

(6) A mortgage is effective as a financing statement filed as a fixture filing from the date of its recording if

(a) the goods are described in the mortgage by item or type; and

(b) the goods are or are to become fixtures related to the real estate described in the mortgage; and

(c) the mortgage complies with the requirements for a financing statement in this section other than a recital that it is to be filed in the real estate records; and

(d) the mortgage is duly recorded.

No fee with reference to the financing statement is required other than the regular recording and satisfaction fees with respect to the mortgage.

(7) A financing statement sufficiently shows the name of the debtor if it gives the individual, partnership or corporate name of the debtor, whether or not it adds other trade names or names of partners. Where the debtor so changes his name or in the case of an organization its name, identity or corporate structure that a filed financing statement becomes seriously misleading, the filing is not effective to perfect a security interest in collateral acquired by the debtor more than four months after the change, unless a new appropriate financing statement is filed before the expiration of that time. A filed financing statement remains effective with respect to collateral transferred by the debtor even though the secured party knows of or consents to the transfer.

(8) A financing statement substantially complying with the requirements of this section is effective even though it contains minor errors which are not seriously misleading.

Note: *Language in brackets is optional.*

Note: *Where the state has any special recording system for real estate other than the usual grantor-grantee index (as, for instance, a tract system or a title registration or Torrens system) local adaptations of subsection (5) and Section 9—403(7) may be necessary. See Mass.Gen.Laws Chapter 106, Section 9—409.*

Part 5 **Default**

§ 9—501. **Default; Procedure When Security Agreement Covers Both Real and Personal Property.**

(1) When a debtor is in default under a security agreement, a secured party has the rights and remedies provided in this Part and except as limited by subsection (3) those provided in the security agreement. He may reduce his claim to judgment, foreclose or otherwise enforce the security interest by any available judicial procedure. If the collateral is documents the secured party may proceed either as to the documents or as to the goods covered thereby. A secured party in possession has the rights, remedies and duties provided in Section 9—207. The rights and remedies referred to in this subsection are cumulative.

(2) After default, the debtor has the rights and remedies provided in this Part, those provided in the security agreement and those provided in Section 9—207.

(3) To the extent that they give rights to the debtor and impose duties on the secured party, the rules stated in the subsections referred to below may not be waived or varied except as provided with respect to compulsory disposition of collateral (subsection (3) of Section 9—504 and Section 9—505) and with respect to redemption of collateral (Section 9—506) but the parties may by agreement determine the standards by which the fulfillment of these rights and duties is to be measured if such standards are not manifestly unreasonable:

    (a) subsection (2) of Section 9—502 and subsection (2) of Section 9—504 insofar as they require accounting for surplus proceeds of collateral;

    (b) subsection (3) of Section 9—504 and subsection (1) of Section 9—505 which deal with disposition of collateral;

    (c) subsection (2) of Section 9—505 which deals with acceptance of collateral as discharge of obligation;

    (d) Section 9—506 which deals with redemption of collateral; and

    (e) subsection (1) of Section 9—507 which deals with the secured party's liability for failure to comply with this Part.

(4) If the security agreement covers both real and personal property, the secured party may proceed under this Part as to the personal property or he may proceed as to both the real and the personal property in accordance with his rights and remedies in respect of the real property in which case the provisions of this Part do not apply.

(5) When a secured party has reduced his claim to judgment the lien of any levy which may be made upon his collateral by virture of any execution based upon the judgment shall relate back to the date of the perfection of the security interest in such collateral. A judicial sale, pursuant to such execution, is a foreclosure of the security interest by judicial procedure within the meaning of this section, and the secured party may purchase at the sale and thereafter hold the collateral free of any other requirements of this Article.

§ 9—503. **Secured Party's Right to Take Possession After Default.**

Unless otherwise agreed a secured party has on default the right to take possession of the collateral. In taking possession a secured party may proceed without judicial process if this can be done without breach of the peace or may proceed by action. If the security agreement so provides the secured party may require the debtor to assemble the collateral and make it available to the secured party at a place to be designated by the secured party which is reasonably convenient to both parties. Without removal a secured party may render equipment unusable, and may dispose of collateral on the debtor's premises under Section 9—504.

§ 9—504. **Secured Party's Right to Dispose of Collateral After Default; Effect of Disposition.**

(1) A secured party after default may sell, lease or otherwise dispose of any or all of the collateral in its then condition or following any commercially reasonable preparation or processing. Any sale of goods is subject to the Article on Sales (Article 2). The proceeds of disposition shall be applied in the order following to

    (a) the reasonable expenses of retaking, holding, preparing for sale or lease, selling, leasing and the like and, to the extent provided for in the agreement and not prohibited by law, the reasonable attorneys' fees and legal expenses incurred by the secured party;

    (b) the satisfaction of indebtedness secured by the security interest under which the disposition is made;

    (c) the satisfaction of indebtedness secured by any subordinate security interest in the collateral if written notification of demand therefor is received before distribution of the proceeds is completed. If requested by the secured party, the holder of a subordinate security interest must seasonably furnish reasonable proof of his interest, and unless he does so, the secured party need not comply with his demand.

(2) If the security interest secures an indebtedness, the secured party must account to the debtor for any surplus, and, unless otherwise agreed, the debtor is liable for any deficiency. But if the underlying transaction was a sale of accounts or chattel paper, the debtor is entitled to any surplus or is liable for any deficiency only if the security agreement so provides.

(3) Disposition of the collateral may be by public or private proceedings and may be made by way of one or more contracts. Sale or other disposition may be as a unit or in

parcels and at any time and place and on any terms but every aspect of the disposition including the method, manner, time, place and terms must be commercially reasonable. Unless collateral is perishable or threatens to decline speedily in value or is of a type customarily sold on a recognized market, reasonable notification of the time and place of any public sale or reasonable notification of the time after which any private sale or other intended disposition is to be made shall be sent by the secured party to the debtor, if he has not signed after default a statement renouncing or modifying his right to notification of sale. In the case of consumer goods no other notification need be sent. In other cases notification shall be sent to any other secured party from whom the secured party has received (before sending his notification to the debtor or before the debtor's renunciation of his rights) written notice of a claim of an interest in the collateral. The secured party may buy at any public sale and if the collateral is of a type customarily sold in a recognized market or is of a type which is the subject of widely distributed standard price quotations he may buy at private sale.

(4) When collateral is disposed of by a secured party after default, the disposition transfers to a purchaser for value all of the debtor's rights therein, discharges the security interest under which it is made and any security interest or lien subordinate thereto. The purchaser takes free of all such rights and interests even though the secured party fails to comply with the requirements of this Part or of any judicial proceedings

    (a) in the case of a public sale, if the purchaser has no knowledge of any defects in the sale and if he does not buy in collusion with the secured party, other bidders or the person conducting the sale; or

    (b) in any other case, if the purchaser acts in good faith.

(5) A person who is liable to a secured party under a guaranty, indorsement, repurchase agreement or the like and who receives a transfer of collateral from the secured party or is subrogated to his rights has thereafter the rights and duties of the secured party. Such a transfer of collateral is not a sale or disposition of the collateral under this Article.

§ 9—505. **Compulsory Disposition of Collateral; Acceptance of the Collateral as Discharge of Obligation.**

(1) If the debtor has paid sixty per cent of the cash price in the case of a purchase money security interest in consumer goods or sixty per cent of the loan in the case of another security interest in consumer goods, and has not signed after default a statement renouncing or modifying his rights under this Part a secured party who has taken possession of collateral must dispose of it under Section

9—504 and if he fails to do so within ninety days after he takes possession the debtor at his option may recover in conversion or under Section 9—507(1) on secured party's liability.

(2) In any other case involving consumer goods or any other collateral a secured party in possession may, after default, propose to retain the collateral in satisfaction of the obligation. Written notice of such proposal shall be sent to the debtor if he has not signed after default a statement renouncing or modifying his rights under this subsection. In the case of consumer goods no other notice need be given. In other cases notice shall be sent to any other secured party from whom the secured party has received (before sending his notice to the debtor or before the debtor's renunciation of his rights) written notice of a claim of an interest in the collateral. If the secured party receives objection in writing from a person entitled to receive notification within twenty-one days after the notice was sent, the secured party must dispose of the collateral under Section 9—504. In the absence of such written objection the secured party may retain the collateral in satisfaction of the debtor's obligation. Amended in 1972.

§ 9—507. **Secured Party's Liability for Failure to Comply With This Part.**

(1) If it is established that the secured party is not proceeding in accordance with the provisions of this Part disposition may be ordered or restrained on appropriate terms and conditions. If the disposition has occurred the debtor or any person entitled to notification or whose security interest has been made known to the secured party prior to the disposition has a right to recover from the secured party any loss caused by a failure to comply with the provisions of this Part. If the collateral is consumer goods, the debtor has a right to recover in any event an amount not less than the credit service charge plus ten per cent of the principal amount of the debt or the time price differential plus 10 per cent of the cash price.

(2) The fact that a better price could have been obtained by a sale at a different time or in a different method from that selected by the secured party is not of itself sufficient to establish that the sale was not made in a commercially reasonable manner. If the secured party either sells the collateral in the usual manner in any recognized market therefor or if he sells at the price current in such market at the time of his sale or if he has otherwise sold in conformity with reasonable commercial practices among dealers in the type of property sold he has sold in a commercially reasonable manner. The principles stated in the two preceding sentences with respect to sales also apply as may be appropriate to other types of disposition. A disposition which has been approved in any judicial proceeding or by any bona fide creditors' committee or representative of creditors shall conclusively be deemed to

be commercially reasonable, but this sentence does not indicate that any such approval must be obtained in any case nor does it indicate that any disposition not so approved is not commercially reasonable.

Appendix C **Restatement of Torts, Second (Excerpts)**

Section 402 A. Special liability of seller of product for physical harm to user or consumer.

(1) One who sells any product in a defection condition unreasonably dangerous to the consumer or to his property is subject to liability for physical harm thereby caused to the ultimate user or consumer, or to his property, if

(a) the seller is engaged in the business of selling such a product, and

(b) it is expected to and does reach the user or consumer without substantial change in the condition in which it is sold.

(2) The rule stated in Subsection (1) applies although

(a) the seller has exercised all possible care in the preparation and sale of his product, and

(b) the user or consumer has not bought the product from or entered into any contractual relation with the seller.

Section 402 B. Misrepresentation by seller of chattels to consumer.

One engaged in the business of selling chattels who, by advertising, labels, or otherwise, makes to the public a misrepresentation of a material fact concerning the character or quality of a chattel sold by him is subject to liability for physical harm to a consumer of the chattel caused by justifiable reliance upon the misrepresentation, even though

(a) it is not made fraudulently or negligently, and

(b) the consumer has not bought the chattel from or entered into any contractual relations with the seller.

Appendix D **The Sherman Antitrust Act (Excerpts)**

The Sherman Antitrust Act (1890, as amended)

Section. 1 Every contract, combination in the form of trust or otherwise, or conspiracy, in restraint of trade or commerce among the several States, or with foreign nations, is hereby declared to be illegal. Every person who shall make any such contract or engage in any such combination or conspiracy shall be deemed guilty of a felony, and, on conviction thereof, shall be punished by fine not exceeding one million dollars if a corporation, or, if any other person, one hundred thousand dollars or by imprisonment not exceeding three years, or by both said punishments in the discretion of the court.

Section 2. Every person who shall monopolize, or attempt to monopolize, or conspire with any other person or persons, to monopolize any part of the trade or commerce among the several States, or with foreign nations, shall be deemed guilty of a felony, and, on conviction thereof, shall be punished by fine not exceeding one million dollars if a corporation, or, if any other person, one hundred thousand dollars or by imprisonment not exceeding three years, or by both said punishments, in the discretion of the court.

Appendix E Clayton Act (Excerpts)

The Clayton Act as Amended

Section 2. This section is also known as the Robinson-Patman amendment to Section 2 of the Clayton Act. (a) That it shall be unlawful for any person engaged in commerce, in the course of such commerce, either directly or indirectly, to discriminate in price between different purchasers of commodities of like grade and quality, where such . . . commodities are sold for use, consumption, or resale within the United States or any Territory thereof . . . and where the effect of such discrimination may be substantially to lessen competition or tend to create a monopoly in any line of commerce, or to injure, destroy, or prevent competition with any person who either grants or knowingly receives the benefit of such discrimination, or with customers of either of them: Provided, That nothing herein contained shall prevent differentials which make only due allowance for differences in the cost of manufacture, sale, or delivery resulting from the differing methods or quantities in which such commodities are to such purchasers sold or delivered: Provided, however, That the Federal Trade Commission may, after due investigation and hearing . . . fix and establish quantity limits, . . . as to particular commodities or classes of commodities, where it finds that available purchasers in greater quantities are so few as to render differentials on account thereof unjustly discriminatory or promotive of monopoly in any line of commerce; and the foregoing shall then not be construed to permit differentials based on differences in quantities greater than those so fixed and established: And provided further, That nothing herein contained shall prevent persons engaged in selling goods, wares, or merchandise in commerce from selecting their own customers in *bona fide* transactions and not in restraint of trade: And provided further, That nothing herein contained shall prevent price changes from time to time where in response to changing conditions affecting the market for or the marketability of the goods concerned, such as but not limited to actual or imminent deterioration of perishable goods, obsolescence of seasonal goods, distress sales under court process, or sales in good faith in discontinuance of business in the goods concerned.

(b) Upon proof being made, at any hearing on a complaint under this section, that there has been discrimination in price or services or facilities furnished, the burden of rebutting the *prima facie* case thus made by showing justification shall be upon the person charged with a violation of this section, and unless justification shall be affirmatively shown, the Commission is authorized to issue an order terminating the discrimination: Provided, however, That nothing herein contained shall prevent a seller rebutting the *prima facie* case thus made by showing that his lower price or the furnishing of services or facilities to any purchaser or purchasers was made in good faith to meet an equally low price of a competitor, or the services or facilities furnished by a competitor.

(c) That it shall be unlawful for any person engaged in commerce, in the course of such commerce, to pay or grant, or to receive or accept, anything of value as a commission, brokerage, or other compensation, or any allowance or discount in lieu thereof, except for services rendered in connection with the sale of purchase of goods, wares, or merchandise, either to the other party to such transactions or to an agent, representative, or other intermediary therein where such intermediary is acting in fact for or in behalf, or is subject to the direct or indirect control, of any party to such transaction other than the person by whom such compensation is granted or paid.

(d) That it shall be unlawful for any person engaged in commerce to pay or contract for the payment of anything of value to or for the benefit of a customer of such person in the course of such commerce as compensation or in consideration for any services or facilities furnished by or through such customer in connection with the processing, handling, sale, or offering for sale of any products or commodities manufactured, sold, or offered for sale by such person, unless such payment or consideration is available on proportionally equal terms to all other customers competing in the distribution of such products or commodities.

(e) That it shall be unlawful for any person to discriminate in favor of one purchaser against another purchaser or purchasers of a commodity bought for resale, with or without processing, by contracting to furnish or furnishing, or by contributing to the furnishing of, any services or facilities connected with the processing, handling, sale, or offering for sale of such commodity so purchased upon terms not accorded to all purchasers on proportionally equal terms.

(f) That it shall be unlawful for any person engaged in commerce, in the course of such commerce, knowingly to induce or receive a discrimination in price which is prohibited by this section.

Section 3. That it shall be unlawful for any person engaged in commerce, in the course of such commerce, to lease or make a sale or contract for sale of goods, wares, merchandise, machinery, supplies, or other commodities, whether patented or unpatented, for use, consumption, or resale within the United States or . . . other place under the jurisdiction of the United States, or fix a price charged therefor, or discount from, or rebate upon, such price, on the condition, agreement, or understanding that the lessee or purchaser thereof shall not use or deal in the goods, wares, merchandise, machinery, supplies, or other commodities of a competitor or competitors of the lessor or seller, where the effect of such lease, sale, or contract for sale or such condition, agreement, or understanding may be to substantially lessen competition to tend to create a monopoly in any line of commerce.

Section 4. That any person who shall be injured in his business or property by reason of anything forbidden in the antitrust laws may sue therefor in any district court of the United States in the district in which the defendant resides or is found, or has an agent, without respect to the amount in controversy, and shall recover threefold the damages by him sustained, and the cost of suit, including a reasonable attorney's fee.

Section 4A. Whenever the United States is hereafter injured in its business or property by reason of anything forbidden in the antitrust laws it may sue therefor in the United States district court for the district in which the defendant resides or is found or has an agent, without respect to the amount in controversy, and shall recover actual damages by it sustained and the cost of suit.

Section 4B. Any action to enforce any cause of action under sections 4 or 4A shall be forever barred unless commenced within four years after the cause of action accrued. No cause of action barred under existing law on the effective date of this act shall be revived by this Act.

Section 4C. (a)(1) Any attorney general of a state may bring a civil action in the name of such State, as parens patriae on behalf of natural persons residing in such State, in any district court of the United States having jurisdiction of the defendant, to secure monetary relief as provided in this section for injury sustained by such natural persons to their property by reason of any violation of the Sherman Act. The court shall exclude from the amount of monetary relief awarded in such action any amount of monetary relief (A) which duplicates amounts which have been awarded for the same injury, or (B) which is properly allocable to (i) natural persons who have excluded their claims pursuant to subsection (b)(2) of this section, and (ii) any business entity.

(2) The court shall award the State as monetary relief threefold the total damage sustained as described in paragraph (1) of this subsection, and the cost of suit, including a reasonable attorney's fee.

(b)(1) In any action brought under subsection (a)(1) of this section, the State attorney general shall, at such times, in such manner, and with such content as the court may direct, cause notice thereof to be given by publication. If the court finds that notice given solely by publication would deny due process of law to any person or persons, the court may direct further notice to such person or persons according to the circumstances of the case.

(2) Any person on whose behalf an action is brought under subsection (a)(1) may elect to exclude from adjudication the portion of the State claim for monetary relief attributable to him by filing notice of such election with the court within such time as specified in the notice given pursuant to paragraph (1) of this subsection.

(3) The final judgment in an action under subsection (a)(1) shall be res judicata as to any claim under section 4 of this Act by any person on behalf of whom such action was brought and who fails to give such notice within the period specified in the notice given pursuant to paragraph (1) of this subsection.

(c) An action under subsection (a)(1) shall not be dismissed or compromised without the approval of the court, and notice of any proposed dismissal or compromise shall be given in such manner as the court directs.

(d) In any action under subsection (a)—

(1) the amount of the plaintiffs' attorney's fee, if any, shall be determined by the court; and

(2) the court may, in its discretion, award a reasonable attorney's fee to a prevailing defendant upon a finding that the State attorney general has acted in bad faith, vexatiously, wantonly, or for oppressive reasons.

Section 6. That the labor of a human being is not a commodity or article of commerce. Nothing contained in the antitrust laws shall be construed to forbid the existence and operation of labor, agricultural or horticultural organizations, instituted for the purposes of mutual help, and not having capital stock or conducted for profit, or to forbid or restrain individual members of such organizations from lawfully carrying out the legitimate objects thereof; nor shall such organizations or the members thereof, be held or construed to be illegal combinations or conspiracies in restraint of trade, under the antitrust laws.

Section 7. That no person engaged in commerce shall acquire, directly or indirectly, the whole or any part of the stock or other share capital and no corporation subject to the jurisdiction of the Federal Trade Commission shall acquire the whole or any part of the assets of another corporation engaged also in commerce, where in any line of commerce in any section of the country, the effect of such acquisition may be substantially to lessen competition, or to tend to create a monopoly.

No person shall acquire, directly or indirectly, the whole or any part of the stock or other share capital and no corporation subject to the jurisdiction of the Federal Trade Commission shall acquire the whole or any part of the assets of one or more corporations engaged in commerce, where in any line of commerce in any section of the country, the effect of such acquisition, of such stocks or assets, or of the use of such stock by the voting or granting of proxies or otherwise, may be substantially to lessen competition, or to tend to create a monopoly.

This section shall not apply to persons purchasing such stock solely for investment and not using the same by voting or otherwise to bring about, or in attempting to bring about, the substantial lessening of competition . . .

Section 8. . . . No person at the same time shall be a director in any two or more corporations any one of which has capital, surplus, and undivided profits aggregating more than $1,000,000 engaged in whole or in part in commerce, . . . if such corporations are or shall have been theretofore, by virtue of their business and location of operation, competitors, so that the elimination of competition by agreement between them would constitute a violation of any of the provisions of the antitrust laws. . . .

Appendix F **The Federal Trade Commission Act (Excerpts)**

The Federal Trade Commission Act (1914) [Excerpts]

Section 5. (a)(1) Unfair methods of competition in or affecting commerce, and unfair or deceptive acts or practices in or affecting commerce, are hereby declared unlawful.

(2) The Commission is hereby empowered and directed to prevent persons, partnerships, or corporations from using unfair methods of competition in or affecting commerce and unfair or deceptive acts or practices in or affecting commerce.

(l) Any person, partnership, or corporation who violates an order of the Commission after it has become final, and while such order is in effect, shall forfeit and pay to the United States a civil penalty of not more than $10,000 for each violation, which shall accrue to the United States and may be recovered in a civil action brought by the Attorney General of the United States. Each separate violation of such an order shall be a separate offense, except that in the case of a violation through continuing failure to obey or neglect to obey a final order of the Commission, each day of continuance of such failure or neglect shall be deemed a separate offense. In such actions, the United States district courts are empowered to grant mandatory injunctions and such other and further equitable relief as they deem appropriate in the enforcement of such final orders of the Commission.

Appendix G **National Labor Relations Act (Excerpts)**

Section 3. National Labor Relations Board. (a) The National labor Relations Board (hereinafter called the "Board") . . . as an agency of the United States, shall consist of five . . . members, appointed by the President by and with the advice and consent of the Senate . . . for terms of five years each, . . . The President shall designate one member to serve as Chairman of the Board. Any member of the Board may be removed by the President, upon notice and hearing, for neglect of duty or malfeasance in office, but for no other cause.

Section 7. Rights of Employees. Employees shall have the right to self-organization, to form, join, or assist labor organizations, to bargain collectively through representatives of their own choosing, and to engage in other concerted activities for the purpose of collective bargaining or other mutual aid or protection, and shall also have the right to refrain from any or all of such activities except to the extent that such right may be affected by an agreement requiring membership in a labor organization as a condition of employment as authorized in section 8(a) (3).

Section 8. Unfair Labor Practice. (a) it shall be an unfair labor practice for an employer—

(1) to interfere with, restrain, or coerce employees in the exercise of the rights guaranteed in section 7;

(2) to dominate or interfere with the formation or administration of any labor organization or contribute financial or other support to it: Provide, that subject to rules and regulations made and published by the Board pursuant to section 6, an employer shall not be prohibited from permitting employees to confer with him during working hours without loss of time or pay;

(3) by discrimination in regard to hire or tenure of employment or any term or condition of employment to encourage or discourage membership in any labor organization: Provide, that nothing in this Act . . . shall preclude an employer from making an agreement with a labor organization . . . to require as a condition of employment membership therein . . . Provided further, that no employer shall justify any discrimination against an employee for nonmembership in a labor organization (A) if he has reasonable grounds for believing that such membership was not available to the employee on the same terms and conditions generally applicable to other members, or (B) if he has reasonable grounds for believing that membership was denied or terminated for reasons other than the failure of the employee to tender periodic dues and initiation fees uniformly required as a condition of acquiring or retaining membership;

(4) to discharge or otherwise discriminate against an employee because he has filed charges or given testimony under this Act;

(5) to refuse to bargain collectively with the representatives of his employees, subject to the provisions of section 9(a).

(b) It shall be an unfair labor practice for a labor organization or its agents—

(1) to restrain or coerce (A) employees in the exercise of the rights guaranteed in section 7: Provided, that this paragraph shall not impair the right of a labor organization to prescribe its own rules with respect to the acquisition or retention of membership therein; or (B) an employer in the selection of his representatives for the purposes of collective bargaining or the adjustment of grievances;

(2) to cause or attempt to cause an employer to discriminate against an employee in violation of subsection (a) (3) or to discriminate against an employee with respect to whom membership in such organization has been denied or terminated on some ground other than his failure to tender the periodic dues and the initiation fees uniformly required as a condition of acquiring or retaining membership.

(3) to refuse to bargain collectively with an employer, provided it is the representative of his employees subject to the provisions of section 9 (a).

(4) (i) to engage in, or to induce or encourage any individual employed by any person engaged in commerce or in an industry affecting commerce to engage in, a strike or a refusal in the course of his employment to use, manufacture, process, transport, or otherwise handle or work on any goods, articles, materials, or commodities or to perform any services; or, (ii) to threaten, coerce, or restrain

any person engaged in commerce or in an industry affecting commerce, where in either case an object thereof is:

(A) forcing or requiring any employer or self-employed person to join any labor or employer organization or to enter into any agreement which is prohibited by section 8 (e);

(B) forcing or requiring any person to cease using, selling, handling, transporting, or otherwise dealing in the products of any other producer, processor, or manufacturer, or to cease doing business with any other person, or forcing or requiring any other employer to recognize or bargain with a labor organization as the representative of his employees unless such labor organization has been certified as the representative of such employees. . . . Provided, that nothing contained in this clause (B) shall be construed to make unlawful, where not otherwise unlawful, any primary strike or primary picketing;

(C) forcing or requiring any employer to recognize or bargain with a particular labor organization as the representative of his employees if another labor organization has been certified as the representative of such employees. . . .

(D) forcing or requiring any employer to assign particular work to employees in a particular labor organization or in a particular trade, craft, or class. . . .

Provided, that nothing contained in this subsection (b) shall be construed to make unlawful a refusal by any person to enter upon the premises of any employer (other than his own employer), if the employees of such employer are engaged in a strike ratified or approved by a representative of such employees whom such employer is required to recognize under this Act: Provided further, that for the purposes of this paragraph (4) only, nothing contained in such paragraph shall be construed to prohibit publicity, other than picketing, for the purpose of truthfully advising the public, including consumers and members of a labor organization, that a product or products are produced by an employer with whom the labor organization has a primary dispute and are distributed by another employer, as long as such publicity does not have an effect of inducing any individual employed by any person other than the primary employer in the course of his employment to pick up, deliver, or transport any goods, or not to perform any services, at the establishment of the employer engaged in such distribution;

(5) to require of employees covered by an agreement authorized under subsection (a) (3) the payment, as a condition precedent to becoming a member of such organization, of a fee in an amount which the Board finds excessive or discriminatory. . . .

(6) to cause or attempt to cause an employer to pay or deliver or agree to pay or deliver any money or other thing of value, in the nature of an exaction, for services which are not performed or not to be performed; and

(7) to picket or cause to be picketed, or threaten to picket or cause to be picketed, any employer where an object thereof is forcing or requiring an employer to recognize or bargain with a labor organization as the representative of his employees, or forcing or requiring the employees of an employer to accept or select such labor organization as their collective bargaining representative, unless such labor organization is currently certified as the representative of such employees:

(A) where the employer has lawfully recognized in accordance with this Act any other labor organization and a question concerning representation may not appropriately be raised under section 9(c) of this Act.

(B) where within the preceding 12 months a valid election under section 9(c) of this Act has been conducted, or

(C) where such picketing has been conducted without a petition under section 9(c) being filed within a reasonable period of time not to exceed 30 days from the commencement of such picketing: Provided, that when such a petition has been filed the Board shall forthwith, without regard to the provisions of section 9(c) (1) or the absence of a showing of a substantial interest on the part of the labor organization, direct an election in such units as the Board finds to be appropriate and shall certify the results thereof: Provided further, that nothing in this subparagraph (C) shall be construed to prohibit any picketing or other publicity for the purpose of truthfully advising the public (including consumers) that an employer does not employ members of, or have a contract with, a labor organization, unless an effect of such picketing is to induce any individual employed by any other person in the course of his employment, not to pick up, deliver or transport any goods or not to perform any services.

Nothing in this paragraph (7) shall be construed to permit any act which would otherwise be an unfair labor practice under this section 8(b).

(c) The expressing of any views, argument, or opinion, or the dissemination thereof, whether in written, printed, graphic, or visual form, shall not constitute or be evidence of an unfair labor practice under any of the provisions of this Act, if such expression contains no threat of reprisal or force or promise of benefit.

(d) For the purposes of this section, to bargain collectively is the performance of the mutual obligation of the employer and the representative of the employees to meet at reasonable times and confer in good faith with respect to wages, hours, and other terms and conditions of employment, or the negotiation of an agreement, or any question arising thereunder, and the execution of a written contract incorporating any agreement reached if requested by either party, but such obligation does not compel either party to agree to a proposal or require the making of a concession: Provided, that where there is in effect a collective bargaining contract covering employees in an industry affecting commerce, the duty to bargain collectively shall also mean that no party to such contract shall terminate or modify such contract, unless the party desiring such termination or modification—

(1) serves a written notice upon the other party to the contract of the proposed termination or modification 60 days prior to the expiration date thereof, or in the event such contract contains no expiration date, 60 days prior to the time it is proposed to make such termination or modification;

(2) offers to meet and confer with the other party for the purpose of negotiating a new contract or a contract containing the proposed modifications;

(3) notifies the Federal Mediation and Conciliation Service within 30 days after such notice of the existence of a dispute. . . .

(4) continues in full force and effect, without resorting to strike or lockout, all the terms and conditions of the existing contract for a period of 60 days after such notice is given or until the expiration date of such contract, whichever occurs later.

. . . .

(e) it shall be an unfair labor practice for any labor organization and any employer to enter into any contract or agreement, express or implied, whereby such employer ceases or refrains or agrees to cease or refrain from handling, using, selling, transporting, or otherwise dealing in any of the products of any other employer, or to cease doing business with any other person, . . . Provided, that nothing in this subsection (e) shall apply to an agreement between a labor organization and an employer in the construction industry relating to the contracting or subcontracting of work to be done at the site. . . .

Section 9. Representatives and Elections. (a) Representatives designated or selected for the purposes of collective bargaining by the majority of the employees in a unit appropriate for such purposes, shall be the exclusive representatives of all the employees in such unit for the purposes of collective bargaining in respect to rates of pay, wages, hours of employment, or other conditions of employment: Provided, that any individual employee or a group of employees shall have the right at any time to present grievances to their employer and to have such grievance adjusted, without the intervention of the bargaining representative, as long as the adjustment is not inconsistent with the terms of a collective bargaining contract or agreement then in effect: Provided further, that the bargaining representative has been given opportunity to be present at such adjustment.

(b) The Board shall decide in each case whether, in order to assure to employees the fullest freedom in exercising the rights guaranteed by this Act, the unit appropriate for the purposes of collective bargaining shall be the employer unit, craft unit, plant unit, or subdivision thereof: Provided, that the Board shall not (1) decide that any unit is appropriate for such purposes if such unit includes both professional employees and employees who are not professional employees unless a majority of such professional employees vote for inclusion in such unit; or (2) decide that any craft unit is inappropriate for such purposes on the ground that a different unit has been established by a prior Board determination, unless a majority of the employees in the proposed craft unit vote against separate representation or (3) decide that any unit is appropriate for such purposes, if it includes, together with other employees, any individual employed as a guard to enforce against employees and other persons, rules to protect property of the employer or to protect the safety of persons on the employer's premises; but no labor organization shall be certified as the representative of employees in a bargaining unit of guards if such organization admits to membership, or is affiliated directly or indirectly with an organization which admits to membership, employees other than guards.

(c) (1) Wherever a petition shall have been filed, in accordance with such regulations as may be prescribed by the Board—

(A) by an employee or group of employees or any individual or labor organization acting in their behalf alleging that a substantial number of employees (i) wish to be represented for collective bargaining and that their employer declines to recognize their representative as the representative defined in section 9(a), or (ii) assert that the individual or labor organization, which has been certified or is being currently recognized by their employer as the bargaining representative as defined in section 9(a); or

(B) by an employer, alleging that one or more individuals or labor organizations have presented to him a claim to be recognized as the representative defined in section 9(a);

the Board shall investigate such petition and if it has reasonable cause to believe that a question of representation affecting commerce exists shall provide for an appropriate hearing upon due notice. Such hearing may be conducted by an officer or employee of the regional office, who shall not make any recommendations with respect thereto. If the Board finds upon the record of such hearing that such a question of representative exists, it shall direct an election by secret ballot and shall certify the results thereof.

(2) In determining whether or not a question of representation affecting commerce exists, the same regulations and rules of decision shall apply irrespective of the identity of the persons filing the petition or the kind of relief sought and in no case shall the Board deny a labor organization a place on the ballot by reason of an order with respect to such labor organization or its predecessor not issued in conformity with section 10(c).

(3) No election shall be directed in any bargaining unit or any subdivision within which, in the preceding twelve-month period, a valid election shall have been held. Employees engaged in an economic strike who are not entitled to reinstatement shall be eligible to vote under such regulations as the Board shall find are consistent with the purposes and provisions of this Act in any election conducted within twelve months after the commencement of the strike. In any election where none of the choices on the ballot receives a majority, a run-off shall be conducted, the ballot providing for a selection between the two choices receiving the largest and second largest number of valid votes cast in the election.

(4) Nothing in this section shall be construed to prohibit the waiving of hearings by stipulation for the purpose of a consent election in conformity with regulations and rules of decision of the Board.

(5) In determining whether a unit is appropriate for the purposes specified in subsection (b) the extent to which the employees have organized shall not be controlling.

(d) Whenever an order of the Board made pursuant to section 10(c) is based in whole or in part upon facts certified following an investigation pursuant to subsection (c) of this section and there is a petition for the enforcement or review of such order, such certification and the record of such investigation shall be included in the transcript of the entire record required to be filed under section 10(c) or 10(f), and thereupon the decree of the court enforcing modifying, or setting aside in whole or in part the order of the Board shall be made and entered upon the pleadings, testimony, and the proceedings set forth in such transcript.

(e)(1) Upon the filing with the Board, by 30 per centum or more of the employees in a bargaining unit covered by an agreement between their employer and a labor organization made pursuant to section 8(a)(3), of a petition alleging they desire that such authority be rescinded, the Board shall take a secret ballot of the employees in such unit, and shall certify the results thereof to such labor organization and to the employer.

(2) No election shall be conducted pursuant to this subsection in any bargaining unit or any subdivision within which, in the preceeding twelve month period, a valid election shall have been held.

Section 19. Individuals with Religious Convictions. Any employee who is a member of and adheres to established and traditional tenets or teachings of a bona fide religion, body, or sect which has historically held conscientious objections to joining or financially supporting labor organizations shall not be required to join or financially support any labor organization as a condition of employment; except that such employee may be required in a contract between such employee's employer and a labor organization in lieu of periodic dues and initiation fees, to pay sums equal to such dues and initiation fees to a nonreligious, nonlabor organization charitable fund exempt from taxation under section 501(c) (3) of title 26 of the Internal Revenue Code.

Appendix H The Federal Civil Rights Laws (Excerpts)

42 U.S. Code, Section 1982. (1866)

All persons within the jurisdiction of the United States shall have the same right in every State and Territory and the District of Columbia to make and enforce contracts, to sue, be parties, give evidence, and to the full and equal benefit of all laws and proceedings for the security of persons and property as is enjoyed by white citizens, and shall be subject to like punishment, pains, penalties, taxes, licenses and exactions of every kind, and no other.

42 U.S. Code, Section 1982. (1866)

All citizens of the United States shall have the same right, in every State and Territory, as is enjoyed by white citizens thereof to inherit, purchase, lease, sell, hold and convey real and personal property.

42 U.S. Code, Section 1983. (1871)

Every person who, under color of any statute, ordinance, regulation, custom, or usage, of any State or Territory, subjects, or causes to be subjected, any citizen of the United States or other person within the jurisdiction thereof to the deprivation of any rights, privileges, or immunities secured by the Constitution and laws, shall be liable to the party injured in an action at law, suit in equity, or other proper proceeding.

Title II of the Civil Rights Act of 1964—The Public Accommodations Section

Section 201. (a) All persons shall be entitled to the full and equal enjoyment of the goods, services, facilities, privileges, advantages, and accommodations of any place of public accommodation, as defined in this section, without discrimination on the ground of race, color, religion, or national origin.

(b) Each of the following establishments which serves the public is a place of public accommodation within the meaning of this title if its operations affect commerce, or if discrimination or segregation by it is supported by State action:

(1) any inn, hotel, motel, or other establishment which provides lodging to transient guests, other than an estab-lishment located within a building which contains not more than five rooms for rent or hire and which is actually occupied by the proprietor of such establishment as his residence;

(2) any restaurant, cafeteria, lunchroom, lunch counter, soda fountain. . . .

(3) any motion picture house, theater, concert hall, sports arena, stadium. . . .

(4) any establishment (A) (i) which is physically located within the premises of any establishment otherwise cov-ered by this subsection, or (ii) within the premises of which is physically located any such covered establishment, and (B) which holds itself out as serving patrons of such cov-ered establishment.

(c) The operations of an establishment affect commerce within the meaning of this title if (1) it is one of the establishments described in paragraph (1) of subsec-tion (b); (2) in the case of an establishment described in paragraph (2) of subsection (b), it serves or offers to serve interstate travelers or a substantial portion of the food which it serves, or gasoline or other products which it sells, has moved in commerce; (3) in the case of an es-tablishment described in paragraph (3) of subsection(b), it customarily presents films, performances, athletic teams, exhibitions, or other sources of entertainment which move in commerce; and (4) in the case of an establishment de-scribed in paragraph (4) of subsection (b), it is physically located within the premises of, or there is physically lo-cated within its premises, an establishment the operations of which affect commerce within the meaning of this sub-section. For purposes of this section, "commerce" means travel, trade, traffic, commerce, transportation, or com-munication among the several States, or between the Dis-trict of Columbia and any State, or between any foreign country or any territory or possession and any State or the District of Columbia, or between points in the same State but through any other State or the District of Columbia or a foreign country.

Section 202. All persons shall be entitled to be free, at any establishment or place, from discrimination or seg-regation of any kind on the ground of race, color, religion, or national origin, if such discrimination or segregation is or purports to be required by any law, statute, ordinance, regulation, rule, or order of a State or any agency or political subdivision thereof.

Section 203. No person shall (a) withhold, deny, or attempt to withhold or deny, or deprive or attempt to deprive, any person of any right or privilege secured by section 201 or 202, or (b) intimidate, threaten, or coerce, or attempt to intimidate, threaten, or coerce any person with the purpose of interfering with any right or privilege secured by section 201 or 202, or (c) punish or attempt to punish any person for exercising or attempting to exercise any right or privilege secured by section 201 or 202.

. . . .

Title VII of the Civil Rights Act of 1964—The Employment Discrimination Section

Section 703. Unlawful Employment Practices. (a) It shall be an unlawful employment practice for an employer—

(1) to fail or refuse to hire or to discharge any individual, or otherwise to discriminate against any individual with respect to his compensation, terms, conditions, or privileges or employment, because of such individual's race, color, religion, sex, or national origin; or

(2) to limit, segregate, or classify his employees or applicants for employment in any way which would deprive or tend to deprive any individual of employment opportunities or otherwise adversely affect his status as an employee, because of such individual's race, color, religion, sex, or national origin.

(b) It shall be an unlawful employment practice for an employment agency to fail or refuse to refer for employment, or otherwise to discriminate against, any individual because of his race, color, religion, sex, or national origin, or to classify or refer for employment any individual on the basis or his race, color, religion, sex, or national origin.

(c) It shall be an unlawful employment practice for a labor organization—

(1) to exclude or to expel from its membership, or otherwise to discriminate against, any individual because of his race, color, religion, sex, or national origin;

(2) to limit, segregate, or classify its membership or applicants for membership, or to classify or fail or refuse to refer for employment any individual, in any way which would deprive or tend to deprive any individual of employment opportunities, or would limit such employment opportunities or otherwise adversely affect his status as an employee or as an applicant for employment, because of such individual's race, color, religion, sex, or national origin; or

(3) to cause or attempt to cause an employer to discriminate against an individual in violation of this section.

(d) It shall be an unlawful employment practice for any employer, labor organization, or joint labor-management committee controlling apprenticeship or other training or retraining, including on-the-job training programs to discriminate against any individual because of his race, color, religion, sex, or national origin in admission to, or employment in, any program established to provide apprenticeship or other training.

(e) Notwithstanding any other provision of this subchapter.

(1) it shall not be an unlawful employment practice for an employer to hire and employ employees, for an employment agency to classify, or refer for employment any individual, for a labor organization to classify its membership or to classify or refer for employment any individual, or for an employer, labor organization, or joint labor-management committee controlling apprenticeship or other training or retraining programs to admit or employ any individual in any such program, on the basis of his religion, sex, or national origin in those certain instances where religion, sex, or national origin is a bona fide occupational qualification reasonably necessary to the normal operation of that particular business or enterprise, and

(2) it shall not be an unlawful employment practice for a school, college, university, or other educational institution or institution of learning to hire and employ employees of a particular religion if such school, college, university, or other educational institution or institution of learning is, in whole or in substantial part, owned, supported, controlled, or managed by a particular religion or by a particular religious corporation, association, or society, or if the curriculum of such school, college, university, or other educational institution or institution of learning is directed toward the propagation of a particular religion.

(f) As used in this subchapter, the phrase ''unlawful employment practice'' shall not be deemed to include any action or measure taken by an employer, labor organization, joint labor-management committee, or employment agency with respect to an individual who is a member of the Communist Party of the United States or of any other organization required to register as a Communist-action or Communist-front organization. . . .

(g) Notwithstanding any other provision of this subchapter, it shall not be an unlawful employment practice for an employer to fail or refuse to hire and employ any individual for any position, for an employer to discharge any individual from any position, or for an employment agency to fail or refuse to refer any individual for employment in any position, or for a labor organization to fail or refuse to refer any individual for employment in any position, if—

(1) the occupancy of such position, or access to the premises in or upon which any part of the duties of such position is performed or is to be performed, is subject to any re-

quirement imposed in the interest of the national security of the United States . . . and

(2) such individual has not fulfilled or has ceased to fulfill that requirement.

(h) Notwithstanding any other provision of this subchapter, it shall not be an unlawful employment practice for an employer to apply different standards of compensation, or different terms, conditions, or privileges of employment pursuant to a bona fide seniority or merit system, or a system which measures earnings by quantity or quality of production or to employees who work in different locations, provided that such differences are not the result of an intention to discriminate because of race, color, religion, sex, or national origin, nor shall it be an unlawful employment practice for an employer to give and act upon the results of any professionally developed ability test provided that such test, its administration or action upon the results is not designed, intended or used to discriminate because of race, color, religion, sex, or national origin. . . .

(j) Nothing contained in this subchapter shall be interpreted to require any employer, employment agency, labor organization, or joint labor-management committee subject to this subchapter to grant preferential treatment to any individual or to any group because of the race, color, religion, sex, or national origin of such individual or group on account of an imbalance which may exist with respect to the total number of percentage of persons of any race, color religion, sex, or national origin employed by any employer, referred or classified for employment by any employment agency or labor organization, or admitted to, or employed in, any apprenticeship or other training program, in comparison with the total number or percentage of persons of such race, color, religion, sex, or national origin in any community. State, section, or other area, or in the available work force in any community, State, section, or other area.

. . . .

Section 704. Other Unlawful Employment Practices.

(a) It shall be an unlawful employment practice for an employer to discriminate against any of his employees or applicants for employment, for an employment agency, or joint labor-management committee controlling apprenticeship or other training or retraining, including on-the-job training programs, to discriminate against any individual, or for a labor organization to discriminate against any member thereof or applicant for membership, because he has opposed any practice made an unlawful employment practice by this subchapter, or because he has made a charge, testified, assisted, or participated in any manner in an investigation, proceeding, or hearing under this subchapter.

(b) It shall be an unlawful employment practice for an employer, labor organization, employment agency, or joint labor-management committee controlling apprenticeship or other training or retraining, including on-the-job training programs, to print or publish or cause to be printed or published any notice or advertisement relating to employment by such an employer or membership or any classification or referral for employment by such a labor organization, or relating to any classification or referral for employment by such an employment agency, or relating to admission to, or employment in, any program established to provide apprenticeship or other training by such a joint-labor-management committee, indicating any preference, limitation, specification, or discrimination, based on race, color, religion, sex, or national origin, except that such a notice or advertisement may indicate a preference, limitation, specification, or discrimination based on religion, sex or national origin when religion, sex, or national origin is a bona fide occupational qualification for employment.

The Federal Civil Rights Act of 1968

Section 803. (a) Subject to the provisions of subsection (b) and section 807, the prohibitions against discrimination in the sale or rental of housing set forth in section 804 shall apply:

(1) . . . to (A) dwellings owned or operated by the Federal Government; (B) dwellings provided in whole or in part with the aid of loans, advances, grants, or contributions made by the Federal Government. . . . (C) dwellings provided in whole or in part by loans insured, guaranteed, or otherwise secured by the credit of the Federal Government. . . . (D) dwellings provided by the development of real property purchased, rented, or otherwise obtained from a State or local public agency receiving Federal financial assistance for slum clearance or urban renewal. . . .

(2) . . . to all dwellings covered by paragraph (1) and to all other dwelling except as exempted by subsection (b).

(b) Nothing in section 804 . . . shall apply to—

(1) any single-family house sold or rented by an owner: Provided, That such private individual owner does not own more than three such single-family houses at any one time: Provided further, That in the case of the sale of any such single-family house by a private individual owner not residing in such house at the time of such sale or who was not the most recent resident of such house prior to such sale, the exemption granted by this subsection shall apply only with respect to one such sale within any twenty-four month period: Provided further, That such bona fide private individual owner does not own any interest in, nor is there owned or reserved on his behalf, under any express or voluntary agreement, title to any right to all or a portion of the proceeds from the sale or rental or, more than three such single-family houses at any one time: Provided further, That . . . the sale or rental of any such single-family house shall be excepted from the application of this Title

only if such house is sold or rented (A) without the use in any manner of the sales or rental facilities or the sales or rental services of any real estate broker, agent, or salesman, or of such facilities or services of any person in the business of selling or renting dwellings, or of any employee or agent of any such broker, agent, or salesman, or person and (B) without the publication, posting, mailing, after notice, of any advertisement or written notice in violation of section 804(c) of this title; . . . or

(2) rooms or units in dwellings containing living quarters occupied or intended to be occupied by no more than four families living independently of each other, if the owner actually maintains and occupies one of such living quarters for his residence.

(c) for the purposes of subsection (b), a person shall be deemed to be in the business of selling or renting dwellings if—

(1) he has, within the preceding twelve months, participated as principal in three or more transactions involving the sale or rental of any dwelling. . . .

(2) he has, within the preceding twelve months, participated as agent . . . in two or more transactions involving the sale or rental of any dwelling. . . .

(3) he is the owner of any dwelling designed or intended for occupancy by, or occupied by, five or more families.

Section 804. Discrimination in the Sale or Rental of Housing. As made applicable by section 803 and except as exempted by sections 803(b) and 807, it shall be unlawful—

(a) to refuse to sell or rent after the making of a bona fide offer, or to refuse to negotiate for the sale or rental of, or otherwise make unavailable or deny, a dwelling to any person because of race, color, religion, sex, or national origin.

(b) To discriminate against any person in the terms, conditions, or privileges of sale or rental of a dwelling, or in the provision of services or facilities in connection therewith, because of race, color, religion, sex, or national origin.

(c) To make, print or publish, . . . any notice, statement, or advertisement, with respect to the sale or rental of a dwelling that indicates any preference, limitation, or discrimination based on race, color, religion, sex, or national origin, or an intention to make any such preference, limitation, or discrimination.

(d) To represent to any person because of race, color, religion, sex, or national origin that any dwelling is not available for inspection, sale, or rental when such dwelling is in fact so available.

(e) For profit, to induce or attempt to induce any person to sell or rent any dwelling by representations regarding the entry or prospective entry into the neighborhood of a person or persons of a particular race, color, religion, sex, or national origin.

Appendix I The Uniform Partnership Act (Excerpts)

Sec. 6. **Partnership Defined**

(1) A partnership is an association of two or more persons to carry on as co-owners a business for profit.

(2) But any association formed under any other statute of this state, or any statute adopted by authority, other than the authority of this state, is not a partnership under this act, unless such association would have been a partnership in this state prior to the adoption of this act; but this act shall apply to limited partnerships except in so far as the statutes relating to such partnerships are inconsistent herewith.

Sec. 8. **Partnership Property**

(1) All property originally brought into the partnership stock or subsequently acquired by purchase or otherwise, on account of the partnership, is partnership property.

(2) Unless the contrary intention appears, property acquired with partnership funds is partnership property.

(3) Any estate in real property may be acquired in the partnership name. Title so acquired can be conveyed only in the partnership name.

(4) A conveyance to a partnership in the partnership name, though without words of inheritance, passes the entire estate of the grantor unless a contrary intent appears.

Sec. 9. **Partner Agent of Partnership as to Partnership Business**

(1) Every partner is an agent of the partnership for the purpose of its business, and the act of every partner, including the execution in the partnership name of any instrument, for apparently carrying on in the usual way the business of the partnership of which he is a member binds the partnership, unless the partner so acting has in fact no authority to act for the partnership in the particular matter, and the person with whom he is dealing has knowledge of the fact that he has no such authority.

(2) An act of a partner which is not apparently for the carrying on of the business of the partnership in the usual way does not bind the partnership unless authorized by the other partners.

(3) Unless authorized by the other partners or unless they have abandoned the business, one or more but less than all the partners have no authority to:

(a) Assign the partnership property in trust for creditors or on the assignee's promise to pay the debts of the partnership,

(b) Dispose of the good-will of the business,

(c) Do any other act which would make it impossible to carry on the ordinary business of a partnership,

(d) Confess a judgment,

(e) Submit a partnership claim or liability to arbitration or reference.

(4) No act of a partner in contravention of a restriction on authority shall bind the partnership to persons having knowledge of the restriction.

Sec. 10. **Conveyance of Real Property of the Partnership**

(1) Where title to real property is in the partnership name, any partner may convey title to such property by a conveyance executed in the partnership name; but the partnership may recover such property unless the partner's act binds the partnership under the provisions of paragraph (1) of section 9, or unless such property has been conveyed by the grantee or a person claiming through such grantee to a holder for value without knowledge that the partner, in making the conveyance, has exceeded his authority.

(2) Where title to real property is in the name of the partnership, a conveyance executed by a partner, in his own name, passes the equitable interest of the partnership, provided the act is one within the authority of the partner under the provisions of paragraph (1) of section 9.

(3) Where title to real property is in the name of one or more but not all the partners, and the record does not disclose the right of the partnership, the partners in whose name the title stands may convey title to such property, but the partnership may recover such property if the partners' act does not bind the partnership under the provisions of paragraph (1) of section 9, unless the purchaser or his assignee, is a holder for value, without knowledge.

(4) Where the title to real property is in the name of one or more or all the partners, or in a third person in trust for the partnership, a conveyance executed by a partner in the partnership name, or in his own name, passes the equitable interest of the partnership, provided the act is one within the authority of the partner under the provisions of paragraph (1) of section 9.

(5) Where the title to real property is in the names of all the partners a conveyance executed by all the partners passes all their rights in such property.

Sec. 13. **Partnership Bound by Partner's Wrongful Act**

Where, by any wrongful act or omission of any partner acting in the ordinary course of the business of the partnership or with the authority of his co-partners, loss or injury is caused to any person, not being a partner in the partnership, or any penalty is incurred, the partnership is liable therefor to the same extent as the partner so acting or omitting to act.

Sec. 15. **Nature of Partner's Liability**

All partners are liable

(a) Jointly and severally for everything chargeable to the partnership under sections 13 and 14.

(b) Jointly for all other debts and obligations of the partnership; but any partner may enter into a separate obligation to perform a partnership contract.

Sec. 16. **Partner by Estoppel**

(1) When a person, by words spoken or written or by conduct, represents himself, or consents to another representing him to any one, as a partner in an existing partnership or with one or more persons not actual partners, he is liable to any such person to whom such representation has been made, who has, on the faith of such representation, given credit to the actual or apparent partnership, and if he has made such representation or consented to its being made in a public manner he is liable to such person, whether the representation has or has not been made or communicated to such person so giving credit by or with the knowledge of the apparent partner making the representation or consenting to its being made.

    (a) When a partnership liability results, he is liable as though he were an actual member of the partnership.

    (b) When no partnership liability results, he is liable jointly with the other persons, if any, so consenting to the contract or representation as to incur liability, otherwise separately.

(2) When a person has been thus represented to be a partner in an existing partnership, or with one or more persons not actual partners, he is an agent of the persons consenting to such representation to bind them to the same extent and in the same manner as though he were a partner in fact, with respect to persons who rely upon the representation. Where all the members of the existing partnership consent to the representation, a partnership act or obligation results; but in all other cases it is the joint act or obligation of the person acting and the persons consenting to the representation.

Sec. 17. **Liability of Incoming Partner**

A person admitted as a partner into an existing partnership is liable for all the obligations of the partnership arising before his admission as though he had been a partner when such obligations were incurred, except that this liability shall be satisfied only out of partnership property.

Sec. 18. **Rules Determining Rights and Duties of Partners**

The rights and duties of the partners in relation to the partnership shall be determined, subject to any agreement between them, by the following rules:

(a) Each partner shall be repaid his contributions, whether by way of capital or advances to the partnership property and share equally in the profits and surplus remaining after all liabilities, including those to partners, are satisfied; and must contribute towards the losses, whether of capital or otherwise, sustained by the partnership according to his share in the profits.

(b) The partnership must indemnify every partner in respect of payments made and personal liabilities reasonably incurred by him in the ordinary and proper conduct of its business, or for the preservation of its business or property.

(c) A partner, who in aid of the partnership makes any payment or advance beyond the amount of capital which he agreed to contribute, shall be paid interest from the date of the payment or advance.

(d) A partner shall receive interest on the capital contributed by him only from the date when repayment should be made.

(e) All partners have equal rights in the management and conduct of the partnership business.

(f) No partner is entitled to remuneration for acting in the partnership business, except that a surviving partner is entitled to reasonable compensation for his services in winding up the partnership affairs.

(g) No person can become a member of a partnership without the consent of all the partners.

(h) Any difference arising as to ordinary matters connected with the partnership business may be decided by a majority of the partners; but no act in contravention of any agreement between the partners may be done rightfully without the consent of all the partners.

Sec. 25. Nature of a Partner's Right in Specific Partnership Property

(1) A partner is co-owner with his partners of specific partnership property holding as a tenant in partnership.

(2) The incidents of this tenancy are such that:

(a) A partner, subject to the provisions of this act and to any agreement between the partners, has an equal right with his partners to possess specific partnership property for partnership purposes; but he has no right to possess such property for any other purpose without the consent of his partners.

(b) A partner's right in specific partnership property is not assignable except in connection with the assignment of rights of all the partners in the same property.

(c) A partner's right in specific partnership property is not subject to attachment or execution, except on a claim against the partnership. When partnership property is attached for a partnership debt the partners, or any of them, or the representatives of a deceased partner, cannot claim any right under the homestead or exemption laws.

(d) On the death of a partner his right in specific partnership property vests in the surviving partner or partners, except where the deceased was the last surviving partner, when his right in such property vests in his legal representative. Such surviving partner or partners, or the legal representative of the last surviving partner, has no right to possess the partnership property for any but a partnership purpose.

(e) A partner's right in specific partnership property is not subject to dower, curtesy, or allowances to widows, heirs, or next of kin.

Sec. 30. Partnership not Terminated by Dissolution

On dissolution the partnership is not terminated, but continues until the winding up of partnership affairs is completed.

Sec. 31. Causes of Dissolution

Dissolution is caused:

(1) Without violation of the agreement between the partners,

(a) By the termination of the definite term or particular undertaking specified in the agreement,

(b) By the express will of any partner when no definite term or particular undertaking is specified,

(c) By the express will of all the partners who have not assigned their interests or suffered them to be charged for their separate debts, either before or after the termination of any specified term or particular undertaking,

(d) By the expulsion of any partner from the business bona fide in accordance with such a power conferred by the agreement between the partners;

(2) In contravention of the agreement between the partners, where the circumstances do not permit a dissolution under any other provision of this section, by the express will of any partner at any time;

(3) By any event which makes it unlawful for the business of the partnership to be carried on or for the members to carry it on in partnership;

(4) By the death of any partner;

(5) By the bankruptcy of any partner or the partnership;

(6) By decree of court under section 32.

Sec. 32. Dissolution by Decree of Court

(1) On application by or for a partner the court shall decree a dissolution whenever:

(a) A partner has been declared a lunatic in any judicial proceeding or is shown to be of unsound mind,

(b) A partner becomes in any other way incapable of performing his part of the partnership contract,

(c) A partner has been guilty of such conduct as tends to affect prejudicially the carrying on of the business,

(d) A partner willfully or persistently commits a breach of the partnership agreement, or otherwise so conducts himself in matters relating to the partnership business that it is not reasonably practicable to carry on the business in partnership with him,

(e) The business of the partnership can only be carried on at a loss,

(f) Other circumstances render a dissolution equitable.

(2) On the application of the purchaser of a partner's interest under sections 28 or 29 [should read 27 or 28];

(a) After the termination of the specified term or particular undertaking,

(b) At any time if the partnership was a partnership at will when the interest was assigned or when the charging order was issued.

Sec. 35. Power of Partner to Bind Partnership to Third Persons After Dissolution

(1) After dissolution a partner can bind the partnership except as provided in Paragraph (3).

(a) By any act appropriate for winding up partnership affairs or completing transactions unfinished at dissolution;

(b) By any transaction which would bind the partnership if dissolution had not taken place, provided the other party to the transaction

(I) Had extended credit to the partnership prior to dissolution and had no knowledge or notice of the dissolution; or

(II) Though he had not so extended credit, had nevertheless known of the partnership prior to dissolution, and, having no knowledge or notice of dissolution, the fact of dissolution had not been advertised in a newspaper of general circulation in the place (or in each place if more than one) at which the partnership business was regularly carried on.

(2) The liability of a partner under paragraph (1b) shall be satisfied out of partnership assets alone when such partner had been prior to dissolution

(a) Unknown as a partner to the person with whom the contract is made; and

(b) So far unknown and inactive in partnership affairs that the business reputation of the partnership could not be said to have been in any degree due to his connection with it.

(3) The partnership is in no case bound by any act of a partner after dissolution

(a) Where the partnership is dissolved because it is unlawful to carry on the business, unless the act is appropriate for winding up partnership affairs; or

(b) Where the partner has become bankrupt; or

(c) Where the partner has no authority to wind up partnership affairs; except by a transaction with one who

(I) Had extended credit to the partnership prior to dissolution and had no knowledge or notice of his want of authority; or

(II) Had not extended credit to the partnership prior to dissolution, and, having no knowledge or notice of his want of authority, the fact of his want of authority has not been advertised in the manner provided for advertising the fact of dissolution in paragraph (1bII).

(4) Nothing in this section shall affect the liability under Section 16 of any person who after dissolution represents himself or consents to another representing him as a partner in a partnership engaged in carrying on business.

Sec. 40. Rules for Distribution

In settling accounts between the partners after dissolution, the following rules shall be observed, subject to any agreement to the contrary:

(a) The assets of the partnership are:

(I) The partnership property,

(II) The contributions of the partners necessary for the payment of all the liabilities specified in clause (b) of this paragraph.

(b) The liabilities of the partnership shall rank in order of payment, as follows:

(I) Those owing to creditors other than partners,

(II) Those owing to partners other than for capital and profits,

(III) Those owing to partners in respect of capital,

(IV) Those owing to partners in respect of profits.

(c) The assets shall be applied in the order of their declaration in clause (a) of this paragraph to the satisfaction of the liabilities.

(d) The partners shall contribute, as provided by section 18(a) the amount necessary to satisfy the liabilities; but if any, but not all, of the partners are insolvent, or, not being subject to process, refuse to contribute, the other partners shall contribute their share of the liabilities, and, in the relative proportions in which they share the profits, the additional amount necessary to pay the liabilities.

(e) An assignee for the benefit of creditors or any person appointed by the court shall have the right to enforce the contributions specified in clause (d) of this paragraph.

(f) Any partner or his legal representative shall have the right to enforce the contributions specified in clause (d) of this paragraph, to the extent of the amount which he has paid in excess of his share of the liability.

(g) The individual property of a deceased partner shall be liable for the contributions specified in clause (d) of this paragraph.

(h) When partnership property and the individual properties of the partners are in possession of a court for distribution, partnership creditors shall have priority on partnership property and separate creditors on individual property, saving the rights of lien or secured creditors as heretofore.

(i) Where a partner has become bankrupt or his estate is insolvent the claims against his separate property shall rank in the following order:

(I) Those owing to separate creditors,

(II) Those owing to partnership creditors,

(III) Those owing to partners by way of contribution.

Appendix J Spanish Equivalents for Important Legal Terms in English

Abandoned property: bienes abandonados

Acceptance: aceptación; consentimiento; acuerdo

Acceptor: aceptante

Accession: toma de posesión; aumento; accesión

Accommodation indorser: avalista de favor

Accommodation party: firmante de favor

Accord: acuerdo; convenio; arregio

Accord and satisfaction: transacción ejecutada

Act of state doctrine: doctrina de acto de gobierno

Administrative law: derecho administrativo

Administrative process: procedimiento o metódo administrativo

Administrator (-trix): administrador (-a)

Adverse possession: posesión de hecho susceptible de proscripción adquisitiva

Affirmative action: acción afirmativa

Affirmative defense: defensa afirmativa

After-acquired property: bienes adquiridos con posterioridad a un hecho dado

Agency: mandato; agencia

Agent: mandatorio; agente; representante

Agreement: convenio; acuerdo; contrato

Alien corporation: empresa extranjera

Allonge: hojas adicionales de endosos

Answer: contestación de la demande; alegato

Anticipatory breach, or anticipatory repudiation: anuncio previo de las partes de su imposibilidad de cumplir con el contrato

Appeal: apelación; recurso de apelación

Appellate jurisdiction: jurisdicción de apelaciones

Appraisal right: derecho de valuación

Abritration: arbitraje

Arson: incendio intencional

Articles of partnership: contrato social

Artisian's lien: derecho de retención que ejerce al artesano

Assault: asalto; ataque; agresión

Assignment of rights: transmisión; transferencia; cesión

Assumption of risk: no resarcimiento por exposición voluntaria al peligro

Attachment: auto judicial que autoriza el embargo; embargo

Bailee: depositario

Bailment: depósito; constitución en depósito

Bailor: depositante

Bankruptcy trustee: síndico de la quiebra

Battery: agresión; física

Bearer: portador; tenedor

Bearer instrument: documento al portador

Bequest or legacy: legado (de bienes muebles)

Bilateral contract: contrato bilateral

Bill of lading: conocimiento de embarque; carta de porte

Bill of Rights: declaración de derechos

Binder: póliza de seguro provisoria; recibo de pago a cuenta del precio

Blank indorsement: endoso en blanco

Blue Sky laws: leyes reguladoras del comercio bursátil

Bond: título de crédito; garantía; caución

Bond indenture: contrato de emisión de bonos; contrato del empréstito

Breach of contract: incumplimiento de contrato

Brief: escrito; resumen; informe

Burglary; violación de domicilio

Business judgment rule: regla de juicio comercial

Business tort: agravio comercial

Case law: ley de casos; derecho casuístico

Cashier's check: cheque de caja

Causation in fact: causalidad en realidad

Cease-and-desist order: orden para cesar y desistir

Certificate of deposit: certificado de depósito

Certified check: cheque certificado

Charitable trust: fideicomiso para fines benéficos

Chattel: bien mueble

Check: cheque

Chose in action: derecho inmaterial; derecho de acción

Civil law: derecho civil

Close corporation: sociedad de un solo accionista o de un grupo restringido de accionistas

Closed shop: taller agremiado (emplea solamente a miembros de un gremio)

Closing argument: argumento al final

Codicil: codicilo

Collateral: guarantía; bien objeto de la guarantía real

Comity: cortesía; cortesía entre naciones

Commercial paper: instrumentos negociables; documentos a valores commerciales

Common law: derecho consuetudinario; derecho común; ley común

Common stock: acción ordinaria

Comparative negligence: negligencia comparada

Compensatory damages: daños y perjuicios reales o compensatorios

Concurrent conditions: condiciones concurrentes

Concurrent estates: condominio

Concurrent jurisdiction: competencia concurrente de varios tribunales para entender en una misma causa

Concurring opinion: opinión concurrente

Condition: condición

Condition precedent: condición suspensiva

Condition subsequent: condición resolutoria

Confiscation: confiscación

Confusion: confusión; fusión

Conglomerate merger: fusión de firmas que operan en distintos mercados

Consent decree: acuerdo entre las partes aprobado por un tribunal

Consequential damages: daños y perjuicios indirectos

Consideration: consideración; motivo; contraprestación

Consolidation: consolidación

Constructive delivery: entrega simbólica

Constructive trust: fideicomiso creado por aplicación de la ley

Consumer-protection law: ley para proteger el consumidor

Contract: contrato

Contracts under seal: contrato formal o sellado

Contributory negligence: negligencia de la parte actora

Conversion: usurpación; conversión de valores

Copyright: derecho de autor

Corporation: sociedad anómina; corporación; persona jurídica

Co-sureties: cogarantes

Counterclaim, or cross-complaint: reconvención; contrademanda

Counteroffer: contraoferta

Course of dealing: curso de transacciones

Course of performance: curso de cumplimiento

Covenant: pacto; garantía; contrato

Covenant not to sue: pacto or contrato a no demandar

Covenant of quiet enjoyment: garantía del uso y goce pacífico del inmueble

Creditors' composition agreement: concordato preventivo

Crime: crimen; delito; contravención

Criminal law: derecho penal

Cross-examination: contrainterrogatorio

Cure: cura; cuidado; derecho de remediar un vicio contractual

Customs receipts: recibos de derechos aduaneros

Damages: daños; indemnización por daños y perjuicios

Debit card: tarjeta de débito

Debtor: deudor

Debt securities: seguridades de deuda

Deceptive advertising: publicidad engañosa

Deed: escritura; título; acta translativa de domino

Defamation: difamación

Delegation of duties: delegación de obligaciones

Demand deposit: depósito a la vista

Depositions: declaración de un testigo fuera del tribunal

Derivative suit: acción judicial entablada por un accionista en nombre de la sociedad

Devise: legado; deposición testamentaria (bienes inmuebles)

Directed verdict: veredicto según orden del juez y sin participación activa del jurado

Direct examination: interrogatorio directo; primer interrogatorio

Disaffirmance: repudiación; renuncia; anulación

Discharge: descargo; liberación; cumplimiento

Disclosed principal: mandante revelado

Discovery: descubrimiento; producción de la prueba

Dissenting opinion: opinión disidente

Dissolution: disolución; terminación

Diversity of citizenship: competencia de los tribunales federales para entender en causas cuyas partes intervinientes son cuidadanos de distintos estados

Divestiture: extinción premature de derechos reales

Dividend: dividendo

Docket: orden del día; lista de causas pendientes

Domestic corporation: sociedad local

Draft: orden de pago; letrade cambio

Drawee: girado; beneficiario

Drawer: librador

Duress: coacción; violencia

Easement: servidumbre

Embezzlement: desfalco; malversación

Eminent domain: poder de expropiación

Employment discrimination: discriminación en el empleo

Entrepreneur: empresario

Environmental law: ley ambiental

Equal dignity rule: regla de dignidad egual

Equity security: tipo de participación en una sociedad

Estate: propiedad; patrimonio; derecho

Estop: impedir; prevenir

Ethical issue: cuestión ética

Exclusive jurisdiction: competencia exclusiva

Exculpatory clause: cláusula eximente

Executed contract: contrato ejecutado

Execution: ejecución; cumplimiento

Executor (-trix): albacea

Executory contract: contrato aún no completamente consumado

Executory interest: derecho futuro

Express contract: contrato expreso

Expropriation: expropriación

Federal question: caso federal

Fee simple: pleno dominio; dominio absoluto

Fee simple absolute: dominio absoluto

Fee simple defeasible: dominio sujeta a una condición resolutoria

Felony: crimen; delito grave

Fictitious payee: beneficiario ficticio

Fiduciary: fiduciaro

Firm offer: oferta en firme

Fixture: inmueble por destino, incorporación a anexación

Floating lien: gravamen continuado

Foreign corporation: sociedad extranjera; U.S. sociedad constituída en otro estado

Forgery: falso; falsificación

Formal contract: contrato formal

Franchise: privilegio; franquicia; concesión

Franchisee: persona que recibe una concesión

Franchisor: persona que vende una concesión

Fraud: fraude; dolo; engaño

Future estate; bien futuro

Garnishment: embargo de derechos

General partner: socio comanditario

General warranty deed: escritura translativa de domino con garantía de título

Gift: donación

Gift *causa mortis:* donación por causa de muerte

Gift *inter vivos:* donación entre vivos

Good faith: buena fe

Good-faith purchaser: comprador de buena fe

Holder: tenedor por contraprestación

Holder in due course: tenedor legítimo

Holographic will: testamento ológrafico

Homestead exemption laws: leyes que exceptúan las casas de familia de ejecución por duedas generales

Horizontal merger: fusión horizontal

Identification: identificación

Implied-in-fact contract: contrato implícito en realidad

Implied warranty: guarantía implícita

Implied warranty of merchantability: garantía implícita de vendibilidad

Impossibility of performance: imposibilidad de cumplir un contrato

Imposter: imposter

Incidental beneficiary: beneficiario incidental; beneficiario secundario

Incidental damages: daños incidentales

Indictment: auto de acusación; acusación

Indorsee: endorsatario

Indorsement: endoso

Indorser: endośante

Informal contract: contrato no formal; contrato verbal

Information: acusación hecha por el ministerio público

Injunction: mandamiento; orden de no innovar

Innkeeper's lien: derecho de retención que ejerce el posadero

Installment contract: contrato de pago en cuotas

Insurable interest: interés asegurable

Intended beneficiary: beneficiario destinado

Intentional tort: agravio; cuasi-delito intenciónal

International law: derecho internaciónal

Interrogatories: preguntas escritas sometidas por una parte a la otra o a un testigo

Inter vivos **trust:** fideicomiso entre vivos

Intestacy laws: leyes de la condición de morir intestado

Intestate: intestado

Investment company: compañia de inversiones

Issue: emisión

Joint tenancy: derechos conjuntos en un bien inmueble

Joint tenancy with right of survivorship: derechos conjuntos en un bien inmueble en favor del beneficiario sobreviviente

Judgment n.o.v.: juicio no obstante veredicto

Judgment rate of interest: interés de juicio

Judicial process: acto de procedimiento; proceso jurídico

Judicial review: revisión judicial

Jurisdiction: jurisdicción

Larceny: robo; hurto

Law: derecho; ley; jurisprudencia

Lease: contrato de locación; contrato de alquiler

Leasehold estate: bienes forales

Legal rate of interest: interés legal

Legatee: legatario

Less-than-freehold estate: menos de derecho de dominio absoluto

Letter of credit: carta de crédito

Levy: embargo; comiso

Libel: libelo; difamación escrita

Life estate: usufructo

Limited partner: comanditario

Limited partnership: sociedad en comandita

Liquidation: liquidación; realización

Lost property: objetos perdidos

Majority opinion: opinión de la mayoría

Maker: persona que realiza u ordena; librador

Mechanic's lien: gravamen de constructor

Mediation: mediación; intervención

Merger: fusión

Mirror-image rule: fallo de reflejo

Misdemeanor: infracción; contravención

Mislaid property: bienes extraviados

Mitigation of damages: reducción de daños

Moral hazard: riesgo moral

Mortgage: hypoteca

Motion to dismiss, or demurrer: excepción parentoria

Municipal law: derecho municipal

Mutual fund: fondo mutual

Negotiable instrument: instrumento negociable

Negotiation: negociación

Nominal damages: daños y perjuicios nominales

Novation: novación

Nuncupative will: testamento nuncupativo

Objective theory of contracts: teoria objetiva de contratos

Offer: oferta

Offeree: persona que recibe una oferta

Offeror: oferente

Order paper: instrumento o documento a la orden

Original jurisdiction: jurisdicción de primera instancia

Output contract: contrato de producción

Parol evidence rule: regla relativa a la prueba oral

Partially disclosed principal: mandante revelado en parte

Partnership: sociedad colectiva; asociación; asociación de participación

Past consideration: causa o contraprestación anterior

Patent: patente; privilegio

Pattern or practice: muestra o práctica

Payee: beneficiario de un pago

Penalty: pena; penalidad

Per capita: por cabeza

Perfection: perfeción

Performance: cumplimiento; ejecución
Personal defenses: excepciones personales
Personal property: bienes muebles
Per stirpes: por estirpe
Plea bargaining: regateo por un alegato
Pleadings: alegatos
Pledge: prenda
Police powers: poders de policia y de prevención del crimen
Policy: póliza
Positive law: derecho positivo; ley positiva
Possibility of reverter: posibilidad de reversión
Precedent: precedente
Preemptive right: derecho de prelación
Preferred stock: acciones preferidas
Premium: recompensa; prima
Presentment warranty: garantía de presentación
Price discrimination: discriminación en los precios
Principal: mandante; principal
Privity: nexo jurídico
Privity of contract: relación contractual
Probable cause: causa probable
Probate: verificación; verificación del testamento
Probate court: tribunal de sucesiones y tutelas
Proceeds: resultados; ingresos
Profit: beneficio; utilidad; lucro
Promise: promesa
Promisee: beneficiario de una promesa
Promisor: promtente
Promissory estoppel: impedimento promisorio
Promissory note: pagaré; nota de pago
Promoter: promotor; fundador

Proximate cause: causa inmediata o próxima
Proxy: apoderado; poder
Punitive, or exemplary, damages: daños y perjuicios punitivos o ejemplares

Qualified indorsement: endoso con reservas
Quasi-contract: contrato tácito o implícito
Quit-claim deed: acto de transferencia de una propiedad por finiquito, pero sin ninguna garantía sobre la validez del título transferido

Ratification: ratificación
Real defenses: defensas legitimas o legales
Real property: bienes inmuebles
Reasonable doubt: duda razonable
Rebuttal: refutación
Recognizance: promesa; compromiso; reconocimiento
Recording statutes: leyes estatales sobre registros oficiales
Redress: reparación
Reformation: rectificación; reforma; corrección
Rejoinder: dúplica; contrarréplica
Release: liberación; renuncia a un derecho
Remainder: substitución; reversión
Remedy: recurso; remedio; reparación
Replevin: acción reivindicatoria; reivindicación
Reply: réplica
Requirements contract: contrato de suministro
Rescission: rescisión
Res judicata: cosa juzgada; res judicata

Respondeat superior: responsabilidad del mandante o del maestro
Restitution: restitución
Restrictive indorsement: endoso restrictivo
Resulting trust: fideicomiso implícito
Reversion: reversión; sustitución
Revocation: revocación; derogación
Right of contribution: derecho de contribución
Right of reimbursement: derecho de reembolso
Right of subrogation: derecho de subrogación
Right-to-work law: ley de libertad de trabajo
Robbery: robo
Rule 10b-5: Regla 10b-5

Sale: venta; contrato de compreventa
Sale on approval: venta a ensayo; venta sujeta a la aprobación del comprador
Sale or return: venta con derecho de devolución
Sales contract: contrato de compraventa; boleto de compraventa
Satisfaction: satisfacción; pago
Scienter: a sabiendas
S corporation: S corporación
Secured party: acreedor garantizado
Secured transaction: transacción garantizada
Securities: volares; titulos; seguridades
Security agreement: convenio de seguridad
Security interest: interés en un bien dado en garantía que permite a quien lo detenta venderlo en caso de incumplimiento

Service mark: marca de identificación de servicios
Signature: firma; rúbrica
Slander: difamación oral; calumnia
Sovereign immunity: immunidad soberana
Special indorsement: endoso especial; endoso a la orden de una person en particular
Specific performance: ejecución precisa, según los términos del contrato
Spendthrift trust: fideicomiso para pródigos
Stale check: cheque vencido
Stare decisis: acatar las decisiones, observar los precedentes
State exemption laws: leyes que exceptúan los estados
Statutory law: derecho estatutario; derecho legislado; derecho escrito
Stock: acciones
Stock split: fraccionamiento de acciones
Stock warrant: certificado para la compra de acciones
Stop-payment order: orden de suspensión del pago de un cheque dada por el librador del mismo
Strict liability: responsabilidad uncondicional
Summary judgment: fallo sumario

Tangible property: bienes corpóreos
Tenancy at will: inguilino por tiempo indeterminado (según la voluntad del propietario)
Tenancy by sufferance: posesión por tolerancia

Tenancy by the entirety: locación conyugal conjunta
Tenancy for years: inguilino por un término fijo
Tenancy in common: specie de copropiedad indivisa
Tender: oferta de pago; oferta de ejecución
Testamentary trust: fideicomiso testamentario
Testator (-trix): testador (-a)
Third-party-beneficiary contract: contrato para el beneficio del tercero-beneficiario
Tort: agravio; cuasi-delito
Totten trust: fideicomiso creado por un depósito bancario
Trade acceptance: letra de cambio aceptada
Trademark: marca registrada
Trade name: nombre comercial; razón social
Traveler's check: cheque del viajero
Trespass to land: ingreso no authorizado a las tierras de otro
Trespass to personalty: violación de los derechos posesorios de un tercero con respecto a bienes muebles
Trust: fideicomiso; trust

Ultra vires: ultra vires; fuera de la facultad (de una sociedad anónima)
Unanimous opinion: opinión unámine
Unconscionable contract or clause: contrato leonino; cláusula leonino
Underwriter: subscriptor; asegurador
Unenforceable contract: contrato que no se puede hacer cumplir

Unilateral contract: contrato unilateral
Union shop: taller agremiado; empresa en la que todos los empleados son miembros del gremio o sindicato
Usge of trade: uso comercial
Usury: usura

Valid contract: contrato válido
Venue: lugar; sede del proceso
Vertical merger: fusión vertical de empresas
Voidable contract: contrato anulable
Void contract: contrato nulo; contrato inválido, sin fuerza legal
Voir dire: examen preliminar de un testigo a jurado por el tribunal para determinar su competencia
Voting trust: fideicomiso para ejercer el derecho de voto

Waiver: renuncia; abandono
Warranty of habitability: garantía de habitabilidad
Warranty of possession: garantía de posesión
Watered stock: acciones diluídos; capital inflado
White-collar crime: crimen administrativo
Writ of attachment: mandamiento de ejecución; mandamiento de embargo
Writ of certiorari: auto de avocación; auto de certiorari
Writ of execution: auto ejecutivo; mandamiento de ejecutión
Writ of mandamus: auto de mandamus; mandamiento; orden judicial

Glossary

A

abandoned property Property discarded by the true owner who has no intention of reclaiming it.

acceleration clause Clause in contract that allows payee or other holder of a time instrument to demand payment of the entire amount due with interest if a certain event, such as a default in the payment of an installment, occurs.

acceptance Voluntary act by word or by conduct of the offeree that shows assent or agreement to the terms of the offer.

accession Something added on, as in value added to a piece of personal property by labor or materials.

accord Agreement to discharge a claim by giving and accepting something different from or less than that to which the party agreeing to accept is entitled.

act of state doctrine Doctrine created by the judiciary that provides that the judicial branch of one country will not examine the validity of public acts committed by a recognized foreign government within its own territory.

actus reus Criminal conduct.

administrative agency Agency of the federal government created by the executive or legislative branch for a specific purpose; endowed with legislative, executive, and judicial powers, agency interprets and enforces congressional statutes and rules.

administrative law Body of law that governs the powers, procedures, and practices of administrative agencies.

Administrative Procedures Act of 1946 (APA) Federal statute that acts as a constitution for administrative agencies; provides standardized administrative agency practices and governs how an administrative agency conducts its business.

ad valorem **tariff** Tax on a percentage of the value of the imported good(s).

adverse possession Means of obtaining title to land without a deed being delivered. To establish title, the adverse possessor must prove nonpermissive use that is actual, open, notorious, exclusive, and adverse for the period prescribed by statute.

affirmative action Remedial step taken to improve work opportunities for women, racial and ethnic minorities, and other people considered to have been deprived of job opportunities in the past.

agency law Body of law that governs the relationship between two parties; one of them, the agent, agrees to represent or act for the other, the principal.

aggravated burglary Burglary with the use of a deadly weapon.

alternative dispute resolution Speedy and just means of resolving a dispute at a reasonable cost to both the parties and to the taxpayers; for example, arbitration, conciliation.

American Arbitration Association Private nonprofit organization established in 1926, whose purpose is to foster study of arbitration, to perfect the techniques of arbitration law, and to advance the science of arbitration for the prompt and economic settlement of disputes.

amicus curiae Friend of the court. A qualified person who is not a party to an action but who gives information to the court on a question of law involved in the case.

analytical school of law Approach to the study of law that uses logical analysis to extract the principles underlying a legal code.

ancillary restraint Trade restraint subordinate to the main lawful purpose of a transaction such as the sale of a business; generally, an ancillary restraint requires one party to refrain from competing with another for a specific period within a particular area.

annual percentage rate (APR) True rate of interest being charged on a yearly basis.

answer Document filed by defendant that answers a complaint and admits or denies the allegations stated in the complaint.

antitrust laws Laws that regulate economic competition in order to prevent monopolists from controlling the economy.

appellate courts Courts of appeal or courts of review; courts whose subject-matter jurisdiction is limited to hearing appeals.

arbitration Procedure in which the parties to a dispute submit their case to an impartial third person (arbitrator).

arbitration clause Clause in a contract that provides for arbitration in the event of a dispute; specifies the expertise of arbitrator, the forum, and the choice of law.

arbitrator Person selected by the parties to a dispute to make a decision based on evidence submitted by both parties.

articles of incorporation Initial incorporation process that provides basic information about the corporation and is the primary source of authority for future operation of the business.

assignment A transfer of all or part of one's property, interest, or rights.

attachment Court-ordered seizing and taking into custody of property that is in controversy over a debt.

automated clearinghouse System of electronic signals that makes money transactions between banks; eliminates paper transfers.

B

bailment Act of delivering personal property without transfer of title from one person (bailor) to another (bailee) under an agreement for a particular purpose on the completion of which the bailee must return the bailed property to the bailor or to a third person or dispose of it as directed.

bankruptcy fraud Dishonesty with the bankruptcy court on the part of the person who has declared bankruptcy.

bilateral contract Contract in which one person makes an offer and receives an acceptance from the offeree; most contracts are of this nature.

bilateral mistake Mistake made by both of the contract parties.

Bill of Rights First ten amendments to the United States Constitution; adopted in 1791; established specific protections for the individual against the federal government.

blank indorsement Signature of the payee or of the person who was specified in a specific indorsement.

bona fide occupational qualification (BFOQ) Job requirement that is unique and specific to a job but that could be discriminatory; for example, the requirement that a wet nurse be female is a BFOQ, and this fact would be a possible defense to an employment discrimination charge.

bond Method of financing (as for a business) that is a long-term commitment in which the loan earns interest at a fixed rate, and repayment to the creditor is commonly secured by property.

breach of contract Failure to perform what a party is under an absolute duty to perform based on an express or an implied-in-fact contract.

brief Method of case analysis and summarization that contains the elements of case citation, facts, issue(s), holding, and reasoning.

burden of proof Requirement that the plaintiff in a lawsuit must prove the truth of the allegations made against the defendant.

burglary Act of entering into the building of another with the intent to commit a felony.

bylaws Statutes of a corporation setting forth the internal rules of management for the corporation.

C

Celler-Kefauver Act Section 7 of the Clayton Act, established in 1950; controls corporate mergers.

certificate of deposit (CD) Acknowledgment by a bank of the receipt of money; carries an agreement to repay the money with interest.

certified check Check that is recognized and accepted by a bank office as a valid appropriation of the specified amount drawn against the funds held by the bank.

chain-style business Type of franchise that operates under a franchisor's trade name and is identified as a member of a select group of dealers engaging in the franchisor's business.

chattel An article of personal property, as opposed to real property; any property other than freehold estates.

chattel real Chattel that concerns real property, such as a lease.

check Paper drawn on a bank, ordering it to pay a sum of money on demand.

choice-of-law clause Clause in an international business contract that designates the forum in which adjudication will take place and the substantive law that will be applied in the event of any dispute.

civil law Body of law that establishes the legal rights and duties existing among individuals or between citizens and their governments.

Clayton Act Federal statute enacted in 1941 to strengthen federal antitrust laws; aimed at restraining specific monopolistic practices.

closed shop Firm that recognizes union membership by its workers as a condition for employment.

Colgate doctrine Rule that resulted from *United States v. Colgate* decision in which the U.S. Supreme Court allowed Colgate to refuse unilaterally to deal with retailers who did not follow suggested retail prices; that is, Colgate can deal with whomever it desires.

collateral note Written promise to pay secured by the payee-creditor in which the maker-debtor creates a lien against his or her personal property.

comity Deference that one nation gives to the laws and judicial decrees of another nation, based on respect.

commerce clause Clause in the U.S. Constitution that gives Congress the power ''to regulate commerce with foreign nations, and among the several states, and with the individual tribes.''

commercial law Body of law that governs commercial actions; business law.

common law Body of judge-made law comprised of principles and the rules of how these principles relate to the government and to the security of persons and property.

common stock Method of financing a business in which stock is held by a shareholder and carries voting rights and the right to a share of the profits of the business if a dividend is declared; has indefinite duration unless redeemed by the corporation.

community property Property of married couples in which each spouse owns an undivided half interest in any property acquired during the marriage.

comparable worth Pay equity; theory that equal pay should be received not just for equal work but also for work of comparable skill, effort, and responsibility.

compensatory damages Award to the injured party as a result of a lawsuit to make up for the monetary loss suffered because the other party breached the contract.

complaint Type of pleading issued by the plaintiff to the defendant that states the purpose of the lawsuit.

computer crimes Crimes committed by use of a computer; for example, electronic thefts of money through issuing an extra paycheck, shaving funds, or depositing funds in personal accounts.

concerted action Action that has been planned, agreed on, and settled between parties acting together pursuant to some scheme.

conciliation Process by which a third party successfully brings together the conflicting parties; this is the process used by the Better Business Bureau.

concurrent jurisdiction Power to hear a case held by both federal and state courts.

confiscation Taking property without proper public purpose or just compensation being awarded.

conglomerate merger Consolidation of two or more firms dealing in unrelated products and operating in markets not horizontally or vertically linked.

consequential damage Foreseeable damage that results when a party breaches a contract.

consideration Something of legal value given in exchange for a promise; essential element of a contract.

constitutional law Public law that involves questions of whether the government has the power to act.

constitutional tort Act by a government official that violates the constitutional rights of a person.

Consumer Credit Protection Act (CCPA) Federal statute that is the primary source of federal law covering credit transactions; enforced by several federal agencies.

contract Promise or set of promises for the breach of which the law gives a remedy, and the performance of which the law in some way recognizes as a duty.

contractual arbitration Arbitration established by contractual agreement entered into either before or after a dispute occurs.

contractual capacity Competence of the parties to a contract.

contributory negligence Negligence on the part of both parties; each party contributes to the negligence.

conversion Taking personal property from its rightful owner or possessor and placing it in the service of another; civil law side of stealing.

copyright Right granted by statute to the author or originator of certain literary or artistic productions.

corporate white-collar crime Crime committed by a complex organization.

corporation Separate legal entity that is owned by shareholders.

counterclaim Claim in which the defendant sets forth allegations against the claims made by the plaintiff in a lawsuit.

counteroffer Rejection of original offer and the simultaneous making of a new offer.

covenant not to compete Clause in an employment contract in which the employee agrees that, if he or she leaves the employment for whatever reason, he or she will not accept employment with a competitor.

covenant running with the land Agreement under which a landowner either acquires certain rights or is under certain obligations based on his or her ownership of the land that is bound by the covenant.

criminal law Body of law that deals with violations of wrongs committed against society as a whole.

D

debenture Form of bond that is unsecured.

debit card Paperless transaction used to obtain a cash advance from an automatic teller machine; the amount is automatically debited from the customer's account.

debt securities Bonds of debentures that represent a loan to the corporation.

deed Writing signed by an owner of property by which title to the property is transferred to another.

defamation Act of making any untrue statement or statements that harm the reputation of another person or corporation.

defamation by computer Production by a computer of erroneous information about a person's credit standing or business reputation that may impair the person's ability to obtain further credit.

defamation of character Act of wrongfully hurting a person's good reputation; results in the tort of slander if spoken or the tort of libel if written.

default Failure to honor the conditions of a contract.

deficiency judgment Award that represents the deficient amount (difference between the mortgage debt and the amount received from the proceeds of the foreclosure sale).

demurrer Defendant's motion to dismiss the complaint, stating that, even if the facts are true, their legal consequences are such that there is no reason to go further with the lawsuit and no need for the defendant to present an answer.

deposition Sworn oral testimony by opposing party or by witness(es) taken by interrogatories, not in open court.

derivative authority Authority accorded the agent by the principal to carry out the principal's business.

discharge To perform a contract fully.

disclosed principal Principle whose identity is known by the third party at the time the contract is made by the agent.

discovery Process of obtaining information from opposing party or from witnesses in a lawsuit.

disparagement of goods False statement made about a person's product.

disparate impact Employment discrimination practice that appears neutral on the surface but that actually affects a protected class adversely.

disparate treatment Employment discrimination practice in which treatment of a certain class differs from the treatment of other employees or applicants.

distributorship relationship Type of franchise where a manufacturing concern (franchisor) licenses a dealer (franchisee) to sell its products; for example, an automobile dealership.

district court Federal trial court of general jurisdiction; the court of original jurisdiction for federal cases.

diversity of citizenship cases Cases involving: (1) citizens of different states, (2) a foreign country as plaintiff and citizens of a state or different states, or (3) citizens of a state and citizens or subjects of a foreign country where the amount in controversy is greater than $10,000 and does not involve a federal question.

doctrine of laches Rule that states that individuals who fail to look out for their rights until after a reasonable time has passed will not be helped.

doctrine of respondeat superior Rule that makes the principal liable for the agent's torts if the torts are committed within the scope of the agency or the scope of employment.

doctrine of sovereign immunity Rule that immumizes foreign nations from the jurisdiction of the United States.

draft Unconditional written order; debt owed by the drawee to the drawer.

drawee Debtor of the drawer.

drawer One who creates or executes the order-to-pay instrument.

duress Compulsion by threat; forcing someone to do something out of fear.

duty of fair representation Implied duty of a union to represent its membership fairly.

E

easement Right of a person to make limited use of another person's property without taking anything from the property.

economic school of law Approach to the study of law that holds that most laws may be evaluated in accordance with economic theory; developed by Richard A. Posner in the 1970s.

electronic funds transfer (EFT) Automatic payment or direct deposit using teller machines, point-of-sale systems, and automated clearinghouses.

eminent domain Power of government to condemn land in order to take it for public use.

employee One employed by the employer to perform services.

Employee Retirement Income Security Act of 1974 (ERISA) Federal statute that established a supplement to social security to be set up by employers for their employees.

employer One who provides a job, and, according to the Fair Labor Standards Act, any person acting directly or indirectly in the interest of an employer in relation to an employee.

employment contract Neutral agreement between employer and employee.

enabling act Congressional legislation that creates an administrative agency, determines its structure, and defines its powers.

Environmental Protection Agency (EPA) Federal agency created in 1970 that assembles various organizations responsible for environmental protection.

Equal Credit Opportunity Act Federal statute that forbids discrimination based on race, sex, religion, national origin, marital status, age, or person's income from public assistance in determinations of creditworthiness.

Equal Employment Opportunity Commission (EEOC) Five-member commission created in 1964 to administer Title VII; members are appointed by the president of the United States with consent of the Senate; issues interpretive guidelines and regulations but does not have force of law; investigates, holds hearings, keeps statistics.

Equal Pay Act of 1963 Amendment to the Fair Labor Standards Act of 1938, administered by the EEOC; prohibits discrimination in wages paid for equal work on jobs whose performance requires equal skills, effort, and responsibility and that are performed under similar conditions (job content rather than job description).

equal protection Legal right that holds that government must treat similarly situated individuals in a similar manner.

equity securities Shares of stock representing an ownership interest in a corporation.

estates Rights of ownership in real property.

exclusive dealing arrangement Legal vertical restraint of trade in which the manufacturer or distributor may require the retailer not to sell products of competing firms, provided there is no boycott but each decision is made on an individual basis.

exclusive jurisdiction Power to hear a case held by only a federal court (as in federal crimes, bankruptcy, patents, copyrights, and suits against the United States) or by only a state court (as in divorce, probate, and adoption cases).

executed contract Contract that is fully performed.

executive agreement Agreement made by the president of the United States without need for the consent of the Senate; used in making treaties with foreign countries.

executive branch Branch of the U.S. government that includes the president and is charged with enforcing the law; the powers of the president, as established in Article II of the Constitution.

executive immunity Doctrine that makes the president of the United States immune from certain lawsuits.

executive order Order or regulation issued under the presidential authority to make rules.

executive privilege Right of the president to keep certain secrets.

executory contract Contract that has not been performed.

express contract Contract in which the terms are stated exactly whether written or spoken.

express warranty Explicit statements made by the seller to the buyer regarding the condition or quality of the goods purchased.

expropriation Government seizure of a privately owned business or goods for a proper public purpose and with just compensation.

extension Increase in length of time (for example, the due date of a note).

extension clause Contract clause that allows the date of maturity to be extended into the future; reverse of acceleration clause.

extraterritorial Beyond the country's borders.

F

fact finding Investigative process by which a third party will investigate the issues and make findings of fact to present to the court or other body charged with ruling on the issues.

Fair Credit Billing Act   Amendment to Truth-in-Lending Act (TILA) that requires creditors to correct errors promptly and without damage to a person's credit rating.

Fair Credit Reporting Act   Title VI of the Consumer Credit Protection Act, which requires that consumers be informed of the nature and scope of a credit investigation, the kind of information that is being compiled, and the names of persons who will be receiving the report.

Fair Debt Collection Practices Act   Part of the Consumer Credit Protection Act; adopted in 1977, it prohibits certain practices in the collection of consumer debt by debt collection agencies.

Fair Labor Standard Act of 1938 (FLSA)   Federal statute that established minimum wage, overtime standards, record-keeping, and child labor prohibitions; provides for administrative procedures for the enforcement of and compliance with these standards as they apply to employees engaged in commerce, production of goods to be placed in commerce, or employees of an enterprise engaged in commerce.

false imprisonment   Intentional confinement or restraint of another person without justification.

Federal Arbitration Act   Federal statute favoring arbitration that withdraws from the states the power to require a judicial forum for the resolution of disagreements if the parties by contract have agreed to solve the problem by arbitration.

Federal Insurance Contribution Act   Federal statute that provides funding for the social security program.

federalism   System of government organization in which state governments and the federal government share powers.

Federal Regulation of Lobbying Act of 1942   Federal statue that requires disclosure law and regulates the activities of lobbyists.

Federal Trade Commission   Bipartisan, independent administrative agency headed by five commissioners authorized to prevent unfair methods of competition in commerce and unfair or deceptive acts or practices in commerce.

Federal Trade Commission Act of 1914   Federal statute that created the Federal Trade Commission.

Federal Unemployment Tax Act (1954) (FUTA)   Federal statute that established a state system of providing unemployment compensation to eligible individuals.

fee simple absolute   Estate in property in which the owner has the greatest aggregation of rights, privileges, and power possible; is indefinite in duration.

felony   Crime punishable by imprisonment in a federal or state penitentiary for more than one year, by fine, or by death.

finance charge   Total amount of interest paid on a loan.

fixture   Object affixed to realty by roots, embedded in it, or permanently attached by cement, nails, bolts, plaster, or screws.

flat rate tariff   Tax on a unit item of goods entering or leaving a country.

force majeure **clause**   Clause in a contract that protects parties from forces beyond their control.

foreclosure   Legal procedure that mortgagee uses to obtain payment in a mortgage default.

Foreign Corrupt Practices Act of 1977 (FCPA)   Federal statute that prohibits bribes given to foreign government officials by representatives of American companies and their directors, officers, shareholders, employees, or agents for the purpose of obtaining or retaining business for the American company.

Foreign Sovereign Immunities Act of 1976 (FSIA)   Federal statute that codifies the law of sovereign immunity.

forgery   Crime of obtaining goods by false pretenses.

formal contract   Written contract between parties.

franchise   Arrangement in which the owner of a trademark, a trade name, or copyright licenses another person under specified conditions or limitations to use the trademark, trade name, or copyright in marketing goods or services.

Freedom of Information Act of 1966 (FOIA)   Amendment to the Administrative Procedures Act that makes all nonexempt information held by federal agencies available to the public.

freehold estate   Estate in real property of uncertain duration.

G

garnishment   Statutory procedure in which a person's property in possession of another is applied to payment of that person's debts.

general jurisdiction   Power to hear almost any subject matter in a lawsuit; authority of the court of original jurisdiction.

general restraint   Illegal restraint of trade used to eliminate competition.

general warranty deed Deed that provides the buyer protection against defects in the title to land.

geographic market Part of the structural analysis tool used by courts to determine whether a monopoly exists; considers whether sellers within an area can raise prices or reduce the supply of products without quantities of lower-priced goods quickly flowing into the regional, national, or local area.

gift Voluntary transfer of ownership of property.

good faith Honesty in a transaction.

government agency Administrative agency created by Congress to administer a quasi-business venture generating its own revenue; for example, U.S. Postal Service.

grand jury A body of people selected to conduct fact finding and based on their conclusions to issue indictments for criminal offenses.

group boycott *Per se* violation of the Sherman Act in which a group refuses to deal with some third party or parties.

H

hardware Computer equipment itself.

Herfindahl-Hirschman Index Statistical formula used by the Department of Justice to determine non-market considerations of a proposed merger, such as the ease of entry into the business and the resulting competitive strength of the merged firms.

historical school of law Approach to the study of law based on the origin and history of the legal system; looks to the past to discover what the principles of contemporary law should be.

holder Person who possesses negotiable instruments drawn, issued, or indorsed to his or her order or to the bearer or in blank.

holder in due course (HDC) Special-status transferee of a negotiable instrument.

homestead exemption Exemption of certain types of real and personal property from levy of execution or attachment in the event of mortgage default and deficiency judgment.

horizontal market division *Per se* violation of the Sherman Act that involves dividing a market for the sale of a specific product among competitors.

horizontal merger Merger of comparable companies.

I

implied-in-fact contract Contract formed in whole or in part from the conduct of the parties.

implied warranty Warranty derived from the facts of the case but not specifically stated.

implied warranty of fitness Warranty that arises when any seller knows the particular purpose for which a buyer will use the goods and knows the buyer is relying on the seller's skill and judgment to select suitable goods.

implied warranty of merchantability Warranty that goods are reasonably fit for the purpose for which they are sold, are properly packaged and labeled, and are of proper quality; arises in the sale of goods by a merchant who deals in goods of that kind.

incorporators People who start the corporation.

independent agency Administrative agency that is not under the control of the president or Congress but is freestanding; has a commission created by Congress and is headed by a commissioner.

independent contractor Person who contracts with another to do something for him or her but who is not controlled by the other or subject to the other's right to control with respect to his or her physical conduct in the performance of the undertaking.

indictment Formal charge of wrongdoing issued by a grand jury prior to trial.

indorsement Signature of the person known as the indorser written on the back of the instrument itself.

infliction of mental distress Intentional act that involves extreme and outrageous conduct and that results in severe emotional distress to another.

informal contract Written or oral contract.

informal rule making Rule making that consists of notice and comment; most commonly used by administrative agencies to promulgate rules.

injunction Equitable remedy in which an order is issued to a person or a business to refrain from doing wrongful act(s).

***in personam* jurisdiction** Jurisdiction over the person.

***in rem* jurisdiction** Jurisdiction over property.

intangible property Property that possesses an invisible value, such as an annuity, checks, or bonds, and is reported by a piece of paper with rights recognized by law.

intentional tort Intentional acts that cause injuries either against the person or against property.

interlocking directorship Situation in which one person is director of two or more competing businesses where one of them has a capital surplus exceeding $1 million.

international custom General practice among nations that is accepted as law.

international law Law considered legally binding among otherwise independent nations.

interpretive rule   Statement by an administrative agency as to how it interprets the statute it is charged with administering; published in the Federal Register.

interrogatories   Written questions sent to the opposing party that must be answered under oath.

intestate   Dying without a will.

J

joint tenancy with right of survivorship   Situation in which two or more persons own an undivided interest in either personal or real property, and, on the death of one of the joint tenants, his or her interest transfers to the remaining joint tenant, not to his or her heirs.

joint venture   Undertaking in which two or more companies join together to conduct business.

judgment   Verdict that has been signed by a judge and that states who won the case and the conditions of the award.

judicial arbitration   Compulsory, court-mandated arbitration.

judicial branch   Branch of the U.S. government that consists of the federal judicial system and its powers as established by Article III of the U.S. Constitution.

judicial review   Process for deciding whether a law is in conflict with the mandates of the Constitution.

jurisdiction   *Juris*: law + *diction*: to speak; the power to speak the law; the authority to interpret and apply the law, to hear cases.

jurisprudence   Science or philosophy of law.

L

Labor Management Relations Act of 1947   Also known as the Taft-Hartley Act; amendment to the Wagner Act that provides protection for employers as well as employees in labor-related issues.

Labor Management Reporting and Disclosure Act of 1959   Also known as the Landrum-Griffith Act; statute that established an employee bill of rights and reporting requirements for union activities; regulates internal union business.

larceny   Wrongful or fraudulent taking and carrying away by any person of the personal property of another.

law   System that gives order to society; a system of moral conduct by which society achieves justice; a body of rules.

law merchant   Rules resulting from the resolution of disputes and from transactions of merchants and other commercial traders; consists primarily of general customs of the trades that remain law unless displaced by specific statutes.

lease   Transfer of real or personal property by landlord or lessor to the tenant or lessee for a period of time in exchange for a consideration (usually payment of rent); on termination, the property reverts to the lessor.

legal realists   Those who stress the pragmatic and empirical sides of law; looking at how well the law meets the needs of society.

legislative branch   Branch of the U.S. government that consists of Congress and its powers as established by Article I of the U.S. Constitution.

legislative immunity   Doctrine that protects members of Congress from being held accountable for their acts and utterances that are part of their legitimate legal duties.

legislative veto   Disapproval of an action by Congress.

letter of credit   Contract used in international business that assures the seller of payment while assuring the buyer that payment will not be made until all terms and conditions of the instrument are complied with.

license   Revocable right of a person to come onto another person's land; for example, a ticket to attend the theater.

licensing power   Authority of governmental body to grant a license to pursue a particular activity.

lien   Type of tangible security beyond the mere promise to pay a debt; uses personal property held in the event of default.

limited jurisdiction   Jurisdiction limited to certain subject matters.

line agency   Administrative agency under the direct control of the president of the United States; for example, the Department of Labor.

liquidated damages   Amount stipulated in a contract to serve as the measure of damages in case of a breach.

lobbyists   Those who attempt to influence lawmakers in favor of certain legislation or special interests.

lost property   Property that is not voluntarily left and forgotten.

M

Magnuson-Moss Warranty Act Federal statute designed to prevent deception in warranties by making them easier to understand; enforced by the Federal Trade Commission.

manufacturing or processing plant Type of franchise in which the franchisor transfers to the franchisee essential ingredients or the formula to make a particular product.

market share Part of the structural analysis employed by courts to determine whether a monopoly exists; considers the market positions of all other firms with which a business competes.

mediation Process of promoting voluntary compromise or resolution of a dispute usually initiated before arbitration.

Medicare Health insurance program administered by the Social Security Administration to people sixty-five years of age and older and for those under sixty-five years of age who are disabled.

mens rea Criminal intent.

merger Combination of two or more firms into one firm.

minor Person less than the legal statutory age.

misdemeanor Crime punishable by a fine or by confinement for up to a year; for example, tresspass or disorderly conduct.

mislaid property Property that has been placed somewhere by the owner voluntarily and then inadvertently forgotten.

mortgagee Creditor or lender; the beneficiary of the mortgage.

mortgage note Type of collateral note used to buy a house.

mortgagor Debtor or borrower who creates a mortgage on real estate.

mutual assent Meeting of the minds of the offeror and the offeree; offer must be made by one person and accepted by another for the same item or service.

N

National Environmental Policy Act (NEPA) Federal statute established in 1970 that created the Council of Environmental Quality and mandated that an environmental impact statement be prepared for every recommendation or report on legislation or major federal action significantly affecting the quality of the environment.

National Labor Relations Act Also known as the Wagner Act; federal statute enacted in 1935 that established rights of employees to engage in collective bargaining and to strike.

National Labor Relations Board (NLRB) Agency created by the Wagner Act to oversee union elections and to prevent employers from engaging in unfair and illegal union-labor activities and practices.

national law Body of law that pertains to a particular nation.

natural law school Approach to the study of law that holds ethics to be the source of legal authority; ethical values are used to make legal decisions.

negligence Conduct that falls below the duty of care and that results in another's personal injury or property damage.

negotiation Process in which two or more people meet to discuss their differences and attempt to arrive at a settlement that is acceptable to both.

nolo contendere Plea by the defendant that does not admit guilt but that allows the court to impose the same penalty as for a guilty plea.

nominal damages Damages awarded when there is a breach of contract and a technical injury has occurred, but where no actual damages are sustained.

nonfreehold estate Chattel real; estate consisting of possession of land without possessing a freehold estate in it.

nonpossessory interests Interests in land that do not include any rights of possession; for example, easements.

Norris-LaGuardia Act Federal statute established in 1932 that permits employees to organize and restricts federal courts from issuing injunctions against unions engaged in peaceful strikes.

novation Written agreement entered into by all the parties in which one party is substituted for another party; that is, one party is completely dismissed, and another party is substituted.

nuisance Improper activity that interferes with another's enjoyment or use of his or her property.

O

obligation to bargain in good faith Requirement of employers and unions to meet at reasonable times and to confer in good faith, but not necessarily to reach an agreement.

Occupational Safety and Health Act of 1970 Federal statute that requires health and safety protections for employees at their place of employment.

Occupational Safety and Health Administration (OSHA)   Organization that promulgates and enforces workers' safety and health standards, conducts inspections and investigations, keeps records, and performs research.

occupational white-collar crime   Crime committed by people through their work; for example, insider trading, bribes.

offeree   Person receiving the offer.

offeror   Person making the offer.

official language clause   Clause in an international business contract that specifies the official language to be used in interpreting the terms of the contract.

order   Decision of the administrative law judge; final disposition of a case between the government and a party in a lawsuit.

order to pay   Document or instrument in which one party (drawer) orders another party (drawee) to pay money to a third party (payee).

P

partially disclosed principal   Principal whose identity is not known by the third party but the third party knows that the agent is acting for a principal at the time the contract is made.

patent   Grant from the government that conveys and secures to an inventor the exclusive right to make, use, and sell an invention for a period of seventeen years.

payee   Bearer of an instrument.

perfection   Legal process by which a secured creditor protects himself or herself against the claims of third parties who may want their debts satisfied out of the same collateral.

per se **illegality**   Illegality that requires for proof only the fact that an agreement existed; for example, pricefixing.

personal property   All property that is basically movable and is not real property.

petty offense   Civil offense not classified as a crime, which is punishable by a fine, imprisonment, or both; for example, a traffic violation.

pleading   Document written by one of the parties to a lawsuit and sent to the other parties and to the court to be included in the judge's case file; provides information to the other parties.

point-of-sale system   Electronic system that allows the consumer to transfer his or her funds from his or her account to the merchant's in order to make a purchase through the use of a debit card.

political action committee (PAC)   Nonpartisan political group whose activities are directed toward raising and spending money to elect lawmakers.

preferred stock   Equity security in a corporation that carries certain preferences, such as dividends at a fixed rate; may or may not carry voting rights and is entitled to preference over common stock in payment of assets in the event the corporation is liquidated.

price fixing   Conspiracy among competitors to fix the price of an item or service.

Privacy Act   1974 amendment to the Administrative Procedures Act that protects individuals who are citizens or legal aliens from uncontrolled transfer of certain personal information to federal agencies for nonroutine uses.

private law   Subdivision of substantive law; addresses direct dealings between persons.

private nuisance   Tort that interferes with the property interest of a limited number of individuals.

privity   Mutual or successive relationship to the same rights of property, or such an identification of interest of one person with another as to represent the same legal right (for example, a lessee is in privity with the lessor).

probable cause   Reasonable ground for supposing that an individual has committed a crime.

procedural due process   Guarantee granted to individuals that requires any government decision to take a person's life, liberty, or property to be made fairly.

procedural law   Established methods or processes of enforcing the rights created by substantive law.

procedural rule   Type of administrative agency rule that governs the internal practices of an agency.

process   Document that is an order coming from the court, signed by the judge or representative; three stages of process exist: issued, served, filed.

professional agent   One who handles contracts in a particular field; for example, real estate broker.

professional association   Organized group of professionals with common interests; subject to antitrust laws.

promisee   Person receiving the promise.

promisor   Person making the promise.

promissory estoppel   Doctrine that prevents the promisor from revoking the offer.

promissory note   Written promise to pay made between two parties; payable at a definite time or on demand.

public law Subdivision of substantive law; addresses the relationship between individuals and their government.

public nuisance Crime that disturbs or interferes with the public.

punitive damages Damages awarded to punish a party for intentional and willful conduct that he or she knew at the time would harm someone.

purchase money security loan Security interest created as part of a purchase agreement.

Q

qualified fee estate Estate in property in which the owner has less rights than with fee simple; qualified, specific conditions exist to the ownership.

qualified indorsement Instrument of indorsement used by the indorser to disclaim or limit liability on the instrument.

quasi-contract Implied-in-law contract in which the parties did not make any promise by word or conduct but the law imposed a promise on the party who benefited.

quasi-executive function Administrative agency power to ensure compliance with the rules and to conduct investigations.

quasi-judicial function Administrative agency power to prosecute cases, render judgments, and impose penalties if violations occur.

quasi-legislative function Administrative agency power to promulgate rules that have the effect of law.

quitclaim deed Deed conveying to the buyer whatever interest the grantor had in the property, if any.

quota Limit, as on the number of goods that can be imported to a country.

R

Racketeer Influenced and Corrupt Organizations Act of 1970 (RICO) Amendment to the Organized Crime Control Act of 1970; designed to control the investment by organized crime into legitimate businesses and to force forfeiture of any profits made as a result of such criminal activity.

raising an affirmative defense Admitting the truth of the complaint but raising new facts that will result in the dismissal of the case.

ratification Express or implied conduct of the principal that binds the principal to the agent's acts and treats the agent's acts or contracts as if they had been authorized by the principal from the beginning.

real estate mortgage Lien that secures repayment of a note given to secure the purchase of real property.

Real Estate Settlement Procedures Act (RESPA) Federal statute that governs the purchase of a house and the borrowing of money to pay for it.

real property Land and the objects permanently attached to it.

reformation of the contract Rewriting of the contract because of errors in the written document.

Regulatory Flexibility Act 1980 amendment to the Administrative Procedures Act that requires an agency to publish in the Federal Register twice each year a special regulatory flexibility agenda.

release Giving up of a right, claim, or privilege by the person in whom it exists or to whom it accrues, to the person against whom it might have been enforced or demanded.

relevant market Part of the structural analysis used by the courts to determine whether a monopoly exists; considers the characteristics of the product, its substitutes, and the geographic area where the product is sold.

remedy Relief provided for an innocent party when the other party has breached a contract.

remedy at law Legal remedy awarded by the court; the harmed party could be awarded land, money, or items of value, or a combination of all three.

remedy in equity Legal remedy granted by the court; an appropriate remedy, based on fairness, justice, and honesty, is awarded to the harmed party in order to correct the situation.

reorganization Also known as Chapter 11 in a business bankruptcy filing; situation in which the creditors and debtors formulate a plan under which the debtor pays a portion of the debts and is discharged of the remainder, and the debtor is allowed to continue in business.

repossession Situation in which the secured party takes possession of the collateral covered by the security agreement in the event of default.

requirement contract Vertical restraint of trade in which either the buyer must purchase all his or her requirements of a particular product for a specific time from the seller or the seller must supply all of the product the buyer requests.

resale price maintenance Vertical restraint of trade in which the buyer and the seller agree to the price at which the buyer will resell the product.

rescission Remedy that cancels the agreement and returns the parties to the contract to the status quo; may be by mutual consent, by conduct, or by decree of a court of equity.

resolution Agreement reached mutually by the disputing parties.

Restatement, Second, Contracts Body of law created by the judiciary and revised in 1979; covers the areas of law regarding property, trusts, torts, and restitution.

restitution Equitable remedy in which a person is restored to his or her original position prior to loss or injury, or is placed in the same position as if a breach had not occurred.

restrictive indorsement Indorsement on an instrument that requires the indorser to comply with certain instructions regarding the funds involved.

revocation Withdrawing of the offer by the offeror.

right-to-work law Statute making it illegal for union membership to be required for employment.

robbery Wrongful or fraudulent taking and carrying away by any person of the personal property of another, involving the use of fear or force.

Robinson-Patman Act Section 2 of the Clayton Act; promotes economic equality in the purchasing and selling of goods; prohibits price discrimination.

rule of reason Doctrine by which the court reviews all the circumstances of a case to decide whether the defendant's practice was an unreasonable restraint on trade.

S

satisfaction Tender of substitute performance in return for the relinquishment of the right of action on a prior obligation; accord is executed.

secured transaction Type of transaction secured by collateral.

service mark Mark used to distinguish the services of one person from those of another; the title, character names, or other distinctive features of radio and television programs may be registered as service marks.

shop right Employer's right to use invention developed during working hours by employee without payment of royalties.

sight (demand) draft Instrument payable on sight when the holder presents it for payment.

slander of title Defaming the title a person has to his or her property and possibly preventing the sale of the property.

Social Security Act of 1935 Federal statute that established a federal insurance program covering the financial impact of retirement, death, disability, hospitalization, and unemployment of a worker through contributions by a worker and his or her employer.

sociological school of law Approach to the study of law that seeks to discover, by observation through social science, what law will work.

software Programming involved with a computer system.

special indorsement Indorsement on an instrument that indicates a specific person to whom the indorser intends to make the instrument payable.

special warranty deed Deed in which the seller warrants that he or she has not previously done anything to lessen the value of the real estate for sale.

specific performance Equitable remedy in which the defendant is ordered to perform the act(s) promised in the contract.

stare decisis "Let the decision stand"; the practice of deciding a case with reference to former decisions.

statutory law Body of law enacted by state and federal legislatures.

stop-payment order Request made by a customer that his or her bank stop payment on an issued check.

straight bankruptcy Bankruptcy in which the debtor lists debts and turns his or her assets over to a trustee for settlement of the bankruptcy action.

strict liability Situation in which no defenses exist; applies to dangerous activities where all risk and responsibility for injury is assumed by the party involved or doing the hazardous activity.

structural analysis Tool used by the courts in determining whether monopoly power exists; involves defining the relevant product, geographic market, and market share.

Subchapter S Voluntary tax status of a small corporation that allows the corporation to be taxed as a partnership; all losses and gains are passed through to the individual shareholders without taxation at the corporate level.

subpoena Process document that secures the attendance of a witness at a trial.

subpoena duces tecum Process document that requires evidence to be brought to court.

substantive due process Doctrine that holds that the content or substance of a piece of legislation must be in compliance with the Constitution.

substantive law   Law that defines, describes, regulates, and creates legal rights and obligations of individuals with respect to each other.

substantive rule   Administrative agency rule that is not procedural or interpretive in nature.

summary judgment   Written request by either party to a lawsuit to the court to grant judgment on grounds that there is no genuine issue of material fact and the requesting party is entitled to judgment as a matter of law.

summons   Process document that requires the defendant to defend against the claim of the plaintiff in a lawsuit.

sunset act   Statute that establishes the automatic expiration date for an administrative agency.

Sunshine Act   Amendment to the Administrative Procedures Act that prohibits administrative agencies from holding secret meetings.

supremacy clause   Clause in the Constitution that governs the relationship between the states and the federal government.

Supreme Court of the United States   Highest level of the federal court system, consisting of nine justices who serve for life, are appointed by the president, and are confirmed by the Senate; primarily an appellate court.

T

tangible property   Visible property that has physical existence; for example, land, cattle, buildings, computers.

tariff   Tax placed on imported goods based on either an *ad valorem* or a flat-rate basis.

tenancy by entirety   Ownership where the husband and wife own property without separate transfer rights.

tenancy by sufferance   Possession of land without right; not a true tenancy.

tenancy for years   Nonfreehold estate created by express contract by leasing property for a specific period of time.

tenancy from period to period   Nonfreehold estate created by a lease that does not specify length of time but states that rent is to be paid at certain intervals.

tenancy in common   Co-ownership in which two or more persons can own an undivided fractional interest in the property, but, on one tenant's death, that interest passes to his or her heirs.

termination statement   Statement showing that a debt has been paid.

time draft   Draft that is payable at a definite future time.

Title VII of the Civil Rights Act of 1964   Federal statute that prohibits discrimination in all areas of employment on the basis of race, color, religion, national origin, sex, including pregnancy, childbirth, and abortion, to state, local, and federal agencies and employers of at least fifteen employees and involved in or a part of interstate commerce (the federal government is exempt); administered by the Equal Employment Opportunity Commission.

tort   French word meaning ''wrong''; wrongdoing for which a civil action in court is possible.

trade acceptance   Draft frequently used with the sale of goods in which the purchaser becomes liable to pay the draft. Equivalent to note receivable of the seller and note payable of the buyer, a trade acceptance permits the seller to raise money on it before it is due.

trade association   Group of organized competitors pursuing a common interest, such as dissemination of information, advertising campaigns, codes of conduct; subject to antitrust laws.

trademark   Distinctive mark, motto, device, or implement that a manufacturer stamps, prints, or otherwise affixes to the goods it produces.

treaty   Agreement or contract between two or more nations that must be authorized and ratified by the supreme power of each nation.

trespass to land   Entering onto land, causing anything to enter onto land, remaining on land, or permitting anything to remain on land owned by another person.

trespass to personal property   Unlawful injury to (or other interference with) the personal property of another that violates that person's exclusive possession and enjoyment of the property.

tribunal administrator   Person who manages the administrative matters and all communication between the parties and the arbitrator in an arbitration.

trust   Legal entity in which a trustee holds title to property for the benefit of another.

Truth-in-Lending Act (TILA)   Title I of the Consumer Credit Protection Act; deals with deceptive credit practices and requires notice and disclosure to prevent sellers and creditors from taking unfair advantage of consumers.

tying arrangement   Arrangement in which the buyer must purchase one item in order to purchase the tied product.

U

unconscionable contract or clause   Clause in a contract, or the entire contract, that is so one-sided as to be unjust after considering the needs of the particular case.

undisclosed principal   Principal whose identity is totally unknown by the third party and the third party has no knowledge that the agent is acting in an agency capacity at the time the contract is made.

Uniform Arbitration Act   Federal statute established in 1955 that is designed to make legislation on arbitration more uniform throughout the country; has been adopted by thirty states and the District of Columbia.

Uniform Commercial Code (UCC)   Uniform act consisting of eleven articles that applies to both interstate and intrastate business transactions governing the conduct of business among individuals and businesses.

Uniform Consumer Credit Code (UCCC)   Comprehensive body of rules governing the most important aspects of consumer credit; has been adopted by only a few states.

unilateral contract   Contract in which a person makes a promise that requires in return an act (not a promise) by the other party; for example, a reward situation.

unilateral mistake   Mistake made by one of the contracting parties.

union shop   Business that does not require union membership of applicants in order to be hired but can and usually does require workers to join the union after a specific period of time on the job.

usury   Rate of interest that is above the amount allowed by statute; applies to cash loans only.

V

valid contract   Contract that meets all requirements of a contract to be enforced in a court.

venue   Particular geographic area within a judicial district where a suit should be brought.

verdict   Decision of the jury.

vertical merger   Merger of a company at one stage of production with another company at a higher or lower stage of production.

vertical restraint   Trade practice that involves firms at different levels of the production and distribution process and that violates antitrust laws.

voidable contract   Situation in which one party to a contract is bound by the other party may disaffirm it; for example, a contract by a minor.

voluntary arbitration   Arbitration entered into voluntarily based on a previous written agreement between the disputing parties to arbitrate when a dispute arises.

W

warranty   Seller's assurance to the buyer that the goods sold will meet certain standards.

warranty to title   Guarantee to the buyer that the goods are not stolen, have no lien against them, and do not infringe a patent or copyright.

white-collar crime   Monetary offense usually against a business; nonviolent crimes committed by corporations or by individuals against corporations.

will   Legal instrument that, on a person's death, directs how the person's property is to be distributed.

writ of certiorari   Order from the Supreme Court to a lower court to send the records of a case to the Supreme Court for review.

writ of attachment   Process document issued after judgment has been made by the court; may take the form of an order to take or seize property or persons to bring them under control of the court.

writ of execution   Process document issued after judgment has been made by the court; puts in force the court's decree or judgment.

writ of garnishment   Process document issued after judgment has been made by the court; garnishes the wages or property of the party at fault.

Z

zoning   Restrictions on land use imposed by the state or local government.

Table of Cases

The principal cases are in bold type. Cases cited or discussed are in roman type. Cases that can also be retrieved on West Publishing's LEGAL CLERK Research Software System are indicated by a color dot. To determine which of the three versions of LEGAL CLERK a particular case appears on, please turn to the text page cited and refer to the color coded computer symbol printed with the case citation.

A blue computer symbol indicates that the case appears on *Uniform Commercial Code Article 2 Sales-Version 1.0*. A black computer symbol indicates that the case is on *Government Regulation and the Legal Environment of Business-Version 1.0*. A black computer symbol with a color background identifies the case as appearing on *Contracts-Version 1.0*.

Index